North Carolina
Extension Gardener
Handbook

Second Edition

AG-831   January 2022

Published by

NC State Extension
College of Agriculture and Life Sciences
NC State University

Visit the digital version of the handbook for the latest updates:
content.ces.ncsu.edu/extension-gardener-handbook

North Carolina
Extension Gardener
Handbook

Editors

Kathleen Moore, Urban Horticulturist, Department of Horticultural Science, NC State University

Lucy K. Bradley, Professor and Extension Specialist, Urban Horticulture; Director, NC State Extension Master Gardener program; NC State University

Authors

Matt Bertone, Extension Associate, Department of Entomology and Plant Pathology

Frank A. Blazich, Distinguished Professor Emeritus, Department of Horticultural Science

Toby Bost, Horticulturist, Author

Mary Jac Brennan, Extension Agent, Forsyth County

Wayne Buhler, Professor and Extension Specialist, Department of Horticultural Science

Hannah Burrack, Associate Professor and Extension Specialist, Department of Entomology and Plant Pathology

Bill Cline, Researcher and Extension Specialist, Department of Entomology and Plant Pathology

Aimee Colf, Extension Agent, Anson County

David Crouse, Professor and Extension Specialist, Department of Crop and Soil Sciences

Christopher DePerno, Professor, Department of Forestry and Environmental Resources; Fisheries, Wildlife, and Conservation Biology

Barbara Fair, Associate Professor and Extension Specialist, Department of Horticultural Science

Gina Fernandez, Professor and Extension Specialist, Department of Horticultural Science

Steven Frank, Associate Professor and Extension Specialist, Department of Entomology and Plant Pathology

Charlotte Glen, Extension Agent, Chatham County

David Goforth, Extension Agent, Cabarrus County

Christopher Gunter, Associate Professor and Extension Specialist, Department of Horticultural Science

Susan Jakes, Associate State Program Leader CRD, Extension Assistant Professor ANR/CRD

Mark Kistler, Associate Professor, Department of Agricultural and Human Sciences

Cyndi Lauderdale, Extension Agent, Wilson County

Anthony V. LeBude, Associate Professor and Extension Specialist, Department of Horticultural Science

Frank Louws, Professor and Extension Specialist, Department of Entomology and Plant Pathology

Diane B. Mays, Department of Horticultural Science

Grady Miller, Professor and Extension Specialist, Department of Crop and Soil Sciences

Christopher Moorman, Professor and Coordinator of the Fisheries, Wildlife, and Conservation Biology Program

Michael Munster, Diagnostician, NC State University Plant Disease and Insect Clinic

Joe Neal, Professor and Extension Specialist, Department of Horticultural Science

David Orr, Associate Professor, Department of Entomology and Plant Pathology

Michael L. Parker, Associate Professor and Extension Specialist, Department of Horticultural Science

Abbey Piner, Urban Horticulturist, Department of Horticultural Science

Kim Richter, Department of Horticultural Science

Julie Sherk, Assistant Professor, Department of Horticultural Science

Rhonda Sherman, Extension Solid Waste Specialist, Department of Horticultural Science

Anne Spafford, M.L.A., Associate Professor, Department of Horticultural Science and Adjunct Faculty Member, Department of Landscape Architecture, NC State University

Sara Spayd, Extension Specialist, Department of Horticultural Science

Michelle Wallace, Extension Agent, Durham County

The North Carolina Extension Gardener Handbook

Published by NC State Extension
ces.ncsu.edu

Portions of this publication are based in part on sections of the 1998 *Extension Master Gardener Manual* prepared by Erv Evans, Extension Associate, Department of Horticultural Science; Peter Bromley, Extension Specialist, Department of Zoology; Stephen Bambara, Extension Specialist, Department of Entomology; James R. Baker, Extension Specialist, Department of Entomology; Ken Sorensen, Extension Specialist, Department of Entomology; L. T. Lucas, Extension Specialist, Department of Plant Pathology; Mike Linker, IPM Coordinator, Department of Crop Science; Steve Toth, Extension Specialist, Department of Entomology; Frank A. Blazich, Professor, Department of Horticulture Science; E. Barclay Poling, Extension Specialist, Department of Horticultural Science; James R. Ballington, Professor, Department of Horticultural Science; Larry Bass, Extension Specialist, Department of Horticultural Science; Doug Saunders, Extension Specialist, Department of Horticultural Science; Jeanine Davis, Extension Specialist, Department of Horticultural Science; Frank Louws, Extension Specialist, Department of Entomology and Plant Pathology; and M.A. Powell, Extension Specialist, Department of Horticultural Science.

Front cover image by therry/iStockphoto.com

Published 2022.
First edition published 2018. Second edition 2022.

ISBN 978-1-4696-6973-1

North Carolina Extension Gardener Handbook
Table of Contents

Acknowledgments

We extend a huge thank you to the many contributors who made this book possible. To all the N.C. Cooperative Extension horticulture agents and Master Gardener[SM] volunteers who contributed countless hours providing content, editing, and technical support; obtaining photographs and graphics; proofreading, and more proofreading; and for their faith and grit in staying engaged throughout this multiyear project. To all the NC State Extension specialists who shared their expertise. To Dr. Tom Melton, Deputy Director, NC State Extension and Agriculture and Natural Resources Extension Program Leader, whose vision and start-up funding made this project possible. To Dr. Richard Bonanno, Associate Dean, College of Agriculture and Life Sciences, and Director, NC State Extension, for helping us identify options for printing. To Dr. Wayne Buhler, Interim Department Head for the NC State Department of Horticultural Science, for his content contributions as well as financial support of the project. To Dr. Brian Whipker, Interim Assistant Department Head for NC State Department of Horticultural Science, for sharing his expertise in developing both Internet and print books. To Dr. Joe Neal, Department Extension Leader, NC State Department of Horticultural Science, for his editing expertise and guidance throughout the process. To Michelle Healy, Business Services Coordinator for the NC State Department of Horticultural Science, for managing the accounting and administrative tasks flawlessly. To Barbara Scott, Wordstone Editing, and Jill Steffey for catching every errant comma and quotation mark, and dutifully checking the spelling of every Latin name. To John Beuttner, Graphic Designer, for his artistic expertise and design skills in transforming the online content into a beautiful book. To Debra Ireland for ensuring conformance with NC State Extension brand requirements and for establishing and managing the partnership with UNC Press. To Justin Moore, Director of Marketing & Communications, NC State Extension, for guiding the process of preparing a printed version of this document. To Sean Munday, Director of Budgets and Planning, NC State College of Agriculture and Life Sciences, for his optimism and skill in finding a way. And, to John McLeod at UNC Press for easing the transition from manuscript to printed handbook.

NC State Extension

NC State University is a land-grant institution charged with serving the people of North Carolina not only through traditional academic and research programs but also through extension, education, and outreach.

NC State Extension builds capacity to create prosperity for all North Carolinians, helping our state's citizens translate research into everyday solutions through educational programs and partnerships focused on agriculture, food and nutrition, and 4-H youth development. It is the largest nonformal educational outreach unit in the 17-campus UNC system. In addition to faculty and staff, more than 70,000 Extension volunteers and citizen advisors donate their time and resources to address local needs. Their involvement in programs like the NC State Extension Master Gardener[SM] program is vital to the success of our efforts across the state.

NC State Extension works in tandem with The Cooperative Extension Program at N.C. A&T State University, as well as federal, state, and local governments, to form a strategic partnership called N.C. Cooperative Extension.

Extension professionals in all 100 counties and the Eastern Band of Cherokee Indians translate research-based information and technology from NC State and N.C. A&T into practical applications that enrich the lives, land, and economy of North Carolinians.

We're honored to be your lifelong partner, helping all North Carolinians put knowledge to work in their communities. We are NC State Extension.

Learn more about the resources and opportunities we provide at ces.ncsu.edu.

The Extension Master Gardener^{SM} Volunteer Program in North Carolina

In 1973 the Extension Master Gardener Program was created in Washington State. The North Carolina program began in Wake County in 1979, and in New Hanover County shortly after. As of September 2021, there are over 3,300 Master Gardener volunteers in North Carolina, each of whom has completed at least 40 hours of training by N.C. Cooperative Extension specialists and Extension agents as well as a 40-hour internship.

Master Gardener volunteers are educators who work on behalf of and under the supervision of NC State Extension. They share unbiased, research-based, environmentally sound information, extending the reach of North Carolina's land-grant universities, NC State University and N.C. A&T University. Master Gardener volunteers focus on garden and landscaping issues important in their local communities, including environmental stewardship, water conservation, water quality preservation, energy conservation, green waste reduction, home food production, wildlife management, sustainable communities, and health and wellness for children and adults.

After completing their first-year, Master Gardener volunteers continue to volunteer in their local communities a minimum of 20 hours a year and expand their gardening knowledge through at least 10 hours of continuing education each year. Volunteers identify opportunities for lifelong learning to make an important contribution and to work with Extension faculty, staff, and volunteers as key benefits of participating in the program.

In 2019, NC State Extension Master Gardener volunteers made cash, in-kind, and service contributions valued at $7.3 million. They documented 229,687 hours of service (the equivalent of 110 full-time employees), recorded 229,687 contacts, and made significant contributions to protecting environmental quality, growing healthy children, and promoting local food security.

If you are interested in becoming a Master Gardener volunteer in your community, you may contact the Extension horticulture agent in your county by visiting ncemgv.org.

Soils & Plant Nutrients

1

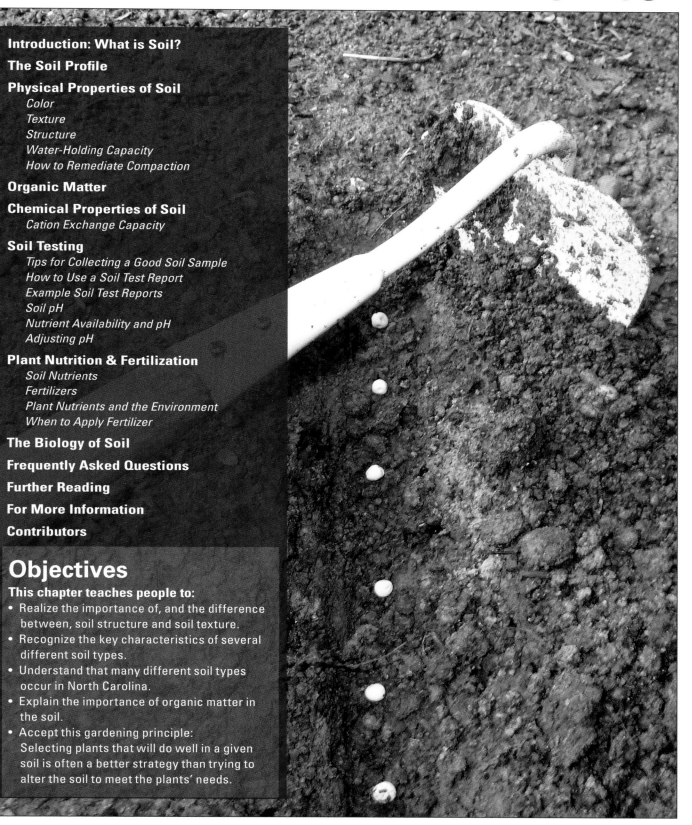

Objectives

This chapter teaches people to:
- Realize the importance of, and the difference between, soil structure and soil texture.
- Recognize the key characteristics of several different soil types.
- Understand that many different soil types occur in North Carolina.
- Explain the importance of organic matter in the soil.
- Accept this gardening principle: Selecting plants that will do well in a given soil is often a better strategy than trying to alter the soil to meet the plants' needs.

Introduction: What is Soil?

Soil is a living, breathing, natural entity composed of solids, liquids, and gases. Soil has five major functions:
- Provides a habitat for organisms
- Recycles waste products
- Filters water
- Serves as an engineering material
- Provides a medium for plant growth

Our focus will be on the fifth function. In this role, soil provides structural stability for plants and retains and relinquishes water and the nutrients necessary for plant growth.

An ideal soil for plant growth contains 50% **porespace** and 50% solids, with the porespace filled with equal parts air and water. This distribution rarely occurs because porespace varies with soil texture and soil management. For example, tilling increases porespace, while poor drainage and compaction reduce it.

Soil solids are a blend of mineral materials and **organic matter**. The mineral materials are typically weathered rock of varying sizes called sand, silt, and clay. The organic matter consists of decaying plant and microbial residues. The relative amounts of porespace and mineral and organic matter vary greatly among different soil types. But for plant growth, most soil scientists agree that 50% porespace, 45% mineral matter, and 5% organic matter make up an ideal ratio. The distribution of solids and porespace in ideal, compacted, and poorly drained soil is illustrated in Figure 1-1a, Figure 1-1b, and Figure 1-1c.

The Soil Profile

Most naturally occurring, undisturbed soils have three distinct layers of variable thicknesses. The layers are the topsoil, subsoil, and **parent material**. Each layer can have two or more sublayers called **horizons**. Collectively, the horizons make up the soil profile. The predominate parent material varies by location in North Carolina. In the NC piedmont and mountains, the parent material is typically weathered bedrock known as saprolite. In the river bottoms and stream terraces of the NC piedmont and mountains, the parent materials are the floodplain sediments delivered from upstream where erosion has occurred. In the NC coastal plain, the parent materials are marine sediments deposited over eons as the oceans go through the natural cycles of advance and retreat. In the easternmost NC coastal plain, the dominant parent material is organic matter. These organic soils are typically found in areas that just 50,000 years ago were below sea level. Such areas are swamps where plants grow and thrive. But these areas are too wet for the plant residues (leaves, branches, roots, trunks, and the like) to efficiently decompose.

Soils' properties vary with the soil depth. The surface soil, or topsoil layer (O and A horizon in Figure 1–2), usually contains less clay, but more organic matter and air, than the lower soil layers. Topsoil is usually more fertile than the other layers and has the greatest concentration of plant roots.

The subsurface layer (B and C horizon in Figure 1–2), known as subsoil, usually has a higher clay content and lower organic matter content than the topsoil.

Soil properties often limit the depth to which plant roots can penetrate. For example, roots will not grow through an impenetrable layer. That layer may be bedrock (Figure 1-3), compacted soil, or a chemical barrier, such as an acidic (very low) **pH**. A high water table can also restrict root growth due to poor soil aeration. Few big trees grow in shallow soils because big trees are unable to develop a root system strong enough to prevent them from toppling over. Shallow soils also tend to be more drought-prone because they hold less water and thus dry out faster than deeper soils. Water lost to runoff on shallow soils would instead be absorbed by a deeper soil. In addition, deep soils allow the roots to explore a greater volume, which means the roots can retain more water and plant nutrients.

Soils change in three dimensions. The first dimension is from the top to the bottom of the soil profile. The other two dimensions are north to south and east to west.

The practical meaning of this three-dimensional variability is that as you move across a state, a county, or even a field, the soils change. Five factors of soil formation account for this variation:

1. Parent material
2. Biological activity
3. Climate
4. Topography
5. Time

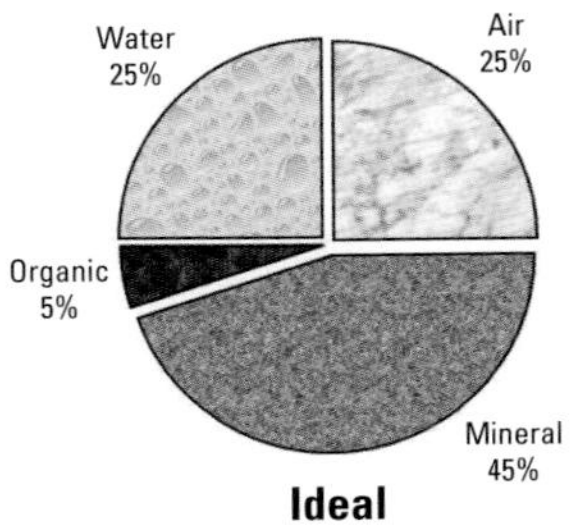

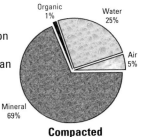

Figure 1–1a. The distribution of solids and porespace in an ideal soil.

Water 25%
Air 25%
Organic 5%
Mineral 45%

Ideal

Organic 1%
Water 25%
Air 5%
Mineral 69%

Figure 1–1b. The distribution of solids and porespace in a compacted soil.

Compacted

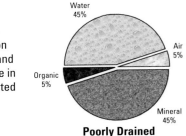

Water 45%
Air 5%
Organic 5%
Mineral 45%

Poorly Drained

Figure 1–1c. The distribution of solids and porespace in a poorly drained soil.

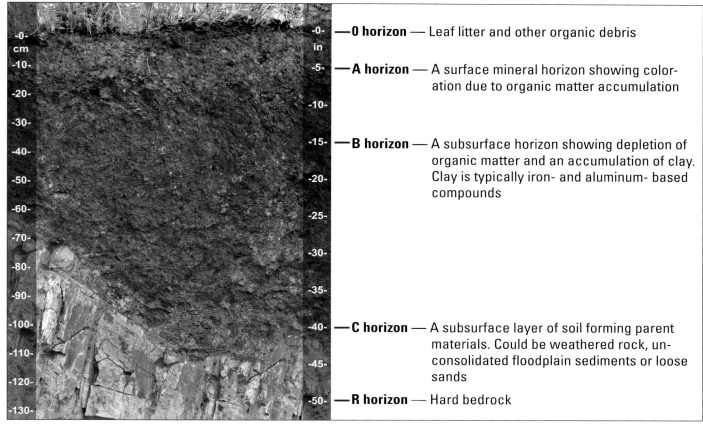

0 horizon — Leaf litter and other organic debris

A horizon — A surface mineral horizon showing coloration due to organic matter accumulation

B horizon — A subsurface horizon showing depletion of organic matter and an accumulation of clay. Clay is typically iron- and aluminum- based compounds

C horizon — A subsurface layer of soil forming parent materials. Could be weathered rock, unconsolidated floodplain sediments or loose sands

R horizon — Hard bedrock

Figure 1–2. Soil horizons.
John A. Kelley, USDA NRCS, Flickr CC BY - 2.0

Figure 1–3. The Craggey soil series; an example of shallow soil.
John A. Kelley, USDA NRCS, Flickr CC BY - 2.0

Differences in even one of these factors will result in a different soil type. Soils forming from different parent materials differ. Soils forming from the same parent material in varying climates differ. Soils at the top of a hill differ from soils at the bottom. The top of the hill loses material due to natural erosion; the bottom gains the material from above. Considering the number of possible combinations of these five factors, it is not surprising that more than 450 unique soil series are currently mapped in North Carolina. Globally, more than 20,000 different soil series occur. Neighborhood-level soil series can be found by typing "Web Soil Survey" into any Internet search engine.

Physical Properties of Soil

The physical properties of soil are characteristics that can be seen, felt, or measured. These include color, texture, structure, and water-holding capacity. Such properties usually determine the suitability of soil as a growth medium. Some physical properties, such as texture, are not economically feasible to change on a large scale.

A soil's fertility, which is a chemical property, is easier to change than the soil's physical properties.

Color

Organic matter, the soil minerals present, and the drainage conditions all influence soil color. Color alone is not an indicator of soil quality, but color does provide clues about certain conditions. For example, light or pale colors in grainy topsoil are frequently associated with low organic matter content, high sand content, and excessive leaching. Dark soil colors may result from poor drainage or high organic matter content. Shades of red indicate a clay soil is well-aerated, while shades of gray indicate inadequate drainage (Figure 1–4). In well-drained soils of the NC mountains and piedmont, the subsoil colors are often shades of red, brown, and yellow. In poorly drained soils, the subsoil is grayer in color.

Texture

Soil texture, which refers to the proportions of sand, silt, and clay, influences nearly every aspect of soil use and management. Sand is the largest particle (at 2.0 to 0.05 mm), silt is much smaller (0.05 to 0.002 mm), and clay is the smallest (less than 0.002 mm) (Figure 1–5). To compare particle sizes, imagine that a sand particle is the size of a basketball. On that scale, a silt particle would be the size

of a marble, and a particle of clay would be a pinpoint. How fine (clayey) or coarse (sandy) a soil is will determine many of the soil's physical and chemical properties.

Much of a soil particle's ability to react with water and nutrients is related to the amount of surface area available (Table 1–1). When the individual particle size is small, more individual particles will fit in a given space, and

Figure 1–4. Color as an indicator of drainage. The soil on the left is the Cecil series, a well-drained mineral soil typical of the NC piedmont. The soil on the right is the Coxville series, a poorly drained mineral soil found in the NC coastal plain.
John A. Kelley, USDA NRCS, Flickr CC BY - 2.0

Figure 1–6. The image on the left shows a close-up of sand particles, which appear grainy as seen by the naked eye. The right image shows the platelike texture of clay visible only under a microscope.
(Left) zoosnow, Pixabay CC0 (Right) Wikimedia, CC0

Figure 1–5.
Relative sizes of sand, silt, and clay.

thus make more surface area available. Clay, with its tiny particle size and platelike structure, holds water and nutrients effectively, while sand, which has a large, chunky structure, does not. In addition to being smaller, clay particles are composed of different minerals than sand and silt, and a clay particle's structure is more like a stack of paper plates than a grain of sand (Figure 1–6).

The relative proportions of sand, silt, and clay determine a soil's textural class (Figure 1–7). For example, a soil that is 12% sand, 55% clay, and 33% silt is in the clay textural class. Soil texture is a permanent feature, not easily changed by human activity. Consider a typical mineral soil that is 6 inches deep on 1 acre. That soil weighs

Table 1–1. Particle Type, Number of Particles per Gram, and the Average Surface Area per Gram.

Particle Type	Diameter (mm)	Number of Particles per gram	Specific surface area (cm²/g)
Clay	< 0.002	90,260,853,000	8,000,000
Coarse sand	1.00-0.50	720	23
Fine sand	0.25-0.10	46,000	91
Medium sand	0.50-0.25	5,700	45
Silt	0.05-0.002	5,776,000	454
Very coarse sand	2.00-1.00	90	11
Very fine sand	0.10-0.05	722,000	227

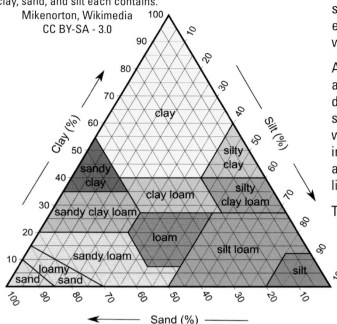

Figure 1–7. Pyramid diagram showing that soil types are based on the percentage of clay, sand, and silt each contains.
Mikenorton, Wikimedia CC BY-SA - 3.0

about 2 million pounds. To change the sand content just 1% would require adding 20,000 pounds (or 10 tons) of sand. A 1% change in sand content would have minimal effect. A significant effect might require a 10% change, which would mean adding 100 tons of sand.

Adding organic matter is a more economically feasible alternative for improving soil. Adding organic matter does not change a soil's texture—the percentage of sand, silt, and clay in the soil—but adding organic matter will alter soil structure by increasing the porespace and improving drainage. Gardeners can be successful with any soil texture, as long as they know the attributes and limitations of that soil.

Typically, laboratory procedures are used to determine the soil texture. It is possible, however, to use the procedure outlined in Figure 1–8 to determine the textural class by the "feel" method. It takes practice and calibration, but it can provide a reasonable estimate of the soil texture.

How Do Soil Types Affect Gardeners?

Compaction. Compaction occurs when pressure is applied to soil particles and the air and water are pushed out of the porespaces. Large, cubic sand particles are not easily compacted. Clay particles, small and platelike, are easily aligned and can compact, especially when wet. Compaction inhibits the movement of water, gases (air), and roots. Compacted soils have less infiltration, greater runoff, a higher risk of erosion, and more restricted root growth than soils without compaction. Water drains slowly, which may increase the likelihood of plant root diseases.

Erosion. Sand particles are heavy, so they are not easily picked up and moved by water or wind. Clay particles are sticky, so they are not easily moved. Silty loam particles are light and not sticky, so erosive forces easily move them. Eroded soils are usually harder to till and have lower productivity than soils without erosion. The main causes of soil erosion in North Carolina are insufficient vegetative or mulch cover, and improper equipment and methods used to prepare and till the soil (Figure 1–9).

Soil erosion can be minimized by following a few preventive measures:
• Choose plants suited to the soil so they establish well.
• Mulch the surface each year with organic materials 1 inch to 3 inches deep.
• Adequately fertilize to promote vigorous, but not excessive, plant growth.
• Create a water diversion, such as a grass waterway, to capture and slow water movement.
• Align rows to follow the land's contour so that water flowing downhill is slowed.
• Use proper tillage methods, such as not tilling when the soil is overly wet and not overtilling.
• Plant a winter cover crop.
• Consider installing rain gardens to capture sediment and runoff.

Surface Area. The most active part of a soil particle is its surface area. A particle's surface is where nutrient exchange takes place. Sand particles have a small surface area relative to their mass, meaning they do not hold on to nutrients well. Clay particles have a large surface area relative to their mass, so a small amount of clay can add a significant amount of surface area to a soil, increasing the nutrient-holding capacity.

Figure 1–8. Feel method for soil textural class determination.

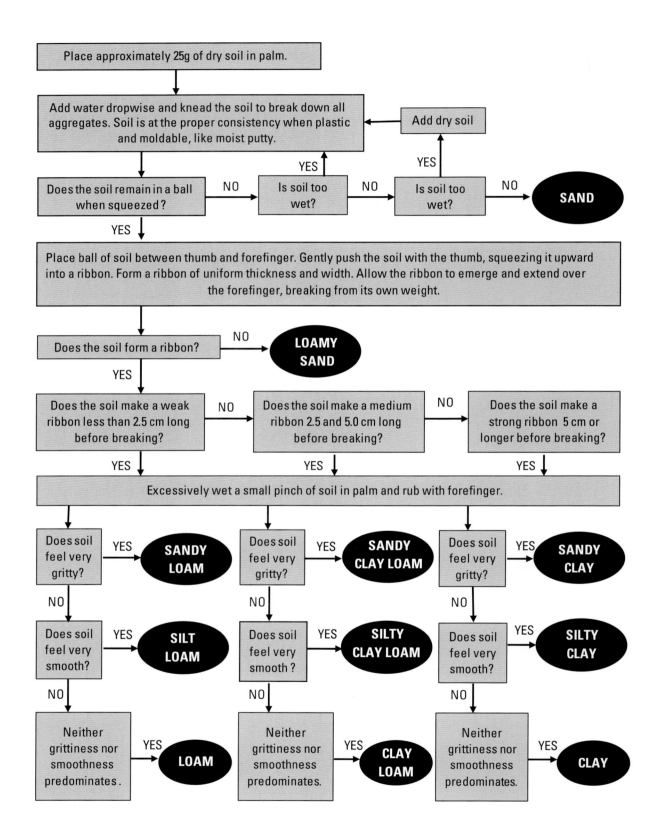

Sandy or Coarsely Textured Soils (Figure 1–10)

- Low in organic matter content and native fertility.
- Rapidly permeable and do not hold soil moisture.
- Nutrient leaching is a concern, so proper fertilization is a must. Apply smaller amounts of nutrients and apply them more frequently.
- Low in **cation exchange** and **buffer capacities**.
- Well-suited for road foundations and building sites.
- Feel gritty.

Loamy or Medium-Textured Soils (Figure 1–11)

- Contain more organic matter.
- Permit slower movement of water and are better able to retain moisture and nutrients.
- Are generally more fertile.
- Have higher cation exchange and buffer capacities.
- Feel crumbly.

Clayey or Finely Textured Soils (Figure 1–12)

- Higher nutrient-holding capacity.
- Higher available water-holding capacity.
- Finely textured soils exhibit properties that are somewhat difficult to manage or overcome.
- Often too sticky when wet and too hard when dry to cultivate.
- May have shrink-and-swell characteristics that affect construction uses.
- Feel slippery.

Structure

Soil structure refers to the grouping of individual soil particles into larger pieces called **peds** or **aggregates**. The structure of topsoil is usually granular and resembles chocolate cookie crumbs (Figure 1–13). Good granular structure allows rapid movement of air and water within the soil. Poor granular structure decreases movement of air and water. Good soil structure allows for extensive root development; poor structure can limit root growth.

Figure 1–9. The soil on this hill eroded because of runoff and lack of vegetation.
John A. Kelley, USDA NRCS, Flickr CC BY - 2.0

Figure 1–10. Sandy soils are low in fertility and do not hold onto soil moisture.
Loretta Sorenson, USDA NRCS South Dakota, Flickr CC BY-SA - 2.0

Figure 1–11. Loamy soils feel crumbly, and generally are darker because they contain organic matter.
Haanala 76, PublicDomainImages CC0

Figure 1–12. Clay soils are sticky when wet and very hard when dry.
D. Lindbo, Soil Science, NC State, Flickr CC BY 2.0

Figure 1–13. Example of granular soil structure (looks like chocolate cookie crumbs) in topsoil.
John A. Kelley, USDA NRCS, Flickr CC BY - 2.0

Supplying an adequate amount of organic matter and working the soil only when it is not excessively wet promotes good topsoil structure.

Water-Holding Capacity

Water enters the soil from precipitation or irrigation. It exits by draining from the soil, evaporating from the surface, and through **transpiration** from plant leaves. Water-holding capacity—the retention of water moving through soil—depends on differences in soil porespace. Ideal soils are half porespace with equal amounts of air and water filling the pores. Too much air means plants will wilt. Too much water means reduced plant vigor and susceptibility to root rot, which occurs due to anaerobic conditions.

Soils differ in the number of large (macro), medium (meso), and small (micro) pores. Macropores, which are more common in sandy soils, take up water more quickly and drain faster than meso- and micropores. This rapid draining from macropores is called "gravitational water" because the weaker forces of **adhesion** and **cohesion** in macropores cannot overcome gravity's pull. Within 24 hours after a saturating rain, gravitational water reaches the lower soil horizons, and the soil is at **field capacity:** the meso-and micropores are still full of water because their adhesive and cohesive forces are stronger than gravity. Water in the mesopores is available to plants. But when the mesopores lose water as the soil dries through plant uptake and transpiration, soil moisture reaches the permanent wilting point. At the permanent wilting point, micropores are still full of water, but this water is so tightly held that it is not plant-available. Note that plants may wilt before the permanent wilting point if the plant transpires water through the leaves faster than it can take water up from the soil through its roots. This is why plants may wilt on hot days and then recover once the sun goes down and why plants can balance uptake with transpiration (Figure 1–14).

Figure 1–14. Plants can wilt during the hot part of the day, but recover once the sun goes down. Plants can balance water uptake with water loss through transpiration.
Scot Nelson, Flickr CC0

How to Remediate Compaction

Compaction is a likely problem if there has been recent construction or other traffic over the area. Deep cultivation, which is mixing the top 6 inches to 2 feet of soil with a tiller, disk, or hand tools, may be needed to loosen the soil. Incorporation of organic matter during deep cultivation can help to rehabilitate soil structure by creating aggregates and both macropores (for drainage) and mesopores (for plant-available water). Digging or cultivating soil when it is wet or excessively dry can destroy structure.

Be wary of quick fixes, such as starting over with a truckload of topsoil. Unfortunately, there are no standards on material sold as "topsoil." New problems may be brought on site, such as weed seeds and disease organisms. Adding new topsoil to existing soil may also create drainage problems when water moves through the purchased topsoil and reaches the compacted layer. The water can pool and create unfavorable conditions for root growth.

Clay soils, which tend to hold excessive amounts of water and become compacted easily, present some tricky problems. Common mistakes are adding sand or peat moss to improve drainage. Adding sand to clay will reduce soil structure, lowering porespace. Adding peat moss will increase the clay soil's high moisture-holding capacity. The best advice is to add smaller amounts of organic matter consistently every year, minimize compaction, and let soil biology naturally improve the structure over time.

Urban Soils

As the locally grown food movement gains momentum, more people are gardening in urban areas. Urban soils can be host to contaminants such as lead, pesticide residue, or petroleum products. Before gardening and especially before producing any food on an urban soil, it is important to understand the history of the land and to properly identify any possible contaminants. *SoilFacts: Minimizing the Risks of Soil Contaminants in Urban Gardens* (NC State Extension publication number AG-439-78) provides in-depth information about risk levels for individual soil contaminants, remediation techniques, and resources for professionals that can assist with analysis and consulting.

Here are some tips for gardening in contaminated soils:

Garden design:
- Plant ornamentals in contaminated areas and locate edibles as far from contaminants as possible.
- Do not plant near roads or buildings.
- Consider using raised beds with imported soil (Figure 1–15).

Soil Management:
- Raising the pH of the soil may help to slow the uptake of some contaminants by a plant.
- Organic matter, such as compost, may bind some contaminants in the soil.
- If large-scale remediation is necessary, contact a professional for help with excavation, washing, or vapor extraction.

Planting Considerations:
- Avoid root crops where edible portions come into direct contact with soil.
- Shoot and leaf crops (lettuce, cabbage, broccoli, celery, rhubarb) will have less of a contamination risk.
- Fruit crops (tomato, zucchini, beans, peppers) will have the least amount of contamination risk.

Garden Hygiene:
- Wear gloves and wash hands and clothes after gardening.
- Do not wear garden shoes in the house.
- Watch children closely so no soil is ingested.
- Wash produce in mild detergent, remove the first leaves of leafy crops (those closest to the ground), and peel root crops.

Rocks and Gravel

Rocks and gravel, which are large, coarse materials, can be found in many soils, but they are not considered when determining soil texture. Although some rocks and gravel in the soil will not affect plant nutrient uptake, they can make the soil difficult to dig. If the garden is mostly rocks or gravel, the soil will have a reduced water- and nutrient-holding capacity, and will be unfit for growing plants. In such a situation, it may be easiest to install raised beds and import soil.

Figure 1–15. Gardening in urban areas requires careful consideration of soil conditions. If contaminated or poorly drained soils are present, raised beds may be necessary.
David Crummey, Flickr CC BY - 2.0

Organic Matter

Organic matter consists of the remains of plants and animals and gives soil a gray to very-dark-brown color. Organic matter is home to many soil organisms.

Earthworms, insects, bacteria, fungi, and animals use organic matter as food, breaking it down to obtain energy and essential nutrients. **Humus** is the portion of organic matter that remains after most decomposition has taken place (Figure 1–16).

Figure 1–16. Humus is the organic matter that remains after most decomposition has occurred.
Kathleen Moore, CC BY - 2.0

When organic matter decomposes in the soil, carbon dioxide is released and replaces some of the oxygen in soil pores. Carbon dioxide is dissolved by water in soil to form a weak acid. This solution reacts with soil minerals to release nutrients that can be taken up by plants. The digested and decomposing organic matter also helps develop good air-water relationships. In sandy soil, organic material occupies some of the space between the sand grains. This binds them together and increases water-holding capacity. In a finely textured or clay soil, organic material creates aggregates of soil particles. This allows water to move more rapidly around soil particles.

The amount of organic matter in the soil depends primarily on rainfall, air temperature, the kinds of plants that have been growing in a soil, management practices, soil temperature, and drainage. Soils that are tilled frequently are usually low in organic matter because tilling decreases residue particle size and increases the amount of air in the soil, increasing the rate of organic matter decomposition. Poorly drained soils tend to have a high percentage of organic matter because low oxygen levels

limit decomposition organisms. To build organic matter in garden soil, till in compost when the garden is first created, but do not till in subsequent years. Instead, apply thin layers (1 inch to 3 inches) of organic mulch or compost to the soil surface each year (Figure 1–17). This material will break down, and the organic matter levels in the soil will gradually increase.

Figure 1–17. Mulching with a 1–3 inch layer of organic material will help to build good air and water relationships in the soil as well as add nutrients for uptake by plants.
Kathleen Moore, CC BY - 2.0

Organic amendments can improve soils that suffer from high compaction, poor drainage, and erosion. Materials such as compost, manures, and pine bark are more effective and economical than vermiculite, peat moss, sand, topsoil, or perlite. Table 1–2 reviews the amounts of organic material to be added to soil per 100 square feet. When working in small areas, a general rule of thumb is to incorporate a 3- to 6-inch layer of organic material into the soil. The organic matter must be decomposed before plants can use the nutrients. The rate of decomposition of organic matter by soil organisms is affected by moisture, temperature, particle size, the carbon-to-nitrogen ratio, and nitrogen availability. The proper balance of carbon and nitrogen is needed for rapid decomposition, as are warm temperatures and adequate moisture. When using straw, leaves, or sawdust (which are high in carbon), add nitrogen fertilizer while the material is decomposing. Soil microbes use nitrogen during decomposition and may deprive plants, resulting in slow or stunted plant growth. Incorporating organic matter some months before planting the garden allows the material time to decompose and have plant-available nutrients in place for good plant growth.

Table 1–2. Organic Materials and Their Application Rates

Organic Material	Amount to be Added per 100 Square Feet
Compost	10–20 cubic feet
Corncobs	50 pounds (2 bushels)
Hay	60 pounds (1 bale)
Leaves	75 pounds (3–4 bushels)
Sawdust	50 pounds (2 bushels)
Straw	60 pounds (1 bale)
Wood chips	50 pounds (2 bushels)

Improving the Soil

Good aeration and drainage, as well as the ability to hold adequate moisture and nutrients, are key components of an ideal soil environment. Although there is no cookbook recipe for creating this ideal environment, these are some of the most important strategies for improving soil quality:

- Minimize soil compaction (do not walk on garden beds or work wet soil) (Figure 1–18).
- Reduce drainage problems.
- Decrease erosion.
- Plant a cover crop (Figure 1–19).
- Incorporate organic matter.
- Provide a 1- to 3-inch layer of organic mulch on the soil's surface.

Chemical Properties of Soil

There are strong relationships between soil physical properties and soil chemical properties. For example, surface area is directly related to chemical reactivity.

Cation Exchange Capacity

The negative ends of two magnets repel each other. The negative end of one magnet attracts the positive end of another magnet. This same principle affects the retention of plant nutrients in soil. Some plant nutrients are **cations**, which have a positive charge, and some are **anions**, which have a negative charge. Just like the opposite poles on magnets, cations will be attracted to anions.

Soil particles are similar to a magnet, attracting and retaining oppositely charged ions and holding them

against the downward movement of water through the soil profile. The nutrients held by the soil in this manner are called "exchangeable cations" and can be displaced or exchanged only by other cations that take their place. Thus, the negative charge of a soil is called the **cation exchange capacity** (CEC). Soils with high CEC not only hold more nutrients, they are better able to buffer or avoid rapid changes in the soil solution levels of these nutrients. A soil test will tell you the CEC number of your soil. Soils high in clay, silt, or organic matter will have a CEC number of 10 or greater, and no remediation is needed. Sandy soils will have a CEC number between 1 and 5. Adding organic matter to these soils will help increase the CEC.

Figure 1–18. To avoid compaction in the vegetable garden, recycled plastic lattice was laid down to walk on.
Sam Saunders, Flickr CC BY-SA - 2.0

Figure 1–19. A cover crop of crimson clover was planted in this annual flower bed. It is being turned under to add nutrients to the soil before planting.
Kathleen Moore CC BY - 2.0

Soil Testing

Soil testing provides valuable information on pH and plant-available nutrients. Test your soil before planting and every two to three years thereafter. Inexpensive soil test kits are unreliable. To accurately determine your soil characteristics and the proper amount of lime and fertilizer to apply, contact the NC Department of Agriculture and Consumer Services (NCDA&CS). The accuracy of these reports, however, depends on the quality of the sample submitted.

Tips for Collecting a Good Soil Sample

- Collect samples with stainless steel or chrome-plated tools. Using brass, bronze, or galvanized materials could contaminate the sample.
- The bucket in which material is collected should be made of plastic.
- Make sure the collection bucket is clean because even small amounts of residual lime or fertilizer can affect the test results.
- Avoid taking samples from areas that are obviously different from the norm, such as wet spots, compost piles, animal urine spots, and brush piles, or from under eaves or sites where trash has been burned.
- Remove large pieces of organic material, such as roots, stalks, and leaves, from the sample.
- For gardens, new lawns, and other cultivated areas, sample to the depth the soil has been, or will be, tilled. For established lawns, collect the sample 2 to 4 inches deep. For trees and shrubs, take a sample to a depth of 6 inches near the plant's drip line. Even if the soil looks the same, take separate samples for flower beds, veg-etable gardens, fruit orchards, shrub borders, and lawn areas.
- If using a trowel or spade, dig a hole, then take a slice of soil down one side. Repeat this procedure in five to eight spots for each area to be tested. Mix these cores together to obtain one composite sample. If the soil is very wet, it could be more difficult to mix, but do not attempt to heat the soil to dry it (Figure 1–20).
- Place about a pint of the composite sample for each area sampled in a soil testing box and label with a return address on the side of the box. Make up a code that will be easy to remember, such as "flawn" for front lawn, "byard" for backyard, or "veg" for vegetable garden. Any combination of letters and numbers can be used. Make notes about where the samples came from so that when you receive the results, you can easily identify how to treat the areas differently based on the results.
- Do not tape the boxes in any way. The lids are removed before the boxes go in the soil lab ovens, and tape makes this process difficult. Do not put the soil in a

Figure 1–20. Collect soil samples using plastic buckets, let soil air dry and screen out any big chunks (rocks, sticks). Mix several soil samples from the same location before sending it in for testing.
Dwight Sipler, Flickr CC BY - 2.0

plastic bag before placing it in the box as doing so will prevent proper drying in the lab oven.

Fill out the soil test report sheet, giving as much information as possible. The required items are name, address, county, sample codes, and the crops planned.

Too Much of a Good Thing: Nitrogen Leaching

Just like magnets, negative charges repel negative charges. Soils with high CEC tend not to hold anions. As a result, water moving through the soil profile will leach negatively charged nutrients, such as chloride, nitrate, and sulfate out of the root zone. This leaching can result in contamination of groundwater, streams, and lakes or have other environmental implications (Figure 1–21). Excess fertilizer becomes a contaminant and can have adverse effects on human health. The U.S. Environmental Protection Agency has set standards for nutrients in groundwater used for drinking water. This is one of many reasons that appropriate levels of fertilization are essential.

Figure 1–21. The milky blue-green swirls are a phytoplankton bloom in Lake Ontario as seen from space. This bloom is, in part, from nutrient loading (nitrogen and phosphorus) and runoff.
Jeff Schmaltz, MODIS Land Rapid Response Team, Flickr CC BY 2.0

Reports are sent by mail only if there is a special request submitted to the lab. Otherwise, provide an email address on the form to receive notification that the report is complete and online. Farmers also use the form, so some of the information requested may not apply to gardeners (pounds of lime per acre, for example). Forms and boxes are available from the NCDA&CS or any county Cooperative Extension center.

Learn more about collecting soil samples in *SoilFacts: Careful Soil Sampling – The Key to Reliable Soil Test Information* (NC State Extension publication number AG-439-30). For detailed information about the soil test results, refer to NCDA&CS Agronomic Division's *Understanding the Soil Test Report*.

How to Use a Soil Test Report

Fertilizing trees and shrubs in a landscape should be based on the amount of rainfall, soil type, the plant's age, the amount of current growth, and desired future growth. Overapplication of fertilizer to home landscapes wastes money, contributes to pollution in our rivers, streams, lakes, and estuaries, and may damage or kill desired plants.

In addition, excess fertilizer can increase the likelihood of disease problems, lead to weak growth, attract pests, and increase the amount of pruning needed to keep mature plants within appropriate boundaries. A soil test report provides accurate guidance for applying fertilizer. Figure 1–22 shows the main components of a soil test report.

Example Soil Test Reports

Depending on the crop indicated when the soil sample was submitted, the soil test report provides results in one of two ways:

- **Home garden scale:** Recommendations for pounds of lime and a rate and grade of fertilizer per 1,000 square feet (for example, an area 50 feet by 20 feet or 10 feet by 100 feet).
- **Farm/Forest scale:** Recommendations for tons of lime and a rate and grade of fertilizer per acre.

At the home gardener scale:

1. Measure the area to be limed or fertilized.
2. Multiply the length by the width to determine the number of square feet.

Main components of a Soil Report

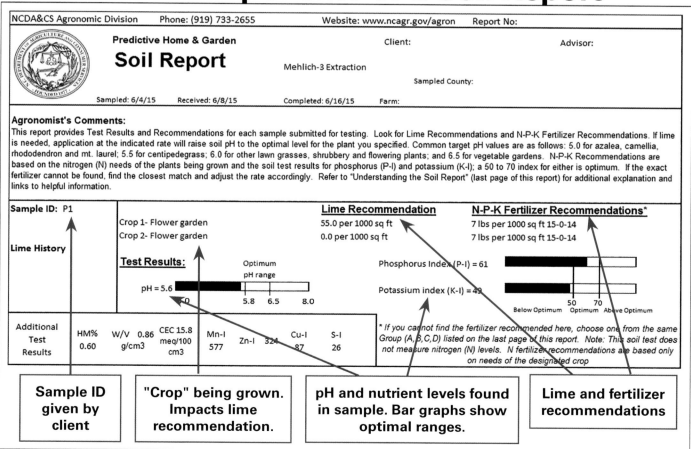

Figure 1–22. The main components of a soil test report.

3. Divide by 1,000 to obtain the number of units to be treated.
4. Multiply the number of units by the pounds of material to treat 1,000 square feet. This calculation will give the amount of fertilizer and lime needed (Figure 1–23).

Example 1: If the area is 500 feet by 20 feet, and the suggested lime or fertilizer treatment is 30 pounds per 1,000 square feet:

1. 500 × 20 = 10,000 square feet
2. Divide 10,000 by 1,000 = 10 units
3. Multiply 30 pounds times 10 units = 300 pounds of material (fertilizer or lime) per 10,000 square feet

Example 2: If the area is 10 feet by 15 feet, and the suggested lime or fertilizer rate is 10 pounds per 1,000 square feet:

1. 10 × 15 = 150 square feet
2. Divide 150 by 1,000 = 0.15
3. Multiply 10 pounds times 0.15 units = 1.5 pounds of material per 150 square feet

Or, look at fertilizer/lime calculations as ratios:

If 5 pounds of fertilizer are applied per 1,000 square feet, how many pounds should be applied to 150 square feet (using the garden size in Example 2)?

5 lb/1,000 sq ft = X lb/150 sq ft
5 lb × 150 sq ft /1,000 sq ft = X lb
750/1,000 = .75 lb

Example soil test reports and their recommended fertilizer applications can be found in Figures 1–24 through 1–27.

Soil pH

Soil pH is a measure of the soil's relative acidity or basicity. The pH scale ranges from 0 to 14. A pH of 7 is a neutral state, representing the value found in pure water. Values above 7.0 are basic, while values below 7.0 are acidic. The pH scale is logarithmic, meaning each unit has a 10-fold increase of acidity or basicity. Thus, compared to a pH of 7.0, a pH of 6.0 is ten times more acidic, and a pH of 5.0 is 100 times more acidic.

North Carolina soils tend to be acidic, as are nearly all soils in the Southeast. These soils were acidified over thousands of years by inputs of acids from atmospheric sources (carbonic, sulfuric, and nitric acid), the decay of

Lime and Fertilizer Recommendations

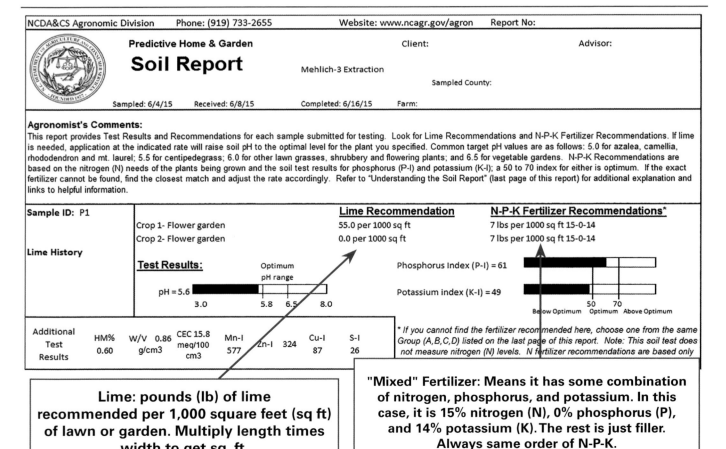

Figure 1–23. Soil test report example showing lime and fertilizer recommendations.

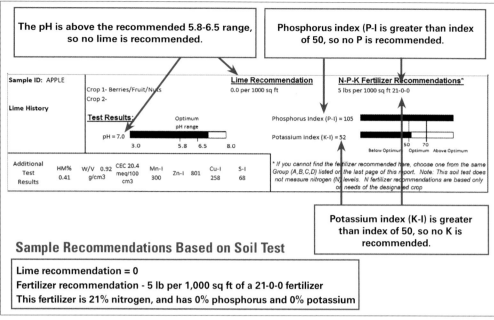

The pH is above the recommended 5.8-6.5 range, so no lime is recommended.

Phosphorus index (P-I is greater than index of 50, so no P is recommended.

Potassium index (K-I) is greater than index of 50, so no K is recommended.

Sample Recommendations Based on Soil Test

Lime recommendation = 0
Fertilizer recommendation - 5 lb per 1,000 sq ft of a 21-0-0 fertilizer
This fertilizer is 21% nitrogen, and has 0% phosphorus and 0% potassium

Figure 1–24. Soil test report example 2.

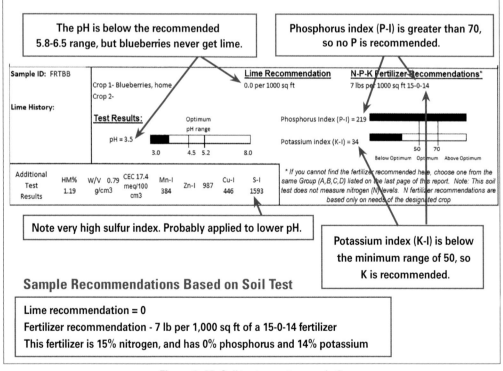

The pH is below the recommended 5.8-6.5 range, but blueberries never get lime.

Phosphorus index (P-I) is greater than 70, so no P is recommended.

Note very high sulfur index. Probably applied to lower pH.

Potassium index (K-I) is below the minimum range of 50, so K is recommended.

Sample Recommendations Based on Soil Test

Lime recommendation = 0
Fertilizer recommendation - 7 lb per 1,000 sq ft of a 15-0-14 fertilizer
This fertilizer is 15% nitrogen, and has 0% phosphorus and 14% potassium

Figure 1–25. Soil test report example 3.

Regardless of the fertilizers used, be aware that excess fertilizer can damage plants and move into our stormwater systems, which can cause serious environmental problems.

Incorporating Soil Amendments

Conditioning soil requires increasing organic matter content to 25% by volume. Incorporating a minimum of 2 inches of material into the top 6 inches of soil will create approximately 8 inches of amended soil. These additions raise the planting bed, improving drainage and making plants more visible. Incorporating more than 50% organic matter may negatively affect plant growth. Be careful when using organic material, making certain that it is fully composted and not merely aged. Microbes attracted to partially decomposed materials will compete with plants for nutrients, especially nitrogen and sulfur, resulting in nutrient deficiencies and poor plant growth.

The best organic matter amendments for clay soils are pine bark (less than ½-inch in diameter) and composted leaf mold. The following amendments are not recommended because they do not adequately improve the physical properties of clay soil: peat moss, sand, hardwood bark, wood chips, and pine straw.

For sandy soils, organic matter amendments, such as pine bark or compost, will improve water retention.

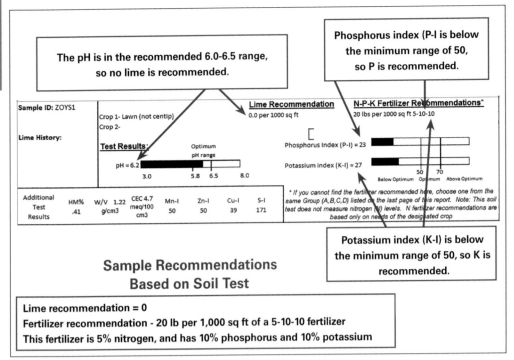

The pH is in the recommended 6.0-6.5 range, so no lime is recommended.

Phosphorus index (P-I is below the minimum range of 50, so P is recommended.

Sample ID: ZOYS1

Crop 1- Lawn (not centip)
Crop 2-

Lime History:

Test Results:

Optimum pH range

pH = 6.2

3.0   5.8   6.5   8.0

Lime Recommendation
0.0 per 1000 sq ft

N-P-K Fertilizer Recommendations*
20 lbs per 1000 sq ft 5-10-10

Phosphorus Index (P-I) = 23

Potassium index (K-I) = 27

50   70
Below Optimum Optimum Above Optimum

| Additional Test Results | HM% .41 | W/V 1.22 g/cm3 | CEC 4.7 meq/100 cm3 | Mn-I 50 | Zn-I 50 | Cu-I 39 | S-I 171 |

*If you cannot find the fertilizer recommended here, choose one from the same Group (A,B,C,D) listed on the last page of this report. Note: This soil test does not measure nitrogen (N) levels. N fertilizer recommendations are based only on needs of the designated crop

Potassium index (K-I) is below the minimum range of 50, so K is recommended.

Sample Recommendations Based on Soil Test

Lime recommendation = 0
Fertilizer recommendation - 20 lb per 1,000 sq ft of a 5-10-10 fertilizer
This fertilizer is 5% nitrogen, and has 10% phosphorus and 10% potassium

Figure 1–26. Soil test report example 4.

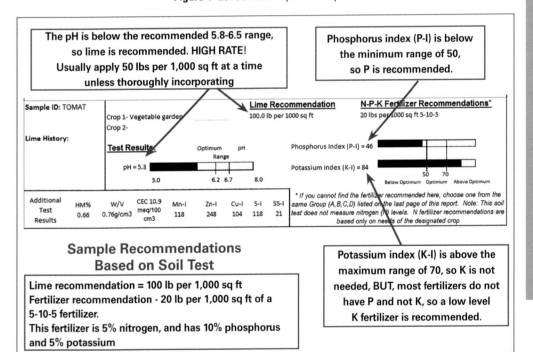

The pH is below the recommended 5.8-6.5 range, so lime is recommended. HIGH RATE! Usually apply 50 lbs per 1,000 sq ft at a time unless thoroughly incorporating

Phosphorus index (P-I) is below the minimum range of 50, so P is recommended.

Sample ID: TOMAT

Crop 1- Vegetable garden
Crop 2-

Lime History:

Test Results:

Optimum pH Range

pH = 5.3

3.0   6.2   6.7   8.0

Lime Recommendation
100.0 lb per 1000 sq ft

N-P-K Fertilizer Recommendations*
20 lbs per 1000 sq ft 5-10-5

Phosphorus Index (P-I) = 46

Potassium index (K-I) = 84

50   70
Below Optimum Optimum Above Optimum

| Additional Test Results | HM% 0.66 | W/V 0.76g/cm3 | CEC 10.9 meq/100 cm3 | Mn-I 118 | Zn-I 248 | Cu-I 104 | S-I 118 | SS-I 21 |

*If you cannot find the fertilizer recommended here, choose one from the same Group (A,B,C,D) listed on the last page of this report. Note: This soil test does not measure nitrogen (N) levels. N fertilizer recommendations are based only on needs of the designated crop

Potassium index (K-I) is above the maximum range of 70, so K is not needed, BUT, most fertilizers do not have P and not K, so a low level K fertilizer is recommended.

Sample Recommendations Based on Soil Test

Lime recommendation = 100 lb per 1,000 sq ft
Fertilizer recommendation - 20 lb per 1,000 sq ft of a 5-10-5 fertilizer.
This fertilizer is 5% nitrogen, and has 10% phosphorus and 5% potassium

Figure 1–27.
Above, soil test report example 5.

Figure 1–28.
At left, a drop spreader has a cylindrical spinning mechanism that releases fertilizer directly below the spreader as it is pushed along.
Chris Alberti, Ira Rozenski, CC BY - 2.0

Calibrating a Spreader

Fertilizers are more effective if they are applied at the proper rate and with uniform coverage. To accomplish this, calibrate the spreader, which requires a little labor and math.

The two types of spreaders used to apply fertilizer and lime are drop spreaders (Figure 1–28) and rotary spreaders (Figure 1–29). The amount of fertilizer that is spread depends on the opening setting, the type of fertilizer, and the speed at which the spreader is pushed. The drop spreader has a series of holes at the base that can be adjusted to apply different amounts of material. With the rotary spreader, the fertilizer falls into a rotating plate and is spread by the centrifugal force of the plate spinning. Instructions for calibrating a spreader should be available on the Internet at the home page for the spreader manufacturer.

Figure 1–29.
Below, a rotary spreader.
Kathleen Moore, CC BY - 2.0

plant and animal residues, and removal of basic cations by the natural processes of leaching. If our native soils are not limed (basic), the pH is often in the 4.5 to 5.5 range.

Nutrient Availability and pH

The optimum pH for a plant varies with organic matter content and plant type. Plant nutrient availability is strongly tied to the pH in the soil solution (Figure 1–30). Decreasing soil pH directly increases the solubility of the plant nutrients manganese (Mn), zinc (Zn), copper (Cu), and iron (Fe). Acidic soils make these nutrients more available. At pH values less than about 5.5, toxic levels of Mn, Zn, or aluminum (Al), a non-nutrient element very common in our southern soils, may be released. The impact of pH on nutrient availability is very important—both for maximum plant availability and to avoid potentially toxic levels at very low or very high pH.

The optimal pH for growth differs among plants. For example, regardless of organic matter content, azaleas and blueberries are well-suited for a soil pH of about 5.0. In contrast, asparagus can tolerate a basic soil with a pH up to 8.0. A soil pH of 6.5 to 7.0 is often considered "ideal" for most plants, but a little research can help you identify the proper pH for the plants you wish to grow. After obtaining a soil test report, you can take measures to adjust soil pH or select plants that will thrive at the current pH. Extreme pH measures of 4.0 (acidic) or 10.0 (basic) will support little plant life and are very difficult to modify.

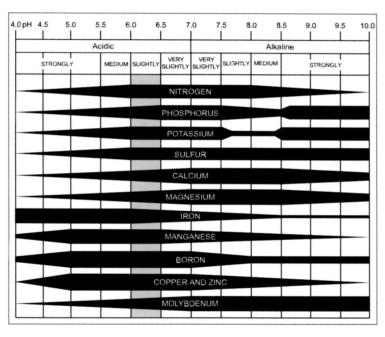

Figure 1–30. Nutrient availability as affected by soil pH. The wider areas represent greater availability.
CoolKoon, Wikimedia CC BY-4.0

Adjusting pH

If the soil pH is too basic for the desired plant, incorporating an acidic soil amendment such as pine bark or compost, or applying elemental sulfur, will lower soil pH. Apply sulfur with caution; too much can harm plants.

If the soil pH is too acidic, apply lime to raise the soil pH. There are two general classes of liming materials: calcitic (without magnesium) and dolomitic (with magnesium). Calcitic lime is composed of calcium carbonate ($CaCO_3$)

and can be used on soils high in magnesium. Dolomitic lime is a mixture of calcium and magnesium carbonates ($CaCO_3$ and $MgCO_3$), which is the preferred liming material for soils low in magnesium.

Knowing the soil type or even the current pH is not enough to determine the amount of lime needed. The texture of the soil, organic matter content, crop to be grown, target pH, level of soil acidity, CEC, type and amount of clay, and the current pH are all factors to consider in adjusting pH. Soils low in organic matter or high in sand content require less lime to change the pH than clay soils or those with high organic matter.

Lime is heavily regulated in North Carolina. Lime must be labeled with a guarantee of percent calcium and magnesium. The percent of calcium carbonate equivalent also must be included on the label, as well as the pounds of material that equal 1 ton of standard lime (Figure 1–31).

Each type of lime must meet a screening requirement for particle size. Lime pellets are formed from lime that has been finely ground. The pelleted product is less dusty and easier to apply, but is slower to react with the soil.

Lime moves slowly in the soil and neutralizes acidity only in the area where it is applied. To be effective, it should be spread and thoroughly incorporated. It takes several months for lime to react in the soil, which is why it is good to soil test and plan for proper soil pH management.

For established lawns, gardens, and ornamentals that require lime, apply the recommended amount up to 50 pounds of lime per 1,000 square feet in one application to the soil's surface. For recommended rates over 50 pounds, wait several months to make a repeat application to avoid a surface buildup of lime. For new plantings where the area will be tilled, apply the entire recommended amount at one time.

Learn more in *SoilFacts: Soil Acidity and Liming: Basic Information for Farmers and Gardeners* (NC State Extension publication number AG-439-51).

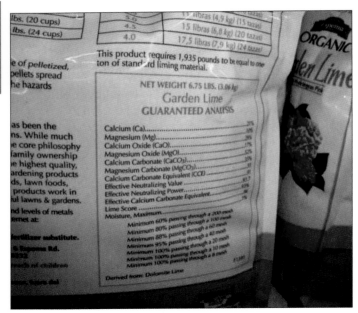

Figure 1–31. Label from a lime bag.
Kathleen Moore, CC BY - 2.0

Plant Nutrition & Fertilization

Many people confuse plant nutrition with fertilization. Plant nutrition refers to the needs of the plant and how a plant uses the basic chemical elements. Fertilization is the term used when these elements are supplied to the soil as amendments. Adding fertilizer during unfavorable growing conditions will not enhance plant growth and may actually harm or kill plants.

To complete their life cycle, plants need 17 essential nutrients, each in varying amounts (Table 1–3). Of these nutrients, three are found in air and water: carbon (C), hydrogen (H), and oxygen (O). Combined, C, H, and O account for about 94% of a plant's weight. The other 6% of a plant's weight includes the remaining 14 nutrients, all of which must come from the soil. Of these, nitrogen (N), phosphorus (P), and potassium (K), the primary **macronutrients**, are the most needed. Magnesium (Mg),

calcium (Ca), and sulfur (S), the secondary macronutrients, are next in the amount needed. The eight other elements — boron, chlorine, copper, iron, manganese, molybdenum, nickel, and zinc — are called **micronutrients** because they are needed in much smaller amounts than the macronutrients.

Soil Nutrients

For a plant to absorb an element, it must be in a chemical form used by the plant and dissolved in the soil water. In addition to those nutrients already dissolved in soil water, nutrients can be present in the soil in these forms:

- Undissolved or granular form, as from newly applied fertilizer
- Chemicals bound to soil particles
- The chemical structure of soil organic matter released by microbial decomposition

Undissolved or granular nutrients, and those that are chemically bound to soil particles, are not immediately useful, although they have the potential to benefit the plant. For many plant nutrients, the soil acts as a bank. Withdrawals are made from the soil solution, much as you would withdraw money from a checking account. The undissolved pool of soil nutrients is like a savings account. When checking funds are low, transfers are made from the savings account to the checking account. When a checking account is flush with money, some can be moved to savings for long-term retention. In the same way, for many plant nutrients, when the soil solution has excess nutrients, some bind to the soil to become temporarily unavailable, and some react with other chemical elements to form insoluble minerals, which can dissolve again later.

Several factors improve a plant's ability to use nutrients:
- **Type of soil:** The more clay and organic matter a soil has, the higher its CEC will be, and the more cationic (positively charged) nutrients it will retain.

Table 1–3. Relative Amounts (out of 100) of the Essential Nutrients Required by Most Plants

Primary Nutrients	Amount	Secondary Nutrients	Amount	Micronutrients	Amount
Carbon (C)	45	Calcium (Ca)	0.5	Iron (Fe)	0.01
Oxygen (O)	45	Magnesium (Mg)	0.2	Chlorine (Cl)	0.01
Hydrogen (H)	6	Sulfur (S)	0.1	Manganese (Mn)	0.005
Nitrogen (N)	1.5			Boron (B)	0.002
Potassium (K)	1			Zinc (Zn)	0.002
Phosphorus (P)	0.2			Copper (Cu)	0.0006
				Molybdenum (Mo)	0.00001
Amounts unknown for Nickel (Ni) and Cobalt (Co)					

- **Soil pH:** The pH affects how tightly nutrients are bound to soil particles. If the soil pH is extremely high (basic) or very low (acidic), many nutrients become inaccessible to the plant because they are no longer dissolved in the soil water.
- **Types of nutrients in the soil:** Some nutrients affect the availability of other nutrients. In fact, an apparent deficiency of one nutrient may actually be caused by a large amount of another.
- **Amount of soil water:** Too much rain leaches nutrients from the soil. If there is too little water, the nutrients cannot dissolve and move into the plant.
- **Anything that affects the plant's growth:** If growing conditions are good, a plant will absorb nutrients from the soil. If the plant experiences extremes in temperature, incorrect light levels, or waterlogged or compacted soil, it will have a limited ability to absorb nutrients. Also, plants in dormant stages absorb few nutrients.

The presence or absence of nutrients can cause outward symptoms to appear on the plant. Table 1–4 reviews the essential nutrients for plant growth and symptoms that may appear if a plant is suffering a deficiency or an excess of that nutrient.

Fertilizers

Fertilizers provide some elements that might be lacking in the soil and stimulate healthy, vigorous growth. How much and when to apply fertilizers should be based on observing plant performance, a reliable soil test, and an understanding of the factors that affect growth: light, water, temperature, pests, and nutrition. Simply applying fertilizer because a plant is not growing adequately will not solve many plant problems (insects, disease, or poor drainage, for example), and, in fact, excess nitrogen can often increase insect and disease infestation.

All fertilizers are labeled with three numbers, giving the percentage (by weight) of nitrogen (N), phosphorus (P), and potassium (K). This is referred to as the fertilizer grade.

A 100-pound bag of fertilizer labeled 0-20-10 has 0 pounds of N, 20 pounds of P (reported as P_2O_5), 10 pounds of K (reported as K_2O), and 70 pounds of filler. Filler is added to make the fertilizer easier to spread and to reduce the likelihood of burning plants with too much fertilizer (the fertilizer salts can pull water out of the plant). A fertilizer may also contain secondary macronutrients or micronutrients not listed on the label because the manufacturer does not want to guarantee their exact amounts.

Fertilizers can be divided into two broad categories: natural and synthetic.

Natural fertilizers are commonly misnamed "organic." "Natural fertilizers" is a more accurate description because these materials can be both complex chemical substances containing carbon (organic materials) or inorganic ores, such as rock phosphate, which are mined. Natural fertilizers containing organic materials include manures and composts, animal byproducts (such as bone meal, blood meal, feather meal), and seed meals. Natural fertilizers that are inorganic ores include potassium and lime.

Natural fertilizers typically release nutrients at a slower rate and over a longer period than synthetic fertilizers because microorganisms are involved in a breakdown and release cycle called mineralization. Moisture, temperature, and the microbial species and populations in the soil affect mineralization. Some water-soluble natural fertilizers, such as fish emulsion, are available when rapid nutrient delivery is desired.

When using natural fertilizers, it is helpful to incorporate them and provide adequate moisture for active microbial populations.

When packaged as fertilizers, natural fertilizers will have the nutrient analysis stated on the labels. How much to use varies with the nutrient content of the material. The age of the material is also a factor. Producers are not required by law to state the nutrient content on bulk organic materials, such as compost, manure, and sludges. The source of these materials should be investigated and possible analysis performed at the Plant, Waste, Solution, and Media Lab at the NCDA&CS Agronomic Division before applying large amounts to a home garden.

The age of the natural fertilizers is another important factor. When natural material decays and is rained on, it loses nutrients, especially potassium and, to some extent, nitrogen. Even natural sources of nutrients can be overapplied and damage plants. Fresh manures, for example, may injure plants by adding excessive nitrogen or potassium, especially when applied in large quantities.

Natural fertilizers can be expensive if applied in amounts adequate to supply nutrients for good plant growth, but have the added benefit of improving soil structure and plant vigor. When applying natural fertilizers, calculate as closely as possible the amounts of nutrients being supplied. Always err on the low side of application rates, then test the soil and augment as recommended on the soil test report. The nutrient content may need to be supplemented with other natural or synthetic materials to achieve a balanced ratio of nutrients.

Synthetic fertilizers are made through industrial processes or mined from deposits in the earth. They are purified, mixed, blended, and altered for easy handling and application. Most are noncarbonaceous chemicals from non- living sources and are usually cheaper than natural fertilizers. In general, nutrients are more rapidly available to plants because they are more water-soluble or in a form plants can use. The disadvantage is that it may be easier to overapply a synthetic fertilizer than a natural one, which may result in fertilizer burn. In addition, synthetic fertilizers may not support beneficial microbial populations to the same extent as natural fertilizers.

Special-purpose fertilizers are packaged for plants such as camellias, rhododendrons, and azaleas (Figure 1–32). Some of the compounds used in these fertilizers have an acid reaction that can be beneficial to acid-loving plants if the soil they are growing in is naturally neutral or alkaline; how-ever, most soils in North Carolina are usually acidic so these special fertilizers are unnecessary.

Fertilizer spikes or pellets are fertilizers compressed into a form placed in the soil or pots (Figure1–33). They are convenient, but are expensive per unit of fertilizer and do not provide uniform distribu-tion. Nutrients are often concentrated around the spikes or pellets.

Figure 1–32.
A fertilizer specially formulated for acidic plants such as azaleas or rhododendrons. These fertilizers are usually unnecessary in North Carolina's acidic soils.
Kathleen Moore, CC BY - 2.0

Liquid fertilizer can be purchased as a dry powder or as a concen-trated liquid (Figure 1–34). Liquid fertilizers are frequently used for houseplants or as a starter solution for transplants. They tend to be more expensive per unit of fertilizer because they are made from refined chemicals.

Figure 1–33.
Fertilizer spikes are compressed fertilizer that can be pushed into the soil.
Kathleen Moore, CC BY - 2.0

Foliar fertilizers are dry powders or concentrated liquids that are mixed with water and sprayed on plants (Figure 1–35). Foliar feeding is used when insufficient fertilizer was applied before planting, when a quick growth response is wanted, when micronutrients are locked in the soil, or when the soil is too cold for the plant to use fertilizer in the soil. Foliar-applied nutrients are ab-sorbed and used by the plant quite rapidly. They are expensive per unit of nutrient and only give short-term fertilization (completely absorbed within one to two days). Relying totally on foliar fertilization can be time consum-ing because the fertilizer must be applied regularly. Improper foliar application of fertilizers can also lead to plant tissue burn. Learn more about fertilizer usage and nutrient concentrations in the *North Carolina Agricultural Chemi-cals Manual*, Chapter IV – Fertilizer Use.

Figure 1–34.
Liquid fertilizer can be found at any local garden center.
Kathleen Moore, CC BY - 2.0

Figure 1–35. Foliar fertilizers are dry powders mixed with liquid and then sprayed on the leaves of plants.
Jerry Norbury, Flickr CC BY-ND - 2.0

Incomplete fertilizers can be used separately or com-bined to supply the needed nutrients, often at a reduced cost compared to using a complete fertilizer. For exam-ple, gardeners who have a soil with sufficient P and K can save money by applying a nitrogen-only fertilizer, such as ammonium nitrate (34-0-0). If a soil test indi-cates N and K are needed, but not P, use an appropriate amount of ammonium nitrate and muriate of **potash** (0-0-60), a naturally occurring material composed almost entirely of potassium, processed to remove impurities and concentrate the product. If a soil needs only P, use triple super phosphate (0-46-0), or for an organic nutrient source apply bone meal (approximately 3-15-0; note that this will add some N) or compost.

Plant Nutrients and the Environment

Fertilizer misuse causes environmental and water quality issues. Nitrogen fertilizers, for instance, break down into ammonium and nitrate. The nitrate form of N, while essential for plant growth, is highly mobile and can move through the soil after rainfall or irrigation and contaminate drinking water supplies. Phosphorus holds tightly to soil particles and does not leach through the soil, but affects water quality through runoff and soil erosion. Excess nitrogen and phosphorus are associated with algal blooms (heavy growth of aquatic plants) and limited oxygen, and cause fish kills in lakes, bays, and non-flowing water bodies.

There are several ways to reduce fertilizers' impacts on water quality:

- Apply only materials that are recommended based on results of a soil test. If possible, use slow-release fertilizers and incorporate into the soil. Avoid applying excess nitrogen and phosphorus fertilizer.
- Calibrate fertilizer spreaders properly and clean spreaders over the lawn area instead of a hard surface.
- Keep the amount of hard surfaces in a landscape to a minimum. When installing a new sidewalk or patio, consider using gravel, porous concrete, stepping stones, wood decking, or bricks on a sand base (Figure 1–36).
- Avoid applying fertilizer to hard surfaces, such as sidewalks, patios, driveways, and streets. Sweep up material that falls on hard surfaces.
- Maximize water absorption by aerating lawns and incorporating organic matter in planting beds and gardens.

Figure 1–36. This homeowner used permeable pavers for their driveway allowing grass to grow in the spaces and reducing runoff from the property. Center for Watershed Protection, Inc., Flickr CC BY - 2.0

- Prevent runoff by turning off irrigation when the soil is no longer absorbing water.
- Avoid applying fertilizer in natural drainage areas or ditches.
- Minimize soil erosion by using ground covers, windbreaks, terraces, and mulches.
- Mulch under trees and shrubs to reduce impact of falling water.
- Maintain a lawn border around planting areas and plant a grass strip between rows in fruit and vegetable gardens.
- Plant cover crops on bare soil, such as barren vegetable gardens.
- Use a rain barrel under drains to collect runoff and direct excess runoff from roofs onto grassy areas (Figure 1–37).

Figure 1–37. A rain barrel catches runoff from a roof top and can be used to water plants in the landscape. Arlington County, VA, Flickr CC BY-SA - 2.0

When to Apply Fertilizer

Soil type affects the frequency of fertilizer application. Sandy soils require more frequent applications of smaller amounts of nitrogen and potash than do clay soils because these nutrients leach more readily in sandy soils. Other factors that affect application frequency include the plant to be grown, the amount of plant growth desired, the amount of water, and the type and release rate of fertilizer applied.

The best time to apply fertilizer and the most effective method of applying it depends on the type of plants being grown. Leafy vegetables require more nitrogen than root crops. Corn is a heavy nitrogen feeder and may require several small nitrogen applications when actively growing. Most established woody plants perform well without fertilization, or with just one application per year. Young plants may benefit from several light applications of fertilizer per year.

Fertilizer is needed when plants are actively growing, never when they are dormant. Nitrogen application will have its greatest effect three to four weeks after application. Excess or improperly timed nitrogen can delay flowering and fruiting or promote tender new growth vulnerable to frost or freeze damage.

Research has shown it is best to broadcast or incorporate fertilizer uniformly over an area rather than concentrating fertilizer in holes or bands in the soil. The most effective method of fertilizing a large area is with a fertilizer spreader; for home gardens, hand fertilization works fine. For new plantings, incorporate fertilizer into the soil and mix it thoroughly. For established plantings, surface application is appropriate.

When fertilizing from overhead, make certain plant foliage is dry and use a broom to brush fertilizer off the foliage, or water thoroughly after applying fertilizer to remove it from plant leaves to prevent burn spots. It is not necessary to remove mulch when fertilizing; irrigation or rainfall will carry fertilizer to the roots. Fertilization should be reduced or delayed during dry weather because the salts in the fertilizer can burn roots if there is inadequate moisture.

Table 1–4. Essential Nutrients for Plant Growth

MACRONUTRIENTS

Nutrient	Why Nutrient is Needed	Deficiency Symptoms	Excess Symptoms	Comments
Nitrogen (N)	Responsible for rapid foliage growth and green color Easily leaches from soil foliage (chlorosis) Mobile in plant, moving to new growth	Reduced growth (Figure 1–38) Light-green to yellow foliage (chlorosis) Reds and purples may intensify with some plants Reduced lateral breaks Symptoms appear first on older growth	Succulent growth; leaves are dark green, thick, and brittle Poor fruit set Excess ammonia can induce calcium deficiency	High N under low light can cause leaf curl Uptake inhibited by high P levels
Phosphorus (P)	Promotes root formation and growth Affects quality of seed, fruit, and flower production Increased disease resistance Does not leach from soil readily Mobile in plant, moving to new growth	Reduced growth Leaves dark-green; purple or red color in older leaves, especially on the underside of the leaf along the veins (Figure 1–39) Leaf shape may be distorted Thin stems Limited root growth	Shows up as micro-nutrient deficiency of Zn, Fe, or Co	Rapidly fixed on soil particles When applied under acid conditions, fixed with Fe, Mn, and Al High P interferes with micronutrient and N absorption Used in relatively small amounts when compared to N and K Availability is lowest in cold soils
Potassium (K)	Helps plants overcome drought stress Improves winter hardiness Increases disease resistance Improves the rigidity of stalks Leaches from soil Mobile in plant	Reduced growth Shortened internodes Margins of older leaves become chlorotic and burned Necrotic (dead) spots on older leaves (Figure 1–40) Reduction of lateral breaks and tendency to wilt readily Poorly developed root systems Weak stalks	Causes N deficiency and may affect the uptake of other nutrients	High N/low K favors vegetative growth Low N/high K promotes reproductive growth (flower, fruit) Calcium excess impedes uptake of K
Magnesium (Mg)	Leaches from sandy soil Mobile in plant	Reduction in growth Yellowish, bronze, or reddish color of older leaves, while veins remain green (Figure 1–41) Leaf margins may curl downward or upward with a puckering effect	Interferes with Ca uptake Small necrotic spots in older leaves Smaller veins in older leaves may turn brown In advanced stage, young leaves may be spotted	Mg is commonly deficient in foliage plants because it is leached and not replaced Epsom salts at a rate of 1 teaspoon per gallon may be used two times a year Mg can be absorbed by leaves if sprayed in a weak solution Dolomitic limestone can be applied in outdoor situations to rectify a deficiency

(Continued)

Figure 1–38. Nitrogen deficiency in Bacopa. Note the severely reduced growth and light green-yellow leaves. Paul Nelson

Figure 1–39. Phosphorus deficiency in lettuce. Scot Nelson, Flickr CC0

Figure 1–40. Potassium deficiency in *Dracaena halapepe*. Scot Nelson, Flickr CC0

Figure 1–41. Magnesium deficiency appears in first in older leaves. On this bean plant, the veins remain green while the rest of the leaf turns yellow. Paul Nelson

Table 1–4. Essential Nutrients for Plant Growth *continued*

MACRONUTRIENTS

Nutrient	Why Nutrient is Needed	Deficiency Symptoms	Excess Symptoms	Comments
Calcium (Ca)	Moderately leachable Limited mobility in plant Essential for growth of shoot and root tips	Inhibition of bud growth Roots can turn black and rot Young leaves are scalloped and abnormally green Leaf tips may stick together Cupping of maturing leaves Blossom end rot of many fruits (Figure 1–42) Pits on root vegetables; stem structure is weak Premature shedding of fruit and buds	Interferes with Mg absorption High Ca usually causes high pH	Ca is rarely deficient if the correct pH is maintained
Sulfur (S)	Leachable Not mobile Contributes to odor and taste of some vegetables	Rarely deficient General yellowing of the young leaves, then the entire plant (Figure 1–43) Veins lighter in color than adjoining interveinal area Roots and stems are small, hard, and woody	Sulfur excess is usually in the form of air pollution	Sulfur excess is difficult to control, but rarely a problem

(Continued)

Table 1–4. Essential Nutrients for Plant Growth *continued*

MICRONUTRIENTS

Nutrient	Why Nutrient is Needed	Deficiency Symptoms	Excess Symptoms	Comments
Iron (Fe)	Accumulates in the oldest leaves and is relatively immobile Necessary for the maintenance of chlorophyll	Interveinal chlorosis primarily on young tissue, which may become white (Figure 1–44) Fe deficiency may occur even if Fe is in the soil when: soil is high in Ca; soil is poorly drained; soil is oxygen deficient; nematodes attack roots; or soil is high in Mn, pH, or P Fe should be added in the chelate form; the type of chelate needed depends upon the soil pH Foliar fertilization will temporarily correct the deficiency May be deficient in centipede grass where pH and P are high	Rare except on flooded soils	
Boron (B)	Important in enabling photosynthetic transfer Very immobile in plants	Failure to set seed Internal breakdown of fruit or vegetable Death of apical buds, giving rise to witches' broom Failure of root tip to elongate normally Young leaves become thick, leathery, and chlorotic (Figure 1–45) Rust-colored cracks and corking on young stems, petioles, and flower stalks (such as heart rot of beets, stern crack of celery) Breakdown occurs at the base of the youngest shoots	Tips and edges of leaves exhibit necrotic spots coalescing into a marginal scorch (similar to high-soluble salts) (Figure 1–46) Oldest leaves are affected first Can occur in low pH soils Plants are easily damaged by excess application Looks like Mg deficiency, green veins on a yellow leaf.	
Zinc (Zn)	Needed for enzyme activity	Young leaves are very small, sometimes missing leaf blades Short internodes Distorted or puckered leaf margins Interveinal chlorosis	Severe stunting, reddening Poor germination Older leaves wilt Entire leaf is affected by chlorosis; edges and main vein often retain more color Can be caused by galvanized metal	

(Continued)

Table 1–4. Essential Nutrients for Plant Growth *continued*

MICRONUTRIENTS

Nutrient	Why Nutrient is Needed	Deficiency Symptoms	Excess Symptoms	Comments
Copper (Cu)	Needed for enzyme activity	New growth small, misshapen, wilted (Figure 1–47) In some species, young leaves may show interveinal chlorosis while tips of older leaves remain green	Can occur at low pH Shows up as Fe deficiency	
Manganese (Mn)	Needed for enzyme activity	Interveinal chlorosis with smallest leaves remaining green, producing a checkered effect (Figure 1–48) Gray or tan spots usually develop in chlorotic areas Dead spots may drop out of the leaf Poor bloom size and color Induced by excessively high pH	Reduction in growth, brown spotting on leaves Shows up as Fe deficiency Found under strongly acidic conditions	
Molybdenum (Mo)	Needed for enzyme activity	Interveinal chlorosis on older or midstem leaves (Figure 1–49) Twisted leaves whiptail Marginal scorching and rolling or cupping of leaves Nitrogen deficiency symptoms may develop	Intense yellow or purple color in leaves Rarely observed	
Chlorine (Cl)	Needed for enzyme activity	Wilted leaves, which become bronze, then chlorotic, then die Club roots	Salt injury Leaf burn May increase succulence	
Cobalt (Co)	Needed by plants recently established Essential for nitrogen fixation	Little is known about its deficiency symptoms	Little is known about its toxicity symptoms	
Nickel (Ni)	Needed by plants recently established Essential for seed development	Little is known about its deficiency symptoms	Little is known about its toxicity symptoms	

Figure 1–42. Calcium deficiency in tomatoes.
Scot Nelson, Flickr CC0

Figure 1–45. This geranium is deficient in boron which is evident by the thick, leathery, chlorotic younger leaves.
Paul Nelson

Figure 1–43. Sulfur deficiency rarely occurs, but on this strawflower it has affected the shoot size and leaves with a yellowing of the veins.
Paul Nelson

Figure 1–46. Boron toxicity on a rose bush. Can look like the inverted "V" of green on a yellow leaf that is characteristic of magnesium deficiency, but uptake of too much boron by theplant often occurs when pH is too low.
Malcolm Manners, Flickr CC BY - 2.0

Figure 1–44. Iron deficiency causing interveinal chlorosis on young leaves.
Scot Nelson, Flickr CC0

Figure 1–47. Copper deficiency in this daisy appears as small misshapen growth.
Paul Nelson

Figure 1–48. Manganese deficiency in a chrysanthemum exhibited as reduced growth while the youngest leaves remain green.
Paul Nelson

Figure 1–49. Molybdenum deficiency on poinsettia.
Paul Nelson

Fertilizer Terms

Fertilizer analysis: The minimum amount of each element in a fertilizer as stated on the label, such as 16-4-8.

Fertilizer ratio: The relative proportion of N, P_2O_5, and K_2O. The ratios of 16-4-8 and 8-2-4 are both 4:1:2, which means 4 parts nitrogen to 1 part phosphorus to 2 parts potassium.

Balanced fertilizer: A fertilizer containing equal parts of each major element, such as 10-10-10.

Complete fertilizer: A fertilizer containing nitrogen, phosphorus, and potassium. Examples of commonly used fertilizers are 10-10-10, 16-4-8, and 12-4-8.

Incomplete fertilizer: A fertilizer missing one or two of the macronutrients, such as 0-20-0.

Weed and feed fertilizers: A combination of fertilizer and herbicide. They are often used on lawns to prevent certain weeds from germinating, or to kill existing broadleaf weeds.

High analysis: A fertilizer containing 30% or more active nutrients, such as ammonium nitrate 33-0-0. The cost per bag is usually more, but the cost per pound of nutrient is less, lowering the cost for fertilizing a given area.

The Biology of Soil

There is more life below the soil surface than there is above. Soil life consists of burrowing animals, such as moles and earthworms, insects, and other soil creatures that are difficult or impossible to see without a microscope, such as mites, springtails, **nematodes**, **viruses**, algae, bacteria, yeast, **actinomycetes**, **fungi**, and **protozoa**. There are about 50 billion microbes in 1 tablespoon of soil. In a typical soil, each gram (what a standard paperclip weighs) likely contains these organisms, listed from largest to smallest:

- Nematodes—10 to 5,000
- Algae—1,000 to 500,000
- Protozoa—1,000 to 500,000
- Fungi—5,000 to 1,000,000
- Actinomycetes—1,000,000 to 20,000,000
- Bacteria—3,000,000 to 500,000,000

Soil-dwellers move through the soil, creating channels that improve aeration and drainage. Nematodes and protozoa swim in the film of water around soil particles and feed on bacteria. Mites eat fungi, and fungi decompose soil organic matter. The microorganisms' primary role is to break down organic matter to obtain energy. Microorganisms help release essential nutrients and carbon dioxide and perform key roles in nitrogen fixation, the nitrogen and phosphorus cycles, denitrification, immobilization, and mineralization. Microbes must have a constant supply of organic matter, or their numbers will decline. Conditions that favor soil life also promote plant growth.

Unfavorable soil conditions, such as high temperatures, compaction, or oversaturation can injure beneficial soil life. This can lead to a proliferation of disease-causing fungi, bacteria, or viruses. To read more about common soil diseases see chapter 5, "Diseases." Plants that are stressed by disease are often more susceptible to insect damage. More information on insects can be found in chapter 4, "Insects." To learn more about managing insects and diseases, please see chapter 8, "IPM."

To promote soil organisms, incorporate organic matter, till as little as possible, minimize soil compaction, maintain favorable soil pH and fertility, and use organic mulch on the soil surface.

Frequently Asked Questions

1. *Do I have to get a soil test report or can you just tell me how much fertilizer to add?*
A soil test is the only accurate way to determine the amount of fertilizer needed for each individual yard. A soil test is a process by which nutrients are chemically removed from the soil and measured for their "plant available content" within the sample. The quantity of nutrients extracted is used to determine the type and amount of fertilizer to be recommended. The pH and acidity of the soil sample is also measured and used to determine if lime is needed and how much. Soil testing is provided by the NCDA&CS. There is a small fee for each soil sample submitted to the NCDA&CS during December through March, which is the peak season for soil testing in North Carolina. There is no fee for soil samples submitted to the NCDA&CS during the rest of the year (April through November). Samples must be mailed in to the NCDA&CS and boxes are available at their main office, 4300 Reedy Creek Road, Raleigh, NC, or at any county Cooperative Extension center. More information and forms are available on the NCDA&CS website.

2. *How often should soil be tested?*
If a soil test report indicates the pH and nutrient levels are in the range needed for plants to be grown, you may not need to sample every year. As a general rule, sandy-textured soils should be tested every two to three years and clay soils every three to four years. However, if nutrient or pH levels are excessively high or low, you should submit a sample every year to determine how much improvement has been achieved and what additional amendments should be made. In addition, if problems occur during the growing season, collect a sample and have it analyzed.

3. *Can I add Epsom salts to my plants?*
Epsom salt (magnesium sulfate) can sometimes be beneficial, especially in sandy soils that may be low in sulfur or magnesium. However, the best recourse is to rely upon a soil test and make adjustments to the soil pH and nutrient content based on the soil test report's lime and fertilizer recommendations.

4. *Why are my (azalea, blueberries, maple, rhododendron) leaves yellow?*
Ruling out water issues, the likely culprit is pH. Azaleas, blueberries, maples, and rhododendrons are acid-loving plants requiring a pH of 4.5–6.0 to thrive. Knowing your soil pH will help you select plants that will thrive in your soil. Altering the pH of a soil is difficult, but can be done in small areas. Refer back to the section on soil pH for more information.

5. *My shrubs/trees are wilting, the leaves are brown on the edges, and are falling off. What is causing this?*
This could be the result of salt injury due to improper application of fertilizer. High salts decrease a plant's ability to extract water from the soil, and salts can move through the plant's vascular system to the leaves where the water evaporates and concentrates the salt to toxic levels. Plants may recover from salt/fertilizer injury if high levels of salts are reduced through repeated, deep irrigation. The best defense against this problem is to obtain a soil test and follow the fertilizer recommendations. Avoid the use of high salt fertilizers such as sodium nitrate; use slow release fertilizers and apply correctly. Azaleas and blueberries are very susceptible to salt/fertilizer injury.

6. *My soil is very heavy clay. What can I do?*
There are several ways you can manage your clay soil.
   - The easiest thing you can do is select plants that perform well in clay soil. Water moves slowly into clay soil so be sure to irrigate slowly. A soaker hose is a good option.
   - Clay soil compacts very easily when wet so keep foot traffic and vehicles away from your garden beds.
   - Adding organic matter like compost or pine bark to the soil is another option. Add a few inches of organic matter to the top of the soil. This will need to be repeated for several years to see results.
   - Build a raised bed on top of the clay soil and bring in soil from a reputable source. Loosen the clay layer in the existing soil before adding new soil to the raised bed so water can adequately drain.

7. *The soil in my lawn is compacted; what can I do to resolve this?*

Foot traffic, mowing, recent home construction, and even rainfall can contribute to soil compaction, which can be especially problematic in clay soils. Turf grass roots need air and water to grow. Core aeration is the removal of small cores from the top few inches of soil to allow air, water, and nutrients to enter the root zone of your turf. The result is reduced water runoff and enhanced water and nutrient uptake, gas uptake, thatch breakdown, and heat and drought tolerance of your turf.

The best time to perform core aeration is when grass is actively growing. That means late spring or early summer for warm-season grasses and fall for cool-season grasses. The soil should be moist, but not wet. Be sure to mark sprinkler heads, shallow lines from the sprinkler, and underground utility, cable, and septic lines to prevent damage. Soil cores should be left on the lawn; they will work their way back into the soil within two to four weeks. Lawns may be fertilized, seeded, or top dressed with a soil amendment immediately after coring, although ensure the timing of fertilization corresponds with the recommendations on the maintenance calendar (**content.ces.ncsu.edu/catalog/series/227**) for your turf. Lawns can be aerated once a year, especially under heavy use conditions and with heavy clay soils. Note that spike aeration is not recommended, as this method of aeration only further compacts the soil.

Further Reading

Brady, Nyle C., and Ray R. Weil. *The Nature and Properties of Soils*. 14th ed. Upper Saddle River, New Jersey: Prentice Hall, Inc, 2007. Print.

Buol, S. W., et al. *Soil Genesis and Classification*. 6th ed. Hoboken, New Jersey: John Wiley & Sons Inc., 2011. Print.

Dunne, Niall, ed. *Healthy Soils for Sustainable Gardens*. Brooklyn, New York: Brooklyn Botanic Garden, 2009. Print.

Maynard, Donald N., and George J. Hochmuth. *Knott's Handbook for Vegetable Growers*. 5th ed. Hoboken, New Jersey: John Wiley & Sons, Inc., 2007. Print.

Soil Fertility Manual. 5th ed. Peachtree Corners, Georgia: International Plant Nutrition Institute, 2003. Print.

For More Information

http://go.ncsu.edu/fmi_soils

Contributors

Author:
Luke Gatiboni, Professor and Extension Specialist, Department of Crop and Soil Sciences

Contributions by Extension Agents:
Jeana Myers

Contributions by Extension Master Gardener Volunteers:
Deborah Green, Kim Curlee, Judy Bates, Jackie Weedon, Karen Damari, Connie Schultz, Edna Burger

Content Editors:
Lucy Bradley, Professor and Extension Specialist, Urban Horticulture, NC State University; Director, NC State Extension Master Gardener program
Kathleen Moore, Urban Horticulturist

Copy Editor:
Barbara Scott

Chapter 1 Cover Photo:
Kathleen Moore, CC BY-2.0

How to Cite This Chapter:
Gatiboni, L. 2022. Soils and Plant Nutrients, Chpt 1. In: K.A. Moore, and. L.K. Bradley (eds). *North Carolina Extension Gardener Handbook,* 2nd ed. NC State Extension, Raleigh, NC. <https://content.ces.ncsu.edu/extension-gardener-handbook/1-soils-and-plant-nutrients>

Composting

2

Objectives

This chapter will teach people to:
- Start a compost pile or worm bin.
- Understand the effects different types and sizes of materials have on the rate of composting.
- Recognize appropriate moisture levels for compost piles and worm bins.
- Effectively manage compost and worm bins.
- Utilize compost, vermicompost, and their extracts (tea).

Introduction

For centuries, gardeners have made compost and used it to improve their garden soil. Today's gardeners also see the importance of composting as an alternative to burning or disposing of organic materials in landfills. Food scraps and yard debris comprise 28% of the solid waste generated in the United States (U.S. EPA, 2011). Many people are surprised that the largest category of waste being thrown away is food residuals—over 21% of the total. Instead of being discarded down sink drains or in the garbage, food waste can easily turn into a valuable soil amendment for a landscape, garden, or lawn.

Compost incorporated into the soil increases the organic matter content, improves the physical properties of the soil, helps roots penetrate more easily, holds moisture, provides aeration to plant roots, suppresses some diseases, and supplies some essential nutrients. Compost can also be applied to the soil surface to conserve moisture, control weeds, reduce erosion, improve appearance, and keep the soil from gaining or losing heat too rapidly.

Composting is a process that controls the decomposition and transformation of biodegradable material into a **humus**-like substance called compost. It can be a fast (hot) or slow (cold) process, depending on the amount of effort put into it. For fast composting, a pile needs a balance of organic materials, moisture, and oxygen to support microorganisms that will heat the pile to 140° to 150°F. At these temperatures, most weed seeds and pathogens will be killed. Organic materials will also break down through slow/cold composting, but the decay will be a lot slower, and seeds and pathogens will not be destroyed.

Many organic materials are suitable for composting. Yard wastes such as leaves, grass clippings, straw, and plant trimmings can be composted. Branches and twigs greater than 1-inch in diameter should be ground up in a shredder or chipper. Kitchen wastes such as vegetable scraps, coffee grounds, and eggshells may also be added.

Slow (Cold) Composting

If hot composting will require too much time or energy, simply gather leaves into a 3 to 4 cubic foot pile or bin, sprinkle them with water, and they will decay on their own. Food wastes may be added, but bury them deep in the pile so they are out of reach of pests. It will take about a year for the leaves to decompose, but eventually rich compost will be ready for landscape use. Disadvantages of slow composting include the length of time it takes for materials to decompose, the possibility of pests being drawn to the decaying matter, and weed seeds and pathogens not being destroyed by high temperatures.

Fast (Hot) Composting

Gardeners who want to produce a higher quality ofcompost more quickly will choose this composting method. It involves aerating the pile, checking temperatures and moisture levels, and getting the right mixture of materials and particle sizes.

A bin is not needed to make compost. Some choose to use a bin to keep the pile neat, help retain heat and moisture, and keep out pests, or they live in a neighborhood where a bin would be more appropriate than an open pile. Many people make their own compost bin using concrete blocks, wooden pallets, mesh fencing, or 55-gallon drums. A three-compartment wooden bin can be constructed using plans from the internet (Figure 2–1).

There are a variety of manufactured composting bins available, including enclosed, spherical, or tumblers (Figure 2–2). Although meat, fish, bones, and dairy should

Figure 2–1. Homemade 3-compartment composting system.
Lucy Bradley, CC BY - 2.0

Figure 2–2. Manufactured composting bin.
Kathleen Moore CC BY 2.0

not be added to a compost pile or bin, they can be placed in an in-ground digester such as the Green Cone.

Composting can be done in a pile or some type of bin, but the size is important for maintaining heat—it should be 27 cubic feet (3 feet wide, deep, and tall). Set it up in a convenient location that is over 6 feet away from the home or other wooden structures. To maximize food safety, the compost should be downhill and as far away as possible from the vegetable garden. Choose a flat space that is protected from flooding or runoff to surface waters or wells. Keep the areas in front of and above the pile or bin clear so it can be worked without difficulty. Place it in a shaded area (to help it retain moisture) and within reach of a garden hose.

There are two basic styles of hot composting: 1) **Single Batch**, where materials are added all at once to form a pile, and 2) **Continuous Pile**, where organic materials are added as they become available. Build a pile 3-feet high and at least 3-feet in diameter so it can become self-insulating to retain heat (Figure 2–3). Add 4-to-5 inches of carbonaceous materials (browns), then two or three inches of nitrogenous materials (greens), and keep alternating the layers. Another method is to mix up browns and greens thoroughly before loading. Be sure to water each layer thoroughly to ensure that moisture is evenly distributed. Toss in a handful of soil on each layer to introduce more microorganisms. Top the pile with 4-to-5 inches of carbonaceous materials to keep out flies and other pests and provide a filter for odors.

Figure 2–3. A large three bin compost system.
Kathleen Moore, CC-BY - 2.0

After the pile is created, it should heat up within a few days and stay hot for several weeks if it is turned weekly. During this time, the pile will shrink and after about a month it may be about half of its original volume.

It will take another four to eight weeks for the pile to cure and be ready for use.

A simple compost recipe is to combine leaves, grass, food scraps, and coffee grounds at a ratio of 2-to-1 mix of "browns" and "greens". There are some additives that

can help to get a compost pile hot. Small amounts of one or more of the following in "meal" form can be dusted on top of the "greens" in a compost pile: alfalfa, bone, hoof, soybean, canola, cottonseed, or blood. A compost pile can also be activated by adding a mixture of water and molasses, sugar, syrups, or flat soft drinks.

Maple leaves have a perfect carbon-to-nitrogen ratio, so with the right moisture and frequent turning, they can break down in several weeks. Oak leaves have less nitrogen (C/N ratio of about 60 to 1) and contain high levels of tannins which are resistant to decay, so they take a lot longer to break down. Mixing oak leaves with high nitrogen materials will accelerate their decomposition.

Decomposition happens on the surface of materials, *so the particle size and shape are very important to the composting process.* By chopping, smashing, grinding-or cutting materials into smaller particles (less than 2-inches in diameter), more surface area is created and decomposition happens faster. Use a chipper/grinder or a machete or place materials in a bucket and use a square-end shovel to chop them into pieces. Do not get carried away because very fine particles will prevent air from flowing into a compost pile. A low-cost method of reducing the size of fallen tree leaves is to run a lawn mower over them before or after raking. The shredded leaves can be collected directly if the lawn mower has an appropriate bag attachment. Rigid particles provide structure and ventilation to a pile, so it is good to layer in small batches.

The decomposition process will slow down if there is too little or too much moisture. Approximately 40% to 60% moisture is needed in the pile. At this moisture level, the pile should feel like a wrung-out sponge. The compost pile is within the right moisture range if a drop or two of water can be squeezed from a handful of material. If no water can be squeezed out, the materials are too dry. If the compost pile is too moist, it will slow the decomposition process and produce unpleasant odors. If that happens, add dry leaves, paper, or sawdust to absorb the excess moisture. Most often, compost piles are too dry, which slows down the composting process. Open piles can be covered with a tarp to hold in moisture.

Compost piles need ventilation. **Anaerobic** (no air) piles smell bad, compost slowly, and produce dense, wet, and smelly compost. Aerobic piles with oxygen throughout will produce little or no odor. To aerate the pile, turn the organic materials with a digging fork or shovel. If turning is not possible, poke it with an aerating device or broom handle to help air flow into the pile. Mixing the pile once a week by moving the material from the outside to the center will hasten the composting process. Turning also exposes seeds, insect larvae, and pathogens to lethal temperatures inside the pile. A pile that is not mixed may take three to four times longer to produce useful compost. During the early phase of decomposition, organic acids are produced and the compost pile becomes more acidic. Some people advocate adding lime during this stage to increase the **pH** of the pile and increase microbial activity. However, lime converts nitrogen to ammonia gas, thus removing nitrogen from the pile. Crushed clam or oyster shells, eggshells, and bone meal tend to reduce the acidity of compost. Over time, the pH in the pile rises so that the acidity of the composted material becomes near neutral.

Heat will be given off as microorganisms feed on waste. Temperatures need to reach over 130°F in the pile to kill most pathogens that are harmful to humans and pets, and over 140°F to destroy most weed seeds. If the temperature of the pile climbs to 160°F, it can kill decomposers and slow the composting process (Figure 2–4).

Figure 2–4. A hot compost pile should reach 140° Fahrenheit to kill off pathogens and weed seeds.
Scot Nelson, Flickr CC BY-0 2.0

Temperatures in the center of the pile will be hottest and they will be cooler on the outer edges. If the pile does not heat adequately, it may be too small, there may not be enough oxygen or nitrogen, or it may be too dry or too wet (Table 2–1). Turn the pile when the center begins to feel cool to the touch. Turning the pile introduces oxygen and undecomposed material into the center, and helps to revive the heating process.

Composting Materials

The organic materials that can be composted are commonly distinguished as "browns" (high in carbon) and "greens" (high in nitrogen). Some examples are in Table 2–2. The "browns" are sugar-rich carbon sources that provide energy to microorganisms, absorb excess moisture, and provide structure to the pile. "Browns" include brown autumn leaves, newspaper, straw, sawdust, napkins, cardboard, twigs, hay, dryer lint, and bark (Figure 2–5).

Figure 2–5. Dead leaves "browns" in the compost pile.
Kathleen Moore, CC BY - 2.0

The "greens" provide protein-rich nitrogen and moisture to microorganisms and include grass clippings, vegetables and fruit, coffee grounds, tea leaves, livestock manures, and alfalfa (Figure 2–6). See Table 2–3 for a more extensive list of raw materials that may be composted.

Figure 2–6. Kitchen scraps "greens" ready for the compost pile.
Chris Alberti, CC BY - 2.0

Food scraps may be stored in a container until they are added to the compost pile (Figure 2–7). Some people like to place food scraps in a container in their freezer until they are taken out to the compost pile. Others reuse a plastic container with a lid or use a purchased compost kitchen container and keep it under their sink or on the kitchen counter. Food scraps should be buried inside the pile to avoid attracting rodents.

Yard waste suitable for composting includes fallen tree leaves, grass clippings, straw, and non-woody plant trimmings. *Leaves are the primary organic waste in most backyard compost piles.* Although grass clippings can be composted, it is better to leave them on the lawn where they will decay and release nutrients, reducing the need for fertilizer (see NC State Extension publication AG-69, *Carolina Lawns*). When adding grass to a compost pile, mix it thoroughly with leaves so it does not compact and restrict airflow.

Newspaper and other types of paper can be composted, but the nitrogen content is low, so it decreases the decomposition rate. If paper is composted, it should make up no more than 10% of the total weight of the material in the compost pile. It is better to recycle paper curbside or take it to a community collection site.

Figure 2–7. Kitchen scraps can be stored in a container (this one is under the sink) until full and ready to be brought out to the compost pile.
Chris Alberti, CC BY - 2.0

2

Table 2–1. Troubleshooting Composting Problems		
Symptom	**Problem**	**Solution**
Pile smells like rancid butter, vinegar or rotten eggs	Too wet or not enough air or too much nitrogen	Turn pile; mix in leaves, straw, sawdust or wood chips
Pile is not heating up	Pile is too small, too dry, or has not enough nitrogen	Make pile larger, provide insulation, add water while turning, add nitrogen sources
Pile is attracting animals	Food scraps are not well covered or meat or dairy products were added	Cover food with brown leaves, wood chips, or finished compost; keep meat and dairy out of pile; enclose pile in ¼-in hardware cloth
Pile is damp but won't heat up	Not enough nitrogen	Mix in grass clippings, food scraps, other sources of nitrogen
Pile is dry	Not enough moisture, too much air flow	Water and mix well; cover loosely with tarp or landscape fabric to help hold in moisture
Pile is damp and warm in middle but nowhere else	Pile is too small	Add more material and moisten
Some people ask "Should I add worms to the pile to help it compost faster?" The answer is no, a compost pile should be too hot for worms to tolerate. During the cooler curing phase of composting, earthworms will naturally be attracted to the pile to help break down the remaining material. Vermicomposting, in which earthworms primarily break down the ingredients, is a different process that is described later in the chapter.		

Table 2–2. Carbon-to-Nitrogen Ratios of Commonly Composted Materials

Materials High in Carbon (Browns)	C:N	Materials High in Nitrogen (Greens)	C:N
Autumn leaves	30 – 80:1	Vegetable scraps	15 – 20:1
Straw	40 – 100:1	Coffee grounds	20:1
Wood chips, sawdust	100 – 500:1	Grass clippings	15 – 25:1
Mixed paper	150 – 200:1	Livestock manure	5 – 25:1
Newspaper, cardboard	560:1		

Source: *Composting to Reduce the Waste Stream: A Guide to Small-Scale Food and Yard Waste Composting.* Northeast Regional Agricultural Engineering Service, Cooperative Extension, #43. 1993.

What NOT to Compost and Common Composting Problems

Some materials may pose a health hazard or create a nuisance and therefore should not be used to make compost. Types of organic materials that should NOT go into compost piles include the following:

- Dog or cat feces and litter, and dirty diapers (may contain parasites and pathogens)
- Meat, fish, bones, fats, grease, lard, oils, eggs, or dairy products such as butter, milk, yogurt, and sour cream (may create odors, attract rodents and flies)
- Yard trimmings treated with chemical pesticides (might kill beneficial composting organisms or not break down in the composting process and affect plants where compost is placed)
- Diseased or insect-infested plants (diseases and insects may survive and be transferred to other plants)
- Black walnut tree leaves or twigs (releases substances that might harm plants)
- Weeds that have gone to seed
- Weeds with invasive roots, such as Dock weed, Alligator weed, or Bermuda grass
- Used facial or toilet tissue (may contain pathogens)
- Charcoal ash or coal (resistant to decay and may contain substances harmful to plants)
- Pressure-treated lumber, pressed wood, plywood (contain toxic chemicals)
- Heavily coated paper (magazines, catalogs, wrapping paper, greeting cards with metallic inks, photographs)
- Wood ash (a handful or two may be added, but more may harm microbes, slow the composting process, cause smelly ammonia gas releases, and leave compost with less nitrogen)
- Pine needles (waxy coating is resistant to decay)
- Contents of swollen cans (could contain botulism)
- Rose thorns and other stickers (take longer to compost and can be painful to handle)

Herbicides may persist during the composting process and harm plants grown in compost-amended soils. Hot composting piles can accelerate the breakdown of most herbicides, and they can also be deactivated by binding with organic matter. The source of herbicides in most home composting piles is usually lawn clippings. However, animal manure may contain composting-resistant herbicides. See NC State Extension publication *Herbicide Carryover in Hay, Manure, Compost & Grass Clippings: Caution to Hay Producers, Livestock Owners, Farmers & Home Gardeners*.

Curing and Using Compost

When heating ceases, cover the pile with a fabric weed barrier and let it cure for 6 to 12 weeks. During that time, mist the compost to keep it slightly damp and poke it occasionally to let in air. As the compost cures, particles will shrink, organic acids will dissipate, and pH will stabilize and move closer to neutral. Compost is basically "done" when the original materials are unrecognizable, the pile temperature is less than 10 degrees warmer than ambient, it is dark brown or black and smells earthy (not like ammonia or rotten eggs). To make sure the compost is fully mature and stable, test it on radish seeds to make sure it does not prevent germination or damage the plants. A sample can be sent to the NC Department of Agriculture & Consumer Services to determine the levels of nutrients, carbon-to-nitrogen ratio, pH, and soluble salts.

For smaller particles of compost, a simple screen can be made with half-inch mesh hardware cloth and a wood frame (Figure 2–8). The screen may be placed on top of a wheelbarrow or inclined at an angle on the ground. Load the screen with compost and use a gloved hand or a square-end shovel to scrape the compost against the screen. Remove the screen to reveal sifted compost.

Organic materials too large to pass through the screen may be added back into the compost pile.

Potted plants, garden and field crops, lawns, shrubs, and trees can benefit from compost. In clay soils, compost improves aeration and drainage and makes it easier to work with hand tools. In sandy soils, compost increases water-holding capacity and increases soil aggregation. Compost may suppress some plant diseases and pests, and it encourages healthy root systems. Although compost contains macro- and micronutrients, it is often not enough to supply all of plants' needs. Thus, lawn and garden soils should be tested and fertilized accordingly. Local Cooperative Extension centers have soil test boxes and instructions.

Figure 2–8. Using a screen to remove larger particles of compost. These large particles can be thrown back in the compost pile. Nadine Ford, CC BY - 2.0

Table 2–3. Organic Materials That Can Be Composted

Nitrogen (Green)	Carbon (Brown)
Grass clippings	Leaves, twigs, yard trimmings
Houseplant leaves	Natural fiber yarn, thread, string, rope
Hair, fur, nail clippings, feathers	Paper rolls (towel, toilet, gift wrap)
Vegetables, fruits	Nut shells (not walnut)
Coffee grounds, filters	Cotton balls, swabs
Tea bags, leaves	Dryer lint from natural fabrics
Egg and crustacean shells (rinsed)	Cotton, wool, silk, felt, hemp, linen, burlap
Old herbs, spices	Vacuum contents, floor sweepings
Flowers, dead blossoms	Straw, hay, corn cobs
Beer, winemaking leftovers	Newspaper, nonglossy paper
Juice, beer, wine, dregs	Brewery hops
Freezer-burned vegetables, fruits	Loofahs
Aquarium water, algae, plants	Paper napkins and bags
Seaweed	Sawdust, wood bark and chips
Herbivorous animal manure (rabbits, cows, sheep, chickens, horses)	Bamboo skewers, toothpicks
	Pizza and cereal boxes, paper egg cartons
	Pencil shavings
	Paper baking cups
	Grains, cereal, crackers

Compost Tea

There is an increasing interest in using compost tea as a drench or foliar spray, as it has similar effects on plant growth, health, and disease resistance as compost. Compost tea brewers may be purchased or made out of a clean 5-gallon bucket, fine mesh fabric, and two sticks. Add 1 part compost to 10 parts water. For example, for 1 gallon of water (128 ounces), use 13 ounces of compost (about 1 ½ cups).

If the water has chlorine in it, first let the chlorine evaporate out by filling the bucket with water and letting it sit for at least 24 hours. Measure the compost to the desired solid-to-water ratio. Place compost inside the mesh fabric so that it can easily be removed later. Place a stick across the top of the bucket and tie the fabric bag into a knot. Submerge the mesh bag in the water in the bucket and tie the fabric bag to the stick (Figure 2–9).

Figure 2–9. Make compost tea in a bucket using one part compost and 10 parts water. Suspend compost in a fine mesh fabric and brew for 48 hours, stirring 12 times.
Kathleen Moore, CC BY - 2.0

Place the bucket out of direct sunlight in an area where the temperatures will remain 60°–80°F (16°–27°C). Do not allow leaves or other debris to fall into the bucket (it is best to keep the bucket indoors). Write down the date and time that the brewing begins. Stir the bucket 12 times over the next 48 hours or run an aquarium pump during that time.

After 48 hours of brewing, remove the bag containing the compost. Pour the yellow-brown "tea" into a watering can or sprayer. Use the tea immediately or within 4 hours after brewing. The tea can be poured into the soil around the base of a plant or sprayed onto the leaves. Do not use the tea on any edible portions of a plant. Spray weekly or every two weeks. To prevent microbe loss from ultraviolet rays, spray early in the morning on a cloudy day before it gets hot, or after irrigation or rain.

Vermicompost

Vermicomposting (earthworm composting) turns many types of kitchen food scraps into nutritious soil amendments or growth media for plants (Figure 2–10). When vermicompost is added to soil, it boosts the nutrients available to plants and enhances soil structure and drainage. Vermicompost helps plants grow bigger, produce higher yields, and it can reduce the impact of some pests and diseases.

Figure 2–10. Vermicomposting.
Oregon State University, Flickr CC-BY-SA

Using earthworms to decompose food residuals offers several advantages:

- Produces less odor and attracts fewer pests than putting food scraps into a garbage container.
- Saves the water and electricity that kitchen sink garbage disposal units consume.
- Reduces garbage disposal costs.
- Produces a free, high-quality soil amendment (vermicompost).
- Requires little space, labor, or maintenance.
- Spawns free earthworms for fishing.

Equipment and Supplies

The materials needed to start a vermicomposting system are simple and inexpensive: a worm bin, bedding, water, composting earthworms, and food scraps (Figure 2–11).

Worm Bin

A suitable bin can be constructed of non-aromatic wood or a plastic container can be purchased. Wooden worm bin construction plans may be found at a number of sites on the internet. Manufactured worm bins can be purchased on-line or at some garden centers. Or one can be made by buying an 18-gallon storage bin with a tight-fitting lid. Make sure the bin is a dark color because earthworms are highly sensitive to light. If a plastic container is used, it should be thoroughly washed and rinsed to remove manufacturing residues before earthworms and bedding are added. Do not use a container that was used to store toxic chemicals. The bin size depends on the amount of food waste produced by a household. The general rule of thumb is one square foot of surface area for each pound of garbage generated per week. So, if a household creates two pounds of food scraps weekly, it will need a 2-foot by 1-foot worm bin.

Homemade worm bins will need holes drilled for aeration and drainage. To provide enough oxygen for earthworms,

drill holes on the upper sides of the bin near the lid. Do not drill holes in the lid, as they would let in light and dry out the bedding. There are three options for drilling holes in the sides of the bin: 1) using a 3-inch hole saw, drill one hole on each upper, narrow end of the bin and insert a 3-inch screened soffit vent (available at hardware stores in the gutter section), OR 2) drill four ½-inch holes on the long sides of the bin and either leave the holes open or glue hardware cloth/screen over them, OR 3) drill a number of tiny holes all the way around the upper sides of the bin. For drainage, drill six ¼-inch holes, equally dispersed, in the bottom of the bin, and place a moisture collection tray under the bin.

There are several suitable locations for a worm bin, such as a garage or carport, porch or deck, kitchen, basement, bathroom, closet, or apartment balcony. Make sure there is room for air to circulate around the bin. If a worm bin is properly maintained, it should not emit odors or attract pests. If the bin is kept outdoors, place it in a location that is always shady. A worm bin should never be placed in the direct sun because it can cause the system to overheat and kill the earthworms. Wherever it is located, the temperature inside the bin should be maintained between 59° and 77°F (15° to 25°C). There are several ways to maintain the bin above the minimum temperature, such as gluing blueboard insulation to the outer walls of the bin or surrounding it with straw or other insulating materials. Alternatively, cut a plastic gallon jug in half, fill it with water, insert an aquarium heater and place it inside the bin. If it is hot and the worm bin needs to be cooled down, mix in some dry bedding or place ice in a container and place it in the bin.

Bedding

To provide a suitable environment for the earthworms to live and to cover food scraps, bedding will need to be added to the worm bin. Bedding should be a non-toxic fluffy material that holds moisture and allows air to circulate. Suitable materials include shredded paper (such as black-and-white newspapers, paper bags, office paper, or cardboard), decaying leaves, or coconut pith fiber (coir). Do not use glossy paper or magazines. For newspapers, fold a section in half and tear off long, half-inch wide strips (go with the grain of the paper and it will tear neatly and easily). Soak any bedding for 5 to 10 minutes in a bucket of water and then wring it out so it is a little wetter than a moist sponge. Aim for the bedding to be very damp, but not soaking wet (only two to three drops of water should come out when squeezed). Fluff up the bedding as it is added to the bin, filling it no more than half way. Mix in a handful of soil from a healthy garden to introduce beneficial microorganisms and aid the earthworms' digestive process. The earthworms will eat the bedding along with the food discards, so more

Figure 2–11. Worm bin
Kathleen Moore, CC BY - 2.0

will need to be added within a couple of months. Use a plant mister to spritz some water on the bedding to keep it moist. Never pour water directly into a worm bin as it can drown the worms.

Also, do not agitate, turn, or stir the contents of the worm bin. It does not need to be aerated like a compost pile, and earthworms can be killed if handled roughly. Earthworm castings should be left undisturbed on the bottom of the worm bin.

Water

Earthworms breathe through their skin, which must remain moist for the gas exchange to take place. Their bedding needs to be at about an 80 percent moisture level. If a worm bin has adequate aeration and it is not over-watered, excess liquid should not puddle or leak out of the bottom of the bin. Excess moisture can be created from wet feedstocks, so limit the amount of coffee grounds and cooked or canned foods that are fed to earthworms.

There is a misconception that the run-off from worm bins (what leaks out of the bottom) can be used to grow plants. It is actually **leachate**—liquid that has passed through unprocessed organic material. Leachate may contain pathogens, phytotoxins, and anaerobic microorganisms that could be harmful to plants. Never use leachate on food crops, houseplants, or sensitive plants. Leachate should be poured on weeds or down a toilet. Use only finished vermicompost to make vermicompost tea.

Composting Earthworms

It is important to use the type of earthworms that will thrive in a worm bin. There are more than 6,000 species of earthworms, but only seven species have been identified as suitable for vermicomposting. Of those, only one species of earthworm is used for vermicomposting by most people worldwide: *Eisenia fetida* (common name: red wiggler). Start with at least one pound (about 1,000) of red wigglers to one square foot of surface area of the worm bin to have a chance of developing a sustainable system.

Do not get the earthworms from a bait shop (that would require 33 to 83 bait cups!) or a yard (there is no way to tell if the species is *Eisenia fetida*). Instead, buy them from a worm grower. Be sure to check around, as prices for earthworms vary significantly. When the red wigglers arrive, gently place them on top of the bedding in

the worm bin. The earthworms will immediately move underneath the bedding to avoid the light, but they need a few days to acclimate to their new home. If the red wigglers try to leave the bin, keep the bin in a bright area around the clock for a few days, while the earthworms are getting used to their new environment.

After a while, other organisms will appear in the worm bin—they come to eat and help break down the organic materials. Most of the organisms will be too small to see, but pot worms, springtails, pill bugs, molds, and mites may be spotted. None of these is harmful to the worms, nor are the organisms an indication there is a problem with your worm bin.

Food Scraps

Once the earthworms have settled into their new home (after a couple of days), add a small amount of food scraps two inches below the surface of the bedding. The amount of food should not exceed 1-inch high. This will prevent the food scraps from building up heat. Feed earthworms any non-meat organics such as vegetables, fruits, crushed eggshells, tea bags, coffee grounds, shredded paper, coffee filters, and shredded garden debris. Red wigglers especially like cantaloupe, watermelon, and pumpkin. Do not add citrus fruits or peels to the bin, as they can cause it to become too acidic. Chop or grind food scraps into small pieces so they break down more easily. Never add meat scraps or bones, fish, greasy or oily food, onions, garlic, fat, tobacco, sugary foods, citrus, salty foods, or pet or human manure. Once the earthworms have been fed, use a three-prong garden tool to cover the food scraps completely with 2 inches of bedding. This will prevent fruit flies from finding the food.

Food scraps can be stored for several days before adding them to the worm bin. Many people store food residuals in a container with a lid next to or under their kitchen sink. Others store their food scraps in a container or bag in the freezer.

One pound of red wigglers will eat up to two pounds of food scraps a week. If more food is added than the earthworms can consume, it will start to rot and become smelly. Ideally, do not add more food until the worms have consumed the last feeding. If more food scraps are produced than one bin can handle, buy more earthworms and start another worm bin. It's a good idea to have a backyard composting bin in addition to a worm bin,

---

Optimal Conditions for Raising Red Wiggler Earthworms

- Temperature: 59°–77°F (15°–25°C) (limits 32°–95°F, 0°–35°C)
- Moisture: 80% (limits 60–90%)
- Oxygen requirement: Aerobicity
- pH: >5 and <9
- Ammonia content of waste: Low; <0.5mg/g
- Salt content of waste: Low; <0.5%

because it can accommodate excess food scraps, along with citrus, onions, and garlic.

The worms may be fed any time of the day. Do not worry about taking a vacation, as the earthworms can be fed as seldom as every three weeks. If extended periods away from the bin are expected, apply ½-inch layer of food scraps across the top of the bin and cover it with two inches of moistened, shredded paper (Table 2–4).

Harvesting Vermicompost

After a few weeks, vermicompost will appear on the bottom of the bin. Vermicompost is a soil-like material containing a mixture of earthworm castings (feces) and partially decomposed bedding and food scraps. In four to six months, it will be time to harvest the vermicompost. It may be harvested by one of three methods:

Method 1: Sideways Separation. Feed the earthworms on only one side of the worm bin for several weeks, and most of the worms will migrate to that side of the bin. Then the vermicompost can be harvested from the other side of the bin where no food scraps have been added.

Fresh bedding should be added where vermicompost was harvested. Repeat this process on the other side of the bin. After both sides are harvested, food scraps can be added to both sides of the bin again.

Method 2: Light Separation. Empty the contents of a worm bin onto a plastic sheet or used shower curtain where there is strong sunlight or artificial light. Wait

Table 2–4. Worm Bin Troubleshooting

Problem	Possible Causes	Solutions
Bin smells bad	Over feeding	Stop feeding for two weeks
	Noncompostables present	Remove noncompostables
	Food scraps exposed	Cover with 2 inches of bedding
	Bin too wet	Mix in dry bedding; leave lid off with strong light overhead
	Not enough air	Drill holes in bin
Bin attracts flies	Food scraps exposed	Bury food completely
	Too much food	Add food after most is eaten
Worms are dying	Bin too wet	Mix in dry bedding; leave lid off
	Bin too dry	Thoroughly dampen bedding
	Extreme temperatures	Move bin where temperature is 55°–77°F
	Not enough air	Fluff bedding; drill holes in bin
	Not enough food	Add more bedding and food scraps
Worms crawling away	Bin conditions not right	See solutions above Leave lid off with light shining into bin (worms will burrow back into bedding)
Bedding is drying out	Too much ventilation	Mist bedding; keep lid on
Liquid collecting in bottom	Poor ventilation	Mix in dry bedding; leave lid off with strong light overhead
	Feeding too much watery scraps	Cut back on coffee grounds and food scraps with high water content; mix with bedding material before feeding

Some people ask "Should I add worms to the pile to help it compost faster?" The answer is no, a compost pile should be too hot for worms to tolerate. During the cooler curing phase of composting, earthworms will naturally be attracted to the pile to help break down the remaining material. Vermicomposting, in which earthworms primarily break down the ingredients, is a different process that is described later in the chapter.

five minutes, and then scrape off the top layer of vermicompost. The earthworms will keep moving away from the light, vermicompost can be scraped off every five minutes or so. After several scrapings, the worms will be in clusters; just pick up the worms and gently return them to the bin in fresh bedding (with the old bedding mixed in).

Method 3: Vertical Separation. Before starting vermicomposting, either buy a manufactured stacking bin or make one by purchasing two identical storage bins and drilling extra holes in the bottoms. Set one bin aside and vermicompost in the other bin for a few months. Periodically try to stack the second bin inside the first one. When the bedding in the first bin is high enough to fit snugly against the bottom of the second bin, add bedding material to the top bin and begin feeding in that bin only for the next several months. Most of the earthworms will move up into the upper bin to eat, and eventually the lower bin will just contain vermicompost.

Be on the lookout for earthworm egg capsules—they are lemon-shaped, about the size of a match head, shiny, and light-brown. A capsule contains two to seven baby earthworms (three on average). Place the egg capsules back inside a worm bin so they can hatch and thrive.

If it appears that there is an overabundance of earthworms in a bin, remove some and start a new worm bin.

Or gift earthworms to others who would like to begin vermicomposting, such as school or church teachers, Cooperative Extension agents, scout clubs, 4-H clubs, etc.

Using Vermicompost

Vermicompost is a fully stabilized organic soil amendment that is much more microbially-active than the original organic material that was consumed. It has a fine particulate structure and good moisture-holding capacity. Vermicompost contains nutrients such as nitrogen, phosphorus, potassium, calcium, and magnesium in forms readily taken up by plants. It also has plant growth hormones and humic acids, which act as plant growth regulators.

Vermicompost can be used immediately or stored for later use. To store vermicompost, dry it to a moisture level of about 35% and place it in a bag or container pricked with a pin to make holes that will allow oxygen in, yet hold in moisture. Store it in a warm, dark place.

The material can be mixed into the soil in a garden and around landscape plants. It can also be used as a top dressing on container plants or sprinkled on a lawn as a conditioner (Figure 2–12). It is best to protect the vermicompost from direct sunlight by incorporating it in soil or covering it with mulch.

Figure 2–12. Top dressing with vermicompost on a lawn.
Diana House, CC BY - 2.0

Summary

Backyard composting and vermicomposting are easy ways to keep food scraps and yard wastes out of landfills or burn piles and convert them into valuable soil amendments. There are many similarities and some differences between the two types of composting. Both compost and vermicompost can enrich soils and increase plant productivity (Table 2–5).

Table 2–5. Differences and Similarities between Composting and Vermicomposting

Attribute	Composting	Vermicomposting
Uses vegetable scraps	Yes	Yes
Uses brown materials, paper, dried leaves	Yes	Yes
Microbes break down materials	Yes	Yes
If managed properly can work quickly	Yes	Yes
Worms break down material	No	Yes
No turning necessary	No	Yes
Hot enough to kill weed seeds	Yes	No
Heat can kill beneficial microbes	Yes	No
Limited by cold weather	No	Yes
Bin can be indoors	No	Yes

Frequently Asked Questions

1. *I have bugs in my compost. Will they hurt my plants?*
   Insects can be an important component in the breakdown of organic material in a compost pile. Very few of these insects are plant pests. If you are trying a "hot compost" method, your pile might not be hot enough; try turning it over and adding more green material. If your pile reaches the correct temperature, insects will stay away. The presence of ants could indicate your pile is too dry and needs to be watered. If your compost is nearing completion and you are noticing insects like sow bugs or earwigs, spread your compost out and let it dry in the sun for a few days before using it in your garden.

2. *I want to compost but I have close neighbors and I am worried my pile will smell.*
   A properly managed compost pile will have a pleasant "earthy" smell when you open the lid to turn it. Your neighbors should not be able to smell it. Your pile will need adequate air incorporated by frequent turning and equal proportions of both green and brown material. A foul odor can come from too much wet green material breaking down in the absence of oxygen. This anaerobic decomposition can produce a strong odor of rancid butter or rotten eggs. To alleviate this, turn the pile over and add straw, wood shavings, or dried leaves.

3. *Can I put weeds in my compost pile?*
   A properly managed hot compost pile will reach 140°F and will easily kill most weed seeds. Unless you are sure your pile is reaching these temperatures, it is best to put only weeds that have not yet gone to seed in your pile.

Further Reading

Appelhof, Mary. *Worms Eat My Garbage: How to Set up and Maintain a Worm Composting System*. 2nd ed. 1997. Kalamazoo, Michigan: Flower Press, 2003. Print.

Bass, Larry, T. E. Bilderback, and M. A. Powell. *Composting: A Guide to Managing Organic Yard Wastes*. Raleigh, North Carolina: North Carolina Cooperative Extension Service, 1992. PDF file. AG-467.

Cogger, Craig, Dan M. Sullivan, and Jim Kropf. *Master Gardener Manual*. Pullman, Washington: Washington State University Extension, 2010. Chapter 22: Composting, pages 22-1 to 22-16. CD file.

Dickson, Nancy, Thomas Richard, and Robert Kozlowski. *Composting to Reduce the Waste Stream: A Guide to Small-Scale Food and Yard Waste Composting*. Ithaca, New York: Northeast Regional Agricultural Engineering Service, 1993. PDF file.

Sherman, Rhonda L. *Backyard Composting of Yard, Garden, and Food Discards*. Raleigh, North Carolina: NC State Extension, 2017. AG-791.

Sherman, Rhonda L. *Worms Can Recycle Your Garbage*. Raleigh, North Carolina: NC State Extension, 2017. AG-473-18 (Revised).

Composting to Reduce the Waste Stream: A Guide to Small-Scale Food and Yard Waste Composting. Northeast Regional Agricultural Engineering Service, Cooperative Extension, #43. 1993.

For More Information

http://go.ncsu.edu/fmi_compost

Contributors

Author:
Rhonda Sherman, Extension Solid Waste Specialist, Department of Horticultural Science

Contributions by Extension Agents:
Pam Jones, Paige Patterson, Peg Godwin, Tim Mathews

Contributions by Extension Master Gardener Volunteers:
Lee Kapleau, Kim Curlee, Jackie Weedon,Karen Damari, Connie Schultz

Content Editors:
Lucy Bradley, Professor and Extension Specialist, Urban Horticulture, NC State University;Director, NC State Extension Master Gardener program

Kathleen Moore, Urban Horticulturist

Copy Editor:
Barbara Scott

Chapter 2 Cover Photo:
Nadine Ford, CC BY - 2.0

How to Cite This Chapter:
Sherman, R. 2022. Composting, Chpt 2. In: K.A. Moore, and. L.K. Bradley (eds). *North Carolina Extension Gardener Handbook*, 2nd ed.NC State Extension, Raleigh, NC. <https://content.ces.ncsu.edu/extension-gardener-handbook/2-composting>

Botany

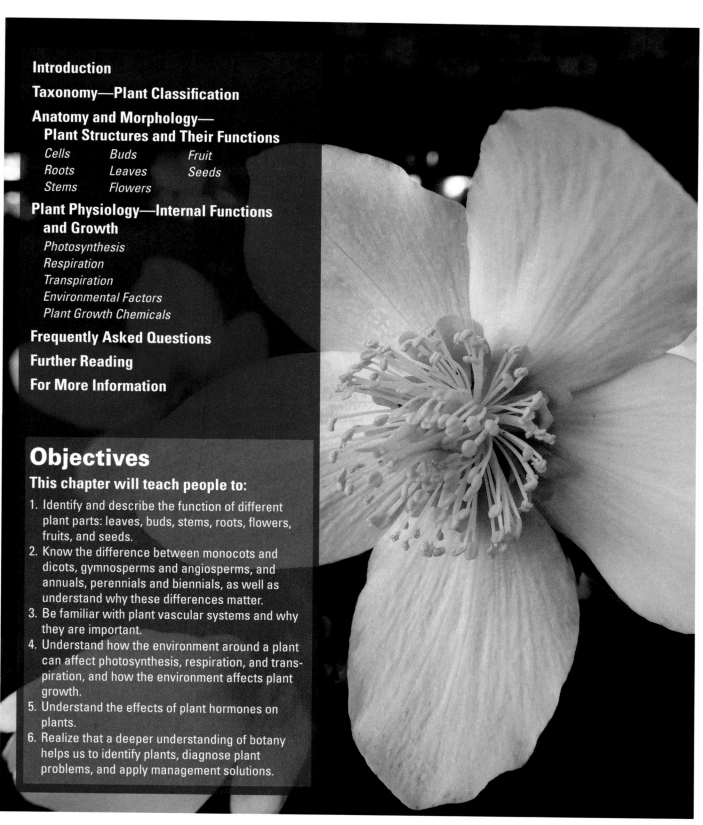

3

Objectives

This chapter will teach people to:

1. Identify and describe the function of different plant parts: leaves, buds, stems, roots, flowers, fruits, and seeds.
2. Know the difference between monocots and dicots, gymnosperms and angiosperms, and annuals, perennials and biennials, as well as understand why these differences matter.
3. Be familiar with plant vascular systems and why they are important.
4. Understand how the environment around a plant can affect photosynthesis, respiration, and transpiration, and how the environment affects plant growth.
5. Understand the effects of plant hormones on plants.
6. Realize that a deeper understanding of botany helps us to identify plants, diagnose plant problems, and apply management solutions.

Introduction

Life on our planet would not be possible, much less enjoyable, without plants. They provide food either directly or indirectly to all animal life. Their leaves create oxygen, and their roots grip the soil and prevent erosion. Their branches shade and cool the ground, and they beautify our surroundings with their interesting shapes, colors, textures, and scents. **Botany** is the scientific study of plants. This chapter will help you understand how plants are classified, the names of their structural and reproductive components, how they grow, including the **physiological** processes, and how plants are influenced by environmental factors. A deep understanding of these topics will help you in diagnosing plant problems and recommending appropriate management techniques.

Botany Encompasses Several Fields

Taxonomy—Plant classification, how plants are named and grouped

Anatomy and Morphology—Plant structures

Physiology—Plant internal functions and growth

Ecology—How plants interact with their environment and each other

Taxonomy—Plant Classification

More than 350,000 different types of plants live on our planet. With new species being discovered regularly and others becoming extinct, that number changes constantly (Kew Gardens). Scientists group plants that share common characteristics to make it easier to identify and study plants. This type of organization based on the characteristics of organisms is called **taxonomy**.

The hierarchy of classification is as follows:

I. **Kingdom**

II. **Phylum**

III. **Class**

IV. **Order**

V. **Family**

VI. **Genus**

   A. **Species**

      1. **Variety or Cultivar**

What's in a name?

All plants have a Latin scientific name consisting of two parts, the **genus** and the **species**. This naming method is called **binomial nomenclature**, and it is the only consistent and dependable way to reference plants. Common names, while popular, have several shortcomings:

1. Some plants have multiple common names and may be called by different common names in different states and regions. For example, the evergreen shrub *Kalmia latifolia* is called mountain laurel, mountain ivy, Virginia ivy, mountain kalmia, and kalmia laurel. The **deciduous** tree *Liquidambar styraciflua* has been called American sweetgum, sweet-gum, red gum, star-leaved gum, or alligator-wood.

2. The same common name is sometimes applied to several different plants. For example, tea or tea plant could be *Camellia sinensis*, *Dysphania ambrosioides*, *Ilex glabra*, or others.

3. Some plants may have no common name.

With binomial nomenclature, it is clear you are referring to a specific plant. The first part is the generic name, which describes the genus, and the second part is the species. For the sweet gum tree *Liquidambar styraciflua*, the genus is *Liquidambar* and the species is *styraciflua*. A genus is a group of related species. **Genera**, the plural of genus, are grouped into **families**, families into orders, and on up the hierarchy of taxonomic classification. The scientific name is underlined or written in *italics* and the genus name is capitalized. In some cases, the genus may be abbreviated to the first letter followed by a period. For example, *Euonymus americanus*, strawberry bush, may be abbreviated as *E. americanus*.

Figure 3–1. A snakeskin liverwort (*Conocephalum conicum*). James St. John, Flickr CC BY - 2.0

Kingdom Plantae is divided into two types of land plants:

Nonvascular—Nonvascular plants are also known as **bryophytes**. These plants have no internal system for moving water and therefore must live in a moist environment. Because they do not have a vascular structure, they are often small. Liverworts (Figure 3–1), hornworts (Figure 3–2), and mosses (Figure 3–3) are bryophytes.

Vascular—Vascular plants contain internal vessels that can move water and **nutrients** throughout the plant. This system allows plants to grow quite large and to survive in many different types of ecosystems. Vascular plants are by far the most abundant type of plant on the planet. Vascular plants can be further divided into seed-producing and non-seed-producing plants. Non-seed-producing vascular plants (such as ferns and horsetails) reproduce through **spores** (Figure 3–4). Seed-producing vascular plants can be further divided into **gymnosperms** and **angiosperms**.

- **Phylum Gymnosperm**—Gymnosperm comes from the Greek word "gymnospermos," which means "naked seed." Gymnosperms produce seeds like angiosperms, but those seeds are not contained in a ripened **ovary**; they form at the tips of **scales** or leaves that are sometimes modified into cones. Conifers are the largest group of gymnosperms, and they bear seeds in cones. Some gymnosperms have fleshy coats or tissues surrounding seeds (yews and ginkgoes, for example).

- **Phylum Angiosperm**—Angiosperms are flowering plants that produce seeds contained in a fruit (a ripened ovary). Fruits have evolved to attract animals that help to disperse seeds. In addition, some fruits decompose, adding organic matter to the soil that the new plant can use to grow. Angiosperms comprise the vast majority of land plants. Flowering plants can be further divided into two classes: **monocots** and **dicots**. Some of their differences are listed in Table 3–1. We will talk more about monocots and dicots when we discuss plant anatomy and reproduction.

3

Figure 3–2. A hornwort.
Miguel Pérez, Flickr CC BY-SA - 2.0

Figure 3–3. Moss, a bryophyte.
Kathleen Moore, CC BY - 2.0

Figure 3–4. Ferns and horsetails (foreground) reproduce by spores.
Kathleen Moore, CC BY - 2.0

Table 3–1. Differences between Monocots and Dicots

Class Monocots	Class Dicots
Embryo with single **cotyledon**	Embryo with two cotyledons
Pollen with single furrow or pore	Pollen with three furrows or pores
Flower parts in multiples of three	Flower parts in multiples of four or five
Major leaf veins parallel	Major leaf veins **netted**
Stem vascular bundles scattered	Stem vascular bundles in a ring
Roots that are **adventitious**	Roots that develop from **radicle**
Secondary growth is absent	Secondary growth often present
Examples: asparagus, corn, ginger, grasses, iris, lilies, onions, palms, tulips	Examples: apples, beans, cabbage, elms, oaks, peppers, peas, potatoes, roses, spinach, squash

The second part of the scientific name is called the **specific epithet**. The epithet describes the species, which is the next level of classification. Individual plants within a species have many common characteristics, yet are distinct from other species in the same genus. Specific epithets are often derived from a description of a flower or leaf, the area where the plant was discovered, or the plant's habitat; sometimes epithets also honor a person. Epithets are written in lowercase letters and are <u>underlined</u> or *italicized* (Table 3–2).

There are several small, inexpensive dictionaries on the market and websites that give a short definition for many Latin terms and many also have audio files that pronounce the names. Understanding the translation makes it easier to remember the scientific name. There are even sites on the Internet that spell botanical Latin names out phonetically. See the "For More Information" section at the end of this chapter for suggestions.

Two additional terms used in identifying plants are **"variety"** and **"cultivar."** A variety is a naturally occurring subset of a species with distinctive features that are true to type, meaning that when **propagated sexually**, through seeds, the offspring have the same characteristics as the parent plant. The varietal name is also an epithet, added after the name of the species and preceded by the abbreviation "var." For example, *Cercis canadensis* var. alba is a white flowering redbud that was discovered in the wild. "Alba" means white, and seeds from this variety grow into plants that have white flowers.

A cultivar, as the name suggests, is a variety that has been cultivated by humans. Cultivars are selected for one or more unique traits and are usually propagated **vegetatively** to maintain these traits. If a new type of tomato were developed by **crosspollination** in a breeding program, it would be a cultivar. A cultivar name follows the species name and is enclosed in 'single quotation marks'; each word begins with a capital letter. For example, *Cornus florida* 'White Cloud' is White Cloud flowering dogwood. It is not necessary to use the single quotes if the word "cultivar" precedes the cultivar name.

Growth Habits
Plants vary with respect to their growth and developmental cycles. **Annuals** complete their entire life cycle, from seed **germination** to seed production, and die in one growing season. Examples of annuals are corn, beans, marigolds, and zinnias. **Biennials** complete their life cycles in two growing seasons. In the first season, they start from seeds and produce vegetative structures and food storage organs. During the winter, a **hardy** evergreen **rosette** of leaves persists. During the second season, they flower, produce fruits and seeds, and die. Some examples of biennials are carrots, hollyhocks, celery, beets, and onions. Annuals and biennials are herbaceous plants, meaning their aboveground tissue dies back and they do not have a persistent aboveground woody stem.

Perennials live for more than two growth seasons, up to several years, decades, or even centuries. After they reach maturity, they can produce flowers and fruit each year.

Table 3-2. Examples of Epithets and Their Translations	
Epithet	**Translation**
grandiflora	large flower
americana	America
wilsoniana	Wilson
autumnale	autumn
parvifolia	small leaves
japonica	Japan
sylvatica	of the forest
praecox	very early

Perennial plants can be either herbaceous or woody plants. Herbaceous perennials die down to the ground each winter and grow new stems from their persistent root system each spring. Several herbaceous perennials that do not tolerate cold are treated as annuals. Many bedding plants are perennial in the wild but are treated as annuals in the garden. Perennial woody plants have stems that live through the winter.

Trees are perennial woody plants that usually have one main **trunk** and are more than 15 feet tall at maturity. Shrubs are perennial woody plants that may have one or several main stems and are usually less than 15 feet tall at maturity.

A vine is a plant that develops long trailing stems that grow along the ground until they become supported by another plant or structure and begin to climb. Some vines have adaptive structures that help them climb: climbing hydrangea (*Hydrangea anomala*) develops **aerial roots**, and garden peas have **tendrils**. Vines can be annuals like sweet peas or perennials like Virginia creeper (*Parthenocissus quinquefolia*).

Anatomy and Morphology — Plant Structure and Their Functions

Cells

Plants, like animals, consist of millions of individual cells. Both plant and animal cells contain a cell membrane, cytoplasm, a nucleus, and other organelles. Plant cells differ from animal cells in that they have a stiff cell wall

How are plants different from animals?

- Plants use pigments in their leaves and stems to capture sunlight and create their own food through a process called **photosynthesis.**
- As a product of this food production (photosynthesis), plants produce oxygen.
- Parts of a plant, like the tips of shoots and roots (**meristems**), are capable of growth throughout the plant's life.
- Plants will respond to environmental stimuli such as animal damage or drought stress, but their response may not be evident immediately. For example, a tree that has been stressed by boring beetles might not show evidence of this infestation for several weeks or even months later.
- Plants will grow to seal off a wound in response to injury, such as removal of a branch or bud.

and a large vacuole for storing water and other nutrients (Figure 3–5). Cell walls consist of cellulose, a type of carbohydrate that helps the plant maintain its structure. Some cells, especially those found in leaves and stems, can contain chloroplasts, which are **organelles** that contain cylindrical stacks called grana. In these grana is a pigment called **chlorophyll** that gives plants a green color and allows them to capture sunlight and turn it into sugar (energy) for the plant.

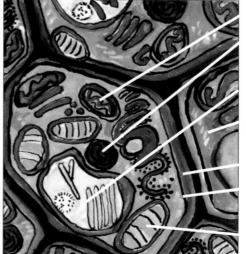

mitochondrion
nucleus
vacuoule
cytoplasm
cell wall
cell membrane
chloroplast

Figure 3–5. Plant cells have rigid cell walls and large vacuole.
Renee Lampila

Groups of cells with similar functions are called tissues. These tissues group together to form the various parts of a plant, including roots, stems, buds, leaves, flowers, and fruits.

Roots

Roots typically develop from the lower portion of a plant or cutting. The principal functions of roots are to absorb nutrients and water, to anchor the plant in the soil or other growing medium, to provide physical support for the stem, and to serve as food storage organs. In some plants, roots are used as a means of propagation—either naturally or through human intervention.

The structure and growth habits of roots have a pronounced effect on a plant's size and vigor, method of propagation, adaptation to certain soil types, and response to cultural practices and irrigation. Roots of certain vegetable crops are also important food sources.

Root Development

A root has three major developmental zones. The zone of cell division includes the **root cap**, which protects the interior cells as the root pushes through the soil, and the root **apical meristem**, an area of division or growth. The root apical meristem produces new cells that contribute to the root cap as well as to the root itself. The second zone, behind the meristem, is called the **zone of elongation**. Here cells take in food and absorb water, thereby increasing in size and pushing the tip of the root through the soil. The third major root zone is the maturation zone, where the majority of absorption occurs and cells undergo changes to become specific tissues, such as **epidermis**, cortex, or **vascular tissue**. The epidermis is the outermost layer of cells surrounding the root. These cells are responsible for absorbing water and minerals dissolved in water. The cortex is the outermost layer of the stem or root of a plant, bounded on the outside by the epidermis and on the inside by the endodermis. Vascular tissue is located in the center of the root and conducts food and water.

Why is it important to know about root hairs?

Root hairs are where the major absorption of water and fertilizer occurs. Watering and fertilizing close to the trunk of a plant are of little use to the plant, though it may help a neighboring plant. It is much more effective to apply water and fertilizer at the dripline of the plant where root hairs are most prolific.

Root hairs begin to emerge in the zone of maturation, developing as outgrowths of the epidermal cells. The majority of the water and nutrients absorbed by the plant enter through the root hairs. Most plants produce root hairs that live only a few days or a few weeks. New root hairs form as roots continue to grow through the soil. Older portions of a root do not have root hairs and cannot absorb water.

Root Systems and Adaptations

Plants generally have one of two types of root systems: **taproot** or **fibrous root**. At the end of the embryo of a seedling, the tip that will develop into a root is called a radicle. A taproot forms when the primary root continues to elongate downward into the soil. The taproot becomes the central and most important feature of the root system (Figure 3–6). Taproots have a somewhat limited amount of secondary (lateral or side) branching. Some trees, such as pecan trees, have a long taproot with very few lateral or finer, fibrous roots. This makes these trees difficult to transplant and necessitates planting in deep, welldrained soil. The taproots of carrots, parsnips, and salsify are the main edible parts of these crops.

Figure 3–6. Example of a taproot: dandelion.
Kathleen Moore, CC BY - 2.0

If plants that normally develop a taproot are undercut so that the taproot is severed early in the plant's life, the root will lose its taproot characteristic and develop a fibrous root system. Undercutting is done intentionally in commercial nurseries to force trees to develop a compact, fibrous root system, which contributes to a higher rate of transplanting success.

A fibrous root system is one in which numerous lateral roots develop. These roots branch repeatedly and form the plant's feeding root system (Figure 3–7).

Fleshy roots become food reservoirs that store surplus food for the winter or other adverse periods to be used by the plant until it is able to renew its growth. Carrots, turnips, and beets have primary or taproots containing food. Sweet potatoes and dahlia tubers are secondary roots transformed into tuberous roots packed with food.

Aerial roots form freely on some land and water plants in a favorable, moist environment (Figure 3–8). These aerial roots enable climbers such as philodendron, orchids, and air plants to attach themselves to a structure for anchorage and support. Aerial roots absorb water from the air. Many aerial roots are also adventitious, meaning they arise from stem tissue. They are often fleshy or semi-fleshy and function as reservoirs for water storage.

Figure 3–7. Grasses typically have a fibrous root system.
Kathleen Moore, CC BY - 2.0

Figure 3–8. Orchids often form aerial roots.
Maja Dumat, Flickr CC BY - 2.0

Factors That Influence Root Growth
- Roots grow best in soil with an adequate balance of moisture and air.
- Soil fertility and pH determine the rate and depth of root growth.
- Lack of oxygen in the soil limits growth, leading to a decrease in overall water and nutrient absorption.
- Soil compaction limits root growth.

Stems
Stems are structures that support buds, flowers, and leaves. The major internal part of a stem is its vascular tissue system, which includes **xylem**, **phloem**, and in most plants, the vascular **cambium**. The vascular tissue system transports food, water, and minerals and provides support for the plant. The conducting elements in xylem transport water and minerals, while those elements in phloem conduct food. Both xylem and phloem can conduct **hormones**.

The two classes of flowering plants, monocots and dicots, both contain xylem and phloem, but they are arranged in different patterns. In a monocot stem, the xylem and phloem are paired into discrete vascular bundles; these bundles are scattered throughout the stem like a bundle of straws (Figure 3–9).

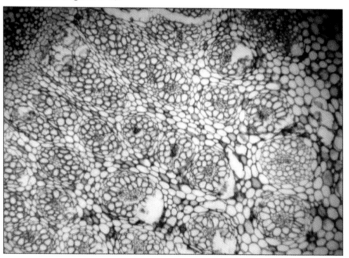

Figure 3–9. Monocot stem cross section showing vascular bundles randomly scattered.
Andrea Scauri, Flickr CC BY - 2.0

In a dicot stem, the vascular system develops in a ring pattern (Figure 3–10). The ring of phloem is near the bark or external covering of the stem and becomes a component of bark in mature stems. In dicot woody plants, just inside the phloem is the vascular cambium, a site of cell division and active growth. The vascular cambium is responsible for a stem's increase in diameter as it produces both secondary phloem and xylem tissues. Xylem tissue forms a ring just inside the vascular cambium, thereby forming the sapwood and heartwood (Figure 3–11).

3

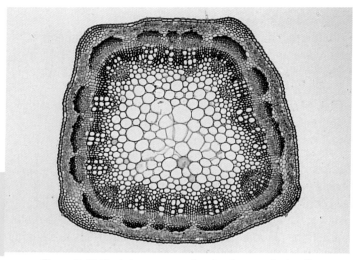

Figure 3–10. Dicot stem cross section showing vascular bundles in a ring.
Berkshire Community College, Flickr CC BY0

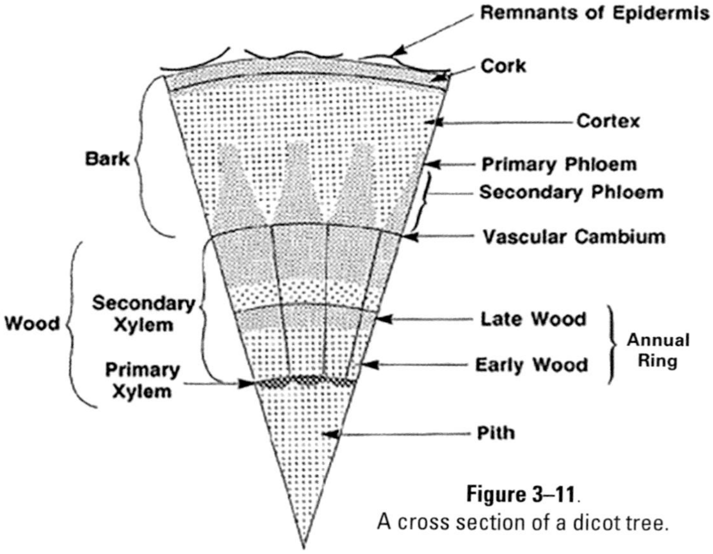

Figure 3–11.
A cross section of a dicot tree.

Understanding the difference between monocot and dicot vascular systems is important to gardeners for several reasons:

- A dicot tree can die if a string trimmer girdles the tree's trunk. This can occur while someone trims the surrounding grass with a Weed Eater or other string trimmer. Such a wound can sever the vascular system just inside the bark. The same treatment of a monocot palm tree does minimal damage because the vascular system is distributed throughout the entire trunk.
- Dicots have multiple meristems, so cutting off a tip just redirects growth. Monocots, however, have only one apical meristem, so cutting the top off a palm kills the tree.
- Monocots do not have secondary meristem cells, so they grow taller but not wider. Dicots with secondary meristem cells grow wider as well as taller.
- Some selective herbicides kill only dicots.
- Other selective herbicides kill only monocots.

The stem area where leaves are attached (or were once attached) is called a **node**. Within the node is a bud, which is an area of great cellular activity and growth. The area between nodes is called an **internode** (Figure 3–12). The length of an internode depends on many factors. Low fertility, for instance, decreases internode length. Too little light causes a long internode and a spindly stem, an occurrence known as stretching or **etiolation**. Growth produced early in the season often results in the greatest internode length; internode length decreases as the growing season nears its end. Vigorously growing plants tend to have greater internode lengths than unhealthy plants. Internode length also varies with competition from surrounding stems or developing fruit. If the energy for a stem has to be divided between three or four stems, or if the energy is diverted into fruit growth, internode length will be shorter.

Stems can be long, with great distances between leaves and buds (such as branches of trees or runners on strawberries), or compressed, with short distances between buds or leaves (such as fruit **spurs**, **crowns** of strawberry plants, or dandelions).

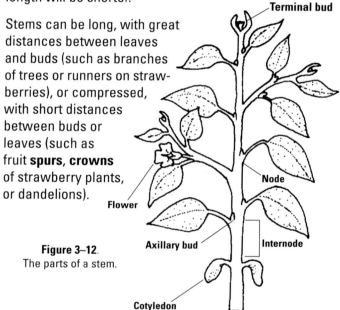

Figure 3–12.
The parts of a stem.

Types of Stems

A shoot is a general term used to describe a young stem with leaves. A **twig** is a woody stem in the current or previous year's growth. A **branch** is a stem that is more than a year old and may have lateral stems. A trunk is the main stem of a woody plant. Woody stems contain relatively large amounts of xylem tissue in the central core and are typical of most fruit trees, ornamental trees, and shrubs.

A **cane** is a stem with a relatively large pith (soft spongy tissue in the center of a stem) and a life expectancy of only one or two years. Examples of plants with canes include roses, grapes, blackberries, and raspberries. Herbaceous stems contain only small amounts of xylem tissue and usually live for one growing season.

Modified Stems

When we think of a stem, we tend to picture typical trunks and branches. Modified stems can be grouped into two categories: aboveground and belowground. Aboveground modified stems are crowns, **stolons**, and spurs. Below-ground stems are **bulbs**, **corms**, **rhizomes**, and **tubers**.

Aboveground Stems
- **Crowns** (on strawberries, dandelions, and African violets) are compressed stems with leaves and flowers on short internodes (Figure 3–13).
- **Stolons** are specialized stems that grow on the soil surface and form a daughter plantlet at one or more of their nodes. Some plants that have stolons, such as periwinkle *Vinca minor*, make good ground covers because they spread easily (Figure 3–14). Stolons are sometimes called runners, but technically runners are a subgroup of

Figure 3–13. This foxglove (*Digitalis purpurea*) has a crown of leaves. The short distance between nodes keeps the leaves near the ground.
Kathleen Moore, CC BY - 2.0

stolons. Examples of plants with runners are strawberries, and spider plants.
- **Spurs** (Figure 3–16) are short, stubby, lateral stems that arise from the main stem and are common on such fruit trees as pears, apples, and cherries. Spurs are where these trees can bear fruit. If severe pruning is done close to fruit-bearing spurs, the spurs can revert to long, non-fruiting stems.

Underground Stems
Many types of modified stems can be found beneath the soil. These belowground stems are often confused with roots. If you find the presence of buds, leaf scars,

Figure 3–14. Buttercups (*Ranunculus sp.*), a common weed, form long stems (stolons) between daughter plantlets making them difficult to remove.
Kathleen Moore, CC BY - 2.0

Are palm trees made of wood? How are they different from other trees?

Along with grasses, palm trees, orchids, bamboo, irises, and yuccas belong to the class **Monocotyledons** (monocots) (Figure 3–15). Monocot plants grow from apical meristems and have only primary growth. Some **Dicotyledons** (dicots), such as oaks, maples, and elms, increase their diameter (experience secondary growth) through lateral meristems, producing wood and bark.

This secondary growth provides structural strength in dicots. How can palm trees get so tall when they do not produce wood? Their vascular bundles are tightly packed and full of cell-strengthening **lignin**. The bundles are surrounded by large numbers of parenchyma cells and other stem-supporting fiber. Palm trees also have leaves that are tightly packed around their stem and prop roots that help support the plant.

There are many differences between palm trees and dicot trees besides the presence of wood in dicot trees. Palms grow from a single point on the plant. If you cut the top off a palm tree, it would not produce more branches as a dicot tree would. The palm tree would die because monocots do not produce wood in concentric circles as dicots do. A monocot's vascular bundles are scattered throughout its stem tissue. Dicot trees can be easily girdled by making a shallow cut into viable vascular bundles found just beneath the bark all the way around the trunk. Girdling can kill a dicot tree. If you made the same girdling cut around a palm tree stem, the tree would continue to live.

Figure 3–15. Palm trees in Wrightsville Beach, NC.
Idawriter, Wikimedia CC BY-SA 3.0

or nodes, you have an underground stem, not a root. These modified stems are energy-storage organs.

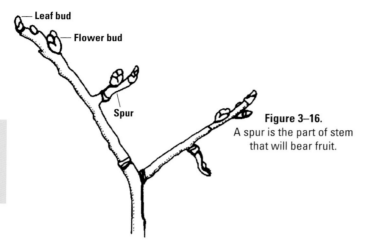

Figure 3–16. A spur is the part of stem that will bear fruit.

Leaf bud

Flower bud

Spur

Woody Stem Parts and Their Functions

Outer bark – Protects the plant from desiccation, insects and disease, excessive heat and cold, and other injuries. Composed of cork cells that are produced from a layer of cells called the **cork cambium**.

Inner bark – The interior portion of the bark, the phloem, carries food produced in the leaves down to the branches, trunk, and roots. Phloem can also move food "upward" (distal movement) to the end of a stem.

Vascular cambium – A single layer of cells between the bark (phloem) and the wood (xylem). This layer is where growth in diameter originates. Annual rings of new wood are produced on the inside of the cambium, and new bark is produced on the outside of the cambium.

Sapwood – The sapwood, or xylem, carries the sap (water plus nitrogen and other essential nutrients) from the roots to the leaves. Xylem also stores food synthesized in the leaves.

Heartwood – A stem's darker-colored center portion that was once sapwood. Heartwood is inactive wood because its cells no longer function. The core of heartwood serves only to structurally reinforce the plant and to keep it upright. Heartwood may decay over time, resulting in hollow centers in living stems.

- **Tubers** are fleshy modified stems with nodes that produce buds (Figure 3–17). A potato is a tuber. The eyes of a potato are actually the nodes on the stem. Each eye contains a cluster of buds. A small piece of potato, as long as it contains an eye, can produce an entirely new potato plant. Some plants, such as begonias and cyclamens, produce an enlarged, modified

underground tuberous stem that is short and flat. Unlike true tubers that have buds scattered on all sides, tuberous stems have shoots only on their tops.

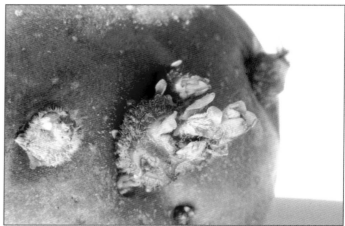

Figure 3–17. A tuber is a fleshy modified stem with nodes that produce leaves.
Steve Johnson, Flickr CC BY - 2.0

- **Rhizomes** are specialized stems that grow horizontally at or just below the soil surface and serve as a storage organ and a means of propagation in some plants (Figure 3–18). Aerial stems with leaves grow from one end of the rhizome, and roots grow from the other end. Some rhizomes are compressed and fleshy, such as those of irises. They can also be slender with elongated internodes as in bent grass. Johnsongrass (*Sorghum halepense*) is a hated weed because of the spreading capability of its rhizomes.

Figure 3–18. A rhizome is a modified stem that grows near the soil surface. It can be thin, as with grasses (left), or thick and fleshy, as with an iris (below).

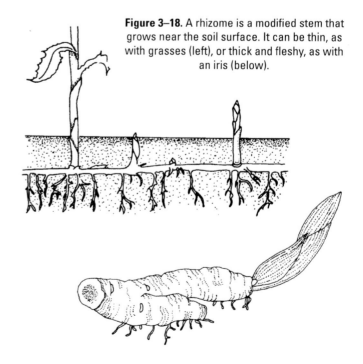

- **Bulbs** are shortened, compressed, underground stems surrounded by thickened, fleshy leaves that envelop a central bud located at the tip of the stem (Figure 3–19). Tulips, lilies, daffodils, and onions are plants that produce bulbs. If you cut through the center of a tulip or daffodil bulb in November, you can see all the flower parts in miniature within the bulb (Figure 3–20).

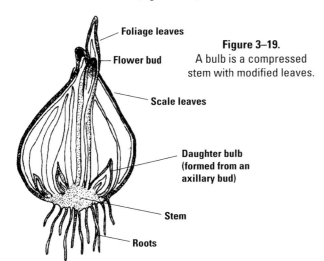

Figure 3–19.
A bulb is a compressed stem with modified leaves.

Foliage leaves
Flower bud
Scale leaves
Daughter bulb (formed from an axillary bud)
Stem
Roots

Figure 3–20. A grape hyacinth (*Muscari armeniacum*) bulb — whole (left) and in cross-section (right).
Kathleen Moore, CC BY - 2.0

- The new stem grows from a bud on top of the corm (Figure 3–21). Some plants produce a modified stem that is referred to as a **tuberous stem.** Examples are crocus, tuberous begonia, and cyclamen. The stem is shortened, flattened, enlarged, and underground. Buds and shoots arise from the crown; fibrous roots occur on the bottom of the tuberous stem.

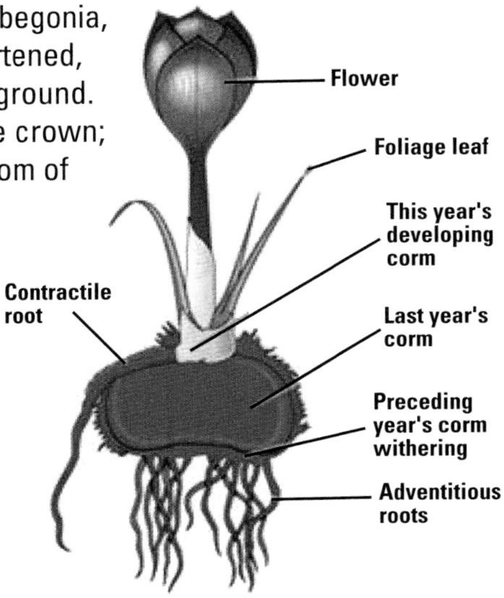

Flower
Foliage leaf
This year's developing corm
Contractile root
Last year's corm
Preceding year's corm withering
Adventitious roots

Figure 3–21.
A corm is a solid, swollen stem without fleshy leaves.

Thorns, **spines**, and **prickles** are terms you may see used interchangeably to describe the sharp projections on plants that protect them from being eaten by herbaceous animals. There are, however, botanical differences between these projections. Thorns are a modification of a stem or branch, which means they can be branched or not, have leaves or not, and they arise from a bud (Figure 3–22). A honey locust tree (*Gleditsia triacanthos*) has thorns. Spines are modified leaves, **leaflets**, **petioles**, or **stipules** (Figure 3–23). Wintergreen barberry (*Berberis juliane*) has spines. Despite the adage, every rose does not have thorns. The sharp projections on roses (*Rosa*) and blackberries (*Rubus*) are modified epidural cells called prickles. Prickles can occur anywhere along the plant and are much easier to remove than thorns or spines (Figure 3–24).

3

Figure 3–22. Thorns come from modified stems as seen here on this honey locust tree (*Gleditsia triacanthos*).
Dick Culbert, Flickr CC BY - 2.0

Figure 3–23. Spines are modified leaf parts. In this example, the spines are modified stipules.
Kathleen Moore, CC BY - 2.0

their location on the stem surface (Figure 3–25). **Terminal buds** are those located at the end of a stem. Lateral buds occur on the sides of the stem. Most **lateral buds** grow in the **axil** of a leaf (the small angle between the plant's stem and the leaf attachment) and are called **axillary buds**. In some instances, more than one bud is formed. **Adventitious buds** are those that arise at sites other than in the terminal or axillary positions. Adventitious buds may develop from the internode of the stem, at the edge of a leaf blade, from callus tissue at the cut end of a stem or root, or laterally—from a plant's roots.

A leaf bud consists of a short stem with immature leaves (Figure 3–26). Such buds develop into leafy shoots. Leaf buds are often more pointed and less plump than flower buds.

Figure 3–24. A prickle arises from an epidermal cell and can appear anywhere along the stem.
Kathleen Moore, CC BY - 2.0

Buds

A bud is an undeveloped shoot from which new leaves or flower parts arise. Buds of trees and shrubs of the temperate zone typically develop a protective outer layer of small, leathery bud scales. Annual plants and herbaceous perennials have naked buds in which the outer leaves are green and somewhat succulent. Buds are named by

Figure 3–25. Types of buds on a stem.
Kathleen Moore, CC BY - 2.0

Figure 3–26. A leaf bud on a stem contains many small leaves (left). Leaves and stem emerge from the bud (right).
Kathleen Moore, CC BY - 2.0

A flower bud consists of a short stem with embryonic floral parts.

Leaves

The primary function of most leaves is to absorb sunlight for the production of plant sugars in a process called photosynthesis. Each leaf develops as a flattened surface that provides a large area for efficient absorption of light energy. The leaf is supported away from the stem by a stem-like appendage called a petiole. The base of the petiole is attached to the stem at the node.

Parts of a Leaf

The **blade** of a leaf is the expanded, thin structure on either side of the midrib (Figure 3–27). The blade is usually the largest and most conspicuous part of a leaf. The petiole varies in length and can be lacking entirely (described as **sessile** or stalkless). Stipules are leaflike structures that often occur in pairs and are sometimes fused. Stipules are usually found at the base of the petiole or on the node of a stem (as on willow, strawberry, and geranium) or occasionally fused to the petiole (as on rose, crabapple, and Callery pear). Stipules often drop as leaves mature, but those that persist or enlarge are good identification features.

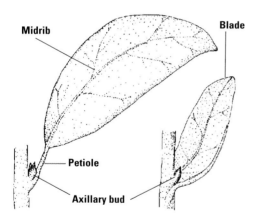

Figure 3–27. The parts of a simple leaf.

The leaf blade consists of several tissue layers (Figure 3–28). The epidermis is the complex tissue layer that covers a leaf's upper and lower surfaces and protects internal tissues. How the cells in the epidermis are arranged determines the texture of the leaf surface.

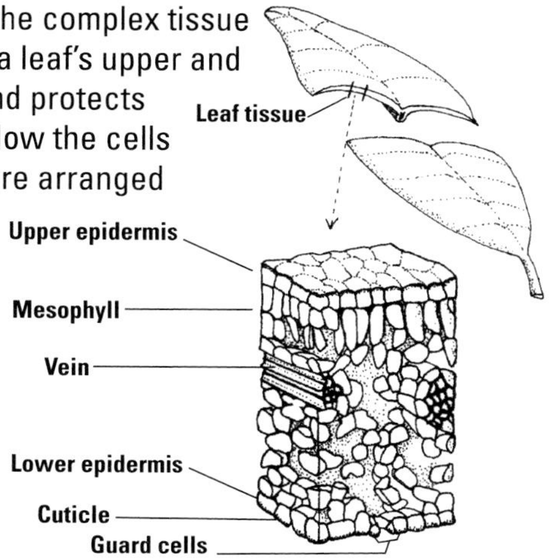

Figure 3–28. A cross-section of a leaf.

Some leaves have hairs, called **trichomes**, that are extensions of certain cells of the epidermis. African violets have so many hairs that the leaves feel like velvet, while other species may have very few to no trichomes.

The **cuticle** is a thin layer covering the epidermis and consists of waxes and a substance called **cutin**. This substance protects the leaf from dehydration and prevents penetration of some disease-causing organisms. The amount of cuticle material produced by epidermal cells correlates to the intensity of sunlight to which leaves are exposed. Plants grown in the shade should be moved into full sunlight gradually to allow the cutin layer to build and protect leaves from the shock of rapid water loss or sunscald. The cuticle also repels water and can shed pesticides if surfactants or soaps are not used as a sticking agent. This is why many pesticide manufacturers include a spray additive that adheres to or penetrates the cuticle.

A leaf's epidermal layer also contains small openings, each of which is called a **stoma**. The plural for stoma is stomata. Each stoma is surrounded by two guard cells. A stoma and its **guard cells** are called a stomatal complex. The bending of the two guard cells regulates the passage of water, oxygen, and carbon dioxide into or out of the leaf (Figure 3–29). The opening and closing of the stomata by their guard cells is determined by the different environmental conditions to which the leaves are exposed. Conditions that would cause a higher rate of water loss from plants (high temperature, low humidity) stimulate guard cells to close. In mild weather, stomata often remain open. With very few exceptions, guard cells usually close the stomata in the absence of light.

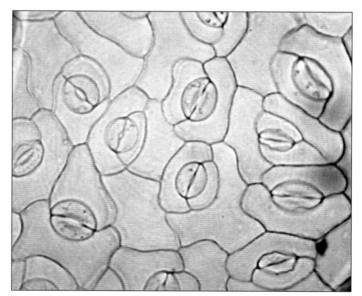

Figure 3–29. This image shows several stomatal complexes-openings on the underside of the leaf surface surrounded by two kidney-shaped guard cells. They control the exchange of gasses (such as carbon dioxide, oxygen, water vapor) by opening or closing.

Andrea Scauri, Flickr CC BY - 2.0

Leaves as a Means of Identifying Plants

Leaves, especially the shapes of their blades and margins (edges), are useful in identifying species and cultivars of horticultural plants. Simple leaves are those in which the leaf blade is a single continuous unit. A compound leaf consists of a blade that is divided into two or more similar structures called leaflets (Figure 3–30). Although compound leaves may resemble a branch stem with several leaf blades attached, leaflets do not have an axillary bud at their base. An axillary bud demarcates the true base of the entire leaf organ structure.

Figure 3–30. A compound leaf has several leaflets. Note the large axillary buds at the base of each leaf.
Kathleen Moore, CC BY - 2.0

Most compound leaves are pinnately compound, which means that the leaf is structured like a feather, with all leaflets arranged on both sides of a central axis, called the **rachis**. Common examples are leaves of ashes, pecans, and Chinese pistache. Some leaves may be doubly (bipinnate) or triply (tripinnate) compound, meaning the leaflets are further divided. Honey locust and nandina (which is triply compound) are examples. Palmately compound leaves are less common than pinnately compound. Palmately compound leaves resemble a hand, with all leaflets emerging from the end of the petiole (Figure 3–31). Examples include buckeye, chaste tree, horse chestnut, and Schefflera species.

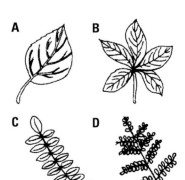

Figure 3–31.
Leaf types:
A) Simple
B) Palmately compound
C) Pinnately compound
D) Bipinnately compound

Some blades are interrupted along the margin and can be mistakenly identified as compound leaves. Lobed leaves, for example, are simple leaves with indentations reaching halfway or less to the center of the leaf, as in a pin oak. Blades with deep indentations reaching close to the midrib yet that are connected by narrow bands of blade tissue (such as ferns) are simple leaves described as pinnatifid.

Leaf Arrangement Along a Stem

Leaves are attached to stems in various patterns, and these patterns can also be used to identify plants (Figure 3–32). Alternate leaves are arranged along the stem with only one leaf at each node, alternating on each side of the stem. This arrangement is most common.

Opposite leaves occur when two leaves at each node are located across from one another. A whorled arrangement is rare and requires three or more leaves at a node. Plants exhibiting whorled leaves may have opposite leaves as well, such as glossy glossy abelia (Linnaea × grandiflora) and cape jasmine (Gardenia jasminodies).

Figure 3–32.
Leaves can be arranged on a stem alternately (top), opposite (middle), or in whorls (bottom).
Kathleen Moore, CC BY - 2.0

Venation

Plants vary with respect to the **venation** pattern in multiple organs, but nowhere are these differences more noticeable than in leaves. Leaves with linear venation are those with numerous lateral veins that run essentially parallel to each other and are connected laterally by minute, straight veinlets. A common type of parallel venation is that found in plants of the grass family, where the veins run parallel from the base to the apex of the leaf. Another type of parallel venation occurs in plants such as bananas, cannas, and pickerel weed. In these plants, the parallel veins run through the center then turn laterally to the margin. Leaves with parallel venation occur in monocot plants. They do not have a midrib but may have one to several larger veins with smaller parallel veins in between them.

Leaves with netted venation (Figure 3–33) have secondary veins that branch from a conspicuous midrib and then subdivide into finer veinlets, which unite into a complicated network. This system of enmeshed veins gives the leaf more resistance to tearing than most parallel-veined leaves. Netted venation may be either pinnate or palmate. In pinnate venation, the secondary veins extend laterally from the midrib to the edge, as in apple, cherry, and peach trees. Palmate venation occurs in grapevine and maple leaves, where several principal veins extend outward, like the ribs of a fan, from the petiole near the base of the leaf blade. Generally, leaves with netted venation occur on dicots.

Several distinct types of leaves occur on plants. Scale leaves or cataphylls are found on rhizomes and are also

the small, leathery leaves that enclose and protect buds. Cotyledons are modified seed leaves that are part of the seed embryo and early seedling. Cotyledons typically serve as energy storage structures for germination and establishment of a seedling's first true leaves. Other specialized leaves include sharp spines that protect the plant and tendrils that assist in supporting stems. Storage leaves are found in bulbous plants and succulents. **Bracts** are specialized leaves that may be brightly colored. The showy structures on dogwoods and poinsettias are not petals. They are bracts, modified to attract **pollinators**.

Figure 3–33. Parallel veins (left) are often seen on monocot plants, netted veins (right) are seen on dicots.
Kathleen Moore, CC BY - 2.0

Leaf Morphology as a Means of Identification

The number of taxonomic terms can be overwhelming at first, but familiarizing yourself with them will help with plant identification. Plant identification is the first step in diagnosing any plant problem (see chapter 7, "Diagnostics"). Careful observation of plants can help us recognize the differences and similarities among plants and plant families.

Leaf Blade
These are some of the most common leaf shapes (Figure 3–34):
- **Linear**—Narrow, five or more times longer than wide; approximately the same width throughout
- **Lanceolate**—Lance-shaped; broadest below the middle and tapering toward the apex
- **Elliptical**—Ellipse-shaped, broadest in the middle, tapering to an acute or rounded apex and base; two or three times longer than wide
- **Ovate**—Egg-shaped, widest below the middle, and tapering toward the apex; two to three times longer than wide
- **Cordate**—Heart-shaped or broadly ovate; tapering to an acute apex, with the base turning in and forming a notch where the petiole is attached

Apexes and Bases
These are some of the most common apex (Figure 3–35) and base (Figure 3–36) shapes for leaves:
- **Acuminate**—A prolonged apex tapering to a long, narrow point
- **Acute**—Ending in an acute angle, with a sharp point
- **Obtuse**—Ending in an obtuse angle
- **Retuse**—A rounded apex with a shallow notch
- **Emarginate**—A deep notch
- **Sagittate**—Arrowhead-shaped, with two pointed lower lobes projected downward
- **Truncate**—Having a relatively square end
- **Attenuate**—A prolonged base with thin tissue extending along part of the petiole
- **Cuneate**—Wedge-shaped, tapering at an acute angle toward the base

Leaf Morphology as a Means of Identification *continued*

Leaf Margins

Leaf margins are especially useful in the identification of some plants (Figure 3–37):

- **Entire**—A smooth edge with no teeth or notches
- **Sinuate**—Having a pronounced wavy margin
- **Crenate**—Having rounded teeth
- **Dentate**—Having large blunt teeth ending in an acute angle, pointing outward
- **Serrate**—Having small, sharp teeth pointing toward the apex
- **Incised**—Margin cut nearly to the midrib into sharp, deep, irregular incisions
- **Lobed**—Incisions extend less than halfway to the midrib
- **Cleft**—Incisions extend more than halfway to the midrib

Leaf Textures

Leaf texture is another way to identify a plant. These are some common leaf textures:

- **Succulent**—Fleshy, soft, and thickened in texture; modified for water storage
- **Coriaceous**—Leather-like, tough
- **Glabrous**—Smooth, shiny, hairless surface
- **Downy**—Covered with very short, weak, and soft hairs
- **Pubescent**—A hairy surface
- **Tomentose**—Covered with matted, wooly hairs
- **Hirsute**—Pubescent with coarse, stiff hairs
- **Hispid**—Rough with bristles, stiff hairs, or minute prickles
- **Scabrous**—Rough to the touch, with the texture of sandpaper

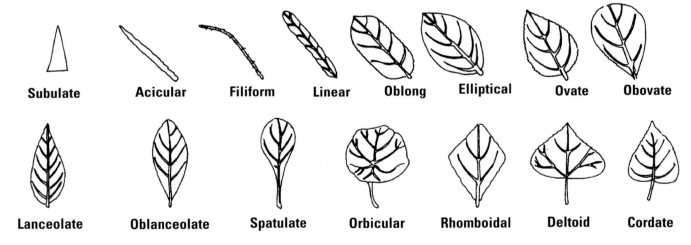

Subulate   Acicular   Filiform   Linear   Oblong   Elliptical   Ovate   Obovate

Lanceolate   Oblanceolate   Spatulate   Orbicular   Rhomboidal   Deltoid   Cordate

Figure 3–34. Common leaf shapes.

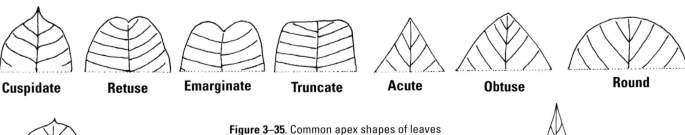

Cuspidate   Retuse   Emarginate   Truncate   Acute   Obtuse   Round

Figure 3–35. Common apex shapes of leaves

Mucronate   Acuminate

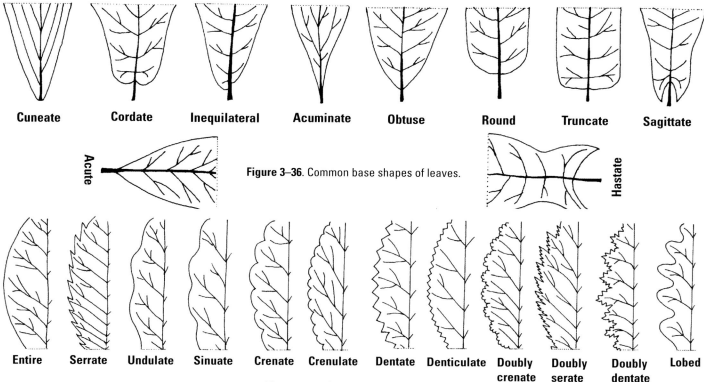

Cuneate   Cordate   Inequilateral   Acuminate   Obtuse   Round   Truncate   Sagittate

Acute   **Figure 3–36.** Common base shapes of leaves.   Hastate

Entire   Serrate   Undulate   Sinuate   Crenate   Crenulate   Dentate   Denticulate   Doubly crenate   Doubly serate   Doubly dentate   Lobed

Figure 3–37. Common leaf margins.

Flowers

Although we appreciate flowers for their beauty and scent, a flower's sole function is sexual reproduction. Plants like grasses and pines that are wind pollinated have no need to attract an insect or animal and so expend little energy on beauty but instead produce copious amounts of pollen for the wind to disperse. Other plants, however, have developed fragrant, pale, night-blooming flowers to attract pollinator moths.

Most fragrant, showy flowers with nectaries have evolved to attract insect pollinators to ensure the reproductive success and continuance of the plant species. Markings on petals signal to insects how to approach and where to land. Bee-pollinated flowers reflect ultraviolet light that is visible to insects but not humans. Some male insects are tricked into transferring pollen by flowers that look and smell like females of an insect species. Fragrant flowers attract bees, butterflies, moths, and other insects. Flowers with foul odors attract flies, beetles, and similar insects.

Other animals, such as birds and bats, also pollinate flowers. Some flowers have landing platforms or nectaries at the end of long tubes to match the body parts of the animals that perform pollination.

Parts of the Flower

As the reproductive structure of the plant, the flower contains pollen-producing structures, **ovule**-bearing structures, and **sterile** structures such as **petals**, **sepals**, and **nectaries** (Figure 3–38).

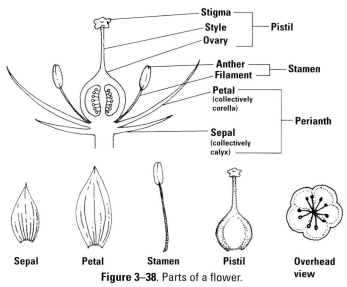

Figure 3–38. Parts of a flower.

A peduncle is a stem that supports the flower or flowers. Sepals are small, usually green, leaf-like structures on the base of the flower. Sepals collectively are called the **calyx**. Petals are usually the highly colored portions of the flower. They may contain specialized structures that produce molecules associated with scent called osmophores, or they may produce nectar in structures known as nectaries. The petals collectively are the **corolla**.

3

The number of petals and sepals on a flower, and the form they take, are often used to identify plant families and genera. The calyx and corolla together are called the **perianth.**

The **receptacle** is the expanded tip of a flower stalk that bears the flower's sexual organs. The **pistil**, located in the center, is the female structure of a flower. Some plants have flowers with no pistil; others have one or more pistils. The totality of the pistils is referred to as a gynoecium ("house of woman"). A single pistil consists of a stigma, **style**, and ovary. The stigma is located at the apex and is the site of pollination. The style is the stalk between the stigma and the ovary. The ovary is the swollen part at the base of the style; it contains ovules, each of which produces a single egg cell. After the egg is fertilized, the ovule develops into a seed, and the ovary matures into the fruit.

The **stamen** is the male reproductive organ. Each stamen consists of an **anther**, containing one to several pollen-producing chambers, and a long, supporting stalk called the **filament**. This filament holds the anther in position so that pollen can be disbursed by wind or carried to the stigma by insects, birds, or other pollinators.

Types of Flowers
A flower that has sepals, petals, stamens, and pistils is called a complete flower. **Incomplete flowers** lack one or more of these parts. Grass plants, for example, typically do not have sepals or petals. If a flower contains both male and female reproductive parts, it is said to be **perfect**. Flowers that lack one of the reproductive structures, either the stamens or pistils, are known as **imperfect flowers**. An imperfect flower is also therefore, by definition, incomplete.

Some plants bear only "male" flowers (**staminate**) or only "female" flowers (**pistillate**). Species in which the sexes are separated into staminate and pistillate plants are called **dioecious** (two houses). Most hollies are dioecious. Therefore, to obtain holly berries, we must plant female plants with a male plant nearby. Plants that have separate male and female flowers on the same plant are **monecious** (one house). Corn, watermelon, and pecan trees are examples of monecious plants. Some monecious plants, such as cucumbers and squash, bear only male flowers at the beginning of the blooming season but later develop flowers of both sexes.

Types of Inflorescences
Some plants bear only one flower per stem or branch; these are called **solitary flowers**. Other plants produce an **inflorescence**, a term that refers to a cluster of flowers and how they are arranged on a floral stem (Figure 3–39). Most inflorescences can be classified into two groups,

indeterminate and **determinate. Indeterminate inflorescences** have an axis terminating in meristematic tissue, which continues to develop until the inflorescence is complete. Flowers bloom in sequence from the bottom to the top of the axis or inward, starting from the outside like *Gladiolus* spp.

There are five basic types of indeterminate inflorescences. A **raceme** has an elongated axis with stalked flowers. A spike has an elongated axis with sessile (stalkless) flowers. A **corymb** has a flat-topped or hemispherical raceme with floral stalks of varying lengths arising up the axis. An **umbel** is similar, but the branches arise from one point at the top of the axis. A **panicle** is a branched raceme.

Determinate inflorescences have a flower that terminates the axis early in its development. Flowers bloom in sequence down from the tip of the axis or progressively outward from the middle. A head has all flowers attached to a disk; examples are sunflowers and Echinacea species. A **cyme** is a broad, flat-topped, or hemispherical inflorescence with flower clusters of threes, in which the floral stalks are similar in length. Some inflorescences can have an indeterminate central axis and determinate lateral branches, such as buckeyes.

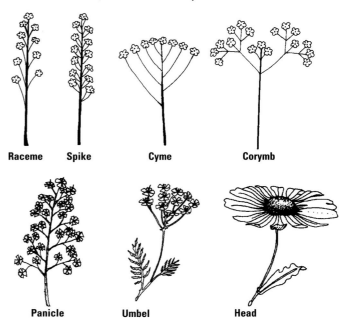

Raceme   Spike   Cyme   Corymb

Panicle   Umbel   Head

Figure 3–39. Types of inflorescences.

Day Length and Flowering
Light duration, or **photoperiod**, refers to the amount of time that a plant is exposed to sunlight. The ability of many plants to flower is controlled by photoperiod. When scientists first recognized the concept of a photoperiod, they believed that the duration of exposure to light triggered flowering. Later they discovered that it is not the light but the uninterrupted dark that triggers floral devel-

opment. Plants can be classified into three categories, depending upon their flowering response to the duration of darkness: short day, long day, or day neutral.

Short-day plants produce flowers only when the period of darkness exceeds a critical minimum called the critical night length. Short-day plants include many spring- and fall-flowering plants such as chrysanthemum and poinsettia. Long-day plants form flowers only when the period of darkness is less than the critical night length. They include almost all of the summer-flowering plants, such as black-eyed Susan (*Rudbeckia fulgida*) and California poppies (*Eschscholzia californica*), as well as many vegetables, including beets, radishes, lettuce, spinach, and potatoes.

Because chrysanthemums flower under the short-day conditions of spring or fall, the method for manipulating the plant into experiencing short days is simple. If long days are predominant, a shade cloth can be drawn over the chrysanthemum for 13 hours daily to block out light until flower buds are initiated. To bring a long-day plant into flower when sunlight is not present longer than a critical minimum, artificial light can be added until flower buds initiate.

Day-neutral plants produce flowers regardless of day length. Some plants do not really fit into any category but can respond to combinations of day lengths. Petunias will flower regardless of day length but will do so earlier and more profusely under long periods of daylight exposure (short periods of darkness).

Fruit
Fruits are important to human nutrition and often have a prominent place in a garden. A fruit is a ripened ovary that contains one or more seed. The fruit functions as protection for the seed until it is ready for dispersal. Many fruits are attractive to animals, thus a fruit's seed can be eaten, pass through a digestive tract, and end up far away from the parent plant, spreading genes and ensuring long-term survival of the plant. Some fruits rely on wind to disperse the seeds like the fluff on dandelion or the winged samara of a maple.

Types of Fruit
Fruits can be simple or compound. Simple fruits are formed in a flower with one ovary or several fused ovaries. Cherries, nectarines, peaches, and plums are **drupes** with a single hard seed in the center (Figure 3–40). Apples, pears, and quince are known as **pomes**. Each is a single fruit, but inside it has five fused ovaries, hence the five-pointed star shape when it is cut around its equator (Figure 3–41). Cantaloupes, cucumbers, eggplant, pumpkins, tomatoes, and watermelons are considered berries; they have several seeds inside a soft outer shell (Figure 3–42). Some

fruits are dry and do not have the typical flesh that comes to mind when one hears the word "fruit." Dry fruits can be either dehiscent and open when ripe or indehiscent and remain closed when ripe. Milkweed, poppies, and legumes are examples of dehiscent fruits (Figure 3–43). Indehiscent fruits remain closed when ripe and depend on some other mechanism, such as decay or predators, to release their contents. Indehiscent fruits include pecans, peanuts, or maples (Figure 3–44).

Compound fruits are either aggregate or multiple. If a single flower has several ovaries that stay together, it forms an aggregate fruit. Raspberries are aggregate fruits, technically aggregate drupes (Figure 3–45). If several flowers are tightly clustered together on one structure and these ovaries remain close together as the fruit ripens, they produce multiple fruits. Pineapples and figs are examples of multiple fruits (Figure 3–46).

Figure 3–40. A drupe like this nectarine has a single hard seed inside the fleshy ovary.
Mayr, Flickr
CC BY - 2.0

Figure 3–41. An apple is an example of a pome. In cross section the seeds form a 5-pointed star.
Denise Cross, Flickr CC BY - 2.0

Figure 3–42. A cantaloupe is an example of a berry, a fleshy ovary with many seeds inside.

Brandon Quester, News 21, Flickr CC BY - 2.0

Figure 3–43. This milkweed is an example of a dehiscent or dry fruit that splits open with seeds inside.

Sarah Nystrom, U.S. Fish and Wildlife Service, Flickr CC0

Figure 3–44. A walnut is an indehiscent fruit, dry outside and remains closed even when ripe. It is broken open either by predation or decay.

Pauline Mak, Flickr CC BY - 2.0

Figure 3–45. A raspberry is an aggregate fruit composed of several drupes fused together.

Ray Bodden, Flickr CC BY - 2.0

Figure 3–46. A pineapple is an example of a multiple fruit where several flowers are fused together to make one fruit.

Ramesh NG, Flickr CC BY-SA - 2.0

Strawberries are not BERRIES

The red part of the strawberry is, technically speaking, not a fruit; it is a ripened receptacle. If you look closely at a strawberry, you can see that each of its seeds is a mini indehiscent fruit called an achene (Figure 3–47). The receptacle ripens upward, softens, and turns red, attracting seed dispersers like birds.

Figure 3–47. A strawberry is a ripened receptacle. Kathleen Moore, CC BY - 2.0

Seeds

Seeds can be a flower's end product. A seed contains three parts (Figure 3–48):

- A miniature plant (embryo) that is in a state of **dormancy**.
- An **endosperm**, which is a stored food source for the embryo that can include proteins, carbohydrates, or fats.
- A **seed coat** or layer around the seed that protects the embryo from diseases, insects, and moisture until it is time for germination.

Germination occurs when the proper temperature, moisture, oxygen, and light conditions are met. As water is drawn in through the seed coat, the radicle is the first part of the seed to appear. The radicle will develop into the primary root and will eventually sprout root hairs and

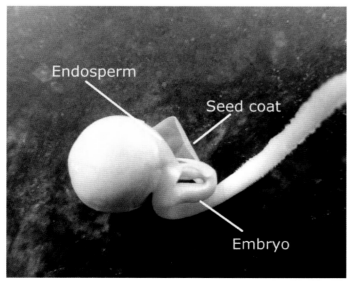

Figure 3–48. The parts of a seed.

lateral roots. The **hypocotyl** will eventually become the stem. The first leaves or cotyledons are usually shaped differently than the leaves the mature plant will produce. Those seeds with two cotyledons are dicots and those with one are monocots.

Plant Physiology—Internal Functions and Growth

Plants perform three basic processes that drive their growth and development:
1. **Photosynthesis**
2. **Respiration**
3. **Transpiration**

Plant growth is affected by how plants balance these three functions to survive in different environmental conditions, including various temperatures, day lengths, weather conditions, and water availability.

Photosynthesis

Unlike animals, plants can internally manufacture their own food. Through a process called photosynthesis, plants use energy from sunlight, carbon dioxide from air, and water from the soil to produce simple carbohydrates. These carbohydrates (such as glucose) are converted by different processes to complex sugars that can be transported to the stems, roots, flowers, and developing tissues for immediate use. These sugars can also be stored (as starch, the primary storage carbohydrate in plants) or used as building blocks for more complicated structures, such as oils, pigments, proteins, and cell walls.

Table 3–3. A Comparison of Photosynthesis and Respiration

At first glance, the equation for respiration appears to be the opposite of that used to depict photosynthesis, but respiration is not photosynthesis in reverse. It is appropriate, however, to think of photosynthesis as a carbon-building process and respiration as a process that breaks down carbon compounds to release the potential energy stored in them.

Photosynthesis	Respiration
uses water	uses food for plant energy
uses carbon dioxide	produces carbon dioxide
releases oxygen	uses oxygen
produces food	produces water
stores energy	releases energy
occurs in cells containing chloroplasts	occurs in all living cells

Photosynthesis

Photosynthesis, which literally means "to put together with light," can be described with the following chemical equation:

Carbon dioxide + Water + Light → Sugar + Oxygen + Water

The chemical notation for that equation is as follows:

$$6CO_2 + 12H_2O + \text{light captured by chlorophyll} \rightarrow C_6H_{12}O_6 + 6O_2 + 6H_2O$$

You can see from the equation above that chlorophyll, a green pigment contained in the chloroplasts, is a necessary ingredient in photosynthesis. Although any green plant tissue can capture light energy and accomplish photosynthesis, leaves are generally the site of most food production because of their specialized structures. Their internal tissues (**mesophyll**) contain cells with abundant chloroplasts in an arrangement that allows for easy movement of air and water. A leaf's stomata allow for the diffusion of carbon dioxide (CO_2) into the leaf, and the CO_2 is used in the manufacture of carbohydrates.

Respiration

The carbohydrates produced by photosynthesis are converted into energy for cellular work via a chemical process called respiration. It is similar to burning wood or coal to produce heat but is instead a slow and controlled release of energy. Respiration results in the formation of **ATP (adenosine triphosphate)**, a molecule used in several metabolic reactions in plant cells to carry out cellular work. ATP is sometimes referred to as the "energy currency of life." Respiration in cells may be shown most simply by this equation:

Sugar + Oxygen → Carbon Dioxide + Water + ATP

$$C_6H_{12}O_6 + 6O_2 \rightarrow 6CO_2 + 6H_2O + \text{ATP (energy)}$$

Respiration occurs in all life forms and in all cells. The release of accumulated carbon dioxide and uptake of oxygen occur at the cellular level. In animals, blood carries both carbon dioxide and oxygen to and from the atmosphere by means of either lungs or gills. In plants, there is simple diffusion of carbon dioxide and oxygen into the open spaces within the leaf, and exchange occurs through the stomata. Respiration continues in flowers, fruits, and vegetables even after they are harvested. That is why refrigeration and humidity control can be used to slow respiration and prolong the shelf life of produce.

Transpiration

We have learned that plants contain vascular tissue called xylem that transports water from the tips of roots to the tips of shoots. This water forms a continuous column in the plant, which helps keep the plant upright and firm or turgid. This cell firmness is called turgor pressure. Transpiration is the process by which a plant loses water, primarily through its stomata, pulling more water up the xylem. Approximately 90% of the water taken up by a plant is lost through transpiration. The other 10% of the water is used in chemical reactions and in plant tissues.

Transpiration is necessary for:
- Transporting minerals from the soil to the plant's parts
- Cooling plant parts through evaporation
- Moving sugars and plant chemicals, such as plant hormones
- Maintaining turgor pressure (wilting is a loss of turgor)

The rate of transpiration depends on several environmental factors. An increase in light, temperature, or wind, or a combination of these factors, increases transpiration to a point. Increases in humidity, however, decrease transpiration.

Leaves of many plants begin to wilt when the rate of water loss by transpiration is greater than the rate of water absorption. As the volume of water in the plant cells is reduced, leaves and herbaceous stems become soft or flaccid. The stomata generally close during drought or high temperature stress, thus reducing further water loss. Wilting reduces transpiration losses to an extent by shrinking the affected leaf surface. The cells will expand and return to their pre-stress size and become turgid (have high turgor pressure) when the plant absorbs sufficient water.

The rate of photosynthesis decreases when stomata are closed due to reduced water availability. Not only is water less available for metabolic reactions, but carbon dioxide cannot diffuse into the leaf tissue from the atmosphere. Cell shrinkage significantly affects other essential metabolic processes as well. Therefore, temporary wilting can be harmful to the plant. Frequent wilting and slow recovery under dry soil conditions can significantly reduce plant growth. This phenomenon accounts for the reduced size of plants when a water shortage occurs. During times of drought, most crops never reach their full potential.

Environmental Factors

Plants balance their basic life functions of photosynthesis, respiration, and transpiration to grow and reproduce. Environmental factors such as light, temperature, humidity, water, carbon dioxide, and oxygen levels can influence how plants perform these life functions. Understanding how these environmental factors can affect plants enables better prediction, prevention, diagnosis, and management of plant problems.

This section will review how the following environmental factors can influence plants:

- Light
- Temperature
- Water
- Oxygen
- Carbon dioxide

Light

Light, for the purpose of photosynthesis, has three main characteristics: duration, quantity, and quality. Duration is the length of time light is present. Light quantity refers to the intensity or concentration of sunlight and varies with the season. Summer brings the most intense light, and winter the least.

Light quality refers to the colors or wavelengths of light reaching the plant surface. Sunlight can be broken up by a prism into the visible color spectrum of red, orange, yellow, green, blue, indigo, and violet (Figure 3–49). Red and blue light have the greatest effect on photosynthesis. Plants mostly reflect green light, resulting in the green color we observe and associate with them. Blue light is primarily responsible for promoting vegetative growth. Red light, when combined with blue light, promotes flowering. Plants also perceive and are affected by wavelengths of light outside of the visible color spectrum, including ultraviolet and far-red.

Fluorescent and incandescent plant lights or "grow" lights have a mixture of red and blue wavelengths that attempt to imitate sunlight as closely as possible. Fluorescent light, particularly cool-white tubes, can be used to encourage leafy growth. Such light is excellent for starting seedlings. Incandescent light is high in the red-orange wavelength ranges but generally produces too much heat.

Figure 3–49. The visible spectrum of sunlight: red, orange, yellow, green, blue, indigo, and violet.
Aiko Van Hulsen, Flickr CC BY - 2.0

Temperature

Temperature affects a plant's productivity and growth by influencing flowering and fruit set, photosynthesis and respiration, water use, and dormancy. **Thermoperiodism** is a term used to describe the length of time that plants require exposure to certain temperatures in order to promote or inhibit different developmental events in the life cycle.

Temperature and Plant Growth

- Photosynthesis increases as temperature increases, to a point.
- Respiration rapidly increases as temperature increases.
- Transpiration increases as temperature increases.
- Flowering can be partially triggered by temperature.
- Sugar storage increases as temperatures cool and the plant uses less energy.
- Dormancy occurs during a period of low temperature. As temperatures warm, the plant will break dormancy and resume active growth.

- **Flowering and Fruit Set** – If temperatures are high and day length is long, cool-season crops such as spinach will flower prematurely (**bolt**) rather than produce the desired foliage. Adverse temperatures can also cause stunted growth and poor quality. For example, the bitterness in lettuce and cucumbers is caused by high temperatures. In addition, at high temperatures pollen may not be **viable**, preventing fruit set. On the other hand, temperatures that are too low for warm-season crops, such as tomatoes, will also prevent fruit set. Manipulating temperature, alone or in connection with day length, can control when certain flowers bloom. Chrysanthemums, for example, will flower for a longer period if daylight temperatures are 50°F. The Christmas cactus forms flowers as a result of short days and low temperatures. Daffodils can be forced to flower by putting bulbs in cold storage in October at 35°F to 40°F.

- **Photosynthesis and Respiration** – Temperature also influences the rates of photosynthesis and respiration; those rates generally increase as the temperature rises. Very high temperatures at night, however, sometimes cause the rate of respiration to surpass that of photosynthesis. When this occurs, the plant is using food faster than it can produce food. For most plants, photosynthesis occurs at its highest rate in the temperature range of 65°F to 85°F and decreases when temperatures are above or below this range. As a result, the most efficient thermoperiod (daily temperature range) for plants is usually when day temperatures are 10°F to 15°F higher than night temperatures. This temperature

3

range allows plants to photosynthesize and respire (break down food) during the day but slows down respiration at night when plants are not getting any light and hence cannot produce food.

- **Water Use** – Extremes in temperature can be detrimental to how plants use water. Very hot temperatures cause plants to lose water faster than they can absorb it, causing wilting and potentially stunting growth. Very low temperatures can freeze the soil, which severely restricts the movement of water into the plant. On a windy, sunny winter day, plants continue to transpire (give off water) and may become **desiccated** (dried out). Freezing temperatures may also result in the formation of ice crystals in and between plant cells, which can cause significant physical damage in addition to dehydration.

- **Dormancy** – Temperature affects plant dormancy. The buds of many plants require exposure to a certain number of days below a critical temperature (chilling hours) before the buds will resume growth in the spring. Peaches are a prime example. Most cultivars require 700 to 1,000 hours below 45°F and above 32°F before they break dormancy and begin to grow. The time period varies for different varieties. During dormancy, buds can withstand very low temperatures. But after the rest period is satisfied, buds become more susceptible to late cold or frost and can be easily damaged by these conditions. So, while very low temperatures can harm nonhardy plants, unseasonably warm winter temperatures can cause premature **bud break** in some plants and consequent bud freezing damage when temperatures dip back to their normal lows.

Water

Water has several important functions in photosynthesis. First, it maintains a plant's turgor, or the firmness or fullness of plant tissue. Turgor pressure in a cell can be compared to air in an inflated balloon. Water pressure, or turgor, is needed in plant cells to maintain shape and ensure cell growth (Figure 3–50). Second, water is split into hydrogen and oxygen by the solar energy that has been absorbed by chlorophyll in the plant's leaves. Oxygen is released into the atmosphere, and hydrogen is used in manufacturing carbohydrates. Third, water dissolves minerals from the soil and transports them upward from the roots and throughout the plant, where they serve as raw materials for the growth of new plant tissues. The soil moisture surrounding a plant should fluctuate. The soil should be well moistened and then allowed to dry out before irrigating again.

Oxygen

Plants use oxygen for respiration to create energy by breaking up the sugars created in photosynthesis. Oxygen is plentiful for the aboveground parts of a plant. Oxygen

can be a limiting factor for a plant's seeds, roots, and other underground parts.

Some soils contain large porespaces that allow air and water to move freely. Well-aerated soils provide the oxygen that seeds need to germinate and roots need to grow.

Some soils are dense, with poor drainage, leaving little to no pore space for oxygen. Soils that are oversaturated with water or compacted can prevent access to oxygen and cause root death (Figure 3–51). Read more about the importance of soil structure in chapter1, "Soils and Plant Nutrients."

Most roots occur in the upper foot or two of soil because that is where the most oxygen is located. The deeper the soil is, the less oxygen there is. Plants grown in saturated soils often have roots growing on the soil surface.

Figure 3–50. Turgor pressure in cells is kept up by adequate water. This peace lily (*Spathiphyllum* spp.) is wilting (loss of turgor pressure) from lack of water.

Cynthia Closkey, Flickr CC BY - 2.0

Figure 3–51. These shrubs are planted in dense soil, causing water to pool after a heavy rain. Oversaturation is detrimental to the shrubs' roots by reducing pore space and oxygen.

Emily LeaAnn, Flickr CC0

Carbon Dioxide

Carbon dioxide is a key component in photosynthesis. Carbon dioxide is plentiful, and its quantity in the air is rarely a limiting factor for plant growth. Most plants take in carbon dioxide through open stomata during the day when sunlight is available and photosynthesis is actively occurring. Carbon dioxide can be a limiting factor if the plant does not open its stomata during the day. Photosynthesis slows and can stop completely when stomata close. Stomata may close during the day to prevent water loss if the plant is drought stressed.

Soil

Another environmental factor is the soil. Soil structure, texture, and nutrient availability each have environmental impacts on plants. For more information about soils, see chapter 1, "Soils and Plant Nutrients."

Exceptions to the Rule:

Some desert-adapted plants, such as cacti and succulents, perform a different type of photosynthesis known as CAM or **Crassulacean acid metabolism** (Figure 3–52). CAM allows plants to keep their stomata closed during the hot part of the day to prevent water loss. These plants open their stomata at night and save the collected carbon dioxide for the next day when sunlight is available.

Figure 3–52. Plants that use CAM metabolism.
Stephen Boisvert, Flickr CC BY - 2.0

Plant Growth Chemicals

Hormones are chemicals that allow a plant to "communicate" with itself in response to the environment. Hormones exist in small concentrations in a plant, but they can have a big impact on its growth, health, and reproduction. Any cell in a plant can produce hormones, but they are typically produced in a plant's meristem. Hormones can travel through cells by **osmosis**, but they often travel down the plant from leaves to roots via phloem cells or up the plants from roots to leaves via xylem cells. Understanding the basics about plant hormones helps us understand why plants react to stimuli and how a change in hormone levels can encourage desired or undesired responses in a plant.

Plant growth is regulated by several classes of hormones: auxins, cytokinins, gibberellins, ethylene, and abscisic acid.

- **Auxins** are produced in the stem tips and promote apical dominance by suppressing the growth of lateral buds. Removing the terminal bud (pinching or pruning back a plant) eliminates the source of auxin, and thus allows lateral buds to grow. In addition, auxins can induce adventitious root formation on cuttings. Auxins differentially support cell division and cell elongation, resulting in directed growth in response to environmental factors. This is called **tropism**. The directional growth response to gravity is called gravitropism, and the growth response to light is called **phototropism** (Figure 3–53). A seed will send its roots down into the soil and its shoots up toward the soil's surface due to gravitropism. A plant will grow away from darkness by elongating cells on the side of the plant in the dark. People often say that plants grow "toward the light," but the elongation of cells is actually a growing away from darkness. Auxins also inhibit the dropping of leaves, flowers, and fruits (a process called **abscission**), and stimulate ethylene production.

Figure 3–53. Phototropism: auxins accumulate on the dark side of a stem, elongating those cells so that the shoot tissues grow towards a light source. Russell Neches, Flickr CC BY0

- **Cytokinins** promote cell division. They enhance shoot growth and counteract the effect of auxins in apical dominance. Cytokinin levels increase in axillary buds when apical dominance is removed. Cytokinins also help tissues delay **senescence**, the aging and maturity of tissues that ultimately results in tissue death. In short, auxins promote vertical (apical) growth; cytokinins promote axillary (lateral) growth.

- **Gibberellins** increase cell division, promote internode elongation, and regulate the production of seed enzymes. These enzymes are important during germination because they break down storage carbohydrates and proteins for use by the embryo. Gibberellins also stimulate flowering and can increase leaf size. Gibberellins can be used to force camellias to bloom out of season and to regulate the production of seedless grapes. A single treatment will more than double the size of Thompson seedless grapes and create a looser cluster of fruits. Gibberellins can be used to coax a plant out of dormancy and to green up a lawn two to three weeks earlier than normally.

- **Ethylene** is the only hormone that is a gas. It speeds aging of tissues and enhances fruit ripening (Figure 3–54). Fruits such as apples and bananas produce large quantities of ethylene. Enclosing a fruit that is a mature size but still gree, such as a tomato, in a bag with some apples will speed the ripening of the tomato. Ethylene is produced in almost every condition in which plant tissues are stressed, physically and chemically. It is also the primary abscission hormone in plants and is responsible for generating an abscission layer at the base of leaves in deciduous species when they drop their leaves. Ethylene is generally associated with senescence of plant tissues and organs.

- **Abscisic acid** (ABA) is considered a "stress hormone." It is a signaling molecule that induces stomatal closure during a drought or high-temperature stress conditions. ABA is involved in dormancy of seeds and buds and promotes abscission (loss of leaves, buds, or fruit). It protects the plant by inhibiting growth during times of stress.

Gardeners can influence plant hormones through plant modification or through the use of plant growth regulators. Any pruning will modify a plant's hormone balance and cause a change in growth pattern. If you remove the leggy stems of a mint plant, you will be cutting back auxin levels from the apical meristem dominance. Cytokinin levels will increase, stimulating "bushy" lateral meristem growth and creating a fuller, more attractive plant. On the contrary, if you pinch back the side branches of your tomato plants, you will reduce the cytokinin levels and encourage apical dominance from auxins. This apical dominance will reduce the number of tomato fruits but will increase fruit size.

A chemical that mimics a hormone is known as a **plant growth regulator**. Plant growth regulators are applied to plants for a specific purpose to achieve a desired result. Many production nurseries use plant growth regulators in their greenhouses, and farmers use them in their agricultural fields to increase plant quality and crop yield. Garden centers sell the following growth regulators:
- Auxin rooting hormone can be used in propagation to stimulate the growth of roots from stem cuttings. These

products are sold as indoleacetic acid (IAA), indolebuytric acid (IBA), or naphthalene acetic acid (NAA). The product for woody plant stem cuttings is 1-napthalene-acetimide (NAD).
- Some auxin products can kill **broadleaf** plants without harming monocots (grass).
- Gibberellic acid is used as a cut-flower preservative and to increase shoot growth, increase fruit size, and hasten maturity.
- Ethylene products enhance fruit color and hasten ripening.

Figure 3–54. These spots indicate stage 7 of ripening (overripe), which can derive from too much exposure to ethylene gas at a ripening facility.
Scot Nelson, Flickr CC BY - 2.0

Notching an Apple Tree to Encourage Lateral Growth

Sometimes young fruit trees need encouragement to produce a quality canopy. If you have a fruit tree with a central leader that could use some more side branches, you can encourage lateral growth by notching. Notching will encourage the canopy to fill in without major branch loss due to heading cuts. Two to three weeks before bloom, find the buds along the leader. Use a small hacksaw to make shallow cuts a third of the way around the branch just above the nodes where branches are desired. Be sure to leave some nodes for later, in case a limb is lost. Cut only through the phloem, not the structural part of the branch. This notching will disturb the flow of auxin hormone from the central leader and cause the axillary meristems to sprout and grow.

Frequently Asked Questions

1. A tree branch grows over my sidewalk, and people keep hitting their head on it. Should I wait for the tree to grow, or should I cut off the branch?

Plants continue to grow throughout their life at places on the plant known as meristems, which are located as follows:

- The tips of branches
- The tips of roots
- In bud tissues at nodes
- The vascular cambium tissue in the trunk (makes the trunk get thicker each year)

If the branch is too low to the ground, none of these meristematic areas of growth are going to raise this branch any higher off the ground. If the branch is a hazard, remove it. Follow the branch back to the union. Remove the branch at its point of attachment so it can compartmentalize the wound. Use sharp, sterilized pruning tools. If it is a large branch, be sure to make a three-point cut. For more information about pruning, see chapter 11, "Woody Ornamentals."

2. My plants didn't flower this year. Why?

A plant may not flower for many reasons:

- The plant has experienced some stress, either lack of water, nutrients, or light.
- It could be immature. Some plants take several years before they reach sexual maturity.
- Excess nitrogen fertilizer can cause leaf growth instead of flower growth.
- Flower buds can be very sensitive to frost. Cold weather during any time of bud development can hinder flowering.
- Incorrect pruning at the wrong time can remove flower buds, especially if a plant flowers on last year's wood. See chapter 11, "Woody Ornamentals," for information on the correct time to prune.

3. My muscadine grapevine does not have any fruit, or my muscadine has small fruit that did not ripen.

There are many reasons for poor yield in grapevines:

- Does it get enough sun? Fruit set and production will be reduced if the vines are shaded for more than several hours a day.
- Have you been giving it a high nitrogen fertilizer, which could cause leaf growth at the expense of fruit development?

Submit a soil sample to obtain specific fertilizer recommendations. Simply adding a balanced fertilizer, without knowing what your soil needs, can lead to high phosphorus in the soil. Boron deficiency may also result in poor fruit set, especially on sandy soils with high pH. Submit a foliar sample to determine boron status.

Figure 3–55.
Spreading lantana
(*Lantana* x 'Moni').

Kathleen Moore,
CC BY - 2.0

Further Reading

Capon, Brian. *Botany for Gardeners*. 3rd ed. Portland, Oregon: Timber Press, Inc., 2010. Print.

Coombes, Allen J. *The A to Z of Plant Names: A Quick Reference Guide to 4000 Garden Plants*. Portland, Oregon: Timber Press, Inc., 2012. Print.

Hodge, Geoff. *Practical Botany for Gardeners: Over 3,000 Botanical Terms Explained and Explored*. Chicago: The University Of Chicago Press, 2013. Print.

Johnson, Arthur T., and H. A. Smith. *Plant Names Simplified*. 2nd ed. Ipswich, England: Old Pond Publishing Ltd., 2008. Print.

Radford, Albert E., Harry E. Ahles, and C. Ritchie Bell. *Manual of the Vascular Flora of the Carolinas*. Chapel Hill, North Carolina: The University of North Carolina Press, 1968. Print.

Stearn, William T. *Botanical Latin*. 4th ed. 1992. Portland, Oregon: Timber Press, Inc., 2004. Print.

Staff of the Liberty Hyde Bailey Hortorium, Cornell University. *Hortus Third: A Concise Dictionary of Plants Cultivated in the United States and Canada*. New York: McMillan Publishers, 1976. Print.

3

For More Information

http://go.ncsu.edu/fmi_botany

Contributors

Contributions by Faculty:
Chad Jordan, Professor, Undergraduate Coordinator Plant Biology

Contributions by Extension Agents: Thomas Glasgow, Amy-Lynn Albertson, Charlotte Glen, Ben Grandon, and Carl Matyac

Contributions by Extension Master Gardener Volunteers: Patty Brown, Karen Damari, Margaret Genkins, Renee Lampila, Edna Burger, Caro Dosé, Connie Schultz, and Jackie Weedon

Content Editors:
Lucy Bradley, Professor and Extension Specialist, Urban Horticulture, NC State University; Director, NC State Extension Master Gardener program
Kathleen Moore, Urban Horticulturist

Copy Editor:
Barbara Scott

Based in part on text from the 1998 Extension Master Gardener manual prepared by:
Erv Evans, Former Extension Associate, Department of Horticultural Science
Paul Fantz, Professor Emeritus, Department of Horticultural Science
James Hardin, Professor Emeritus, Department of Botany

Adapted in part from the Virginia Gardener Handbook.

Chapter 3 Cover Photo: Kathleen Moore, CC BY - 2.0

How to Cite This Chapter:
Moore, K.A. and L.K. Bradley (eds). 2022. *North Carolina Extension Gardener Handbook*, 2nd ed. NC State Extension, Raleigh, NC. <https://content.ces.ncsu.edu/extension-gardener-handbook/3-botany>

Insects

4

Objectives

This chapter teaches people to:

- Recognize the value of insects in the garden.
- Identify insect structures and understand how to use structure in insect identification.
- Understand insect life cycles and how they influence the timing of insect management.
- Know insect classification and important orders.
- Identify all life stages of common beneficial insects found in home landscapes in North Carolina.
- Identify symptoms and signs of plant damage caused by insects.
- Differentiate between damage caused by biotic (insects, disease) and abiotic (environmental) factors.
- Distinguish between plant damage caused by piercing-sucking insects and chewing insects.

Introduction

Insects thrive in more environments than any other group of animals. They live in the air, on and in the soil, and in water. Insects and mites are among the oldest and most numerous animals on earth, with an estimated 100,000 different insect species in North America alone. A typical backyard contains 1,000 or more different insect species. Some estimates say there are 10 quintillion (10,000,000,000,000,000,000) individual insects on earth at any given time. That means there are approximately 300 pounds of insects for every human pound. With that many insects, how is it possible for plants and animals to survive? The vast majority of insects are harmless or even beneficial; less than 1% are considered pests. For example:

- Insects aid in the production of fruits, seeds, and vegetables by pollinating blossoms. Seventy-five percent of the world's crops (for food, beverages, fiber, medicine, and spices) and up to 30% of the American diet are the direct result of insect pollination, including many fruits (such as apples, blueberries, and raspberries) and vegetables (such as melons, peppers, and squash).
- Insects improve the soil's physical condition by burrowing throughout the surface layer. The dead bodies and droppings of insects serve as fertilizer.
- Insects consume or process dead plant matter, joining fungi and bacteria in recycling waste in our environment.
- Insects are valuable scavengers, devouring the bodies of dead animals and burying carcasses and dung (animal waste).
- Some insects parasitize or prey on harmful insects.
- Some insects are important because they feed on weed plants and seeds, helping to keep populations low.
- Insects serve as food sources for birds, fish, mammals, reptiles, and other animals.
- Some insects produce products humans use, such as honey, wax, silk, and dyes.
- Many insects such as butterflies and beetles can add beauty to a garden.

This chapter covers insects' biological structure, insect life cycles, insect classification, noninsect arthropods, strategies for identifying insect problems, symptoms and signs of plant damage caused by insects, the cultural and biological management of insects, and beneficial insects relevant to horticultural plants in North Carolina.

Insect Structures

Adult insects have an **exoskeleton**, three body regions, three pairs of legs, one pair of antennae (absent in Protura, a type of soil insect), and zero to two pairs of wings. Because legs and other appendages vary greatly to suit the insect's environment, they are often used to classify insects. Immature insects lack wings.

Exoskeleton

Unlike humans, insects do not have bones or a skeleton but rather a tough outer body wall, called an exoskeleton. The exoskeleton provides support for the internal organs and serves as a barrier to prevent water loss. Once it hardens, the exoskeleton restricts growth of the insect and must be molted so that the insect can continue to grow.

The exoskeleton is made of a sheet of cells covered by layers of **cuticle**. The cuticle contains wax that keeps the insect from drying out and determines how permeable the exoskeleton will be to water. Insects' bodies are separated into segments, and the cuticle of each segment is formed into several hardened plates called **sclerites**. These plates are joined together by flexible portions that enable the insect to move. The exoskeleton can be covered with hair, scales, spines, or spurs. The adult insect's body is made of three main parts: head, thorax, and abdomen (Figure 4–1), but the division between the thorax and abdomen is not always obvious.

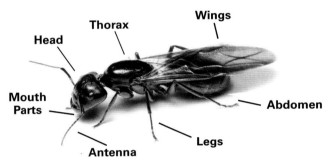

Figure 4–1. Parts of an insect.
Matt Bertone

Head

The main features of the adult insect's head are the eyes, antennae, and mouthparts.

1. Eyes – There are two types of insect eyes: simple and compound. Simple eyes (called **ocelli**) have one lens that perceives light intensity but does not produce an image. Compound eyes are usually large and composed of many small lenses; they can detect movement quite well but do not produce a particularly detailed image. The eyes of most insects are sensitive to color, which helps them to both select flowers to pollinate and detect mates. Some insects can also see ultraviolet light. Insect larvae, such as caterpillars, have only simple eyes or lack eyes, while adults often have both ocelli (lacking in most beetles) and compound eyes.

2. Antennae – Adult insects have one pair of antennae. Antennae, often referred to as horns or "feelers," are primarily organs of smell but can serve other functions, such as helping insects perceive humidity changes, vibrations, and wind direction and velocity. Segmented antennae vary greatly in form and complexity and are often useful in identifying insects (Figure 4–2).

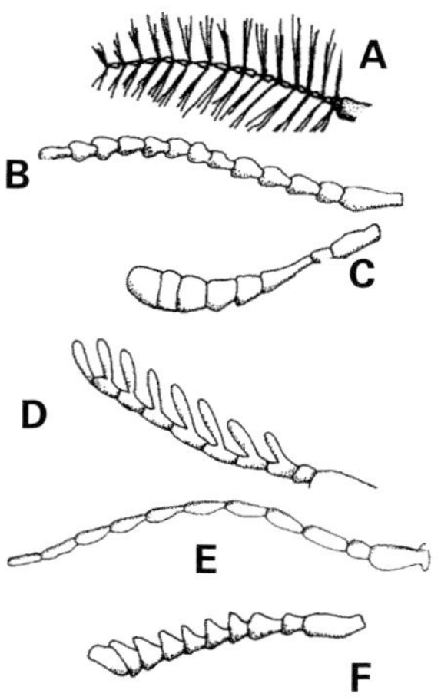

Figure 4–2. Antennae can be used to identify insects.
A. Plumose
B. Moniliform
C. Clavate
D. Pectinate
E. Filiform
F. Serrate

3. Mouthparts – While insect mouthparts differ considerably in appearance, the same basic parts are found in most types of insects (Figure 4–3a and Figure 4–3b). Mouthparts can be used to identify insects, the type of insect that caused plant damage, and the type of insecticide that would be effective in managing an insect problem. There are many types of mouthparts, but most insects fall into one of four categories: chewing, piercing-sucking, siphoning, and sponging.

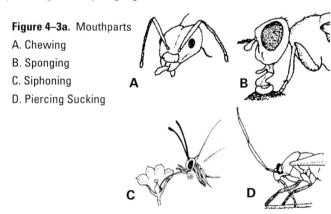

Figure 4–3a. Mouthparts
A. Chewing
B. Sponging
C. Siphoning
D. Piercing Sucking

There are also intermediate types, including rasping-sucking (thrips) and chewing-lapping (honeybees, wasps, and bumblebees). In some adult insects, the mouthparts are vestigial and the insect does not feed. The mouthparts of immature insects may vary from those of adults. Larval forms of insects that **pupate** generally have chewing mouthparts, regardless of the kind possessed by the insect in its adult stage; for example, caterpillars (larval form) generally possess chewing mouthparts while butterflies and moths (adult form) have siphoning mouthparts. However, **nymphs** (immature forms of insects that morph slightly with each molt, gradually maturing to the adult form) usually maintain the same mouthparts as adults.

Chewing mouthparts leave noticeable holes in leaves, wood, or fruit. Beetles (Coleoptera), caterpillars (Lepidoptera), crickets, grasshoppers, and katydids (Orthoptera), termites (Isoptera), and many other insect orders have chewing mouthparts.

Piercing-sucking mouthparts are a straw-like tube that punctures tissue and sucks fluids from the host, while also injecting saliva. Both plant pests and insect predators can have piercing-sucking mouthparts. They are typical of Hemiptera—(true bugs, aphids, scales, mealybugs, etc.), bloodsucking lice, fleas, and mosquitoes. Plant damage caused by piercing-sucking mouthparts includes stippling, spotting, stunting, yellowing, distorted growth, and **honeydew** (excrement produced by some sucking insects), which can lead to sooty mold. In addition, insects with piercing-sucking mouthparts can transmit diseases when they feed. Pesticides applied to the surface of the leaf are less likely to kill sucking insects because they feed inside the leaf.

4

Figure 4–3b Mouthparts
A. Chewing B. Sponging C. Siphoning D. Piercing Sucking
Matt Bertone

Siphoning mouthparts include a long tube adapted to draw nectar from flowers. While they also work like straws, they do not penetrate the plant like piercing-sucking mouthparts. Many moths and butterflies have siphoning mouthparts that may be up to several inches long. When not in use, the tubes are coiled under the head.

Sponging mouthparts are found in house flies, flesh flies, and blow flies, which all have mouthparts with a spongy tip (called a labellum) to suck up liquids or readily soluble food.

Thorax
The thorax is made up of three segments (prothorax, mesothorax, and metathorax). Each segment has a pair of legs, and the wings are attached to the last two seg-

ments, which also have **spiracles** or circular openings used for breathing.

1. Wings—Most adult insects have two pairs of wings. Wings are membranous outgrowths of the body wall and contain no muscles. Movement, direction, and folding of the wings are controlled by special muscles and **sclerites** of the thorax. Wings are supported by reinforcing structures called veins. Venation (the arrangement of veins in wings) is different among many groups of insects, even species, and serves as a useful means for insect identification (Figure 4–4).

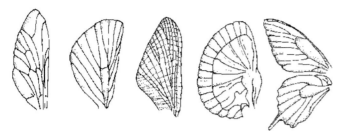

Figure 4–4. Wing venation can be used to help identify an insect.

Wing surfaces may be bare or covered with fine hairs or scales. The names of many insect orders end in *-ptera*, which comes from the Greek word meaning "wing." Thus, each of these names denotes some feature of the wings. Hemiptera means "half-winged," Hymenoptera means "membrane-winged," Diptera means "two-winged," and Isoptera means "equal wings." If the order ends in *-aptera*, it means the adult has "no wings."

2. Legs—The most important characteristic of an insect is the presence of three pairs of jointed legs. In addition to walking and jumping, insects use their legs for digging, grasping, feeling, swimming, carrying loads, building nests, cleaning parts of the body, and even making noise. Legs vary greatly in size and form and can help determine classification (Figure 4–5).

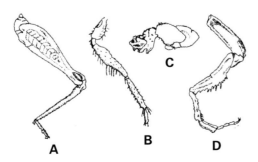

Figure 4–5. Legs can be used to identify insects.

A. Jumping (grasshopper)   C. Digging (mole cricket)
B. Running (beetle)   D. Grasping (praying mantid)

Abdomen

The abdomen contains digestive and reproductive organs as well as spiracles. The abdomen may have 11 or 12 segments, but in most cases they are difficult to distinguish. Some insects have a pair of appendages at the tip of the abdomen called cerci, which are used as sensory structures to help insects detect and identify their environments. They may be short, as in grasshoppers, termites, and cockroaches; to extremely long, as in mayflies. In earwigs and some diplurans they are modified as forceps to grip prey or defend from attackers.

In addition to six legs, caterpillars may have five (occasionally fewer) pairs of false legs (**prolegs**) that enable them to move. Prolegs are plump, fleshy, and often hooked to allow the caterpillar to hold onto a plant (Figure 4–6). Sawfly larvae (Hymenoptera) have six or more pairs of prolegs that lack hooks. This is an important distinction to note when looking to manage a caterpillar-like pest as proper identification of the larvae will aid in selecting an appropriate treatment. For example, some pesticides such as Bt (*Bacillus thuringiensis*) will work only on lepidopteran larvae and will not work on sawflies.

Figure 4–6. The prolegs are fleshy appendages visible on the left side; true legs are visible on the thorax (right side) of both larvae. Top: sawfly with 8 pairs of prolegs that lack hooks. Bottom: unicorn caterpillar.

Matt Bertone

Insect Life Cycle

A better understanding of insect life cycles will help guide proper identification. Positive identification can help determine if there is a need for management and if so, the best timing for that management. Knowledge of insect life cycles can help identify:

1. The life stage(s) of an insect that may cause plant damage.

4

2. The life stage of the insect that is easiest to manage.
3. Cultural choices such as choosing resistant varieties or adjusting planting times to insure plants are not in a susceptible stage when a pest is most active.
4. How local climate and ecological conditions may affect insect life cycles.

For example, seeing caterpillars defoliating a passion-flower vine may be alarming until those caterpillars are recognized as the larval form of the Gulf Fritillary butterfly (Figure 4-7). If the caterpillars are treated with insecticide, the beautiful adult stage of this beneficial pollinator would never be enjoyed. Cutworms overwinter as eggs on landscape debris, so their numbers can be significantly reduced by properly disposing of weeds and other landscape debris in the fall. The larval form is much more difficult to manage in the spring. Cabbage loopers can devour vegetables in their larval form, but securing row covers when the adult moths are flying around will significantly reduce the number of eggs laid. Insects may look different in various stages of their development, and being able to recognize those stages will guide decisions about when management is necessary and the appropriate timing of that management.

Figure 4–7. Gulf Fritillary caterpillars can destroy passion flower vines but they will turn into beautiful butterflies.

Devra, Flickr, CC BY - 2.0

The process by which insects change throughout their life is called metamorphosis. The term is a combination of two Greek words: *meta* meaning "change" and *morphe* meaning "form." Metamorphosis is a marked or abrupt change in form or structure. Some primitive orders of insects, such as springtails and silverfish, do not go through true metamorphosis but increase in size while maintaining the same characteristics.

"Gradual" (incomplete) and "complete" are descriptions of how many distinct parts there are in the metamorphosis. Insects that undergo gradual, or incomplete, metamorphosis get larger but do not generally change their appearance dramatically as they mature. The three stages of gradual metamorphosis are egg, nymph, and adult (Figure 4–8). The nymphs (immature insects) have eyes and antennae, resemble the adults, and often have similar feeding habits;

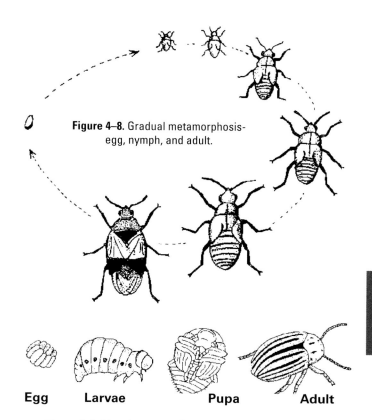

Figure 4–8. Gradual metamorphosis-egg, nymph, and adult.

Egg   Larvae   Pupa   Adult

Figure 4–9. Most insects undergo complete metamorphosis from an egg, larva, pupa, to adult.

however, nymphs are smaller and have no wings. They may have wing pads, which are developing wings in later nymphs. As nymphs grow into adults, they undergo a series of molts, where old exoskeleton sheds and new exoskeleton forms. This new exoskeleton expands and then hardens. The stage of life between each molt is an **instar**. The number of instars, and frequency of molts, varies considerably with species and to some extent with food supply, temperature, and moisture. Examples of insects that undergo gradual metamorphosis include earwigs, grasshoppers and their kin, bugs and their kin, cockroaches, and termites. Adults are usually short-lived.

Most insects undergo complete metamorphosis, passing through four distinct stages: egg, larva, pupa, and adult (Figure 4–9). A larva may or may not have legs, antennae, or eyes. Sometimes they appear wormlike or are covered with spines or tufts of hair. Larvae may molt several times but generally do not change their form until they reach the pupal stage. During the pupal stage, the insect becomes inactive and does not eat but undergoes a profound change. Some insects spin a cocoon or web, or roll a leaf around their bodies for protection. During pupation many tissues and structures are completely broken down and structures of the adult are formed. The adult has little or no resemblance to the larval stage and may be associated with an entirely different habitat. The adult insect spends its often short adulthood reproducing. Its food is often entirely different from that of the larval stage. Insects that undergo complete metamorphosis include beetles, butterflies, ants, bees, moths, wasps, flies, and fleas.

Insect Classification

Identification of the thousands of species of insects would be impossible if we did not organize a standard classification system. Like the plant kingdom, the animal kingdom has major divisions known as phyla. Several of the phyla that contain horticultural pests include:

- Arthropoda (insects, spiders, crayfish, millipedes)
- Nematoda (roundworms, nematodes, trichina)
- Platyhelminthes (flatworms, flukes, tapeworms)
- Mollusca (snails, slugs, clams)

More than three-fourths of the animals known to exist belong to the phylum Arthropoda. *Arthro* means "jointed" and *poda* means "foot." Characteristics common to arthropods include paired, jointed appendages; **chitinous** exoskeleton; segmented bodies; and bilateral symmetry. The phylum Arthropoda is divided further into different classes. Table 4–1 describes a few of the more important classes and presents some characteristics that are used to distinguish insects from other arthropod classes. For an arthropod to be further classified into the Insecta class, it must have three body segments and three pairs of legs.

Families are further divided into genera and species. These are the most specific levels of the classification system. The house fly, *Musca domestica*, serves here as an example of classification:

Phylum	Arthropoda
Class	Insecta
Order	Diptera
Family	Muscidae
Genus	*Musca*
Species	*domestica*

Insects often acquire common names; sometimes one species may have several common names. For example, *Helicoverpa zea*, when found on corn, is called the corn earworm, but when found on tomatoes it is called the tomato fruitworm. Common names are often used to refer to large groups of insects, such as families or orders. The term "beetle" refers to the entire order Coleoptera, which includes thousands of different species. The term "moth" refers to thousands of species in the order Lepidoptera.

When to space…
When a common name includes the type of insect, the name is two words, for example "honey bee." However, if the common name includes the name of another order (not the one in which the insect is classified), the name is one word–for example, "ladybug" (also called "lady beetle") because the insect is actually a beetle rather than a true bug.

Insect Orders Important to Gardeners

The ability to classify an insect to the correct order gives access to valuable information about the biology of the insect in question. Knowing its biology can reveal the insect's habitat, how it feeds, and its life cycle and gives clues about useful management strategies, including proper timing for best control.

COLEOPTERA
(from Greek koleos = "sheath" + ptera = "wings")

Coleoptera—including beetles, weevils, and soft-bodied larvae called grubs—is the largest order of insects (Figures 4–10 a-b). These insects vary greatly in size, diet, and habitat. They can feed on agricultural, horticultural, and weed plants. Beetles can be predators, scavengers, parasites,

---

Table 4–1. Classes of the Phylum Arthropoda

Class	Examples	Major Body Regions	Pairs of Legs
Malacostraca	crayfish, sowbugs	2	5
Arachnida	spiders, mites, ticks	1 or 2	4
Symphyla	symphylans	2	12
Insecta	bugs, beetles, butterflies	3	3

Classes are further divided into orders. The more important orders of the class Insecta are listed in Table 4–2. Insect orders are broken down into groups known as families of very closely related insects. Family names end with *idae*. Aphididae (aphids), Muscidae (house flies), and Blattidae (cockroaches) are examples of insect families.

Table 4–2. Some Orders of the Class Insecta and Their Characteristics

Order	Common Name	Metamorphosis	Adult Mouth Parts	Wings[1]
Coleoptera	beetles, weevils	complete	chewing	2 pairs
Collembola	springtails	none	chewing	none
Dermaptera	earwigs	gradual	chewing	2 pairs
Diptera	flies	complete	chewing, piercing-sucking or sponging	1 pair
Hemiptera	true bugs, aphids, scales	gradual	piercing-sucking	2 pairs
Hymenoptera	bees, wasps, ants	complete	chewing	2 pairs
Isoptera	termites	gradual	chewing	2 pairs
Lepidoptera	butterflies, moths	complete	chewing or siphoning	2 pairs
Neuroptera	lacewings, antlions, dobsonflies	complete	chewing	2 pairs
Orthoptera	crickets, grasshoppers	gradual	chewing	2 pairs
Siphonaptera	fleas	complete	chewing or rasping-sucking	none
Thysanoptera	thrips	gradual	rasping-sucking	2 pairs
Thysanura	silverfish	gradual	chewing	none

[1] Many orders that have wings have short-winged or wingless forms. Also some insect body modifications such as beetle elytra may look similar to wings but are not used for flying.

or decomposers. They may also be pests of stored grain products. Coleopterans occupy almost every habitat in which insects are found. Almost 40% of all insects are beetles. In some species only the adult or the larval stage damages plants; in other cases, both the adult and the larval stages cause harm. In still other cases, neither the larva nor adult causes harm. Larvae may feed on roots, stems, foliage, buds, seeds, fruit, or woody tissue. Coleopteran larvae can be distinguished from other insect larvae by their hardened, often dark head, chewing mouthparts, and the presence of **spiracles** along their bodies. Some common examples of beetles include Japanese beetles, wireworms, June beetles, rootworms, striped cucumber beetles, plum curculios, pea weevils, Mexican bean beetles, Colorado potato beetles, flea beetles, weevils, cane borers, and lady beetles. Several characteristics are common to most beetles:

- Adults have a hardened, dense exoskeleton; size and shape vary greatly.
- Adults have two pairs of wings; the outer pair, called elytra, is hardened or leathery. The inner pair is membranous, folds under the front wings, and is used to fly.
- Adults and larvae have chewing mouthparts.
- Adults usually have noticeable antennae, which can be club shaped, serrated, feathery, bead-like or threadlike.

Figure 4-10a. Japanese beetle (Scarabaeidae). Laura Wolf, Flickr, CC BY - 2.0

Figure 4–10b. Bark weevils (Cossoninae), order Coleoptera. Matt Bertone

- Soft-bodied larvae have three pairs of legs on the thorax and no legs on the abdomen. Weevil larvae and a few other groups of beetle larvae lack legs on the thorax.
- All Coleoptera undergo complete metamorphosis.

DERMAPTERA
(from Greek derma = "skin" + ptera = "wings")

Dermaptera (Figure 4–11), known as earwigs, are **nocturnal** insects that hide during the day in leaf litter, mulch, and under bark. They are generally scavengers or predators. They are believed to be good nocturnal feeders on aphids. Earwigs share several common traits:
- Adults are moderately sized, elongated, flat, brown insects.
- They have two pairs of wings: front wings that are short and leathery and leave the abdomen exposed and a hind pair that is membranous and folds under the front pair.
- Adults have movable forceps (cerci) on the abdomen.
- Their antennae are threadlike.
- Adults and nymphs have chewing mouthparts.
- They metamorphose gradually. Nymphs resemble adults, only smaller or lacking true wings. Their forceps are also softer.

Figure 4–11. Female earwig guarding and caring for her eggs, order Dermaptera.
Matt Bertone

DIPTERA
(from Greek, di = "two" and ptera = "wings")

This is the order of true flies (Figure 4–12). Most insects have four wings, but dipterans have only two. The size of the adult varies from less than 1/8-inch to more than 1 inch. They range in color, and most are soft bodied. Some adults feed on nectar, some are blood feeders, some are parasites of other insects, and many are predators. Although they are less known than bees, flies are important pollinators. Fly larvae occur in a wide variety of habitats, though many live in some sort of aquatic environment. Plant-feeding larvae generally feed within the plant tissue—for example, leaf miners, borers, and

gall formers. Many species feed during the larval stage on decaying plant or animal matter. Common traits for the order include the following:
- Two adult forewings are membranous and clear.
- Hind wings are modified to small knobs called **halteres**, which are used for stabilization during flight.
- Larvae are legless and wormlike (maggots) or can be aquatic forms.
- Adults lack chewing mouthparts; they are either piercing or sponging. Larval mouthparts are variable, but many (especially maggots) have simple mouth hooks. They can cause plant damage, but most do not.
- They undergo complete metamorphosis.

Figure 4–12. A blow fly (*Calliphora livida*), order Diptera.
Matt Bertone

HEMIPTERA
(from Greek, hemi = "half" and ptera = "wings")

This order includes true bugs and sucking insects in the former order Homoptera (mealybugs, whiteflies, leafhoppers, aphids). This order includes stink bugs, plant bugs, squash bugs, boxelder bugs, chinch bugs, damsel bugs, predaceous assassin bugs (Figures 4–13 a-f), scale insects, cicadas, planthoppers, treehoppers, spittlebugs, wooly aphids, and psyllids (Figure 4–14 a-i; Figure 4–14e appears on page 4-20).

Figure 4–13a. Chinch bug (*Blissus insularis*), a true bug in the order Hemiptera.
Matt Bertone

Both hemipteran nymphs and adults feed on plants by puncturing seeds, stems, foliage, flowers, or fruit and then sucking the sap. Some hemipterans may inject a toxin into the plant, which causes further damage. Injury to plants is characterized by mottled gray spots on foliage, deformed buds or fruit (catfacing), wilting, or death. They may also carry plant diseases. Some Hemiptera, howev-

Figure 4–13b. Plant bug, a true bug in the order Hemiptera.

Matt Bertone

Figure 4–13c. A member of the squash bug family, a true bug in the order Hemiptera.

grassrootsgroundswell CC BY - 2.0

Figure 4-13d. A damsel bug, predatory beneficial insect, a true bug in the order Hemiptera.

Matt Bertone

Figure 4–13e. Predatory assassin bug, a true bug in the order Hemiptera.

John Flannery (DrPhotoMoto), Flickr CC BY - ND 2.0

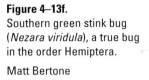

Figure 4–13f.
Southern green stink bug (*Nezara viridula*), a true bug in the order Hemiptera.

Matt Bertone

Figure 4–14c. Whitefly, order Hemiptera.
Greenhouse and citrus whiteflies are among the pest species in NC.
Matt Bertone

Figure 4–14d. Aphids, both adult and nymphs, order Hemiptera.

Matt Bertone

Figure 4–14e appears on page 4-20.

Figure 4–14a. Scale insect, order Hemiptera.
USGS Bee Inventory and Monitoring Lab, Sam Droege, Flickr public domain

Figure 4–14b. Mealybug, order Hemiptera.
Eran Finkle, Flickr CC BY - 2.0

Figure 4-14f. Leafhopper (*Sibovia occatoria*), order Hemiptera.
Matt Bertone

Figure 4-14g. Flatid planthopper, order Hemiptera.
Matt Bertone

er, are helpful predators of other insects. Common traits among hemipterans include:

- Adults and nymphs usually resemble one another.
- Adults and nymphs have piercing-sucking mouthparts that can cause damage to plants.
- If pests, both adults and nymphs cause damage.
- They undergo incomplete metamorphosis; the stages are egg, nymph, and adult. Scales and whiteflies go through a type of "pupal" stage, though it is not exactly the same as in insects that have complete metamorphosis.
- Adults usually have two pairs of wings. The first pair are "halfwings" (leathery at the base and nearly transparent at the tip). The second pair is membranous and smaller; at rest, the transparent tips overlap.
- Many true bugs give off an unpleasant odor when disturbed.
- Many secrete "honeydew," especially certain scales, aphids and whiteflies.

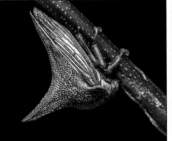

Figure 4-14h. Thorn treehopper (*Umbonia crassicornis*), order Hemiptera.
Matt Bertone

Figure 4-14i. Hop-hornbeam psyllid, order Hemiptera.
Matt Bertone

4

HYMENOPTERA
(from Greek, hymen = "membrane" and ptera = "wings")

Hymenoptera (Figures 4–15 a-e; Figure 4–15e appears on page 4-20) includes bees, ants (Figure 4–1), beneficial predatory and parasitic wasps, sawflies, and horntails. Their egg-laying organ (ovipositor) is well developed; some are modified into stingers for subduing prey or defense. Males, however, cannot sting. In adult form, hymenopterans can often be found around flowers. Common traits include:

- Most adults have two pairs of membranous wings (hind wings are smaller).
- Most adults have a pinched waist.
- Adults have rather soft or only slightly hard bodies.
- Some species organize into societies.
- Larvae are grublike or maggotlike. They have either no legs (wasps, bees, ants) or three pairs of legs on their thorax and six pairs of prolegs (without hooks) on their abdomen (some sawfly larvae).
- Most have chewing mouthparts, although some adults have chewing-lapping mouthparts.
- They undergo complete metamorphosis.

Figure 4–15a. A worker honey bee (*Apis mellifera*), order Hymenoptera.
USGS Bee Inventory and Monitoring Lab, Sam Droege, Flickr public domain

Figure 4–15b. A beneficial braconid wasp, order Hymenoptera.

Matt Bertone

Figure 4–15c.

A parasitoid wasp (Pteromalidae), order Hymenoptera, checking out freshly peeled bark on *Pinus taeda*.

Matt Bertone

Figure 4–15d. Female horntail (*Tremex columba*), order Hymenoptera.
Matt Bertone

Figure 4–15e appears on page 4-20.

Figure 4-16. Orange sulphur butterfly, order Lepidoptera.
John Gerwin

LEPIDOPTERA
(from Greek, lepid = "scale" and ptera = "wings")

Lepidoptera (Figure 4–16) is composed of butterflies, moths, and skippers. Not all adults feed, but those that do, feed on nectar or other liquid food. Adults do not harm plants, but they lay eggs that hatch into plant-eating larvae with chewing mouthparts called caterpillars. Most larvae feed externally on plant materials; others are leaf miners, borers, or gall makers; a few are predators. We classify larvae based on the damage they cause to different plants. Some of the names for lepidopteran larvae include budworms, cutworms, borers (potato tuberworm, peach tree borer, European corn borer), fruitworms (codling moth, oriental fruit moth, pickleworm, tomato pinworm, squash vine borer), webworms (fall webworm, Eastern tent caterpillar), leaf miners, leaf rollers, leaf folders, and leaf crumplers. Other Lepidopterans include loopers, corn earworms, monarch butterflies, cankerworms, redhumped caterpillars, imported cabbageworms, and parsleyworms. Many will pupate in silk cocoons; some do not. Injury to plants is characterized by tears, tunnels, or ragged holes in the affected plant part.

Common lepidopteran traits include:
- Adults are soft-bodied, with four well-developed membranous wings covered with small scales.
- Larvae are wormlike caterpillars, variable in color, and voracious feeders.
- Larvae generally have three pairs of segmented legs on the thorax and five or fewer pairs of prolegs on the abdomen.
- The adult's mouthpart is a coiled, sucking tube.
- Larvae have chewing mouthparts that cause damage to plants.
- Lepidopterans undergo complete metamorphosis and have one or more generations per year.

NEUROPTERA
(from Greek, neuro = "veined" and ptera= "wings")

Neuroptera (Figure 4–17 a-c) includes lacewings, antlions, mantispids, and dustywings. Many are terrestrial, but some are aquatic. As far as we know, all larvae are predators, and many adults are also predators. Some adults may take only pollen, nectar, or honeydew. Antlion larvae live in the sand and construct pit falls to trap prey. Lacewing larvae prey on aphids, mites, and scale insects. Some species are available commercially for biological control. Common traits include:

- Adults have two pairs of membranous wings with an extensive pattern of veins and cross veins.
- At rest, wings are held flat to the body or held up to resemble a tent.
- Most are weak fliers.
- Their antennae are long.
- Larvae have piercing sucking mouthparts and are predatory. They do not cause damage to plants.
- They undergo complete metamorphosis.

Figure 4–17a. Ant lion larvae (top) build small dirt cone traps that prey fall into and cannot get out of. The larva will wait at the bottom with its large mouthparts. The adult ant lion is pictured at the bottom, order Neuroptera.
Matt Bertone

Figure 4–17b. Dustywing, order Neuroptera.
Matt Bertone

Figure 4–17c. Mantispid, order Neuroptera.
Matt Bertone

Figure 4–18a. Eastern lubber grasshopper (*Romalea microptera*), order Orthoptera.
Matt Bertone

Figure 4–18b. Female katydid (*Conocephalus*), order Orthoptera.
Matt Bertone

ORTHOPTERA
(from Greek, ortho = "straight" and ptera = "wings")

Examples of insects in Orthoptera (Figures 4–18 a-b) include grasshoppers, crickets, mole crickets, and katydids. Food and habitat vary, depending on species. Most orthopterans are plant feeders, but they can be predators, scavengers, or omnivores. Orthopterans share the following traits:

- Adults are moderate to large and often have rather hard bodies.
- Adults have two pairs of wings. The front wings are elongated, narrow, and thickened; hind wings are broad, many-veined, membranous, and usually fold under front wings when at rest. Some have small wings or lack them altogether.
- Enlarged hind legs are common and assist in jumping.
- Many rub their wings together to make noise.
- Both adults and nymphs of pest species cause damage to plants.
- Nymphs resemble adults, but they have wing pads or are wingless.
- They have chewing mouthparts and can damage plants, but some are predators.
- They metamorphose gradually.

THYSANOPTERA
(from Greek, thysano = "fringe" and ptera = "wings")

Thysanoptera (thrips, singular and plural) are thin, tiny insects with four narrow, fringed wings in the adult stage (Figure 4–19). During their life, they change gradually in size and slightly in form. Several generations occur each year if conditions are favorable. They do not fly well but can travel great distances by wind. Some thrips feed on other insects or mites and are beneficial, but many cause damage to commercial crops. Discolored and distorted flowers and buds or gray speckled areas on fruit or foliage characterize injury to plants. Thrips scrape the feeding surface and suck up the plant's fluids. Thrips can transmit tomato spotted wilt virus (TSWV). Common traits of thrips include:
- Adults are small insects (around 1 mm in length) and have soft bodies.
- They are often present on flowers or leaves.
- They have two pairs of wings that are slender and featherlike with fringed hairs.
- They have rasping-sucking mouthparts that can cause damage to plants.
- Thrips' metamorphosis is intermediate (between simple and complete).

Figure 4–19. Thrips, order Thysanoptera.

Matt Bertone

Common Noninsect Arthropod Pests of Plants or People in the Garden

SPIDER MITES
Spider mites are tiny, soft-bodied arachnids with two body regions. They do not have a thorax. They have three (larvae) or four (nymphs and adults) pairs of legs, and no antennae (Figure 4–20). Larvae, nymphs, and adults have sucking mouthparts. They are so small that they are often not discovered until after they have damaged the plant. Foliage, buds, stems, and fruit of infected plants may become red, bronze, rusted, yellow, white, or brown from feeding damage. Spider mites spin light, delicate webs over buds and between leaves where they feed. Mite populations are favored by hot, dry conditions and can spread from field or road margins by wind currents.

There are several common species:
- Two-spotted spider mites and near relatives can be clear, green, orange, or reddish. They have two small spots on the back that are difficult to see without a magnifying glass.
- Southern red mites are dark red.
- Clover mites are larger, brown or gray, flat, and have very long front legs.

Some mites are beneficial predators that eat other mites. They generally move faster than the damaging mites and are often less hairy.

Figure 4–20.
Spider mites.
Matt Bertone

SPIDERS
Spiders have two body regions clearly distinct from one another, separated by a thin waist. Most spiders are beneficial predators. North Carolina has two dangerous spiders: the black widow and the brown recluse. The black widow spider is shy, likes dark places, and spins a characteristically messy web. The female is normally a shiny, black, moderate-sized spider with a red or orange hourglass marking on the underside of the abdomen (Figure 4–21). Males and immature females can have stripes of red, yellow, and black on the abdomen. Brown recluse spiders are only found natively in the far western tip of the state; they are extremely rare in most of North Carolina. Wolf spiders and other hunting spiders are often confused with brown recluses. A brown recluse has six eyes arranged in pairs and a dark brown fiddle- or violin-shaped mark on its head-thorax. The spider is light brown or gray with long, delicate legs and is about the size of a quarter when mature (Figure 4–22).

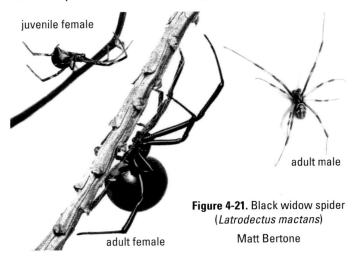

juvenile female

adult male

adult female

Figure 4-21. Black widow spider (*Latrodectus mactans*)

Matt Bertone

Figure 4–22. A female brown recluse spider (*Loxosceles reclusa*). Note the fiddle-shaped marking on the cephalothroax.

Matt Bertone

TICKS

Ticks are parasitic blood feeders of animals and humans. Larvae have six legs; nymphs and adults have eight legs. All stages lack antennae (Figure 4–23). Many can carry diseases. Hard ticks have a hard dorsal plate called a scutum and mouthparts that are visible from above. Soft ticks lack a scutum, are soft-bodied, and have mouthparts visible from below.

Figure 4–23. Female lone star tick (*Amblyomma americanum*) seeks out vertebrates to suck their blood.
Matt Bertone

MILLIPEDES

Millipedes are slender, somewhat wormlike animals, with two pairs of legs on most of their body segments. Very young millipedes have only six legs, but as they grow, they gain more pairs of legs with each molt. This is why millipedes have garnered the nickname "thousand leggers." Millipedes lay their eggs in damp places. They usually eat decaying plant matter but sometimes feed on the roots of ornamental plants to obtain moisture when the weather gets dry. Ordinarily, more complaints about millipedes occur during wet weather (millipedes like dampness but not long rainy periods), when they may invade people's homes. When disturbed, some millipedes curl up and secrete a foul-smelling fluid containing cyanide compounds. (Figure 4–24)

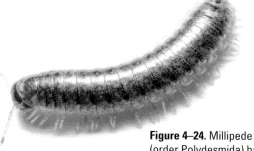

Figure 4–24. Millipede (order Polydesmida) has two pairs of legs for every body segment.

Matt Bertone

CENTIPEDES

Centipedes strongly resemble millipedes, except they have longer antennae, a flat cross section, and only one pair of legs on each body segment (Figure 4–25). They are beneficial predators of other arthropods, and they do no damage to plants.

Figure 4–25. A stone centipede. Centipedes (order Chilopoda) are beneficial arthropods that have only one pair of legs per body segment.
Matt Bertone

PILLBUGS AND SOWBUGS

These insects are similar to millipedes in biology and in the damage they cause to ornamental crops, but they differ in that they have only one pair of legs per body segment, for a total of seven pairs (Figure 4–26). Pillbugs can roll up into small spheres; sowbugs usually cannot roll up. Pillbugs and sowbugs are crustaceans (akin to crayfish) and typically live in damp areas under stones, boards, and dead leaves. Pillbugs and sowbugs sometimes crawl into the drainage holes of houseplant pots to feed on decaying organic matter. They work the potting mix out of these holes as they crawl in and out at night. In dry weather, they sometimes feed on tender plants, fruits, or roots to obtain moisture.

Figure 4–26. Sowbugs (order Oniscidea) have one pair of legs per body segment for a total of seven pairs of legs. They are similar to pill bugs but cannot roll up when touched.

Matt Bertone

Table 4–3. A diagnostic tool to help determine the cause of plant damage.

Biotic problems include insects, diseases, weeds, nematodes, parasitic plants, animals, and other living organisms. Abiotic problems include water issues, compacted soil, nutrient deficiencies and toxicity, salinity, pH, temperature, sunburn, light, wind, pollution, lightening, root girdling, mechanical injury, chemical injury, and other nonliving plant problems.

| | BIOTIC (Living) | | ABIOITIC (Nonliving) |
	Insect	Disease	Weather, Mechanical, Chemical
Location	Generally limited to one type of plant (specific host)	Generally limited to one type of plant (specific host)	Affects multiple types of plants in a specific location
Progression	Over time progresses on plant and to similar plants	Over time progresses on plant and to similar plants	Does not progress
Signs	Frass, cast skins, insect	Fungal spores, bacterial ooze	No signs of living pathogen

Identifying Insect Problems

A detailed picture or an actual specimen is generally necessary for proper insect identification. Photographs can be helpful if they include critical elements. Ensure the subject is in focus as well as large enough to see important features such as legs and mouthparts. Include a scale item such as a finger or a coin in the same focal plane as the subject. Taking several photographs from different angles is helpful.

Avoid answering identification questions over the telephone. Describing what an insect looks like over the telephone can be challenging. Ask as many questions as possible to help identify the problem. For example, ask the following: When did it start and for how long has it been an issue? What was the insect feeding on? How many were there? How were they distributed? Does it appear to be mobile or stationary? Does the insect have wings? Try to get as many facts from the client and consult resources before making any decisions on whether the situation warrants intervention. If a specific pest is suspected, look at online pictures. Pesticide recommendations are in the *North Carolina Agricultural Chemicals Manual*. When in doubt, ask an Extension agent to help positively identify the insect. If the Extension agent is unsure, a sample may need to go to the Plant Disease and Insect Clinic at NC State University.

Indices
Pests can be indexed by name and by host plant in pest publications. Cynthia Westcott's *The Gardener's Bug*

Book has one of the more complete pest indices by host plant. *IPM for Shrubs in Southeastern U.S. Nursery Production: Vol. I* also lists insect pests by shrub, shows timing of incidence, and offers management strategies. If the host plant is known, indices can be used to narrow down the list of possible pests. Asking more questions about the size, shape, damage, and byproducts of a pest, can further limit the list of potential culprits.

Keys
Entomologists have designed keys to identify insects. A key is a step-by-step process of elimination using morphological characteristics—such as mouthparts, leg parts, or wing veins—that narrow the choices until an identification is determined. Use of these keys depends on knowledge of basic insect structure. NC State Extension resources such as *Insects and Related Pests of Shrubs* (AG-189) and NC State Extension TurfFiles: Insects and Other Pests contain introductory keys to pest identification on the family level. By keying a pest to a family and using the indices of pests by host plant, a pest can usually be identified correctly.

Pest Calendars
Many pests occur on plants only at certain times of the year. Pest calendars provide approximate dates when certain insects attack plants and in what stage of life the insects will be. Armed with this information, the field of potential pests can be narrowed. For example, a pest is discovered in a lawn in July. It appears to be an immature insect. According to the *Turfgrass Pest Management*

Submitting Insect Samples to the Plant Disease and Insect Clinic

If insect identification is not possible, consult the Extension agent in your county. If you still need help, submit a specimen to the Plant Disease and Insect Clinic at NC State University.

Follow these instructions:
- Most insects—cockroaches, termites, bugs, beetles, flies, wasps, ants, maggots, and spiders: preserve in 70% alcohol.
- Mites, scales, aphids, and thrips—Send in alive on some part of the affected plant. Place the plant in a plastic bag or preserve some specimens in alcohol.
- Butterflies and moths—Send in dead. Adults can be frozen.
- Caterpillars—Send in alive on some part of the host plant in a plastic bag.
- Grubs—Send in alive in a pint or two of soil enclosed in a plastic bag.
- When in doubt, put specimens in 70% alcohol.
- Collect several specimens if possible.

If a specimen cannot be collected, take digital pictures of the insect and damage to the plant. Tips for good photographs:
- Be sure to include a "scale" item in images, such as a coin or a thumb.
- Take many photos from several angles with the flash both on and off.
- Use the "macro" feature (usually a flower symbol) on a camera to zoom in on the details of the insect. A hand lens can sometimes be put in front of the camera lens to increase magnification.
- Be sure to take close-up images of the head, thorax, and legs, as well as the underside of the insect.
- Take images of the insect on the plant if possible as well as on a white or dark sheet of paper.
- If different life stages of the insect are present, take images of all of them.

Fill out an insect identification form. Provide all of the following information:
- Date specimen was collected. (Date actually found, not the date submitted.)
- Town and county where specimen was collected. If not found in a town, give the nearest town. This may or may not be the same as the gardener's address.
- Name of collector, the person who captured or collected the insect.
- What was the insect feeding on when collected? If on a plant, specifically name the plant. If not on a plant, name the location, such as windowsill, carport, or closet.
- List the severity of the damage or infestation.

4

Manual (AG-348), white grubs are usually not a problem in July, so those can be eliminated as a possibility. Refer to NC State's Ornamental and Turf Pest Calendars for more information.

Symptoms and Signs of Plant Damage Caused by Insects

Symptoms are descriptions of how the plant reacts to insect damage, whereas signs are the actual evidence that insects leave behind—including **frass**, feeding traces, castings, dead bodies, and nests. All of this information is used to identify whether the damage was done by insects and if so, what kind of insect.

Feeding Habits: The location of insect feeding damage and the types of damage (tissue bitten and chewed versus tissue pierced and sucked) are valuable information in identifying the responsible insect. Types of damage and examples of insects that could be responsible are listed below.

Chewing Damage
- Entire leaf consumed (with the possible exception of tough midvein): caterpillars like cankerworms, and webworms (Figure 4–27).
- Distinct sections of leaf missing. Notches cut from leaf margin (black vine weevil adult); circular holes cut from margin of leaf (leaf cutter bees)(Figure 4-28); small randomly scattered holes in leaf (beetles, chafers, weevils, grasshoppers).
- Leaf skeletonized: slugs, beetles, pear slug (pear sawfly larvae), elm leaf beetle.
- Leaf rolled into tube or tied together with silken threads: leafrollers and leaftiers (caterpillars of moths). Tunnels between the upper and lower leaf surfaces (Figure 4–29).
- Insect or frass visible in tunnels when leaf is held up to the light: leaf miners.
- Leaf falls in early summer. Slicing petiole lengthwise

reveals insect larva: leaf stalk borers, larva of small moth or sawfly, maple petiole borer.

- Girdled twigs: vine weevil and twig girdling beetle.
- General decline of the entire plant or a specific branch. Holes in the bark, accumulation of frass, sawdust or pitch: borers, bark beetles, pitch moths.
- General decline of plant, chewed areas of roots: root feeders—larval stages of weevils, beetles, and moths, including sod webworm, Japanese beetle, root weevil.

Figure 4–27. Fall webworms completely consume leaves.

U.S. Fish and Wildlife Service - Midwest Region, Courtney Celley, Flickr public domain

Figure 4-28. Leaf cutter bees have chewing mouth parts they use to cut semi-circles out of leaves, roll them up, and use them to line their tubular nesting sites. They are beneficial insects and do not damage enough plant tissue to be of concern.

Bob Peterson
CC BY - 2.0

Figure 4–29. Leaf miners tunnel through the upper and lower leaf surfaces.

Scot Nelson, Flickr CC BY 0 - 1.0

Sucking Damage

- Spotting or stippling on leaf resulting from localized destruction of chlorophyll: aphids, leafhoppers, lygus bugs, thrips (Figure 4–30).
- Random stipple pattern on leaf: leafhoppers, mites.
- General/uniform stippling, flecking, bronzing, or chlorotic pattern on leaf: adelgids, lace bugs on azalea, some thrips (Figure 4–31).
- Leaf curling or puckering: severe aphid infestations, thrips.
- Reduced growth and chlorosis: psyllid yellows on potatoes and tomatoes, scale, mealy bugs.
- Leaf and stem distortion associated with off-color foliage: aphids (distortion often confused with growth regulator injury).
- General decline of entire plant or section of a plant as indicated by poor color, reduced growth, dieback: scales, mealy bugs, other root, stem, and branch feeders.
- In addition to direct mechanical damage, some piercing-sucking insects cause additional damage when feeding by injecting toxic substances or diseases. They can cause a range of symptoms.

Figure 4–30. Aphid damage created areas of bleached stippling on this leaf.

Scot Nelson, Flickr CC BY 0 - 1.0

Other Damage

- Galls, swellings on leaf and stem tissue: aphids, wasps, midges.
- Damaged or split twigs: egg laying (oviposition), treehoppers and cicadas.

Table 4–4. Some Plant Diseases Carried by Insects

Disease	Insect Carrier
Dutch elm disease (fungus)	elm bark beetles
Fire blight (bacterial)	pollinating insects
Tomato curly top (virus)	beet leafhopper
Tomato spotted wilt (virus)	Western flower thrips
Watermelon mosaic virus	aphids

Figure 4-31. Hemlock woolly adelgid (*Adelges tsugae*).
Nicholas A. Tonelli, Flickr CC BY - 2.0

Table 4–5. Plants That Attract Beneficial Insects

Plant	Insects
Black locust	Lady beetles
Caraway	Lacewings, hover flies, insidious flower bugs, spiders, parasitic wasps
Common knotweed	Big-eyed bugs, hover flies, parasitic wasps, soft-winged flower beetles
Cowpea	Parasitic wasps
Crimson clover	Minute pirate bugs, big-eyed bugs, lady beetles
Flowering buckwheat	Hover flies, minute pirate bugs, predatory wasps, tachinid flies, lacewings, lady beetles
Hairy vetch	Lady beetles, minute pirate bugs, predatory wasps
Queen Anne's lace	Lacewings, predatory wasps, minute pirate bugs, tachinid flies
Spearmint	Predatory wasps
Subterranean clover	Big-eyed bugs
Sweet alyssum	Tachinid flies, hover flies, chalcids, wasps
Sweet fennel	Parasitic wasps, predatory wasps
Tansy	Parasitic wasps, lady beetles, insidious flower bugs, lacewings
White sweet clover	Tachinid flies, bees, predatory flies
Wild buckwheat	Hover flies, minute pirate bugs, tachinid flies
Yarrow	Lady beetles, parasitic wasps, bees

a Other plants that attract a variety of beneficial insects include sage, wallflower, salvia, nasturtium, poppy, zinnia, dill, anise, fennel, coriander, parsley, marigold, aster, daisy, coneflower, bee balm, basil, oregano, mint, cosmos, lovage, wild mustard, and canola.

4

Distinguishing Between Plant Damage Caused by Insects, Diseases, and Environmental Stress

One way to begin the diagnostic process is to determine if the problem stems from biotic (living) factors, including insects and diseases, or abiotic (nonliving) factors including environmental stress. Examine the patterns of damage, location, and progression to determine whether the cause is biotic or abiotic. Look for signs of a living culprit to distinguish between insect and disease causal agents. Use Table 4–3 as a diagnostic tool.

Common Mistakes in Pest Diagnosis

If all plant pests were always in the most easily identifiable stage, diagnosis would be simple. However, all 1,700 potential pests of ornamentals in North Carolina have egg stages and immature stages that may be difficult to identify. Following are two examples of common mistakes.

Lady beetle pupa—The pupae of lady beetles attach themselves by the hind end to leaves or twigs. These pupae do not resemble adult lady beetles (Figure 4–32). A home gardener might assume that they are "sucking the life" out of the plant. Quite to the contrary, however, lady beetles help the plant by eating harmful aphids. Each pupa destroyed by a mistaken diagnosis allows thousands of aphids to survive.

Figure 4–32.
Lady beetle pupa.

Matt Bertone

Seed-corn maggot flies—Each spring home gardeners discover dead flies on the tips of dogwood and crape myrtle twigs. These flies are infested with an *Entomophthora* fungus, which "programs" the fly to land or crawl onto a prominent perch (such as a dead twig) to die. Then the fungus fruits (sporulates) and the spores disperse to infect other flies. The fungus is beneficial because it attacks seed-corn maggots, which consume the inside of seeds, forcing many gardeners to replant. Because the flies often select bare twigs on which to make their last landing, home gardeners sometimes jump to the conclusion that the fly is harming the twig.

Types of Insect Injury

Chewing Insects
Some insects feed by chewing external parts of a plant. To get an idea of how prevalent this type of insect damage is, try to find leaves of plants that have no sign of injury from chewing insects. Cabbageworms, armyworms, grasshoppers, Colorado potato beetles, and fall webworms are common examples of insects that cause injury by chewing.

Piercing-Sucking Insects
Another way insects feed on growing plants is by piercing the epidermis (skin) and sucking sap from the vascular system or individual cells. These insects have a slender, sharp, pointed portion of their mouthparts that they thrust into the plant and suck up plant sap. The hole is so small it is not easy to see. The withdrawal of sap causes minute white, brown, or red spots on leaves, fruits, or twigs. This may result in curled leaves; deformed fruits; or general wilting, browning, or death of the entire plant. The spots remain after management, but new foliage should be normal. Aphids, scale insects, squash bugs, leafhoppers, and plant bugs are examples of piercing-sucking insects. The difference between chewing and piercing-sucking damage can be seen in Figure 4–33.

Internal Feeders
Some insects feed within plant tissues during all or part of their destructive stages. They gain entrance to plants in the egg stage either when their mothers deposit eggs into the plant tissue or the immatures, after hatching from the eggs, eat their way into the plant. In either case, the hole of entry is usually minute. A large hole in a fruit, seed, nut, twig, or trunk generally indicates where the insect has come out, not where it entered.

Common group names for internal feeders include borers in wood or pith; worms or weevils in fruits, nuts, or seeds; leaf miners; and gall insects. Nearly all of the internally feeding insects live inside the plant during only part of their lives and usually emerge as adults. Leaf miners are small enough to find comfortable quarters and an abundance of food between the upper and lower epidermis of a leaf. Management strategies are most effective when aimed at emerging adults (Figure 4–34) or during the immature stages before they enter the plant.

Below-ground Feeders
Below-ground feeders include chewers, sap suckers, root borers, and gall insects. Their attacks are the same as above-ground pests, except that they harm plant

Figure 4–33. Chewing damage to a kale leaf, likely from the chewing mouthparts of a beetle (left), and stippling on a bean leaf from the piercing-sucking mouthparts of a lace bug (right).
Scot Nelson, Flickr CC BY-0- 1.0

Figure 4–34. Stages of a leafminer. Eggs are deposited on the surface of a leaf, and they become larvae that tunnel through the leaves leaving frass (middle). They pupate and emerge as adult flies.
Martin Cooper Ipswich, Flickr CC BY - 2.0

parts below the soil surface. The woolly apple aphid, for example, as both nymph and adult, sucks sap from roots of apple trees, causing the development of tumors and subsequent decay of the tree's roots. With other below-ground insects, the larvae are root feeders, but the adults live above ground. Examples of below-ground feeders include wireworms, root maggots, pillbugs, strawberry root weevils, and grape and corn rootworms.

Egg Layers

Insects can damage plants by laying eggs in critical plant tissues. The periodic cicada, for instance, deposits eggs in one-year-old growth of fruit and shade trees, splitting the wood so severely that the entire twig often dies. As soon as the young hatch, they leave the twigs. Although the dead branches can seem alarming, most established trees will withstand the damage. Pruning out damaged branches would be the only management necessary.

Some insects and mites cause plants to produce a structure of deformed tissue called a gall (Figure 4–35). The organisms then find shelter and abundant food inside this plant growth. The growth of the gall occurs when an adult lays an egg inside plant tissue; the gall develops through reactions with the secretions of the developing larva. If several species of gall-forming insects attack the same plant, the galls that form will differ in appearance. Although the gall is made entirely of plant tissue, the insect controls and directs the form and shape the gall takes as it grows. While galls may be unsightly, they generally do not cause problems for healthy plants.

Figure 4–35. Galls on cherry leaves caused by the mite *Eriophyes tiliae*.
Jason Hollinger, Flickr CC BY - 2.0

Nesting Insects

Besides laying eggs in plants, insects sometimes remove parts of plants for the construction of nests. Leaf-cutter bees nip out neat, circular pieces of foliage, which they carry away and fashion together to form thimble-shaped cells. Some insects fold, roll, or tie leaves together for a protective cover. While it may be disturbing to see some leaves cut or missing from a plant, the damage is often minimal and does not require management.

Vectors of Plant Disease

There is evidence that insects spread more than 200 plant diseases. Of these, about 150 diseases are caused by viruses, 25 or more by parasitic fungi, 15 or more by bacteria, and a few are caused by protozoa. Insects may spread plant diseases in the following ways:

- Indirectly when they feed, lay eggs, or bore into plants, creating an entrance point for a disease present in the environment.
- Directly on or in their bodies as they move from one infected plant to another susceptible plant.
- Directly as they feed on susceptible plants; they infect them with the disease organism.
- Indirectly as an essential host for some part of the pathogen's life cycle, where the disease could not complete its life cycle without the insect host.

Honeydew Producers

Honeydew is a sweet, sticky liquid excreted by insects that feed on sap from the phloem tissue of plants. Aphids, mealybugs, soft scales, and leafhoppers feed on phloem by sucking with slender, threadlike mouthparts. Sap from phloem is rich in sugar but poor in other nutrients, so these insects consume large amounts of sap to obtain enough minor nutrients. The pests, therefore, excrete copious amounts of honeydew. Unless washed off by rain, honeydew clings to the plant and surfaces below it.

Honeydew itself is not a harmful substance. However, spores or fragments of dark fungi called sooty mold are blown or carried to the honeydew, and new colonies of sooty mold develop. Many times the tiny strands of sooty mold become so abundant that infested plants appear dark and sooty or almost charcoal gray. The mold can block sunlight to the point that photosynthesis is no longer possible. Heavily infested leaves often die. Feeding by a large number of aphids or scales combined with the heavy coating of sooty mold may drastically reduce the vigor and beauty of ornamental plants.

Encouraging Beneficial Insects

Take advantage of biological management in a garden by encouraging natural predators such as praying mantids, lady beetles, lacewings, and ground beetles. Increase their populations by providing shelter, food, moisture, and overwintering sites. Some beneficial insect suppliers offer a formulation for feeding and attracting the beneficials to keep them in the garden longer.

Learn to recognize the eggs and larvae of beneficial insects, and avoid harming them. Praying mantid egg cases are often found in weedy lots. Carry the twig with the cluster attached into the garden and set it in a place where it will not be disturbed. Learn to recognize parasites and their pupal cases. For example, a tomato hornworm often has a number of white cocoons, a little larger than grains of rice, on its back. These are from a parasitic wasp. The hornworm will die, and more wasps will emerge. Obviously, it is to a gardener's advantage to leave that caterpillar in the garden.

Another possibility is to increase the type and number of plants in a landscape that will attract beneficial insects. Search for beneficial insects in the NC State Plant Database. Most composite and umbel plants attract beneficial insects by providing nectar and pollen that prolong the insect's life. Cosmos and marigolds attract a few beneficial insects, and tansy attracts large numbers. Best results come from planting the attractant plants on the edges of the area instead of interplanting them in the garden.

Insecticides often kill beneficial insects. A selective insecticide has less adverse effect than a broad--spectrum insecticide. Stomach poison insecticides are less likely to harm beneficial insects. Apply insecticides at dusk, as this is the time when most beneficial insects are done foraging for nectar or pollen.

Think IPM— A Cantaloupe Problem

You are concerned about your cantaloupe plant. The vines are doing poorly, some of the fruit has scarring, and you are concerned you will lose the whole crop. You think about the five steps for IPM:
1. Monitor and scout insects to determine insect type and population levels.
2. Accurately identify pest and host.
3. Consider economic or aesthetic injury thresholds. A threshold is the point at which action should be taken.
4. Implement a treatment strategy using physical, cultural, biological, and/or insecticide control.
5. Evaluate success of treatments.

Monitor and determine insect type
You have noticed the plants doing poorly for a few weeks. An insect that looks like a beetle has been flying around the crop. The plants have been in the ground for a few months (are mature) and they appear to have insect damage to their leaves. A younger planting of the same crop suffered from severe damage, and the stems appeared chewed through. Cantaloupe has been planted in the same spot for many years. You feel the insect population is high enough and damage is severe enough to warrant further investigation. You take a sample of the leaves, getting leaves that are healthy, partially affected and completely affected by damage. You also try to capture the insect if possible or at least get some good photographs. You review the sample collection information found in the "Submitting Insect Samples to the Plant Disease and Insect Clinic" section of this chapter.

Accurately identify the pest and host
Using the samples you research this problem. The leaves appear to be missing sections, especially along the margins, which leads you to believe an insect with chewing mouthparts was present. You carefully examine the sample to see if any insects are still present. You see a yellow and black insect and remove it from the plant for further investigation. The insect is quite active, so you put it in a jar and freeze it to slow it down. Looking at it with your hand lens, you determine it is in the order Coleoptera, or a beetle, because you see two pairs of wings; the outer pair is hardened or leathery with yellow and black stripes, and the inner pair is membranous and folds under the front wings. You also see chewing mouthparts and long jointed antennae. You consult some insect identification guides at the Extension office and discover a photo that looks like your insect (Figure 4–36). You read that cucumber beetles can attack all plants in the cucurbit family and that cantaloupe is in that family. Now that you have a positive ID, you do more research on this insect. You type in "cucumber beetle + extension" into your Internet search engine.

Figure 4-36. A striped cucumber beetle, order Coleoptera.

Matt Bertone

Consider economic or aesthetic injury thresholds
The injury to these vines and their fruit is severe enough to warrant management. It may be too late for this year's crop, but you can research how best to avoid this problem in future plantings.

Implement a treatment strategy using physical, cultural, biological, and/or insecticide control

You research cultural strategies to discourage cucumber beetles. Cucumber beetle eggs often overwinter in discarded plant material, so removal of plant material after the growing season and plowing or turning the planting bed will help disrupt this part of the beetle's life cycle. Crop rotation can be an effective means of managing soil fertility and pest problems. Ideally, plant a different crop family in the spot, waiting at least three years before returning to a cucurbit-family crop. The use of resistant varieties is perhaps the most important management tactic. The following cucurbit varieties are resistant to cucumber beetles as seedlings and also have resistant foliage later in the season: Blue Hubbard (squash); Ashley, Chipper, Gemini (cucumber). Use of resistant varieties may not give complete control where infestations are heavy. The NC State Extension publication AG-295, *Insect and Related Pests of Vegetables*, gives additional cultural management strategies.

Delaying planting times for more favorable germinating conditions and heavy seeding rates will ensure a good stand. For young seedlings, wire or cloth screen protectors shaped like cones will keep beetles off home plantings until plants are established.

If this combination of management strategies is not enough, insecticides may be needed. In that case, a foliar insecticide applied at the cotyledon stage will retard cucumber beetle feeding and encourage plant establishment. Where insects are abundant, additional foliar applications may be needed to prevent beetles from spreading bacterial wilt and squash virus. For recommended insecticides and rates, consult the current *North Carolina Agricultural Chemicals Manual*.

Evaluate success of treatments

You decide to keep a garden journal or notes about management strategies tried and their results. You realize that it may take more time to see the results of some strategies than others.

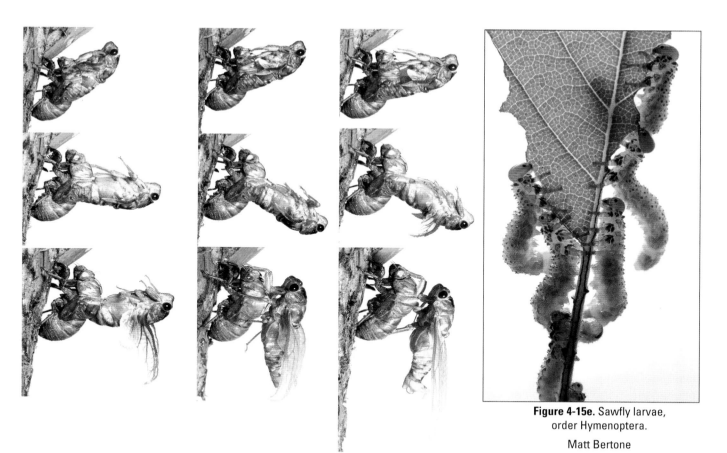

Figure 4-14e. Cicada molting, order Hemiptera.

Matt Bertone

Figure 4-15e. Sawfly larvae, order Hymenoptera.

Matt Bertone

Frequently Asked Questions

1. There are spots on my leaves. How can I tell if they are caused by an insect or disease?

The first step is accurately identifying the plant. Many insects and diseases are host specific. It is also important to consider any abiotic factors that could cause damage to your plant or leave it susceptible to insects or disease. Is it possible the plant is drought stressed or had herbicide overspray contact the leaves? Has anything in the environment changed recently? Was the plant recently fertilized? Where are the damaged leaves–all over the plant or only on new growth? Are there any wounds on the plant? Ask probing questions and find out as much history on the plant as you can. Insect damage to plants comes from either chewing, sucking, or boring. Indications that insects with chewing mouthparts are feeding on your plants include missing chunks of leaves or stems, skeletonization of leaves or leaf mining. Insects with sucking mouthparts remove sap from plant cells, which can cause stippling (spotting), discoloration, or drooping of leaves, or lead to honey dew. Boring insect larvae tunnel into the plant beneath the bark, leaving sawdust toothpicks on tree trunks or sawdust mounds below. Their adult forms can feed on leaves or twigs. You may look for the insects themselves, insect parts, or frass (excrement). Some fungal diseases can leave spots on leaves. The diseases generally produce "target-like" spots, each with a dark center, yellowing ring, and a brown or red margin between the dead tissue and the live green tissue of the plant.

2. There are small bumps on the leaves of my hackberry, is it going to die?

This is most likely insect galls. Galls are abnormal growth of plant cells due to an injection of a chemical by an adult or larval form of an insect. These chemicals cause the plant tissue to swell and become misshapen, forming the bumps you see. Insects often live inside the galls for a short period of time, gaining shelter from predators and feeding off the swollen plant tissue. Galls are quite common on plants like hackberry and oaks. The damage, generally cosmetic, will not kill the plant.

3. There are many black bugs with orange stripes on their backs flying around in my grass. It looks like somebody spit on my grass in spots.

These are most likely two-lined spittlebugs. Both adults and nymphs damage turf by sucking out the plant juices from leaves and stems. They also produce a spittle mass, which is nothing more than a nuisance. In late summer adults can also fly to hollies to feed and cause holly leaves to drop prematurely. Following good turf management practices, reducing excessive thatch, and avoiding overwatering will help manage spittlebugs. Plant a more tolerant turfgrass species such as St. Augustinegrass or zoysiagrass, and avoid centipedegrass if possible. On ornamentals and grape vines, a strong spray of water may be sufficient for management.

4. How do I get rid of fire ants?

Red imported fire ants expand naturally and steadily in our area because their reproductive rates are high and our winters are mild. The mounds are unsightly, and their stings are painful. Both baits and contact insecticides are effective management tools. Common active ingredients are hydramethylnon, spinosad, methoprene, and pyriproxyfen. In bait formulations the active ingredients are shared by the ants in a mound, including the queen (which is the only ant in the colony that can lay eggs), usually resulting in more effective management. Contact products containing the active ingredients acephate, carbaryl, or pyrethroids produce management in a few days if broadcast over the landscape, or in a few hours if applied to individual mounds. Both require water (rainfall or irrigation) to become active. An exception is a product with the active ingredient fipronil, which produces long lasting effects when broadcast in late May to early June. Fipronil will provide five to six months of management. Repeat treatment in November if ant mounds reappear in the fall, as sometimes happens. Be sure to read and follow product labels closely before application in order to achieve desired results. To determine if you have fire ants, look for two nodes between the thorax and abdomen. Other ants only have one. For more information regarding fire ant management in the home landscape type "fire ants + extension" into your internet search engine.

Further Reading

Bellows, Thomas S. and T. W. Fisher, eds. *Handbook of Biological Control: Principles and Applications of Biological Control*. San Diego, California: Academic Press, 1999. Print.

Brandenburg, Rick L. and Callie P. Freeman, eds. *Handbook of Turfgrass Insects*, Second Edition. Annapolis, Maryland: Entomological Society of America, 2012. Print.

Bruneau, Arthur H. and Gail G. Wilkerson, eds. *Turfgrass Pest Management Manual: A Guide to Major Turfgrass Pests & Turfgrasses*. Raleigh, North Carolina: NC Cooperative Extension Service, 2006. PDF file.

Capinera, John L. *Handbook of Vegetable Pests*. San Diego, California: Academic Press, 2001. Kindle file.

Clark, Christopher A., et al., eds. *Compendium of Sweetpotato Diseases, Pests, and Disorders*. 2nd ed. St. Paul, Minnesota: The American Phytopathological Society, 2013. Print.

Common Tree Fruit Pests. Columbia, Missouri: University Of Missouri Extension, 1993. Print. North Central Regional Publication NCR 63.

Cottam, Clarence, and Herbert S. Zim. *A Golden Guide from St. Martin's Press: Insects*. New York: St. Martin's Press, 2002. Print.

Cranshaw, Whitney. *Garden Insects of North America*. Princeton, New Jersey: Princeton University Press, 2004. Print.

Davidson, Ralph H., and William F. Lyon. *Insect Pests of Farm, Garden, and Orchard*. 8th ed. Hoboken, New Jersey: John Wiley & Sons Inc., 1987. Print.

Dreistadt, Steve H. *Pests of Landscape Trees and Shrubs: An Integrated Pest Management Guide*. 2nd ed. Davis, California: University of California Division of Agriculture And Natural Resources, 2004. Print. Publication 3359.

Eiseman, Charly and Noah Charney. *Tracks and Signs of Insects and Other Invertebrates: A Guide to North American Species*. Pennsylvania: Stackpole Books, 2010. Print.

Ellis, Barbara W. and Fern Marshall Bradley, eds. *The Organic Gardener's Handbook of Natural Insect and Disease Control: A Complete Problem-Solving Guide to Keeping Your Garden and Yard Healthy without Chemicals*. Emmaus, Pennsylvania: Rodale Press, Inc., 1996. Print.

Ellis, M. A., et al., eds. *Compendium of Raspberry and Blackberry Diseases and Insects*. St. Paul, Minnesota: The American Phytopathological Society, 1991. Print.

Elzinga, Richard J. *Fundamentals of Entomology*. 6th ed. Upper Saddle River, New Jersey: Prentice Hall, Inc., 2004. Print.

Fisher, Brian L., and Stephan P. Cover. *Ants of North America: A Guide to the Genera*. University of California Press, 2007. Print.

Horst, R. Kenneth, and Raymond Cloyd. *Compendium of Rose Diseases and Pests*. 2nd ed. St. Paul, Minnesota: The American Phytopathological Society, 2007. Print.

Johnson, Warren T., and Howard H. Lyon. *Insects That Feed on Trees and Shrubs*. 2nd ed. Ithaca, New York: Cornell University Press, 1991. Print.

Jones, Jeffrey B., et al., eds. *Compendium of Tomato Diseases and Pests*. 2nd ed. St. Paul, Minnesota: The American Phytopathological Society, 2014. Print.

Leahy, Christopher. *Peterson First Guide to Insects of North America*. New York: Houghton Mifflin Company, 1998. Print.

Mitchell, Robert T., and Herbert S. Zim. *Butterflies and Moths: Revised and Updated*. New York: St. Martin's Press, 2002. Print.

Pirone, Pascal P. *Diseases and Pests of Ornamental Plants*. 5th ed. New York: John Wiley & Sons, Inc., 1978. Print.

Schultz, Warren, ed. *Natural Insect Control: The Ecological Gardener's Guide to Foiling Pests*. 1995. Brooklyn, New York: Brooklyn Botanic Garden, 1999. Print.

4

Schwartz, Howard F. and S. Krishna Mohan, eds. *Compendium of Onion and Garlic Diseases and Pests*, 2nd ed. St. Paul, Minnesota: The American Phytopathological Society, 2008. Print.

Solomon, J. D. *Guide to Insect Borers in North American Broadleaf Trees and Shrubs*. Washington, DC: United States Department of Agriculture Forest Service, 1995. PDF file. *Agriculture Handbook* AH-706.

Sutton, Turner B., et al., eds. *Compendium of Apple and Pear Diseases and Pests*. 2nd ed. St. Paul, Minnesota: The American Phytopathological Society, 2013. Print.

Wagner, David L. *Caterpillars of Eastern North America: A Guide to Identification and Natural History* (Princeton Field Guides) 1st ed. Princeton, New Jersey, Princeton University Press 2005. Print.

Weinzierl, Rick, and Tess Henn. *Alternatives in Insect Management: Biological and Biorational Approaches*. Urbana, Illinois: University of Illinois at Urbana-Champaign, 1991. PDF file. North Central Regional Extension Publication 401.

Weinzierl, Rick, and Tess Henn. *Alternatives in Insect Management: Microbial Insecticides*. Urbana, Illinois: University of Illinois at Urbana-Champaign, 1989. PDF file. Circular 1295.

Weinzierl, R., et al. *Insect Attractants and Traps*. Gainesville, Florida: University of Florida Institute of Food and Agricultural Science, 2005. PDF file. Publication ENY-277.

Westcott, Cynthia. *The Gardener's Bug Book* .New York, New York. Doubleday. 1973. Print

White, Sarah et. al. *IPM for Shrubs in Southeastern U.S. Nursery Production*: Vol. I. Southern Nursery IPM Working Group. 2018. PDF File

Yepsen, Roger B, ed. *The Encyclopedia of Natural Insect and Disease Control: The Most Comprehensive Guide to Protecting Plants, Vegetables, Fruit, Flowers, Trees and Lawn*. Emmaus, Pennsylvania: Rodale Press, Inc., 1984. Print.

For More Information

http://go.ncsu.edu/fmi_insects

Contributors

Authors:
Hannah Burrack, Associate Professor and Extension Specialist, Department of Entomology and Plant Pathology
Matt Bertone, Extension Associate, Department of Entomology and Plant Pathology

Contributions by Extension Agents: Sam Marshall, Mary Hollingsworth, Peg Godwin, Kerrie Roach, Julie Flowers, David Goforth

Copy Editor: Barbara Scott

Contributions by Extension Master Gardener Volunteers:
Louise Romanow, Linda Alford, Jackie Weedon, Karen Damari, Connie Schultz, Patty Brown, Sue Davis, Barbara Goodman, Edna Burger

Content Editors:
Lucy Bradley, Professor and Extension Specialist, Urban Horticulture, NC State University; Director, NC State Extension Master Gardener program
Kathleen Moore, Urban Horticulturist

Based in part on text from the 1998 Extension Master Gardener manual prepared by:
Stephen Bambara, Extension Specialist, Department of Entomology
James R. Baker, Extension Specialist, Department of Entomology
Erv Evans, Extension Associate, Department of Horticultural Science
Ken Sorensen, Extension Specialist, Department of Entomology

Chapter 4 Cover Photo Credit: Brown Lacewing. Matt Bertone, Author

How to Cite This Chapter:
Burrak, H.J., and M. Bertone. 2022. Insects, Chpt 4. In: K.A. Moore and L.K. Bradley (eds). *North Carolina Extension Gardener Handbook*, 2nd ed. NC State Extension, Raleigh, NC. <https://content.ces.ncsu.edu/extension-gardener-handbook/4-insects>

Diseases and Disorders

5

Objectives

This chapter teaches people to:

• Identify certain plant diseases and disorders using a step-by-step process.
• Recognize when a laboratory diagnosis for a plant problem is warranted.
• Describe and explain the differences between the major categories of plant diseases.
• For each plant disease, explain the implications for plant health.
• Explain how the host plant and environmental conditions affect disease development.
• Recommend preventive strategies and management techniques for the most common plant diseases in North Carolina.
• Distinguish between plant damage caused by diseases, insects, and environmental conditions.

Introduction

The term plant disease refers to an impairment in the structure or function of a plant that results in observable symptoms. In this chapter the focus will be on infectious diseases—those that result from an attack by a **fungus**, **bacterium**, **nematode**, **virus**, or another organism. Other disorders can be caused by abiotic (environmental and cultural) factors, such as compacted soil, excess water, nutrient deficiencies, chemical injury, or air pollution. Many of these factors produce symptoms similar to those caused by infectious agents. Some detective work is often necessary to figure out what is wrong with a particular plant. This chapter provides an introduction to the causes of plant diseases, their diagnosis, and the methods used to prevent and control them. For information on particular diseases, refer to the chapters on specific types of plants.

Figure 5–1. A variegated loquat (*Eriobotrya japonica*) that could be mistaken for a disease.
Megan Hansen (MeganEHansen), Flickr CC BY-SA - 2.0

Healthy and Unhealthy Plants

To recognize a plant problem, you must first know what the healthy plant looks like. Although this may seem obvious, some plants have characteristics or habits at certain stages of growth that can be mistaken for symptoms of disease. For instance, patterns of light and dark colors on foliage can sometimes indicate disease, but color patterns can also be normal variegation in certain varieties of ornamentals (Figure 5–1). A deodar cedar might appear to be suffering from a nutrient deficiency because it has yellow-green leaves, but this coloring is normal for this cultivar (Figure 5–2). The spore-bearing **sori** on the underside of a fern frond might be mistaken for insects (Figure 5–3). The female cones on the tips of arborvitae foliage look somewhat like **galls** (Figure 5–4). Leaves on some evergreen trees (such as some hollies and magnolias) drop in the spring as new leaves expand; homeowners new to

North Carolina might become concerned if they expect leaves to shed only in the fall. None of these examples are diseases. Instead, all are normal plant structures and responses.

Figure 5–2. A sunburst honeylocust has naturally yellow-green leaves.
Famartin, Wikimedia Commons CC BY-SA - 3.0

Figure 5–3. Spores on the underside of fern leaves can sometimes be confused with insects.
honey-bee, Flickr CC BY - 2.0

Figure 5–4. Unripe female cones of oriental arborvitae (*Platycladus orientalis*).
Daniel Fuchs, Wikimedia Commons CC BY-SA - 2.5

In order to talk about diseases and disorders, we need a set of terms to describe plant abnormalities and **pathogen** structures. These are detailed in Tables 5–1a, 5–1b and 5–2.

Table 5–1a. Common Symptoms of Plant Diseases

Symptoms are not unique to a particular disease as a specific symptom can be caused by a variety of pathogens.

Chlorosis (adj. chlorotic) (Figure 5–5): Yellowing of a normally green plant part. If it is more pronounced between veins it is called "interveinal chlorosis."
PDIC

Necrosis (adj. necrotic) (Figure 5–6): Death of plant tissue. A necrotic leaf blotch is pictured. Note that any well defined dead area of a leaf, stem, or root can be called a "necrotic lesion."
PDIC

Example of necrotic (dead) leaf spots with chlorotic (yellow) halos (Figure 5–7).
PDIC

Shot-hole (Figure 5–8): Clean-edged, round to oval holes in leaves where necrotic spots have fallen out.
PDIC

Wilting (Figure 5–9): Loss of **turgor** in all or part of a shoot.
PDIC

Scorch (Figure 5–10): Necrosis and desiccation of leaf tissue, starting at the margins.
PDIC

Mosaic or **mottle** (Figure 5–11): Patchwork of colors, usually light-green, yellow, or dark-green, against the normal green background color of the leaf.
PDIC

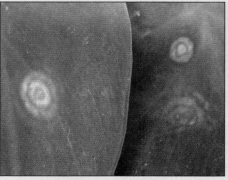

Ringspot (Figure 5–12): Chlorotic or necrotic rings or arcs surrounding healthy tissue.
PDIC

Water-soaking (Figure 5–13): A dark, "wet" appearance to a spot, best seen by holding the leaf up to a light source.
PDIC

Flecking or **stippling** (Figure 5–14): Numerous very small chlorotic or necrotic points.
PDIC

Blight (Figure 5–15): Extensive and rapid death of plant tissue.
Mike Munster

Dieback (Figure 5–16): Death of a branch from the tip down.
PDIC

Canker (Figure 5–17): Sharply-defined dead area on a woody plant part.
PDIC

Example of a canker visible only under the bark (Figure 5–18).
PDIC

Root rot (Figure 5–19): Decay of roots. The exterior portion is easily pulled off the central core of vascular tissue.
PDIC

Brown rot or fruit rot (Figure 5–20): Decay of fruit. May be firm or soft.
Mike Munster

Mummy (Figure 5–21): A dried, shriveled fruit.
Ron Jones, NC State Deptartment of Plant Pathology

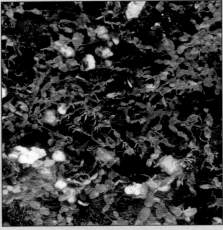

Damping off (Figure 5–22): Death of seedlings, before or after emergence from the soil.
PDIC

5

Malformation (Figure 5–23): Any deviation from the normal shape of a plant organ.
PDIC

Leaf galls (Figure 5–24): Swellings on leafy tissue.
PDIC

Stem galls (Figure 5–25): Swellings, usually woody, on stems.
PDIC

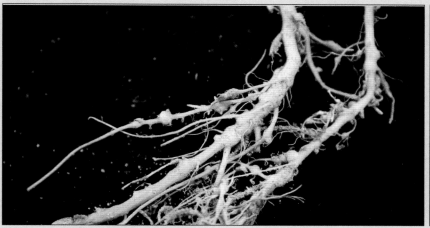

Root galls (Figure 5–26): Swellings on root tissue.
PDIC

Gummosis (Figure 5–27): Exudation of sticky sap. In conifers, this is known as "resinosis."
PDIC

Witch's broom (Figure 5–28): Abnormal proliferation of shoots on one area of a stem.
PDIC

Vascular discoloration (Figure 5–29): Darkening of the plant's conductive tissue. Visible after cutting along or into the stem.
PDIC

Table 5–1b. Stand Symptoms in Turfgrasses

Specific terms are used to describe the overall patterns of death or discoloration in turf, independent of what the symptoms may be on individual leaves, **stolons**, and other parts. These are known as stand symptoms. Several of the most important are illustrated below. All photos are courtesy NC State University.

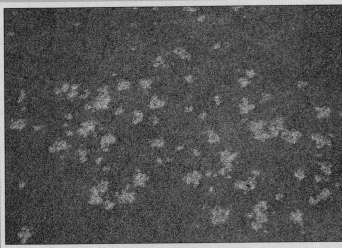

Spots (Figure 5–30): Each area of affected turf is less than 4" in diameter.

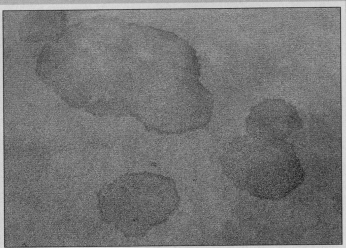

Patches (Figure 5–31): Irregularly shaped areas greater than 4" in diameter.

Circle (Figure 5–32): Perfectly circular areas greater than 4" in diameter.

Rings (Figure 5–33): Surrounded by healthy turf to the inside and outside of the affected area.

Irregular (Figure 5–34): No visible pattern.

Table 5–2. Common Signs of Plant Pathogens

Here we see the **causal organism** itself, usually a fungus.

Mycelium (Figure 5–35): The visible vegetative body of a fungus, made up of threads called **hyphae**. (sing., hypha).

Gray mold (Figure 5–36): Fungal surface growth, gray in color.

Powdery mildew (Figure 5–37): White surface growth on living leaves, stems, flowers, or fruit. With time this can turn gray or develop minute black flecks within.

Downy mildew (Figure 5–38): Group of diseases characterized by white, bluish, or gray sporulation on the underside of leaves.

Sclerotium (pl. sclerotia) (Figure 5–39): Hardened brown or black fungal survival structure. May be round or irregular.

Rust (Figure 5–40): One of a group of important fungal diseases with multiple stages, at least one of which typically produces dry yellow to orange spores.

Rust (see above) (Figure 5–41). Example of the aecia of quince rust on ornamental pear fruit. Note the tubular white membranes that cover the spore-producing pustules in this species.

Rust (see above) (Figure 5–42). Example of the gelatinous telia of cedar apple rust.

Fruiting body (Figure 5–43): Any spore-producing structure of a fungus. Many are small and dark. Some grow on the surface of leaves or stems.

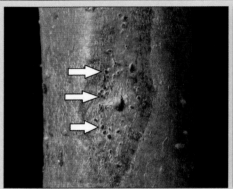

Canker (Figure 5–44): Fruiting bodies that develop in a canker, below the bark, and break through the surface.

Mushroom (Figure 5–45): A soft, stalked fungal fruiting body. One genus—Armillaria—is a plant pathogen.Most are mycorrhizal or aresecondary decomposers.

Conk (Figure 5–46): A tough, often shelf-like fungal fruiting body emerging from standing, fallen, or buried wood. Sign of wood decay in progress

Dodder (Figure 5–47): A parasitic plant with yellow to orange string-like stems and inconspicuous flowers.

Slime mold (Figure 5–48): A group of soil-, litter-, or bark-dwelling organisms, usually unnoticed until the conspicuous spore-producing phase develops.

Abiotic Disorders of Plants

When the cause of a problem is an environmental condition, cultural practice, or chemical exposure, the causal agent is *abiotic* (nonliving). Disorders caused by abiotic factors are not contagious, but such disorders can severely damage plants. In these cases, it is more appropriate to use the term *injury* or *disorder* rather than disease. Most environmental problems are caused by deficiencies or excesses of factors that support life (including soil moisture, light, and temperature). Simple actions such as soil testing, finding out if a plant prefers sun or shade, loosening the edges of the root ball when planting, watering during dry weather, mulching, and knowing when to lime, fertilize, and prune are major factors in preventing many plant problems. Symptoms such as leaf yellowing, poor vigor, and dieback are the plant's signal something is wrong with its environment.

Moisture

Both excess moisture and lack of moisture can damage plants (Figure 5–49). Extreme waterlogging results in root death because of reduced oxygen levels in the root zone. More commonly, excess soil moisture is a contributing factor to root disease. Another disorder that sometimes occurs under high moisture conditions is edema, which appears as numerous swollen bumps on the lower side of leaves (Figure 5–50). These swellings later turn brown and

Figure 5–49. Hellebores thrive in drier soils than average. The poor growth at one end of this bed is probably due to the higher than average water content of the soil there.

PDIC

corky (Figure 5–51). Edema is common on certain thick-leaved herbaceous and woody plants such as geraniums, camellia, and euonymus. At the other extreme, insufficient moisture can result in **scorch** symptoms on foliage, stunting, leaf yellowing, leaf drop, and abortion of flowers and fruits. **Necrosis** can occur on the tips, margins, and interveinal regions of leaves, for example, on sycamore and dogwood trees. Under certain circumstances, potting mixes, mulches, or soils can become **hydrophobic** (water-repellent). Rain and irrigation will not be effective at getting water to the roots once a hydrophobic condition has occurred. Another type of moisture problem is winter burn. Roots cannot extract water from frozen soil, so foliage of evergreen trees and shrubs can get a scorched appearance when winter winds dry them out.

Plant Nutrition

Excessive fertilization can result in root burn and plant damage from high concentrations of soluble salts. Lower-than-optimum levels of nutrients usually result in diminished growth and a wide variety of foliar symptoms, depending on the nutrients involved. Even when nutrients are present in the soil, they may be unavailable to plants if the soil pH is not in the correct range. One common nutritional problem that can be mistaken for a disease is blossom end rot of tomatoes and peppers. Flattened, tan-colored dead spots appear on the fruit, around the point where the flower was attached (Figure 5–52). This often happens on the first cluster produced on a given tomato plant. In peppers, the damage can also appear elsewhere on the fruit (Figure 5–53). The affected areas may become dark if secondary molds develop in the affected tissue (Figure 5–54). The cause is a localized calcium deficiency in the developing fruit. It can be brought on by water stress or by low levels of calcium in the soil. High levels of fertilizer salts—especially ammonium nitrogen—can also contribute to the disorder. For more information on nutrient deficiencies, see chapter 1, Soils and Plant Nutrients.

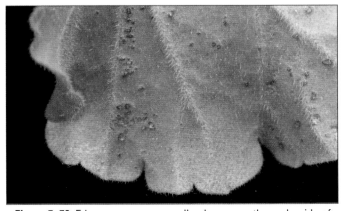

Figure 5–50. Edema, numerous swollen bumps on the underside of leaves.
PDIC

Figure 5–51. Edema bumps turning brown and corky.
PDIC

Figure 5–52. Blossom end rot starts with flattened dead spots where the flower was attached.
Mike Munster

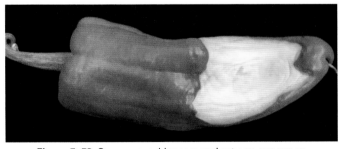

Figure 5–53. On peppers, blossom end rot can appear on other sides of the fruit.
PDIC

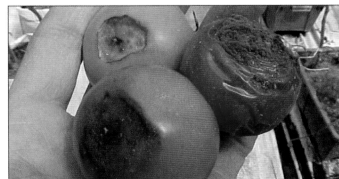

Figure 5–54. Secondary molds can sometimes infect areas with blossom end rot damage.
Mike Munster

5

Light, Temperature, Wind, and Weather

Some plants require shade. Sensitive plants such as aucuba can show burn on those leaves most exposed to the sun. Fleshy vegetables such as peppers and tomatoes can show sunscald on fruit (Figure 5–55). If a large tree is removed from a landscape, the sudden increase in sunlight can damage previously shaded plants. Other plants require sunlight. When planted in shade they have spindly growth until they reach adequate light.

Figure 5–55. Sun scald on a tomato.
Scot Nelson, Flickr CC BY - 0 1.0

Cold can damage plants that are grown out of their area of adaptation or plants exposed to rapid drops in temperature. Tropical indoor plants are prone to injury from low temperatures—both in the home and while in transport. This kind of chilling injury usually shows up as a blackening of plant tissues soon after the exposure.

Perennial and woody plants develop some tolerance to cold as fall and winter progress but lose this hardiness with the onset of spring. In the fall, cold hardiness first occurs in the terminal buds. The last tissues to go dormant are at the base of the main stem. An early freeze in the fall or late freeze in the spring results in bark splitting or loss in those lower stems. The plant may not show distress until the heat of summer when the damaged stems are unable to move sufficient water to the foliage. Late frosts often damage the flower buds of peaches, cherries, apricots, and strawberries. Frost damage to new conifer needles will uniformly kill all needles of the same age back to the same point.

Dry winds can pull moisture from leaves, resulting in a scorched appearance. Heavy winds can remove leaves and limbs and effectively sandblast plants. Ice storms can result in broken limbs. Hail can punch holes in leaves or knock plants down. In addition, lightning strikes, fire, and high temperatures can damage or even kill a plant.

All of the abiotic plant problems described above occur naturally. Several other abiotic problems are caused by humans. Examples include air pollution, herbicide injury, and mechanical damage (for example, when a lawn mower, or weed trimmer hits a tree). Other human-caused abiotic problems include root girdling on plants left too long in a small pot and compacted soil.

All of these abiotic injuries may attract insects and become entry points for diseases.

Plant Pathogens

We can classify diseases according to the symptoms they cause on particular plant parts. For example, there are leaf spots, fruit rots, petal blights, and other diseases named after plant parts. As a general rule, leaf spot diseases are the least serious because the plant can compensate. Exceptions occur when leaves are killed quickly, as with late blight, or when leaves drop off in large numbers, as with black spot of rose or boxwood blight. Canker diseases on woody plants are more serious because entire limbs can sometimes be affected. Root and crown rots are even more serious because a compromised root system will weaken or even kill entire plants. To make matters worse, the soil inhabitants that attack roots tend to persist from year to year. Perhaps the most destructive group of plant diseases are vascular wilts such as Dutch elm disease or fusarium wilts. In these cases the water-conducting vessels of the plant are impaired, and decline is rapid and irreversible. One of a gardener's challenges is to identify whether the disease will affect a plant's long-term health and if not, whether management is necessary.

An alternate way to classify plant diseases is according to their cause. We use the term pathogen to refer to any organism that can cause a disease. Some pathogens affect only a single kind (**genus**) of plant. Others can infect many members of a single plant family, and still others have an extensive host range and can attack plants across multiple families. Examples of pathogens include fungi, bacteria (including **phytoplasmas**), nematodes, viruses, and parasitic plants.

Fungi
Fungi are a diverse group of organisms that include everything from mushrooms to molds. In most cases the

What's in a Name?

Some disease names are confusing simply because the names resemble one another. S*ooty mold* is a fungal growth on insect honeydew (easily rubbed off), while *sooty blotch* is a fungal infection of the surface layer of apple fruit. Likewise, *slime mold* refers to a group of harmless organisms living in mulch or soil, while *slime flux* is the discharge of a fermenting liquid from trunks of hardwood trees in midsummer.

At other times confusion can arise when a single name is used in different ways. There's no problem with "black root rot," a disease of plants such as carrot, pansy, Japanese holly, and many herbaceous perennials, caused by the fungus *Thielaviopsis basicola*. Drop the middle word, though, and you have "black rot," a term used for a disease of crucifers caused by the bacterium Xanthomonas, a disease of grape caused by the fungus *Phyllosticta*, and a disease of sweetpotato caused by the fungus *Ceratocystis*. Another example, black leg of geranium, is caused by the water mold *Pythium*, while black leg of crucifers is caused by the fungus *Phoma*.

The use of scientific names of pathogens can help avoid some of these problems. Some fungi have traditionally borne more than one name, depending on whether the sexual or asexual form is observed. Scientists are in the process of sorting this out, so stay tuned.

fungal "body" consists of fine microscopic threads that grow and branch out through substrates, such as soil, plant parts, foods, or even skin (in the case of the athletes' foot fungus). There are almost 100,000 described fungal species. Estimates of the total number of fungi on earth range upwards of 5 million. Fungi lack **chlorophyll** and thus cannot manufacture their own food. Instead they "feed" by using enzymes to break down organic compounds produced by plants and animals.

Although some fungi are plant pathogens, the vast majority are harmless or even beneficial. For example, *saprobic* (also known as ***saprophytic***) fungi obtain nourishment from dead plants and animals. In the process, they decay wood, leaf litter, and other debris. This is a part of the earth's nutrient cycle—a beneficial service unless the wood happens to be part of your home! Other important functions of fungi include flavoring some cheeses, causing bread to rise, fermenting beer and wine, and producing certain antibiotic precursors.

Examples of common fungal foliar diseases are black spot of rose, powdery mildew, downy mildew, brown patch, and oak leaf blister. Botryosphaeria and Phomopsis species are fungi that commonly cause cankers in woody plant parts. More serious canker diseases include chestnut blight and thousand cankers disease of walnut. Pythium, Phytophthora, and Armillaria species are important causes of root rots. Dutch elm disease and fusarium wilt, already mentioned above, are caused by fungi, as are verticillium wilt, laurel wilt, and oak wilt. Abnormal growth incited by fungi can include twisting and curling of leaves, stunting, or galling, as in the case of black knot or cedar apple rust.

The life of a fungus may include some time on a plant, in the soil, or on plant debris. Survival and growth of the fungus depends on favorable temperatures and moisture levels. Fungi can be spread by one or more of the following: wind, water, insects, soil, or people. A few have more exotic means of transport, such as via birds or on seeds. Figure 5–56 shows the life cycle of the fungus that causes brown rot on peaches.

The microscopic threads that make up the fungal body are called hyphae, a term that comes from the Greek word for "web." A visible mass of hyphae is called a **mycelium**. At some stage in their development, the hyphae of many fungi group together to produce other visible signs, such as powdery mildew, conks, or mushrooms. Table 5–2 illustrates a number of these fungal signs.

Some fungi, such as *Rhizoctonia solani,* spread mainly by the growth of hyphae. But most fungi reproduce via spores. Spores are formed either directly on specialized hyphae or within a fruiting body of some kind. Spore shapes and spore-bearing structures are unique to particular species and can be used to identify fungi under a microscope. Fungal spores almost always require free (liquid) water for a period of time before they can germinate. If foliage stays wet for a certain number of hours at a sufficiently warm temperature, spores of fungal pathogens will germinate, forming hyphae that grow into the plant. Spores that land on dry plant tissue may lie there for several days until moisture becomes available. Depending on the particular fungus, entry into plants can be directly through the **cuticle**, through **stomata**, or via pruning cuts, leaf scars, or other wounds.

Some fungal spores are thick-walled and can tolerate dry or cold conditions, but some fungi survive these hardships by forming **sclerotia**. These small, hard bodies survive in plant tissue or in the soil. Examples include the sclerotia of the fungus *Sclerotium rolfsii*, which resemble radish seeds in size and color (Figure 5–39), and those of *Sclerotinia sclerotiorum* which are black, irregular, and look rather like mouse droppings.

Bacteria

Bacteria are microscopic, single-celled organisms with no organized nucleus. They live in incredibly diverse environments where they have many ecological roles. Plant pathogenic bacterial species number in the hundreds (versus thousands for fungi). Because bacteria look a lot alike under the microscope, they are usually identified by isolating them from plant tissue. Then differences in colony characteristics, biochemical properties, and DNA are used to make the identification.

Unlike many fungi, bacteria cannot penetrate plant cuticles. Rather, they enter through wounds (either caused by human activity or by insect feeding) or through natural openings such as **lenticels**, **hydathodes**, and stomata. Bacteria can be spread from plant to plant by way of soil, insects, splashing water, infected seeds, or pruning tools. The bacterium that causes fire blight can be spread by bees. Bacteria do not have specialized survival structures, so many will not survive in infected plant debris once it decays. Unfortunately, some bacteria can survive long-term in the soil or in cankers of woody plants.

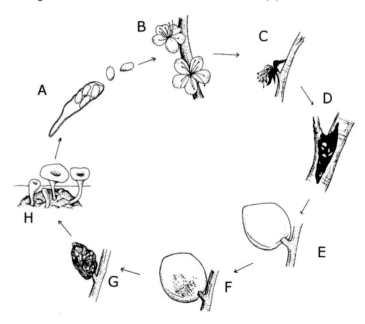

Figure 5–56. Life cycle of *Monilinia fructicola*, Brown Rot. A. Spores in the wind, B. Spores infect blossom, C. Blossoms killed, D. Canker develops, E. Fruit infected by spores, F. Fruit rots during summer, G. Fruit mummifies, H. Fruit produces spores early spring.

Bacteria can cause leaf spots, blights, cankers, and wilts, as well as fruit, stem, and crown rots. Many leaf spots caused by bacteria are angular or linear and have straight edges because spots expand easily between but not across leaf veins (Figure 5–57). They may also have a water-soaked appearance when held up to the light. With some bacterial leaf spots, a yellow halo surrounds the lesion. Bacterial rots often lead to a slimy texture and a foul odor. How much a disease develops and how quickly it spreads depends on temperature, humidity, maturity of the plant tissue, and susceptibility of the plant. Although there can be distinctive characteristics of bacterial disease, it can sometimes be difficult to distinguish bacterial diseases from those caused by fungi. For example, bacterial leaf spot of English ivy looks a lot like anthracnose, and alternaria leaf spot of zinnia can be mistaken for bacterial leaf spot of that same host.

Figure 5–57. Leaf spots caused by bacterium tend to be angular because they are initially limited by the veins on leaves.
PDIC

The bacterium that causes southern bacterial wilt of tomatoes and several other plants is soilborne. The bacteria enter the roots and multiply in the **xylem** tissue. As these water-conducting channels become clogged, plants wilt and die.

Phytoplasmas are an unusual group of bacteria that lack cell walls. They inhabit the **phloem** of plants and have been associated with several plant diseases. The best known of these is aster yellows, a disease that can infect many other host species besides asters. The aster yellows phytoplasma are spread by leafhoppers. The phytoplasma cause symptoms that include yellowing of foliage, abnormal green color of flower petals, and shoot proliferation. *Xylella fastidiosa* is another unusual sort of bacterium. It causes the bacterial scorch diseases of sycamore and oak, and Pierce's disease of grapes. While not a phytoplasma, *Xylella fastidiosa* is likewise spread by leafhoppers.

Rose Rosette Disease

It is not easy to determine whether a rose bush has rose rosette disease (RRD), which is caused by the *Rose rosette virus*. Symptoms vary among different rose cultivars and can change as the disease progresses.

- Excessive (hyper-) thorniness (Figure 5–28) is a sure sign of *RRD*, but thorniness does not always occur.
- Abnormal elongation of shoots, with a retention of the juvenile red coloration (Figure 5–59) in the mature leaves, is a strong indicator of RRD, but it can be hard to be sure you are not looking at normal coloration, especially when presented a single cane.

- Shoot proliferation (witches'-broom) can occur with RRD, but this symptom can also be caused by exposure to low doses of the herbicide glyphosate.
- A bright yellow mosaic without leaf deformation represents a much less serious disease called rose mosaic (Figure 5–60).

Because laboratory confirmation of RRD is time-consuming, diagnosticians at the PDIC (Plant Disease and Insect Clinic at NC State University) usually rely on an array of symptoms and the presence of the microscopic eriophyid mite vector when making a diagnosis. For additional information, see Pest News article (Volume 27, number 21, page 10-12).

Figure 5–59. Elongated new shoots that retain their red color is often an early indication of rose rosette disease.
PDIC

Figure 5–60. This bright yellow mosaic, often in an "oak leaf" pattern, is typical of rose mosaic. This is not the same as rose rosette.
NC State University Deptartment of Plant Pathology
Slide Collection

Nematodes

Nematodes are tiny roundworms (Figure 5–58). Some are famous for causing human and animal diseases such as hookworm, river blindness, and heartworm. Others are beneficial, for example, those used to control fungus gnats in greenhouses. Several hundred species of nematodes—all of them microscopic—are parasites of plants. Most of these are soil inhabitants and feed on plant roots. Nematodes can cause economic losses on everything from turfgrass to peach trees. The host range of individual nematode species can be fairly narrow or tremendously wide. Some nematodes remain outside the root while feeding, while others actually enter it. Once inside the root, some types migrate, while others become sedentary at a particular feeding site. All plant-parasitic nematodes have a needlelike mouth structure called a **stylet**. The stylet is used to puncture plant cells so that the nematode can obtain food or inject substances into the plant. The direct damage caused by nematodes is not only harmful,

the damage also can predispose the host to other kinds of diseases.

Figure 5–58. Root-knot nematode magnified.
USDA (William Wergin and Richard Sayre; Colorized by Stephen Ausmus), Wikimedia Commons CC BY - 2.0

Nematode damage interferes with root uptake of water and nutrients. This is why the above-ground symptoms resemble those of other stresses. Nematode symptoms include poor growth, small leaves, wilting, and off-color foliage. Examination of the roots may reveal stunted root systems, dark lesions on roots, or galls (Figure 5–26). The root-knot nematodes (genus *Meloidogyne*) are the most destructive plant-parasitic nematodes in North Carolina, in part due to their wide host range. They inject growth-regulating substances into root cells that stimulate the formation of galls or knots that are visible to the unaided eye. The size of the gall varies with the host. The adult nematodes themselves remain hidden within the gall. These galls should not be confused with the nitrogen-fixing nodules formed on the roots of legumes (Figure 5–61) or with the normal swellings on the roots of plants such as liriope, mondograss, and daylily.

The amount of damage caused by nematodes depends on four factors:

1. The particular species of nematodes present
2. The population levels of the nematodes
3. The particular species of plant involved
4. Growing conditions, such as moisture levels and nutrient status

The plant-nematode combination is critical. For example, we worry about spiral, lesion, and root-knot nematodes on boxwoods. But our major nematode concern for azaleas is the stunt nematode.

All nematodes reproduce by eggs. Juveniles hatch from the eggs and develop into adults after a series of molts. Many nematode species can survive and complete their life cycles on weeds. In addition, many nematode species are able to survive long periods even in the absence of a plant host. Egg masses are an important overwintering stage for root-knot nematodes, and the eggs of cyst nematodes are protected in a sort of shell formed from the dead body of the female that produced the eggs. These cysts are just barely large enough to be visible on the surface of the roots if you look closely. Fortunately, we seldom see problems with cyst nematodes in North Carolina, except on soybeans.

On their own, nematodes can travel horizontally in soil only inches to a foot or so per year. For long-distance spread, nematodes rely on the movement of soil clinging to boots, tools, or equipment, and on the shipment of transplants. Once introduced into a new site, it may take years for populations to build to the point where plant injury is noticed.

If you suspect that your soil has plant-parasitic nematodes, submit a sample to your county's Extension center or to the NC Department of Agriculture & Consumer Services for testing.

Two important kinds of nematodes do not fit the general pattern described. Foliar nematodes directly enter leaf tissue, where they cause yellowing and then necrosis. As with bacterial leaf spots, these affected areas tend

Figure 5–61. Nitrogen-fixing nodules (left) and nematode swellings on roots (right).
Harry Rose, Flickr CC BY- 2.0 and Scot Nelson, Flickr CC BY- 0 1.0

to be limited by the veins in the leaf and so are angular (as for example in butterfly bush) or linear (as in the case of hosta). Foliar nematodes are particularly a problem in greenhouses and nurseries. The pine wilt nematode is destructive to nonnative trees in the pine family. The pine wilt nematode lives within the wood of the trees and is transmitted by a type of longhorn beetle. In North Carolina, the greatest problem with pine wilt nematode is on Japanese black pine along the coast.

Viruses

Plant viruses are very small particles of either DNA or RNA wrapped in a protein coat. They can be visualized only with the aid of powerful electron microscopes. Approximately a thousand plant viruses have been described, with more being discovered continually. Viruses enter plant cells and multiply by using the plant's own enzymes to manufacture more virus particles. Damage to plant cells occurs because normal cellular processes are disrupted.

Viruses are diagnosed by using knowledge of the viruses affecting certain hosts, observing plant symptoms, and conducting laboratory tests. Symptoms of virus infection are extremely diverse. They can include green and yellow mottling or mosaic (Figure 5–11), ringspots (Figure 5–12), color break on flowers (Figure 5–62), and sometimes necrotic spots (Figure 5–6). With some viruses, vein clearing (veins are lighter than normal) or vein banding (Figure 5–63) (leaf tissue alongside veins is a darker green than the rest) develops. Stunting of leaves, flowers, and entire plants is not uncommon. With a few viruses, leaf malformation (Figure 5–64) or shoot proliferation (witches'-broom) (Figure 5–28) can occur.

Care must be taken when interpreting some symptoms.

Figure 5–62. Color break on a Camellia sp.
PDIC

Figure 5–63. Vein banding means that the darker green areas follow the veins.
PDIC

Figure 5–64. Distorted leaves on Nandina sp. infected with *cucumber mosaic virus.*
PDIC

Chimeras—genetic aberrations in chlorophyll production—look at first glance like a virus-induced mosaic (Figure 5–65). A "shoestring" distortion of tomato leaves can be caused both by *Cucumber mosaic virus* (CMV) and by exposure to synthetic **auxin** herbicides. Witches'-broom in rose can be caused by *Rose rosette virus* or by exposure to the herbicide glyphosate. Care should also be taken when interpreting virus names. *Rose rosette virus* infects only roses, but *Cucumber mosaic virus* has hundreds of hosts.

5

Figure 5–65. A chimera in tomatillo leaves.
PDIC

Viral infections of plants are incurable and also **systemic**, meaning that the virus occurs throughout the plant. Any plant that is vegetatively propagated from a virus-infected mother plant will also be infected. This includes propagation by **division**, **cuttings**, **air-layering**, **tubers**, and **grafting**. On the other hand, relatively few viruses are transmitted by true seed and a very few via pollen. A handful of extremely hardy viruses can be "mechanically" transmitted on hands or tools. These include **Tobacco mosaic virus** and its relatives, as well as **Hosta virus X**. Many viruses are transmitted by arthropods, such as aphids, thrips, whiteflies, leafhoppers, and eriophyid mites. These insects and mites are referred to as **vectors** of the virus. For example, thrips are the vector of *Tomato spotted wilt virus*. So-called "soilborne" viruses are actually spread by nematodes and fungi in the soil. Most viruses die quickly outside a living cell, but they can overwinter in perennial or woody plants and in weeds.

Viroids are virus-like particles consisting of RNA but with no outer protein coat. They cause diseases similar to those caused by viruses and are spread mechanically or

Figure 5–66. Mistletoe.
bobistraveling, Flickr CC BY - 2.0

Parasitic Plants

Parasitic plants include dodder, mistletoe, witchweed, and broomrape. Parasitic plants derive nourishment from the host plant's vascular system. Dodder (Figure 5–47) and mistletoe (Figure 5–66) attach themselves to aboveground portions of a plant, whereas witchweed and broomrape attach themselves to plant roots. Dodder produces twining yellow to orange stems that resemble spaghetti. Witchweed is a serious pest of corn and has been the subject of quarantine efforts over the last several decades. Native to Africa and Asia, here it is restricted to only a few counties in southeastern North Carolina.

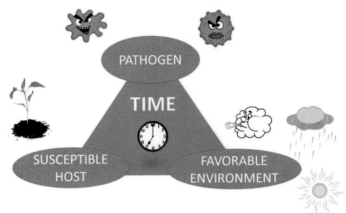

Figure 5–67. The disease triangle represents the fact that disease occurs only when a pathogen, a susceptible host, and a favorable environment are all present together, and a sufficient period of time has elapsed.
Gloria Polakof CC BY - 2.0

Disease Development

Although we consider pathogens as the causes of plant diseases, the development of a disease is not automatic. It also depends on the plant and the environment. Each species of plant is capable of being infected by only certain pathogens. A plant is considered *susceptible* when a pathogen can cause infection. If a pathogen cannot infect a plant, even under conditions favorable for disease development, the plant is considered resistant to that pathogen. Plants have varying degrees of resistance, which can change with each plant's growth stage. For example, brown rot will develop only on maturing fruit, but peach scab develops on younger fruit. The **virulence** (aggressiveness) of pathogens can also vary. The environment, especially temperature and the presence or absence of water, will determine how much disease develops. By a long tradition, this relationship is depicted as the disease triangle. Because the process requires time—usually days to weeks—the time element is also included in the diagram. In some versions, the influence of a vector or of human activity is depicted as a fourth corner, making it a disease pyramid (Figure 5–67).

The beauty of the disease triangle is that it provides a *framework* for disease management strategies. You can grasp it at one or more of the corners. For example, *modifying the environment is* one method of controlling disease development. The goal is to make the environment unfavorable for the pathogen, favorable for the plant, or preferably both. You can adjust planting dates, change the spacing between plants, provide good drainage, and avoid wetting leaves during irrigation. *Using resistant plants* is another strategy, based on the next corner of the triangle. *Addressing the pathogen* can be key, for example, because some diseases occur only during certain well-defined periods of the year.

Spread and Survival of Pathogens

Another important consideration in disease control is how pathogens move around and how they survive when there is no host plant available. Some examples were mentioned above in the section on pathogen groups. Fungi, especially in the form of spores, can move via wind, water, insects, and human activity. Some species of fungi are so versatile that they produce different kinds of spores that may disperse in different ways. Bacterial cells are very often water-splashed from diseased to healthy plants. There they may colonize plant surfaces without immediately causing an infection. Working among plants while they are wet is a good way to spread both fungi and bacteria. Viruses often rely on an insect or mite vectors for dispersal and for entry into a plant. Nematodes and their eggs move wherever soil is moved.

It is critical to understand where and how pathogens overwinter. Many pathogens survive in plant parts that remain alive over the winter, such as roots, bulbs, stems, and buds. Soilborne diseases such as *southern bacterial wilt* survive in the garden soil. Once a given piece of ground is infested with the causal bacterium, known as *Ralstonia solanacearum*, it will remain infested indefinitely. Tomatoes planted there will succumb to the bacteria as soon as hot weather arrives. On the other hand, the occurrence of *Tomato spotted wilt virus* is a game of chance each year, depending on the survival of the virus in weeds and the movement of the thrips vectors. At the farthest extreme are diseases such as downy mildew of cucurbits. This pathogen can overwinter only in warm climates like Florida's. The spores are blown long distances on wind currents, reaching North Carolina in late May or June each year. The disease can arrive earlier if spores hitchhike a ride on infected transplants.

The Diagnostic Process

Before making a hasty diagnosis and planning action to correct a plant problem, we must identify the cause. Some plant diseases are easily recognizable based on a specimen or photograph, but others may be difficult to identify. We recommend a structured diagnostic process. As you work through the steps below, be aware that a definitive diagnosis is not always possible or even necessary. In some cases, you will simply narrow the list of possibilities to the point where an informed management decision can be made. In other cases, you will need the assistance of an extension agent or the resources of the Plant Disease and Insect Clinic.

Step 1: Gather as much information as you can and take notes. You may want to use the PDIC sample submission form as a guide. Also think of the "three Ws **(where, when, what)** and H **(how)**" of good reporting.

- **Where** is the problem occurring? Be sure to confirm that the plant was actually growing in your county. Plants brought from elsewhere could have problems that are uncommon in your area. In what setting is the plant growing, such as in a hanging basket, in vegetable garden, or on a north-facing slope?
- **When** did the problem first occur? Has it progressed quickly or slowly? Has it spread? When were the plants sown or transplanted to their current site? When was the sample collected?
- **What** kind of plant is affected? Is just one species or variety affected, or are there many affected? What kinds of plants were grown in this location last year?
- **How** was the plant managed in terms of water, mulch, compost, fertilizer, lime, irrigation, and pesticides? How was the weather in the weeks before the problem appeared?

Step 2: Observe the specimen or photos from the site, or both.

- First verify that the plant has been identified correctly. Then look at the entire plant: roots, stems, leaves, flowers, and fruit. Does it seem to be the right size and color for a plant of the reported age?
- Do you notice any of the other symptoms listed in Tables 5–1a and 5–1b? If so, do they occur in the upper portion of the plant, the lower portion, or toward the middle?
  Are the symptoms or signs different on the upper surface of the leaf versus the lower? If there are color changes, are they generalized across the foliage, or are they mainly between or along the veins? If there are leaf spots, what are their size and shape? If the plant appears wilted, was it that way in the garden? Or did wilting occur since the plant was dug or pulled?

How does the leaf look when held up to the light? Are any parts of the plant missing?

- Look for signs of insects or mites. Their damage is sometimes mistaken for disease. Have leaves or flowers dropped off? What is the distribution of affected plants: scattered, grouped, or otherwise distributed?

- With turf problems, note carefully both the symptoms on the individual grass plants and whether the "stand symptoms" consist of small spots, larger patches, rings, or just scattered plants. See the TurfFiles glossary for more information.

- In all cases, see if there are any signs of the **causal organism**, such as those listed in Table 5–2. Be aware that many fungi are secondary and grow on plant parts damaged or killed by another pathogen.

Step 3: Compare your observations with the easily recognized diseases and disorders described in Table 5–3a – f and come up with a diagnostic hypothesis. Be aware that some symptoms are unique to particular diseases, whereas other symptoms can be caused by a wide range of factors. Wildly excessive thorn production on roses is a foolproof indicator of *Rose rosette virus*, but not every rose-rosette-infected bush shows this symptom. Mosaics (Figure 5–11) are usually the result of a viral infection, as are ringspots (Figure 5–12). The famous exception to this is that African violets will develop ringspots when cold water contacts the leaves. Leaf spots with an angular or linear shape because the spots stop abruptly at the major veins often indicate a bacterial infection, downy mildew, or foliar nematodes. Wilting, on the other hand, can have many causes. See the special section on page 5–36, "**When Plants are Wilted.**"

Step 4: Double-check your diagnosis. Once you have a short list of possible causes, look for photos and descriptions in NC State Extension publications or other references you may have on hand or online. Is there anything that can help rule out one or more of the possibilities? Make more observations if needed. With experience you will be able to confidently identify a number of diseases. If you cannot reach any conclusions, show the sample to an Extension agent or the PDIC.

Step 5: Make recommendations, if possible, based on what you were able to determine from the suggestions presented above and consult available NC State extension publications for recommended ways of managing the problem. Sometimes there is nothing that can be done to alleviate a problem in a home garden situation. In other cases, cultural practices can reduce the impact of the disease this year or in the future. In a few cases, **fungicide** applications may be worthwhile. Always encourage an integrated pest management (IPM) approach. A study of plant pathogens and the disease development and spread will give you a better understanding of how diseases occur, which management strategies are helpful, and when there are no effective manangement strategies.

> **Some example diagnostic scenarios are given at the end of this chapter.**

Although many diseases can be confidently diagnosed in the Extension center (Table 5–3a-f), other cases will require specialized testing or expert examination. Be especially careful about the following situations:

Vegetables

- Necrotic spots or blotches on the leaves of crucifers (including cabbage, collards, and broccoli). These spots may be the result of *black rot*, caused by the bacterium *Xanthomonas campestris*. The typical V-shaped lesions are not always present, making diagnosis difficult at times. This disease has a high destructive potential.

- Wilting of tomato plants in the garden without a visible sign of fungal activity. (See page 5–36, "**When Plants are Wilted**.") Whether the cause is nematodes, southern bacterial wilt, the early stages of southern stem blight, or something else entirely, wilting can have serious long-term implications for the garden.

- Leaf spots on tomatoes and peppers. Spots caused by bacteria, fungi, or even *Tomato spotted wilt virus* can look surprisingly similar. Some are more serious than others, and control measures are quite different.

- Large areas of tomato or potato foliage turning gray or gray-green and withering in a short period of time, often accompanied by large rotted spots on tomato fruit. These symptoms can indicate *late blight*, a very destructive disease that the PDIC helps to monitor. The timing of its appearance in North Carolina varies from year to year.

- Stem rots, leaf spots, and blights of cucurbits. *Downy mildew*, several true fungi, and two kinds of bacteria can cause leaf spotting in cucurbits. In addition, *downy mildew* is subject to monitoring because it shows up at different times and in different places each year. When stems are involved, the laboratory can help to differentiate between the various possible causes. Note that *gummosis* (Figure 5–27) on stems is a response to a number of kinds of stress, not just the disease known as "gummy stem blight."

- Anything involving leaf distortion or **dwarfing**. These symptoms can be caused by viruses, mites, or insects, or by chemical injury.

Fruit and Nut Trees

- Fruit and nut trees in the home orchard present particular challenges for diagnosis. Refer anything to the PDIC that does not fit the pattern of one of the diseases described in Table 5–3c.

Other Trees and Woody Ornamentals
- Table 5–3d mentions a number of diseases of woody ornamentals. When none of those seems to fit, the PDIC can be of assistance. It is important to get a good sample that includes sufficient roots in soil, plus the right parts of branches and foliage. It normally is not enough to have just detached leaves, or stems that are completely dead.
- If dieback symptoms are present, carefully cut away a strip of outer bark from an affected branch. If you find a very clear boundary between live and dead cambium (or inner bark), it is likely a *canker* (Figure 5–68).

Herbaceous Ornamentals
- Table 5–3e reviews many diseases that affect herbaceous ornamentals.
- **Root and stem rots**—For confident diagnosis of root rots in bedding plants, a microscope and selective media are often needed. The results are important because they affect the choice of replacement plants. (See page 5–36, **"When Plants are Wilted."**)
- **Blights**—When large areas of foliage die in a short period of time. Even when lower stems, roots, rhizomes, and other plant parts look good, then a laboratory diagnosis is helpful.

For more information on diagnosing plant problems, see chapter 7, "Diagnostics."

Figure 5–68. Camellia stem canker.
PDIC

Principles of Plant Disease Management

Although homeowners and growers are sometimes simply curious to know the cause of a particular disease, most are interested in controlling it. Often no acceptable measures are available that will halt the disease, and the affected plant or plants must be removed. Sometimes the only thing that can be done is to redouble preventive efforts for the next growing season. In other cases the affected plant will recover by putting out new roots and leaves with or without the application of management measures. Diagnosis of the disease is very important in deciding whether the problem is serious and what measures, if any, will be helpful and cost-effective. The choice of management measures is influenced by where the pathogen overwinters, how it spreads, its host range, and how the conditions favor infection. See the previous sections on Disease Development and Spread and Survival of Pathogens.

In many cases, it is not realistic to talk about disease *control*. We do not have complete control over nature, even in our own backyards. Thus, the sections that follow will discuss the two main types of disease management strategies: cultural and chemical. Many homeowners and growers today are interested in biological methods of dealing with pests. Unfortunately, there are very few biological options for plant disease management in the yard and garden at the present time. Later in this chapter, we will pull these ideas together within the framework of integrated pest management using a case study model.

Cultural Management
We often hear these sayings about managing problems: "A stitch in time saves nine." Or "An ounce of prevention is worth a pound of cure." Taken literally, this means that what we do to prevent disease is 9 to 16 times more effective than dealing with a disease after it has become established. Many of these preventive measures fall under the category of cultural practices, the actions we take every day as part of growing plants. A summary of the top practices for disease management in the garden is given in the highlighted box on page 5–19. Notice that all but one are cultural methods.

Besides adaptability to your soils and climate, look for plants that are not susceptible to common diseases. Even within susceptible species, look for varieties and hybrids that offer resistance to key diseases. For example, there are apple cultivars that are resistant to *cedar apple rust*, dogwood cultivars resistant to *powdery mildew*, rose cultivars resistant to *black spot* and *cercospora leaf spot*, and tomato cultivars resistant to nematodes and some fungal wilts. Heirloom tomato varieties have become

Top Strategies for Preventing Plant Diseases in the Home Garden

1. Choose the right plants (adapted species and resistant varieties).
2. Rotate sites in the vegetable garden among different plant families.
3. Start with healthy seeds, transplants, shrubs, and trees.
4. Do not move pathogens around on tools, with soil, or on shoes and clothing.
5. Plant correctly, in season, and into a properly prepared site.
6. Do not overwater, or wet foliage as nighttime approaches.
7. Clean up diseased material during and after the growing season.
8. Use mulches effectively.
9. Optimize fertility.
10. Avoid unnecessary injury to plants.
11. Manage weeds and insects.
12. Apply pesticides only when the benefits outweigh the costs.

increasingly popular, but may lack resistance to soilborne diseases. In this case, grafting is an option. For more information, see the *Grafting for Disease Resistance in Heirloom Tomatoes* by Cary Rivard and Frank Louws (AG-675), and keep an eye out for a grafting workshop near you.

Plant with an eye toward diversity. If all the plants in the vicinity are of the same type, a disease can spread quickly. Diversified plantings are less likely to suffer major disease problems. You could, for instance, use groups of different shrubs for a screen rather than just Leyland cypress or Japanese cedar.

Rotate crops to try to break the disease cycle. Change the location in the garden where crops are planted from one year to the next. Vegetable crops in the same family, such as cabbage and broccoli, should not follow each other in the same spot in the garden. The length of an effective rotation will depend on the disease involved, so get a diagnosis. Some pathogens, unfortunately, do not disappear over time. An example is *Ralstonia solanacearum*, the cause of *southern bacterial wilt*. Once introduced it will remain in the soil indefinitely.

Improving the soil will reduce plant stress and decrease soilborne diseases. Good soil drainage, proper soil pH, and optimum fertility produce healthy plants that are more resistant to insects, diseases, and environmental stresses. Soil testing will reveal pH and nutritional problems that can reduce growth and lead to plant stress. Learn more about soil testing in chapter 1, Soils and Plant Nutrients. Planting in beds raised 6 to 8 inches above grade and adding organic amendments to the soil can significantly reduce problems with *phytophthora root rot*.

Buy seed from a reputable source, and inspect all transplants, including the roots, before planting. *Boxwood blight* finds its way into landscapes in North Carolina by the installation of new, infected plants.

Among plant pathogens, most nematodes, many fungi, some bacteria, and a few viruses are soil inhabitants. Take care not to move soil among landscapes or gardens on borrowed or rented tools or equipment. For the same reason, transplanting shrubs or perennials from one location to another risks transplanting pathogens as well as the plant.

Plant and harvest at recommended times, to give every advantage to the plant. For example, Madagascar periwinkle (*Catharanthus roseus*) should not be planted until the soil has warmed in the spring. Planting when the soil is cold and wet can also cause okra seeds to rot in the ground. While late plantings of squash are very likely to suffer from powdery mildew, pansies should not be transplanted until the soil temperature has cooled in the fall.

Because water is the major limitation for bacteria and most fungi, be careful with irrigation. Overwatering favors water mold species like *Phytophthora* and *Pythium* and the root rots they cause. Avoid wetting leaves and stems if possible to prevent foliar diseases. If overhead watering cannot be avoided, at least water during times that will not add hours to the natural nighttime leaf wetness period. Space and prune plants properly to improve air circulation and help the foliage dry quickly.

In some cases, prompt removal of diseased plants or plant parts can reduce the amount of a pathogen in the vicinity. For example, the removal of diseased tomato leaves can slow the progress of septoria leaf

Follow the **"right-plant-right-place"** approach. Before planting, carefully study the site. Does it have the appropriate sun exposure, drainage, and soil for a chosen plant to thrive? Boxwoods and dogwoods, for instance, prefer light shade. Although they may appear to tolerate full sun, it predisposes them to problems. Azaleas and daphne need good drainage to avoid root rot.

spot. If a tree or shrub in a hedge planting has been diagnosed with armillaria root rot, the individuals on either side should also be removed, because they have likely been infected via fungal growth through the soil. The same strategy would be of little benefit with *phytophthora root rot* because the spores of *Phytophthora* species can move far beyond the initial infection in water runoff.

Remove plant debris in the fall to reduce pathogen populations. Many fungal foliar pathogens overwinter in dead leaf litter. In the case of fallen camellia blossoms, rake them up in the spring. Sclerotia of the camellia petal blight fungus, *Ciborinia camelliae*, survive the whole year on the ground's surface after the blossoms rot away. The sclerotia resume growth and release spores in the spring, to coincide with the emergence of camellia blossoms. In the vegetable garden, remove roots if they were infested with nematodes or root rot pathogens. Liriope (*Liriope muscari*) should be trimmed close to the ground in late winter to reduce carryover of anthracnose on foliage from one year to the next. Fire blight, brown rot, and many other fruit diseases overwinter in cankers. Even the fungus that causes black spot of rose can overwinter on canes as well as fallen leaves. Prune and remove cankers during the dormant season by removing 4 to 6 inches into clean wood. When pruning out active fire blight infections in the spring, be more aggressive, going 10 to 12 inches below the visible damage. Destroy the clippings, or at least remove them from the site, and sanitize shears frequently. See the *NC State Extension sanitizers* table for more information.

When composting, turn the pile thoroughly so it reaches a high enough temperature to kill pathogenic fungi, bacteria, and nematodes. Even though compost pile temperatures might get high enough to kill pathogens, you should never knowingly place infected plant material in the compost pile. Read more about composting in chapter 2.

If pathogens are present, cultivate flower beds and vegetable gardens. Cultivation can expose soil insects and disease organisms to desiccation, cold temperatures, and predation.

A 2-to-3-inch layer of mulch acts as a barrier between the soil and the plant and may prevent inoculum-infested soil from splashing onto the plants during watering or heavy rain. Mulching will also enhance the total health and vigor of most plants. Late winter mulching can reduce camellia petal blight and the early infections of black spot of rose. In both cases, the mulch covers overwintering fungal structures so that spores are not released into the air.

Many pathogens take advantage of wounds to enter, so avoid any unnecessary injury. This is especially important with trees, where roots are often disturbed by digging, and the consequences may take years to develop.

Remove weeds while they are young. Some weeds can harbor diseases and arthropod vectors. Mow or destroy weeds from ditch banks and other nearby areas. Till the planting area early, so weeds that might carry pests have time to die before you plant.

A physical barrier can protect certain plants. Tomatoes, peppers, and eggplants benefit from this technique; they can be protected from cutworms and the soilborne disease southern blight. Wrap the stem of transplants with a 4-by-4-inch strip of aluminum foil so that 2 inches of the stem is protected above and below the ground.

A solid planting of French marigolds (*Tagetes patula*) will give good control of many kinds of root-knot nematodes. Details of the practice can be found in the NCDA&CS publication *NemaNote 1*. A common misconception is that a sprinkling of marigolds can discourage nematodes. In fact, planting only a few marigold plants in a vegetable garden will provide little or no control.

Solarization is an approach that involves heat-treating the soil using energy from the sun to reduce populations of nematodes, weeds, and soilborne fungi. It has potential benefits in approximately the eastern half of North Carolina. The soil should be covered with plastic for at least four weeks, preferably longer, during a hot and sunny time of the year. Frequent cooling by rain and cloudy periods will reduce the benefits. To achieve maximum results, follow these recommendations:

- Till the soil well before covering it with plastic to destroy clods and plant debris, which might interfere with uniform conduction of heat through the soil and protect some organisms from the full effects of the treatment.
- Make sure the soil is moist when you apply the plastic cover. Wet soil conducts heat better than dry soil. Also, most pest organisms are more susceptible to lethal effects of heat in moist soil; they may be dormant if dry.
- Raise the center of the bed so that it forms a small crown or peak to enable the plastic to shed water. Water standing on the plastic will absorb some of the heat intended for the soil.
- Use clear plastic instead of black plastic. Clear plastic produces higher temperatures faster than black plastic.
- Use thin plastic (1 to 2 millimeters), which permits more sunlight to penetrate to the soil and has been reported to accomplish more rapid and deeper control for soil borne fungi than thicker plastic (6 millimeters).
- Leave the plastic cover on until planting time. It has no detrimental effects on the soil and will reduce chances of recontamination before planting.

- Avoid bringing contaminated plants or untreated soil into the treated bed when planting, and do not till or otherwise disturb treated soil. Deep tillage can bring soil up from depths that were not adequately heated.

Chemical Management

Prevention and sanitation are the most practical approaches to disease control and have been detailed in the previous section. Home gardeners have few alternatives for chemically controlling plant diseases, and almost all of those alternatives are directed against fungi. Although the products used are called fungicides, they slow down rather than eliminate fungi. There are few, if any, chemical options for consumers to use against bacteria, nematodes, and viruses.

Fungicides are often unnecessary because many diseases cause only minor aesthetic damage. In other cases, fungicides may be impractical to apply. They are of no value against cankers or root rots in trees and shrubs. However, fungicides can be an important component of IPM in some situations. It is impossible to control black spot in susceptible rose cultivars without fungicides. A homeowner with a peach or apple tree will need a high tolerance for damaged fruit if he or she chooses not to spray. Fungicides can also be important tools in the management of certain turfgrass diseases.

No single fungicide will control all fungi, though some have a wider spectrum of activity than others. Most fungicides are protectants and should be applied before a pathogen infects a plant. Furthermore, many do not move within the plant and so must

> For a fungicide to be a useful tool, the disease must be properly diagnosed and the right chemical must be applied in a timely manner, at the correct dose, with good coverage, and at the necessary intervals.

be applied repeatedly to protect new growth. Some fungicides are systemic and can cure early infections.

Do not expect miracles from fungicides. For example, fungicides applied after powdery mildew is present on a leaf will not return the leaf to its original green color. A fungicide can, however, protect new growth from becoming infected.

Fungicide Classification

Fungicides can be classified by their topical mode of action (how they interact with the plant) or their biochemical mode of action (how they affect the target fungus). There are four basic topical modes of action.

1. **Contact fungicides.** These are strictly protectants and must be on the surface of the plant before infection takes place. They break down and wash off over time and so must be reapplied fairly frequently, usually every

7 to 10 days. Reapplication is also necessary because new growth is not protected.

2. **Translaminar fungicides** (local penetrants). These compounds will move into and across a leaf but not up or down in the plant.

3. **Acropetal penetrants.** These fungicides will enter the plant and move from the point of entry in an upward direction only, with the transpiration stream.

4. **True systemics.** Only one group of fungicides—the phosphonates—will move downward from the point of application. One implication is clear: For most fungicides, if you want activity in the crown or roots, you have to apply to the crown or roots!

There are dozens of biochemical modes of action, but they can be conveniently grouped into two groups: "multisite" and "single-site" modes of action. Fungicides classified as having "multisite" modes of action are all broad-spectrum protectants with a contact topical mode of action. These chemicals disrupt a wide array of life processes in the fungal cell. On the other hand, fungicides with "single-site" modes of action affect very specific biochemical processes in the fungal cell. They usually have a narrower spectrum of activity and are often—but not always—local or acropetal penetrants. One limiting factor in using these compounds is that some fungal populations can evolve to be less sensitive, or have a resistance to a compound after repeated use (see below).

Recent years have shown increased interest in chemicals that have fungicidal activity but are not fungicides in the traditional sense. Examples in this category include petroleum-based horticultural oils, neem oil (derived from the neem tree), and potassium bicarbonate (a relative of baking soda, used primarily against powdery mildew). When used against certain diseases, these chemicals can be adequate alternatives to conventional fungicides when the disease pressure is not too great. Keep in mind that neem is toxic to bees.

The repeated use of pesticides can lead to the evolution of insensitive pest populations, whether they are fungi, bacteria, insects, weeds, or rodents. In such cases, individual pests are not becoming stronger. Instead, chance mutations result in resistant individuals, which are the ones that survive and reproduce. Whether and how fast resistance becomes widespread enough in a population to result in loss of control depends on the biochemical mode of action of the pesticide, the life history of the pest, its reproductive rate, and the intensity of pesticide use.

Fungicide Timing

Timing of fungicide applications is an important component in chemical disease control. Fungicides should be applied when conditions favoring disease development are present.

Rainy, foggy, warm, and humid weather conditions generally favor disease development. Whenever possible, spray schedules should be adjusted to provide fungicide protection before rainy periods, and fungicides should be reapplied after heavy rains if the label so indicates.

When using chemical management, we need to know the life cycle of the disease organism and when it is most susceptible. Many fruit diseases are best managed when the fruit is very young, or even in the blossom stage; once the fruit starts to rot, it is too late. A diagnosis at that time can at least help a gardener plan management strategies for the next season.

Always carefully read and follow the label when using any pesticide.

Case Study—Think IPM: Cucumbers in Distress

Something is not right with your cucumbers. You wonder if they are suffering from a disease and what you should do. You review the diagnostic procedures from chapter 7, Diagnostics, and think about the five steps for IPM:

1. Monitor and scout to determine pest type and population levels.
2. Accurately identify host and pest.
3. Consider economic or aesthetic injury thresholds. A threshold is the point at which action should be taken.
4. Implement a treatment strategy using physical, cultural, biological, or chemical management, or combine these strategies.
5. Evaluate success of treatments.

1. Monitor and scout to determine pest type and population levels.

You grow a wide range of vegetables at home for personal use and to give to friends. Everything looked great this year, but now about half of the cucumber plants are wilting. Before sending a sample to the PDIC, you decide to do some sleuthing on your own.

2. Accurately identify the host and pest.

STEP 1. Identify the plant: *I see on my garden plan that the affected plants are 'Straight 8' cucumber plants.*

STEP 2. Describe the problem: *Almost half of my cucumbers are wilting. At first the leaves would droop a little during the heat of the day, so I started watering more. The problem only got worse.*

STEP 3. Identify what is normal:

What does the healthy part of the plant look like? *The stems still look good and so do the youngest leaves. The unaffected plants on the other side of the garden are green and happy and seem to be growing faster than these.*

What does the unhealthy part of the plant look like? *Besides the general wilting, I notice that the lower leaves have large tan spots between the veins and burned looking edges.*

Have you had a soil test? *Yes. Last year I had a soil test done. I put on dolomitic lime in the fall according to the report recommendations. (For information on how to submit a soil test see chapter 1, Soils and Plant Nutrients.)*

STEP 4. Consider cultural practices:

Age and history of plants: *These plants were direct-seeded in mid-April. They came up slowly because of cool weather, but then really took off in May.*

Irrigation: *If it does not rain, the vegetables get watered about twice a week. I put the lawn sprinkler on them for about an hour when I come home from work. The leaves dry off before sunset.*

Fertilizer: *We added about an inch of compost a couple of weeks before planting, along with some calcium nitrate and muriate of potash, but no phosphorous, because the soil test was high. My brother-in-law always brings over his tiller and works up the ground for us. The good and bad plants all got the same compost and fertilizer. There has been no fertilizer side-dressing.*

Maintenance: *I have been diligent about hand hoeing and careful not to cut the vines. No herbicides have been used in the area.*

STEP 5. Consider environmental conditions:

Are there any significant water issues? *We have had fairly good rains, but no flooding and no standing water.*

What is the soil like? *This garden is on pretty sandy soil. Come to think of it, the worst plants are on the sandiest, best-drained part.*

Describe the light near this garden bed. How many hours of sunlight? *This bed gets about 8 hours of full*

5

sun a day, with some morning shade from the neighbor's pine trees.

Describe any recent changes or events: *None. We have had veggies here since the year 2000.*

STEP 6. Look for signs of pathogens and pests:

On the leaves: *There are no squash bugs or eggs or other insects that I can see. When I look at the spots with a magnifying glass, I do not see any mold or dark specks, even on the underside.*

On the vines: *Vines look good. There are no insects or frass to be seen.*

On the roots and in the soil: *I do not see any wireworms or cutworms or any other pests, but they are awfully good at hiding.*

STEP 7. Describe the symptoms:

On the leaves: *The lower leaves have brown spots or blotches and some scorched edges. New growth looks green, just wilted.*

On the buds and flowers: *Plants are just starting to flower. The blossoms look normal.*

On the stems: *There are no holes or rotten areas on the stems, even at the soil line.*

On the roots: *There are not a lot of roots, but they are white and firm. Parts of the root system do look "lumpy." There is no bad odor.*

STEP 8. Distribution of damage in the landscape:

Are other plants in the landscape affected?
The problem is just in the cucumbers. The sweet corn next to them and the tomatoes on the other side of the corn all look fine.

STEP 9. Distribution of damage on the plant and specific plant parts:

Where is the damage seen on the plant?
Lower leaves, mostly, are showing symptoms. Scattered roots show the lumpiness.

STEP 10. Timing:

When did you notice this problem?
Starting the first week of June some of the plants looked "off." The wilting started in mid-June.

Based on your observations, you hypothesize that this cucumber problem is a disease, not an insect because there were no insect signs. Though there are symptoms on both leaves and roots, you suspect that it is fundamentally a root or soil problem because it is happening in just one patch in the garden. Based on the other facts gathered, you doubt it is anything you did because fertilization and other practices were carefully planned and uniform. The sandier soil could be the problem, but then the plants should have responded to increased irrigation. Given that wilting is a primary symptom, you work through the key in this chapter entitled "**When Plants Are Wilted**." The answer to the first couplet leads you to choice 2, which leads to choice 4, which leads to choice 5, which leads you to the disconcerting conclusion that the problem is root-knot nematodes. In fact, the roots look just like Figure 5–26, and Table 5-3b indicates that root knot can occur on cucumbers in the summer. It also gives the scientific name of the pathogen as Meloidogyne. Now that you have a positive ID, you do more research on this disease. You search extension. org or type in "Meloidogyne vegetables +edu" into your Internet search engine to find university-based resources. This yields several helpful links, including information from the mid-Atlantic and Southeast. You also check out the NCDA&CS note mentioned earlier in this chapter.

3. **Consider economic or aesthetic injury thresholds.**
Root-knot nematodes can cause severe yield losses on many plants in the vegetable garden. You want to try and salvage what you can of this year's crop and to prevent problems for the future.

4. **Implement a treatment strategy using physical, cultural, biological, or chemical management, or combine these strategies.**
Physical management. You remove the affected plants, including the roots and the soil immediately around those roots. You bag them up and send them off to the landfill. These plants should not go into the compost pile. You take care in the process not to spread contaminated soil on the shovel or your boots into the other areas of the garden. You realize that the nematodes may have come into your garden on your brother-in-law's tiller, or that he may have picked them up from you. Your other research shows you that solarization can work in your area, but you decide it is too tricky with the shade from the corn and other factors, so you opt for frequent tilling of the soil this summer to expose the nematodes to desiccation.

Cultural management. You provide extra care to the remaining cucumbers, optimizing watering and fertilizer, hoping to get a harvest before they succumb to the nematodes, powdery mildew, downy mildew, and other late-summer pathogens. Given the wide host range and persistence of these nematodes, you would like to move the garden to another location next year. But there is no other suitable location in your small yard. You decide to dedicate the affected area next year to a solid planting of French marigolds, and to avoid cucurbits, tomatoes, beets, okra, spinach, and sweet potatoes for several years afterward. In the fall before going back to these susceptible crops, you will send a soil sample to the NCDA&CS Nematode Assay Laboratory to see if it is safe to plant susceptible crops in this location. In other areas of the garden, you will go with either sweet corn or look for resistant varieties. Unfortunately, there are no salad-type cucumbers with resistance to root-knot nematode, but there are a few resistant varieties of other vegetables. You decide to try those in the future. As a back-up, you will try a few favorite heirloom veggies in containers.

Chemical management. There are no chemical controls for nematodes in the home garden at this time.

5. Evaluate success of treatments.

Keeping a garden journal or notes about the management strategies tried and their results will help make decisions much easier in the future. Some of the management strategies you researched may take time to see results, and having a written record will help jog your memory, as well as help you keep the rotation straight and remember which species and varieties do well.

Table 5–3a.

Easily Recognized Plant Diseases and Disorders of NC Homes and Gardens

Important: Problem names can vary, depending on the host plant and the plant part affected.

GENERAL

Problem	Occurs on	Season*	Hallmarks	Cause
Artillery fungus	Leaves, walls, windows, cars	(W, Sp) Su, F	Circular, dark raised specks about one-tenth of an inch across. When scraped off, a persistent stained spot remains.	Spore balls shot from the fungus Sphareobolus growing on mulch.
"Dog-vomit" slime mold (Figure 5–48)	Mulch, walls, tree trunks, and other wood surfaces	Su	Yellow frothy masses several inches to a foot wide, developing a pink crust over dusty dark spores.	*Fuligo septica*, a harmless organism unrelated to fungi.
Sooty mold	Any plant	Su, F	Black mold on upper surface of leaf is easily wiped off with fingers (Figure 5–69).	Fungi growing on insect honeydew. Not damaging except blocking photosynthesis.
Stinkhorns	Mulched beds	Su, F	Foul-smelling, horn shaped fungi with dark sticky tops and tan or orange stalks, developing from egg-like structures in the ground.	Several fungi that develop in decaying plant material. (Some differ from the description at left)

*Time of year encountered in field and garden: Sp—Spring, Su—Summer, F—Fall, W—Winter.

Table 5-3b.
Easily Recognized Vegetable Diseases and Disorders of NC Homes and Gardens

VEGETABLES

Problem	Occurs on	Season	Hallmarks	Cause
Blossom-end rot	Tomato, pepper	Su	Flattened dead areas on blossom ends of fruit (Figure 5–52). Tan colored, becoming dark (Figure 5–54) if secondary fungi invade. In pepper (Figure 5–53), can occur on sides of fruit.	Calcium deficiency in developing fruit due to lack of Ca in soil or moisture fluctuations
Common smut	Sweet corn	Su	Ears or other parts develop whitish galls that fill with dusty black spores.	*Ustilago maydis* (fungus) organism unrelated to fungi.
Glyphosate injury	Tomato is very sensitive, but any plant can be affected	Su, F	In tomato: bright yellow coloration of youngest leaves, often at the base of leaflets. At higher doses plant death occurs.	Drift of spray droplets from nearby application of glyphosate herbicide.
Powdery mildew	Many species (Figure 5–70)	Sp, Su, F	White to gray fungal growth on upper and/or lower leaf surfaces.	Different fungi, each specific to a group of plants, e.g., *Podosphaera xanthii* on cucurbits
Root-knot nematode	Cucurbits (Figure 5–70) tomato, beet, okra, spinach, others	Su, F	Swellings not easily detached from roots. Size variable.	Nematodes in the genus Meloidogyne.
Rust	Sweet corn	Su, F	Small pustules break through leaf surface, producing dry spores that are brick-red or orange.	Two fungi in the genus Puccinia cause common and southern rusts.
Southern blight, Southern stem rot	Many species (not corn)	Su	Rot on lower stems and other parts in contact with soil. In moist weather a felt-like fan of white fungal growth on stem (Figure 5–71). Round sclerotia (Figure 5–39) are white at first, turning into tan to brown "bb's".	*Sclerotium rolfsii* (fungus)
**White mold, Sclerotinia blight Sclerotinia rot, "Drop" (lettuce)	Crucifers, lettuce, sometimes others	F, W, Sp	Usually light-brown rot of stems and leaves (Figure 5–72). Fluffy white fungal growth. Irregular black sclerotia - similar in shape and color to mouse droppings - eventually form on or within stems.	*Sclerotinia rolfsii sclerotiorum* (fungus)

** Until and unless fungal structures develop, stem rots are difficult to distinguish from one another.

Table 5–3c.
Easily Recognized Fruit Diseases and Disorders of NC Homes and Gardens

FRUITS (TREE AND SMALL)

Note: A wide variety of problems can occur on fruits, and some resemble each other (for example, copper injury, bacterial leaf spot, and scab on peach fruit). Anything beyond the easily recognized diseases on this list should be referred to an experienced agent or to the PDIC. For more information, including recommendations on preventive sprays, see Disease and Insect Management in the Home Orchard at content.ces.ncsu.edu/disease-and-insect-management-in-the-home-orchard.

Problem	Occurs on	Season	Hallmarks	Cause
Bitter rot	Apple	F	Circular rotten spots have a V-shaped profile when the apple is sliced. Cream-colored to orange spores may exude from tiny dark fruiting bodies.	Two species of the fungus *Colletotrichum*
Black knot	Stone fruits, esp. plum and cherry	All	Segments of twigs, branches, or trunks become swollen, black, and roughened (Figure 5–73).	*Apiosporina morbosa* (fungus)
Brown rot (Figure 5–20)	Stone fruits	Su	Smooth, brown rotted areas expand rapidly as fruit mature. Fuzzy gray or tan fungal sporulation develops on the surface.	Species of the fungus *Monilinia*
Cedar-apple rust	Apple	Late Sp to Su	Bright yellow and orange leaf spots (Figure 5–74). Small yellow blisters on upper leaf surface turn dark. Later, spore-producing pustules with frilled edges form on leaf under-sides (Figure 5–42). (Use hand lens to confirm)	*Gymnosporangium juniperi-virginianae*
Fly speck	Apple	Su, F	Dark flecks, each the size of a period, in clusters on the surface of developing and and mature fruit.	*Schizothyrium pomi* (fungus)

chart continues next page

Figure 5–69. Sooty mold on *Danae racemosa.*
PDIC

Figure 5–70. Powdery mildew on calabash squash (*Lagenaria siceraria*)
PDIC

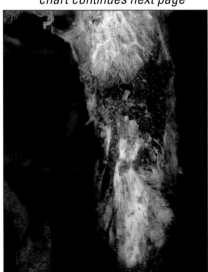

Figure 5–71. Southern blight (*Sclerotium rolfsii*) on Canada goldenrod (*Solidago canadensis*).
PDIC

Table 5–3c. *continued*

Gray mold Also called botrytis blight on many plants	Strawberry	Sp	Fuzzy gray mold on rotting fruit (Figure 5–75) Caution: Can be confused with several other problems if the mold is not yet present.	*Botrytis cinerea* (fungus)
Leaf curl	Stone fruits (not corn)	Sp to early Su	Expanding leaves become twisted and ruffled, often with reddening. (Figure 5–76).	*Taphrina deformans* (fungus)
Mummy berry	Blueberry	Su	Ripening berries turn cream to pink (Figure 5–21) instead of blue. They fall from the plant and eventually shrivel into a dry pumpkin-shaped "mummy".	*Monilinia vaccinii-corymbosi* (fungus)
Powdery mildew	Many species	Sp, Su, F	White to gray fungal growth on upper and/or lower leaf surfaces. Can also occur on fruit (e.g., peaches, grapes).	Multiple fungi, esp. *Podosphaera* (rosaceous hosts) and *Uncinula* (grape)
Sooty blotch	Apple	Su, F	Superficial, irregular dark areas on the skin of developing and mature fruit.	Various fungi

Figure 5–72. Sclerotinia blight on collards. PDIC

Figure 5–74. Cedar apple rust on a leaf. Matt Bertone

Figure 5–73. Black knot. PDIC

Table 5–3d.
Easily Recognized Tree and Shrub Diseases and Disorders of NC Homes and Gardens

		TREES AND SHRUBS		
Problem	Occurs on	Season	Hallmarks	Cause
Black spot	Rose	Sp, Su F	Dark leaf spots with "feathered" borders. Also yellowing and leaf drop. (Figure 5–77)	*Diplocarpon rosae* (fungus)
Boxwood blight (If suspected send to PDIC for confirmation)	All boxwood species; also sweetbox and pachysandra	All	On boxwood: Dark-brown leaf spots, dark streaks on green stems, extensive leaf drop starting at bottom of the plant. On pachysandra, leaf spot.	*Calonectria pseudonaviculata* (fungus)
Camellia petal blight	Camellia japonica	Sp	Petals turn brown and blossoms drop off. When base of flower is removed, a ring of white fungal growth is visible on petal bases.	*Ciborinia camelliae* (fungus)
Cedar apple rust	Apple, crabapple	Su	On these hosts, mostly affects leaves. See section on fruit diseases, above.	*Gymnosporangium juniperi-virginianae* (fungus)
Cedar apple rust	Eastern red cedar	Sp	Woody, round galls on branches sprout orange gelatinous telial horns in mid-spring after warm rains. Comparison with quince rust (Figure 5–78).	*Gymnosporangium juniperi-virginianae* (fungus)
Cold Injury	Gardenia (Figure 5–79), pittosporum (Figure 5–80), boxwood (Figure 5–81), others	All	Not the same as frost damage to foliage or blooms. Typically, bark loosens or splits, often near soil line. Dieback and decline may go unnoticed until shrub is stressed by summer heat.	Extremely low temperatures in late fall or early spring, when stems are not completely dormant
Exobasidium leaf gall	Camellia (Figure 5–24), azalea (Figure 5–82), rhododendron	Sp	Thickening or bulbous growths on new leaves. Whitish-green at first; may darken over time.	Species of Exobasidium (fungus)
Entomosporium leaf spot	Red-tip photinia, Indian hawthorn, (Figure 5–83), sometimes pear	All	Bright red leaf spots, whose centers turn gray over time and develop tiny blisters where spores are produced. Leaf drop can be severe.	*Diplocarpon mespili* (fungus)
Lichens	All trees and shrubs	All	Flat (Figure 5–84), flaky (Figure 5–85), or hairy (Figure 5–86) growths on the bark of branches and trunks (also on rocks). Typically gray to grayish-green in color.	Lichens are symbioses between algae and fungi. They're often seen on declining plants, but do not cause direct damage.

(chart continues on next page)

5

Table 5–3d. *continued*

Problem	Occurs on	Season	Hallmarks	Cause
Normal leaf drop	Southern Magnolia, American holly (Figure 5–87), pines	Sp, Su F	Pines as well as broadleaved evergreens shed their 2+ year-old leaves or needles. The time of year depends on the tree species.	Natural ageing. No cause for concern unless leaves formed during last two years are dropping.
Oak leaf blister	All oaks	Sp, Su	Yellow-green to white puckered spots on newly expanded leaves. Spots turn brown in early summer.	*Taphrina caerulescens* (fungus)
Powdery mildew	Euonymus (Figure 5–37), rose (Figure 5–88) saucer magnolia, dogwood, Leucothoë, spiraea, tulip poplar, many others	Sp, Su F	White fungal growth on leaf and stem surfaces ranges rom thin to felt-like. Dogwoods in midsummer get brown blotches on leaves (Figure 5–89). (hold edgewise to see the fungus) Leucothoë develops red leaf spots where infected (Figure 5–90).	Multiple fungi, esp. Erysiphe and Podosphaera
Quince rust	Eastern red cedar (Figure 5–91)	Sp	Needles or slight branch swellings develop small orange telia in early spring. Comparison with cedar-apple rust and Quince rust on eastern red cedar. (Figure 5–78)	*Gymnosporangium clavipes* (fungus)
Quince rust	Ornamental pear (Figure 5–92)	Su	Pustules (aecia) or orange spores develop on fruit or swollen twigs. Tubular white membranes over the aecia are obvious on fruit.	*Gymnosporangium clavipes* (fungus)
Shot-hole	Cherry-laurel and flowering cherry	Su, F (All, if on evergreen species)	Leaf spots turn from green to brown and drop out, leaving holes with clean edges (Figure 5–8).	Several fungi and bacteria
Slime flux	White oak, elm, other hardwoods	Su	In the heat of summer, fermented sap oozes from crack in bark (Figure 5–93). On white oak this is usually close to the soil line. The sour odor attracts a variety of insects. (Figure 5–94)	Anaerobic bacteria cause a condition called wet wood. Gas from fermentation forces sap out.
Spot anthracnose (not the same disease as dogwood anthracnose)	Flowering dogwood	Sp	Small red or tan spots develop on showy bracts (Figure 5–95). Bract can be deformed if spots are numerous.	*Elsinoë corni* (fungus)

Figure 5–75. Gray mold on a strawberry.
Ron Jones, NC State Dept. of Plant Pathology

Figure 5–76. Peach leaf curl.
Scot Nelson, Flickr CC BY 0 1.0

Figure 5–77. Black spot on a rose.
PDIC

Figure 5–78. Left arrow is quince rust, right arrow is cedar-apple rust.
PDIC

Figure 5–79. A gardenia with cold injury.
PDIC

Figure 5–80. Cold injury on Pittosporum sp.
PDIC

Figure 5–81. Cold injury on boxwood.
PDIC

5

Figure 5–82. Exobasidium galls on *Azalea* spp.
PDIC

Figure 5–83. Entomosporium leaf spot on Indian hawthorn (*Rhaphiolepis* sp.)
PDIC

Figure 5–84. Lichens on an *Azalea spp.*
PDIC

Figure 5–85. Foliose lichen on bark.
PDIC

Figure 5–86. Usnea lichen.
PDIC

Figure 5–87. Normal defoliation of magnolias and hollies.
PDIC

Figure 5–88. Powdery mildew on a rose.
PDIC

Figure 5–89. Powdery mildew exhibits as brown leaf spots on dogwood leaves.
PDIC

Table 5–3e.
Easily Recognized Herbaceous Ornamental Diseases and Disorders of NC Homes and Gardens

HERBACEOUS ORNAMENTALS (ANNUAL AND PERENNIALS)

Problem	Occurs on	Season	Hallmarks	Cause
Dodder	Many hosts	Su, F	Masses of thin, orange strands grow among and attach to stems of host plant (Figure 5–47). Inconspicuous white flowers may be present.	Parasitic plants in the genus Cuscuta
†Impatiens downy mildew	Standard impatiens and its hybrids (not New Guinea)	Su	Leaves yellow and drop (Figure 5–96), leaving only stems that eventually rot. Velvety layer of white spores (Figure 5–97) develops on underside of leaves in humid weather.	*Plasmopara obducens* (fungus-like organism)
Leaf streak	Daylily	Su	Leaves turn brown from the tip (Figure 5–98). The leading edge of the dead tissue is in the form of a narrow "V" along the midrib.	*Aureobasidium microstictum* (fungus)
‡Phytophthora aerial blight	Madagascar periwinkle (annual vinca)	Su	Leaves on individual stems wilt and die, turning gray-green and brown. Leaves do not stick together. Often there are distinct brown or purple lesions on stems (Figure 5–99)	*Phytophthora nicotianae* (fungus-like water-mold)
Powdery mildew	Coreopsis, gerbera, monarda, sedum, zinnia, and others	Sp, Su, F	White to gray fungal growth on upper and/or flower leaf surfaces (Figure 5–100).	Several different fungi, each specific to a group of plants
Root-knot nematode	Begonia, impatiens, liriope, others	Sp, Su, F	Swellings not easily detached from roots. Galls tend to be large and numerous in begonia and impatiens (Figure 5–101) but can be small (e.g. in liriope).	Nematodes in the genus Meloidogyne
Rust	Aster, daylily, hollyhock, Jack-in-the-pulpit, oxalis, St. John's-wort, others	Su, F	Yellow or orange spots on upper leaf surface (Figure 5–102). Pustules of yellow to orange to reddish brown, dry (often dusty) spores on the underside (Figure 5–103) of each spot.	Many fungi including Puccinia, Uromyces, and Coleosporium; specific to their hosts

† A similar disease affects basil and cucurbits, but we recommend diagnosis at the PDIC when there are foliar problems in those plants.

‡ On other hosts, Phytophthora is more difficult to diagnose.

5

Figure 5–90. Powdery mildew exhibits as red leaf spots on leucothoë.
PDIC

Figure 5–91. Quince rust on eastern red cedar (*Juniperus virginiana*).
PDIC

Figure 5–92. Quince rust on a Callery pear (*Pyrus calleryana*).
PDIC

Figure 5–93. Trunk of white oak (*Quercus alba*), stained by slime flux.
Matt Bertone

Figure 5–94. Fresh slime flux visited by flies.
Matt Bertone

Figure 5–95. Spot anthracnose on dogwood (*Cornus* sp.)
PDIC

Figure 5–96. Impatiens downy mildew, leaves yellow and drop.
PDIC

Figure 5–97. Downy mildew on impatiens leaf.
PDIC

Figure 5–98. Leaf streak on a daylily.
PDIC

Table 5–3f.
Easily Recognized Turfgrass Diseases and Disorders of NC Homes and Gardens

TURFGRASS IN HOME LAWNS

Problem	Occurs on	Season	Hallmarks	Cause
Brown patch	Tall fescue and other cool-season turf	Late Sp to early F	Browning out of circular patches of turf. Distinct necrotic lesions on individual grass blades.	*Rhizoctonia solani* (fungus)
Fairy ring	Any turf	All	Arcs or rings of dark green or dead grass, expanding slowly over time. No lesions visible on leaves. Mushrooms or puffballs may develop in the ring.	Several species of fungi that decay thatch and soil organic matter.
Gray leaf spot	Tall fescue, perennial ryegrass, St. Augustine grass	Late Su	Distinct necrotic spots on blades. Similar to brown patch except stand symptoms are irregular across the turf instead of distinct circular patches.	*Pyricularia grisea* (fungus)
Large patch	Bermudagrass, Centipedegrass, other warm-season turf	Sp, F	Large patches of dead turf. Lesions primarily on the leaf sheaths in contact with the soil. Often there are distinct brown or purple lesions on stems.	*Rhizoctonia solani* (fungus)
Pythium blight	Cool-season grasses	Sp to F	Dead patches of matted-together leaves; a heavy webbing of mycelium forms in humid weather.	*Pythium aphanidermatum* (fungus-like water-mold)
Slime mold	Any turf	Sp to early F	Many forms. The most common appears as gray powdery granules on leaves, stems, and other surfaces. See also the "General" table above.	Physarum and other genera of bacteria - and detritus-feeding organisms
Spring dead spot	Bermudagrass, some zoysiagrass	Sp	Sharply-defined circular patches of turf fail to turn green in the spring. Roots and stolons die and decay.	Species of Ophiosphaerella (fungi)

Figure 5–99.
Phytophthora blight
(left and right).
PDIC

Figure 5–100. Powdery mildew on a coreopsis.
PDIC

Figure 5–102. Rust on St. John's wort (*Hypericum* sp.)
PDIC

Figure 5–103. Rust on the underside of a St. John's wort
(*Hypericum* sp.) leaf.
PDIC

Figure 5–101. Root-knot nematodes
on impatiens.
PDIC

5

When Plants Are Wilted

A plant can wilt (droop) during all or part of the day. This is often accompanied by a loss of luster in the green color. When wilting occurs within individual leaves, you may see large tan-colored dead areas between the veins, sometimes extending to entire leaves.

Several problems can lead to wilting. It may be an indication of the following:

- The plant lacks sufficient water in the root zone, either because of a lack of rain or irrigation, excessive drainage, or hydrophobic (water-repellent) soil.
- Heat and low humidity are causing a plant to transpire moisture more quickly than it is able to pull water from the soil.
- Excess soluble salts in the soil—usually because of excess fertilizer applications—are limiting water uptake.
- Decay has affected roots or lower stems. Root rot often starts in wet weather, but the wilting may not be apparent until hot, dry weather sets in. At that point there are not enough healthy roots left to supply the plant's water requirements.
- Root-feeding nematodes have compromised the root system. One common group of nematodes causes visible swellings on roots, but many kinds do not. Nematode feeding may or may not be accompanied by noticeable root decay.
- A vascular disease such as southern bacterial wilt or fusarium wilt is interfering with water transport. In these cases the xylem vessels in the roots or stems are unable to move water up to the leaves, fruits, and other plant parts.
- Wilting caused by insect attack or infectious disease often starts with just a few plants, or even one side of a plant. If most or all plants of a certain kind are affected in a short period of time, it is likely a cultural or environmental issue.

When an herbaceous plant has wilted in the vegetable garden or flower bed in spite of adequate soil moisture in the root zone, the following schematic can be used. It is set up in the format of a **"dichotomous key."** Starting at the top, decide whether statement 1a or statement 1b better applies to the situation. Depending on the answer, you will either be directed to a diagnosis or to another set of numbered comparisons. Repeat the process until you reach a diagnosis or recommendation.

1a. Evidence of insect tunneling in stem (insect, webbing, frass, shed skin) insect injury ....
.... see chapter 4, "Insects"

1b. No sign of insects feeding in or on stems 2

2a. Visible decay at the base of the main stem, near the soil line (also check roots) 3

2b. No visible decay at the base of the main stem.. 4

3a. Visible fan of white fungal mycelium (Figure 5–35) and/or small, round,
tan sclerotia (Figure 5–39) .... southern stem blight

3b. Little or no evidence of fungal growth ....unidentified stem rot; submit sample to PDIC

4a. Roots darkened, decaying, or missing† .... root rot, submit sample to PDIC

4b. Good number of roots present, neither darkened nor decayed 5

5a. Areas of roots swollen into knots that do not easily detach‡ ....root-knot nematode

5b. No swellings on roots .... vascular wilt, nematodes, or excess fertilizer; submit sample

Note: This text refers to symptoms seen in herbaceous plants in the garden or flower bed.
Trees and shrubs can respond differently to the kinds of stresses listed here.

† Normal roots of some plants are naturally dark. A good test for root rot is to tug on a root to see whether the outer portion can be easily pulled off of the central core of vascular tissue.

‡ Root knots are reliably large in some plants such as tomato, cucumber, impatiens and begonia. They may be small and hard to see in some kinds of plants, in which case a clinic diagnosis will be needed.

Frequently Asked Questions

1. My petunias are wilting and dying and the roots have rotted off.

Petunias are susceptible to several root, crown, and stem rots, especially if planted in poorly drained soils or watered too often. The most common cause of this problem in North Carolina is phytophthora root rot, but *Rhizoctonia* species can also infect petunia stems. A plant sample along with soil and roots should be submitted to the NC State's PDIC to confirm the type of fungus involved. Chemical management of these root rot diseases is generally not practical or economical in the home landscape. It is best to correct the wet soil condition. Ensure the site has good drainage by amending the soil and raising the level of the bed. Avoid overwatering and overfertilizing. It also helps to periodically rotate petunias with other annuals. If phytophthora is confirmed, there are many plants that are potentially susceptible and should be avoided. Consult publication AG-747, *Suggested Plant Species for Sites with a History of Phytophthora Rot or Crown Rot*, for more information. Furthermore, many diseases are introduced into our gardens on the plants we purchase. Therefore, be sure to inspect plants before purchase, and avoid buying plants that appear unhealthy.

2. My roses have black spots on the leaves, which are turning yellow and falling off.

You suspect that this is black spot. Consulting Table 5–3d, you see that the dark spots, yellowing, and leaf drop are typical of this disease, and that a diagnostic feature is the irregular or "feathered" edges on the spots. Confirm that the spots on her roses do have this characteristic, and you are now confident in the diagnosis. Your research shows that defoliation will continue if the disease is not controlled, reducing flower formation and weakening the plant. You also learn that the causal fungus can also infect canes. With susceptible cultivars, a number of cultural practices will help against black spot. Prune out cane infections in the winter, mulch around shrubs in the late winter, improve air circulation by proper pruning, keep fallen leaves cleaned up, and water at the base of the plants, in such a way as to not extend the nighttime leaf wetness period into the morning or evening. Even with these cultural measures, sprays may be necessary to keep the disease in check on susceptible cultivars. For specific fungicide recommendations, see the *North Carolina Agricultural Chemicals Manual*. Start spraying when leaves first appear, and continue at label-specified intervals and after heavy rains throughout the growing season. For organic management, use copper-based fungicidal soaps. Be sure to follow label directions, as these products may burn leaves if used in cool wet weather. You may also read about using baking soda to control black spot, but this is ineffective, at least in the southern United States.

When it comes time to add or replace a rose bush, there are a number of less susceptible cultivars, such as Knock Out roses or the Easy Elegance series. Other varieties that have shown good resistance are 'Bonica', 'Carefree Beauty', 'Carefree Wonder', 'Cuddles', 'Playboy', 'Simplicity', 'The Fairy', and 'Topaz Jewel'. This does not mean these cultivars are resistant to all diseases. The shrub roses chapter of the publication *IPM for Shrubs in Southeastern US Nursery Production*, Vol. 1, has a table listing relative susceptibilities of a large number of cultivars to three important diseases.

3. Many of the leaves on my boxwoods are falling off. Does it have boxwood blight?

Boxwood blight is slowly becoming more and more widespread in North Carolina since its first occurrence in October of 2011. The first step is to be sure that the shrub in question is a boxwood and not a Japanese holly or dwarf yaupon. Boxwood leaves are arranged in pairs opposite one another on the stem, while the hollies (including yaupon) have alternate leaves. Once this is established, look for the three hallmarks of boxwood blight: clearly defined dark-brown leaf spots, dark streaks on the green twigs, and defoliation, usually starting near the bottom of the bush. In some cases, the leaves will shrivel without the brown spotting. As of this writing, all suspected cases of boxwood blight should be referred to the PDIC for confirmation, but check with your local Extension agent to see whether this is still the case. Be sure to collect a complete sample that includes roots and soil, so that problems other than boxwood blight can be diagnosed as well.

4. There is a dark, wet-looking area on the side of my tree, and the area has a foul odor.

If it is midsummer and the tree is a mature hardwood, this is likely a bacterial disease called slime flux or wet wood. Check if the odor is of fermentation, and whether insects are attracted to it. The bacteria enter the tree through wounds, usually in the roots. The disease is most common in oaks, but also occurs in elms, maples, tulip poplars, and other species. With white oak, the fluxing normally occurs on the lower portion of the trunk, near the ground. Slime flux is not a serious problem if the tree is otherwise healthy. A given tree may flux some years and not others. There are no curative or preventative measures except to maintain trees in a good state of vigor and minimize wounds and other injuries. You may remove loose or dead bark to allow the affected area to air dry. Do not apply a wound dressing such as pruning sealer or paint or attempt to seal the cavity with concrete or a similar material, as this does more harm than good to the tree.

5. My tomato plant wilted suddenly and died. What happened?

Southern bacterial wilt (caused by the soilborne bacterial pathogen *Ralstonia solanacearum*) and southern stem rot or southern blight (caused by the soilborne fungal pathogen *Sclerotium rolfsii*) are the most common diseases causing sudden wilting of tomatoes in North Carolina. See the special section earlier in the chapter "**When Plants are Wilted.**" Southern bacterial wilt causes a brown discoloration in the vascular tissue, visible after slicing off the outer portion of the stem, but is not the only disease that does this. Southern bacterial wilt can sometimes be confirmed using the following simple test. Hang a 4-inch to 6-inch stem piece cut from the base of the affected plant in a glass of water, such that the cut end is an inch or so from the bottom of the glass. If it is a sufficiently advanced case of bacterial wilt, milky strands of bacterial cells will start streaming from the cut end within a minute or so. With southern stem rot, a white covering of fungal mycelium is often visible at the base of the plant. Small round sclerotia may also be visible; these begin as white "pills" on the mycelium and later turn a tan-to-brown color. When mature, the sclerotia are about the size, shape, and color of radish seeds. Unfortunately there is no cure for either of these diseases. Dig up and destroy the affected plants including the roots. Because both of these disease organisms live in the soil for years, rotate your plantings within the garden, or even better, relocate your garden spot. Note that crop rotation is generally not an option with southern stem rot due to the large number of plants susceptible to this pathogen (corn is a major exception). You may also consider growing tomatoes in containers. Be sure that the container soil does not come in contact with native soil, and take care not to spread infested soil to other parts of your landscape. There are no resistant tomato varieties available to homeowners for either of these diseases, though an aluminum foil stem wrap (for southern stem blight) and grafted tomatoes (for southern bacterial wilt) can be tried.

6. There is a fungus that looks like a shelf coming out of my tree trunk. Is my tree dying?

Any mushroom, shelf fungus, or conk emerging from under the bark of a tree is an indication of decay within. Even if the crown looks healthy, the strength of the wood can be compromised. This is especially critical when buttress roots are involved. Because diseased trees can cause possible damage to homes or property it is important to have the tree evaluated by a certified arborist. Use the International Society of Arboriculture's search tool to find a certified arborist in good standing in your area.

5

Further Reading

Agrios, George N. *Plant Pathology*. 5th ed. Burlington, Massachusetts: Elsevier Academic Press, 2005. Print.

Blancard, D., H. Lecoq, and M. Pitrat. 1994. *A Colour Atlas of Cucurbit Diseases*. Manson Publishing, Ltd. Limoges, France.

Blancard, Dominique, H. Lot, and B. Maisonneuve. *A Colour Atlas of Diseases of Lettuce and Related Salad Crops*. San Diego, California: Academic Press, 2006. Print.

Blancard, Dominique. *Tomato Diseases: A Color Handbook*. 2nd ed. San Diego, California: Academic Press, 2012. Print.

Bruneau, Arthur H. and Gail G. Wilkerson, eds. *Turfgrass Pest Management Manual: A Guide to Major Turfgrass Pests & Turfgrasses*. Raleigh, North Carolina: North Carolina Cooperative Extension Service, 2006. PDF file.

Chase, A. R. *Foliage Plant Diseases: Diagnosis and Control*. St. Paul, Minnesota: The American Phytopathological Society, 1997. Print.

Compendium Series. St. Paul, Minnesota: The American Phytopathological Society, Print.

Datnoff, Lawrence E., Wade H. Elmer, and Don M. Huber, eds. *Mineral Nutrition and Plant Disease*. St. Paul, Minnesota: The American Phytopathological Society, 2007. Print.

Ellis, Barbara W. and Fern Marshall Bradley, eds. *The Organic Gardener's Handbook of Natural Insect and Disease Control: A Complete Problem-Solving Guide to Keeping Your Garden and Yard Healthy without Chemicals*. Emmaus, Pennsylvania: Rodale Press, Inc., 1996. Print.

Gladders, Peter and Albert O. Paulus. *Vegetable Diseases: A Color Handbook*. Ed. Steven T Koike. Burlington, Massachusetts: Elsevier Academic Press, 2006. Print.

Gleason, Mark L., et al. *Diseases of Herbaceous Perennials*. St. Paul, Minnesota: The American Phytopathological Society, 2009. Print.

Horst, R. Kenneth. *Westcott's Plant Disease Handbook*. 8th ed. Dordrecht, Netherlands: Springer, 2013. Print.

Jones, Ronald K. and D. Michael Benson, eds. *Diseases of Woody Ornamentals and Trees in Nurseries*. St. Paul, Minnesota: The American Phytopathological Society, 2001. Print.

Koike, Steven T., Peter Gladders, and Albert O. Paulus. *Vegetable Diseases: A Colour Handbook*. San Diego, California: Academic Press, 2007. Print.

Lucas, George B., Lee Campbell, and Leon T. Lucas. *Introduction to Plant Diseases: Identification and Management*. 2nd ed. New York: Chapman & Hall, 1992. Print.

Pirone, Pascal P. *Diseases and Pests of Ornamental Plants*. 5th ed. New York: John Wiley & Sons, Inc., 1978. Print.

Pleasant, Barbara. *The Gardeners Guide to Plant Diseases: Earth Safe Remedies*. North Adams, Massachusetts: Storey Publishing, 1995. Print.

Sherf, Arden F., and Alan A MacNab. *Vegetable Diseases and Their Control*. 2nd ed. Hoboken, New Jersey: John Wiley & Sons Inc., 1986. Print.

Shigo, Alex L. *Tree Decay: An Expanded Concept*. Information Bulletin Number 419. Washington, DC: United States Department of Agriculture Forest Service, 1979. PDF file.

Sinclair, Wayne A., and Howard H. Lyon. *Diseases of Trees and Shrubs*. 2nd ed. Ithaca, New York: Cornell University Press, 2005. Print.

Skelly, John M, et al., eds. *Diagnosing Injury to Eastern Forest Trees*. Washington, DC: The Pennsylvania State University, for the USDA Forest Service, 1987. PDF file.

Yepsen, Jr., Roger B, ed. *The Encyclopedia of Natural Insect and Disease Control*. Emmaus, Pennsylvania: Rodale Press, Inc., 1984. Print.

For More Information

http://go.ncsu.edu/fmi_diseases

See appendix C, "Diagnostic Tables."

Contributors

Author: Michael Munster, Diagnostician, NC State University Plant Disease and Insect Clinic

Contributions by Extension Agents: Randy Fulk, Matt Jones, Carl Maytac, Danny Lauderdale, Jeana Meyers, Charlotte Glen

Contributions by Extension Master Gardener Volunteers: Jackie Weedon, Kim Curlee, Connie Schultz, Karen Damari, Marjorie Rayburn, Linda Alford, Joanne Celinski, Edna Burger, Caro Dosé

Content Editors: Lucy Bradley, Professor and Extension Specialist, Urban Horticulture, NC State University; Director, NC State Extension Master Gardener program; Kathleen Moore, Urban Horticulturist

Copy Editor: Barbara Scott

Based in part on text from the 1998 Extension Master Gardener manual prepared by:
Erv Evans, Extension Associate, Department of Horticultural Science
L. T. Lucas, Extension Specialist, Department of Plant Pathology

Chapter 5 Cover Photo: NC State Plant Disease and Insect Clinic

How to Cite This Chapter:
Munster, M. 2022. Diseases Chpt 5. In: K.A. Moore, L.K. Bradley (eds). *North Carolina Extension Gardener Handbook*, 2nd ed. NC State Extension, Raleigh, NC. <https://content.ces.ncsu.edu/extension-gardener-handbook/5-diseases-and-disorders>

5

Weeds

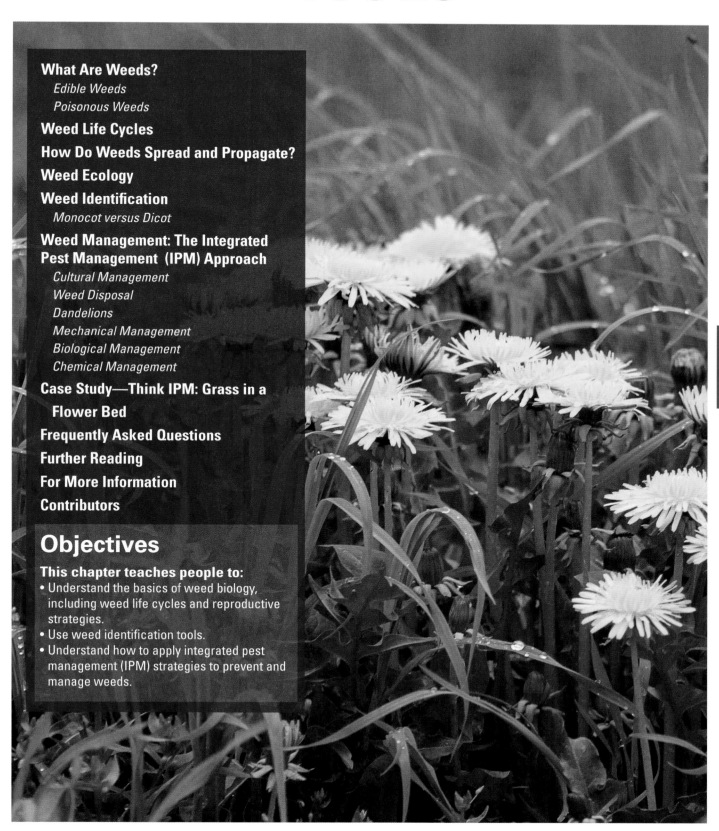

Objectives

This chapter teaches people to:
- Understand the basics of weed biology, including weed life cycles and reproductive strategies.
- Use weed identification tools.
- Understand how to apply integrated pest management (IPM) strategies to prevent and manage weeds.

6

What Are Weeds?

A weed is, in essence, "a plant out of place." Some plants (such as poison ivy, poison oak, and poison sumac) are easily recognized as harmful. Other plants, however, may or may not be considered weeds depending on one's viewpoint. Dandelions, wild violets, and goldenrod, for example, may be weeds to one person but attractive wildflowers or food to another. Many of our most common weeds were accidentally introduced with crop plants our ancestors brought to this country. Other plants were intentionally introduced, and only later were categorized as weeds. Crabgrass, for example, was among the first grains cultivated in Europe during the Stone Age and was probably introduced to the United States in fodder. Some varieties were later introduced here as forage crops and continue to be cultivated. Similarly, kudzu was introduced for soil stabilization and as a possible pasture plant, and the multiflora rose was introduced and promoted as a living hedge. Some ornamentals, such as English ivy, bamboo, Japanese knotweed, and water hyacinth, have been intentionally planted in landscapes only to "escape" and become invasive weeds in natural areas.

Weeds compete with crop and landscape plants for water, nutrients, and sunlight. Weeds can reduce crop yield, affect the aesthetic qualities of landscapes and the functionality of sports turf, and displace native flora in natural areas. Weeds sometimes attract or harbor harmful insects or serve as alternate hosts for plant pathogens. Many weeds, such as ragweed, are wind-pollinated and produce copious amounts of pollen, which can cause hay fever.

Many weeds are ornamental, some are edible, but certain ones can be poisonous. Regardless of their other qualities, by definition all weeds are plants growing where they are unwanted.

Edible Weeds

Edible weeds can be delicious, home-grown, and economical additions to any dinner table. We have been conditioned to think of weeds as pests to be eradicated from tidy landscapes. In fact, some weeds are nutritional powerhouses containing vitamins, minerals, and fiber. Eating weeds from your yard can motivate you to weed and take advantage of growing food that does not require planting, watering, or fertilizing.

Although many weeds are edible (Table 6–1), many are not. It is important to correctly identify any weed you plan to eat and also which parts of each weed are edible. While some parts may be edible, others can be toxic. Edible weeds can be enjoyed in a variety of ways. Leaves can be eaten raw and added to salads, or sautéed, steamed, or

boiled. Roots can be boiled or roasted. Teas can be made from dried flowers, leaves, or roots. Edible flowers can adorn salads or desserts or be infused to make tasty oils or vinegars.

Here are some guidelines for eating weeds:
- Proper identification is essential.
- Use plants that have not been sprayed with fertilizer, pesticides, herbicides, or fungicides.
- Avoid weeds growing on roadsides where exhaust from vehicles can leave residues on foliage.
- Young tender weeds are usually less bitter than mature weeds.
- After harvesting, wash weeds thoroughly with cool soapy water and rinse before eating them.
- Limit consumption to small amounts of one type of weed at a time to be able to pinpoint any allergic reactions.

Figure 6–1. Jimsonweed flower, fruit capsule, and seeds.
Forest and Kim Starr, Flickr CC BY - 2.0

Poisonous Weeds

Serious illness or even death can result when poisonous weeds are eaten. The plant may be poisonous, or the toxins may be confined to only specific parts (leaves, roots, fruit, or seeds). In addition, the plant may be toxic throughout its entire life cycle or only at certain stages. It is primarily young children who are poisoned by plants. Prone to put everything in their mouths, children are particularly attracted to colorful berries and seeds. No one should ever put any part of a plant in his or her mouth unless the plant has first been identified as edible. Cocklebur seeds and young seedlings are poisonous to humans and livestock, but burdock seedlings are edible. All parts of jimsonweed (*Datura stramonium*) (Figure 6–1) contain toxic alkaloids that cause hallucinations, convulsions, or death; contact with jimsonweed sap causes a skin rash on some people. Pokeweed (*Phytolacca americana*) leaves are poisonous unless carefully prepared (harvest only young leaves and change the water when cooking). Pokeweed roots are quite poisonous, and the berries, though less poisonous, also contain the toxin.

For additional information on poisonous plants, refer to NC State Extension Gardener Plant Toolbox. Another helpful guide to poisonous plants is *Plants Poisonous to Livestock and Pets in North Carolina*, Bulletin Number 414, available through NC State Extension.

Possible poisoning cases should be referred to the nearest Poison Control Center. The Carolinas' Poison Control Center can be reached by phone at 1-800-222-1222.

Table 6–1. Edible Weeds[1]

Common Name	Botanical Name	Edible Part
Burdock	*Arctium* L.	Roots
Chickweed	*Stellaria media*	Young shoots and tender tips of shoots raw, cooked, or dried for tea
Chicory	*Cichorium intybus*	Leaves and roots
Clover	*Trifolium* L.	Leaves sautéed; flowers raw, cooked, or dried for tea
Creeping Charlie	*Pilea nummulariifolia*	Leaves, often used in teas
Dandelion	*Taraxacum officinale*	Leaves, roots, and flowers
Garlic mustard	*Alliaria petiolata*	Roots and young leaves
Japanese knotweed	*Reynoutria japonicaa*	Young shoots less than 8 inches long and stems (Do not eat mature leaves.)
Lambsquarters	*Chenopodium album*	Young leaves and stems
Little bittercress or shotweed	*Cardamine breweri*	Whole plant
Mallow	*Malva neglecta*	Leaves and seeds
Nettle	*Urtica dioica*	Young leaves (must be cooked thoroughly or dried for tea) and seeds
Pigweed or wild amaranth	*Amaranthus* L.	Leaves and seeds
Plantain	*Plantago major*	Leaves (remove stems) and seeds
Purslane	*Portulaca* L.	Leaves, stems, and seeds
Sheep's sorrel	*Rumex acetosella*	Leaves
Violets	*Viola sororia*	Young leaves and flowers
Wild garlic	*Allium canadense*	Leaves and roots

[1]For images and descriptions, see plants.ces.ncsu.edu

Weed Life Cycles

There are four basic weed life cycles: *winter annual, summer annual, biennial, and perennial*. Each life cycle has weak links that can be exploited in control programs. Seed-propagated weeds can be managed by preventing **germination** or survival of young seedlings. Perennial and biennial weeds are generally more difficult to control because they have vegetative structures that are persistent and more resilient, making these species resistant to mechanical and chemical measures. Perennial weeds in particular have varied means of reproduction that must be considered when developing management plans. In all cases, effective weed management includes preventing reproduction by removing flowers before they can set seed.

Annual weeds germinate from seeds, grow, produce seeds, and die in one season. There are two types of annual weeds. **Winter annuals,** such as annual bluegrass, chickweed, and henbit, germinate in the fall or early spring when soil temperatures are cool, then flower and die in late spring or summer (Table 6–2). **Summer annuals,** such as crabgrass, spurge, and pigweed, germinate when the soil warms in the spring and summer, then set seed and die in late summer or fall (Table 6–2). As with any rule, exceptions occur. For example, horseweed is a winter annual that can germinate in the fall or the spring. It then

Weed Management through the Year

Winter
- Top-dress mulch in planting beds. Mulch will help smother weeds that will germinate in the spring (Figure 6–2) . Do not be tempted to use mulch excessively. The mulch layer should be 3 to 4 inches deep. Do not pile up mulch around the base of trees or shrubs.

Spring
- In early spring before seeds germinate, a preemergence herbicide could be applied. This will stop seeds of desired plants as well as weed seeds from germinating. Therefore, **preemergence** herbicides are best used in established lawns or planting beds where no desired plants will be sprouted from seed.
- Waiting for a flush of weeds to germinate and then controlling them with minimal soil disturbance can be an effective way to suppress weed populations. Emerged weeds can be burned by a flame weeder or an herbicide (natural or **synthetic**) applied before planting with desired seeds or plants. With minimum soil disturbance, the amount of new weed germination is reduced. This method is often referred to as a "stale seedbed" technique.
- Hand-pulling weeds when they are small (Figure 6–3) is not only easier but will remove them before they have had a chance to produce reproductive structures (flowers and seeds).

Summer
- For **fallow** planting beds, solarization by using clear plastic is an option when temperatures are high (Figure 6–4). Solarization kills small seeds near the soil surface but does not affect weed seeds deeper in the soil and does not control perennial weeds.
- Continuously mow and prune the foliage. This will reduce the leaf surface area that can produce food for underground storage and will also remove reproductive parts (flowers and seeds).
- Hand-pull or kill weeds before they flower.

Fall
- Hand-pull weeds so their storage organs are not left in the ground over winter.
- In early fall before seeds germinate, a preemergence herbicide could be applied if winter weeds were prevalent the previous spring. This will stop all seeds from germinating, so do not use this strategy in beds where you will be planting desirable plants from seed. This strategy is best used in established lawns or planting beds.
- If chemical treatment is deemed necessary to control perennial weeds, early fall is the optimal time of year to control many weeds with **systemic herbicides**. This will ensure systemic herbicides are translocated to the storage areas of the plant as temperatures cool and plants get ready for winter.

grows through the summer and produces seeds in mid-to-late summer. In shady or irrigated landscapes or in cooler mountain regions, soil temperatures stay cool, allowing some winter annual weeds (such as chickweed) to germinate and grow during summer.

Figure 6–2. A 3- to 4-inch layer of mulch will help reduce weeds in planting beds.
Emily May, Flickr CC BY - 2.0

Figure 6–3. Hand-pulling weeds before they have flowered or set fruit will help disrupt their life cycle.
Tony Fischer, Flickr CC BY - 2.0

Biennial weeds germinate from seed and produce a cluster (rosette) of leaves near the soil surface during the first year of growth. During the second year, biennial weeds flower, produce seeds, and die. Examples of biennial weeds include Queen Anne's lace (*Daucus carota*) and bull thistle (*Cirsium vulgare*). Biennial weeds are best managed in the early growing stage of the first year.

Perennial weeds grow for many years, producing seeds each year. Perennial weeds that reproduce exclusively by seed are called "simple perennials." Examples include dandelion, plantain, dogfennel, and curly dock. Simple perennials usually die back to the ground during the

winter and resprout from the hardy crown or root system in the spring. Many other perennials also have vegetative reproductive organs: **tubers, bulbs, or stolons**. These perennials are often referred to as tuberous, bulbous, stoloniferous, or rhizomatous, respectively. Woody shrubs and vines are also perennials but are usually categorized separately as "woody weeds."

The growth of perennial weeds is influenced by climate and season. As days shorten and nights get cooler in late summer or fall, food reserves move to the underground and overwintering reproductive plant parts. Production of tubers or bulbs is often seasonal. Time any management procedures to reduce the production of overwintering reproductive plant parts and to attack the weed at its most susceptible growth stages. For example, chemical control of perennials is often more effective in early fall, when stored food is moved to the root system, carrying with it systemic herbicides. Early-season growth of perennial weeds is rapid—neither chemical nor mechanical controls are very effective. However, repeated mowing or pruning of the foliage during summer removes flowers before they can set seed, removes leaves and thus reduces photosynthesis, and causes the plant to draw on stored resources to regrow, reducing the amount of food available for production of reproductive plant parts.

Figure 6–4. If temperatures are high enough, solarizing the soil with clear plastic will kill some weed seeds in the top few inches of soil.
Chris Alberti, CC BY - 2.0

How Do Weeds Spread and Propagate?

Almost all weeds reproduce by seed. Some perennial weeds may also reproduce and spread vegetatively by creeping stems or roots, bulbs, **corms**, or tubers (Figure 6–5). Seeds may germinate shortly after being shed or may have mechanisms to prevent germination until conditions (sunlight, water, and temperature) are conducive to germination and growth. This **quiescent** state is referred to as **dormancy**. For example, seeds of many summer weeds require some cold temperatures before they will germinate. Cold keeps the seeds dormant until after winter, preventing them from germinating only to be killed by winter frosts prior to completing their life cycle and producing more seeds. Dormancy is a useful adaptation for survival because delaying germination until spring will give the new plants the best chance to grow, flower, and reproduce.

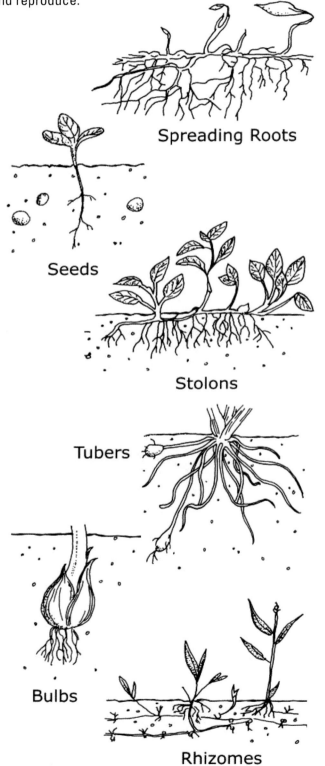

Figure 6–5. The different methods by which weeds spread.

Weed seeds can be blown into a landscape by wind, washed in by rain runoff, or deposited in animal feces. Weed seeds can be carried in on clothing, shoes, or tools, or brought in by gardening activities such as **cultivation**, mowing, or adding topsoil or compost. And weed seeds can be in the root balls of purchased plants (Figure 6–6). Additionally, many common landscape weeds have means of self-dispersal. Yellow woodsorrel (*Oxalis grandis*), for example, has evolved a mechanism to forcefully expel its seeds up to 12 feet from the plant. Once introduced to a site, weeds can spread rapidly, and they are remarkably persistent. Pigweed and ragweed seeds can germinate after remaining in the soil for 40 years or more; mustard and knotweed seeds 50 years or more; and evening primrose, curly dock, and common mullein for 70 years or more. Each time the soil is cultivated, dormant seeds are brought to the surface where sunlight stimulates their germination. As a result, it can take years to reduce the weed seed "reserve" already existing in the soil.

Figure 6–6. Weeds can hide in rootballs of purchased plants. This sapling has a thistle and some grass growing in the pot.
Kathleen Moore, CC BY - 2.0

Weed Ecology

Every plant has a function and niche in biological ecosystems. Plants we call "weeds" are part of the natural growth process that reclaims an open area. Open areas become populated by annual grasses and **broadleaf plant** species, followed by perennial grasses and biennial and perennial broadleaf species, then **brambles** and vines, and eventually trees. This succession in plant communities also occurs in residential gardens and lawns. Whenever a garden is cultivated, the site is essentially disturbed, which allows natural succession processes to start over again and again. We also create opportunities for undesirable species to become established when we move plants from one environment to another or when we disturb the plant community or the soil.

Weeds, like any other plant, require light, moisture, nutrients, and a suitable substrate for growth. So, what makes weeds so "weedy?" Weed species have developed a variety of ways to outcompete other plants for resources, including light, water, nutrients, and physical space. Because weeds can reproduce vigorously, and access and use available resources efficiently, weeds outcompete other plants.

One trait that allows weedy plants to be so successful is their astonishing ability to reproduce. For example, nutsedge tubers planted one every square foot on an acre of land can produce over 3 million plants and 4 million tubers

Table 6–2. Some Common Annual, Biennial, and Perennial Weeds

		Lawns	Gardens	Ornamentals
Summer Annuals	**Broadleaves – Dicots**	Black medic, chamberbitter, lespedeza, prostrate knotweed, spurge	Cocklebur, lambsquarters, pigweed, prostrate knotweed, prostrate spurge, purslane, ragweed	Carpetweed, chamberbitter, mulberry weed, sida, spurge, Virginia copperleaf
	Grasses – Monocots	Crabgrass, goosegrass, Japanese stiltgrass	Crabgrass, foxtail, goosegrass	Crabgrass, goosegrass, Japanese stiltgrass
Winter Annuals	**Broadleaves – Dicots**	Asiatic hawksbeard, bittercress, chickweed, henbit, horseweed, lawn burweed, speedwell, vetch	Chickweed, henbit, sowthistle, vetch	Asiatic hawksbeard, bittercress, Carolina geranium, chickweed, common groundsel, henbit, horseweed, shepherd's purse, sowthistle, speedwell, vetch
	Grasses – Monocots	Annual bluegrass, annual ryegrass	Annual bluegrass	Annual bluegrass
Biennials	**Broadleaves – Dicots**	Wild carrot	Bull thistle, musk thistle	Bull thistle, musk thistle
	Simple	Aster, curly dock, dandelion, dogfennel, plantain, Virginia buttonweed, wild violet	Curly dock	Dandelion, dogfennel, pokeweed, Virginia buttonweed, wild violet
Perennials	**Creeping Broadleaves – Dicots**	Dollarweed[a], ground ivy, white clover, woodsorrel	Woodsorrel	Dollarweed[a], hedge bindweed, mugwort, white clover, woodsorrel
	Creeping Grasses – Monocots	Bermudagrass, nimblewill	Bermudagrass, johnsongrass	Bamboo, bermudagrass
	Tubers	Florida betony, nutsedge	Florida betony, nutsedge	Florida betony, nutsedge
	Bulbs	Wild garlic, wild onion	Wild garlic, wild onion	Wild garlic, wild onion
	Woody		Japanese honeysuckle, poison ivy	English ivy, Japanese honeysuckle, poison ivy, smilax, wisteria

[a]Sandhills – coastal plain

6

in one season. Weeds can also produce a tremendous number of seeds (Table 6–3). The top inch of soil in an acre contains an estimated 3 million weed seeds. In addition to sexually reproducing by seeds, many weeds reproduce asexually via tubers, corms, bulbs, and stem and leaf rooting.

Many weeds use the available resources more efficiently than other (often more desirable) plants. Weedy plants may germinate more rapidly than desirable species (think about those pesky weeds coming up in the garden before the squash germinated). Fast germination gives weeds a jump-start on growing leaves that then block slower plants from sunlight. Similarly, the root systems of some weed species are quicker to claim space in the soil. Other weed species grow more rapidly than surrounding vegetation, such as some pigweeds that grow at twice the rate of most garden plants. Weedy vines grow over the tops of more desirable plants, capturing all of the available sunlight.

Table 6–3. Number of Seeds Produced by Select Weeds

Common Name	Scientific Name	Approximate Number of Seeds Produced per Plant
Sandbur	*Cenchrus longispinus*	1,110
Black mustard	*Brassica nigra*	13,400
Curly dock	*Rumex crispus*	40,000
Common lambsquarters	*Chenopodium album*	72,000
Palmer's pigweed	*Amaranthus palmeri*	117,000
Evening primrose	*Oenothera biennis*	118,000

Table 6–4. Using Weeds as Clues

Variable	Condition	Weeds
pH	Acidic (pH < 5)	Broomsedge, Carolina geranium, red sorrel
		Appear pale and stunted: chickweed, dandelion, redroot pigweed, wild mustard
	Slightly acid (pH 5.2)	Acceptable to most weeds, including jimsonweed and morning glory
	pH 5.8 – 6.0	Appear lush and green: chickweed, dandelion, redroot pigweed, wild mustard
	Alkaline (pH > 7)	Buckhorn plantain, clover
Soil structure	Compacted soil	Annual bluegrass, annual lespedeza, annual sedge, broadleaf plantain, corn speedwell, goosegrass, prostrate knotweed, prostrate spurge
Soil moisture	Moist soil	Alligatorweed, annual bluegrass, liverwort, moneywort, moss, pearlwort, rushes, sedges
	Dry soil	Annual lespedeza, birdsfoot trefoil, black medic, goosegrass, bracted plantain, prostrate knotweed, spotted spurge, yellow wood-sorrel
Management	Infrequent mowing	Biennial and perennial weeds, such as aster, brambles, chicory, ogfennel, goldenrod, thistle, and wild carrot
	Mowing too low	Annual bluegrass, chickweed, crabgrass, goosegrass
	Fall cultivation of the soil	Winter annual weeds, such as henbit, horseweed, and pepperweed

Many weeds are better adapted to grow under adverse conditions, such as compacted, saturated, or nutrient-poor soils. Consequently, the presence of certain weeds may be used as an indicator of soil or management problems that need to be addressed. For example, some weeds are opportunistic, establishing in the worn or thin spots in a lawn. Be cautious, however, of making quick assumptions. Just because red sorrel is often associated with acidic soil does not automatically mean the soil it is growing in is acidic. Red sorrel can survive in very alkaline soils as well.

Weed Identification

While weed control by hand or by mechanical or cultural methods can be accomplished without knowing the name of a weed, it is still useful to identify the weeds because some are actually spread by cultivation rather than discouraged by it. Where herbicides are used, correct identification of a weed becomes even more critical because no herbicide kills all plants. Even nonselective herbicides have varying degrees of effectiveness on weeds. Comparing a weed to a photograph is the easiest way to identify an unknown weed. Remember that weeds can appear to be different from a picture when the weed has been mowed or has been growing under less than ideal conditions (such as shade or moisture stress).

Identifying unknown weeds is easiest when plants are in flower. But by the time plants are flowering, the damage from weed competition has already occurred. Fortunately, most weed books (see "Further Reading" section) also include vegetative characteristics, photographs, and keys to aid in identification. When trying to identify an unknown weed, look for unique characteristics—such as **thorns** or **spines**, square or winged stems, compound leaves, **whorled leaves**, and milky sap—that can often help narrow the search.

Monocot vs. Dicot

Weeds can be separated by species into broad categories based on the number of **cotyledons** (seed leaves). Seedlings have either one or two cotyledons, and plants are termed **monocots** (one cotyledon) and **dicots** (two

Weeds as Clues: The type of weeds growing in an area can help you to identify soil conditions. Weeds can also offer clues that point to poor management of a garden or lawn (Table 6–4).

Figure 6–7. Crabgrass is a monocot with a fibrous root system and long narrow leaf blades with parallel veins.
Harry Rose, Flickr CC BY - 2.0

cotyledons). Read more about what defines a monocot or dicot plant in "Botany," chapter 3.

Monocot weeds—Monocots typically have long, narrow leaf blades with parallel veins. Grasses, onions, garlics, sedges, rushes, lilies, irises, and daylilies are all monocots. For management purposes and because they can look very similar, it is important to differentiate between *grasses, sedges,* and *rushes.*

Grasses have rounded or flattened stems. Leaves are generally narrow and upright with parallel veins. Grasses have fibrous root systems, but may also produce rhizomes or stolons for reproduction. The growing point of a seedling grass is sheathed and located at or below the soil surface, protecting plants from such control measures as mowing, flame weeders, and herbicides. Examples include crabgrass (Figure 6–7), goosegrass, and dallisgrass. The most reliable way to identify grasses is by their floral characteristics. Most weedy grasses, however, can be identified with relative ease before flowering. Vegetative identification of unknown grasses relies on a few structures: leaf bud (folded or rolled), **ligule** (absent, hairy, or membranous), **auricles** (absent or present), hairs on the leaf blade or sheath and growth habit (clump-type or spreading by stolons or rhizomes) (Figure 6–8). The TurfFiles website at NC State contains an online key to help identify weeds and grasses, as well as weed profiles with images, descriptions, and management recommendations.

Sedges (Figure 6–9) and *rushes* are also monocots. Sedges are not grasses or broadleaf plants but are sometimes listed with grasses on the pesticide label. They have triangular, solid stems without **nodes**, and have parallelveined leaves that occur in threes. The perennial sedges—purple nutsedge, yellow nutsedge, and kyllinga—are particularly difficult to control.

Yellow nutsedge is the most commonly encountered sedge. It grows in nearly all crops and landscape settings; has grasslike, glossy, light-green leaves; and has yellow to tan seed heads; it spreads by rhizomes and produces tubers

6

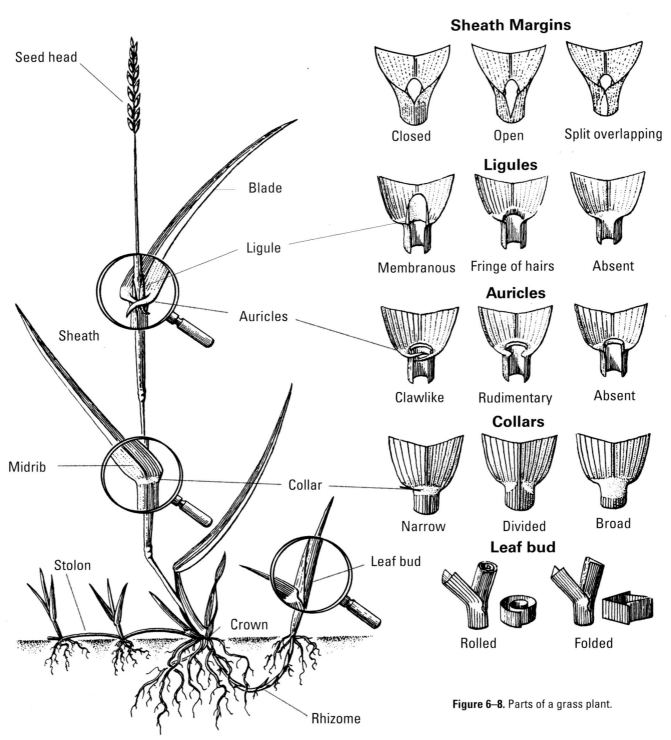

Sheath Margins

Closed Open Split overlapping

Ligules

Membranous Fringe of hairs Absent

Auricles

Clawlike Rudimentary Absent

Collars

Narrow Divided Broad

Leaf bud

Rolled Folded

Seed head

Blade

Ligule

Auricles

Sheath

Midrib

Collar

Leaf bud

Stolon

Crown

Rhizome

Figure 6–8. Parts of a grass plant.

at the tips of rhizomes. Purple nutsedge is usually smaller and deeper green than yellow nutsedge, has reddish-purple seed heads, and produces "chains" of tubers on rhizomes. One of the easiest ways to distinguish between yellow and purple nutsedge is to look at the leaf tip.

Yellow nutsedge has a very sharp, needlelike point at the leaf tip. The leaf tip of purple nutsedge is boatshaped and resembles that of bluegrass. Green kyllinga is much shorter than nutsedges, has finer leaf blades, and spreads by rhizomes that do not produce tubers. The seed head of kyllinga

is globe- or cylinder-shaped, in contrast to the branched seed heads of nutsedges. Sedges are particularly important to identify because many herbicides and cultural procedures that are effective on grassy weeds do not control sedges. Additionally, sedges differ in their susceptibility to many herbicides.

Rushes have rounded, hollow stems (Figure 6–10), and their leaf blades are round in cross section (grass and sedge leaf blades are flat). The presence of large populations of rushes usually indicates drainage problems resulting in wet soil.

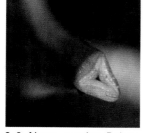 

Figure 6–9. Above, a sedge. Below, examples of triangular stems and parallel veins in sedges.
Forest and Kim Starr, Jerry Kikhurt, and John Tan, Flickr CC BY - 2.0

versus compound leaves, overall leaf shape, leaf margins (toothed, entire, lobed, or deeply cut), **petiole** length, and hairs on leaves or other plant parts. Drawings of leaf margins and orientation are provided in "Botany," chapter 3, of this handbook.

Weed identification references are listed in the "For More Information" section at the end of this chapter.

Figure 6–10. This slender rush (*Eleocharis equisetina*) has rounded hollow stems.
Mcleay Grass Man, Flickr CC BY - 2.0

Dicot weeds—Broadleaf weeds, or dicots, are a highly variable group, but sometimes they have brightly colored, showy flowers. As they emerge, dicot seedlings have two seed leaves. Leaves are diverse but generally broad with **netted veins**. Broadleaf weeds may have a **taproot** or a coarse, branched root system. All broadleaf plants have exposed growing points at the end of each stem and in each leaf axis. Perennial broadleaf weeds may also have growing points (that can produce new shoots) on roots and stems below the soil surface. Because there is much diversity among broadleaf weeds, accurate identification is necessary to select appropriate control procedures.

Some vegetative characteristics useful in identifying broadleaf weeds include growth habit (Figure 6–11), leaf orientation (opposite, alternate, or whorled), simple

Figure 6–11. Growth habit can be a useful characteristic in identifying weeds. This spurge (left) growing along the ground, is an example of prostrate growth form. The thistle (right) is an example of an erect weed.
Kathleen Moore, CC BY - 2.0

Weed Management: The Integrated Pest Management (IPM) Approach

Weed management consists of limiting weed infestations so that other plants can grow efficiently. Eradication is the elimination of weeds, weed parts, and weed seeds in a particular area. Eradication of all weeds is a nearly impossible goal (even fumigation does not control all weeds). For certain species that do not have long seed dormancy, eradication in a small area is possible. For the majority of weeds, however, an integrated management approach—with a goal of managing rather than eradicating weeds—is most appropriate. Integrated weed management uses one or more methods to achieve the maximum control with minimum inputs and as few adverse environmental effects as possible.

Cultural Management

Cultural methods limit the introduction, establishment, reproduction, survival, and spread of specific weed species into areas not currently infested. Cultural methods of weed management in the landscape include cultivating plants adapted to the site conditions; installing transplants rather than seeds; optimizing plant health through best management practices for plant spacing, watering, fertilizing, use of cover crops and compost; avoiding or containing potentially weedy plants; and sanitation.

Give desirable plants a competitive advantage over weeds by providing the best possible growing conditions. Use adapted plants and cultivars, maintain adequate soil fertility, plant at the proper date, and seed or plant at the correct depth and rate. Transplants have a greater competitive edge over weeds than plants started from seeds. When using seeds, however, a uniform, well-prepared seedbed will result in quick establishment, enabling desirable plants to better compete with weeds. Plant-spacing techniques can also reduce weeds. For example, if flowers are planted close enough that they grow to touch the adjoining plant, weeds will have less room and light to grow. Vegetables can be planted in wide beds or multiple rows instead of single rows (Figure 6–12); this planting strategy shades more of the soil surface, thus reducing weed seed germination and helping plants compete more effectively with emerged weeds. If greater than 80% of the soil surface is shaded, weeds will seldom become a problem.

Drip or trickle irrigation discourages weed growth because these methods place water only near desired plants, not in other spaces where weeds might grow. Fertilizer placed in bands near desired plants instead of broadcast widely helps the desired plants grow without

promoting weeds. A **cover crop** like clover, vetch, or annual ryegrass between garden rows (Figure 6–13) helps reduce weed seed germination and competes with weeds that do germinate. Cover crops planted when an area is not in production also limit weed growth.

Figure 6–12. By planting lettuce intensively instead of in single rows, weed growth is greatly reduced.
NC.Hort, Flickr

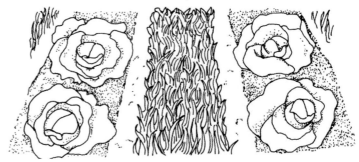

Figure 6–13. A cover crop between vegetable beds can prevent weeds.

Proper composting procedures, which include reaching a temperature of 140°F and turning the pile often, kill most weed seeds and vegetative structures. The longer the pile remains at 140°F, the more weed seeds will be killed. Always inspect composts and mulches that have been stockpiled outdoors; the presence of weeds, seeds, or material that has not decomposed is a sign that the compost pile has not been properly maintained.

Weed Disposal

Weeds can be disposed of in a variety of ways. If they are dead (left in hot sun to dry) and do not contain weed seeds, they can be used as mulch around trees and shrubs. Nutsedge, bermudagrass, quackgrass, and Canadian thistle do not lose their viability until their moisture content drops below 20%. Landscape debris with weed seeds should not be used as mulch or put in a compost pile unless the compost reaches a temperature of 140°F to 160°F. The longer the pile remains at this temperature, the more likely it is that weed seeds will be destroyed. If weeds are added to compost piles, turn the pile frequently to disturb and kill any weed seedlings. Properly composted landscape debris will not be a source of weeds. But if the debris is not fully composted, many weeds can be introduced to garden or landscape beds.

Pruning certain weeds can help limit their spread. Some ornamental plants can become invasive weeds if allowed to grow unchecked. Trumpet creeper (*Campsis radicans*), for example, is a perennial woody vine that has beautiful flowers but also an ability to self-seed. To limit its spread, prune off all of the green seed pods before they mature and produce seeds. Tansy, an herb, is useful for attracting beneficial insects but can be invasive. Cut the plant back after it flowers but before it produces seed. Many other self-seeding herbaceous perennials need to be cut back before producing and shedding seeds. Remove and destroy seed heads to prevent these ornamental plants from becoming weeds in another part of the garden.

Avoid planting potentially invasive plants, or install some type of control. For example, mints spread (by rhizomes) several feet per year and are easier to manage if planted in containers. If morning glories are planted, locate them away from the vegetable garden or flower beds. Jerusalem artichokes should be planted only in an isolated area, with precautions taken to prevent the spread of roots, rhizomes, and tubers. Tilling the area spreads the underground roots. Some types of bamboo are also weedy plants and are almost impossible to contain. Flowers that naturally reseed can sometimes become weeds in landscape beds. Use such plants only in areas where self-seeding is desirable, or remove spent flowers before seedpods form.

On-site sanitation is another effective cultural control method. Clean equipment after each use because weed seeds can be moved on rototillers and mowers.

Dandelions

Dandelions (*Taraxacum officinale*) get a bad rap. Their image is featured on many herbicide labels, and homeowners go to great lengths to eradicate them. Dandelions thrive in sunny environments and can be found in the United States and Europe. Their leaves are long and toothed, they produce taproots that have light-colored flesh, and their yellow flowers are actually a composite of many **ray flowers**. Dandelions produce seeds that are attached to a tiny fluff that creates the iconic "puff ball" familiar to children everywhere. The dispersal of these seeds is one of the great milestones of childhood. Dandelions have many positive features, including these:

- As one of the first plants to bloom in the spring, the dandelion provides nectar and pollen to honeybees and other beneficial insects

- Every part of the plant is edible. Roots are used to make a coffee substitute. Tender, highly nutritious leaves can be sautéed and eaten like spinach. Flowers can be added to salads or used to make wine. Their roots can break up compact soils.

Mechanical Management

Mechanical management is used to kill weeds directly or to make the environment unsuitable for them. Mechanical methods include selectively excluding weeds, creating barriers, and such practices as hoeing, cultivating, mowing, and pruning. Mechanical methods that are not as effective include hand-weeding, covering, and solarizing undesirable plants.

Purchase weed-free seeds and plants (or at least as weed-free as possible). State and federal laws regulate the presence of certain weed species in crop seeds. Information about the kind and percentage of weed seeds is required by law to be listed on the seed packet label. Also, check container-grown and balled-and-burlapped plants for weeds before purchasing or planting; pay particular attention to perennial weeds such as nutsedge, bindweed, and bermudagrass (Figure 6–14).

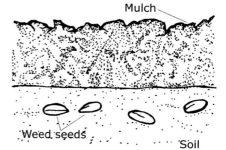

Figure 6–14. A layer of mulch can stop weed seeds from germinating.

Mulch

Weed seeds

Soil

Maintain weed-free borders, including underground barriers, to prevent underground encroachment by perennial weeds. Seeds from weeds in a vacant lot or along a fence row or ditch bank can be blown or washed into a landscape, so mow the weeds before they go to seed.

Mulching, another type of barrier, is by far the most common and reliable tool for preventing annual weed emergence in home landscapes. Mulch can prevent light from reaching weed seeds and thus prevent germination (Figure 6–14). In addition, weeds that do germinate under mulch may die because they do not have enough stored energy in their seeds to enable them to grow through 3 inches of mulch to reach sunlight and produce leaves. Newspapers, cardboard, bark, wood chips, shredded leaves, and pine needles are common mulching materials. Be aware that synthetic mulching materials like plastic and geotextile fabrics can become an unattractive maintenance problem as they degrade (Figure 6–15). In addition, as a layer of organic material builds up on top of these materials, weed seeds can germinate on top of the barrier and can create holes. Be careful not to introduce seeds or weed plant parts with mulch. Many mulching materials have not been completely composted and may contain weed **propagules**. Free sources of mulch are more likely to contain weed seeds than mulch purchased from certified suppliers. Mulches do not control creeping perennial weeds and may even enhance their growth.

Figure 6–15. Over time landscape plastics can degrade, become unsightly, and allow weeds to come through.
Chris Alberti, CC BY - 2.0

Hand-pulling weeds as they appear is an effective, but only temporary, way of controlling annual weeds. Minimize soil disturbance when hand-weeding. Remember that each time the soil is disturbed, new weed seeds are brought to the soil surface to germinate. Weeds are easier to pull when the soil is moist, so try to pull them after a rain or irrigation. Pulling is less effective and more difficult for creeping perennial weeds because it is usually impossible to pull out all the underground reproductive structures. Hoeing should be done when the weeds are tiny. Hoe three to four days after a rain. Weed seeds will be swollen and ready to germinate or will already be coming up. A shallow hoeing at this time dries out the soil surface and prevents weeds from becoming established.

Lightly scraping the soil surface is the best method to control small weeds. The hoe cuts weeds just below the soil surface and brings few or no weed seeds to the surface. Many people end up with more weeds after they hoe than before they started because they use the hoe to dig rather than to skim the soil, and thus bring many more weed seeds to the surface than they killed.

The kind of hoe selected affects the success rate in controlling weeds. The blade of a chopping hoe, for instance, tends to dig holes rather than sliding across the soil surface. Soil builds up behind the blade and moves weed seeds to the soil surface. A chopping hoe may be the only practical tool if the soil is rocky. A Warren hoe is ideal for making shallow trenches for planting but is poorly designed for severing weeds. The best hoes (Figure 6–16) for weeding are the scuffle hoe and the onion hoe (also called the tobacco hoe). These hoes allow scraping of the soil surface, and, if held at the right angle, cause the soil to flow over the hoe.

Rototillers can be used to destroy small weeds in row middles. Set the rototiller depth to about 1 inch, otherwise weeds may be transplanted rather than eliminated. Because tilling exposes seeds to sunlight and stimulates germination, be ready to manage the seedling weeds that will emerge shortly after tillage.

	Contact	**Systemic**
Selective	Rapid action, visible within hours	Takes days or weeks to translocate
	Affects only the area where applied	Affects the entire plant
	May require repeat applications	Affects only certain types of plants
	Affects only certain types of plants	Apply when plants are actively growing
		Works best when plants are not stressed
Non-Selective	Rapid action, visible within hours	Takes days or weeks to translocate
	Affects only the area where applied	Affects the entire plant
	May require repeat applications	Affects all plants
	Affects all plants	Apply when plants are actively growing
		Works best when plants are not stressed

Table 6–5. The Difference between Contact and Systemic, Selective and Nonselective Herbicides

6

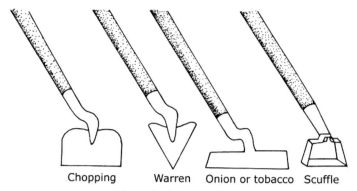

Chopping   Warren   Onion or tobacco   Scuffle

Figure 6–16. Types of hoes.

Another option is to till the seedbed several weeks before planting and allow weeds to germinate. Use a nonselective herbicide or flame weeder to kill the emerged weeds before planting the desired plants. After killing any weeds, avoid disturbing the soil to prevent weed seeds from germinating. This is often referred to as a "stale seedbed" technique.

Tilling is rarely effective on creeping perennial weeds and can make them worse by cutting and spreading the roots, rhizomes, or stolons. But weeds such as bermudagrass, johnsongrass, or goldenrod can be reduced by tilling during the winter and exposing the underground reproductive structures to freezing temperatures. Nutsedge can also be reduced by tilling and leaving the tubers exposed during the month of August when new tubers are normally formed.

Some gardeners cover small areas with shingles or boards in hopes of weakening weeds, but this is not an effective or recommended control method. Likewise, soil solarization, the process of harnessing the sun's energy to heat the soil, is not recommended. Solarization can heat the soil enough to control some disease organisms. But in North Carolina, it usually does not produce temperatures high enough to control weeds effectively.

Leaves are the food factories of plants. Through the process of photosynthesis, leaves create energy from sunlight. Removing leaf tissue requires the plant to use up stored reserves and can eventually starve the plant to death. Mowing, one way of removing leaf tissue, can suppress many erect weeds, reduce the food reserve of many perennial weeds, and reduce seed production in many others. However, most grassy weeds, prostrate annual broadleaves, and many creeping perennial weeds will not be eliminated by mowing. Nor does mowing reduce competition from these types of weeds. In addition, mowers and string trimmers often cause severe damage to landscape plants by wounding the bark (often referred to as lawn mower blight). This damage is completely avoidable if areas around the base of trees and shrubs are mulched and weeded by hand.

Biological Management

Biological weed management relies on the use of beneficial living organisms, such as insects, **nematodes, bacteria, fungi,** or animals, to manage weeds. A benefit to using biological management versus broad-spectrum herbicides is its relative safety and low impact on the environment.

Weeds can become invasive in new environments where they have no natural predators, but weeds often have natural enemies that keep their populations in check in their place of origin. Scientists must carefully weigh the benefits and possible problems of introducing biological management measures to a new environment. Not many biological weed management options are readily available to a home gardener. Using goats to eat English ivy, kudzu, blackberries, and other weeds is one example.

Chemical Management

Chemical management of weeds relies on the use of herbicides. In IPM, herbicides are used only when needed, and the type of herbicide, timing, and placement of application are optimized to maximize benefit and minimize possible harm to people and the environment. Herbicides are used in combination with other IPM approaches for effective, long-term management.

Herbicides are chemicals used to control, suppress, or kill plants by interrupting normal growth processes. One of the greatest challenges of using herbicides is choosing the best one for the specific weed and site. Several factors affect this decision, including the weed and desired plant species, the season, weed growth stage, soil type, proximity of susceptible species, application method (spray or granular), cost, and potential environmental risks. Lists of weeds that herbicides control and which plants they can be safely used on are included in NC State Extension publications such as the *North Carolina Agricultural Chemicals Manual* and various crop production guides. No herbicide is safe for all horticultural plants—always read the label carefully.

To be effective, herbicides must be applied at the proper time in relation to the growth stages of the weed and the desirable plant. Newly transplanted ornamentals are often more easily injured than established plants. The length of time each herbicide will control weeds and persist in the soil depends on its mode of action, rate of application, and the soil type.

Herbicide Safety Tips

Keep new or unused herbicides in their original containers and store away from children. Do not allow herbicides to contact the skin or eyes. Change clothes and wash skin thoroughly after spraying. Do not smoke, eat, or drink while using any herbicide. Additional information

6

on safety, storage, and use of pesticides can be found in Appendix B.

Types of Herbicides

Herbicides may be grouped or classified based on their general mode of action, or how they are used (Table 6–5). Selective herbicides control certain plant species without seriously affecting the growth of others. Some control grasses without harming broadleaf plants; others do just the opposite. For example, some herbicides will selectively control dandelions without harming tall fescue growing around them. The majority of herbicides used are selective. Nonselective herbicides control or kill green plants regardless of species, controlling or damaging almost any plant contacted by the spray. Because nonselective herbicides indiscriminately control all plants, use them only to kill plants before renovating and planting an area, as a spot treatment (avoiding contact with desirable plants), or on a driveway or sidewalk where no vegetation is the desired end result.

Herbicides may also be categorized as contact or systemic action. Contact herbicides affect only the portion of the green plant tissue that is directly contacted by the spray solution. These herbicides do not move through the vascular system of plants, do not kill the underground plant parts of perennials, and may only kill the top growth of annual weeds. Adequate spray coverage—and often repeat applications—are necessary for effective management.

Contact herbicides can be selective or nonselective. For example, there are selective contact herbicides that can control yellow nutsedge in turfgrass.

Systemic herbicides are absorbed by the foliage and translocated, or moved, into the plant's vascular system. These chemicals move to and accumulate in the plant's active growth centers, where a chemical can block or interfere with an important growth process (such as photosynthesis or respiration). Systemic herbicides kill plants over a period of days or weeks rather than immediately. It may not be obvious, however, that anything is happening. If a systemic herbicide is applied and it frustrates the gardener because it does not appear to be working quickly enough, applying a contact herbicide on the same plant may be counterproductive. The contact herbicide, while having a dramatic visual impact, can actually serve to protect the plant by preventing the translocation of the

systemic herbicide. The plant may be more likely to come back than if the contact herbicide had not been sprayed. Systemic herbicides can also be classified as selective or nonselective. Selectivity results from the ability of some plants to deactivate or not absorb the herbicides or from a plant's inherent insensitivity to the herbicide. Selective systemic herbicides are most effective when applied during times of active vegetative growth when the poison is most effectively translocated throughout the plant.

Knowing what type of herbicide you are using is very important if you compost any vegetation that may have been sprayed. Some herbicides for broadleaf plants are persistent. If turfgrass is sprayed and then the clippings are added to a compost pile, the herbicide may not break down sufficiently in the composting process. Herbicides can also carry over in manure. If you plan to add manure to your compost, ask your supplier about any herbicides used on the grazing pastures. Those herbicides can negatively affect desirable plants when that compost containing herbicide residues is added (Figure 6–17). Read more in chapter 2, "Composting," or see this NC State Extension publication: *Herbicide Carryover in Hay, Manure, Compost, and Grass Clippings: Caution to Hay Producers, Livestock Owners, Farmers, and Home Gardeners.*

Time of Application

Preemergence—Preemergence herbicides do not kill existing plants or dormant seeds, nor do they prevent germination. They do, however, kill seedlings during germination. So they must be applied to a site (lawn, garden, flower bed) before weed seeds emerge. If the weed seedling can be seen, it is too late to apply a preemergence herbicide. Preemergence herbicides are effective in controlling most annual grasses and some small-seeded broadleaf weeds. In turfgrasses and ornamentals, preemergence herbicides are applied in late summer to early fall to control winter annuals such as annual bluegrass, henbit, and common chickweed. Preemergents may also be applied in early spring (before dogwoods start blooming), to control summer annuals, such as crabgrass. Preemergence herbicides remain effective for 6 to 12 weeks (varies with the chemical). A second application may be required for season-long control.

For a list of preemergence herbicides, see the *North Carolina Agricultural Chemicals Manual.* Relatively few

---

Adjuvants and Surfactants

Products can be added to herbicides or pesticides that can improve their performance. **Adjuvants** may be included in the herbicide, or they may be separate chemicals that are added to a spray tank at the time of application. Some examples of adjuvants include suspension aids, spray buffers, drift retardants, compatibility agents, and surfactants. A **surfactant** is a type of adjuvant that helps enhance the herbicide's dispersion (spreading), adhesion (sticking), and plant tissue penetration. Surfactants are often used to help herbicides penetrate a waxy cuticle or a hairy leaf surface.

6

Figure 6–17.
A healthy tomato plant (left) and a tomato plant planted in soil that contains pine bark mulch previously contaminated with a synthetic auxin herbicide.
Joe Neal

preemergence herbicides, however, are readily available to homeowners. Preemergence herbicides require rainfall or irrigation to move the herbicide into the upper 1 to 2 inches of soil. Most require ¼-inch to ½-inch of rainfall or irrigation within seven days of application to activate the herbicide. If the soil does not receive adequate water in this time frame, the herbicide will not be activated, and, therefore, weed control will generally be poor.

Postemergence—Postemergence herbicides are applied directly to the foliage of emerged weeds. In contrast to preemergence herbicides, the majority of postemergence herbicides do not provide residual control; that is, they control emerged weeds only and do not prevent weeds from emerging afterwards. Most postemergence herbicides are systemic but, as previously noted, some have only contact action. Apply the herbicide until just before the point when spray runs off the plant. Any spray that drips from the leaf surface is wasted and increases the expense and the environmental impact without increasing control. Postemergence herbicides are less effective when the weed is under stress (drought, cold), has begun to seed, or has been mowed within a few days before or after application. Postemergence herbicides also require a rain-free period after application. To determine the required rain-free period, read the label for each product.

Herbicide movement within a weed is slower during cool, cloudy weather. Some postemergence herbicides are temperature sensitive. The activity of these herbicides is reduced when daily temperatures are less than 60°F for several days before treatment. High temperatures (85°F or above) cause some herbicides to volatilize and move as an invisible gas to nontargeted plants and can cause excessive burn to plants in the treated area. Some postemergence herbicides are not greatly affected by low temperatures, making them an effective product for winter annual weed control in late fall through early spring in landscape plantings. Check the label of each product before using.

Nonselective herbicides must be applied in a manner that avoids contact with desirable plants. But selective herbicides to control weedy grasses (such as crabgrass and bermudagrass) may be used as broadcast sprays over broadleaf landscape plants. These selective herbicides are most effective when grasses are less than 6 inches tall.

Factors Affecting Chemical Management
Generally, the more similar the desired plant is to the weed species (in life cycles, foliar characteristics, and herbicide susceptibilities), the more difficult or impossible selective weed management becomes. It is important to identify and exploit any differences between the weed and the desired plant.

Some factors affecting chemical management include the following:
- **Growing points**—Points that are sheathed or located below the soil surface are not contacted by herbicide sprays.
- **Leaf shapes**—Herbicides tend to run off narrow upright leaves. Broad and flat leaves tend to hold herbicide spray longer than narrow leaves.
- **Wax or a thick cuticle layer on the leaf surface**—Either characteristic prevents herbicides from entering the leaf. The waxy surface also tends to cause a spray solution to form droplets and run off the leaf.
- **Leaf hairs**—A dense layer of leaf hairs holds the herbicide droplets away from the leaf surface, whereas a thin layer causes the chemical to stay on the surface longer than normal.
- **Plant's age**—Young, rapidly growing plants are often more susceptible to herbicides than larger, more mature plants.
- **Special properties**—Some plants can deactivate herbicides and are thus less susceptible to injury.
- **Growth stage**—Seedlings are very susceptible to most herbicides. Plants in the vegetative and early bud stages are very susceptible to translocated herbicides. Young, rapidly growing plants are often more susceptible to herbicides than larger, more mature plants.
- **Application rate and uniformity**—Application errors are the primary cause of poor herbicide performance.
- **Season of application**—When selecting herbicides,

planning when to use them, and applying them, consider the season, weed growth stage, life cycle, and time of germination (relative to herbicide application).

- **Weather conditions before and after application**— Preemergence herbicides must be watered-in, but too much or too little water reduces their efficacy. Conditions that are too wet or too dry reduce the effectiveness of postemergence herbicides. Also, weeds must be actively growing when postemergence herbicides are applied.
- **Temperature**—Air temperature can have a critical effect. Some herbicides should be applied only in cool weather.Warm temperatures make some chemicals more volatile and speed up the biological and physical processes that break down herbicides in the soil.
- **Species of weed to be managed**—Identify the weed to select the most appropriate herbicide. Some weeds may require repeat applications.
- **Soil type and organic matter**—Organic matter, pH, and clay content may affect, for some preemergence herbicides, the dose required for adequate weed management.
- **Cultivation**—Disturbing the soil by cultivating deeply after applying preemergence herbicides reduces their effectiveness and can bring a new crop of weed seeds to the soil surface.

Herbicide Injury

Herbicide injury to plants can often be traced to application of the wrong herbicide for the site, improper application, or application under less than optimum conditions. Herbicides applied on windy or hot days can drift from the area where they were sprayed. Some formulations are especially volatile, and the vapors or fumes can drift to susceptible plants. Fine spray droplets (caused by high spray pressure) have a greater potential for drifting than sprays applied at low pressure. High temperatures (85°F or higher) during or immediately after herbicide application may cause some herbicides to vaporize and drift.

The possibility of root uptake of soil-applied herbicides depends on the herbicide, the type of soil, and its moisture content. Some herbicides are relatively mobile and move rapidly in sandy or porous soils.

Diagnosis of herbicide injury is often difficult at best. Injury often occurs within several days, but symptoms may take several weeks to appear. Some plants that are especially sensitive to herbicides include grapes, tomatoes, elms, sycamores, petunias, roses, apples, dogwoods, redbuds, forsythias, and honey locusts.

In general, broadleaf herbicide (synthetic auxin) injury appears as a strapping of the leaf with veins becoming parallel or close together. Twisting and distortion are usually associated with this narrowing and thickening of the leaf (Figure 6–18). With dicamba injury, there is usually more

cupping and less leaf strapping. Symptoms from many residual herbicides are usually seen as **chlorosis** and death of the area between the veins. Other herbicides affect root growth, and the casual observer usually notices only a more generalized decline of the plants. These symptoms may appear on lower leaves before new growth occurs, or about evenly over the entire plant. For a more detailed list of injury symptoms see Table 6–6.

Figure 6–18. Glyphosate injury showing interveinal chlorosis.
Scot Nelson, Flickr CC BY - 2.0

Several resources are available online focusing on herbicide injury symptoms in agronomic crops and a few focusing on horticultural crops and landscape plants. In addition, fact sheets are available from NC State to aid in diagnosing herbicide injury symptoms.

Diagnosing Herbicide Injury

- Do not make snap decisions. Gather all possible information before drawing conclusions.
- Consider planting details, such as date of planting, area planted, desired plant cultivar, seed treatment, spraying details (including chemical used, date of treatment, equipment used, spray pressure, total amount used, and total area sprayed), stage of desired plants and weeds at time of treatment, weather conditions (before, during, and after spraying), and soil conditions.
- Look for patterns in types of plants affected, location of damage (in rows, along edges, in low lying areas), differences between treated and untreated plants, and progression of symptoms.
- Watch for evidence of alternate causes for similar symptoms, such as nutrient deficiency, fertilizer burn, improper pH, pest damage (insect, mite, or disease), air pollution, weather (wind, frost, hail, drought, sun), root damage, or improper cultural practices.

Herbicide Use Guidelines

- Identify the desirable plants to be protected and the problem weeds to be killed.
- Select an appropriate herbicide. Information identifying which plants an herbicide may be used on and which weeds it will control is listed on the label and in the *North Carolina Agricultural Chemicals Manual*.

6

- Thoroughly read and understand the entire herbicide label. The label is the best reference on how to use an herbicide effectively and safely.
- Follow all directions on the label, including rate of application, instructions for mixing, time of application, application methods, interval between application and harvesting fruits or vegetables, storage and disposal of the empty herbicide container, and personal protective equipment.
- Never apply more herbicide than is recommended on the label. Applying more than the recommended amount does not improve weed control but may increase the risk of injury to desirable plants.
- Purchase and maintain proper herbicide application equipment.
- Do not use an herbicide on a plant that is not listed on the label.
- Do not use weed-and-feed lawn herbicides in other areas, such as landscape beds or vegetable gardens.

Cautions about Long-lasting Herbicides

Some herbicides contain products that remain active in the soil for years. These materials are rarely appropriate for use in urban areas and should be used only with extreme caution. Never apply them in areas where possible surface runoff may wash them into unintended areas. Do not apply them in areas where soil may contain tree or shrub roots. Tree roots often extend twice as far as the branches and may extend out beneath turf and be harmed by herbicides applied to lawns. Other herbicides have little or no persistence in the soil (see the *North Carolina Agricultural Chemicals Manual* for additional information).

Table 6–6. Symptoms of Herbicide Injury

Plant Part Affected	Injury Symptoms	Possible Causes and Comments
Entire plant	Reduced plant growth and vigor while producing no other acute symptoms	Causes include low doses of herbicides sprayed over the top of plants when new growth is present, poor drainage, root-feeding insects, competition from weeds, low fertility, and water stress; look for untreated plants growing in similar conditions and carefully evaluate all potential causes
Leaves	Feathering of leaves; strap-shaped leaves	Leaf malformations are induced by translocated herbicides
	Fiddlenecking in young growing points of plants; upward curling of older leaves	Symptoms are produced by growth-hormone herbicides
	Cupping of leaves	Distinct cupping (usually upward) is caused by growth-hormone herbicides; also may be caused by root uptake of ALS-inhibitor herbicides
	Crinkling of leaves; in grass species such as corn, leaves fail to emerge normally from the sheath and the plant remains in a stunted condition with twisted and crinkled leaves	Caused by thiocarbate herbicides
	Leaf rolling	Injury symptom on grasses can be caused by an herbicide but is more commonly caused by leaf-rolling arthropod pests
	Tip chlorosis (yellowing in the actively growing regions of plants); chlorotic areas may appear yellow, white, or pinkish	Typical of translocated herbicides
	Veinal chlorosis (yellowing of leaf veins)	Usually results from root uptake of herbicides

continued

6

Table 6–6. Symptoms of Herbicide Injury *continued*

Plant Part Affected	Injury Symptoms	Possible Causes and Comments
Leaves	Interveinal chlorosis (yellowing of tissues between leaf veins)	Typically is caused by root uptake of herbicides but is also caused by some nutrient disorders, such as Fe deficiency
Stems	Marginal chlorosis (a narrow, yellow band almost entirely around the leaf margin; sometimes called a "halo effect")	Can be caused by root or foliar uptake of herbicides
	Mottling (chlorosis that occurs randomly on the leaf); parts of the leaf remain green while others are chlorotic, sometimes puckered	Rarely associated with herbicide injury; sometimes preemergence herbicides applied over very young plant tissues can cause puckering and mottled leaves in susceptible species such as hydrangea, heuchera, and *Euonymus alatus compacta*; may also be injury from foliar nematodes
	Marginal **necrosis** (death of isolated tissues, often following chlorosis) on the leaf margins; develops on older leaves after they have exhibited a chlorotic condition	Several herbicides labeled for use in turf may cause these symptons; some bacterial infections may mimic these symptoms
	Necrosis occurring in small spots scattered through the leaf	An overdose of a herbicide can cause these symptoms
	Epinasty (bending and/or twisting that occurs in either the stem or petioles of plants)	Response often occurs within a few hours after exposure to growth-hormone herbicides
	Abnormal stem elongation	Stem elongation of broadleaved plants may be enhanced (at low concentration) or inhibited (at high concentrations) by growth-hormone herbicides
	Stem cracking; stems become brittle and may break off in heavy winds; stems often crack near the soil line	Symptoms are typical of injury from growth-regulator herbicides
	Adventitious root formation	Can be caused by growth-hormone herbicides
	Swelling of coleoptiles, **hypocotyl**, and/or stem	Caused by growth-hormone herbicides; also a common result of stem girdling at the soil line (resulting in stem swelling above the soil line)
Flowers	Changes in size, shape, or arrangement of various flower parts; branched flowers; multiple spikelets; some spikelets missing; flower partly or completely enclosed in the leaf; opposite instead of alternating spikelets along the rachis (axis of an **inflorescence**)	Usually caused by growth-hormone herbicides; delay in flowering due to herbicide injury is common
Fruit	Changes in size, shape, and appearance of fruit or abortion of fruit	Often associated with growth-regulator-type herbicides, spray drift or misapplication of contact-type herbicides
Roots	Development of primary and/or lateral roots is inhibited; thickened and shortened roots; usually leads to stunting of plants	Some herbicides are effective inhibitors of root growth; growth-hormone herbicides may cause swelling of roots in some plants

Case Study—Think IPM: Grass in a Flower Bed

No single herbicide or management method will control all weeds. However, by integrating cultural, mechanical, biological, and chemical methods into a weed management system, the goal of growing a relatively weed-free, aesthetically pleasing landscape or productive garden may be realized. Integrated weed management depends on correctly identifying the weed and understanding available weed management options.

It is September, and the goal is to eliminate grass growing in a flower bed (Figure 6–19). Review the steps of integrated pest management:

• Monitor and scout to determine pest type and population levels.
• Accurately identify host and pest.
• Consider economic or aesthetic injury thresholds. A threshold is the point at which action should be taken.
• Implement a treatment strategy using cultural, mechanical, biological, or chemical management, or a combination of these methods.
• Evaluate success of treatments.

Figure 6–19. The iris bed and adjacent grass.
F.D. Richards, Flickr CC BY-SA - 4.0

1. **Monitor and scout to determine pest type and population levels.**
   Where is the grass growing? In how large an area?
   This grass is part of the lawn, but it is growing out of bounds into an adjacent 15-foot by 20-foot iris bed.

   When did you first notice grass in the iris bed? There were a few blades of grass in the iris bed last year, but this summer the grass is coming on strong. It is beginning to choke out the iris plants.
   How important is this particular planting bed?
   These are grandmother's irises and have high sentimental value.

2. **Accurately identify host and pest.**
   You examine the grass and its seed head, which resembles a helicopter blade. The blades are smooth, pointed, and green. It has wiry stolons, and you see a ring of tiny hairs where the blade meets the sheath. The flowering structure has a whorl of five to seven seed heads at the top of stalk. You confirm the sample is that of bermudagrass, *Cynodon dactylon*.

3. **Consider economic or aesthetic injury thresholds. A threshold is the point at which action should be taken.**
   You research bermudagrass and find it grows by both above and below the ground by stolons and rhizomes and it also reproduces by seed. It does well with heavy foot traffic and a hot dry climate, but it can easily become an invasive weed. It is difficult to remove when it is growing in an unwanted location. The longer you wait, the worse the problem will become. Any piece of the stolon or rhizome that is left in the soil can produce a new plant. Most of the management strategies will require removing the iris and then replanting once the bed is clear of bermudagrass.

4. **Implement a treatment strategy using physical, cultural, biological, or chemical management, or a combination of these methods.**

   Cultural management—Mulching will prevent bermudagrass seedlings from establishing but will not prevent bermudagrass from reestablishing via rhizomes or stolons left in the soil. Mulching will suppress most annual weeds, conserve water, and generally improve the growth of the iris plants.

   Biological management—No recommended strategies exist.

6

Mechanical management—Physically removing as much of the bermudagrass from the iris bed as possible will reduce the bermudagrass population. Iris rhizomes may need to be removed from the soil to achieve this. *Any* piece of the bermudagrass left in the soil can produce a whole new plant. Rototill the bed to break up stolons and bring rhizomes to the surface. Any plant material should be raked up, picked up, and disposed of. This may need to be repeated several times throughout the summer. Never till the soil when it is damp or when any broken pieces of the grass that are not removed can sprout. Seeds will remain viable in the soil for several years. Installing a weed barrier of landscape fabric can keep any bermudagrass shoots from emerging.

Chemical management—There are several postemergence herbicide options for bermudagrass suppression—both selective herbicides that specifically target grasses and nonselective herbicides that are broad spectrum (kill any living plant). It is best to apply a chemical when the grass is actively growing. For the most effective application, the grass should not be drought stressed or dusty and should not have been recently mowed so there is plenty of leaf surface area to absorb the chemical. A broad-spectrum systemic herbicide is translocated to the rhizomes and roots. It is best to apply a systemic herbicide in the fall when the plant is moving nutrients to its roots. Preemergence herbicides are not effective on bermudagrass from rhizomes or stolons but will control bermudagrass from seed.

Integrated Weed Management Options

Option 1. Cultural and Mechanical Management. Dig up the iris rhizomes and store them in a cool, dry place for the winter. Gently remove the soil and pieces of grass from the rhizomes to ensure the grass parts will not be transplanted elsewhere. Dig the bed to expose the grass rhizomes and stolons to winter temperatures and desiccation. In the spring, prepare the planting bed. Remove as much of the remaining grass rhizomes and stolons as possible. Remember bermudagrass rhizomes may grow 6 to 8 inches deep. Replant the iris rhizomes, and then mulch the bed to control annual weeds from seed (Figure 6–20). Consider installing a root barrier around the bed to prevent bermudagrass encroachment from the lawn. Hand-weed the bed every two weeks to remove bermudagrass before it can reestablish.

Option 2. Chemical Management. Because bermudagrass goes dormant in the fall, top-dress the bed with new mulch to improve the appearance. In spring, watch the bed carefully for bermudagrass emergence. When you see it emerge, begin treatment with a selective herbicide to control grasses. Spot spray as you see the bermudagrass emerging. Edge the bed with a contact herbicide to prevent encroachment from the adjacent lawn area.

Remember cultural, mechanical, and chemical options are not mutually exclusive. You may want to divide the iris plants. Periodic division and replanting invigorates iris plants and offers a chance to amend the soil. Control bermudagrass with a nonselective herbicide.

5. Evaluate success of treatments.
Keep a garden journal of photos, dates, and descriptions of management strategies to evaluate which are most effective. See Appendix A, "Garden Journaling," for more information.

Figure 6–20. Use straw as a mulch to prevent bermudagrass from invading planting beds.
kenny_point, Flickr CC BY-SA - 2.0

Frequently Asked Questions

1. There are weeds in my lawn. How do I get rid of them?

A healthy lawn can outcompete many weeds. Review your watering, fertilizing, and mowing practices. Refer to "Lawns," chapter 9, for recommendations. Be sure to properly identify the weed. Hand-weeding may be an option. Many effective herbicides are available for broadleaf weed control in lawns; these products are available in "ready to use" and concentrate formulations.

2. How do I control bamboo?

Clumping-type bamboos can be removed by digging up the plants. Creeping, spreading-type bamboos are very weedy once established and are extremely difficult to control. Begin with removing as much of the bamboo growth, rhizomes, and root system as possible. This may require the use of power equipment for large infestations. Follow-up treatments with herbicides are usually required. As shoots resprout, control can be obtained by applying a systemic herbicide to the new shoots before leaves open (when 12 to 24 inches high). Wear rubber gloves; wipe the entire shoot with a sponge dampened with herbicide. Avoid contact with desirable vegetation or the grass. Another option is to put the affected area into turf, as bamboo does not tolerate frequent mowing. If the bamboo is encroaching from an adjacent area, install a root-barrier 12 to 18 inches deep. The best way to control bamboo is not to plant it in the first place. If you desire to plant bamboo in the landscape, hedge bamboo (*Bambusa multiplex*) is a tall, tightly clumping bamboo species that can be grown in our area.

3. How do you kill Japanese honeysuckle (Lonicera japonica) vines?

For small infestations, vines in the home landscape can be cut back to ground level in late summer. Treat the cut ends with herbicide. For thickets, cut all stems to the ground with a mower or string trimmer. Let the stems resprout, and then spot-spray the ends with a ready-to-use brush control herbicide. If mechanical vine control is impractical, you may still spray the honeysuckle with an herbicide, but remember that any other desirable species in the area will likely be injured. Note: Japanese honeysuckle (*Lonicera japonica*), an invasive plant of the Southeast, is often confused with two native vines in our area: Carolina jessamine (*Gelsemium sempervirens*) and coral honeysuckle (*Lonicera sempervirens*). If you are unsure which vine is in your yard, bring a sample to your local Cooperative Extension center for identification before using chemical control.

4. How do I control kudzu?

Kudzu can be managed by grazing. In fact, some entrepreneurs have started businesses to control invasive species like kudzu with goats. Remember, do not allow goats to graze on plants that have been treated with herbicides, and do not allow goats near any prized plantings. Goats are nonselective and will graze on all vegetation. However, where kudzu grows, there is usually very little else growing. Kudzu can also be managed with herbicides, but it may take several years of follow-up applications to eradicate this vine from your yard. Before applying herbicide, cut off vines at ground level, and, if possible, use a mower or string trimmer to cut patches to ground level during the growing season so that root crowns are visible. Allow vines to resprout. Then in late summer, spot-spray the ground level foliage at the root crowns with herbicide that includes a surfactant solution. If mechanical control is impractical, you can still spray the kudzu with an herbicide that includes surfactant solution. But spray carefully. Do not spray in windy conditions because these herbicides are not selective and will injure or kill any green plant tissue.

5. Can I spray a nonselective herbicide to kill weeds on my bermudagrass lawn when it is dormant?

A healthy lawn will outcompete most weeds, so one option would be to wait until spring and encourage the lawn to come out of dormancy with proper irrigation and fertilization. A second option would be to use a selective herbicide for broadleaf weeds. If your goal, however, is to kill grass weeds that are actively growing when your lawn is dormant and if it is not possible to wait, a nonselective herbicide applied at the labeled rate can be used on bermudagrass that is fully dormant. If applied at the right time and in the right concentration, a nonselective herbicide can be effective at managing many winter broadleaf and grassy weeds. The efficacy of the herbicide is much greater when temperatures rise above 60°F. The challenge lies in timing the application so the temperature is warm enough but the bermudagrass is still dormant. Some winters are very mild or have fluctuating temperatures. Under those conditions, bermudagrass never goes completely dormant. Although the application at labeled rates will not completely kill semidormant bermudagrass, it may delay spring green-up. Common bermudagrass is slightly more tolerant to herbicides than hybrid bermudagrass varieties such as 'Tifway'.

6. Can I spray a broadleaf herbicide in my flower bed for weeds and not hurt my flowers?

The simple answer is "no." Broadleaf herbicides target dicot plants. Many flowers are dicots, so blanket spraying flower beds for weeds is not recommended. Hand-pulling weeds is the safest option for surrounding plants, but you need to be sure to get the entire root of the weed. If hand-pulling is not an option, target specific weeds by protecting other plants. Use a can or milk jug (or other plastic container) with both ends cut off to make a "collar." Place this collar over the weed, and spray only inside of the collar. Alternatively you can paint herbicide on the leaves of weeds with a foam applicator brush. There are often weed seeds in the soil that will continue to germinate. By applying mulch or a preemergence herbicide, you can stop those seeds from emerging.

Further Reading

Baldwin, Ford L., and Edwin B. Smith. *Weeds of Arkansas Lawns, Turf, Roadsides, Recreation Areas: A Guide to Identification.* Pine Bluff, Arkansas: University Of Arkansas Division of Agriculture Cooperative Extension Service, 1981. Print. Publication MP 169.

Bryson, Charles T. and Michael S. DeFelice, eds. *Weeds of the South.* Athens, Georgia: The University of Georgia Press, 2009. Print.

Marinelli, Janet, ed. *Invasive Plants: Weeds of the Global Garden.* Brooklyn, New York: Brooklyn Botanic Garden, 1996. Print.

Murphy, Tim R. *Weeds of Southern Turfgrasses.* Gainesville, Florida: University Of Florida Institute Of Food And Agricultural Science, 2004. Print.

Pleasant, Barbara. *The Gardener's Weed Book: Earth-Safe Controls.* North Adams, Massachusetts: Storey Publishing, 1996. Print.

Uva, Richard H., Joseph C. Neal, and Joseph M. DiTomaso. *Weeds of the Northeast.* Ithaca, New York: Cornell University Press, 1997. Print.

Wax, L. M., R. S. Fawcett, and D. Isely. *Weeds of the North Central States.* 1981. Urbana, Illinois: University Of Illinois At Urbana-Champaign, 2011. Print. North Central Regional Publication NCR281.

For More Information

http://go.ncsu.edu/fmi_weeds

6

Contributors

Author: Kathleen Moore, Urban Horticulturist, Department of Horticultural Science
Joe Neal, Extension Weed Specialist, Department of Horticultural Science
Lucy Bradley, Extension Specialist, Urban Horticulture, Department of Horticultural Science

Contributions by Extension Agents: Joanna Radford, Jessica Strickland, Susan Brown, Kelly Groves, Donna Teasley, Shawn Banks, Danelle Cutting

Contributions by Extension Master Gardener Volunteers: Jackie Weedon, Karen Damari, Connie Schultz, Kim Curlee, Lee Kapleau, Judy Bates, Chris Alberti, Kristen Monohan

Content Editors: Lucy Bradley, Professor and Extension Specialist, Urban Horticulture, NC State University; Director, NC State Extension Master Gardener program; Kathleen Moore, Urban Horticulturist

Copy Editor: Barbara Scott

Based in part on text from the 1998 Extension Master Gardener manual prepared by:
Erv Evans, Extension Associate, Department of Horticultural Science

Chapter 6 Cover Photo: Pixabay CC BY0

How to Cite this Chapter:
Moore, K.A., J. Neal and L.K. Bradley. 2022. Weeds Chpt 6. In: K.A. Moore, and. L.K. Bradley (eds), *North Carolina Extension Gardener Handbook*, 2nd ed. NC State Extension, Raleigh, NC. <https://content.ces.ncsu.edu/extension-gardener-handbook/6-weeds>

6

Diagnostics

Objectives

This chapter teaches people to:

- Effectively use a 10 step strategy to diagnose plant problems.
- List 3 normal plant characteristics commonly misidentified as plant problems.
- Describe 5 common distributions of plant damage and identify potential causes for each.
- List 3 common criteria you can use to separate biotic and abiotic problems.

7

Introduction

Every gardener will eventually encounter plant problems. This chapter reviews a systematic approach to plant problem diagnostics. This approach does not require vast knowledge of every plant pest or pathogen. Instead it helps gardeners identify a pest or pathogen based on cultural practices, environmental conditions, signs, symptoms, distribution of the problem in the landscape and on the plant, and timing of the problem. Often pests or pathogens are blamed for the decline of plants but this chapter discusses the links between cultural or abiotic factors and how pathogens or pests can be secondary problems. By following the steps in this chapter, garden investigators will feel more confident in their diagnosis of plant problems.

10 Steps for Gathering Facts to Understand the Problem

The answers to each of the questions below help to either indicate or rule out specific causes of plant problems.

Step 1. Identify the Plant
Some plants are predisposed to certain types of problems to which other plants are immune. Some plants are normally a color that on another plant would indicate a nutrient deficiency or disease. Some plants thrive in conditions that would stress another type of plant. Correctly identifying the plant is key to successful plant problem diagnosis. There are a variety of online tools and books to help with identification, or you can send in a photo or take a sample to your local Cooperative Extension center for assistance.

Step 2. Describe the Problem
Specifically identify what appears to be wrong. Is there a change in leaf color? If so, where? Is the change on the entire plant or just certain parts? On new growth or old growth? The entire leaf or just between the veins? Is there tissue damage? If so, is it in the center of the leaves or the edges? Is it circular or irregular? Observe carefully and gather detailed information that will help to identify the cause.

What is Normal?
Fall needle color in white pine (*Pinus strobus*) is often submitted as a plant problem because it is unusual for pine needles to turn yellow and drop in the fall and it is also unusual for a plant to shed only half its leaves in the fall. But that is normal for a white pine. Each fall, half of its needles turn yellow and drop off while the other half stays green (Figure 7–9).

Step 3. Identify What Is Normal
Determine if the described observations are normal for this plant. Normal characteristics that are sometimes confused with problems are:

1. Spore-bearing structures on ferns (Figure 7–1)
2. Stem growth on certain plants including sweetgum (*Liquidambar styraciflua*) and winged elm (*Ulmus alata*) (Figure 7–2)
3. Silvery stem and leaf characteristics on Russian olive (*Elaeagnus angustifolia*) (Figure 7–3)
4. Leaf spot on Japanese aucuba (*Aucuba japonica* 'Variegata') (Figure 7–4)
5. Pollen-bearing structures (strobili) on some conifers (Figure 7–5)
6. Normal fall leaf and needle color (Figure 7–6)
7. Normal leaf or needle drop, which can be in the spring for some plants (*Magnolia grandiflora*, *Ilex opaca*)
8. Variegation or coloration selected as a desirable plant characteristic (Figure 7–7)
9. Raised lenticels on certain woody stems (Figure 7–8)

Figure 7–1. These sori are the reproductive structures on ferns, but their appearance can be alarming for those who do not know what they are.
Ruth Hartnup, Flickr CC BY - 2.0

Figure 7–2. The corky growth on sweetgum is often mistaken for a problem. This growth causes the tree no harm.
Trish Walters, Flickr CC BY - 2.0

Figure 7–3. The healthy leaves and stems on *Elaeagnus angustifolia* have a silvery color that can sometimes be confused with a sick plant.

Matt Lavin, Flickr CC BY-SA - 2.0

Figure 7–4. The yellow spots on this Japanese aucuba *(Aucuba japonica* 'Variegata'*)* are perfectly normal.

Julie Anne Johnson, Flickr CC BY - 2.0

Figure 7–5. Male strobili are normal pollen-producing cones on conifers. This is a *Cupressus macrocarpa.*

Forest and Kim Starr, Flickr CC BY - 2.0

Figure 7–6. This maple is going through a fall color change.

Kathleen Moore, CC BY - 2.0

Figure 7–7. Variegation can be a desirable selection. The leaves of this loquat plant (*Eriobotrya japonica* 'Variegata') are variegated, not suffering from a nutrient problem.

Megan Hansen, Flickr CC BY-SA - 2.0

Figure 7–8. Lenticels are raised growths on woody stems.

Shihchuan, Flickr CC BY-SA - 2.0

7

Figure 7–9. Normal fall leaf color of white pines (*Pinus strobus*). This can be confused with a problem because only some of the needles change color while others remain green.

Jay Cross, Flickr CC BY - 2.0

Figure 7–10. The leaves on this maple tree (*Acer* spp.) show leaf burn from underwatering and drought.

Robert L. Anderson, USDA Forest Service, Bugwood CC BY - 3.0

Step 4. Review Cultural Practices

Review plant care and other human impacts. When was the plant transplanted? If the plant hasn't been moved within the past 12 months, it is probably not a transplanting error. However, consequences from excessive root damage or planting too deeply may not become visible until the plant is stressed. What fertilizers and pesticides have been applied recently, in what quantities, and under what conditions? Applying too much, or in the heat of the day, can cause damage. When and how has the plant been pruned? Each pruning cut creates a potential entry for insects and diseases. What other activity, such as construction or trenching, has taken place within the root zone of the plant?

- Damage to roots during transplant may result in wilting and marginal leaf burn due to water stress. Often these symptoms show up almost immediately; however, in some cases the plant stays stunted for a year or more before dying.
- Planting too deeply may result in pale yellow discoloration on the interior portion of the leaf blade or needle. Sometimes the leaves on these plants will droop like they are wilting. They may also **flag,** which means certain branches will die back.
- Improper watering can cause plant damage. Overwatering causes symptoms identical to being planted too deeply. This problem shows up the first growing season after transplanting. Underwatering causes wilting and marginal leaf burn. The effects of underwatering will be evident the first time the plant gets dry (Figure 7–10).

Step 5. Identify Environmental Conditions

What recent environmental conditions could have affected the plant, for example: excessive cold, heat, drought, rain, lightning, wind, or hail (Figure 7–11)? What chronic environmental conditions could be affecting the plant, for example: too much or too little sunlight, soil pH, soil compaction?

Figure 7–11. Hail damage to an eggplant (*Solanum melongena*).
Forest and Kim Starr, Flickr CC BY - 2.0

Step 6. Look for Signs of Pests and Pathogens

Look for signs of insects, mites, other animals, or pathogens. There may be physical evidence of a pest, including the actual animal, cast skins, egg casings, excrement, **frass**, silken threads, slime trails, tracks, holes, or teeth marks. Make a note of where the evidence of a pest is seen on roots, stems, or the top or the bottom of leaves. Plant pathogen signs include **mushrooms, conks, rust, ooze, slime mold, powdery mildew, sooty mold,** and **smut**. The presence of a sign is not proof that the animal or pathogen that left the sign is the cause of the problem, but it does make them a suspect. Some signs are easy to identify, but look online or in common reference books for help identifying others.

Step 7. Identify Symptoms of Pathogens

Look for symptoms of insects, animals, or pathogens. Symptoms are physical plant responses to the insect, animal, or pathogen.

Symptoms include:

- **Blight** — A nonspecific term, applied to a wide variety of symptoms, that usually refers to rapid death of leaves and other plant parts (Figure 7–12).

Figure 7–12. This tomato (*Solanum lycopersicum*) had a rapid death of leaves and stems.
Scot Nelson, Flickr CC0

- **Canker** — A plant lesion where part of the plant quits growing and the surrounding parts continue to grow. There may be sunken, discolored, dead areas on twigs or branches, usually starting from an injury, wound, or pathogen (Figure 7–13).
- **Chlorosis** — A yellowing or whitening of normally green tissue (Figure 7–14).
- **Dieback**—- Progressive death of shoots, branches, or roots, generally starting at the tips and moving back toward the roots.
- **Distorted growth** — Twisted or misformed growth (Figure 7–15).

- **Gall** — An abnormal growth or swelling in the plant (Figure 7–16).
- **Leaf Drop** — Leaves fall off the plant.
- **Mosaic**- Nonuniform foliage coloration with a more or less distinct intermingling of normal green and light green or yellowish patches (Figure 7–17).
- **Rot (fruit, root)** — Soft spoiling or decomposing of stems, crowns, and fruit, often accompanied by strong and unpleasant odors.
- **Spot (leaf, fruit)** — May be dry and colorful, may have a yellow circle inside the spot, may have small structures inside the spot, may be tan and have a water-soaked appearance (Figure 7–18).
- **Smut** — A specific type of fungus that produces black masses of spores that may form on stems or ears (such as corn), or grain heads. (Figure 7–19).
- **Wilt** — Leaves appear limp or droopy.
- **Witches'-broom** — All buds in a certain part of the plant start growing, resulting in a lot of tiny stems; abnormal brush-like development of many weak shoots (Figure 7–20).

Figure 7–13. Cankers are sunken, discolored, dead areas on twigs or stems.
Mike Ostry, USDA Forest Service, Bugwood CC BY - 3.0

Figure 7–14. Interveinal chlorosis is the yellowing of leaves between green veins.
Scot Nelson, Flickr CC0

Figure 7–15. Distorted growth on a pepper.
Dave, Flickr CC BY-ND - 2.0

Figure 7–16. A wool sower gall on an oak (*Quercus* sp.) tree.
Connie Schultz, CC BY - 2.0

Figure 7–17. Mosaic presents as light green and yellow patches dispersed across the leaf surface.
Scot Nelson, Flickr CC0

Figure 7–18. Leaf spot on a hibiscus.
Scot Nelson, Flickr CC0

Figure 7–19. Smut usually affects members of the grass family.
Maja Dumat, Flickr CC BY - 2.0

Figure 7–20. Witches'-broom is abnormal growth.
Carol Kwan, Flickr CC0

Step 8. Determine Distribution of Damage in the Landscape

Is more than one plant affected? If so, are different types of plants affected or only one type? What is the pattern of distribution of affected plants (uniform, random, hot spots, linear, high areas, low areas, and increasing or originating from a specific point or direction)?

If the problem is focused on a single plant family, consider theories involving living animals or pathogens. Living organisms have often co-evolved with one particular plant family. If more than one plant family is showing the same symptom in the same location, environmental or nonliving problems are more likely to be the culprit. Common environmental problems include temperature extremes, drought, soluble salt damage, air pollution, herbicides, and pesticides.

The distribution of damage among plants in the landscape can provide useful clues to the cause. Distribution among the same species may indicate:

- **Uniform**—likely an abiotic problem (even more likely when all plant parts are affected within a short period of time)
- **Random**—often caused by a living pathogen
- **Hot spots**—generally caused by a living pathogen, occasionally caused by nutrition
- **Linear**—likely man-made, possibly trenching
- **High areas**—problems associated with limited water
- **Low areas**—problems associated with excess water
- **Originating from a specific direction or source**—problem is toward the direction of the most damage (examples include a point source of air pollution or insects dispersing from overwintering sites in nearby woodlands)

Step 9. Examine Distribution of Damage on the Plant and Specific Plant Parts

Look at the distribution of damage on the individual plant. Does it affect the entire plant or just specific limbs or leaves? Is the problem random across the canopy or does it occur mostly on the outside of the canopy or inside the canopy? Is the damage restricted to new growth or old growth? Does it affect this year's needles/leaves, or older ones? What do the roots look like? Is there evidence of a canker, a sharply delineated dead area of wood or cambium on a branch or main stem (it may require a shallow cut below the bark to reveal this)?

Look for patterns on specific plant parts. On the leaves, does the pattern affect the inside of the leaf, the margin of the leaf, randomly across the leaf, the veins or between the veins? Is the problem limited by veins or does it go across the veins? On needles, are all needles affected at the same length, or is there a random variation in how much of the needle is affected? On the flowers or the fruit, is the problem distributed randomly or is it concentrated on the distal (blossom) end, or only on the stem end?

- If the entire plant is affected, the problem is likely either environmental or from a pathogen that has compromised the root system, lower stem, or vascular system.
- If random above-ground parts of the plant are affected, the problem is likely a living airborne pathogen or pest. If only the lower parts are affected, consider shade or temperatures. Often fungal and bacterial diseases are progressively less severe as you move up the plant. Viruses, on the other hand, are systemic and can affect new growth as well as old.
- If only the upper parts are affected, again it may relate to temperature.

7

- If only the interior parts of evergreens are affected, the problem most likely relates to something that occurred last year. Consider secondary leaf spot. However, Rhizosphaera needlecast and Passalora needle blight affect lower and interior portions of a plant first.
- When looking at a leaf, a marginal leaf burn usually indicates lack of water, too much soluble salts, or a problem with the transport system, such as xylem-inhabiting bacteria.
- A random pattern on the leaf indicates an airborne pathogen or pollutant.
- Uniform patterns between the veins are typically nutritional problems, although spider mites can also bleach out the interveinal area while leaving the veins green.
- Vein clearing patterns are typically caused by specific pesticides and certain viruses.
- Most fungal leaf spots will often cross the veins, while bacteria leaf spots, downy mildew, and foliar nematodes are often limited by the veins. When veins limit the advance of a leaf spot, the resulting pattern is called "angular" in dicots or a "streak" in monocots.
- On needles, compare adjacent needles. If all the needles are damaged at the same length, this is typically an environmental problem. If some needles have extensive damage while other needles are not damaged, this is typically an airborne pathogen.
- On flowers or fruit, a random pattern is typically an airborne problem. Problems on the blossom end of a fruit are typically nutrition-related.
- Nonliving problems do not spread; for example, when a lightning strike occurs, the damage is done all at once and shows up over a short period of time.
- Living problems generally start small and spread. In addition, they are usually season-specific.

Step 10. Review Timing
When did the symptoms first appear? What season? Did more plants and plant parts become affected over time?

> A large enough sample of a woody ornamental can sometimes give clues to the previous growth history. Compare the distance between terminal bud scale scars on the branches. In Figure 7–21, the branch on the top is from a plant that grew under normal conditions. Note the shorter distance between the terminal bud scale scars on the bottom branch, denoting that the tree suffered from severe drought stress in Years 1 and 3, less so in Year 2.

Secondary Problems and their Abiotic or Cultural Start

Why is this (insect, fungus, disease) killing my plant?
Insects and pathogens rarely attack healthy plant tissue. Often a plant has been stressed by abiotic or cultural factors before insects and diseases move in. However, when a gardener finally notices that a plant is suffering, these pests and pathogens are easy to spot and are wrongly blamed for the entire problem.

Abiotic, or nonliving, factors that can affect a plant include: sunlight, temperature, wind, and precipitation. Too much sunlight can burn plant tissue while too little can prevent the plant from photosynthesizing properly. High temperatures can scorch a plant while freezing temperatures can damage plant tissue. High winds can break branches and stems or cause a plant to transpire and lose water. Too little precipitation can stunt growth or cause plant tissues to dry out. Too much precipitation can lead to root rot.

Cultural factors such as humans planting, irrigating, fertilizing, or pruning plants can also have a large impact on plant health. Selecting the "right plant for the right place" goes a long way in ensuring a plant stays healthy. A proper irrigation schedule of deep, infrequent waterings will help establish a plant so it does not suffer drought or overwatering. Fertilizing based on recommendations from a soil test will allow for healthy growth. Excess fertilizer initiates a spurt of new growth, which may be more susceptible to pests and diseases or can cause fertilizer burn. Read more about fertilizing and soil testing in chapter 1, "Soils and Plant Nutrients." Proper pruning at the right time of year will help wounds close over and not leave the plant open for pathogens to enter. Read more about proper pruning in chapter 11, "Woody Ornamentals."

By taking care to ensure abiotic and cultural factors support plant health, secondary problems of pests and pathogens can be greatly reduced.

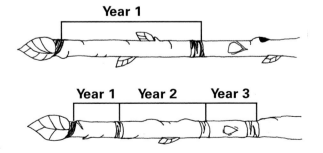

Figure 7–21. The terminal bud scar is a way to determine tree vigor. The top branch shows much greater growth in year 1, the bottom branch suffered from drought stress.

Develop a hypothesis

Use the information gathered in the 10 steps to rule out those insects, other animals, and pathogens that could not have caused the problem and focus in on the likely culprits.

Symptoms and Potential Causes:

- **Blight** — Fungal, bacterial, or environmental condition (Figure 7–12).
- **Canker** — Bacteria and fungi. Mechanical injury may look similar (Figure 7–13).
- **Chlorosis** — Poor nutrition, overwatering, some insects, some pesticides (Figure 7–14).
- **Dieback** — Insect, fungi, bacteria, or pesticides.
- **Distorted growth** — Pesticide, virus, insect, or gene mutation (Figure 7–15).
- **Gall** — Fungus, bacteria, or insect (Figure 7–16).
- **Leaf Drop** — Typically drought; less commonly, toxic chemicals and certain diseases.
- **Mosaic** — Virus or genetic mutation (Figure 7–17).
- **Rot (fruit, oot)** — Fungi or bacteria. Bacteria do not decay roots, but can cause soft rots of stems, crowns, and fruit.
- **Spot (leaf, fruit)** — Spots that are dry and colorful are typically fungal, though yellow halos can be present around bacterial or fungal spots. Spots with small structures inside the spot are fungal. Spots that start out water-soaked and turn tan are often caused by bacteria (Figure 7–18).
- **Smut** — Fungal pathogen that most commonly affects members of the grass family (Figure 7–19).
- **Wilt** — Drought, root rot, or anything interfering with the plant's water transport system (xylem) will cause plants to wilt.
- **Witches'-broom** — Virus, possibly genetic mutation (Figure 7–20).

Figure 7–22. Secondary leaf spot on a maple. These leaves are old and are going to die and drop off anyway. You will know it is secondary leaf spot because there will be no spots on new growth.
Emily Carlin, Flickr
CC BY-ND - 2.0

Secondary Leaf Spot

Evergreen leaves do not stay on the plant forever. Most of the broadleaf evergreens will hold their leaves for 14 to 18 months. By the time these leaves drop, the plant usually has new leaves. So the plant always appears green, but individual leaves get old and drop. With both evergreens and deciduous trees and shrubs, it is not uncommon for leaves to get fungal spots as they approach the end of their life. Sometimes the leaves may get the spots in early spring before the new leaves arrive. There may be as many as 50 different fungi that can infect old azalea or rhododendron leaves. As a simple description, plant pathologists call this phenomenon "secondary leaf spot" (Figure 7–22). There is no need to worry about these leaf spots or attempt to identify them or to treat them. The leaf has already contributed to the plant and is going to fall off in a few months anyway. Secondary leaf spots will not attack the new growth.

Table 7–1. Comparison of Symptom Distribution for Living and Nonliving Factors

Living Insect or Pathogen	Nonliving (Environmental)
Not widespread	Widespread
Species specific	Several species
Hot spots	100% of vulnerable parts affected
Progressive with time	Sudden death or decline
Occurs in specific seasons	Not necessarily limited to specific seasons

Submitting Samples

Good samples or photographs will make it much easier to identify a problem.

Some tips for bringing in live samples to your local Cooperative Extension center:

Plant Samples

1. Gather samples from the healthy part of the plant as well as the damaged or diseased sections. This will help identify what the "normal" growth looks like next to the problem. If possible, it is helpful to gather samples from older growth and new growth. If multiple plants of the same type are present, taking samples of plants in various stages of the problem will be helpful.
2. Take a large enough sample that leaves are still attached to stems. Pulling a few individual leaves from the plant will not provide as much information as intact stems.
3. Look for evidence of cankers along the stem and gather a sample.
4. For roots, remove sections of healthy, as well as diseased root tissue, along with some of the surrounding soil.
5. Bring samples in immediately. If they do need to be stored, put them in a dry plastic bag in the refrigerator or cooler.

Insect Samples

1. Collect any insects present; looking for adult as well as immature forms.
2. Be sure to collect any samples of the damage the insects are believed to have caused.
3. Place insects in a tightly lidded glass jar and fill with rubbing alcohol or put in the freezer for several hours.

If it is not possible to bring in a sample, quality photographs can be submitted.

Quality Photographs

1. To help identify a plant, document the leaf pattern (alternate, opposite), leaf margins, bark, and flowers or fruits if present. See chapter 3, "Botany", to help identify plant anatomy and structure.
2. To identify an insect, look for both mature and immature forms. Close-ups of legs and antennae can be particularly helpful. Images of damage they have done, frass, or casings can also help with identification. See chapter 4, "Insects."
3. To diagnose a problem, be sure to capture healthy parts of the plant, as well as parts that are damaged. Include an image of the entire landscape, the entire plant, as well as close-up images of the problem area, and an image that shows both the problem area and healthy tissue if possible. If symptoms are occurring on leaves, take pictures of both the top and the underside of a leaf.
4. Take multiple shots with different camera settings to help ensure the best shot.
5. Use a scale object like a coin or a thumb (Figure 7–23).
6. Use a fast shutter speed for moving insects and animals to lessen blurring.
7. Use macro settings to ensure an in-focus image when taking close-ups.
8. For birds, butterflies, or other fast-moving subjects, set the camera up on a tripod, turn it on, focus and wait for a good shot.

For more detailed information about gathering samples for submittal, please review the steps on the North Carolina Plant Disease and Insect Clinic's (PIDC) website.

7

Figure 7–23.
Use a scale item when capturing images like the penny used in this stag beetle photo.

Jim Champion,
CC BY-SA - 2.0

Case Studies

Case Study 1 – Wilted Tomato

Presenting Problem: Tomato plant wilted.

Step 1. **Identify the plant:** Tomato

Step 2. **Describe the problem:** Wilting

Step 3. **Identify what is Normal:** While it is normal for tomatoes to wilt in the middle of a hot summer day, they generally regain **turgor** in the evening. Extended wilting is not normal for tomatoes.

Step 4. **Cultural Practices:** The tomato was transplanted several weeks ago. It was hand watered once but it has not been sprayed, fertilized, or pruned.

Step 5. **Environmental conditions:** Within the last two weeks, it has rained twice. No other relevant environmental conditions.

Step 6. **Signs of Pathogens:** A close examination of the plant reveals no obvious signs of pest or pathogens.

Step 7. **Symptoms:** The only symptom is the wilting.

Step 8. **Distribution of Damage in the Landscape:** No other types of plants in the garden are affected. Cucumbers and green beans are doing fine. Three of nine tomato plants in the garden have wilted and there does not appear to be a uniform, linear, and high or low pattern to the arrangement of the plants.

Step 9. **Distribution of Damage on the Plant and Specific Plant Parts:** All the above ground portions of the plant are affected and all parts are affected equally.

Step 10. **Timing:** Two plants were wilted on one day and the third plant about a week later.

Figure 7–24. Fusarium wilt on a tomato.
F.D. Richards, Flickr CC BY-SA - 2.0

Steps 4, 5, 6, and 7 were inconclusive, but steps 8, 9, and 10 indicate a living pathogen. Consult chapter 5, "Diseases and Disorders," and chapter 16, "Vegetable Gardening," or use a reference book or online tool to identify living pathogens that cause wilt on tomatoes: (Fusarium wilt, Verticillium wilt, Southern blight, bacterial wilt, root-knot nematodes, and Tomato spotted wilt virus). Nematodes would – eventually – affect the cucumbers and beans, as well as tomato. Cutting into the lower stem reveals darkening of the vascular tissue, which makes Fusarium, Verticillium, or bacteria a suspect. Verticillium wilt of tomato would be found only in the cooler portions of the state of North Carolina.

A review of the literature reveals that both Fusarium and Verticillium cause some yellowing and curling of the leaves (Figure 7–24), while Tomato spotted wilt virus causes some **necrotic** spotting on the foliage and fruit (Figure 7–25).

Figure 7–25. Tomato spotted wilt virus causes spotting on foliage and fruit.
Scot Nelson, Flickr CC0

Southern blight causes a dark spot encircling the stem at the base of the plant (Figure 7–26). Since these leaves and stem are completely green, each of these are ruled out, leaving bacterial wilt. A reference book may explain a test for bacterial wilt of suspending a stem in clean water and seeing if the water turns murky from the bacteria (Figure 7–27). This test confirms bacterial wilt (Note: the streaming may not be visible if populations of the bacteria are low). An internet search for "bacterial wilt site:ncsu.edu" finds a blog from the Plant Disease and Insect Clinic that states, "if your plants have bacterial wilt, there is nothing you can do to save them. Infected plants will not recover and should be removed and destroyed."

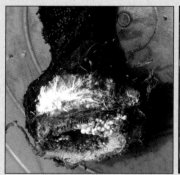 

Figure 7–26. Southern blight on a taro plant.
Glenn Teves, Flickr CC0

Figure 7–27. The severed stem of an infected ginger rhizome placed in clean water. Moments later, bacteria can be seen streaming out of the rhizome.
Scot Nelson, Flickr CC0

Case Study 2 – Pine Tree Death

Presenting Problem: Twenty to 30 mature native pines died over a few months (Figure 7–28).

Step 1. Identify the plant: Native pines may mean several species. For most of the state, the identification to species level isn't necessary. In places where both white pines and yellow pines are native, you should further identify the pine since the major problems are different.

Step 2. Describe the problem: A whole group of trees died within a few months.

Step 3. Identify what is Normal: Plants do not have indefinite life spans so the death of one individual may be normal. However, the rapid death of 20 or 30 adjacent pines is abnormal.

Step 4. Cultural Practices: No recent cultural management.

Step 5. Environmental Conditions: No environmental conditions out of the ordinary; however, it has been dry.

Step 6. Signs of Pathogens: An examination of the pines showed no signs of insects, animals, or pathogens.

Step 7. Symptoms: The needles are brown and are clinging to the tree. The wood inside a broken branch is dark. Remember that pathogens are not always visible, so they cannot be ruled out based on their absence to the unaided eye.

Step 8. Distribution of Damage in the Landscape: Under the pines, there was Japanese honeysuckle that showed some dieback. In addition, there was an understory dogwood that showed some dieback. So other types of plants were affected. The distribution of damage on the pines was uniform.

Step 9. Distribution of Damage on the Plant and Specific Plant Parts: Every plant that was dead, the entire plant was affected.

Step 10. Timing: All the pines died within a few months.

Steps 8, 9 and 10 show the uniform nature of the problem across the plant, the fact that additional plants families were affected, and the rapid onset of symptoms. This suggests an abiotic problem, like drought.

Figure 7–28. Mature dead pine tree that died over the period of a few months.
Dirk, Flickr CC BY - 2.0

Case Study 3 – Orange Growth on Cedar Tree

Presenting Problem: Orange jelly-like growth on the needles, branches, and trunk of a mature cedar tree (Figure 7–29).

Figure 7–29. Orange jelly-like growth on a cedar tree.
Mike Lewinski, Flickr CC BY - 2.0

Step 1. **Identify the plant:** Native red cedar (*Juniperus virginiana*).

Step 2. **Describe the problem:** Orange jelly-like growth on the needles, branches, and trunk of a mature cedar tree.

Step 3. **Identify what is Normal:** Orange jelly is not normal.

Step 4. **Cultural Practices:** No cultural issues.

Step 5. **Environmental Conditions:** No specific environmental conditions identified.

Step 6. **Signs of Pathogens:** The orange jelly-like growth is a sign.

Step 7. **Symptoms:** No noticeable exterior change to the branches, needles, or bark itself.

Step 8. **Distribution of Damage in the Landscape:** No plants other than cedars exhibit this sign and only some of the cedar trees exhibit this sign. The location of orange jelly on the trees appears random, with no apparent patterns connecting the affected trees.

Step 9. **Distribution of Damage on the Plant and Specific Plant Parts:** Only one side of the tree's needles, branches, and trunk is affected, the rest of the tree still looks healthy.

Step 10. **Timing:** The orange jelly appeared rapidly, shortly after some spring rains.

With the exception of Step 10 stating the rapid appearance of the substance, all indications point toward a living, airborne pathogen. A review of references for diseases of cedar that fits this pattern identifies cedar-quince rust as a possibility. Examining pictures and a description identifies cedar-quince rust as the likely pathogen. A search of available references indicates there are no recommended control measures for this problem.

Case Study 4 – Katsura Tree Stunted Growth

Presenting Problem: Katsura tree is not growing (Figure 7–30 and Figure 7–31).

Step 1. **Identify the plant:** Katsura Tree (*Cercidiphyllum japonicum*)

Step 2. **Describe the problem:** Not growing properly. It is growing slowly and has small leaves.

Step 3. **Identify what is Normal:** Larger leaves and faster plant growth is normal. There is a problem with this Katsura tree.

Step 4. **Cultural Practices:** Tree has been in the landscape for four years. No cultural practices identified that would cause problems.

Step 5. **Environmental Conditions:** No adverse environmental conditions noted.

Step 6. **Signs of Pathogens:** No signs.

Step 7. **Symptoms:** Smaller than normal leaves and short stature of plant.

Step 8. **Distribution of Damage in the Landscape:** Liriope (*Liriope muscari*) in the same area is growing well.

Step 9. **Distribution of Damage on the Plant and Specific Plant Parts:** Entire plant affected.

Step 10. **Timing:** Symptoms observed over the past four years.

No obvious answer, take plant sample to your local Cooperative Extension center for assistance.

Figure 7–30.
A katsura tree
(*Cercidiphyllum japonicum*)
trunk.
Harum Koh, Flickr
CC BY-SA -2.0

Figure 7–31. Katsura tree (*Cercidiphyllum japonicum*) leaves.
Wendy Culter, Flickr CC BY - 2.0

Frequently Asked Questions

1. *My plants have some black spots on them, what can I spray?*
   Before even thinking about chemicals, the host and pest or pathogen must be identified. Using the 10 steps outlined in this chapter, work to identify the plant and develop a theory. Once the plant and issue have been identified, use IPM strategies from chapter 8, to manage the problem.

2. *What do I do when I cannot identify the pest or pathogen?* If you go through the diagnostic steps and are unable to develop a sound theory, use the directions to take both samples and photographs to Master Gardener volunteers at the local Cooperative Extension center. If the volunteers and the county agent are unsure, samples can be sent in to NC State's Plant Disease and Insect Clinic. A fee may apply. Processing times vary depending on the volume of samples. A report will be emailed to you if you provide an address.

7

Further Reading

Brown-Rytlewski, Diane, ed. *A Pocket Guide for IPM Scouting of Woody Landscape Plants.* East Lansing, Michigan: Michigan State University Extension, 2008. Print.

Byrne, Jan, and Raymond A. Cloyd. *A Pocket Guide for IPM Scouting in Herbaceous Perennials.* East Lansing, Michigan: Michigan State University Extension, 2007. Print.

Carr, Anna. *Rodale's Color Handbook of Garden Insects.* Emmaus, Pennsylvania: Royale Press, Inc., 1983. Print.

Horst, R. Kenneth. *Westcott's Plant Disease Handbook.* 8th ed. New York: Springer Publishing Company, 2013. Print.

Narayanasamy, P. *Plant Pathogen Detection and Disease Diagnosis.* 2nd ed. New York: Marcel Dekker, Inc., 2001. Print.

Pirone, Pascal P. *Diseases and Pests of Ornamental Plants.* 5th ed. Hoboken, New Jersey: John Wiley & Sons, Inc., 1978. Kindle file.

Schumann, Gail L. *Essential Plant Pathology.* 2nd ed. St. Paul, Minnesota: American Phytopathological Society, 2009. Print.

For More Information

http://go.ncsu.edu/fmi_diagnostics

Contributors

Authors:
Mike Munster, Diagnostician, NC State Plant Disease and Insect Clinic
David Goforth, Extension Agent, Cabarrus County

Contributions by Extension Agents:
Jeana Myers, Julie Flowers, Kerrie Roach

Contributions by Extension Master Gardener Volunteers:
Kim Curlee, Jackie Weedon, Karen Damari, Ann Barnes, Lee Kapleau, Chris Alberti

Content Editors:
Lucy Bradley, Professor and Extension Specialist, Urban Horticulture, NC State University;
Director, NC State Extension Master Gardener program; Kathleen Moore, Urban Horticulturist

Copy Editor:
Barbara Scott

Chapter 7 Cover Photo: Kathleen Moore, CC BY - 2.0

How to Cite This Chapter:
Munster, M. 2022. Diagnostics, Chpt 7. In: K.A. Moore, and. L.K. Bradley (eds). *North Carolina Extension Gardener Handbook*, 2nd ed. NC State Extension, Raleigh, NC. <https://content.ces.ncsu.edu/extension-gardener-handbook/7-diagnostics>

7

Integrated Pest Management–IPM

Objectives

This chapter will teach people to:
- Be able to analyze pest problems, determine if management is necessary, and make appropriate recommendations using IPM techniques.
- Be familiar with different methods of pest management - their benefits and limitations.
- Understand the value of beneficial insects.

8

Introduction

It is not possible—or even desirable—to rid gardens of all pests. Monitoring and managing pest levels instead of eliminating pests can preserve the environment, reduce costs, protect the health of humans and animals, and maintain beneficial organisms such as birds, bees, butterflies, predaceous bugs, and other pollinators. This chapter discusses **integrated pest management** (IPM), an approach that uses knowledge about pests and their **life cycles**, **cultural practices**, nonchemical methods, and pesticides to manage pest problems. Additional information about IPM for specific plants is included in chapters that concentrate on those plants. Nonchemical pest control measures are stressed in chapter 17, "Organic Gardening." Managing birds and mammals is covered in chapter 20, "Wildlife." Managing **weeds** in the yard and garden is covered in chapter 6, "Weeds."

Pests as Part of a Natural System

Pests in a garden or landscape may include insects and mites, weeds, **plant diseases**, mammals, and birds. It can be tempting to look for a quick solution to an insect feeding on a garden plant. Many people hurry to pull, hoe, or spray every weed they see. Insects and weeds, however, play a role in the **ecosystem**. After planting a garden or establishing a lawn, the natural process of plant succession begins to reestablish **native** and **nonnative** plants. A weed growing in a lawn represents the first stage in a sequence of events that, if allowed to continue, could eventually result in a forest. Many cultivated plants are not as competitive as many of our natives, weeds, or pests; cultivated plants survive only with the constant help and intervention of the gardener.

What we call "pests" are part of a natural system at work. An ecosystem has no pests. Only humans consider certain species pests when they occur where they are not wanted. We will be more successful in managing unwanted species when we realize that these organisms follow predictable patterns that we can use to our advantage.

IPM Approach

When modern pesticides were first developed, they were used extensively. Pests susceptible to a pesticide were quickly killed, leaving resistant ones to breed and multiply. It became clear that pesticides alone would not solve all pest problems. Instead, overuse of pesticides caused the development of resistant pests. Scientists began to develop a new approach to pest control. This new approach was described as integrated pest management

(IPM). Integrated refers to the fact that all control measures (mechanical, cultural, biological, and chemical) are considered and used as appropriate. An IPM plan allows some level of pests in the environment. Pests are much less likely to survive a program that uses many different methods of reducing their populations.

Integrated pest management was first suggested by entomologists because insects were the first group of pests to prove difficult to manage with chemicals alone. Early proponents of IPM suggested using five basic strategies to improve insect management:

Step 1: Monitor and scout insects to determine insect types and population levels.
Step 2: Identify pest and host accurately.
Step 3: Assess and consider economic or aesthetic injury thresholds. A **threshold** is the point at which action should be taken.
Step 4: Implement a treatment strategy using mechanical, cultural, biological, or chemical controls, or a combination of these strategies.
Step 5: Evaluate success of treatments.

IPM has extended beyond insects to management of all pest populations: weeds, disease organisms, and mammals. Integrated pest management regulates pests by using a variety of control measures, including physical, mechanical, cultural, biological, and chemical. Management rather than eradication of pests is the goal.

An IPM plan begins with a careful evaluation of each pest infestation. Only then can one decide about the appropriate tactics necessary to suppress pest activities. The life cycle of the pest, possible damage, natural enemies, and effects of weather, among other factors, are considered before a control plan is implemented. For example, weeds like Queen Anne's lace (*Daucus carota*) or London rocket (*Sisymbrium irio*) can harbor **beneficial insects** such as lacewing or lady beetle larvae that help keep aphid and other pest populations at acceptable levels (Figure 8–1). Clover growing in a lawn may be viewed as an unwanted weed, but as a legume it is synthesizing nitrogen for the soil and the flowers are providing nectar to honey bees and other **pollinators**. Tolerance for some weeds may be part of an IPM plan. **Caterpillars** may be eating the leaves of a plant, but when they are identified as the larvae of Eastern tiger swallowtail butterflies, their damage may be tolerated so we can enjoy the beautiful butterfly. A woodpecker may be creating holes in the trunk of a peach tree, but at the same time it is eating insect **larvae** that may do more damage to the tree. See "Weeds," chapter 6; "Insects," chapter 4; and "Wildlife," chapter 20, for more information.

Pesticides may be an attractive option for homeowners because the formulations can be inexpensive, easy to use, and can provide quick results. An IPM plan may be slower to show results and could require more effort than spraying a chemical, but the reduced impact on the environment can be worth the investment. The more gardeners learn about biological and ecological processes, the more imaginative they will be in formulating and implementing IPM plans.

Figure 8–1. Brown lacewing larva (Hemerobiidae family).
Matt Bertone

Pest Management

Prevention is the first tool in pest management because it is the most effective, least expensive, most environmentally friendly solution. Choosing a healthy plant that will thrive in the desired location with the available light, planting it carefully, and ensuring that it has adequate water and nutrients will prevent stress and minimize pest problems. *Stressed plants can attract pests*. The second most important tool in pest management is *early intervention*. Being present and observant in the garden ensures early detection. Reacting to problems quickly, before they have time to multiply, will require a less dramatic intervention. The third most important tool is recordkeeping; tracking what happens in the garden enables a gardener to recognize patterns and make informed decisions. Record planting dates, varieties, purchase location, dates of problem onset, weather conditions, management strategies and their effectiveness, and other kinds of information that help you to recognize relationships and form gardening strategies.

Many safe, practical, nonchemical methods of plant protection and pest management may reduce or eliminate the need to spray. Other methods are most beneficial when used with pesticides. To implement management practices correctly and to minimize losses, gardeners should be aware of the types of pests that attack plants and understand pest biology. Scouting methods, equipment selection, timing, and other pest management practices all depend on an accurate knowledge of the pest. Pest management methods fall into four groups: cultural, mechanical, biological, and chemical.

Cultural Management

Keeping plants healthy and preventing plant stress helps plants to better withstand and repair the damage caused by an insect or mite pest. Some evidence indicates that healthy plants resist infestation by pests better than plants with low vigor. The most effective and most important of all practices is to observe what is going on in the garden. Many serious disease or insect problems can be halted or slowed by regularly visiting the garden, knowing what to look for, recognizing potential problems, and intervening early. Cultural methods of suppressing insect and mite problems in the landscape include *preparing the soil*; *choosing plants* that are adapted to the site conditions, that are not attractive to pests, and that are tolerant of insects and diseases; *rotating crops*; *interplanting*; *timing planting dates* to avoid pests; *managing weeds*; and *planting "trap" crops*.

Soil Preparation

Providing a favorable soil environment encourages the growth of healthy roots, increasing access to water and nutrients, preventing stress, and making the plant more resistant to pests and diseases than plants in poor soil. Conducting a soil test and applying only the recommended amount of fertilizer and lime maximizes the benefit to the plant while minimizing problems related to excessive use of fertilizer. Covering the soil with several inches of **organic** mulch will protect the plant in several ways: reducing soil water loss to evaporation, minimizing weed competition, providing nutrients, and creating a suitable environment for earthworms and microorganisms that keep the soil loose for roots and break down organic material to release nutrients. Keep organic mulch, pine straw, or wood chips a few inches from the trunk of a plant when the mulch is installed (Figure 8–2). If mulch touches the trunk, it can create a way for voles, bacteria, and fungi to attack the plant. Do not use manure or compost that has not *thoroughly decomposed* as a top dressing because it can encourage undesirable pests.

Figure 8–2.
Leave a few inches of space around the trunk of the plant when mulching.
hardworkinghippy : La Ferme de Sourrou, CC BY SA- 2.0

Research suggests that tilling the soil is detrimental to soil structure. Read more about tilling in "Soils and Plant Nutrients," chapter 1. If tilling is deemed necessary, consider doing it in the fall when the life cycles of many pests brings them near the surface. At the surface, pests become exposed to the weather as well as birds and other natural enemies. Fall tilling can also destroy insects in crop residues.

Plant Selection

Use disease-free and insect-free certified seeds and plants if available. Select plants that are sturdy and have well-developed root systems. Diseases and insects in young seedlings can start in greenhouses or plant beds and later cause heavy losses in the garden when the pests are introduced along with the seedlings. White-flies are an example of an insect that is easy to overlook on nursery stock (Figure 8–3). Always buy plants from a reputable grower who can assure their plants are healthy. Avoid accepting plants from friends if there is any chance of also getting insects or diseases. Examine plants carefully (tops of leaves, bottoms of leaves, stems, and soil) before planting to be sure they are clean. Consider planting **cultivars** identified as resistant to pests.

Resistant cultivars are those that repel, are unattractive to, or otherwise are unsuitable as food for certain pests or that will withstand feeding by certain pests with little reduction in yield or quality. Some cultivars may not taste as good to the pest. Some may possess certain physical or chemical properties that repel or discourage insect feeding or egg laying. Genetic engineering offers potential for incorporating genes into plants that reduce a plant's susceptibility to insect attacks.

Figure 8–3. Always check the undersides of leaves at the nursery. There are lots of whiteflies under this tomato leaf.
Scot Nelson, Flickr CC 0 1.0

By choosing plants carefully, gardeners can avoid some common pest problems. For example, when choosing hollies for landscaping, one could choose native hollies such as yaupon (*Ilex vomitoria*), winterberry (*Ilex verticil-lata*), or American holly (*Ilex opaca*) instead of Japanese hollies, which are much more susceptible to southern red mites. When selecting a squash to grow in a vegetable garden, butternut squash is a good option because it is resistant to squash vine borer. If deer are a problem in a garden, choose a plant that is naturally resistant to deer predation over a plant that is more attractive to deer. For example, a native downy hawthorn (*Crataegus mollis*) would be a better choice than an Eastern redbud (*Cercis canadensis*).

Rotation

Planting two similar crops in successive years tends to increase pest problems. Many vegetables are closely related and have the same pests and diseases. Some insects hibernate in the soil or litter around plants, or lay eggs in or on the host plant. Do not grow the same kind of vegetable in the same place each year (Figure 8–4). Use related crops in a site only once every three or four years. The rotation period for avoiding some tomato diseases may be five to seven years. Another type of crop rotation is to avoid planting root crops in consecutive years in the same row. Crop rotation is most effective on pests that develop on a few plants.

Figure 8–4. Crop rotation is important. Corn had been planted in the garden shown here in the same spot for several years. The soil has been depleted of nutrients, and pest and weed problems have built up.
Danelle Cutting

Interplantings

Avoid placing all plants of one kind together; instead spread them throughout the garden (Figure 8–5). Consider alternating groups of different plants within rows or patches. Insects that become severe on cabbage will probably also infest nearby mustard, broccoli, and collards, but they may not spread to cabbage planted on the other side of the garden. If an insect lays eggs or otherwise attacks a species, the presence of unrelated plants in the area can interrupt the attack's progress by diluting the attractive odor of the preferred plants. Interplanting can also slow the spread of diseases, giving the gardener more time to develop a management strategy. Marigolds and garlic are two plants recommended as insect repellants; however, most of these recommendations are unproven. In some cases, the evidence indicates these plants are not effective repellents.

Figure 8–5. Interplanting chard, kale, and basil with herbaceous ornamentals helps reduce pest and disease build up.
Dinkum, Wikimedia Commons CC0 1.0

Planting Dates
Some insects do not overwinter locally but migrate from more southern states each year. Time plantings so that most of the crop will avoid the peak of insect infestations. Early squash should reach maturity before the pickle-worm arrives. Plant squash seeds or seedlings as early as possible in the season to avoid borers, which lay eggs in July. Early plantings of sweet corn may reduce occurrence of corn earworm, especially if crops are harvested before July 15. Delay planting warm weather crops until after the soil has warmed to avoid seed and root rots and promote vigorous growth. Keep a record of planting dates, where plants or seeds were purchased, and the dates insect problems occur.

Weed Management
Weeds and grasses can harbor both pests and beneficial insects. Spider mite problems are fewer, for example, if broadleaf weeds near fruit trees are removed. If the weeds are closely related to the crop plants, they can harbor pest insects and should be removed. Pests with a wide host range — such as armyworms, crickets, cutworms, flea beetles, grasshoppers, lygus bugs, slugs, snails, stink bugs, and thrips — often inhabit weedy areas and can move to nearby desirable plants. Before planting, mow weedy areas and continue to mow on a regular basis. It is important to mow weeds before a crop is established to prevent insects from moving to the desirable plants. Weeds can be a forage, nectar, or pollen source for beneficial organisms. Milkweed (*Asclepias* spp.) is the larval plant to the monarch butterfly. Weeds that attract insects can be a feeding ground for birds. Finches and pine siskins eat the seeds of goldenrod (*Solidago* spp.) as well as any insect this plant attracts. The flowers of thistle, plantain, knotweed, and dandelion are important to honey bee populations. Removing weeds after flowering but before seed set will provide food for the honey bees but keep the weeds from continuing to spread.

Trap Crops
Another way to manage insect pests is to plant a crop that is very attractive to insects and then treat the trap crop with an insecticide. Trap crops for Japanese beetles include soybeans, zinnias, or white roses. Radishes, turnips, or mustard plants will attract harlequin bugs; radishes attract corn and cabbage maggots; and sunflowers attract *Lygus* plant bugs.

Limitations of Cultural Management
The use of cultural controls for pest management requires advanced planning on the gardener's part. Although it may sound simple to plant resistant landscape plants or vegetable varieties, these varieties must be located and purchased in advance. In some cases, varieties may not be available locally, but special orders can sometimes be placed at a nursery or ordered online.

Crop rotation is a valuable cultural method for reducing insect and disease issues, but many gardeners do not have the room to sufficiently implement this practice. Where space is limited, it may be best to allow the garden to lie fallow for a year or two or more. Consider raised beds with new soil or plant in containers when you know a disease problem exists. At the very least, skip growing the crops, and crop families, that have experienced pest issues.

Mechanical Management

Handpicking
Inspect plants regularly for eggs, immatures, or adults. Many insects are beneficial (Figure 8–6). If they are identified as harmful to the plant handpick as many as possible (Figure 8–7). Almost any large, non-venomous pest can be picked off at any stage. To avoid the task of hand-squashing the pests, knock the insects and egg clusters into a coffee can or quart jar with a small amount of water and a bit of dish detergent.

Traps
Insect traps can assist with detection and management. Use caution, however, as many traps are of limited use

8

or may lure pests to the garden. Light traps, particularly black light or blue light traps (which emit ultraviolet light that is highly attractive to nocturnal insects), are good insect monitoring tools but provide little or no protection for the garden. While they usually capture a tremendous number of insects, a close examination of light-trap collections shows that light traps attract both beneficial and harmful insects that would ordinarily not be found in that area. Those insects attracted but not captured remain in the area, and the destructive ones may cause damage. Also, these traps do not catch some wingless species, as well as those species active only during the day (diurnal) as opposed to active during the night (nocturnal).

Figure 8–6. These tiny white eggs suspended on a stalk are laid by lacewings. Lacewings are beneficial insects whose larvae voraciously consume aphids and other soft-bodied pests.
JKehoe_Photos, Flickr CC BY - 2.0

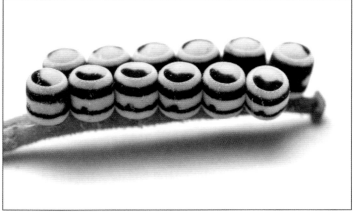

Figure 8–7. Harlequin bug eggs on the underside of a leaf. Harlequin bugs are a pest to the cabbage family and their eggs should be removed.
Matt Bertone

Pheromone traps are used for detecting the presence of pests or sometimes for disrupting insect mating habits. Adult females produce and release a chemical odor attractive to males of the same species. Traps are "scented" with these odors. Rainfall, cool temperatures, wind speed, and wind direction can reduce the lures' effectiveness. Heat, sunlight, or improper storage can damage scented lures. The best success occurs when the pest density is low and movement into the area is minimal.

Some physical traps are easy to make from materials around the home. A shallow tin of beer partially embedded in the soil makes an effective trap for slugs and snails (Figure 8–8). Slugs hiding under slightly propped boards during the daylight hours should be removed and disposed of daily. Yellow plastic dishpans filled with soapy water can attract aphids.

Yellow sticky traps made with boards painted yellow and lightly coated with oil or grease will catch whiteflies and cucumber beetles (Figure 8–9). Commercial sticky traps are available through some catalogs.

Figure 8–8. A beer trap set out to catch slugs and snails.
SteveR-, Flickr CC BY - 2.0

Figure 8–9. A yellow sticky trap captures the adults of whiteflies, cucumber beetles, fungus gnats, and other winged insects. This interrupts their life cycle and helps manage these pests.
Mike Linksvayer, Flickr CC0

8

Barriers

Mechanical barriers can help to exclude some pests but will not be effective if the pest population is large. Aluminum foil and other reflective mulches can repel aphids. Crushed eggshells or hydrated lime spread around plants discourages slugs. Copper tape can be an effective barrier for slugs (Figure 8–10). While heavy mulch is good for weed management, it gives slugs a place to hide.

Figure 8–10. Copper tape can be an effective barrier for slugs, but beware of sharp edges. This is most practical for small garden beds or containers.
Kathleen Moore, CC BY - 2.0

Collars made of cardboard, tin cans, or aluminum foil and inserted halfway into the soil are effective barriers to cutworms (Figure 8–11). They prevent cutworms from being able to feed on seedling stems. Use of screening around potato storage areas can prevent the entry of tuberworm moths. Mounding soil around grapevines can prevent the emergence of grape root borer moths.

Figure 8–11. Cardboard plant collars are effective barriers to cutworms.
Kathleen Moore, CC BY - 2.0

Cheesecloth screens for **cold frames** and **hot beds** prevent insects from laying eggs but also reduce light. **Floating row covers** of spun polyethylene are a little more expensive, but they can be quite effective at excluding insects (Figure 8–12). Many commercial growers use them, particularly on cole crops and strawberries. Sticky barriers on the trunks of trees and woody shrubs prevent damage from some crawling insects.

Figure 8–12. Floating row covers prevent some adult insects from flying around to deposit eggs on new plants.
Scot Nelson, Flickr CC 0 1.0

Kaolin clay, sometimes referred to as "China clay," can be used to form a thin film on leaves and fruit and can protect plants from Colorado potato beetle, tarnished plant bug, leafhopper, mite, thrips, flea beetle, and Japanese beetle damage. This film irritates the bodies of insects and reduces their feeding. Mix 1 quart of clay with 2 gallons of water and 1 tablespoon of liquid soap in a sprayer. Continuously agitate the sprayer to prevent clumping of the clay. Reapply every one to three weeks. This barrier is preventive; it will not work if an insect pest is already established.

Net-covered cages over young seedlings help prevent insect, bird, and rabbit damage. Using wire collars around tree trunks may prevent damage from bark eating mammals such as voles. Bird netting can be draped over fruiting plants to prevent predation when fruit is ripe. Use paper bags to cover ears of corn to keep birds and insects out. Be sure to wait until pollination is complete before bagging ears. Electric fence barriers will prevent large mammals such as deer or raccoons from feeding on plants, though fences can be expensive and time consuming to install.

Pruning and Raking

Some pests, such as the azalea stem borer and the dogwood club gall (Figure 8–13), can be managed by pruning

8

infected twigs out of infested plants and destroying them. If twigs infested with dogwood twig borers are pruned in late spring or early summer, the plants should still bloom without any problem the following spring. However, if infested twigs are removed in late summer, a larger portion of the branch must be removed (the larvae bore inside the stem), and the plant will not have time to set new flower buds before winter. Raking the fallen twigs of pecans, oaks, elms, hickories, and other shade trees in the fall removes the larvae of twig girdlers. These long horned beetles overwinter as eggs or grubs in fallen twigs. New beetles emerge during the following fall to lay eggs. Camellia leaf gall, caused by *Exobasidium camelliae*, is kept under control by removing infected leaves before the fungus matures to its reproductive stage.

Figure 8–13. Dogwood club galls should be pruned off and destroyed as a means of managing midges.
Sally Jennings (NATT-at-NKM), Flickr CC BY- 2.0

Water Sprays and Irrigation

Aphids and other insects often feed on the underside of leaves. Spraying infested plants with a strong stream of water dislodges and kills many spider mites, aphids, and other relatively fragile insects. Rain is one of the greatest natural management strategies for spider mites; populations tend to build up during dry weather. Cool, cloudy weather promotes fungal pathogens which attack chinch bugs, spider mites, aphids, and other pests, keeping populations low. Proper irrigation can help reduce the likelihood of pest problems.

Hose adapters can be purchased that have a motion sensor and can spray a stream of water at an animal such as a squirrel, deer, or raccoon. These are most effective if pointed at a specific area needing protection, such as a vegetable garden bed.

Properly irrigated plants will be able to better withstand damage from pests. A well-watered, healthy lawn will be able to naturally out-compete weeds. A tree that is not experiencing water stress will be able to withstand some root predation from voles or twig predation from deer.

Heat Treatment

It is possible to use propane flamers to kill Colorado potato beetle larvae on potatoes without killing the plant. In addition, flames can be used to kill annual weeds. Extreme caution should be used when using fire in the garden. Some hot water treatments can be used to reduce disease when saving seed.

Frightening Devices

Frightening is a tool that can vary greatly in its effectiveness. It requires knowledge of the pest and vigilance so the pest is not desensitized to any one technique. Frightening devices include: reflective objects, noise makers, human or **predator effigies**, lights, lasers, pyrotechnics, guard animals, and ultrasonic devices. When using a frightening device, it is important to consider the pest's ability to see or hear the stimulus. Many birds have excellent eyesight, so a scarecrow may deter starlings from a yard if moved frequently (Figure 8–14). Lighting a garden at night and playing a radio can be effective in deterring raccoons but does little to stop small rodents. Insects do not register sight and sound the way birds and mammals do, so frightening is not a technique used in insect management.

Figure 8–14. A scarecrow is one type of frightening device. For it to be effective, it needs to move around the garden often.
Kathleen Moore, CC BY - 2.0

Limitations of Mechanical Management

Mechanical methods require time and can be more practical for small gardens. For example, the use of row covers to exclude pests can be effective. Depending on the size of the garden, however, it may be a large expense and time investment to place the row covers, remove them to allow for pollination, and replace after pollination. Handpicking also has limitations. Once crop damage is noticeable, it might be too late for handpicking to be effective. This is why observing is so important to any IPM strategy. Actively monitoring the crops and looking for the first signs of damage will keep the insect populations at a level that will allow handpicking to be successful.

Biological Management: Use of Predators, Parasitoids, and Pathogens

Biological management is the process of reducing a pest population by using predators, **parasites**, or disease organisms that ordinarily occur in nature. The greatest single factor in keeping plant-feeding insects from overwhelming the rest of the world is that they are food for other insects.

Insect and mite populations are usually relatively concentrated. Thus, one or two lawns in a neighborhood may have copious numbers of millipedes or green June beetle grubs while a lawn two houses away may have almost none. When pests become numerous, parasitoids and predators are attracted to them and reduce the pest species in that area. The parasitoids and predators then disperse to seek out more prey.

Parasitoids and **predators** are available through garden catalogs and gardening magazines, but some insects sold as biological control agents—such as praying mantises and lady beetles—are not very effective for home gardeners. This is because they are either highly mobile (lady beetles) or nonselective, eating as many **beneficial insects** as pests, and potentially cannibalistic (praying mantises). It is far more effective to create an environment that attracts and supports naturally occurring predators and parasitoids. Tolerate some pests in the yard; look at them as food for the beneficial insects. If beneficial insects have no food, they will move to another location. Minimize the use of pesticides that can kill beneficial insects as well as pests.

Predators are insects (or other animals, such as spiders, frogs, and birds) that catch and devour other creatures (called prey), usually killing and consuming them in a single meal. The prey are generally smaller and weaker than the predators. Predators are typically very active and have long life cycles. Some examples include ground beetles, lady beetles, lacewings, wheel bugs (Figure 8–15), hover flies, and predatory mites.

Figure 8–15. A wheel bug is a predatory insect that helps to naturally manage insect populations in a garden.
Danelle Cutting

Parasites are organisms that live on or in the body of a living organism (called a **host**) from which they get their food during at least one stage of the parasite's existence. The parasite can gain enough nutrients and resources to survive without killing the host or preventing it from reproducing. Parasites tend to have a very short life cycle. Some examples include nematodes, fleas, and ticks. Biological control parasites are quite different: they are close in size to their hosts, they live about the same length of time, most are incapable of reproducing in or on their hosts (they require a free-living period), and they usually kill their hosts. For this reason, the term parasitoid was coined in 1913 to describe those insects, such as ichneumonid wasps and tachinid flies, that parasitize and kill other insects.

A **parasitoid** is an organism that gains nutrients and resources from a host and ends up killing or sterilizing the host in the process. There are two major categories of parasitoids. Ectoparasitoids attach themselves to the outside of a host and feed by sucking body fluids through the host's skin (Figure 8–16). Endoparasitoids have eggs that are deposited by an adult female inside the body of a host. The eggs hatch, and the larvae consume the host from the inside (Figure 8–17). The most common parasitoids are found in the Hymenoperta and Diptera orders. Some examples of parasitoids are parasitic wasps, bees, and tachinid flies (Figure 8–18). The adults will feed on nectar, pollen, or honeydew. Many adult parasitoids are very tiny, so they may be overlooked in a garden. But they play an

8

important role in keeping some pests populations under control. Sometimes parasitoids fail to appear even when many pests invade a landscape, several acres, or even hundreds of acres. This happens when environmental conditions are favorable for the pests but not the parasitoids, or when new pests invade a region where there are few or no natural predators. Japanese beetles and gypsy moths, for instance, are harder to manage because they are introduced insects that do not have naturally occurring predators, parasitoids, or pathogens to keep their populations under control.

Beneficial nematodes feed on insects such as cutworms, squash vine borers, pillbugs, grubs, fungus gnats, root weevils, and armyworms. Effective use of beneficial nematodes requires knowledge of the nematode and the insect that warrants management. Producers ship beneficial nematodes in the form of gels, dry granules, clay, and water-filled sponges.

All of these forms dissolve in water. Nematodes are sensitive to ultraviolet light, heat, and dehydration. The best time to apply is early morning or late afternoon when light and temperatures are lower. Because nematodes move in the soil on the film of water that surrounds soil particles, the area should be watered before releasing nematodes or lightly watered afterward. High-nitrogen fertilizer can reduce nematode effectiveness, so manufacturers recommend not applying fertilizer for two weeks before or after releasing nematodes.

Pathogens are disease-causing organisms, including viruses, bacteria, and fungi that kill or debilitate their hosts. They are usually specific to certain insects.

Figure 8–16. Braconid wasps pupating on a hornworm larva.
Connie Schultz

Figure 8–17. A tiny parasitic wasp, *Aphidius*, injecting its egg into an aphid. This endoparasitoid consumes the aphid and then emerges from an aphid mummy as an adult. The lime green aphids are free of parasitoids, while the bloated brown ones are parasitized.
Debbie Roos

Figure 8-18. Adult tachinid flies (left) and a tachinid fly egg on the head of a leaf-footed bug (*Leptoglossus* spp.) (right). Some species of tachinids lay eggs that are eaten by a host and emerge in the host's stomach while others inject eggs directly into a host's body.
Matt Bertone

The most successful example of biological management is the use of bacteria to kill caterpillars. ***Bacillus thuringiensis*** (Bt) is a bacterium that produces a toxin that destroys the midgut of an insect. Several formulations are available that provide effective management of more than 400 insect species without harming people or domestic animals. For example, Bt *Israelenisis* works on mosquitos and Bt *Kurstaki* works on Lepidopterans. Be sure to use the proper strain for the pest under management.

Bacillus thuringiensis is quite slow in its action. For example, caterpillars that consume some of the spores will stop eating within two hours, but may continue to live and move around until they die, which may be 72 hours later. When this occurs, the untrained gardener may assume the material was ineffective because of the continued pest activity and impatiently apply a chemical pesticide. Some insects have developed resistance to Bt because of its overuse on some crops.

Nosema locustae is a disease organism that shows some promise for managing grasshoppers. There are claims that these fungal microsporidum may be effective for up to five years after initial application. In some areas, this pathogen is available commercially under different trade names. It is still too early to make extensive claims about its effectiveness in home gardens.

Limitations of Biological Management
Biological management can be an effective means of killing harmful pests. Timing, however, can be a challenge. For instance, a pest may be identified for which a predator is commercially available, but by the time the predator arrives and the plant is treated, an unacceptable amount of damage may have already occurred. If the predator is ordered beforehand, it must be stored until the pest appears, and the predator may have a short shelf life.

Purchased natural predators are often effective for only a short period because they tend to move out of the area in which they are released. For example, some species of the western lady beetles sold for biological management instinctively fly long distances after hibernation to reach a source of aphids. Thus, when lady beetles from California find themselves released into a yard in North Carolina, they automatically fly far away before they begin to feed. Natural predators can be very effective in greenhouses where they are held captive.

Chemical Management

If the pest has been correctly identified and is still a problem after other management strategies have been implemented, chemical options may be considered as a last resort. Herbicides are available to kill weeds, insecticides to kill insects, and fungicides and antibiotics to manage diseases. It is imperative that the chemical is labeled both for management of the offending pest and for use on the specific type of plant upon which it is to be sprayed. All users are legally required to follow the instructions on the pesticide label including the amount and timing of application.

Pesticides and pesticide safety are covered in Appendix B.

Limitations of Chemical Management
Misuse of pesticides can result in killing all of the insects vulnerable to the active ingredients, leaving only the strongest to mate and reproduce. This results in pests quickly evolving resistance to the chemicals. In addition, pesticides can kill beneficial insects as well as pest species. Because pest populations generally recover more quickly, the pest problem may soon be much worse than it was initially. Pesticide applications can also lead to outbreaks of secondary pests and can have adverse impact on nontarget organisms that eat insects or leaves contaminated with pesticide. Pesticides may be carried into streams by stormwater runoff and cause unintended consequences. Further potential problems with chemical management are direct hazards to the user and secondary exposure of family, friends, and pets to pesticide residue.

Formulating an IPM Plan

IPM combines background information about a pest problem with a strategy that fits the situation. It will help a gardener decide:
1. Which pests are present and if they are in high enough concentrations to cause problems.
2. Which control measures should be taken to manage a problem.
3. How to evaluate the success of the control measures.

An IPM plan has five steps:
Step 1: Monitor. Inspect plants on a regular basis.
Step 2: Identify. Accurately diagnose the problem using information about the plant, the environment, and the pest.
Step 3: Assess. Use thresholds to determine if action is necessary. Will the plant survive? Will yield decrease or will the appearance be compromised beyond your threshold level?
Step 4: Implement. Formulate an action strategy based on all options available. This is the "integrated" part of IPM. Consider what will be economical, physically feasible, effective, and least toxic.
Step 5: Evaluate. What were the results of the action? Did it produce the desired results?

8

Follow the steps listed here to create an IPM plan.

Step 1: Monitor

One of the great joys of gardening is observing changes through the seasons. To effectively monitor a garden, it is important to conduct a complete survey identifying all the plants, including cultivars. Walking through the yard at least twice a month or as often as twice a week in warm weather can help a gardener recognize problems as soon as they arise and before they become difficult or impossible to control. A "monitoring kit" (Figure 8–19) consisting of a garden journal, pencil, camera, hand lens, gloves, and pruners will make it easy for a gardener to conduct regular inspections. Garden journals help gardeners document changes in the landscape. See Appendix A for more information on how to create an effective garden journal. Monitoring documentation should include overall conditions and any abnormalities. If a plant looks different from acceptable norms, evaluate the irrigation schedule, fertility, soil pH, and other factors that might be responsible for the change before assuming there is a pest problem. Examine plants carefully for developing infestations. If any pests are observed, take note of what kind of damage is occurring. If there is a history of pest problems, keep a close watch on those plants for any sign of reoccurrence. Gardeners often use pesticides when problems seem to occur "overnight." Many of these overnight events actually take two to three weeks to develop but seem to occur rapidly because no one noticed initial signs. A regular, systematic check for pests helps avoid such situations.

The effort devoted to monitoring for pests should be proportional to the value of the plants, the time available, the life cycle of the pest (that is, its potential damage if left unchecked), and the skill level of the observer. For example, a privacy hedge would have a less frequent monitoring plan than a planting of prize-winning roses.

Step 2: Identify

The only way to effectively combat a problem is to diagnose it properly. See "Diagnostics," chapter 7, for help with diagnosing plant problems.

Step 3: Assess

Several factors should be weighed before deciding if action should be taken, including the value of the plant in question, the likelihood the problem could spread to other plants, and the cost to treat the problem.

Figure 8–19. An IPM monitoring kit, including hand pruners, a plastic bag for collecting samples, gloves, pencils, a garden journal, a hand lens, a camera, and a bag for easy transport to and from the garden.
Jim Janke

It is easy to understand that if an insect eats a leaf, less photosynthesis takes place and the plant will grow more slowly. Plants can often withstand a great deal of **defoliation**, however, before serious problems occur because the sunlight going through a hole at the top of the plants will hit a lower leaf and increase photosynthesis there. Heavy feeding on woody ornamentals early in the season is more damaging to plants than heavy feeding in early autumn when leaves are about to fall anyway. The level of injury a plant can withstand without unacceptable harm is called a threshold. A level of plant damage perceived to be unacceptable by the owner is called an aesthetic threshold. Below a threshold, no pest control action is required; above a threshold, corrective action should be taken. That said, to keep damage below the threshold requires action before the threshold is reached.

Homeowners can set their own thresholds by determining the level of acceptable damage to the plant's health and visual appeal. The next step is to approximate the number of pests that cause the level of damage homeowners can tolerate. Making this estimate requires monitoring, recording pest counts, and deciding whether unacceptable damage is occurring or whether the pest population is going to reach damaging levels. Some pests have several generations a year, while others have a few generations or only a single generation. It is important to accurately identify the pest to determine if population levels will increase until food sources are exhausted or when weather conditions might limit population growth. Diseases are treated differently than insects because remedial action is not available. Still, it makes sense to tolerate low levels of disease. Tolerance levels for weeds and aesthetic thresholds are mostly a matter of individual preference.

Defoliation does not necessarily threaten the life of most landscape plants, but it is unsightly. Even in this situation, thresholds may vary. For example, a foundation plant next to an entrance will likely have an aesthetic threshold that is lower than plants on the side of the yard. Some plants do not lend themselves to thresholds. Roses, which are highly valued for their appearance, are also highly susceptible to several pests. The threshold for these plants may be zero, but most plants in an urban landscape will tolerate some damage.

Using a threshold to make pest control decisions supports the idea that a healthy urban ecosystem contains a diversity of species. A diverse species community is more likely to stabilize at a desirable level and less likely to suffer major pest outbreaks. Recognizing and supporting the beauty of the system as a whole rather than intervening heavily on behalf of individual elements allows for balance rather than perfection.

Some problems may be so severe that little can be done to save the plant. For example, if a tree located next to a new patio has a shelf fungus and oozing cracks in the bark, it could have internal decay because of root loss and might need to be removed.

Step 4: Implement
Healthy plants are better able to resist pests. In many urban environments, selection of the wrong cultivar, improper placement, or poor maintenance contribute to pest problems. For example, sun-loving plants placed in the shade will be weak and more susceptible to pests. Plants watered too much or too little will be more vulnerable to certain diseases. Weeds in a lawn often suggest problems such as soil compaction, mowing too short, or a pH imbalance. Overfertilizing can lead to lush growth that is more easily attacked by insects. Changing conditions in the landscape to improve plant health will help eliminate or reduce pest problems.

The saying "the best defense is a good offense" could not be more true for integrated pest management. The objective is to deny pests the food, shelter, proper temperature, and other elements they need. Denying pests the basics reduces their growth or reproduction. It is important to understand a bit about pest biology, behavior, and ecology. For example, certain weeds need full sunlight for germination, so mulching around plants can deprive weed seeds of the sunlight required. Locating sun-loving plants where they receive full sun encourages leaves to dry quickly and deprives the fungal organisms that cause leaf diseases of the moisture they require to infect leaves. By knowing when a certain insect flies around in its reproductive stage, gardeners can set up sticky traps to interrupt the breeding cycle. Gardeners who use their knowledge of site selection and management practices can limit pests to small populations that cause little damage.

Some pests have natural enemies—either predators or parasitoids—that can be established, enhanced, or conserved in an area or purchased for release. Many beneficial species provide at least partial control of native pests. To support a population of beneficial insects in a yard, gardeners must tolerate a few pests. This "food" will ensure that beneficial insects stay rather than move to better feeding grounds. Established plantings that attract beneficial insects also reduce the use of pesticides that can kill beneficial organisms as well as the pests they feed upon. Deliberate release of predators and parasitoids is not a casual effort. Success requires careful study. Before using this strategy, find a reliable source of beneficial insects, learn when, where, and how to release them, and know which pest species they target.

8

Step 5: Evaluate

Once implemented, an IPM plan must be constantly reevaluated. Because biological systems can behave in unexpected ways, always check the effectiveness of a decision and make changes if needed. Also, as landscape plants mature, roots will occupy more area, shading may increase, and other changes can take place that alter the relationship between plants and pests. It is important to keep records of pest problems, actions taken, and other factors that will help inform a pest management strategy in the future.

Case Study—Think IPM: Failing Juniper

Step 1: Monitor

Using a notebook, journal, or spreadsheet you frequently visit your yard and make notes about the condition of the landscape plants and any insect or disease activity you see. In June you noticed that a juniper tree in the backyard was starting to look sick, and by August the needles look chewed and part of the tree is defoliated. You also see several small 1- to 3-inch-wide brown, carrot-shaped bags hanging from the branches.

Step 2: Identify

Use the diagnostic procedures from chapter 7, "Diagnostics," to identify the pest as bagworms *Theridopteryx ephemeraeformis* (Figure 8–20).

Step 3: Assess

You might consider replacing the juniper with a dwarf magnolia *(Magnolia grandiflora 'Little Gem')* or Eastern arborvitae *(Thuja occidentalis)*, both of which are resistant to bagworms. However, the expense of removal and replacement, along with the years needed for the new tree to grow to maturity, inspire you to review treatment options for your existing tree instead.

- Type "bagworms site: ncsu.edu" into your Internet search engine to get research-based information about this pest from NC State University.

- From your research, you discover that healthy plants can overcome a bagworm infestation, even if the plant has been severely defoliated. Bagworms are usually found on conifers such as arborvitae, spruce, juniper, cedar, and Leyland cypress, so you go back into the landscape to check other plants for infestation. Information on their life cycle is useful in determining the best strategies and timing for management. Female bagworms never leave their bag, and after mating, they lay eggs inside the bag and die. The eggs overwinter inside these bags and hatch in May and June. The larvae will then either catch the wind and "balloon" over to another plant or begin feeding on the plant where they hatched. They create their own bags out of plant foliage. As the caterpillars grow, they expand their bags. If a bag is cut open during this larval stage, a tan or blackish caterpillar will be found inside. The larvae feed on the plant until pupating into moths in August and September.

- Some management options include cultural (physical removal of the bags), biological (using natural predators), and chemical control. Physical removal of the bags is a possibility, but if bags are too high they may be difficult or dangerous to reach. Another method is encouraging natural predators, such as tachinid flies, parasitoid wasps, sparrows, and finches. Plant beneficial flowers, such as asters (*Aster* spp.), which are nectar plants for insect predators, and fruiting shrubs such as service berry (*Amelanchier canadensis*) to attract birds. Another option according to the *North Carolina Agricultural Chemicals Manual* would be management using Bt (*Bacillus thuringiensis*). Note that applications are most effective when larvae are young, in the early summer. Bt management is not effective other times of the year.

Figure 8–20. Bagworms *(Thyridopteryx ephemeraeformis ephemeraeformis)* on a juniper.
Delaware Cooperative Extension, Flickr CC BY 2.0

8

Step 4: Implement

Mechanical management by physically removing every bag you can reach may be your best option. In addition, biological management by planting asters along the fence line near the juniper will attract natural predators. Cultural management is another important strategy. Keeping trees well-watered and avoiding pruning will minimize stress.

Step 5: Evaluate

In the spring evaluate the tree's health. Continue to monitor the tree weekly and remove any bags that you see. If bagworms reoccur early in the spring, consider bacterial management, like Bt (*Bacillus thuringiensis*), which is effective in the larval stage.

Frequently Asked Questions

1. *How can I reduce pesticide use in my yard?* (Figure 8–21)

Prevention is the key: Select plants adapted to our environment, plant them in locations where they can thrive, and ensure they have adequate water and nutrients. Follow the IPM strategies outlined in this chapter. Make a habit of monitoring the yard and taking note of any changes. If a pest is discovered, accurately identify both the pest and the host plant. Work through a treatment strategy, starting with correcting any cultural issues such as plant placement, irrigation, or fertilizer issues. If treatment is deemed necessary, start with mechanical or biological controls. Evaluate the success of treatment. If cultural changes or mechanical or biological controls are ineffective, consider chemicals specifically labeled for the problem. Carefully follow the label instructions for timing and application amounts.

2. *I wish to release ladybugs in my garden this year. When do I buy them?*

Lady beetles/ladybugs have a limited shelf life, and once released tend to fly a distance before they settle down somewhere far from where they were released. A much more effective strategy is to create a healthy environment in your yard to attract native beneficial insects. If you build it, they will come. Tolerate some pests in your yard; look at them as food for the beneficial insects. Minimize your use of pesticides. Add flowering plants that attract beneficial insects. Plants can be found by searching the NC State Extension Gardener Plant Toolbox.

Figure 8–21. Using IPM techniques can help many gardeners avoid the use of pesticides.
Kathleen Moore, CC BY - 2.0

8

Further Reading

Citizen's Guide to Pest Control and Pesticide Safety. Washington, DC: United States Environmental Protection Agency, 1995. PDF file. EPA 730-K-95-001.

Cloyd, Raymond A., Philip L. Nixon, and Nancy R. Pataky. *IPM for Gardeners: A Guide to Integrated Pest Management.* Portland, Oregon: Timber Press, Inc., 2004. Print.

Marshall Bradley, Fern, Barbara W. Ellis, and Deborah L. Martin, eds. *The Organic Gardener's Handbook of Natural Pest and Disease Control: A Complete Guide to Maintaining a Healthy Garden and Yard the Earth-Friendly Way.* New York: Rodale Press, Inc., 2009. Print.

Olkowski, William, et al. *The Gardener's Guide to Common-Sense Pest Control: Completely Revised and Updated.* Newtown, Connecticut: The Taunton Press, Inc., 2013. Print.

Applying Pesticides Correctly: (Virginia Core Manual): *A Guide for Private Applicators, Commercial Applicators, and Registered Technicians in Virginia.* Blacksburg, Virginia: Virginia Cooperative Extension Service, 2012. Print. Publication 456-210.

Wamsley, Mary Ann, and Donna M. Vermeire, eds. *Ornamental and Turfgrass Pest Control.* Washington, DC: United States Environmental Protection Agency, 1976. PDF file. EPA 730-R-76-104.

For More Information

http://go.ncsu.edu/fmi_ipm

Contributors

Authors:
Steven Frank, Professor and Extension Specialist, Department of Entomology and Plant Pathology
Lucy Bradley, Professor and Extension Specialist, Urban Horticulture, NC State University; Director, NC State Extension Master Gardener program
Kathleen Moore, Urban Horticulturist, Department of Horticultural Science

Contributions by Extension Agents: David Goforth, Danelle Cutting, Tim Mathews, Alison Arnold, Pam Jones, Peg Godwin

Contributions by Extension Master Gardener Volunteers: Louise Romanow, Linda Alford, Patricia Brown, Marjorie Rayburn, Jackie Weedon, Karen Damari, Connie Schultz, Sue Davis, Edna Burger, Kim Curlee, Caro Dosé

Copy Editor: Barbara Scott

Chapter 8 Cover Photo: Kathleen Moore, CC BY - 2.0

Based in part on text from the 1998 Extension Master Gardener manual prepared by:
Erv Evans, Extension Associate, Department of Horticultural Science
Mike Linker, IPM Coordinator, Department of Crop Science
Steve Toth, Extension Specialist, Department of Entomology
Stephen Bambara, Extension Specialist, Department of Entomology
James R. Baker, Extension Specialist, Department of Entomology
Ken Sorensen, Extension Specialist, Department of Entomology

How to Cite this Chapter: Frank, S., L.K. Bradley and K.A. Moore. 2022. Integrated Pest Management, Chpt 8. In: K.A. Moore, and. L. K. Bradley (eds). *North Carolina Extension Gardener Handbook*, 2nd ed. NC State Extension, Raleigh, NC. <https://content.ces.ncsu.edu/extension-gardener-handbook/8-integrated-pest-management-ipm>

Lawns

Objectives

This chapter will teach people to:
- Understand the basic functions of turfgrass in the landscape.
- Select the best turfgrass for a given home lawn setting.
- Establish a lawn from seed or sod.
- Implement environmentally friendly maintenance practices: watering, mowing, aerating, and fertilizing.
- Use IPM techniques to determine pest problems and their management.
- Become familiar with lawn alternatives.

9

Introduction

Lawns are smooth, living carpets that add beauty and recreational space to a home. As grass grows, it helps the environment by stabilizing soil and reducing air pollution, noise, heat, dust, and glare. Surveys show that an attractive, well-landscaped lawn can even add to a home's value. By choosing well-adapted grasses and planting them in the right location, a lush lawn will grow with minimal maintenance and pesticide use.

What to Plant

Whether you are establishing a new lawn or renovating an existing one, deciding which type of grass to plant is the first step. A number of factors should be considered, including region, climate, intended use or wear at the site, and desired appearance. Different types of grass thrive in different conditions, so it is important to pick a variety adapted to your location.

North Carolina is divided into three major regions: coastal plain, piedmont, and mountains (Figure 9–1). Both cool-season (northern) and warm-season (southern) grasses are grown in North Carolina (Table 9–1). Cool-season grasses grow best in the spring and fall and less actively in the summer. They stay reasonably green in the winter. Tall fescue, Kentucky bluegrass, fine fescue, and perennial ryegrass are common types of cool-season grasses. Table 9–2 lists ratings for the performance of various cultivars of these grasses in North Carolina. Warm-season grasses are slow to green up in the spring, grow best in the summer, and go dormant after the first heavy frost. Table 9–3 lists many warm-season cultivars. Consider each site's characteristics and your goals for the site to determine which types of grass are appropriate. Choose a grass that best meets color, density, and texture preferences. Choose a tough, aggressive, wear-tolerant grass where heavy traffic is expected. When making a selection, remember to consider the amount of time, effort and money needed for turfgrass maintenance.

Table 9–1. Characteristics of Principal Lawn Grasses Grown in North Carolina

Region	Lawn Grass	Can Be Seeded	Shade	Heat	Cold	Drought	Wear	Color	Texture	Preferred Season	Rate of Establishment[a]	Cutting Height (in.)	Fertilizer (lb N/1,000 sq ft/yr)	Mowing Frequency[b]
			Tolerance Ratings					**Appearance**					**Maintenance**	
MOUNTAINS-FOOTHILLS	Kentucky bluegrass	Yes	4	3	5	4	4	Medium-Dark	Medium	Fall	Moderate	1.5–2.5	2–3	Med
	Kentucky bluegrass/ fine fescue mix	Yes	4	3	5	4	3	Medium-Dark	Fine-Medium	Fall	Moderate	1.5–2.5	2–3	Med
	Kentucky bluegrass/ perennial ryegrass mix	Yes	4	3	5	4	5	Medium-Dark	Medium	Fall	Fast	2–3	2.5–3.5	Med-High
	Kentucky bluegrass/ tall fescue mix	Yes	4	4	5	5	5	Medium-Dark	Medium-Coarse	Fall	Fast	2.5–3.5	2–3	High
	Kentucky bluegrass/ tall fescue/fine fescue mix	Yes	5	4	5	5	5	Medium-Dark	Medium-Coarse	Fall	Fast	2.5–3.5	2–3	High
	Tall fescue	Yes	4	4	5	5	5	Medium	Medium-Coarse	Fall	Fast	2.5–3.5	2.5–3.5	High
	Zoysiagrass	Yes	4	5	4	6	4	Medium	Fine	Spring-Summer	Very slow	0.75–2	1–3	Low

Key for tolerance ratings: 6—Excellent, 5—Very good, 4—Good, 3—Fair, 2—Poor, 1—Very poor

Note: Some improved cultivars are better adapted and more pleasing in appearance than the comparison rating provided for a given lawn grass. Check with your local Cooperative Extension center concerning specific cultivars that have characteristics of interest to you. See Table 9–4 for suggested months of establishment.

[a] Establishment rate is dictated by planting dates, seeding and planting rate, intensity of culture, and environment.

[b] Mowing frequency is dictated by season, intensity of management, and use.

9

Table 9–1. Characteristics of Principal Lawn Grasses Grown in North Carolina

Region	Lawn Grass	Can Be Seeded	Tolerance Ratings					Appearance		Preferred Season	Rate of Establishment[a]	Maintenance		
			Shade	Heat	Cold	Drought	Wear	Color	Texture			Cutting Height (in.)	Fertilizer (lb N/1,000 sq ft/yr)[a]	Mowing Frequency[b]
PIEDMONT	Bermudagrass (common)	Yes	1	5	1	6	6	Medium	Medium	Spring-Summer	Fast	0.75–2	4–4.5	Med-High
	Bermudagrass (hybrid)	No	1	5	2	6	6	Light-Dark	Fine	Spring-Summer	Moderate	0.75–2	3–6	High
	Bahiagrass	Yes	4	4	2	6	4	Medium-Dark	Coarse	Spring-Summer	Moderate	2–4	1	High
	Centipedegrass	Yes	4	4	2	4	1	Light	Coarse	Spring-Summer	Slow	1–1.5	1–2	Low
	Kentucky bluegrass/ tall fescue mix	Yes	4	4	5	5	5	Medium-Dark	Medium-Coarse	Fall	Fast	2.5–3.5	2–4	High
	Kentucky bluegrass/ tall fescue/ fine fescue mix	Yes	5	4	5	5	5	Medium-Dark	Medium-Coarse	Fall	Fast	2.5–3.5	2–4	High
	St. Augustine grass	No	5	5	2	4	1	Medium-Dark	Coarse	Spring-Summer	Moderate	2.5–4	2–3	Med-High
	Tall fescue	Yes	4	4	5	5	5	Medium	Coarse	Fall	Fast	2.5–3.5	2–4	High
	Zoysiagrass	Yes	4	5	4	6	4	Medium-Dark	Fine-Medium	Spring-Summer	Very slow	0.75–2	1–3	Low-Med
SANDHILLS-COASTAL PLAIN	Bermudagrass (common)	Yes	1	5	1	6	6	Medium	Medium	Spring-Summer	Fast	0.75–2	3–4.5	Med-High
	Bermudagrass (hybrid)	No	1	5	2	6	6	Light-Dark	Fine	Spring-Summer	Moderate	0.75–2	3–6	Very High
	Bahiagrass	Yes	4	5	2	6	4	Medium-Dark	Coarse	Spring-Summer	Moderate	2–4	1	High
	Centipedegrass	Yes	4	4	2	4	2	Light	Coarse	Spring-Summer	Slow	1–1.5	1–2	Low
	St. Augustinegrass	No	5	5	2	4	2	Medium-Dark	Coarse	Spring-Summer	Moderate	2.5–4	2–4	Med-High
	Tall fescue	Yes	4	4	5	5	5	Medium	Coarse	Fall	Fast	2.5–3.5	2–4	High
	Zoysiagrass	Yes	4	5	4	6	4	Medium-Dark	Fine-Medium	Spring-Summer	Very slow	0.75–2	2–4	Low-High

Key for tolerance ratings: 6—Excellent, 5—Very good, 4—Good, 3—Fair, 2—Poor, 1—Very poor

Abbreviations: Med—Medium, Spr—Spring, Sum—Summer

Note: Some improved cultivars are better adapted and more pleasing in appearance than the comparison rating provided for a given lawn grass. Check with your local Cooperative Extension center concerning specific cultivars that have characteristics of interest to you. See Table 9–4 for suggested months of establishment.

[a] Establishment rate is dictated by planting dates, seeding and planting rate, intensity of culture, and environment.

[b] Mowing frequency is dictated by season, intensity of management, and use.

Figure 9–1. A regional map showing the mountain, piedmont, and coastal plain regions of North Carolina.

Mountains · Piedmont · Coastal Plain

Cool-Season Grasses

Tall fescue, Kentucky bluegrass, fine fescues, and perennial ryegrass are cool-season perennial grasses used for lawns, mostly in the mountain and piedmont regions of North Carolina (Table 9–1). Unlike warm-season grasses, cool-season grasses remain green throughout most of the winter. They are better adapted to the mountains and piedmont and suffer more stress in the coastal plain. These grasses perform best in spring and fall and have a tendency to show signs of stress in the summer. Cool-season grasses are best seeded in early fall, but fair results may be obtained from seeding in early spring (mid-February to late March in the North Carolina piedmont). Generally, late winter or spring seeding of these grasses is not recommended.

Tall Fescue

Tall fescue is best adapted to the NC mountains and piedmont but can be successfully maintained on the heavy silt loams in the coastal plain (Figure 9–2). It is a reliable performer and easily started from seed. It is the best grass to plant for a green lawn year-round. Tall fescue thrives in sun or medium shade in the mountains and piedmont. It will not perform well in full sun in the coastal plain, especially if the soil is sandy. It can be seeded by itself or mixed with Kentucky bluegrass or fine fescue, or both, particularly where shade is a concern. Tall fescue is a bunch-type grass, so damaged or bare areas will need to be re-seeded. It exhibits good disease resistance, drought tolerance, and cold tolerance. It tolerates moderate traffic and persists with minimum care. Several improved tall fescue cultivars have been developed that are more shade tolerant, denser, and finer textured than Kentucky 31, a commonly used older cultivar. These characteristics become more evident as the turf matures and the maintenance level increases. Research has shown that some of these improved

cultivars also have darker green color, improved disease and drought tolerance, hold up to wear better, and have a lower growth habit.

Figure 9–2. Tall fescue.
Matt Lavin, Flickr CC BY-SA - 2.0

Experts recommend planting a blend of two or three cultivars rather than seeding just a single cultivar. This broadens the genetic base and gives the turf a better chance of withstanding a variety of challenges. Use a seeding rate of 6 pounds per 1,000 square feet (sq ft). Do not assume more seed is better. Higher seeding rates can result in weak, thin stands that are more susceptible to disease and high temperature stress.

Tall fescues perform best when mowed at a height of 3.5 inches, and should never be mowed shorter than 2.5 inches. Tall fescue may turn brown but will often survive short periods of drought. Under certain circumstances, some tall fescue may be lost if a drought exceeds three weeks. To maintain a green lawn, it is best to irrigate, if possible, during periods of drought.

Kentucky bluegrass

Kentucky bluegrass produces a high-quality, medium- to fine-textured turf when grown in the right climate (Figure 9–3). In North Carolina, it is well suited for the mountains and can be grown in combination with tall fescue in the piedmont. It is not suitable for use in the coastal plain. Kentucky bluegrass prefers fertile, limed, well-drained soils in sun or light shade. Excellent sod results from rhizomes (underground stems) that spread, with most cultivars recuperating from and tolerating pest control measures and moderate levels of traffic. Many new cultivars with improved color, texture, and pest resistance are now commercially available.

Figure 9–3. Kentucky bluegrass.
NC State University

As with most cool-season grasses, it is best to broaden the genetic base by planting a blend of two to three cultivars rather than seeding a single cultivar. It is also common for Kentucky bluegrass to be seeded in combination with tall fescue. Tall fescue enhances drought and heat tolerance, whereas the Kentucky bluegrass provides finer texture and greater recuperative potential. Generally, Kentucky bluegrass grows better than tall fescue in moderate shade. When mixed with tall fescue, Kentucky bluegrass tends to dominate where the soil is limed, the turf is adequately fertilized, and the grass is kept mowed fairly short.

Kentucky bluegrass should be mowed at a height of 1.5 to 2.5 inches when planted alone. It should be mowed at 2.5 inches or higher when mixed with tall fescue. Seeding rates range from 1 to 2 pounds per 1,000 square feet. Higher rates can result in weak, thin stands that are more susceptible to disease and high temperature stress.

Even though Kentucky bluegrass may turn brown during a two- to four-week summer drought, it is not necessary to irrigate. Letting the grass go dormant will prevent it from becoming stressed by drought conditions. Kentucky bluegrass recovers well from most droughts, and watering will often increase disease problems.

Fine Fescues

Fine fescues include creeping red, chewings, and hard fescue. The name is derived from the very finely textured leaves, which are almost as fine as pine needles (Figure 9-4). Noted for tolerance to shade, drought, and poor soil conditions compared to other cool-season grasses, fine fescues are often included with tall fescue or Kentucky bluegrass when planted in the shade or when the grass will be subject to low maintenance. They are best adapted to the mountains but can be grown in the piedmont. They should not be used in the coastal plain. They may not persist in sunny locations exposed to high temperature extremes, excessive soil moisture or humidity, or heavy traffic.

Figure 9–4. Fine fescue.
NC State University

Fine fescue seed should be mixed with Kentucky bluegrass because most of the fine fescues are bunch type and do not have the ability to spread. New seedlings establish quickly due to excellent seedling vigor. Seed fine fescue at 1.5 pounds per 1,000 square feet when mixed with either tall fescue or Kentucky bluegrass.

Fine fescue should be mowed at 1.5 to 2.5 inches when mixed with Kentucky bluegrass but at 2.5 inches or higher when mixed with tall fescue. Fine fescues generally do well in more natural areas with infrequent mowing.

9

Perennial Ryegrass

Perennial ryegrass is similar in appearance to Kentucky bluegrass but is only adapted to the mountains (Figure 9–5). In North Carolina it is never seeded alone but always mixed with Kentucky bluegrass. These grasses complement each other because perennial ryegrass establishes faster than Kentucky bluegrass, and Kentucky bluegrass has the ability to spread and fill in damaged areas.

A mix of Kentucky bluegrass and perennial ryegrass should be seeded at the rate of 2.5 pounds per 1,000 square feet, with Kentucky bluegrass making up 60 percent of the mix by weight. Perennial ryegrass should be mowed at 1.5 to 2.5 inches when mixed with Kentucky bluegrass.

Figure 9–5. Perennial ryegrass.
Grady Miller, NC State University

Annual Ryegrass

Annual ryegrass (Figure 9–6) is used only when a temporary turf cover is needed. It is never recommended for permanent lawn mixtures because it dies in late spring when temperatures approach 80°F or higher. It is sometimes found in inexpensive commercial seed mixtures, and those should be avoided. Because annual ryegrass is an annual, it must be reseeded each fall. Annual ryegrass has been used by some homeowners to provide winter

Figure 9–6. Annual ryegrass.
NC State University

color for bermudagrass lawns. It is never recommended for overseeding other warm-season grasses.

Warm-Season Grasses

Bermudagrass, zoysiagrass, centipedegrass, St. Augustine-grass, carpetgrass, and bahiagrass are classified as warm-season perennial grasses. All except bahiagrass and carpetgrass are recommended for lawns in the North Carolina piedmont and coastal plain (Table 9–3). They grow best in the summer, go dormant in the fall at the first heavy frost, turn brown, and then green up slowly the following spring. For these reasons, warm-season grasses usually perform better farther east and south in these regions. Warm-season grasses are best planted in late spring and early summer. Unlike cool-season grasses, some warm-season grasses must be planted either by sod or other vegetative means because seeds either are not available or do not result in uniform stands. Warm-season grasses are usually seeded or planted as a single variety (monoculture) rather than in blends and mixtures.

A comparative chart of principal lawn grasses used in each region is provided in Table 9–1. Study the chart to help select the appropriate grass for the site and the intended use of the lawn. This information is based on cultivar (variety) trials and observations by turfgrass researchers at NC State University. Cultivar performance recommendations are based on overall quality ratings for each of these commercially available varieties. The National Turf Evaluation Program (NTEP) trial research results have been consolidated into an easy-to-use question-and-answer program that provides proven grass types and cultivars suitable for each region and use.

The release and evaluation of turfgrass cultivars changes rapidly, so contact a local Cooperative Extension center for the latest information on grass characteristics and selection.

Bermudagrass

Bermudagrass spreads by **stolons** and **rhizomes**. It can invade flowerbeds and other areas because its runners spread rapidly both above and below ground (Figure 9–7). Bermudagrass is, however, extremely drought tolerant and grows rapidly on any type of soil except where drainage is poor. It makes a good turf when fertilized and mowed low and often. Cultivar textures range from coarse to fine, forming a dense, durable surface when grown in full sunlight. It will not tolerate shade. Bermudagrass is well adapted to sandy soils, establishes quickly, withstands wear and traffic, and recovers rapidly from injury.

Most finely textured, high-quality turf-type bermudagrasses are planted using **sod**, **sprigs**, or **plugs**. Common bermudagrass, which is the most coarsely textured (that is, it has wide leaf blades), can be seeded. Several newer cultivars with a medium texture can also be seeded.

Bermudagrass should be seeded at 1 to 2 pounds per 1,000 sq ft. If the seed is coated, the seeding rates may need to be doubled.

Good performance can be achieved with a rotary mower with sharp blades set as low as possible without scalping. Uneven ground can make mowing below 1 inch difficult. For this reason, a 1- to 2-inch mowing height is recommended when using a rotary mower. For best results, bermudagrass should be mowed often during its peak growth in mid-summer (at least twice per week), especially at the lower mowing heights.

Figure 9-7. Bermudagrass.
Scot Nelson, Flickr CC0 1.0

Zoysiagrass
Zoysiagrass spreads by stolons and rhizomes, but it is easier to keep out of flowerbeds than bermudagrass (Figure 9–8). It produces a very dense, wear-tolerant lawn that grows well in full sun and light shade. It has stiff leaves that produce a very dense turf, which people often describe as feeling like "walking on a cushion." Zoysiagrass grows more slowly than bermudagrass, rebounds more slowly from damage, and thus requires less frequent mowing. The leaves are stiff, making mowing difficult unless the mower blades are sharp. Zoysiagrass is very drought resistant. Once fully established, it rarely needs irrigation to survive in North Carolina.

Zoysiagrass was once limited to two cultivars: Meyer and the finer textured Emerald. These low, slow-growing cultivars cannot be planted from seed and must be planted vegetatively (sod, stolon, plug, or sprig). They are very slow to establish from plugs, often taking three years for total coverage when planted on 12-inch centers. These older cultivars can become **thatchy**—puffy due to an accumulation of dead, dying, decaying plant residue at the soil surface. This happens especially when these

grasses are mowed high and infrequently or heavily fertilized. Thatch may need to be removed every two to three years, but care should be taken due to the slow recovery rate of these cultivars.

In the last 20 years, a number of zoysiagrass cultivars have been released. These new cultivars, including El Toro, Crowne, Palisades, Empire, and Jamur, are coarser in texture (similar to newer tall fescues) and are quicker to establish and recover from injury. They are not as cold tolerant as Meyer and should not be mowed as short as Emerald and Meyer. Cavalier, Zeon, and Zorro are new zoysiagrass cultivars with a moderate growth rate and a fine texture similar to Emerald. Cold tolerance of zoysia is not a problem in North Carolina's piedmont and coastal plain.

A few cultivars of zoysiagrass, such as Compadre, Zenith, Zen 100, and Zen 300CS, can be seeded. These coarse-textured zoysiagrasses are typically mowed with a rotary mower.

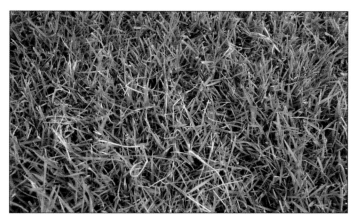

Figure 9-8. Zoysia grass.
Forest and Kim Starr, CC BY - 2.0

Centipedegrass
Centipedegrass is a slow-growing, **stoloniferous**, apple-green, coarsely leaved turfgrass that is best used as a low maintenance, general purpose turf (Figure 9–9). It requires little fertilizer once established (0.5 to 1 pound of nitrogen per 1,000 sq ft per year) and infrequent mowing. It grows well on acidic soils in full sun to partial shade. It does not tolerate traffic, compaction, high soil pH, high soil phosphorus, excessive thatch, drought, or heavy shade.

Centipedegrass is slow to establish and may take two to three years when seeded. It should be mowed when it attains 1 inch in height and no higher than 2 inches. Centipedegrass can become thatchy, especially when mowed high and infrequently or when heavily fertilized. Thatch may need to be removed every two to three years, but care should be taken because the stems can easily be torn from the ground, leaving bare spots. TifBlair, an improved cultivar from the University of Georgia, is quicker

9

to establish and more cold tolerant then common centipe-degrass. It also retains its green color later in the fall.

Figure 9–9. Centipedegrass.
Grady Miller, NC State University

St. Augustinegrass

St. Augustinegrass is a fast-growing, stoloniferous turf-grass best adapted to the North Carolina coastal plain (Figure 9–10). It has a medium- to dark-green color and very coarsely textured leaves. With proper maintenance, it will provide a dense, lush lawn. St. Augustinegrass is very shade and salt tolerant but is considered the least cold tolerant lawn grass. The cultivar Raleigh has the best cold tolerance and is well adapted for the eastern side of the piedmont and the western side of the coastal plain. Seed is unavailable, so cultivars must be vegetatively planted. St. Augustinegrass grows best in fertile, well-drained soils.

This fast-growing grass needs to be mowed frequently at 3 to 4 inches during the growing season using a rotary mower. It should never receive more than 4 pounds of ni-trogen per 1,000 sq ft annually. At high rates of fertilization and irrigation, thatch buildup may become a problem. St. Augustinegrass is not tolerant of heavy traffic, compaction, or cold weather.

Figure 9-10. St. Augustinegrass.
Grady Miller, NC State University

Carpetgrass

Carpetgrass is a slow and low-growing, stoloniferous, medium-green, coarsely textured lawngrass (Figure 9–11). It produces a low maintenance, general purpose turf. Carpetgrass resembles St. Augustinegrass and centi-pedegrass and is often mistaken for centipedegrass but has broader leaves. It grows well in full sun to moderate shade and performs well in wet, shaded, acid soils where other lawngrasses may not grow. It grows best in full sunlight when daytime temperatures are between 60° and 90°F, and does not tolerate cold, drought, salt, or traffic. Carpetgrass requires only 1 pound of nitrogen per 1,000 sq ft annually. It needs to be mowed only infrequently at 2 inches. It can be seeded, but it is not commonly avail-able in most retail outlets. It is considered a minor use grass in North Carolina.

Figure 9-11. Carpetgrass.
Grady Miller, NC State University

Bahiagrass

Bahiagrass spreads by stolons and rhizomes (Figure 9–12). Bahiagrass is never recommended as a lawn grass because of its open canopy, unsightly seedheads, and difficulty in mowing. It is best used on roadsides where appearance is not a concern and low maintenance is the priority. Bahiagrass can be seeded, but seed is not commonly available at retail outlets. It is often considered a weed in improved turfgrasses.

Figure 9–12. Bahiagrass.
Harry Rose, Flickr CC BY - 2.0

9

Table 9–2. Cool-season Grass Cultivars with Excellent Performance in North Carolina

Grass Type	Cultivar Name				
Tall fescue	2nd Millennium	Dominion	Inferno	Padre	Serengeti
	Avenger	Dynasty	Jaguar 3	Picasso	Signia
	Barlexas	Endeavor	Justice	Plantation	Silverstar
	Barlexas II	Escalade	Kalahari	Proseeds 5301	Southern Choice II
	Barrera	Falcon II	Kitty Hawk 2000	Prospect	Stetson
	Barrington	Falcon IV	Legitimate	Pure Gold	Tarheel
	Biltmore	Fidelity	Lexington	Quest	Titan Ltd.
	Bingo	Finesse II	Magellan	Rebel Exeda	Titanium
	Bonsai	Fireaza	Masterpiece	Rebel IV	Tracer
	Bravo	Firebird	Matador	Rebel Sentry	Ultimate
	Cayenne	Focus	Millennium	Regiment II	Watchdog
	Constitution	Grande II	Millennium SRP	Rembrandt	Wolfpack
	Coyote	Greenkeeper	Mustang	Rendition	
	DaVinci	Greystone	Mustang 3	Rhambler	
	Desire	Hunter	Olympic Gold	Scorpion	
Kentucky bluegrass	Alpine	Blackstone	Eagleton	Liberator	Rugby
	Apollo	Blueberry	Envicta	Limousine	Showcase
	Arcadia*	Bodacious	Everest	Midnight	Skye
	Arrow	Boomerang	Everglade	Moonlight	Sonoma
	Award	Bordeaux	Excursion	NuGlade	Total Eclipse
	Awesome	Boutique	Freedom II	Odyssey	Unique
	Bariras	Brilliant	Hallmark	Prosperity	Washington
	Baronie	Cabernet	Impact	Quantum Leap	
	Bedazzled	Champagne	Jefferson	Rambo	
	Bewitched	Champlain	Jewel	Rita	
	Beyond	Chicago	Langara	Royce	
Fine fescue	Ambassador	DP	Jasper II	Quatro	Spartan II
	Berkshire	Edgewood*	Musica*	Razor*	Zodiac
	Cardinal	Firefly	Oxford	Reliant IV*	
	Class One	Fortitude	Pathfinder	Scaldis	
	Compass*	Garnet Gotham	Predator*	Seabreeze	
Perennial ryegrass	Accent II	Derby Extreme	Keystone II	Panther GLS	Quicksilver
	Allstar 3	Fiesta 4	Line Drive GLS	Paragon GLR	Repel GLS
	Apple GL	Fiji	Majesty II	Pentium	Revenge GLX
	Brightstar SLT	Goalkeeper II	Manhattan 5 GLR	Phenom	Secretariat II
	Caddieshack II	Grand Slam 2	Monterey 3	Pianist	Silver Dollar
	Charismatic II	Harrier	Nexus	Pinnacle II	Top Gun II
	Citation Fore	Headstart 2	Palace	Pizzazz	Transformer
	Dart	Homerun	Palmer III	Premier	Zoom
	DCM	Inspire	Palmer IV	Primary	

These cultivars have not been tested in North Carolina but have performed well in surrounding states.

Table 9–3. Performance of Warm-season Grass Cultivars in North Carolina

Grass Type	Cultivar	Comments
Bermudagrass, seeded cultivars	Arizona Common Mohawk Numex Sahara Princess 77 Riviera Savannah Southern Star Sunbird Sundevil II Sunstar Transcontinental Yukon	• These cultivars are available as seed and produce acceptable quality under proper management. They closely resemble common bermudagrass in its coarse texture and light-green color. • Transcontinental, Yukon, Riviera, and Princess are finer textured and denser than other seeded cultivars. • Riviera and Yukon are noted for cold tolerance and are more likely to survive in the western and northern parts of the state. • Note: Seeded cultivars are grasses that do produce viable seed, which can be harvested and sold for use.
Bermudagrass, vegetative cultivars	Celebration GN-1 Patriot Premier TifGrand Tifsport Tifton 10 TifTuf Tifway	• These cultivars produce excellent quality grass under proper management. They possess dark-green color, fine leaf texture, and dense growth habits. They are typically considered as high maintenance grasses and must be mowed with a reel mower at a height of 0.5 to 1 inch to achieve high quality. These grasses are primarily suited for use on golf courses as well as high-end athletic fields and home lawns. • Tifsport performs best at 1 to 2 inches. • Note: Vegetative cultivars are only available as sprigs, plugs, or sod. This is because they are either sterile grasses that do not produce viable seed or they may produce seed that does not retain characteristics true to the cultivar. Vegetative cultivars must be purchased from a sod farm that carries the variety.
Centipedegrass	Common Tifblair	Tifblair is an improved cultivar that exhibits better cold tolerance compared to Common.
St. Augustine-grass	Common Raleigh	Raleigh is noted for its improved cold tolerance compared to Common St. Augustinegrass.
Zoysiagrass, coarsely textured varieties	Compadre Crowne El Toro Empire Jamur Meyer Palisades Zenith	Seed is available for Compadre and Zenith.
Zoysiagrass, finely textured varieties	Cavalier Diamond Emerald Zeon Zorro	*Because the release and evaluation of turfgrass cultivars changes rapidly, you are encouraged to contact the Cooperative Extension center in your county for the latest information on grass characteristics and selection (www.turfselect.ncsu.edu).*

9

Establishing a New Lawn

Establishing a healthy, attractive lawn means planting the best grass for the site at the right time and in a careful manner. Grass can be seeded or established using vegetation in the form of sprigs, plugs, or sod. The type of grass and the planting method selected will determine the best time of year to plant. Site and soil preparation, including fertilization, are especially important.

Site Preparation

Preparing the site involves removing weeds and debris, planning for drainage, and grading the site. Insist that the builder not use the site as a dumping ground for paint, concrete, and other materials. Think about how the lawn will be accessed for mowing and fertilizing. Avoid terraces, steep grades, poorly drained areas, and heavily shaded spots. Perennial weeds may need to be managed with a nonselective herbicide. Hard-to-control weeds may require the services of a professional.

Install tile drains in poorly drained areas. Get professional advice about the type of drain and installation. Remove the topsoil (usually four to eight inches) and stockpile it nearby if grading is needed. If topsoil is brought from other sites, be cautious. It may contain diseases and hard-to-control weeds or weed seeds.

Complete site preparation by following these steps:

1. Build protective walls to maintain the existing grade out to the edge of the canopy of trees if the final grade is to be appreciably higher or lower than the present level.
2. Shape the underlying subsoil to the desired contour, and redistribute topsoil uniformly above the subsoil. A 2 to 3 percent slope is needed for proper drainage away from buildings. Make certain the soil is firmed after shaping. There should be no footprints visible after walking on the prepared soil.
3. Water the area to enhance settling. Fill areas that settle unevenly to avoid standing water.
4. If possible, mix 1 to 2 cubic yards of compost per 1,000 square feet into the top 6 to 8 inches of subsoil if planting in heavy clay or very sandy soils. Clay soils are prone to compaction and require frequent **aerification** (removal of soil cores).

Soil Preparation

Well-prepared soil with adequate nutrients for growing grass encourages the development of a healthy lawn.

Take soil samples from the front yard and the backyard to determine soil pH and nutrient requirements. A single soil test may be all that is necessary if there are no obvious differences in soil texture or terrain of the front yard and backyard. If the soils seem different, collect soil samples

to a depth of 3 to 4 inches from several (10 to 15) locations and mix them together to produce a composite sample. Send approximately 1 cup of the air-dried soil sample to the NC Department of Agriculture and Consumer Services Agronomic Division Soil Testing Services, 1040 Mail Service Center, Raleigh NC, 27607. Boxes and forms can be obtained at a local Cooperative Extension center or at the Agronomic Division office in Raleigh. Allow several weeks for the results to be posted.

If recommended by the soil test report or the fertilization guidelines presented below, incorporate lime and fertilizer into the top 6 to 8 inches of the soil using a disk or rototiller. Regardless of the region, grass with a deeper root system is able to extract more moisture and nutrients from the soil, improving drought tolerance and overall health of the plant.

Rake or **harrow** the site to establish a smooth and level final grade (Figure 9–13). Soil particles should be no larger than marble size, and pea gravel size is even better. Hand raking is the best way to level the soil and work out hills and hollows. Allow time for rain or irrigation to settle the soil, and roll or **cultipack** lightly to firm the soil before planting seed, sprigs, plugs, or sod. Hand rake again to break up the crusty surface before planting.

Figure 9–13. Give the grass a good start with a properly prepared seedbed. Lucy Bradley, CC BY - 2.0

Fertilization

As recommended above, it is best to submit a soil sample for testing when establishing a new lawn to determine which, if any, nutrients should be added. This is especially important when planting centipedegrass. It prefers acidic soils and low levels of phosphorus and may not require the addition of lime and phosphorus.

Fertilize before planting. Apply fertilizer and lime when the soil is prepared based on these guidelines:

If a soil test was conducted, apply the amount of lime and fertilizer recommended by the soil testing laboratory. For additional information about fertilizer components and interpreting a soil test, see "Soils and Plant Nutrients", chapter 1, or visit the NCDA&CS webpage.

If no soil test was conducted, follow these recommendations for all grasses except centipedegrass:
1. Apply 75 pounds of ground limestone per 1,000 square feet.
2. Apply a starter-type fertilizer (one that is high in phosphorus) based on the type of grass and the planting method.
3. Fertilizer bags have a three-number system such as 8-8-8 or 5-10-10. These numbers indicate the percent, by weight, of the primary nutrients Nitrogen (N), Phosphorus (P), and Potassium (K). The percentages are always noted in the following order:
   N **Nitrogen** for green color and growth.
   P_2O_5 **Phosphorus** for good establishment and rooting.
   K_2O **Potassium** to enhance pest and environmental stress tolerance.

Some common examples of starter fertilizers for a 1,000 square foot area include 40 pounds of 5-10-10, 20 pounds of 10-20-20, or 16 pounds of 18-4-6 . For sandy soils, typical to the North Carolina coastal plain and sandhills, fertilizer rates should be increased by 20 percent.

Apply fertilizers uniformly and with care using a centrifugal (rotary) or drop-type spreader. Apply half the fertilizer in one direction and the other half moving at right angles to the first pass to ensure thorough and uniform coverage (Figure 9–14).

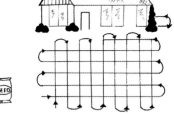

Figure 9–14. Suggested pattern for applying seed and fertilizer.
Renee Lampila

For seeded lawns: Fertilize the new seedlings approximately six to eight weeks after emergence. For more specific maintenance information on a particular grass type, refer to the NC State TurfFiles web page. Use a complete N-P-K turf-grade fertilizer that provides about 1 pound of nitrogen per 1,000 sq ft or the amount recommended on the soil test. The fertilizer should have a 3-1-2 or 4-1-2 analysis (for example, 12-4-8 or 16-4-8), and one-fourth to one-half of the nitrogen should be a slow-release form.

Encourage faster spread of vegetatively planted warm-season grasses by fertilizing every three to four weeks with 0.5 to 1 pound of nitrogen per 1,000 sq ft throughout the first growing season or until the plants have completely covered the desired lawn area. To help reduce turf loss, avoid high nitrogen fertilization of cool-season grasses in the late spring or summer and of warm-season grasses in the fall or winter. If higher nitrogen fertilization is applied, there may be a greater occurrence of diseases.

When to Plant Cool- and Warm-season Grasses
Seeding: Cool-season grasses are best seeded from mid August to early October, depending on location. Seeding beyond these dates increases the chance of failure caused by winter injury. Spring or late-winter seedlings are often less than satisfactory because the seedling roots do not have time to become well established before the heat and drought of summer. If seeding of a cool-season grass is not accomplished in the fall, the best alternative date for the North Carolina piedmont is mid-February to early March. Coastal plain areas would be seeded two weeks earlier, whereas the mountain areas would be seeded two weeks later.

If a cool-season grass will be seeded in the fall, such as tall fescue or Kentucky bluegrass, and the lawn site is ready for seeding in late March, April, May, or June, temporary cover can be obtained by seeding annual ryegrass at 1.5 to 2 pounds per 1,000 square feet, and then amending the soil based on your soil test report. It is also possible to go ahead and seed the desired cool-season grass. This procedure may succeed in some years. In any event, it will provide ground cover until fall. And even if all of the grass dies, it will prevent erosion and weeds.

Warm-season grasses may be seeded successfully between March 1 and July 1, depending on the species used and the location.

Sodding: Cool-season grass sod may be installed successfully anytime in the cooler portions of the growing season when the ground is not frozen. Warm-season grasses are best established by sodding at the same dates suggested for seeding, about March 1 until July 1. Warm-season sod will not produce roots unless the soil temperature exceeds 55°F for several weeks. Professional sod installers have been successful in establishing lawns beyond those dates, but care must be given to ensure that the soil does not dry out.

Vegetative: Warm-season grasses may be planted vegetatively (by sprigs or plugs) from March 1 through July 1.

How to Plant
Lawns can be established by seeding, sodding, or vegeta-

9

tive planting (sprigs or plugs). Buying poor-quality seed or plants often results in less-than-satisfactory performance, pest problems, and general disappointment. Selection of seeds or plants is especially important when establishing a lawn. Read the information on the seed tag carefully, and make sure there are no noxious weed seeds and low levels of other crop seed. One way to be sure a seed or planting material is true to type, free of noxious weed seed, and contains low levels of other crop seed is to purchase certified seed or sod. A blue certified tag indicates that the seed or plants have met certain standards to assure high quality and low levels of contaminants. The NC Crop Improvement Association (NCCIA) offers a list of certified sod producers on its website.

Seeding is the most economical method of establishing grasses. To ensure uniform coverage, use a centrifugal (rotary) or drop-type spreader. Apply half the seed in one direction and the other half moving at right angles to the first pass (Figure 9–14). Lightly cover the seed by hand raking or dragging with a mat or span of chain-link fence. Roll the soil lightly to firm the surface and provide good seed-to-soil contact.

Mulch grass seed with weed-free small-grain straw or hay. Use one bale per 1,000 square feet for warm-season grasses and one to two bales for cool-season grasses. This will help conserve moisture, control erosion, and reduce surface crusting until establishment. Once in place, stabilize the mulch by rolling or watering. Twine netting can be used if wind displacement is a problem. If applied evenly and lightly, these materials need not be removed.

Vegetative planting is necessary for some grasses that do not produce viable seed (seed that will germinate). When this method is used, the planting material must be kept fresh and moist from the time it is harvested until established in the new site. Fertilize with 0.5 to 1 pound of nitrogen per 1,000 square feet every one to three weeks for the fastest spread.

Space planting is the planting of separate shoots or sprigs (runners, cuttings, or stolons) at regular spacings. This labor-intensive method is best used for planting small areas. Spacing is determined by how fast the grass will spread, the amount of material, and how much time is available. The closer the spacing, the faster the lawn will become established (Figure 9–15).

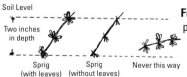

Soil Level

Two inches in depth

Sprig (with leaves)   Sprig (without leaves)   Never this way

Figure 9–15. Cross section of space planting. In space planting, always leave some part of the plant or sprig aboveground.
Renee Lampila

Broadcasting is the uniform distribution of sprigs (cut stems) over the entire area. The sprigs are pressed into the top 0.5 to 1 inch of soil by hand or by using an old disk set straight, special planter, cultipacker, or roller. Large areas planted with bermudagrass or zoysiagrass sprigs require a minimum of 3 to 5 bushels (yards) of sprigs per 1,000 sq ft and 5 to 10 bushels (yards) for extremely fast cover. St. Augustinegrass is seldom established through broadcasting because the stems are too sensitive.

Plugging is planting individual pieces (2 inches or larger) of sod (or plugs) on 6-inch or 12-inch centers. This is an excellent way to introduce a more adapted lawn grass into an old lawn in an effort to replace old grass by crowding it out. Zoysiagrass, St. Augustinegrass, and centipedegrass are often planted by plugging.

Sodding is placing sod stripped from one site to another for an "instant" lawn. Lay sod as soon as possible after it has been harvested to prevent injury (Figure 9–16).

Figure 9–16. Install sod as soon as possible after it has been harvested to prevent injury to the turf.
slgckgc, Flickr CC BY - 2.0

1. Make sure the soil is moist (but not overly wet) before laying sod. Irrigating the soil several days before delivery is often adequate.
2. Install the sod within 24 hours of delivery. Plan to unstack and unroll the sod if it cannot be laid within 48 hours.
3. While installing, keep sod in the shade to lessen the chance of heat buildup.
4. Start sodding from a straight edge (driveway or sidewalk), and butt strips together, staggering them in a bricklike pattern (Figure 9–17).
5. Avoid stretching sod. Use a knife or sharp spade for trimming to fit irregularly shaped areas.

Figure 9–17. Start sodding from a straight edge and butt strips together in a bricklike pattern.

9

6. Lay sod lengthwise across the face of slopes, and peg or stake the pieces to prevent slippage.

7. After the sod has been placed, roll the lawn to ensure good sod-to-soil contact. Then begin watering.

Again, to ensure high quality and better chance for success, it is highly recommended that certified sod be used. A list of producers growing certified sod, and the varieties they carry, can be found on the NCCIA website.

Caring for a New Lawn

Irrigation
To prevent drying of planting material, keep the top 1.5 inches of the soil moist. This may require light watering two or three times a day for 7 to 21 days. Bluegrass takes 7 to 14 days longer to germinate than other cool-season grasses. As the seedlings grow and root, water less often but for longer periods. For mixtures containing bluegrass, do not make the mistake of decreasing water as soon as the first seedlings appear. Continue watering until the bluegrass seedlings emerge. After the third mowing, water to a depth of 6 to 8 inches about once a week or when needed.

Mowing
Begin mowing as soon as the grass is 50 percent higher than the desired height. For example, mow tall fescue back to 3 inches when it reaches 4.5 inches. The frequency of mowing is governed by the amount of growth, which depends on temperature, fertility, moisture conditions, the season, and the natural growth rate of the grass. The suggested height of cut is given in Table 9–1. Cut often enough that less than one-third of the total leaf surface is removed. Use a mower with a sharp blade. To reduce the danger of spreading disease and injuring the turf, mow when the soil and plants are dry. If clippings are heavy enough to hold the grass down or shade it, catch them or rake and remove them. Otherwise, do not bag the clippings. Allow them to fall into the turf where they will decay and release nutrients. This may reduce the need for fertilizer by 20 to 30 percent.

Pest Management
Fungicides and insecticides are rarely needed on new lawns. Weeds are common and it is environmentally responsible to have some tolerance of weeds in a lawn. If weeds are deemed a problem, be aware that different planting methods require different management methods. If any pesticides or herbicides are used, always read and follow label directions.

Seeding: Broadleaf weeds are common in new seedings. Many will be controlled with frequent mowing at the proper height. Selective preemergence herbicides may be used to manage some annual grassy weeds such as crabgrass. Other herbicides may be applied to young seedlings during establishment. Get the latest recommendations by visiting the NC State TurfFiles web page.

Planting sprigs, broadcasting sprigs, and plugging: Herbicides may be applied for control of certain annual grasses and broadleaf weeds when sprigging bermudagrass, centipedegrass, St. Augustinegrass, and zoysiagrass. Do not apply these herbicides over the rooting areas of trees and ornamentals that are not listed as being tolerant on the herbicide label.

Sodding: Preemergence herbicides can be applied for annual weedy grass control after sodding cool- and warm-season grasses.

Maintaining an Established Lawn

A lawn is considered established when it has been mowed three times. Lawn Care Maintenance Calendars for specific grass types are available online through the NC State TurfFiles website.

Irrigation
Improper irrigation of lawns results in wasted water, added cost, and unhealthy plants. Water should be applied only when a reasonable portion of the lawn shows signs of moisture stress. A dark bluish-gray color, footprints that remain for some time after walking, and wilted, folded, or curled leaves are indications that it is time to water (Figure 9–18).

Figure 9–18. Footprints that remain sometime after walking indicate irrigation is needed.
Glenn Fleishman, Flickr CC BY - 2.0

9

Table 9–4. Planting Dates and Rates for Cool- and Warm-season Grasses in North Carolina

Lawn Grass	Optimum Planting Date[a]	Planting Rate per 1,000 Square Feet		
		Seed (pounds)	Sprigs for Space Planting (bushels)[c]	Sprigs for Broadcast (bushels)[c]
Mountains-Foothills				
Kentucky bluegrass	Aug. 15 – Sept. 1	1.5–2	–	–
Kentucky bluegrass/ fine fescue mix	Aug. 15 – Sept. 1	1.5+1.5	–	–
Kentucky bluegrass/ tall fescue mix	Aug. 15 – Sept. 1	1+5	–	–
Kentucky bluegrass/ tall fescue/fine fescue mix	Aug. 15 – Sept. 1	1+5+1	–	–
Kentucky bluegrass/ perennial ryegrass mix	Aug. 15 – Sept. 1	1.5+1	–	–
Tall fescue	Aug. 15 – Sept. 1	6	–	–
Piedmont				
Bermudagrass	April – July[b]	1–2	0.75	3–10
Bermudagrass (hybrid)	April – July	–	0.75	3–10
Bahiagrass	March – June	5	–	–
Centipedegrass	March – July	0.25–0.50	1–2[d]	–
Kentucky bluegrass/ tall fescue mix	Sept. 1 – Sept. 15	1+5	–	–
Kentucky bluegrass/ tall fescue/fine fescue mix	Aug. 1 – Sept. 1	1+5+1	–	–
St. Augustinegrass	April – July	–	1	1
Tall fescue	Sept. 1 – Sept. 15	6	–	–
Zoysiagrass	April – July[b]	1–2	1–2[d]	3–10
Sandhills-Coastal Plain				
Bermudagrass	April – July	1–2	0.75	3–10
Bermudagrass (hybrid)	March – July[b]	–	0.75	3–10
Bahiagrass	March – June	5	–	–
Centipedegrass	March – July	0.25–0.50	1–2[d]	–
St. Augustinegrass	April – July	–	–	–
Tall fescue	Sept. 15 – Oct. 15	6	–	–
Zoysiagrass	March – July[b]	1–2	1–2[d]	3–10

[a] Seeding beyond these dates increases the chance of failure. Sod consisting of cool-season grasses can be installed any time the ground is not frozen. Warm-season grasses can be installed as long as soil temperature exceeds 55°F.

[b] For best results, choose earlier dates when using vegetative material.

[c] 1 square yard of turf pulled apart is equivalent to 1 bushel of sprigs.

[d] Often plugged using 3 square yards of turf cut into 2-inch squares on 12-inch centers to plant 1,000 square feet.

If irrigation is not available or desirable, then an alternative to irrigating is to allow the turf to go semi-dormant. Tall fescue, bermudagrass, and zoysiagrass are tolerant of drought if allowed to go dormant. See Extension publication AG-661, *Water Requirements of North Carolina Turfgrasses*, for additional information. General watering recommendations include the following:

1. Water in the early morning if possible. This is the preferred time to water because it reduces the risk of disease, water loss through evaporation, and improper water distribution. Also, the demand for water by industry and municipalities is usually low at this time.

2. Water established lawns to a depth of 6 to 8 inches to encourage deep rooting. Usually, 1 inch of water per week is adequate. Ideally, this would not be applied in one application. Applying 0.5 inch of water every three to four days is adequate for most situations.

3. Use cans or a rain gauge to determine how much water is being delivered in a certain period of time. It takes 640 gallons of water to apply 1 inch of water per 1,000 sq ft. Because clay soils accept water slowly, water should be measured to prevent wasteful runoff. Water clay soils until runoff is about to occur. Wait 30 minutes for the water to be absorbed. Then apply more water until the desired depth or amount is achieved. This same technique can be used on slopes and compacted soils. Few lawns established on clay soils can absorb more than 0.5 inch of water per hour. Sandy soils require more frequent watering. Applying 0.5 inch of water every third day is usually sufficient. Adjust any automatic irrigation system to supplement rainfall so that the lawn is not over-watered.

Take certain precautions if there will be no irrigation throughout the summer. Slowly ease a lush, actively growing lawn into dormancy. This can be accomplished by allowing the drought stress symptoms to appear between infrequent irrigation cycles, by mowing high, and by not over-fertilizing with nitrogen. Brown, withered leaves are normal signs of dormancy, so do not be alarmed by them. If the lawn is conditioned for this stress and has a reasonable level of maintenance, it should survive without permanent damage. Most turfgrasses can withstand three to six weeks (or longer) without rainwater or irrigation and exhibit minimal or no damage, depending on the situation.

In the absence of rain, water dormant lawns with a minimal amount (about 0.25 inch) every three weeks to keep the growing points hydrated. It is difficult to maintain vibrant green color in cool-season grasses during the summer. Irrigation helps maintain color, but may also increase the risk of disease. For this reason, it is particularly important that cool-season grasses not be overwatered.

Be vigilant about checking irrigation systems for overspray and be sure to direct heads so they are not hitting tree trunks, plant foliage, fences, buildings, or other hardscape elements. Repeated overspray can cause salt buildup and can damage plants and structures (Figure 9–19). It is also important to check irrigation timing so water does not run off the lawn and onto a sidewalk or street (Figure 9–20).

Figure 9–19. Sprinklers that overspray and hit trees, shrubs, or other structures can cause salt buildup and damage to plant tissue.
RonPorter, Pixabay CC BY 0

Figure 9–20. Water running off onto the sidewalk from an irrigation system that was set to run too long.
FFamartin, Wikimedia Commons CC BY-SA-4.0

Mowing

Use either a rotary (centrifugal) or reel (cylinder) mower. The reel mower is preferred if grasses are cut to less than 1 inch (Figure 9–21).

1. Keep the mower blades sharp and balanced. The cleanest cut and best mowing are obtained when the mower blades are sharp. Dull mower blades reduce lawn quality by tearing instead of cleanly cutting the grass. Tearing creates many ragged leaf ends that quickly wither and bleach and are easy ports of entry

for disease. Using a sharp mower is especially important for difficult-to-mow grasses, such as zoysiagrass, bahiagrass, and certain perennial ryegrass cultivars. A properly sharpened and balanced mower blade will also reduce mower vibration, lengthen mower life, and reduce fuel consumption by as much as 22 percent.

Figure 9–21. Reel lawn mower.
rseigler0, Pixabay CC BY0

2. Mow at the proper height. The frequency of mowing is governed by the desired grass height and by the amount of growth, which depends on temperature, fertility, moisture conditions, season, and the natural growth rate of the grass. In most instances, this may amount to biweekly and weekly mowing. To maintain a high-quality lawn, turfgrass should be cut often enough that no more than one third of the leaf surface is removed with each mowing. The proper mowing heights are presented in Table 9–1. If the lawn gets too high during wet seasons, raise the mower height and cut off a fourth to a half of the present growth. Then lower the mower to its proper height and mow again in a day or two.

3. Leave clippings to decompose when they are short. Some homeowners bag lawn clippings because they think that the clippings add to the buildup of thatch, which can be harmful to the lawn. Actually, thatch is made up of roots, stems, and the lower portions of leaves that are below the mower blade. Frequent mowing, mowing when the grass is dry, and proper fertilization are the best ways to reduce thatch buildup. Though studies have shown that a lawn of 1,000 square feet can produce 500 pounds of clippings in one growing season, these clippings contribute very little to thatch. In fact, clippings that remain on the lawn quickly decompose and release valuable nutrients. Fertilizer use can be reduced by 20 to 30 percent.

4. Rake, bag, and remove the clippings when mowing is delayed. If prolonged periods of rainfall prevent mowing, clippings may be long enough to shade or smother the grass. Collected clippings can be used as mulch around trees and shrubs or added to compost. If persistent herbicides have been used on your lawn, however, do not use the clippings as mulch or in a compost pile as

the herbicides may not break-down and they can impact desired plants. Because yard trash accounts for 20 percent of the waste in our overflowing landfills, legislation has been passed that bans depositing yard trash in most public landfills. Homeowners must now look for other alternatives. Contact the local local Cooperative Extension center for information about composting yard trash and other uses for this material.

Fertilizing

A soil test should be made at least every two to three years to determine the amounts of lime, phosphorus, and potassium needed by an established lawn. Failure to test can result in under- or overfertilization that can lead to plant damage, contamination of storm water, and unnecessary expense. A complete fertilizer with an N-P-K ratio of 4:1:2 or 4:1:3 can be used in lieu of a soil test, but it is not advised.

Cool-season grasses: Avoid any nitrogen fertilization of cool-season grasses, such as tall fescue, after the February application until September for the NC central piedmont. If one additional application of nitrogen is made between these dates to improve the color, the rate should not exceed 0.5 pound of nitrogen per 1,000 sq ft. This nitrogen should be applied in the central piedmont no later than April 15 (two weeks earlier in the coastal plain and two weeks later in the mountains). This application will not improve the longevity of tall fescue but will enhance its green color.

The application of high rates or repeated low rates of nitrogen to cool-season grasses in the spring or summer greatly increases the severity of brown patch (*Rhizoctonia* spp.), which can kill the grass. If nitrogen is applied to tall fescue in spring or summer, or both, fungicide applications may be necessary to reduce disease symptoms.

Warm-season grasses: Avoid fall or winter applications of nitrogen to reduce winter injury.

Lime

Most soils in North Carolina are acidic and just right for centipedegrass, which requires a pH close to 5.5. Most turfgrasses, however, prefer a soil pH between 6.5 and 7.0 for optimum nutrient availability. Lime may be applied any time during the year. Winter is usually best, however, because there is less traffic. Gentle winter rains minimize runoff, and alternate freezing and thawing help incorporate lime into the soil.

Fertilizers and lime should be applied uniformly with a centrifugal (rotary) or drop-type spreader. Apply half the fertilizer in one direction and the other half moving at right angles to the first pass to ensure uniform coverage (Figure 9–14).

9

How to Determine Fertilizer Requirements

The three-number ratio on the fertilizer bag tells you how much of an element is present by weight.
A 10-10-10 bag of fertilizer contains 10% Nitrogen, 10% Phosphorus, and 10% Potassium. A 100 lb bag of this fertilizer contains 10 lb of nitrogen, 10 lb of phosphorus, and 10 lb of potassium. If more nitrogen is desired, look for a formulation that has a higher ratio of nitrogen to phosphorus or potassium such as 16-6-12. In this case, 16 lb would be nitrogen, 6 lb phosphorus, and 12 lb potassium. The percentages never add up to 100% because the remainder of the bag is a mixture of **secondary nutrients** such as calcium, magnesium, and sulfur, **micronutrients**, and fillers such as sand or granular limestone.

Example: a 50 lb bag of 16-4-12 has 8 lb of N, 2 lb of P and 6 lb of K.
Bag Weight × % of Nutrients = lb of Nutrients
50 lb × .16 = 8.0 lb of nitrogen
50 lb × .04 = 2.0 lb of phosphorus
50 lb × .12 = 6.0 lb of potassium

Example: a 4 lb bag of 8-4-0 has about 5 oz* of N, 2.5 oz of P, and zero K
*Changing the weight to the equivalent in ounces makes it easier to work with bags containing smaller amounts.
Bag Weight × % of Nutrients = oz of Nutrients
64 oz × .08 = 5.12 oz nitrogen
64 oz × .04 = 2.5 oz phosphorus
64 oz × 0.0 = 0.0 oz potassium

Fertilizer recommendations are usually in lb/sq ft. To apply 1 pound of nitrogen per 1000 sq ft of lawn: Divide 100 by the first number on the fertilizer bag to determine the amount of product to be used per 1000 sq ft.

Example: Apply 1 lb of nitrogen per 1,000 square feet of a 16-4-8 fertilizer. 100 divided by 16 equals 6.25 pounds of fertilizer, which delivers 1 pound of nitrogen per 1,000 sq ft.

To apply 0.5 pounds of nitrogen per 1,000 sq ft of lawn, divide 50 by the first number on the fertilizer bag. 50 divided by 16 equals 3.13 lb of fertilizer. Therefore 3.13 lb of fertilizer delivers 0.5 lb of nitrogen per 1,000 sq ft.

Example: Apply 0.5 lb of nitrogen per 1,000 square feet of a 10-10-10 fertilizer. 50 divided by 10 equals 5 lb of fertilizer. Therefore, 5 lb of fertilizer per 1,000 sq ft delivers 0.5 pounds of nitrogen per 1,000 sq ft.

Weed Management

Weeds will occur in any lawn, but a thriving turfgrass lawn will naturally crowd out most weeds. Choosing a proper location and turfgrass variety and preparing the site before planting will give the lawn the best possible start. Once established, paying close attention to adequate moisture, proper fertilization, and frequent mowing (at no more than 50 percent of the height of the grass blades) will keep the turfgrass in top condition. Frequent mowing will also stop weeds from flowering and going to seed. Turfgrass that is stressed from drought or overwatering, burned from too much fertilizer, or stressed from scalping will be much more likely to struggle with weed populations. Compaction can also negatively affect turfgrass, causing weeds to more easily establish themselves.

Having many weeds in your lawn can be frustrating, but having some tolerance for weeds will keep chemical use to a minimum. Tolerating some weeds can also improve soil conditions and help support the ecosystem. Weeds like dandelion have taproots that break up heavy clay soil. Their blooms are food for many pollinators such as honey bees and butterflies. Clover is a legume and so has nitrogen-fixing bacteria in the roots, and its blossoms are a favorite of honey bees.

If herbicides are deemed necessary, use them as part of an integrated plan based on good cultural practices. No one herbicide is going to be effective to manage all weeds in a lawn. Being able to properly identify weeds and understand their life cycle is essential to their management. Read more about common weeds and management techniques in chapter 6, "Weeds."

Young and actively growing weeds are easiest to manage. Removing weeds by hand as they appear, and before they flower and set seed, can be an effective technique for a small area. If an herbicide is used, make sure that the soil is moist several days before application. Carefully read and follow directions and precautions on the herbicide labels. Treat only those areas that need it.

To help control weeds that may have gone to seed in the lawn, use a preemergence herbicide. Pre-emergent herbicides stop all seeds from emerging from the soil, so do not apply them when trying to renovate a lawn with new grass seed.

Postemergence herbicides are used for actively growing weeds that have emerged from the soil. Postemergent herbicides can be either **selective** or **nonselective**, **contact**, or **systemic**. *Selective* means the herbicide will affect only certain types of plants (usually **monocots** or **dicots**). *Nonselective* herbicides will kill any growing plant, so these should be used with great caution. *Contact* herbicides will damage any tissue they come into contact with,

9

while *systemic* herbicides will translocate through a plant and can be more effective against older weeds. Selective broadleaf post-emergence herbicides should be used four to six weeks before seeding with grass. Most selective post-emergent herbicides that control annual grassy weeds, such as crabgrass, should also be applied at least four weeks before seeding with the desired grass.

Weed and feed products contain a preemergence or postemergence broadleaf herbicide, and sometimes both. These products should be used only when a high number of weeds is present and treatment is necessary—not every time the lawn is fertilized. Certain broadleaf herbicides can be absorbed by tree and shrub roots and can cause damage if applied too close to the drip line.

Coring (Aerification)
Soils that are subject to heavy traffic are prone to compaction. Coring will alleviate this condition. Use a device that removes soil cores. Chop up the cores, and, if possible, distribute them by dragging with a span of chain-link fence or a mat. Coring should be accomplished when the lawn is actively growing so that it can recover from any injury. Core cool-season grasses in fall or early spring. Core warm-season grasses in late spring or early summer. Some lawn care and landscape companies offer coring services if rental equipment is not available.

Power Raking (Verticutting)
Sod-forming grasses, such as Kentucky bluegrass, bermudagrass, zoysiagrass, St. Augustinegrass, and centipedegrass, tend to build up thatch when they are heavily fertilized and watered. When thatch exceeds 0.75 inch, lawns should be power raked and cored. A light **power raking** is better than trying to remove too much debris at one time. When not excessive, thatch buildup can be removed from warm-season grasses by cutting as closely as possible at spring green-up and then raking by hand. To avoid seriously injuring the lawn, a 3-inch blade spacing is required to remove thatch from centipedegrass and St. Augustinegrass. Some lawn care and landscape companies have specialized equipment and offer power raking services.

Renovating a Lawn

Lawn renovation refers to any procedure beyond normal maintenance (short of soil modification) required to upgrade an existing lawn. A deteriorated lawn is often a symptom of some underlying problem. Failure to identify and correct the exact problem can lead to further lawn deterioration and the need for repeated renovation. These are some of the major causes of turf deterioration:
- improper site location
- poor establishment procedures
- improper lawn management (irrigation, fertilization, mowing)

- poorly adapted lawn grasses
- excessive thatch buildup
- disease, insect, or weed infestation

The problems that caused the lawn to deteriorate must be corrected before the renovation process begins.

When to Renovate
Late summer to early fall is the best time to renovate cool-season lawns. Warm-season lawns are best renovated in late spring to early summer. Attempts to upgrade existing lawns when conditions are not conducive to good growth are difficult at best.

Considerations
When renovating a lawn, the first step is the management of undesirable vegetation that will compete with newly planted grasses. Some weeds growing in small areas may be removed by hand weeding or by using a small hoe, rake, or shovel. Hard-to-control weeds, such as perennial grasses with underground shoots or weeds in large areas, may be controlled with herbicides.

To control perennial grassy weeds, undesirable turfgrasses, annual grasses, and broadleaf weeds, spray a nonselective herbicide. It will take several applications spaced three to four weeks apart to completely control bermudagrass. If perennial grassy weeds like bermudagrass are scattered throughout, consider killing the entire lawn.

When using an herbicide that translocates from the leaves to the roots of the plant, do not disturb the soil or plants before treatment. Tillage or renovation techniques, such as vertical mowing, coring, or slicing, should be delayed for seven days after application to allow proper movement of the herbicide into the weeds' underground parts.

Preparation for Seeding
Preplanting renovation procedures are designed to create the optimum environment for the establishment of newly planted grasses. This process includes the following steps:
1. Reduce competition from existing grasses and remove unwanted vegetation, including thatch.
2. Apply the required fertilizer and lime.
3. Prepare a good seedbed.

Reduce competition. Set the rotary or reel mower at the lowest setting, mow, and collect the clippings. Remove all undesirable vegetation, dead grass, thatch, and weeds so that the soil is exposed. This may not be necessary if a **slit seeder** is used. A rake or hoe is ideal for small areas. Several passes with a dethatcher (power raker or **vertical mower**) is usually the best choice for large areas. If thatch is excessive, it may be necessary to make another pass with a dethatcher after mowing. Both mowing and dethatching reduce plant competition and enhance light penetration for good germination and fast establishment.

Apply fertilizer and lime. Uniformly apply needed fertilizer and lime based on soil test results. Hand application is fine for small areas, but a rotary or drop-type spreader should be used on large areas to ensure uniform application.

Prepare a good seedbed. In small bare spots, loosen the top 4 to 6 inches of the soil with a rake, hoe, or shovel. On soils difficult to loosen with hand equipment, loosen the top 2 to 3 inches for good results. Fill in low areas, and smooth the surface so clods are smaller than marbles. Large areas and areas that contain 50 percent desirable grasses are best prepared for seeding by using a piece of equipment (such as an aerator or coring machine) that brings small soil cores to the surface. This will bring soil to the surface with minimal disruption and create an environment for good seed-to-soil contact. Core in several directions, allow plugs to dry, and then pulverize them with a mower, dethatcher, or by dragging a span of weighted-down chain-link fence behind a tractor or lawn mower. Because tines have a difficult time penetrating dry, compacted soils, coring is best achieved when the soil is damp.

Seeding
Bare spots larger than 4 inches in diameter should be replanted. Smaller areas tend to fill in naturally, provided the lawn grass is capable of spreading. Tall fescue and perennial ryegrass exhibit a bunch-type growth habit and are incapable of spreading. Choose a blend or mixture that is compatible with the environment and the existing lawn. To ensure uniform coverage, use a rotary or drop-type spreader, applying half the seed in one direction and the other half at right angles to the first pass. Incorporate seed and fertilizer into the top 1/8-inch of soil by lightly pulling a leaf rake over loosened soil or running a vertical mower over areas that were just power raked and cored.

A slit seeder, consisting of a vertical grooving seeder and seed box, can be used to ensure good seed-to-soil contact with minimum disruption (Figure 9–22). Seed should be drilled in a diamond-shaped pattern. Dry, compacted soils, obstructions such as rocks and trees, and excessive slopes may limit the usefulness of a slit seeder. Bare areas that are seeded should be mulched to enhance germination.

Plugging
Plugging can be used for those grasses that spread laterally—not bunch-type grasses such as tall fescue, ryegrass, bahiagrass, and fine fescue. Place plugs on either 6-inch or 12-inch centers, depending on the desired establishment speed. Use a plugging device to remove plugs of soil from bare areas, and switch them with plugs collected from healthy areas. Apply a starter-type fertilizer, such as 10 pounds per 1,000 square feet of 5-10-10 fertilizer.

Sprigging Large Areas
Large areas of 15,000 sq ft or more can be sprigged using this method, which is often reserved for bermudagrass. Rototill the recommended amount of fertilizer and lime, indicated by soil test results, or apply lime at 75 pounds per 1,000 sq ft and 10-10-10 fertilizer at 20 pounds per

Figure 9–22. A core aerator (left) pulls plugs of soil out of the ground, which makes it better for soil compaction. A slitseeder (right) has disks that make slices in the soil, a hopper feeds seed into the slits, and then a roller behind rolls it in.

1,000 sq ft to the area to be sprigged. Spread sprigs over the surface using rates provided in Table 9–4 for new areas. Press them into the top 0.5 to 1 inch of soil using a cultipacker, or roller (Figure 9–23). Roll the area to firm the soil and ensure sprig-to-soil contact.

Care After Planting

Keep renovated areas moist with light sprinklings several times a day. As the seedlings, plugs, or sprigs grow, continue to decrease the frequency of watering while increasing the duration to promote deep rooting. After the third mowing, water to a depth of 6 inches.

Mow the area as normal, using a sharp blade. But continue to severely stunt existing vegetation by mowing short until desirable grasses have germinated and the desired mowing height is achieved. This will reduce the competition for new seedlings.

Fertilize the new seedlings of cool-season grasses as described for "fertilize after planting" in the section on fertilization on page 9-16. Use the example provided in that section to determine how much fertilizer to use.

Warm-season grasses can be fertilized every four weeks until coverage is complete. Use a complete N-P-K fertilizer that provides about 1 pound of nitrogen per 1,000 sq ft. Twice-monthly applications of a nitrogen-only fertilizer that provides about 0.5 pound of nitrogen per 1,000 square feet may help warm-season grasses fill in more rapidly. Keep unnecessary traffic off the renovated lawn until it is well established.

Figure 9–23. A cultipacker or roller ensures the seeds have good soil contact to help with germination rates.
Kerry Garratt, Flickr CC BY SA 2.0

Integrated Pest Management

People are becoming more concerned about the potential effects of chemicals on our environment. Research indicates that pesticide use poses a minimal threat to the health of humans, animals, and the environment. But because we cannot be certain, many people choose to avoid pesticides. What is the best way to handle a pest problem that is destroying the appearance of a lawn? Should pesticides be used, cultural practices changed, or both?

The balanced use of all available control methods is called integrated pest management (IPM). The idea is simple. All available prevention and control methods are used to keep pests from reaching damaging levels. Pesticides are used only when necessary. Read more in chapter 8, "IPM."

Planting the best-adapted grass and then watering, mowing, and fertilizing it properly form the basis for integrated pest management. Keeping the lawn healthy enables it to tolerate low levels of diseases and pests and makes the area a good habitat for beneficial organisms that help control pests.

Properly identifying an insect or disease will help guide appropriate management strategies. Table 9–5 lists common turf insects and diseases. The Turffiles web page is an invaluable tool in giving background information on common turf insects and available treatment options. The TurfFiles page also has background information on common turf diseases, a tool to help you identify diseases based on signs and symptoms in your lawn, and several strategies for managing those diseases.

To best use natural controls, it is important to develop a sound understanding of the biology and ecology of the lawn environment. Fortunately, many books and other educational materials are available to assist the homeowner. There is also an increasing number of offerings from companies that specialize in organic lawn care. These range from organic fertilizers, nematodes or bacteria that attack caterpillars, to traps, and nontoxic repellents. Some are quite effective, whereas the effectiveness of others has not been well documented. As each product is tested and proven to be effective, it will be added to the list of available options for turf pest management. In the meantime, if chemical control is necessary, select the safest effective pesticide and closely follow label recommendations.

Chemicals should be applied when the pest is most susceptible. Treat only those areas in need, and regard pesticide use as only one of many tools available in lawn care. Integrated pest management can be successful, but homeowners must realize that more time and labor are required and high expectations may not be met when pest issues and environmental conditions are severe. Read more about some of the common insects and diseases that affect turfgrass in chapter 4, "Insects," and chapter 5, "Diseases and Disorders."

Table 9–5.
Common Turf Insects and Diseases

Insects	Diseases
Beneficial	Anthracnose
Cicada Killer Wasps	Brown Blight
Formica Ants	Brown Patch
Scoliid Wasps	Copper Spot
Solitary Bees	Damping Off
People Pests	Dollar Spot
Fire Ants	Fairy Ring
Hornets	Gray Leaf Spot
Yellowjackets	Gray Snow Mold
Plant Pests	Large Patch
Chinch Bugs	Leaf Spot/Melting Out
Crane Fly Larvae	Microdochium patch (Pink Snow Mold)
Cutworms	Net Blotch
Fall Armyworms	Powdery Mildew
Ground Pearls	Pythium Root Rot
Hunting Billbugs	Red Leaf Spot
Japanese Beetles	Red Thread
Mole Crickets	Rust
Rhodesgrass Mealybugs	Slime Mold
Sod Webworms	Spring Dead Spot
Springtails	Summer Patch
Sugarcane Beetles	White Patch
Twolined Spittlebugs	Yellow Patch
White Grubs	Yellow Tuft

Lawn Alternatives

Turfgrass is the best choice for areas of the landscape that are heavily used by family and pets for play and sports activities. However, lawns can require significant time and money for maintenance, water, and fertilizer. There can be an environmental impact from the air pollutants released by gas lawn mowers and the fertilizer nutrients and pesticides that make it into water sources. If there are turf areas in a landscape that are underused, consider one of the many attractive, wildlife-supporting lawn alternatives (Figure 9–24).

Not all turfgrass needs to be removed at one time. Try starting with a small patch of grass, perhaps on the side of a home. Or carve out an area at the edge of an existing turf patch. Some lawn alternatives can take a few seasons to become established, so be patient.

Figure 9–24. The turfgrass in this front yard was underused (above). The homeowner decided to remove the grass and replace it with perennial plants, a spiral garden, and vegetable beds adding diversity and increasing functionality (below).
Kate Ware

To remove some existing turfgrass, try one of these methods:

Layer it: This method requires the least muscle by smothering the grass in place, but it does take time. Place six to eight layers of newspaper or one layer of cardboard on top of the grass with a 3-inch layer of weed-free mulch or compost to keep it in place (Figure 9–25). Water it down and wait. It can take between three months and a year to kill the grass beneath the mulch. Once the grass is dead, the nutrient-rich soil will be ready to plant. It works most quickly to start in summer months when the grass is actively growing versus in the fall when the grass is starting to store energy in its roots.

Figure 9–25. To remove existing turfgrass, put wet newspaper (several sheets thick) or cardboard down and then cover it with a 3-inch layer of weed-free compost or mulch. It can take between three months to a year to kill the grass underneath.
Kathleen Moore, CC BY - 2.0

Turn it over: Turn the soil over and break up the grass roots using a power tiller weekly for six weeks. Be sure to remove from the site any roots or stems that are pulled up, as even a small piece of root can resprout (Figure 9–26).

Cut it out: Use a flat shovel or sod cutter to remove the grass in chunks. **Cold compost** these pieces of sod over the next year. There is no need to turn the pile; the sod will gradually turn into usable compost for the yard or garden.

Conducting a soil test of the planting area will give insight into plants that are well adapted to this soil type and will allow for the addition of amendments if they are needed. Incorporating a 1-to 2-inch layer of compost into the soil will help plants become established quickly.

Figure 9–26. Turning the soil over using a power tiller every week for six weeks helps to remove grass from a site. Even small parts of the root or stem can resprout, so be sure to rake those up.
Ash901, Wikimedia Commons CC BY SA 4.0

Choosing a Ground Cover

Many different ground covers are available from local and mail-order nurseries. Choosing one that will thrive in the given site conditions will offer a low-maintenance alternative to turfgrass. Native ground covers will be well-adapted to the climate, and they are a great choice for supporting local biodiversity.

For a list of specific ground covers that perform well, check the NC State Extension Gardener Plant Toolbox and search for "Native Plants."

Here are some ground covers to consider:

Clover *(Trifolium repens)*. A member of the legume family, clover can thrive in sun to partial shade and needs no fertilizing (Figure 9–27). Clover is well adapted to acidic soils. It is more forgiving of foot traffic than moss, but will not appreciate heavy running and playing. If animals and children will frequently use the area, an alternative plant may be more suitable. Sow seeds in the spring after nighttime temperatures are consistently higher than 40°F. Keep the soil moist until the clover germinates. While white flowering clover is a favorite of honey bees, red clover (*Trifolium pratense*), has petals that are too long for a honey bee's tongue. Bumblebees and other pollinators will frequent red clover.

Figure 9–27. White clover (*Trifolium repens*), makes an excellent ground cover and pollinator plant.
Kathleen Moore, CC BY - 2.0

9

Mondo grass (*Ophiopogon japonicus*). This evergreen ground cover is an easy maintenance alternative to a traditional grass lawn (Figure 9–28). Regular mondo grass grows up to 6 inches tall if a taller look is preferred. Dwarf mondo grass grows to just 2 inches tall and more closely resembles a turfgrass lawn. Regular mondo grass should be mowed annually in late winter to promote new growth. Mondo grass is native to Asia, but is adapted to North Carolina's climate. Mondo grass is a good choice for areas that receive regular foot traffic. Plant mondo grass in the spring or fall using plugs spaced 6 inches apart. Placing a light layer of mulch between the plugs will discourage weeds and keep the roots moist.

Figure 9-28. Mondo grass (*Ophiopogon japonicus*).
Forest and Kim Starr, Flickr CC BY - 2.0

Lilyturf (*Liriope muscari*). Lilyturf, also known as liriope, is native to Eastern Asia. This evergreen ground cover features dark green strappy leaves and grows well in North Carolina. It is similar in appearance to mondo grass, but it has wider leaves and it grows to a height of 1- to 1½-feet tall (Figure 9–29). Liriope tolerates a wide range of soil conditions and will grow well in sun to light shade. It is considered drought tolerant when established but it looks most attractive when it has consistent irrigation.

Figure 9–29. Liriope, a little taller than mondo grass, is a lawn alternative. It flowers best in full sun.
Syrio, Wikimedia Commons CC BY-SA - 4.0

It handles occasional light foot traffic. Place plantings 1 foot apart and lightly mulch between them to discourage weeds until the ground cover is filled in. It does well in the planting strip between sidewalks and streets or for planting on steep banks. Lilyturf is listed as a "Rank 3 - Lesser Threat" on the North Carolina Native Plant Society's weedy plant list. Because of its weedy nature, it is best planted in contained areas.

Moss (*Hypnum* or *Thuidium* spp.). Moss is a great grass alternative for damp spots (Figure 9–30). It thrives in North Carolina's acidic soil. Moss grows very low to the ground and does not need mowing. The fine texture of moss balances beautifully with nearby flowering perennials and evergreens. Moss needs very little water once it is established, and fertilizer is not needed. Be advised that it does not handle heavy foot traffic well. If landscape traffic patterns will lead to walking through a moss planting on a daily basis, a flagstone or paver walkway will help keep the moss in good condition. In the spring after the last frost, plant moss by pressing chunks into freshly raked soil. Keep it moist for the first three weeks. Depending on the growing conditions and spacing when planted, a moss lawn could take up to a year to fill in.

Figure 9-30. Moss (*Thuidium* spp.).
John Game, Flickr CC BY - 2.0

Sedge (*Carex* spp.). Sedges have grass-like leaves and grow in clumps. They come in many sizes and textures, and grow in several different kinds of soils. They can closely resemble a grass lawn, but need to be mowed only a few times a year (Figure 9–31). If a taller, more meadow-like look, is preferred, leave sedge unmowed. Sedge can handle light foot traffic and can be planted in either spring or fall. Letting the seeds drop after flowering will fill in any spaces and thicken the planting. If the sedge suffered any frost damage, be sure to mow it in the spring.

9

Figure 9-31. Sedge (*Carex* 'Sunny Blue').
Susan Harris, Flickr CC BY - 2.0

Sedum (*Sedum* spp.). There are many sedums, so look for a creeping variety that will reach only about 4 inches tall (Figure 9–32). Sedums transplant well, so pieces of the plant can be dug up and moved around to new locations. They are drought tolerant and will not need fertilizing. By the second year in the ground, sedums will become dense enough to out-compete weeds. Blooms that occur in the late spring attract pollinators. Despite their short root systems, sedums do very well when planted along banks or hillsides. Consider planting different varieties in the same area for an extended bloom. Sedums will take only light foot traffic.

Figure 9-32. Sedum (*Sedum* spp.) used as a low-maintenance alternative in a roadway median.
Megan Hansen, Flickr CC BY-SA - 2.0

Thyme (*Thymus* spp.). Thyme is well known for its culinary uses because of its pungent aroma and flavor. Thymes are slow spreading and drought tolerant. Thyme does best with fast-draining soil, so amendments such as compost may be needed to improve drainage. Each plant will grow about 6 inches a year. Planting from pots can be an expensive option for a large area. Expect to be on top of weeding the first year. During the second year, thyme will begin to out-compete new weed seeds, and by the third or fourth season, it will reach full coverage (Figure 9-33). To speed up the process, divide larger clumps to fill in any gaps. Once filled in, thyme is close to trouble-free. It doesn't require mowing or fertilizing and only needs water in drought conditions. It can handle moderate (once or twice a day) foot traffic, and it releases a lovely fragrance when strolled over.

Figure 9–33. Wooly thyme (*Thymus pseudolanuginosis*) and Turkish Speedwell (*Veronica liwanensis*) are planted between the stones and withstand foot traffic very well.
Patrick Standish, Flickr CC BY - 2.0

Installation

Once appropriate plants have been selected (Figure 9–34), it is time for installation. Planting in the fall will give roots time to become established in warm soils while the cool air temperatures put a lower demand on shoot growth.

Adequate rainfall will also help reduce supplemental irrigation to help the plants become established. Spring, with

9

its mild temperatures and adequate rainfall, would be the second best time to plant.

Dig planting holes wider than the size of the root ball. Try digging a trench for planting large areas. Spacing depends on the number of plants and their growth rate. Install root balls at the same depth they were growing in their containers, filling any remaining space with soil and tamping it down to press out air pockets. Water new plantings as soon as possible to minimize transplant shock.

A 1- to 1½-inch layer of mulch will conserve soil moisture, prevent erosion, suppress weeds, and help buffer the soil from air temperature fluctuations. As plants mature and their canopy expands, the need to mulch will be greatly reduced. Depending on the size of the plants and planting area, it may be easier to spread mulch prior to planting. Irrigate regularly for the first three months or until established. Choose plants with moisture requirements that match the climate's natural rainfall, and the plants probably will not need supplemental irrigation after the first year, except perhaps during extreme drought (Figure 9–35).

Maintenance

The need for weed control will be highest during the first year or two and diminish as plantings spread to completely cover the ground. Application of a slow-release fertilizer once or twice annually will encourage good plant coverage. Use fertilizers at appropriate levels for lowest environmental impact.

Few ground cover shrubs require pruning, though some gardeners employ it as a technique for stimulating new growth or neatening the appearance of a plant grouping. Prune spring-flowering plants after they bloom and summer- and fall-flowering plants in early spring before new flower buds form. Pruning in late summer or fall is not recommended because it stimulates new growth that could be injured by the winter elements.

Use IPM for disease or pest control. Selecting ground covers appropriate to the site conditions generally translates to well-adapted, healthy plants with minimal pest or disease problems. On the other hand, if a plant is stressed by failure to have its requirements met, it may experience increased susceptibility to pests and disease. Practice IPM to monitor potential problems and minimize harm to the environment. Incorporating a diverse array of native plants into a landscape design may aid in pest management. Native plants will attract a diverse population of native insects, which will in turn attract native predators.

Figure 9-34. A diverse border planting provides habitat for beneficial insects.
Kathleen Moore, CC BY - 2.0

Figure 9–35. Left: The front yard before. Right, after: Mondo grass planted between pavers provides interest in this turfgrass-free front yard. Once established, the mondo grass receives only rainwater.
Barbara Goodman, CC BY - 2.0

9

Case Study—Think IPM: A Brown Area in the Lawn

You have noticed that a brown area appears in the middle of your tall fescue lawn each year. This year the area seems to be even bigger. You worry about it spreading and wonder if there is anything you can do to treat it.

Review the five IPM steps summarized in this section and conduct some background research on tall fescue grass.

1. Monitor and scout to determine pest type and population levels.

The grass grew well for the first five years after planting. Last year you noticed a small brown area that appeared as the weather heated up in the summer. This year the area has grown and is now about 4 feet in diameter (Figure 9–36). A sample could be sent to a diagnostic lab to determine if a disease may be causing the problem. But a more cost-effective response simply requires digging a little deeper to reach the root of the problem.

Figure 9-36. A brown area on tall fescue grass.
NC State Turf Pathology

2. Diagnostics: Accurately identify host and pest.

The following diagnostic steps and questions will help you accurately identify the problem. Responses are included in italics.

Step 1. Identify the plant: Review images and descriptions and select the one most like your turf.
Tall fescue.

Step 2. Describe the problem: Examine both the healthy and damaged leaves carefully.
There is a 4-foot wide, irregular area of dead brown grass in the middle of the yard.

Step 3. Identify what is normal: What does the healthy part of the plant look like?
Dark green thin blades. This is seen on edges of the lawn.

Have you had a soil test?
No (For information on how to submit a soil test, see "Soils and Plant Nutrients," chapter 1.)

Step 4. Describe cultural practices: Describe the age and history of the plant. *The grass was installed as seed five years ago.*

Irrigation. *It is watered three times a week for 45 minutes.*

Fertilizer. *It was fertilized at the beginning of the summer. I do not remember what type, but I followed the label for the amount.*

Maintenance. *It is mowed two times a week during the growing season with a push mower, and the mower is set to remove only a third of the blade of grass so grass blades are more than 1 inch tall after mowing. The clippings are left on the lawn.*

Step 5. Review environmental conditions: What is the yard's topography?
The backyard is fairly flat.

Are there any significant water issues?
It has not rained for three and a half weeks, and it has been very hot for the past two months. There is never any standing water when it rains.

Describe the light near this plant. How many hours of sunlight?
There is a large maple tree on the west side of the yard and a large elm on the south side, so it stays shaded for most of the day. Maybe two hours of full sun per day.

Describe any recent changes or events.
My neighbor lost a tree last winter on the west side of the yard, so there is slightly more light on that side. I had a party two months ago and there were a lot of people walking on the lawn.

Step 6. Identify signs of insects and pathogens: On the leaves?
No insects are visible, and no fungus can be seen.

On the roots?
No insects are visible, and no fungus can be seen.

Step 7. Identify symptoms of pathogens: On the leaves?
There is no evidence of insect feeding.
Some of the leaf blades are all brown, and some have irregular brown spots with a dark halo around them (Figure 9–37).

On the roots? *There is no evidence of insect feeding. Roots look pretty normal, but some are a little brown.*

© 2008 Lane Tredway

Figure 9–37. Irregular brown spots with a dark outline around them on the grass blades.
NC State University

Step 8. Describe distribution of damage in the landscape:
Are other plants in the landscape affected?
No other types of plants in the yard are affected.

Step 9. Describe distribution of damage on the plant and specific plant parts:
Where is the damage seen on the plant?
On the aboveground portions of the grass, some leaves are all brown and some have spots.

Step 10. Identify the onset of the problem:
When did you notice this problem?
The spot appears in the heat of the summer; it appeared last year and is bigger this year.

Brown patch. You can confirm this diagnosis by comparing your responses during the diagnostic steps to the disease description. For example, see Step 2: The size of the damage matches. In Steps 7 through 10, the responses match the description of brown patch.

3. Consider economic, aesthetic, and injury thresholds.
The lawn is vital to your enjoyment of the landscape. The disease is severe enough to warrant investigation. The grass will continue to decline without intervention.

4. Implement a treatment strategy using physical, cultural, biological, or chemical control, or combine these strategies.
From the information found on the TurfFiles web page you learn brown patch is a common disease of tall fescue in North Carolina. Tall fescue is a cool-season grass that does not grow well in our summers. Unfortunately, there is no possible way to get "rid" of the disease. There are, however, many ways to manage the disease effectively.

Physical: This disease is most problematic when lawns have poor air movement and significant shade. Anything to promote more sunlight and air movement will help minimize brown patch development. Pruning up the bottom limbs on the maple and elm trees will help.

Cultural: Aggressive fertilization before the onset of summer stress will promote brown patch. Light, frequent fertilizer applications should be conducted during the summer. Some cultivars of tall fescue have partial resistance to the brown patch fungus. This means the grass will still get the disease, but it will be less severe.

Biological: There are no known biological treatments for brown patch.

Chemical: Fungicides are effective for brown patch management. Check the *North Carolina Agricultural Chemicals Manual* for recommendations. Many of these products are not available to the public, so a contract with a landscape company may be necessary.

5. Evaluate treatment success.
The improved light from pruning the maple and elm trees seem to have kept the spot from growing larger. You are careful to apply only light amounts of fertilizer in the summer. You started a garden journal (Appendix A) to keep track of weather patterns, maintenance, and fertilizer applications so you have records to look back on when future problems occur.

9

Frequently Asked Questions

1. *Should I bag my grass clippings?*

Generally the answer is no. The clippings produced by properly maintained and mowed turf break down rapidly because they are 75 to 85 percent water. Research has shown that a fourth of a lawn's fertilizer needs can be met by recycling grass clippings. If you have a problem with large patch (*Rhizoctonia solani*) or another disease, then bag clippings to lessen spread of the disease. Do not compost diseased clippings.

2. *How do I control excessive thatch buildup in my lawn?*

As turfgrass grows, it produces new roots, leaves, and stems. As older roots and shoots die and slough off, they accumulate on the soil surface as thatch. All healthy turf has some thatch, and appropriate amounts of thatch (¼- to ½-inch) make a lawn more tolerant to traffic, decrease soil compaction, protect grass crowns from temperature extremes, decrease water loss from the soil surface, and return nutrients to the soil environment. Excessive thatch, however, limits turfgrass rooting, attracts insect pests, encourages fungal growth, and can prevent water from penetrating into the soil. Mechanical dethatching is usually recommended when thatch build-up is thicker than ½-inch. Routine hand raking of thatch is effective in small areas; vertical mowers or power rakes may be used in larger areas. Note that centipedegrass and St. Augustinegrass may not tolerate vertical mowers or power raking, so ensure that your type of turf will not be seriously injured by a particular method of thatch removal before beginning. Thatch removal can be performed on our warm-season grasses in late winter when they are dormant, or in the spring after green-up when the grasses are actively growing.

3. *Weeds have taken over my lawn. What can I do?*

The most effective way to achieve long-term weed control is by promoting and maintaining a healthy and vigorously growing lawn. Weakened or slowly growing turf allows sunlight to penetrate the soil surface, encouraging weeds to invade and become established in the landscape. The correction of management practices, such as improper mowing height and poor fertilization, will reduce weeds in the home lawn. Some weed species can become established even with good turf management practices. Hand-pulling is an option in some cases; in others, herbicides can be used as a short-term aid in weed management. There are several pre- and post-emergence herbicides on the market that help control broadleaf weeds in the lawn. Ensure that the active ingredient is labeled for use on the weed(s) you are trying to control. Your county Extension center can provide assistance in weed identification if needed. Always read the label carefully, and be sure your species of turfgrass is tolerant of a particular herbicide.

4. *The soil in my lawn is compacted. What can I do to resolve this?*

Foot traffic, mowing, recent home construction, and even rainfall can contribute to soil compaction, which is especially problematic in clay soils. Soil compaction prevents air and water from penetrating the soil. Grass roots need air and water to grow, so soil compaction results in weaker, thinner turf and more weeds. Core aeration, which is the removal of small cores of soil from the top few inches of soil, allows more air, water, and nutrients to enter the root zone of your turf, helping to alleviate this condition. The results include reduced water runoff; enhanced water, nutrient, and gas uptake; faster thatch breakdown; and better heat and drought tolerance in your turf area.

The best time to perform core aeration on our warm-season grasses is in late spring or early summer when the grass is actively growing. The soil should be moist, but not wet. Be sure to mark sprinkler heads, shallow lines from the sprinkler, and underground utility, cable, and septic lines to prevent damage. Soil cores should be left on the lawn; they will work their way back into the soil within two to four weeks. Lawns may be fertilized, seeded, or top-dressed with a soil amendment immediately after coring. Be sure the timing of fertilization corresponds with the recommendations on the maintenance calendar for your particular turf. The county Extension center has maintenance calendars for our warm-season grasses, or you may access them online. Lawns can be aerated once a year, especially under heavy use conditions and with heavy clay soils. If core aeration equipment is not available for rent or purchase, some lawn care companies may offer this service. Note that spike aeration is not recommended, as this method of aeration only further compacts the soil.

9

5. *When can I plant a fescue lawn?*

If sodding, tall fescue can be planted any time the ground is not frozen. If you are planting from seed, the ideal time is between August 15 and September 1 in the NC mountains, September 1 to September 15 in the piedmont, and September 15 to October 15 in the coastal plain. Seeding beyond these dates increases the chance of failure. Spring-seeding tall fescue is not recommended, especially outside North Carolina's mountain region.

6. *My neighbor's lawn seems to always look greener than mine. What can I do and when should I do it to keep my lawn looking green?*

Just because a grass is greener does not mean the grass is healthier. It may be a species or grass cultivar that is genetically darker than yours. Moisture stress also affects leaf color. In addition, two fertilizers, nitrogen (N) and iron (Fe), are the most commonly used nutrients for deeper turfgrass color. The application of high rates or repeated low rates of nitrogen to cool-season grasses in the spring or summer greatly increases the severity of brown patch.

7. *What is the best grass to plant in my area?*

There is no one best grass to plant in any area of North Carolina. The decision should be based on region, microclimate, intended use or wear at the site, and desired appearance. Over the last several years, zoysiagrass lawns have become increasingly popular. Each grass has its merits and disadvantages. Other lawn grasses found in the area to a lesser degree are centipedegrass, bermudagrass, fine fescues, and tall fescue + Kentucky bluegrass mixes. All of these grasses are used across much of the state, although some species lend themselves more to certain regions.

8. *There are mushrooms in my lawn. Should I worry about them?*

Many homeowners become worried when a prolific group of mushrooms develops in their yard. There is no need to worry about mushrooms with respect to your turf's health. Mushrooms are fungi—ubiquitous organisms that grow and thrive in many turf systems. Typically mushrooms appear after a rain when the weather is warm. Spore germination during warm, moist conditions is how fungi reproduce. Mushrooms are lawn allies in that they feed on the organic material (such as thatch, buried wood, and tree roots) present in the yard, breaking it down into nutrients available to turf. Even when mushrooms develop into what is sometimes called a fairy ring, there is no need to fret. These types of fungi rarely damage turf used for home lawns. If substantial mushroom formation has developed, however, it may be time to consider a lawn aerification program. Aerification can help minimize the buildup of thatch, and it can also slow the development of mushrooms in the lawn. The best recommendation for managing mushrooms is to mow them. Fungicides are typically not effective against these fungi in a landscape.

9. *I noticed some orange stuff on my shoes after I walked through the grass. What is it?*

That depends on the tint of the orange color. In North Carolina, some of our soils are highly oxidized and have a reddish-brown or reddish-orange tint. This could be a possible reason for the orange stuff on the bottom of shoes. Another cause could be a disease called rust. This disease is caused by a fungus that produces many different spore types, and one of those types is a rust color, hence the name of the disease. In North Carolina we see rust on zoysiagrasses, Kentucky bluegrass, and tall fescue. Typically this disease is most active in spring and fall and can produce copious amounts of spores. The spores can develop into orange clouds after mowing and most certainly can turn shoes orange. Although a lot of spores are produced, rust is rarely more than a cosmetic issue.

9

Further Reading

Bruneau, Arthur H. and Gail G. Wilkerson, eds. *Turfgrass Pest Management Manual: A Guide to Major Turfgrass Pests & Turfgrasses*. Raleigh, North Carolina: North Carolina Cooperative Extension Service, 2006. PDF file.

Daniels, Stevie, ed. *Easy Lawns: Low Maintenance Native Grasses for Gardeners Everywhere.* Brooklyn, New York: Brooklyn Botanic Garden, 2001. Print.

Ortho All about Lawns. 2nd ed. Hoboken, New Jersey: John Wiley & Sons Inc., 2008. Print.

Penick, Pam. *Lawn Gone!: Low-Maintenance, Sustainable, Attractive Alternatives for Your Yard.* New York: Ten Speed Press, 2013. Print.

For More Information

http://go.ncsu.edu/fmi_lawns

Contributors

Author: Grady Miller, Professor and Extension Specialist, Department of Crop and Soil Sciences

Contributions by Extension Agents: Shawn Banks, Sam Marshall, Jessica Strickland, Mary Hollingsworth, Peg Godwin, Kerrie Roach

Contributions by Extension Master Gardener Volunteers: Linda Alford, Jacquelyn Weedon, Lee Kapleau, Karen Damari, Judith Bates, Barbara Goodman, Chris Alberti, Connie Schultz, Renee Lampila

Content Editors:
Lucy Bradley, Professor and Extension Specialist, Urban Horticulture, NC State University; Director, NC State Extension Master Gardener program
Kathleen Moore, Urban Horticulturist

Copy Editor: Barbara Scott

Chapter 9 Cover Photo Credit: Skitterphoto, Pixabay CC BY0

Text adapted in part from *Carolina Lawns* (AG-69), NC State Extension.

How to Cite This Chapter:
Miller, G. 2022. Lawns, Chpt 9. In: K.A. Moore, and. L.K. Bradley (eds). *North Carolina Extension Gardener Handbook*, 2nd ed. NC State Extension, Raleigh, NC. <https://content.ces.ncsu.edu/extension-gardener-handbook/9-lawns>

9

Herbaceous Ornamentals

Objectives

This chapter teaches people to:

- Identify why annuals are a better choice in some situations than perennials and vice versa.
- Select appropriate herbaceous plants from garden centers.
- Perform seasonal maintenance requirements for herbaceous plants.
- Incorporate herbaceous plants into a landscape design.
- Recognize and manage the most common problems with herbaceous plants.

10

Introduction

Herbaceous ornamentals are plants that have flexible stems and die back to the ground each year. Unlike woody ornamentals, they do not develop persistent woody tissue that lasts through the winter and develops new buds in the spring. Herbaceous ornamentals are divided into **annuals**, **biennials**, or **perennials** based on their life cycles. Annuals die after a growing season. They are sensitive to temperatures that are either too hot or too cold. With biennial and perennial plants, the stems die back, but the crown of each plant survives to produce new growth the following season (Figure 10–1). These life cycles can be influenced by geography. In the cooler mountain region of the state, a plant may grow as an annual. But in the coastal region, it may grow as a perennial.

Herbaceous ornamentals provide interest and contrast that make a landscape lively and interesting (Figure 10–2). These plants also add depth, dimension, form, and texture to the landscape. Their flowers are often the stars of the garden, providing enchanting colors and fragrances. This chapter provides information on how to select, install, and maintain herbaceous ornamentals, and how to address common problems associated with these plants.

Figure 10–1. This biennial foxglove dies back to a rosette of leaves at the crown. The crown is the transition between the leaves and the root and can be found at or just below ground level.

Barbara Goodman, CC BY - 2.0

Figure 10–2. A perennial bed.
NC.Hort, Flickr

10

Annuals

Annuals are plants that are transplanted or direct-seeded each year because once they bloom and set seed, they die. Annuals bloom more quickly and for a longer period than any other group of plants. They are versatile, easy to grow, and relatively inexpensive. They offer the gardener a chance to experiment with color, height, texture, and form. Annuals provide a massive display of color when used in beds, planters, window boxes, and hanging baskets, or they can be used to fill in spaces where a perennial has died or where spring-flowering bulbs have died back (Figure 10–3). Plant breeders have produced many new and improved cultivars that have a more compact form, produce more flowers, tolerate more sun or shade, or are resistant to insect and disease damage.

Figure 10–3. Annual color, a massing of pansies (*Achimenes* spp.). Kathleen Moore, CC BY - 2.0

As with all plants, it is important to place annuals where there is adequate sun or shade and space for growth. Small plants purchased in 4-inch pots may grow to fill a space 2-feet-square by the end of the growing season.

Annuals that perform well can be found online in the NC State Extension Gardener Plant Toolbox.

Some plants like alyssum (*Lobularia maritima*), ageratum (*Ageratum houstonianum*), cleome (*Cleome houtteana*), impatiens (*Impatiens walleriana*), melampodium (*Melampodium divaricatum*), nasturtium (*Tropaeolum majus*), petunia (*Petunia* ×*hybrida*), and vinca (*Catharanthus roseus*)

naturally reseed themselves. The ability to reseed varies with the cultivar and the severity of the winter. Reseeding is not always desirable. Volunteer plants are often scattered or located in a clump instead of growing in their designated spot. Some hybrid varieties are developed to be sterile and do not reseed, or their seedlings do not have the same flower quality as their parents.

Types of Annuals

Annuals are sometimes categorized as cool-season or warm-season. Cool-season annuals, such as geraniums (*Pelargonium* × *hybridum*), petunias (*Petunia* ×*hybrida*), and snapdragons (*Antirrhinum majus*), grow best when the temperatures are in the 70s°F and 80s°F during the day. The best flower production is in the spring and fall, while flower production declines in the middle of a hot summer. Warm-season annuals, such as cosmos (*Cosmos* spp.), four-o'clocks (*Mirabilis jalapa*), and pentas (*Pentas lanceolata*), perform well when the daytime temperatures are in the 80s°F and 90s°F and the nighttime temperatures are in the 60s°F and 70s°F.

Annual flowers differ in their tolerance to cold weather and frost. Hardy annuals are the most cold-tolerant. They tolerate light frost and some freezing weather without being killed. In most cases, hardy annuals are planted in the fall or in the spring before the last frost date. Hardy annuals include calendula (*Calendula officinalis*), cornflower (*Centaurea cyanus*), foxglove (*Digitalis purpurea*), larkspur (*Delphinium* spp.), pansy (*Viola* × *wittrockiana*), sweet alyssum (*Lobularia maritima*), stock (*Matthiola incana*), viola (*Viola cornuta, V. tricolor*), and many *Dianthus* cultivars. Most hardy annuals are not heat-tolerant and usually decline and die with the onset of hot summer temperatures.

Half-hardy annuals tolerate periods of cold damp weather but are damaged by frost. Most half-hardy annuals are seeded outdoors in early spring because they do not require warm soil temperatures to germinate. Seeds or plants are normally planted after the last spring frost. Examples of half-hardy annuals include baby's breath (*Gypsophila elegans*), bells of Ireland (*Moluccella laevis*), blue sage (*Salvia uliginosa*), candytuft (*Iberis amara, I. umbellata*), cleome (*Cleome houtteana*), forget-me-nots (*Myosotis sylvatica*), love-in-a-mist (*Nigella damascena*), snow-on-the-mountain (*Euphorbia marginata*), strawflower (*Xerochrysum bracteatum*), and torenia (*Torenia fournieri*). Many half-hardy annuals decline in the midsummer heat but may re-bloom in late summer or fall.

Tender annuals are native to warm tropical regions of the world. They are sensitive to fall temperature drops and cold soil temperatures and are easily damaged by frost. Plant tender annuals after the threat of frost is past. Tender annuals include ageratum (*Ageratum houstonia-*

10

num), balsam (*Impatiens balsamina*), begonia (*Begonia (Semperflorens-Cultorum Group)*), plumed cockscomb celosia (*Celosia argentea* var. *plumosa*), coleus (*Coleus scutellarioides*), colocasia (*Colocasia* spp.), globe amaranth (*Gomphrena globosa*), impatiens (*Impatiens walleriana*), marigold (*Calendula officinalis*), morning glory (*Ipomoea purpurea*), nasturtium (*Tropaeolum majus*), nicotiana (*Nicotiana alata*), petunia (*Petunia* × *hybrida*), purple heart (*Tradescantia pallida* 'Purple Heart'), Persian shield (*Strobilanthes auriculata* var. dyeriana), scarlet sage (*Salvia splendens*), moss verbena (*Verbena aristigera*), vinca (periwinkle) (*Catharanthus roseus*), and zinnia (*Zinnia angustifolia, Z. elegans*).

Winter-flowering annuals, such as pansies (*Viola* × *wittrockiana*), violas (*Viola cornuta*), and flowering cabbage, are planted in the fall, flower in the winter and early spring, and die during the summer.

Some flowers that might otherwise be classified as perennial, such as begonias (*Begonia* spp.) and snapdragons (*Antirrhinum majus*), are classified with annuals because they do not consistently survive the winter in a specific location.

Biennials

The life cycle of biennial plants is completed over two growing seasons. During the first season they produce only leaves, usually in a rosette. Following a winter cold period, they flower in the second growing season, produce seeds, and then die. Popular biennials include foxglove (*Digitalis purpurea*), hollyhock (*Alcea rosa*), stock (*Matthiola incana*), and sweet William (*Dianthus barbatus*). Cultural practices are basically the same as for annuals, except that the plants are alive for two growing seasons and produce no flowers the first season.

If biennial seeds are sown in midsummer, however, the plants develop during the summer and fall. After exposure to the winter cold, they develop flowers in the spring.

New cultivars of plants traditionally referred to as biennials are being developed that produce flowers the first season. 'Foxy' is a cultivar of foxglove (*Digitalis purpurea*) that blooms the first year. Annual cultivars of sweet William (*Dianthus barbatus*) and hollyhock (*Alcea rosea*) are also available.

Perennials

Many perennials flower for only a few weeks each year. But with careful planning, a gardener can grow perennials that produce a succession of flowers for most of the season. As one type of perennial finishes, another begins to bloom.

Although trees, shrubs, vines, and many ground covers are perennials, gardeners usually use the term perennial to refer to herbaceous perennial flowering plants. Most herbaceous perennials grow and flower for several years, although some perennials survive for only three or four years. In the fall, the tops of herbaceous perennials (leaves, stems, and flowers) die down to the ground, while the root system persists through the winter. In the spring the plant grows a new top from its crown or roots. Plants that grow from bulbs and bulblike structures (**corms, tubers, rhizomes**) are also herbaceous perennials, but are often classified separately as flowering bulbs.

Perennial classifications are based on hardiness. Hardy perennials normally survive the winter with little or no protection. Tender or half-hardy perennials can survive a mild winter, but may not survive a severe winter without protection. In colder climates, tender perennials are often grown as annuals, including snapdragons (*Antirrhinum majus*) and four-oclocks (*Mirabilis jalapa*). Microclimates and soil drainage are factors in determining how hardy and long-lived a perennial is at any particular site.

Perennials have some advantages over annuals:
- There is a wider diversity of perennials to choose from, which allows for more colors, textures, and fragrances.
- It is easier to find a perennial that thrives under differing sun exposures, soil types, and moisture levels. If annuals cannot grow in a particular location, a perennial is often a good option.
- Perennials survive for several years without replanting.
- They grow quickly, reaching their mature size in just a few years.
- They often divide easily for spreading around the landscape or to share with friends, thereby reducing a garden's overall cost.

Is It an Annual, a Biennial, or a Perennial?

Local climatic conditions, development of new cultivars, and new uses for specific garden flowers have blurred the distinctions among annuals, biennials, and perennials. Annuals have traditionally been referred to as plants that complete their life cycle in one growing season. Some perennials that bloom quickly, such as moss verbena (*Verbena aristigera*) and Jerusalem cherry (*Solanum pseudocapsicum*), are grown as annuals and discarded at the end of one season. Some of our so-called annuals, including begonias (*Begonia* spp.), impatiens (*Impatiens* spp.), and snapdragons (*Antirrhinum majus*), are actually perennials in warmer climates or mild winters as found in the NC coastal plain.

Garden Design and Implementation

Site Selection

A successful and beautiful herbaceous ornamental garden takes planning by the gardener before the first seed or plant hits the soil. Finding an appropriate site and finding the types of plants that thrive in that site are the first steps. Consider the amount of sunlight, microclimate temperature, competition from tree roots, soil drainage, and aeration.

Herbaceous ornamentals are showy, so place them where they can be seen and enjoyed. Will you look out from inside the home at these plants, or do you wish them to welcome visitors to your home? If the plants are fragrant, consider a location where you linger, such as near a patio or front porch. Herbaceous ornamentals are very flexible and can be planted in the ground, in raised beds, and in containers, including hanging baskets.

Will this garden area be brand new, or is this an older planting bed that needs some renovation? Are there woody plants in the area to consider?

These factors affect site selection:

• **Sunlight.** Examine the type of light available, from full sun to partial sun, and heavy shade. How many hours a day is the site in full sun? When evaluating light exposure, note the duration and intensity of sunlight the site receives. Four hours of full sun during the morning is very different from 4 hours of stronger, more intense afternoon sun. There are also many types of shade, and the amount of light in a shaded location varies with the type, number, and size of trees in the area. If the site receives more than 3 hours of unfiltered midday sun, treat it as a "full sun" site. "Partial shade" is defined as receiving unfiltered morning sun but shade during the afternoon hours, or moderate shading throughout the entire day. A "heavily shaded" site would receive very little direct midday light and less than 60% of the sun's intensity during the remainder of the day. Few flowering plants do well in deep shade. Introducing more light to a shaded location can greatly increase flower production. Removing some tree limbs can allow more light to reach the ground below. Plants preferring partial shade may tolerate more sunlight if temperatures are moderate and adequate water is provided.

• **Water.** Annuals and perennials need about an inch of water per week during the growing season. If summers are particularly hot, plants may need more water. Deep infrequent irrigations are better than light, frequent watering. Locating the plantings near a water source makes it easier to water the beds. A soaker hose, drip irrigation system, or careful hose watering at the base of the plants helps to keep the foliage dry and to avoid disease problems. If overhead watering is unavoidable, water in the morning so the foliage has time to dry before nightfall.

• **Slope angle and exposure.** The steeper the angle of the slope is, the greater the runoff and potential for erosion. Plants on slopes need to be watered more frequently. North- and east-facing slopes are cooler than south- or west-facing slopes.

• **Temperature.** Very few plants look attractive and flower profusely from early spring through late fall. Cool-season flowers such as dianthus (*Dianthus* sp.), pansies (*Viola × wittrockiana*), and snapdragons (*Antirrhinum majus*) grow best when the temperatures are mild; they slow or stop flowering when exposed to high summer temperatures. It is possible to extend the flowering season of cool-season annuals by placing them in a protected location, shaded from direct sunlight from about noon to 4:00 p.m. Plants adjacent to a paved surface or brick wall experience warmer temperatures, and their flowering period is shortened. Choose heat-loving plants such as gaillardia (*Gaillardia pulchella*), portulaca (*Portulaca grandiflora*), and moss verbena (*Verbena aristigera*), for locations next to walls, driveways, or other locations with reflected heat. On the contrary, planting these heat-loving plants on the north side of the house in light shade delays and reduces their flower production.

• **Weeds.** Select a site without a severe weed problem. Avoid sites with hard-to-control weeds such as bermudagrass and nutsedge. A site that has been cultivated for several years probably has fewer weeds. Manage weeds prior to planting. Read more about weed management in chapter 6, "Weeds."

• **Soil type.** The soil type, whether sand, silt, or clay, affects moisture and drainage of the planting site. Soil pH requirements vary among annuals and perennials, but most prefer a pH between 5.5 and 6.5. Conduct a soil test and review chapter 1, "Soils and Plant Nutrients." Apply lime to the soil prior to installing plants that need a higher pH. Soil improvement for perennial beds is similar to that for annuals. Fall is the best time to incorporate organic matter, but any time is better than not using organic matter at all. Add a 3-inch to 4-inch layer of pine bark mulch on top of the soil before planting. If the soil is not suitable, consider creating raised beds and importing soil.

• **Soil moisture.** Many perennials need well-drained soil. Although many plants tolerate a wet site for a short period of time, most are killed by extended periods of wet feet. So do not locate a perennial border in a low-lying area that is subject to standing water. Examine the site's interrelated factors of drainage, moisture retention, and soil aeration. Frequent heavy

10

rains in combination with poorly drained soils causes excessive soil moisture and limited air space in the soil, thus reducing plant growth and increasing the chances of root-rot problems. One way to check for adequate drainage is to dig a hole 10 inches deep and fill it with water. After it drains, refill it with water. If the water drains in 8 to 10 hours, the site has adequate drainage for most herbaceous plants. If the water drains in an hour or less, add organic matter to slow percolation. If it takes longer than 10 hours to drain, subsoil compaction or the presence of a hardpan beneath the bed may be to blame. Deep tillage of the beds is sometimes needed to break up the subsoil and increase the drainage rate.

Garden Design

Select plants for a specific purpose—such as edging, accents for evergreens, masses of color, or rock garden specimens—so that each plant's characteristics match the site and your objectives. Observe flowering times to find plants that flower together and plants that are showy when little else is in bloom. To obtain details on particular plants or groups of plants, consult plant societies, specialty books, nurseries that specialize in herbaceous perennials, and local botanical gardens. Information about recommended perennials is also on the NC State Gardener Plant Toolbox website.

Identify the roles the plants will play in the garden. This is especially important with perennials because they grow in the same location for several years. Add plants that provide contrast in height, form, and texture. Keep color combinations in mind when designing a bed or border. In general, it is best to plant in groups or drifts rather than using single plants. Groups or drifts are normally repeated several times throughout the landscape to provide unity. Read more about designing planting beds in chapter 19, "Landscape Design."

Designing a garden with plants that exhibit many different colors requires some coordination. Consider the color of the house and any other fixed structures, such as fences or utility buildings. Using pink flowers against a brick house with orange tones would not produce a pleasant combination. Try to use masses of a single color instead of mixing colors in a flower bed (Figure 10–4). A mass planting of a single color or planting in bands of colors produces a stronger impact.

Consider location and how the flowers will be viewed. Bright colors stand out and appear closer, while dark colors appear farther away and tend to fade into the background. For example, a bed of red flowers is easily seen from a distance, but blue and purple flowers are best enjoyed up close (Figure 10–5). Bright colors draw attention to an area, so do not use red and yellow flowers near an eyesore or unattractive area. White is the last color to fade from sight as darkness falls and thus is good for areas used at night.

Figure 10–4. A mass planting of milkweed (*Asclepias tuberosa*) makes a visual impact and also supports wildlife. Blanket flower (*Gaillardia pulchella*) is seen in the foreground.
Mark Levisay, Flickr CC BY - 2.0

Figure 10–5. Blue or purple flowers like this stock (*Centaurea cyanus*) are best viewed up close.
Kathleen Moore, CC BY - 2.0

Colors that look good together are said to be in harmony. There are four basic color schemes to choose from: complementary, monochromatic, analogous, and triadic. Colors opposite on the color wheel (Figure 10–6) are complementary and look good when used together. Examples include red and green, yellow and violet, orange and blue. Monochromatic color schemes use lighter and darker shades of a single color. For an analogous harmony, use any three colors next to each other on the color wheel; for example, orange, yellow-orange, and yellow. A triadic harmony is achieved by combining three colors that are equal distances apart—for example, yellow, red, and blue. Read more about harmony in chapter 19, "Landscape Design."

Colors also affect how people feel. Colors on the right-hand side of the color wheel are considered warm colors (yellow to red); colors on the left side are considered cool colors (green to violet). Planting warm-colored flowers around a deck or patio make it seem warmer. Red tends to excite people. Research has also shown that food tastes better around red colors. Pink is perceived as being sweet and fragrant. Yellow is associated with liveliness and exuberance. White gives the feeling of neatness, cleanliness, and orderliness. Green helps eyes to recover quickly from strain. Blue is perceived as cool and calming. Gray is said to promote creativity.

Preparing the Soil

Good soil is the foundation of healthy plants. Study "Soils and Plant Nutrients," chapter 1, in this manual to learn how to test soil for deficiencies and how to properly amend it for greatest success.

Plant Selection

Herbaceous ornamental plants and seeds are available from a wide variety of sources. If possible, buy named cultivars selected for their known characteristics of disease resistance, heat and cold tolerance, growth habit, and color. Garden centers provide plants in a variety of container sizes. These plants are often in flower when they are offered for sale, which allows selection of the desired colors and often gives an instant color effect in the garden. Although it is possible to transplant perennials in flower, it is much better to transplant prior to flowering.

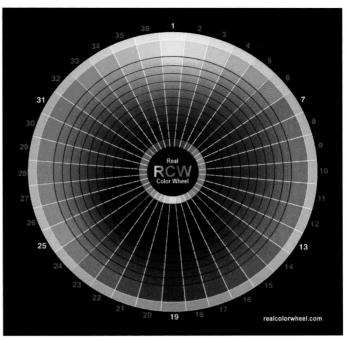

Figure 10–6. The color wheel.
Donald Jusko, CC BY - 2.0

Landscaping with Perennials

Traditionally, perennials were planted in formal gardens in large beds or borders 6-feet to 12-feet wide. Perennials are used in a wide variety of ways—in island beds, rock gardens, woodland plantings, or even in bog gardens.

Ideally a perennial border includes a background, such as a wall or hedge, against which perennials stand out while in flower (Figure 10–7). In island beds, perennials can provide their own background if the tallest plants are planted in the center and low-growing plants are located toward the edges. In designing long borders or beds, group plants according to their height. Verify bloom times to have plants blooming at different times of the year. Do not forget that perennials with colorful or interesting foliage provide interest even when the plants are not in flower (Figure 10–8). Combine annuals with perennials to fill in bloom-time gaps and produce a continuous colorful show. Figure 10–9 shows an example of how to design a bed using height and bloom time to provide year-round interest. Figures 10–10 and 10–11 illustrate designs for sun and shade respectively. Learn more about "Landscape Design" in chapter 19.

Figure 10–7. Flowers from this perennial border stand out because of the fence background element.
Patrick Standish, Flickr CC BY - 2.0

Figure 10–8. When you design a bed, group plants together, placing the tallest plants toward the back, and remember to use plants that are interesting even when not in bloom like grasses and evergreen shrubs.
Kathleen Moore, CC BY - 2.0

10

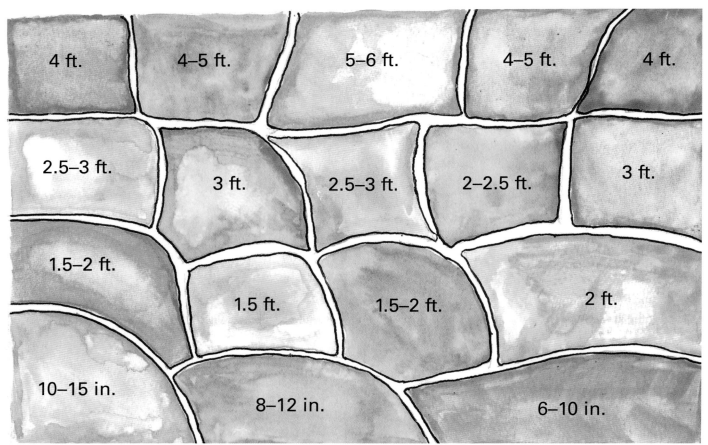

Figure 10–9. A perennial bed designed by height of the plants and to provide for year-round bloom. Pink = spring blooming, Green = summer blooming, and Yellow = fall blooming.
Renee Lampila

Plants sold in cell packs are less expensive than plants grown in larger containers, and their roots usually grow into the surrounding soil more quickly. Select plants that are compact and have normal color. Plants in cell packs dry out quickly, so keep them moist until they are planted.

Discount chain stores and grocery stores often sell plants in cardboard boxes, tubes, or plastic bags. These plants were dormant when shipped but may have started growth while on display. If purchased soon after the plants arrive at the merchant, such plants often grow satisfactorily. But they seldom do well if they have dried out or have produced new stems and leaves that are thin, yellow, or pale-green. If only a small amount of new growth has occurred, these plants may grow satisfactorily but should be hardened off before planting outdoors (Figure 10–12).

Mail-order companies offer a wider selection of plants than most local nurseries. While most mail-order companies are reputable, a few are misleading in their claims and specialize in offering small, lower-grade plants. Most mail-order companies guarantee their plants and offer to replace those that arrive in poor condition or fail to grow

Importing Soil

Sometimes it is necessary to import soil to fill a raised bed, but there are several potential problems. Consider using imported soil only as a last resort. Imported soil is often harvested from subsoil sources rather than top soil. Subsoil is not ideal for plant growth as it does not contain adequate supplies of organic matter or nutrients.

Imported soils may contain insect pests, soilborne diseases, organisms such as nematodes, or weed seeds. Pollutants, including toxic metals such as lead, are other potential contaminants. It is challenging to obtain accurate historical information on imported soils, making it difficult to evaluate potential problems. Often, improving the existing soil through composting, mulching, and fertilizers is a better option.

properly. Most companies ship plants bare-root or in small containers. Shipping dates vary with each company's location. Northern nurseries often ship only in the spring. When the plants arrive, check to see that they are moist.

Figure 10–10. An example of a perennial bed designed for full sun and contains the following plants:

Number	Common Name	Latin Name
1.	Elderberry	*Sambucus canadensis*
2.	Weigela	*Weigela florida*
3.	Milkweed	*Asclepias tuberosa*
4.	Coral bells	Heuchera 'Palace Purple'
5.	Black-eyed Susan	*Rudbeckia fulgida*
6.	Ox eye	*Heliopsis helianthoides*
7.	Sneezeweed	*Helenium autumnale*
8.	Calico aster	*Symphyotricum lateriflorum*
9.	Cranesbill	*Geranium manculatum*
10.	Mealy cup sage	*Salvia farinacea*
11.	Tulips 40 bulbs	Tulipa hybrids
12.	Monkshood	*Aconitum* spp.
13.	Delphinium	*Delphinium* spp.

Renee Lampila

Figure 10–11. A bed designed for shade from existing evergreen trees and contains the following plants:

Number	Common Name	Latin Name
1.	Existing long-leaf pines	*Pinus palustris*
2.	Dwarf rhododendron	*Rhododendron minus*
3.	Wild columbine	*Aquilegia canadensis*
4.	Lenten rose	*Helleborus orientalis*
5.	Hosta	*Hosta* 'Blue Mammoth'
6.	Hosta	*Hosta* 'Francee'
7.	Lady's mantle	*Alchemilla mollis*
8.	Bugle weed	*Ajuga reptans*

Renee Lampila

Starting From Seeds

Start herbaceous ornamentals indoors from seeds or sow them directly in the garden.

Indoor Sowing

Start seeds eight to 10 weeks before the last spring frost. Harden off seedlings by exposing them to outside conditions before planting in their intended site. Read more about starting plants from seeds in chapter 13, "Propagation."

Direct Sowing

Wait two to three weeks after the last spring frost before sowing. If sowed directly in the garden when soil temperatures are below 60°F, most seeds do not germinate well or can rot.

Annuals seeded in the garden sometimes fail to germinate properly because the soil surface crusts and prevents water entry. One way to overcome this is to make a furrow in the soil about ½-inch deep and fill it with vermiculite (if the soil is dry, water the furrow before filling with vermiculite).

Figure 10–12. Harden off plants by placing them in a protected area outdoors.
Lucy Bradley, CC BY - 2.0

Then sow the seed at the rate recommended on the package. Cover the seeds with vermiculite, and use a nozzle adjusted to a fine mist to water the seeded area thoroughly. Keep the seedbed well-watered, or cover with

10

All-America Selections

Plant breeders are constantly developing new and improved cultivars of bedding plants. Some of the outstanding new cultivars are designated as All-America Selections Winners. The All-America Selections is an industry-sponsored organization composed of a council of judges and over 50 official test gardens across the country.

NC State University has a test garden at the J. C. Raulston Arboretum (JCRA) in Raleigh. April is the best time to see winter annuals; July and August are the best months for summer annuals. Trial reports summarizing the results of bedding plant and perennial research conducted are posted on the JCRA website.

mulch such as newspaper to prevent excessive evaporation. Remove the mulch promptly after germination begins so young seedlings receive adequate sunlight.

Seeds that are particularly susceptible to damping-off fungal disease, such as sweet alyssum (*Lobularia maritima*), should be sown in hills. Zinnias (*Zinnia elegans*) are another exception to the traditional planting recommendations. In many cultivars of zinnias, some flowers may appear with a large, nearly naked **corolla** and few colorful petals. This phenomenon is sometimes referred to as "Mexican hats." To eliminate undesirable plants without leaving holes in the garden bed, sow two or three seeds at each location, wait until the plants start flowering, and then remove plants with undesirable characteristics. Thin the remaining plants to the recommended 8-inch to 12-inch spacing.

When most outdoor-seeded annuals develop their first pair of true leaves, it is time to thin seedlings to the recommended spacing. Transplant the excess seedlings to another spot. Many perennials are hybrids that do not grow true to type when propagated from saved seed; off-types of color, flower form, and plant habit are common. Although some perennial seeds can be sown directly in the beds where they are to flower, it is usually best to start plants indoors or in a cold frame and set them out in beds after the weather warms. An alternative to spring seeding is to sow seeds in flats or seedling beds during the summer for fall transplanting.

Working With Transplants

Transplants produce a display of flowers several weeks earlier than direct-seeded plants. This is especially true for annuals such as scarlet sage (*Salvia splendens*) and common lantana (*Lantana camara*), which germinate slowly or need several months to bloom from seeds.

Annual flowers are available at a variety of retail businesses in the spring. Buy only healthy plants, free of insects and diseases. Retailers often purchase flowering plants or bedding plants from a wholesale grower instead of growing the plants themselves. While the quality of these plants is often excellent when they first arrive,

some retailers are not plant experts, nor are equipped to properly care for plants. Do not purchase plants that have not been watered properly or that have been stored under stressful conditions (as on hot, paved surfaces) for extended periods. Ask when the plants arrived or if a new shipment is expected soon. Freshly stocked plants are preferable to plants held for several weeks. Choose plants with compact foliage, side branches, and good color. It is tempting to select the plants that are in bloom, but younger, nonflowering plants are often better choices because they establish in the landscape more quickly.

Bare-root plants are normally transplanted in early spring. In theory, container-grown plants can be transplanted any time of the year. But in reality, plants set out during hot, dry weather or the cold of winter, require more pampering to survive. Container-grown perennials that flower in late summer or fall are normally planted in the spring, while spring-flowering perennials are planted in late summer or early fall. Regardless of the time of planting, allow perennials sufficient time to establish before flowering or before the onset of cold or hot, dry weather. Many gardeners prefer fall planting because the plants develop an extensive root system before new foliage growth occurs. The ideal weather for transplanting is cool and overcast. Wait until the proper planting time to purchase plants even though transplants are often available sooner. Do not plant tender annuals before the danger of frost has passed. Do not plant hardy annuals, such as pansies, until the soil has cooled because planting too early can result in heat damage and disease in the fall. Likewise, setting out transplants too early in spring, before the soil has warmed, results in cold damage. Do not set out new plants immediately after purchase. Give them time to acclimate by keeping plants outdoors for a few days in a partially shaded location. Check them daily and water as needed. Because the soil volume is limited in small containers, roots dry out quickly. Although plants may appear to recover fully, wilting stunts their potential growth.

Soak bare-root plants in water for about a half hour before planting. Water container-grown plants before removing them from their pots. A damp root ball is less likely to fall apart. Do not pull plants from their containers.

Remove plants from individual containers by tipping each container and tapping the bottom. To remove plants from cell packs, turn the pack upside down and squeeze the bottom of each cell to force the root ball out of the pack (Figure 10–13). If the plants are in fiber pots, remove the fiber from the outside of the root mass. When setting out plants in peat pots, remove the upper edges of the pot so that the lip of the peat pot is not exposed above the soil level—where it acts as a wick and pulls water away from the plant (Figure 10–14). Remove the bottom of the peat pot to encourage better rooting and drainage (Figure 10–15).

Figure 10–13. Remove plants from individual plastic pots by tipping the pot and tapping the plant until it falls into your hand; do not pull a plant out by the stem. Turn plants in cell packs over, and push out from the bottom.
Chris Alberti, CC BY - 2.0

Figure 10–14. Remove the top lip of the peat pot so there is no wicking of water.
Kathleen Moore, CC BY - 2.0

Figure 10–15. Remove the bottom of a peat pot to encourage drainage.
Kathleen Moore, CC BY - 2.0

Review the information provided when plants are purchased, or check references such as the NC State Gardener Plant Toolbox to determine optimum spacing between plants. Crowding plants increases the likelihood of disease and insect problems. Plant tall, upright plants such as snapdragons about one-fourth as far apart as their mature height. Space tall, bushy plants about one-half as far apart as their mature height and rounded, bushy annuals about as far apart as their mature height. To make beds look more uniform, use staggered spacing instead of setting plants in straight rows.

Once the soil in a planting bed is amended, water it until it is slightly damp. Dig a hole for each plant as deep as the plant's root ball and twice as wide. Prior to planting, drench the soil around the planting hole with a liquid fertilizer (16-12-10 or 20-20-20 mixed 1 tablespoon per gallon of water) to stimulate root growth.

Turn the pot upside down and slide the root ball out. Roots may have difficulty growing into the surrounding soil unless the roots and soil mixture are cut or loosened. Loosen the roots around the bottom and sides of the root ball and spread them out. Fill the hole and firm the soil lightly around the plant, making sure the crown is at the soil line. This is sometimes difficult to determine for dormant bare-root plants. Set the plants at the same depth or just slightly higher than they were growing in the container. When filling the hole, firm the soil lightly. If plants must be transplanted during hot or windy periods, provide some shading after planting.

After planting, apply a 2-inch to 3-inch layer of mulch, such as pine bark nuggets or pine straw. Because most perennials grow from the crown, do not cover the crown. Mulches help keep the soil surface from crusting, reduce soil temperature, conserve moisture, and prevent weed seed germination. When organic mulches break down,

10

they add humus to the soil. Avoid using pine straw around pansies (*Viola ×wittrockiana*) and violas (*Viola cornuta*) as it can reduce their growth and flowering. Pine straw has also caused problems with other bedding plants.

Monitor transplants frequently, and prevent moisture stress until new roots have had time to grow into the surrounding soil. Remember that the root mass is initially only as large as the original container, so apply irrigation water toward the base of the plant until it becomes established.

Maintenance of Annuals and Perennials

Watering

Although some herbaceous plants tolerate moderate periods of dry weather, others must have a continuous supply of water. Flowering of most annuals slows or stops during extended hot, dry summer weather. To minimize the need for watering, select drought-tolerant annuals such as globe amaranth (*Gomphrena globosa*), blue blazes hyssop (*Agastache* 'Blue Blazes'), Dahlberg daisy (*Thymophylla*),, gazania (*Gazania rigens*), portulaca (*Portulaca grandiflora*), and creeping zinnia (*Zinnia angustifolia*).

Supplemental irrigation probably will be necessary at some point during the growing season. Soil type, as well as growth stage and temperature, influence watering frequency. Bedding plants grown in a properly watered clay soil may need watering only once a week. Bedding plants grown in a sandy soil may need watering several times a week. This varies with the time of year, amount of sunlight or shade, plant growth, and other environmental factors. Most plants need 1 inch of water per week but may require more when flowering or when exposed to high temperatures or windy conditions. Moisten the entire bed thoroughly, but do not water so heavily that the soil becomes soggy. After watering, allow the soil to dry moderately before watering again.

A soaker hose is excellent for watering flower beds. Water seeps directly into the soil without waste and without wetting leaves and flowers. The slow-moving water does not disturb the soil or reduce its capacity to absorb water. Sprinklers wet the flowers and foliage and make them more susceptible to diseases. The impact of water drops falling on the surface may change soil structure and cause it to puddle or crust, preventing free entry of water and air.

The least effective method for watering is with a hand-held nozzle. Watering with a nozzle has all the disadvan-

Care of Cut flowers (Figure 10–16)

Extend the longevity of cut flowers by cutting them in the morning when their water content is high. Select flowers that are not yet in full bloom. Use a clean sharp knife or clippers, and place the cut stems immediately into a bucket of warm water. Moving the stems quickly into water prevents bubbles from blocking the vascular system in the stem. Leave them in the warm water for 2 hours to soak up as much water as possible before arranging. To hold the flowers longer, place them in fresh warm water, cover them with plastic to prevent water loss, and set them in a refrigerator.

When flowers are arranged, remove any foliage that will be below the water line in the vase. Cut the stem again, but make the cut at an angle to maximize the area available to take up water and cut the stem underwater to prevent air bubbles. Arrange flowers in a clean container that has been washed with one part household bleach to nine parts water and allowed to dry. This should kill bacteria that could clog the stems and reduce water uptake.

A commercial flower preservative added to the water lengthens the flowers' vase life by providing nutrients and killing bacteria. Do not reuse florist foam as it is sometimes contaminated with bacteria. Place the arrangement in a cool, draft-free location out of direct sunlight. Recut the stems every third day, change the water, and add fresh preservative.

Note that daffodils and other jonquils have a sap that is toxic to other cut flowers. If you want to use daffodils in a mixed arrangement, place them in a vase of cool water overnight so most of the sap is released before mixing them with other flowers.

Figure 10–16. Properly cared for cut flowers last a long time in a vase.
Erin Downey, Flickr CC BY-SA - 2.0

10

tages of watering with a sprinkler. Additionally, gardeners seldom are patient enough to do a thorough job of watering with a nozzle so they do not apply enough water and do not distribute it evenly over the bed.

Fertilizing

Nitrogen is the nutrient that most frequently limits plant growth. Unfortunately, nitrogen is the most difficult nutrient to manage. Soil tests for nitrogen are not dependable, and nitrogen is easily leached from the soil. The challenge is to maintain adequate nitrogen levels to meet the plants' requirements without damaging the plants or the environment.

Follow the fertilizer recommendations provided with the soil test results. In addition, growth rate and foliage color are the primary guides for determining whether additional fertilizer should be applied during the growing season. A plant growing well may not need fertilizer, and too much fertilizer promotes excessive foliage growth without necessarily promoting flower production. Too much fertilizer may also stimulate disease and pest problems. Always follow the recommendations on your soil test results. It is not necessary to remove the mulch before fertilizing. Watering after applying fertilizer washes fertilizer off the foliage, prevents foliage burn, and makes the fertilizer available to the plants more quickly.

Do mulches affect soil pH?

While oak leaves and pine needles are acidic when fresh, as they break down they become neutral or even slightly alkaline. In addition, except in sand, soil pH is strongly buffered and difficult to change. In fact, mulches have very little impact on soil pH and almost none below 2 inches deep.

Mulching

A mulched garden has an orderly look, requires less weeding, and better maintains uniform soil moisture. In addition, mulches help insulate roots during cold periods and keep roots cool during warm periods. Furthermore, mulches reduce the spread of soilborne diseases by preventing soil from splashing onto leaves There are two types of mulches: organic and inorganic. Organic mulches include bark, grass clippings, leaves, pine needles, shredded hardwood, straw, and wood chips. Inorganic mulches include landscape fabrics, plastic, rocks, and rubber. Organic mulches have the advantage of adding nutrients and humus to the soil as they decompose, improving soil tilth and moisture-holding capacity. In addition, using yard waste, like compost, leaves, or grass clippings, as a mulch reduces waste disposal costs.

Figure 10–17. Pine needles are a great mulch for perennial beds.
Malcolm Manners, Flickr CC BY - 2.0

10

Apply mulch containing small pieces of matter sparingly to avoid forming a layer that water cannot penetrate. Be aware that mulch with large pieces of matter, placed in thick layers, may provide habitat for voles and cause crown rot.

Organic mulches are almost always the better choice for herbaceous ornamental beds. Apply most organic mulches after plants are well-established and when there is reasonably good soil moisture. Replenish mulch in early spring to maintain the desired mulch depth. Mulch the entire bed except for the crowns and stems of the plants.

Organic Mulches

- **Bark (pine bark nuggets).** Use 2 inches to 3 inches of this dark-brown mulch. Various sizes are available, from shredded to large chunks. Be aware that a thick layer of shredded bark becomes impermeable to water, and larger bark pieces may float away during heavy rains.
- **Grass clippings.** Grass is best left on the lawn to naturally decompose and supply nutrients. Only use dry grass for mulching planting beds, and slowly build up to a layer of 2 inches. A thick layer of grass clippings is impenetrable to water. Be wary of weed seeds and herbicides that may have been used on the lawn as they can have a negative effect on sensitive plants.
- **Leaf mold.** Leaf mold consists of fallen leaves that are starting to decompose. Use a 2-inch to 3-inch layer of leaves under plants for a natural look. Leaf mold mulch needs to be replaced each year. If the leaves are already well decomposed, they may be better used as a soil amendment than a mulch.
- **Pine needles.** Use a 2-inch to 3-inch layer of this red-brown mulch (Figure 10–17). It allows water and air to penetrate to the soil easily. And because it has an interlocking habit, it is effective for use on slopes. There are many grades available, with long-leaf pine (*Pinus palustris*) being the most expensive and "cleanest" in appearance. Loblolly pine (*Pinus tinea*) needles are the most common and least expensive pine straw. Pine needles can lower soil pH, but only very gradually over many years. Inspect needles for mold or heavy dirt or other particulate contamination before purchasing. Do not use pine straw mulch around pansies as it can reduce the number of flowers in the spring. In addition, to minimize risk of fire, some cities have banned the use of pine straw as a ground cover within 10 feet of multi-family dwellings.
- **Shredded hardwood.** This mulch usually comes in a ground or double-ground form and should be spread thinly, in a 1-inch to 2 inch layer, to avoid creating an impermeable layer. Hardwood mulches decompose slowly and do not need to be replaced as often as some other mulches.

- **Straw.** Straw is not the most attractive mulch, so it may be a better option for vegetable beds or new lawns than for ornamental beds. It decomposes quickly, so replenish a 2-inch to 3-inch layer regularly. Never use hay as it contains too many weed seeds.
- **Wood chips.** Use a 2-inch to 3-inch layer of this mulch, which consists of bark and various sizes of ground-up or chipped wood. Wood mulches are generally less expensive than pine needle or hardwood mulches. Wood mulch may need to be replaced every two years, depending on the particle size.

Colored Wood Mulch

There is no evidence that dyes used in coloring wood mulch are toxic. The wood chips themselves, however, may contain toxic substances. Much of the wood in colored mulch came from chipped scraps, pallets, and construction waste. Some of this wood is contaminated with creosote or chromated copper arsenate (CCA)—both chemicals used in pressure-treating lumber. Although the sale of CCA lumber has been banned, some older decks and fences still contain CCA-treated lumber, which can make its way into the recycling stream. In addition, pallets used to transport chemicals can become contaminated by spills. CCA and other toxic chemicals have been found in soil where colored wood chip mulch had been applied. Not all colored wood mulch is contaminated. Recycled construction and demolition wood have the highest rate of CCA contamination. Check the source of the wood used in the mulch prior to purchase.

Weeding

Using mulch and spacing plants so they produce a solid canopy are the best ways to minimize weed problems. Some weeds can be managed by cultivation or use of an herbicide, but some still need to be pulled by hand. Weeds are easier to pull after a rain or irrigation.

Cultivation is most effective as a weed management strategy early in the season. As annual plants grow, the feeder roots that spread between plants are likely to be injured by cultivation. In addition, cultivation stirs the soil and uncovers weed seeds that then germinate.

Any herbicide used in flower beds must be chosen carefully. Read the label: No one herbicide is safe for use on all herbaceous ornamentals. Time and rate of application varies with the herbicide selected. A **preemergence** herbicide is used to disrupt the germination process. Some preemergence herbicides are applied before planting; others are applied after planting but before weeds emerge. Make sure the planting bed is weed-free when the preemergence herbicide is applied. Only a few postemergence herbicides are labeled for use on grassy weeds after herbaceous plants have become established. For additional information on weed management, refer to chapter 6, "Weeds."

Staking

Many tall annuals and perennials—such as cosmos (*Cosmos* spp.) and cleome (*Cleome houtteana*)–may need support to protect them from strong winds and rain (Figure 10–18). Begin staking when plants are about one-third their mature size. Many materials can be used for staking: wire cages, bamboo stakes, tomato stakes, twiggy brushwood, or wire rings.

Figure 10–18. Many tall perennials, such as peonies (*Paeonia* hybrids), need support like this wire cage.
Kathleen Moore, CC BY - 2.0

Make the staking material 6 inches to 12 inches shorter than the height of the mature plant. Place stakes close to the plant, but take care not to damage the root system. Sink stakes into the ground far enough to be firm. Loosely tie plants to the stakes.

Tie the plant by making a double loop with one loop around the plant and the other around the stake to form a figure-eight (Figure 10–19). Never loop the tie around both the stake and plant. The plant hangs to one side, and the stem may become girdled. Support plants with delicate stems (like cosmos) with a frame-work of stakes and strings in crisscrossing patterns.

Figure 10–19.
A stake used to support tall perennials. Use soft twine or strips of cloth for ties. Loop the tie around the stem in a figure-eight pattern.

Deadheading and Pruning

Deadheading is the removal of dead or faded flowers and seed pods. When annuals and perennials expend energy to produce seeds after the flower fades, flower production often decreases. To maintain vigorous growth and assure neatness, remove spent flowers and seed pods (Figure 10–20a and Figure 10–20b).

Figure 10–20a. Deadheading, or removing dead flowers from this big-leaf hydrangea (*Hydrangea macrophylla*).
Kathleen Moore, CC BY - 2.0

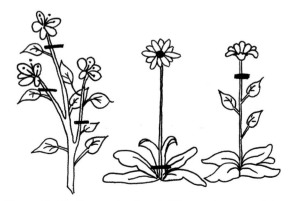

Figure 10–20b. How to deadhead different plant growth forms. A) Cut just above the leaves, B) Cut at base of flower stalk, C) Cut above a leaf.
Renee Lampila

10

Although this step is not necessary for all flowers, it is a good practice with ageratum (*Ageratum houstonianum*), calendula (*Calendula officinalis*), celosia (*Celosia argentea*), coleus (*Coleus × hybridus*), cosmos (*Cosmos bipinnatus*), geraniums (*(Pelargonium × hybridum)*), marigolds (*Tagetes erecta, T. patula*), scabiosa (*Scabiosa atropurpurea*), salvia (*Salvia argentea*), black-eyed Susan (*Rudbeckia fulgida*), and zinnias (*Zinnia elegans*). Check plants weekly. Many modern cultivars are self-cleaning; their spent flowers drop off quickly. Some cultivars are sterile and do not produce seeds.

Some bedding plants, such as polka dot plant (*Hypoestes phyllostachya*) and impatiens (*Impatiens* spp.), may benefit from pruning back for size control and rejuvenation. Pruning can stimulate greater flowering of some cultivars of petunias. Cut back plants as needed, leaving approximately one-half of the shoot.

Heavy rains and wind may cause herbaceous plants to split or drop over. Remove any damaged stems by cutting them back to a foot aboveground. Water carefully, and be watchful for signs of disease as the plant regrows.

Fall Cleanup

Remove and compost annuals after they die, but do not simply mow perennials to the ground after the first frost. Not only does this create a barren spot in the landscape; it also robs wildlife of valuable winter food, nest supplies, and shelter (Figure 10–21). Many beneficial insects hibernate in dead plant material or leaf litter.

Figure 10–21. Leaving perennial plant skeletons, like these *Hosta* spp., through the winter provides valuable wildlife food and habitat.
Chris Alberti, CC BY - 2.0

Some perennials—such as lavender (*Lavandula* spp.), Russian sage (*Salvia yangii*), and candytuft (*Iberis simpervirens*)—have woody bases and are severely set back or can even die if heavily pruned in the fall. Wait until spring, and scratch some of the twigs at the plant's base to find white or green living tissue to prune back to. Some peren-

nials are semi-evergreen or evergreen, and their foliage should be maintained to bring some welcome green to the barren winter landscape. However, if the bed contains nonwoody perennials and is in a highly visible area—or if it has become clear that birds and other wildlife have used the winter bounty you provided—prune stems to just above ground level and remove and compost any dead plant tissue. If any plants were prone to disease the previous growing season, remove and dispose of them immediately instead of composting the material. Fall is a great time to re-apply a layer of mulch to help protect the root zone through the winter.

Specifics for Perennials

Division

Many perennials left in the same place for more than three years are likely to become overcrowded and need to be divided. Some perennials, however, are best left in place and not divided; this is true of baby's breath (*Gypsophylla elegans*), blue wild indigo (*Baptisia australis*), gas plant (*Dictamnus albus*), goat's beard (*Aruncus dioicus*), globe thistle (*Echonops ritro*), and sea holly (*Eryngium planum*).

The best time to divide most perennials is in the spring when new shoots are 2 inches to 3 inches tall, or in the fall when the foliage starts to die back. Most plants that are divided during an active growth period in the summer are slower to reestablish. Daylily (*Hemerocallis* spp.) and bearded iris (*Iris (Iris × germanica)*) are among those perennials that can be divided after their flowering period, even during the summer. Division is usually done by digging the plant up and dividing it into several smaller sections. An alternative for vigorous clumps is to slice off a section with a sharp spade while leaving the main clump in the ground.

Some plants like chrysanthemums (*Chrysanthemum* spp.) or iris (*Iris* spp.) exhibit a decline in vigor as a clump grows. Transplants from the center often grow poorly and flower sparsely. To divide mature clumps, select only the vigorous side shoots from the outer edges of the clump and discard plants from the center. Divide the plant into clumps of three to five shoots each. Be careful not to overdivide; a clump that is too small does not give much color the first year after replanting. Do not put all the divisions back into the space that contained the original plant; that would place too many plants in a given area. Exchange extra plants with a friend, plant them elsewhere in the yard, or discard them.

Pinching

Some plants produce thicker and fuller growth if the shoot tips are pinched back to promote growth of side (axillary) shoots. Plants that respond to pinching include chrysanthemums (*Chrysanthemum* spp.), asters (*Aster* spp.), and phlox (*Phlox* spp.). Start pinching in early spring when the shoots are several inches long, and discontinue by early July. This reduces the height and decreases the likelihood of blow-over by wind and rain or from the weight of large, heavy flowers. The result is a more compact plant with more, but sometimes smaller, flowers. Pinching off buds also delays flowering.

Winter protection

In colder parts of the country, perennial beds are often mulched with an extra 2-inch to 4-inch layer of organic material to provide winter protection. For most perennials and most areas of North Carolina, this practice is not necessary. Dead foliage can provide winter protection for the plant and cover for wildlife, but old foliage can also harbor disease-causing organisms and insects. If dead foliage is left over the winter, it should be removed quite early in the spring.

Alternate freezing and thawing can cause plants to be heaved out of the soil, which causes root damage. Apply mulch to plants that are growing at the upper limits of their normal range to help keep them dormant. Apply mulch only after the soil temperature has cooled following several killing frosts. If winter mulch is applied too early, the warmth from the protected soil could cause growth to continue and increase winter injury. Do not pile mulch heavily over the crowns, as this would encourage rotting. Reduce the mulch depth to 2 inches to 3 inches as soon as growth starts in the spring.

Flowering Bulbs

A wide variety of bulbs is grown in North Carolina (Figure 10–22). Most are grown for their flowers, but some are grown for their foliage. Most flowering bulbs are perennial plants and require little maintenance. Some bulbs provide weeks or months of color; others flower for only a few weeks each year. Bulbs are broadly grouped into spring-flowering (January through May) and summer-flowering or fall-flowering (June through October) plants.

Bulb types used for gardens and landscapes include true bulbs, corms, tubers, tuberous roots, enlarged hypocotyls, and rhizomes. All are commonly called "flower bulbs." A true bulb, however, is a modified stem surrounded by scalelike, modified leaves that contain stored food for the shoots. Tulips (*Tulipa* hybrids), daffodils (*Narcissus* spp.), hyacinths (*Hyacinthus orientalis*), and lilies (*Lilium* Asiatic hybrids) are examples of true bulbs. There are two types of true bulbs: tunicate and imbricate. The outermost scales of a tunicate bulb are dry and papery. Tulips (*Tulipa* hybrids), daffodils (*Narcissus* spp.), hyacinths (*Hyacinthus orientalis*), grape hyacinths (*Muscari armeniacum*), and alliums (*Allium aflatunense*) grow from tunicated bulbs. An imbricate bulb has thick, loosely arranged scales that lack a protective covering. Lilies (*Lilium* spp.) produce imbricate bulbs.

Figure 10–22. Many bulbs grow well in North Carolina.
Petr Kratochvil, Pixabay CC0

10

A corm is the swollen base of a stem that contains stored nutrients; it does not have fleshy scales. Corms are tunicated or imbricate. On top of the corm are one or more "eyes" from which new shoots develop. The corms of crocuses and gladioli disintegrate as the stored food within is used to produce roots and shoots. A new corm forms on top of the remains of each original corm. In addition, stolonlike structures bearing miniature corms (called cormels) develop on the tip.

A tuber is a thickened underground stem swollen with food reserves. It differs from a true bulb or corm in that it has no covering of dry leaves and no basal plate from which roots grow. Usually short, fat, and rounded, tubers have a knobby surface with growth buds, or eyes, from which the shoots of the new plant emerge. Caladiums (*Caladium* spp.) grow from tubers.

Tuberous roots are true roots. Their food supply is stored in root tissue, not in stem or leaf tissue as with other "bulbs." Buds are produced only on the crown or stem end of the tuberous root. Fibrous roots develop on the opposite end. Tuberous roots are biennial; they are produced in one growing season and go dormant when the herbaceous shoot dies. In the spring, buds from the crown produce new shoot growth using energy from the old root. Dahlia (*Dahlia hortensis*), anemone (*Anemone* spp.), and ranunculus (*Ranunculus* spp.) produce tuberous roots.

In some plants, the hypocotyl (the portion of the stem below the cotyledon and above the roots) enlarges to become a fleshy storage site. This enlarged hypocotyl is perennial and continues to enlarge laterally each year. Cyclamen (*Cyclamen* spp.), gloxinia (*Incarvillea* spp.), and "tuberous" begonia (*Begonia* spp.) have enlarged hypocotyls.

A rhizome is a modified stem that grows horizontally just above or below the soil surface. Roots grow from the lower surface, while shoots develop from buds on the upper surface or sides, usually at the tips. Canna (*Canna* spp.), bearded iris (*Iris* × *germanica*), calla lily (*Zantedeschia* spp.), and oxalis (*Oxalis* spp.) produce rhizomes.

Spring-flowering Bulbs

Spring-flowering bulbs provide color before most annuals and perennials (Figure 10–23). Some crocuses (*Crocus* spp.) begin flowering in January; some daffodils (*Narcissia* spp.) begin flowering in February. Spring-flowering bulbs are planted in the fall, produce foliage and flowers in the spring, then die back and remain dormant during the summer months. It is usually best to plant spring-flowering bulbs in groups of 12 to 25 instead of planting in rows. Note that some bulbs in the eastern regions of North Carolina are grown as annuals because chilling hour requirements are too high for mild winters.

Types of Spring-flowering Bulbs

Tulips (*Tulipa* hybrids), daffodils (*Narcissus* spp.), and hyacinths (*Hyacinthus orientalis*) are referred to as the major spring-flowering bulbs. Minor spring-flowering bulbs include aconite (*Aconitum* spp.), anemone (*Anemone* spp.), crocus (*Crocus* spp.), cyclamen (*Cyclamen* spp.), fritillaria (*Fritillaria meleagris*), glory-of-the-snow (*Chionodoxa luciliae*), grape hyacinth (*Muscari armeniacum*), Dutch iris (*Iris hollandica*), lily-of-the-valley (*Convallaria majalis*), and snowdrops (*Galanthus nivalis*). Species in this group of bulbs are often quite easy to grow and produce massive flower displays.

Tulips (*Tulipa* hybrids) are one of the most popular spring-flowering bulbs. They are sold by type and cultivar. Some of the most common types are single, cottage (late-blooming), Darwin (tallest), parrot (twisted, ruffled petals), and double (two or more rows of petals). Species tulips are the wild forerunners of today's hybrid tulips. Species tulips are generally smaller than hybrid tulips, and they sometimes naturalize where growing conditions are favorable. Popular species tulips include *Tulipa fosteriana, T. greigii,* and *T. kaufmanniana.*

Traditionally, tulips were treated primarily as annuals in the South because few—if any—flowered the second year. The lack of flowering is often due to poor site selection and preparation. Many of the tulip cultivars available in garden centers and mail-order catalogs are unsuitable for our heat. Tulips are a short-lived perennial at best. Here in the southern states, tulip cultivars are generally considered successful perennials if they survive for three years. To increase the likelihood of perennialization, plant the bulbs in well-drained soil. Amending heavy clay soils with organic matter, planting on a slope, adding drainage tiles, and constructing raised beds are all methods that will improve drainage. If the bed is not prepared properly, no cultivar will perennialize. Fertilize the bulbs twice a year or use a slow-release fertilizer once a year. For a list of recommended tulip cultivars for North Carolina, refer to Table 10–1.

Daffodils (*Narcissus* species—Hardy II) are more hardy than tulips in North Carolina and usually come back year after year with minimum care. *Narcissus*, daffodils, and jonquils are classified into twelve divisions based on the length of **corolla** in relation to **perianth** segments. They come in a variety of colors, including white, yellow, peach, and bicolor. They are sold as single-, double-, or triple-nose bulbs (from smallest to largest bulb size). As a group they are easy to grow, multiply rapidly, and do well in naturalized settings. The terms "daffodils" and "narcissus" are often used interchangeably. *Narcissus* is the genus name for all daffodils. Daffodil is the common name for all members of the genus *Narcissus*. In some parts of the country, any yellow-flowering daffodil is called a jonquil. Technically, however, jonquils are characterized by having several yellow flowers with a strong scent and rounded foliage.

Table 10–1. Tulip Cultivars for North Carolina

Season	Color	Cultivar	Hardiness Zone	Color	Cultivar	Hardiness Zone
VERY EARLY	Purple	Demeter	6 – 8	Yellow	Bellona	8
	Red	Showwinner	8		Candela	6 – 8
	Red/Yellow	Stresa	8		Golden Apeldoorn	6 – 7
EARLY	Orange	Dillenberg	6		Golden Parade	6 – 7
		Orange Emperor	6		Hoangho	6
	Pink (Rose)	Christmas Marvel	8		Monte Carlo	7
	Red	Toronto	6 – 8		Yellow Dover	6 – 8
	Red/Yellow	Queen of Sheba	8		Golden Oxford	6 – 8
	White	Purissima (White Emperor)	7 – 8	Yellow/Red	Gudoshnik	6 – 7
	Yellow	Yokohama	6 – 8		Jewel of Spring	6 – 7
MID	Orange	Juan	6		Striped Apeldoorn	6 – 8
		Orange Emperor	8		Oranjezon	6 – 8
	Pink (Rose)	Blenda	6		Don Quichotte	8
		Preludium	6	Purple	Negrita	6
	Red	Apeldoorn	8		Diplomat	6 – 8
		Frankfurt	6		Holland's Glorie	6 – 7
		Ile de France	6		Margaret Herbst	8
		Oscar	6		Oxford	6 – 8
		Parade	7 – 8	Red/White	Leen van der Mark	6
		Lucky Strike	7		Merry Widow	6 – 7
		Princess Victoria	6		Spring Song	6 – 8
	Red/Yellow	Beauty of Apeldoorn	6 – 8		Kiezerskroon	6
		Los Angeles	6		Thule	6
	White	Kansas	6			
LATE	Orange	Jimmy	6 – 7		Orange Bouquet	7
	Pink (Rose)	Angelique	8		Gordon Cooper	6 – 7
	Purple	Prince Charles	6	Purple/White	Arabian Mystery	6
		Dreaming Maid	6	Red	Balalaika	8
		Bing Crosby	6		Dyanito	6
		Oriental Beauty	6		Red Matador	7
		Renown	8		Rosy Wings	7
	Red/Yellow	Ad Rem	6		Kees Nelis	6 – 7
	Red/White	Ballade	6		Karel Doorman	6
	White	Maureen	7	White/Pink	Douglas Baader	6
		Make Up	6	Yellow	West Point	6 – 7
VERY LATE	Orange	Orange Favourite	7 – 8			
	Red (Wine)	Burgundy Lace	7			
	Pink (Rose)	Sorbet	7			

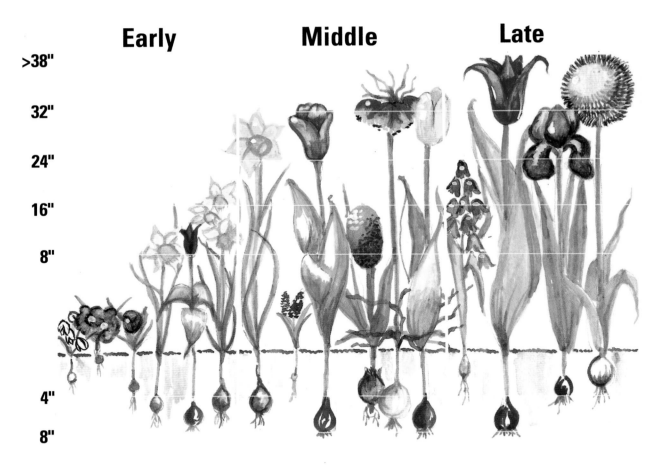

Early　　**Middle**　　**Late**

>38"

32"

24"

16"

8"

8"

4"

8"

Snowdrops (*Galanthus nivalis*)
Crocus (*Crocus* spp.)
Anemone (*Anemone* spp.)
Mini daffodils (*Narcissus asturiensis*)
Greigii tulips (*Tulipa greiggi*)
Emperor tulips (*T. fosteriana*)

Daffodils (*Narcissus species–Hardy II.*)
Grape hyacinth (*Muscari latifolium*)
Mid-season tulips
Hyacinths (*Hyacinth orientalis*)
Crown imperial (*Fritillaria imperialis*)

Cottage tulips
Lilies (*Lilum* spp.)
Lily flowering tulips
Dutch iris (*Iris hollandica*)
Giant onion (*Allium giganteum*)

Figure 10–23. Examples of early, mid, and late-season spring-flowering bulbs. Their mature height and planting depth are indicated on the left side.
Renee Lampila

Hyacinths (*Hyacinth orientalis*) produce a large, single spike of many small, fragrant flowers that come in a wide range of colors. Traditionally, hyacinths flower for only one year in North Carolina, but repeat blooming can be encouraged by paying special attention to site preparation and fertilization after blooming.

Planting Dates

Plant spring-flowering bulbs in the fall to promote good root development and to satisfy the cold requirement. The cold requirement ranges from six weeks to 20 weeks depending on the species or cultivar. The exact time to plant depends on the prevailing soil temperature. In general, it is advisable to wait until the soil temperature is below 60°F (at the optimal planting depth). The optimal planting time in Zone 6 is October. In Zones 7 and 8, it is better to wait until November or early December. Root growth starts in the fall and continues through the winter.

Bulb Selection and Preplanting Care

Selecting high-quality spring-flowering bulbs is important because the flower bud has already developed before the bulb is sold. Size is important. Generally, larger bulbs produce better flowers. Select bulbs that are plump and firm. Small nicks and loose skins do not affect the quality. Beware of bargain bulbs that are often too small to flower the first year.

If you buy bulbs well before planting time, keep them in a cool, dry place. A temperature of 60°F to 65°F is cool enough to prevent bulbs from drying out before planting.

Temperatures higher than 70°F can damage the flower inside spring-flowering bulbs. Rhizomes, tubers, and tuberous roots dry out faster than bulbs and corms and survive best if stored in peat, perlite, or vermiculite.

10

Do not store spring-flowering bulbs near fruits that produce ethylene (such as apples or pears). Ethylene is a gas that can cause "flower abortion" and other problems with flowering. Store the bulbs in open trays, and if they are stored in a refrigerator, ventilate frequently. Unless specified, do not store bulbs in paper or plastic bags.

Summer-flowering and Fall-flowering Bulbs

Summer-flowering and fall-flowering bulbs come in a wide range of flower colors, shapes, and heights, and many do well in North Carolina.

Purchase bulbs that are healthy and disease-free. Diseased bulbs look moldy or discolored, or feel soft and rotted. Site preparation is essentially the same as for other herbaceous plants and spring-flowering bulbs (see section on soil preparation).

Good drainage is essential for most bulbs. Most summer-flowering and fall-flowering bulbs require a soil pH between 6.0 and 7.0. Apply fertilizer and lime according to a soil test report. Planting times and depths vary greatly for different species. Plant bulbs upright and rhizomes and tuberous roots on their sides. Firm the soil around them, and water thoroughly after planting to settle the soil.

During the growing season, most bulbs benefit from a light application of fertilizer, but not heavy applications of nitrogen. Apply a light application in the spring before growth begins. Some plants, such as cannas, are heavy feeders and require additional fertilizer during the growing season. Use soil test results, foliage color, and growth rates to determine the need to make subsequent fertilizer applications.

Most bulbs prefer to be moist, but not wet, during the growing season, especially if temperatures exceed 80°F. A 2-inch to 3-inch layer of mulch reduces water needs and helps manage weeds. Plants that grow over 2 feet tall and have large blooms require staking. When flowers fade, cut them off to prevent seed formation. Seed production diverts food that would otherwise be stored in the bulb for next year's growth. Cannas produce flowers up until frost if they are deadheaded. When the foliage dies back in the fall, cut and destroy the old foliage, which can harbor disease and insect problems.

If summer-flowering bulbs need dividing, do so in the spring just prior to planting or before new growth begins on established plants. Use a sharp knife to cut roots and tubers, and make sure that each division contains at least one growing shoot or eye.

True bulbs and corms produce offsets called bulblets or cormels (Figure 10–24), which can be pulled from the parent and planted separately. Bulblets or cormels are usually too small to flower the first year.

Site Selection for Bulbs

In selecting a site for planting, consider light, temperature, soil texture, and function. Most bulbs prefer full sun. Select a planting site that provides at least 5 to 6 hours of direct sunlight a day. Bulbs left in the ground year after year should have 8 hours to 10 hours of daily sunlight for good flowering. This requirement should not restrict planting to areas that receive full sun year-round. Many bulbs flower and produce foliage before deciduous trees leaf out in the spring. A few bulbs, such as daffodils (*Narcissus*—Hardy I and II), crocus (*Crocus* spp.), squill (*Puschkinia libanotica*), and wood hyacinths (*Hyacinthoides hispanica*), tolerate partial shade.

Consider microclimate conditions when selecting spring-flowering bulbs for specific locations. A microclimate is a local modification of the general climate. It is influenced by topography, the ground surface, plant cover, and man-made conditions. The microclimate produced by screening with tall evergreens provides a windbreak and possibly shade. Bulbs planted in a southern exposure near a building or wall bloom earlier than bulbs planted in a northern exposure. Because daffodil flowers always face the source of strongest light, they are best planted with shrubs, a wall, or fence as a background.

Most bulbs and bulblike plants do not tolerate poor drainage; they grow best in deep, well drained loam or sandy soils. This is especially true for tulips and hyacinths. The easiest method to determine if the site drains well is to observe the proposed planting area the day after a heavy rainfall. If water remains in the site, then the soil does not drain adequately. A better method is to dig a hole about a foot deep and fill it with water. The next day fill the hole with water again. If the water drains away in 8 hours to 10 hours, the soil is sufficiently well-drained to grow most bulbs. If the water does not drain adequately, select another site, improve the drainage, or create a raised bed using landscape timbers, stacked stone, brick, or other suitable materials.

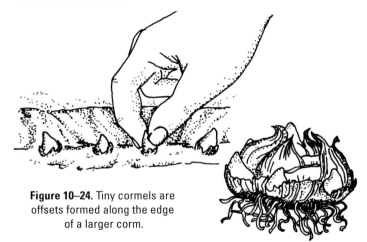

Figure 10–24. Tiny cormels are offsets formed along the edge of a larger corm.

Planting Bulbs

The simplest method for planting bulbs is to dig individual planting holes. Loosen the soil below the depth of the planted bulbs (Figure 10–25). Add fertilizer according to the soil test report, then cover with a layer of soil (bulbs should not come into direct contact with fertilizers). Set bulbs upright in the planting hole with the roots facing down and cover with amended soil.

Figure 10–25. A hole for planting a bulb.
Kathleen Moore, CC BY - 2.0

A better method for planting bulbs is to dig and remove the soil to a depth of 8 inches to 12 inches over the entire bed (Figure 10–26). Dig bulb beds when the soil is fairly dry because wet soil packs tightly. Remove large stones and building trash, but turn under all leaves, grass, stems, roots, and anything else that decays. Incorporate into the soil fertilizer, amendments, and organic matter as recommended by a soil test report. A soil pH between 6.0 to 7.0 is ideal for most bulbs. If the pH level needs to be raised, apply lime at the prescribed rate. Never apply more than 40 pounds of lime per 1,000 square feet per application. Because both lime and phosphorus move slowly when applied on the soil surface, thoroughly incorporate them into the soil when preparing the bed prior to planting. In many situations, incorporating 30% to 50%, by volume of composted pine bark or composted yard waste greatly improves soil drainage. Refill the planting site with several inches of the prepared soil.

Arrange the bulbs at the recommended depth and spacing. Bulb catalog and reference recommendations for planting may be either too shallow or too deep depending on soil conditions. As a general rule, plant bulbs at a depth 2½ to 3 times as deep as the diameter of the bulb. To provide winter protection and to reduce mechanical damage to the flower bulbs, plant most small bulbs 5 inches deep and large bulbs 8 inches deep. Because a surface mulch of 2 inches to 3 inches is advised, calculate this amount in the planting depth. Bulbs planted at

shallower depths experience wide temperature shifts in the winter and earlier warming in the spring. Early spring warming leads to smaller bulbs and poorer flowering the following year. Cover the bulbs with amended soil, water to remove air pockets and to settle the soil, and apply a 2-inch to 3-inch layer of mulch. Mulch keeps the soil temperature more uniform and delays warming of the soil in the spring. To root properly and grow well, most flower bulbs require a soil that is moist, but not wet.

Planting in Poorly Drained Soil

Till the site 4-inches deep and space the bulbs properly on the soil surface. Cover with 5 inches to 8 inches of ½-inch, screened pine bark mulch (amended with lime at the rate of 5 pounds per cubic yard). Roots will grow and position the bulbs at the optimal depth for subsequent growth and development. The mulch also provides winter protection.

Animals such as voles, mice, rabbits, squirrels, and deer eat spring-flowering bulbs such as crocuses and tulips. Daffodils and hyacinths are usually not bothered. Although no system can totally exclude animals, in some cases, covering the bulbs with heavy ½-inch wire mesh screening at planting affords some protection and still allows the shoots to grow through. For more information, see Chapter 20, "Wildlife."

Figure 10–26.
A) Remove soil from the entire bed first, B) Lay out bulbs,
C) Cover bulbs, D) Enjoy the flowers.
Kathleen Moore, CC BY - 2.0

10

Figure 10–27.
Daffodil foliage emerging from the soil in early spring.
Alex O'Neal, Flickr CC BY-SA - 2.0

Care After Planting Bulbs

Shoot elongation occurs during mid to late winter, and shoots appear above the ground by late winter (Figure 10–27). The foliage is quite cold hardy and normally does not need to be protected.

Mulching

After soil has cooled in winter, mulch bulbs with 2 inches to 3 inches of an organic material such as straw, pine bark, hay, or shredded leaves in order to manage weeds and to prevent premature warming of the soil. Do not use large leaves because they may mat too tightly on the ground and keep shoots from pushing aboveground.

Fertilization

Do not fertilize bulbs after they flower as this can cause disease problems. Fertilize according to soil test recommendations when foliage is 1 inch to 2 inches tall (about six to eight weeks before flowering). Keep fertilizer off the leaves and away from roots so that it does not burn the plants. An alternative is to use a single fall application of a slow-release fertilizer at planting and each fall thereafter at the normal planting time. Many references suggest using bone meal as a bulb fertilizer; however, research at NC State University has found that the phosphorus from bone meal is released very slowly and does not

move through the soil very well. It often stays within a few inches of where it is applied. Use foliage color and growth rates to determine the need to make subsequent applications of fertilizer.

Pruning

After spring-flowering bulbs finish flowering, remove faded blooms to prevent seed development, which reduces food storage in the bulb for next year's growth (Figure 10–28). The foliage should be allowed to dry naturally. Green leaves produce food for plant growth the following year. During this period the mother bulbs enlarge or produce offsets, or they are replaced by daughter bulbs. Removal, braiding, or bending of the fading and dying foliage markedly reduces future bulb size. The undesirable appearance of dying foliage should be considered when selecting a site for bulb plantings. When bulbs are used around a mailbox or walkway, the dying foliage is more visible than when bulbs are used on the sides of the yard or in natural areas. After the foliage turns yellow, falls over, and comes loose when slightly tugged, it can be removed and destroyed. Remove dead foliage so that any diseases present do not infect new growth the following year.

10

Figure 10–28. Remove faded blooms after flowering so energy goes into the bulb for next year, rather than into making seeds. If this tulip is left alone, the green ovary will grow, diverting energy from root storage into seed development.
Ruth Hartnup, Flickr CC BY - 2.0

Replanting
If the bulbs flower satisfactorily, leave them in the ground. If tulips and hyacinths fail to flower, remove them and replant with new bulbs in the fall. The flowering of daffodils decreases over time if they become crowded. If this happens, dig them up, divide, and replant. Often the flowering of recently divided daffodils is poor the first year. The bulbs are small and must go through a season of good growing conditions before they produce enough stored food to flower satisfactorily. If bulbs need to be moved from one place to another, wait until after the foliage has faded before digging and replanting.

Pest Problems
Several insects and related pests can attack flowering bulbs. The most common are aphids, thrips, and mites. Use "Diagnostics" and "Integrated Pest Management" strategies from chapters 7 and 8 to correctly identify the problem and implement management techniques.

Although it is possible for flowering bulbs to become infected by a wide range of diseases, most flowering bulbs are selected for some tolerance or resistance to most of the serious soil-borne diseases. The most prevalent foliar disease of bulbs is caused by a species of *Botrytis*, also known as "tulip fire." Symptoms of this fungal disease, which spreads quickly in warm, wet weather, include yellowing and shriveling of the leaf tips, followed by development of spots near the leaf margins that increase in size and merge. Spots appear on petals followed by rotting and a mushy, gray mold. A preventive measure includes planting on a well-ventilated site in full sun. Remove and destroy any heavily infested bulbs.

In the spring rabbits, voles, and deer may feed on the new foliage of tulips and lilies. Refer to "Wildlife," chapter 20, for management strategies.

Winter Hardiness and Storage
Traditionally, bulbs are classified as "hardy," "semi-hardy," or "tender." The degree of hardiness varies with soil drainage, winter severity, hardiness zone, depth of planting, and the presence or absence of mulch. Hardy bulbs are left in the ground year round. Semi-hardy bulbs are left in the ground in mild climates but are not reliably hardy in colder climates without applying a 2-inch to 3-inch layer of mulch. In the eastern part of North Carolina, dahlias (*Dahlia hortensis*) survive in the ground through the winter, but they must be dug and stored in the state's piedmont and mountain regions. Tender bulbs do not tolerate severe freezing and can be left in the ground only in warm climates. Normally they are dug in the fall after frost, stored, and replanted in the spring. Caladiums are very sensitive to cold weather and must be dug in all parts of the state. Refer to Table 10–2 for recommended storage conditions for selected bulbs.

Why Bulbs Fail to Perennialize:

Failure of spring-flowering bulbs to perennialize may be related to several factors.

- **Plant selection**
  Bulb species or cultivar may not be hardy in the climate zone.

- **Site conditions and physical damage**
  Poor drainage
  Attack by voles or squirrels
  Exposure to air from tunneling moles
  Drought
  Competition from roots of other plants
  Sunlight too limited for adequate photosynthesis
  Disease

- **Management errors**
  Planted too deep or too shallow
  Inadequate or excess water

- **Produced bulbs below minimum size required for flowering**
  pH too low or too high
  Bulbs not properly fertilized
  Foliage not left to dry naturally after flowering

Table 10–2. Storage Conditions for Selected Bulbs

Bulbs	Harvest and Storage	Temperature
Achimenes (*Achimenses* spp.)	Store rhizomes in pots	50°F to 70°F
Amaryllis (*Hippeastrum* spp.)	Bring container plants indoors in early fall. Keep them growing at 55°F for 8 weeks to 10 weeks to force reflowering.	It is not necessary to let the plants go dormant.
Begonia (*Tuberosa group*)	Harvest in fall; dry, and store in dry peat	35°F to 45°F
Caladium (*Caladium bicolor*)	Harvest in fall; dry, and store in mesh bag or in dry sphagnum moss	70°F to 75°F
Calla lily (*Zantedeschia* spp.)	Store dry	50°F to 55°F
Canna (*Canna* spp.)	Harvest in fall; dry, and store in dry peat or vermiculite	41°F to 50°F
Crinum (*Crinum* spp.)	Not commonly stored, but if so in slightly moist sand	35°F to 45°F
Crocosmia (*Crocosmia* hybrids)	Store so corms do not dry out	35°F to 41°F
Dahlia (*Dahlia* spp.)	Harvest in fall; dry (do not wash), and store in dry vermiculite or sand	35°F to 45°F
Elephant's ear (*Colocasia* spp.)	Store dry	70°F to 75°F
Gladiolus (*Gladiolus byzantinus*)	Harvest after the foliage dies back; store in mesh bags with good air circulation	41°F
Gladiolus (*Gladiolus spp.*)	Store in dry peat moss	60°F to 70°F
Tritonia (*Tritonia* sp.)	Harvest rhizomes and store	35°F to 41°F
Tuberose (*Agave amica*)	Store in plastic bag containing sand or vermiculite	55°F to 65°F

Digging is done in the fall when the foliage turns yellow after a frost. Use a spading fork to gently lift the bulbs from the ground. Brush but do not wash off soil that clings to the bulbs. Spread the bulbs in a shaded place to dry. When dry, store them away from sunlight in a cool, dry basement, closet, or garage. Be sure that air circulates around stored bulbs.

Never store bulbs more than two or three layers deep, as they generate heat and may decay. Leave the soil on achimenes (*Achimenes* spp.), begonia (*Begonia grandis*), canna (*Canna americanallis*), caladium (*Caladium bicolor; Caladium × hortulanum*), dahlia (*Dahlia hortensis*), and ismene (*Hymenocallis* spp.) bulbs. Store these bulbs in clumps on a layer of peat moss or sawdust in a cool place. Clean and separate them just before planting.

Wildflowers

North Carolina has an abundance of wildflowers and native plants. Wildflowers can be found in pastures, woodlands, wetlands, along beaches and roadways, and on rocky slopes (Figure 10–29). While many wildflowers can be found growing throughout the state, others naturally occur in only a few isolated locations.

"Wildflower" refers to a plant native to the region that has not undergone any major change or improvement by humans. Many wildflowers are not true natives, but plants that have naturalized after being introduced (accidentally or on purpose) from other parts of the country or world. Cultivars of native wildflowers have also been developed for use in gardens.

10

While some wildflowers are hardy and easy to grow, others need very specific growing conditions or they decline and die. Some wildflowers are quite weedy and should be avoided except in meadow gardens. Success depends on matching the needs of each type of wildflower to specific site conditions. The NC State Extension Gardener Plant Toolbox has more information about specific wildflower plants and their preferred conditions. Select a location that closely resembles the growing conditions in nature; examine sunlight, moisture, and drainage conditions.

Wildflowers can be used in combination with other perennials and annuals in flower beds and borders. Plants that prefer wet conditions can be used in a bog garden, rain garden, or on the edge of a pond or stream. A woodland or informal shade garden is probably the best option for a wooded site. If a site is sunny and dry, a meadow garden may be the best choice. The placement of plants in a design can be very formal, or plants can be grown in a naturalistic setting. Clusters or drifts of wildflowers are quite effective.

Figure 10–29. Wildflowers.
Bobistraveling, Flickr CC BY -2.0

Obtaining Plants

Wildflowers can be started from seeds, stem cuttings, division, or root cuttings, or purchased from a nursery as bare-root or container-grown plants. An often overlooked strategy is to identify and preserve any native plants that occur naturally in your landscape.

Collecting plants from the wild may seem like an inexpensive method of obtaining plants, but may be illegal and the result is often less than satisfactory. Some wildflowers are endangered or threatened and should never be collected from the wild. The USDA Forest Service does offer limited collection permits for wildflowers. Costs and stipulations vary by region and time of year. For more information see Chapter 12, "Native Plants".

Woodland and Shade Gardens

Native woodland wildflowers have evolved a life cycle that coincides with available sunlight. Rapid growth and flowering occurs from late March through May, then tree leaves develop and significantly reduce sunlight available to plants on the forest floor. As tree leaves develop, wildflower growth and flowering are greatly reduced. Some early spring woodland wildflowers such as mayapple (*Podophyllum peltatum*) become dormant by midsummer and do not reappear until the following spring.

Shade-loving, summer-blooming, and fall-blooming wildflowers occur along forest edges in filtered or dappled shade; they do not grow in dense shade. To increase the amount of available sunlight for a shade garden, remove some undergrowth and undesirable trees. It is easier to grow wildflowers under some trees than others. Oaks, maples, beeches, and sweetgums have shallow roots and produce heavy shade; only early spring flowers do well near these trees. Wildflowers growing under pine trees are often quite different from those growing under deciduous trees. While the shade from pine is year-round, it is a filtered or dappled shade.

Shade-loving wildflowers have several basic needs: light shade, adequate moisture, soils high in organic matter, and leaf mulch that persists throughout the year. Most woodland wildflowers prefer an acidic soil that is rich in humus. In general, the soil should have adequate moisture but be well-drained. However, wildflowers differ in their moisture needs and tolerance of adverse moisture conditions. Some wildflowers like cardinal flower (*Lobelia cardinalis*), jewelweed (*Impatiens capensis*), and forget-me-not (*Myosotis sylvatica*) actually need boglike conditions. Mayapple (*Podophyllum peltatum*) and foam flower (*Tiarella cordifolia*) prefer uniform moisture.

Woodland wildflowers naturally grow in areas where leaves and other plant debris accumulate and become part of the soil environment. Organic matter as mulch is critical for their growth; it helps hold moisture, keeps the soil cool, and helps the soil stay loose and well-aerated. Adding a 3-inch to 5-inch layer of organic matter or leaf compost is ideal. It is usually not necessary to apply lime to raise the soil pH because most North Carolina wildflowers tolerate acidic soils. In woodland settings, it is best to plant container-grown plants. Dig individual holes instead of preparing an entire bed; this minimizes damage to established trees. Fertilizing wildflowers is rarely necessary and can be harmful. Mulching and adding compost is usually adequate.

Each year, the deciduous forests of North Carolina put on a generous display of wildflowers (Figure 10–30). To preserve these woodland wildflower displays for everyone to enjoy, it is important not to illegally harvest plants from the wild.

Meadow Gardens
Meadow gardens have increased in popularity, but claims that they need no maintenance and that masses of color appear after simply broadcasting seeds from a mixture are very misleading. Unfortunately, most such attempts at meadow gardening have produced a weed garden because of inadequate site preparation or sowing seeds of wildflowers that were not suitable for local growing conditions. Many of the prepackaged seed mixtures contain mostly annual wildflowers. Read the label closely.

A field or meadow garden is very different from a woodland garden. Meadow wildflowers need full sun for at least 6 to 8 hours a day, adequate moisture early in the year, and a well-drained soil. Soils are generally less fertile and lower in organic matter than the soils in woodland gardens.

Weeds can be a major concern. Select a site that has been cultivated as a lawn or garden. Eliminate weed problems a year before planting. Frequent mowing and hand pulling will eliminate many problem weeds.

Ideally, prepare the site in midsummer for a fall planting. Spray with a nonselective, nonresidual herbicide in August, and allow the weeds to die before cultivating.

Soil preparation includes cultivation, incorporation of a 2-inch to 4-inch layer of organic matter (such as pine bark or composted yard waste), and a soil test. Amend according to the soil test results. Do not incorporate fertilizer unless the soil is low in nutrients because excessive nitrogen stimulates weeds more than wildflowers. Tilling the soil brings more weed seeds to the soil surface where they can germinate. A few weeks after tilling, lightly till the soil again (1 inch to 2 inches deep) or use a nonselective herbicide to kill newly sprouted weeds. This process may need to be repeated several times to reduce the weed population. The use of a preemergence herbicide is not recommended because it also prevents wildflower seeds from germinating.

Because some seeds require chilling conditions before they germinate, October and November are the best months for seeding a wildflower meadow in North Carolina. Lightly rake the soil surface after seeding to cover the seeds. A light layer of weed-free straw is a good mulch to reduce erosion, improve soil moisture retention, and

Figure 10–30. A woodland shade garden.
Stephen Bowler, Flickr CC BY - 2.0

10

shade the soil from hot, drying sunlight. Germination of some species occurs within a few weeks after seeding, so water to keep the soil surface moist.

Meadow wildflowers are of two basic types: perennials and annuals that reseed themselves. Allow those that reseed to finish flowering, and the seeds need to become fully mature before the foliage is mowed. Without management, a "natural" planting of wildflowers eventually reverts to a succession of weeds, vines, and volunteer trees. Weed management consists of hand-weeding, fall mowing, and possibly spot treating of weeds with a nonselective, nonresidual herbicide.

Insects and Diseases of Herbaceous Ornamentals

Although in general herbaceous plants are not insect or disease prone, they do experience occasional problems, and some plants are likely to develop problems every year. To reduce potential problems, select disease-resistant cultivars when possible. Choose a site that is optimal for plant growth, and prepare the soil according to soil test results. Allow adequate spacing between plants, and install a 1-inch to 3-inch layer of organic mulch.

Keeping plants healthy through good cultural practices avoids many pest and disease problems. Most insect pests in the garden do not cause appreciable damage, especially if they are caught early or if natural predators and parasites are allowed to keep a balance. Practice integrated pest management (IPM) strategies to minimize problems. See chapter 8, "IPM," for specific strategies. Use of a pesticide should be a last resort after all other options have been exhausted. Before using any pesticide, be certain that the pest and the plant species are indicated on the label. Read and follow all directions, including precautions, shown on the label. Read more about pesticide safety in appendix B, "Pesticides and Pesticide Safety."

Familiarize yourself with the major insect and disease pests of your plants as many insect and disease problems are limited to specific plant species. Soilborne diseases are not as serious a problem for annuals as they are for perennials because annuals grow in the garden for only one season.

Insects and related pests
Spider mites become abundant during dry weather. Their piercing-sucking mouthparts cause stippled spots on the leaf surface as they remove plant fluids from the underside of the leaf. Aphids are found during periods of warm temperatures when rapid, tender growth occurs. The green peach aphid is the most widespread of the many types of aphids. Leaves, stems, and flowers become distorted because the piercing-sucking mouthparts of aphids damage leaf cells when they are young. As the leaf cells expand, leaves appear deformed. Aphids also spread virus diseases and produce honeydew that leads to sooty mold development. Spraying the foliage with a strong stream of water helps to manage spider mites and aphids.

Various plant bugs attack herbaceous plants. Some of the most common ones are four-lined and tarnished plant bugs. Borers tunnel within the stems of some herbaceous plants and cause the stems to be stunted or to fall over. Among the borers that occur most frequently are the burdock borer, European corn borer, iris borer, and stalk borer. Other insects that occur on herbaceous ornamentals include beetles, leaf miners, mealy bugs, thrips, various caterpillars, and whiteflies. Some plants have unique insect problems that do not occur on other plants—for example, the snapdragon lace bug or phlox plant bug. Monitor for insects and related pests during the season when pests normally occur. Remove insects by hand if they are adversely affecting a plant's appearance. Most insects are not present in sufficient numbers to cause significant damage.

Do not treat for soil insects unless large numbers of cutworms, white grubs, or wireworms are observed when the soil is prepared for planting. Read more about managing insect problems in "IPM," chapter 8.

Foliage diseases
Although leaf spot diseases caused by fungi are not normally fatal to herbaceous plants, specific cultivars or species can be greatly disfigured. Crowded plants are more likely to develop foliar diseases. Cultural practices are the best preventive measures for disease management. Select resistant plants when possible, remove severely damaged plants, and destroy plant residue in the fall. Improve air circulation and sunlight, and keep water off foliage when irrigating.

Rust is a fungal disease that appears as pale spots on a plant's upper leaf surfaces and as orange, yellow, or brown pustules on leaf lower surfaces. Many rusts must have an alternate host for survival. Elimination of infected foliage is the best management strategy.

Botrytis blight is a fungal disease caused by *Botrytis cinera*. It attacks leaves, stems, and flowers, covering them with fuzzy, grayish-black tissue.

Some leaf spots are caused by bacteria; the management is the same as for fungal leaf spots except chemical options are less effective. To help manage bacterial diseases, improve air circulation, reduce overcrowding, and remove and destroy infected foliage.

Powdery mildew appears as a powdery, gray, or almost white growth on the leaves that is easily rubbed off. Some relief is achieved with fungicidal sprays. Downy mildew occurs on the lower sides of leaves, causing pale-green or yellow spots to appear on the upper leaf surfaces. Remove affected foliage, remove weeds, and keep the foliage dry by watering the soil with a soaker hose instead of an overhead sprinkler. Read more about "Diseases" in chapter 5.

Soil diseases

Herbaceous ornamentals commonly develop several soil or root diseases. Damping-off disease causes young seedlings to collapse when a fungus attacks the stem near the soil line. Sanitation and well-drained soils help to prevent the disease. Crown gall is caused by bacteria that enter through a wound and is characterized by galls forming on the roots or at the base of the stems. Chemical management is not effective; remove and destroy infected plants.

A number of soilborne fungi can cause stem and root rots. Feeder roots attacked by *Pythium* species become gray or brown. *Rhizoctonia* species cause the stem at the soil line to turn brown and shrivel. Avoid planting too deeply and improve soil aeration and drainage. A species of the fungus *Sclerotinia* causes brown stem cankers. Stems develop round black knots of fungal tissue on the stem surface and in the pith, and a white cottony fungus is often visible at the soil line. Remove and dispose of plants exhibiting root diseases to reduce the spread of infection to nearby plants. Also remove soil adjacent to the roots.

Some herbaceous plants are susceptible to wilts caused by species of two other soilborne fungi: *Fusarium* and *Verticillium*. An infected plant often appears healthy until subjected to drought or hot temperatures. While the roots remain viable, the vascular system becomes clogged, and the plant may be stunted, develop yellow foliage, or wilt and die. Select resistant cultivars if possible, keep foliage dry, and remove infected plants and debris.

Case Study—Think IPM: Bee Balm in Distress

Some of your bee balm plants (*Monarda didyma*) look sick. You wonder what is wrong with them and what you can do to improve their appearance. You review the diagnostic procedures from chapter 7, "Diagnostics," and think about the five steps for IPM:

1. Monitor and scout to determine pest type and population levels.
2. Accurately identify host and pest.
3. Consider economic or aesthetic injury thresholds. A threshold is the point at which action should be taken.
4. Implement a treatment strategy using physical, cultural, biological, or chemical management, or combine these strategies.
5. Evaluate success of treatments.

1. Monitor and scout to determine pest type and population levels.

You have several bee balm plants in your landscape. It is early fall, and you have noticed that two of your bee balm plants are declining. There is a white powdery substance on the leaves (Figure 10–31). A sample could be sent to the Plant Insect and Disease Clinic at NC State, but a cost-effective approach involves digging into some diagnostic questions.

2. Accurately identify the host and pest.
Step 1. Identify the plant: *You look through your garden journal and verify on your landscape design that the affected plants are bee balm (*Monarda didyma*).*

Figure 10–31. Powdery substance on bee balm (*Monarda* spp.) leaves.
Kathleen Moore, CC BY - 2.0

Step 2. Describe the problem: *Two of the 10 bee balm plants have a white powder on the leaves and stems. Some of the leaves look disfigured.*

Step 3. Identify what is normal:
What does the healthy part of the plant look like?
The healthy bee balm in the same bed has bright-green leaves. The parts of the affected plant that still look healthy are the older growth.

10

What does the unhealthy part of the plant look like? *The new growth has smaller leaves that are distorted. A white powdery substance is visible, mostly concentrated on the younger leaves and on some stems.*

Have you had a soil test? *Yes, and it showed I needed to add lime, which I did add to the bed along with compost at the time of planting.* (For information on how to submit a soil test see chapter 1, "Soils and Plant Nutrients.")

Step 4. Cultural practices:

Describe the age and history of plant: *The bee balm plants are three years old and have been growing well since they were planted.*

Irrigation: *Now that the weather has cooled off, they are watered once a week with a soaker hose for 2 hours after the sun rises.*

Fertilizer: *I have added a 2-inch layer of compost every fall plus fertilizer recommended on my soil test results.*

Maintenance: *I have been diligent about keeping weeds out of the bed, pruning, deadheading, and removing any fallen material.*

Step 5. Environmental conditions:

Are there any significant water issues? *It was a very hot, dry summer. We did go on vacation, and the bee balm looked a little wilted when we returned. The soil absorbs water readily; there is no standing water when irrigating or after rain.*

Describe the light near this garden bed. How many hours of sunlight? *This bed gets about 6½ hours of full sun a day. There is a maple tree nearby that does shade the bee balm in the afternoon. The plants that are affected are the ones that receive the most shade.*

Describe any recent changes or events: *We put in a new paver patio that is adjacent to this bed.*

Step 6. Signs of pathogens:

On the buds/flowers: *There is some of the powdery white substance on some of the buds.*

On the leaves: *No insects are visible, white powdery substance is visible on the leaves and some stems.*

On the stems: *There is some of the powdery white substance on some of the stems.*

On the roots: *Nothing visible.*

On the soil: *No insects are visible. No pathogens are visible on the soil.*

Step 7. Symptoms:

On the leaves: *The new leaves are disfigured.*

On the roots: *No foul odor is detected coming from* the soil. *(Looking for a root pathogen at this point would require digging up the plants. Because this is a destructive procedure, it was not attempted.)*

Step 8. Distribution of damage in the landscape:

Are other plants in the landscape affected? *The zucchini plants in the garden have the same white powdery substance on the leaves.*

Step 9. Distribution of damage on the plant and specific plant parts:

Where is the damage visible on the plant? *On the aboveground portions of the plant on new leaves and buds.*

Step 10. Timing:

When did you notice this problem? *Yesterday when I went out to water. The bee balm plants looked good last week when I checked on them.*

You hypothesize that this is a disease rather than an insect and that it is a foliar problem and not a root problem. You look up the disease section in a resource guidebook and discover a photo that looks like your powdery leaves (Figure 10–32). Now that you have a likely identification, you do more research on this disease. You search extension. org or type in "powdery mildew + edu" into your Internet search engine to find university-based resources. The first few links that come up name powdery mildew as a common fungal disease.

Figure 10–32. Powdery mildew on a zucchini plant.
Scot Nelson, Flickr CC0

10

Steps 6 and 7 lead us to believe we are dealing with a pathogen. Steps 2, 4, 5, 9, and 10 support our theory that this is powdery mildew.

3. **Consider economic or aesthetic injury thresholds.**

   Powdery mildew is not fatal, and with some management strategies, the bee balm can move into spring with a fresh start.

4. **Implement a treatment strategy using physical, cultural, biological, or chemical management, or combine these strategies.**

   You research strategies to manage powdery mildew.

   • **Physical.** You discover powdery mildew thrives in warm, humid, shady locations with poor air circulation. Planting in sunny locations with plenty of room around the plants for air to move is less favorable for disease. The current location of the bee balm is not ideal with the close proximity of other shrubs and shade from the maple tree. The planting bed cannot be moved, but the maple tree can be pruned up to increase sunlight and the bee balm can be pruned to help airflow. You read that powdery mildew on deciduous plants can come on late in the growing season and that it is generally not fatal. Powdery mildew is dormant in the winter. In the dormant season, all infected branches, buds and plant material can be removed and disposed of so as to not spread spores. You will carefully remove all infected material later this fall. In the spring, close monitoring of plants that have been infected previously can help identify any re-infections early. If it is early in the growing season, affected leaves can be removed and disposed of.

   • **Cultural.** You find that fertilizers high in nitrogen can cause a flush of new growth, making plants more susceptible, so careful monitoring of fertilizer application is important. You recall not exactly following the soluble fertilizer label directions and just adding a "scoop" to their watering can a few months ago. You plan to avoid doing that in the future. You discover there are many powdery-mildew-resistant varieties of bee balm, such as 'Purple Mildew Resistant' and 'Marshalls Delight', which can be planted if this plant does not survive or if you are interested in planting any new bee balm plants.

   • **Chemical.** For recommended fungicides and rates, consult the current *North Carolina Agricultural Chemicals Manual*. Given that it is late in the season, that powdery mildew is not usually serious, and that other measures are being taken, fungicide applications are not justified, saving you time and money.

5. **Evaluate success of treatments.**

   Keeping a garden journal or notes about the management strategies tried and their results provides valuable data for making garden decisions in the future. Some of the management strategies you researched may take more time to see results, and having a written record helps to jog your memory. If the problem continues in the spring or the plant is declining further, you can reevaluate your management strategies and even consider additional diagnostic work.

Frequently Asked Questions

1. *How do I fertilize my bulbs so they return every year?*

   To encourage spring-flowering bulbs to bloom subsequent years, apply a complete nitrogen fertilizer in the fall and again in the spring when shoots appear. Fertilize summer-flowering bulbs when shoots appear in the spring. A second application may be needed in mid to late summer. Be sure to follow the recommendations on the soil test report and manufacturer's directions. Water in the fertilizer so that it becomes available to the plant. For additional reference, refer to NC State Extension publication HIL 551, *Bed Preparation and Fertilization Recommendations for Bedding Plants in the Landscape*.

2. *Can you suggest some annuals that tolerate hot, dry sites?*

   No site is without stress, but a few things can be done to minimize stress. Begin with evaluating the soil texture. If it is sandy, then the addition of pine bark humus, composted leaf mold, or peat moss improves water retention. Adding lime and nutrients to the bed based on a soil test also improves plant nutrition. Bedding plants grown in sandy soils may require watering as frequently as two to three times per week. Use heat-loving, drought-tolerant annuals—such as Mexican heather (*Cuphea hyssopifolia*), blanket flower (*Gaillardia pulchella*), lantana (*Lantana camara*), red fountain grass (*Pennisetum setaceum*), mealycup sage (*Salvia farinacea*), moss rose or purslane (*Portulaca grandiflora*), creeping zinnia (*Zinnia angustifolia*), globe amaranth (*Gomphrena globosa*), celosia (*Celosia argentea* var. *plumosa*), cosmos (*Cosmos sulphureus*), verbena (*Verbena ×hybrida*), and Madagascar periwinkle (*Catharanthus roseus*). For additional reference, refer to NC State Extension publication HIL 552, *Selection and Use of Stress-Tolerant Bedding Plants for the Landscape*.

10

3. When is the best time to plant annuals?

Annuals, as their classification implies, complete their entire life cycle in one year and are classified by horticulturists as hardy, half-hardy, or tender. Plant hardy plants in late fall to early spring. Plant half-hardy plants after the last frost date in spring. Wait to plant tender annuals until soil is warm. To expand your selection of annuals, consider starting plants from seed. Study seed packets for recommended planting dates. Zones recommended for planting apply to heat as well as frost dates.

4. My petunias are wilting and dying, and the roots have rotted off. What should I do?

Petunias are susceptible to several root and crown rot diseases if planted in poorly drained soils or watered too often. Two common crown rots are caused by species of *Phytophthora* and *Rhizoctonia*. To confirm the pathogen, submit a plant sample along with soil and roots to the NC State Plant Disease and Insect Clinic. Chemical management of these diseases is generally not practical or economical in the home landscape. It is best to correct the wet soil condition. Ensure the site has good drainage by amending the soil, and avoid overwatering and overfertilizing. Rotate petunias with other annuals to prevent disease build-up. Furthermore, many diseases are introduced into our gardens on the plants we purchase. Therefore, be sure to inspect plants before purchase, and avoid buying plants that appear unhealthy.

Further Reading

Adams, Denise Wiles. *Restoring American Gardens: An Encyclopedia of Heirloom Ornamental Plants, 1640-1940.* Portland, Oregon: Timber Press, Inc., 2004. Print.

Armitage, Allan M. *Armitage's Garden Perennials.* 2nd ed. Portland, Oregon: Timber Press, Inc., 2011. Print.

Armitage, Allan M. *Herbaceous Perennial Plants: A Treatise on Their Identification, Culture and Garden Attributes.* 3rd ed. Champaign, Illinois: Stipes Publishing L.L.C., 2008. Print.

Ball, Jeff, and Liz Ball. *Rodale's Flower Garden Problem Solver.* Emmaus, Pennsylvania: Rodale Press, Inc., 1990. Print.

Bryan, John E. *Timber Press Pocket Guide to Bulbs.* Portland, Oregon: Timber Press, Inc., 2005. Print.

Chaplin, Lois Trigg. *The Southern Gardener's Book of Lists: The Best Plants for All Your Needs, Wants, and Whims.* Lanham, Maryland: Taylor Trade Publishing, 1994. Print.

Cox, Jeff. *Perennial All-Stars: The 150 Best Perennials for Great-Looking, Trouble-Free Gardens.* Emmaus, Pennsylvania: Rodale Press, Inc., 1998. Print.

Darke, Rick. *The Encyclopedia of Grasses for Livable Landscapes.* Portland, Oregon: Timber Press, Inc., 2007. Print.

DeWolf, Jr., Gordon P, ed. *Taylor's Guide to Ground Covers, Vines, and Grasses.* New York: Houghton Mifflin Company, 1987. Print.

DiSabato-Aust, Tracy. *The Well-Tended Perennial Garden: Planting and Pruning Techniques.* Expanded Edition. Portland, Oregon: Timber Press, Inc., 2006. Print.

Dole, John M., and Harold F. Wilkins. *Floriculture: Principles and Species.* 2nd ed. Upper Saddle River, New Jersey: Prentice Hall, Inc., 2004. Print.

Ellis, Barbara. *Taylor's Guide to Annuals: How to Select and Grow More than 400 Annuals, Biennials, and Tender Perennials.* New York: Houghton Mifflin Company, 1999. Print.

Ellis, Barbara. *Taylor's Guide to Perennials: More than 600 Flowering and Foliage Plants, Including Ferns and Ornamental Grasses.* New York: Houghton Mifflin Company, 2000. Print.

Hanson, Beth, ed. *Spring-Blooming Bulbs: An A to Z Guide to Classic and Unusual Bulbs for Your Spring Garden.* Brooklyn, New York: Brooklyn Botanic Garden, 2002. Print.

Hanson, Beth, ed. *Summer-Blooming Bulbs: Scores of Spectacular Bloomers for Your Summer Garden.* Brooklyn, New York: Brooklyn Botanic Garden, 2001. Print.

Hessayon, D. G. The Bulb Expert. London: Expert Books, 1995. Print.

10

Hodgson, Larry. *Making the Most of Shade: How to Plan, Plant, and Grow a Fabulous Garden That Lightens up the Shadows.* Emmaus, Pennsylvania: Rodale Press, Inc., 2005. Print.

Hudak, Joseph. *Gardening with Perennials Month by Month.* 2nd ed. 1993. Portland, Oregon: Timber Press, Inc., 2000. Print.

Johnson, Eric A., and Scott Millard. *The Low-Water Flower Gardener.* Littleton, Colorado: Ironwood Press, 1996. Print.

MacKenzie, David S. *Perennial Ground Covers.* 1997. Portland, Oregon: Timber Press, Inc., 2003. Print.

McGary, Jane, ed. *Bulbs of North America.* Portland, Oregon: Timber Press, Inc., 2001. Print.

McKinley, Michael, ed. *Ortho's All about the Easiest Flowers to Grow.* Des Moines, Iowa: Meredith Books, 2001. Print.

Mickel, John T. *Ferns for American Gardens.* 1994. Portland, Oregon: Timber Press, Inc., 2003. Print.

Ogden, Scott. *Garden Bulbs for the South.* 2nd ed. Portland, Oregon: Timber Press, Inc., 2007. Print.

Peace, Tom. *Sunbelt Gardening: Success in Hot-Weather Climates.* Golden, Colorado: Fulcrum Publishing, 2000. Print.

Phillips, Ellen, and C. Colston Burrell. *Rodale's Illustrated Encyclopedia of Perennials: 10th Anniversary Revised and Expanded Edition.* Emmaus, Pennsylvania: Rodale Press, Inc., 2004. Print.

Rogers, Ray. *The Encyclopedia of Container Plants: More than 500 Outstanding Choices for Gardeners.* Portland, Oregon: Timber Press, Inc., 2010. Print.

Schmid, W. George. *An Encyclopedia of Shade Perennials.* 2002. Portland, Oregon: Timber Press, Inc., 2003. Print.

Schrock, Denny, ed. *Ortho All about Perennials.* Hoboken, New Jersey: John Wiley & Sons Inc., 2007. Print.

Still, Steven M. *Manual of Herbaceous Ornamental Plants.* 4th ed. Champaign, Illinois: Stipes Publishing L.L.C., 1994. Print.

Sullivan, Barbara J. *Garden Perennials for the Coastal South.* Chapel Hill, North Carolina: The University Of North Carolina Press, 2002. Print.

Sunset Annuals and Perennials. Menlo Park, California: Sunset Publishing Corporation, 2002. Print.

Welch, William C. *Perennial Garden Color.* 1989. College Station, Texas: Texas A&M University Press, 2012. Print.

For More Information

http://go.ncsu.edu/fmi_herbaceousornamentals

10

Contributors

Author: Toby Bost, Horticulturist, Author

Contributions by Extension Agents: Cyndi Lauderdale, Debbie Dillion, Sam Marshall, Susan Brown, Pam Jones, Ben Grandon, Paige Patterson

Contributions by Extension Master Gardener Volunteers: Renee Lampila, Barbara Goodman, Sue Davis, Jackie Weedon, Karen Damari, Connie Schultz, Bethany Sinnott, Gloria Polakof, Cynthia Wagoner, Linda Mahoney, Kim Curlee, Caro Dosé

Content Edits: Lucy Bradley, Professor and Extension Specialist, Urban Horticulture, NC State University; Director, NC State Extension Master Gardener program
Kathleen Moore, Urban Horticulturist

Copy Editor: Barbara Scott

Based on text from the 1998 Extension Master Gardener manual prepared by:
Erv Evans, Extension Associate, Department of Horticultural Science

Contributions from:
Doug Bailey, Extension Specialist, Department of Horticultural Science
Gus De Hertogh, Professor, Department of Horticultural Science

Chapter 10 Cover Photo: Pixabay CC BY0

How to Cite This Chapter:
Bost, T. 2022. Herbaceous Ornamentals, Chpt. 10, In: K.A. Moore, and. L.K. Bradley (eds). *North Carolina Extension Gardener Handbook*, 2nd ed. NC State Extension, Raleigh, NC. <https://content.ces.ncsu.edu/extension-gardener-handbook/10-herbaceous-ornamentals>

Woody Ornamentals

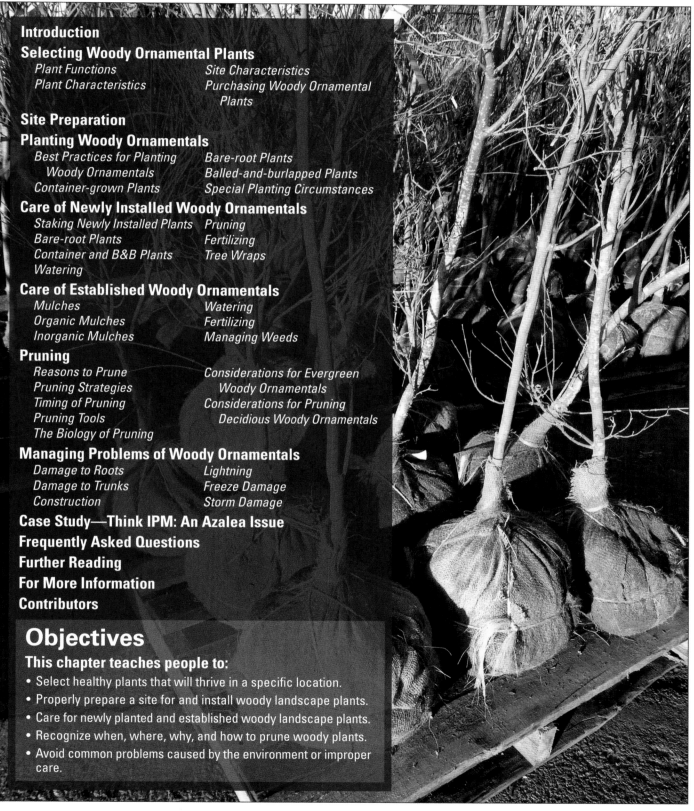

Objectives

This chapter teaches people to:
• Select healthy plants that will thrive in a specific location.
• Properly prepare a site for and install woody landscape plants.
• Care for newly planted and established woody landscape plants.
• Recognize when, where, why, and how to prune woody plants.
• Avoid common problems caused by the environment or improper care.

11

Introduction

Woody ornamental plants are the living, structural components of a well-landscaped yard. They are long-lived perennials with stems and **branches** that increase in girth and height each growing season. Unlike **herbaceous** plants that die back to the ground in winter, woody ornamentals remain aboveground year-round. In the landscape, woody ornamentals serve many essential functions. Individual specimens provide a focal point, while groups establish a framework. Woody plants create vertical layering from the ground up, affording a host of **ornamental** and environmental benefits. Shrubs help define areas of the landscape. Flowering woody plants add color and fragrance to a yard, especially in the spring (Figure 11–1). Many **deciduous** woody plants offer fall color from foliage, **berries**, or **twigs** to brighten autumn landscapes, while **evergreens** provide winter interest (Figure 11–2). Environmental benefits include wildlife habitat, wind screens, shade (Figure 11–3), and erosion control. This large group of plants is divided into three basic categories: vines, shrubs, and trees. Each of these categories can be subdivided into evergreen and deciduous plant varieties, and evergreens can be further divided into broad-leaved (broadleaf) and narrow-leaved (narrowleaf) plants.

Figure 11-1. Flowering woody ornamentals add color to the landscape, especially in the spring.
emetzner130, Pixabay CC BY0

Figure 11-2. Many deciduous woody plants offer fall color from foliage, berries, or twigs to brighten up an autumn landscape, while evergreens provide winter interest.
Robert Lyle Bolton, Flickr CC BY - 2.0

Figure 11-3. Shade trees like this evergreen wax myrtle (*Morella cerifera*), cool houses with their shade.
Margaret Genkins

Vines are **climbing** or **crawling** woody plants without self-supporting stems. When allowed to crawl along the ground, woody vines can be used as ground covers. However, providing vertical support for vines makes them versatile, interesting aspects of the landscape and reduces their footprint, making them very useful in small spaces. When trained over an arbor, vines create shade; when encouraged to grow up a trellis or fence, vines screen unwanted views or define garden spaces. Deciduous or evergreen vines add interest when trained against the wall of a building or when used to frame a doorway. Vines relieve the monotony of a large expanse of fencing and can hide a chain-link fence with a mass of green foliage. Many woody vines offer seasonal color with blooms, foliage, or berries.

Types of Vines

Vines are generally divided into four groups based on their method of climbing.

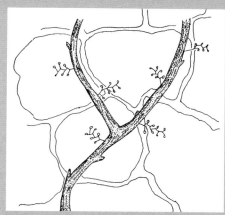

Figure 11-4. Boston ivy (*Parthenocissus tricuspidata*) climbs using disc-like adhesive tips for support.

Clinging vines produce short rootlike growths that serve as adhesive pads (Figure 11–4). They easily climb trees, walls, and wood fences with little assistance. These vines should not be allowed to grow on houses or eaves. As such a vine matures, its **canopy** becomes dense and traps moisture against the home leaving it susceptible to rot. The vine can work its way into cracks and crevices, destroying masonry or pulling down window frames or gutters. Vines with rootlets growing on tree trunks do not harm the tree unless they grow to cover the tree's foliage. Examples of this type of vine are Japanese hydrangea vine (*Hydrangea hydrangeoides*) and climbing fig (*Ficus pumila*).

Twining vines make up the largest group of vines. They climb by wrapping their stems around and through their support structure (Figure 11–5). They grow well on lattice, chain-link fencing, or any structure they can weave through, but usually need help becoming established. Avoid planting twining vines near small trees and shrubs because these vines may become difficult to control. Examples of this type of vine are American wisteria (*Wisteria frutescens*) and Carolina jessamine (*Gelsemium sempervirens*).

Scrambler vines produce long, supple stems that can be woven through the same type of support structures as twining vines (Figure 11–6). They generally need to be trained to climb up and through their support structures. Examples of this type of vine are climbing aster (*Ampleaster carolinianus*) and greenbriar (*Smilax laurifolia*).

Tendrils are short curly stems that wrap around narrow structures like wire or bamboo (Figure 11–7). These vines need a support structure with small diameter elements and do very well on chain-link fences or wires. Examples of this type of vine are grape (*Vitis* spp.), evergreen clematis (*Clematis armandii*), Virginia creeper (*Parthenocis quinquefolia*), and crossvine (*Bignonia capreolata*).

Figure 11-5. Twining vines like American wisteria (*Wisteria frutescens*) wrap their stems around a support structure.

Figure 11-6. Scrambler vines like greenbriar (*Smilax laurifolia*) need to be wound around a support like this chain-link fence.

Figure 11-7. Tendril vines like Passion flower (*Passiflora* spp.) climb by twining stems and tendrils.

11

Shrubs are woody plants that grow up to 12 feet tall with foliage extending to the ground. They often have multiple trunks. Deciduous and evergreen (both broadleaf and narrowleaf or coniferous) shrubs are versatile in the landscape, creating structure as ground covers, hedges, screens, and borders. Woody shrubs offer focal points as specimen plantings and provide a wide variety of seasonal interest via blooms, fruit, foliage, or twigs that offer color, texture, or scent.

Trees are woody plants that typically grow more than 12 feet tall and usually have only one main trunk. Deciduous and evergreen (both broadleaf and narrowleaf or coniferous) trees are key components in a well-planned landscape, creating vertical shape and architecture. Working as specimen plants or in groups, trees contribute a strong vertical element to the landscape. Trees also offer a wide spectrum of foliage, both evergreen and deciduous, and provide interest via blooms, fruit, and twigs. Trees are environmental workhorses that create cooling shade, detain stormwater runoff, remove air pollutants, sequester carbon, and host many species of wildlife.

Selecting Woody Ornamental Plants

Selecting the "right plant for the right place" is the most important step in creating a healthy, vibrant landscape. Thousands of different kinds of plants are grown in North Carolina, and the number of options at a nursery can be overwhelming. Begin by identifying the site characteristics (sun, soil, available space), and limit your search to plants that thrive in those conditions. Next, consider the role you want the plant to play in the landscape design, and narrow your search further to plants that can fulfill those requirements. See "Landscape Design," chapter 19, for more information about the site, and see the NC State Extension Gardener Plant Toolbox for detailed information about specific plants or to search for plants with specific characteristics.

Consider the following factors as you choose woody ornamentals to become the architectural framework for a healthy, beautiful landscape:

Plant Functions
Plants serve many functions in the landscape—from increasing comfort and beauty, to creating physical barriers, to providing wildlife habitat, to protecting the soil. Select plants that can fulfill the desired functions.

- **Climate.** Provide shade, modify humidity and air temperature, and divert breezes or block wind. Providing shade usually requires tall, sturdy, long-living tree species. Place deciduous trees to shade south-facing windows of a home in the summer, and allow the sun

to help heat the home in winter. Windbreaks must be able to survive rigorous climatic conditions.

- **Visual.** Provide screening or privacy and reduce glare. For screening, select an evergreen tree or shrub with dense foliage that grows quickly to the desired height.

- **Physical.** Direct or limit movement of people or animals. Barrier plantings may require sturdy plants with dense growth and possibly thorns or spines.

- **Environmental.** Control erosion, prevent stormwater runoff, and filter air and water.

- **Ecological.** Contribute multiple **ecosystem services**, such as attract and host **pollinators** (including birds, bats, butterflies, bees, beetles, and moths) and provide habitat for songbirds and other native wildlife. Native woody trees and shrubs can be particularly effective. For example, some oak trees host more than 500 moth and butterfly species.

- **Aesthetic.** Fulfill landscape design criteria through colorful fruits and flowers, interesting foliage, fall colors, attractive bark, winter appeal, fragrances, textures, and pleasing forms.

Plant Characteristics
There are many plant characteristics to consider when selecting a plant for the landscape: mature size, mature form, foliage, bloom, fruit, seeds, cones, bark, growth rate, hardiness, water needs, insect and disease resistance, air pollution tolerance, and **weediness**.

- **Mature size.** Consider size at maturity, and carefully survey the landscape to consider both the horizontal and vertical space available. Evaluate the plant's impact on buildings, rooflines, fences, patios, sidewalks, and power lines. Consider how shading from the mature tree canopy and the extensive **feeder roots** might affect plants or **hardscape** beneath the canopy.

- **Mature form.** Forms include low-spreading, round or oval, vase, pyramidal, columnar or **fastigiate**, upright, and **pendulous** or weeping (Figure 11–8). Choose plants that provide the desired functions and visual appeal in their mature size and form.

- **Foliage.** Consider all aspects of foliage, including color in all seasons, texture, size, and whether deciduous or evergreen. Plan for leaf drop as all plants shed leaves. Deciduous plants drop all their leaves in a short period of time, whereas evergreen plants shed throughout the year.

- **Bloom.** Consider color, fragrance, duration, season, and bloom time within season (early, mid, or later).

- **Fruit, seeds, and cones.** Consider beauty and color as well as potential messiness and weediness of each plant's fruiting and seed dispersal habits.

- **Twigs and bark.** Consider beauty, color, and texture, as well as potential messiness. **Exfoliating** bark, while

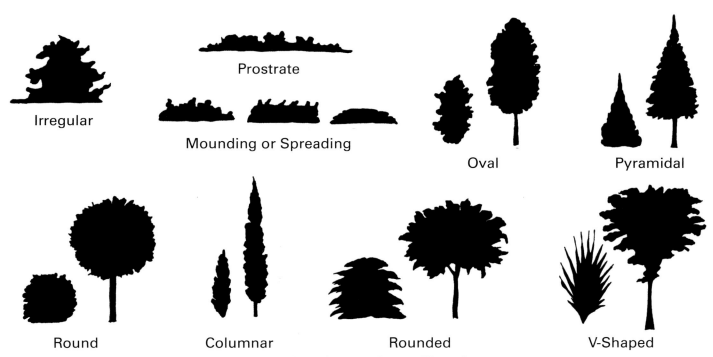

Irregular

Prostrate

Mounding or Spreading

Oval

Pyramidal

Round

Columnar

Rounded

V-Shaped

Figure 11–8. Woody plants grow in many different forms.

visually interesting on the trunk, may become undesirable once it falls to the ground.

- **Growth rate.** Plants grow at varying rates. Although it may be appealing to purchase a "fast-growing" tree in hopes of instant shade, sometimes that speed comes at a cost to strength. Many fast-growing trees have weak wood that breaks easily. Evaluate both your immediate landscape goals and the plant's long-term impact on the mature landscape.
- **Hardiness.** Consider cold and heat tolerance of plant selections.
- **Water needs.** Consider drought and wet tolerance. Plants vary widely in their adaptation to soil moisture. Most plants need to dry out slightly between watering and can tolerate neither drought nor standing water for extended periods. The lack of oxygen in saturated soil causes the roots of many plants to die. Some plants, however, like bald cypress (*Taxodium distichum*), grow in the middle of a river. Other species, like eastern red cedar (*Juniperus virginiana*), survive months without rain. Select and group plants that have similar water needs to increase survival and improve watering efficiency.
- **Native.** See "Native Plants," chapter 12, for guidance in selecting native plants adapted to the site conditions and supportive of native wildlife for an environmentally friendly landscape.
- **Insect and disease resistance or susceptibility.** Check with your local N.C. Cooperative Extension Center for plants to avoid because of poor adaptability to pests in your region.

- **Air pollution tolerance.** If air pollution is a problem in your area, conduct some research before selecting plants for your yard. Plants like arborvitaes (*Thuja* spp.), ginkgos (*Ginkgo biloba*), sugar maples (*Acer saccharum*), and red oak have a higher tolerance for air pollution.
- **Weediness.** Some plants produce seeds that germinate quickly and prolifically or have root systems that invade planting beds and send up new plants. Research the potential weediness of plants such as Algerian ivy (*Hedera canariensis*), bamboo, cottonwood (*Populus* spp.), English ivy (*Hedera helix*), periwinkle (*Vinca major*), privet (*Ligustrum* spp.), tree of heaven (*Ailanthus altissima*), trumpet creeper (*Campsis* spp.), and willow (*Salix* spp.). Some research is being done to produce seedless versions of weedy woody ornamental plants.

Site Characteristics

Consider the following site characteristics to select a plant that will thrive in a particular setting: size of available space, sunlight, soil characteristics, climate, microclimate, moisture, slope, hardscapes, water, and existing vegetation.

- **Size of available space.** Width and height aboveground and available root space belowground.
- **Sunlight.** Duration, timing, intensity, and direction of exposure. Some plants require shade or filtered light, while others require full sun for best growth. Before choosing plants for the landscape, observe how many hours of sun and shade various parts of the landscape receive. Plants requiring full sun need at least 6 hours of direct sun each day. Many shade-loving plants tolerate exposure to early morning sun but may suffer

if exposed to 2 hours of direct sunlight at midday or afternoon.

Shade Characteristics

Not all shade is the same. There is filtered shade, partial shade, open shade, and dense shade. **Filtered shade (dappled sunlight)** occurs under trees with smaller leaves or leaflets (Figure 11–9) and is suitable for growing many plants—even plants that prefer full sunlight, such as service berry (*Amelanchier alnifolia*) or staghorn sumac (*Rhus typhina*). **Partial shade** indicates that the area may be in shade a portion of the day and then receive full sun at another time. **Open shade** occurs where there is an obstacle, such as a building, blocking the plant so that it does not receive direct sunlight but does receive indirect light. **Deep shade** is the most restrictive and is found in heavily wooded areas and in landscapes under large evergreens or broadleaf deciduous trees (maple, oak, hickory, beech). Deep shade also occurs in a narrow side yard when another building is close or in a recessed entryway on the north side of the house.

Figure 11–9. This honeylocust (*Gleditsia triacanthos*) has small leaflets that provide filtered shade.
Leonora Enking, Flickr CC BY-SA 2.0

Shade and light intensity changes with the time of day, the season, the slope, and over time as trees grow. Sites that might be in full sun in winter may become heavily shaded as the season changes and trees leaf out. Light is also influenced by topography. For example, a south-facing slope receives more light than a north-facing slope. As trees grow taller and wider, they cast larger shadows and less light penetrates the increasingly dense shade. It is possible to admit more light under the canopy of trees or large shrubs by removing lower limbs. Removal of too

many limbs, however, stresses the plant. Selecting plants that thrive in dense shade is a better option than attempting to alter the environment by **thinning** the canopy of otherwise healthy plants.

- **Soil characteristics.** *Moisture, drainage,* **pH**, *texture, and structure.* Identify the soil moisture and drainage characteristics of your site by digging a hole 12-inches to 15-inches deep where you intend to place the plant. Fill the hole with water. If the water remains in the hole after 24 hours, the soil is poorly drained. For poorly drained sites, select plants that tolerate wet conditions. Winter daphne (*Daphne odora*) prefers uniform moisture but not wet soil. Bald cypress (*Taxodium distichum*) grows in a range of moisture situations from very wet sites to moderately dry sites. If the site is dry, select plants that thrive in dry conditions like santolina (*Santolina virens*) or plan to irrigate. Most woody plants grown in NC landscapes thrive in a pH range from 6.0 to 7.0, but there are exceptions. So before selecting a plant, review its soil pH requirements to ensure it will thrive in the intended site. Read more about pH in "Soils and Plant Nutrients," chapter 1, and have a soil sample tested to determine pH for different planting areas in the landscape.

  Plants such as Japanese pieris (*Pieris japonica*), azaleas, blueberries, camellias, mountain laurel, and rhododendrons grow best in soil with a pH of 5.0 to 5.5. In soils with a pH of 6.0 or higher, these acid-loving plants may become yellow and grow poorly. Soil texture or the amount of sand, silt, and clay in any given soil is extremely difficult to change on a large scale. Work with your soil's given texture to choose plants that thrive in that soil type. Plants that are native to your region are already well-adapted to a given soil texture. Read more in chapter 12, "Native Plants." Changing the structure of the soil or how well it holds and releases nutrients and water can be managed over several seasons by the repeated addition of organic matter.

- **Climate.** *Temperature highs and lows, air movement, rainfall, and length of growing season.* The climate varies significantly within North Carolina, and plants that flourish in the mountains may do poorly or fail in the coastal plain. This is due, in part, to the variation in temperature. Use the USDA Plant Hardiness zone map to determine which plants are hardy in your location. The map is based on the average annual minimum winter temperature and is divided into 13 zones, each covering a range of 10°F. Each zone is subdivided into five degree bands indicated by "a" and "b". In North Carolina, the zones tend to be aligned with elevation and transition—from 6a in the mountains to 8a on the coast. A plant is said to be hardy if it tolerates the average annual minimum winter temperatures that occur in a zone. Cold tolerance is an important limiting factor, but one of the biggest challenges for plants in the South is warm nights. High night temperatures increase respiration and deplete food reserves, leading to a greater incidence of plant stress. The American Horticultural Society has developed a national Plant Heat Zone Map that includes 12 zones based on the number of days the temperature rises above 86°F. North Carolina has four zones represented. The zoning map provides guidelines, but it is important to evaluate your own specific site. Characteristics of a specific location can cause it to be warmer or colder than other locations within the same zone. Here are some examples of **microclimates**:

- **Radiated heat.** The south side of a building and hardscapes (rocks, paved surfaces, and brick walls) absorb heat during the day and radiate heat at night.
- **Enclosure.** Evergreen trees keep the area beneath their canopy warmer by holding the heat from the ground.
- **Shade.** The north side of a house and beneath the canopy of a tree are protected from the sun and so are cooler during the day.
- **Slope.** Gravity takes rainfall away from plants on hills before it has time to soak in. Plants at the bottom of hills or near gutter downspouts, however, may get much more than the reported rainfall. Like water, cold air also flows down. So in winter, low spaces at the bottom of hills are colder.
- **Vegetation.** A high concentration of plants leads to increased humidity and increased competition for water, nutrients, and sunlight. In forests, cooler temperatures and less wind exposure decrease water loss. Competition from tree roots, however, causes some shady areas to be quite dry.
- **Overhangs.** Plants under eaves, awnings, or branches may receive no rain.
- **Moisture.** Humidity, the amount and timing of rainfall, and the soil texture and structure affect the amount of moisture available to plants.
- **Water.** Proximity to a large body of water can moderate temperature and humidity.

Purchasing Woody Ornamental Plants

Plants can be purchased as container-grown, **bare root**, or **balled-and-burlapped (B&B)**. Always purchase plants from a reputable source (such as a nursery, garden center, botanical garden, or Extension Master Gardener Volunteer plant sale). Select healthy, vigorous plants that are uniformly shaped with no thin areas or broken or damaged limbs. Compact, full foliage is more important than height. Examine the trunk for **cankers** and split bark, especially after a severe winter (Figure 11–10). Examine both the tops and the bottoms of leaves, and reject plants that show signs or symptoms of insect or disease problems.

Small trees (less than 2-inch caliper trunks, measurement taken 6 inches from the ground) do not have to look like a miniature of a mature tree. Select trees with foliage evenly distributed in the entire upper two-thirds of the tree (Figure 11–11). This distribution of limbs and foliage supports the development of **trunk taper** and strength as the tree matures.

Figure 11–10. This newly installed tree has a stem canker. Do not purchase plants that have split bark or cankers. Scot Nelson, Flickr CC BY0

Figure 11–11. Branches lower on the trunk help develop trunk taper. The tree on the left would be a better option; the tree on the right has been pruned up too high. Kathleen Moore, CC BY - 2.0

The root system is just as important, if not more important, than the top of the plant. Check the bottom of the container for roots growing out of drainage holes. It is fine if a few small roots are sticking out of the holes. But if large roots have to be cut off to remove the plant from the container, choose a different plant. Severe root pruning stresses the plant and reduces growth. If you suspect a plant may be root bound, gently slide the root ball out of the container. The root ball should stay together but be somewhat pliable. If the root ball is very hard or many roots are circling the root ball, purchase a different plant. A mass of circling roots acts as a physical barrier to root growth into the soil after transplanting. The circled or **girdled roots** also choke and kill the plant as it grows (Figure 11–12). Examine the root system for small white roots along the exterior of the root ball indicating a healthy plant and root structure (Figure 11–13).

Figure 11–12. A parking lot tree that died from girdling roots.
Kathleen Moore, CC BY - 2.0

Figure 11–13. This Scotch heather (*Calluna vulgaris*) has many feeder roots at the edge of the pot but no woody roots wrapping around. Slice and loosen the roots in several places before planting.
Kathleen Moore, CC BY - 2.0

Small plants are easier to transplant, more economical, and adjust to transplant shock more quickly than large plants.

Large plants are more expensive and take longer to become established.

Cover plants placed in the back of a truck to prevent wind exposure from **desiccating** and damaging foliage during transport home. Ideally, transplant plants soon after they are purchased. If there is a delay, keep the plants in a protected, shaded area and check for moisture frequently to prevent the root ball from drying out. Avoid placing plants on paved surfaces that absorb and radiate heat. Keep the plants out of the sun because the dark-colored root balls and containers also absorb heat, causing the temperature inside the root ball to be higher than the air temperature. Do not lay a tree down on its side for extended periods of time unless the trunk is wrapped or covered to prevent **sunscald**. Low temperatures are also dangerous to plants that have not been **hardened off**. Expect root injury if temperatures drop below 23°F unless soil or **mulch** is used to insulate the outside of the root ball or container.

Site Preparation

Proper site preparation is a good investment in the long-term health of woody ornamental plants. The work put into preparing the site can significantly improve root growth, leading to a healthy plant, resistant to stresses that might otherwise create problems. Based on recommendations from soil test results, add amendments and address fertility issues to improve soil prior to planting.

If the existing soil is **compacted** and poorly drained, tilling or digging to improve aeration and drainage is essential for satisfactory plant growth. If deep tilling or ripping is necessary to eliminate a **hardpan** that was formed below the soil surface during construction, consider hiring a professional with appropriate equipment. If drainage is a problem, consider installing a **drain tile system** to evacuate excess water or creating raised beds.

Rather than creating individual planting holes, prepare the entire bed when possible. When preparing the bed, incorporate 1 inch to 3 inches of organic matter, such as compost, into the top 12 inches of soil. Ensure that organic matter is well composted or aged.

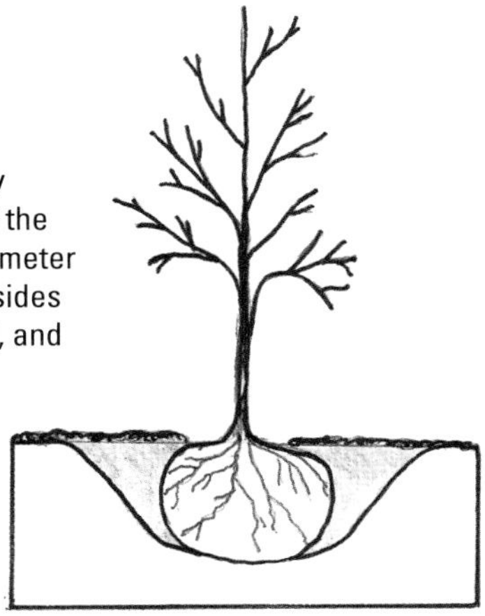

Planting Woody Ornamentals

Careful attention to proper planting techniques prevents future problems. Although planting procedures vary depending on whether the plant is container-grown, bare-root, or balled-and-burlapped (B&B), there are some best practices that apply to all three.

Best Practices for Planting Woody Ornamentals

Consider timing. Most container plants can be transplanted at any time of year but do best, and require the least attention to watering, if transplanted in late fall or early spring. This planting time also provides plants with time to begin to become established before low or high temperatures occur.

Prepare. Move plant to the planting location and remove trunk wrap if present. Remove twine from crown and any labels. At time of planting, prune only broken or dead branches, or those that are rubbing. For trees, if there is more than one central leader, select the healthiest one and remove the other, making a proper pruning cut. Determine how big the hole should be by measuring the root ball. You can use a measuring tape, yardstick or the shovel handle for a good approximation.

Dig the hole. An ideal planting hole is only as deep as the root ball and at least two to three times wider, with roughened sides sloping in toward the bottom (Figure 11–14). Reserve the soil removed to refill the hole. The sides of a hole dug in heavy soil can become slick, especially if the soil is somewhat wet. Slick sides can act as physical barriers to root growth and moisture movement. Use a shovel to make the sides of the hole rough and irregular (Figure 11–15). Loosened soil below the root ball can settle, resulting in the plant being too deep. If the hole is dug too deep, firm the bottom of the hole to reduce settling. Because most new roots grow horizontally from the side of the root ball, soil firmed at the bottom of the hole does not substantially affect root growth. In many urban soils, root growth from the bottom of the root ball is limited by inadequate aeration and excessive moisture.

Figure 11–14. Diagram of a properly planted tree. Note that the width of the hole is more than two times the diameter of the root ball with gently sloping sides tTe rootball sits on undisturbed soil, and the trunk flare is just above grade.

Figure 11–15. Rough up the sides of a planting hole.
Luke McGuff, Flickr CC BY-ND - 2.0

Position the plant. Carefully place the plant in the hole. For B&B trees gently roll them into the hole. Position the tree so it is straight, and the "best side" faces out. Make sure to plant at or slightly above grade. If your soil is very poorly drained, create a small mound (about 6 inches in height) in the middle of the hole and set the root ball on this mound. This allows water to collect beneath the roots.

Attend to the roots. For B&B trees, remove any twine wrapped around the base of the trunk. Remove the top 1/3 to 1/2 of the wire basket using wire cutters. Pull the burlap down away from the top of the ball and cut off. For container-grown trees, use a shovel to shave off roots around the edge and bottom of the root ball. Slice down into the root ball in a radial manner.

Refill the hole. Loosen and break up any clods in the excavated soil before backfilling because clods can create air pockets around the root ball. Do not amend the backfill. Fill the planting hole about halfway and then water-in. Finish adding soil to the hole so it is level with the surrounding grade. Chop the soil in the hole with the end of a shovel to minimize air pockets, taking care not to chop the roots. Do not tamp the soil too firmly, as this will compact the soil making it harder for growing roots to penetrate.

11

Water. After planting, construct a ring of soil 2 inches to 3 inches high to form a water basin just beyond the outside edge of the hole (plants in beds probably do not require a water basin). This permits water to soak into the root zone rather than running off the surface. Water the plant to eliminate air pockets around the roots. The water basin can be expanded as the plant grows or removed after the plants become established.

Mulch. Apply 2 inches to 3 inches of organic mulch in an area that extends to several inches beyond the plant canopy. Keep mulch at least 6 inches away from the trunk or crown of the plant to improve air circulation and discourage insect and mammal activity (Figure 11–16). The root zone of trees and shrubs grows to extend beyond the drip line—two to three times the distance between the trunk and the edge of the canopy. Increase the mulch zone outward as plants mature to continue to protect the roots. The mulch helps to maintain moisture and reduce fluctuations in soil temperature. Mulch inhibits weeds and breaks down over time, improving the soil.

Figure 11–16. Mulch is placed 6 inches from the crown of this heavenly bamboo (*Nandina domestica*) shrub.
Kathleen Moore, CC BY - 2.0

Container-Grown Plants

Container-grown plants have become the most popular method of growing plants for sale by the nursery industry. Water plants thoroughly before transplanting. For smaller plants, remove each plant from its container by turning the plant upside down and giving the top edge of the container a sharp rap. Catch the root ball as it slips from the container. For larger plants, turn each plant on its side and gently press on the container; then holding on to the base of the plant, gently slip the root ball out of the container. Always pick the plant up by the root ball, never by the trunk or stem as it could split or break.

Bare-Root Plants

Mail-order companies often sell bare-root plants because it is more economical to ship plants without soil. Bare-root plants are usually the least expensive but require more care during and after planting. These plants were grown in a field nursery and dug during the dormant season. Soil was removed from their roots before they were put into cold, moist storage. At shipping, the roots are covered with damp peat moss or sawdust and wrapped with plastic or cardboard (Figure 11–17). Most bare-root plants are deciduous trees or shrubs. Evergreen plants are rarely sold bare-root. Plants with a long tap root, such as nut trees and some fruit and shade trees, are often sold bare-root because they are not well-suited to B&B or container production.

Figure 11–17. Bare-root tree with sawdust wrapped in plastic.
Kathleen Moore, CC BY - 2.0

Install bare-root plants while they are dormant. When plants arrive, check them for moisture and do not let the roots dry out. Keep roots wrapped in wet paper or sphagnum moss and covered with plastic until it is time to install. Keep plants in a cool (not freezing) location; roots can be easily damaged by freezing temperatures.

Before planting, soak the roots in water for at least an hour but not more than 24 hours. Longer soaking can drown the roots from lack of oxygen. Remove any broken or damaged roots before planting. Never leave the roots exposed to wind or sun even during the planting process; keep the roots protected by wrapping in moist burlap or place them in a bucket of water.

Build a mound of soil in the center of the planting hole and spread the roots around it. Gently work the soil in and around the roots while the plant is being supported to ensure good soil-root contact.

Balled-and-Burlapped Plants

Most of the trees and shrubs sold B&B have been grown in field nursery rows, dug with soil intact, wrapped with burlap, and tied with twine (Figure 11–18). The size of the root ball varies with plant size. Select a plant with a sound, firm root ball, 10 to 12 times the diameter of the tree trunk measured 6 inches off the ground.

Figure 11–18. Balled-and-burlapped trees.
Kathleen Moore, CC BY - 2.0

Most B&B plants are root pruned for several years to create a compact and fibrous root system. But even with the best nursery efforts, up to 95% of the roots are lost in the digging process. The remaining small portion of the plant's former root system has difficulty absorbing enough water to meet the plant's needs. Take extra care to ensure the roots never dry out and are not exposed to hot summer or freezing winter temperatures for an extended period of time before planting.

Handle B&B material carefully; on most species if the soil ball is broken, many of the small roots are severed and the plant will die. Always pick the plant up by the soil ball, never by the trunk or stem.

Natural burlap that has not been treated or dyed can be buried with the plant because it is biodegradable, but remove all synthetic material from a root ball. To determine the difference between a natural and a synthetic material, hold a lit match to a small portion of the material. Natural materials burn while synthetics melt.

After positioning the plant in the hole, remove any straps, ties, strings, or wires secured around the root ball. Wire baskets are often used to reinforce the root ball during shipping. Experts disagree on possible harm that the wires might cause if left in the planting hole. If possible, cut and remove the top portion of the basket. Removing the entire wire basket can cause the root ball to be damaged. Remove natural burlap from the top one-half to one-third of the root ball. Cut the burlap on top of the root ball, roll it back, and cover with soil. If part of the burlap is exposed above the soil line, it acts as a wick, removing moisture from the root ball. B&B plants usually need little pruning at planting but may need careful watering during the summer.

Special Planting Circumstances

When planting under a shade tree, do not till within the drip line. Tilling would damage tree roots, possibly resulting in slow decline and eventual death. Instead, dig individual holes for a few spreading plants. Install young plants (quart-sized containers versus gallon-sized) so only small holes are needed. Smaller holes are easier to dig and are less disruptive to the tree. Choose long-lived plants to minimize disturbance to the roots.

Care of Newly Installed Woody Ornamentals

Staking Newly Installed Plants

Staking Vines

Newly transplanted vines often need guidance to reach the intended support. Use a short piece of string, netting, or stake to guide growth to the lower portions of the trellis or fence. To prevent vines from growing upright with a mass of foliage at the top and little at the base, train the vine horizontally at first, forcing the upward growth to develop from lateral shoots. Moderate pruning in the first few years also encourages low branching.

Staking Trees and Shrubs

In some situations, staking can provide stability to the roots and trunk of a tree while allowing it to develop a healthy root system, strong trunk, and strong branches. Avoid staking trees and shrubs if possible as it is a labor-intensive, costly procedure that can easily do more harm than good. Most plants less than 6 feet tall with less than a 1-inch trunk do not need to be staked. As nursery stock gets larger, the root ball may not be large enough to keep the stem from tipping once planted. Environmental factors at the planting site—such as wind exposure, topography, surrounding plantings, and soil conditions—also play a role in the decision to stake. Plant and observe the tree or shrub for a day; if it leans, it may need staking. Drive the first stake at least 2 feet down into native soil,

11

outside the root ball on the side of the prevailing winds. Set the other stake in on the opposite side. Use broad, smooth strapping material to avoid abrasion, and place the strapping at the highest point on the trunk where the crown stands upright. Place straps using a "figure 8" crossing pattern wrapped around the trunk and securely fastened to the stake. Never use wire, even if it is placed in old garden hose, as this can girdle the plant. Tighten straps so they are firm enough not to contact the stakes but loose enough to allow slight (two to three times the trunk diameter) movement, which increases trunk taper and strength (Figure 11–19). Check the strapping regularly to ensure it is not causing trunk injury. It may be possible to remove stakes for fall-planted trees by midspring. Remove all staking within one year after planting or growth may be reduced.

Figure 11–19. This mature pine tree has developed good trunk taper, flaring out at the soil line.
J. Triepke, Flickr CC BY - 2.0

Bare-Root Plants
Drive a single stake about three-fourths the height of the tree at a distance of 2 inches to 4 inches from the center of the planting hole on the southwest side of the tree trunk (Figure 11–20). Fasten the tree to the stake with nylon tape or strapping formed in a loose loop just above the lowest scaffold branches, or 6 inches above the lowest point at which you can hold the tree upright.

Figure 11–20. Staking a bare-root tree.

Container and B&B Plants
Use as few stakes as possible to keep the plant upright. Start with a stake placed outside the root ball and upwind from the prevailing winds. Drive the stake into the ground 2 feet. Create a loop, and wrap one end of a nylon tape or strapping two-thirds of

the way up the trunk. Securely fasten the other end to the stake without putting a strain on the trunk. If one stake is not sufficient to keep the plant upright, run another stake into the ground parallel to the prevailing winds (Figure 11–21). In some cases, three stakes may be needed to keep the plant upright. Drive three stakes an equal distance from the planting hole and from each other 2 feet into the ground.

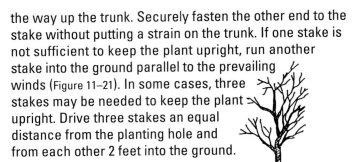

Figure 11–21. Staking a small tree using two parallel stakes.

Watering
Depending on the season and current weather conditions, recently installed plants may be subject to drought stress until roots grow into the surrounding soil. The well-drained planting mix of container-grown

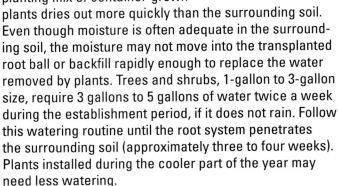

plants dries out more quickly than the surrounding soil. Even though moisture is often adequate in the surrounding soil, the moisture may not move into the transplanted root ball or backfill rapidly enough to replace the water removed by plants. Trees and shrubs, 1-gallon to 3-gallon size, require 3 gallons to 5 gallons of water twice a week during the establishment period, if it does not rain. Follow this watering routine until the root system penetrates the surrounding soil (approximately three to four weeks). Plants installed during the cooler part of the year may need less watering.

Check the root ball for moisture by putting a finger in the soil. If the root ball is dry, increase the amount or the frequency of watering, or both. Care must be taken to prevent the transplanted root ball from drying out because the organic mix is very difficult to rewet once it becomes dry. Water applied after a root ball has become very dry may run off rather than soaking in. If this happens, apply water two or three times each day until the root ball is wet.

Pruning
Newly installed plants typically need only light pruning to remove damaged or broken branches. To prevent future structural problems, however, also remove at planting, or within the first year or two, any serious branch problems, such as a tight v-crotch (Figure 11–22). Maintain the natural growth habit of shrubs, and do not remove the central leader of shade trees. Do not remove the lower branches of trees following transplanting. The foliage is needed to shade the trunk and for food production, and these laterals help produce trunk taper. Because the signal that initiates new root growth originates in shoot tips, removing the ends of branches reduces root development. Pruning reduces the leaf area; while this reduces **transpiration**, it also reduces **photosynthates** for root growth.

Figure 11–22. A tight v-crotch. The smaller branch should be removed to prevent structural problems later on.
Kathleen Moore, CC BY - 2.0

Fertilizing

Before using fertilizer, conduct a soil test to determine which nutrients are needed. Always follow fertilizer package instructions. Applying more than the recommended amounts can damage plants. Remember that natural fertilizers, like slowly decomposing compost, do not have the same issues with salt buildup that some commercial fertilizers have. Wait until spring to fertilize trees and shrubs that were planted in the fall. Wait six weeks to eight weeks to fertilize plants installed in the spring. Roots are actively growing two to three times the diameter of the canopy. Fertilizer placed too far away from actively growing roots is wasted (Figure 11–23).

Tree Wraps

Research regarding the use of tree wraps is inconclusive, but most experts agree tree wrapping is not necessary. However, landscape professionals often wrap the trunks of newly transplanted trees that have thin bark. The intent is to prevent trunks from cracking when direct sunlight shines on the lower trunk in cold weather. In winter, the sun is at a lower angle, so more light hits the trunk on the south and southwest sides than it does during the summer. Newly planted trees that have thin bark, such as red maple and ornamental cherry, planted in high-heat sites

(near hard-surface materials such as brick, concrete, or asphalt that reflect or absorb heat) are often wrapped. To wrap a tree, begin at the soil line and spiral the wrapping material around the trunk up to the first major branches. Overlap each layer by half a width. Tree wraps are applied in the fall and removed the following spring. If left on too long, wraps encourage insect and disease problems.

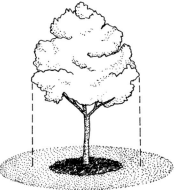

Figure 11–23.
Place fertilizer where roots are growing, or two to three times the canopy's diameter.

Care of Established Woody Ornamentals

There is no such thing as a "no maintenance" landscape. Good maintenance practices include mulching, irrigation, fertilizing, weeding, and pruning. These practices lead to higher vigor and resistance to insects and diseases. Different types of woody ornamentals require different levels of maintenance.

Mulches

Mulch is a material applied to the soil surface for protection or improvement of the area covered. Mulch is not worked into the soil. Mulching conserves soil moisture and prevents weed seed germination. Mulch also reduces runoff, helps maintain uniform soil temperatures, prevents soil and fungi from splashing onto the foliage (thus reducing the potential of soilborne diseases), and adds to the aesthetic appearance of landscape plantings.

Mulch can be applied at any time of the year, but the best time to apply mulch to established plantings is in spring after soil has started warming and plants are beginning to grow but before weed seeds start to germinate. Apply mulch to the entire bed, or for individual trees, from 6 inches away from the trunk to at least 6 inches to 12 inches beyond the drip line of the tree. Renew as needed to maintain a 2-inch to 3-inch depth.

Organic Mulches

As organic mulches break down, they provide organic matter and nutrients to the soil. For maximum benefit, extend the mulched area to include as much of the root zone as possible. Pull mulch 6 inches away from the base of plants to prevent bark decay and vole damage.

11

Select organic mulching material that is readily available, easy to apply, and weed-free. Fine-textured mulches have more surface area and less airspace and therefore retain more moisture than coarse-textured materials. See Table 11–1 for pros and cons of some organic mulch materials.

Potential Problems from Mulch

- Too much of a good thing. Excessive application of mulch can result in roots growing in the mulch rather than the soil. In addition, overmulched plants are easily damaged when herbicides and fertilizers are applied and during periods of drought stress or extreme cold.
- Mulching an area that is poorly drained can aggravate the condition.
- Thick piles of unshredded leaves or uncomposted grass clippings form a thick mat that inhibits water penetration. Run the lawn mower over dry leaves to shred before using them as mulch. Leave grass clippings on the lawn.
- If mulch is too deep and too close to the trunk, mice and voles may tunnel in undetected and cause damage by chewing the bark. Moisture trapped by the mulch may also cause decay and can eventually lead to death of the plant (Figure 11–24). Keep the mulch back 6 inches from the stems. A circle of crushed stone about 6 inches wide around the stems may also be helpful.

Figure 11–24. The mulch is mounded up like a volcano against the trunk of the tree, which can cause pest and disease problems.

NY State IPM Program at Cornell University, CC BY - 2.0

Inorganic Mulches

Gravel, rock, plastic, and landscape fabric can be used as mulches, but applying these materials requires extra time and expense. Replanting is also difficult once these materials are in place, and they are difficult to remove. Rock materials absorb and re-radiate heat from the sun and thus increase water loss from plants and soil. Black plastic mulch interferes with the normal oxygen and water supplies to the root system, restricting gas and water exchange to only the places where holes were cut for planting. A very shallow root system develops, leaving the plant susceptible to drought stress. Landscape fabrics allow normal water and oxygen exchange while preventing the growth of most weeds that germinate beneath the fabric, excluding sedges and some grasses, which grow right through landscape fabric. Weed seeds germinate

and grow on soil that accumulates on top of the fabric and plastic. Black plastic and landscape fabric also degrade over time, becoming unsightly, and small pieces are difficult and time-consuming to remove from garden beds (Figure 11–25).

If landscape fabric is used, apply it on bare soil before or immediately after planting. Fasten the material to the soil to prevent weeds from pushing the material up. Cut an "x" in the material, lay the flaps back, and plant a shrub in the opening. Once the plant is installed, lay the flaps back to cover the opening. Avoid getting soil on top of the material. Be sure to expand the hole as the plant grows so the landscape fabric does not **girdle** the trunk.

Some attractive results have been obtained by using a combination of landscape fabric covered with an organic material. As the mulch decomposes, however, it produces a layer of "soil" in which weeds can grow. Coarse-textured mulch materials, such as pine-bark nuggets, decompose more slowly.

Figure 11–25. Landscape fabric degrades over time and becomes visible and unsightly in the landscape.

Lucy Bradley, CC BY - 2.0

Watering Established Plants

Most plants can withstand short periods of drought without significant damage, but excessive water, even for relatively short periods, causes oxygen depletion, root decay, and root-rot diseases. Overwatering is much more common than underwatering. The key to irrigation success is to water the entire root zone deeply and infrequently.

The amount of water needed is influenced by several factors, including soil texture, slope, drainage, mulch, weather, shade, plant type, plant size, location, time since transplant, fertilization, pruning, and competition.

Soil texture. Soils differ in how much water they absorb and how quickly they dry out after a rain or watering. Water percolates rapidly into and through sandy soil, so plants can be watered quickly and must be watered frequently. Because water applied to a clay soil runs off the surface and is slow to percolate, clay soils must be watered slowly, allowing the water to be absorbed into the soil. Because clay soils may also drain slowly, they may not need to be watered as frequently.

Slope. Water plants on slopes more slowly and more frequently as gravity pulls the water down the slope away from the root zone.

Drainage. The faster the drainage, the more frequently plants need irrigation.

Mulch. Mulches help keep the soil cool and reduce water loss through evaporation, thus extending the time between watering.

Weather. The more sunlight, the longer the day length, the higher the temperature, the higher and drier the wind, and the lower the humidity, the more watering is needed.

Shade. The denser the shade, the less radiant heat from the sun, the cooler the temperature, the less watering is needed. In addition, the object that is creating the shade may also be creating a microclimate. For example, the canopy of a tree over the top of a plant may block wind and prevent evaporation of soil moisture in a way that shade produced by an adjacent building would not.

Plant type. Some plants have specific adaptations of their structure and physiology that allow them to use less, or tolerate more water. For example, desert plants tend to have smaller leaves with a waxy **cuticle** or **trichomes**. Many desert plants can store water in their leaves, trunks, or roots. On the other hand, plants with large leaves (hydrangea) or with shallow root systems (dogwood) are usually the first to suffer during drought periods.

Plant size. Large plants need more water over a wider area than small plants. Apply water from the trunk outward, two to three times the distance to the drip line.

Location. Shrubs under large trees are especially susceptible to drought because of the large volumes of water taken up by tree roots.

Time since transplant. Late spring or summer transplants are the most susceptible to drought because their roots have had a shorter time to become established prior to summer stress.

Fertilization. Recently or heavily fertilized plants easily suffer root damage if water becomes depleted. In addition, new growth stimulated by fertilizing is vulnerable to drought stress.

Pruning. Severe pruning results in vigorous, tender growth that is more dependent on uniform moisture.

Competition. Weeds and landscape plants compete for water. The denser the planting, the more watering is needed.

It is important to water thoroughly and then allow the soil to dry between waterings. Frequent light watering wastes water, does little to satisfy the water requirements of

Table 11–1. Pros and Cons of Some Organic Mulch Materials

Organic Mulch Materials	Pros	Cons
Pine-bark nuggets	attractive, long lasting	expensive; floats and washes away in rain storms; thick layers can provide habitat for voles and other pests
Shredded or chipped wood/bark/fines	readily available, attractive	splintery to work with; decomposes rather quickly and needs to be reapplied
Pine straw	readily available, remains in place even on slopes	stunts the growth of some annuals like pansies, highly flammable
Leaves and twigs	readily available	can mat and prevent water penetration unless shredded
Grass clippings	readily available, free	herbicides sprayed on the lawn could affect broadleaf woody ornamentals; if applied too thickly, can mat and prevent water penetration, or can mold or heat up as it breaks down; best left on the lawn where clippings are a huge asset
Straw	readily available	frequently contains seeds that germinate in landscape; needs to be reapplied frequently; not as attractive as other mulches

11

most plants, and leads to development of a shallow root system, increasing susceptibility to drought. Allowing the soil surface to dry out somewhat between watering encourages root development at greater depths where soil moisture is higher. During prolonged dry spells, water well-established woody plants every 10 days. During cool seasons, less watering is necessary because evaporation from the leaves and soil is slower.

When watering woody ornamentals, especially trees, the goal is to wet the soil 1 foot to 3 feet deep. The best way to determine if adequate water has been applied is to dig in the soil and check how far the water has moved. Wetting the soil to a depth of 12 inches requires about 3 inches of surface water (varies with soil type, compaction, and slope). This may seem like a lot, but when applied slowly you give the water time to move down through the soil profile. This takes time, particularly in a clay-type soil. The most efficient time to water trees and shrubs is between 9 p.m. and 9 a.m. During this time, there is generally less wind, lower temperatures, and higher humidity, so less water is lost through evaporation. If water is being applied directly to the soil through an irrigation system, there is no increased risk of disease. However, if water is applied via a sprinkler that wets the leaves, water early in the morning to promote quicker leaf drying to reduce the spread of disease.

Hand-watering is ineffective for watering woody ornamentals because water is applied at a rate that exceeds the soil's ability to absorb the water. Hand-watering also may not supply enough water. To reduce runoff, use a water-breaker nozzle that divides the spray into rain-size droplets (Figure 11–26). Apply a minimum of 5 gallons of water per 10 square feet, which is approximately the amount delivered by a 5/8-inch hose operating for 1 minute at medium pressure (water pressure from municipalities range from 30 to over 100 pounds of pressure per square inch). To determine how much water comes out of a hose, use a 5-gallon bucket and time how long it takes to fill to the top. Apply 5 gallons (which usually takes about a minute) to small shrubs (under 4 feet tall). Larger shrubs need more water; add 15 seconds of watering for each foot of height exceeding 4 feet. For large trees, apply 6 to 7 gallons (usually takes 1½ minutes to 1¾ minutes) for each 10 square feet of canopy area. If runoff occurs before the correct amount has been applied, move to another spot and come back after the water has soaked in.

Sprinklers come in a variety of sizes and spray patterns. Hose-end sprinklers are easy to move and come in many sizes and shapes. But because of their limited range, hose-end sprinklers are not convenient for watering large areas. In addition, much of the water sprayed into the air is lost to evaporation. Hose-end sprinklers increase disease pressure by splashing disease **propagules** from

Figure 11–26. Use a water-breaker nozzle instead of a trigger-type nozzle when watering plants by hand.
Chris Alberti, CC BY - 2.0

the soil onto leaves. Wetting leaves also increases the opportunity for those disease propagules to infect leaf tissue. Pop-up rotary sprinkler heads are for turf—not ornamental plantings.

Drip irrigation systems have several key components: a controller that regulates when, where, and for how long water is distributed; a pressure regulator to control the water pressure going into the system; a filter to prevent debris from clogging the emitters; tubing to distribute the water; and emitters to regulate the flow of water onto the soil (Figure 11–27). Some emitters are embedded into the tubing. Others are attached. Sensors are available to shut the system off when it rains. Modular aboveground systems that attach to a hose or water spigot are also available. Be sure to distribute enough emitters to irrigate the soil under the canopy of the plant and to add emitters as the plant and its root zone grow. Emitters come in a variety of flow rates. The most common flow rates are ½ gallon/hour, 1 gallon/hour, and 2 gallons/hour. To wet the soil 12 inches deep, you must apply approximately 3 inches of surface water. So if you use 1-gallon-per-hour emitters, you need to run your system for 3 hours when you irrigate. A drip irrigation system is expensive to install, and in many cases it may be best to hire a professional. But a drip system may save money in time by using

Figure 11–27. A drip irrigation system has emitters that place water at each plant's root zone.
Alice Welch, USDA, Flickr CC0

water more efficiently. Rabbits, squirrels, and chipmunks sometimes chew on the tubing.

Soaker hoses emit water directly to the soil, slowly and economically (Figure 11–28). They do not wet the foliage or disturb the soil structure because water does not hit the ground with any force. Many gardeners leave the hoses in one location for an entire season or longer.

Figure 11–28. A soaker hose emits water slowly.
Kathleen Moore, CC BY - 2.0

Most plants wilt when they experience inadequate moisture. If they wilt in the middle of the day and then recover at night, they probably have plenty of water in the soil but their roots are not able to take it up quickly enough to keep up with transpiration in the middle of the day. In this case, irrigating the soil does not help. If the plant is wilted in the morning, check the soil moisture. If the soil is dry 3 inches down, apply water. Wilt can be caused by various factors. So if the soil is moist, look for other causes. Drought stress is also expressed by a change in leaf color or leaf drop. Leaves on river birch and poplar trees turn yellow and drop. Sycamore leaves turn brown and fall, while other trees develop premature fall color or shed small branches.

Leaf scorch develops when a plant's root system cannot replenish moisture as fast as it is lost from foliage. This disorder is caused by a limited or damaged root system, drought, soil compaction, or hot, windy conditions. The leaf tissue on the edges and between the main veins dies and turns brown. Eventually the entire leaf dies except for a narrow band along the veins. Plants can be affected uniformly or only on one side. Plants growing near reflective surfaces such as hardscapes, as well as recent transplants, are more likely to be affected. Desiccation also occurs in the winter, so be sure to water evergreen plants prior to high winds or a severe freeze.

Fertilizing Established Plants

Applying too much fertilizer contributes to polluting our rivers, streams, lakes, and estuaries and kills plants and animals that rely on these water resources. In addition, excess fertilizer increases the likelihood of some plant diseases. Further, overapplying fertilizer creates more work and wastes money. Applying fertilizer in the wrong place and at the wrong time—including just before a rainstorm—also contributes to pollution and wastes resources.

A moderate rate of growth and healthy green color are desired for most woody plants. Excessive vigor, which is evident by lush, abnormally deep green leaves and long shoot growth, is weak and undesirable. Fertilizing plants that have outgrown their allotted landscape space leads to more pruning, which is work for you and creates wounds on the plant. All too often, gardeners assume fertilizing is the answer for any plant problem. Lack of fertilizer, however, is rarely the cause of poor growth. Fertilizer may be helpful, but only after the problem causing poor growth has been identified and corrected. Symptoms of poor plant growth include the following:
• Abnormally light-green or yellow leaves
• Leaves smaller than normal
• Fewer leaves and/or flowers than normal
• Shorter-than-normal annual twig growth
• **Dieback** of branches at tips
• Foliage **wilt**

Lack of nutrition is only one of many causes for poor plant growth. Other causes include inadequate soil aeration or moisture, adverse climatic conditions, pH not matched to a plant's need, pests, and diseases. In addition, transplanting woody ornamentals initially results in slow growth, but the normal growth rate resumes after the root system is reestablished. Another cause of shock and limited new growth is construction disturbance within the past five to 10 years. Determine the specific cause of poor growth in each situation; then identify appropriate corrective measures, if needed. Fertilizer is not the remedy for all plant problems. In many cases, fertilizer makes existing problems worse.

Conduct a soil test and follow the resulting fertilizer recommendations. Consider current and desired growth rate, any visible symptoms of deficiency, and the plant's age, type, and location. The fertilization rate is also influenced by rainfall, irrigation, and soil type. A wet season often increases the need to fertilize, especially in sandy soils. During periods of dry weather, reduce the amount of fertilizer. Both natural (organic) or synthetic fertilizers are appropriate for use on woody ornamentals; chapter 1, "Soils and Plant Nutrients," provides detailed information on different types of fertilizers. Fertilizer encourages water-demanding new growth and can injure roots of

11

ornamentals under drought stress. Here are points to consider when deciding when, where, how, and how much to fertilize.

When to Fertilize

- **Foliage.** Growth can be used as a guide to determine fertilizer needs. When plants exhibit off-colored leaves, smaller-than-normal leaf size, or premature fall color or leaf drop, the plants may need fertilizer. These signs, however, may also indicate a root problem or the need for water. Deficiency symptoms do not indicate how much fertilizer is needed, only that fertilizer may be needed.

- **Plant age.** Give newly installed plants time to reestablish their root systems before applying a high-nitrogen fertilizer to push new growth. To accelerate the growth of a young plant, several light applications of fertilizer per year (March, May, and July) may be made. As woody plants mature, the need for nitrogen decreases; rapid growth is no longer needed or desired. Most established woody plants perform well with just one application every two to three years.

- **Temperature.** Woody plants can absorb nutrients as long as the soil temperature is above 40°F, but absorption slows during hot summer weather. Root growth is most active during cool weather in fall and late winter to early spring and can occur even when the foliage appears dormant. Fertilize trees and shrubs in the fall after the first frost and in early spring before new growth begins.

Where to Apply Fertilizer

- Dumping fertilizer in one spot causes the roots below the fertilizer to burn and die.

- Spread the fertilizer on top of the soil or mulch, and water well. Because the fertilizer quickly moves through the mulch, there is no need to remove it or to place the fertilizer below it.

- Keep fertilizer off the stems of shrubs and at least a foot away from tree trunks.

- Do not get dry fertilizer on the leaves of plants. If this happens, use a broom to brush the fertilizer off or rinse it off with water.

- Because feeder roots are within the top foot of soil and lateral fertilizer movement in the soil is very limited, a broadcast surface application of fertilizer is preferable to the use of fertilizer spikes, stakes, or to placing fertilizer in holes spaced around the tree.

- Feeder roots normally grow two to three times the size of the canopy (Figure 11–29). Ornamentals located near a lawn or planting bed that is fertilized regularly do not need additional fertilizer because many of their roots extend into those areas and absorb nutrients.

- **Weed-and-feed** fertilizers should not be used under trees or shrubs unless the label says doing so is safe.

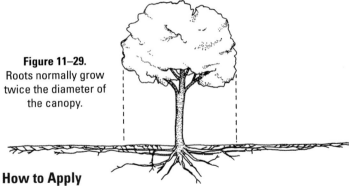

Figure 11–29. Roots normally grow twice the diameter of the canopy.

How to Apply

- **Liquid** foliar fertilizer sprays can temporarily correct deficiencies of minor elements such as iron or manganese. Do not use this method to provide all of a plant's fertilizer needs because the benefits of foliar sprays are short-lived. Nutrient deficiencies are often caused by a disease or improper soil condition (pH, drainage, soil compaction) affecting the roots. Foliar sprays give only temporary relief and do not correct the main problem.

- **Tree injection** of micronutrients is a last resort. Trees can be permanently injured by drilling holes, and the decay that could develop may outweigh any benefit the fertilizer might provide. Any benefit from the fertilizer is temporary at best.

How Much Fertilizer to Apply

- **Soil test.** The results include specific fertilizer recommendations. Have the soil tested before planting and every two to three years thereafter. Information on taking a soil test and interpreting the results can be found in "Soils and Plant Nutrients," chapter 1.

- **Plant type.** Plants with a fibrous root system, such as azaleas, rhododendrons, and blueberries, can be easily damaged by fertilizer. It is important to fertilize only when needed and never to overfertilize.

Managing Weeds

A 2-inch to 3-inch layer of mulch suppresses most annual weed seeds and makes it easy to hand-pull any that do germinate. However, perennial weeds that propagate from roots in addition to seeds, such as bermudagrass, sedges, and nut grass, are more difficult to control.

If needed, **herbicides** are available to aid in weed control.

Preemergence herbicides work by interrupting seed germination; they do not work after the seedling has emerged. If summer or winter annual weeds are identified as a problem, apply a **preemergent** as directed on the product label. Apply in spring before summer annual weed seeds germinate or in late summer to early fall prior to winter weed germination.

11

Postemergence herbicides kill growing weeds, but may also damage trees or shrubs if not applied with extreme care. The younger and smaller the weeds are, the more effective the control is. Treat weeds before they flower or fruit. As most woody ornamentals are **dicots**, use a **postemergence** herbicide that kills only monocots. These chemicals do not control dicot weeds but do kill **monocot** ornamental plants such as ornamental grasses, irises, and lilies. Furthermore, although intended for monocot eradication, any herbicide contact with the green bark or foliage could result in plant injury or death. For more information on weeds and weed management, refer to "Weeds," chapter 6.

Pruning

Reasons to Prune

Pruning involves the selective removal of specific plant parts. There are several reasons to prune:

- **To train young trees.** Select strong scaffolding branches, and eliminate competing branches, double leaders, crossing, or broken branches.
- **To maintain plant health.** Remove damaged, diseased, dying, or dead branches, as well as crossing branches that may rub together and injure bark.
- **To improve ornamental aesthetics.** Selective pruning that thins crowded branches opens up the canopy for better light penetration. This increases flowering and fruiting and may make attractive bark more visible. Remove **water sprouts** (Figure 11–30) and **suckers** (Figure 11–31). Selective pruning includes training to a specific shape, for example **espaliered** along fences or walls.

Figure 11–30. Water sprouts are shoots that arise from latent buds on the trunk or stems of a plant and are often the result of heavy pruning.
Kathleen Moore, CC BY - 2.0

Figure 11–31. Suckers on a weeping Siberian pea tree (*Caragana arborescens* 'Pendulua').
Jonathan Teller-Elsberg, Wikimedia CC BY-SA 3.0

- **To manage growth and size.** Minimize the need to control size by installing plants where they can grow to their mature size unimpeded by buildings or other plants (right plant for the right place).
- **To increase light under the tree canopy.** Raise the tree's canopy by removing lower branches to allow better light penetration to turfgrass or ornamentals under a canopy. Selecting plants that can survive dense shade, however, is a better option than attempting to alter the environment by thinning the canopy of otherwise healthy plants.
- **To improve safety.** Remove branches that block driveways, impede traffic on sidewalks or neighbors' yards, or interfere with important site lines. Pay special attention to any plants that have damaged branches that may fall on people or property. Trees that grow near power lines need to be pruned but only by a certified arborist from a utility company. Never attempt to prune a tree that touches a power line.

11

Pruning is frequently misunderstood and incorrectly practiced. Some mistakenly view pruning as an annual spring ritual and prune whether it is needed or not. Others resort to severe pruning to manage the problems created by overplanting or installing a plant that grows too large for the site.

Pruning Strategies

Five basic techniques are used for pruning woody ornamental trees and shrubs: pinching, heading back, thinning, renewal pruning, and shearing. Some plants require more of one method than another, but good pruning is usually a combination of several methods.

- **Pinching** is the removal of the terminal portion of a succulent, green shoot before it becomes woody and firm (Figure 11–32). Pinching greatly reduces the need for more dramatic pruning later. Whenever a shoot becomes excessively long (except late summer), simply pinch or cut the shoot to reduce its length and to promote side branching. Cut back long, vigorous shoots into the canopy.

Figure 11–32. Pinching back.
Kathleen Moore, CC BY - 2.0

- **Heading back** involves removing the terminal portion of a woody branch by cutting it back to an arbitrary location on the branch without regard for buds or lateral branches (Figure 11–33). Heading back stimulates shoot growth below the cut, thus making the plant denser. Repeated heading back with no thinning cuts results in a top-heavy plant. Dense top growth reduces sunlight and results in the loss of foliage inside the plant canopy.

- **Thinning** is the least conspicuous method of pruning and results in a more open plant without stimulating excessive new growth. Considerable growth can be removed without changing the plant's natural appearance or growth habit. With thinning cuts (Figure 11–34), a branch is cut off at its point of origin from the parent

stem (branch collar), to a lateral side branch, or to the "Y" of a branch junction. Prune to a lateral that is one-third the diameter of the branch being removed. Thin out the oldest and tallest stems first, allowing vigorous side branch development. This method of pruning is best done with a handsaw, pruning shears, or loppers, not hedge shears. Almost all plant species can be thinned. Repeated thinning with no heading back results in plants with long, spindly branches.

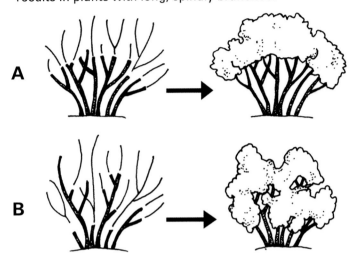

Figure 11–33. Heading back involves removing the terminal portion of woody branches without regard to buds or lateral branches.
A) A shrub with shoots headed back to the same height.
B) A shrub with shoots headed back to different heights.

Figure 11–34. With thinning cuts, branches are removed at their point of origin.

- **Renewal pruning (rejuvenation)** involves removing the oldest branches of a shrub by pruning them near the ground, leaving only the younger, more vigorous branches, which also may be cut back (Figure 11–35). Remove small stems (less than pencil size). Plants pruned by renewal include azalea (*Rhododendron* spp.), deutzia (*Deutzia* spp.), forsythia (*Forsythia* spp.), mock orange (*Pittosporum tobira*), spirea (*Spirea* spp.), and weigela (*Weigela florida*). On some species, the entire top portion of the plant can be removed close to the ground. A variation of renewal pruning involves cutting branches back to a predetermined height each year. Butterfly bush (*Buddleja davidii*) is often pruned back to a woody framework (Figure 11–36). With time the framework becomes congested and requires some slight thinning. Yellow (*Cornus sericea* 'Flaviramea') and red twig dogwood (*Corunus sericia* 'Cardinal') and beautyberry (*Callicarpa americana*) are severely pruned almost to the ground each year to promote the growth of more colorful twigs or berries.

- **Shearing** involves cutting the terminal of most shoots with shearing or hedge clippers. Only use this method to create formal hedges. Shearing is a form of heading back. If done correctly, shearing does lead to the development of a "veneer" of foliage on the outside edges of the plant (Figure 11–37). This results in a reduction of leaves in the interior. Every three years to five years perform a thinning to open the plant up and allow light to enter the interior. In many cases, a plant that has been sheared for many years may benefit from a late winter rejuvenation pruning to allow new growth.

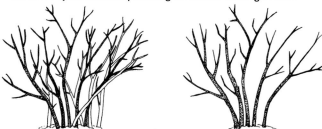

Figure 11–35. Renewal pruning involves cutting the oldest branches back to the ground leaving the younger, more vigorous branches.

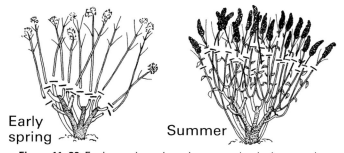

Early spring   Summer

Figure 11–36. Each year in early spring, prune back plants such as butterfly bush to a framework. In late summer, remove the faded blooms to promote further flowering.

Figure 11–37. A hedge trimmer got a little too close and removed the veneer of foliage.
Kathleen Moore, CC BY - 2.0

For heading, thinning and rejuvenation pruning, cut back to a bud making the cut at a slight angle ¼ inch above the bud (Figure 11–38). The angle will allow moisture to flow off the cut. Avoid making the cut at a sharp angle because it produces a larger wound. When making cuts back to buds, lateral branches, or the trunk of the plant, the wounds seal quickly. Pruning the middle of a branch will leave a stub which cannot seal over. While pruning is done to reduce the overall size of the plant, remember that the growth of shoots near the pruning cuts are invigorated. Severely pruning back strong shoots produces vigorous growth.

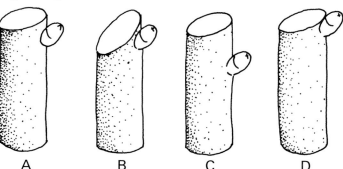

A   B   C   D

Figure 11–38. A) Proper location and angle of a pruning cut; B) Too slanted; C) Too far from the bud; D) Too Close to the bud.

Timing of Pruning

Pruning at the wrong time of year rarely kills a plant immediately. Doing so, however, may remove flower buds or make the plant more susceptible to frost damage, sunscald, insects, or disease. Light corrective pruning can be done at any time of year and reduces the need for severe pruning, which can weaken the plant and reduce its natural beauty. Base the selection of when to prune on the pruning objectives, when the plant flowers, and how extensive the pruning should be. Start pruning and training when trees are quite young. This prevents many serious problems before they develop. Older, neglected trees are more difficult, dangerous, and expensive to prune.

Consider the life cycle of insects and disease when choosing the time to prune. Do not prune plants in the genus Prunus in fall or early winter when bacterial cankers are reproducing. Do not prune dogwoods in May, June, and July when borers are most active.

Late winter or early spring. Before new growth begins in spring, prune summer-flowering and fall-flowering shrubs that bloom after May, including abelia (*Abelia* spp.), beautyberry (*Callicarpa americana*), butterfly bush (*Buddleja davidii*), rose of Sharon hibiscus (*Hybiscus syricsus*), crape myrtle (*Lagerstroemia indica*), and summersweet (*Clethra alnifolia*). These plants flower on new growth produced in the current growing season. If necessary, do any extensive pruning in late winter to early spring when bare branches are lighter and the tree structure is visible. Pruning wounds created in late winter or early spring seal off quickly, and insect and disease organisms are not as prevalent. **Callus** cells that gradually grow over each wound occur rapidly just prior to the onset of new growth in the spring. New growth is greatest after late-winter or early-spring pruning because all the stored energy from the full-size plant is channeled into the smaller pruned plant.

Spring. Spring-flowering shrubs flower before May, including forsythia (*Forsythia* spp.), deutzia (*Deutzia* spp.), lilac (*Syringa* spp.), viburnum (*Viburnum* spp.), mock orange (*Pittosporum tobira*), and spiraea (*Spiraea* spp.). These shrubs flower on buds formed the previous summer or fall. If these shrubs are pruned during late summer, fall, winter, or early spring, many of the flower buds are removed. To ensure maximum flowering, prune these shrubs as soon as possible after flowers fade in the spring.

Summer. Do little or no pruning after July 4th because new growth may not have time to mature before cold weather. Callus cells also grow rapidly just after maximum leaf expansion in early summer.

Fall. Prune hydrangeas (*Hydrangea* spp.) after flowering. They are an exception to the customary practice for shrubs that bloom in summer.

Winter. Prune older deciduous trees in late winter when they are dormant so limbs are not obscured by leaves. Wood around winter-pruned cuts is more susceptible to desiccation. Some trees—such as birch, honey locust, maple, dogwood, elm, and walnut—exude excessive sap from the wound when pruned in late winter or early spring. Although this bleeding does not hurt the tree, it can be alarming to many gardeners. These trees do not ooze sap if pruned in late spring, summer, or fall.

Sometimes pruning is necessary regardless of the time of year.

- **Damaged or dead wood.** If there are only a few damaged or dead branches, remove them as soon as they are noticed. If the damage is extensive, however, pruning may need to be done in stages, with follow-up work distributed over several months or years.
- **Diseased or insect-infected wood.** Properly identify the insect or disease before branches are pruned. Remove small insect infestations (like **scales** or webworms) by pruning the areas of the plants where the insects are attached. Cut back to healthy wood to remove all diseased tissue. When working with diseased wood, use sterilized pruning tools. A bleach solution (9 parts water to 1 part bleach) is often used, but it can corrode pruning tools. Household disinfectant sprays are easier on tools and clothing, as is rubbing alcohol.

Pruning Tools

Efficient pruning requires quality, sharp tools that are designed for the specific task. Useful tools include hand clippers, lopping shears, and pruning saws . Optional equipment includes hedge shears, pole pruners, and chainsaws. Neither wound sealant (Figure 11–39) nor anvil clippers (Figure 11–40) are recommended. Clean and oil tools regularly. After use, wipe blades with an oily cloth to prevent rusting. Keep cutting edges sharp with several passes with a good oilstone. Pruning cuts made with a sharp blade close more quickly than cuts made with a dull blade. Paint, varnish, or regularly treat wooden handles with linseed oil. Use tools properly; don't twist or strain pruners or loppers. Don't cut wire with pruning tools.

Figure 11–39. Wound sealants over pruning cuts are not recommended. They only serve to "seal in" pathogens and interfere with a plant's natural ability to seal over a wound.
Kathleen Moore, CC BY - 2.0

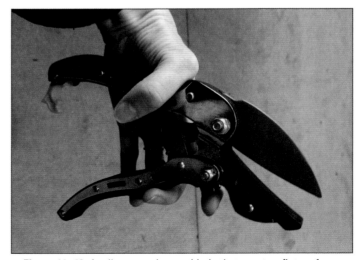

Figure 11–40. Anvil pruners have a blade that meets a flat surface. These types of pruners can crush stems as they cut.
Kathleen Moore, CC BY - 2.0

11

Hand clippers, sometimes called hand shears or pruners, are effective on branches less than ½-inch in diameter. Attempting to cut larger branches risks damaging the plant and the clippers. The two types of hand clippers are anvil and bypass (scissor). Anvil clippers have one sharp top blade that cuts against an anvil of softer metal. The branch is cut on one side and crushed and torn on the other side. Although anvil clippers are lighter and less expensive than bypass clippers, they are not recommended for pruning woody ornamentals. Bypass clippers have one sharp blade that "by-passes" a softer metal anvil in making a cut (Figure 11–41). They usually cost more, but make cleaner, closer cuts.

Figure 11–41. Bypass pruners.
Kathleen Moore, CC BY - 2.0

Hedge shears have long blades that are flat, or wavy and relatively short handles—one for each hand (Figure 11–42). Gas- or electric-powered hedge shears are also available (Figure 11–43). Shears are designed for clipping small-leaved plants to create a formal appearance, such as a topiary. Hedge shears are sometimes misused to prune shrubs with large leaves into round balls and squares that do not enhance shrub growth or appearance.

Figure 11–42. Hedge shears.
Kathleen Moore, CC BY - 2.0

Figure 11–43. Gas-powered hedge shears.
Kathleen Moore, CC BY - 2.0

Lopping shears have long handles to provide the leverage needed to cut through branches up to 1¾-inch in diameter. Handles vary in length from 20 inches to 36 inches (Figure 11–44). Lopping shears are useful for pruning overgrown shrubs and small tree branches. Ratchet and gear-type loppers exert more leverage for cutting thicker branches, but are more expensive.

Pole pruners are used to cut overhead branches that might otherwise be difficult to reach. They have a cutter with a hooked blade above and a cutting blade below, and some include a saw (Figure 11–45). The pole is either in sections that fit together or that telescope. Wooden poles are heavy; aluminum poles are lighter but conduct electricity if they touch an overhead wire. Fiberglass or plastic is probably the best material. Wear head and eye protection when using pole pruners, as branches cut overhead might fall.

11

Figure 11–44. Loppers.
Kathleen Moore, CC BY - 2.0

Figure 11–45. A pole pruner with a cutter on one side and a pruning saw on the other allows for cutting high branches from the ground.
Kathleen Moore, CC BY - 2.0

Pruning saws are used on branches ½-inch in diameter and above (Figure 11–46). They make a cleaner and often more accurate cut than hand pruners or loppers. There are many makes and models of pruning saws. Most are "tri-cut" types that cut only on the pull, which allows greater strength and control. A narrow, curved pruning saw fits well into most branch crotches, ensuring a better angle of the cut. Pruning saws allow access to areas that might otherwise be too dense or crowded to prune. They have narrower blades and coarser teeth than carpenter saws. Fineness of the cutting edge is measured in points (teeth per inch). An 8-point saw is for delicate, close work on small shrubs and trees. Average saws are about 6 points, while 4½-point saws are for fairly heavy limbs.

Figure 11–46. A pruning saw.
Kathleen Moore, CC BY - 2.0

Chainsaws are most appropriate for cutting trees down or for firewood (Figure 11–47). Some arborists use chainsaws to prune large branches, but it is not advised for homeowners to use chainsaws on live wood. It is too difficult to make accurate pruning cuts. Chainsaws come in a variety of sizes and can be electric or gas powered. Generally, the longer the blade, the stronger the motor and the heavier the saw. Protective clothing along with eye and ear protection are recommended. Chainsaws should be used only with the operator standing on the ground. The chainsaw should never be lifted over the head.

Figure 11–47. Use a chainsaw on downed wood only.
Kathleen Moore, CC BY - 2.0

The Biology of Pruning

Examine plant structure to identify optimal locations for pruning cuts.

- **Branch bark ridge:** the location where the bark from the trunk joins the bark from the branch forming a dark line, sometimes resembling a tiny mountain range that extends from the branch union (crotch) a short way down both sides of the trunk, parallel to the side branch.
- **Branch collar:** the slightly swollen area just outside the connection between the branch and the trunk (Figure 11–48). It is more noticeable on some types of plants than others.
- **Branch defense zone:** a cone of cells inside the branch collar that activates a reaction zone that inhibits the spread of decay organisms into the trunk and also initiates the growth of **woundwood**, the callus tissue that grows to seal off wounds.

Figure 11–48. Branch collar is the slightly swollen area just outside the connection between the branch and trunk.
Chris Alberti, CC BY - 2.0

When the cut is properly placed, between the branch bark ridge and just outside the branch collar, the woundwood grows inward from all edges in a doughnut shape, ultimately sealing off the entire wound (Figure 11–49). However, no woundwood grows from areas where the branch collar was damaged. If the branch collar is injured during pruning, neither the branch defense zone nor woundwood will be activated to protect the tree, so it is essential to leave the branch collar intact.

> *Do NOT apply wound dressing to a pruning cut. In most cases, sealing wounds promotes decay by creating an environment favorable to disease. Some wound dressings kill **cambial** cells and cause the wound to remain open for years longer than if no treatment had been applied.*

Figure 11–49. Callus tissue covering a correctly pruned branch.
Kathleen Moore, CC BY - 2.0

Tree Wound Response

Trees have a natural defense response to wounding. They form two types of walls- chemical (fungi-toxic compounds) and physical (gums or plugs) that close off or "compartmentalize" four sides of a wounded area, thus preventing the potential spread of decay organisms (Figure 11–50). The decay or injury remains but is sealed off and does not increase in size if the walls remain intact. The storage capacity and function of the injured part is lost forever, however.

1. The first wall is formed by plugging the vertical **vascular (xylem)** cells. This is the weakest wall but slows the vertical spread of decay.
2. The second wall is formed at the outer edge (late wood initiation) of a growth ring. It is a weak barrier but does offer resistance to inward spread of decay by producing fungi-toxic chemicals.
3. Each growth ring is subdivided into compartments with a radial, or third wall. It is a very strong wall and provides resistance to lateral spread. It presents a chemical barrier.
4. The fourth wall is a barrier wall. While it is the strongest of all the walls, it can be broken by outside forces, such as woodpeckers or mechanical injury. Internally, it separates the wood present at the time of injury from new wood formed as the tree grows.

11

The ability of a tree to compartmentalize depends on its species, age, vigor, and the size and location of the wound.

Separate from the four internal walls, is wound closure. Callus tissue develops around the external injury or pruning cut and can eventually cover the wound by growing over the dead wood (Figure 11–50).

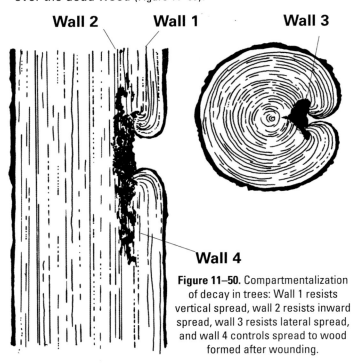

Wall 2   **Wall 1**   **Wall 3**

Wall 4

Figure 11–50. Compartmentalization of decay in trees: Wall 1 resists vertical spread, wall 2 resists inward spread, wall 3 resists lateral spread, and wall 4 controls spread to wood formed after wounding.

Prune to Promote "Sealing" of Wounds

When humans are injured, like a skinned knee, a scab forms over the wound. Skin cells are regenerated, and eventually the scab falls off—revealing a knee that looks the same as it did before it was injured. While humans are able to produce new cells and heal over wounds on any part of our bodies, plants are only capable of "sealing" or encapsulating wounds. This sealing process is possible only in certain areas of the plant, which is why it is important to identify these areas when making pruning cuts. The areas capable of growth or sealing are called meristematic tissue. Meristematic tissue occurs in the tips of roots and shoots, in buds, or at the outer edge of trunk and stem tissue just below the bark. Branches that are less than 2 inches in diameter seal over well if cut off at a point of attachment or just beyond a bud because they are made up of mostly decay-resistant sapwood (active xylem). Large branches are made up of more **heartwood** (dead xylem tissue) that is slow to seal over and more susceptible to decay and disease.

To create the smallest wound for a plant to seal over, use the three-cut method for branches larger than 2 inches in diameter (Figure 11–53).

1. The first cut is an undercut, made 4 to 6 inches from the branch collar, which prevents bark from ripping down the trunk when the limb is removed.
2. The second cut, made further out on the branch from the first cut, removes the weight of the branch.

Tree Anatomy

Properly pruning a tree requires a basic understanding of tree structure. A cross section of a tree trunk reveals it is composed of many layers (Figure 11–51). Each year a tree essentially grows a new "layer of wood" or sapwood over the older wood, or heartwood. The outside layer of the tree is dead bark that provides protection from the environment. Between the bark and wood is the cambium layer, which is responsible for increases in tree diameter (by creating annual rings) and responds to injury by producing callus tissue.

Branches are attached to the tree trunk by interlocking branch and trunk tissue. A new layer of interlocking tissue is produced each year. Branches with a 45-degree to 60-degree angle of attachment are considered the strongest. When branches on the main trunk have a narrow angle of attachment, as they increase in diameter, they eventually run out of room to grow. The branch bark becomes surrounded by woody trunk and branch tissue. The bark that becomes overgrown is referred to as **included bark** (Figure 11–52). The union is weak and likely to split.

Figure 11–51. Cross section of a tree trunk.
Forest and Kim Starr, Flickr CC BY - 2.0

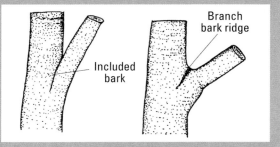

Branch bark ridge

Included bark

Figure 11–52. V-shaped crotches lead to included bark.

11

3. The third cut, the precision cut, is made at the branch collar. Care must be taken to leave the collar intact so callus tissue can form. If the third cut is made too close to the trunk, it is known as a flush cut (Figure 11–54). This removes the tissue that would have formed the callus, thus preventing the wound from sealing.

For very large branches, it is best to contact a certified arborist. An arborist has the equipment and expertise to remove large branches safely with the least amount of damage to the tree.

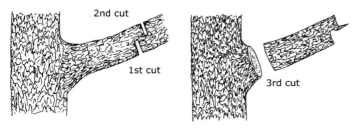

Figure 11–53. A three-point cut. The first cut is an undercut to prevent bark ripping. The second cut, further out on the branch removes the weight. The third cut is made outside the branch collar to remove the limb protecting the meristematic tissue.

Figure 11–54. A flush cut made too close to the trunk, removing the branch collar and leaving an oval-shaped wound.
Kathleen Moore, CC BY - 2.0

Topping and Flush Cuts

Tree topping is not a recommended practice. Topping, also called shearing, heading back, or **dehorning**, involves cutting back main branches and the central leader to a specific height without regard to the location of lateral branches (Figure 11–55). This practice is mistakenly thought to reduce the risk of property damage during a storm. Topping, however, actually makes trees more dangerous by creating wounds that do not close, thus allowing decay organisms to enter the tree. In addition, the new growth that sprouts in response to topping is attached weakly and is easily damaged during storms. Thinning is an alternate way to reduce wind resistance without damaging the tree.

Flush cuts or cuts that go beyond the branch bark collar are also not recommended. Flush cuts open up larger wounds than are necessary that are also difficult for trees to close over. Large wounds make the tree susceptible to entry by decay organisms.

Figure 11–55. Topped trees where major branches have been removed. The large wounds are subject to decay. Water sprouts have grown from the cuts but are poorly attached. As they get larger, the sprouts become a hazard.
Kathleen Moore, CC BY - 2.0

11

Considerations for Evergreen Woody Ornamentals

Pruning Broadleaf Evergreens

The term "**broadleaf evergreen**" is somewhat misleading because it is used to describe evergreens with large leaves such as Japanese aucuba (*Aucuba japonica*). It is also used to describe evergreens with small leaves, such as boxwood (*Buxus sempervirens*), Japanese hollies (*Ilex crenata* cultivars), and scarlet pyracantha (*Pyracantha coccinea*). The term "broadleaf" is used here to include all evergreens except conifers, which have needlelike or scalelike leaves.

General maintenance. The minimal pruning needed by broadleaf evergreens is best done in early spring, but can be done any time of year. Selectively cut back branches that are damaged, diseased, dying, or dead. Also cut back branches that are headed into the center of the canopy, and branches that extend far beyond the canopy of the rest of the plant. A compact plant results when branches are pruned back to an outward facing lateral within the plant canopy.

Some plants, such as azalea (*Rhododendron* spp.) and abelia (*Abelia* spp.), produce long, vigorous shoots that extend well beyond the natural canopy and well above a lateral branch. Cut these back severely within the canopy; try to leave a few leaves on the stem. When needed, moderate to heavy pruning should be done in late winter or early spring before new growth begins. Rejuvenate both species after flowering in the spring.

Evergreens that flower in early spring should not be pruned in late summer, fall, or winter because doing so reduces the number of flowers. Wait to prune until immediately after they finish flowering. The best time to prune is after berries drop in the spring. Cut back a few of the tallest and oldest branches to achieve a layered look. For multistemmed plants, such as leucothoe (*Leucothoe* spp.), completely remove a few of the oldest branches to the ground each year for two to three years. Because boxwood is grown for its foliage rather than flowers, it should be rejuvenated in late winter. It is best pruned by cutting only the tips of stems. The center of older plants often has little or no green foliage. Avoid severe pruning if possible as the plants are slow to recover. If heavy pruning becomes necessary, do so over a period of several years.

Experts differ on the importance of **deadheading** broadleaf evergreens such as rhododendron and mountain laurel. Some find that allowing the seed capsules to develop reduces flower and shoot development the following year. To deadhead as soon as the flowers fade, hold the branch with one hand and snap the faded flower **truss** with the other (Figure 11–56). Use care to prevent damaging the new shoots that form directly below the flower cluster.

Figure 11–56. This rose bush is being deadheaded by snapping off the faded flower truss.
Chris Alberti, CC BY - 2.0

Severe pruning. If broadleaf evergreens become too large for their location, severe pruning is an option. To successfully rejuvenate healthy evergreens, prune in late winter or early spring just before new growth begins. Cut back overgrown shrubs, such as hollies (*Ilex* spp.), camellia (*Camellia* spp.), and mountain laurel (*Kalmia latifolia*), to bare branches 2 feet to 4 feet (or even lower) from the ground (Figure 11–57). Plants recover in two to three years depending on plant health and cultural practices such as fertilization, mulching, watering, and insect and disease control. After severe pruning, new growth is slow because dormant buds must become active. In midsummer, thin and head back excessively vigorous new shoots when they reach 6-inches to 12-inches long.

Figure 11–57. Severe pruning of an overgrown (*Vitex agnus-castus*) shrub.
Chris Alberti, CC BY - 2.0

Hedges

Begin pruning hedge plants soon after they are transplanted to ensure they do not become leggy and that branches go all the way to the ground. A dense hedge must be developed slowly, and severe pruning may be required the first two years. Never try to make a hedge reach the desired height in a single season or it will be thin and open at the base.

Subsequent pruning depends on the formality of the hedge. Formal hedges are often sheared in the spring after the main flush of growth has fully elongated. Because any new growth that occurs appears out of place, numerous shearings are required throughout the growing season. An informal hedge is usually pruned only one or two times per year. Any significant pruning is done in late winter to early spring before new growth begins. A follow-up pruning is usually done in midsummer. Allow informal hedges to grow following the natural shape of the plant but conforming to the size and shape of the desired hedge. It is important that the top of the hedge be narrower than its base to prevent the upper branches from shading out the lower branches (Figure 11–58).

Figure 11–58. Pruning of a formal (left) and naturally shaped (right) hedge to allow sunlight to reach the lower foliage. The top of the hedge must be narrower than its base to prevent the upper branches from shading the lower branches.

Pruning Narrowleaf Evergreens
Narrowleaf evergreens are plants that have needles, awls, or scales, such as juniper, pine, cedar, spruce, and yew. Although some dwarf forms are available, most cultivars require some pruning to control size, shape, and density. Enhance the natural shape of the plant through maintenance pruning. The timing of selective pruning is less critical for narrowleaf evergreens because they are normally grown for their foliage and not for their flowers. Prune in the winter and use the cuttings for holiday decorations, or prune in early spring before new growth starts. A second light pruning (thinning and heading) is often done in late June to early July after new growth is completed. Remove long, out-of-scale branches by cutting back to a lateral or just above a vigorous side shoot on two- or three-year-old wood. Start at the top of the plant and work down, removing branches that extend out and over lower shorter branches. Do not cut all branches back to the same length, or the natural shape of the plant is lost. Hide pruning cuts under an overlapping branch.

Many conifers, such as arborvitae, develop an area on the inside of the plant canopy that has little or no foliage. Avoid cutting back to bare branches; they seldom develop new growth. Yews on the other hand sprout new growth wherever cuts are made.

Pines are unique because buds for new growth occur only on branch terminals. Prune back to a branch or to the main trunk. An exception to this rule is in the spring when new shoots called candles develop. When the candle has extended to its full length and the needles are still soft, remove about half the length of the candle to reduce growth (Figure 11–59).

Figure 11–59. Prune pines by cutting back half of the new growth.

Severe pruning. Heavy pruning kills most narrowleaf evergreens because most narrowleaf evergreens do not have dormant buds on old wood. If narrowleaf plants become too large for their location, it's best to remove them and replant with a smaller variety.

Considerations for Pruning Decidious Woody Ornamentals

Deciduous Vines
Prune vines to limit vigorous growth, clear around windows and doors, enhance flower production, thin branches, and remove dead or damaged wood. The best time to prune depends on when the vine flowers. Spring-flowering vines are usually pruned after they finish flowering, while most other vines are pruned during the dormant season. Twining vines initiate most of their growth from the upper buds; if the lower portions of the vine become leafless, promote new, low-growing foliage by pruning severely and then removing all but the strongest new shoots. Keep vines that produce long, vigorous shoots, such as Carolina jessamine (*Gelsemium sempervirens*), in bounds by shearing and training several times a year. Specific pruning practices for commonly planted vines are provided below.

Wisteria (*Wisteria* spp.) easily becomes stem heavy, producing few flowers. To promote profuse flowering never prune heavily during the dormant season. Instead prune in late summer and early fall before flower bud development. Reduce the spur-bearing shoot length by onehalf or greater, leaving about six short nodes with spurs that will bear next year's flowers. Remove excessively vigorous shoots entirely or train to fill voids.

Clematis (*Clematis* spp.) vines are thicker and more vigorous if pruned to the lowest pair of strong buds when newly planted. There are three types of Clematis; those that bloom on new wood, those that bloom on one-year-old wood, and those that bloom on both. Those that flower on the current season's wood (*Clematis × jackmanii, C. tangutica,* and *C. viticella*) should be severely pruned in late winter to early spring to promote new growth. Prune clematis that flower on one-year-old wood (*C. armandii, C. montana*) by cutting away all flowering wood to within a few inches of the main framework immediately after flowering. Most of the popular, large-flowering cultivars—such as 'Nelly Moser', 'Henry', 'Duchess of Edinburgh', and 'William Kennett'—flower both in the spring on one-year old wood, and also produce side shoots that provide further displays of medium-size flowers during late summer. Only lightly prune these. Regardless of the species flowering habit, after five or more years some clematis vines may become too tall or leggy. Prune severely in late winter to early spring to rejuvenate. Spring flowers are eliminated that year, but late summer flowers develop. An alternative is to severely prune a fourth to a third of the oldest shoots back to within a foot of the ground each year for several years.

Climbing and rambling roses are pruned differently, but both flower more heavily when new canes are trained in a somewhat horizontal position rather than allowed to grow in a vertical position.

Climbing roses flower on the current season's growth. This group of roses is not particularly vigorous and little pruning is required. Examples of climbing roses include 'Iceberg', 'Meg', 'Handel', and 'Marigold', as well as roses derived from hybrid tea cultivars, such as climbing 'Peace' or climbing 'Crimson Glory'. Cut dead or weak wood flower stems back to a vigorous bud. In the winter, shorten flowering laterals to three or four buds. After several years, some of the old canes may be removed at the base to produce new vigorous canes. Lady Banks rose (*Rosa banksiae*) and Mermaid rose (*Rosa* 'Mermaid') are pruned like climbing roses, but do not prune the flowering laterals in winter.

Rambling roses are vigorous growers that flower only once in the spring. Ramblers derived from *Rosa wichuraiana* flower on one-year-old wood. After flowering, cut the old canes to the ground and leave the new vigorous shoots to flower the following year. Another group of ramblers flowers on new canes but not those that primarily arise from the base; new flowers develop on new growth midway up on old canes. Remove some of the old flowering canes where new vigorous shoots have started growing.

Deciduous Shrubs
General maintenance. Remove small branches that do not conform to the natural shape. Use thinning and heading cuts when removing larger branches. Plants vary in how often older branches should be removed. Prune forsythia (*Forsythia* spp.) annually, while viburnum (*Viburnum* spp.)

and witch hazel (*Hamamelis* spp.) may not need this type of pruning more than once every three to five years.

Severe pruning. Older shrubs that have outgrown their location may need more severe pruning to reduce plant size. If they are healthy and receive adequate sunlight, they respond well to renewal pruning. Prune all the branches near the ground and then remove some of the excessive number of new upright shoots that develop from the base by midsummer. Head back the shoots you leave when they reach their full length. To prevent the inner portion of a plant from becoming overly dense, prune to the outward-growing buds.

An alternative is to selectively remove up to half of the branches at the base. This would include the removal of older, unproductive wood, inward-growing branches, and any other growth that detracts from the natural form of the plant. Also remove any extremely vigorous, unbranched suckers. Examine the remaining branches and head back those that detract from the intended size or appearance. In midsummer, new shoots develop quickly. Remove some of the new basal shoots. A less dramatic method is to annually remove a fourth to a third of the oldest branches for several years until all of the old branches are removed. This method also requires the removal of excessive basal shoots in midsummer.

Roses. Prune hybrid tea, floribunda, grandiflora, hybrid perpetual, and polyantha roses in early spring as the buds are swelling, but before growth has started. Remove all dead wood by cutting at least an inch below the dead area. Select three to five of the strong canes; the rest are completely removed. Cut the remaining canes back to a height of 18 inches to 24 inches (Figure 11–60). Cut just above a large, strong, outward-facing bud. Prune shrub roses that bloom only in spring after they have flowered by removing old canes, dead wood, and dead flowers. Prune shrub or landscape roses back to 6 inches to 10 inches above ground either in fall or spring.

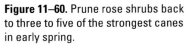
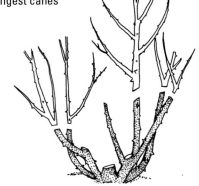

Figure 11–60. Prune rose shrubs back to three to five of the strongest canes in early spring.

Deciduous Trees
Young Trees

Begin training young trees the first year after transplanting. Train gradually over a period of several years. Limit pruning to enhancing the natural shape or structural strength of the tree. The objective in the first few years is to identify and correct problems with the main framework of the tree. Lower branches are left on the trunk to manufacture food and to shade the lower bark (which is often quite thin) and to promote trunk taper.

The height of a branch does not increase as the tree grows but remains at the same height for life. With time, some of the lower branches need to be removed as they increase in length, create unwanted shade, or interfere with gardening activities or traffic.

Most ornamental trees are grown with one central leader (the topmost vertical branch). A single-trunk tree with evenly spaced branches is structurally stronger than one that has multiple trunks or branches clustered together (Figure 11–61). Exceptions are trees such as crape myrtles and river birches that are grown for their interesting bark color and have been pruned to develop multiple trunks. A tree that grows to more than 40 feet should have a single trunk well up into the canopy, but the trunk does not have to be perfectly straight. When a young tree has two competing leaders, remove the weaker of the two. If they are essentially equal, either can be removed. Trees with several trunks often develop included bark in the crotch that eventually causes one of the trunks to split from the rest of the tree during a storm.

Figure 11–61. A single-trunk tree with evenly spaced branches (left) is structurally stronger than one that has multiple trunks or has branches clustered together (right).

Ideally, select **scaffold branches** (primary branches that make up the tree's framework) emerging from the trunk with a 45-degree to 70-degree angle of attachment (Figure 11–62). Generally, branches with angles less than 45 degrees become weaker as they grow longer and increase

in diameter. Branch angles of less than 30 degrees result in a very high percentage of limb breakage, while those between 60 degrees and 70 degrees have a very small breakage rate.

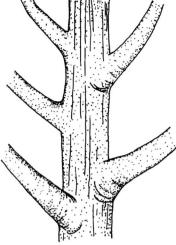

Figure 11–62. Optimum angle of attachment of scaffold branches (45 degrees).

Choose scaffold branches that form ascending spokes around a central axle (Figure 11–63). This provides a structurally strong tree that is attractive, balanced, and allows sunlight to penetrate and wind to pass through the canopy. Space major scaffold branches at least 8 inches and preferably 20 inches apart vertically. Closely spaced scaffolds have fewer lateral branches. The result is long, thin branches with poor structural strength. Good radial spacing prevents one limb from overshadowing another. Branch arrangement and spacing is more critical for large shade trees than for small flowering trees.

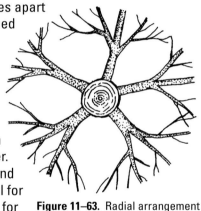

Figure 11–63. Radial arrangement of scaffold branches.

Established Trees

For pruning older trees that are typically large, it is best to call a certified arborist. If you must do it yourself, first remove damaged, diseased, dying, or dead branches. Selectively remove limbs from the perimeter of the canopy, especially those growing close together or beyond the desired size. Also, remove branches with narrow angles of attachment. Remove branches at their point of origin, or cut back to laterals that are at least one-third the diameter of the limb being removed. To locate the appropriate angle to make a pruning cut, identify the branch bark ridge on the limb in question. The angle created by the branch bark ridge and an imaginary line flush with the tree trunk is the approximate angle at which to make the pruning cut (Figure 11–64). Never remove more than 25% of the total foliage at one time.

11

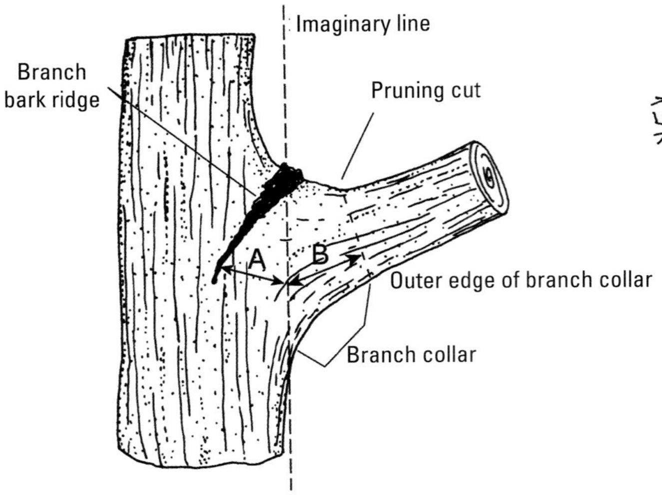

Branch bark ridge

Imaginary line

Pruning cut

Outer edge of branch collar

Branch collar

A B

Figure 11–64. The angle (A) created by the branch bark ridge and an imaginary line flush with the tree trunk is the approximate angle (B) at which to make the pruning cut.

Thinning techniques are used to improve the appearance or function of a tree in a landscape. Thinning does not significantly reduce the overall size of a tree but opens up its canopy to allow more sunlight to penetrate the interior of the tree (Figure 11–65). Prune laterals that have grown taller than the terminal leader or beyond the canopy of the tree. Remove laterals that have grown inward toward the center of the tree at their point of attachment (Figure 11–66). Remove water sprouts; they are structurally weak and lead to overly dense growth in the interior of the tree. Branches that are less than half the diameter of the trunk are stronger than those that grow larger than half the trunk diameter. Thinning is sometimes used to open the canopy to allow the wind to blow through (rather than blowing the tree over) and to reduce stress during drought periods or following construction damage, but thinning is rarely necessary and if done improperly harms the tree. Trees vary in the amount of thinning they tolerate without suffering ill effects. An overthinned tree responds by producing numerous water sprouts and suckers. Sunscald occurs on trees with thin bark.

Heading reduces the overall size of a tree. Cut back to good lateral branches and possibly head the tips of the laterals (Figure 11–67). It is better to cut back over a period of several years than to attempt dramatic pruning in one year. When cutting back to an intersecting lateral branch, choose a branch that forms an angle of no more than 45 degrees with the branch to be removed and that has a diameter at least half that of the branch to be removed.

When cutting branches over 1 inch in diameter, use the three-cut method (Figure 11–53) to avoid tearing the bark of the trunk. Make slanting cuts when removing limbs that grow upward; this prevents water from collecting in the cut and speeds sealing.

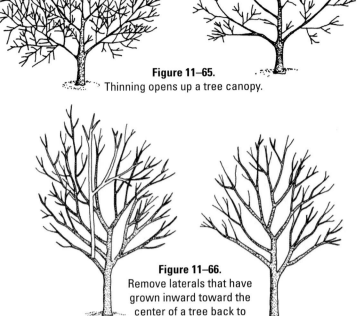

Figure 11–65.
Thinning opens up a tree canopy.

Figure 11–66.
Remove laterals that have grown inward toward the center of a tree back to their point of origin.

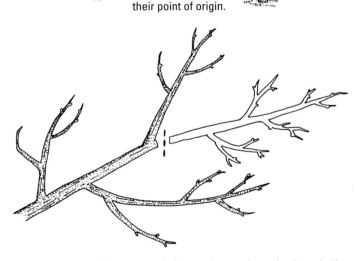

Figure 11–67. Heading cuts made by pruning to a lateral at least half the the diameter of the branch being removed.

Arboriculture

Arboriculture is the art and science of planting and caring for trees. If a tree is too large to prune from the ground or has experienced extensive damage, it is best to hire a certified arborist (someone who is trained to work on trees). While many people advertise that they prune trees, not all of them are trained in proper tree care. A certified arborist has passed a tree knowledge exam from the International Society of Arboriculture (ISA) and is required to earn continuing education credits to maintain certification. Obtain several bids for tree work, ask for, and check out references.

Managing Problems of Woody Ornamentals

Woody ornamentals make up the vast majority of landscape plants. They suffer from environmental stresses such as drought, low temperatures, too much or too little sunlight, or cultural problems such as improper plant selection and poor location or maintenance techniques. Insects and diseases affect woody ornamentals but are usually secondary problems that appear after an environmental or cultural stress. Properly identifying the plant is the first step in solving a plant problem. Knowledge of the plant type helps rule out some insect or disease problems.

One of the challenges when diagnosing problems with woody plants is their longevity. Problems that manifested years ago may only now be showing symptoms. A pot-bound plant might not show the effects of girdled roots until the roots grow larger and start restricting water and nutrients. A particularly dry summer might not affect a mature tree immediately, but symptoms may appear in the following seasons. Problems caused by tree root damage during construction may not manifest themselves in the canopy for several years. A plant that was improperly pruned may not cause a problem until a wind- or ice storm causes it to shed branches. Evergreens are particularly challenging. A cut Christmas tree tossed out into the yard can remain green for several months, giving us an idea of how long it can take for stresses to appear on the leaves of a living tree.

The sheer size of a mature tree or shrub makes it difficult to diagnose a problem. Often problems are seen on the newest growth. On a large tree this would be at the tips of branches that may be high in the air. Management may be delayed simply because a homeowner is unaware of the problem.

Gather information through observation and asking questions before diagnosing a plant problem. What type of plant is it? Has a soil test been completed? What is the soil pH? Is the soil compacted or poorly drained? How much sunlight does the plant receive? Has soil drainage been tested? Has the plant suffered from hot, dry, or freezing weather? Was the plant recently transplanted? How and when was it watered and fertilized? Has an herbicide been used in the area recently? Has the plant been pruned recently? Has there been any tilling, construction, or disturbance of the soil around the plant?

This section examines plant problems, starting with roots, trunk, branches, and leaves. In all cases, proper selection, planting, and care of a plant are the most important factors for plant health. It is much easier and less expensive to properly care for a plant than remediate a problem.

What are the signs that woody ornamentals are under duress?

- Change in leaf color from green to yellow, orange, or brown. This often starts as blotches or on the margins.
- Leaf drop, especially on lower branches.
- New leaves are smaller than normal.
- Branch or twig dieback.
- Poor yearly growth increment. Has it been growing well for a number of years, but the last year or two the amount of growth has greatly decreased?
- The presence of lichens on the branches. Something may be happening that is weakening the plant.

Damage to Roots

Plant roots develop and survive where there is adequate oxygen and moisture. Most active roots are in the top 3 feet of soil, with the majority in the top 12 inches. The more compacted or poorly drained the soil is, the closer the roots are to the soil surface. Roots grow most of the year, stopping only when soil temperatures are around 40°F to 45°F. Roots occur as perennial woody roots and as annual absorbing roots. Woody roots become thicker each year; absorbing roots die but are replaced by new absorbing roots. Annual absorbing roots form shallow, horizontal fans that take up water and nutrients. A few woody support roots grow downward and outward to anchor the plant in place. Most plants do not have a deep tap root. Although a tap root may develop on trees growing in the woods in well-drained soils, tap roots generally do not develop on plants transplanted into the landscape or grown in compacted or poorly drained soil.

- **Exposed surface roots.** These roots become unsightly or in the way. Roots do not suddenly grow on the soil surface. Roots increase in diameter over a period of years. Soil erosion speeds their exposure. Exposed roots need protection from pedestrian and vehicle traffic, including lawn mowers. Mulching exposed roots physically protects them as well as conserving soil moisture and preventing direct sunlight from heating the roots. Cutting off or covering roots with top soil are temporary solutions that cause long-term damage to tree roots.
- **Septic system.** Root problems occur around septic fields and sewer lines. Do not plant trees such as willow, maple, and elm species near a septic field. Tree roots are often incorrectly blamed for plugged and broken

pipes actually caused by natural settling, age, and wear. Leaking pipes encourage roots to grow into the area and to move into and through the cracks. As roots increase in size, cracks widen and more breaks occur.

- **Cracked sidewalks and pavement.** As roots increase in diameter, they crack or lift sidewalks, asphalt driveways, and other paved surfaces. Severe pruning of tree roots leads to major decline or tree death. The best solution is to select trees that are less likely to become a problem or to plant further away from paved surfaces.
- **Tree stumps.** Consider leaving stumps as wonderful wildlife habitat for birds and beneficial insects. If it is not possible to leave a stump, remove it by digging (difficult at best), burning (not recommended), or by hiring a tree company to grind out the stump. Another method is to encourage or speed up the natural decay process. The length of time varies with tree species, moisture, temperature, and size of the stump. To expedite the decay process, cut the stump as close as possible to the ground and cover it with soil, or drill holes in the stump about an inch in diameter, 6 inches to 12 inches deep, and spaced about a foot apart.
- **Trenching.** Digging trenches for installation of water, sewer, telephone, cable, or gas lines, or for building foundations, damages the root systems of nearby trees and shrubs. To minimize potential damage, attempt to locate trenching in areas that cause the fewest roots to be damaged or near areas that have already been trenched.
- **Roots covered by pavement.** Roots that are covered by pavement may be deprived of air and moisture, which are essential for growth. If the covered area involves only a small portion along one side of the plant, satisfactory growth will continue. If the entire area around the plant is to be paved, use a porous material to allow water and air to penetrate. If brick or flagstone is used, do not mortar the joints. When pavement is nonporous, leave a 6-foot-diameter opening around the trunk of small trees and a larger opening for large trees. It the roots extend beyond the pavement into uncovered soil, the opening does not need to be as large.
- **Changes in soil grade.** Even a few inches of fill added or soil removed causes extensive root damage. If possible, never remove soil from or add large amounts of soil within the drip line. Symptoms may appear within months or years after filling has occurred. The extent of injury from fills varies with the species, age, and condition of the plant; the depth and type of fill; and drainage. The base of an established tree flares at the soil line (wider than the tree's trunk a foot above the soil line). If the tree does not have a flare but enters the ground in a straight line, fill dirt has been added. Gently remove soil at the base of the tree to reveal the depth of the fill (Figure 11–68). Other visible symptoms include small

leaves, many dead twigs, and the presence of numerous suckers along the main trunk and branches.

Figure 11–68. Fill dirt covered over the trunk taper of this tree.
Kathleen Moore, CC BY - 2.0

Damage to Trunks

Woody plants have a thin layer of living tissue just beneath the bark. Damage to this growing cambium causes serious problems for a tree. Avoid injury by preventing grass and weeds from growing at the base of the plant or by hand-trimming or hand-clipping them. Wounds are serious enough by themselves, but a wounded plant must also protect itself from pathogens that invade the wound.

These microorganisms often attack the injured bark and invade adjacent healthy tissue, greatly enlarging the affected area. Woody plants can be completely girdled from microbial attack following injury. Decay fungi also become active on the wound surface, and structural deterioration of the woody tissues beneath the wound often occurs.

Hollow trees result from a tree injury when walls 1, 2, and 3 fail to stop the spread of decay. Wall 4 remains intact so new growth continues to occur on the outer part of the trunk. When there is evidence of decay in a tree, contact a certified arborist for a consultation (Figure 11–69).

Figure 11–69.
Conks are a sign that a tree has internal decay—even if the outside appears healthy.
Scot Nelson, Flickr CC0

Construction

Protect trees and large shrubs on a construction site from the devastating effect of grade changes, fill, soil compaction, and building construction. Damage to plants during construction usually involves impairment of the water and nutrient supply system. Plan protective measures before construction begins. Simply placing a barrier around the trunk of a plant does not protect the root system. Place tall, conspicuous stakes and fencing at the ends of the branches on the sides where trucks or bulldozers are operating. Groups of trees or shrubs usually stand a better chance of survival than individual specimens (Figure 11–70).

Figure 11–70. Protect trees and large shrubs during construction. A simple barrier is not enough.
Chris Alberti, CC BY - 2.0

Many roots are destroyed when the soil is compacted by construction equipment driving over the root zone. Minimize construction traffic to a few paths that are covered with 6 inches to 10 inches of mulch, and do not allow parking under desirable trees. Do not spread soil beneath the canopy of plants that are to be saved. In addition, be sure that grading changes do not cause water to be channeled toward plants.

Trees may respond quite differently to various types of construction damage. Under some circumstances, death may occur soon after the tree is damaged. In most cases, the tree appears to stabilize but grows little for years. Often insects and disease invade the weakened tree and lead to gradual deterioration. During periods of stress (high temperatures and drought) the trees may go through a rapid decline and die. Young trees are normally able to recover more quickly than old or middle-aged trees.

Lightning

Lightning strikes vary in their severity (Figure 11–71). A lightning bolt passing through a trunk may cause internal damage, but the tree may not develop visible symptoms until years later. Severe strikes cause loosened bark that hangs in strips, or the tree may even catch fire.
If only a small amount of damage occurred, remove loose

bark and damaged branches and provide excellent care (mulch, water, and fertilize) to minimize stress. Have an arborist assess the tree.

Figure 11–71. A severe lightning strike.
Brandon Blahnik, Flickr CC BY - 2.0

Freeze Damage

- **Leaves and stems.** Injuries can occur from desiccation and ice crystals.
  - **Desiccation:** During the winter, evergreen plants continue to lose water through transpiration—particularly during periods of strong winds and on bright, sunny days. However, root absorption is reduced or prevented when the soil is cold or frozen. Desiccation occurs when water leaves the plant foliage faster than the roots can replenish it. The foliage of plants such as camellia (*Camellia* var.) and boxwood (*Buxus* spp.) may turn yellow or orange due to mild desiccation or excessive sunlight. In severe cases, the branches also become dehydrated and die. Damage is normally worse on the side of the plant facing the wind or sun or near a reflective surface (white house, concrete paving, and snow cover).
  - **Ice crystals:** Ice crystals rupture cell walls. This damage shows up as discolored leaves and dead branch tips.

- **Flowers and leaf buds.** Alternating or unseasonably warm temperatures in late winter prematurely stimulate the opening of flowers or leaf buds, which might then be killed by a late freeze. Many spring flowering shrubs, including quince (*Chaenomeles speciosa*), forsythia (*Forsythia* spp.), and camellia (*Camellia* var.), flower over an extended period of time with only a small portion of their flowers open at one time. The open flowers may be killed, but the unopened buds normally go unharmed. If the leaf buds are killed, the plant is often delayed in resuming spring growth but eventually puts out new growth from dormant buds.

Preventing Freeze Damage

- **Plant selection.** Choose plants known to be winter hardy.
- **Plant placement.** Use hardscaping and exposure to prevent freeze damage.
  - Place frost-sensitive plants in sheltered locations with western or southern exposures; near block walls, rocks, and patios that collect and reflect the heat of the sun; or in full sun, which is warmer than shaded locations during the day. It is, however, night temperatures that usually cause frost damage. The worst place to plant a frost-tender plant is the south side of the landscape with no shade or protection from wind. Avoid planting tender plants in locations that are likely to experience rapid fluctuations in temperature.
  - Place frost-tolerant plants that bloom early, such as some cultivars of gardenia (*Gardenia* spp.), azalea (*Rhododendron* spp.), camellia (*Camellia* var.), and daphne (*Daphne* spp.), in cold spots protected from wind and sun on the north, northeast, or east side of a building or near some other barrier to prevent a premature break of dormancy and risk flower and fruit damage.
- **Fertilization.** Avoid late-summer fertilization because it stimulates new growth in early fall that may not have time to harden off prior to sudden temperature drops in late fall and early winter.
- **Weather.** Know the average first and last frost dates for your area. Keep an eye on the weather forecast. Cool, clear nights with low humidity, often following a cold front, are signs of an impending frost.
- **Water** the soil prior to a freeze. Compared to dry soil, moist soil absorbs and holds four times more heat, conducts that heat to the surface faster, and radiates 5°F warmer throughout the entire night. In addition, watering reduces desiccation. Avoid antidesiccant products as they reduce transpiration for only a short period, and research has shown them to be ineffective for use over the winter.
- **Protect.** Shade plants from direct winter sun and wind because plants that freeze and thaw slowly suffer less damage. Protect small evergreens by both reducing the force of the wind and providing shade with windbreaks created by attaching burlap or canvas to a frame on two sides of the plant. Plants under trees are protected by the canopy, which both provides shade that delays vulnerable spring growth and traps heat radiated from the soil. Cover plants with burlap, sheets, plastic, or frost cloth. Do not allow the covering to touch the foliage. Extend the covering to the ground to trap heat radiating off the soil at night. A light bulb placed near the ground, well away from the trunk, offers additional protection, as does placing 5 gallon buckets full of water inside the covering. Remove the covering every morning to prevent overheating, which can cause premature bud break, increasing susceptibility to a late frost or even killing the plant.
- **Mulch.** Provide a 3-inch layer of mulch to reduce water loss and maintain uniform soil moisture and temperature around roots.

Managing Freeze Damage

Wait until new growth starts in the spring to prune winter-damaged plants. Plants and branches that look dead may still be alive. In addition, dead branches create a protected air space around the living tissue, preventing future frost damage. Also, pruning may stimulate new growth that is vulnerable to freeze damage. Spring growth may be delayed in damaged plants, and only when new growth starts will the extent of winter damage become apparent.

- **Split bark.** A rapid nighttime drop in temperature can freeze water within branches or the trunk of a tree, causing it to explode or split open along frost cracks (Figure 11–72). If not severe, these cracks appear to close when warm weather arrives. The wood fibers within, however, may not actually grow back together. This is commonly found on the southwest side of young shade trees where warm afternoon sun creates greater extremes in the day and night temperatures. Protect the trunk by planting evergreens on the south and southwest side of the tree, or wrap the trunk in white tree wrap for the winter.

Figure 11–72. Frost crack.
Lucy Bradley, CC BY - 2.0

- **Snow and ice damage.** The weight of accumulated snow and ice on branches can cause them to bend or break, and high winds compound the damage, resulting in misshapen plants with broken, split branches (Figure 11–73). Snow can be removed with a broom. But when branches are frozen, they are quite brittle. So always sweep upward, lifting snow off. Plants bent out of shape by snow or ice often straighten up on their own in a few days, but prune broken branches as soon as possible. Minimize damage from ice and snow by preventive pruning, including the removal of weak, narrow-angled, v-shaped crotches.

Figure 11–73. Snow and ice damage.
Kaarina Dillabough, Flickr CC BY-SA 2.0

Storm Damage

Care for damaged large trees is best left to professionals. Wise decisions and prompt action are required to minimize the impact of storm damage. First decide if the tree is worth saving. Consider replacing plants that do not serve a needed function or do not have any sentimental or historical value. Also consider replacement when a plant has already been stressed or is old or had low vigor prior to the storm. A tree with severe damage to the trunk or more than 30% of the main branches should be replaced. Also consider replacing a damaged shrub or tree if other, more desirable species or varieties are available.

Repairs to damaged trees come in two stages:
(1) first aid for immediate attention and
(2) follow-up work to be distributed over several months or years.

Uprooted small trees. Remove any damaged roots or branches. Straighten and stake immediately because exposure to sun and wind severely damages any upturned roots and trunks.

Prune broken and split branches and eliminate breeding grounds for insects and diseases by promptly removing all debris, including broken branches and pruned limbs. Delay pruning to reshape the tree because removal of more than a fourth of the canopy in one year may result in sunscald, weak branching habits, and sucker growth.

Minimize stress by keeping the tree mulched and watered, removing suckers, and managing insect and disease problems. Gradually prune and reshape trees for balance and general appearance over a period of three to five years. When they begin to grow again, a light application of fertilizer may be helpful. But too much fertilizer applied too early can cause further damage.

Natural characteristics or plant problems?

Some characteristics of plants are often incorrectly diagnosed as a disease or plant problem. Some of the most common are listed below:

Yellow leaves or leaf drop in fall. Many narrowleaf evergreens and some broadleaf evergreens, including azaleas (*Rhododendron* spp.), develop yellow leaves in the fall (Figure 11–74). This is the normal shedding of the oldest leaves. The yellowing is uniform from the top to the bottom of the plant. The newest leaves or needles on the tips of branches remain green.

Figure 11–74. Normal yellowing of azalea (*Rhododendron* spp.) leaves in the fall.
Katja Schultz, Flickr CC BY - 2.0

Bark shedding. Tree bark sheds as the tree grows. Bark shedding of some trees, including sycamore (*Platanus occidentalis*), maple (*Acer* spp.), and crape myrtle (*Lagerstroemia indica*), tends to be very noticeable (Figure 11–75). If the bark sheds off and exposes more bark, there is no need to be concerned. If bare wood is exposed, sunscald, lightning, or winter damage could be a serious problem.

Spring leaf drop. Some broadleaf evergreens, including holly (*Ilex* spp.), camellia (*Camellia* var.), and magnolia (*Magnolia* spp.), shed their oldest leaves in the spring as new growth begins. The yellowing is uniform from top to bottom of the plant, and new growth is not affected.

Gummosis. Plum and cherry trees may exude a clear to yellowish gum to seal off injuries (Figure 11–76). It may be related to pruning or mechanical injury.

Figure 11–76. Gummosis on a peach tree is the result of injury.
Carroll E. Younce, USDA Agriculture Research Service, Bugwood CC BY - 3.0

Figure 11–75. Natural shedding of sycamore (*Platanus occidentalis*) bark.
Judy Gallagher, Flickr CC BY - 2.0

11

Case Study—Think IPM: An Azalea Issue

Something is wrong with your azalea shrub. The branches seem to be dying back.

You review the diagnostic procedures from chapter 7, "Diagnostics," and think about the five steps for IPM:

1. Monitor and scout to determine pest type and population levels.
2. Accurately identify host and pest.
3. Consider economic or aesthetic injury thresholds. A threshold is the point at which action will be taken.
4. Implement a treatment strategy using physical, cultural, biological, or chemical management, or a combination of these strategies.
5. Evaluate success of treatments.

1. Monitor and scout to determine pest type and population levels.

You have an azalea that was planted seven years ago and has been blooming beautifully for the past three years. But this spring there were fewer blossoms, and now the leaves on half the shrub are wilted. Before sending a sample to the Plant Disease and Insect Clinic at NC State, you decide to do some sleuthing on your own (answers to questions are in italics).

2. Accurately identify the host and pest.

Step 1. Identify the plant: *The shrub is a 'Pink Ruffles' Southern Indica azalea with large pink blossoms.*

Step 2. Describe the problem: *The shrub had fewer blooms this spring, and in the summer it began to look unhealthy. A few of the branches are dying back, and the leaves on those branches are dry and brown* (Figure 11–77).

Figure 11–77. An overall view of the azalea shrub.
Plant Disease and Insect Clinic (PDIC)

Step 3. Identify what is normal:
What does the healthy part of the plant look like?
The unaffected branches have glossy, deep-green leaves.

What does the unhealthy part of the plant look like?
The affected branches have wilted or dead leaves some of which are still attached to the stem (Figure 11–78).

Figure 11–78. A branch with dead and missing leaves.
PDIC

Have you had a soil test? *No.* (For information on how to submit a soil test, see chapter 1, "Soils and Plant Nutrients.")

Step 4. Identify cultural practices:
Age and history of plants: *This shrub was purchased seven years ago from a local nursery. The first few years it did not bloom much, but then it became a beautiful shrub. This spring there were few blossoms.*

Irrigation: *It is watered with a hose every other week in the winter and once a week during the warmer months depending on the rain.*

Fertilizer: *This shrub has not been fertilized.*

Maintenance: *In the early summer it was pruned because the branches were getting tall. The surrounding area was weeded, and a layer of pine needle mulch was added. No pesticides or herbicides have been added.*

Step 5. Identify environmental conditions:
Are there any significant water issues? *There is no standing water in this area. It has been a hot, dry summer. The shrub did appear drought stressed a few times but seemed to perk up after being watered.*

What is the soil like? *The soil is red and seems claylike. It holds water well.*

Describe the light. How many hours of sunlight does this shrub get? *The shrub gets filtered shade most of the day from a large tulip tree.*

What happened over the winter? Did frost damage occur? Were any melting salts used? *It was a mild winter, so there was no frost damage. Salts were used on the walk and driveway twice, but that is 25 feet from this plant.*

Describe any recent changes or events: *Nothing has changed near this shrub recently.*

Step 6. Identify signs of pathogens and pests:
On the leaves: *There are no missing pieces of leaf, no spots, insect eggs, frass, or webbing. There was a small black beetle on one of the leaves, and there were a few small flies.*

On the stems: *There are no insects, eggs, frass, webbing, or missing chunks.*

On the crown, roots and in the soil: *The crown of the plant shows some dead and dying branches* (Figure 11–79). *There is no smell coming from the roots. There were no visible signs of any fungus, eggs, or frass. There were some ants crawling around in the soil around the plant.*

Figure 11–79. The crown of the plant shows some dead and dying branches.
PDIC

Step 7. Identify symptoms:
On the leaves: *The leaves on the affected branches are brown and wilted, and many are falling off.*

On the stems: *The healthy branches do not have splitting or peeling bark. They are white inside with green when I scratch the outer surface of a twig. The dead branches are only dead on the tips. Toward the base they have healthy foliage . At the tips of the damaged branches, when I scratch the bark, I see reddish-brown streaking in the wood* (Figure 11–80). *There are no holes on the stems.*

On the roots: *The roots appear somewhat yellow and well-hydrated, but it is difficult to tell if they are healthy.*

Figure 11–80. Scraping the bark of damaged branches reveals dark spots in the wood.
PDIC

Step 8. Identify distribution of damage in the landscape:
Are other plants in the landscape affected? *This is the only azalea shrub and the other shrubs—boxwoods and hollies—do not appear to be affected. No other plants in the landscape appear to be affected.*

Step 9. Identify distribution of damage on the plant and specific plant parts:
Where is the damage seen on the plant? *Scattered branches on the shrub.*

Step 10. Identify timing:
When did you notice this problem? *The branches started dying back this July. Now in August, dieback occurs on almost half the shrub.*

You hypothesize this is a disease because there were signs of disease and no signs of insects or insect damage. Because the symptoms appear on the stems affecting the leaves, you suspect this is a vascular problem. The branches die back but not to the base, and there is still live tissue on the branches. Doing the scratch test and seeing the transition zone between the dead and healthy green tissue (Figure 11–80) leads you to believe this is not a root problem. Based on the other facts gathered, the cultural practices of infrequent watering—especially in dry conditions—could have caused stress to the shrub, making it susceptible to disease. You look at a cross section of an unhealthy branch (Figure 11–81) and see a triangular dark area of dead tissue surrounded by lighter living tissue. This sharp distinction between dead and live tissue is a clue this may be a canker disease.

You search extension.org or type in "azalea+canker+edu" into a search engine to find university-based resources on the Internet. Several resources discuss a twig blight called *Phomopsis* sp. that causes the same reddish-brown

11

streaking you saw on the stems. It is a common fungal problem among mature azaleas, particularly 'Indica' cultivars. It would be impossible to confirm this fungus without laboratory diagnosis, but you feel confident enough in your diagnosis to research the ways to manage this pathogen.

Phomopsis sp. is worse following heat or drought stress and follows a poor pruning job.

Figure 11–81. A cross-section of branches also reveals dark spots in the wood.
PDIC

3. Consider economic or aesthetic injury thresholds.

This mature shrub is just to the left of your front door. It is a beautiful addition to the landscape, and it is important to save it.

4. Implement a treatment strategy using physical, cultural, biological, or chemical management, or combine these strategies.

Physical: Promptly prune out branches at least 6 inches below any discoloration. Be sure to use good pruning practices by always pruning back to a bud, not leaving any stubs. Practice hygienic pruning by spraying the shears with isopropyl alcohol between cuts to prevent spreading the disease. Dispose of all affected material; do not compost.

Cultural: Keep the shrub well-watered in warmer months but do not overwater. Mulch around the plants with an acidic mulch like pine needles, wood chips, or bark.

Biological: There are no recommended biological treatments at this time.

Chemical: Fungicides are not affective in treatment of *Phomopsis* sp.

5. Evaluate success of treatments.

Keeping records in a garden journal, or notes about the appearance of wilting branches helps to identify if your management strategies are affective. Documenting the strategies implemented and their success or failure helps you make better management decisions in the future.

Frequently Asked Questions

1. Do I need to prune my woody ornamentals, and if so, how do I do it?

Pruning is the removal of plant parts to accomplish any or all of the following goals: to train the growth habit of the plant; to maintain plant health; to improve the quality of flowers, fruits, foliage, and stems; to control growth. Pruning can also enhance the natural beauty of a plant and accentuate its features. Based on the needs of the specific plant, use the proper tools effectively at the optimal time of year to achieve the desired effect. Some plants only require pruning to remove damaged, diseased, dying, or dead branches or other plant parts, and heavy pruning may actually kill some plants. Refer to the following publications, all of which are available online.

Pruning Trees and Shrubs Series

- AG-780-01, *Before the Cut*
- AG-780-03, *General Pruning Techniques*
- AG-780-02, *How to Make the Cut*
- AG-780-04, *How to Prune Specific Plants*

2. Why didn't my big leaf hydrangea bloom this year?

There are many factors that affect flowering in shrubs. Big leaf hydrangea (*Hydrangea macrophylla*) flower buds are particularly notorious for not forming in weather that is too cold and for dying off if there is a sudden cold snap after bud development. These hydrangeas bloom on old wood, so pruning in the fall or spring could remove all the flower buds and prevent blooming.

3. Should I use wound paint after pruning a tree or shrub?

Wound paint is not recommended and may even hinder the plant's ability to seal off (compartmentalize) the pruning injury. A better strategy, especially on trees, is to make proper pruning cuts, either at the point of attachment or just beyond a bud, early in the life of a plant. This results in small wounds (less than 4 inches in diameter) near tissue that is capable of growing to seal off the wound naturally. This pruning, done in the first few years of a plant's life to direct future growth, is called "training."

4. My variegated dogwood has a branch with all green leaves. What should I do?

The branch with all green leaves has reverted back to its original form. These nonvariegated branches grow more quickly than variegated ones. Remove them immediately by cutting back to a branch union.

Further Reading

Armitage, Allan M. *Armitage's Vines and Climbers: A Gardener's Guide to the Best Vertical Plants.* Portland, Oregon: Timber Press, Inc., 2010. Print.

Batdorf, Lynn R. *Boxwood Handbook: A Practical Guide to Knowing and Growing Boxwood.* 3rd ed. Boyce, Virginia: American Boxwood Society, 2005. Print.

Bitner, Richard L. *Conifers for Gardens: An Illustrated Encyclopedia.* Portland, Oregon: Timber Press, Inc., 2007. Print.

Brickell, Christopher, and David Joyce. *American Horticultural Society Pruning and Training.* New York: DK Publishing, 2011. Print.

Callaway, Dorothy J. *The World of Magnolias.* 1994. Portland, Oregon: Timber Press, Inc., 1999. Print.

Church, Glyn. *Complete Hydrangeas.* Cheektowaga, New York: Firefly Books Ltd., 2007. Print.

Dirr, Michael A. *Dirr's Encyclopedia of Trees and Shrubs.* Portland: Timber Press, Inc., 2011. Print.

Dirr, Michael A. *Manual of Woody Landscape Plants: Their Identification, Ornamental Characteristics, Culture, Propagation and Uses.* 6th ed. Champaign, Illinois: Stipes Publishing L.L.C., 2009. Print.

Gardiner, Jim. *The Timber Press Encyclopedia of Flowering Shrubs.* Portland, Oregon: Timber Press, Inc., 2011. Print.

Gregory, Peter, and J. D. Vertrees. *Japanese Maples: The Complete Guide to Selection and Cultivation.* 4th ed. Portland, Oregon: Timber Press, Inc., 2009. Print.

Jaynes, Richard A. *Kalmia: Mountain Laurel and Related Species* (Third Edition). Portland, Oregon: Timber Press, Inc., 2009. Print.

Ortho *All about Roses.* 2nd ed. Hoboken, New Jersey: John Wiley & Sons Inc., 2007. Print.

O'Sullivan, Penelope. *The Homeowner's Complete Tree & Shrub Handbook: The Essential Guide to Choosing, Planting, and Maintaining Perfect Landscape Plants.* North Adams, Massachusetts: Storey Publishing, 2007. Print.

Simeone, Vincent A. *Great Flowering Landscape Shrubs.* Chicago: Chicago Review Press, 2005. Print.

Simeone, Vincent A. *Great Flowering Landscape Trees.* Chicago: Chicago Review Press, 2007. Print.

Simeone, Vincent A. *Great Landscape Evergreens.* Chicago: Chicago Review Press, 2008. Print.

Toomey, Mary K., and Everett Leeds. *An Illustrated Encyclopedia of Clematis.* Portland, Oregon: Timber Press, Inc., 2001. Print.

Towe, L. Clarence. *American Azaleas.* Portland, Oregon: Timber Press, Inc., 2004. Print.

Trehane, Jennifer. *Camellias: The Gardener's Encyclopedia.* Portland, Oregon: Timber Press, Inc., 2007. Print.

For More Information

http://go.ncsu.edu/fmi_woodyornamentals

11

Contributors

Authors
Lucy Bradley, Professor and Extension Specialist, Urban Horticulture, NC State University; Director, NC State Extension Master Gardener program
Barbara Fair, Associate Professor and Extension Specialist, Department of Horticultural Science

Contributions by Extension Agents:
Tim Mathews, Matt Jones, Danelle Cutting, Katy Shook, Paul McKenzie, Allison Arnold, Deborah Dillion

Contributions by Extension Master Gardener Volunteers:
Barbara Goodman, Margaret Genkins, Kristen Monahan, Chris Alberti, Linda Alford, Jackie Weedon, Karen Damari, Connie Schultz, Bethany Sinott, Kim Curlee, Edna Burger, Caro Dosé

Content Editor:
Kathleen Moore, Urban Horticulturist

Copy Editor:
Barbara Scott

Based in part on text from the 1998 Extension Master Gardener manual prepared by:
Erv Evans, Extension Associate, Department of Horticultural Science

Chapter 11 Cover Photo:
Kathleen Moore, CC BY 2.0

How to Cite this Chapter:
Bradley, L., B. Fair. 2022. Woody Ornamentals, Chpt. 11, In: K.A. Moore, and. L.K. Bradley (eds). *North Carolina Extension Gardener Handbook*, 2nd ed. NC State Extension, Raleigh, NC. <https://content.ces.ncsu.edu/extension-gardener-handbook/11-woody-ornamentals>

Native Plants

Objectives

This chapter teaches people to:

• Explain why the term "native" is of no value without specifying time and location

• Define the ecological regions of North Carolina

• Recognize the connection between native plants and native wildlife

• Appreciate the importance of native plants in an ecosystem

• Describe the principles of gardening with native plants

• Select appropriate native plants for a given landscape

Introduction

Landscaping with native plants empowers gardeners to care for nature and enhance the local environment while adding beauty and diversity to their homesites. By planting natives, gardeners support native pollinators and connect with the natural heritage of a region. Gardeners and the environment reap the most benefits from natives when gardeners understand key concepts related to the meaning of the words "**native plant**," the value of incorporating native plants into landscapes, and principles of gardening with native plants.

What Are Native Plants?

Native plants are those species that evolved naturally in a region without human intervention. Red maple (*Acer rubrum*), flowering dogwood (*Cornus florida*), and butterfly weed (*Asclepias tuberosa*) are examples of the over 3,900 species of plants the U.S. Department of Agriculture (USDA) PLANTS Database lists as native to North Carolina. These plants developed and adapted to local soil and climate conditions over thousands of years and are vital parts of local ecosystems necessary for the survival of pollinators, insects, birds, mammals, and other wildlife.

Plants are not considered native to a region within decades or even centuries after introduction. To be native, they must originate in the region and co-evolve with other species over thousands of years. As these species evolve together, they adapt to the physical environment formed by local climate and weather conditions, soil types, topography, and hydrology.

Native plants form interdependent, highly specialized relationships with other organisms that are necessary for each other's survival. Replacing natives with plants from other regions cannot replicate the complex interactions that naturally occur.

North Carolina's Ecological Regions

Climate, geology, and evolutionary history determine the distribution of plants, animals, and other organisms in complex ways. In large areas with similar climate, ecosystems recur in predictable patterns. These patterns, known as ecological regions or ecoregions, provide the boundaries for a meaningful definition of the term "native."

"Ecoregions of North America" was developed by the U.S. Environmental Protection Agency (EPA) to provide a framework for the environmental study and conservation of the continent's ecosystems; this system also provides a useful framework for gardeners when selecting native plants.

"Ecoregions of North America" has four levels, each progressively more refined. Level III is probably the best reference for gardeners to use to define regions for selecting native plants. This level subdivides North America into 182 ecoregions and is used to define regions within which plant material can be transferred with little risk of it being poorly adapted to the new location. The four Level III ecoregions found in North Carolina align with our state's physiographic regions as follows:

- Middle Atlantic coastal plain and Southeastern plains ecoregion (combined) align with the NC coastal plain, including the NC sandhills region.
- Piedmont ecoregion aligns with the NC piedmont.
- Blue Ridge ecoregion aligns with the NC mountains.

Level IV further subdivides each Level III ecoregion into smaller areas that more fully reflect the enormous biological and ecological diversity of our state. This level is of interest to gardeners seeking a more local, specialized, frame of reference. Ecoregion maps are available to download from the EPA.

Selecting native plants begins with defining the ecoregion of the property to be landscaped and then identifying plants native to that ecoregion. Choosing plants native to the local region will provide the greatest benefits to wildlife and the environment.

Native Plant Terminology

Many terms describe native plants and where they occur. The term "indigenous" is synonymous with native, but neither term specifies where a plant is native. Native range describes the area over which a plant naturally occurs.

Native Range

Although it is convenient to refer to a plant's native range using political boundaries, such as county or state names, soil and climate conditions determine plant distribution (native range). It is more important to know a plant's adaptation to the ecoregion and growing conditions than whether or not a species occurs within a specific county.

What Are Wildflowers?

The term wildflower is often used to describe native plants, but may also refer to naturalized plants that are not indigenous to the region. In addition, wildflower plantings and seed mixes often include species from other parts of the country or world. Don't assume plants or seeds labeled as wildflowers are native to your region; when purchasing wildflowers, identify the species, then determine if it is native to your region.

Figure 12–1. Venus flytrap (*Dionaea muscipula*). This plant's native range is restricted to several counties in southeastern North Carolina and coastal South Carolina.
Charlotte Glen

Figure 12–2. Red maple (*A. rubrum*).
Alex Lomas, Flickr CC BY - 2.0

Plants limited to one region are said to be **endemic** to that region and often occur on sites with specialized soils and hydrology. For example, Venus flytrap (*Dionaea muscipula*) is endemic to a small portion of North Carolina's and South Carolina's coastal plain (Figures 12–1 and 12–18). This well-known carnivorous plant grows in nutrient-poor, highly acidic, sandy soils with a high water table that impedes drainage. Plants with such a limited native range that are adapted to very specific growing conditions are less likely to survive in the typical landscape.

Plants with a broad native range may occur in each of North Carolina's ecoregions, as well as in other states. For example, red maple (*A. rubrum*, Figure 12–2) has a native range that extends along the Atlantic seaboard and well into the center of the country. Such plants typically adapt to a variety of habitats and are more likely to survive in conditions found in residential landscapes. The USDA's PLANTS Database is an excellent resource for determining a plant's native range.

Natural Communities

Native plants occur within natural communities, which are defined by the NC Natural Heritage Program as "distinct and reoccurring assemblages of populations of plants, animals, bacteria, and fungi naturally associated with each other and their physical environment." Within North Carolina, 30 natural communities have been identified, each with multiple subtypes related to the dominant plant species and conditions—soil, hydrological, and geological—that shape that community. A plant's inclusion in a natural community is not exclusive; many native plant species are components of several natural communities.

Knowing the natural communities within a region helps gardeners identify plants that will thrive in that region's landscapes, and better match a given plant to a suitable site. One resource that gardeners can use to learn about the natural communities in their region is the Guide to the Natural Communities of North Carolina, Fourth Approximation, written by Michael Schafale. It is available from the NC Natural Heritage Program.

What Is Provenance?

Provenance refers to where, within a plant's native range, seed or propagation materials, such as cuttings, were collected. For example, red maple (*A. rubrum*) trees grown from seed collected near Pittsboro, North Carolina, have an NC piedmont provenance. The characteristics of plants with a broad distribution can vary from one area of their range to another. Red maple trees grown from seed collected in the northern part of the red maple's range, for example, produce fall color two to three weeks earlier than trees grown from seed collected in the southern part of its range, even when trees grown from northern seed are planted in the South.

Try to locate plants of local provenance when creating habitat or restoring disrupted natural areas. Plants sourced within the same ecoregion ensure the best possible fit with local conditions and wildlife.

Naturalized and Invasive Plants

Not all plants growing wild in a region are natives. Nonnative, or exotic, plants that reproduce and establish outside their native range are described as **naturalized**. According to the USDA PLANTS Database, over 1,100 species of naturalized plant species grow in North Carolina. Examples include many common weeds and wildflowers, such as chickweed (*Stellaria media*), white clover (*Trifolium repens*), Queen Anne's lace (*Daucus carota*), and orange daylily (*Hemerocallis fulva*), all of which were introduced from Eurasia.

Weeds are nuisance plants that interfere with human activities, such as farming, gardening, and turf maintenance. When cultivated areas are abandoned, most common lawn and garden weeds disappear after a few years, allowing native plants and the many wildlife species that rely upon them to re-establish.

A small percentage of plants introduced to North Carolina have become exceptionally persistent and damaging. These extra-aggressive nonnative species, capable of invading natural areas and destroying ecosystems, are known as **invasive species**. The USDA's National Invasive Species Information Center characterizes invasive species as adaptable, aggressive, and having a high reproductive capacity. Because they did not evolve locally, invasive species lack the natural enemies that limit aggressive spreading in their native habitat, resulting in rampant, uncontrolled population growth that can threaten the health of humans, livestock, wildlife, and ecosystems.

Figure 12–3. Chinese privet (*Ligustrum sinense*) is an invasive plant in North Carolina.
Melissa McMasters, Flickr CC BY - 2.0

Invasive species are one of the greatest threats to ecosystems worldwide. Many invasive plants in the United States were originally introduced for agricultural or ornamental use. For example, kudzu (*Pueraria montana* var. *lobata*) was introduced to the Southeast in the 1930s for erosion control and animal fodder. Invasive plant species that were introduced as landscape plants, but have become too well-adapted to local conditions, include Japanese honeysuckle (*Lonicera japonica*), autumn olive (*Eleagnus umbellata*), Chinese privet (*Ligustrum sinense*, Figure 12–3), English ivy (*Hedera helix*), and Asian wisterias (*Wisteria floribunda* and *Wisteria sinensis*).

Exotic plants are most likely to become invasive in regions with soil and climate conditions similar to those of their native habitat. Plant species that are invasive in one ecoregion of the state may not be invasive in others. For example, the invasive species Oriental bittersweet (*Celastrus orbiculatus*) is particularly problematic in the Blue Ridge Mountains, but not in the NC coastal plain. One of the most important things gardeners can do to protect local ecosystems is to identify and remove invasive plants from their property and avoid planting species that have a high potential to become invasive. Resources to help gardeners and landowners in North Carolina identify and manage invasive plants are available from the NC Invasive Plant Council, NC Native Plant Society, and NC Forest Service.

Why Should Gardeners Plant Natives?

Including native plants in the landscape helps gardeners create visually appealing outdoor spaces and build healthier local ecosystems. The key to understanding why natives are so important in our gardens lies in recognizing the essential role plants play in supporting biodiversity and the ecosystem services needed to sustain our environment.

The Need for Biodiversity

Biodiversity refers to the variety of living organisms. It can describe the number of different ecosystems or habitats within a region, the number of species within an ecosystem, as well as the genetic diversity within a species. Biodiversity sustains the natural processes that support all life on earth, known as ecosystem services. According to the Ecological Society of America, healthy ecosystems are needed to provide services that accomplish these functions:

- Pollinate crops and natural vegetation (Figure 12–4)
- Disperse seeds (Figure 12–5)

Figure 12–4. Squash bees (*Peponapis pruinosa*) are important pollinators of cucurbits such as squash, pumpkins, and gourds, and are one of many native insects that provide vital pollination services.
Ilona Loser, CC BY-SA 4.0

- Balance agricultural and garden pest populations
- Regulate disease-carrying organisms
- Generate soils
- Cycle and move nutrients
- Purify the air and water
- Detoxify and decompose wastes
- Contribute to climate stability
- Moderate weather extremes and their impacts including drought and floods
- Protect streams, river channels, and coastal shores from erosion (Figure 12–6)

The destruction of natural habitat is the greatest threat to biodiversity worldwide. In fast-growing regions, development often fragments remaining natural habitats into smaller pieces that are less likely to support the needed range of ecosystem services. As natural areas disappear, residential landscapes become more important sources of nourishment and habitat for the many species needed to support healthy ecosystems.

North Carolina's population is increasing. Each year new homes and communities are constructed, removing natural habitat and native plants from local ecosystems. Many communities scarcely resemble the natural areas they replace, and nonnative turfgrasses, shrubs, and flowers often dominate residential landscapes. These plants are unable to perform the same ecological roles as the native plants they replaced. As a result, other species native to the region cannot survive, diminishing the biodiversity of the community. By restoring native plants to landscapes, gardeners help preserve biodiversity and create opportunities to interact with birds, butterflies, bees, and other species in their yards.

The Role of Plants in Ecosystems
Plants, animals, and microbes interact with nonliving elements, such as air, water, and minerals to form ecosystems. Each element—living or nonliving—is integral to the system, and changes to any component have the potential to affect all other parts of the system. This definition extends to residential landscapes, which are part of the local ecosystem. Everything that happens in a landscape, from plant selection and landscape design, to pesticide and fertilizer applications, can either help or harm the local ecosystem.

Figure 12–5. A healthy ecosystem supports life forms that help disperse seeds like these cedar waxwings are doing on a juniper tree.
Del Green, Pixabay CC0

Figure 12–6. A stream bank protected from erosion with plant material.
Jindřich Škrla, Pixabay CC0

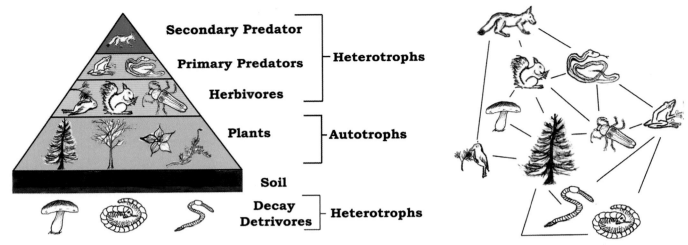

Figure 12–7. Examples of a food web.
Tompsma, Wikipedia CC BY - 3.0

Figure 12–8. A bluebird with a caterpillar for its nestlings.
Kansasphoto, Flickr CC BY - 2.0

Living organisms within an ecosystem connect through a food web: a complex, overlapping series of pathways that move energy and nutrients through the ecosystem (Figure 12–7). Trophic levels describe the position an organism occupies in a food web—what the organism eats and what eats it. As one species eats another, energy moves from one trophic level to the next. Plants are the first trophic level in almost every food web on earth.

Within most food webs, plant-eating insects make up the second trophic level. A significant percentage of the world's animals depend on insects to access the energy plants store. For example, insects are a critical food source for the survival of most bird species. Adult birds may feed on insects, seeds, and berries, but juvenile birds require a diet of insects to provide the protein for development (Figure 12–8). Large numbers of caterpillars feeding on native tree leaves are the food source that sustains the nestlings of many bird species. Just consider this:

6,000 to 10,000 caterpillars are needed to successfully raise a single nest of chickadees!

In any ecological region, the coevolution of plant and insect species over thousands of years includes plant defenses against insect predation and insect processes to counteract those defenses. In many cases, an insect's adaptation focuses upon a limited range of closely related plants that occur within that insect's native range. Insects that evolved to feed upon specific plant species cannot survive if those plants are not available. This is particularly true for leaf-feeding insects, such as butterfly and moth larvae (caterpillars).

Figure 12–9. Monarch caterpillars feeding on *Asclepias* sp.
Vladeb, Flickr CC BY-ND 2.0

Monarch butterflies are a well-known example of such specialized adaptation. The survival of monarch butterflies depends on plants in the genus *Asclepias*, commonly known as butterfly weed or milkweed. Monarch caterpillars cannot feed on any other plant genus; if *Asclepias* sp. disappear from a region, so do monarchs (Figure 12–9). This is true for other insects that rely upon specific plant species: If their host plants disappear, these insects cannot survive, which reduces the food supply for other organisms in the food web.

Gardeners play a valuable role in helping the environment by putting native plants to work in their landscapes. Landscaping with native plants sustains native insect populations, ensuring these insects are available for the birds, mammals, and other organisms that rely on insects for food. Gardeners may be reluctant to intentionally select plants for insects to feed upon, but native plants and native insects evolved together and established native plants can withstand the minor injury these insects cause. Researchers conclude that gardeners don't even notice such damage until insects injure up to 10% of a plant's foliage, so a few nibbled leaves are not likely to detract from the landscape's appearance. In a balanced ecosystem, species further up the food chain eat plant-feeding insects before the insects cause serious harm.

Additional Reasons to Plant Natives
Creating an ecologically balanced landscape that attracts

a multitude of birds and pollinators is not the only reason to use native plants in landscapes. Within North Carolina's ecoregions, approximately 3,900 species of native plants have been identified—from towering, graceful trees to striking shrubs and perennial wildflowers. The selection of native plants from any of our state's ecoregions is diverse and offers numerous varieties that are sure to enhance the beauty of all types of gardens—from more traditional, formal designs to free-form natural gardens. Whatever the style of a landscape or garden, the inclusion of native plants can contribute to its visual appeal.

Landscapes that include diverse regional flora provide a connection to the area's natural history. Such landscapes harmonize with their natural surroundings, creating a sense of place often lost when a limited selection of exotic species that can be grown from coast-to-coast dominates landscapes.

Incorporating native plants also commemorates the gardening history of a region. Many native plants used

Are Hybrids and Cultivars Native?

Do cultivars and hybrids of native plants support ecological functions as well as their wild relatives? Should we label such cultivars and hybrids, sometimes called "**nativars,**" as native plants? There are no decisive answers to these complex questions.

Cultivars are varieties of a species that are selected because they have larger flowers, shorter stature, extended bloom times, different colored petals or leaves, or some other feature gardeners find desirable. For example, 'Shamrock' is an inkberry holly (*Ilex glabra*) cultivar selected because it is more compact and holds its color better in winter than the wild species.

Hybrids are the result of two closely related plants, typically from the same genus, cross-pollinating and producing a viable offspring. Hybrids inherit genes from both parents and typically exhibit traits that are intermediate of the parent species. Hybrids can occur in nature where the distribution ranges of closely related plants overlap. *Vernonia × georgiana* is an example of a naturally occurring hybrid between *Vernonia acaulis*, stemless ironweed, and *Vernonanthura nudiflora,* narrow-leaf ironweed. All species of Vernonia are highly attractive to bees, so this hybrid may also occur in gardens where these species are grown together.

Gardeners and plant breeders intentionally cross two species to create hybrids. Some common reasons landscape plants are intentionally hybridized are to develop disease-resistant strains, to create novel flower or foliage colors, and to improve growth habit or performance in nursery production systems. Many of the new coneflower (*Echinacea* spp.) varieties with orange, yellow, and red flowers are hybrids between purple coneflower, *Echinacea purpurea*, and other *Echinacea* species, including *E. angustifolia*, *E. paradoxa*, *E. laevigata*, and *E. tennesseensis* (Figure 12–10). Although we can bring together two species that do not have overlapping native ranges, we cannot cross species that would not naturally do so.

Figure 12–10. Coneflower hybrid, 'Mango Meadowbrite'.
SB Johnny, Wikimedia CC BY-SA - 3.0

in southern gardens since the colonial period have long horticultural histories. Examples include southern magnolia (*Magnolia grandiflora*), flowering dogwood (*Cornus florida*), wax myrtle (*Myrica cerifera*), redbud (*Cercis canadensis*), cardinal flower (*Lobelia cardinalis*), oakleaf hydrangea (*Hydrangea quercifolia*), and foamflower (*Tiarella cordifolia*).

Cultivars or hybrids of wild species do not necessarily show diminished ecological performance. In some cases nativars are more attractive to pollinators or leaf-feeding insects than their wild parents and in others they are less so, according to Doug Tallamy's research at the University of Delaware. Characteristics that reduce plant attractiveness to pollinators or leaf-feeding insects include:

- **Having extra petals or fully double flowers.** Pollen and nectar are less accessible to pollinators; pollen and nectar-bearing structures are absent in fully double flowers.
- **Being sterile.** Sterile plants do not produce seeds or fruits. In some plants, sterile varieties do not even produce pollen. Planting a sterile selection of a native plant reduces food resources available to pollinators and birds.
- **Having purple or highly variegated leaves.** Purple leaves are higher in anthocyanins than green leaves, while variegated leaves contain less chlorophyll. Both of these characteristics can deter leaf-feeding insects.
- **Earlier or later blooming or fruiting times than wild species.** Altered bloom or fruiting times may not be in sync with local wildlife populations.

Although nativars with these characteristics may not perform the same ecological function as wild species, they may have a place in sustainable landscapes along with noninvasive, nonnative species, when sited appropriately and used in moderation alongside species native to a region.

Principles of Gardening with Native Plants

Native plants require thoughtful selection and care for long-term success. Choosing species adapted to the site conditions, preparing the soil, helping plants establish, and following ecological design principles ensures the gardener and the local ecosystem gain the most benefit from including native plants in landscapes.

Choose the Right Plant for the Site

North Carolina's amazing diversity of natural habitats ranges from coastal dunes and saltwater marshes, flat woods and inland swamps, rolling hills and highland meadows, to steep slopes and rich mountain coves. This variety of habitats means North Carolina has one of the most diverse floras in North America, offering numerous species of beautiful native plants well-suited to landscaping. The first step in selecting the right species for the site is performing a site analysis to assess these attributes:

- Soil texture, drainage, and pH
- Intensity and timing of direct sun and shade during the growing season
- Amount of horizontal and vertical growing space

A detailed site analysis helps you choose species adapted to the site's growing conditions. While plant tags often include sun or shade requirements, soil texture, drainage, and pH are equally important for success. Plants requiring well-drained conditions die quickly in wet areas; wetland plants may adapt to drier sites, but appreciate supplemental watering during dry spells. Choosing the right plant for the site is the most practical, economical, and sustainable approach to plant selection.

Many urban landscape conditions do not resemble natural habitats found in North Carolina. This is particularly true for parking lots and street tree plantings, which have highly disturbed soils and drainage patterns. Paved surfaces also reflect heat, creating extra stress. In planting sites surrounded by impervious surfaces, choose plants that can tolerate these harsher conditions (Figure 12–11).

Figure 12–11. A parking lot planting has reflected heat, reduced water infiltration, and limited soil volume, and is surrounded by impervious surfaces unlike conditions found in most natural areas.
LEEROY Agency, Pixabay CC0

Many genera native to the state include multiple species, each adapted to different growing conditions. For example, there are 16 species of *Asclepias* found in North

Carolina—some growing in wetland habitats, and others found only in upland areas. All species are larval hosts of the monarch butterfly. The two most common landscape species, butterfly weed (*Asclepias tuberosa*) and swamp milkweed (*Asclepias incarnata*), are found in each of the state's ecoregions, but grow in very different habitats. As its common name implies, swamp milkweed prefers consistently moist sites and tolerates shallow flooding; butterfly weed thrives in well-drained soils and is exceptionally drought-tolerant. Using these plants successfully and sustainably in the landscape requires matching the right species to the site.

Choose Natives Suited for Landscape

Not all native plants are good candidates for landscaping. Some are too vigorous, producing rhizomes or stolons that quickly dominate smaller planting beds. Examples include obedient plant (*Physostegia virginiana*), hardy ageratum (*Conoclinium coelestinum*), and tall goldenrod (*Solidago altissima*). These plants are best reserved for large-scale plantings, such as meadows or natural areas.

Some of North Carolina's most spectacular native plants require very specific soil and moisture conditions not found in most landscapes. This limits their usefulness as landscape plants. Examples include the beautiful, yet notoriously difficult to cultivate, pink lady's slipper orchid (*Cypripedium acaule*), and the striking lady lupine (*Lupinus villosus*), which grows in areas of deeply sandy, extremely well-drained soil found only in the counties of the NC southern coastal plain (Figure 12–12). For most plants from very specialized habitats, it is better to admire them in the wild rather than waste resources attempting to grow them in the landscape.

Figure 12–12. Lady lupine (*Lupinus villosus*).
Charlotte Glen

To determine if a native species is a good fit for a landscape, consider these factors:
- Growth habit in relation to available space, including height, width, and if the plant is a vigorous spreader
- Adaptability to the growing conditions found in the landscape, including sun or shade exposure, soil type, and drainage
- How well the plant fits the purpose for which it is planted
- If the plant is commercially available or sustainably propagated

Prepare the Soil and Help Plants Establish

Even though native plants survive in natural areas without care, this trait does not mean the plants will be able to do the same in a yard—even when you select the right plant for the site. Construction and development alter soil conditions, and almost everyone's landscape was a construction site at some point. Removal of organic matter and soil compaction are the two most damaging construction-related changes to natural soil conditions.

During construction, removing the top layer of soil, commonly known as the topsoil, is a typical first step. Topsoil contains more organic matter than the layers below, so removal strips away organic matter needed to support the healthy growth of plant roots and beneficial soil microbes. Heavy equipment traffic in and around the construction site compacts the soil (Figure 12–13), compressing pore spaces that allow water to infiltrate and percolate through the soil profile. This diminishes drainage and reduces soil oxygen that most plant roots and soil microbes require to survive.

Figure 12–13. A new home construction site with compacted soil.
Chris Alberti, CC BY - 2.0

Alleviating soil compaction before planting gives any plant, including native species, the best chance to thrive. Incorporating a 1-inch to 3-inch layer of compost into the soil before planting adds organic matter back to the soil, helps reduce compaction, and restores soil structure. Always test soil before planting to determine if nutrient levels and soil pH are in the appropriate range for the desired plants. If lime or nutrients are recommended, incorporate them into the soil before planting. Amend the soil over the entire planting area rather than amending individual planting holes.

As with all plants, keep newly planted natives well-watered for the first few weeks after planting, or until their roots establish into the surrounding soil. Depending on soil texture, microclimate conditions, and plant species, native plantings may or may not require additional irrigation and fertilization after planting. Plants growing in locations where buildings and hard surfaces interfere with rainfall infiltration are more likely to require additional watering after establishment.

In addition to soil test results, let plant growth and appearance be the guide to determining nutrient needs. If plants are growing at a satisfactory rate and have plenty of healthy green leaves, you do not need to fertilize. Maintaining a 2-inch to 3-inch layer of mulch around plants helps conserve soil moisture, moderates soil temperatures, prevents weeds from self-seeding, and slowly adds organic matter to the soil. In areas where deciduous trees are established, allow leaves to serve as natural mulch by leaving them in place when they fall.

Maximize Wildlife and Ecological Value

Different species of birds, pollinators, and other creatures have distinct preferences for where they nest, what they eat, and when they are active. A landscape that maximizes biodiversity and benefits the local ecosystem relies on planting a diverse mixture of species to create a variety of habitats and provide flowers, fruits, and seeds throughout the year.

Figure 12–14. Typical southern landscape.
Hottholler, Flickr CC BY - 2.0

Plan for Diversity

Many southern landscapes are primarily composed of common nonnative plants, such as 'Bradford' pear (*Pyrus calleryana*), Leyland cypress (× *Hesperotropsis leylandii*), Chinese (*Ilex cornuta*) and Japanese hollies (*Ilex crenata*), Asian azaleas (*Rhododendron* spp.), daylilies (*Hemerocallis* spp.), and large areas of turfgrass. These landscapes lack the diversity necessary to support biodiversity and a wide range of ecosystem services (Figure 12–14).

Figure 12–15. A diverse landscape.
Charlotte Glen

An easy way to increase the diversity of any yard is to limit lawn areas to sites where turfgrass is the most functional choice, such as outdoor recreation areas and areas that need to be kept low to preserve visibility and for access routes to other parts of the property. Excess turf areas can be converted into woodland or meadow-style plantings (Figure 12–15), or used to grow edible plants. Within turf areas, tolerating some flowering broadleaf weeds can increase diversity and provide important resources for pollinators (Figure 12–16).

Figure 12–16. The common meadow violet (*Viola sororia*), a larval host of fritillaries, makes an attractive and functional addition to turfgrass in the landscape.
James Steakley, Wikimedia CC BY-SA - 3.0

Create a variety of habitats and maximize diversity by including plants that mature at different heights, produce flowers and fruit throughout the growing season, and include both deciduous and evergreen species. Provide multiple areas in the landscape where birds and pollinators can gather nectar, pollen, and seeds from flowers. Within these areas, include groups of at least three to five plants of each species. This allows bees, butterflies, and other species to forage more efficiently by minimizing the distance they must move from plant to plant.

To create a continuous food supply, aim to have at least three different species native to the region in bloom during each growing season, from early spring through late fall. Provide nesting habitats for a variety of species by including both shade and understory trees. Adding birdhouses, birdbaths, snags, and brush piles further supports wildlife. Include habitat signs (Figure 12–17) to communicate to friends and neighbors that this landscape supports local wildlife, and inspire others to install similar plantings.

Figure 12–17. Pollinator habitat sign.
Chris Alberti, CC BY - 2.0

Plant in layers
Creating vertical layers in the landscape is important for sustaining diversity and maximizing ecological function. Vertical layers include different plant heights, from tall canopy trees to low-growing ground covers. As part of the Eastern Temperate Forest, natural plant communities within North Carolina may include five distinct layers: canopy, understory, shrub, herbaceous, and ground layer. Designing landscapes so that each layer is represented with native plants provides the most benefit to the local ecosystem and supports the widest array of species.

Canopy Layer
The tallest trees in a forest or landscape create the canopy. Canopy species typically mature at 40-feet to 80-feet tall, or more. The nuts and seeds of canopy trees such as oak (*Quercus* spp.) and hickory (*Carya* spp.) are important food sources for many mammals. Tree foliage supports

a wide range of caterpillars that birds eat. Although few canopy trees have spectacular flowers, the blossoms of trees such as red maple (*A. rubrum*) and tulip poplar (*Liriodendron tulipifera*) provide important nectar sources for bees.

In a landscape setting, we often describe canopy trees as shade trees, in reference to the important cooling service they provide. From a design standpoint, canopy trees give a landscape structure and are major design elements in any yard. Most canopy trees are deciduous, and their annual cycle of growing and shedding leaves is a dynamic landscape element, reflecting the changing seasons. Fallen leaves left in place on the ground return nutrients to the soil and serve as a natural mulch layer that provides habitat to firefly larvae, click beetles, and other ground-dwelling species. Table 12–1 lists some of the commercially available native canopy trees suitable for NC landscapes.

Understory Layer
In most forests, trees that mature from 20-feet to 40-feet tall make up the understory. Many understory trees produce showy blossoms in spring and are important early nectar sources for pollinators. Because they evolved to grow beneath taller trees, understory trees typically tolerate shade. When grown in sunnier sites, their flower production is more prolific and growth habit denser and more compact. Like their taller canopy counterparts, understory trees provide many resources for insects, birds, and other wildlife. In the landscape, plant understory trees in combination with canopy trees, or on their own where a smaller stature tree is desired. See Table 12–2 for suggestions of native understory trees.

Shrub Layer
Many shrubs produce flowers, seeds, or fruits that support birds and insects and provide color and interest in the landscape. Shrubs are an important component of NC forests where moisture is abundant, but may be sparser or noticeably absent in drier habitats. Table 12–3 lists a few of the many native shrubs suitable for NC landscapes.

Herbaceous Layer
The herbaceous layer, which is composed of plants lacking woody stems, includes wildflowers, grasses, sedges, and ferns and is the most diverse layer in most natural communities and landscapes. Although some herbaceous natives have annual or biennial life cycles, most are perennials. Those with showy flowers are favorites with gardeners and landscape designers.

There are hundreds of native perennials suitable for landscapes. You can find herbaceous plants for sun or shade, wet or dry conditions, with mature heights ranging from a few inches to several feet. To support local pollinators, select at least three different plant species to bloom in each growing season: spring, summer, and fall. Tables 12–4, 12–5, and 12–6 provide examples of spring-, summer-, and fall-blooming native perennials for NC landscapes. See Table 12–7 for examples of native grasses and sedges, and Table 12–8 for native ferns.

Ground Layer

The ground layer is the lowest layer in any planting, composed of plants and materials extending just a few inches above the soil surface. In nature, the ground layer is most often made up of fallen leaves in various states of decay that provide critical habitat to ground-foraging birds, along with the insects the birds hunt. In most landscapes, mulch or turfgrass dominates the ground layer. Where possible, allowing leaves to remain on the ground where they fall helps restore the natural ground layer and provides natural mulch.

None of the commonly cultivated turfgrass varieties are native to North Carolina, but there are native alternatives for areas that do not receive frequent traffic. Moss is one alternative for areas where gardeners desire a very low-growing ground cover. Moss thrives in shady areas unsuited to lawn growth, as well as in moist, acidic soils, providing a low-maintenance, attractive alternative to turf. Low-growing, spreading perennials are effective ground covers. Adding a path of mulch or stepping stones through ground cover areas will allow people to pass through without damaging these plantings. See Table 12–9 for suggestions of native ground covers for NC landscapes.

Figure 12–18. Venus flytrap (*Dionaea Muscipula*) is native to both Native North Carolina and South Carolina.
Charlotte Glen

Summary

Native plants contribute to the health of the local ecosystem through complex relationships with native insects and wildlife that have evolved over thousands of years. Native plants help create healthy, sustainable, low-maintenance landscapes that are likely to thrive over the long term. Select the right native plants, plant them in the right place, and care for them until the plants are successfully established. That is how gardeners create resilient landscapes capable of enhancing local ecosystems and supporting their community's environment.

Table 12–1. Examples of Native Canopy Trees for NC Landscapes

Common Name	Scientific Name	NC Regions Native
Red maple	*Acer rubrum*	Mountains, piedmont, coastal plain[1]
River birch	*Betula nigra*	Mountains, piedmont, coastal plain
Persimmon	*Diospyros virginiana*	Mountains, piedmont, coastal plain
American beech	*Fagus grandifolia*	Mountains, piedmont, coastal plain
Black gum	*Nyssa sylvatica*	Mountains, piedmont, coastal plain
Loblolly pine	*Pinus taeda*	Piedmont, coastal plain
White oak	*Quercus alba*	Mountains, piedmont, coastal plain
Pin oak	*Quercus palustris*	Piedmont
Willow oak	*Quercus phellos*	Piedmont, coastal plain
Shumard oak	*Quercus shumardii*	Mountains, piedmont, coastal plain
Live oak	*Quercus virginiana*	Coastal plain
[1] *The NC sandhills are part of the NC coastal plain.*		

Table 12–2. Examples of Native Understory Trees for NC Landscapes

Common Name	Scientific Name	NC Regions Native
Red buckeye	*Aesculus pavia*	Piedmont, coastal plain
Downy serviceberry	*Amelanchier arborea*	Mountains, piedmont, coastal plain
Ironwood	*Carpinus caroliniana*	Mountains, piedmont, coastal plain
Redbud	*Cercis canadensis*	Mountains, piedmont, coastal plain
Flowering dogwood	*Cornus florida*	Mountains, piedmont, coastal plain
Carolina silverbell	*Halesia carolina*	Mountains, piedmont
American holly	*Ilex opaca*	Mountains, piedmont, coastal plain
Sourwood	*Oxydendrum arboreum*	Mountains, piedmont, coastal plain

Table 12–3. Examples of Native Shrubs for NC Landscapes

Common Name	Scientific Name	NC Regions Native
American beautyberry	*Callicarpa americana*	Piedmont, coastal plain
Buttonbush	*Cephalanthus occidentalis*	Mountains, piedmont, coastal plain
Sweet pepperbush	*Clethra alnifolia*	Piedmont (eastern), coastal plain
Dwarf fothergilla	*Fothergilla gardenii*	Coastal plain
Inkberry	*Ilex glabra*	Piedmont (eastern), coastal plain
Winterberry	*Ilex verticillata*	Mountains, piedmont, coastal plain
Yaupon holly	*Ilex vomitoria*	Coastal plain
Virginia sweetspire	*Itea virginica*	Mountains, piedmont, coastal plain
Wax myrtle	*Morella cerifera*	Piedmont (eastern), coastal plain
Catawba rhododendron	*Rhododendron catawbiense*	Mountains, piedmont
Arrowwood	*Viburnum dentatum*	Mountains, piedmont, coastal plain
Possumhaw	*Viburnum nudum*	Mountains, piedmont, coastal plain

Including native plants in the landscape helps gardeners create visually appealing outdoor spaces and build healthier local ecosystems. The key to understanding why natives are so important in our gardens lies in recognizing the essential role plants play in supporting biodiversity and the ecosystem services needed to sustain our environment.

Table 12–4. Examples of Native Spring-Blooming Perennials for NC Landscapes

Common Name	Scientific Name	NC Regions Native
Eastern bluestar	*Amsonia tabernaemontana*	Mountains, piedmont, coastal plain
Eastern columbine	*Aquilegia canadensis*	Mountains, piedmont, coastal plain
White false indigo	*Baptisia alba*	Piedmont, coastal plain
Green and gold	*Chrysogonum virginianum*	Mountains, piedmont, coastal plain
Lanceleaf coreopsis	*Coreopsis lanceolata*	Mountains, piedmont, coastal plain
Trailing phlox	*Phlox nivalis*	Mountains, piedmont, coastal plain
Sundrops	*Oenothera fruticosa*	Mountains, piedmont, coastal plain
Pink beardtongue	*Penstemon australis*	Piedmont, coastal plain

Table 12–5. Examples of Native Summer-Blooming Perennials for NC Landscapes

Common Name	Scientific Name	NC Regions Native
Swamp milkweed	*Asclepias incarnata*	Mountains, piedmont, coastal plain
Butterfly weed	*Asclepias tuberosa*	Mountains, piedmont, coastal plain
Threadleaf coreopsis	*Coreopsis verticillata*	Piedmont, coastal plain
Swamp rosemallow	*Hibiscus moscheutos*	Mountains, piedmont, coastal plain
Wild bergamot	*Monarda fistulosa*	Mountains, piedmont
Summer phlox	*Phlox paniculata*	Mountains, piedmont, coastal plain
Mountain mint	*Pycnanthemum tenuifolium*	Mountains, piedmont, coastal plain
Green-headed coneflower	*Rudbeckia laciniata*	Mountains, piedmont, coastal plain

Table 12–6. Examples of Native Fall-Blooming Perennials for NC Landscapes

Common Name	Scientific Name	NC Regions Native
Joe-pye weed	*Eutrochium fistulosum*	Mountains, piedmont, coastal plain
Narrow leaf sunflower	*Helianthus angustifolius*	Mountains, piedmont, coastal plain
Grass-leaf blazing star	*Liatris pilosa*	Mountains, piedmont, coastal plain
Cardinal flower	*Lobelia cardinalis*	Mountains, piedmont, coastal plain
Narrow-leaf silkgrass	*Pityopsis graminifolia*	Mountains, piedmont, coastal plain
Wrinkle-leaf goldenrod	*Solidago rugosa*	Mountains, piedmont, coastal plain
Calico aster	*Aster lateriflorus*	Mountains, piedmont, coastal plain
New York ironweed	*Vernonia noveboracensis*	Mountains, piedmont, coastal plain

Table 12–7. Examples of Native Grasses and Sedges for NC Landscapes

Common Name	Scientific Name	NC Regions Native
Southern waxy sedge	*Carex glaucescens*	Piedmont, coastal plain
Gray's sedge	*Carex grayi*	Piedmont, coastal plain
River oats	*Chasmanthium latifolium*	Mountains, piedmont, coastal plain
Pink muhly grass	*Muhlenbergia capillaris*	Piedmont, coastal plain
Switchgrass	*Panicum virgatum*	Mountains, piedmont, coastal plain
Little bluestem	*Schizachyrium scoparium*	Mountains, piedmont, coastal plain

Table 12–8. Examples of Native Ferns for NC Landscapes

Common Name	Scientific Name	NC Regions Native
Northern maidenhair	*Adiantum pedatum*	Mountains, piedmont
Southern lady fern	*Athyrium asplenioides*	Mountains, piedmont, coastal plain
Marginal wood fern	*Dryopteris marginalis*	Mountains, piedmont
Cinnamon fern	*Osmunda cinnamomea*	Mountains, piedmont, coastal plain
Christmas fern	*Polystichum acrostichoides*	Mountains, piedmont, coastal plain
New York fern	*Thelypteris noveboracensis*	Mountains, piedmont, coastal plain

Table 12–9. Examples of Native Ground Covers for NC Landscapes

Common Name	Scientific Name	NC Regions Native
Pussytoes	*Antennaria plantaginifolia*	Mountains, piedmont, coastal plain
Pennsylvania sedge	*Carex pensylvanica*	Mountains, piedmont
Green and gold	*Chrysogonum virginianum* var. *brevistolon*	Mountains, piedmont
Partridgeberry	*Mitchella repens*	Mountains, piedmont, coastal plain
Allegheny spurge	*Pachysandra procumbens*	Mountains
Creeping phlox	*Phlox stolonifera*	Mountains, piedmont
Heartleaf foamflower	*Tiarella cordifolia*	Mountains, piedmont
Creeping blueberry	*Vaccinium crassifolium*	Piedmont, coastal plain

Frequently Asked Questions

1. What is a native plant?

There are many definitions, but native plants are those that have evolved naturally in a region without human intervention. Because they have evolved over thousands of years with the elements, animals, insects, and other plants, native plants make up an integral part of the survival of our ecosystem.

2. Are native plants better than "regular" plants I can buy at a nursery?

From a landscape design perspective, native plants are not necessarily better than traditional nursery stock. Some nonnative plants may have more colorful blooms or foliage than their native counterparts. A native wildflower garden may appear understated compared to a bed planted with petunias, lantana, or caladiums. However, native plants are well-adapted to the environment and have co-evolved with organisms in the local ecosystem. They provide more ecosystem services, such as food and shelter for pollinators and wildlife, than nonnative plants. If you appreciate the elegance and value of native plants, you strengthen your local ecosystem network.

3. If I plant natives, will I have to water and fertilize them?

Native plants in a residential landscape are in far different conditions than in their natural habitat. Compacted soils from construction, removal of top soil, reflected heat from buildings, runoff from paved surfaces, shade or lack of it, can all affect how a native plant performs in a landscape. Native plants are not maintenance-free, especially new plantings. A soil test will help you identify any problem areas where topsoils were removed. Leaving fallen leaves as natural mulch will help supply slow-release nutrients to your native plants. New plants require water to establish and, depending on the location, may need supplemental irrigation through hot dry periods.

4. Can I just dig up plants or collect seeds I find in the wild?

Harvesting plants from the wild can diminish natural populations, reducing diversity and putting pressure on other organisms that rely on the plants. Removing a plant from a natural environment leaves a void that is often filled with a weedy plant or invasive. Plants harvested from the wild often die after transplanting, or they perform poorly. The easiest way to have a successful native garden is to identify and preserve native plants that appear in your landscape, or purchase native plants propagated from local cuttings or seed. In addition, the NC Plant Protection and Conservation Act, administered through the Plant Conservation Program in the NC Department of Agriculture & Consumer Services, identifies legally protected plants that may not be harvested in the wild. Instead of trying to transplant a wild plant, purchase one and support nurseries propagating native plants from cuttings or seed. The USDA Forest Service does offer limited collection permits for wildflowers. Costs and stipulations vary by region and time of year.

5. My neighbor's yard looks like a weed patch. He says the plants are native plants. Will they always look this way?

Native plant landscapes can range from formal, highly structured plantings to more natural, low-care designs. Converting a yard from turfgrass to a naturalized native garden can take several years, and some stages may appearweedier than others. Your neighbor needs to ensure the planting consists of native plants rather than invasives. Along with providing many ecological benefits, established native gardens are a rich source of colors and textures and can be quite beautiful. Incorporating design elements such as pathways, benches, fencing, or other decorative features into naturalized landscapes can provide structure and communicate that the yard is being maintained.

6. Are there any grasses native to North Carolina that can be cultivated for lawns?

While many native grasses make beautiful additions to NC landscapes, only carpetgrass (*Axonopus fissufolius*) tolerates frequent mowing and can be grown as a lawn grass. Carpetgrass is native to several counties in the coastal plain, where it grows in moist, open wooded areas. Carpetgrass is less wear, drought, and cold tolerant than popular nonnative warm season turfgrasses such as zoysia and bermuda. Described as coarse textured and greenish yellow in color, carpetgrass is mainly used for low maintenance areas that do not receive heavy traffic.

7. What percent of plants in a landscape should be native to the local ecoregion?

The ratio of native to nonnative plants necessary to sustain ecosystem services in residential landscapes has not been determined. Increasing the number and diversity of native plants in your landscape will increase its value to wildlife, but landscapes do not have to be 100% native to be ecologically functional. To design an aesthetically pleasing, sustainable landscape that benefits the local environment, select a diversity of plants suited to the site's growing conditions. Incorporate plants native to the region along with noninvasive plants from other regions where needed to fulfill the landscape design purpose.

8. Why are some native plants not available from nurseries?

Traditional nurseries may not carry native plants that are difficult to propagate, are slow-growing, or are not well-adapted to nursery production systems. Some nurseries, however, specialize in native plants and carry native azaleas (*Rhododendron* spp.) and spring ephemerals such as trillium (*Trillium* spp.). While it is possible to include slow growers in landscapes, they are expensive and may be hard to find. Other native plants are not offered due to low demand or because they do not perform well in landscape settings.

9. Are native plants pest free?

Native plants can have serious pest and disease issues, especially from introduced pests to which they have no resistance. Examples include the emerald ash borer, a fatal pest of ash trees (*Fraxinus* sp.), and Dutch elm disease, a fungal disease that has decimated American elm (*Ulmus americana*) populations. Other introduced pests, such as Japanese beetles, can cause cosmetic damage to native plants, but rarely threaten the long-term health of established plantings.

Native insects can also become pests in unnatural conditions where the insects are not kept in check by predators and parasites. Gloomy scale on red maple (*A. rubrum*) is one example. In forests, gloomy scale occurs on red maples, but the pest's populations remain low. In parking lots where the red maple is often planted, there are few natural scale predators or parasites. Reflected heat boosts the pests' reproduction rate on already stressed trees, leading to their decline and death. Gloomy scale is such a serious problem on red maple trees in urban areas that these trees are not recommended for sites surrounded by impervious surfaces (Figure 12–19).

Figure 12–19. Gloomy scale (*Melanaspis tenebricosa*) on a maple.
Matt Bertone

10. Are native plants deer resistant?

Native plants are not necessarily deer resistant. As with all plants, deer prefer to browse some native plants while they leave others alone. In areas where deer populations are high, some native plants that are frequently browsed include phlox (*Phlox* spp.), strawberry bush (*Euonymus americanus*), and Virginia sweetspire (*Itea virginica*). Unless they are very hungry, deer tend to avoid green and gold (*Chrysogonum virginianum*), blue star (*Amsonia tabernaemontana*), inkberry (*Ilex glabra*), and buckeyes (*Aesculus* spp.). Deer damage is more likely to occur in urban and suburban areas where natural habitat is limited and there are few predators to balance deer populations.

12

Further Reading

Armitage, Allan M. *Armitage's Native Plants for North American Gardens*. Portland, Oregon: Timber Press, Inc., 2006. Print.

Beaubaire, Nancy, ed. *Native Perennials: North American Beauties*. Brooklyn, New York: Brooklyn Botanic Garden, 2001. Print.

Bir, Richard E. *Growing and Propagating Showy Native Woody Plants*. Chapel Hill, North Carolina: The University Of North Carolina Press, 1992. Print.

Burrell, C. Colston, ed. *Native Alternatives to Invasive Plants*. Brooklyn, New York: Brooklyn Botanic Garden, 2006. Print.

Burrell, C. Colston, ed. *Wildflower Gardens: 60 Spectacular Plants and How to Grow Them in Your Garden*. Brooklyn, New York: Brooklyn Botanic Garden, 2007. Print.

Cullina, William. *Native Ferns, Moss, and Grasses: From Emerald Carpet to Amber Wave, Serene and Sensuous Plants for the Garden*. New York: Houghton Mifflin Company, 2008. Print.

Darke, Rick. *The American Woodland Garden: Capturing the Spirit of the Deciduous Forest*. Portland, Oregon: Timber Press, Inc., 2002. Print.

Darke, Rick, and Doug Tallamy. *The Living Landscape*. Portland, Oregon: Timber Press, Inc., 2014. Print.

Druse, Ken. *The Natural Habitat Garden*. 1994. Portland, Oregon: Timber Press, Inc., 2004. Print.

Dunne, Niall, ed. *Great Natives for Tough Places*. Brooklyn, New York: Brooklyn Botanic Garden, 2009. Print.

Hightshoe, Gary L. *Native Trees, Shrubs, and Vines for Urban and Rural America: A Planting Design Manual for Environmental Designers*. Hoboken, New Jersey: John Wiley & Sons Inc., 1988. Print.

Jones Jr., Samuel B., and Leonard E. Foote. *Gardening with Native Wild Flowers*. 1990. Portland, Oregon: Timber Press, Inc., 2010. Print.

Mellichamp, Larry. *Native Plants of the Southeast: A Comprehensive Guide to the Best 460 Species for the Garden*. Portland, Oregon: Timber Press, Inc., 2014. Print.

Nelson, Gil. *Best Native Plants for Southern Gardens: A Handbook for Gardeners, Homeowners, and Professionals*. Gainesville, Florida: University Press Of Florida, 2010. Print.

Phillips, Harry R. *Growing and Propagating Wild Flowers*. Chapel Hill, North Carolina: The University of North Carolina Press, 1985. Print.

Schafale, Michael. *Guide to the Natural Communities of North Carolina, Fourth Approximation*. 2012. North Carolina Natural Heritage Program, Department of Environment and Natural Resources.

Stein, Sara. *Noah's Garden: Restoring the Ecology of Our Own Backyards*. 1993. New York: Houghton Mifflin Company, 1995. Print.

Sternberg, Guy, and Jim Wilson. *Native Trees for North American Landscapes*. Portland, Oregon: Timber Press, Inc., 2004. Print.

Summers, Carolyn. *Designing Gardens with Flora of the American East*. New Brunswick, New Jersey: Rutgers University Press, 2010. Print.

Tallamy, Douglas W. *Bringing Nature Home: How You Can Sustain Wildlife with Native Plants, Updated and Expanded*. 2007. Portland, Oregon: Timber Press, Inc., 2009. Print.

Wasowski, Sally. *Gardening with Native Plants of the South*. 1994. Lanham, Maryland: Taylor Trade Publishing, 2010. Print.

Wells, B. W. *The Natural Gardens of North Carolina, Revised Edition*. Chapel Hill, North Carolina: The University of North Carolina Press, 2002. Print.

Wilson, Jim. *Landscaping with Wildflowers: An Environmental Approach to Gardening*. New York: Houghton Mifflin Company, 1992. Print.

12-17

Native Plant Identification

Adkins, Leonard M. *Wildflowers of Blue Ridge and Great Smoky Mountains.* Birmingham, Alabama: Menasha Ridge Press, 2005. Print.

Alderman, J. Anthony. *Wildflowers of the Blue Ridge Parkway.* Chapel Hill, North Carolina: The University of North Carolina Press, 1997. Print.

Carman, Jack B. *Wildflowers of Tennessee.* Tullahoma, Tennessee: Highland Rim Press, 2001. Print.

Justice, William S., C. Ritchie Bell, and Anne H. Lindsey. *Wild Flowers of North Carolina.* 2nd ed. Chapel Hill, North Carolina: The University of North Carolina Press, 2005. Print.

Kirkman, Katherine, Claud L. Brown, and Donald J. Leopold. *Native Trees of the Southeast: An Identification Guide.* Portland, Oregon: Timber Press, Inc., 2007. Print.

Nelson, Gill. *Atlantic Coastal Plain Wildflowers.* Guilford, Connecticut: Falcon Guide, 2006. Print.

Porcher, Richard Dwight, and Douglas Alan Rayner. *A Guide to the Wildflowers of South Carolina.* Columbia, South Carolina: The University of South Carolina Press, 2001. Print.

Sorrie, Bruce A. *A Field Guide to the Wildflowers of the Sandhills Region.* Chapel Hill, North Carolina: The University of North Carolina Press, 2011. Print.

Spira, Timothy P. *Wildflowers and Plant Communities of the Southern Appalachian Mountains and Piedmont: A Naturalist's Guide to the Carolinas, Virginia, Tennessee, and Georgia.* Chapel Hill, North Carolina: The University of North Carolina Press, 2011. Print.

Weakley, Alan S. *Flora of the Southern and Mid-Atlantic States.* Chapel Hill, North Carolina: The University of North Carolina Press, 2012. PDF file.

For More Information

http://go.ncsu.edu/fmi_nativeplants

Contributors

Author:
Charlotte Glen, Extension Agent, Chatham County

Contributions by Extension Agents:
David Goforth

Contributions by Extension Master Gardener Volunteers:
Margaret Genkins, Deborah Green, Lee Kapleau, Karen Damari, Chris Alberti, Jackie Weedon

Content Editors:
Lucy Bradley, Professor and Extension Specialist, Urban Horticulture, NC State University; Director, NC State Extension Master Gardener program;
Kathleen Moore, Urban Horticulturist

Copy Editor:
Barbara Scott

Chapter 12 Cover Photo:
Charlotte Glen

How to Cite This Chapter:
Glen, C.D. 2022. Native Plants, Chpt 12. In: K.A. Moore, and. L.K. Bradley (eds). *North Carolina Extension Gardener Handbook*, 2nd ed. NC State Extension, Raleigh, NC. <https://content.ces.ncsu.edu/extension-gardener-handbook/12-native-plants>

Propagation

Objectives

This chapter teaches people to:
• Understand the basic principles of sexual and asexual propagation.
• Be familiar with common methods of sexually and asexually propagating plants.
• Know the recommended timing for propagating plants.

Introduction

Plant propagation is the process of producing a new plant from an existing one. It is both art and science requiring knowledge, skill, manual dexterity, and experience for success.

To understand the science of why, when, and how to propagate requires basic knowledge of plant growth and development, plant anatomy and morphology, and plant physiology.

There are two general types of propagation: **sexual** and **asexual**. **Sexual propagation** is the reproduction of plants by seeds. The genetic material of two parents is combined by pollination and fertilization to create offspring that are different from each parent. There are several advantages of sexual propagation:

- It may be quicker and more economical than asexual propagation.
- It may result in new cultivars and vigorous **hybrids.**
- For some plants, it may be the only means of propagation.
- It provides a way to avoid transmission of particular diseases, such as viruses.
- It maintains genetic variation, which increases the potential for plants to adapt to environmental pressures.

Asexual propagation, sometimes referred to as **vegetative propagation**, involves taking vegetative parts of a plant (stems, roots, and/or leaves) and causing them to regenerate into a new plant or, in some cases, several plants. With few exceptions, the resulting plant is genetically identical to the parent plant. The major types of asexual propagation are cuttings, layering, division, separation, grafting, budding, and micropropagation. Advantages of asexual propagation include:

- It may be easier and faster than sexual propagation for some species.
- It may be the only way to perpetuate particular cultivars.
- It maintains the juvenile or adult characteristics of certain cultivars.
- It allows propagation of special types of growth, such as weeping or pendulous forms.
- It may more quickly result in a large plant (compared to one propagated by seed).

A form of asexual reproduction in plants, in which multicellular structures become detached from the parent plant and develop into new individuals that are genetically identical to the parent plant.

Sexual Propagation

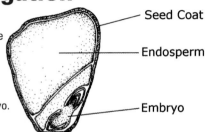

Figure 13–1. The three parts of a seed: (1) The protective tissue or seed coat; (2) the embryo, which grows into a new plant; and (3) the endosperm, which is the nutritive or food storage, supplying nutrients to the embryo.

Seed Coat

Endosperm

Embryo

Seeds

Most seeds are composed of three major parts: embryo, endosperm (food storage) tissue, a seed coat (protective tissue) (Figure 13–1). The embryo is a miniature plant in a resting (dormant) state. Most seeds contain a built-in food supply called the endosperm. The protective outer covering of a seed is called the **seed coat**. It protects seeds from mechanical injury and from diseases and insects. Also, the seed coat usually prevents water from entering the seed until time to germinate. The seed coat in many cases allows seeds to be stored for extended periods. The seed leaves, cotyledons, differ in shape from the true leaves. Monocots (such as corn) produce only one **cotyledon**; dicots (like beans) produce two cotyledons (Figure 13–2). Some gymnosperms, like pines, have many cotyledons.

Figure 13–2.
Seed germination of a dicot seedling.

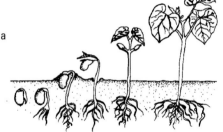

To obtain vigorous plants from seeds, start with high-quality seeds from a reliable source. Select cultivars that provide the desired size, color, and growth habit. Choose cultivars adapted to your area. Many vegetable and flower cultivars are hybrids that may cost more than open-pollinated types, but they usually have more vigor, more uniformity, and better growth than nonhybrids.

Purchase only enough seed for one year because the likelihood of germination decreases with age. The seed packet label usually indicates essential information about the cultivar or species, such as the year in which the seeds were packaged, the germination percentage, and whether the seeds have received any chemical treatment.

If seeds are obtained well ahead of the actual sowing date (or are surplus seeds), store them in a cool, dry place. Laminated or foil packages help ensure dry storage. Paper packets are best kept in tightly sealed containers and maintained around 40°F in low humidity. A good storage location would be an airtight jar in the refrigerator. Gardeners can save money and cultivate a

Table 13–1. Germination Information for Selected Plants.

Plant	Approximate Time to Sow Before Last Frost (weeks)	Time Seeds Take to Germinate (days)	Temperature (°F)	Light/Dark Requirement
Ageratum	8	5–10	70	Light
Alyssum	8	5–10	70	Either
Aster	6	5–10	70	Either
Balsam	6	5–10	70	Either
Begonia	12 or more	10–15	70	Light
Broccoli	8	5–10	70	Either
Browallia	12 or more	15–20	70	Light
Cabbage	8	5–10	70	Either
Cauliflower	8	5–10	70	Either
Celosia	8	5–10	70	Either
Centaurea	6	5–10	65	Dark
Coleus	8	5–10	65	Light
Cosmos	4 or less	5–10	70	Either
Cucumber	4 or less	5–10	85	Either
Dahlia	8	5–10	70	Either
Dianthus	10	5–10	70	Either
Eggplant	8	5–10	70	Either
Geranium	12 or more	10–20	70	Light
Impatiens	10	15–20	70	Light
Larkspur	12 or more	5–10	55	Dark
Lettuce	8	5–10	70	Light
Marigold	6	5–10	70	Either
Muskmelon	4 or less	5–10	85	Either
Nicotiana	8	10–15	70	Light
Pansy (Viola)	12 or more	5–10	65	Dark
Pepper	8	5–10	80	Either
Petunia	10	5–10	70	Light
Phlox	8	5–10	65	Dark
Portulaca	10	5–10	70	Dark
Snapdragon	10	5–10	65	Light
Squash	4 or less	5–10	85	Either
Tomato	6	5–10	80	Either
Verbena	10	15–20	65	Dark
Vinca	12 or more	10–15	70	Either
Watermelon	4 or less	5–10	85	Either
Zinnia	6	5–10	70	Either

13

rewarding hobby by saving seeds from plants in their own gardens. Seeds that have been produced through insect, animal or wind, or other natural pollination methods are known as open-pollinated. Open-pollination can increase biodiversity, and plants may display different characteristics than the parent plants. This is especially true when saving seed from hybrids.

Germination

Germination is the resumption of active embryo growth after a dormant period. Three conditions must be satisfied for a seed to germinate:

- The seed must be viable; that is, the embryo must be alive and capable of germination.
- Internal conditions of the seed must be favorable for germination; that is, any physical, chemical, or physiological barriers to germination must have disappeared or must have been removed by the propagator.
- The seed must be subjected to appropriate environmental conditions, including water (moisture), proper temperature, oxygen, and, for some species, light (Table 13-1).

The first step in germination is absorption of water. An adequate, continuous supply of moisture is important to ensure germination. Once germination has begun, a dry period can kill the embryo.

Light can stimulate or inhibit seed germination of some species. Plants that require light for germination include ageratum, begonia, browallia, impatiens, lettuce, and petunia. Other plants germinate best in the dark. These include calendula, centaurea, phlox, and verbena. Some plants germinate in either light or dark. Seed catalogs and seed packets often list germination and cultural information for particular plants. When sowing light-requiring seeds, sow them on the soil surface. Supplemental light can be provided by fluorescent fixtures suspended 6 to 12 inches above the soil surface for 16 hours a day.

Respiration in dormant seeds is low, but they do require some oxygen. Respiration rate increases during germination. The medium in which the seeds are sown should be loose and well aerated. If the oxygen supply during germination is limited or reduced, germination can be severely retarded or inhibited.

Temperature affects the germination percentage and the rate (speed) of germination. Some seeds germinate over a wide range of temperatures; others have a narrow range. Many species have minimum, maximum, and optimum temperatures at which they germinate. For example, tomato seeds have a minimum germination of 50°F, a maximum of 95°F, and an optimum germination temperature of 80°F. When germination temperatures are listed, they are

usually optimum temperatures. For most plants, 65 to 75°F is best.

Seed Dormancy

Viable seeds that do not germinate are dormant. Dormancy can be regulated by the environment or by the seed itself. If a seed is not exposed to sufficient moisture, proper temperature, oxygen, or for some species, light, the seed will not germinate. In this case, the seed's dormancy is caused by unfavorable environmental conditions.

Some seeds may not germinate because of some inhibitory factor of the seed itself. This kind of dormancy consists of two general types: (a) seed coat (or external) dormancy and (b) internal (endogenous) dormancy. A seed can also exhibit both kinds of dormancy.

Techniques to Break Dormancy

Seed Scarification

External dormancy results when a seed's hard seed coat is impervious to water and gases. The seed will not germinate until the seed coat is altered physically. Any process of breaking, scratching, or mechanically altering the seed coat to make it permeable to water and gases is known as scarification. In nature this may occur during the winter, when freezing temperatures crack the seed coat or while microbial activities modify the seed coat as the seed lies in the soil. Scarification may also occur as the seed passes through the digestive tract of an animal.

Scarification can be forced, rather than waiting for nature to alter the seed coats. Commercial growers scarify seeds by soaking them in concentrated sulfuric acid. Seeds are placed in a glass container, covered with sulfuric acid, gently stirred, and allowed to soak for 10 minutes to several hours, depending on the species.

Reference books give appropriate concentrations and durations. When the seed coat has been modified (thinned), the seeds are removed, washed, and sown. Sulfuric acid can, however, be very dangerous for an inexperienced individual and should be used with extreme caution. Vinegar is safer and can be used for some species; the technique is the same as with sulfuric acid.

With mechanical scarification, seeds are filed with a metal file, rubbed with sandpaper, or cracked gently with a hammer to weaken (break) the seed coat. Another method is hot water scarification. Bring water to a boil (212°F), remove the pot from the stove, and place the seeds into the water. Soak the seeds until the water cools; then remove them and let them dry.

Seed Stratification

The second type of imposed dormancy, internal dormancy, is regulated by the inner seed tissues. This dormancy prevents seeds of many species from germinating when environmental conditions are not favorable for survival of the seedlings. There are several different types of internal dormancy. "Shallow" dormancy, displayed by many vegetable seeds, simply disappears with dry storage. No special treatment is necessary. However, other types require a particular duration of moist-chilling or moist-warming periods, or both.

Cold stratification (moist-chilling) involves mixing seeds with an equal volume of a moist medium (sand or peat, for example) in a closed container and storing them in a refrigerator. Periodically, check to see that the medium is moist but not wet. The length of time required to break (remove) dormancy varies by species; check reference books for recommended times. This type of dormancy may be satisfied naturally if seeds are sown outdoors in the fall. Warm stratification is similar except temperatures are maintained at 68 to 86°F depending on the species.

Seeds of some species exhibit double dormancy. This is a combination of two types of dormancy, such as external and internal dormancy. To achieve germination with seeds having both external and internal dormancy, the seeds must first be scarified and then stratified for the appropriate length of time. If the treatments are administered in reverse order, the seeds will not germinate. After completing these treatments, plant the seeds under the proper environmental conditions for germination.

Growing Plants from Seeds

Media

A wide range of media can be used to germinate seeds. With experience, you will learn to determine what works best for you. The germinating medium should be fine and uniform yet well aerated and loose. It should be free of insects, disease organisms, nematodes, weeds, and weed seeds. It should also be of low fertility and capable of holding moisture but be well drained. Purchase commercial potting media containing fine-particle pine bark, sphagnum peat moss, and perlite, or prepare a combination of equal parts (by volume) of these materials. Do not use garden (mineral) soil to start seedlings; it is not sterile, it is too heavy, and it does not drain well. Soil mixes have little fertility, so seedlings must be watered with a dilute fertilizer solution soon after germination and emergence.

Containers

Plastic cell packs can be purchased or reused if sterilized. In this system, each cell holds a single plant. This method reduces the risk of root injury when transplanting. Peat pellets, peat pots, or expanded foam cubes can also be used for producing seedlings. Resourceful gardeners often use cottage cheese containers, the bottoms of milk cartons, bleach containers, or pie pans. Just make certain that adequate drainage holes are made in the bottoms of the containers and that the containers are sterile.

Sterilizing Containers

The importance of using sterile medium and containers cannot be overemphasized. Before using the containers, wash them to remove any debris, immerse them in a fresh solution of one part chlorine bleach to nine parts water for five minutes, and allow them to dry.

Sowing Seeds

Seedlings are often started indoors 4 to 12 weeks before the last spring frost (Table 13–1). A common mistake is to sow the seeds too early and then attempt to hold the seedlings under poor environmental conditions. This usually results in tall, weak, spindly plants that do not perform well in the garden. The following paragraphs give general guidelines for sowing seeds for transplants. Nevertheless, it is important to refer to the instructions on the seed packet for more specific information.

When sowing seeds, fill the container to within 3⁄4-inch of the top with moistened growing medium. For very small seeds, use a fine, screened medium such as a layer of fine vermiculite for the top 1⁄4-inch. Firm the medium at the corners and edges with your fingers or a block of wood to provide a smooth and level surface.

For medium and large seeds, make furrows 1 to 2 inches apart and 1⁄8-inch to 1⁄4-inch deep across the surface of the planting medium. Sowing in rows improves light and air movement. If **damping-off** (read more in chapter 5, "Diseases and Disorders") disease occurs, there is less chance of it spreading. Seedlings in rows are easier to label and handle at transplanting time than those that have resulted from broadcasting seeds. Sow the seeds thinly and uniformly in the rows by gently tapping the packet of seed. Cover the seeds lightly; a suitable planting depth is usually about two to four times the minimum diameter of the seeds.

Extremely fine seeds such as carrot, petunia, and snapdragon should not be covered, but simply dusted on the surface of the germinating medium and watered with a fine mist. If these seeds are broadcast, strive for a uniform stand by sowing half the seeds in one direction, then sowing the remaining seeds in the other direction.

Large seeds are frequently sown directly in a small container or cell pack, which eliminates the need for early transplanting. Usually, sow two or three seeds per cell. Later, thin them to allow only the most vigorous seedling per cell to grow.

Most garden stores and seed catalogs offer indoor and outdoor seed tapes. Seed tapes have precisely spaced seeds enclosed in an organic, water-soluble material. When planted, the tape dissolves and the seeds germinate normally. Seed tapes are convenient for extremely small, hard-to-handle seeds. Seed tapes allow uniform emergence, eliminate overcrowding, and permit sowing in perfectly straight rows. The tapes can be cut at any point for multiple row plantings, and thinning is rarely necessary. Tapes are more expensive per seed.

Water and Light

Moisten the planting medium thoroughly before planting. After seeding, spray with a fine mist or place the containers in a pan or tray that contains about 1 inch of warm water. Avoid splashing or excessive flooding, which might displace small seeds. When the planting mix is saturated, set the container aside to drain. The soil should be moist but not overly wet.

The seed flats should remain sufficiently moist during the germination period. Excessive moisture, however, can lead to damping-off or other disease or insect problems. Place the whole flat or pot into a clear plastic bag to maintain moisture. The plastic should be at least 1 inch above the soil. Keep the container out of direct sunlight; otherwise, the temperature may increase and injure the seeds. Many home gardeners cover their flats with panes of glass instead of using a plastic bag. Be sure to remove the plastic bag or glass cover when the first seedlings emerge.

After the seeds have germinated, move the flats to a well-lighted location; the temperature should be 65 to 70°F during the day and 55°F to 60°F at night. This prevents soft, leggy growth and minimizes disease problems. Some crops, of course, may grow best at different temperatures.

Seedlings must receive bright light after germination. Place them in a south-facing window. If a large, bright location is not available, place the seedlings under fluorescent lights. Use two 40-watt, cool-white fluorescent tubes or special plant growth lamps. Position the plants 6 inches below the light source and provide 16 hours of light daily. As the seedlings grow, the lights should be raised. A more detailed discussion of lighting is covered in chapter 18, "Plants Grown in Containers."

Transplanting Seedlings

Plants not seeded individually must eventually be transplanted into their own containers as seedlings to give them proper growing space. A common mistake is to leave the seedlings in the flat too long. The ideal time to transplant young seedlings is when the first true leaves appear.

Dig up the small plants carefully with a knife or plant label. Let the group of seedlings fall apart and pick out individual plants. Gently ease them apart to avoid root injury in the process. Handle small seedlings by their leaves, not their delicate stems (Figure 13–3). Using a small tool or your finger, punch a hole in the medium. Plant a seedling at the same depth at which it was growing in the seed flat.

Examples of Seed Treatments

Camellia—Collect and plant in the fall before the seed coat hardens. If seeds are dry, soak them in warm water for 24 hours before planting. Some people pre-chill the seeds until **radicle** emergence and then plant the sprouted seeds.

Crabapple—Collect fruits as they begin to soften and when the seeds are brown. Remove the fruit pulp. Provide one to four months of cold-moist stratification. Seeds will germinate in 30 to 60 days.

Dogwood—Collect fruits (drupes) when they are red and when seeds are mature; if collection is delayed too long, birds may eat the fruit. Remove the pulp, clean, and air dry, then moist-chill them in a refrigerator for three to four months. Seeds can be planted in the fall, but they will not germinate until spring.

Goldenrain tree—Collect fruits when capsules turn brown but before they open. Extract seeds, dry, and store. Seed coats are very hard, and seeds will require scarification before germination.

Holly—Germinating holly seeds can be very difficult and extremely slow. It may take two to three years because of the holly's hard seed coat and an immature (rudimentary) embryo.

Maple—Variation in dormancy exists with different species of maples. Spring-maturing seeds of species such as red and silver maple should be collected immediately when mature, not permitted to dry, and sown immediately. For seeds of other maple species that mature in the fall, such as southern sugar maple, stratification for 90 to 120 days is necessary.

Oak—Acorns of white oak do not become dormant. When planted in the fall, roots will emerge during winter; shoots will emerge in the spring. On the other hand, acorns of black oak germinate best if stratified for one to three months (if not planted in the fall). Acorns of red oaks should be planted in the fall or stratified for one to three months. Check references for individual species.

Redbud—Germination is inhibited by an impermeable seed coat and embryo dormancy. Soak for 30 minutes in concentrated sulfuric acid or vinegar, and then follow up with three months of cold stratification.

Southern magnolia—Remove the fleshy pulp from around the seeds. Moist pre-chilling for two to four months is needed unless planted in the fall.

Firm the soil and water gently. Keep newly transplanted seedlings in the shade for a few days, or place them under fluorescent lights. Locate them away from sources of direct heat. Continue watering and fertilizing as in the seed flats.

Containers for seedlings should be economical, durable, and make efficient use of available space. Individual pots or plastic cell packs can be used. Another possibility is compressed peat pellets, which expand to form compact individual pots when soaked in water.

Figure 13–3. Remove seedlings from the tray and place them in a pile. Tease individuals out gently holding them by their leaves.

They waste no space, do not fall apart as easily as peat pots, and can be set out directly in the garden. If you wish to avoid transplanting seedlings altogether, compressed peat pellets are excellent for direct sowing.

When setting plants outdoors that were grown in peat pots, be sure to break the sides of the pot and to cover the pot completely. If the top edge of the peat pot extends above the soil level, it may act as a wick and draw water away from the soil in the pot. Tear off the top lip of the pot and plant flush with the soil surface.

Asexual Propagation Cuttings

Asexual propagation is the process of taking vegetative pieces of a desirable plant and reproducing new plants from these tissues. Asexual propagation permits cloning of plants, meaning the resulting plants are genetically identical to the parent plant. The major methods of asexual propagation are cuttings, layering, division, separation, budding, grafting, and micropropagation (tissue culture).

CUTTINGS

Propagation by cuttings involves rooting a severed piece of the parent plant or, in some cases, producing new plants from severed pieces of tissue (leaf cuttings). A greenhouse is not necessary for successful propagation by cuttings.

If rooting only a few cuttings, you can use a flowerpot or small flat (Figure 13–4). Maintain high humidity by covering the cuttings with a bottomless milk jug or by placing the pot into a clear plastic bag. Cuttings can also be placed in plastic trays covered with clear plastic stretched over a wire frame.

Containers must have holes in the bottoms for drainage. The plastic helps keep the humidity high and reduces water loss from the plant. If a more elaborate structure is needed, construct a small hoop frame or use an intermittent mist system. NC State Extension publication AG-426, *A Small Backyard Greenhouse for the Home Gardener*, may be helpful.

The rooting medium should be sterile, low in fertility, well drained to provide sufficient aeration, and moisture-retentive so that watering does not have to be done too frequently. Materials commonly used are coarse sand, a mixture of one part peat and one or two parts perlite (by volume), or one part peat and one part sand (by volume). Various commercial potting media may also be used. Vermiculite by itself is not recommended because it packs and tends to hold too much moisture. Media should be watered well before use.

There are several different kinds of cuttings. Which type you use depends on the kind of plant and, often, the plant's growth stage.

Some plants can be propagated from only a leaf, but most plants produce only a few roots or simply decay. Because leaf cuttings do not include an **axillary bud**, they can be used only for plants that are capable of forming adventitious buds. Leaf cuttings are used almost exclusively for propagating some indoor plants.

Figure 13–4. A small flat can be used to start cuttings.
Chris Alberti, CC BY - 2.0

Leaf Cuttings
Leaf petiole—Remove a leaf and include up to 1½-inches of the petiole. Insert the lower end of the petiole into the medium (Figure 13–5). One or more new plants form at the base of the petiole. The leaf may be severed from the new plants—when they have their own roots—and then reused. Examples of plants that can be propagated by this method include African violet, peperomia, episcia, hoya, and sedum.

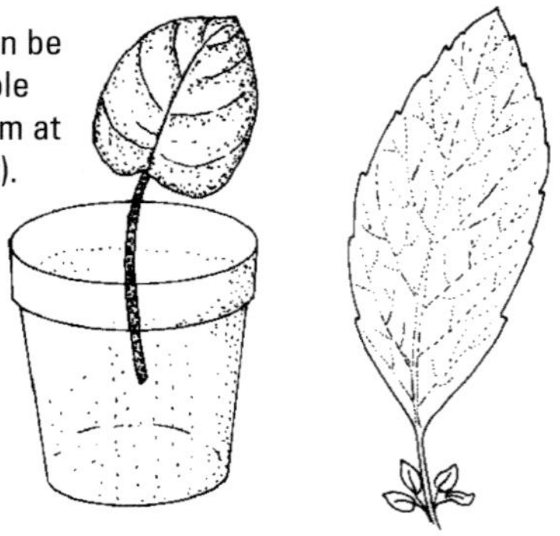

Figure 13–5. Some plants can be propagated from a leaf petiole cutting (left). New plants form at the base of the petiole (right).

Leaf without a petiole—This method is used for plants with thick, fleshy leaves. The snake plant (*Sansevieria trifasciata*), a monocot, can be propagated by cutting the long leaves into 3-inch to 4-inch pieces (Figure 13–6). Insert the cuttings vertically into the medium. African violets (dicot) can also be propagated this way. Cut a leaf from a plant and remove the petiole. Insert the leaf vertically into the medium, making sure that the midvein is buried in the rooting medium. New plants form from the midvein.

Figure 13–6. *Sanseviera trifasciata* (snake plant) leaves that were cut and placed in rooting medium.
Chris Alberti, CC BY-2.0

Split-vein—Detach a leaf from the plant and remove the petiole. Make cuts on several prominent veins on the underside of the leaf (Figure 13–7). Lay the cutting, lower side down, on the medium. New plants form at each cut. If the leaf curls up, hold it in place by covering the margins with rooting medium. A variation of this method is to cut the leaf into wedges so that each piece has a main vein.

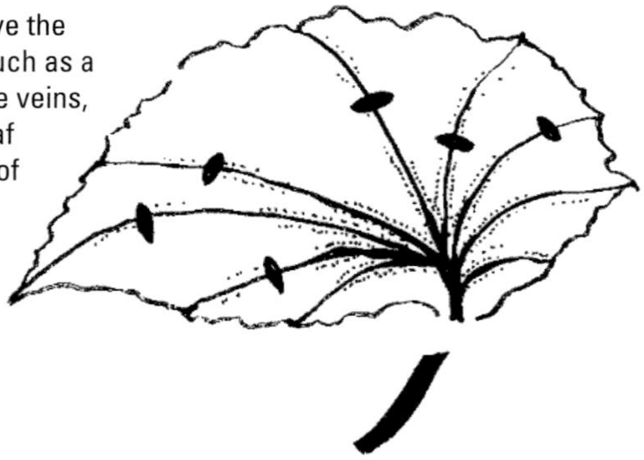

Figure 13–7. Remove the petiole of a plant such as a rex begonia, cut the veins, and then lay the leaf flat on the surface of the media.
Renee Lampila

Leaf-Bud Cuttings

Leaf-bud cuttings are used for many trailing vines and when space or cutting material is limited. Each node on a stem can be treated as a cutting. The cutting consists of a leaf blade, **petiole**, and a short piece of stem with an attached **axillary bud**. Place cuttings in the medium with the bud covered (to 1 inch) and the leaf exposed (Figure 13–8). A modified version of a leaf-bud cutting, referred to as a single node cutting, can be prepared simply by cutting the stem below and above the leaf petiole having a well-developed axillary bud. Examples of plants propagated this way include blackberry, camellia, clematis, devil's ivy, dracaena, grape ivy, heart-leaf philodendron, jade plant, mahonia, rhododendron, and rubber plant.

Figure 13–8. Many plants can be propagated by leaf-bud cuttings.
Renee Lampila

Cane Cuttings

A cane cutting is an easy way to propagate some overgrown, leggy houseplants such as dumbcane, corn plant, Chinese evergreen, and other plants with thick stems. Leafless stem sections (2 to 3 inches long) are cut from older stems. Each cane should contain one or two nodes (Figure 13–9). Lay the cutting horizontally on the medium, or insert it vertically with about half of the cutting below the surface of the medium, and leave a bud facing upward. Cane cuttings are usually potted when roots and new shoots appear.

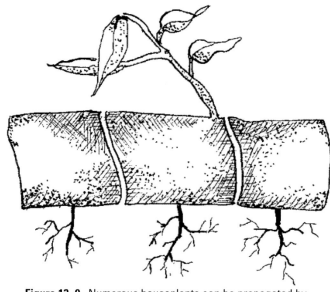

Figure 13–9. Numerous houseplants can be propagated by cane cuttings.
Renee Lampila

Stem Cuttings

Propagation by stem cuttings is the most commonly used method for many woody ornamental plants. Typically, stem cuttings of tree species are more difficult to root successfully; however, cuttings from trees such as crape myrtles, some elms, and birches can be rooted.

Types of Stem Cuttings

The four main types of stem cuttings are herbaceous, softwood, semi-hardwood, and hardwood. These terms reflect the growth stage of the stock plant, which is one of the most important factors influencing whether cuttings produce roots. Calendar dates are useful only as guidelines. Refer to Table 13–2 for more information on optimum growth stages for rooting stem cuttings of various woody ornamentals.

Herbaceous cuttings are made from nonwoody, herbaceous plants such as coleus, chrysanthemums, and dahlia. A 3-inch to 5-inch piece of stem is cut from the parent plant. The leaves on the lower one-third to one-half of the stem are removed, and the cutting is placed in the rooting medium. A high percentage of the cuttings root, and they do so quickly.

Softwood cuttings are prepared from soft, succulent, new growth of woody plants, just as it begins to harden (mature). Shoots are suitable for making softwood cuttings when they can be snapped easily when bent and when they still have a gradation of leaf size (oldest leaves are mature whereas newest leaves are still small). For most woody plants this stage occurs in May, June, or July. The soft shoots are quite tender, and extra care must be taken to keep them from drying out. The extra effort pays off, though, because they root quickly.

Semi-hardwood cuttings are usually prepared from partially mature wood of the current season's growth, just after a flush of growth. This type of cutting normally is made from mid-July to early fall. The wood is reasonably firm and the leaves of mature size. Many broadleaf evergreen shrubs and some conifers are propagated by this method.

Hardwood cuttings are taken from dormant mature stems in late fall, winter, or early spring. Plants are generally fully dormant with no obvious signs of active growth. The wood is firm and does not bend easily. Hardwood cuttings are most often used for deciduous shrubs but can be used for many evergreens. Examples of plants propagated at the hardwood stage include fig, forsythia, grape, privet, and spirea. The three types of hardwood cuttings are straight, heel, and mallet (Figure 13–10). A straight cutting is the most commonly used stem cutting. For the heel cutting, a small section of older wood is included at the base of the cutting. For the mallet cutting, an entire section of older stem wood is included.

13

Propagating Ferns by Spores

Although ferns are propagated more easily by division, some gardeners like the challenge of raising ferns from spores. Spores are the fern's means of sexual propagation, equivalent to seeds. The following is one proven method for germinating small quantities of spores.

Place a solid, sterilized brick in a pan, add water to cover the brick, and bake at 250°F for 30 minutes. When the brick is wet throughout, remove it from the water and place a thin layer of moist soil and peat (1:1 by volume) on top of the brick. Dust spores on the medium. Cover with plastic (not touching the spores) and place the brick in a warm place with indirect light. It may take up to a month for the spores to germinate. Keep moist at all times.

A small, heart-shaped structure, about 1/8-inch across (called a prothallus) develops first from each spore, forming a light green mat. Mist lightly to maintain high surface moisture because sperm must be able to swim to the archegonia (female organ). After about three weeks, fertilization should have occurred.

About two months later, pull the mat apart with tweezers in 1/4-inch squares and space them 1/2-inch apart in a flat containing a 2-inch bottom layer of sand, a 1/4-inch layer of charcoal, and a top 2-inch layer of a mixture of potting soil and peat (1:1 by volume). Cover with plastic and keep moist. When fronds (fern "leaves") appear, transplant to small pots. Reduce humidity gradually until plants can survive in less humid conditions. Light exposure may be increased at this time.

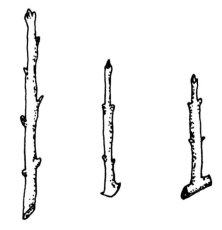

Figure 13–10. The three types of hardwood cuttings are straight, heel, and mallet.

Table 13–2. Optimum Stage(s) of Tissue (Wood) Maturity for Rooting Stem Cuttings of Selected Evergreen Woody Ornamentals.

Common Name	Scientific Name	Type of Cutting[a]
Abelia	*Abelia* spp.	SW, SH, HW
Arborvitae, American; Northern white-cedar	*Thuja occidentalis*	SH, HW
Arborvitae, Oriental	*Platycladus orientalis*	SW
Azalea (evergreen & semi-evergreen)	*Rhododendron* spp.	SH
Barberry, Japanese[b]	*Berberis thunbergii*	SH, HW
Barberry, Mentor	*Berberis x mentorensis*	SH
Barberry, Wintergreen	*Berberis julianae*	HW
Bayberry; Wax myrtle	*Myrica* spp.	SW
Boxwood, Common	*Buxus sempervirens*	SH, HW
Boxwood, Littleleaf	*Buxus microphylla*	SH, HW
Camellia	*Camellia* spp.	SH, HW
Ceanothus	*Ceanothus* spp.	SW, SH
Cedar	*Cedrus* spp.	SH, HW
Cedar, Eastern red	*Juniperus virginiana*	HW
Cotoneaster	*Cotoneaster* spp.	SW, SH
Cryptomeria, Japanese	*Cryptomeria japonica*	SW, SH, HW
Cypress, False	*Chamaecyparis* spp.	SH, HW
Cypress, Leyland	x *Cupressocyparis leylandii*	SW, HW
Daphne	*Daphne* spp.	SH
Eleagnus, Thorny; Silverthorn	*Elaeagnus pungens*	SH, HW
Euonymus[b]	*Euonymus* spp.	SH
Fir	*Abies* spp.	SW, HW
Gardenia, Cape jasmine	*Gardenia jasminoides*	SH, HW
Heath	*Erica* spp.	SW, SH, HW
Heather, Scotch	*Calluna vulgaris*	SH, HW
Hemlock	*Tsuga* spp.	SW, HW
Holly, American	*Ilex opaca*	SH, HW
Holly, Chinese	*Ilex cornuta*	SH, HW
Holly, English	*Ilex aquifolium*	SH, HW
Holly, Foster's	*Ilex x attenuata* 'Fosteri'	SH, HW
Holly, Japanese	*Ilex crenata*	SH, HW
Holly, Yaupon	*Ilex vomitoria*	SH
Ivy, English[b]	*Hedera helix*	SH, HW
Jasmine	*Jasminum* spp.	SW, SH, HW
Juniper, Chinese	*Juniperus chinensis*	SH, HW
Juniper, Creeping	*Juniperus horizontalis*	SH, HW
Juniper, Shore	*Juniperus conferta*	SH, HW
Loropetalum	*Loropetalum* spp.	SW
Magnolia	*Magnolia* spp.	SW, SH
Mahonia[b]	*Mahonia* spp.	SH, HW

(*Continued*)

Table 13–2. continued

Common Name	Scientific Name	Type of Cutting[a]
Oleander	*Nerium oleander*	SH
Osmanthus, Holly; False holly	*Osmanthus heterophyllus*	SH, HW
Photinia	*Photinia* spp.	SH, HW
Pieris, Japanese; Japanese Andromeda	*Pieris japonica*	SW, SH
Pine	*Pinus* spp.	SW, HW
Pine, Mugo	*Pinus mugo*	SH
Pittosporum	*Pittosporum* spp.	SH
Podocarpus	*Podocarpus* spp.	SH
Privet [b]	*Ligustrum* spp.	SW, SH, HW
Pyracantha; Firethorn	*Pyracantha* spp.	SH
Rhododendron	*Rhododendron* spp.	SH, HW
Spruce	*Picea* spp.	SW, HW
Viburnum	*Viburnum* spp.	SW, HW
Yew	*Taxus* spp.	SH, HW

[a] SW = softwood, SH = semi-hardwood, HW = hardwood

[b] Plants considered moderately weedy in the eastern United States. Unless working with either a sterile or demonstrated functionally sterile cultivar, use care when distributing.

- Barberry, Japanese *Berberis thunbergii*
- Ivy, English *Hedera helix*
- Privet, Chinese *Ligustrum sinense*
- Euonymus Burning Bush *Euonymus alatus*
- Mahonia, Leatherleaf *Mahonia bealei*
- Privet, Japanese *Ligustrum japonicum*

Figure 13–11. A stem cutting is prepared for rooting by removing the leaves from the lower one-third to one-half of the cutting; large leaves should be cut in half perpendicular to the midvein.

Procedures for Rooting Woody Stem Cuttings

Cuttings should generally consist of the current or past season's growth. Avoid material with flower buds. Remove any flowers and flower buds when preparing cuttings so the cuttings' energy can be used in producing new roots rather than flowers. Take cuttings from healthy, disease-free plants.

The fertility status of the stock (parent) plant can influence rooting. Avoid taking cuttings from plants that show symptoms of nutrient deficiency. Conversely, plants that have been fertilized heavily, particularly with nitrogen, also may not root well. The stock plant should not be under water stress. In general, cuttings taken from young plants root quicker than cuttings taken from older, more mature plants. Cuttings from lateral shoots often root better than cuttings from terminal shoots.

Early morning is the best time to take cuttings because the plant is fully **turgid.** It is important to keep the cuttings cool and moist until they are stuck. An ice chest or a dark plastic bag with wet paper towels may be used to store cuttings. If there will be a delay in sticking cuttings, store them in a plastic bag in a refrigerator.

While terminal bud ends of the stem are best, a long shoot can be divided into several cuttings. Cuttings are generally 4 to 6 inches long. Use a sharp, thinbladed pocketknife or sharp pruning shears. Dip the cutting tool in rubbing alcohol or a mixture of one part bleach to nine parts water to prevent transmitting diseases from infected plant parts to healthy ones.

Remove the leaves on the lower one-third to one-half of the cutting (Figure 13–11). On large-leafed plants, the remaining leaves may be cut in half perpendicular to the midvein to reduce moisture loss and conserve space in the rooting area.

During preparation of stem cuttings of particular woody species, the lower portion of the stem that is inserted into

Table 13–3. Optimum Stage(s) of Tissue (Wood) Maturity for Rooting Stem Cuttings of Selected Deciduous Woody Ornamentals.

Common Name	Scientific Name	Type of Cutting[a]
Azalea (deciduous)	*Rhododendron* spp.	SW
Basswood, American, American linden	*Tilia americana*	SW, SH
Beautyberry	*Callicarpa* spp.	SW
Birch	*Betula* spp.	SW
Bittersweet [c]	*Celastrus* spp.	SW, SH, HW
Blueberry	*Vaccinium* spp.	SW, HW
Broom	*Cytisus* spp.	SW, HW
Catalpa	*Catalpa* spp.	SW, HW
Cherry, Flowering	*Prunus* spp.	SW, SH
Clematis	*Clematis* spp.	SW, SH
Crabapple	*Malus* spp.	SW, SH
Crapemyrtle, Crape Myrtle	*Lagerstroemia indica*	SW, HW
Deutzia	*Deutzia* spp.	SW, HW
Dogwood	Cornus spp.	SW, SH
Elderberry	*Sambucus* spp.	SW
Elm	*Ulmus* spp.	SW
Euonymus	*Euonymus* spp.	SH, HW
Forsythia	*Forsythia* spp.	SW, SH, HW
Fringe tree; Fringetree	*Chionanthus* spp.	SW
Ginkgo; Maidenhair tree	*Ginkgo biloba*	SW
Goldenrain tree	*Koelreuteria* spp.	SW
Hibiscus, Chinese	*Hibiscus rosa-sinensis*	SW, SH, HW
Honeylocust; Honey locust	*Gleditsia triacanthos*	HW
Honeysuckle [c]	*Lonicera* spp.	SW, SH, HW
Hydrangea	*Hydrangea* spp.	SW, SH, HW
Ivy, Boston	*Parthenocissus tricuspidata*	SW, HW
Larch	*Larix* spp.	SW, HW
Lilac	*Syringa* spp.	SW
Maple	*Acer* spp.	SW, SH
Mock orange	*Philadelphus* spp.	SW, HW
Mulberry	*Morus* spp.	SW, SH, HW
Pear, Callery [b]	*Pyrus calleryana*	SH
Poplar, Aspen, Cottonwood	*Populus* spp.	SW, HW
Poplar, Yellow; Tulip poplar	*Liriodendron tulipifera*	SH
Quince, Flowering	*Chaenomeles* spp.	SW, SH
Redbud	*Cercis* spp.	SW, SH
Redwood, Dawn	*Metasequoia glyptostroboides*	SW, HW
Rose	*Rosa* spp.	SW, SH, HW
Rose-of-Sharon, Shrub-althea	*Hibiscus syriacus*	SW, HW
Russian olive, Oleaster	*Elaeagnus anugustifolia*	SH

(Continued)

Table 13–3. *continued*

Common Name	Scientific Name	Type of Cutting[a]
Serviceberry	*Amelanchier* spp.	SW
Smoketree; Smokebush	*Cotinus coggygria*	SW
Spirea	*Spiraea* spp.	SW
St. John's Wort	*Hypericum* spp.	SW
Sumac	*Rhus* spp.	SW
Sweetgum	*Liquidambar styraciflua*	SW
Trumpet creeper	*Campsis* spp.	SW, SH, HW
Virginia creeper	*Parthenocissus quinquefolia*	SW, HW
Weigela	*Weigela* spp.	SW, HW
Willow	*Salix* spp.	SW, SH, HW
Wisteria [b]	*Wisteria* spp.	SH, HW

[a] SW = softwood, SH = semi-hardwood, HW = hardwood

[b] Plants considered moderately weedy. Unless working with a sterile variety use care when distributing.
Pear, Callery *Pyrus calleryana*   Wisteria, Chinese *Wisteria sinensis*   Wisteria, Japanese *Wisteria floribunda*

[c] Plants considered highly invasive. Unless you are working with a sterile variety do not distribute.
Bittersweet, Oriental *Celastrus orbiculatus*   Honeysuckle, Japanese *Lonicera japonica*

the rooting media is deliberately wounded, which is done to stimulate rooting. Most species do not require wounding, but some benefit greatly from this practice.

There are two general types of wounds, light and heavy. A light wound consists of two or four equidistant vertical cuts, administered with a knife or single-edge razor blade, to the lower portion (approximately 1 to 1½-inches) of the cutting. The cuts go through the bark into the wood but are not deep enough to split the stem. Many conifer cuttings respond to light wounds. On the other hand, a heavy wound consists of removal of a thin strip of bark on one or opposite sides of the lower 1 to 1½-inches of a cutting, exposing the green tissue just beneath the bark termed the cambium. Be careful when applying a heavy wound not to remove (scrape) all the bark from the lower portion of the stem as this kills the cutting or prevents it from rooting. Species that respond to heavy wounding include magnolias and evergreen rhododendrons. As mentioned previously, most species do not require wounding. There is nothing wrong, however, with using wounding, whether it be light or heavy, on all species provided it is done properly. Also, wounding by itself is of no benefit unless cuttings are treated with root-promoting compounds after wounding.

Treating cuttings with root-promoting compounds (chemicals), particularly for difficult-to-root species, is a common practice when rooting woody stem cuttings because these compounds increase the percentage of cuttings that form roots, speed up the rooting process (make the cuttings root faster), increase the uniformity of rooting, and lastly increase the number and quality of roots produced per cutting. Root-promoting compounds are generally available commercially in two forms, powders or liquids.

When treating cuttings with root-promoting compounds, prevent possible contamination of the entire supply (stock) of formulation by putting some in a separate container before treating cuttings. Any material remaining after treatment should be discarded and not returned to the original container. Be sure to tap the lower portion of the cutting to remove excess material when using a powder formulation. If the base of the cutting is not moist, moisten it with water before applying a powder formulation so the powder adheres to the base. Once the cuttings have been treated with a powder formulation, use a dibble for inserting them into the rooting medium so the powder stays on during insertion. When treating cuttings with a liquid formulation of a root-promoting compound, dip the lower ½-inch to 2 inches of a cutting into the solution for 1 to 2 seconds followed by 15 to 20 minutes of air drying; then insert the cutting into the rooting medium without the use of a dibble.

Use a rooting medium such as coarse sand, pine bark, or a mixture of one part peat and one or two parts perlite (by volume), or peat and sand (1:1 by volume). The rooting medium should be sterile, low in fertility, sufficiently well drained to permit aeration, and moisture retentive enough so that it does not have to be watered too frequently. Moisten the medium before inserting cuttings.

Various commercial potting mixes can be used. Insert the cuttings one-third to one-half of their length into the medium with the buds pointing upward. Do not insert the stem upside down. Space cuttings just far enough apart to allow all leaves to receive sunlight. Water again after inserting the cuttings if the containers or frames are 3 or more inches deep. Cover the cuttings with plastic and place in indirect light. Keep the medium moist until the cuttings have rooted. Rooting is improved if the plants are misted on a regular basis.

Rooting time varies with the type of cutting, the species being rooted, and environmental conditions. Conifers require more time than broadleaf plants. Late fall or early winter is a good time to root conifers. Once rooted, conifer cuttings may be left in the rooting structure until spring.

Root Cuttings

Some plants can be propagated from a section of a root. Root cuttings are usually taken from 2- to 3-year-old plants during the dormant season when carbohydrate levels are high. Root cuttings of some species produce new shoots, which then form their own root system, whereas root cuttings of other plants develop root systems before producing new shoots. Examples of plants that can be propagated from root cuttings include blackberry, apple, fig, lilac, phlox, raspberry, rose, sumac, and trumpet vine.

Plants with large diameter roots are normally propagated outdoors. The root cuttings should be 2 to 6 inches long. Make a straight cut on the proximal end (nearest the crown of the parent plant) and a slanted cut on the distal end (farthest from the crown) of each root cutting. Tie the cuttings in bundles with all the same ends together. It is important to maintain the correct polarity of the cuttings. Store about three weeks in moist sawdust, peat moss, or sand at 40°F. Remove from storage. Plant the cuttings distal end pointed down, about 2 to 3 inches apart in well-prepared garden soil. The tops of the cuttings (proximal ends) should be the shallowest part of the planting at 2 to 3 inches below the soil surface.

For plants with small diameter roots, cut the roots into 1-inch to 2-inch sections. Lay the cuttings horizontally on the medium surface in a flat and cover with about ½-inch of soil or sand. Place the flat inside a plastic bag or cover with a pane of glass. Place the flat in the shade and remove the protective cover after new shoots appear.

Asexual Propagation— Other Methods

LAYERING

Stems still attached to their parent plant may form roots where they come in contact with a rooting medium. This method of vegetative propagation is generally successful because water stress is minimized and carbohydrate and mineral nutrient levels are high. The development of roots on a stem while the stem is still attached to the parent plant is called layering. A layer is a rooted stem after it has been removed from the parent plant. Some plants propagate naturally by layering, but sometimes plant propagators assist the process. Layering is enhanced by wounding the side of the stem where the roots will grow or by bending the stem very sharply. The rooting medium should always provide aeration and a constant supply of moisture. Some common forms of layering are as follows. However, keep in mind these protocols are sometimes modified.

Tip layering. Dig a hole 3 to 4 inches deep in the rooting medium. Insert the tip of a current season's shoot and cover it with soil. The tip grows downward first, then bends sharply and grows upward (Figure 13–12). Roots form at the bend. The recurved tip becomes a new plant. Remove the tip layer and plant it in late fall or early spring. Examples of plants propagated this way include purple and black raspberries, trailing blackberries, and dewberries. The aforementioned plants also do this naturally.

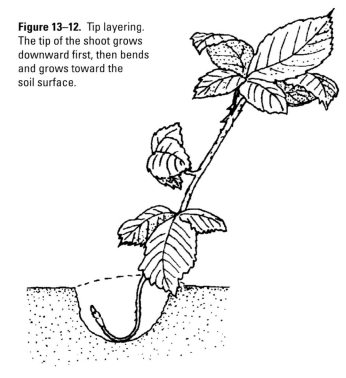

Figure 13–12. Tip layering. The tip of the shoot grows downward first, then bends and grows toward the soil surface.

Simple layering. Bend the stem to the ground. Cover part of it with soil, leaving the remaining 6 to 12 inches above the soil. Bend the tip into a vertical position and stake in place (Figure 13–13). The sharp bend often induces rooting, but wounding the lower side of the bent branch may help. Simple layering can be done on most plants that have low-growing branches. Examples include azalea, forsythia, boxwood, honeysuckle, rhododendron, and wax myrtle.

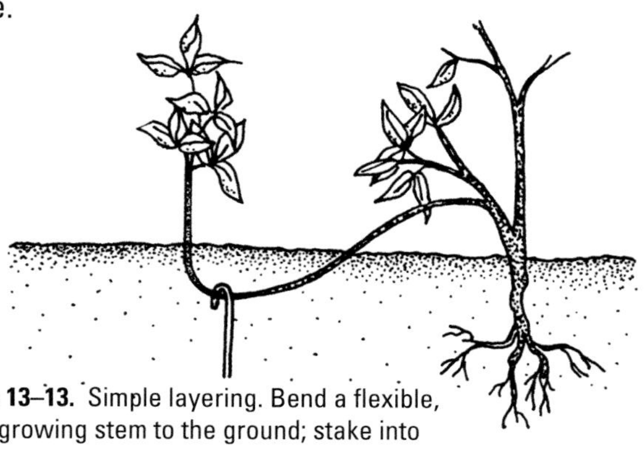

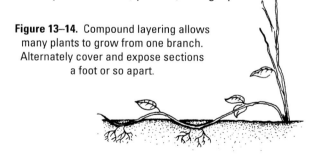

Figure 13–13. Simple layering. Bend a flexible, low-growing stem to the ground; stake into place; cover with soil.

Compound (serpentine) layering. Bend the stem to the rooting medium as for simple layering, but alternately cover and expose stem sections. Wound the lower side of the stem sections to be covered (Figure 13–14). This method works well for plants producing vinelike growth such as heart-leaf philodendron, pothos, and grape.

Figure 13–14. Compound layering allows many plants to grow from one branch. Alternately cover and expose sections a foot or so apart.

Mound (stool) layering. Cut the plant back to 1 inch above the ground in the dormant season. Dormant buds produce new shoots in the spring. Mound soil over the new shoots as they grow (Figure 13–15). Roots develop at the bases of the young shoots. Remove the layers in the dormant season. Mound layering works well on apple rootstocks, cotoneaster, daphne, quince, and spirea.

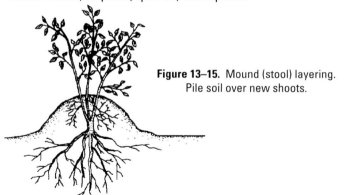

Figure 13–15. Mound (stool) layering. Pile soil over new shoots.

Air layering (pot layering, circumposition, marcottage, Chinese layering, gootee). Air layering can be used to propagate large, overgrown houseplants (such as rubber plants or dieffenbachia that have lost most of their lower leaves) as well as some woody ornamentals such as camellias. The process varies depending on whether the plant is a monocot or dicot. For monocots, such as *Dracaena fragrans* 'Massangeana' (corn plant), make an upward cut about one-third of the way through the stem. This is normally done on a stem about 1 foot from the tip. The cut is held open with a toothpick or wooden matchstick. . Dust the wound with rooting hormone and surround with damp, unmilled sphagnum moss. Wrap the moss with plastic and hold in place with twist ties or electrician's tape. Aluminum foil can also be used; it does not require twist ties or tape to hold it in place.

The process for dicots is similar except a 1-inch ring of bark is removed from the stem. Scrape the newly bared ring to remove the cambial tissue in order to prevent callus from forming. Wrap and cover using the same procedure as that described for monocots (Figure 13–16).

After the rooting medium is filled with roots, sever the stem below the medium. The new plant requires some pampering after planting until the root system becomes more developed.

Natural forms of layering. Sometimes layering happens without the help of a propagator. Runners and offsets are specialized structures that facilitate propagation by layering.

A runner produces new shoots where it touches the growing medium. Plants that produce stolons or runners are propagated by severing the new plants from their parent stems. Plantlets at the tips of runners may be rooted while still attached to the parent or detached and placed in a rooting medium. Examples include strawberry and spider plants (Figure 13–17).

Plants with a rosetted stem often reproduce by forming new shoots, called offsets (offshoots), at their base or in the leaf axil. Sever the new shoots from the parent plant after they have developed their own root system. Unrooted offsets of some species may be removed and placed in a rooting medium. Some of these must be cut off, whereas others may simply be lifted from the parent stem. Examples include date palm, haworthia, bromeliads, and many cacti.

SEPARATION AND DIVISION

Separation and division are the easiest and quickest ways to propagate many plants. Separation uses naturally occurring vegetative structures such as bulbs and corms. Individual bulbs or corms are separated from a clump.

Figure 13–17. Some plants, such as the spider plant, produce runners that are propagated easily.
Chris Alberti, CC BY - 2.0

Most of the spring- and summer flowering bulbs are propagated this way. Division involves digging up the plant or removing it from its container and cutting (dividing) the plant into separate pieces. Division uses specialized vegetative structures such as rhizomes and tubers. Indoor plants that can be propagated by division include ferns, snake plant, prayer plant, and African violet. Outdoor plants that can be divided include many perennials such as daylily, hosta, iris, liriope, and verbena. Separation and division are normally done in the fall or early spring.

BUDDING AND GRAFTING

Budding and grafting are methods of asexual propagation that join parts of two or more different plants together so they unite and grow as one plant. These techniques are used to propagate cultivars that do not root well from cuttings, or to alter some aspect of the plant (for example, to create weeping or dwarf forms), or to increase disease resistant plants. Most fruit and nut trees are propagated by budding or grafting.

The scion consists of a short stem piece with one or more buds and is the part of the graft that develops into the

Figure 13–16. Air layering. Remove a 1-inch strip of bark around the stem, dust rooting hormone on the cut surface, cover with moist sphagnum moss, enclose in plastic or aluminum foil. Rooting hormone is not always necessary.
Velacreations, Flickr CC BY - 2.0

top of the grafted plant. The rootstock (also called stock or understock) provides the new plant's root system and sometimes the lower part of the stem. Seedling rootstocks are used commonly.

Six conditions must be met for bud grafting to be successful:
1. The scion and rootstock must be compatible (capable of uniting).
2. The scion and stock plant must be at the proper physiological stage of growth.
3. The cambial region of the scion and the stock must be in close contact—touching if possible.
4. Proper polarity must be maintained (the buds on the scion must be pointed upward).
5. Immediately after grafting, all cut surfaces must be protected from drying out.
6. Proper care must be given to the graft after grafting. (See "Care of Buds and Grafts", p. 13–17.)

Once the bud has healed and broken to form a shoot, the top of the stock plant is cut back (removed) to the bud union.

Not all plants can be grafted. The two plants should be closely related taxonomically. Grafting between clones and seedlings of the same species is usually successful.

Budding

Budding, or bud grafting, is the union of one bud, with or without a small piece of bark, from one plant (scion) onto a stem of a rootstock. It is especially useful when scion material is limited. Budding is usually done during the growing season when the bark is slipping (soft and easy to peel back from the cambium), June through August in the Southeast United States, but it can also be done in late winter or early spring.

T-budding—This is the most commonly used budding technique (Figure 13–18). When the bark is slipping, make a vertical cut (same axis as the rootstock) through the bark of the rootstock, avoiding any buds on the stock.

Make an intersecting, horizontal cut at the top of the vertical cut (forming a "T" shape), and loosen the bark by twisting the knife slightly at the intersection. Remove a shield-shaped piece of the scion, including a bud, some bark, and a thin section of wood. Push the shield under the loosened stock bark at the "T." Wrap the union, leaving the bud exposed. Many fruit trees are propagated by this method.

Chip budding—This method can be used when the bark is not slipping. Although all the basics in handling budwood and stock are the same for chip budding and T-budding, the cuts made in chip budding differ radically. The first cut on both stock and scion is made at a 45° to 60° downward angle to a depth of about ⅛-inch (Figure 13–19). After making this cut on a smooth part of the rootstock, start the second cut about ¾-inch higher and draw the knife down to meet the first cut. (The exact spacing between the cuts varies with species and the size of the buds.) Then remove the chip. Cuts on both the scion (to remove the bud) and the rootstock (to insert the bud) should be exactly the same size. Although the exact location is not essential, the bud is usually positioned one-third of the way down from the beginning of the cut. If the bud shield is significantly narrower than the rootstock cut, line up one side exactly. Wrapping is extremely important in chip budding. If all exposed edges of the cut are not covered, the bud dries out before it can "take." Chip budding has become more popular over the past five years because of

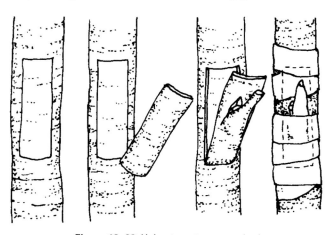

Figure 13–19. Chip budding can be done when the rootstock bark is not slipping.

the availability of thin (2 mil) polyethylene tape as a wrapping material. This tape is wrapped to overlap all of the injury, including the bud (Figure 13–20), and forms a miniature plastic greenhouse over the healing graft.

13

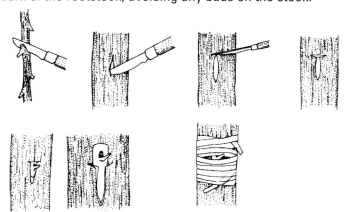

Figure 13–18. Many fruit trees are propagated by budding a scion onto a seedling rootstock, using a process called T-budding.

Figure 13–20. Using tape to wrap a bud.

Grafting

Grafting is the union of the stems of two plants to grow as one. There are several kinds of grafting; which method to use depends on the age and type of plants involved.

Whip or tongue grafting—This method is often used for stems ¼-inch to ½-inch in diameter. The scion and rootstock are usually of the same diameter. This graft provides excellent cambial contact and heals quickly. Make a sloping cut 1-inch to 2½-inches long at the top of the rootstock and a matching cut on the bottom of the scion. On the cut surface, slice downward into the stock and up into the scion, so the pieces will interlock when brought together. Fit the pieces together such that the cambium matches on at least one side, and then wrap and tie or wax the graft union (Figure 13–21).

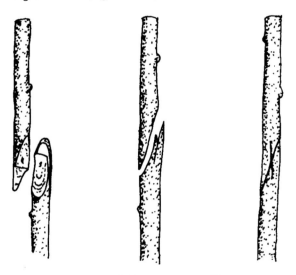

Figure 13–21. Whip or tongue grafting.

Cleft grafting—Cleft grafting is one of the oldest and most widely used methods of grafting. The two most common circumstances when one would use this technique are (1) when creating a weeping ornamental tree and (2) when upgrading an older cultivar of a fruit tree to a newer, improved one while maintaining the existing root system. Cleft grafting is best done in early spring when the buds on the stock plant are beginning to swell but before active growth has begun. The scions, however, must be fully dormant. Collect scion wood ⅜ to ⅝ inch in diameter during the dormant season and refrigerate it until needed.

Cut the limbs to be reworked at a right angle to the main axis of the branch. Use a heavy knife to split the branch, making a 2-inch vertical cut through the center of the stub to be grafted. Be careful not to tear the bark. Keep this cut wedged apart. Prepare two scion pieces 3 to 5 inches long; cut the lower end of each scion piece into a wedge. Insert the scions at the outer edges of the cut in the stock. Tilt the top of the scion slightly outward and the

bottom slightly inward to be sure the cambial layers of the scion and stock touch. Remove the wedge propping the slit open, and cover all cut surfaces with grafting wax (Figure 13–22). If both scions grow, one can be removed later.

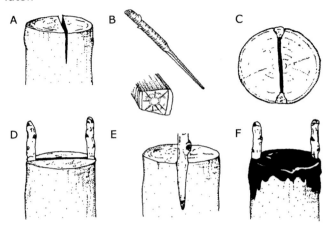

Figure 13–22. Cleft grafting. A) Split the branch of the rootstock to be grafted with a 2-inch vertical cut. B) Prepare two scion pieces 3 to 5 inches long with wedge-shaped ends. C) and D) Insert the scions into the outer edges of the stock. E) Make sure the cambial layers of the scion and stock touch. F) Cover all cut surfaces with grafting wax.

Some other types of grafting include splice, side, stub, side veneer, and side tongue. Check reference books for additional information. Each method has advantages for special situations.

Care of Buds and Grafts

Propagation is not likely to be successful unless you properly care for the grafted plants for a year or two after budding or grafting. If you use binding materials such as waxed string or nursery tape, remove them shortly after growth starts to prevent girdling. Rubber budding strips have some advantages over other materials. They expand with growth and usually do not need to be removed because they deteriorate after several months. Inspect the grafts after two or three weeks to see if the grafting wax has cracked and, if necessary, rewax the exposed surface. After this, the union will probably have healed and no more waxing will be necessary. Limbs on the old cultivar (rootstock) that are not selected for grafting should be cut back at the time of grafting.

The total leaf surface of the old cultivar should be reduced gradually as the new one increases for one or two years; by this time, the new cultivar (scion) has had adequate time to grow. Completely removing all the limbs of the old cultivar at the time of grafting increases the shock to the tree and causes excessive suckering. Also, the scions may grow too fast, making them susceptible to wind damage.

MICROPROPAGATION

Micropropagation involves the application of tissue culture techniques to propagate plants from very small plant parts (parts of leaves, stems, shoot tips, root tips, single cells, and pollen grains). The small plant part is grown (cultured) in a test tube, petri dish, or other sterilized container with a culture medium and precise environmental conditions. The container and growing medium must be sterilized. Because plants often harbor bacterial and fungal spores, the plant tissue must also be disinfected.

Micropropagation is a rapidly growing part of the plant propagation industry. It is not practical for most home gardeners because of the very specific requirements of the culture media and the constant efforts that must be made to avoid possible contamination from disease organisms. For nurseries, special care must be taken in transporting micropropagated plants from the lab to the store because they are not acclimated to outdoor growing conditions.

Hardening Plants

Hardening is the process of conditioning a plant for growth outdoors. If plants produced inside are planted outdoors without a hardening period, their growth could be severely limited. Hardening is most critical with early crops, when adverse climatic conditions can be expected.

Hardening is accomplished by decreasing temperature and relative humidity gradually, and reducing water. This procedure results in the accumulation of carbohydrates and the thickening of cell walls. A change from a soft, succulent type of growth to a firmer, harder type is desired.

The process should be started at least two weeks before plants are to be planted in the garden. Place seedlings outside in a protected area on warm days (Figure 13–23). Increase the length of exposure gradually. Do not put tender seedlings outdoors on windy days or when temperatures are below 45°F. Even cold-hardy plants will be injured if exposed to freezing temperatures before they are hardened.

The hardening process is intended to slow plant growth. Carried to an extreme, however, hardening can cause significant damage. For example, cauliflower produces thumb-sized heads and fails to develop further if hardened too severely; cucumbers and melons stop growing entirely.

Figure 13–23. Tomatoes hardening off under cover and near the wall of a building.
Cristina Sanvito, Flickr CC BY - 2.0

Genetically Modified Organisms (GMOs)

Genetically modified organisms (GMOs) have their DNA manipulated through the introduction of genes from other organisms or through the rearrangement of their own genes. These changes are made to produce an organism with a desired trait that is not naturally occurring. Genetic modifications to plants can include resistance to insect pests or diseases, the ability to grow faster, the ability to use less water, or increased resistance to pesticides or herbicides. Three federal agencies currently regulate GMOs: the U.S. Department of Agriculture (USDA), the Food and Drug Administration (FDA), and the Environmental Protection Agency (EPA). Much debate exists over the sustainability and environmental impact of these genetic modifications, and the jury is still out. Currently, in the United States, food and seeds are not required to be labeled if they contain GMOs. The only label that guarantees no GMOs is the "USDA Certified Organic" label (Figure 13–24).

If you see either of these labels, you can be sure the product is at least 95% organic.

Figure 13–24. Organic labeling.

Figure 13–25. New plants are forming at the base of these rooted hens and chicks (*Echeveria* spp.) leaves.
Kathleen Moore, CC BY - 2.0

Frequently Asked Questions

1. When should I collect oak acorns and other shade tree seeds to grow them, and how should I handle the seeds to get them to germinate?

Seeds that mature and drop from trees in the fall should be collected in the fall and sown immediately in tilled and prepared beds or into containers. They generally germinate the following spring. Before planting, place acorns in water. Sound acorns sink; unviable acorns float. Discard the floaters. The cap should also be removed from the acorn. Dogwood and magnolia seed should have the outer red covering removed; these seeds can be soaked to ferment the pulpy flesh from the seed. Red maple seeds ripen in spring and should be collected and sown immediately after removing the dry samaras in prepared beds or into pots. Check references on handling woody species from seeds. *The Manual of Woody Landscape Plants: Their Identification, Ornamental Characteristics, Culture, Propagation and Uses* by Michael A. Dirr is a highly recommended source of information. Another excellent source for the propagation of woody species is *The Reference Manual of Woody Plant Propagation: From Seed to Tissue Culture*, by Michael A. Dirr and Charles W. Heuser Jr. For showy native woody plants, consult *Growing and Propagating Showy Native Woody Plants* by Richard E. "Dick" Bir (available from The University of North Carolina Press; or call 1-800-848-6224 to order).

2. My jade plant is dying. Can I propagate it and keep it alive?

Cuttings from healthy plants work best; sometimes, cuttings from plants that are struggling will not take root. Jade plants can be propagated by stem or leaf cuttings. If it is a variegated jade, use a stem cutting to ensure you are preserving the genetic material that leads to the variation in leaf color.

3. I planted seeds for some annual flowers, but none of them came up. Why?

There could be several reasons your seeds failed to germinate.
- The seeds were never viable.
- They were planted too deep or too shallow.
- The seedbed was kept too wet or too dry.
- They died shortly after germinating.
- The seeds or seedlings were eaten by an insect or animal.
- The seeds or seedlings were killed by a disease.
- A weather event such as frost killed the seedlings.

4. How do I propagate azaleas?

One of the most reliable ways to propagate azaleas is to layer some of the lower branches in the soil and weigh them down with a brick (wounding and applying a rooting hormone also helps the process). If cuttings are to be used, best success is achieved on evergreen azaleas with semi-hardwood cuttings (they break with a snap), taken late June through August. Again, wounding the lower stems and applying a rooting hormone increases success rates. Be sure to use a well-drained medium and provide partial shade. Roots should form in four to six weeks. These Horticulture Information Leaflets from NC State Extension are excellent references: HIL 8701, *Plant Propagation by Layering: Instructions For the Home Gardener*, and HIL 8702, *Plant Propagation by Stem Cuttings: Instructions For the Home Gardener.*

5. My irises are about 10 years old, and they are not blooming well any more. What is wrong with them?

Irises produce leaves and flowers from thick rhizomes beneath the ground. In time the rhizome produces side shoots and the original rhizome withers and dies. The smaller side shoots need to be broken off and planted separately so they can mature into a new plant. Irises should be divided every three to four years for the plants to remain healthy and vigorous. Read more about irises and their propagation in NC State Extension publication HIL-8506, *Bearded Iris for the Home Landscape.*

Further Reading

Beyl, Caula A. and Robert N. Trigiano, eds. *Plant Propagation: Concepts and Laboratory Exercises*. Boca Raton, Florida: CRC Press, 2008. Print.

Bir, Richard E. *Growing and Propagating Showy Native Woody Plants*. Chapel Hill, North Carolina: The University Of North Carolina Press, 1992. Print.

Bonner, Franklin T. and Robert P. Karrfalt, eds. *The Woody Plant Seed Manual*. Washington, DC: United States Department of Agriculture Forest Service, 2008. Print and PDF file. Agriculture Handbook 727.

Bryant, Geoff. *Propagation Handbook: Basic Techniques for Gardeners*. Mechanicsburg, Pennsylvania: Stackpole Books, 1995. Print.

Dirr, Michael A. *Manual of Woody Landscape Plants: Their Identification, Ornamental Characteristics, Culture, Propogation and Uses*. 6th ed. Champaign, Illinois: Stipes Publishing L.L.C., 2009. Print.

Dirr, Michael A., and Charles W. Heuser, Jr.. *The Reference Manual of Woody Plant Propagation: From Seed to Tissue Culture*. 2nd ed. Cary, North Carolina: Varsity Press, Inc., 2006. Print.

Hartmann, Hudson T., et al.. *Hartmann & Kester's Plant Propagation: Principles and Practices*. 8th ed. Upper Saddle River, New Jersey: Prentice Hall, Inc., 2010. Print.

Hill, Lewis. *Secrets of Plant Propagation: Starting Your Own Flowers, Vegetables, Fruits, Berries, Shrubs, Trees, and Houseplants*. North Adams, Massachusetts: Story Publishing, 1985. Print.

Phillips, Harry R. *Growing and Propagating Wild Flowers*. Chapel Hill, North Carolina: The University of North Carolina Press, 1985. Print.

Royal Horticultural Society Propagation Techniques. London: Octopus Publishing Group Ltd, 2013. Print.

Thompson, Peter. *Creative Propagation*. 2nd ed. Portland, Oregon: Timber Press, Inc., 2005. Print.

Toogood, Alan, ed. *American Horticultural Society Plant Propagation: The Fully Illustrated Plant-by-Plant Manual of Practical Techniques*. New York: DK Publishing, Inc., 1999. Print.

For More Information

http://go.ncsu.edu/fmi_propagation

Contributors

Authors:

Anthony V. LeBude, Associate Professor and Extension Specialist, Department of Horticultural Science

Frank A. Blazich, Distinguished Professor Emeritus, Department of Horticultural Science

Contribution by Extension Agents: Jessica Strickland, Mary Hollingsworth, Shawn Banks, Mack Johnson, Paige Patterson, Peg Godwin

Contributions by Extension Master Gardener Volunteers: Patty Brown, Renee Lampila, Jackie Weedon, Karen Damari, Connie Schultz

Content Editors:

Lucy Bradley, Professor and Extension Specialist, Urban Horticulture, NC State University; Director, NC State Extension Master Gardener program;

Kathleen Moore, Urban Horticulturist

Copy Editor: Barbara Scott

Chapter 13 Cover Photo: Kathleen Moore, CC BY - 2.0

Based on text from the 1998 Extension Master Gardener manual prepared by:

Erv Evans, Extension Associate, Department of Horticulture Science

Frank A. Blazich, Professor, Department of Horticulture Science

How to Cite This Chapter:

LeBude, A.V., F.A. Blazich, 2022. Propagation, Chpt 13, In: K.A. Moore, and. L.K. Bradley (eds). *North Carolina Extension Gardener Handbook*, 2nd ed. NC State Extension, Raleigh, NC. <https://content.ces.ncsu.edu/extension-gardener-handbook/13-propagation>

13

Small Fruits

Objectives

This chapter will teach people to:

- Become familiar with recommended cultivars of small fruit.

- Understand important considerations in selecting fruits and fruit cultivars for home landscapes.

- Select a good site for planting small fruit.

- Be aware of the common pests and diseases associated with growing small fruits.

14

Introduction

Berries and grapes, when properly tended, are well-suited to the home garden. A small planting can produce an abundance of fruit to eat fresh, make juice and bake with, and can, freeze, or dry for future enjoyment. The most popular small fruits in North Carolina are strawberries, grapes, blackberries, raspberries, and blueberries. Small fruits have several advantages over tree fruits. Most small fruits bear fruit in less time, require less room, and suffer from fewer insect and disease problems than tree fruits. A blueberry hedge, a strawberry border, or a grape arbor can also enhance the beauty of a landscape. With a little creativity, fruit can be incorporated into an edible landscape. This chapter provides information on the establishment and care of small fruits in home gardens. Table 14–1 summarizes the characteristics of small fruits commonly grown in North Carolina gardens.

Currants and gooseberries cannot be grown legally in North Carolina. Both serve as alternate hosts for diseases that affect important economic crops in our state. For further clarification, contact the NC Department of Agriculture and Consumer Services, Plant Protection Division.

Strawberries

First among small fruits to produce berries after planting, strawberries are also the first fruit to ripen in the spring. From just 25 plants and their resulting runner plants, 25 quarts of berries can be harvested. Strawberries can be raised throughout North Carolina, are relatively easy to grow, and require a minimum of space. They can be grown in the home garden with virtually no pesticides. When grown commercially, however, strawberries are in the top 12 types of produce with pesticide residue, according to the U.S. Department of Agriculture. If you would like to reduce your pesticide exposure, consider growing your own strawberries.

Types of Strawberries

The small wild strawberry often found along roadsides and at woodland edges is one of the parents of today's hybrid strawberries. The yellow-flowered plant with strawberry-like fruits found in our lawns and gardens is the Indian or false strawberry (also called snake berry). These plants are not poisonous, but their fruits have little flavor and a pulpy texture. True wild strawberries have white flowers.

The cultivars recommended for home gardens in North Carolina are June-bearing strawberries such as 'Galletta', 'Chandler', and 'Jewel'. June-bearing cultivars produce a single crop of fruit in the spring. The name "June-bearing" is somewhat confusing because these cultivars bear most of their crop in May (although in more northern climates, they do produce fruit in June). June bearers are short-day plants, which means they start forming flower buds when days are less than 12 hours long. Runner production is a long-day response; it occurs only when day length is more than 12 hours.

The so-called everbearing strawberry is one that produces a crop in spring and another crop in late summer to early fall. This type initiates most of its flower buds under **long-day** conditions. All of the everbearing strawberries adver-

Table 14–1. Bearing Age, Average Yield, Plant Quantity, and Life Span of Small Fruits

Fruit	Type	Bearing Age	Average Annual Yield (pounds/plant)	Number of Plants for Four People	Life Expectancy (years)
Blueberry	Highbush	3	8	6	20–30
	Rabbiteye	3	12	4	20–30
Blackberry	Erect	2	4	6	5–12
	Semi-trailing	2	20	2	5–20
Raspberry	Red & black	2	2–4	6	5–10
Grape	Bunch	3	15	4	15–20
	Muscadine	3	25–50	2	15–30
Strawberry	Everbearing	1	1/3	50	2–3
	June-bearing	2	1/2	50	3–4

tised in nursery catalogs originated in the northern states; they are poorly adapted to southern heat. But 'Albion', a cultivar from California, has done well in the NC mountains.

Strawberry cultivars best adapted to North Carolina are listed in Table 14–2. 'Galletta' strawberry was developed in North Carolina and is well-adapted to our climate. Strawberries developed for other regions of the country are generally poorly adapted here. Exceptions are the cultivars 'Chandler', 'Albion', and 'Jewel', which have a wide area of adaptation.

Choose disease-free, certified plants from a reliable nursery. Cornell University maintains a list of nurseries and cultivars. The harvest season can be extended with a mix of early, midseason, and late cultivars. Early cultivars are more subject to frost damage because they bloom earlier in the spring. The open blossom stage of development is the most susceptible to cold injury.

Site Selection, Preparation, Planting, and Maintenance

Strawberries grow best in full sun but tolerate light shade (with decreased yields). A southern exposure encourages earlier blooming and earlier fruit, but this may not be desirable in locations where late spring frosts often damage the flower buds. Strawberries can be grown in most garden soils. But because they are very shallow-rooted, they grow best in sandy loam soils with good drainage. Because clay soils drain poorly, they are not the best choice; poorly drained soils induce small root systems and encourage the proliferation of many fungal diseases. Planting in raised rows or beds and incorporating organic matter can help overcome this problem. The raised row should be 6 inches to 9 inches high and 15 inches wide. Leaves, chopped straw, rotted sawdust, and pine bark mulch can be used to improve soil texture. Manure (two to three bushels per 100 square feet) is a good source of organic matter. Incorporate the organic matter in the fall, so the material will be partially decomposed by spring planting.

Kill perennial weeds the season before planting. Do not plant strawberries on a site that has recently grown sod as the grubs and weevils that feed on grass roots can also feed on strawberry roots.

Have a soil test done to determine the amount of lime and fertilizer that may be needed. The pH should be between 6.0 and 6.5.

If you purchase bare root strawberries and plan to plant soon after they arrive, keep them in a cool, moist place. If they cannot be planted immediately, moisten the plants and place them in a plastic bag in the refrigerator. Set plants any time from October to March in the NC coastal plain, and during March or April in the NC piedmont and western North Carolina. In the spring, the temperature should be 40°F to 50°F; a spring frost generally does not harm the vegetative growth of new strawberry plants.

Spread out the roots and set the plants so the midpoint of the crown (the point where the stem and root merge) is level with the soil (Figure 14–1). If they are set too deep, the growing point of the crown may be damaged or may rot. If they are set too shallow, the crown and the tops of the plants may dry out. Water newly set plants, and press the soil firmly around the roots. Remove flower buds that develop on new plants (first year only) so the plant's energy can go into runner production. The runners that form early produce more fruit than runners that form late in the season.

Figure 14–1. Set strawberry plants so the crown is level with the soil line. The plant on the left is too shallow. The plant on the right is too deep.

Cultivar	Area[a]	Season	Berry Size	Yield	Fresh	Processing	Comments
Albion	M	Spring–fall	Medium	Medium	Good	Good	Everbearing
Chandler	All	Mid–late	Large	High	Good	Good	Commercial standard
Galletta	All	Early	Large	High	Good	Poor	Glossy fruit
Jewel	P, M	Late	Medium	High	Good	Good	Rot resistant

Table 14–2. Recommended Strawberry Cultivars for North Carolina

[a] S = sandhills-coastal plain; P = piedmont; M = mountains-foothills

Training Systems

The matted row system is the easiest to follow. Set plants 1½ feet to 2½ feet apart in the row. Space the rows 3 feet to 4 feet apart. Allow most of the runners from mother plants to grow during the first season, but keep them in a band 24-inches wide. The ideal plant density is four to six plants per square foot.

The hill system is ideal for most everbearing cultivars. Set plants 12 inches apart in double rows, leaving 2 feet to 3 feet between double rows. Remove all runners that form during the summer. Large individual hills can produce abundant crops of excellent quality fruit.

The annual hill system is the type of planting system that is used by many commercial growers in North Carolina. In this system, plants are set in the ground in the fall and harvested in the following spring. This system is more costly as new plants have to be set each year. The disease and insect pressure, however, is not as significant. In this system, plants are set on a 12-inch staggered span in 3-foot-wide raised beds. This system has been used in the schools as part of the Strawberries in Schools project.

Fertilization

Before planting, follow the soil test recommendations. One month after planting, fertilize each newly planted strawberry with 2 teaspoons of fertilizer containing 16% nitrogen (N). Apply the fertilizer at least 4 inches from the plant crown. Apply 16% nitrogen fertilizer again between August 15 and September 15. Three pounds of a 16% nitrogen material, 2½ pounds of 20%, or 1½ pounds of a 33% nitrogen material are adequate for each 100 feet of row (Table 14–3). Scatter the material over the top of the plants while they are dry and use a soft broom to brush it off the foliage.

Very sandy coastal soils usually need additional nitrogen again in late January or early February. The rate suggested is half that of the fall application. Measure and apply nitrogen carefully; too much causes rank top growth and soft berries that rot easily. For mature plantings, use the same amounts and same timing as for new plantings.

Mulching

Mulching helps to manage weeds, conserves water, and keeps the fruit clean. In eastern and central North Carolina, spread pine needles or grain straw in February before new growth starts. Scatter over the plants and in the middle of the rows so only a few strawberry leaves show. The plants grow easily through the straw.

In the western part of the state, mulch is also used to protect plants during the winter. In December when the night temperature drops to 20°F, broadcast pine needles or grain straw in the row middles and around the plants to protect the crowns. At high elevations, cover plants with

Strawberry Pyramids

A strawberry pyramid is an easy-to-build planter that can grow lots of strawberries in a limited space (Figure 14–2).

Materials Needed

- 4 boards – 6 feet long and 6 inches wide
- 4 boards – 5 feet long and 6 inches wide
- 4 boards – 4 feet long and 6 inches wide
- 4 boards – 3 feet long and 6 inches wide
- 10 feet of 2-inch by 2-inch boards for corners
- 1 lb of sixpenny galvanized nails
- 33 bushels of soil
- 2 lb of 8-8-8 fertilizer
- 6 lb of lime

Instructions

- Nail four 6-foot boards together to make a square.
- Place the 6-foot square on the ground and fill with good garden soil. Use a 2-inch by 2-inch stake in each corner to add stability. Add 1 ounce of 8-8-8 fertilizer and 3 ounces of lime for each bushel of soil and mix well.
- Build a 5-foot square to set on top of the 6-foot square. Then fill the 5-foot square. Continue the process for each square.
- Place the first plants 3 inches from any corner. Set the rest of the plants 6 inches apart. Fill all tiers this way. Mulch the plants.
- Remove runners as they form during the summer.
- Apply 1 teaspoon of sodium nitrate or 10-10-10 around each plant after new growth starts and again in August.
- Mulch again heavily in December to protect the plants during the winter.

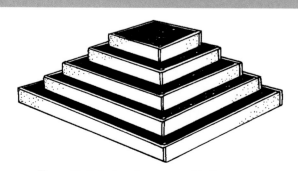

Figure 14–2. A strawberry pyramid allows many strawberry plants to be grown in a limited space.

2 inches of mulch. Remove half of the straw in the spring; rake the excess straw into the row middles (Figure 14–3).

Strawberry plants have a shallow root system and cannot withstand severe drought. Plants need a total of 1 inch of water per week (rain plus irrigation). It is critical that plants receive adequate moisture at the following times:

- When plants are first set and during dry periods after setting.
- Just before harvest and during harvest when berry size appears to be suffering.
- After renovation, to encourage new runner plants.
- In late August, September, and early October, when fruit buds are forming for next season's crop.

Fruit size can be increased by watering. Excessive water, however, can result in diluted flavor and increased fruit rot.

Weed Management

Because strawberries are shallow-rooted plants, they do not compete well against weeds. Weeds can be managed by mulching, **cultivating**, hoeing, or pulling by hand. Chemical herbicides can be used to manage many grasses and some broadleaf weeds. Consult the *North Carolina Agricultural Chemicals Manual* for recommendations. Herbicides should not be applied when plants are blooming, when runner plants are taking root, or during late summer and early fall, when fruit buds are forming. See "Weeds," chapter 6, for more information on weed management.

Frost Protection

Spring, with its temperature swings, is a likely time for frost to damage strawberry blooms. When the flower is completely open, a temperature of 30°F at plant level can cause some damage. A temperature of 28°F can cause considerable damage. In earlier stages, before the flower

Table 14–3. Strawberry Fertilization Schedule for North Carolina

	Before Planting	One Month After Planting	Between August 15 and September 15	Between Late January and Early February (only in Sandy Soils)
Per plant	Follow recommendations from soil test	2 tsp of 16% N applied 4 inches from the crown	2 tsp of 16% N applied 4 inches from the crown	1 tsp of 16% N applied 4 inches from the crown
Per 100 ft row	Follow recommendations from soil test	3 lb of 16% N	3 lb of 16% N	1.5 lb of 16% N

Figure 14–3. Straw used as mulch around strawberries. Andrew Watson, Flickr CC BY-SA - 2.0

is fully open, the plants can withstand these temperatures but are still at risk if lower temperatures occur. After a frost or freeze, the flower petals may still be white. But if the center of the flower has turned brown, it will not produce fruit. Some protection from frost can be obtained by covering plants with 2 inches to 3 inches of straw, old cloth, paper, or row covers of materials that block the loss of heat. It is best to tent the material over the plants, because damage is likely where the material touches the plant (Figure 14–4). Placing the blanket over the strawberry bed during the peak afternoon heat helps to trap heat overnight.

Figure 14–4. Tent row covers over strawberry plants. Stakes are used to keep the material from touching the plants.
Scot Nelson, Flickr CC0

Harvest

Harvest normally begins 30 days after bloom. For strawberries, this period usually starts in the latter part of April in eastern North Carolina, early May in the NC piedmont, and late May in the NC mountains. Harvest strawberries every other day or three times a week. Pick the fruit with about a fourth of the stem attached. The best time to pick is early morning when berries are still cool. Not all berries ripen at the same time; pick only those that are fully red.

Renovation

Matted row strawberry plantings can bear fruit for more than one season, although yield and berry size decrease after the first year. Renovation helps renew the strawberry planting by keeping plants from becoming too crowded. Do not attempt to renew strawberry beds heavily infested with weeds, diseases, or insects; it is better to set a new planting. To renew a planting, follow these five steps immediately after harvest:
- Manually remove all broadleaf weeds. Then mow the leaves off with a lawn mower or weed trimmer. Be careful not to damage the crowns. Rake the leaves away and dispose of them.

- Reduce the row width with a rototiller or hoe to a strip 12 inches to 18 inches wide.
- Thin the plants, leaving only the most healthy and vigorous. Plants should be about 6 inches apart in all directions.
- Fertilize and water to promote new runner production.

Insects and Diseases

Although strawberries can have their share of insect and disease problems, most homeowners ignore these problems unless they become serious. Appendix C, "Diagnostic Tables," reviews common problems associated with strawberries. If the plants' symptoms are serious, visit NC State University's Strawberry Portal.

Following these six precautions should minimize insect and disease problems:
- Use only certified, disease-free plants. Do not use plants from a neighbor or an existing planting.
- Plant in well-drained soil, follow **crop rotation** recommendations, and have the soil tested for nematodes.
- Remove berries damaged by insects and diseases as the damage occurs (Figure 14–5).
- Properly renovate beds to remove older, diseased foliage and to keep plants from getting too crowded.
- Do not keep a planting in production too long; start a new planting to replace old plantings after their second or third crop.
- Do not allow insects and diseases to build up. Follow the NC State University recommendations.

Figure 14–5. Removing strawberries suffering from anthracnose fruit rot.
USDA, Flickr CC BY - 2.0

Blackberries and Raspberries (Brambles or Caneberries)

Brambles are any plant belonging to the genus Rubus. They have an average life expectancy of 5 years to 8 years. Raspberries and blackberries are the most commonly grown brambles. Other types of brambles include tayberries, tummelberries, loganberries, and boysenberries, all of which are hybrids between red raspberries and blackberries. These fruits are often scarce in local markets, and homeowners may have to grow them or do without.

Brambles

Although the term "bramble" is well known in the South, raspberries and blackberries are often called "caneberries" in other parts of the country. The term "bramble" has a negative connotation for some folks. In Latin, bramble means thorny shrub. However, most of the new blackberry cultivars and many of the raspberries are now essentially thornless.

BLACKBERRIES

Types and Growth Habits of Blackberries

Blackberries are classified as **trailing**, **semi-trailing**, and **erect**. Trailing blackberries (dewberries) produce **canes** that are not self supporting and have low yields. Boysenberry is the main trailing cultivar currently available. Semi-trailing (semi-erect) types (Table 14–4) are fully trailing the first year but become more erect the following year. Current cultivars are thornless and include 'Chester' and 'Triple Crown'. Their fruit ripens about one month after that of the erect type. The semi-trailing and trailing types should not be grown in areas where winter temperatures may drop below 0°F. Erect blackberries (Figure 14–6) have arching, self-supporting canes; some cultivars can tolerate temperatures of 10°F to 15°F without significant injury. Cultivars include 'Arapaho', 'Apache', 'Ouachita', and 'Navaho'.

Recently a new type of blackberry has been released. **Primocane**-fruiting blackberries produce fruit on the first year (primo) canes. Fruit can be produced well into the fall, and this type of plant does well in the foothills and lower elevations of western North Carolina.

Table 14–4. Recommended Blackberry Cultivars for North Carolina

Cultivar	Area[a]	Season	Hardiness	Yield	Fruit Character
Erect					
Apache	All	Mid	Good	Moderate	White drupelets
Arapaho	All	Early	Good	Moderate–high	Earliest thornless; sweet
Cheyenne	All	Mid	Good	Moderate	Large, firm fruit, good for processing
Choctaw	M, P	Early	Moderate	High	Smaller seeds than most cultivars
Navaho	All	Mid-late	Good	Moderate	Sweet; aromatic; large seeds; thornless; rust susceptible
Ouachita	All	Mid	Good	High	Very sweet; large
Shawnee	All	Mid	Good	Moderate–high	Produces heavily for several weeks
Semi-trailing					
Chester	All	Mid-late	Moderate	High	Semi-tart; large
Triple Crown	All	Mid	Moderate	High	Semi-tart; large
Primocane-fruiting					
Freedom	All	Very late	Good	High	Tart, thornless canes
Prime-Jan	M	Very late	Good	Moderate	Tart

[a] S = sandhills-coastal plain; P = piedmont; M = mountains-foothills

Most bramble plants take two years to bear fruit. They produce new **shoots** from the crown of the original plant and from buds on the roots (shoots from the roots are called suckers). Shoots grow for one season and produce **laterals** (side branches). The second year, shoots and flowers develop from buds on the laterals. Fruit is borne on the tips of these new shoots (Figure 14–7). The canes (2-year-old shoots) are biennial and die after bearing fruit. However, some raspberry cultivars (such as 'Heritage') and blackberry cultivars (such as 'Prime-Jan') can produce fruit on the tips of first-year canes.

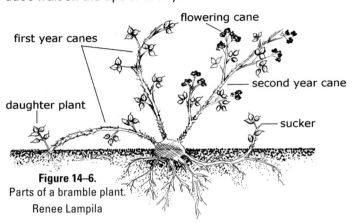

Figure 14–6.
Parts of a bramble plant.
Renee Lampila

Site Selection, Planting, and Maintenance
Blackberries grow best in full sun but can tolerate light shade. Good **air drainage** is preferred because it helps protect the fruit from frost damage, but air drainage is not critical because blackberries bloom later than most fruits. Blackberries grow in a variety of soil types but prefer a well-drained soil. Have a soil test conducted to determine lime and fertilizer needs. The pH should be between 5.8 and 6.8.

Destroy perennial weeds and sod before planting. Avoid a site previously planted in peaches, apples, grapes, or brambles because of potential *crown gall* infection. Avoid planting within 600 feet of wild blackberries, which can spread *double-blossom* and *orange-rust diseases*.

For all types of blackberries, allow at least 10 feet between rows. Erect blackberries can be set as close as 3 feet apart in the row. Semi-trailing plants are very vigorous and should be spaced 6 to 10 feet apart in the row. Less vigorous trailing plants can be set 4 to 6 feet apart. Align plants carefully within a trellis, or build the trellis first.

Early spring is the best time to plant **dormant** plants. If the plants are dry when they arrive, soak the roots in water for several hours. Keep plant roots moist until planting time by either temporarily placing them in a shallow trench and loosely covering with soil or wrapping them in wet burlap. Prepare a planting hole large enough to allow the roots to spread out naturally. Do not prune the roots

except to remove damaged ones. Plant so the crown is 1 inch below ground level; tissue culture plants should be set at ground level. Be sure to ask at the nursery if the plants were produced through the tissue culture process. Tamp the soil firmly to remove air pockets around the roots. Water all new plantings immediately.

Figure 14–7. Fruit is borne on the tips of blackberry branches.
Deborah Austin, Flickr CC BY - 2.0

Training and Pruning
Erect blackberries develop many root **suckers** in addition to new shoots that arise from the crown during the first and subsequent years. If all the suckers were allowed to develop, the planting would soon become a tangled thicket. Let the suckers grow in a band 12 inches wide; remove all others. Erect blackberries can be grown with or without a trellis, but tying the shoots to a trellis yields more berries. A single wire attached to posts about 3 feet above the ground can serve as a quick, easy trellis (Figure 14–8). When the new shoots reach a height of 30 inches to 36 inches in the summer, cut off the tips. This makes the canes branch and grow stout.

During late winter, prune the laterals back to 12 to 18 inches for convenient harvesting and larger berries. Remove any dead and diseased wood. Thin the canes and leave the most vigorous ones spaced to leave about six canes per plant. After harvest, remove all the fruiting canes and burn them or throw them away; this helps manage disease. Be careful not to damage the new green shoots because they will produce next year's crop.

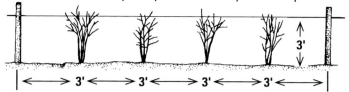

Figure 14–8. A single wire and post trellis for brambles.

During their first year, allow semi-trailing blackberry shoots to grow on the ground without trellising or tie them to bamboo stakes to keep them out of the way. The following spring, tie the shoots to the trellis. In the second and succeeding years, the shoots are more vigorous and upright. Tie them to a trellis as soon as they reach a height of 4 feet to 6 feet and then tip them (cut the tips off) to encourage lateral shoot growth.

Construct the blackberry trellis by stretching a wire between posts set 20 feet to 30 feet apart in the row. End posts should be 8 feet long and set 2 feet into the ground. For semi-trailing blackberries, use two wires at heights of 3 feet and 5 feet from the ground. The wire should be stapled loosely to allow for contracting in cold weather and manual tightening in the spring.

When primocanes reach 3 feet to 5 feet tall, they need to be pinched or tipped. Pinching does two things. First, it maintains a manageable **canopy** height. Second, it enables the canes to produce laterals. These laterals will produce fruit next year.

The ideal diameter to pinch is small enough to remove easily by hand and not use a pruner. Wider diameter cuts that need a pruner create larger wounds. These large wounds do not heal as quickly and are therefore more prone to infection. Figure 14–9 shows a cane before tipping and the same cane after it has been tipped.

The primary disease that occurs as a result of large pruning wounds is cane blight. Cane blight of blackberry is caused by *Leptosphaeria coniothyrium*. For more information on cane blight, see University of Georgia Extension Plant Pathologist Dr. Phil Brannen's interview and publication.

In the spring of the second season, prune the laterals back to 12 inches to 18 inches tall. This greatly increases fruit size. After harvest, remove all the old fruiting canes. Do not remove the new shoots that have started in the spring except to thin them to four to six shoots per crown. The best shoots should be trained to the trellis.

Allow first-year shoots on trailing blackberries to grow along the ground. In late winter or early spring, remove weak canes. Spread the remaining canes along the ground parallel to the trellis, with half the canes going in one direction and half in the other. Each group of canes should be divided again into two groups, one group twisted along the top trellis wire and the other group along the lower trellis wire, and tied securely to the wires. Then tip the canes back to no more than 10 feet in length to improve fruit size.

As with other types of blackberries, remove all the old fruiting canes after harvest.

Fertilization

A blackberry plant requires ½ ounce to 1 ounce of nitrogen per year depending on soil fertility. Well-balanced fertilizers such as 10-10-10 or 16-16-16 are well-suited to blackberries. To calculate the amount of fertilizer to apply, divide the desired amount of nitrogen you wish to apply by the percentage of nitrogen in the fertilizer (for a 10-10-10, the percentage of nitrogen is 10%, or for 16-16-16 it is 16%).

Figure 14–9. Blackberry primocane before and after tipping.
Gina Fernandez

If you wanted to apply ½ ounce of N using a 10-10-10 fertilizer, this formula would apply:

$$\frac{0.5 \text{ ounce}}{0.10 \text{ percent}} \text{ N} = 5 \text{ ounces}$$

If you wanted to apply 1 ounce of N using a 16-16-16 fertilizer:

$$\frac{1 \text{ ounce}}{0.16 \text{ percent}} \text{ N} = 6.25 \text{ ounces}$$

The fertilizer amount should be broken up, with half being applied in early spring when growth starts and half applied in summer just after harvest. Spread the fertilizer in a 12-inch radius around the base of each plant. For late-ripening thornless blackberries, apply the fertilizer no later than July to avoid forcing late-season growth that would be subject to winter injury.

Weed Management
Blackberry plantings should be cultivated frequently or mulched well to manage grass and other weeds. Once they get started, weeds are difficult to control. Begin cultivating in the spring as soon as the soil is workable. Avoid deep cultivation that may cut the blackberry roots; undesirable suckers develop when roots are damaged. Herbicides can be useful on established blackberry plantings; consult the *North Carolina Agricultural Chemicals Manual*.

Irrigation
Young plants may need to be irrigated throughout the first season to improve survival and to promote root development. Blackberries require abundant moisture while the berries are growing and ripening. Moisture stress at that time can reduce both yields and the production of shoots for the following year. If rainfall is less than 1 inch per week, provide supplemental water.

Figure 14–10. A soaker hose on these newly planted raspberry and blackberry plants conserves water.
Lucy Bradley, CC BY - 2.0

Using drip irrigation or a soaker hose rather than over-head irrigation reduces the total amount of water needed and minimizes the potential of fruit rot (Figure 14–10). A minimum rate of drip irrigation for mature blackberry plants is 2 gallons of water per day per plant while berries are developing.

Mulching reduces watering frequency and aids in the management of weeds and grasses that compete for moisture and nutrients. Good mulching materials include pine straw, wood chips, and seed-free grain straw, such as wheat or rye.

Harvesting
The harvest of trailing and some erect thorny blackberries begins about a week or two after the strawberry season (about the first of June in the NC piedmont). Semi-trailing thornless types usually do not begin ripening until mid-summer. For direct-marketed berries that are not shipped, do not harvest fruit when it first turns black; wait until the fruit is dull black in appearance. Sugar levels increase as the berry becomes dull colored.

For more information on blackberries, see NC State Extension's Blackberry and Raspberry Information web page.

RASPBERRIES
Raspberries grow best in cool climates and are not well-suited for hot, humid southern weather. The cultivar 'Dormanred' is an exception that does reasonably well in the South (Table 14–5).

Types and Growth Habits of Raspberries
Like blackberries, raspberries have a biennial growth habit and can be divided into two groups based on their fruiting pattern. Primocane-fruiting types produce fruit on the first-year canes in late summer through fall and on those same canes the next spring. **Floricane**-fruiting types produce fruit on the second-year canes in early summer.

Raspberries may or may not need trellising depending on whether they have an erect, semi-erect, or trailing habit. 'Dormanred' has a trailing habit and 'Mandarin' a semi-erect habit. Black raspberries (blackcaps) have arching canes that root at the tip; they do not require trellising.

Purple and yellow raspberries are less common (Figure 14–11). Though they are not very productive, they can provide a range of fruit color to harvest.

Site Selection, Planting, and Maintenance
Site selection, planting, and maintenance are basically the same as for blackberries (see Site Selection, Planting, and Maintenance for blackberries). In the NC piedmont and NC coastal plain, however, raspberries do best when planted in partial shade provided by a canopy of medium-tall trees (30 feet to 40 feet tall).

Figure 14–11. Yellow raspberries.
Gina Fernandez

Plant Selection and Installation

Plants grown from tissue culture are preferred as they should be free of viruses and phytophthora root rot.

Plant red raspberry cultivars 2 inches to 3 inches deeper than they grew in the nursery. Space them 2 feet to 3 feet apart in the row. Set black raspberry cultivars at the same depth they grew in the nursery, and space plants 2½ feet apart. Rows should be 8 feet to 10 feet apart. The middles can be planted in sod. Cut off all canes to ground level at planting to help manage disease.

Training and Pruning

Black raspberries: They have arching canes so they do not need to be trellised. The plants, however, can benefit from a trellis. Black raspberries are treated much the same as erect blackberries (see above). Summer prune by pinching them back when new shoots reach 18 to 24 inches. It is sometimes necessary to do this a number of times, as not all shoots will be tall enough for pinching on the same date. The three to five buds below the pinched area develop vigorous lateral growth; this allows the canes to become self-supporting. In the spring, prune the laterals back to 12 to 18 inches (Figure 14–12).

Red Raspberries: Because the most productive portion of red raspberry canes is the top third of the cane, trellising is strongly recommended rather than pruning the plants into hedgerows. Space posts 20 feet to 30 feet apart and attach wires at a 4-foot to 5-foot height (Figure 14–13). For the 'Dormanred' cultivar, use two wires located 5 feet above the ground. A single wire can be used (for cultivars other than 'Dormanred'), and the canes should be loosely tied to the wire.

Allow root suckers to develop in a 12-inch to 15-inch band in the row; all other shoots should be removed. Do not pinch the tips of new shoots in the summer. During late February, thin the canes to 4 inches to 6 inches apart along the width of the row. Be sure to select healthy canes and remove weaker ones. Head the canes back to about 5 feet tall.

Remove all fruiting canes after harvest; make cuts close to the ground. Thin new shoots, leaving three to four shoots per foot of row. If a trellis is used, tie the new shoots loosely to it.

Primocane-fruiting types may be grown exclusively for a late-summer crop. For the trellis, use a cross bar or horizontal trellising system. Two-foot cross arms are attached to the posts at a height of 4 feet, and two wires are secured at the ends of the cross arms. The new canes grow between and are supported by the wires with a minimum of tying. Cut the canes to within 2 inches of the ground before new growth starts in the spring. This does not work with other, nonprimocane red raspberry cultivars because it would eliminate the wood that bears fruit.

Researchers have found that yields on raspberries double when grown under a high tunnel. Tunnels also allow for an extended harvest season.

Harvesting

Raspberries can have a long fruiting season. Floricane-fruiting types ripen soon after the strawberry season finishes, whereas primocane-fruiting types can be harvested until a hard frost occurs in the NC mountains. Ripe berries should be rolled off the plant rather than squeezed or pulled. Raspberries are notorious for their poor shelf life. Pick them in the morning after the dew has dried and when the air is cool. Refrigerate or use promptly.

For more information on raspberries, see NC State Extension's Blackberry and Raspberry Information web page.

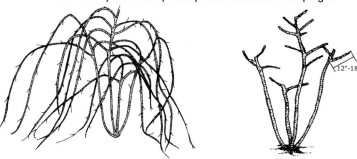

Figure 14–12. Left: Black raspberry plant before spring pruning. Right: The same plant after pruning.

Table 14–5. Recommended Raspberry Cultivars for North Carolina
(Yield in the NC piedmont may decline in time due to stress.)

Type	Cultivar	Season	Region*	Yield	Berry Size	Flavor	Remarks
Red Cultivars	Dormanred	Summer	CP, P, M	Medium	Medium	Fair	Shiny fruit, good for jams
Red Cultivars	Latham	Summer	P, M	Medium	Medium	Fair	Fruit can be soft, plant is vigorous
Red Cultivars	Joan J	Everbearing	M	High	Large	Good	Early everbearing season
Red Cultivars	Caroline	Everbearing	M	High	Large	Good	Mid everbearing season
Red Cultivars	Nantahala	Everbearing	M	Medium	Medium	Excellent	Sold as 'Sweet Repeat' in some catalogs, late everbearing season
Black Cultivars	Allen	Summer	M	Medium	Large	Good	Good adaptation, early to midseason
Black Cultivars	Bristol	Summer	M	Medium	Large	Good	Disease susceptible, midseason
Black Cultivars	Jewell	Summer	M	High	Large	Excellent	Firm berry, hardy, most widely adapted and reliable yield, midseason

* M = Mountain, P = Piedmont, CP = Coastal Plain

Figure 14–13. To trellis raspberries, space posts 20 feet to 30 feet apart and attach wires at a 4-foot to 5-foot height.
Lucy Bradley, CC BY - 2.0

Figure 14–14. Nantahala and Heritage raspberries.
Gina Fernandez

Table 14–6. Raspberry Cultivation in North Carolina

	REGION			Fruit Production	Trellis	Prune
	Coastal Plain	Piedmont	Foothills & Mountains			
Primocane	None recommended	None recommended	Caroline, Heritage, Nantahala (Figure 14–14), Autumn Britten, Himbo Top, Joan J, Anne	First-year canes, late summer, and second year	Cross bar or horizontal	
Floricane	Dormanred	Dormanred, Mandarin if available	Dormanred, Lauren, Moutere, Nova, Latham	Second-year canes, early summer		Summer prune new shoots at 18 to 24 inches

Blueberries

Blueberries (Vaccinium species) are native to North America, and several species may be found growing wild in North Carolina. These wild-growing bushes are well-known to hikers and other outdoor enthusiasts, but their berries are not often harvested due to the small berry size and sparse yield. Economically important types of blueberries grown in North Carolina are improved cultivars (cultivated varieties) of three types: highbush (*Vaccinium corymbosum*), southern highbush (*V. corymbosum* interspecific hybrids), and rabbiteye (*V. virgatum*, syn. *V. ashei*).

Other well-known Vaccinium species that are not grown in North Carolina due to lack of sufficient winter chilling include lowbush blueberries (*V. angustifolium* and *V. myrtilloides*) and the cranberry (*V. macropcarpon*).

Blueberries are relatively easy to grow but demand special site and soil preparation. They are acid-loving, wetland plants requiring a well-drained, highly organic soil with constant moisture. Blueberries do not grow well under conditions where other plants may be expected to thrive. They can be grown successfully throughout the state if the grower has a clear understanding of the crop requirements. Large-scale commercial production, however, is limited to certain soils in the southeastern NC coastal plain. Despite their name, highbush and southern highbush plants (6 feet to 8 feet tall) are not as tall as rabbiteye plants (15 feet tall). Bushes are fully mature by year 8 and can remain productive for 20 years or more with proper care.

Highbush blueberries, sometimes called "northern highbush blueberries," were first selected from the wild in New Jersey (Figure 14–15). They are well-adapted to colder climates and are the best species for the western NC mountains at higher elevations (>2500 ft). Highbush cultivars often do not grow well in the NC piedmont and NC coastal plain because highbush blueberries are not adapted to those soils. Often the NC coastal plain does not receive enough winter chilling to allow highbush plants to leaf and flower normally the following spring.

Southern highbush blueberries are intermediate between highbush and rabbiteye in their chilling requirements, winter hardiness, and soil adaptability (Figure 14–16). Southern highbush cultivars account for a large proportion of new commercial acreage in the Southeast, but many cultivars are early blooming and are not suitable for home garden use because of the increased risk of crop loss due to spring freezes.

Rabbiteye blueberries get their name from the immature fruit; the light color and pink blush on the blossom end look like a rabbit's eye (Figure 14–17). The rabbiteye blueberry is a southern species native to the Gulf Coast states. Rabbiteye blueberries are well-known for their vigor and productivity. They ripen later and over a longer period than highbush berries. The fruit has a slightly tougher skin and better storage life than highbush. Rabbiteyes are more tolerant of drought, heat, and a wider range of soil types than highbush.

Figure 14–15. Highbush blueberry.
Bill Cline

Figure 14–16. Southern highbush blueberry.
Bill Cline

Figure 14–17. Rabbiteye blueberry.
Bill Cline

Table 14–7. Blueberry Cultivation in North Carolina

	Mountains	Piedmont	Coastal Plain
Does Well	Highbush, Rabbiteye (at elevations below 2,000 ft to 2,500 ft, depending on site)	Rabbiteye	Rabbiteye
Can Survive		Highbush, Southern highbush	Highbush, Southern highbush

Cultivar Selection

Cultivars vary in their ability to grow on different soil types and also vary in their need for cold winter temperatures (hours below 45°F). For instance, in the NC coastal plain, cultivars with a chill requirement between 350 hours and 1,000 hours do best. Cultivars that require fewer than 350 hours often bloom too early and are damaged by a late frost, while those requiring more than 1,000 hours may not receive enough chilling to leaf and bloom normally. You must plant at least two different varieties of blueberry for pollination and fruit set. There are many cultivars that thrive in North Carolina (Table 14–8).

Table 14–8. Recommended Blueberry Cultivars for North Carolina[a]

Highbush[b]	Rabbiteye[c]	Highbush and Southern Highbush[d]
Duke	Robeson[e] (early pentaploid)	O'Neal (begins May 15 in sandhills-coastal plain)
Sunrise	Climax	Star[e]
Draper[e]	Premier	Duke
Bluecrop	Columbus[e] (mid-season)	New Hanover[e]
Echota	Ira	Legacy (begins June 1 in sandhills-coastal plain)
Blueray	Tifblue	
Toro	Powderblue	
Berkeley	Onslow[e]	
Jersey		
Patriot		
Liberty[e]		
Elliott		
Aurora[e]		

[a] Listed in order of ripening, earliest to latest. You must plant at least two different varieties of blueberry for pollination and fruit set.

[b] For the western mountains above 2,500 feet or with extended winter temperatures below 10°F.

[c] For most sandhills-coastal plain, piedmont, and foothills sites below 2,500 feet with minimum winter temperatures usually above 10°F.

[d] For sand-based, high-organic soils in the sandhills-coastal plain; on a trial basis only for well-drained, amended, mulched, and irrigated sites in the piedmont and foothills.

[e] Trial basis only.

Growth Cycle

Blueberries are upright, deciduous, thornless woody perennials, forming multi-trunked bushes.

Winter. Blueberries lose their leaves in winter. Healthy new canes have smooth red bark, while older wood is gray (Figure 14–18). Winter pruning is performed every year to remove some gray, older canes and encourage new growth. Bushes that are not pruned eventually become less productive, with smaller, less flavorful fruit.

Spring. Flower buds formed the previous fall open in spring, and flowers are pollinated by both native insects (bumblebees, solitary bees) and honey bees (Figure 14–19);

Figure 14–20. Blueberry buds for future flowers and leaves.
Bill Cline

Figure 14–18. Newer wood is reddish and older wood is gray.
Helena Jacoba, Flickr CC BY - 2.0

Figure 14–19. Blueberry digger bee (*Habropoda laboriosa*) pollinating a Highbush blueberry flower.
Judy Gallagher, Flickr CC BY - 2.0

Figure 14–21. Blueberries develop attractive fall color.
Orionpozo, Flickr CC BY - 2.0

most blueberry cultivars cannot form fruit without insect pollination. Flower buds open sequentially in the spring, from the tip down. The flowers within a bud open in a similar manner, with the flowers nearest the tip opening first. Flower bud age affects blooming; buds on older, thinner fruiting twigs open before buds on younger, thicker wood.

Summer. Berries develop and ripen 45 to 80 days after bloom, depending on the cultivar, and ripen over a period of three weeks to five weeks. Throughout the year, leafy blueberry shoots grow in flushes of rapid growth, stopping as the uppermost (**apical**) leaf bud aborts, causing the very tip of the shoot to stop growing. Then, another leaf bud near the tip of the shoot opens, and another flush of growth begins. Each shoot may have several of these growth flushes during the season, and each may grow 6 inches to 10 inches long. Extensive growth usually ceases in midsummer as flower buds begin forming in leaf **axils** at the tips of twigs (Figure 14–20).

Fall. Most healthy shoots develop three to eight flower buds; each flower bud can produce up to 10 flowers the following spring. Blueberries develop attractive fall colors (mostly deep reds, but some yellows), and the leaves drop in early winter (Figure 14–21).

Site Selection, Planting, and Maintenance

Site Selection

Free air movement is especially important in the spring when late spring freezes can kill the emerging flowers. Low-lying planting sites with poor air movement tend to be colder than surrounding higher areas. Avoid areas surrounded by trees. Trees provide too much shade, compete with plants for water and nutrients, and interfere with air movement around the plants. Highbush blueberries should be planted in areas that have 800 to 1,200 hours below 45°F each winter and a minimum winter temperature of not less than -10°F. In North Carolina, highbush blueberries can be grown in the coastal plain, piedmont, and mountains, but they are more difficult to grow than rabbiteyes. Rabbiteyes generally need 400 to 600 hours of winter chilling and a minimum temperature not below 5°F to 10°F. They can be grown in the NC coastal plain, piedmont, and in the mountains at elevations below 2,500 feet.

Blueberries require soil that is acidic and well-drained but with good moisture retention. Have a soil test taken in the fall before planting. The optimum pH for blueberries is around 4.5. Poor growth and leaf chlorosis can be expected when the pH is above 5.0 for highbush and above 5.3 for rabbiteye.

Preparation

Many home garden soils have a pH that is too high for blueberries. If the pH is above 6.0, planting is not recommended. If sandy soil has a pH below 6.0 but above 5.3, apply wettable sulfur (90% S) at the rate of 1 pound (2½ cups) per 100 square feet to lower the pH by one unit (from 6.0 to 5.0, for example). On soils containing silt, clay, or more than 2% organic matter, apply 2 pounds per 100 square feet for the same pH reduction. Some soils in the NC mountains are very high in manganese. When growing blueberries on such soils, keep the pH around 5.0. Any sulfur applications should be made a year before the anticipated planting time. Check the pH one or two times during the first year (after applying sulfur) to determine if

more sulfur is needed. Do not plant in high pH soils without first lowering the pH and adding acidifying organic matter.

Prior to planting, all blueberries benefit from the incorporation into the soil of organic materials such as peat moss, composted pine bark, or decomposed softwood sawdust into the soil. Hardwood sawdust is not recommended because it is often attacked by decay fungi. Do not use undecomposed sawdust or wood chips to amend soil. Instead, compost the sawdust and use wood chips as a surface mulch to suppress weeds.
A blueberry plant's root system is shallow, fibrous, and lacks **root hairs.** Often 90% of the root system is in the top 6 inches of soil. Highbush blueberry roots do not penetrate tight, clay soils easily and require a loose, crumbly soil to develop an extensive root system. For heavier soils, incorporate organic materials such as composted pine bark or decomposed softwood sawdust to improve soil aeration.

Blueberry roots cannot tolerate standing water for extended periods during any part of the year. Check for drainage problems before planting; dig a hole 6 inches to 8 inches deep and observe the water level after heavy rains. Water should not remain for more than 24 hours. If the drainage is not good, choose another planting site or prepare a 4-foot-wide raised bed.

Blueberries grow best in soils with high levels of organic matter (3% or more), such as those found in areas of the southeastern NC coastal plain where the commercial blueberry industry is located and in certain high-elevation sites in the NC mountains. Most mineral soils in the NC piedmont contain less than 1% organic matter. To increase the organic matter content, apply and incorporate a 3-inch to 4-inch layer of organic matter in a band 36 inches to 48 inches wide.

Planting

Do not plant in heavy clay soil; raised beds are necessary on most of these sites. Apply the band of organic material on the soil surface and rototill into the surface soil, but make sure to form a mound (for single plants) or ridge (for rows of plants) at least 10 inches to 12 inches above the surrounding soil surface. The mound or ridge ensures adequate drainage, but it still needs to be watered thoroughly two to three times per week during drought periods.

Two-year-old potted or bare root nursery plants (12 inches to 36 inches tall) are generally used. Bare root plants should be transplanted in late winter to early spring. Roots must be kept moist at all times. Plants more than 3 years old or less than 2 years old may die from water stress the first growing season. Potted plants can be transplanted in the late fall or spring. Problems with survival and growth often occur if plants are pot-bound. With container plants it is essential to score (cut with a knife) the root ball several times to prevent the roots from growing in a circular manner.

Space rabbiteye plants 6 feet apart in the row; rows should be 10 feet to 12 feet apart. Space highbush plants 4 feet to 5 feet apart; rows should be 8 feet to 10 feet apart. Plant in a raised bed at the same depth as the plants grew in the nursery, and apply a 3-inch to 5-inch layer of pine bark, wood chips, aged sawdust, or pine needle mulch. Leave at least 3 inches around the trunk clear of mulch to prevent insect, disease, and pest problems. Avoid using fine hardwood sawdust as it may form a crust that prevents water from entering the soil.

Prune the plant to leave only the strongest three or four shoots. The plant has the best chance of survival and subsequent development if two-thirds of the top growth on bare root and one-half on potted plants is removed. Also, after planting, remove all flower buds to stimulate good shoot and root development (Figure 14–22). Blueberry flowers and fruits drain considerable energy from the plant; fruit yields in subsequent years can suffer because of poor plant development in the first two establishment years.

Setting out new plants (Figure 14–22) — Always prune or rub off all flower buds and cut back 1/2 to 2/3 of the height at the time of planting. For potted plants, gently separate and spread out the roots so that the root mass is no longer the shape of a pot.

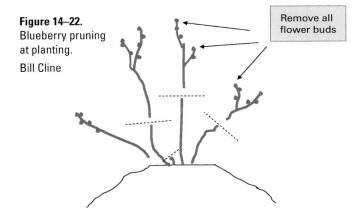

Figure 14–22.
Blueberry pruning at planting.
Bill Cline

Remove all flower buds

Fertilization

Blueberries are easily damaged by excess fertilizer. Fertilizer dropped in lumps or piles under the bush can cause serious root damage or death. Do not fertilize immediately after planting; wait until the first leaves have emerged, then apply 1 tablespoon of an azalea fertilizer or 10-10-10 in a circle 1 foot from the plants. Repeat at approximately six-week intervals before rainfall or irrigation until mid-August in the NC coastal plain and mid-July in the NC mountains. Use ½ tablespoon of ammonium nitrate

(33-0-0) instead of a complete fertilizer for the second and subsequent applications if the phosphorus index was above 60 on the soil test.

For the second year, double the first year's rates and increase the circle around the plants to 1½ feet. Make the first application when new growth begins in spring. For bearing plants, apply 1 cup of a complete fertilizer such as 10-10-10 in a circle 3 feet from the plant as new growth begins. If more vigorous growth is desired, **side-dress** with ¼ cup of ammonium nitrate at six-week intervals until July 1. For mature plants, 6 inches to 12 inches of new growth per year is adequate; if the plant has grown beyond this range, decrease the fertilizer rate.

Ammonium nitrate (33-0-0) may be difficult to obtain due to security concerns about its explosive properties. If necessary, urea (46-0-0) can be used as a substitute for ammonium nitrate.

If the soil pH is 5.0 to 5.5 in an established planting, side-dress with ammonium sulfate (21-0-0) rather than ammonium nitrate (33-0-0). If the pH is above 5.5, apply wettable sulfur in a narrow band under the drip line of the bush at the rate of 1/10 pound per bush to lower the pH by one unit (for instance, 6.0 to 5.0). Do not overapply sulfur, and use only after soil testing to determine pH. Sulfur requires months of warm weather to break down and reduce pH and should not be applied every year.

Mulching
If mulch is applied after planting and replaced at the rate of 2 inches per year, few weed problems should develop. Hand pull the occasional weeds that do grow. Try to avoid using a hoe around blueberries as they are shallow rooted and easily damaged. If row middles are in sod, mow often to prevent running grasses and weed seeds from invading the mulched area

Irrigation
Blueberries are very sensitive to drought, and supplemental irrigation is absolutely essential the first and second years after planting. Hand watering the soil around the plant with a hose is possible for a few bushes; a soaker hose usually gives more uniform watering for maximum yield. Large-scale plantings are most often watered with drip irrigation lines using pressure-compensated emitters. In the southeastern NC coastal plain where surface and well water is abundant, overhead irrigation is used both for drought relief and for freeze protection.

Pruning
All cultivated species require annual pruning to remove dead, diseased, or insect-infested wood and to manage bush height and shape. Pruning stimulates new, vigorous growth on which the next year's fruit is borne. And

pruning helps to manage fruit production by increasing berry size and preventing overcropping, which can result in small, poor-quality fruit and may shorten the life of the plant.

The following steps can be used at each bush to rapidly eliminate undesirable growth and to select for flexible, upright, and productive canes.

Tools and Techniques

Most blueberry pruning is done during the dormant (winter) season after the leaves have fallen. Mature canes can be up to 2 inches in diameter, so long-handled loppers capable of cutting large stems are essential. Smaller one-handed pruners are used for finish work and for shaping young bushes. Avoid leaving stubs and do not treat pruning cuts.

Steps in Winter Pruning (November – March)
(Figure 14–23)

- Define the crown. Pruning starts at the ground, not at the top of the bush. Visualize a circle 12 to 18 inches in diameter around the crown of the bush, and remove ALL shoots of any age that have emerged from the ground outside the circle. This narrows the base of the bush to facilitate hand-harvesting.

- Remove low-angled canes and crossovers. Low-angled canes that are too close to the ground are undesirable because the fruit is more likely to contact the ground, or to be contaminated by rain-splashed soil. Remove these low-lying branches, and also any canes that angle through the bush (crossovers). What remains is a narrower bush consisting of the most upright canes.

- Open the center. If needed, remove one to three large canes from the center of the bush to reduce crowding, improve air circulation and phase out older canes. The older canes to target for removal are larger and grayer in color, and are more likely to be covered with a fuzzy growth of foliose lichens.

- **Thinning** and **heading** back. As a blueberry cane ages, it branches repeatedly, resulting in smaller and smaller diameter lateral twigs in successive years. If left unpruned, this results in excessive numbers of unproductive, matchstick-sized shoots, each with a few tiny berries. To avoid reaching this stage, thin canes by making cuts to selectively remove clumps of twiggy, brushy-looking, matchstick-sized laterals (Figure 14–24). At this time also cut (head back) any long whips or canes to a convenient height for picking.

These basic hand-pruning steps can be used with any blueberry bush. Every cultivar has a slightly different growth habit, and only experience will guide how to manage each one. Some cultivars produce too many new shoots from the ground and require a lot of thinning,

while others are less prone to sprouting. The goal should be to have a multi-trunked bush with strong canes of all different ages emerging from the ground, so as each older cane is removed, a younger cane is already there to replace it.

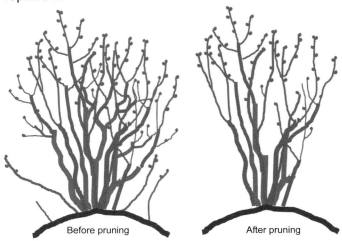

Figure 14–23. Properly pruning a blueberry bush November – March.
Bill Cline

Figure 14–24. Healthy branches on the left, "matchstick" branches on the right.
Bill Cline

About Flower Buds

Yield reduction via flower bud removal occurs when winter pruning is done properly. Flower buds are readily visible during winter pruning, and it is tempting to leave too many, which is a mistake. Expect to remove at least a third of the flower buds during pruning to prevent the bush from being overloaded with fruit in one year. This results in plant stress that causes reduced yields in the following years. Several years of this type of stress eventually requires even more severe pruning to bring the bush back into production.

Pruning Young Blueberry Plants

Young blueberry bushes are usually planted in late winter (February or early March) while fully dormant and leafless. During the first year, flower buds are removed by pruning, or by stripping off flowers by hand after the blooms emerge. In subsequent years, flower buds must be thinned to prevent overcropping and to promote vegetative growth vital to the establishment of a full-sized bush.

The following diagrams show the growth of a single blueberry bush for the first three years, with "before" and "after" pruning comparisons each February.

Year one (Figure 14–25) — The goal is to avoid fruit production entirely. With removal of all flower buds at the beginning of year one, the bush grows vegetatively, and by fall of the first year has increased in size and produced more flower buds.

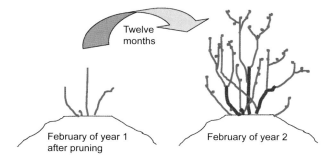

Twelve months

February of year 1 after pruning

February of year 2

Figure 14–25. Growth during the first year after pruning.
Bill Cline

Year two (Figure 14–26) — In year two, remove low-lying or weak shoots and cross-overs, keeping the healthiest, large upright canes. Some flower buds may be allowed to produce fruit in year two if the bush grew vigorously in year one.

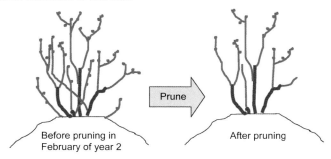

Prune

Before pruning in February of year 2

After pruning

Figure 14–26. Growth February of the second year.
Bill Cline

First crop? (Figure 14–27) — The bush may be allowed to produce a few berries in year two; however, the goal is still to promote vegetative growth that will build the structure of the bush for years to come.

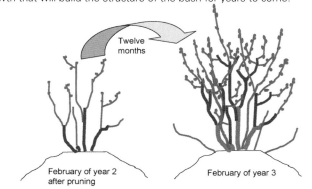

Twelve months

February of year 2 after pruning

February of year 3

Figure 14–27. Growth during the second year.
Bill Cline

Year three (Figure 14–28) — The bush is well established and capable of producing a significant crop. However, routine pruning should still remove 40% to 50% of the flower buds. Begin selecting new basal shoots that will replace older canes.

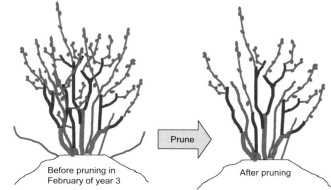

Prune

Before pruning in February of year 3

After pruning

Figure 14–28. Growth during the third year.
Bill Cline

Harvest

Blueberry fruit ripens approximately two months after blooming, although harvest time varies with cultivar, weather conditions, and plant vigor. Plants should produce about ½ pound per bush in the third year, and 1 pound to 2 pounds per bush in the fourth year.

Highbush cultivars begin ripening in mid-May in the southeastern NC coastal plain and in early July in the NC mountains. Highbush blueberries are the best quality when picked every five to seven days, depending upon temperature. With good care, mature highbush plants should produce more than 8 pounds of fruit each year.

Rabbiteye harvest begins in mid-June in the southeastern NC coastal plain. Rabbiteye fruit continues to increase in size and flavor for some time after berries turn blue and appear to ripen. Allow the fruit to become fully ripe before picking (three to six days after turning blue). Rabbiteye cultivars can produce 12 to 25 pounds per year.

Birds also harvest blueberries. Nylon netting draped over the bushes or supported on a framework is usually the best method, but is not practical for large plantings. Some success with bird management is achieved with scare devices and electronic bird distress calls.

Insects and Diseases

Blueberries have historically been grown successfully in North Carolina without using insecticides or fungicides. In 2009, however, a new exotic fruit fly, the spotted wing drosophila (SWD), became a problem. Most sites are affected by this insect and some may require the use of organic or conventional insecticides. Some homeowner sites may also require fungicide sprays to manage mummy berry and other fungal diseases. See Appendix C "Diagnostic Tables," for common problems that affect blueberries. For more information, see the NC State Extension Blueberry Portal.

14

Figure 14–29. Many cultivars of grapes can be grown successfully in North Carolina.
Bill Cline

Grapes

Growing grapes in North Carolina home gardens can be challenging, but also rewarding and tasty. Careful selection of cultivars that are well-adapted to your specific soil conditions and climate ensures success. Bunch grapes perform well in the NC piedmont and NC mountains, while the NC coastal plain can support muscadine grapes. One grapevine can produce up to 10 pounds of fruit. Though grapevines are **self-fertile**, planting multiple cultivars extends your harvest season (Figures 14–29).

Parts of a Grapevine

Trunk – the main perennial, woody part of the vine.

Buds – the conical swellings found at each node on shoots and canes.

Shoots – the current season's growth; as they mature, they are called canes.

Canes – the mature shoots of the current season or the dormant growth of the preceding season that have five or more nodes.

Arms or cordons – the horizontal perennial part of the vine along which fruiting spurs are distributed.

Renewal spurs – canes pruned to two or three buds; canes from these spurs are selected for fruit production the following season when vines are cane pruned.

Bunch and Wine Grapes

Bunch grapes are one of the most difficult fruits to grow in North Carolina due to disease susceptibility. They also have very specific soil requirements. Success depends on attention to the details of cultivar and rootstock selection, soil management and amendment, training, pruning, and particularly pest and disease management. All bunch grapes are self-fertile and may be planted alone or with other cultivars

Cultivar Selection

Bunch Grapes: There are three basic types of bunch grapes grown in North Carolina. American bunch grapes produce small clusters with big berries and have moderate yields, good disease resistance, and cold hardiness. They grow best in the lower elevations of the NC mountains and NC piedmont. In the NC coastal plain, *Pierce's disease* kills or shortens the life expectancy of bunch grapes. Some of the newer cultivars are seedless for fresh consumption, but they are also susceptible to *Pierce's disease*. Most American grapes are grown on their own roots, although they may benefit from being grafted on rootstock. The bunch grapes listed in Table 14–9 are the most suitable for growing in the NC piedmont and in western North Carolina. Six grapevines should furnish enough fruit for most families. A mature vine can yield 10 to 20 pounds or more of fresh fruit. Early-season table grapes begin ripening in midsummer.

Table 14–9. American Bunch Grapes Recommendations for North Carolina[a]
(These cultivars are suitable for home production in the NC piedmont and NC mountains.)

Cultivar	Season	Color	Berry Size	Best Use[b]	Skin	Comments
Catawba	Late	Red	Medium	F, J, W	Slipskin	All purpose grape; thick skin; seeded
Concord	Early-Mid	Black	Medium	F, J	Slipskin	Ripens unevenly within the cluster in warm to hot climates; thick skin; seeded
Delaware	Mid	Red	Small	F, J, W	Slipskin	Excellent wine quality for American type; good flavor; thick skin; seeded
Faith	Early	Blue	Medium	F	Non-slipskin	Seedless though occasional seed traces can be found; uneven fruit set some years; occasional slight skin astringency
Gratitude	Mid-Late	White	Medium	F	Non-slipskin	Seedless; exceptionally thin skin; very tight clusters; occasional winter injury
Hope	Mid	White	Small – Medium	F	Non-slipskin	Seedless; thin skin; slight fruit cracking after rain; tight clusters
Joy	Early	Blue	Small – Medium	F	Non-slipskin	Seedless; thinnest skin of University of Arkansas cultivars; soft texture; occasional variable berry set (some shot berries) and shatter of ripe berries in some years
Jupiter	Very early	Blue	Large	F	Non-slipskin	Semi-crisp; seedless with some small soft seed traces
Mars	Early	Blue	Medium	F	Slipskin	Thick skin; seedless with occasional seed traces; very winter hardy
Neptune	Early-Mid	White	Medium	F	Non-slipskin	Seedless though some soft seed traces can be found
Niagara	Mid	White	Medium	F, J	Slipskin	Harvest early if a reduction in foxy (musty odor flavor) character is desired; thick skin; seeded
Norton	Late	Black	Medium	W	Slipskin	High acid, high pH fruit; small clusters; very vigorous; also known as Cynthiana
Reliance	Early	Pink	Medium	F	Slipskin	Hardiest of University of Arkansas cultivars; seedless and seed trace free; susceptible to fruit cracking with rain near maturity
Saturn	Early	Red	Medium	F	Non-slipskin	Crisp texture; moderately hardy; seedless but small seed traces observed
Sunbelt	Early-Mid	Blue	Large	F, J	Slipskin	Nicknamed "Southern Concord"; characteristics very comparable to Concord grapes, however, it is more adapted to hot weather; ripens more evenly than Concord; thick skin; seeded
Venus	Very early	Blue	Medium	F	Slipskin	Seed traces often noticeable

[a] For successful production, all of these cultivars will need a regular control program for fungal diseases and insects.

[b] F = fresh fruit, J = juice, jams, jelly, W = wine

Table 14–10. Wine Grape Recommendations for North Carolina[a]
(These cultivars are suitable for home production in the NC piedmont and NC mountains.)

Cultivar	Season	Color	Berry Size	Skin	Comments
French-American Hybrids					
Chambourcin	Late	Blue	Small	Non-slipskin	Wine can have herbaceous flavors if fruit is under ripe or with poor wine-making techniques; otherwise, excellent wine quality; cold tender; more disease resistant than European cultivars
Chardonel	Early-Mid	White	Small	Non-slipskin	Excellent wine quality; flavor similar to Chardonnay; has similar disease susceptibility as Chardonnay
Seyval	Late	White	Small	Non-slipskin	Good wine; crop reduction required to achieve good quality
Traminette	Early-Mid	White to pink	Small	Non-slipskin	Fruit and wine flavor similar to Gewürztraminer ("spicy"); more disease resistant than its Gewürztraminer parent, but still susceptible to downy mildew
European Wine Grapes (*Vitis vinifera L.*)[b]					
Cabernet Franc	Mid	Blue	Small	Non-slipskin	Performs better than Cabernet Sauvignon
Cabernet Sauvignon	Very Late	Blue	Small	Non-slipskin	Wine can be herbaceous if vegetative growth is not controlled
Chardonnay	Early-Mid	White	Small	Non-slipskin	Early bud break, frost problems; very susceptible to foliar diseases; excellent wine quality

[a] For successful production, all of these cultivars will need a very regular control program for fungal diseases and insects.

[b] This is a small selection of the hundreds of European grape cultivars that are available. There are other cultivars that are grown in NC with varying degrees of success.

Wine Grapes: The European grapes or *Vitis vinifera* are wine-type grapes. *V. vinifera* have poor disease resistance and lower cold tolerance than most American bunch grapes. Hybrid bunch grape cultivars resulting from crosses of *V. vinifera* and native American cultivars are known as French-American hybrids. Many of these hybrid cultivars are more resistant to common diseases of grapes than the pure *V. vinifera* cultivars. They are primarily bred for winemaking. *V. vinifera* and French-American hybrids require very intensive cultural practices and must be grafted on rootstock (Couderc 3309, 101-14 MGT, Riparia Gloire). Both types require frequent and careful spraying for disease and insect pests. Ripening begins in late summer and continues into fall depending upon the variety.

V. vinifera and French-American hybrids are very susceptible to *Pierce's disease*. Wine grapes that are suitable for growing in the NC piedmont and NC mountains are listed in Table 14–10.

Planting and Maintenance
Planting
Plant grapevines in late winter and early spring. Vigorous 1-year-old plants are best. Two-year-old plants cost more and do not start bearing any earlier than 1-year-old plants. Set bunch grapes 5 feet to 6 feet apart. If there are enough vines to use a tractor, allow row widths wide enough to accommodate it (about 10 feet apart). Otherwise, ideal row width is no less than a 1:1 ratio of row width to canopy height. For example, if a trellis allows for a canopy height of 6 feet, the narrowest the row can be is 6 feet. Dig a hole large enough to let the roots spread out naturally (root pruning is not recommended except to remove damaged roots). Plant the vines the same depth or slightly deeper than they grew in the nursery. If the vine is grafted, the graft union must be 3 inches to 4 inches above the soil line. Do not place fresh manure or fertilizer in the hole. Tamp the soil firmly around the roots and water plants. Eliminate air pockets but do not compact the soil or drown the roots.

Training and Pruning

Erect the trellis before planting or as soon as possible after planting (Figure 14–30). Use 8-foot treated posts 3 inches to 4 inches in diameter. Set the posts 2 feet into the ground and allow for two vines per panel to provide adequate support for a mature vine's fruit and foliage in a high wind. End posts should be 8 feet apart, 3 feet into the ground, and braced. This bracing system is commonly used in fencing. Regardless of species, 3 feet to 4 feet of canopy are required to properly ripen fruit and sustain the grapevine. A three-wire to five-wire vertical trellis can be used for *V. vinifera* and French-American hybrid cultivars that have an erect growing habit. The fruiting wire should be about 40 inches above the soil. Foliage wires are equally spaced alternately or in pairs to within a foot of the top of the trellis post. For American and French-American hybrid cultivars with a pendulous growth habit, only one fruiting wire is needed, and no foliage wires are required. The wire should be about 5 feet to 6 feet above the soil surface to provide room for sufficient foliage to support the crop and for ease of weed management under the vine. Use 9-gauge or 11-gauge high tensile wire for the fruiting wire stretched horizontally on firmly set posts. A lighter gauge, galvanized wire can be used for foliage management. If using metal line posts, they must be hot-dipped galvanized posts.

Year 1. During the first season, the primary objective for grapevine growth is the development of a healthy root system. Weed management around the vine during the first growing season is critical in development of a long-lived, productive grapevine. After setting the vine, prune to two or three stems and cut back to two buds each (Figure 14–31). In the first growing season, the vine may be kept upright by loosely tying shoots to a training stake. Most of the training work, however, is done in the second growing season.

Pinch lateral shoots back to the leaf growing on the main shoot. This allows the main shoot to grow more rapidly, possibly saving as much as a year in establishing a healthy vine. Do not pinch laterals at or just below the fruiting wire, however, as these laterals provide the future cordons for the vines.

For best yield, quality, and disease management, grapes should be pruned every year. A vine stores a limited amount of food in its roots, trunk, and canes during the winter. In the spring, food reserves are directed to buds for shoot growth. If left unpruned, those reserves must be distributed to numerous buds. As a result, the vine produces many weak shoots and small, poorly ripened fruit clusters. Pruning reduces the number of buds so the food reserves are concentrated in those that remain. Grapes are borne on the current season's wood that grows from buds formed on last season's growth.

Year 2. The goal for the second year of the vine's life is to establish the permanent wood and lay a groundwork for the fruiting structures of the vine. In the spring following planting, leave one or two shoots to form trunks. On each future trunk leave two buds. Select the strongest shoots from the previous growing season. When new growth begins and the first shoots from the two-bud stem reach 6 inches to 10 inches in length, select the one or two most vigorous and prune off the others. Again, tie the shoot gently to a training stake (tomato or bamboo stake).

After the shoot reaches pencil size at the fruiting wire, tip the shoot to force laterals. As the new shoots begin to grow, support their upright growth for as long as possible. This allows for stronger growth and more rapid filling of the fruiting wire (Figure 14–32). When appropriate, orient the lateral shoots or cordons horizontally on the fruiting wire with one cordon in each direction. To support the cordon, at most, loop the shoot 1.5 times for every linear 3 feet of fruiting wire. Once the cordon has filled the allotted space, allow the shoot tip to drop below the fruiting wire. This allows for more uniform bud break of laterals along the horizontal cordon. If the shoot drops too close to the ground for weed management, it is time to cut it back to the fruiting wire. Leave about one hand-width of separation between cordons on adjacent grapevines. Remove any fruit that may develop as it weakens the vine's vegetative growth. The second winter, prune the laterals back to one-bud "spurs" spaced about one hand-width apart.

Year 3. There is now a small production of fruit on vines that have filled the allotted trellis area. For shoots that are 1 foot or less long, remove fruit from that shoot. For shoots greater than 1 foot long and up to 2 feet long, leave two clusters on that shoot. For shoots greater than 2 feet in length, leave two clusters on those shoots. Follow this basic rule for the life of the vine to maintain long-term health. Shoots should be about a hand-width apart. In the third winter, if cordon training with spur pruning is the selected method, prune back to two buds per cane.

Long-cane training and pruning

Some cultivars respond better to annual long-cane pruning rather than the cordon-and-spur system. There are at least two reasons to cane prune rather than cordon train and spur prune. First, completely replacing the fruiting arm annually can reduce disease pressure within the canopy. Second, some cultivars do not have fruitful base buds (the buds left in normal spur pruning). For this training system, no cordons are established. Each year a new cane is laid down as a replacement for the previous year's cane (one in each direction). There should be about five buds per foot, and the cane should be long enough to fill the allotted trellis space. In addition to the new fruiting wood, a two-bud renewal spur is left at the head of the vine to develop the fruiting cane for the next year. Cane pruning should be used for the American bunch grape and some European wine grape cultivars.

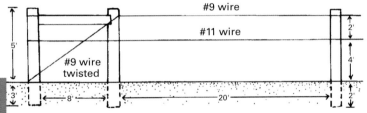

Figure 14–30. Trellis for grapes using a two-wire system.

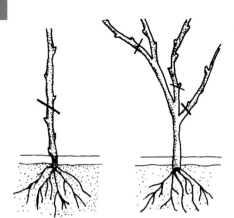

Figure 14–31. Pruning of bare root grape vines after planting.

Figure 14–32. Train the young shoots to a training stake. Remove any side shoots that develop. Pinch off the growing tip when the vine reaches the top of the trellis.

Shoot Tucking

Once European grape vines are established and are producing the vertical shoots off of the fruiting wire, the shoots must be tucked or trapped between the foliage wires. This supports the canopy in an erect configuration, reduces insect and disease pressure, and increases fruitfulness of the buds in the subsequent year. Shoots should be topped during the growing season to maintain a 3-foot to 4-foot length of the shoots in order to reduce shading. One leaf layer captures about 90% of the sunlight striking the vine. The canopy should be no more than two to three leaves in depth.

High-Wire Cordon System

This system is often used with American bunch grapes and French-American hybrids with a pendulous growth habit. The initial training of the trunk is the same as that for the vertical shoot position (VSP) trellis except a longer trunk is needed. With the high-wire system, however, cordons are trained along the one wire at the top of the trellis with no foliage catch wires (Figures 14–33 , 14–34, 14–35). The fruiting wire is about 5 feet or 6 feet in height. For American bunch grapes, vines can be either cordon trained—and either spur or cane pruned—or cane

"trained." For the first scenario, which for simplicity we will call short-cane pruning, cordons are established as described for the VSP trellis. In the third and subsequent years, however, rather than pruning back the permanent fruiting positions to two-bud spurs, five to six bud canes are left at each position on the cordon. The number of these short canes left depends on the annual vigor of the vine. The more vigorous the vine, the more short canes can be left and vice versa. For example, a very weak plant might have only 30 buds left on six to eight five-bud short canes, while a very vigorous vine might have 100 buds left on 20 five-bud short canes. For the second scenario, follow the description of long-cane pruning under VSP.

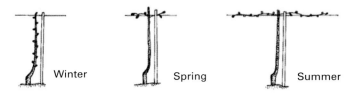

Figure 14–33. High-wire cordon system.
Winter: Tie the cane to the wire. Cut it off just at or below the wire.
Spring: Select two strong shoots near the wire and remove all others.
Summer: Tie both shoots along the wire in opposite directions.

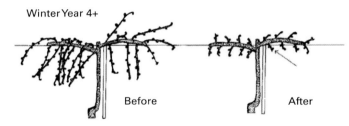

Figure 14–34. High-wire cordon system, fourth year and beyond.
Winter: Shorten the canes from each cordon to two buds (these are fruiting spurs). Keep 8 to 15 spurs on each cordon and prune the rest. The spurs should be spaced 3 inches to 8 inches apart.

Fertilization

After setting and just before growth starts, apply ½ cup (¼ pound) of 10-10-10 in a 20-inch circle around each vine. If the vine grows vigorously, no other fertilizer is needed. If growth is poor, repeat monthly until mid-July. The second year, double the first-year amounts; follow the same schedule as for the first year. Apply nitrogen fertilizer sparingly to grapevines as it promotes excessive vegetative growth, can reduce fruit set, and promote foliar and fruit diseases. If vines are in or near a lawn that is being fertilized, it is likely that the vines are already receiving more fertilizer than is needed for good vine health. On mature vines (5 years old or older), if leaves become pale green and shoot growth and fruit production are reduced, apply N in a split application of ½ cup pre-bloom and ½ cup post-bloom per vine. Nitrogen fertilization may not be necessary each year. Continue to monitor soil pH and phosphorus status of the soil around the vine. If there is

Figure 14–35. Grape vines before pruning (left) and after pruning (right).
Bill Cline

marginal leaf reddening in July, soil phosphorous may be limiting either due to unavailability because of soil pH or phosphorous deficiency in the soil.

Weed Management

For at least the first two years, an area 1 foot to 2 feet around each vine should be kept weed free by hoeing or with a heavy mulch (4 inches to 6 inches deep). Black plastic is a satisfactory mulch material, but it does not add to the humus content of the soil. When using a mulch other than black plastic, care should be taken to maintain the graft union at least 3 inches to 4 inches above the mulch or soil line to prevent **scion** rooting. Once established, the shade of the vine suppresses weed growth. Again, use organic mulches with discretion as they add nitrogen to the soil. Grapevines use superfluous nitrogen to produce lots of vegetative growth and can reduce fruit production.

Recommended chemical herbicides may also be used for weed management in grapes, but mulching is the preferred management practice. Certain types of herbicides should not be used near grapes because grapes are very sensitive. Do not use the combination of fertilizer plus weed killer on lawns near a grapevine. Weed killer may be picked up by the grape roots and cause vine injury. Vapor from herbicides can also cause foliar symptoms on grapevines. Avoid using herbicides after midsummer as the material is absorbed and moved into the permanent wood. Symptoms of such uptake will appear the following growing season. Grapevines are very sensitive to 2,4-D. Systemic herbicides should not be used after mid-July.

Insects and Diseases

Bunch grapevines require frequent and thorough spraying to avoid diseases and insects; this is especially true of wine-type grapes. Current recommended spray programs are given in the *North Carolina Agricultural Chemicals Manual.*

Harvest

Acceptable taste is the main criterion for table use. As they ripen, the grapes of black grapevine cultivars lose their red color, and those of white grapevine cultivars change from green to golden-yellow. Ripe grapes become soft, and seeds become brown. Determining the harvest time of wine grapes requires either experience or a means of measuring both sugar and acid content.

MUSCADINE GRAPEVINES

Muscadine grapevines are native to the southern United States. They are known by several common names, such as bullace, scuppernong, and fox grapes. Scuppernong was the first cultivated muscadine cultivar. Many people incorrectly refer to all muscadine grapes as being scuppernong. Some muscadine grapevine cultivars are **perfect-flowered** (male and female parts in one flower), while others are female and require a perfect-flowered cultivar for pollination. Many wild grapes are male vines and do not produce fruit.

The grapes have a distinct fruity or musky aroma, and the juice by itself is sweet with a light taste and aroma. The fruit can be used for making wine, pies, and jellies and for eating fresh from the vine.

Muscadine grapevines are well adapted to the NC coastal plain, where temperatures seldom fall below 10°F. Considerable injury generally occurs where winter temperatures drop below 0°F. Muscadines have a high degree of tolerance to insects and diseases.

Cultivars

Recommended cultivars are listed in Table 14–11. The old traditional cultivars, 'Scuppernong' (bronze) and 'Thomas' (black), are the most widely known and asked for by the public. Some of the more hardy cultivars, such as 'Magnolia' and 'Carlos' (Figure 14–36) survive northward to Virginia and westward to the foothills of the Blue Ridge Mountains.

Table 14–11. Recommended Muscadine Grapevine Cultivars
(All recommended cultivars are perfect-flowered.)

Cultivar	Season	Color	Berry Size	Stem Scar	Use
Carlos	Mid	Bronze	Medium	Very dry	Good fresh or for wine
Doreen	Very late	Bronze	Medium	Dry	Good fresh or for wine
Magnolia	Early	Bronze	Medium to large	Wet	Excellent fresh flavor; wine and juice
Nesbitt	Early	Black	Large	Dry	Good fresh; poor wine color
Noble	Early	Black	Small	Wet	Good fresh; wine and juice
Regale	Mid	Black	Medium	Wet	Good fresh; wine and juice
Scarlett	Mid	Bronze-pink	Very large	Dry	Good fresh
Southern Home	Mid	Black	Medium	Dry	Hybrid, ornamental, home winemaking
Tara	Early	Bronze	Very large	Dry	Good fresh
Triumph	Early	Bronze	Large	Dry	Good fresh; fair wine

All of the cultivars listed are perfect-flowered (have both male and female flower parts), so a single vine will produce fruit. Other available cultivars such as 'Fry', 'Higgins', 'Scuppernong', and 'Jumbo' have flowers with only female flower parts and must be planted near a perfect-flowered cultivar. 'Southern Home' is a new cultivar with attractive, unusual fig-shaped leaves. The fruit has a non-muscadine flavor and may be useful in home winemaking.

Figure 14–36. 'Carlos' cultivar, the best for making wine.
Bill Cline

Site Selection, Planting, and Maintenance
Plant grapevines in full sun. Fruit set and production is reduced if the vines are shaded for several hours each day during the growing season. Muscadine grapevines can survive and produce a crop on a wide range of soils as long as drainage is good. Plants are likely to die in locations where water stands for even short periods after heavy rains.

Soils with a hard, compacted layer below the surface should be avoided, as well as those high in organic matter. Active growth late in the growing season makes vines susceptible to winter injury on soils with more than 1% organic matter content. Apply and work in dolomitic lime at the rate recommended by the soil test to bring the pH to 6.0 before planting.

The best time to plant is late winter after the danger of freezing has passed. One-year-old container-grown plants are preferred. Two-year-old bare root plants are satisfactory. Keep the roots moist (not wet) until planted. Never allow the roots to dry or freeze. Plant at the same depth as or slightly deeper than the previous growing depth. Vines should be set 15 feet to 20 feet apart in the row. Distance between rows can depend on the equipment used for mowing, but they should be at least 10 feet apart.

Training Systems
Provide a space at least 12 feet to 14 feet long by 6 feet wide for each vine. Decide on the trellis system and complete the construction before planting. Many types of

trellising are not practical for long-term management. For example, growing muscadine grapevines over a garden arch or a pergola can be aesthetically pleasing and provide shade. But if individual cordons are not maintained, management is likely to be difficult, neglect is likely, and fruit production declines.

A practical system allows for establishing permanent cordons (arms) that can be easily reached for the required annual pruning (Figure 14–37). This requires training the cordons to single strands of high tensile wire (number 12 is recommended). A single wire 5 feet to 6 feet above the ground is the easiest trellis to construct and maintain. Four-foot cross arms of 2-inch by 6-inch treated lumber can be attached to treated posts to support double wires. The double-wire system yields about 30% more than the single-wire system.

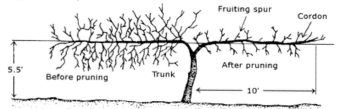

Figure 14–37. Trellising system for muscadine grapes. A one-wire or two-wire system can be used. Prune back all shoots to 4 inches to 5 inches in length, but leave the main arms (cordons).

Muscadine training is the same as for bunch grapes (see above). Select the most vigorous shoot to become the main trunk; remove all other shoots. A bamboo stake beside the plant is convenient for attaching the growing vine. Tie the shoot to the stake. Paper-covered wire ties that are wrapped around the vine and stake work well; to avoid **girdling**, do not twist the ties. As the shoot grows it produces side shoots; they should be removed to promote faster growth of the main trunk. When the vine is just below the top trellis wire, cut the growing tip to force lateral buds. Select four shoots to train down the wire to form the cordons. The goal should be to get the vine on the wire the first growing season and to full length in the second season. After the cordon has developed to full length, allow side shoots to develop on the cordon.

Pruning
An unpruned muscadine vine can quickly become a tangled mess. Annual pruning is required to maintain productive vines. Late February or early March is the best time to prune. Remove any dead, damaged, or undesirable wood.

The current season's shoots bear the fruit. These shoots must arise from buds set on last season's growth. Shoots from older wood are nonproductive. Prune back the canes from the previous summer to spurs with three to four buds (4 inches to 6 inches long). The main cordon is left unpruned. After four to five years, the spurs need

thinning. Spurs should be spaced about a hand-width apart. This thinning forces new spur growth. Also cut off shoots that arise along the main trunk. Vines that are pruned in late winter or early spring exude sap or "bleed." This is normal and does not harm the vines. If there is no sap flow, the vine is probably dead.

Fertilization
Apply ¼ pound of 10-10-10 in an 18-inch circle around each vine after planting (late April to early May). Repeat every six weeks until early July. The second year, apply in early March, May, and July at double the first year's rate (or ½ pound per vine). On bearing vines, scatter 1 pound to 2 pounds of 10-10-10 uniformly under the vine (60 square feet to 120 square feet) in early to mid-March. Apply another pound in mid-June. If the average length of new vine growth exceeds 3 feet to 4 feet during the season, reduce the amount of fertilizer the following year by 20%. Continue adjusting the fertilizer rate until the desired vigor (based on vine length) is obtained. To minimize winter injury, do not apply any fertilizer after early July. Again, excessive nitrogen fertilizer leads to shaded, crowded canopies that result in reduced fruit production and increased insect and disease incidents.

Weed Management
Keep an area 1 foot to 2 feet in diameter around each vine free of weeds by practicing shallow cultivation for the first two years. Avoid mulching materials such as compost or grass clippings that release nitrogen late in the season and cause increased susceptibility to winter damage. A coarse, non-nitrogen-releasing mulch such as bark helps manage weeds and reduce moisture loss from the soil. Water during dry periods the first two years. After establishment, muscadine grapevines are quite drought-tolerant.

Harvest
Muscadine grapes ripen in August through early October. Muscadine clusters are small compared to those of bunch grapes. Clusters ripen in the order they bloomed; the first are the ones nearest the base of the shoot. Fully mature grapes will fall from the vines. Cultivars with a wet scar (end of grape attached to the vine) do not store well and should be used soon after harvest. Cultivars with a dry stem scar keep well for a week in the refrigerator.

Insects, Disease, and Wildlife
Muscadine grapevines can often be grown successfully without insecticides or fungicides. Japanese beetles feed on the young shoot tips mid to late summer. If the vines are healthy, the beetles may have little impact on overall health and fruit ripening. Japanese beetle management is necessary in all species when vines are young to establish healthy, mature vines.

Selecting cultivars with some disease resistance, such as 'Carlos', 'Nesbitt' (Figure 14–38), 'Noble' (Figure 14–39), 'Triumph' (Figure 14–40), and 'Regale', reduces the need for fungicide applications. See appendix C, "Diagnostic Tables," for problems that are common to grapes.

Netting is required to protect the bunch grapes from birds (Figure 14–41). Turkeys eat fruit regardless of netting. Muscadines are less prone to bird damage. Raccoons and opossums eat all types of grapes. Deer eat vines and fruit, even in backyards. Rabbits sometimes eat young vines. Voles feed on the roots of grapevines and can be disguised by mulch. Monitor the vines regularly for any evidence of root-feeding mammals. See chapter 20, "Wildlife," for more information on protecting crops from wildlife.

Figure 14–38. 'Nesbit' cultivar, perfect flowered, medium large size, good vigor.

Bill Cline

Figure 14–39. 'Noble' grapes, self fertile and very productive.

Bill Cline

Figure 14–41. Netting over grapes can protect against bird predation.

Kathleen Moore, CC BY - 2.0

Figure 14–40. 'Triumph' is an early-ripening cultivar that suffers from few rots.

Bill Cline

Kiwis

Cold weather is the limiting factor in growing kiwi vines in North Carolina. During 12 years of testing at the Horticultural Crops Research Station near Wilmington, only one crop of fruit was produced. Three times the vines were killed to the ground. The main site of the winter injury occurred from ground level up to about 18 inches on the plant. Spring freezes also resulted in shoot and blossom damage.

Kiwi flowers develop on shoots that come from buds that formed the previous year. This is similar to the fruiting habit of grapes. Unlike grapes, however, if there is any damage to the new shoots in the spring, no additional flower buds develop or produce flowers.

The commercial kiwi is *Actinidia deliciosa*. Another species, *A. arguta*, is often advertised as hardy. Survival in the test planting was much better for *A. arguta* (Figure 14–42) than for *A. deliciosa*.

The fruit characteristics of the two species differ in the following ways:

- *A. arguta* has much smaller fruit.
- The skin surface of *A. arguta* is smooth, unlike the hairy skin of *A. deliciosa*.
- *A. arguta* ripens in August, while *A. deliciosa* does not mature until late October or early November.
- *A. arguta* must soften on the vine. The fruit does not soften and develop normal flavor and sugar content if picked when still hard. *A. deliciosa* can be harvested in the mature hard stage and held in cold storage for up to six months. After storage, the fruit softens and develops full sugar content more rapidly in a high ethylene environment.
- *A. arguta* fruit is less crisp when it is ready to eat than fruit of *A. deliciosa*.
- In trial plantings, each *A. arguta* vine had a total yield of only five to 20 fruits each.

14

Figure 14–42. An *Actinidia arguta* kiwi.
Björn Appel, Wikimedia CC BY-SA - 4.0

Case Study—Think IPM: Berry Problems

Something is wrong with your raspberries. Though the plants appear healthy, the fruit is damaged.

You review the diagnostic procedures from chapter 7, "Diagnostics," and think about the five steps for IPM:

1. Monitor and scout to determine pest type and population levels.
2. Accurately identify host and pest.
3. Consider economic or aesthetic injury thresholds. A threshold is the point at which action should be taken.
4. Implement a treatment strategy using physical, cultural, biological, or chemical management, or combine these strategies.
5. Evaluate success of treatments.

1. Monitor and scout to determine pest type and population levels.

You have 10 raspberry plants that produce enough fruit for fresh eating and freezing. You have had great success since planting seven years ago. But now the ripe fruit on half of the raspberries appears wilted and damaged. You notice tiny white worms inside some of the fruit (Figure 14–43). Before sending a sample to NC State's Plant Disease and Insect Clinic, you decide to do some sleuthing on your own.

Figure 14–43. A tiny worm inside a raspberry fruit.
Hannah Burrack

2. Accurately identify the host and pest.
Step 1. Identify the plant: *They are raspberry plants (Rubus sp.).*

Step 2. Describe the problem: *About half of my ripe fruit is damaged. I thought the birds might be damaging it. But I added netting, and the damage was not reduced.*

Step 3. Identify what is normal:
What does the healthy part of the plant look like? *The stems and leaves of the plant look healthy. The unaffected plants at the south end of the planting bed have plump ripe fruit.*

What does the unhealthy part of the plant look like? *The berries appear wrinkled and deflated with soft areas as if something has been eating them. Some of the berries have dark spots.*

Have you had a soil test? *Yes. Two years ago I had a soil test done. I put on dolomitic lime in the fall according to the report recommendations. (For information on how to submit a soil test, see chapter 1,"Soils and Plant Nutrients.")*

Step 4. Cultural practices:

Age and history of plants: *These were transplants from a neighbor. The canes were planted three years ago. The canes were a little slow producing during the first year, but they have been going strong up until now.*

Irrigation: *I water about once or twice a week depending on the rain. I have a soaker hose around the base of the plants that I run for about two hours. I do not do any overhead watering so the leaves and fruit do not get wet.*

Fertilizer: *We added about 3 inches of composted leaves and chicken manure mixed with wood shavings last fall as a top-dressing. This spring (in March and then in May) I fertilized with 10-10-10 at a rate of 8 pounds per 100 square feet as indicated by NC State's Hort Leaflet 8204, "Raspberries in the Home Garden."*

Maintenance: *I have not been great about weeding, so the area has more weeds than it should. No herbicides or pesticides have been used in the area.*

Step 5. Environmental conditions:

Are there any significant water issues? *None that I can think of. This spring was pretty wet. The area drains well, so no standing water occurs.*

What is the soil like? *This garden is on acidic clay soil. All parts of this bed have similar soil.*

Describe the light near this garden bed. *How many hours of sunlight? This bed gets about seven hours of full sun a day, with some afternoon shade from the house.*

Describe any recent changes or events: *Nothing has changed in this bed in the last three years other than I have added bird netting.*

Step 6. Signs of pathogens and pests:

On the leaves: *There are no missing pieces of leaf and no discolored spots, insect eggs, frass, or webbing that I can see. I did see a beetle on one of the leaves, and there were a few small flies crawling around* (Figure 14–44). *The leaves appear healthy.*

On the canes: *There are no insects, eggs, frass, webbing, missing chunks, or discoloration seen.*

On the roots and in the soil: *The small roots appear white and healthy, and the base of the plant also appears firm. I did not see any eggs or frass. There was an earthworm and a small white grub in the soil.*

On the fruit: *Some of the fruits have dark spots. There are some small white worms inside some of the fruits* (Figure 14–43).

Step 7. Symptoms:

On the leaves: *The leaves appear green and healthy.*

On the buds/flowers: *Some plants are still flowering. The blossoms look normal.*

On the canes: *There are no holes or rotten areas on the canes, even at the soil line.*

On the roots: *The roots are white and firm.*

On the fruit: *The fruit is discolored and wrinkled and appears rotten in some spots* (Figure 14–45). *There is no bad odor.*

Figure 14–44. A fly on a raspberry leaf.
Hannah Burrack

Figure 14–45. The fruit appears discolored and malformed. Another fly is seen on this fruit.
Hannah Burrack

Step 8. Distribution of damage in the landscape:

Are other plants in the landscape affected? *The black-berry canes on the back side of the property that border a greenbelt also appear to have the same problem with the fruit. So far, the other plants in the yard that are bearing fruit right now (two peach trees and a muscadine grape-vine) do not appear to be affected.*

Step 9. Distribution of damage on the plant and specific plant parts:

Where is the damage seen on the plant? *On the ripe fruit. Unripe fruit appears okay.*

Step 10. Timing:

When did you notice this problem? *Starting the first week of June. When the first raspberries ripened, a few of the berries appeared damaged. Now in mid-July, half of the berries appear damaged.*

You hypothesize this is an insect, not a disease, because there were insect signs and no disease signs. Because there are no symptoms on the leaves, stems, or roots, you suspect that it is fundamentally a fruit problem. It is affecting the blackberries as well, so you hypothesize that the problem is something that affects caneberries. Based on the other facts gathered, your cultural practices seem to support healthy plants.

You decide to start investigating the insect you saw on both the fruit and the leaf. It reminds you of a fruit fly so you search extension.org or type "fly+raspberry+edu" into an internet search engine to find university-based resources. You find links to several articles that discuss a fly called the spotted winged drosophila (*Drosophila suzukii*), or SWD. It is one of the few pests that can bother soft-skinned fruits such as strawberries, blueberries, and caneberries. Female SWD lay their eggs on ripe and ripening fruit. This is unusual because most *Drosophila* species lay their eggs on rotting fruit. The larvae that emerge damage the fruit by feeding on it and may be present when it comes time to harvest. SWD has caused the most damage with caneberries, but it has also been occasionally found in figs, peaches, grapes, and other fruit. SWD takes advantage of other damage to firmer-skinned fruit like grapes or peaches and may not be the primary pest.

SWD are small (2 mm to 3 mm) light-brown flies. Males have a distinctive spot on the end of their wings and dark bands of bristles around the base of the last segment on their front legs (Figure 14–46). Females do not have spots on their wings but can be distinguished by their large, blade-like ovipositor (egg-laying appendage) at the end of their abdomen (Figure 14–47).

Larvae are 3 mm long, are tapered at both ends, and do not have a distinguishable head. True fruit fly (Tephritidae) larvae are larger and have a flat rear end. It is possible to have Tephritidae in blueberries or apples, but they will not be present in caneberries, strawberries, grapes, peaches, or figs.

3. Consider economic or aesthetic injury thresholds.
Spotted winged drosophila can cause significant damage to fruit harvests. The problem is likely to worsen over time and spread to other fruits in the yard.

4. Implement a treatment strategy using physical, cultural, biological or chemical management, or combine these strategies.

While SWD-infested fruit may be unpalatable, larvae are not harmful if consumed. Good cultural practices can limit SWD damage.

Physical. The fruit should be harvested frequently and completely. Any fruit containing larvae should be disposed of off-site or "baked" in clear plastic bags in the sun. When harvesting is complete, strip any unwanted fruit and destroy it. Cover fruits with a fine mesh bag prior to ripening to exclude egg-laying flies.

Cultural. Prune plants to maintain an open canopy. Do not overwater plants. Fruit should be observed regularly for infestation before and during harvest. Placing berries in the refrigerator or freezer immediately after picking helps to slow or stop larval development.

Biological. Research is being done on parasitic wasps and other parasitoids that may prove helpful in managing SWD, but there are no recommended biological controls at this time.

Chemical. There are insecticides registered for use against SWD. See the *North Carolina Agricultural Chemical Manual* for recommendations.

5. Evaluate treatment success.
Keeping a record, garden journal, or notes about the appearance and numbers of SWD helps you identify patterns that can assist with management strategies. Documenting the strategies implemented and their success or failure helps you make management decisions in the future.

Figure 14–46. A male spotted winged drosophila.
Matt Bertone

Figure 14–47. A female spotted winged drosophila.
Matt Bertone

Frequently Asked Questions

1. What type of small fruit should I plant?

Your family members' tastes, the amount of space available, microclimate conditions, and soil type are all factors that can help you narrow down fruit selections. Specific recommended cultivars vary by region, but a general list of small fruits is offered below. Also see this NC State Extension publication: AG-15, *Grapes and Berries for the Garden*.

NC mountains: Blackberries, highbush blueberries, bunch grapes, raspberries

NC piedmont: Blackberries, rabbiteye blueberries, bunch grapes, muscadine grapes, raspberries

NC coastal plain: Blackberries, rabbiteye blueberries, muscadine grapes

Growing gooseberries and currants is illegal in North Carolina. They are alternate hosts for certain fungi that attack some trees grown for timber.

2. How do I fertilize blueberries? When and with what?

Always begin with a soil test to get specific recommendations for your property.

First year: Use caution. Excess fertilizer can easily damage blueberries. Do not fertilize immediately after planting. Wait until the first leaves have reached full size, then apply 1 tablespoon of an azalea fertilizer, 12-12-12 or 10-10-10, in a circle 1 foot from the plants. Repeat at six-week intervals until mid-August. Substitute ½ tablespoon of ammonium nitrate (33-0-0) for the second and subsequent fertilizer applications if the phosphorus index level is above 60 on a soil test.

Second year: Double the first year's rates and increase the circle to 1½ feet around the plants. Apply the first application when new growth begins in the spring.

Bearing plants (three years to four years old): When growth begins in the spring, apply 1 cup of a complete fertilizer such as 10-10-10 in a circle 3 feet from the plants. Side-dress with ¼ cup of ammonium nitrate (33-0-0) at six-week intervals if desired, but no later than mid-August. On mature bushes (5 years old or more), 6 inches to 12 inches of new growth is adequate. Desirable pH is 5.0 to 5.3. Mulching is very beneficial to blueberries.

3. When do I fertilize muscadines and with what?

Apply ¼ pound of 10-10-10 in an 18-inch circle around each vine after planting (late April to early May). Repeat every six weeks until early July. The second year, apply in early March, May, and July at double the first year's rate (½ pound total per vine) at least 21 inches away from the trunk. On bearing vines, scatter 1 pound to 2 pounds of 10-10-10 uniformly under the vine (60 sq ft to 120 sq ft) in early to mid-March. Apply another 1 pound in mid-June. If the average length of new vine growth exceeds 3 feet to 4 feet during the season, reduce the amount of fertilizer the following year by 20%. Continue adjusting fertilizer rate until the desired vigor (based on vine length) is obtained. To minimize winter injury, don't apply any fertilizer after early July. Avoid mulching materials that release nitrogen late in the season and cause increased susceptibility to winter damage.

4. There is a white foamy substance on my muscadine grapevines, almost as if someone had been spitting on them. What is it?

The cause of this white foamy substance is the spittlebug. The larvae produce this substance to protect themselves from other insects and predators while developing into adults. The spittlebug is a vector for *disease* in both muscadine and bunch grapes. Unlike bunch grapes, muscadines appear to tolerate the disease with little reduction in yield, and spittlebugs are not known for causing any other injury to muscadines. Therefore, no management is needed. Pesticide use is not recommended because the larvae are protected by the white foamy substance. If you find the appearance of the white foam to be unsightly, hose down the plant early in the morning to wash it away, or wait for the next rainfall to take care of it.

14

5. My muscadine vine does not have any fruit, or my muscadine has small grapes that did not ripen. What am I doing wrong?

There are many reasons for poor yield in the home garden:

Are you sure you have a perfect-flowered (male and female) cultivar?
- Some cultivars ('Fry', 'Higgins', 'Scuppernong', and 'Jumbo') have only female flowers and must be planted near a perfect-flowered cultivar to produce fruit. 'Carlos' is a perfect-flowered variety that is fairly common and good for fresh fruit or winemaking.

Does it get enough sun?
- Fruit set and production can be reduced if the vines are shaded for more than several hours a day.

Have you been giving it a high nitrogen fertilizer, which could cause leaf growth at the expense of fruit development?
- Use a balanced fertilizer such as 10-10-10. Submit a soil sample to obtain specific fertilizer recommendations. Boron deficiency may also result in poor fruit set, especially on sandy soils with high pH. Submit a foliar sample to determine boron status.
- Poor pollination can occur in adverse weather.
- Drought stress can cause fruit drop.
- Powdery mildew is a fungal disease that can infect blossoms, reducing fruit set.
- A late frost can also kill primary fruit buds. If this happens, vines often set fruit on secondary buds. This fruit usually fails to ripen and is small.
- Bitter rot can cause fruit drop near harvest.
- Improper pruning causes reduced harvests.
- Some heirloom cultivars are low producers, even with the best of care.
- Japanese and June beetles may have fed directly on flowers and small berries.
- Stink bugs can cause severe fruit drop.

Further Reading

Gough, Robert E. and E. Barclay Poling, eds. *Small Fruits in the Home Garden*. Binghamton, New York: Food Products Press, 1996. Print.

For More Information

http://go.ncsu.edu/fmi_smallfruits

Contributors

Authors:
Gina Fernandez, Professor and Extension Specialist, Department of Horticultural Science
Bill Cline, Researcher and Extension Specialist, Department of Entomology and Plant Pathology
Sara Spayd, Extension Specialist, Department of Horticultural Science
Hannah Burrack, Extension Specialist, Department of Entomology and Plant Pathology

Contributions by Extension Agents:
John Vining, Susan Brown, Jessica Strickland, Cyndi Lauderdale, Danny Lauderdale, Mack Johnson

Contributions by Extension Master Gardener Volunteers:
Jackie Weedon, Karen Damari, Lee Kapleau, Sandy Quinn, Patty Brown, Connie Schultz, Judy Bates, Caro Dosé

Content Editors:
Lucy Bradley, Professor and Extension Specialist, Urban Horticulture, NC State University; Director, NC State Extension Master Gardener program
Kathleen Moore, Urban Horticulturist

Copy Editors:
Barbara Scott, Debbi Braswell

Chapter 14 Cover Photo: Kathleen Moore, CC BY - 2.0

Based in part on text from the 1998 Extension Master Gardener manual prepared by:
Erv Evans, Extension Associate, Department of Horticultural Science
E. Barclay Poling, Extension Specialist, Department of Horticultural Science
Ken Sorensen, Extension Specialist, Department of Entomology and Plant Pathology
James R. Ballington, Professor, Department of Horticultural Science

How to Cite This Chapter:
Fernandez, G.E., B. Cline, S.E. Spayd, H.J. Burrack. 2022. Small Fruits, Chpt 14, In: K. A. Moore, and. L. K. Bradley (eds), *North Carolina Extension Gardener Handbook*, 2nd ed. NC State Extension, Raleigh, NC. <https://content.ces.ncsu.edu/extension-gardener-handbook/14-small-fruits>

14

Tree Fruits and Nuts

15

Objectives

This chapter teaches people to:
- Select varieties of fruit and nut trees that thrive in specific environmental conditions.
- Select quality sites for planting fruit and nut trees.
- Plant and prune fruit and nut trees.
- Identify and manage common fruit and nut tree pests and diseases.

Introduction

Growing a crisp apple, juicy peach, or a perfect pecan is the dream of many gardeners. Backyard gardeners can grow varieties not available in the market. And unlike commercial producers who must harvest and ship weeks before the fruit is ripe, gardeners can harvest fruit and nuts at their peak. Fruit and nut trees, however, require ample garden space, annual maintenance, and plenty of patience because many do not produce a crop for several years. If properly maintained, fruit and nut trees are productive for many years. This chapter explains some of the challenges and opportunities that gardeners encounter when selecting, planting, and maintaining fruit and nut trees in North Carolina.

Selecting and Placing Fruit and Nut Trees in a Home Landscape

Site Selection

Select the site carefully to ensure your fruit or nut trees will thrive for years to come. Begin by identifying what your site has to offer such a tree. How big a space is available with at least six hours or more of sunlight, and how much of that sunlit space is free from the interference of walls, eaves, sheds, fences, or powerlines? If you have less than 10 square feet, consider a berry bush instead. If you have a 10-to-20-square-foot area, you can grow a self-pollinating dwarf fruit tree, fig, or persimmon. With more than 20 square feet you can grow a **self-pollinating** apple, pear, peach, or plum tree. Pecan trees require 70 square feet of space. Fruit trees that require **cross-pollination** need at least twice as much space to accommodate the two or more different varieties needed to get fruit set. If you plant a fruit or nut tree in a space that's too small, you must prune to contain size rather than to promote fruiting. That kind of pruning will stress the trees, making them more susceptible to insect and disease damage and rarely productive. With limited space, consider trees **grafted** on dwarfing **rootstock**, container trees, or **espalier** trees.

Regional Considerations

More than 200 soil types occur in North Carolina, which stretches 503 miles from the Appalachian Mountains to the Atlantic Coast and ranges in elevation from 6,684 feet on the top of Mount Mitchell to sea level on the beach. Altitude has the greatest influence on climate in North Carolina, and year-round there is a 20-degree difference in temperature between the highest and lowest elevations. November is the driest month, while July is the wettest, and all of North Carolina's rivers are likely to flood. In addition, all areas of the state are subject to wind, hail, and ice damage. Each of these factors affects which fruit and nut trees thrive and what weeds, pests, and diseases present challenges. Because of these considerations, gardeners need region-specific information regarding fruit tree cultivation in North Carolina.

Location

Eastern North Carolina

The NC coastal plain elevation is generally less than 200 feet. Relatively uniform soils of soft sediment occur here, with high sand content (generally referred to as "light soils"), and little or no hard rock near the surface. The NC coastal plain includes the NC tidewater area, which is flat and swampy, and the gently sloping, well-drained interior area.

Where the cold Labrador Current flows between the warm Gulf Stream and the North Carolina coast, the two divergent currents create major storms, causing rain along the coast. Tropical cyclones in the fall can cause severe floods. Temperatures range from 20°F in the winter to 89°F in summer. Average annual rainfall ranges from 40 to 55 inches.

These fruit and nut tree crops are recommended for eastern North Carolina: apples, chestnuts, figs, pears (Asian and European), pecans, persimmons (American and Asian), and plums.

Gardeners must confront several challenges to growing fruit trees in the NC coastal plain. **Nematodes** are more common in sandy soils; use nematode-resistant Guardian™ rootstock in the light sandy soils of eastern North Carolina. In addition, there are several variety-specific issues with apples. For example, difficult-to-grow varieties, such as 'Pink Lady', do not produce good color in the NC coastal plain. In the eastern part of the state, *peach tree short life* (PTSL) complex causes sudden death of young peach trees in the spring.

Central North Carolina

The NC piedmont has hard rock near the surface, and the elevation rises from 200 feet to 1,500 feet. Elevation changes consist primarily of gently rolling hills. Much of the subsoil in the NC piedmont has high clay content—commonly called "heavy" soil. Floods covering a wide area do occur, most likely in winter. Temperatures range from 10°F in winter to 100°F in summer. Average annual rainfall ranges from 40 to 55 inches.

Recommended fruit and nut tree crops for central North Carolina include apples, chestnuts, figs, pears (Asian and European), pecans, persimmons (American and Asian), and plums. 'Lovell' and 'Halford' rootstocks work well for peaches in the NC piedmont.

Western North Carolina

The elevation in the NC foothills and mountains ranges from 1,000 to 6,684 feet. The soils consist of eroded, rocky materials, with rocks on the surface. Like the subsoil in the NC piedmont, much of the subsoil in the NC foothills and mountains has high clay content. Temperatures range from 0°F in winter to 80°F in summer. Depending on the location, average annual rainfall ranges from more than 90 inches to less than 37 inches. Flash floods on small streams in the mountains most commonly occur in spring, when thunderstorm rain falls onto saturated or frozen soil.

Recommended fruit and nut tree crops for western North Carolina include apples, chestnuts, pears (Asian and European), and plums.

Temperature
Chilling Hours

In order to bloom and set fruit, deciduous fruit and nut trees require a certain number of winter hours below 45°F. Inadequate chilling can result in little or no fruit. Different types of fruit and different varieties of the same fruit require different numbers of chilling hours. For example, peach trees may require as little as 200 hours to as much as 1,000-plus hours. The lower the chilling-hours requirement, the earlier the tree will begin growing once temperatures are warm enough. In North Carolina, wide fluctuations occur in winter and spring temperatures, and the requirements of low-chilling-hour varieties may be met early in the winter. When that happens, any warm period during the remainder of the winter will cause the tree to bloom prematurely. The next freezing temperature will kill those blossoms. Likewise, varieties that require a high number of chilling hours will suffer if the chilling requirement is not met. Trees will bloom erratically, produce deformed leaves, and have little to no fruit set in the spring. Typically, throughout North Carolina, gardens receive in excess of 1,000 chilling hours annually, so insufficient chilling rarely occurs. To minimize frost and freeze crop losses, plant varieties with a chilling requirement of 750 hours or greater. In North Carolina, varieties with chilling requirements of less than 750 hours suffer frequent crop losses.

Frost

Select species and varieties that are hardy at the lowest temperatures in your yard.

Air Drainage

Cold air is heavier than warm air and thus drains down and settles in low spots at the bottoms of hills. Adequate air drainage is as important as proper water drainage. In North Carolina, spring frosts and freezes are common, and a small difference in elevation can mean the difference between a full crop and no crop at all. For example, a 10-foot difference in elevation may equate to a difference of 1°F during a spring freeze event. Select a higher site with an unobstructed, gradual slope that allows cold air to flow downhill away from the trees. Avoid low sites, which are commonly known as "frost pockets."

Sunlight

Fruit and nut trees need at least 6 hours of sunlight during the growing season. Avoid areas shaded by taller trees, houses, or buildings. Avoid direct southern exposure because the warmer temperatures on a southern slope can cause early blooming and exposure to frost damage.

Light penetration is essential for flower bud development and optimal fruit set, flavor, color, and quality. Fruit tree buds require direct sunlight to initiate flowers and for high-quality fruit production. Shaded branches do not develop flower buds. Although the exterior of a tree may receive full sun, light penetration is reduced by as much as half just 18 inches into the tree's canopy. Pruning to allow sunlight into the canopy is essential—both for fruit production and to prevent pest problems.

Soils

Soil consists of minerals, organic matter, air, and water. For more information about soil structure, texture, and profiles, see chapter 1, "Soils and Plant Nutrients."

Soil Type and Drainage

Fruit trees must be planted in well-drained soil to prevent standing water from drowning the roots. Even though a tree is dormant in the winter, its root system is still growing and it is susceptible to damage from poor drainage. Water standing in the root zone for two to three days could result in tree death. Poorly drained soils also promote the growth of pathogens that infect roots.

When poorly drained soils are difficult to avoid, minimize problems by planting the trees in raised beds or berms. Form beds and berms by shaping well-drained topsoil from the surrounding area. Raised beds should measure 18 inches to 24 inches high and 4 feet to 5 feet wide.

Soil Fertility

To determine fertility needs, collect soil samples for analysis. Detailed directions can be found in chapter 1, "Soils and Plant Nutrients." Instructions and sample boxes are available through N.C. Cooperative Extension centers. Take soil samples from two depths: the first from the top 6 inches to 8 inches of soil and the second from the lower profile, 16 inches to 18 inches in depth. Samples are analyzed by the N.C. Department of Agriculture and Consumer Services, which provides a detailed analysis and specific recommendations for improving fertility. A soil **pH** of approximately 6.0 to 6.5 is optimum for fruit tree growth. North Carolina soils, however, are typically more acidic (lower pH). Follow the directions included with your soil test results to adjust your pH, if recommended, by adding lime to a depth of 16 inches to 18 inches, preferably before planting. Note that in acidic soils, even when nutrients are present, they may be locked up in the soil and unavailable to roots. In this case, additional fertilizer does not benefit the tree but may run off or leach to pollute storm water.

Tree Selection

Whether a fruit or nut tree thrives in a particular location or not depends upon the site's climate and soil, and the tree's rootstock and **cultivar**. Because it is virtually impossible to change the climate or soils, always select cultivars known to thrive in the given conditions. Fruit and nut trees that look promising on the glossy pages of mail-order catalogs are destined to fail if grown in incompatible climates and soils. Climatic conditions and soils vary greatly from one region to another in North Carolina, so the best way to minimize stress and limit pesticide use is to choose plants that are well-adapted to the particular environment.

Another factor to consider when selecting fruit and nut trees is the level of management required. Low-maintenance crops, such as pecans, figs, and persimmons, grow with little attention to training, fertility, or insect and disease management. Conversely, peaches, nectarines, and plums require intensive management.

Table 15–1 lists fruit trees that grow well and produce reliable crops in North Carolina. Table 15–2 includes often-overlooked native fruit crops that grow well in North Carolina. Tree fruits not included on the lists may grow in North Carolina, but few produce quality fruit on a regular basis. Apricot and cherry trees grow in certain areas where the climate is favorable, but need careful management and will not consistently bear fruit. Most tropical fruits do not grow outdoors anywhere in North Carolina. Edible bananas, for example, need a longer growing season to produce fruit and cannot survive NC winters.

Cultivar Selection

After selecting the planting site and type of fruit or nut crop, identify a cultivar that thrives in your particular landscape conditions. Novice growers often try to plant the same cultivars they find in their local grocery stores. These cultivars, however, are often grown far away in different climates. Instead, plant cultivars that are known to flourish in local conditions and are resistant to local insects and diseases. Select peach varieties that require at least 750 chilling hours in order to delay spring bloom and minimize frost damage to the flowers and fruit. Chilling hours are not an important consideration in North Carolina with other types of fruit and nut trees.

Figure 15–1. Apples.
Włodek, Pixabay CC0

Figure 15–2. Chestnuts.
Mike Parker

Figure 15–3. Brown turkey figs.
Dan, Flickr CC BY-ND 2.0

Figure 15–4. Nectarines.
Shinya Suzuki,
Flickr CC BY-ND - 2.0

Figure 15–5. Peaches.
Danelle Cutting

Figure 15–6.
A Bartlett pear.
Kathleen Moore, CC BY - 2.0

Table 15–1. Fruit Cultivar Recommendations for North Carolina

Fruit	Recommended Cultivars	Pollination Notes	Disease Notes	Other Considerations
Apples *Malus domestica* (Figure 15–1)	Empire, Gala, Ginger Gold, Jonagold, Red Delicious, Golden Delicious, Crispin (Mutsu), Stayman, Rome, Fuji	Requirements vary. Some cultivars are **self-fruitful**. Others require a pollinator.[a]	Summer rots are the most serious disease problems and can destroy an entire crop. No cultivars are resistant. Some cultivars are resistant to apple scab, powdery mildew, cedar apple rust or fire blight. These include Redfree, Prima, Priscilla, Jonafree, and Liberty (which performs poorly in North Carolina).	In warmer regions, red cultivars may not color well.
Chestnuts *Castanea* (Figure 15–2)	*Chinese:* Nanking, Meiling, Kuling, Abundance, Crane; *Chinese-American Hybrid:* Revival, Carolina, Willamette	All require pollination from another cultivar. Plant at least two cultivars of the same type to ensure optimal size and production.	Most Chinese and hybrid chestnuts are highly resistant to the chestnut blight fungus.	Many people prefer the hybrid chestnut cultivars, citing superior quality over the Chinese cultivars.
Figs *Ficus carica* (Figure 15–3)	Celeste, Brown Turkey, Brunswick/Magnolia (for preserves), Greenish, Marseille	Only cultivars that do not require pollination can be grown in North Carolina.	Few serious disease problems except nematodes.	Fruit may drop prematurely because of drought or excessive shade, moisture, or fertilization.
Nectarines *Prunus persica* (Figure 15–4)	Summer Beaut, Sunglo, Redgold, Flavortop, Fantasia, Carolina Red [b]	Self-fruitful. Do not require pollination by other cultivars.	Plant nectarines and peaches only on Lovell or Halford rootstocks to avoid premature death. Hairless nectarines are more susceptible to diseases than peaches so require a multipurpose fungicide and insecticide spray program.	Many cultivars were developed in California and may not do well in North Carolina.
Peaches *Prunus persica* (Figure 15–5)	Redhaven, Norman, Carolina Belle (white-fleshed), Winblo, Contender, Summer Pearl (white-fleshed), China Pearl, Cresthaven, Encore. Many cultivars were developed for North Carolina by the peach breeding program at NC State [b]	Self-fruitful. Do not require pollination by other cultivars.	Needs a multipurpose fungicide and insecticide spray program during the growing season.	Choose cultivars requiring at least 750 hours of chilling
Pears *Pyrus communis* (Figure 15–6)	Moonglow, Magness (not a pollen source), Kieffer, Harrow Delight, Harrow Sweet, Harvest Queen, Seckel	At least two cultivars are recommended to ensure adequate pollination.	Plant only fire blight-resistant cultivars.	Plant pears on higher sites than apples; they bloom earlier.

Table 15–1. Fruit Cultivar Recommendations for North Carolina *continued*

Fruit	Recommended Cultivars	Pollination Notes	Disease Notes	Other Considerations
Pears, Asian *Pyrus pyrifolia* (Figure 15–7)	Twentieth Century (Nijisseiki), Nititaka (pollen source), Shinseiki (New Century),Chojuro	At least two cultivars are needed to ensure adequate pollination.	Fire blight is the biggest concern.	Fruit needs to be thinned heavily. Flower is very susceptible to frost damage.
Pecans *Carya illinoinensis* (Figure 15–8)	Type I: Cape Fear, Pawnee; Type II: Chickasaw, Elliot, Forkert, Gloria Grande, Kiowa, Stuart, Sumner	Pollination requires two cultivars.	Scab is the most serious disease in North Carolina. A fungicide spray program is usually not practical.	Careful cultivar selection is essential to avoid frost or freeze problems and to allow a long enough season for maturation.
Persimmons *Diospyros* (Figure 15–9)	Fuyu, Jiro, Hanagosho (very good pollen source). For North Carolina plant only large-fruited Asian persimmons.	For best fruit set, plant two cultivars.	No serious disease problems.	Fruits of non-astringent cultivars may only be suitable for eating when fully mature and flesh is soft.
Plums *Prunus domestica* (Figure 15–10)	*Japanese:* Methley (self-fruitful), Byrongold, Burbank, Ozark Premier (may bloom early); *European:* Bluefre, Stanley, Shropshire (Damson) [b]	Some cultivars are self-fruitful, but planting two cultivars is recommended.	Needs a multipurpose fungicide-insecticide spray program during the growing season.	Select later-blooming cultivars to avoid damaging temperatures.

a Apple pollination requirements vary with cultivar. For cultivars requiring cross-pollination, plant at least two cultivars with overlapping bloom periods. For self-fruitful cultivars, pollination by another cultivar will increase yield and quality.

b Peaches, nectarines, and plums have a chilling requirement: a certain number of hours in temperatures in the 40°F range during the dormant season to break bud and grow properly in spring. In North Carolina, select cultivars with chilling requirements of at least 750 hours to prevent trees from blooming too early in the spring, which risks frost/freeze damage and resultant crop loss.

Figure 15–7. Asian pears.
Krzysztof Jaracz, Pixabay CC0

Figure 15–8.
Pecans.
Tseiu, Pixabay CC0

Figure 15–9.
A Fuyu persimmon.
Manseok Kim, Pixabay CC0

Figure 15–10.
Methley (cherry) plums.
Forest and Kim Starr,
Flickr, CC BY - 2.0

Table 15–2. Tree Fruits and Nuts Native to North Carolina

Fruit	Varieties	Advantages	Disadvantages
American persimmon *Diospyros virginiana* (Figure 15–11)	C-100, Killen, Meader, Morris Burton, Prok	Tough tree; grows in a variety of locations	Wild trees are either male or female and thus usually not self-pollinating.
Chinquapin *Castanea pumila* (Figure 15–12)	Fuller, Rush	Grows more like a shrub than a tree; a good producer of sweet nuts reminiscent of American chestnut	Nuts are covered in prickly burrs that can be a nuisance; birds and small mammals love them; somewhat difficult to harvest; susceptible to problems that attack chestnut trees.
Mulberry, Red *Morus rubra* (Figure 15–13)	Collier, Hicks Everbearing, Illinois Everbearing, Silk Hope, Townsend, Travis	Tasty fruit similar to that of blackberry; tolerant of dry, poor soil; cold hardy; can grow near the shore with protection from wind	For fruit production, choose a self-pollinating variety.
Pawpaw *Asimina tribola* (Figure 15–14)	Allegheny, NC-1, Overleese, Potomac, Shenandoah, Sunflower, Susquehanna, Wabash	Can be grown on the border of the forest line or in partial shade; high nutritional value compared to apples, peaches, and grapes	Deer love fruit; tree requires some chilling, so may not be adapted to some coastal areas.
Plum, Chickasaw *Prunus angustifolia* (Figure 15–15)	Guthrie	Tolerates high humidity; great for jelly	Tends to bloom early so fruit can be killed when there is a late spring freeze; plant has spines or sharp edges.
Walnut, Black *Juglans nigra* (Figure 15–16)	Black Gem, Kwik-Krop	Bears nuts most years	Thousand cankers, new to the South in 2011, will kill the tree; nuts have a gamey taste; walnut tree roots produce juglone, an allelopathic chemical that can injure or kill some nearby plants.

Note: This table was prepared by John Vining.

Figure 15–11. American persimmon. Katja Schultz, Flickr, CC BY - 2.0

Figure 15–12. Chinquapin oak (*Castanea pumila*). Fritz Flohr Reynolds, CC BY-ND - 2.0

Figure 15–13. Red mulberries. Famartin, Wikimedia CC BY-SA - 4.0

Figure 15–14. Pawpaws. Scott Bauer, USDA Agricultural Research Service, Wikimedia CC0

Figure 15–15. Chickasaw plums. Couleur, Pixabay CC BY0

Figure 15–16. Black walnuts (*Juglans nigra*). Katja Schultz, Flickr CC BY - 2.0

Rootstock Selection and Spacing

Almost all commercially available fruit trees have their top portions, or scions, of the desired fruit cultivar grafted or budded onto a root system. **Scions** are selected based on desirable factors, such as tasty fruit, large size, or extended shelf life. The rootstock is selected for its effect on the mature size of the tree (dwarfing to full size), resistance to certain pest problems, or performance in certain soil conditions. Fruit trees are commonly available with a scion from one tree grafted to the rootstock of another tree because most fruit trees do not come true from seed due to cross-pollination. Grafting is also beneficial because grafted trees bear fruit more quickly than seed-grown trees.

Apple trees, for example, grow on many different cultivars of rootstocks (Figure 15–17). Some rootstocks limit growth, resulting in dwarf trees, while others produce trees that crop early and are easier to manage than full-sized trees. Fruit size is not significantly affected by the rootstock. Two categories of growth habit are included in Table 15–3: **spur** and nonspur. Spurs are short, stubby, slow-growing branches that support multiple fruit blossoms and remain fruitful for 7 to 10 years. Spur-type cultivars have more fruiting spurs and a more compact growth habit. Generally, spur strains of a cultivar result in trees that are only 60% to 70% as large as nonspur types.

Because the choice of rootstock affects a tree's size, it also affects the optimum spacing between trees. Table 15–4 gives the recommended distance between trees for both spur and nonspur cultivars. Note that vigorous cultivars should be spaced farther apart.

Apple trees on rootstocks of a size class smaller than M.7 bear fruit earlier. Stakes or a trellis system support the fruit load in the early years and help to optimize growth. Use 10-foot stakes and drive them 2 feet into the ground. Stakes are commonly made from 1-inch-diameter aluminum electrical conduit or ½-inch angle iron. Tie the trees to the stake. Strips of plastic or heavy-duty canvas or cloth work as well for staking as ties do. Do not use materials that restrict tree growth and/or **girdle** the tree, such as wire, rope, or twine.

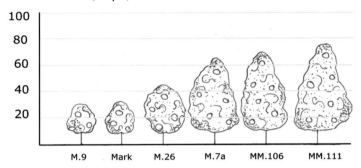

Figure 15–17. Size of trees grown on commercially available rootstocks shown as a percentage of the size they would reach if grown from a seedling.

Peaches, nectarines, and plums are also affected by rootstock. In the Southeast, trees are susceptible to peach tree short life (PTSL), a condition that causes sudden death of the tree after only four or five years of growth. Proper rootstock selection, nematode suppression, and cultural practices minimize the threat of PTSL.

Spacing recommendations for various fruit trees are given in Table 15–5.

Table 15–3. Commercially Available Apple Rootstocks and their Characteristics

Rootstock	Tree Size as Percentage of Seedling (Nonspur)[a]	Tree Size as Percentage of Seedling (Spur)[a]	Fruit-Bearing Age (Years)	Resistance to Crown Rot	Resistance to Fire Blight
Seedling	100	80	6 – 10	Medium	High
MM.111	85	70	4 – 6	Medium	Low
MM.106	80	70	3 – 4	Very low	Low
M.7 [a]	70	60	3 – 4	Medium	High
M.26	50	40	2 – 4	Medium	Very low
Mark	35	20	2 – 3	Medium	Low
M.9	35	20	2 – 3	Medium	Low

[a] **See Figure 15–17.**

Tree Quality

Once you select a fruit or nut tree type, and its cultivar and rootstock, it is time to shop and carefully evaluate tree quality. Keep the following criteria in mind:

- Look for trees at least 4 feet to 6 feet tall, with a ½-inch or greater trunk caliper at the base, and a healthy root system.
- Choose a smaller tree with a good root system rather than a large tree with a poor root system.
- Check the label for the desired cultivar and rootstock.
- Avoid trees that appear stunted, poorly shaped, diseased, or injured by insects.
- Many healthy fruit trees are shipped as **bare roots**.

Cultural Practices

Planting

The best time to plant a fruit or nut tree in North Carolina is late fall or early winter. When trees are planted in the fall, the roots grow through the winter, resulting in greater tree growth during the first season—which ultimately leads to faster vigorous growth. Young fruit trees are commonly shipped bare root with the exposed roots wrapped in moist sawdust. Plant trees as soon after purchase as possible.

To plant a tree, dig a hole twice as wide as the root system and as deep as the root ball, making sure not to pack down the soil (Figure 15–18). Rough up the sides of the hole with a trowel or your fingers to avoid glazing (hardening) the hole's sides with the shovel. Cut off any damaged roots at the point of injury. Shorten roots that are especially long and do not fit in the hole. Roots that are not shortened or spread out can wrap around the tree hole and girdle the root system, eventually resulting in tree death.

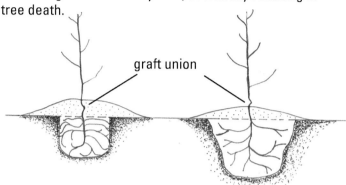

Figure 15–18. On the left is an improperly planted fruit tree. The hole is too narrow and shallow, forcing the roots to wrap inside the hole. The graft union is below the soil surface, negating the effect. The figure on the right is properly planted.

When planting a grafted tree, ensure that the graft union is at least 2 inches above the soil. When graft unions are planted below the soil surface, the top portion, or scion, often grows roots and negates the effect of the grafted root system.

Table 15–4. Recommended Planting Distances for Apple Trees Grown on Size-controlling Rootstocks

Rootstock Cultivars	Distance Between Trees (feet)		
	Nonspur Cultivars	Spur Cultivars [a]	Very Vigorous Cultivars [b]
Seedling*	18 – 25	12 – 16	25 – 35
MM.111	14 – 18	9 – 12	20 – 25
MM.106	12 – 16	8 – 11	17 – 22
M.7 [a]	10 – 14	7 – 9	14 – 20
M.26**	8 – 12	5 – 8	11 – 17
Mark**	4 – 8	3 – 5	6 – 11
M.9**	4 – 8	3 – 5	6 – 11

* Mature tree is 12 – 20 feet tall, depending on variety.

** Trees should be staked and tied to the stake at planting.

[a] For spur-type cultivars such as Red Chief Red Delicious, Starkrimson Red Delicious, Lawspur, Rome, and Oregon Spur

[b] For very vigorous cultivars such as Rome Beauty, Granny Smith, and Jonagold

Table 15–5. Spacing Requirements for Various Fruit and Nut Trees

Fruit Crop	Minimum Spacing Between Trees (feet)
Black Walnut	10–12
Chestnuts	40
Figs	10
Red Mulberry	20–30
Pawpaw	10
Peaches	18–20
Pears	20
Pears, Asian	20
Pecans	70 [a]
Persimmons	15
Plums	20

[a] At maturity, approximately 20 years

After the tree is in place, fill the hole with native soil. Never add fertilizer to the planting hole. Fertilizers are very caustic and can burn and kill the roots of young trees. After the hole is backfilled, water the area well.

Nutrient Management
Applying fertilizer routinely without knowing whether it is needed results in poor fruit quality and excessive tree growth. Over-fertilization also wastes money and contributes to environmental pollution.

Biennial soil analyses will keep you informed about the soil's nutrients and acidity. In addition to soil analyses, simple observation of the amount of vegetative growth helps in managing fertilizer needs. Trees with less than 10 inches to 12 inches of current season's growth on lateral branches may need fertilizer. On the other hand, trees with greater than 18 inches of growth may not need fertilizer for several years. Excessive tree growth can promote weak wood and pest problems.

Broadcast the fertilizer on the soil surface, both inside and outside the **dripline** of the tree. Keep fertilizer at least 6 inches away from tree trunks. Apply fertilizer in late winter. In areas with sandy soils, apply half of the recommended amount of fertilizer in late winter and the remainder in May. If the crop is lost due to frost, do not apply the second half.

Mulch
Organic mulch applied 4 inches to 6 inches deep in a doughnut shape—with the trunk at its center and stretching to the dripline—is an excellent strategy for improving the soil and creating an environment for roots to promote plant growth. Mulch suppresses weeds, improves water penetration and retention, encourages earthworms and beneficial microbes, and insulates the soil, protecting a tree's roots from both heat and cold.

Pruning and Training
Pruning is removing a portion of a tree to correct or maintain its form and structure. Training incorporates pruning but also involves manipulating a tree's branches and leaders early in the growth process to direct tree growth into a desired shape and form, rather than just correcting problems after they occur.

Pruning and training create a strong tree framework that supports fruit production. Improperly trained fruit and nut trees generally have very upright branches with narrow **crotch angles** (Figure 15–19). These limbs are more likely to break under a heavy fruit load. Another goal of annual pruning and training is to remove dead, diseased, or damaged limbs. See chapter 11, "Woody Ornamentals," for more information about pruning.

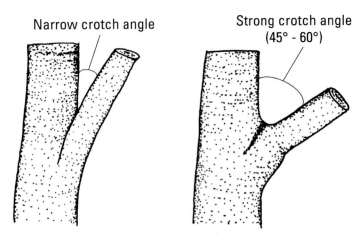

Figure 15–19. Narrow crotch angles are not as strong and can lead to included bark.

The following sections describe the basic types of pruning cuts, the differences between dormant and summer pruning, and several training systems that include these pruning methods.

Types of Pruning Cuts
When making pruning cuts, it is important to use techniques that promote rapid healing of the cut surface, which minimizes the opportunity for disease and insect infection. Without leaving stubs, make pruning cuts at the point of attachment to a larger branch or trunk. When making large horizontal cuts, make them at a slight angle so water does not sit on the cut surface. Standing water on a cut surface can result in rot and disease. Do not use wound dressing or pruning paints. The best treatment is to make proper pruning cuts and allow natural healing.

- **Thinning Cuts.** Remove a shoot back to a side shoot (Figure 15–20). Thinning cuts do not invigorate the tree as much as other types of pruning cuts.

Figure 15–20. Thinning cut.
Kathleen Moore, CC BY - 2.0

• **Heading Cuts.** Remove only the terminal portion of a shoot (Figure 15–21). This type of cut promotes the growth of lower buds, as well as several terminal buds below the cut. Heading cuts made on lateral branches into one-year-old wood invigorate the area near the cut. The headed branch is stronger and more rigid, resulting in lateral secondary branching. Hold older trees in their allotted space by mold-and-hold cuts (Figure 15–22), which are devigorating heading cuts made into two-year-old wood.

Figure 15–21. Heading cut.
Kathleen Moore, CC BY - 2.0

Figure 15–22. A mold and hold cut can be made on older trees to help them maintain their shape. The wrinkle that goes all the way around the stem marks the second year wood.
Kathleen Moore, CC BY - 2.0

• **Bench Cuts.** Remove vigorous, upright shoots back to side branches that are relatively flat and outward-growing (Figure 15–23). Bench cuts are used to open up the center of the tree and spread the branches outward. This is a major cut and used only when necessary.

Proper tree training opens up the canopy to maximize light penetration during the growing season. This is important because most deciduous fruit and nut trees form flower buds the summer before they bloom. Opening the tree canopy also permits air movement through the tree. Good air flow promotes rapid drying to minimize diseases and allows pesticides to penetrate thoroughly. Finally, a well-shaped fruit or nut tree is aesthetically pleasing, whether in a landscaped yard, garden, or commercial orchard.

Figure 15–23. A bench cut removes a vertical branch back to a horizontal branch of equal thickness.
Kathleen Moore, CC BY - 2.0

Initial Pruning

After planting young trees, prune the top of each tree to promote vigorous growth in the spring. When working with unbranched trees, cut the tree off at approximately 30 inches to 34 inches tall, 12 inches to 18 inches above where lateral branches are desired. For larger trees, remove approximately one-third of the treetop to form a whorl of **scaffold branches** (Figure 15–24).

Figure 15–24.
Pruning a pecan tree at planting, cutting off about one-third of the height.
Mike Parker

Dormant and Summer Pruning

Trees respond very differently to winter, dormant pruning than to summer pruning. Dormant pruning is an invigorating process. During the fall, energy is stored primarily in the trunk and root system to support the top portion of the tree. If a large portion of the tree is removed during winter dormancy, the tree's energy reserve is unchanged. In the spring, the tree responds by producing many new vigorous upright shoots, called water sprouts. This uses a large portion of the tree's energy, leaving little for fruit growth and development. Done correctly, however, light dormant pruning improves the tree's shape, allowing light to penetrate interior branches, and increases fruit production.

Pruning may temporarily and slightly reduce cold hardiness. So avoid winter injury by delaying dormant pruning until late winter. Because pruning is least likely to break their dormancy, prune the latest blooming trees first and the earliest blooming last. For example, prune apple and pecan trees first, followed by cherry, peach, and plum trees. Tree age also affects cold hardiness. Younger trees are more prone to winter injury from early pruning. Within a particular fruit type, prune the oldest trees first.

Summer pruning eliminates the energy or food-producing portion of the tree and results in reduced tree growth. Pruning begins as soon as the buds start to grow, but it is generally started after vegetative growth is several inches long. For most purposes, summer pruning is limited to removing the upright and vigorous current season's growth, using only thinning cuts. To minimize the potential for winter injury, do not summer prune after the end of July.

General Pruning Guidelines

- Remove dead, diseased, and broken branches.
- Remove water sprouts (excessive vegetative growth at the top) and suckers (excessive vegetative growth at the bottom of the tree).
- Remove shoots emerging from the rootstock.
- Eliminate competition between branches that grow into each other or toward the center of the tree.
- Eliminate narrow or sharp-angled branches.
- Remove growth that is below horizontal (anything angled toward the ground).
- Remove low branches that touch the ground.

Training Systems

One of the most frequently asked questions is this: "To what shape should I train a fruit tree?" The objectives of training and pruning are to achieve maximum tree life and productivity. There are many different training shapes and forms with multiple variations on each form. Three of the most common systems are "central leader," "modified central leader," and "open center."

Central Leader Training—Apple, Pear, Pecan, Plum

A central leader tree is characterized by one main, upright trunk, referred to as the **leader** (Figure 15–25). Branching generally begins on the leader 24 inches to 36 inches above the soil surface to allow movement under the tree. The first year, three to four branches, collectively called a "scaffold whorl," are selected. Space the selected scaffolds around the trunk, not directly across from or above one another. Above the first scaffold whorl, leave an area of approximately 18 inches to 24 inches without any branches to allow light into the center of the tree. This light slot is followed with another whorl of scaffolds. Alternating **scaffold whorls** and light slots are maintained up the leader to the desired maximum tree height.

Figure 15–25. Apple, pear, pecan, and plum trees should be trained to a central leader.

Mike Parker

Figure 15–26 shows (A) First year pruning, remove leader 30–34 inches above ground; (B) Dormant pruning, remove leader 24–30 inches above first set of branches; (C) First summer after planting, determine proper leader (a) and prune off other wood around the leader (b and c); (D) The shape of a properly trained central leader tree is like that of a pyramid with 18–24 inches between branches; (E) Top view of central leader system showing ideal branch spacing around the tree.

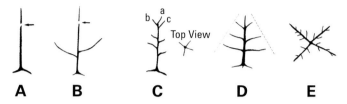

Figure 15–26. Pruning a central leader tree.

Pruning at Planting

Fruit trees are frequently purchased as whips, which are unbranched trees ranging from ½-inch to ¾-inch in diameter. Just before the buds start to grow in the spring, head the tree, at 30 inches to 34 inches above the soil surface, 12 inches to 18 inches above where the first whorl of lateral branches is desired. Once the tree is headed, permanent branches are selected from buds growing within 4 inches to 12 inches below the heading cut.

First-Year Summer Pruning

The first summer after planting is the optimal time to select the leader and the scaffold branches and to remove undesirable growth. Prune just enough to develop an optimal tree structure. Keep summer pruning to a minimum.

Select the leader after the new vegetative growth has reached 3 inches to 4 inches in length. Choose one upright shoot near the top of the tree, usually one growing into the prevailing winds. Cut the tree back to just above where this leader branches out from the trunk (Figure 15–26 C), and remove all competing shoots to approximately 4 inches below it.

During the first year, limit additional summer pruning to removing vigorous shoots growing upright and branches growing toward the ground. Branches that grow toward the ground will affect future maintenance under the tree canopy. Train and prune young trees every six to eight weeks, May through July (June through July in the NC mountains), to remove unwanted growth and to properly orient young branches. Summer pruning greatly reduces the amount of dormant pruning needed. Failure to summer prune the first year may result in an improperly trained tree that requires drastic dormant pruning to correct tree structure.

Spreading

All lateral branches should have a wide angle (45 degrees to 90 degrees) between the leader and the side shoots. This angle is referred to as the crotch angle. Branches that do not have a wide crotch angle are often overly vigorous and have a weak union. These branches frequently break under a heavy fruit load and injure the trunk, reducing tree life and productivity. Spreading the lateral branches slows the growth of the branches to a manageable level and promotes the development of secondary or side shoots on the scaffolds.

When growth is only 3 inches to 4 inches long, use toothpicks (Figure 15–27) or spring-loaded clothespins between the trunk and the branch to develop wide crotch angles (Figure 15–28). After a branch grows to a proper angle, move the clothespins to the ends of longer limbs to weigh down the branches as they start to grow upward. Extreme care must be taken when using the clothespins as weights.

Figure 15–27. A toothpick helps maintain a wide crotch angle.
Kathleen Moore, CC BY - 2.0

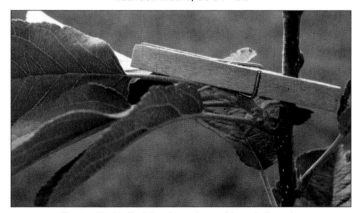

Figure 15–28. Training branches with a clothespin.
Mike Parker

Periodic checking is essential to assure that the scaffold angles are not too flat.

Spreaders are another option. Construct your own spreader by measuring the distance between the trunk and lateral shoot you wish to spread. Cut 1-inch-square wood pieces a few inches longer than your measured distance, and angle the spreaders at both ends. Drive finishing nails into each end (Figure 15–29). Lateral branches are spread for about the first five years, using a larger spreader each year.

Figure 15–29. Lateral spreaders using 1-inch square pieces of wood with finishing nails on either end.
Mike Parker

Spreading branches in later years reduces vigor and promotes fruit development on the lateral branches. The reduced growth rate and the weight of the crop load also help pull the branches down to a proper angle. It is important that the young tree is not allowed to crop too heavily while the branches are young and weak. If the weight of the fruit pulls the branches below horizontal, the branches become weak and nonproductive and must be removed.

Succeeding Years

- **Dormant pruning.** Managing the central leader is one of the most important aspects of dormant pruning. Head the leader at approximately 24 inches to 30 inches above the highest whorl of scaffolds to promote continued branching and scaffold whorl development. Dormant pruning should also eliminate dead, diseased, and damaged wood. Remove unwanted growth, such as upright growing shoots and laterals with sharp branch angles not removed during summer pruning. Head unbranched lateral branches back by approximately one-fourth of their length to encourage side branches and to stiffen lateral branches (Figure 15–30).

Figure 15–30. A heading cut encourages side shoot development.
Mike Parker

Another objective of dormant pruning is to control the length of the lateral branches. In order to maintain the pyramidal tree shape, lateral branches need to be cut back. Once the tree has reached its desired height and lateral spread, it is necessary to mold and hold the lateral branches and the central leader with heading cuts. This is done by cutting the laterals and leader back to a side-growing shoot on two-year-old wood. Two-year-old wood can be anywhere from a couple of inches to a few feet back from the tips of the branches. Follow the branch toward the trunk and look for a wrinkly scar that goes all the way around the branch (Figure 15–22). The shoot should be the same diameter as the leader being removed.

- **Summer pruning.** Eliminate competing shoots where dormant heading cuts were made (on the central leader and laterals) as in the first year. Summer is also the optimal time to remove unwanted side shoots and excessive growth.

Initial Steps in Pruning a Tree to a Central Leader:

- Leave only one trunk for the central leader.
- Remove branches with crotch angles of less than 60 degrees.
- Remove all branches directly across from one another on the leader.
- Space lateral branches uniformly around the leader to prevent crowding as the limbs grow in diameter.

Mature Central Leader Trees

Mature trees that have been properly trained and summer pruned require minimal pruning. The first step is to remove dead, diseased, and damaged wood and then upright shoots and shoots below horizontal. To prevent shading, it is important to maintain the pyramidal tree shape by heading lateral branches with mold-and-hold cuts (Figure 15–22). For quality fruit production, it is also essential to maintain the light slots between the scaffold whorls.

Neglected Central Leader Trees

Mature fruit trees that have not been properly trained frequently do not have a true central leader shape (Figure 15–31). For those trees, consider your objectives in pruning and training. In many cases, too many lateral branches and upright limbs were left and now must be removed to allow proper light penetration. This type of pruning is done during the dormant season.

15

Figure 15–31. An untrained pear tree.
Chris Alberti, CC BY - 2.0

Neglected trees often have overgrown tops that act as an umbrella, shading the rest of the tree. Cut back or remove the tops of these trees to allow better light penetration. Do not remove more than 30% of the tree's top to avoid shifting the tree into an excessively vegetative state with little fruit development.

Modified Central Leader Training

This method of training a tree uses the central leader concept on multiple branches based on the best shape for optimum production.

Example of a Modified Leader: Pecan Trees

Train pecan trees to a central leader with the lateral branches attached to the main trunk in a spiral (like a circular stairway). Leave approximately 12 inches to 15 inches between branches, initially, for adequate light penetration. As the tree matures it is necessary to remove branches to prevent crowding and provide continued light penetration (Figure 15–32).

Figure 15–32. Properly trained pecan trees.
J. M. Villarreal, USDA, Flickr CC BY - 2.0

Multileader System—Pear

For pear varieties subject to fire blight, a multileader tree is the goal of another training system. With a multileader tree, if one leader is infected with fire blight, it is safe to remove the infected leader without compromising the tree's health. The multileader system uses the same concept as the central leader system except that pruning creates several leaders in the center of the tree. In the first and second year, instead of removing the competing leaders, leave several leaders. Maintain each leader to the same shape as an individual central leader tree. On the tree in Figure 15–26 C, it is necessary to leave shoots a, b, and c for a multileader tree. Spreaders between the selected leaders are necessary to get the proper shape of the tree.

Open-Centered or Vase System—Peach, Nectarine, Plum

With the open-center system, the leader is removed, leaving an open center (Figure 15–33, Figure 15–34, and Figure 15–35). Instead of having a central leader, the open-center tree has three to five major limbs, called scaffolds, coming out from the trunk. This training system allows for adequate light penetration into the tree, which minimizes the shading problem prevalent in higher vigor trees, such as peach trees.

Figure 15–33. A heading cut should be made just above the selected branches that will form the whorl for the peach tree.
Mike Parker

Figure 15–34. A heading cut should be made just above the selected branches that will form the whorl for the peach tree.
Mike Parker

Figure 15–35. This mature peach tree shows the open center style of pruning. Prune in February and thin the blossoms after the trees are in full bloom.

Mike Parker

Pruning at Planting

As the buds begin to swell, head whips at approximately 30 inches to 34 inches above the soil surface. As discussed with the central leader system, new branches will come from buds 6 inches to 9 inches below the heading cut. For branched trees, consider the work that needs to be done under the tree, such as weeding, mowing, and harvesting to determine the appropriate height for branching. This is usually 24 inches to 32 inches. Remove branches that are too low. Select three to four uniformly spaced branches around the tree as scaffolds, and head the tree just above the highest selected scaffold. Remove any remaining branches not selected as scaffolds. If it is not possible to have three or more scaffolds, cut the tree back to a whip and remove the side branches.

First-Year Summer Pruning

For trees that started as whips, select the shoots that will become the major scaffolds after the new vegetative growth is approximately 3 inches to 4 inches long. The lowest scaffold should be 24 inches to 32 inches above the soil surface to allow for cultural practices. It is best to select three to four scaffolds that are uniformly spaced around the tree, with wide branch angles, and not directly across from another scaffold.

During the summer, spread the shoots out to a 45-degree to 60-degree angle and hold each shoot in place with a toothpick or clothespin. Remove all other upright growth. Every month during the summer remove upright growth shading the primary scaffolds, and make sure that the scaffolds have been spread to a proper angle. Many times the crotch angle is proper initially, but as the scaffolds grow, they turn upright. A spring-loaded clothespin placed on or near the end of a shoot can pull the scaffold down to a proper angle.

Succeeding Years

After the first year of growth, continue to train the primary scaffolds outward.

- **Dormant Season.** Head the scaffolds for the first three years to promote continued lateral branching on the scaffolds and to stiffen and strengthen the scaffolds. Head the scaffolds to outward-growing shoots similar in angle to those being removed. Avoid bench cuts. For bearing trees, the goal of dormant pruning is to remove vigorous upright growth on the scaffolds and trunk. The upright growth left in the tree during the growing season may shade out lateral growth near the trunk, preventing lateral fruiting wood except on the outer ends of the scaffolds. The resulting heavy fruit load on the tips of the branches can break scaffolds. Ensure that light penetrates the canopy so the fruiting wood on the scaffolds stays as close to the tree trunk as possible to reduce tree breakage and to produce the highest quality fruit.

  Also remove damaged, dead, and diseased wood, such as cankers. Remove mummies, or shriveled and dried fruits from the previous season, to reduce disease pressure for the coming season.

- **Summer pruning.** Remove undesirable growth as soon as shoots are 4 inches to 6 inches long. Use summer pruning to direct scaffold growth outward to the desired growing points.

Factors Affecting Fruiting

Pollination

Fruit and nut trees rely on pollination to reproduce. Pollen must travel from the **anther** (male organ) of one flower to the **stigma** (female organ) of a receptive flower, where the pollen germinates, fertilizes the egg, and creates a seed or seeds. Many fruit and nut trees rely on honey bees, mason bees, or bumble bees to move pollen from one flower to another. Pollinators are very sensitive; suspend any type of chemical management when they are active.

Some fruit trees, such as peaches and nectarines, are self-pollinating. Even with self-pollinating trees, it is always beneficial to have more than one cultivar to help with pollination. Self-pollinated trees produce less fruit than trees that require cross-pollination.

Most apples, pawpaws, pears, and plums require another cultivar of such a tree to pollinate flowers. This cross-pollination ensures genetic diversity and, generally, a larger crop. To cross-pollinate each other, cultivars must bloom at the same time: early season, midseason, or late season. Ideally, plant trees 50 feet to 100 feet apart. Some cultivars are better producers of pollen. For example, crabapple trees produce copious amounts of pollen and are often planted in orchards to help with apple pollination. Pear trees bloom earlier in the spring when bees are less active. Pear trees have paler blossoms and are not as fragrant as apple trees so are less attractive to bees. Planting multiple cultivars will help with pear tree pollination. Some growers resort to hand-pollination with a paintbrush.

Most fruit trees are "diploid:" having two sets of chromosomes—one set from the mother plant and one set from the father. Some apples and pears are listed as "triploid"—having three sets of chromosomes. Triploid trees will accept pollen from other trees of the same species, but they do not produce viable pollen for cross-pollination. If you plant a triploid pear or apple, you need to plant two other diploid pears or apples to ensure adequate pollination. **Monoecious** trees—pecans, for example—have both male and female imperfect flowers on the same tree. When male flowers (long, drooping structures called catkins) release pollen, the female flowers may not be at a stage of development where pollination is possible. Pecan trees are divided into two pollination types. A Type I tree releases pollen before its female flowers are ready. A Type II tree releases its pollen after the female flowers are receptive. To ensure adequate pollination, plant at least one tree of each type.

Pruning Fruiting Wood

Knowing where a tree forms flowers and bears fruit is crucial in understanding how to prune the tree. **Stone fruit** trees (such as peach and plum trees) bloom before leaves appear, while pome fruit trees (including apple and pear trees) generally bloom two weeks to three weeks after leaves appear.

Pome fruit trees produce fruit on the tips of shoots or spurs (very short branches that grow less than an inch a year) located on wood that is at least two years old (Figure 15–36). As a result, very light crops are produced if these trees are pruned by heading back all the branches because most of the fruiting wood is removed. Some cultivars, called spur-type, produce fruit perennially on spurs rather than longer branches. 'Red Delicious' is an example of a spur-type cultivar. Individual spurs live for many years, but their productive life is usually not more than 8 to 10 years. Spur-type cultivars produce smaller trees and should not be pruned as vigorously as non-spur-type cultivars.

Stone fruit trees, such as peaches, differ from pome fruit in that they bear most fruit from flower buds on one-year-old shoots. At least 12 inches to 18 inches of new growth is essential to ensure adequate fruit.

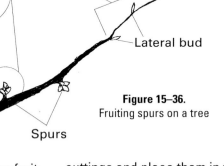

Figure 15–36.
Fruiting spurs on a tree

Weather

Midwinter temperatures of 0°F or below may kill some fruit buds on peaches, plums, cherries, and apricots and possibly result in tree injury. Such low temperatures, however, are rare in North Carolina. A greater risk comes from early and late frosts.

In the fall, if a cold snap comes suddenly and the plant has had no opportunity to "harden off" with a gradual drop in temperature in the weeks before, there is greater risk of damage from an early frost. If temperatures were already low before the cold snap, much less bud injury and tree death may occur. Buds and flowers can survive slightly lower temperatures if the temperature drop is gradual and if the minimum temperature occurs for only a short period.

On the other hand, in the spring, as the buds swell and develop, they become less cold hardy and more prone to injury. Spring injury from a late freeze is the greatest threat to fruit tree buds in North Carolina, with a temperature difference of 3°F to 4°F being the difference between a full crop and no crop. The stage of bud and flower development is significant in cold hardiness. Before the blossoms open, flower buds may survive temperatures down to 20°F to 23°F. Flower buds showing color, however, may only survive temperatures down to 25°F to 28°F. At full bloom, and with small developing fruit, damage may occur below 27°F to 28°F. Apple trees send out green leaves first, followed two to three weeks later by blossoms. Peach, plum, and apricot trees are very vulnerable because the first growth to emerge in the spring is the blossoms. However, even if 80% of the flowers are damaged, the remaining 20% can still result in a full crop of fruit that requires minimal thinning. To determine the extent of blossom injury after a cold snap, take shoot cuttings and place them in water to open and bloom. If the center of the flower (**pistil**) is brown, the blossom is damaged and cannot bear fruit.

Fruit Thinning

Thin apples, nectarines, peaches, and pears early in the season to prevent overproduction, which results in small fruits and increased problems with insects, diseases, and tree breakage (Figure 15–37). A heavy crop also reduces the chances for an adequate crop the following year.

Table 15–6. Fruit and Nut Harvesting Guidelines

FRUIT YEARS TO HARVEST	APPROXIMATE HARVEST DATES	SKIN COLOR	GROUND COLOR stem end, bottom, or shaded side of the fruit	SEED OR PIT	FLESH TEXTURE and/or FIRMNESS	REMARKS
Apples *2 – 6*	August to November	Light conditions and position in the canopy may affect color. Red apples: Blush or stripes change from dull red to bright red. Yellow apples: Skin turns from green to yellow.	Turns from green to yellow or green to yellow-green	Turns from greenish-white to dark brown when ripe	Crisp and juicy	Fruit should release easily from tree with the **pedicel** (stem) intact. Taste to confirm that apples have reached optimal tree-ripened maturity. Fruit lasts longer stored at 32°F. Red apples may not color as well in warmer regions.
Chestnuts, chinquapin *3 – 6*	September	N/A	N/A	Spiny husks separate to reveal shiny brown seeds. Ripe nuts will fall to ground. Harvest promptly as nuts quickly decay.	Kernel is rubbery, cream to yellow in color. Chestnuts fresh from the tree are not as sweet as they are after they have been cured for 7 to 10 days.	To peel, score bottom with 'X'. Boil or roast. Fresh, unpeeled chestnuts stored in an airtight container last one month in the refrigerator and a year or more in the freezer. Dehydrated peeled nuts have a longer storage life but lose some flavor. Soak nuts in cold water 3 to 4 hours to rehydrate.
Figs *3 – 4*	June to August	Turns from green to purple-brown or coppery-brown, depending on variety	Yellow-green	N/A	Flesh turns to strawberry-pink or amber, depending on variety. Fruit bends downward at pedicel (stem).	Pick fresh figs with stems attached. Fresh figs last only a few days; dry or make preserves or jam for long-term storage.
Mulberry, Red *8 – 10*	May to June	Turns red, deep purple, or black, depending on species	N/A	N/A	Soft, sweet, and juicy	Ripe berries fall off the tree; pick or shake the tree. Plant away from sidewalks and driveways because fallen fruit causes stains. Fruits are a bird favorite. White mulberry can be weedy.

15

Table 15–6. Fruit and Nut Harvesting Guidelines *continued*

FRUIT *YEARS TO HARVEST*	APPROXIMATE HARVEST DATES	SKIN COLOR	GROUND COLOR stem end, bottom, or shaded side of the fruit	SEED OR PIT	FLESH TEXTURE and/or FIRMNESS	REMARKS
Nectarines *2 – 4*	May to July	Yellow-orange to dark orange, red, or reddish pink. Even-colored or patch.	Green changes to creamy-yellow. All green disappears before fully ripe.	N/A	Fruit softens and yields to hand pressure. Flesh color is yellow-orange with red around the pit; juicy, developed flavor.	Sample ripening fruit to determine suitability for picking. Chill fruit after picking.
Pawpaw *5 – 7*	August to September or to first frost	Turns lighter green, or a little yellow when ripe. Overripe fruit turns yellow with brown splotches and streaks like a banana.	Green	Seeds are easy to separate and remove before eating.	Fruit begins to soften like an avocado.	Ripe fruit has a fruity, floral aroma. Fruit picked before fully mature will ripen at room temperature like a peach or pear.
Peaches *2 – 4*	June to August	Yellow-orange to dark orange, red, or reddish pink. Can be even-colored or patchy.	Green changes to creamy yellow. All green disappears before fully ripe.	Flesh does not adhere to pit in ripe freestone peach varieties. Flesh adheres to pit in ripe cling varieties.	Fruit yields to gentle hand pressure along the crease. Flesh color is yellow-orange with red around the pit; juicy, developed flavor.	Fruits on the ends of branches and those high in the tree ripen first. Ripe fruit becomes uniformly shaped on both sides of the suture. Taste fruit as it ripens to desired sweetness. Chill fruit after picking.
Pears, Asian *2 – 3*	August to October	Most varieties change from green to yellow-brown or yellow-green	Changes from green to yellow	Brown to dark brown	Very crunchy and juicy	Asian pears have tender skin that bruises and marks easily. Store under refrigeration for a few weeks. Will become spongy after 7 to 14 days at room temperature.

Figure 15–37.
This apple tree fruit was not thinned so there are too many apples on this spur. This risks breakage and small fruit size.
Kathleen Moore,
CC BY - 2.0

Figure 15–38.
Thin fruit a hand width, or 6 to 8 inches apart.
Lucy Bradley,
CC BY - 2.0

Table 15–6. Fruit and Nut Harvesting Guidelines *continued*

FRUIT *YEARS TO HARVEST*	APPROXIMATE HARVEST DATES	SKIN COLOR	GROUND COLOR stem end, bottom, or shaded side of the fruit	SEED OR PIT	FLESH TEXTURE and/or FIRMNESS	REMARKS
Pears, European 4 – 6	August to October	Harvest when green, but at fully mature size	Green with yellowish tinge	Light-brown to brown	Ripe pears yield to gentle hand pressure on the neck just below the pedicel (stem)	Maximum flavor and quality develops when picked mature, but not tree-ripened. Tree-ripened pears are mealy. Harvest when green color turns lighter green or yellow. Ready-to-pick pears detach when lifted horizontally. Refrigerate after picking; ripen at room temperature several days.
Pecans 4-8 *(grafted)* 8-10 *(seedling)*	October to December	N/A	N/A	N/A	Pecan kernels are brittle when adequately dry	Harvest pecans when the shuck (outer fruit wall) opens and releases the nut. Before storing, dry pecans in paper or burlap bags hung in an area with good air movement. Freeze for long-term storage.
Persimmons, American and Asian 3 – 7	September to November	Orange to reddish-brown on native varieties, orange-red to red on Asian varieties	N/A	N/A	Fruit of native and astringent Asian varieties must be soft before eating. Nonastringent Asian varieties can be eaten when fruit is still firm.	Persimmon fruit continues to ripen after picking. Frost may ruin native and astringent Asian varieties.
Plums 4 – 6	June to August	Turns from green to yellow, red, or dark purple, depending on variety	Yellow to yellow-green	N/A	Flesh is firm but yields to gentle pressure	Chill ripe fruit after picking
Walnut, Black 4 – 7 *(small crop)* 20 – 30 *(large crop)*	August to September	N/A	N/A	Press thumb into husk: if it yields and makes a dark mark, nuts are ready to harvest. Nuts will fall from the tree when ripe. Pick up and husk promptly.	Kernel should be creamy-white and firm	Wear rubber gloves as husks can irritate skin. Rinse and dry nuts after removing husks.

Thin fruits when they are about the size of a nickel. Remove enough fruit so that the remaining ones are spaced approximately 6 inches to 8 inches apart along the branch (Figure 15–38). Even though it may look as though very few fruit remain, the fruit size at harvest more than compensates for the reduced number of fruit.

Harvest Guidelines

Harvest guidelines for various fruits and nuts are outlined in Table 15–6.

Integrated Pest Management

Weeds, insects, and diseases cause tree stress and crop damage. Most pests can be managed using integrated pest management (IPM) techniques. Proper identification of the pest is the first step in any IPM program, and identification leads to identifying appropriate management strategies. Review the chapters on IPM, Insects, and Diseases for specific information on how to manage pest problems.

To minimize pest problems:
- Select resistant cultivars.
- Provide optimum growing conditions: proper soil pH, drainage, light, and spacing.
- Prune correctly to provide maximum sunlight and air.
- Clean up and destroy plant litter and damaged fruit.
- Fertilize according to recommendations on a soil test report and the amount of new growth.
- Correctly identify and manage weed, insect, disease, and animal pest problems.

If spraying is warranted:
- Choose only a product that is labeled specifically for both the pest problem and the plant.
- Mix the product according to the labeled instructions.
- Use a good sprayer, and spray to achieve maximum coverage.
- Time sprays for maximum benefit.

Time early spray applications according to fruit bud development—not the calendar (Figure 15–36). Dormant applications minimize pest pressure later in the season. During the growing season, begin pesticide applications after the petals fall off the blossoms (petal fall). Do not apply any insecticides during bloom because this harms the insects required for pollination.

Weeds
Weeds or grasses growing between or under fruit and nut trees compete for soil nutrients and moisture and reduce tree growth. Remove all vegetation under the trees, and place a 3-inch to 4-inch layer of mulch from just outside the trunk to the dripline (the circle formed by the tips of the outermost branches of the tree). Mulch suppresses weed growth and conserves soil moisture, but it may also provide cover for voles or mice. These rodents burrow under the mulch and gnaw tree trunks or roots, killing the tree or impeding its growth. Minimize aboveground damage by placing a guard around the base of each tree, and use traps to manage these pests. Keep mulch back 12 inches from the tree trunk to force voles out into the open and allow natural predators to help manage populations.

Avoid mechanical cultivation—hoes, tillers or discs—to eliminate weeds because tree roots near the surface are destroyed during cultivation. Weed trimmers are especially harmful. If the cutting line strikes the bark of the tree, the line crushes layers of cells under the bark and girdles the tree. Herbicides are an effective alternative, but be careful to follow the label directions and keep the herbicides off a tree's foliage and green bark.

Insects
Codling moth larvae (*Cydia pomonella*) overwinter behind loose bark or in loose soil around the base of the tree in thick silken cocoons. The adult moths are ½-inch to ¾-inch long with mottled gray wings and a coppery-brown band at the wingtips (Figure 15–39). Moths lay many eggs on fruits, leaves, or nuts soon after petal fall. Larvae are light-pink worms with a dark-brown head. They tunnel inside the apple and pear fruits leaving **frass**-filled holes (Figure 15–40). Codling moths produce two to three generations per year and are particularly damaging to late-ripening fruit. Prevention is the best management, as codling moths can be difficult to manage if populations have built up over several years. Choose late-ripening apple or pear tree varieties, or late-leafing walnut trees, as they are most resistant. Prune trees to a low height for easy access to fruit and braches. Remove infected fruit immediately from the tree and the ground to maintain orchard sanitation. Bagging individual fruit four weeks to six weeks after bloom provides excellent control, but bagging is a labor-intensive process only practical for small trees. Hanging sticky traps to catch adult codling moths can be part of an overall management protocol, but traps are not effective on their own. Tolerating some level of damage is also

Figure 15–39. Adult codling moth.
gailhampshire, Flickr CC BY - 2.0

recommended, as the codling moth is nearly impossible to completely eradicate. Infected parts of the fruit can be cut away, and the rest is still edible. If chemical management is warranted, apply when larvae have just emerged from the eggs. If the larvae have already entered the fruit, they will be protected from pesticides. Trees can also be infected from neighbors' yards even if you are treating, so a neighborhood-wide effort is advised.

Figure 15–40. Codling moth damage to apples.
Patrick Clement, Flickr CC BY - 2.0

Oriental fruit moths (*Grapholita molesta*) attack peach, plum, cherry, and apple trees (Figure 15–41). The first-generation larvae tunnel into the ends of new shoots, causing shoot dieback (Figure 15–42). Later generations feed inside the fruit. Fruits near the top of a tree that are beginning to color are the first to be attacked, so take samples from there. Placing pheromone traps in the orchard in early spring to disrupt mating is the preferred treatment strategy. The braconid wasp (*Macrocentrus ancylivorus*) is a natural parasite to oriental fruit moth and peach tree borer larvae. Planting sunflowers will encourage the braconid wasp population. Avoid broad-spectrum insecticides, which negatively affect populations of *Macrocentrus ancylivorus*.

Figure 15–41. Adult Oriental fruit moth.
Matt Bertone

Figure 15–42. Oriental fruit moth larva.
Matt Bertone

Plum curculio (*Conotrachelus nenuphar*) attack several soft fruits, including plums and apricots, and can cause superficial damage to apples (Figure 15–43). Adults are brown, black, and gray mottled weevils that overwinter in wooded areas and become active at bloom time. Eggs are laid in crescent-shaped flaps cut in the fruit skin shortly after petal fall. Larvae hatch and feed inside the fruit. Sanitation is important. Remove and dispose of damaged or fallen fruit. In early morning, place a tarp under trees and shake branches. The adult weevils are slow-moving in the morning and will fall from the tree where they can be crushed. Use a registered insecticide after petal fall to ensure pollinators are not affected.

Figure 15–43. An adult plum curculio weevil.
Matt Bertone

Peach tree borers (*Synanthedon exitiosa*) attack the trunk and lower branches of stone fruit trees and other members of the Prunus genus, causing sap to ooze from the wounds. Adults are black and orange moths but look and behave like wasps (Figure 15–44). The cream-colored larvae have a brown head and can reach 1½ inches in length. They tunnel under the bark, and over several years they can girdle the tree. Parasitic nematodes are a treatment option, but results vary. A registered insecticide will be most effective against egg-laying and will kill tiny larvae when they hatch. Apply it at the base of the trunk several times throughout the growing season, especially in early September when adult moths emerge.

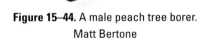

Figure 15–44. A male peach tree borer.
Matt Bertone

San Jose (*Quadraspidiotus perniciosus*) and white peach scales (*Pseudaulacaspis pentagona*) (Figure 15–45) overwinter as nymphs and start feeding as soon as sap begins flowing in the tree. The young crawlers feed on branches, leaves, and fruit, causing red, spotted areas (Figure 15–46). Infested leaves usually drop, and branches lose vigor and die. Biological predators, such as the twice-stabbed lady beetle (*Chilocorus stigma*), or parasites like chalcid and aphelinid wasps, are effective against scale insects. Use a dormant oil spray at two-week intervals with good spray coverage just before bud break, or treat with registered insecticide when crawlers are active.

Figure 15–45. White peach scale (*Pseudaulacaspis pentagona*) on a branch.

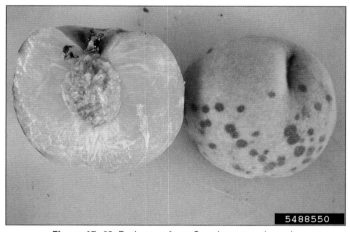

Figure 15–46. Red spots from San Jose peach scale.

Spider mites (*Tetranychus urticae*) suck juice from peach tree leaves, creating stippling and causing leaves to turn yellow or red (Figure 15–47). Spider mites produce webbing colonies, especially on the undersides of leaves. Hot, dry weather that causes water stress encourages their development. Spider mites have many natural enemies, including predatory mites and thrips that, if supported by limiting broad-spectrum insecticides, naturally keep populations in check. A strong water spray, **horticultural oil**, or soap spray are other management strategies. Be sure to reach the undersides of leaves.

Figure 15–47.
Spider mite damage appears as stippling and bleaching.

Catfacing is the pitting and fruit deformity caused by adult insects with piercing-sucking mouthparts, such as lygus bug, stink bug, tarnished plant bug, and boxelder bug. These insects damage both pome and stone fruits (Figure 15–48). Weeds are the primary food source for these insects, so keeping weeds to a minimum around the orchard will help manage populations. Several parasitic wasps and predatory insects, such as big-eyed bugs, assassin bug, damsel bugs, and crab spiders, attack these insects. Reducing the use of broad spectrum insecticides helps these biological predators keep pest populations in check. Use of an insecticide is a last resort to prevent substantial fruit damage.

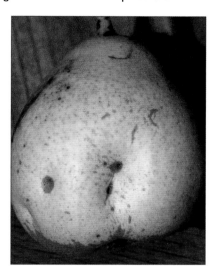

Figure 15–48. Catfacing damage on a pear.

Diseases

Bacterial spot (*Xanthomonas arboricola*) is a bacterial disease on peach trees that results in irregularly shaped lesions on the leaves (Figure 15–49) and sunken lesions on the fruit. Prevent it by growing resistant cultivars and spraying dormant trees with copper bactericides.

Figure 15–49. Bacterial spot of peach leaves.

15

Common Pecan Tree Insect Problems

Pecan weevils (*Curculio caryae*) attack the nut (Figure 15–50). The weevil punctures the nuts in early August (Figure 15–51); the larvae feed within the nut, causing some nuts to fall in a few days. Pecans damaged early in the season fall off with the shuck attached. Nuts damaged later in the season fall from the shuck with a small hole in the shell where the larvae have exited.

Stink bugs (*Pentatomidae*) puncture nuts before and after nut hardening. This puncture causes nut drop or black-spotted bitter kernels (Figure 15–52).

Twig girdlers (*Oncideres cingulate*) cut off the vascular system of twigs and small branches, causing them to drop in September. The branches appear as if cut with pruners (Figure 15–53). Dispose of fallen shoots because they contain eggs for the next generation of twig girdlers.

Insect Management Measures for Pecan Trees

- Plant at least 200 feet from wooded areas.
- Do not grow vegetables or soybeans near pecan trees (these crops are alternate hosts for stink bug pests).
- Manage broadleaf weeds under the trees.
- Gather and destroy fallen twigs and nuts.
- When other options have been exhausted, use registered insecticides labeled for use on pecan trees to treat the specific insect pest.

Figure 15–50. Damage to pecans from pecan weevils.
Jerry A. Payne, USDA Agricultural Research Service, Bugwood CC BY - 3.0

Figure 15–51. An adult female weevil using her piercing mouthpart to feed on a pecan.
JJerry A. Payne, USDA Agricultural Research Service, Bugwood CC BY - 3.0

Figure 15–52. Stink bug damage to a pecan kernel.
Jonas Janner Hamman, Universidade Federal de Santa Maria (UFSM), Bugwood CC BY - 3.0

Figure 15–53. A twig girdler.
Clemson University - USDA Cooperative Extension Slide Series, Bugwood CC BY - 3.0

Brown rot (*Monilinia fructicola*) is the most common problematic fungus and occurs during bloom. It kills blossoms and then reoccurs two weeks to three weeks before harvest on ripening stone fruits. The rotted areas are soft and brown. Brownish-gray mold covers the rotted areas (Figure 15–54). Infected fruits often shrivel, gradually turning into hard, wrinkled black mummies. To avoid brown rot, plant resistant cultivars. If trees become infected, remove and destroy infected fruit and branches. Prune the trees to improve air flow, and avoid overhead watering to keep foliage dry. If problems persist, use a registered copper-based fungicide.

Figure 15–54. Brown rot.
University of Georgia Plant Pathology, University of Georgia, Bugwood CC BY - 3.0

Cedar apple rust (*Gymnosporangium juniperi-virginianae*) occurs on apple and crabapple trees. It causes small bright-yellow spots on the leaves in early summer that enlarge and turn orange with black specks in the center (Figure 15–55). A cup-shaped structure forms on the under side of each infected leaf (Figure 15–56). The disease organism spends part of its life on cedar trees, where it produces structures that release spores from orange gelatinous appendages in the spring (Figure 15–57). Cedars as much as ¼-mile away can serve as alternate hosts so if infestation is severe remove all cedars in a ½-mile radius. Apply a registered fungicide from early pre-pink through petal fall for fruit infections and from pre-pink through second cover for leaf infections.

15

Figure 15–55.
Cedar apple rust on
apple leaves.

Figure 15–56.
Cup-shaped structures on the
underside of apple leaves.

Figure 15–57. The gelatinous orange appendages of cedar apple rust
as it appears on cedar trees.

Fire blight (*Erwinia amylovora*) is a bacterial disease that is spread by bees during bloom on pome fruit trees and their relatives. New shoots rapidly turn black at the tips and die, with blackened leaves remaining attached to the stem (Figure 15–58). Newly infected wood has pink-orange streaks. Watery brown sap oozes from cankers or damaged tissue, created by previous years' infections. Fire blight is most easily spread when temperatures are between 75°F and 85°F with high humidity or precipitation. Choose resistant cultivars. Avoid heavy pruning and high nitrogen fertilizers, which cause rapid, tender growth that is most susceptible to fire blight. Do not irrigate trees during bloom, and remove and discard any infected tissue in summer or winter when the disease is inactive. Copper products are the only chemical management available to homeowners, and they are difficult to time and apply effectively.

Figure 15–58.
Fire blight on an apple tree. Branches die back from the tips and leaves remain attached.

Peach leaf curl (*Taphrina deformans*) occurs just after bloom and causes unfolding terminal leaves to blister, swell, and curl. The stunted leaves turn reddish-purple and fall off (Figure 15–59). New stems are stunted and distorted. Cool, wet weather when leaves are emerging favor the disease. To avoid peach leaf curl, plant resistant varieties. For already infected trees, treat with a registered fungicide yearly after leaf fall.

Figure 15–59.
Peach leaf curl.

Peach scab (*Cladosporium carpophilum*) causes small, round, dark, olive-green-to-black spots to form near the stem end on nearly full-grown fruit (Figure 15–60). Severely infected fruit can crack, shrivel, or not ripen. The fungus overwinters in light-brown lesions appearing on new twig growth. Water splashes these lesions and moves spores onto the fruit. Spring and early summer in North Carolina provide ideal growing conditions. All peach varieties are susceptible to scab, though some more than others. The worst infection usually occurs during the first fruiting season, or around the third

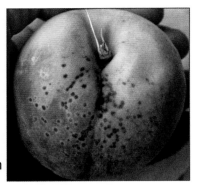

Figure 15–60. Peach scab.
Mike Parker

growing season after planting. Avoid low-lying planting sites, and prune trees to maintain good air circulation.

Powdery mildew (*Golovinomyces cichoracearum*) is a whitish-gray powdery mold that occurs on buds, young leaves, and green twigs (Figure 15–61). Leaves may be crinkled or cupped upward, dwarfed, narrow, and erect. Plant resistant varieties and maintain good cultural practices. Prune out infected areas during dormant season and use a registered fungicide if necessary.

Figure 15–61. Powdery mildew.
Benjamin Vanegtern, Flickr CC0

Apple scab fungus (*Venturia inaequalis*) causes dull, smoky spots on young leaves and petioles (Figure 15–62). The spots later turn olive-green, then blacken and drop off the tree. The secondary infection on the apple fruit produces lesions that cause the fruit to become deformed, knotty, and cracked (Figure 15–63). This fungus over-winters in fallen leaves on the ground. Cool, wet weather favors infection, and new leaves are most susceptible. Avoid overhead watering, and prune trees to promote good air circulation. In autumn, remove any fallen leaves, spray trees with urea to hasten leaf fall, and apply lime to fallen leaves to prevent the spread of infection. Use a registered fungicide at the first sign of greening leaves in the spring.

Figure 15–62. Apple scab lesions on leaves.
Joseph OBrien, USDA Forest Service, Bugwood CC BY - 3.0

Figure 15–63. Apple scab on fruits.
University of Georgia Plant Pathology, University of Georgia, Bugwood CC BY - 3.0

A Year in the Life of a Deciduous Tree

Winter
The tree has shed its leaves and remains dormant until spring. It is possible to see the entire tree structure and make informed decisions about where to prune. Fertilize in late winter.

Spring
During early spring, gradually increase irrigation as temperatures rise. Add a new layer of mulch around the base of the tree, avoiding the trunk, to help conserve water and manage weeds. Fertilize trees only if they show pale leaves and weak growth. Be sure to follow label directions; do not fertilize young fruit trees as this can slow their maturation. Flowering, pollination, fruit set, and abundant vegetative growth occur in spring. Thin fruit, and remove unwanted vigorous shoots to begin summer pruning. Scout for any insect or disease problems, and address them promptly.

Summer
Monitor rainfall and irrigate trees deeply if necessary. Some varieties of tree fruits ripen in summer. Taste fruit to check for ripeness, and harvest if necessary. If fruit spurs and leaves are breaking off when you pick the fruit, it is not ready to harvest. Continue to shape the tree with summer pruning, removing unwanted vigorous shoots. Scout for any insect and disease problems, and address them promptly.

Fall
Harvest varieties of tree fruit that ripen in fall. Do not leave fruit on the tree too long before picking, as this can attract pests and diseases. **Chlorophyll** production ends, and as it disappears from the leaves, other pigments become visible with a color display prior to leaf drop. Water trees into October so they are not drought-stressed going into winter. Avoid pruning in fall when fire blight is active. Add a layer of mulch to insulate the roots from cold temperatures. Rake up and dispose of any diseased or insect-infested leaves, twigs, and fruits to avoid spreading problems to healthy trees.

15

Case Study—Think IPM: Unhealthy Peach Tree

It is June, and your four 'Winblo' peach trees have fruit that is starting to rot on the tree before completely ripening. Some of the peaches are shriveled.

1. Monitor and scout to determine pest type and population levels.
2. Accurately identify host and pest.
3. Consider economic or aesthetic injury thresholds. A threshold is the time to take action.
4. Implement a treatment strategy using cultural, mechanical, biological, or chemical management, or a combination of these methods.
5. Evaluate success of treatments.

Sample responses are included in italics.

1. **Monitor and scout to determine pest type and population levels.**
   You have noticed that the peach trees have had this condition in the past and it seems to get worse every year.

2. **Accurately identify host and pest.**
   Use the steps outlined in chapter 7, "Diagnostics" to help you identify the problem. The following questions will help.
   Step 1. Identify the plant: *'Winblo' peach trees.*
   Step 2. Describe the problem: *Many of the peaches are rotting on the trees. Some are wrinkly with a fuzzy substance covering them and some have brown spots on them.*

Step 3. Identify what is normal:
What does the healthy part of the plant look like? *Healthy peach fruit from 'Winblo' peach trees have a reddish tint with an orange-to-yellow background when ripe.*
What does the unhealthy part of the plant look like? *The unhealthy fruit has brown, fuzzy spots, and is rotten and shriveled.*
Have you had a soil test? *No.* (For information on how to submit a soil test see "Soils and Plant Nutrients," chapter 1.)

Step 4. Cultural practices:
Age and history of plant: *The trees are five years old.*
Irrigation: *Trees are not watered unless there is a drought.*
Fertilizer: *The trees have never been fertilized.*
Maintenance: *The trees have never been pruned.*

Step 5. Environmental conditions:
Are there any significant water issues? *Yes. A lot of rainfall occurred in early spring. There was standing water around the trees for several days at a time.*
What is the soil like? *It is a clay soil, very red.*
Describe the light. How many hours of sunlight? *The peach trees receive 9 hours of full sun.*
Describe any recent changes or events: *A lot of rain occurred in early spring. Now in June the rain is intermittent. There have been no other changes around these trees.*

Step 6. Signs of pathogens and pests:

On the leaves: *I do not see signs of insects, a fungus, or a disease. There are no spots or missing pieces of the leaves.*

On the stems: *I do not see signs of insects, a fungus, or a disease.*

On the roots and in the soil: *I do not see anything near the roots. Some dried or rotting fruits are on the ground, and some have flies and fly larvae on them.*

On the fruit: *I saw some stink bugs feeding on some of the fruit.*

Step 7. Symptoms:

On the leaves: *The leaves appear healthy.*

On the buds/flowers: *The peaches flowered in the spring, and many blooms died during a frost and turned a brownish color. More blooms died and turned brown during the spring rains.*

On the stems: *Most stems have smooth reddish-brown bark. Some of the stems are dead with dark-gray lesions.*

On the roots: *Roots are creamy-white and look healthy. There is no odor coming from them.*

On the fruit: *About 40% of the fruits are damaged. Some are dried and shriveled and have remained on the tree* (Figure 15–64), *while the majority have fallen to the ground. There are some fruits with brown mushy spots on them.*

Figure 15–64.
Dried shriveled fruits that remain on the tree.
Clemson University - USDA Cooperative Extension Slide Series, Bugwood CC BY - 3.0

Step 8. Distribution of damage in the landscape:

Are other plants in the landscape affected? *This is widespread among the four peach trees. I also see some wild plums in the greenbelt behind my home with the same wrinkly, rotten fruit.*

Step 9. Distribution of damage on the plant and specific plant parts:

Where is the damage seen on the plant? Is it evenly distributed around the tree or localized? Inside the canopy or on the edges? High in the canopy or near the ground? *The flowering and fruiting wood seems most affected, so the damage is on the outer edge of the canopy.*

Step 10. Timing:

When did you notice this problem? *A few fruits started looking like this two years ago. Last year the damage was on a few more fruits, and this year it is much worse.*

You saw stink bugs and flies on the fruit, which are signs of a possible insect problem. You learned in "Insects," chapter 4, that stink bugs are a true bug in the order Hemiptera. They have piercing-sucking mouthparts. There was no stippling on the leaves or fruit to support these insects as the problem. You also learned in "Insects," chapter 4, that the flies are in the Diptera order and that they have either piercing, sucking, or sponging mouthparts and are often seen as secondary pests when there is rotting fruit. There is no evidence to support flies as the cause of damage to the tree.

Because there were symptoms on the fruit—wrinkly brown or rotting spots—and because some stems were damaged with brown streaks inside the twig wood, you hypothesize this plant is suffering from a disease. You decide to research peach diseases by typing "peaches +disease +nc state" into your search engine. You learn that peaches are not well-adapted to North Carolina's climate and often struggle to produce a reliable crop. You discover the Extension publication *Growing Peaches in North Carolina*, which covers all the major diseases. From the signs and symptoms noted in the diagnostic steps, you determine that your peaches have brown rot (*Monilinia fructicola*).

You could send a sample to the NC State Plant Disease and Insect Clinic for a confirmation of diagnosis. But after carefully reviewing the diagnostic steps, you are confident you have identified the problem. The poor cultural practices of never pruning, soil sampling, or removing shriveled and mummified fruit are the primary causes of the disease having spread. The dead limbs most likely died due to cankers forming and girdling the limbs. The spores on the fruit and the mummified fruit being left on the tree or on the ground increased the pathogen, so that all of the trees now have brown rot. You also learned from *Growing Peaches in North Carolina* that the wild plums behind your home can also be a vector of the disease.

3. Consider economic or aesthetic injury thresholds. A threshold is the point at which action should be taken.

After researching brown rot, you learn that without proper sanitation, pruning, and chemical control, the disease can quickly reduce peach yields. Brown rot on the fruit is also unsightly, and the smell of rotting fruit is not the most appealing. These trees provide shade in your backyard and, in previous years, provided a modest harvest of delicious peaches. You would like to save these trees, but also recognize that peach trees can struggle in North Carolina and they will always require a high level of maintenance. You decide to try some management techniques for the next two years to see if the problem decreases.

4. Implement a treatment strategy using physical, cultural, biological, or chemical management, or a combination of these methods.

Physical—First, you clean up any mummified or rotten fruit left on the ground from previous years and dispose of it off-site. You maintain a pruning schedule to remove any diseased limbs in the spring, before bloom. You pick fruit regularly so that it does not become overripe before harvesting. You are sure to remove and discard off-site any fruit left over after the last harvest, including mummified fruits that are still hanging on the trees. You consider talking to your homeowners association to see if it is possible to remove the wild plum trees, which are vectors of brown rot.

Cultural management—You obtain a soil test and amend the soil according to the test results. You address the heavy clay soil by applying a 3-inch layer of organic mulch around the trees every fall. You maintain a proper irrigation schedule, making sure the trees receive at least 1 inch of water per week during the dry period.

Biological management—No recommended strategies exist.

Chemical management—There are several fungicides to manage brown rot; they must be applied at a timely interval because the infection can start when trees are in bloom. If conditions are dry between fruit set and ripening, brown rot is not usually a problem. If there is rain, apply fungicide at the first sign of fruit color development. This is usually around three weeks before harvest. It is also important to remember to rotate fungicides to reduce resistance.

5. Evaluate success of treatments.
Keeping a garden journal or notes about the management strategies tried and their results will help make future decisions easier. Some of the management strategies may take time to produce results, and having a written record will help to jog your memory.

Frequently Asked Questions

1. Why is my tree not producing fruit?
Your tree may not produce fruit for many reasons. The tree's age is important; a tree less than three years old may not produce a reliable crop, and old trees may not support a good crop. Frost can also be a culprit. Flowers do not have to be in full bloom to be affected by frost. As soon as flower buds begin to swell, temperatures below 29°F cause the buds to turn black and die. Lack of pollination also affects fruit production. Avoid spraying your trees during the day when pollinators are most active. Be sure you have planted any trees needed for cross-pollination. Finally, vigorously growing trees put more energy toward leaf, trunk, and root production than flower and fruit production. Shoot growth on bearing fruit trees should average 12 inches to 18 inches a year. What causes trees to grow too vigorously? Over fertilization and over pruning. Heavy nitrogen application favors wood over flower growth. Fertilizing the grass or other plants surrounding the trees may affect fruit trees. If you have not over fertilized you could be overpruning. Fruit trees need to be pruned each winter, but heavy heading cuts can cause a tree to produce leaves and branches instead of fruit.

2. I have a large overgrown pear tree that does not produce very well. How do I get it to fruit for me again?
Restorative pruning of a large fruit tree takes a few years and quite a bit of work. You never want to remove more than 25% of a tree's canopy in one year. For the first year or two, remove dead wood, suckers, water sprouts, or crossing branches. Next, make two to four cuts of major branches. This helps decrease the height to a more manageable size and allows for better light penetration.

3. Last year I had a ton of apples and this year not nearly as many. Is there something wrong with my tree?
Many apple trees have a natural biennial cycle of alternate bearing habits. They produce more fruit in one year and less the next. Years with heavy fruit set signal to the tree to have a subsequent year with lighter fruit. This is mitigated by thinning the fruit in years with heavy fruit set three weeks after the fruit has set.

Further Reading

Childers, Norman F. *Modern Fruit Science.* 10th ed. Gainesville, Florida: Horticultural Publications, 1995. Print.

Westwood, Melvin Neil. *Temperate-Zone Pomology: Physiology and Culture.* 3rd ed. Portland, Oregon: Timber Press, 2009. Print.

For More Information

http://go.ncsu.edu/fmi_treefruit

Contributors

Author: Michael L. Parker, Professor and Extension Specialist, Department of Horticultural Science

Contributions by Extension Agents: Danelle Cutting, John Vining, Matt Jones, Colby Griffin, Mary Hollingsworth

Contributions by Extension Master Gardener Volunteers: Barbara Goodman, Jackie Weedon, Karen Damari, Kim Curlee, Chris Alberti, Edna Burger, Connie Schultz, Lee Kapleau, Debbie Green, Caro Dosé

Content Editors: Lucy Bradley, Professor and Extension Specialist, Urban Horticulture, NC State University; Director, NC State Extension Master Gardener program;
Kathleen Moore, Urban Horticulturist

Copy Editors: Barbara Scott, Debbi Braswell

Chapter 15 Cover Photo: Krzysztof Jaracz, Pixabay CC0

Based in part on text from the 1998 Extension Master Gardener manual prepared by:
Ken Sorensen, Extension Specialist, Department of Entomology
Erv Evans, Extension Associate, Department of Horticultural Science

How to Cite This Chapter:
Parker, M. 2022. Tree Fruits and Nuts. Chpt 15. In: K.A. Moore and L.K. Bradley (eds.). *North Carolina Extension Gardener Handbook*, 2nd ed. NC State Extension, Raleigh, NC. <https://content.ces.ncsu.edu/extension-gardener-handbook/15-tree-fruit-and-nuts>.

Vegetable Gardening

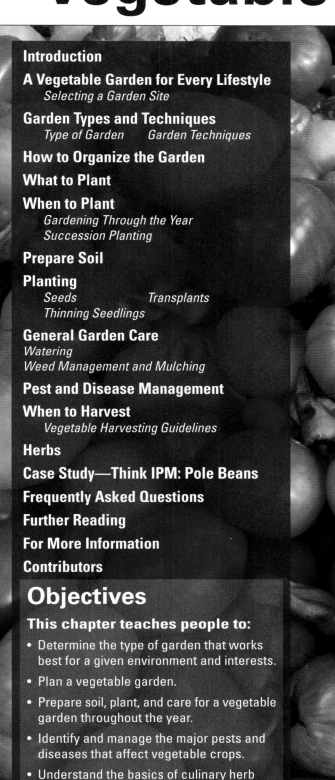

16

Objectives

This chapter teaches people to:

- Determine the type of garden that works best for a given environment and interests.
- Plan a vegetable garden.
- Prepare soil, plant, and care for a vegetable garden throughout the year.
- Identify and manage the major pests and diseases that affect vegetable crops.
- Understand the basics of culinary herb cultivation in the home garden.

Introduction

Many gardeners grow vegetables for the outstanding flavor and freshness of homegrown produce or to reduce the family food budget. Others are inspired by the wide variety of options and easy access to hard-to-find and unusual varieties. For example, a grocery store may have only three types of squash, whereas a seed catalog may have 49 or more (Figure 16–1). Still others view vegetable gardening as a relaxing escape from everyday pressures. The food they produce may be secondary to the sense of joy and accomplishment they get from tending the garden and sharing produce with neighbors and friends.

Successful vegetable gardening begins with selecting a site, planning what to grow, and preparing the soil. Once the garden area is ready, vegetables are selected, planted, and nurtured until the produce is ready to harvest. Vegetable gardening can be accessible to anyone with a sunny space, some seeds, water, fertilizer, and patience (Figure 16–2).

Figure 16–1. A wide variety of squash can be grown in a home garden.
Tony Austin, Flickr CC BY - 2.0

Figure 16–2. Gardens can be any size. This patio garden provides enough produce for the owner to have a salad every day.
Jeremy Keith, Flickr CC BY - 2.0

A Vegetable Garden for Every Lifestyle

Before donning garden gloves and putting seeds in the soil, give careful thought to the type or types of vegetable gardens that work best for your lifestyle. Consider the size of your family, the vegetables you wish to grow, the health of the soil, and how much time and money you have to invest in a vegetable garden.

If you have a sunny backyard with space to spare and good quality soil, you have the option of planting a traditional in-ground vegetable garden. If your soil is poor, you may wish to consider planting in raised beds. Front yards are often overlooked—underused spaces that could provide food if located in a neighborhood with no restrictions. Many vegetable plants are beautiful. If your landscape is already well-established and you have no room for a traditional vegetable garden, interplanting vegetables in your ornamental beds is a great option. Interplanting is also an easy first step to try vegetable gardening if you are unsure about dedicating a new space to vegetables.

Many vegetables thrive in containers, and container gardening is ideal for those with limited outdoor space. Vegetables cannot survive indoors without supplemental light, but growing plants indoors hydroponically is an option that is gaining popularity (Figure 16–3). Hydroponics allows the gardener to control temperature, light, and nutrients, all without as many pathogen pressures as plants grown outdoors. It can involve a large initial investment, so it may not be the best choice for someone new to growing plants.

Figure 16–3. Hydroponically grown lettuce.
Chris Alberti, CC BY - 2.0

These methods are not mutually exclusive. For example, you could grow cucumbers and corn in a traditional in-ground garden bed in your backyard while growing carrots and broccoli in a raised bed in your front yard. At the same time, you could interplant a perennial border with kale and Swiss chard, grow herbs in containers on your back patio, and produce microgreens hydroponically inside your home.

Selecting a Garden Site

Prior to selecting a site, consider previous uses of the land and potential contaminants. Review NC State Extension publication AGW-439-78, *Soil Facts: Minimizing Risks of Soil Contaminants in Urban Gardens*, which provides indicators for concern, guidelines for when to have the soil tested for contaminants, directions for how to interpret the results, and strategies for minimizing risks—for example, using containers or raised beds with imported soil.

The most important factor to consider when selecting a garden site is sunlight. The garden must receive at least 6 hours of direct sunlight each day; 8 to 10 hours is ideal. Vegetables should be planted away from the shade of buildings, and the shade and competing root systems of trees and shrubs. Some vegetables tolerate shade better than others. Those vegetables that produce edible stems and leaves (such as broccoli, cabbage, collards, kale, lettuce, parsley, and spinach) as well as those that produce edible roots (such as beets, carrots, radishes, and turnips) are more tolerant of shade. Plants that flower and set fruit, such as eggplants, melons, peppers, and tomatoes, require more light.

Good soil drainage is also very important. Observe your yard after a rain. Areas where water pools have poor drainage and without serious remediation would not be a good site for a garden (Figure 16–4). Chapter 1, "Soils and Plant Nutrients," provides more information about the soil in your garden as well as soil testing. Learn about amending your soil in chapter 2, "Composting." More about preparing garden soil is covered in the following sections.

Placing a garden near the home or near a pattern of foot traffic through the yard ensures easy access for garden tasks and facilitates frequent inspections. Consider convenient availability to clean water sources when locating your garden. Access to a hose bib or irrigation system saves the effort of hauling water during dry months.

Another important consideration is good air movement. Avoid locating the garden in a low spot, such as at the base of a hill. These areas are slow to warm in the spring, and frost forms more readily in them because cold air cannot drain away. Vegetable gardens located on high ground are more likely to escape light freezes, which may

permit an earlier start in the spring and a longer harvest in the fall. If access to land is a problem, explore opportunities at a community garden. Visit the NC Community Gardens Directory for a list of active community gardens.

Figure 16–4. Examine potential vegetable garden sites after a heavy rainfall. The lower part of this yard would not be an ideal location because there is standing water.
Kathleen Moore, CC BY - 2.0

Got Shade?

Very few plants grow well in dense shade. If you have partial, filtered, or high shade, however, you may be able to grow vegetables. Select large-leafed plants from which you harvest the roots, stems, or leaves. Producing flowers, fruits, and seeds (part of a plant's reproductive process) requires more sunlight. In shade, try collards, spinach, cabbage, carrots, kale, turnips, parsley, radishes, and lettuce. Avoid planting tomatoes, beans, eggplant, and other plants from which you harvest flowers, fruit, and seeds.

Garden Types and Techniques

There is a garden type, or a combination of types, to fit each gardener's needs. Gardens can be grown in-ground, in a raised bed, or in containers. In addition, a variety of techniques can be used to manage the garden. Plants can be laid out in traditional rows or intensely planted, or can take advantage of vertical spaces. Review the following types and techniques, and select the strategies that work best for your unique situation.

Garden Types

In-ground Gardens

In-ground gardens are less expensive, the water does not drain away as quickly, and the roots stay cooler in the summer. While water does not drain as quickly from in-ground beds, it can be difficult to supply water only to planting beds and not to adjoining areas. An in-ground garden generally requires more space than raised bed or container gardens. Care must be taken to create paths for traffic to avoid compaction of planting areas. Weeds from adjacent pathways can be challenging to manage (Figure 16–5).

Figure 16–5. Weeds can be a challenge with in-ground garden beds. Straw is used here as a mulch to help suppress weeds.
Chris Alberti, CC BY - 2.0

Raised Bed Gardens

Raised beds are garden spaces elevated 6 to 8 inches or more aboveground (Figure 16–6). They are connected to the native soil beneath them and they may or may not have constructed sides. They can simply consist of soil piled high with a flattened top, or they can be framed with logs or rocks, constructed out of lumber boards, or made of straw bales (Figure 16–7). Raised beds, arranged just wide enough to reach to the center, are ideal for growing vegetables. Having defined beds not only makes a garden

attractive, it also limits foot traffic in the bed, which can compact soil. Soil raised aboveground will likely drain well and warm up earlier in the spring. Raised beds do require more frequent irrigation than those planted in a traditional in-ground garden. As a higher percentage of the available growing space is used, there is less room for weeds to grow and water can be used more efficiently. When planted properly, one 4-foot by 8-foot raised bed can supply the majority of produce during the growing season for one or two people. Raised beds are generally 8 to 12 inches high, 3 to 4 feet wide, and as long as desired or as dictated by the materials used.

Figure 16–6. Raised bed gardens.
Kathleen Moore, CC BY - 2.0

Figure 16–7. Raised bed made with straw bales.
Ruth Temple, Flickr
CC BY - 2.0

16

If the raised bed has sides, they should be made of a rot-resistant material. Wood products can be naturally rot-resistant or can be comprised of wood shavings mixed with synthetic materials such as plastic. Naturally rot-resistant woods include Eastern red cedar (*Juniperus virginiana*), redwood (*Sequoia sempervirens*), and black locust (*Robinia pseudoacacia*).

Container Gardens

Growing edibles in containers is a popular way to produce food for the home. Many vegetables can be grown in containers deep enough to support their roots (Figure 16–8). Container size is directly related to gardening ease and success—larger is better. Vegetables that thrive in containers include beans, beets, carrots, collards, cucumbers, eggplants, garlic, kale, leeks, lettuces, mustard greens, peas, peppers, potatoes, spinach, squash, Swiss chard, and tomatoes. Gardening in containers is particularly useful for people with limited space, soil problems, or heavy wildlife pressure. Containers can be placed on a rooftop, balcony, patio, deck, entrance area, or walkway. Containers should be placed in locations that favor the growth of the crop being grown. For instance, a container can be moved to a sunny spot if growing tomatoes, a partly shady area when growing lettuce, or a protected microclimate during the winter for growing year-round kale. Container gardening of edibles offers more flexibility than traditional gardening and is great for children,

renters, new gardeners, people with physical limitations, or experienced gardeners wanting to downsize. With container gardening, there is no digging or tilling and crops are virtually weed-free. Container gardening can also be a way of containing aggressive herbs, such as mint, that may otherwise take over traditional garden spaces. Vegetables grown in containers do require more care than plants grown in traditional garden beds in the ground. Learn more about growing edibles in containers in chapter 18, "Plants Grown in Containers."

Figure 16–8. Growing vegetables in containers is a popular option. Here vegetables are grown in old water troughs. Make sure that any containers used have good drainage.
Kathleen Moore, CC BY - 2.0

16

Where do I get soil for my raised beds?

Raised beds can take many forms, and so can the soil used inside the beds. For shallow beds with no support, use topsoil from neighboring pathways and mix it with existing soil and organic matter. Soil can be piled up and flattened to make a raised bed less than 6 inches high. To prevent soil erosion, gently slope the sides of the bed.

If making a taller raised bed or one in a framed box, you may need additional soil. If your soil is good quality loam, you can screen your soil into the raised bed and add 50% **finished compost**. You can also purchase raised garden soil blends bagged from a nursery. Or soil can be ordered by the cubic yard from a landscape company. To calculate how many cubic yards of soil you need, consider that one cubic yard of soil is:

3 feet × 3 feet × 3 feet = 27 cubic feet

To find out how many cubic feet you need in a raised bed, multiply the length by the width and depth of your raised bed (convert all measurements to feet). If your bed is 4 feet wide by 10 feet long by 18 inches deep, that would be:

4 feet × 10 feet × 1.5 feet = 60 cubic feet

Divide the number of cubic feet by the number of feet in a cubic yard (27):

60 cubic feet / 27 cubic feet = 2.22 cubic yards of material

Be sure to ask about the components of the blend. A quality blend consists of topsoil, compost, and a soilless mix, such as vermiculite. Are the materials organic? What is the source? Is this blend high in animal manures? Have they been fully composted? Is it guaranteed to be topsoil free of pollutants, weeds, insect pests, diseases, and pathogenic nematodes? Simply purchasing a raised bed mix is not enough to maintain a garden over the long term.

To keep nutrient levels high in the soil, raised beds need to be amended after each growing season by adding a 1-inch to 4-inch layer of organic material.

Treated Lumber and Pallets

Several concerns exist about the safety of using treated lumber in food gardens.

Avoid using creosote-treated railroad ties. Freshly treated creosote lumber can leach into the soil for several years and continue to give off vapors for seven to nine years. Pressure-treated lumber using chromated copper arsenate (CCA) as a preservative is a concern because of the carcinogenic potential of leached arsenic. CCA manufacturers no longer manufacture products for residential uses, but the U.S. Environmental Protection Agency (EPA) has not banned CCA and does not require the removal of existing structures made with CCA-treated wood or the surrounding soil. Do not use any remaining stock in raised beds for growing food crops. Alkaline copper quaternary (ACQ) is another preservative choice for pressure-treated lumber. Although AQC does not contain arsenic or chromium, it does contain copper, which can leach into the soil from treated lumber. Although copper is an essential element for both plants and animals, excessive amounts can be harmful.

Pallets have become a popular choice for garden construction because they are inexpensive and readily available, but exercise caution before using wood pallets in a garden. Understanding the stamps and markings on a pallet helps in making an educated choice.

Pallets are marked with these identifiers (Figure 16–9):
1. Country of origin
2. An International Plant Protection Convention (IPPC) logo, for pallets that are used and shipped internationally
3. How the pallet was treated (HT: heat treated, DB: debarked, KD: kiln dried, MB: methyl bromide, or a combination of these)
4. Possibly a numerical code and a logo identifying the inspector

If a pallet is unmarked, it may be safe to use. It is better, however, to reject a pallet without origin and treatment information.

Pallets that are safe for use in vegetable gardens

HT: Heat-treated wooden pallets manufactured in Canada or the United States undergo HT pest control treatment, which involves heating the pallet to a minimum core temperature of 56°C (132°F) for softwoods and 60°C (140°F) for hardwoods, for a minimum of 30 minutes in a kiln.

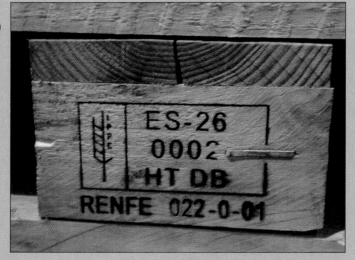

Figure 16–9. A pallet stamp gives information about the pallet's origin and how the wood was treated. This pallet has the IPPC logo, ES is the abbreviation for Spain, and was heat treated and debarked. It is safe for garden use.

Oaktree Brian, Wikimedia CC BY-SA 2.5 CA

DB: Debarked pallets means that the bark was cut off the wood using a scraping tool before the pallets were constructed. This has no effect on the wood of the pallet. Some pallets may be marked DB-HT.

KD: Kiln-dried pallets have the moisture in the wood reduced to a level below 19%. This helps control warping and some fungal problems. The kilns do not necessarily reach the same temperatures (132°F) as wood that is labeled as HT.

Pallets that should not be used in vegetable gardens

MB: Methyl bromide is a pesticide used to treat pallets that ensures insects, weeds, pathogens, and rodents do not travel on shipped items. This pesticide has been linked to human health problems and ozone depletion. Dispose of them at a hazardous waste facility.

Gardening Techniques

Row Gardening

Single-row planting started when mules were used to cultivate the garden. Out of habit, many gardeners still use this system for in-ground, and even some raised beds. If space is not an issue, a traditional row garden is an option. Row gardens allow for the use of a tractor and tiller for garden chores (Figure 16–10). Create planting "beds" with rows planted close together, or use wide rows to shade out weeds.

If you are making traditional garden rows, make them straight to aid in cultivation, weed management, and harvesting. In traditional beds with rows, the entire garden is amended—both the rows and the pathways. To make a straight row, drive a stake into the ground at each end of the row and draw a string taut between the stakes.

Intensive Gardening

The purpose of an intensively grown garden is to harvest the most produce possible from a given space. Intensive gardening has become a popular model as urban areas have become more crowded and yards have become smaller. Many home landscapes cannot accommodate the traditional row garden, and intensive gardening provides a viable alternative. Intensive gardens optimize the use of space and use succession planting to maximize production, but they require careful planning. Although intensive gardens are often in raised beds, they can also be in-ground gardens or even in large containers. One method of **intensive planting** is "square foot garden-

ing," an approach that was formalized by Mel Bartholemew in his 1981 book *Square Foot Gardening* and his subsequent 2006 *All New Square Foot Gardening*. The French were using these intensive gardening techniques in the late 1800s, but Bartholemew popularized the concept. Vegetables are grown in 1-foot by 1-foot squares within a raised bed (Figure 16–11). Beds are designed to be no more than 4 feet across so they can be managed from the outside. The gardener never compacts the soil by stepping where the vegetables grow. Gardeners can arrange their square-foot beds in multiple ways to fit the available space. Beds are marked in 1-foot squares using a wood lattice, string, plastic tape, or re-used slats from window blinds. These markings help clearly define planting spaces and make it easy to follow planting density recommendations. Within each square, many vegetables can be grown. The spacing is determined by the ultimate size of the vegetables grown within

Figure 16–11. Square foot gardening.
Karen Jevsevar

that square. Large plants, such as broccoli or tomatoes, may require multiple squares to allow each plant to grow to full size. Smaller plants (like beets) can be planted up to 16 plants per square, while others (such as carrots) can have 32 per square.

Figure 16–10. A traditional row garden.
Paulo O, Flickr CC BY - 2.0

Table 16–1.
Intensive Vegetable Planting Guide

Plant	Intensive Planting Distance (inches) Between Plants
Asparagus	12
Bean, bush	2–3
Bean, lima	4–6
Bean, pole	6–12
Beets	2–3
Broccoli	6–12
Brussels sprouts	14–18
Cabbage	9–12
Carrot	2–3
Cauliflower	15–18
Chard, Swiss	4–6
Collards	12–15
Corn, sweet	12
Cucumber	12
Eggplant	18–24
Endive	8–12
Kale	6
Kohlrabi	4
Leek	3–4
Lettuce, head	10
Lettuce, leaf	4–6
Mustard	4–6
Okra	12–18
Onion	2–4
Pea	1–3
Pepper	9–12
Potato	10–12
Pumpkin	24–36
Radish	1–2
Southern pea	3–4
Spinach	4–6
Squash, summer	18–24
Squash, winter	24–36
Tomato	18–24
Turnip	3–4

16

Unlike in traditional row gardens, where there is generally as much empty space as plant-occupied space, no wasted space occurs within a square-foot garden. In intensive gardens, the fertilization, watering, and management efforts are concentrated on the planting beds. See Table 16–1.

Another method of intensive gardening is **interplanting**, or growing two or more types of vegetables in the same place at the same time (Figure 16–12). This technique has been practiced for thousands of years by American Indians, but is now regaining widespread support in this country. The benefits include increased production and a decrease in weeds. Proper planning is essential to obtain high production and improved quality of the crops planted. Another type of **interplanting** is to grow flowers among vegetable plants. This brings pollinators and predators, may deter pests, and adds color to a vegetable garden (Figure 16–13).

Figure 16–12. Three sisters intensive planting technique. The corn provides a trellis for the beans, the beans give nitrogen to the corn, and the squash sprawls out, conserving water and suppressing weeds.
Garlan Miles, CC BY-SA 4.0

Figure 16–13. Zinnias interplanted with kale.
Kathleen Moore, CC BY - 2.0

The following factors must be considered for each plant combination:

- The length and pattern of growth. Is the vegetable tall, short, belowground, or aboveground?
- Allelopathy or the possible negative effects of one crop on another. Some plants, such as sunflowers, produce toxins that impede the growth of other crops.
- The length to maturity. Mixing up maturity dates helps to extend harvesting.
- Light, nutrient, and moisture requirements of the plants. Using plants with like cultural requirements promotes optimal health of all the crops.

Possible plant combinations include planting long-season, slow-maturing plants and short-season, quick-maturing ones at the same time. An example of this combination would be peppers and radishes. The radishes are harvested before peppers begin to crowd them. Another example of combining growth patterns is planting smaller plants close to larger plants, such as radishes at the base of beans or broccoli. Shade-tolerant species, such as lettuce, spinach, and celery, can be planted in the shadow of taller crops, like beans or squash.

Interplant by alternating rows within a bed (plant a row of peppers next to a row of onions), by mixing plants within a row (leeks and parsley), by distributing various species throughout the bed, or by planting edibles among ornamentals. Swiss chard could be planted between azalea shrubs, or carrots could pop up along a walkway between perennial beds.

Vertical Gardening

The use of trellises, nets, strings, cages, or poles to support growing plants constitutes vertical gardening (Figure 16–14). This technique is especially suited to gardeners with only a small garden space. Vining and sprawling plants, including cucumbers, tomatoes, melons, and pole beans, are obvious candidates for this type of gardening. Some plants twine themselves onto the support; others require tying.

Vertical plantings cast a shadow, so place them on the north side of a garden bed to reduce shading, and plant shade-tolerant crops near the vertical ones. Plants grown vertically take up much less ground, and though the yield per plant may be less, the yield per square foot is much greater. Because vertically growing plants are more exposed, they dry out faster and require more water than if they were spread over the ground. This fast drying is advantageous to plants susceptible to fungal diseases. Vertical gardening is often used with raised beds.

In summary, any of these garden types and techniques can be used in isolation or combined to create a garden that works best for a given space. A raised bed can be planted intensively, or a container garden may use vertical gardening to its advantage. Whichever garden type or combination of types and techniques you choose, remember to start small, select plants appropriate for the season that thrive in the light you have, make amendments to the soil based on your soil test report, manage the weeds and diseases, and only plant what you can manage easily and joyfully. As your interests and skills expand, so can your garden space.

Figure 16–14. A garden taking advantage of vertical space.
Shizzi, Flickr CC BY-ND - 2.0

For a family of four, an area of 1050 square feet should be adequate space to provide most of the produce needs during the growing season. Start small and expand the garden as you have time and interest. Be careful not to start with too large a space; it is easy to become overwhelmed by the weeds and work of creating a new garden. Once you get started, it is easy to expand.

How to Organize the Garden

Once you have decided on the space and the type of garden that best suits your needs, a diagram helps you organize the garden. There are several things to consider when creating a garden diagram.

- Use graph paper or a scale so you can accurately draw the size of the garden bed and plants.
- Draw a north arrow and make note of the sun's pattern throughout the day.
- Note water access and composting locations.
- Use a different color or shape for each type of vegetable.
- Review planting dates of each crop to help you plan for succession throughout the growing season. Ideally, once a crop has been harvested, another crop is ready to be planted in its place.
- Plant north to south to make the best use of sunlight.
- Group tall crops (corn, okra, sunflowers) and trellised vines (peas, beans, squash) together on the north side of the garden to avoid shading shorter plants. Follow this principle unless you are planting crops that are marginal in the summer, like lettuce, that can take advantage of the shade.
- Leave pathways so you can easily access the plants or beds from multiple sides.
- Show the plant size at maturity to ensure adequate space is allotted.

What to Plant

The simple answer to that question is this: "Grow what your family likes to eat and what you have space for." Consult your garden plan. If you are planting in a limited space, consider vegetables that give the highest yield for the least amount of space, such as leafy greens, root crops, pole beans, and tomatoes. If you have plenty of square footage in your garden, you can plant crops like pumpkin, squash, and corn. If you are an adventurous chef, try planting vegetables that are unusual or expensive to buy at the market, such as broccolini, kale sprouts, or shallots. If your family hates zucchini, by all means, avoid planting any.

Be sure to consider the growing season when deciding what to plant. What to plant is influenced by when you plant and vice versa. Most vegetables are annuals and reach maturity in one growing season. They are grouped according to the season that best meets their growth requirements. Spring and fall have short, cool days, so vegetables that do best during these times are called "cool-season annuals." Summer is hot with long days, and vegetables that do best during this season are called "warm-season annuals."

Cool-season annuals include beets, broccoli, Brussels sprouts, cabbage, carrots, cauliflower, collards, kale, kohlrabi, lettuce, mustard, onions, peas, potatoes, radishes, rutabagas, spinach, Swiss chard, and turnips. These vegetables grow well and produce leaves and roots in the cool temperatures of early spring and fall. Some cool-season annuals can be planted in the late summer and if they are well established, can survive the winter and continue growing again in the early spring. Warm-season annuals include beans, corn, cucumber, eggplant, melons, peppers, squash, sweet potatoes, and tomatoes. These vegetables grow best when the weather and soils warm up in the late spring and summer.

Warm-season vegetables are generally not planted in the ground until after the last frost date. Check the days until fruit production and maturity on each variety you select. It may be necessary to plant starts instead of seeds, or start seeds early in a greenhouse, to get the highest yield. Some crops live for more than one season or year.

Biennial crops, such as artichokes and parsley, grow in the first year, and flower, fruit, and die in the second year. **Perennials** live for many years once established. Examples include asparagus, horseradish, and rhubarb.

When to Plant

With proper planning, your vegetable garden can provide produce almost year-round. Keeping track of planting and harvest dates, however, can be a challenge without an effective system. Writing planting and harvest dates on a calendar is a tactic many farmers and gardeners use. If you have a garden diagram, adding planting and harvesting dates can make it an even more powerful tool. By careful planning, even a small space can realize its full potential for vegetable production.

Gardening Through the Year

Spring. Cool-season annuals are cold-hardy plants that thrive in the early spring and fall when temperatures fall below 70°F. To get a jumpstart on the spring season, use a cold frame, low tunnel, or frost cloth. Warm-season annuals are frost-sensitive crops that grow well in the late spring when temperatures are above 70°F and soils have warmed up.

Summer. As temperatures rise, cool-season crops bolt and become bitter. Use shade cloth or taller crops to provide shade and extend cool-season crops into summer. Warm-season crops planted in late spring grow until the first frost. Late summer is the time to plant cool-season annuals for a fall harvest.

Fall. Cool-season annuals that are well-established grow through cold temperatures and sometimes even moderate freezing.

Winter. Crops considered cold hardy (such as collards, kale, turnip greens, spinach, and Swiss chard) planted in fall may live through the winter or may go dormant for a period in the winter and flourish again in early spring. A cold frame or frost cloth can help protect and extend this growing season. Many of these plants bolt quickly in the spring.

For specific planting dates, consult the North Carolina Planting Calendar for Vegetables, Fruits, and Herbs. To help extend the garden season, see Appendix E.

Succession planting

Succession planting is a technique in which vegetables are planted at staggered intervals to extend the harvest. If you want to have a huge harvest of tomatoes all at once so you can do all your canning in one weekend, this strategy is not for you. In addition to enabling an extended harvest, succession planting also buffers against total crop failure as another group of plants is in the queue. The easiest strategy for succession planting is to plant different varieties of the same vegetable that have different days to maturity. These crops naturally stagger their harvest times. The second strategy is to plant the same variety multiple times. The interval of time between planting should be as long as the harvest time for each particular vegetable. Filling in with a new vegetable in place of a vegetable that was harvested is also a way to make sure the garden stays in production for a longer period. When a head of lettuce is harvested in May, plant some carrots in the space that is made. If you remove a tomato plant because it has finished producing in the early fall, plant kale or rutabaga in its place to grow through the late fall and perhaps even overwinter. If you start some seeds in trays about four to five weeks ahead of the planned harvest schedule, you can get an even bigger jumpstart on your garden's production. See Table 16–2.

Prepare Soil

To grow quality vegetables you need a soil that is fertile, deep, easily crumbled, well-drained, and high in organic matter. If you are gardening in containers, purchase potting soil or make your own mix by combining equal parts of compost, shredded pine bark, and vermiculite. Never use soil from your yard in containers. Using yard soil in a container, will likely result in poor drainage and may introduce pathogens that thrive in enclosed environment. For more about outdoor container gardening, read chapter 18, "Plants Grown in Containers."

To plant in raised beds or in-ground gardens, start by amending the soil with 2 inches to 3 inches of homemade or certified compost. Then take a sample and submit it to the NC Department of Agriculture & Consumer Services (NCDA&CS) for a soil test. The soil test gives you information about the makeup of your soil (mineral or organic), the pH (acidity or alkalinity), the nutrient content, and the amounts of lime or fertilizer per 1,000 square feet of growing area that might be needed to correct pH or nutrient levels.

A soil test should be repeated every two to three years. The ideal **pH** range for most vegetables is between 6.0 and 6.5. If lime is needed, try to apply it several months before planting. Lime reacts relatively slowly in soil; therefore, a fall application of lime can correct soil acidity before spring planting. Read more about soils and soil testing in chapter 1, "Soils and Plant Nutrients."

The fastest way to improve sandy soil or heavy clay soil is by repeatedly adding organic matter. You can incorporate a 2-inch to 3-inch layer of well-rotted leaves or compost in the spring before preparing the soil and again in the fall after harvest. **Green manure crops**—such as winter rye, ryegrass, or wheat—can be planted in the garden in the fall and turned under in the spring when growth is about knee-high. For best results, seed fall **cover crops** between September 15 and October 20 in the NC piedmont (one to two weeks later in the NC coastal plain, and one to two weeks earlier in the NC mountains). Cover crops are not limited to fall planting. Clover or buckwheat can be planted after harvesting early spring vegetables like lettuce or spinach and turned under in time to plant a frost-tolerant crop in the late summer. Seeding rates per 1,000 square feet for winter rye are 1 to 2 pounds, and for ryegrass and wheat, 3 to 4 pounds. Read more information about cover crops in "Organic Gardening," chapter 17.

Apply fertilizer, if recommended by a soil test, shortly before or at planting time. The best way to fertilize a traditional row garden is to broadcast half to two-thirds of the total amount and apply the remainder by banding. To broadcast, spread the fertilizer over the top of the soil with a cyclone or drop spreader in an east-west and north-south movement with half of the broadcast amount in each direction. Then till the fertilizer into the soil to a depth of 3 to 4 inches. For banding, apply fertilizer in furrows 3 inches from the center of the row and slightly below the level of the seed (Figure 16–15). For raised beds, sprinkle fertilizer evenly over the bed and scratch or rake it in. Water the soil before planting.

Some garden vegetables, such as beans, cabbage, peppers, potatoes, squash, and sweet corn, need extra nitrogen applied to the soil in the form of a side-dressing to keep them growing rapidly and continuously. See the NCDA&CS publication *Note 4: Fertilization of Lawns, Gardens, and Ornamentals* for more information.

Figure. 16–15. Fertilizer applied by banding 3 inches from the center of the row and slightly below the seed.
Chris Alberti, CC BY-ND - 2.0

Side-dress individual plants or hills with 1 level tablespoon of a high nitrogen fertilizer per plant (Figure 16–16). For organic fertilizer alternatives and application rates, see chapter 17, "Organic Gardening." For widely spaced plants, such as cucumbers or cantaloupe, place the side-dressing fertilizer in bands 6 inches from the plant's base. Vegetable plants should be side-dressed about midway through their maturity cycle, except when grown on sandy soils and during periods of excessive rainfall; these conditions require more frequent side-dressing applications. Crops such as tomatoes, eggplant, and okra require two or three side-dressings per season because of their long growth cycles. For more information on fertilization, refer to chapter 1, "Soils and Plant Nutrients."

Figure 16–16. Side-dressing a potato plant with 1 tablespoon of high nitrogen fertilizer.
Kathleen Moore, CC BY - 2.0

Using Composted Manure in the Garden

Manure can be a valuable addition to any garden soil, supplying nitrogen, potassium, and phosphorus. But take the following precautions before adding it to a vegetable garden:

- Use manure from vegetarian animals, including cows, horses, chickens, goats, or sheep.
- Make sure you know if any herbicides or other chemicals were used where the animals were grazing. Some herbicides can persist through an animal's digestive tract, through the composting process, and remain active in the vegetable garden, where they affect your lettuce and tomatoes the same way they affected the broadleaf weeds they were initially purchased to manage.
- Avoid manures from animals kept in a confined area; these manures may contain high amounts of salts from urine.
- Fresh is not best. Use manure in a garden only after it ages for at least six months in an open pile or after the manure is composted (Figure 16–17). To compost, mix fresh manure with a high carbon source, such as straw or dried leaves, rather than adding to an existing compost pile. Or mix fresh manure into a garden bed that will remain fallow for an entire growing season.
- Kiln-dried manure that has been heated to kill any pathogens can be purchased from a garden center.

Figure 16–17. Age manure in an open pile for at least six months.
Lucy Bradley, CC BY - 2.0

Table 16–2. Succession Planting Template for Large Traditional Row Garden

The 25-foot by 42-foot garden below could produce the majority of the vegetables needed for canning, freezing, and fresh use for one year for a family of four. In most of the rows, as soon as one crop is harvested, another is planted so that two crops can be grown in succession during the growing season. Because sweet corn requires a large space, the overall yield from the garden would be higher if lima beans or snap beans were planted in place of corn. Find out more about yield amounts in the "When to Harvest" section of this chapter.

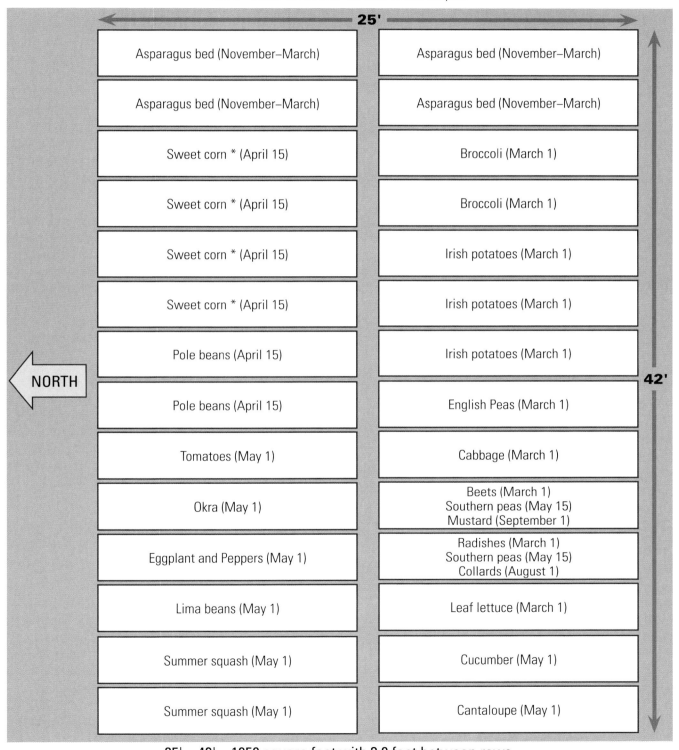

25'

Asparagus bed (November–March)	Asparagus bed (November–March)
Asparagus bed (November–March)	Asparagus bed (November–March)
Sweet corn * (April 15)	Broccoli (March 1)
Sweet corn * (April 15)	Broccoli (March 1)
Sweet corn * (April 15)	Irish potatoes (March 1)
Sweet corn * (April 15)	Irish potatoes (March 1)
Pole beans (April 15)	Irish potatoes (March 1)
Pole beans (April 15)	English Peas (March 1)
Tomatoes (May 1)	Cabbage (March 1)
Okra (May 1)	Beets (March 1) / Southern peas (May 15) / Mustard (September 1)
Eggplant and Peppers (May 1)	Radishes (March 1) / Southern peas (May 15) / Collards (August 1)
Lima beans (May 1)	Leaf lettuce (March 1)
Summer squash (May 1)	Cucumber (May 1)
Summer squash (May 1)	Cantaloupe (May 1)

NORTH

42'

25' × 42' = 1050 square feet with 3.0 feet between rows.

*Lima and snap beans can be planted in place of sweet corn if desired. All planting dates are for NC upper coastal plain and lower piedmont.

16

Planting

Seeds

Old seeds bought on sale may not be a bargain because their **germination** rate may be reduced and the resulting seedlings can be weak and grow very slowly. Check the date stamped on the seed packet to make sure the seeds were produced for the current gardening year. Many vegetable seeds, however, are viable for three to five years if kept in a dark dry place that stays below 85°F. Seed packets can be a wealth of information, and it is worth becoming familiar with all of the information on the back (Figure 16–18).

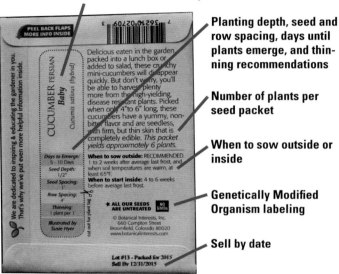

Common name and Latin name of plant

Planting depth, seed and row spacing, days until plants emerge, and thinning recommendations

Number of plants per seed packet

When to sow outside or inside

Genetically Modified Organism labeling

Sell by date

Figure 16–18. The back of seed packets contain a lot of information. Brook Williams

Bulk vegetable seeds sold by the ounce or pound in garden centers and farm supply stores are shipped to the store in a container or bag with a date and germination rate label attached. Look for the information before making a purchase. Seeds with high germination rates should be the first choice.

Review the North Carolina Planting Calendar for information on the crops that are best started as seeds in the ground, rather than as transplants. To be successful with directly sowing seeds, the garden soil should contain enough moisture at seeding to initiate germination. If it does not, water the soil thoroughly (4 to 6 inches deep) and allow the surface to dry before seeding. If preferred, the open furrow can be watered directly before depositing the seeds in the soil and covering firmly with dry soil. In the spring when the soil is cool, vegetable seeds are much less likely to germinate if they are planted too deeply. As a general rule, in the spring and summer plant the seeds 1 to 2 times their greatest diameter; in fall plant them 1½ to 2 times deeper.

Small seeds like lettuce and carrot can be difficult to distribute thinly and evenly. To sow small seeds, tear off a corner of the seed packet, then move the packet along the furrow while tapping it with an index finger. You can also mix the seeds with dry sand or dry, pulverized soil to help with even distribution.

Seeds that are large enough to handle can be planted by **hilling** or by row planting (**drilling**). Hilling is placing several seeds in one spot at definite intervals. Squashes, pumpkins, and melons are often planted this way. Once the seeds germinate, the hills are thinned, leaving one or two plants per hill, depending on the vegetable. Drilling is spacing seeds more or less evenly down the row. Beans and peas are planted this way. Plant them closer than the desired final spacing because after germination, extra plants can be removed. Planting extra seeds compensates for poor germination and loss of seedlings to disease and insects. If seeds are one year old or older, plant them thicker than fresh seeds.

Once the seeds are placed, cover them with soil. Firm the soil, but do not pack it, around the seeds with the flat blade of the hoe or your hands. Be careful to plant seeds at the recommended depth; seeds covered with too much soil may rot before germinating or the seedling may use up all of its stored energy before it grows to the surface and can produce food by **photosynthesizing**. On the other hand, seeds planted too close to the surface may die from overheating or drought.

The formation of a hard layer, or crusting, of the soil's surface developing shortly after seeding can prevent seedlings from emerging. Heavy rains or use of overhead sprinklers may cause soil crusting. To avoid this problem, incorporate 2 to 4 inches of organic matter into the soil, cover the seeds with the newly amended soil, and use a soaker hose instead of an overhead sprinkler.

Transplants

Seedlings may be referred to as starts, sets, or transplants. They are started in containers indoors or in a greenhouse (see Appendix E) and can help plants get a jumpstart on growth when weather outside is unfavorable.

Warm-season plants can be transplanted to the garden when the danger of frost has passed. Starting cool-season crops, like lettuce and spinach, from seed in a greenhouse can help them mature before high outdoor temperatures can cause **bolting**. See Table 16–3 for temperatures and times to germinate vegetable seeds for later planting outside. Chapter 13, "Propagation," provides additional information on starting transplants from seed. The North Carolina Planting Calendar gives suggested outdoor planting dates, cultivars, and spacing distance between plants. See Table 16–4 at the end of this chapter.

16

Contaminants in the Garden

Soil testing for contaminants is essential prior to gardening in an urban setting. If high levels are found, consider gardening in an alternate spot. If moderate levels are found, consider gardening in containers or take steps to minimize exposure and prevent health risks.

Garden design. If the contamination is in only one part of the garden, avoid those areas. Consider planting contaminated areas with non-edible ornamental perennials, shrubs, and trees to minimize soil disturbance. Consider installing raised beds with imported healthy soil. Seal off the bottom of the bed with an impermeable barrier so roots do not penetrate contaminated soil. Be sure to drill holes near the bottom of the raised beds to allow for drainage.

Soil management. Maintain a neutral soil pH of 6.5 to 7.0 by incorporating organic matter. This neutral pH chemically binds contaminants and makes them less available to plants. Mulch the soil to reduce contaminated dust being picked up by the wind.

Plant selection. Avoid root crops that have their edible parts in contact with the soil. Even though peeling reduces some risk, beets, carrots, onions, parsnips, potatoes, radishes, and turnips, should not be planted in high-risk soils. Shoot and leaf crops, such as asparagus, broccoli, cabbage, celery, lettuce, and spinach, represent an intermediate level of risk. Fruit crops, such as beans, cucumbers, eggplant, peas, pumpkins, and tomatoes, have the lowest contaminant concentrations.

Food safety. Remove outer leaves of leafy crops, and wash all produce with a mild detergent to remove dirt and dust. Conduct plant tissue testing to assess the level of contaminants actually in the produce.

Personal hygiene. Wear gloves and wash your hands well after working in the garden. Remove shoes outside to avoid tracking soil into the house.

Read NC State Extension publication AG-439-78, *Minimizing Risks of Soil Contaminants in Urban Gardens,* for additional information.

The most common vegetables bought as young plants for transplanting are broccoli, cabbage, cauliflower, celery, eggplant, lettuce, peppers, and tomatoes. If you buy vegetable transplants, larger and taller are not necessarily better. Tomato plants that have already started to flower are not optimal, because flowering places the plant under stress. Good-quality transplants are stocky and medium size with a healthy appearance and good green color (not too pale and not too dark), are free from insects and diseases, and have a well-developed root system (Figure 16–19). Allow the transplants to harden off gradually, acclimatizing them to the conditions in the garden prior to planting.

Before transplanting to the garden, make sure the soil has been prepared and determine that the timing is appropriate for the crop. To prevent wilting, try to transplant on a cloudy day or in early evening. Check the weather forecast for the days after you intend to plant to avoid conditions like extreme heat, heavy rain, or hail, that could harm new transplants (Figure 16–20). Handle the plants carefully to avoid disturbing the roots and bruising the stem.

For container-grown plants, dig a hole large enough to accommodate the container. Peat and other biodegradable pots can be set directly in the planting hole. Although the pots eventually disintegrate in the ground, remove any part that is above the ground as it may wick water away from the roots. For most vegetables, place the transplant

in the ground at the same depth as it grew in the container. Tomato plants are exceptions: they do develop roots all along buried stem tissue, dramatically expanding their root system (Figure 16–21). Plant by removing all but the top three sets of leaves, laying them sideways in a 3-inch to 4-inch-deep trench and burying all but the leaves (Figure 16–22).

Figure 16–19. Choose transplants that are stocky, have good color, well-developed roots, and have not gone to flower.
Lucy Bradley, CC BY - 2.0

If cold or windy conditions threaten spring transplants, place **row covers**, boxes, baskets, plastic milk jugs, or flower pots over the new transplants. Try to keep the covers from touching the plants, and do not leave them over the plants longer than necessary. If it gets warm during the day, remove the covers to provide proper ventilation. Summer transplants may need protection from heat for several days after they have been planted. A piece of wood or cardboard stuck in the ground at a slant on the south side of a plant can serve as a sunshade. Irrigation also helps to lower the air and soil temperature.

Figure 16-20. Hail damage to a pumpkin seedling.
Greg Younger, Flickr CC BY-SA - 2.0

Figure 16–21. Tomatoes grow roots along their stems.
Kathleen Moore, CC BY - 2.0

Table 16–3. Temperatures and Time Required to Grow Plants for Transplanting into the Garden

Vegetable	Optimum Temperature Day (°F)	Night (°F)	Growing Time from Seed Weeks
Asparagus	70–80	65–70	8–10
Broccoli	60–70	50–60	5–7
Brussels sprouts	60–70	50–60	5–7
Cabbage	60–70	50–60	5–7
Cauliflower	60–70	50–60	5–7
Corn, sweet	70–75	60–65	3–4
Cucumber	70–75	60–65	2–3
Eggplant	70–80	65–70	6–8
Lettuce	55–65	50–55	4–5
Muskmelon	70–75	60–65	3–4
Onion	60–65	55–60	10–12
Pepper	65–75	60–65	6–8
Summer squash	70–75	60–65	3–4
Tomato	65–75	60–65	5–7
Watermelon	70–80	65–70	3–4

Table 16–4 is located on page 16-30.

16

Figure 16–22. Plant tomatoes by digging a shallow trench and laying the stems down to promote more root growth.
Kathleen Moore, CC BY - 2.0

Table 16–5. Effective Crop Rotation

(By selecting plants from different families, you can avoid pathogen and pest buildup that can occur if the same type of plant is used in the same place year after year.)

PLANT FAMILY	VEGETABLES & COVER CROPS
Carrot, Parsley (Apiaceae)	Caraway, carrots, celery, chervil, cilantro, coriander, dill, fennel, parsley, parsnips
Composite, Sunflower (Asteraceae)	Artichoke, chamomile, chicory, dandelion, echinacea, endive, escarole, Jerusalem lettuce, radicchio, safflower, salsify, sunflowers, tarragon
Goosefoot (Chenopodiaceae)	Beets, spinach, sugar beets, Swiss chard
Grass (Poaceae)	Barley, corn, fescue, lemon grass, millet, oats, rice, rye, ryegrass, sorghum, sorghum-sudangrass, sugar cane, timothy, wheat
Knotweed (Polygonaceae)	Buckwheat, rhubarb
Legume, Pea (Fabaceae)	Alfalfa, bean, birdsfoot trefoil, black medic, clovers, cowpeas, edamame, fava beans, garbanzo bean, garden peas, green/string beans, hairy vetch, lentil, peanuts, southern peas, soybeans, vetches
Lily (Liliaceae)	Asparagus, chives, garlic, leeks, onions, shallot
Mallow (Malvaceae)	Okra
Morning-glory (Convolvulaceae)	Sweet potatoes
Mustard (Brassicaceae)	Arugula, bok choi, broccoli, broccoli raab, broccolini, Brussels sprouts, cabbage, cauliflower, Chinese cabbage, collards, cress, horseradish, kale, kohlrabi, mizuna, mustard, mustard greens, pak choi, radishes, rape, rutabagas, tatsoi, turnips, watercress
Nightshade (Solanaceae)	Eggplant, peppers (bell and chile), potatoes, tobacco, tomatillo, tomato,
Squash, Gourd, Melon (Cucurbitaceae)	Cantaloupe, cucumber, gourd, luffa, muskmelon, pumpkin, squash (summer and winter), watermelon, zucchini

Thinning Seedlings

Anytime seedlings grow too close together, thinning can benefit the plants selected to remain. Thinning is the process of reducing the number of seedlings in the soil or container media, giving those that remain more room to grow (Figure 16–23). If seeds are sown at the desired rate from the beginning, as with square foot gardening, thinning may not be necessary.

Thinning is a valuable practice for several reasons:
- It reduces competition among the seedlings for soil nutrients, sunlight, and water.
- It can reduce some early disease problems by providing better air circulation around the plants.
- It contributes to higher yields by giving plants the proper amount of space in which to flourish.

Leaf lettuce, beets, radishes, carrots, spinach, turnips, and other plants with small seeds are easily overplanted. Start thinning when the plants have one or two pairs of true leaves. Evening is a good time to thin because the remaining plants have the cool, dark night to recover from any disturbance. Pinch or cut out seedlings rather than pulling them out of the soil to avoid potentially damaging nearby root systems. The cut seedlings may be edible and tasty.

Figure 16–23. Thin seedlings by snipping with scissors rather than pulling.
Brook Williams

Fall Gardening

Growing a productive fall vegetable garden takes thoughtful planning and good cultural practices. August is the main planting time for fall gardens. Vegetables that have a 60-day to 80-day maturity cycle should be planted around August 1 in the NC piedmont. Seeding of shorter-season vegetables, such as turnips and leafy greens, can be delayed until September 1 in the NC piedmont. Keep in mind that the planting dates can be as much as 10 to 20 days earlier in western North Carolina and 7 to 14 days later in the NC coastal plain. Be sure to adjust the planting dates for a specific location by noting the frost date and counting backward on the calendar the days to maturity of the vegetables.

Before preparing the soil for a fall garden, remove the remains of the spring garden. In most cases, the spring-planted crops have already matured and the warm-season vegetables are beginning to decline.

Vegetables that can be grown in the fall garden include beets, beans, broccoli, Brussels sprouts, cabbage, cauliflower, carrots, collards, kale, kohlrabi, leaf lettuce, mustard, radishes, rutabagas, spinach, turnips, southern peas, and sugar snap peas.

Seeds should be planted deeper in the fall because the moisture level is lower in the soil and the soil surface temperatures are higher. In many cases, the planting depth may be 1½ to 2 times as deep as for spring planting of the same crop. The seeded area may need to be covered with burlap, newspaper, or boards to keep the soil cool and moist. Remove covers as the seeds begin to germinate.

Direct seeding is often used in the fall for crops such as broccoli and collards. The success of this planting method, however, depends on having enough moisture available to keep the young seedlings actively growing after germination. If there is no irrigation source, buy vegetable transplants from a local garden center instead of seeding. Most fall vegetables benefit from an application of nitrogen three and six weeks after planting.

Some Hints about Hybrids

Hybrids are the result of intentionally crossing (breeding) two or more plants. Hybrid **cultivars** are often superior to older, nonhybrid cultivars because they combine such desirable traits as consistency of plant and fruit type, uniform maturity, disease resistance, improved quality, and vigor. Seeds saved from hybrids do not "come true": appear and perform the same as the hybrid parents. Seeds from hybrids are either sterile or express a range of parental characteristics. Hybrid seeds are often more expensive than open-pollinated seeds.

Open-pollinated seeds are those that are naturally pollinated through wind, birds, insects, or other natural mechanisms. Open-pollinated cultivars do "come true" from seed in the same way that children resemble their parents. "Heirloom varieties" refer to historically grown seeds that were prized for their superior taste and texture. By saving seeds from the healthiest plants that produce the best tasting fruit, gardeners gradually create their own cultivars. If plants are selected over time in a region, those cultivars are specially adapted to a particular region's climate, soil, and pests. Heirloom crops keep the gene pool rich and can offer gardeners a taste of the past.

Heirloom vegetables come in a variety of colors, tastes, and textures.
Cody Maureen, Flickr CC BY - 2.0

16

General Garden Care

Watering

On average, vegetable gardens need 1 inch of water per week; provide only what is not supplied by rain. Keep a rain gauge in the garden to track precipitation, and adjust your watering times accordingly. Water the soil, not the plant. Many diseases are spread by water splashing from the soil up on the leaves or from a diseased leaf to a healthy one. Organic mulches (straw, leaves, or compost) help conserve moisture and prevent splash.

When providing an inch of water to the garden, the goal is to wet the soil to a depth of 6 inches. After some experimenting it is easy to tell how long it takes for water to reach that depth. One way to check is to dig into the soil with a long trowel or shovel to see how far the water has penetrated into the root zone. Another way is to measure how long it takes to apply 1 inch of water (which can moisten the soil to 6 inches deep, depending on soil type) by placing small, straight-sided containers in a grid pattern over the area being watered. Check the containers every 30 minutes until they contain l inch of water. As a general guide, the average house spigot must be left running approximately l½ to 2 hours to apply 1 inch of water to 1,000 square feet. Gardens with sandy soil must be watered more frequently than those with a high percentage of clay. Failure to provide adequate moisture stresses the plants and reduces yields. On the other hand, overwatering can lead to insect and disease problems, as well as wash nutrients away, converting a valuable garden resource into pollution in nearby streams.

From a water conservation perspective, the most efficient time to water plants is at night. During a hot, dry, summer, this may be ideal as night-time temperatures remain high. Cooler night temperatures in the spring or fall, however, can keep water from evaporating. The longer water stays on the leaves, the higher the likelihood of disease problems. If it is cool and wet enough for dew to form on plants, the best time to water is mid-morning after the dew has dried. Watering the soil directly instead of overhead not only promotes water conservation but also saves money on your water bill and reduces chances of water-borne diseases reaching leaves because they remain dry. Drip and trickle irrigation systems allow a gardener to irrigate slowly and efficiently. A soaker hose is the least expensive and easiest to use. It operates at low pressure and delivers small amounts of water to the soil very slowly. A full drip irrigation system provides water to individual plants and can be controlled by a timer. Gardeners can install these systems or hire a contractor. Periodically check the emitters to ensure all the heads are functioning properly.

A portable lawn sprinkler is also an option, but be sure to keep the application rate low enough that water does not run off the soil. Also make sure that the vegetable plants themselves do not interfere with the application pattern. Often this requires mounting the sprinkler on a small platform above the plants.

Avoid frequent shallow watering, which promotes the development of roots in the top 1 to 2 inches of soil rather than at a greater depth.

Weed Management and Mulching

As you recall from chapter 6, "Weeds," weeds compete for available soil nutrients, water, air and sunlight, and provide a home for insects and diseases. A steel hoe is one of the most effective weapons in fighting the war against weeds. When used regularly, it is effective and inexpensive. It is not possible, however, to control all weeds with a hoe alone. Weeds at the base of the plant should be pulled by hand rather than running the risk of damaging the roots (Figure 16–24). Do not allow weeds to become well-established before they are removed because pulling large weeds can damage the root system of vegetable plants. Mulch can significantly decrease the amount of hoeing needed.

Figure 16–24.
When cultivating around plants, be careful not to disturb the roots. Consider weeding by hand.
Brook Williams

Mulches help retain soil moisture and reduce weed growth. They fall into two categories—organic types that decompose naturally in the soil and inorganic types that do not decompose and, therefore, must be removed after serving their purpose.

Organic mulches are by far the most common. Typical examples are bark chips, compost, ground corncobs, chopped cornstalks, grass clippings, leaves, newspapers, peanut shells, pine needles, sawdust, and grain straw. Organic mulches conserve soil moisture and reduce the soil temperature by 8°F to 10°F during the summer. For this reason, they should not be used too early in the spring. If mulches are applied to cold garden soils, the soil warms up slowly, causing plant maturity to be delayed. After the soil warms in the spring, organic mulch may be applied to a depth of 2 to 4 inches around well-established plants. Be sure that there is adequate moisture in the soil before applying the mulch as dry mulch can pull moisture out of the soil.

Inorganic mulches, such as plastic sheeting that comes in good contact with the soil, can increase soil temperature early in the growing season and reduce the weed

population by excluding light. Install plastic mulch after fertilization, but before planting, when the soil is neither too wet nor too dry. Bury the edges to prevent the wind from blowing it away (Figure 16–25). Make short slits in the material with a pocketknife when planting seeds or transplants. Black plastic, which can raise soil temperatures by 5°F to 6°F, is recommended for crops that produce fruit on the ground, such as melons, cucumbers, squash, and tomatoes, because diseases are reduced when plant foliage has no contact with the soil. Clear plastic allows sun rays to penetrate and can increase the soil temperature more than any other type of mulch—by 8°F to 14°F.

Because light can penetrate clear plastic, it is possible for weeds to grow underneath if temperatures do not get high enough. Plastic mulches have hidden financial and labor costs. Plants mulched with plastic need supplemental water as roots do not receive water from rainfall, and irrigation needs to be monitored carefully. Plastic mulches degrade and should be removed and replaced regularly. Unintended environmental cost is disposal in a landfill.

Herbicides are chemicals that kill existing weeds or interrupt the germination. No single herbicide controls all weeds or can be safely used for all vegetable crops. It is difficult to apply relatively small amounts of the herbicide evenly to the garden surface. Miscalculation or faulty calibration of the application equipment can cause some

Figure 16–25.
Black plastic mulch keeps squash leaves off the ground, helping to reduce diseases.
Lance Cheung, USDA
CC0

Record Keeping

As with other hobbies and important tasks, keeping a journal or record of what was done and how it worked is helpful. See Appendix A to this handbook for more information on keeping a garden journal. Information from previous years helps to assess what to do better when planning next year's garden. Records can be kept in a notebook or on a garden calendar. Items that can be included are a diagram of the garden, plant varieties, dates of planting, how many transplants were planted and how many survived, descriptions of diseases or pests with any action taken and its effect, dates of harvest, amount of rain, amount and type of fertilizer used, evaluation of overall results, ideas for next year, and photographs of plants.

areas of the garden to be treated with too much or too little herbicide, leading to growth problems for some vegetables. Consult "Weeds," chapter 6 of this handbook, or the *North Carolina Agricultural Chemicals Manual* for more information.

Appendix D reviews tools that can be used while tending a garden.

Pest and Disease Management

Integrated Pest Management in the vegetable garden involves the same practices we learned about in chapter 8, "IPM":

- **Cultural management.** Practices include planting on the recommended dates, spacing plants properly, rotating crops, mulching, providing good soil fertility, and removing debris.
- **Mechanical management.** Uses strategies such as installing physical barriers like mulch or placing plastic collars to protect vegetable stems.
- **Biological management.** Practices include planting resistant vegetable cultivars or using natural predators for plant pathogens.
- **Chemical management.** Involves the use of herbicides and pesticides.

Many of the cultural practices that help prevent disease also discourage pest infestations. Interplanting can help keep insect and disease problems under control. Pests are usually crop-specific; they prefer vegetables from one plant family. Mixing plant families breaks up expanses of pest-preferred crops and confines early pest damage within a small area, thus allowing more time to manage the pests. Avoid overcrowding of vegetables, which decreases air movement and increases humidity, the perfect conditions for many diseases.

Because many insects and diseases have preferred host plants within the same plant family, **crop rotation** helps prevent the buildup of insects and disease problems. Table 16–5 provides information about which vegetables are related. Avoid planting related vegetables (same family) in the same location more often than once every three years. Rotation also keeps plants healthy and less prone to insect and disease problems by managing soil structure and fertility. Planting crop families with varying root depths helps keep soil structure loose. Plant families have different nutrient requirements, so a good plan would be planting legumes, which replace nitrogen in the soil through nitrogen-fixing bacteria in their roots, after a heavy nitrogen feeder like broccoli or cabbage. Leaving garden beds fallow or planting with a green manure for a season is another method for breaking an insect or disease cycle and a chance for soil nutrients to be replenished.

Insects and diseases can be more abundant and difficult to control in a fall garden. Most insect and disease problems result from a buildup of their populations during the previous spring and summer. Pests can be kept at tolerable levels by managing irrigation and fertilization to optimize plant health. Plants under stress are more susceptible to insect and disease development. Check the plants frequently for insect and disease damage. If sufficient damage is detected, use Integrated Pest Management strategies to manage the pest (see chapter 8, "IPM").

As with most gardening practices, preventing insects from damaging crops is partly a matter of timing. Some of the most common vegetable insects are discussed in Appendix C—Diagnostic Tables. AG-295 *Insect and Related Pests of Vegetables* and the *NC State Vegetable Pathology Lab Disease Fact Sheets* are other sources of information. Read more about "Diseases" in chapter 5 and "Insects" in chapter 4.

When to Harvest

Vegetable nutritional content, freshness, and flavor depend on the stage of maturity and time of day that vegetables are harvested. Overly mature vegetables are stringy and coarse. When possible, harvest vegetables during the cool part of the morning and process them as soon as possible.

Vegetable Harvesting Guidelines

Some guidelines for harvesting vegetable crops based on average yield expected per square foot are provided below.

Asparagus (0.08 to 0.1 pound). Harvest the spears when they are at least 6 to 8 inches tall by snapping or cutting them at ground level. Up to eight spears per plant may be harvested the second year after planting. A full harvest season lasts four to six weeks during the third growing season (Figure 16–26).

Figure 16–26. Asparagus.
Rob Ireton, Flickr CC BY - 2.0

Beans, lima (0.08 to 0.17 pound shelled). Harvest when the pods first start to bulge with the enlarged seeds. Pods must still be green, not yellowish (Figure 16–27).

Beans, snap (0.38 to 0.6 pound). Begin harvesting before seeds develop in the pod (when pods are about the diameter of a pencil). Beans are ready to pick if they snap easily when bent in half (Figure 16–28).

Figure 16–27. Lima beans.
Ton Rulkens, Flickr CC BY-SA - 2.0

Figure 16–28. Snap beans.
Rob Bertholf, CC BY - 2.0

Broccoli (0.33 to 0.5 pound). Harvest the dark-green, compact cluster or head (about 6 inches in diameter) while the buds are tight, before any yellow flowers appear. Smaller side shoots develop later, providing a continuous harvest (Figure 16–29).

Brussels sprouts (0.25 to 0.38 pound). Harvest the lower sprouts (small heads) when they are about 1 to 1½ inches in diameter by twisting them off. Remove lower leaves along the stem to hasten maturity (Figure 16–30).

 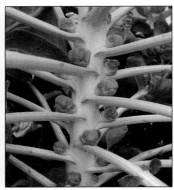

Figure 16–29. Broccoli.
Chris Alberti, CC BY - 2.0

Figure 16–30. Brussels sprouts.
Kathleen Moore, CC BY - 2.0

Figure 16–31. Red cabbage.
Kathleen Moore, CC BY - 2.0

Cabbage (0.5 to 0.75 pound). Harvest when the heads feel hard and solid (Figure 16–31).

Carrots (0.5 to 0.8 pound). Harvest when the roots are ¾-inch to 1 inch in diameter. The largest roots generally have the darkest tops. Mulched fall carrots can be left in the ground all winter and harvested as needed (Figure 16–32).

Cauliflower (0.33 to 0.5 pound). Exclude sunlight (blanch) when the curds, or heads, are 1 to 2 inches in diameter by loosely tying together the outer leaves above the curd with a string or rubber band. Some varieties are self-blanching. Harvest the curds when they are 4 to 6 inches in diameter but still compact, white, and smooth. The head should be ready 10 to 15 days after tying (Figure 16–33).

Figure 16–32. Purple carrot.
Lucy Bradley, CC BY - 2.0

Figure 16–33. Cauliflower.
Kathleen Moore, CC BY - 2.0

Collards (0.33 to .67 pound). Harvest older, lower leaves when they reach a length of 8 to 12 inches. New leaves grow as long as the central growing point remains, providing a continuous harvest. Whole plants may be harvested and cooked if desired (Figure 16–34).

Corn, sweet (n/a). Silks begin to turn brown and dry out as the ears mature. Check a few ears for maturity by opening the top of the ear and pressing a few kernels with a thumbnail. If the liquid exuded is milky, rather than clear, the ear is ready for harvest (Figure 16–35).

Figure 16–34. Collards.
Tim Sackton, Flickr CC BY-SA - 2.0

Figure 16–35. Sweet corn.
Alice Henneman, Flickr
CC BY - 2.0

16

Herbs

Herbs are plants that add interest and flavor to our foods and perfume our homes (Figure 16–61). Herbs are pest-resistant plants that are relatively easy to grow. If you are adding herbs to your garden, start with the herbs that are used the most. For example, choose basil, fennel, and oregano for Italian cooking; lavender and lemon verbena for making potpourri; or chamomile and mints to make teas.

Some of the herbs familiar to North Americans, such as bay laurel, dill, lavender, marjoram, oregano, rosemary, and thyme, are native to the Mediterranean region. These herbs grow best in soils with excellent drainage, bright sun, and moderate temperatures.

Figure 16–61. An herb garden.
Maggie Hoffman, Flickr CC BY - 2.0

When growing herbs, follow these basic guidelines:
- Plant herbs in average garden soil with organic matter added to improve texture and drainage.
- Choose a site that receives at least 6 hours of direct sun each day.
- Avoid ground where water stands or runs during rains.
- Compensate for poor drainage with raised beds.
- Apply balanced fertilizers sparingly to leafy, fast-growing herbs. Heavy applications of fertilizer, especially those containing large amounts of nitrogen, may decrease the concentration of essential oils in the lush green growth.

Most herbs require little special care after being established. Plan an herb garden by grouping herbs according to light, irrigation, and soil requirements. Most herbs enjoy full sun, but a few tolerate shade. Herbs can be classified as either annual, biennial, or perennial. Be aware of the growth habits of the plants before purchasing them. Some herbs—such as anise, borage, caraway, chervil, coriander, dill, and fennel—should be direct-seeded because they do not transplant well. Other herbs, such as mints, oregano, rosemary, tarragon, and thyme, should be transplanted to ensure production of the right plant and to obtain desired growth the first year. Additional information on specific herbs can be found in the NC State Extension Gardener Plant Toolbox.

To conserve moisture and prevent splashing mud on the plants, mulch an herb garden after planting. If you are planting from seed, wait until germination and establishment of the plants and then mulch. Use 1 to 2 inches of organic material. Many growers mulch with hardwood bark or a mixture of bark and sawdust.

When grown outdoors and given ample air circulation, sunlight, and water drainage, herbs rarely suffer severe disease or insect damage. Natural predators and parasites usually keep mite and aphid populations low. Traditional pesticides are not labeled for use on culinary herbs, so rely on cultural, biological, and physical management techniques. Insecticidal soap is useful against severe outbreaks of aphids, mites, and whiteflies. Hand-pick larger pests such as beetles and caterpillars.

Growing a diverse group of herbs can be attractive. Herbs provide color, fragr-ance, and interest throughout the season, and they help to keep pest problems at a minimum.

Harvesting Herbs

Most herbs grow healthier and fuller if they are harvested frequently. The method of harvesting depends on which herbs and their use.

- Begin harvesting herb leaves when the plants are well-established, but before flowering to keep leaf production high.
- Harvest up to three-quarters of the current season's growth.
- Harvest early in the morning, after the dew dries but before the sun becomes hot.
- Herb flowers have their most intense oil concentration and flavor when harvested after flower buds appear but before they open.
- Herb flowers harvested to dry for craft purposes should be picked just before they are fully open.
- Annual herbs can be harvested until frost.
- Perennial herbs can be clipped until late August. Stop harvesting about one month before the frost date. Later pruning could encourage frost-tender growth.
- Harvest lavender flowers in early summer, and then shear the plants to half their height to encourage a second flowering period in the fall.

Preserving Herbs

Herbs acquire their fragrance and flavor from oils that evaporate into the air when the leaves are crushed. Ideally, use fresh herbs for cooking. But to preserve and retain quality for later use, freezing is one of the easiest methods. Rinse the herbs quickly in cold water, shake off excess moisture, and chop coarsely. Freeze generous pinches of herbs in filled ice cube trays to prevent freezer burn, or loosely spread the herbs onto a cookie sheet to freeze. Then transfer the herbs into a large plastic bag and seal. Thawed herbs are unsuitable for garnish, but they can be used in cooking.

Drying is the traditional method of herb preservation. Simply tie fresh herb stems into small bundles and hang upside down in a dark, warm, airy place (Figure 16–62). UV rays from the sun and moisture from dew and frost can discolor and severely reduce the quality of many herbs. Shade drying allows the crop to be dried more slowly and uniformly than in direct sun.

When the leaves are dry, separate them from their stems and package in rigid, light-proof containers. To preserve full flavor, avoid crushing the stems. Sage, thyme, summer savory, dill, and parsley are easy to dry. Basil, French tarragon, and mints mold if not dried quickly. An alternative method of drying is to spread the herbs out on window screens. Keep them out of the sun and turn them often.

Herbs can also be dried in a microwave. Lay a single layer of clean, dry leaves between dry paper towels and put them in the microwave for 1 minute to 2 minutes on high power. Let the leaves cool. If they are not brittle, reheat for 30 seconds and retest. Repeat as needed, until they are brittle.

Store dry herbs ready for cooking in an airtight bottle, preferably brown glass, in a cool place out of direct sunlight and away from heat. Use for cooking within a year for maximum freshness.

To air dry herbs for seeds, tie the herbs in small bundles and suspend inside a paper bag with holes. Suspend the bag in a dark area that has good air circulation. Collect the seeds when they are dry, and store in rigid, light-proof containers.

Figure 16–62. Preserving herbs by drying them upside down in a warm place.
Caitlin Regan, CC BY - 2.0

Case Study—Think IPM: Pole Beans

You have noticed your pole bean plants looking damaged and unhealthy. You are wondering what is causing the damage and if there is anything you can do to prevent it.

Review the five Integraded Pest Management (IPM) steps summarized in this section, and conduct some background research on problems with pole beans.

1. **Monitor and scout to determine pest type and population levels.**
   You have planted a vegetable garden in the same location for the past five years. This June, you noticed your pole beans looking sick. You inspect the plants and see an olive-green square-shaped insect congregating in large groups on the plants. You notice it has a strong foul aroma. You take pictures of the insect (Figure 16–63).

2. **Diagnostics: Accurately identify pest and host.**
   The following diagnostic steps and questions will help you accurately identify the problem. Responses are included in italics.

Figure 16–63. Adult kudzu bug.
Matt Bertone

Step 1. Identify the plant: *Green pole beans*

Step 2. Describe the problem: *About half of my pole beans (10 plants) are showing signs of damage and look very unhealthy. The leaves have chunks missing, and some of them are turning brown.*

Step 3. Identify what is normal:
What does the healthy part of the plant look like? *The healthy beans are dark-green and have no damage on the leaves.*
Have you had a soil test? *No.* (For information on how to submit a soil test see chapter 1, "Soils and Plant Nutrients.")

Step 4. Cultural practices:
Describe the age and history of the plants: *The bean plants are about seven weeks old. I have planted beans in this spot for the last five years.*
Irrigation: *I water the garden with a soaker hose so it gets 1 inch of water a week.*
Fertilizer: *I amended my garden soil with compost before planting the beans this spring.*
Maintenance: *I have monitored the beans every other day, kept weeds to a minimum, and have put a 2-inch layer of compost on top of the soil.*

Step 5. Environmental conditions:
Are there any significant water issues? *It has been a warm summer, but I have been diligent about watering.*
Describe the light near this garden bed. How many hours of sunlight? *The garden gets about 7 hours of full sun a day.*
Describe any recent changes or events: *I did expand my garden by 10 feet this year just to the south of this bed.*

Step 6. Signs of pathogens:
On the leaves: *Many small, square, mottled olive and brown insects (about the size of a ladybird beetle) are clumped together. On the underside of the leaves, tiny oval-shaped tan eggs are visible. The insects emit a strong odor. There is a whitish looking substance on the leaves.*
On the stems: *There are some slightly smaller, hairy, greenish insects on the stems.*
On the roots: *No insects are visible; no other pathogens are visible on the roots.*
On the soil: *A few dead insects are on the soil; no other pathogens are visible on the soil.*

Step 7. Symptoms of pathogens:
On the leaves: *Some of the leaves are missing completely, and some appear mottled.*
On the stems: *The stems show some damage and scraped missing tissue.*
On the roots: *Roots are yellowish-white and appear healthy.*

Step 8. Distribution of damage in the landscape:
Are other plants in the landscape affected? *My wisteria (Wisteria fructescens) vine at the front of the garden also has these insects on it.*

Step 9. Distribution of damage on the plant and specific plant parts:
Where is the damage seen on the plant? *On the leaves (aboveground portion).*

Step 10. Timing:
When did you notice this problem? *Yesterday when I did my routine garden check. I did not see any insects or insect damage a few days ago.*

16

Steps 6 and 7 lead you to believe you are dealing with a pathogen. Based on the description of damage to the leaves and of the insect present (Steps 2, 9), we form a hypothesis that this is a kudzu bug (*Megcopta cibrara*) (Figure 16–63). Though it looks like a beetle, kudzu bugs are more closely related to a stink bug (Step 6). They are an olive-green to brown square-shaped insect (Step 6) native to Asia and first seen in North Carolina in 2011. They attack members of the bean family including kudzu, wisteria, soybeans, peanuts, butter beans, green beans, and field peas (Step 8). Their nymph form is quite hairy (Step 6) as seen in Figure 16–64. Sooty mold commonly follows damage by kudzu bugs, hence the white substance seen on the leaves (Step 6).

3. Consider economic, aesthetic, and injury thresholds.

Half of your beans are affected. Considering the numbers of insects, the likelihood is high that your entire bean crop will be lost. You are also concerned about the wisteria plant that is a focal point of the arbor at your garden entrance. The problem is severe enough to warrant management.

Figure 16–64. Kudzu bug nymph.
Matt Bertone

4. Implement a treatment strategy using physical, cultural, biological, or chemical control, or combine these strategies.

From the information found by searching "kudzu bug + extension" on the Internet, you learn that kudzu bugs appear in the spring but can overwinter in homes causing damage by staining and leaving behind a strong foul odor.

Physical. This insect is difficult to manage when it is in full reproductive swing, but hosing off adults, nymphs, and eggs into a bucket of soapy water can help to disrupt reproduction. Do not remove the insects by hand as they can release a yellow substance that can cause skin irritation. Removing all foliage from the wisteria in the fall and disposing of it also helps break the cycle. Monitor any bean family plants in the immediate area. You notice your neighbor has a kudzu vine on his fence, and you plan to work with him to remove that vine as well. To prevent the insects from overwintering in a home, all cracks should be sealed with caulk. Vents, windows, and doors should also be checked and sealed.

Cultural. To help break the cycle, do not plant any bean family crops next year. Keep the wisteria vine well-watered and fertilized to keep it as healthy as possible.

Biological. Some beneficial insects, such as assassin bugs and predatory stinkbugs, have been seen feeding on kudzu bugs. Some research is being conducted on the use of predatory wasps.

Chemical. Identify insecticides that are labeled for use on kudzu bugs on beans. Check the *North Carolina Agricultural Chemicals Manual* for an up-to-date list. Only spray affected bean family plants and follow label directions. Check the label for information on when, or if, the beans can be eaten after the plant is sprayed.

5. Evaluate treatment success.

You removed as many insects as possible with the soapy water method and decided not to plant beans in your garden next year and not to plant them in that location again for at least five more years. You disposed of all the bean family plant material in the fall and helped your neighbor manage his kudzu vine. You plan to plant some native wildflowers to attract more beneficial insects to your yard and have decided against spraying insecticides as this time. You have sealed up any cracks in the windows and doors around your home to prevent them from overwintering there. You started a garden journal to keep track of the insect sightings and other events in your garden so you have records to look back on when future problems occur.

Rob Bertholf, CC BY - 2.0

Table 16-4. Garden Planting Calendar for Annual Vegetables, Fruits, and Herbs in North Carolina

Fruit, Herb, or Vegetable	Days to Harvest (from seed unless otherwise noted)	Distance Between Plants	Jan		Feb		Mar		Apr		May		Jun		Jul		Aug		Sep		Oct		Nov		Dec	
			1	15	1	15	1	15	1	15	1	15	1	15	1	15	1	15	1	15	1	15	1	15	1	15
Artichokes, globe	T = 1 year	30 in																						E P	E P	E P
Artichokes, Jerusalem (Best grown in a pot because plants can spread aggressively.)	Tu = 6 – 8 months	9 – 12 in						E P W	E P W	W																
Arugula	40 – 50	6 – 9 in			E P	E P	E P	W	W	W								E P W	E P W	E P W	E					
Asparagus	C = 2 years	18 in				E P	E P	W	W																	
Basil	T = 14 – 35 / S = 50 – 75	2 – 8 in									E P W	E P W	E P W	E P	E P	E P										
Beans, lima/bush	65 – 80	6 in									E P	E P W	E P W	W												
Beans, lima/pole	75 – 95	6 in									E P	E P W	E P W	W												

E = Eastern, **P** = Piedmont, **W** = Western

B = Bulbs; C = Crowns; S = Seeds; T = Transplants; Tu = Tubers

*Start seeds indoors for later transplant in the garden. Do not plant seeds directly in the garden.

16

Table 16-4. Garden Planting Calendar for Annual Vegetables, Fruits, and Herbs in North Carolina *continued*

Fruit, Herb, or Vegetable	Days to Harvest (from seed unless otherwise noted)	Distance Between Plants	Jan 1	Jan 15	Feb 1	Feb 15	Mar 1	Mar 15	Apr 1	Apr 15	May 1	May 15	Jun 1	Jun 15	Jul 1	Jul 15	Aug 1	Aug 15	Sep 1	Sep 15	Oct 1	Oct 15	Nov 1	Nov 15	Dec 1	Dec 15
Beans, snap/bush	50 – 55	2 in						E P	E P	E P	E P	E P	E			P	E P	E P	E P	E P	E					
Beans, snap/pole	65 – 70	6 in						E	E P	E P	E P W	E P W	E P W	W	W	E P	E P	E P	E P	E P	E					
Beets	55 – 60	2 in					E P	E P	E P	W				W	W	E P	E P	E P	E P							
Broccoli	T = 70 – 80	18 in				E P	E P	E P	W	W	W					E W	E P W	E P	E P							
Brussels sprouts	T = 40 – 50 S = 90 – 100*	14 – 18 in							W	W	W	W			E P	E P	E E	P								
Cabbage	T = 63 – 75 S = 90 – 120*	12 in			E P	E P	E P W	E P	E P	E P					E P	W	E	E	E P	E P						
Cabbage, Chinese	T = 45 – 55 S = 75 – 85	12 in					E	P		W	W					W W	W				P P					
Carrots	75 – 80	2 in				E P	E P	W	W	W	W	W	E P	E P	W	W	E P	E P	E P							

E = Eastern, **P** = Piedmont, **W** = Western

B = Bulbs; C = Crowns; S = Seeds; T = Transplants; Tu = Tubers

*Start seeds indoors for later transplant in the garden. Do not plant seeds directly in the garden.

Table 16–4. Garden Planting Calendar for Annual Vegetables, Fruits, and Herbs in North Carolina *continued*

Legend: **E** = Eastern, **P** = Piedmont, **W** = Western
B = Bulbs; C = Crowns; S = Seeds; T = Transplants; Tu = Tubers
*Start seeds indoors for later transplant in the garden. Do not plant seeds directly in the garden.

Fruit, Herb, or Vegetable	Days to Harvest (from seed unless otherwise noted)	Distance Between Plants	Region	Jan 1	Jan 15	Feb 1	Feb 15	Mar 1	Mar 15	Apr 1	Apr 15	May 1	May 15	Jun 1	Jun 15	Jul 1	Jul 15	Aug 1	Aug 15	Sep 1	Sep 15	Oct 1	Oct 15	Nov 1	Nov 15	Dec 1	Dec 15
Cauliflower	T = 55–65; S = 85–95	18 in	E				E	E	E									E	E	E	E	E	E				
			P					P	P	P								P	P	P	P						
Celery	T = 60–70; S = 120–150*	6–8 in	E				E	E	E							E	E	E									
			P					P	P	P							P	P	P								
			W								W	W				W											
Chard, Swiss	T = 32–42; S = 60–70	6 in	E				E	E	E										E	E							
			P					P	P	P									P	P							
			W						W	W	W	W	W	W													
Cilantro	50–55	2–4 in	E			E	E	E	E											E	E	E					
			P			P	P	P	P											P	P						
Collard greens	T = 32–72; S = 60–100	18 in	E				E	E	E	E	E					E	E	E	E	E							
			P					P	P	P	P	P				P	P	P	P								
			W								W	W	W	W	W	W	W										
Corn, sweet	85–90	12 in	E						E	E	E	E															
			P							P	P	P	P														
			W									W	W	W													
Cucumbers	T = 28–37; S = 56–65	12 in	E								E	E	E	E	E	E	E	E	E								
			P									P	P	P	P	P	P	P	P	P							
			W										W	W	W	W	W										
Dill	40–55	2–4 in	E						E									E	E	E							
			P							P									P	P							
			W								W	W	W														

16

Table 16–4. Garden Planting Calendar for Annual Vegetables, Fruits, and Herbs in North Carolina *continued*

Fruit, Herb, or Vegetable	Days to Harvest (from seed unless otherwise noted)	Distance Between Plants	Jan 1	Jan 15	Feb 1	Feb 15	Mar 1	Mar 15	Apr 1	Apr 15	May 1	May 15	Jun 1	Jun 15	Jul 1	Jul 15	Aug 1	Aug 15	Sep 1	Sep 15	Oct 1	Oct 15	Nov 1	Nov 15	Dec 1	Dec 15
Eggplant	T = 90 – 95 S = 150 – 155*	24 in								E	E P	E P W	E P W				E P	E								
Florence fennel	60 – 90	6 – 12 in					E P	E P	E P W	E P W	W	W	W		W	E P	E P	P								
Garlic	B = 180 – 210	4 – 6 in																	W	E P W	E P W	P W	E P W	E P W		
Kale	T = 14 – 22 S = 40 – 50	6 in			E P	E P	E P W	E P W	E P W	E P W	E P	E P	E P	E			E P	E P W	E P W	E P W	E					
Kohlrabi	T = 22 – 32 S = 50 – 60	4 in			E P	E P	E P	E P	E P W	E P W	E P W	E P W	E P	E			E P	E P W	E E P	P						
Leek	T = 50 – 80 S = 120 – 150	4 in			E P	E P	E P	E P	E P W	E P W	E P W	E P W	E W	W	W		W	W								
Lettuce, head	T = 45 – 60 S = 70 – 85	10 in		E P	E P	E P	E P	E P W	E P W	E P W	E	E					E P	W	E P	E P	E	P				
Lettuce, leaf	T = 15 – 25 S = 40 – 50	6 in		E P	E P	E P	E P W	E P W	E P W	E P W	W					W	E P	P W	E P	E P	E	P				

E = Eastern, **P** = Piedmont, **W** = Western
B = Bulbs; C = Crowns; S = Seeds; T = Transplants; Tu = Tubers
*Start seeds indoors for later transplant in the garden. Do not plant seeds directly in the garden.

Table 16–4. Garden Planting Calendar for Annual Vegetables, Fruits, and Herbs in North Carolina *continued*

Fruit, Herb, or Vegetable	Days to Harvest (from seed unless otherwise noted)	Distance Between Plants	Region	Jan 1	Jan 15	Feb 1	Feb 15	Mar 1	Mar 15	Apr 1	Apr 15	May 1	May 15	Jun 1	Jun 15	Jul 1	Jul 15	Aug 1	Aug 15	Sep 1	Sep 15	Oct 1	Oct 15	Nov 1	Nov 15	Dec 1	Dec 15
Melons, cantaloupe	T = 57 – 62 / S = 85 – 90	24 in	E								E	E	E	E	E	E											
			P								P	P	P	P	P	P											
			W									W	W	W	W	W											
Melons, watermelon	T = 62 – 72 / S = 90 – 100	60 in	E								E	E	E	E	E												
			P								P	P	P	P													
			W									W	W	W	W												
Mustard	30 – 40	2 in	E				E	E	E	E	E	E	E	E				E	E	E		E					
			P				P	P	P	P	P	P	P	P				P	P	P							
			W						W	W	W	W	W	W	W	W	W	W	W								
Okra	T = 18 – 28 / S = 60 – 70	12 in	E									E	E	E	E			E	E								
			P									P	P	P	P			P	P								
			W													W	W										
Onions, bulb	B = 75 – 105 / S = 90 – 120	4 in	E	E	E	E	E	E	E	E	E	E	E					E	E	E	E	E	E	E	E	E	E
			P	P	P	P	P	P	P	P	P	P	P					P	P	P	P	P	P	P	P	P	P
			W				W	W	W	W	W	W	W	W	W												
Onions, green	T = 42 – 50 / S = 60 – 70	1 – 2 in	E			E	E	E	E	E									E	E							
			P				P	P	P	P								P	P	P							
			W				W	W	W	W								W	W	W							
Pac choi, bok choy	T = 30 – 75 / S = 45 – 90*	7 – 12 in	E			E	E	E	E	E	E								E	E	E	E					
			P				P	P	P	P	P							P	P	P	P						
			W					W	W	W								W	W	W							
Parsley	T = 33 / S = 75	9 – 12 in	E															E	E	E							
			P															P	P	P							
			W							W	W	W	W			W	W	W									

E = Eastern, **P** = Piedmont, **W** = Western

B = Bulbs; C = Crowns; S = Seeds; T = Transplants; Tu = Tubers

*Start seeds indoors for later transplant in the garden. Do not plant seeds directly in the garden.

Table 16–4. Garden Planting Calendar for Annual Vegetables, Fruits, and Herbs in North Carolina *continued*

Fruit, Herb, or Vegetable	Days to Harvest (from seed unless otherwise noted)	Distance Between Plants	Jan 1	Jan 15	Feb 1	Feb 15	Mar 1	Mar 15	Apr 1	Apr 15	May 1	May 15	Jun 1	Jun 15	Jul 1	Jul 15	Aug 1	Aug 15	Sep 1	Sep 15	Oct 1	Oct 15	Nov 1	Nov 15	Dec 1	Dec 15
Parsnips	100–130	3–4 in			E	E P	E P	E P										E P	E P	E P	E	E				
Peanuts	145–160	6–8 in								W	E W	P W	W	W	W	W	W									
Peas, dwarf/bush	54–60	4 in	E P	E P	E P	E P	E P W	E P W	P W	W	W						E	E P	E P	E P	E					
Peas, vining	54–72	2–3 in	E P	E P	E P	E P	E P	E P W	P W	W		W	W				E	E P	E P	E P						
Peas, field/southern	55–65	4 in						E	E P	E P	E P W	E P W	E P W	E W			E	E P								
Peppers	T = 75–80 / S = 145–150*	18 in								E P	E P	E P W	E W	W												
Potatoes, Irish	Tu = 95–120	10 in				E	E P	E P	W	W																
Potatoes, sweet	T = 95–125	10 in									E	E P	E P W	E P W	E P											

E = Eastern, **P** = Piedmont, **W** = Western

B = Bulbs; C = Crowns; S = Seeds; T = Transplants; Tu = Tubers

*Start seeds indoors for later transplant in the garden. Do not plant seeds directly in the garden.

Table 16–4. Garden Planting Calendar for Annual Vegetables, Fruits, and Herbs in North Carolina *continued*

Legend of cell codes: **E** = Eastern, **P** = Piedmont, **W** = Western. Each crop row shows up to three region timelines (Eastern, Piedmont, Western). Month columns are divided into "1" and "15" (first and middle of month). Jan, Nov, and Dec are blank for all crops.

Fruit, Herb, or Vegetable	Days to Harvest (from seed unless otherwise noted)	Distance Between Plants	Feb 1	Feb 15	Mar 1	Mar 15	Apr 1	Apr 15	May 1	May 15	Jun 1	Jun 15	Jul 1	Jul 15	Aug 1	Aug 15	Sep 1	Sep 15	Oct 1	Oct 15
Pumpkin	115–120	48 in				E	E	E	E,P	E,P	E,P,W	E,P,W	E							
Radishes	20–25	1 in		E,P	E,P	E,P	E,P,W	E,P,W	W						P,W	E,P	E,P	E,P	E	
Rutabaga	70–80	4 in			W	W	W	W	W					W	W		E	E	E	
Spinach	50–60	6 in		E,P	E,P,W	E,P,W	E,P,W	W	W						E,P,W	E,P,W	E,P	E,P	E,P	E
Squash, summer	T = 30–40; S = 50–60	24 in					E	E,P	E,P,W	E,P,W	E,P,W	E,P,W	E,P	E,P	E					
Squash, winter	T = 42–67; S = 70–95	36 in						P	E,P,W	E,P,W	E,P,W	E,P,W	E,P	W	E,P					
Sunflower	55–110	9–24 in				E	E,P,W	E,P,W	E,P,W	E,P,W	E,P	E,P	E,P		E					
Tomatoes	T = 75–85; S = 125–135*	18 in					P	P,W	E,P,W	E,P,W	E,P,W	W			E,P					

E = Eastern, **P** = Piedmont, **W** = Western

B = Bulbs; C = Crowns; S = Seeds; T = Transplants; Tu = Tubers

*Start seeds indoors for later transplant in the garden. Do not plant seeds directly in the garden.

16

Table 16–4. Garden Planting Calendar for Annual Vegetables, Fruits, and Herbs in North Carolina *continued*

Fruit, Herb, or Vegetable	Days to Harvest (from seed unless otherwise noted)	Distance Between Plants	Jan 1	Jan 15	Feb 1	Feb 15	Mar 1	Mar 15	Apr 1	Apr 15	May 1	May 15	Jun 1	Jun 15	Jul 1	Jul 15	Aug 1	Aug 15	Sep 1	Sep 15	Oct 1	Oct 15	Nov 1	Nov 15	Dec 1	Dec 15
Turnips	55–60	2 in			E	E	E	E	E	E	E	E	E	E				E	E							
					P	P	P	P	P	P	P	P	P	P				P	P							
							W	W	W	W					W	W	W									

E = Eastern, **P** = Piedmont, **W** = Western

B = Bulbs; C = Crowns; S = Seeds; T = Transplants; Tu = Tubers

*Start seeds indoors for later transplant in the garden. Do not plant seeds directly in the garden.

For more information on gardening in North Carolina, see **go.ncsu.edu/eg – handbook** and **gardening.ces.ncsu.edu**.

Acknowledgments: This publication is based on prior work by Charlotte Glen, Danny Lauderdale, Kerrie Roach, Donna Teasley, Debbie Roos, Doug Jones, Erv Evans, and Larry Bass. The authors would like to thank Jeanine Davis, Bill Jester, Issac Lewis, Jonathan Schultheis, Allan Thornton, Kathleen Moore, and Debra Ireland for their assistance with this publication.

Prepared by: Lucy K. Bradley, Extension Specialist, Urban Horticulture; Christopher C. Gunter, Extension Specialist, Vegetable Crop Production; Julieta T. Sherk, Assistant Professor; and Elizabeth A. Driscoll, Extension Associate

Frequently Asked Questions

1. *My tomatoes, peppers, or melons have dry rotten spots on the ends.*

Blossom-end rot occurs on tomatoes, peppers, squash, eggplant, and watermelons from a lack of calcium in the developing fruits. It can be caused by fluctuations in the soil moisture, rapid early-season growth followed by extended dry weather, excessive rain, excess soil salts caused by overfertilization (especially with high nitrogen fertilizers), and improper soil pH. Fungi or bacteria that invade the damaged tissue may cause moldy growths on the rotted area. The rotten area looks unsightly, but the rest of the fruit is edible. Applying preventive sprays of calcium chloride to the tomatoes is not very effective. To prevent the problem in the future, maintain an even moisture level by regular watering and using good mulch. Plant in well-drained soil and avoid using high nitrogen fertilizers. Do not cultivate deeply close to the plant. Test soil and use lime as recommended to bring the pH up to 6.5 to 6.8. Smaller-fruited varieties, such as cherry tomatoes, are less susceptible to blossom-end rot.

2. *My tomatoes do not set fruit.*

This may be due to extreme temperatures causing blossoms to drop without setting fruit. This occurs when night-time temperatures fall below 55°F or stay above 70°F, or daytime temperatures rise above 90°F for extended periods. Recently, new "hot-set" varieties of tomatoes, such as Sun Leaper and Solar Set, have been developed that continue to set fruit at high temperatures. There could be other explanations.

- Does the plant get enough sun? Tomatoes need at least 6 hours of sunlight per day.
- If there is vigorous leafy growth but no fruit, there may be too much nitrogen in the soil, which stimulates leaf production at the expense of fruit formation.
- Drought also causes tomato plants to not set fruit, so make sure the tomato plant is getting 1 inch to 2 inches of water per week and is kept evenly moist.

3. *Can my vegetables cross-pollinate each other?*

Pollination is the transfer of pollen from the anther to the stigma (ovary) of a flower that results in seed and enlargement of the ovary producing a fruit. Cross-pollination is the transfer of pollen from a flower on one plant to a flower of another plant. Different varieties of the same vegetable can cross-pollinate (yellow and white corn) and some closely related species in the same family (squash and pumpkins), but not species in different families (corn and melons). Even if your pumpkin and squash or cantaloupe and Crenshaw did cross-pollinate, however, the fruit would still look the same. Only if the seeds from the fruit produced were saved and planted the next season would you possibly see differently colored or shaped fruit produced. There are some exceptions, such as planting hot and sweet peppers near each other. The gene for hotness is dominant, and insect cross-pollination can occur in peppers. Therefore, the seed produced in the current season's sweet pepper may contain capsaicin, which causes heat, and your sweet pepper could taste hot. Corn kernels are seeds, and planting white and yellow corn near each other can result in cobs with mixed yellow and white kernels. Likewise, a supersweet corn planted near a traditional corn cultivar does not develop its sweet flavor.

4. *Why is my broccoli, spinach, lettuce, or other cool-season crop flowering? Can I still eat it?*

Cole crops or cold weather crops thrive in cooler temperatures. When the weather warms up in the spring, it can signal to cole crops that it is time to flower and reproduce. This rapid growth of flowering structures is often called bolting. While you can still eat plants that have bolted, they often contain a bitter sap that makes them unpalatable. Consider planting cole crops in the fall rather than the spring.

5. *Why do my cucumbers taste bitter?*

Cucumbers grown under environmental stress—such as a lack of water, uneven watering practices, high heat or cool conditions, wide temperature swings, low soil fertility, or low soil pH—produce increased levels of chemicals called cucurbitacins. These compounds are bitter and concentrated in the cucumber's skin. Misshapen fruit from poor pollination can also be bitter. Bitterness also varies to some degree with the particular variety of cucumber grown. Overly mature or improperly stored cucumbers may also develop a mild bitterness.

16

6. My tomato starts from the nursery do not have many leaves on the lower stem, but they do have a few blossoms and one tiny tomato. How deep should I plant?

Good early root establishment makes for the most prolific tomato plants. Tomato plants can produce **adventitious** roots all along their stem (see Figure 16–21), so burying the plant up to the first set of leaves can allow the plant to produce the most roots. If your plant is more than 6 to 7 inches tall, the soil below that depth could be too cool to promote the best root growth. In this case, consider digging a shallow trench and laying the tomato plant on its side (see Figure 16–22). Gently bend up the tip of the plant so it is above the soil line and cover the rest of the stem. Any blossoms or fruits should be pinched off because they can take energy away from developing roots.

7. Why are my broccoli or cauliflower heads small? And why is my cauliflower turning green?

When small heads form on broccoli or cauliflower, the condition is called "**buttoning**". Excessive cold, nutrient deficiency, or drought stress (usually soon after planting) can cause buttoning. Large transplants are much more susceptible to buttoning, so look for plants with no more than four to six leaves. Cauliflower heads begin to turn green because they are starting to photosynthesize due to light exposure. When your head is approximately 3 inches across, you can keep light off of it by pulling leaves up and tying them together. This is known as "**blanching**". Be sure to check on your plant frequently. If you notice it starting to bolt or elongate, harvest the entire head immediately.

8. There is a little tomato growing on my potato plant. Did they cross-pollinate?

Potatoes, tomatoes, eggplants, and peppers are in the Solanaceae or nightshade family. This family is self-pollinating, so unlikely to cross-pollinate. What you are seeing is the true fruit of a potato, which contains many tiny seeds. Do not eat the fruit, which is poisonous.

9. My zucchini plant has only produced a couple of fruits this summer. What is wrong with it?

Zucchini are members of the cucurbits family, along with squash, melons, and cucumbers. Cucurbits produce separate male and female flowers. The male flowers produce large, sticky, yellow pollen that is not easily transferred by wind. The most effective pollinators for cucurbits are bees. Encourage native and honey bees in your yard by not spraying insecticides and by planting other nectar-producing plants. If you are in an urban area and have not seen many bees working your plants, try hand pollination. First distinguish male flowers from female flowers: Both have yellow petals, but female flowers have a tiny fruit at their base. Use an artist's brush to collect some pollen from the stamen of a male plant, or remove the male flower, pull off the petals to expose the **stamen**, and place the pollen from the stamen or from your brush directly on the stigma of the female plant. It is best to try this technique early in the morning. It is important to use freshly opened flowers as they are only receptive for one day.

Further Reading

Adams, William D., and Thomas LeRoy. *The Southern Kitchen Garden: Vegetables, Fruits, Herbs and Flowers Essential for the Southern Cook.* Lanham, Maryland: Taylor Trade Publishing, 2007. Print.

Coleman, Eliot. *The Winter Harvest Handbook: Year Round Vegetable Production Using Deep Organic Techniques and Unheated Greenhouses.* White River Junction, Vermont: Chelsea Green Publishing Company, 2009. Print.

Harrington, Geri. *Growing Chinese Vegetables in Your Own Backyard.* North Adams, Massachusetts: Storey Publishing, 2009. Print.

Kemble, J. M, ed. *Southeastern U.S. 2014 Vegetable Crop Handbook.* Lincolnshire, Illinois: Vance Publishing Corporation, 2014. PDF file. Publication AREC-63NP.

Kowalchik, Claire and William H. Hylton, eds. *Rodale's Illustrated Encyclopedia of Herbs.* 1987. Emmaus, Pennsylvania: Rodale Press, Inc., 1998. Print.

Maynard, Donald N., and George J. Hochmuth. *Knott's Handbook for Vegetable Growers.* 5th ed. Hoboken, New Jersey: John Wiley & Sons, Inc., 2007. Print.

Raymond, Dick. *Garden Way's Joy of Gardening.* North Adams, Massachusetts: Storey Publishing, 1982. Print.

Rogers, Marilyn K, ed. *All about Vegetables.* Des Moines, Iowa: Meredith Books, 1999. Print.

Rubatzky, Vincent E., and Mas Yamaguchi. *World Vegetables: Principles, Production, and Nutritive Values.* 2nd ed. New York: Chapman & Hall, 1997. Print.

Specialty and Minor Crops Handbook. 2nd ed. Davis, California: University of California Division of Agriculture and Natural Resources, 1998. Print.

Van Wyk, Ben-Erik. *Food Plants of the World: An Illustrated Guide.* Portland, Oregon: Timber Press, Inc., 2005. Print.

Wallace, Ira. *The Timber Press Guide to Vegetable Gardening in the Southeast.* Portland, Oregon: Timber Press, Inc., 2013. Print.

16

For More Information

http://go.ncsu.edu/fmi_vegetablegardening

Contributors

Author: Christopher Gunter, Associate Professor and Extension Specialist, Department of Horticultural Science

Contributions by Extension Agents: Lisa Rayburn, Donna Teasley, Julie Flowers, Danny Lauderdale, Silas Brown

Contributions by Extension Master Gardeners: Deborah Green, Margaret Genkins, Barbara Goodman, Jacquelyn Weedon, Karen Damari, Connie Schultz, Judith Bates, Chris Alberti, Brook Williams, Karen Jevsevar, Kim Curlee, Caro Dosé

Content Editors: Lucy Bradley, Professor and Extension Specialist, Urban Horticulture, NC State University; Director, NC State Extension Master Gardener program;
Kathleen Moore, Urban Horticulturist

Copy Editor: Barbara Scott, Debbi Braswell

Chapter 16 Cover Photo: Cody Maureen, Flickr CC BY - 2.0

Based in part on text from the 1998 Extension Master Gardener manual prepared by:
Larry Bass, Extension Specialist, Department of Horticultural Science
Erv Evans, Extension Associate, Department of Horticultural Science
Ken Sorensen, Extension Specialist, Department of Entomology
Doug Saunders, Extension Specialist, Department of Horticultural Science
Jeanine Davis, Extension Specialist, Department of Horticultural Science
Frank Louws, Extension Specialist, Department of Plant Pathology

How to Cite This Chapter:
Gunter, C. 2022. Vegetable Gardening, Chpt 16. In: K.A. Moore, L.K. Bradley (eds). *North Carolina Extension Gardener Handbook,* 2nd ed. NC State Extension, Raleigh, NC. <https://content.ces.ncsu.edu/extension-gardener-handbook/16-vegetable-gardening>

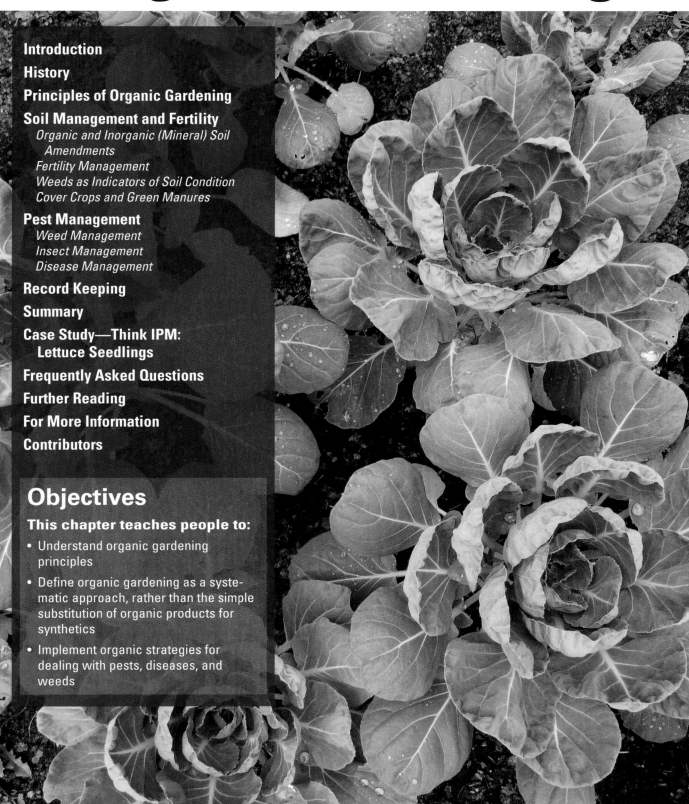

Organic Gardening

Objectives

This chapter teaches people to:

- Understand organic gardening principles

- Define organic gardening as a systematic approach, rather than the simple substitution of organic products for synthetics

- Implement organic strategies for dealing with pests, diseases, and weeds

17

Introduction

Interest in home gardening, sustainable use of natural resources, and organic practices continues to rise with increasing concern about the health and safety of families, pets, and the environment. Generally, organic gardeners focus on practices that enhance soil health and plant nutrition, as well as suppress weeds. Organic gardeners manage weeds and other pests (including disease organisms) without the use of synthetic fertilizers or pesticides. Organic and conventional gardening share many similarities, so other chapters in this manual provide more in-depth information on many of the topics included here.

The definition of organic methods varies because there is no organic gardening standard for home gardens. Certified organic farmers must meet the U.S. Department of Agriculture's National Organic Program (NOP) Organic Standards and use the National List of Allowed and Prohibited Substances. The Organic Materials Review Institute (OMRI) is a nonprofit organization that provides professional, independent reviews of materials and processes for suitability in organic food and fiber production (Figure 17–1). Home gardeners can consult the *OMRI Products List* © to find products that OMRI has determined are allowed for use under NOP organic standards.

Figure 17–1. OMRI's logo.

Figure 17–2. An organic vegetable garden that is just as productive as a conventionally grown garden.
NC.Hort, Flickr

History

Organic gardening began in 1940s wartime England when Lord Walter Northbourne coined the phrase "organic farming" in his book, *Look to the Land*. Publication of Sir Albert Howard's *An Agricultural Testament* and Lady Eve Balfour's *The Living Soil* during the same decade inspired J.I. Rodale, who popularized organic gardening in the United States (Figure 17–2). Rodale's books and magazines promoted the theory that we must restore and protect soil health to preserve and improve human health.

In 1962, Rachel Carson's book *Silent Spring* increased public awareness of the impact of pesticides such as DDT on nontargeted organisms, including birds, fish, mammals, and beneficial insects. During the 1970s and 1980s, increasing concerns about industrial agricultural practices led to interest in "alternative agriculture." By the end of the 1980s, the phrase "sustainable agriculture" came into popular use to describe a movement to restore the ecology in socially responsible, economically viable ways.

Principles of Organic Gardening

Organic gardeners generally subscribe to the following principles, each of which will be discussed in greater detail in subsequent sections of this chapter:

- A strong emphasis on building healthy garden soil, which has a diverse microbial population, adequate organic matter, proper pH, and good fertility
- Building a nutrient reservoir into the soil, as opposed to relying heavily on fertilizer applications
- A holistic approach to pest management
- Use of only naturally-derived fertilizers and pest control products, and using them sparingly

Soil Management and Fertility

Rather than a traditional approach of applying fertilizers to feed plants, the foundation of successful organic gardening is building healthy soils. Healthy organic garden soils have a strong nutrient reservoir and proper pH for plant growth, which are provided by adding organic matter rather than traditional fertilizers. Refer to chapter 1, "Soils and Plant Nutrients," and chapter 2, "Composting," for more in-depth information.

Organic and Inorganic (Mineral) Soil Amendments

Soil amendments are used to improve soil health and condition. Incorporating organic matter into tight clay, for example, lowers soil bulk density, creates pore spaces for air and water, and improves soil structure and tilth, allowing expansion of roots. Adding organic matter to sandy soil improves water-holding and nutrient-holding capacity, feeds soil microbes, and improves soil structure.

In the warmer North Carolina piedmont and coastal plain, higher temperatures lead to faster rates of decomposition, and soils can require up to twice as much organic material compared to cooler environments. If practical, it is a good idea to mulch areas after adding organic matter. Mulch is material layered over the soil surface to reduce evaporation and keep roots cool. Mulch also reduces weed emergence, soil compaction, and erosion. In the case of plant-based mulches, the addition of mulch further contributes to soil organic matter content.

Many organic and inorganic, or mineral, materials increase a soil's pore space or improve water-holding capacity. Most of the amendments listed in Table 17–1 will improve a clay or sandy soil. Peat and sand, however, are two amendments that warrant caution. As the product of wetland ecosystems, sphagnum peat and sedge peat are not renewable at the current rate harvested to satisfy horticultural market demands. Coir dust, derived from coconut husks, may be a more sustainable alternative to peat, and more consistent in pH and quality (Figure 17–3). Coir dust performs better in light, sandy soils where its moisture retention qualities are appreciated. Like peat, however, coir may overwhelm clay soils, making a saturated native soil even stickier.

Heavy clay soils always benefit from the addition of compost. Fine sand is not recommended as a clay conditioner because small clay particles mixing with fine sand particles cause compaction and a loss of aeration, resulting in a concrete-like soil. For heavy clay, rocky, poorly drained, or contaminated soils, create raised beds.

Figure 17–3. Coconut husk coir can be used as a soil amendment as a replacement for sphagnum peat moss.
Matis Miika, Flickr CC BY - 3.0

Herbicide Carryover

Some gardeners have seen damage to their plants or crops after the application of hay, manure, compost, or grass clippings. This is due in part to the persistence of some herbicides that were used on the plant materials before they became **mulch**. It is important to know the source and chemical history of any green material before it is used in the garden. Learn more in the NC State Extension publication *Herbicide Carryover in Hay, Manure, Compost, and Grass Clippings*.

17

Table 17–1. Soil Amendments and Mulch [a]

Organic

Chopped straw	Green manures	Vermicompost	Leaf mulch
Composted fruit wastes	Municipal compost	Composted kitchen scraps	Peanut hulls
Composted manure	Pecan hulls	Composted sawdust	Coir dust
Composted seaweed	Pine straw	Composted wood chips	Corn cobs
Shredded newspaper	Cotton gin compost	Pine bark (¼"-½" pieces)	Yard waste

Mineral

Medium or coarse sand	Gravel (pea-sized)	Gypsum	Perlite
Vermiculite	Agricultural-grade expanded shale		

[a] Starbuck, Christopher J. 2008. *Mulches*. G6960. Columbia, MO: University of Missouri Extension.

Fertility Management

Rather than relying primarily on applied fertilizers, many organic gardeners seek to build a nutrient reservoir in the soil through the periodic addition of organic soil amendments and the use of **green manures** (cover crops that are incorporated back into the bed). As with any gardening project, start with a soil analysis to determine initial nutrient and pH levels, and monitor with follow-up sampling at least every three years.

Organic Fertilizers

Use organic materials listed in Table 17–2 to address soil test recommendations. Note that some materials are not allowed by OMRI for use as crop fertilizers, but may be considered for household use. Nutrients listed are averages. Because nutrient composition of animal manures and composts vary widely, send a sample to the NC Department of Agriculture & Consumer Services, Agronomic Division, for nutrient analysis before use.

Weeds as Indicators of Soil Condition

As you refine your observation skills regarding soil type and quality, you may be able to identify soil conditions and estimate soil pH by the plants growing in it. Weed seeds prosper in niches with the light, water, and soil conditions that each weed prefers. The presence of some weeds can indicate certain soil conditions (Figure 17–4). Table 17–3 includes information on some weeds' preferred soil conditions.

Figure 17–4. This compacted soil is a favorite of broadleaf plantain.
Kathleen Moore, CC BY - 2.0

Cover Crops and Green Manures

Cover crops, or green manures, are plants grown specifically for incorporation into the soil to improve fertility and add organic matter, which in turn improves soil structure. Cover crops reduce erosion, suppress weeds, and aerate compacted soils. It is common to combine cover crops such as rye and vetch in the winter with soybean and pearl millet in the summer (Figure 17–5). Examples of common cover crops are found in Tables 17–4 and 17–5.

Figure 17–5. A cover crop of clover in this vegetable garden provides nutrients to the soil when it is tilled under.
Graibeard, Flickr CC BY-SA - 4.0

17

Table 17–2. Organic Fertilizers [abc]

Items below are generally acceptable under the NOP for commercial organic farmers, unless otherwise noted.

Fertilizer	Primary Benefit	Average Analysis	Notes
Alfalfa meal	Organic matter	5–1–2	Contains triacontanol, a natural fatty acid growth stimulant, and trace minerals.
Algae	Organic matter	N/A	Includes photosynthetic organisms of the Kingdom Protista typically found in aquatic or shoreline environments. Algae do not have true roots, stems, or leaves. Organic Materials Review Institute (OMRI) approved.
Amino acid (nonsynthetic)	Chelating agent	N/A	A chelating agent improves plant uptake of a nutrient. Also used as a plant growth regulator.
Ash	Liming effect, source of calcium, micronutrients	25% calcium carbonate; 9% potash	Ash from plant or animal sources only. Ashes from burning minerals, manure, or other substances are prohibited.
Basalt dust	Micronutrients	N/A	Improves cation exchange capacity.
Blood meal (dried)	Nitrogen	10–0–0	Dried blood collected from slaughtered animals. One of the highest non-synthetic forms of nitrogen. Over-application can burn plants with too much ammonia.
Bone meal (steamed)	Phosphate	3–15–0; 20% total phosphate; 24% calcium	Ground animal bones that have been steamed under pressure, heated, or rendered sterile. Bone meal phosphorus is only plant-available in soils lower than pH 7. Widely available at feed stores.
Borax	Trace minerals	10% boron	Also known as sodium tetraborate.
Calcitic limestone	Calcium	65%–80% calcium carbonate	Mined calcium carbonate.
Coffee grounds	Nitrogen	2–0.3–0.2	Acid-forming soil amendment. Needs limestone supplement.
Colloidal phosphate	Phosphate	0–2–2	
Compost (commercial or homemade)	Organic matter	Varies with components added	The product of a managed process through which microorganisms break down plant and animal materials into plant-available soil nutrients. Composted materials produced in vessels or static aerated piles must be maintained at a temperature between 131° F to 170° F for three days. Windrow systems must maintain at the above temperature for 15 days and turned at least five times. NCDA&CS waste analysis recommended if fertilizer content unknown.
Corn gluten meal	Nitrogen	9–0–0	Allelopathic properties may inhibit seed germination for one to four months, however there is no danger to established or transplanted plants; can reduce weed seed germination. Cannot come from genetically modified corn.
Cottonseed meal	Nitrogen	6–4–1.5	Cannot come from genetically modified cotton. Must be free of prohibited pesticide residues.

17

Table 17–2. Organic Fertilizers *continued*

Cotton gin trash	Nitrogen, phosphorus, potash	14–10.5–41	Cannot come from genetically modified cotton. Must be free from prohibited residues.
Dolomite (mined or fired)	Balancer, calcium, magnesium	51% calcium carbonate; 40% magnesium carbonate	May cause buildup of magnesium.
Eggshell meal	Calcium	1.2–0.4–0.1	Contains trace minerals.
Elemental sulfur	Balancer, nutrient	99.5% sulfur	Used as a fertilizer and soil amendment. Not plant-available until soil bacteria oxidize it to the sulfate form. OMRI restricts use, but does not prohibit.
Epsom salts	Balancer, magnesium	10% magnesium; 13% sulfur	Also known as mined magnesium sulfate or kieserite.
Feather meal	Nitrogen	11–0–0	Slow-release nitrogen source.
Fish emulsion	Nitrogen	5–2–2	Contains 5% sulfur. Foul odor. Emulsions are soluble liquid fertilizers.
Fish meal	Nitrogen	10–6–2	Ground and heated dried fish waste. Includes cannery waste and pomaces.
Fish powder	Nitrogen	12–0.25–1	Heat-dried into a water-soluble powder. Can be injected into an irrigation system for immediate to 1-month release.
Fur	Nitrogen	12–0–0	
Granite dust	Potash	4% potash	Contains 67% silicas and 19 trace minerals. Cannot use sources mixed with petroleum products such as from stone engraving.
Greensand	Potash	7% total potash	Glauconite. Contains trace minerals.
Gypsum, mined	Calcium, balancer	22% calcium; 17% sulfur	Also known as calcium sulfate. Do not apply for pH < 5.8. OMRI-approved, but prohibits Gypsum produced as a manufacturing byproduct.
Hair	Nitrogen	12%–16% nitrogen	
Hoof and horn meal	Nitrogen	12–2–0	Slow-release nitrogen source.
Horse manure	Organic matter	1.7–0.7–1.8	Be sure that manure is composted when applied to plants for human consumption to prevent burning plants and cross-contamination of edible portions by pathogens. OMRI restricts, but does not prohibit, animal manure.
Kelp meal	Potash	1.5–0.5–2.5; trace minerals	Dried marine algae derived from the botanical divisions of Rhodophyta (red algae), Phaeophyta (brown algae), and Chlorophyta (green algae). Combined with fishmeal to provide NPK.

Table 17–2. Organic Fertilizers *continued*

Fertilizer	Primary Benefit	Average Analysis	Notes
Leaf mulch	Organic matter	0.5–0.1–0.5	Uncomposted plant material.
Magnesium rock	Magnesium	32%–35% magnesium	Mined substance.
Milk	Nitrogen	0.5–0.3–0.2	Dry and liquid forms.
Oyster shells	Calcium	33.5% calcium	Also known as oyster shell lime from ground shells.
Peanut meal	Nitrogen	7.2–1.5–1.2	
Peat moss	Organic matter	pH range 3.0–4.5	Use around acid-loving plants. Must not contain synthetic wetting agents.
Potassium sulfate	Potassium, sulfur	22% potash; 23% sulfate	Langbeinite or non-synthetic sources.
Poultry manure	Organic matter	4–4–2	Be sure that manure is composted when applied to plants for human consumption to prevent burning plants and cross-contamination of edible portions by pathogens.
Rabbit manure	Organic matter	1.5–1–1	Be sure that manure is composted when applied to plants for human consumption to prevent burning plants and cross-contamination of edible portions by pathogens.
Rock phosphate	Phosphate	0–3–0	Source of slow-release phosphate. Contains trace minerals and 32% calcium.
Sawdust (untreated)	Organic matter	0.2–0–0.2	Be sure sawdust is well composted before incorporating. Untreated, unpainted wood only.
Sheep manure	Organic matter	4–1.4–3.5	Be sure that manure is composted when applied to plants for human consumption to prevent burning plants and cross-contamination of edible portions by pathogens.
Soybean meal	Nitrogen	7–0.5–2.3	Not OMRI approved.
Straw	Nitrogen, potash	0.2–0–0.2	May be from nonorganic sources. Must be from non-genetically modified plants.
Sulfur	Sulfur	50%–100% sulfur	Can be used to lower pH. Elemental sulfur.
Sul-Po-Mag	Potash, magnesium	0–0–22; 11% magnesium; 22% sulfur	Do not use if applying dolomitic limestone. Substitute greensand or other potassium source. Sul-Po-Mag from langbeinite or other nonsynthetic mineral sources.
Wood ashes	Potash, micronutrients	0–2–6	Do not use ash from colored paper, plastic, or other prohibited materials. Ashes derived from coal, cardboard, household trash, or stained, painted or treated woods contain elements toxic to plant growth. Do not use ash on acid-loving plants or tender seedlings[d.] Apply no more than 20 lbs. per 100 square feet annually. May be used to temporarily repel slugs and snails[e.]
Wood chips	Phosphorus	0–0.4–0.2	From untreated, unpainted materials.

17

Table 17–2. Organic Fertilizers *continued*

Fertilizer	Primary Benefit	Average Analysis	Notes
Worm castings	Organic matter	0.5–0.5–0.3	50% organic matter, plus trace minerals. Must be made from feedstock; no raw manure feedstock or synthetic feedstock.[f]

[a] Zublena, J. P., J. V. Baird, and J. P. Lilly. 1991. *SoilFacts: Nutrient content of fertilizer and organic materials* (AG-439-18). Raleigh, NC: North Carolina Cooperative Extension Service.

[b] Carr, P. M., G. R. Carlson, J. S. Jacobsen, G. A. Nielson, and E. O. Skogley. 1991. "Farming soils, not fields: A strategy for increasing fertilizer profitability." *Journal of Production Agriculture*, 4(1): 57-61. Madison, WI: American Society of Agronomy, Crop Science Society of America, Soil Science Society of America.

[c] Items listed are generally acceptable under the National Organic Program for commercial organic farmers, unless otherwise noted.

[d] Herring, Peg. 2011 Jan 1. *Use caution with wood ash on your lawn and garden.* Corvallis, OR: Oregon State University Extension Service.

[e] Lerner, B. Rosie. 2006, April 10. *Wood ash in the garden.* LaFayette, IN: Purdue University Consumer Horticulture, Department of Horticulture and Landscape Architecture.

[f] For information regarding other benefits of worm castings, see the NC State University website for vermicomposting in North Carolina.

Table 17–3. Soil Indicator Weeds

Soil Condition	Weeds
Dry soil	Prostrate and spotted spurge, black medic, yellow woodsorrel, goosegrass, mustards, annual lespedeza, birdsfoot trefoil, prostrate knotweed, bracted plantain, silvery cinquefoil, yarrow
Wet soil	Moneywort, annual bluegrass, alligatorweed, pearlwort, moss, liverwort, rushes, sedges, plantains, oxeye daisy, meadowsweet, docks, coltsfoot, kyllinga, goosegrass, algae, henbit, woodsorrel, dollarweed
Compacted or clay soil	Annual bluegrass, annual sedge, annual lespedeza, broadleaf plantain, corn speedwell, goosegrass, prostrate knotweed, prostrate and spotted spurge, common sow thistle, quackgrass, plantain, pennycress, mustards, dandelion, coltsfoot, chickweed
Light or sandy soil	Common sheep sorrel, horsetail, field bindweed, sandspur, poorjoe, quackgrass
Low fertility	Birdsfoot trefoil, broomsedge, hawkweed, moss, legumes (clover spp., chickweed, speedwell spp., black medic, chicory), bitter sneezeweed, crabgrass, common mullein, yarrow
High fertility	Annual bluegrass, chickweed, ryegrass, pigweed, lamb's quarter, moss
Acid soil	Silvery cinquefoil, common sheep sorrel, red sorrel, plantain, oxeye daisy, nettles, common mullein, moss, knotweed, horsetail, docks, coltsfoot
Alkaline soil	Pennycress, broad plantain
Saline soil	Shepherd's purse
Plant-parasitic nematodes	Prostrate knotweed, spotted spurge, Florida pusley, sedges

17

Table 17–4. Winter Cover Crops for North Carolina (Evans, 2012; Hamilton, 2005)

Crop	Planting and Growth	Seeding Rate	Comments
Austrian winter pea (legume)	Sow Sept – Oct	1 lb. per 1,000 ft^2	Grows well in combination with oats, barley, rye, or wheat. Decomposes quickly, therefore not a good choice as surface mulch. Unreliable growth in western half of NC.
Barley	Sow Aug – Oct	4 – 6 lb. per 1,000 ft^2	Typically planted as a smother crop to supress winter annuals.
Crimson clover (legume)	Sow Sept – Nov	½ – 1 lb. per 1,000 ft^2	Can be seeded into fall vegetable crops.
Rye	Sow Sept – Oct	2 – 3 lb. per 1,000 ft^2	Good nitrogen scavenger.
Ryegrass	Sow Sept – Nov	1 lb. per 1,000 ft^2	High water and nitrogen needs.
Triticale	Mid Aug – Early Dec	2.5 lb. per 1,000 ft^2	Can be grown earlier than wheat to produce more winter growth.
Hairy vetch	Sow Sept – Nov	12 oz. per 1,000 ft^2	Does well planted in combination with grasses. Easily killed in mid-bloom by mowing.
Wheat	Late Sept – Early Dec	2.75 lb. per 1,000 ft^2	Can also be seeded in April to be incorporated as a green manure.

Table 17–5. Summer Cover Crops for North Carolina (Evans, 2012; Hamilton, 2005)

Crop	Planting and Growth	Seeding Rate	Comments
Buckwheat	Spring, summer, fall *Seed formation four to six weeks*	1.5 lb. per 1,000 ft^2	Frost sensitive. Effective phosphorus scavenger. Decomposes rapidly. Do not allow to go to seed.
German (foxtail) millet	Mid May – Aug. *Seed formation 75 – 90 days*	11 oz. per 1,000 ft^2	Small-seeded grass crop. Best if planted in stale seedbed. Avoid coarse sands.
Japanese millet	April to July *Seed formation around 45 days*	11 oz. per 1,000 ft^2	Rapid growth. Does not perform well in sandy soils.
Oats	Spring and Fall	3 – 4 lb. per 1,000 ft^2	Provides rapid groundcover. Fall planted oats will be winter killed.
Pearl millet	April – July *Seed formation around 60 – 70 days*	11 oz. per 1,000 ft^2	Summer annual bunchgrass. Grows well in sandy loam or poor, sandy soils.
Sorghum-Sudangrass	Mid May – July *Frequent mowing prevents seeding*	1 lb. per 1,000 ft^2	Plant in mixtures to support climbing legumes like velvetbean. Scavenges nitrogen. Mowing at 3" promotes root growth.
Southern peas (legume)	May – Aug. *Seed formation around 60 days*	2 – 4 lb. per 1,000 ft^2	Also known as cowpeas, blackeye, and crowder peas. Wide soil and drought tolerance.
Soybeans (legume)	April – June *Seed formation around 90 days*	2 lb. per 1,000 ft^2	Will grow on nearly all soils. Late-maturing varieties generate more biomass and fix more nitrogen. Inexpensive choice.
Velvetbean (legume)	May – June *Seed formation around 100 days*	1 lb. per 1,000 ft2	Does well in poor, sandy soils. Can be planted with sorghum-sudangrass. Good green manure crop.

Pest Management

Organic gardeners rely on methods other than synthetic pesticides to manage weed, insect, and disease pests. Organic gardening, however, is more than simply substituting a naturally derived pesticide for a synthetic one. Organic gardeners must take a holistic approach to pest management and focus on using all available methods to support plant health, including good fertility, proper irrigation, crop rotation, conserving beneficial insects, and mulching. This approach requires the extensive use of integrated pest management strategies (refer to chapter 8, "IPM," for more information). Even those who do not strictly follow organic gardening practices benefit from following this holistic approach. Organic pesticides should be handled with the same care and caution as synthetic pesticides because even naturally derived products may pose risks to health and the environment.

Weed Management

Weeds are a mixed aspect of the landscape. Weeds compete with desirable plants for water, nutrients, and sunlight. Some harbor insect pests and diseases, cause allergies, or are poisonous. Nevertheless, weeds also make many positive contributions. Weeds are indicators of soil problems, such as compaction. Weeds return nutrients to the soil when pulled and composted, and weed roots can help break up compacted soil. Weeds provide habitat, shelter, pollen, and nectar for beneficial organisms, such as spiders (Figure 17–6), praying mantises (Figure 17–7), beetles (Figure 17–8), predatory wasps (Figure 17–9), syrphid flies (Figure 17–10), and bees (Figure 17–11). Many weeds are edible, such as the greens from chickweed, cress, dandelion, lamb's quarters, mustard, and purslane. Some weeds serve as "**trap crops**" that lure insect pests away from desirable plants (Figure 17–12). It may be advantageous to permit certain weeds during the season, but prevent them from going to seed. As you learn more about the different weed species and the benefits of having some weeds in your garden, you may even learn to regard some of them as allies to promote soil and plant health. Weed management is most effective if you know what species of weed you are fighting and how it spreads, so proper identification is important. See chapter 6, "Weeds," for further information on identification and management strategies.

Tillage and Mechanical Management

Repeated cultivation with hand tools or powered tillage equipment is very effective on many annuals and biennial weeds, but less so on many perennial weeds. Many perennial weeds have underground structures such as tubers and **rhizomes** that allow the weeds to regrow (Figure 17–13). Such structures are easily spread to new areas if tillage equipment is not cleaned after use. Most perennial weeds are well-managed in small gardens, ornamental beds, and turf by hand-pulling or digging the roots out and removing new sprouts. Larger areas may require hoe or rotary cultivation. Take care when using these tools to avoid damaging the roots of nearby desirable plants.

Cultivation is best done one or two days after watering when the soil is still damp, but not wet. Working wet soil degrades soil structure, especially that of heavy soils. When the soil is too dry, weeds are hard to pull and hoeing is difficult. Weeds that have been pulled, but have not yet gone to seed, can be used to return organic matter to the soil. Hand-pulled weeds may be laid on top of the soil to dry out, with the exception of rhizomatous grasses, such as Kentucky bluegrass, Canada bluegrass, and creeping red fescue. Succulent weeds, such as purslane, and weeds that have gone to seed, which may inadvertently reestablish, should be completely removed from the garden. Reducing weed growth in the surrounding yard by mowing or other means also helps prevent the spread of weeds in the garden.

Hand-pulling

Pulling weeds by hand is a necessary part of maintaining any garden, organic or not. As with tillage, pulling weeds is easiest when the soil is slightly moist and when the weeds are young and small. Scouting beds on a weekly basis makes this routine chore easier.

Mulch

Organic mulch prevents most annual weeds. Applied annually in late winter before deciduous plants leaf out and before summer annual weeds germinate, mulch covers winter weeds, suppresses germination of summer annual weeds, holds soil moisture, and improves aesthetics. For best results, remove existing weeds before applying the mulch.

Select the type of mulch based on availability, cost, aesthetics, and personal preference. Examples include shredded hardwood, pine straw, pine bark, and cedar. Maximum weed management benefits can be seen with 3 inches to 4 inches of organic mulch. In general, 1 cubic yard covers 100 square feet to a depth of 3 inches.

These are suggested mulch depths:
- 3 inches for woody and perennial landscape beds
- About 1 inch of mulch on annual color beds—just enough to cover the surface

Materials such as newspaper or cardboard that are covered with an attractive mulch (such as pine bark, shredded hardwood, or pine straw) provide excellent weed suppression (Figure 17–14). Some gardeners use living grass as a weed barrier between raised beds. Fescue works well because it does not spread into adjacent beds (Figure 17–15).

Figure 17–6. A spider on a stinging nettle (*Urtica dioica*) leaf. Spiders prey on many insects in the garden.

Kathleen Moore, CC BY - 2.0

Figure 17–7. A praying mantis on an amaranth (*Amaranthus* sp). Mantises are ambush predators that eat crickets, grasshoppers, and frogs.

Nikolaj Potanin, Flickr CC BY-SA - 4.0

Figure 17–8. A soldier beetle on a Japanese knotweed (*Reynoutria japonica*) leaf. Soldier beetle larvae eat eggs and larvae of other beetles, moths, and other insects while adult beetles feed on aphids and other soft-bodied insects.

Cheryl Moorehead, Flickr CC BY - 2.0

Figure 17–9. A braconid wasp on rambling dock. Braconid wasps are parasitoids or parasites that kill their hosts, which include aphids, beetles, caterpillars, squashbugs, and stinkbugs

John Tann, Flickr CC BY - 2.0

Figure 17–10. A syrphid fly, resting on a thistle blossom. Syrphid fly larvae feed on aphids, scales, thrips, and caterpillars, while the adults are important pollinators.

Shenandoah National Park, Flickr CC0

Figure 17–11. A bumblebee pollinating a creeping Charlie weed (*Pilea nummulariifolia*).

Bob Peterson, Flickr CC BY - 2.0

17

Figure 17–12. A trap crop—goldenrod (*Solidago* sp.)—is attracting aphids so they stay away from garden vegetables.
rockerBoo, Flickr CC BY-SA - 2.0

Figure 17–13. Nettles (*Urtica dioica*) spread via its creeping, connected roots called rhizomes.
Rasbak, Wikimedia CC BY-SA - 4.0

Cover Crops

Planting cover crops, also called **green manures**, is another effective strategy for weed management (Table 17–4). Oats, a widely grown cereal grass, is a winter cover crop (Table 17–5) that does not pose a weed problem upon maturation (Figure 17–16). Left over the winter, winter-killed oat grass creates a thick mat of mulch that prevents soil erosion and suppresses late-fall and early-spring weeds. Rye is a good winter cover crop for late-season plantings. Rye typically establishes better than wheat and is thought to be **allelopathic**, inhibiting the growth of other plant species.

Green manures are also used as **living mulches**, meaning that they are planted among crops where they help to fill the open spaces, reduce weeds and erosion, and conserve water. For example, late-season broccoli benefits from underseeding with a winter-hardy legume like hairy vetch. To do this, maintain a weedfree seedbed for one month after the broccoli is planted by cultivating or pulling weeds in and between rows, being careful not to disturb the roots of your garden plants. When plants are 6 inches to 8 inches tall, spread the mulch crop seed over the entire area. By the time the broccoli is ready for

harvest, the vetch can be walked on without being damaged. Turn under the vetch several weeks before planting the following spring so that the vetch does not go to seed and become a weed itself.

Figure 17–14. Cardboard laid down before mulch is used to suppress weeds.
Kathleen Moore, CC BY - 2.0

Figure 17–15. Fescue grass works well planted between garden beds because it does not spread.
Kathleen Moore, CC BY - 2.0

Figure 17–16. Oats (*Avena sativa*) are sown in February or March. After the corn is harvested in June the oats grow as a cover crop until the next planting season.
Allan Manson, Wikimedia CC BY-SA - 4.0

Thermal

Thermal weed management, using either flame weeders or hot water, is most effective on young broadleaf weeds that are 1 inch to 2 inches tall. Perennial weeds and grasses may require repeat treatments. Hand-held propane gas burners, which produce a carefully controlled and directed flame, sear leaves, causing the plant to wilt and die (Figure 17–17). High temperature water or steam eliminates the hazard of flame application. It is possible for hot water to infiltrate to the roots or move across the soil surface, so only use it in open areas where there is less contact with roots and crowns of desirable plants.

Figure 17–17. A hand-held propane gas burner used for weed management in a gravel driveway. Exercise caution and always carry a bucket of water.
Kathleen Moore, CC BY - 2.0

Spacing

Spacing of vegetable garden plants is an effective weed suppression tool. Establish transplants or plant seeds close together so that a foliar canopy quickly develops (Figure 17–18). This shades the soil and prevents the growth of many weed seedlings, giving crop plants a head start. As vegetable plants become larger and require more room, they can be thinned to maintain the canopy and plant health. Note that excessively close spacing reduces yields and increases insect and disease pressure.

Organic Herbicides

Vinegar (acetic acid), salts of fatty acids, the soap-based herbicide ammonium nonanoate, lemongrass oil, eugenol oil (clove oil), cinnamon oil, and corn gluten are examples of chemical organic weed managment.

Figure 17–18. These Brussels sprouts were planted close together so their canopy shades out weeds.
Kathleen Moore, CC BY - 2.0

Insect Management

Organic pest management places an emphasis on biodiversity and optimal growing conditions to build the garden's natural resistance to pests. Enhancing habitat attracts and sustains beneficial organisms in the garden. Pest problems in the garden and landscape may indicate less than optimal growing conditions or an ecological imbalance. However, some familiar pathogens, such as tomato early blight (Figure 17–19), that spread by insects, irrigation, or garden tools, may always be a threat in North Carolina.

See chapter 8, "IPM," for more information.

17

Figure 17–19. Tomato early blight is caused by a fungus, *Alternaria solani*, that overwinters in the soil.
Dwight Sipler, Flickr CC BY - 2.0

Ways That Home Gardeners Deviate from the NOP Rules for Commercial Production and Sales

Although commercial growers who wish to sell produce labeled as "organic" are under strict guidelines and require third-party certification, home gardeners are not regulated and have more flexibility. For example, most home gardeners do not keep the extensive records that commercial organic growers must maintain.

Here are some other differences between certified commercial organic growers and home organic gardeners:

Seed purchases. The NOP requires organic farmers to purchase organic seed when available (Figure 17–20). There is no evidence that organic seed is any better than conventional seed. The current rules probably originated as a way to support the organic industry. So some gardeners buy nonorganic seed. Gardeners should make sure, however, that the seed has not undergone synthetic seed treatment or been pelletized with nonapproved seed coats.

Transplant purchases. The NOP requires commercial farmers to purchase or grow certified organic transplants. This insures that no synthetic pesticides, synthetic fertilizer, or unapproved wetting agent comes in contact with the transplant. (Although unapproved, the wetting agent frequently used is a product of the yucca plant and is acceptable to some gardeners.) Organic transplants are sometimes hard for home gardeners to find and can be expensive. Some transplants may have been grown without synthetic pesticides, fertilizers, or wetting agents, but simply have not been certified.

Manures. The NOP requires manure on organic farms to be applied no later than 120 days before harvest. Conventional farms require only 90 days between manure application and crop harvest to reduce pathogens. There is no scientific support for the 120 days, and that length of time may have been chosen simply because it was longer than the length of time used by conventional growers. A 90-day period between manure application and crop harvest may be acceptable to some home gardeners.

Compost. The NOP requires compost to meet strict criteria, including temperature guidelines. Home-produced compost does not meet NOP guidelines, but most organic gardeners consider home-produced compost acceptable to use.

Figure 17–20. Organic seed.
Chris Alberti, CC BY - 2.0

Genetically modified organisms. The NOP contains rules prohibiting the use of genetically engineered crops, or materials derived from such crops. Very few genetically engineered crops are available for home gardeners, so this is rarely a consideration in home gardens.

In summary, home organic gardeners are not certified and so are not required to adhere to the NOP guidelines. Many gardeners fall somewhere on the spectrum between conventional gardening and organic gardening.

Take note of the insect pests you have struggled with in the past and concentrate on techniques to manage those. Be aware of recent climatic conditions. For example, Colorado potato beetles may be more numerous after a mild winter (Figure 17–21). Unusually wet springs favor slugs (Figure 17–22), and dry summers favor spider mites.

For more information on insect identification, please refer to chapter 4, "Insects."

Figure 17–21. Colorado potato beetle.
Matt Bertone

Figure 17–22. Wet springs favor slugs.
Kathleen Moore, CC BY - 2.0

The integration of cultural, biological, physical, and chemical management methods help prevent many problems from becoming serious enough to affect plants or yields.

Cultural management

Emphasize plant health. That is the basis for cultural management, which relies on inexpensive measures to prevent infestations. This includes choosing well-adapted cultivars with insect and disease resistance, choosing the proper planting location, planting seeds or transplants during the weak point of a pest's life cycle, and practicing good garden sanitation. Other cultural management strategies include managing soil fertility, cultivating and hand-pulling to manage weeds, and mulching to reduce pests.

Biological Management

Blend natural defenses into your management plan. One example is parasitic wasps, which seek host insects for larval development (Figure 17–23). It is possible to enhance the habitat for beneficial insects so they do much of the pest management for you. Learn more about the beneficial insects you want to attract, the plants they prefer, and their life-cycle needs as they emerge and scout for prey. Be aware that microbial sprays also negatively affect some beneficial insects.

Figure 17–23. A beneficial parasitic wasp laying eggs on a tomato horn worm.
Connie Schultz, CC BY - 2.0

Physical Management

Physical management strategies include basic handpicking (Figure 17–24), water sprays (Figure 17–25), floating row covers (Figure 17–26), tree bands (Figure 17–27), cutworm collars (Figure 17–28), and diatomaceous earth (Figure 17–29). Copper strips (Figure 17–30), sticky traps (Figure 17–31), wrapping fruit in cloth or paper bags (Figure 17–32), wrapping stems in fabric or foil (Figure 17–33), covering fruit in kaolin clay (Figure 17–34), and pheromone traps (Figure 17–35) are other types of physical barriers. Pheromone traps are not effective at significantly reducing larval populations but may be helpful in monitoring movements of adult insects. Place pheromone traps far away from the garden to avoid luring pests into the garden.

Figure 17–24. Hand-picking large insects like caterpillars and throwing them in a bucket of soapy water is an effective physical management technique.
Kathleen Moore, CC BY - 2.0

17

Figure 17–25. A strong spray of water can dislodge many plant pests.

Gloria Polakof, CC BY - 2.0

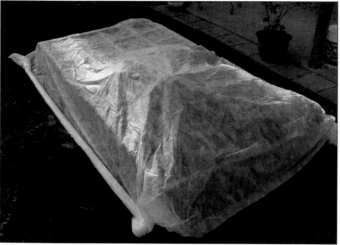

Figure 17–26. A floating row cover can protect crops from flying insects.

Aaron Baugher, CC BY - 2.0

Figure 17–27. Sticky tree bands catch fall cankerworm caterpillars before they can completely defoliate the tree.

Steven Frank

Figure 17–28. Cutworm collars constructed out of foil to protect cabbage seedlings.

Karen Jevsevar, CC BY - 2.0

Figure 17–29. A scanning electron microscope image of diatomaceous earth showing the sharp edges that get in between insects exoskeleton and cause them to dry out and die.

Dawid Siodłak, Wiki Commons CC BY-SA - 4.0

Figure 17–30. Copper tape along beds can keep slugs and snails out.

Kathleen Moore, CC BY - 2.0

Figure 17–31. A sticky trap can help monitor insect populations as well as disrupt the life cycles of certain pests by catching flying or jumping forms. Be aware that sticky traps are indiscriminate. A honey bee flew too close (right).
Kathleen Moore, CC BY - 2.0

Figure 17–34. Kaolin clay on a pear provides a barrier that prevents insect damage and sun burn.
Kathleen Moore, CC BY - 2.0

Figure 17–32. Wrapping fruit in individual cloth bags can be time consuming but worth protecting the fruit from insects, birds, or mammal predators.
Jim Epler, Filckr CC BY - 2.0

Figure 17–35. This trap uses chemicals that mimic insect pheromones and also has a solar-powered light to attract insects.
Scot Nelson, Flickr CC BY - 2.0

Knee hi hose wrapped around stem

Foil wrapped over hose

Figure 17–33. This squash plant has its stem wrapped in nylon stockings and foil to protect from vine borers.
Karen Jevsevar, CC BY - 2.0

17

Chemical management

All pesticides are chemical (whether they are categorized as botanical, inorganic, microbial, or petroleum-based). Chemical controls can be integrated into a management plan if garden pests are out of balance and overwhelming other management options.

There are three categories of approved organic pesticides of *natural origin*:

1. Plant-derived products that contain the active ingredients pyrethrin, rotenone, nicotine, or other botanical chemicals

2. Inorganic products, such as sulfur, copper, diatomaceous earth, kaolin clay, and boric acid

3. Microbial products, such as beneficial nematodes, *Bacillus thuringiensis*, and spinosad

In addition, OMRI lists a select few synthetic pesticide products derived from fatty acids of potassium salts, such as insecticidal soap, and petroleum-based horticultural and dormant oils, used to smother scale and other soft-bodied insects. Horticultural oil in combination with bicarbonate salts, such as baking soda, may also be used to prevent powdery mildew on crops such as cucurbits. Organic pesticides are not necessarily safer than synthetic insecticides, either to the user or the environment. For instance, products containing rotenone or pyrethrins are extremely toxic to fish. Insecticidal soaps are phytotoxic to some crops, and many organic pesticides are harmful to some beneficial insects. All pesticides, natural or synthetic, are toxins designed to kill pests, and should be treated as poisons. Read the label carefully and use the product only as directed.

OMRI

The **Organic Materials Review Institute** (OMRI) is a nonprofit organization that provides independent reviews of products based on organic standards. It provides the results for organic certifiers, growers, manufacturers, and suppliers. If the products pass the review, they are **OMRI Listed**®. OMRI also provides technical support and training for professionals.

Disease Management

Prevention is the key strategy for managing diseases in an organic garden:

- Select disease-free plants and disease-resistant cultivars.
- Select varieties that have been grafted onto disease-resistant rootstock.
- Practice garden sanitation.

- Wash hands after working with soils or plant material.
- Do not transfer garden soil from other gardens.
- Dispose of infected plants.
- Sterilize tools with 10 percent bleach solution.
- Avoid wounding plants. Wounds create entryways for pathogens.
- Maintain vigorous plants.
- Thin plants when they become crowded.
- Practice crop rotation. Rotate crop families so that they are planted in the same plot no more than once every three years.
- Avoid working around wet plants, which favors spread of pathogens.
- Water plants in the morning versus other times of the day.
- Use physical strategies.
- Burn, bury, or dispose of, but do not compost, diseased plant residues.
- Solarize soil.
- Protect plants with row covers.
- Prune and remove diseased plant parts.

Organic fungicides

Occasionally cultural practices are not enough, especially with fungal diseases, and a preventive chemical is necessary. Sulfur, copper sulfate, and lime-sulfur are OMRI allowed for the following fungal diseases: rusts, black spot on roses, and powdery mildew. Bordeaux mixture is not allowed by OMRI because it contains hydrated lime, in addition to copper sulfate.

One tablespoon of baking soda plus 1 tablespoon of summer horticultural oil mixed with a gallon of water prevents the following fungal diseases: black spot, powdery mildew, botrytis, alternaria leaf spot, and many others. The oil acts as a sticker-spreader, or **surfactant**, and can be replaced by insecticidal soap. Mixing the ingredients in higher concentration than recommended may result in leaf scorch. Spray as a preventive every three to five days for best results.

Neem oil prevents fungal infections such as powdery mildew on grapes and cucurbits and black spot on roses, as well as being a miticide and insecticide that kills aphids, white flies, and eggs of other insect pests. Neem does not persist on foliage. Water and sunlight break it down after 100 hours; therefore, it must be reapplied frequently.

Bacillus subtilis, a biofungicide, contains beneficial organisms that attack and control foliar diseases. It suppresses many different diseases on roses, vegetables, fruits, flowering plants, trees, and shrubs.

Record Keeping

Record keeping is critical in evaluating the success or failure of any activity. Garden size, crop rotation, fertilization source and rate, pest management (including insects, diseases, and weeds), and postharvest garden sanitation are all practices to monitor and record throughout the season. See Appendix A, "Garden Journaling," for more information.

Summary

Organic gardeners strive for a biologically balanced ecological system containing diverse insects, microorganisms, animals, and plants. By carefully nurturing the soil environment with proper cultural practices, enhancing biodiversity, and managing problematic weeds, insects, and diseases, organic gardeners maintain thriving and attractive landscapes. These healthy landscapes have a minimized need for the use of synthetic fertilizers and pesticides.

The transition from conventional to organic and sustainable practices includes learning to read the soil environment to identify if a site requires more frequent irrigation, soil amendments, mulching, or other practices. Selecting disease-resistant, climate-adapted cultivars and being aware of appropriate planting times further boost plant health. A final recommendation is to become familiar with common insect pests and diseases for the plants in the garden to stay a step ahead of potential problems.

Gardeners have various levels of commitment when gardening organically. Initially, it may require greater inputs of time to learn how to identify and address the needs of the landscape in new ways. Take time and set reasonable goals to avoid becoming overwhelmed. After a yearly organic maintenance routine is established, a successful and thriving organic garden is the reward.

Crop Rotation

Growing the same crop in the same location year after year not only decreases yields. It sets a gardener up for weed, insect, and disease problems. By establishing a three-year or four-year rotation sequence and diversifying the crop (and the crop family), gardeners can avoid many problems with soil fertility, weeds, insects, and diseases. Rotate crops by the type of food that is produced (such as fruit, root, stem, or leaves). For example, a gardener may choose to rotate a garden bed for four years beginning with tomato (fruit), followed by beets (root), followed by celery (stem), followed by spinach (leaf). Planting cucumbers followed by cantaloupes and then corn would not be a good option because cantaloupes and cucumbers are both in the cucurbit family, and they are also fruit crops. Tomatoes, eggplants, peppers, and potatoes are all in the nightshade family. Rotating beans, or legumes, through a plot naturally adds nitrogen to the soil through nitrogen-fixing bacteria in the legume roots. Keeping a plot fallow for a year can break an insect or disease cycle. Sowing a cover crop is one way to add nutrients to the soil. If cucumber beetles have been a problem in the past year, select another crop family to plant in that spot and plant cucumbers as far away from the original plot as possible. This prevents the adult beetles that overwinter nearby from spreading to the new crop of cucumbers. Read more about crop rotation in the The Center for Environmental Farming Systems publication *Crop Rotation on Organic Farms*.

17

NC.Hort, Flickr

Case Study—Think IPM: Dead Lettuce Seedlings

Your lettuce seedlings have died, and you are wondering what is causing this and if there is anything you can do to prevent it.

Review the five IPM steps summarized in this section and the diagnostic procedures from chapter 7, "Diagnostics:"

1. Monitor and scout to determine pest type and population levels.
2. Accurately identify host and pest.
3. Consider economic or aesthetic injury thresholds. A threshold is the point at which action should be taken.
4. Implement a treatment strategy using physical, cultural, biological, or chemical management, or combine these strategies.
5. Evaluate success of treatments.

1. Monitor and scout to determine pest type and population levels.

You have planted lettuce in this raised bed for the past three years, and it has grown fine. This year, after one week in the ground, all but a few of the seedlings have died. There is no evidence of insects. A sample could be sent to a diagnostic lab to determine which disease might be causing this, but a more cost-effective approach requires digging a little deeper to reach the root of the problem.

2. Accurately identify pest and host.

After looking at the seed packet and reference books and reviewing the Lettuce Horticultural Information Leaflet from NC State, you confirm that you have the Romaine lettuce 'Romulus'. Reading about disease problems with lettuce, you see damping off is a serious fungal disease that affects seedlings.

The following steps and questions from chapter 7, "Diagnostics," will help you accurately identify the problem. Responses are included in italics.

Step 1. Identify the plant: *Romaine lettuce (cultivar 'Romulus').*

Step 2. Describe the problem: *All but about five of my 40 lettuce seedlings have died after a week in the ground. There is a fuzzy whitish mold on the top of the soil in some spots.*

Step 3. Identify what is normal:
What does the healthy part of the plant look like? *The healthy seedlings are bright-green and have held their shape.*

Have you had a soil test? *Yes, and I have amended my garden soil with compost and bone meal.* (For information on how to submit a soil test, see chapter 1, "Soils and Plant Nutrients.")

Step 4. Cultural practices:
Describe the age and history of plant: *The seedlings are a week old. I have planted lettuce in this bed for the past three years.*
Irrigation: *It is watered twice a day for about 5 minutes.*
Fertilizer: *I amended the soil beds before I planted with compost and bone meal.*
Maintenance: *I have been diligent about keeping weeds out of the bed.*

Step 5. Environmental conditions:
Are there any significant water issues? *It has not rained for three and a half weeks, and it has been very hot for the past two months. There is never any standing water when it rains.*
Describe the light near this garden bed. How many hours of sunlight? *This bed gets about 5 hours of full sun a day.*
Describe any recent changes or events: *None that I can think of.*

Step 6. Signs of pathogens:
On the leaves: *No insects are visible; no pathogens are visible on the leaves.*
On the roots: *No insects are visible; no pathogens are visible on the roots.*
On the soil: *There are fuzzy white patches on the soil.*

Step 7. Symptoms of pathogens:
On the leaves: *Some of the leaves are yellow-brown.*
On the stems: *Stems are shrunken and black and appear almost girdled.*
On the roots: *Roots are brown and slimy.*

Step 8. Distribution of damage in the landscape:
Are other plants in the landscape affected? *No other vegetables in the garden are affected.*

Step 9. Distribution of damage on the plant and specific plant parts:
Where is the damage seen on the plant? *On the aboveground and belowground portions of the plant.*

Step 10. Timing:
When did you notice this problem? *This morning when I went out to water. The seedlings were fine yesterday.*

Steps 6 and 7 lead us to believe we are dealing with a pathogen. Steps 2, 4, 5, 9, and 10 support our theory that this is damping off.

3. Consider economic, aesthetic, and injury thresholds.

The lettuce is a small part of your overall vegetable garden, and you have other lettuce varieties planted in different locations. You do not wish to have this problem in the future, so the disease is severe enough to warrant investigation.

4. Implement a treatment strategy using physical, cultural, biological, or chemical control, or combine these strategies.

From the information found by searching "damping off + NCSU or Extension" on the internet, you learn damping off is a fungus and its spores are naturally present in the soil. It is a common disease of many seedlings but is often a problem when seeds are sowed indoors. Because the fungus is naturally occurring in the soil, there is no way to get "rid" of the fungus. There are, however, many ways to manage it effectively.

Physical. This fungus is most problematic when humidity and temperatures are high, and air moves poorly. Growing seedlings in a cool, well-ventilated greenhouse helps. Thin seedlings so there is good air movement around them. Rotating crops so the same crop is not grown in the same bed stops the buildup of this fungus.

Cultural. Letting soil dry out between watering and not watering on cool sunless days helps keep damping off spores at bay. Heating soil in an oven before sowing seeds may kill off the spores. Covering the seeds with compost or sphagnum moss may also help.

Biological. There are no known biological treatments for damping off.

Chemical. Sulfur powder has been shown to be effective at treating small areas and preventing this fungus from spreading.

5. Evaluate treatment success.

You decided to rotate the lettuce out of this bed and not plant it there again for at least four more years. You heat your soil medium in the oven before starting any seedlings now, and you make sure the windows on your greenhouse allow for good airflow. You are careful to thin out seedlings and water them thoroughly, but you let them dry out before watering again. You started a garden journal to keep track of the rotation of crops in your garden so you have records to look back on when future problems occur.

Frequently Asked Questions

1. Are all animal manures safe for organic gardens?

Manure from vegetarian animals is generally recommended because it composts faster and has less nitrogen. Fresh manures are very high in nitrogen, so composting the manure rather than applying it directly is recommended. Mixing the high nitrogen compost, which is "green," with some "browns," such as dried leaves, straw, or untreated sawdust, makes balanced compost. The microbes present and the nitrogen content of the manure heats up your compost pile quickly. Keep your pile at 140°F for several days to kill weed seeds. The National Organic Program (NOP) specifies that all manures are spread 120 days or more prior to harvest to reduce pathogens. Beware of using manure from animals that have been fed on hay grown in a field where persistent broadleaf herbicides were used to manage weeds. The herbicides can persist through the animal's digestive tractk and through the composting process and kill plants where the compost is applied.

2. How do I start a vegetable garden on a former lawn without using chemicals?

Smother the grass by laying wet cardboard or several layers of newspaper on the ground, making sure to overlap any seams. On top of the cardboard or newspaper start layering organic material, such as compost, straw, leaf mulch, shredded paper, sawdust, or other organic material. Plant your seedlings by placing potting mix in the planting holes. Or if seeding crops, put a 1-inch to 2-inch layer of potting soil on top of your beds. Another option is to wait for the bed to compost over the next year and then plant directly in the amended soil.

Further Reading

Bowe, Alice. *High-Impact, Low-Carbon Gardening: 1001 Ways to Garden Sustainably.* Portland, Oregon: Timber Press, Inc., 2011. Print.

Bradley, Fern Marshall, ed. *Rodale's Garden Answers: Vegetables, Fruits, and Herbs: At-A-Glance Solutions for Every Gardening Problem.* Emmaus, Pennsylvania: Rodale Press, Inc., 1995. Print.

Damping-off in Flower and Vegetable Seedlings, NC State Extension Horticulture Information Leaflet ODN-14.

Deardorff, David, and Kathryn Wadsworth. *What's Wrong with My Plant? (And How Do I Fix It?): A Visual Guide to Easy Diagnosis and Organic Remedies.* Portland, Oregon: Timber Press, Inc., 2009. Print.

Hanson, Beth, ed. *Natural Disease Control: A Common-sense Approach to Plant First Aid.* Brooklyn, New York: Brooklyn Botanic Garden, 2001. Print.

Lettuce, NC State Extension Horticulture Information Leaflet.

For More Information

http://go.ncsu.edu/fmi_organic

Contributors

Authors:
Aimee Colf, Extension Agent, Anson County
Lucy Bradley, Professor and Extension Specialist, Urban Horticulture, NC State University; Director, NC State Extension Master Gardener program
Frank Louws, Professor and Extension Specialist, Department of Entomology and Plant Pathology
David Orr, Associate Professor, Department of Entomology and Plant Pathology

Contributions by Extension Agents: Paul McKenzie, Cyndi Lauderdale, Danny Lauderdale, David Goforth, Colby Griffin

Contributions by Extension Master Gardener Volunteers: Deborah Green, Bethany Sinnott, Karen Damari, Connie Schultz, Lee Kapleau, Katie Maynard

Copy Editors: Barbara Scott, Debbi Braswell

Chapter 17 Cover Photo: Kathleen Moore, CC BY-2.0

How to Cite This Chapter:
Rankin, A., L. K. Bradley, F. Louws, D. Orr. 2022. Organic Gardening, Chpt 17, In: K. A. Moore, L.K. Bradley (eds), *North Carolina Extension Gardener Handbook,* 2nd ed. NC State Extension, Raleigh, NC. <https://content.ces.ncsu.edu/extension-gardener-handbook/17-organic-gardening>

Plants Grown in Containers

18

Objectives

This chapter teaches people to:

- Understand the differences between growing plants outdoors in containers versus indoors.
- Properly water, fertilize, prune, and repot container-grown plants.
- Recognize and manage common abiotic problems of container-grown plants.
- Identify and manage common pests and diseases of container-grown plants.
- Select houseplants that are appropriate for various home environments.
- Select outdoor plants that are appropriate for containers in various landscape environments.

Introduction

Plants grown in containers offer homeowners flexibility, whether the plants are houseplants indoors or colorful annuals on an outdoor patio. Planting in containers allows a gardener to easily make changes in location if sunlight or temperatures do not encourage plant growth. Indoor container plants not only improve air quality but also help to enhance the visual interest of a home (Figure 18–1). Outdoor containers offer people without a large yard or garden the opportunity to grow vegetables, herbs, or flowers for personal enjoyment (Figure 18–2). Gardeners with physical limitations may find that plants in raised containers are easier to maintain than those planted in the ground. The possibilities are endless—with new exciting plant varieties that thrive in containers and the bounty of beautiful containers that can be found at local retailers and garden centers.

Figure 18–1. An indoor hanging basket.
Kathleen Moore, CC BY - 2.0

All plants need the same basic environmental conditions to survive. Correct management of growth factors—light, water, temperature, air movement, **relative humidity**, and fertilization—and the proper growing medium are the keys to success with container-grown plants. Indoor and outdoor container-grown plants share many characteristics, but each situation also has some unique needs. This chapter first explores what all container-grown plants have in common and then reviews the differences between outdoor and indoor container gardening.

Figure 18–2. Vegetables and herbs grown in outdoor containers.
Lucy Bradley, CC BY - 2.0

Start With High-Quality Plants

The first step toward successful container gardening is to start with healthy, attractive, high-quality plants. When shopping for a new plant, pick up the pot and view it from all sides. Plants should be full and lush with no empty areas or dead material. Plant growth should be stocky and sturdy, not spindly. The potting mix or media should be weed-free. The foliage should be **turgid**, with no **necrosis**, **chlorosis**, tears, or holes. The colors should be true to type. (If solid green, the foliage should not be faded or "washed out." If variegated, the leaves' colors should contrast and not be reverting back to solid green.) Evaluate whether the plant is properly potted in its container. It should fit snuggly in its pot, and its roots should not be pushing out of the pot. Next, examine the plant's roots. Gently slide the plant out of the pot to examine the roots. For most species, a healthy root system has white or tan roots. The roots should be growing towards the bottom or sides of the pot but not circling horizontally around the inside. **Girdled roots** indicate that the plant has been confined in a pot for too long, which can stunt its growth (Figure 18–3). And finally, inspect **leaf-axils** and the undersides of the leaves for signs of insects or diseases.

Many houseplants are sprayed with "leaf shines" to make them more attractive. Leaf shines, however, consist of an unnatural polish that clogs **stomates**. These plants should be avoided.

Transporting Plants

After selecting healthy plants, protecting them from light, temperature, or wind extremes during transport is vital.

When bringing plants home for the first time, the following guidelines provide the best transportation care.

In the summer, heat can build up quickly in a closed vehicle. So avoid leaving plants in a car for an extended period. Sun shining directly on delicate leaf tissue can burn leaves, even if the overall inside temperature is comfortable. Place plants out of direct sunlight to prevent sunburn. If plants must be transported in the back of a truck, be sure to cover them with a tarp to prevent wind damage, which can result in broken limbs and torn and **desiccated** leaves.

In winter, many tropical plants can incur damage at temperatures below 50°F. This damage is called **chilling injury**. Depending on the temperature and the exposure time, plants may quickly show signs of chilling injury, or damage may not appear for several weeks. To protect tropical plants from cold temperatures when transporting, wrap them thoroughly in newspaper, paper bags, or plastic sleeves before leaving the store. Warm up the car ahead of time, and place plants inside the passenger compartment. The trunk of most cars is too cold to transport plants safely.

restricted root growth, or roots sitting in water and developing root rot.

Container materials can be divided into these basic categories:
1. Nonporous: plastic, metal, fiberglass, glazed (Figure 18–4)
2. Semi-porous: wood, pressed fiber (Figure 18–5)
3. Porous: clay, unglazed ceramic, terracotta (Figure 18–6)

Figure 18–4. Nonporus glazed containers.
Kathleen Moore, CC BY - 2.0

Figure 18–3. Girdled roots.
Brendan Landis, Flickr CC BY-SA - 2.0

Selecting a Container

Plants can be grown in containers that are purchased, built, or recycled. Four important aspects to consider are container material, size, color, and drainage. By choosing the proper container, you protect the plant from stress that results from the container drying out too quickly,

Figure 18–5. Semi-porous wood barrel container.
Kathleen Moore, CC BY - 2.0

18

Figure 18–6. Porous terracotta pots.
Sharon_K, Flickr CC BY-SA - 2.0

Choose containers made out of materials that suit your growing purposes. Porous and semi-porous containers lose moisture more quickly and require more frequent watering than nonporous containers. So porous and semi-porous pots are best used to grow plants that do not require a lot of water. The increased moisture loss is advantageous for species such as cacti and succulents.

Material

When container gardening outdoors, unglazed ceramic pots should not be used for plants that remain outside during the winter. These pots absorb water, which will freeze and crack the pot. The growing medium in out-door pots fluctuates in temperature by as much as 30°F between day and night. This problem can be exacerbated when metal pots and small containers are placed in the sun. Wood and plastic containers can safely remain outside year-round. Cedar and redwood are naturally resistant to decay and can last around 10 years without staining or painting. Heavy-duty plastic containers are the most lightweight of all containers, retain moisture well, and can easily be moved near a protective wall when overwintering plants, but their colors can fade when exposed to direct sunlight for long periods. All containers should be cleaned with soapy water and disinfected with a non-bleach household disinfectant product before use.

Weight

When container gardening, we usually select containers for aesthetic appeal rather than horticultural practicality. The weight of the pot, however, should be considered for plants that are top-heavy, plants that will be subjected to wind, or plants that are moved around frequently to give them the proper interior environments.

Color

Dark-colored containers absorb more heat than light-colored ones, causing the potting media to dry out faster and the potting mix temperatures to rise. When gardening outdoors, this temperature change can be an asset in the winter. In the summer, however, the increased heat can burn fragile roots. Therefore avoid placing dark containers in full sun.

Trick of the trade: Whether growing containerized plants outdoors or indoors, double-potting can reduce moisture loss. Double-potting is placing a slightly smaller pot inside a larger one and filling the space between them with mulch or Styrofoam. (Figure 18–7)

Figure 18–7. Double-potted plant. Renee Lampila

Drainage

Drainage holes are necessary in all containers to prevent plant roots from standing in water and developing root rot. If the container sits flat on a solid surface such as a paved patio, place drainage holes along the side of the container, ¼-inch to ½-inch from the bottom (Figure 18–8). If herbs or a fruit tree are to be showcased in an attractive pot that does not have drainage holes, the plant needs to be double-potted (Figure 18–7). In addition, the pot's porosity is important. If someone tends to overwater their container plants, a porous container should be used. Container gardeners who underwater their plants should choose nonporous containers that help to hold moisture in the potting mix. Never put a layer of gravel or rocks in the bottom of a container beneath the potting mix in an effort to improve drainage. Doing so causes the water to collect in the potting mix just above the gravel. Only when no air space is left in the potting mix will the water drain into the gravel below. So gravel in the bottom does little to keep soil above it from being saturated by overwatering.

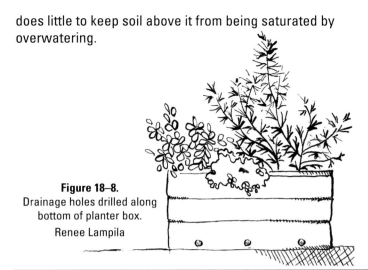

Figure 18–8.
Drainage holes drilled along bottom of planter box.
Renee Lampila

Size

A container's size should match the plant's growth requirements for two reasons. First, restricted root growth results in decreased plant growth. Root restriction is a physical stress on the plant that causes a pronounced decrease in root and shoot growth. Second, flowering and fruiting is also reduced for plants in small pots. Consider both depth and total volume of the container. The minimum recommended container size per plant is listed for vegetables in Table 18–1 and fruit in Table 18–2. Choosing larger containers is beneficial, however, as they do not dry out as quickly and require less frequent watering. Shallow-rooted annual plants and vegetables—such as lettuce, radishes, and scallions—need a minimum potting mix depth of 6 inches to 8 inches, whereas carrots grow

Table 18–1. Minimum Container Size Needed for Vegetables

Vegetable	Minimum Size Container	Spacing	Minimum Container Depth
Beans	2 gallon	2–3 inches	8–10 inches
Beets	2 quart	2–3 inches	8 inches
Bok choy	1 gallon	6 inches	20 inches
Carrots	2 quart	2–3 inches	10 inches
Collards	3 gallon	12 inches	12 inches
Cucumbers	1 gallon	1 plant per container or 12–16 inches	8 inches
Eggplant	5 gallon	1 plant per container	12–16 inches
Green garlic	2 quart	4 inches	4–6 inches
Kale	3 gallon	6 inches	8 inches
Lettuce	2 quart	4–5 inches	6–8 inches
Mustard greens	3 gallon	6 inches	4–6 inches
Peas	2 gallon	2–3 inches	12 inches
Peppers	2 gallon	1 plant per container or 14–18 inches	12–16 inches
Potatoes	30 gallon	5–6 inches	
Radishes	2 quart	2–3 inches	4–6 inches
Scallions	2 quart	2–3 inches	6 inches
Spinach	1 gallon	2–3 inches	4–6 inches
Squash	2 gallon	1 plant per container	12–24 inches
Swiss chard	2 quart	4–5 inches	8 inches
Tomatoes	5 gallon	1 plant per container	12–24 inches

18

better with a potting mix depth of 10 inches to 12 inches. Most herbs can be grown in a 4-inch to 6-inch diameter pot. Some herbs with a large taproot, however, need a 12-inch deep container. (Refer to the recommendations for success with herbs in the NC State Extension Publication AG-748, *Container Garden Planting Calendar for Edibles in the NC Piedmont*.) Perennial plants and fruits require large containers (Table 18–2) for adequate root growth. Interior plants grow best in pot sizes that are one size larger than their root system. For small pots, 8 inches in diameter or less, a pot that is 1-inch to 2-inches wider than the current root ball works well. For large pots, 10 inches or wider in diameter, 2-inches to 3-inches wider than the plant's root ball is ideal.

Table 18–2.
Minimum Container Size
Needed for Fruit

Fruit	Minimum Container Size
Apples	20–25 gallon
Blueberries	2 feet × 2 feet × 2 feet
Figs	10 gallon
Grapes	15 gallon
Peaches	20–25 gallon
Strawberries	8-inch deep container

Potting Mixes, Substrates, or Growing Media

The potting "soil" used to grow container plants is really not soil at all. True soils are field soils that often retain too much water, have too little pore space (for oxygen), are too heavy, and potentially harbor harmful diseases, insects, and weeds. Because of these drawbacks, field soils are no longer used for growing plants in containers.

Instead, materials called "**soilless substrates**" (also referred to as "**substrates**," "**media**," or "**potting mixes**") are used when growing container plants. Most soilless potting mixes are free of insects, diseases, and weeds and are ready to use immediately. The most common ingredients are perlite, pine bark, sand, sphagnum peat moss, and vermiculite——or combinations of these components.

- **Perlite** is a white, heat-treated, expanded volcanic rock used to improve drainage. It has replaced pea-gravel because it is lighter, making it easier to move potted plants. A word of caution: Avoid breathing perlite dust. Wear a dust mask or wet the perlite down. Perlite contains some fluoride, so do not include it in the potting mix used to grow fluoride-sensitive species such as spider plants or dracaenas.

- **Pine bark** has large particles, making it good for aeration in a potting mix. It is difficult to re-wet, however, if allowed to dry out.

- **Sand** was once used extensively but is now often replaced with lighter-weight products, such as perlite. Sand has low water-holding capacity and provides little aeration, but is useful (in moderate percentages) in providing a counterweight to top-heavy plants, preventing them from tipping over. Do not use fine playground sand. Instead, use coarse builder's sand, which is a nutrient-poor material that has a large particle size and heavy weight. The potting mix must be almost 50% sand by total volume to drain quickly.

- **Sphagnum peat moss** is the decaying matter in a peat bog. Peat increases the nutrient and water-holding capacity of media, but it is not a sustainable resource. Fortunately, there is current ongoing research at NC State's Horticultural Science Substrate's Lab looking into peat alternative materials. The researchers are looking for alternatives that are local, regional, environmentally friendly, and economical.

- **Vermiculite** is a heat-treated, expanded clay mineral that absorbs water and attracts nutrients when wet.

Potting mixes sometimes include other ingredients:
- **Compost** benefits include good water-holding capacity, disease suppression, and the addition of nutrients and organic matter. The nutritional value of compost varies, depending on the plant matter or animal waste that was used to make it. Because many types of compost have a pH over 7.0, it is best to limit the amount of compost to between 15% and 40% of the total container mix. Do not use composted grass clippings from lawns treated with herbicides as some of the chemicals can persist through composting cycles and affect plants.

- **Pasteurized soil** has been heated to 180°F for 30 minutes to kill most diseases, weed seeds, and insects. Be aware that when soil is heated in a home oven, it does emit an odor.

- **Sedge peat** is a granular material made of partially decomposed sedges. Avoid using this in containers as it compacts easily and drains poorly.

There are many combinations of soilless potting mix components that make great growing mixes.

Common mixtures consist of these proportions:
- 50% peat and 50% perlite
- 60% peat, 20% perlite, and 20% vermiculite
- 60% pine bark, 20% peat, and 20% sand

Qualities of Good Growing Media
Because plants grown in containers are restricted to the limited amount of media available within each pot, high-quality potting mixes are essential to supply the roots with nutrients, air, and water. A potting mix, regardless of the components, should have these characteristics:
- **High permeability to water and air:** Larger particles and pore spaces allow rapid percolation of water and air.
- **Water-holding capacity:** Small particles and pore spaces and high quantities of organic matter increase water retention.
- **Drainage:** Large particles and pore spaces allow water to drain quickly, but a compacted growing medium does not.
- **Aeration:** Large particles and organic matter create air space, providing roots with access to the oxygen that is necessary for a plant to grow, take up nutrients, and absorb water.
- **Light weight:** The lighter a mix is, the easier it is to move the container. Likewise, a lighter mix has lower bulk density and more air space than a heavier mix.
- **Fertility:** A fertile mix is necessary for healthy growth. Plants need nutrients to thrive.
- **Pasteurized:** A mix that is mostly free of weed seeds, insects, and diseases.

Selecting Potting Mixes
There are many commercial soilless mixes developed through scientific research that provide optimum water and nutrient properties. Most commercial mixes combine finely textured and coarsely textured components to create a balance of water retention and drainage qualities. When considering commercial mixes, read each mixture's label to identify and evaluate the components. It may be necessary to experiment with several mixes to find one that works in the desired setting. For example, a sandier mix is appropriate for cacti, while orchids prefer a large textured mix. Both require minimal nutrients while container-grown tomatoes require frequent applications of fertilizer in order to provide good quality fruit, necessitating a mix that retains water, allowing the nutrients to stay in solution longer and not drain out the bottom of the pot.

Many high-quality commercial potting mixes have a small quantity of fertilizer mixed in to give newly potted plants a surge of nutrients to jump-start their growth. In most cases, these nutrients last only a couple of weeks and often do not supply the full spectrum of nutritional elements needed for long-term growth, so an on-going fertilizer regime is also necessary. Examine whether your container plant is foliage, flower, or fruit, and research its nutrient requirements appropriately.

In most situations, it is faster, easier, and more precise to purchase a commercial soilless mix than to make your own mix. Sometimes, however, specific needs occur that make a custom potting mix ideal, such as growing root rot–sensitive plants that need a well-drained potting mix, growing high-water-using plants without an automatic irrigation system, or gardening on a windy rooftop (which makes a heavy mix ideal). Choose components based on the specific needs of each situation. For root rot–sensitive plants or plants that prefer dry conditions, such as succulents, cacti, and herbs, limit potting mix and sand to no more than a third of the total mixture and include perlite to achieve a blend with greater air space. For plants with a high water requirement, such as coleus or tomatoes, the mixture should include vermiculite and compost for a greater water-holding capacity. For a blend with greater bulk density to prevent container blow-down in windy conditions, increase sand (more than a third of the mixture should be soilless potting mix and sand) and limit perlite.

No single potting mix is ideal for all container-grown plants. Often a ready-made bag mix can be improved by adding components. A garden center or an Internet search can provide information regarding the best mixes in which to grow particular species.

Potting Plants

Potting media should be moist before potting. Moist media should be slightly damp to the touch but not wet, meaning no water is draining from the media. Pre-moistened potting mix makes watering-in newly potted plants more effective. Peat or pine bark that is excessively dry is very difficult to rehydrate.

When potting a plant, the crown of the plant must not be buried below nor exposed above the top of the media. This zone, where crown meets media, is called the "substrate-line." Planting too deeply below the substrate-line can smother the plant's growing point, which can kill the crown. Planting too shallowly exposes roots to the air's drying effects, which can lead to root desiccation.

To allow for proper watering, sufficient space is needed between the top of the potting mix and the top of the pot. This space is known as the "reservoir" and provides space to apply water and soluble fertilizer. When watered, the various soilless potting mix components settle (or compact) differently. Therefore the reservoir depth is measured after the initial watering (Figure 18–9).

Experiment with your media to obtain the optimal reservoir depth. Approximately ¼-inch to 3 inches of reservoir space is needed, depending on the diameter of the pot; larger pots require deeper reservoirs.

Figure 18–9. Reservoir space is measured after initial watering.
Kathleen Moore, CC BY - 2.0

To successfully pot your container plants, loosely fill the pot with media approximately a third full. Do not pack down the media. Center the plant in the pot, positioning its substrate-line slightly above the ideal reservoir depth. Fill media in around the roots, lining up the existing substrate-line with the new substrate-line. At this point, both the plant and the potting mix are positioned slightly above the desired reservoir depth. Shake the pot gently back and forth to evenly spread out the potting mix around the crown. Watering-in settles the plant and the new potting mix together to the correct reservoir depth.

Avoid pressing the media down around the crown or tamping the container, which cause compaction. If additional support is needed, consider staking the plant. Water thoroughly. Occasionally water makes a channel through the container mix and leaves dry areas. Fill the channel with potting mix and water again. The potting mix moistens faster with warm water than with cold water. A drop of dishwashing soap in the water allows for more uniform wetting because it decreases the cohesive and adhesive properties of the water. Depending on the composition of the container mix, the amount of water needed to fully wet the media in a container is normally between 45% and 60% of the container volume. So for a 5-gallon container, that would be 2½ gallons to 3 gallons of water.

If planting seeds in the container, sow them after the potting mix has been added and thoroughly watered.

Repotting

Repotting (or transplanting) is the transfer of a plant from one container to another. Transplanting is necessary to increase the root system's growing space, to replenish nutrients, improve aeration, and alleviate fertilizer salt buildup. Plants that are healthy and grown under optimal conditions should be repotted annually using fresh potting mix (Figure 18–10). Repotting is best done in the early spring, before plants start actively growing.

Figure 18–10. This pothos (*Epipremnum aureum*) is at the optimal stage for repotting.
Diane Mays, CC BY - 2.0

There are, however, various signs that repotting may be necessary at other times throughout the year.

- **Stunting:** Plants that are not growing during their active growth period may be outgrowing their pots. If the root system is constricted, roots do not have room to expand. An overabundance of roots quickly uses up the available water and nutrients in the potting mix.
- **Wilting:** When the leaves of a potted plant wilt frequently, yet rehydrate after watering, the roots are not getting enough water, often because the plant is in too small a pot (Figure 18–11). "Up-potting" the plant increases the amount of water available to the root system. If a plant's leaves remain wilted after watering, most likely the roots are rotted. The continuous wilting means the roots are unable to absorb water. Reduce the amount of water given to the plant or "down-pot" (or do both) to balance the root size and potting mix volume ratio.
- **Escaping:** Plants that have roots pushing out of their pots should be repotted in a larger container (Figure 18–12).
- **Surface exposure:** When a plant's crown or roots become exposed on the potting mix surface, it could indicate that the media has settled or been washed over to one side of the pot. In this case repotting may not be necessary. **Top-dressing,** (applying additional potting mix to the media surface), may be all that is needed.

18

Figure 18–11. A plant wilting between waterings.
Diane Mays, CC BY - 2.0

Figure 18–12. A spider plant (*Chlorophytum comosum*)
with roots escaping the pot.
Keith Williamson, Flickr CC BY - 2.0

Repotting Techniques

Start repotting by removing the plant from its old pot. While securing the plant with one hand, turn the pot upside-down and gently tap the rim of the container on the edge of a table. If the plant does not slide out easily, its roots might be attached to the inside walls of the container. To detach, carefully run a straight knife between the root ball and container walls. Examine the root ball. A dense root ball is an indication that the plant needs to be potted up into a larger pot. Roots that are so intertwined they retain the shape of the old pot do not develop properly and hinder plant growth if left entangled. Break this encircling growth pattern by teasing the roots apart or by cutting the roots vertically along the side of the root ball.

The container selected for potting-up should be one size larger in diameter than the pot in which the plant is currently growing. For vigorously growing species, two pot sizes larger may be required. If down-potting is necessary, the container size should accommodate the size of the root system. At this stage it is crucial not to overwater nor let the few remaining roots dry out.

Whether potting or repotting, it is always important to use pots that are void of diseases, insects, weed seeds, or build-up of salts from fertilizers (Figure 18–13). Wash previously used pots in a solution of non-bleach household disinfectant. Rinse the solution off thoroughly prior to use. Scrub clay pots with water and a wire brush to remove salts.

Figure 18–13. Soluble salts build up on containers. Wash them off before using the container again.
Diane Mays, CC BY - 2.0

Reusing Container Media

Container media can be reused as long as no soilborne disease problems have occurred, such as Verticillium or Fusarium wilt, in the previous season. If disease was present, the media needs to be discarded or added to an area in the yard or garden that has resistant plants—such as grasses, lilies, or ferns. When reusing container media from year to year, organic matter breaks down and decomposes, causing a decrease in the size of particles and pore space, resulting in reduced drainage and aeration. Emptying out the container mix, breaking up the material and any old roots, and re-blending keep the media from getting too compacted. Because many of the nutrients are used by plants or leached out during the previous growing season, add additional media, compost, and fertilizer.

Nutrient Management

A regular fertilization schedule must be followed to maintain healthy plants.

18

Fertilizer Types

Controlled-release, slow-release, or liquid fertilizers are the preferred ways to supply nitrogen, potassium, and phosphorous to container plants. These fertilizers can be used independently or in combination. Plants also require micronutrients such as copper, zinc, boron, manganese, and iron; these can be supplied with a micronutrient solution.

- **Controlled release:** Controlled-release fertilizers are synthetic fertilizers that have been coated by materials to reduce their immediate solubility and availability to plants. Controlled-release fertilizers are expensive but offer several advantages: avoidance of high initial salt levels in the growing media, availability of nutrients for several months, and reduction of nutrient losses from the container by leaching and runoff. Higher summer temperatures and increased moisture in the growing media increase the rate of nutrient release. Top-dressing, rather than incorporating fertilizer, typically results in reduced nutrient losses, as the nutrients have to travel throughout the growing medium, which increases their chance of being absorbed by the plant. Intermittent drying of top-dressed fertilizer between watering may also slow down the leakage of nutrients through the fertilizer coating. If containers are subject to blow-over due to being placed in a windy area, however, the fertilizer should be mixed in prior to potting rather than applied to the surface.

- **Slow release:** Slow-release fertilizers come in both organic and synthetic forms. Organic fertilizers have low water solubility, prolonged nutrient release rates (over years), and are less concentrated per unit weight than synthetic fertilizers. The main disadvantage to slow-release fertilizers is the release rate may be too slow for fast growing crops, and supplementation with liquid fertilizer may be needed. Three factors affecting the release of nutrients in slow-release fertilizers are particle size, media moisture content, and microorganisms present in the medium (organism numbers increase with warmer temperatures). The smaller the particle size is, the higher the moisture content. And the warmer the temperatures are, the faster the rate of nutrient release.

- **Liquid:** Liquid fertilizers are quick-release, water-soluble fertilizers. Water-soluble fertilizers are most desirable after plants are growing, and these fertilizers can quickly replace nutrients lost from the potting mix during a prolonged rainfall or period of rapid plant growth. They have minimal temperature dependence and are cheaper in cost per unit of nitrogen than slow-release fertilizers.

- **Granular:** Granular fertilizer that is not time-released is generally not recommended as a supplemental fertilizer for container gardening. It can be worked into the top few inches of potting mix around plants in containers, but the fertilizer can burn plant roots if it comes into contact with them.

- **Foliar:** Foliar fertilizer is the spraying of nutrients onto plant leaves and stems for subsequent nutrient absorption. The solutions are very dilute to avoid burning plant foliage. Absorption is increased when the sprays reach the leaf undersides where the stomata are located. Foliar fertilization can be used as a way to supplement nutrients but should not be a substitute for a potting mix fertility program.

Timing

There are no hard-and-fast rules for fertilizing container gardens. How much and how often to fertilize depend on such factors as the type of plants grown, each plant's growth stage, the type of fertilizer used, and the irrigation method. Some basic principles, however, can be followed.

Pre-plant fertilization allows for a successful start to plant growth. If the fertilizer used before planting is a controlled-release fertilizer, additional fertilizer is needed in eight to 10 weeks. If the potting mixture is amended with slow-release fertilizer, transplants can be fertilized again three weeks after planting, seedlings three weeks after the plants have two sets of leaves, and fruit trees when new growth starts.

Nutrient levels usually drop because plants take up the nutrients and nutrients are leached from the potting mix. Additional time-release fertilizer can be applied, or liquid fertilizers can be used once a week at half strength or every two weeks at full strength. When using liquid fertilizers, salt accumulation can sometimes be a problem and is evident by a white crust on top of the potting mix. If salt accumulation is observed, the media should be leached to remove excess nutrients by slowly running water through the media for several minutes.

Fertilize indoor houseplants once a month from March to October. Do not fertilize from November to February unless deficiency symptoms appear.

Outdoor Container Gardening

Growing plants in outdoor containers provides color and interest in a landscape. Container gardens can produce food or herbs for cooking and make an ideal choice for those with limited space, soil problems, or woodland creatures that eat their plants. Containers can be placed on a rooftop, balcony, patio, deck, entrance area, or walkway (Figure 18–14). Containers are mobile and can be moved to a sunny spot if growing tomatoes or petunias, a partly shady area when growing lettuce or impatiens, or a protected microclimate during the winter for growing year-round rosemary. Container gardening offers more

18

flexibility than traditional gardening and is great for people with physical limitations, children, renters, new gardeners, or even experienced gardeners wanting to downsize. Container gardening requires no digging or tilling, and it is virtually weed-free. Container gardening can also be a way of containing aggressive plants, such as mint, that may otherwise take over traditional garden spaces. Plants grown in containers, however, do require more care than plants grown in traditional garden beds in the ground. The medium in the containers drains easily, leaching nutrients, and it becomes warmer than soil in the ground—causing it to dry out faster and necessitating more frequent applications of fertilizer and water. These small hurdles can be overcome to allow the gardener to harvest fresh vegetables, herbs, and fruits practically year-round.

Figure 18–14. A container garden on a tiny patio.
Aehdeschaine, Flickr CC BY-ND - 2.0

Plant Varieties
Outdoor plants grown in containers need to have a confined or compact growth habit. Most annual plants and flowers are suitable for growing in containers. Perennial varieties should be chosen that are labeled bush, dwarf, or miniature, or ones that have been especially bred or hybridized for container growing. Nearly all leafy green vegetables do well in containers, but corn and most large-fruited vining crops—such as full-sized pumpkin and watermelon—cannot be grown in containers. There are bush-type squash, cucumbers, and melons, however, that are ideal for small-space and container gardening. When growing fruit trees such as apples, peaches, and figs, the amount of fruit produced is proportional to the plant's size, so large yields should not be expected. Fruit production is possible in containers but will not equal the quantity produced on trees planted in the ground.

Planting Calendar
See the container gardening planting calendar for vegetables in Table 18-3, fruit in Table 18-4, and herbs in Table 18-5. See AG-748, *Container Gardening Planting Calendar for Edibles in the NC Piedmont*, for guidance in scheduling container plantings for optimal performance.

Combinations that Work
A container can hold more than one type of plant if all the plants have similar requirements for light, water, and nutrients (Tables 18–6, 18–7, and 18–8). For example, lavender (*Lavandula angustifolia*), thyme (*Thymus vulgaris*), and oregano (*Origanum vulgare*) require a loose growing medium, dry conditions, and very little fertilization. They can be planted together in a porous clay pot or in a semiporous or nonporous container with some perlite added to the potting mix. Growing requirements are not the only consideration. Plants can also be combined in containers based on harvesting time, form, size, texture, color, or ingredients for favorite recipes to create a themed garden. Place the tallest plant either in the center of the container or toward the back if it will be up against a wall. Plants that cascade should be placed closest to the edge of a container, whereas medium height plants can go in the middle. Depending on the size and shape of the container, consider planting odd numbers, with one tall plant, three medium, and five smaller.

- For a spring vegetable garden, choose an 18-inch diameter container and place a trellis in the center. Direct sow bush peas in the center and 'Black-Seeded Simpson' and 'Red Deer Tongue' lettuce around the edges.
- Create a hummingbird garden using a hanging basket. Plant the basket with flowers that have staggered bloom times to extend nectar availability. A red-colored pentas (*Pentas lanceolata*) works well as a center plant. Cascading plants like lantana (*Lantana* sp.), verbena (*Verbena* × *hybrida*), and trailing petunias (*Petunia* × *hybrida*) are particularly attractive in hanging baskets and give birds easy access to blooms.
- A full-sun container garden may need additional insulation in the pot to protect the roots from getting too hot. Setting browallia (*Browallia speciosa*) in the center of the pot works well because of its upright growth habit. Add some cape daisies (*Arctotis stoechadifolias*) that bloom into the fall for long-lasting color, and plant a coordinating color of million bells (*Calibrachoa* × *hybrida*) around the outer edge to cascade down the container.
- Another full-sun option is placing the upright striking copper plant 'Margarita' (*Acalypha wilkesiana*) in the center, angel wing begonias (*Begonia* 'Argenteo-guttata') and weeping sedge (*Carex oshemensis*) fill out the middle, and sweet potato vines in green and black (*Ipomoea batatas*) and blue scavola (*Scalova aemula* 'Blue Fan') cascading down the sides (Figure 18–15).

Table 18–3. Container Garden Planting Calendar for Vegetables

Vegetable	Days to Harvest	Jan 1	Jan 15	Feb 1	Feb 15	Mar 1	Mar 15	Apr 1	Apr 15	May 1	May 15	Jun 1	Jun 15	Jul 1	Jul 15	Aug 1	Aug 15	Sep 1	Sep 15	Oct 1	Oct 15	Nov 1	Nov 15	Dec 1	Dec 15
Beans, lima (bush)	65–80									S	S	S	S												
Beans, lima (pole)	75–95									S	S	S													
Beans, snap (bush)	50–55								S	S	S	S	S	S											
Beans, snap (pole)	65–70								S	S	S	S	S												
Beets	55–60				S	S	S										S	S							
Bok choy	45–60						T										T	T	T						
Carrots	75–80			S	S										S	S									
Collards	90–120														ST	ST									
Cucumbers	60–65								ST	ST						ST									
Eggplant	80–85									T	T	T	T												
Endive	80–90			S	S	S												S	S						
Green garlic	30–35						B	B	B	B															
Kale	50–60				ST	ST	ST										S	S							
Leeks	70–100								T	T								T	T						
Lettuce, head	75–85				ST	ST	ST										ST								
Lettuce, leaf	45–50				ST	ST	ST										ST	ST							
Mustard greens	30–45			ST	ST	ST	ST										S	S	S						
Peas, garden	65–70			S	S																				
Peas, snap	65–70			S	S																				
Peas, snow	65–70			S	S																				
Peppers	75–80									T	T														
Potatoes	100–120					T	T	T	T	T															
Radishes	20–25			S	S	S	ST	S									S	S	S						
Scallions	60–80			B	B	B												B	B	B					
Spinach	45–50			S	S	S																			
Squash, summer	50–60									T	T														
Squash, winter	85–95									S	S					S									
Swiss chard	60–70						ST	ST	ST																
Tomatoes	75–85								T	T	T	T	T	T											

B = bulbs, S = seeds, T = transplants

Table 18–4. Container Garden Planting Calendar for Fruits

Fruit / Pollination	Jan		Feb		Mar		Apr		May		Jun		Jul		Aug		Sep		Oct		Nov		Dec	
	1	15	1	15	1	15	1	15	1	15	1	15	1	15	1	15	1	15	1	15	1	15	1	15
Apples *Cross-pollination needed*	P	P	P	P	P	P								H	H	H	H	H	H	H				P
Blueberries *Partially self-fertile[a]*	P	P	P	P								H	H	H	H	H	H			P	P	P	P	P
Citrus *Self-fertile*								P	P	P				H	H	H	H	H	H	H	H	H		
Figs *Self-fertile*	P	P	P	P	P	P								H	H	H	H	H	H	H			P	P
Grapes *Most varieties self-fertile*				P	P	P	P	P						H	H	H	H	H	P	P	P			
Peaches *Most varieties self-fertile*	P	P	P	P	P	P						H	H	H	H	H	H							P
Strawberries[b] *Self-fertile*				P	P				H	H	H									P	P			

H = harvest, P = plant

[a] Partially self-fertile means cross-pollination. It is not necessary but will result in increased yield and berry size.

[b] Strawberries planted in late February or early March will produce a very limited crop in May or early June. Plant in late October or early November for a better yield.

Note: blueberries, grapes, and most fruit trees will take several years to bear full crops.

Figure 18–15. A full-sun container.
Gloria Polakof, CC BY - 2.0

- A container in the shade needs plants that can tolerate low light levels and still produce beautiful foliage and blooms. Give some height to the container with the arrow-shaped leaves of a caladium (*Caladium bicolor*) or porcupine grass (*Miscanthus sinensis* 'Strictus'). Add some contrast with the grassy golden leaves of (*Hakanechola macro* 'Aureola') and fill in with some cascading bacopa (*Chaenostoma cordatum*).
- For a pink-colored garden in the summer, place 'Marshall's Delight' monarda (*Monarda didyma*) in the center of a large container surrounded by 'Ruby' Swiss chard alternating with 'Forescate' chives (*Allium schoenoprasum*). On the outer edge of the container, mix in tricolor sage (*Salvia officinalis* 'Tricolor') and scented geraniums (*Pelargonium* spp.).
- An Italian-themed garden needs a container at least 2 feet in diameter. At the three corners of a triangle, plant a plum tomato and two 'Giant Marconi' roasting red peppers. The tomato needs to be trellised, and the peppers may also benefit from some support. Marjoram (*Origanum majorana*), parsley (*Petroselinum crispum*), and basil (*Ocimum basilicum*) can be planted to fill in the spaces around the three main plants.

Table 18–5. Container Garden Planting Calendar for Herbs

Herb	Harvest Season	Jan 1	Jan 15	Feb 1	Feb 15	Mar 1	Mar 15	Apr 1	Apr 15	May 1	May 15	Jun 1	Jun 15	Jul 1	Jul 15	Aug 1	Aug 15	Sep 1	Sep 15	Oct 1	Oct 15	Nov 1	Nov 15	Dec 1	Dec 15
Basil	Summer							T	T	T															
Bay	Continuous							T											T	T	T	T			
Borage	Spring to fall								S	S															
Chamomile	Late summer to early fall								S	S															
Chervil	Late summer into winter							S	S	S							S	S							
Chives	Spring to fall							T	T	T															
Cilantro	Early summer			S	S	S																			
Dill	Summer to fall								S	S								S	S						
Fennel	Late summer								S	S															
Feverfew	Summer						ST	ST																	
Lavender	Summer						T	T	T																
Lemongrass	Late summer			T		T																			
Lemon verbena	Summer								T	T															
Marjoram	Summer						ST	ST																	
Mint	Spring to fall						T	T	T																
Monarda[a]	Summer to fall								T	T															
Oregano	Summer to fall						T	T	T																
Parsley	Summer to fall							T	T	T										T	T				
Rosemary	Continuous							T	T	T															
Saffron crocus	Fall							B	B																
Sage	Summer to fall								T	T															
Salad burnet	Spring to early summer						ST	ST																	
Scented geranium	Spring to fall								T	T															
Stevia	Continuous								T	T															
Tarragon	Spring to fall								T	T															
Thyme	Summer						ST	ST	ST	ST															

B = bulbs, S = seeds, T = transplants

[a] Also known as bee balm, oswego tea, or bergamot, because the fragrance resembles the bergamot orange.

Planting

With some plants, seeds are placed directly in the container, and with others, like annual flowers, transplants are usually used. When using seeds, always plant more than needed because there is seldom 100% germination and emergence. After the seeds have sprouted, seedlings can be thinned to the desired number. For example, beets, carrots, and radishes can be thinned to 2 inches apart (Figure 18–16), but Swiss chard and lettuce should be thinned to 4 inches to 6 inches apart (Table 18–1). When thinning, cut or pinch off the unwanted seedlings near the base rather than pulling them out, as the roots may be intertwined with neighboring seedlings and the other plants can be damaged. With transplants, the potting mix should be broken up around the root ball and the roots loosened before the plant is put into the new container. The plant should be positioned at the same depth as in its original container, planted in a large enough container so that there is at least 3 inches of potting mix under the root ball for further root growth, and watered in thoroughly. A support or trellis is required for vines or vining vegetables (such as beans, cucumbers, eggplant, peas, peppers, tomatoes). The support should be put in place at the same time as seeding or transplanting to minimize disturbance to the plant roots. When planting blueberries, grapes, and most fruit trees, be aware that it will be several years before they bear full crops.

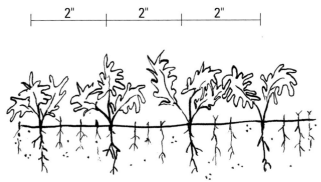

Figure 18–16. Thinned carrots.
Renee Lampila

Container Location

Most flowers, vegetables, and fruits do best in full sun—in locations that get at least 6 to 8 hours of sunlight a day (Tables 18–6 and 18–7). Most herbs and cool-season vegetables—such as beets, carrots, kale, lettuce, radish, and spinach—tolerate partial shade and need only 3 to 5 hours of direct sun a day (Tables 18–6 and 18–8). Containers allow a gardener to take advantage of microclimates, such as an area cooled by shading from an overhang, or an area warmed by a building's reflective surface or by heat held in brick or concrete. Southern and western exposures are the sunniest and warmest, while northern and eastern exposures are shadier and cooler.

Irrigation

Plants in containers can readily receive water from several sources, but the method of irrigation significantly affects the leaching of nutrients. Watering requirements can vary considerably and are affected by several variables, including wind, light (full sun versus cloudy conditions), temperature, humidity, container size and type, the composition of the media, the amount of media in a pot compared to the amount of roots, the type of plant, and the stage of plant growth (seedling versus mature plant producing fruit). A top dressing of mulch over the potting mix surface significantly reduces moisture loss.

Methods

Water can be supplied to containerized plants with a watering can, a garden hose, a series of drip emitters on a timer, or by using self-watering containers. Each method has benefits and drawbacks, and the choice of which method to use should be made based on the situation (Table 18–9).

Frequency

The amount of water a containerized plant requires increases if the weather is hot and windy or if the pot is small, dark-colored, or placed in full sun. Easy access to water is crucial because most containers will need to be watered at least once a day when plants are mature. Containers should never be allowed to dry out completely between watering as doing so damages feeder roots and leads to flower and fruit drop. When the plant finally receives water, its energy goes toward growing new feeder roots, resulting in a slowing down of overall plant growth. To avoid drought stress and wilting, stick a finger 2 inches to 3 inches into the potting mix, and if the mix is dry, the plant should be watered. At the other extreme, avoid overwatering, as the water fills all of the pore space in the potting mix and the roots are unable to get enough oxygen. Water only when needed, and water pots until the water starts to come out the bottom of the container. If there is a saucer under the pot, remove the water from the saucer after watering the plant. This prevents root rot, prevents a build-up of salts that would occur if the water evaporated and left the salts in the saucer, and prevents mosquitoes from breeding there.

Moisture Retention

To retain moisture in the potting mix, place mulch on the media's surface. After planting, 1 inch of mulch can be added to the surface of the potting mix of each container. The mulch should be pulled back about 1 inch from the base of the plant to prevent moisture from building up next to the stem and causing disease. Water-holding polymers (*Polyacrylamide hydrogels*) are not recommended, as they have not proven to be effective tools for water management.

Table 18–6. Light, Water, and Nutrient Requirements for Vegetables

Vegetable	Light			Water			Nutrients		
	Full Sun	Tolerates Partial Shade	Partial Shade	Moist	Slightly Dry	Dry	Light[a]	Medium[b]	Heavy[c]
Beans	X			X				X	
Beets		X		X				X	
Carrots			X	X				X	
Cucumbers	X			X					X
Eggplant	X			X					X
Green garlic		X		X				X	
Kale			X	X				X	
Leeks	X			X				X	
Lettuce			X	X				X	
Peas		X		X					X
Peppers	X			X				X	
Potatoes	X			X			X		
Radishes		X		X			X		
Scallions		X		X				X	
Spinach			X	X			X		
Squash, summer	X			X					X
Squash, winter			X	X					X
Swiss chard			X	X				X	
Tomatoes	X			X				X	

[a] Fertilize at planting or for established plants fertilize once early in the growing season.
[b] Fertilize monthly with a liquid fertilizer or every 12 weeks with a timed-release fertilizer.
[c] Fertilize every 2 weeks with a liquid fertilizer and every 8–10 weeks with a timed-release fertilizer.

Nutrient Management

The frequent watering required by container gardening flushes out nutrients from the potting mix. For example, nitrogen is water-soluble and is easily lost in the water that drains from the bottom of the container. As plants set fruit, their demand for nutrients increases, and nitrogen is pulled out of the leaf tissue for this purpose. Fish emulsion or compost may be used, but fish emulsion does have a strong odor and may attract cats, dogs, raccoons, and other pests to the containers. Apply foliar fertilizer during the early morning hours when the plant stomata are open.

The temperature should be under 80°F, the wind minimal, and the air humid. The main concern with continuous use of liquid fertilizer in containers is nutrient runoff. To limit the environmental impact of runoff, always follow the label's recommended rate. Too much fertilizer promotes vegetative growth at the expense of flowering and fruit production. Overapplication not only increases nutrient runoff but can greatly increase the amount of money spent on fertilizer. Overapplication also can be harmful to the plant by damaging roots through excess salt accumulation.

Fruit	Light			Water			Nutrients		
	Full Sun	Tolerates Partial Shade	Partial Shade	Moist	Slightly Dry	Dry	Light[a]	Medium[b]	Heavy[c]
Apples		X		X				X	
Blueberries	X			X					X
Citrus	X			X					X
Figs		X			X			X	
Grapes		X			X			X	
Peaches		X		X				X	
Strawberries	X			X				X	

Table 18–7. Light, Water, and Nutrient Requirements for Fruits

[a] Fertilize at planting or for established plants fertilize once early in the growing season.

[b] Fertilize monthly with a liquid fertilizer or every 12 weeks with a timed-release fertilizer.

[c] Fertilize every 2 weeks with a liquid fertilizer and every 8–10 weeks with a timed-release fertilizer.

Overwintering

The weight of an empty plastic container gives the impression that it can be easily moved, but a 20-inch diameter container filled with potting mix and plants can weigh 100 pounds. Place container gardens on a rolling platform to be more easily moved indoors (Figure 18–17). If a container garden contains cold-hardy plants, overwinter them outside in the pot or in a cold frame.

Figure 18–17. Place heavy pots on a rolling surface to easily move them.
Kathleen Moore, CC BY - 2.0

Inside

Bring tender plants inside for the winter once nighttime temperatures drop to 55°F and well before the heat in the house is turned on. Plants need to adapt to the indoor conditions of reduced light and humidity. Over the period of a week, gradually reduce light levels by moving the container from sun to light shade to heavy shade, and finally indoors. If a porch or shed is available, move the plants there for a week before moving them inside. Once indoors, place the containers away from cold drafts caused by outside doors and the drying air of heating ducts. In the spring, once daytime temperatures are around 65°F and nighttime temperatures above 50°F, move plants outdoors again. Gradually expose them to sunlight by placing them in a shaded area for a few days and then gradually moving them into brighter sunlight.
Do not leave them outside if the forecast calls for nighttime temperatures below 50° F.

Outside

Many hardy perennials, vegetables such as collards or kale, and some herbs such as bay and rosemary tolerate cold weather. If possible, move these plants close to the house or to a sheltered area. These containers, along with pots containing fruit trees or bushes that remain outside during winter, may need insulation to protect the root balls from freezing. (Refer to the recommendations for success with fruits in the NC State Extension publication AG-748, *Container Gardening Planting Calendar for Edibles in the NC Piedmont.*) Root damage can occur because the root system is not as well-insulated from cold in a container as it would be in the ground. The container can be loosely wrapped with chicken wire and the area between the pot and the wire filled with inches of leaves or straw for insulation. Alternatively, several materials

Table 18–8. Light, Water, and Nutrient Requirements for Herbs

Herb	Full Sun	Tolerates Partial Shade	Partial Shade	Moist	Slightly Dry	Dry	Light[a]	Medium[b]	Heavy[c]
Basil		X			X		X		
Bay		X				X	X		
Borage		X			X		X		
Chamomile		X		X			X		
Chervil			X	X			X		
Chives		X		X			X		
Cilantro		X		X			X		
Dill		X		X			X		
Fennel	X					X	X		
Feverfew		X			X		X		
Lavender		X				X	X		
Lemongrass	X			X					X
Lemon verbena	X			X				X	
Marjoram	X					X		X	
Mint	X	X	X	X			X		
Monarda		X		X				X	
Oregano	X					X	X		
Parsley			X		X		X		
Rosemary	X				X		X		
Sage		X				X	X		
Salad burnet		X			X		X		
Scented geranium	X				X		X		
Stevia		X			X			X	
Tarragon	X					X			X
Thyme		X				X	X		

[a] Fertilize at planting or for established plants fertilize once early in the growing season.

[b] Fertilize monthly with a liquid fertilizer or every 12 weeks with a timed-release fertilizer.

[c] Fertilize every 2 weeks with a liquid fertilizer and every 8–10 weeks with a timed-release fertilizer.

18

are available that can be used to directly wrap the pots. These include a frost blanket, bubble wrap, closed cell foam (1-inch thick), quilt batting, household insulation, or a blanket (Figure 18–18). If using quilt batting or household insulation, cover with a layer of plastic to keep it from getting soaked during wet weather. When overwintering plants, the moisture in the potting mix should be periodically checked and dry containers watered if the temperatures are going to be above freezing. Keeping the plants watered can help protect them from frost damage.

Figure 18–18. Insulating a container using closed cell foam.
Kathleen Moore, CC BY - 2.0

Indoor Containers— Houseplants

People are spending more time indoors than ever before. It is estimated that many of us spend as much as 90% of our time inside. Even so, we have an innate need to be intimately connected with the outdoor world. Decorating our interior living and work spaces with live plants gives us an instant connection with nature.

Benefits of Houseplants

Plants make almost any interior more pleasant and attractive. Homes, offices, banks, commercial buildings, shopping malls, and restaurants are so much more inviting when living plants are part of the setting. Plants add warmth, color, texture, scent, and beauty to cold, uninviting indoor spaces.

Their beauty and warmth is not the only reason to grow plants indoors. Indoor air pollution, a particular problem in sealed-off, energy-efficient buildings, consists of particles and gases trapped in building air that are not circulated or filtered properly. Research by the National Aeronautics and Space Administration (NASA) has proven that houseplants have the ability to improve indoor air quality by reducing air pollution from chemicals such as formaldehyde and benzene. Further research is under way to determine the efficiency of indoor plants in reducing common indoor air pollutants such as asbestos, pesticides, carbon dioxide, carbon monoxide, and chemicals released from detergents, solvents, cleaning fluids, clothing, furniture, carpets, and insulation.

Growing houseplants is a great way to bring our outdoor gardens indoors, enabling us to garden year-round.

In addition, work environments that incorporate interior plants into the décor have increased employee productivity. When surrounded by plants, workers tend to be more relaxed and their mental and physical well-being enhanced. Houseplants beautify our interior spaces, improve indoor air quality, and give us an energy boost.

Challenges of Growing Plants Indoors

Most species that are sold as houseplants are native to the many tropical regions of the world. The tropics are warm all year with average temperatures between 65°F to 80°F, with no threat of freezes. Plants that originate from tropical rainforests are accustomed to high humidity, filtered light, ambient temperatures, and evenly moist potting mixes.

Our temperature preferences are very similar to those of tropical plants so it is logical that we have chosen these plants to share our indoor spaces. Even though we find the same temperatures agreeable, the available light intensities and humidity in our indoor spaces are often too low for most tropical plant species. Plants are adaptable to a degree, but the closer the indoor environment is to their native habitat, the more they flourish. The key then is to choose plants that match the environmental conditions already available and learn the possibilities and limitations of altering the environment to suit each plant's needs.

18

Table 18–9. Container Watering Methods and Their Pros and Cons

Watering Type	Pro	Con
Watering Can	Least expensive. Can use water from rain barrels.	If watered too heavily, soil nutrients are washed out the bottom of the container. If the foliage gets wet, it is more susceptible to sunscald as well as to disease.
Garden Hose	Lightweight compared to carrying a watering can. One hose will likely reach all containers on a patio.	If hose sits in the sun, water may be hot and can stunt root development. Sunscald and powdery mildew can occur after inadvertently wetting foliage.
Drip Irrigation System	Convenient and timesaving. Ensures the plants get watered in a timely manner. Decreased water volume per irrigation cycle results in less nutrient runoff. Can purchase a timer with a rain delay so that the system can be turned off when it rains.	Initial cost of purchasing the system and the time to install it. Requires routine maintenance to be sure all parts remain in good working order.
Self-Watering Containers	Draws water from a bottom reservoir into the soil by capillary action through small soil columns or rope wicks without causing the soil to become too wet. Useful for people maintaining weekend cottages, doing balcony gardening where draining water would be a problem, or taking summer vacations.	Purchasing multiple containers at one time can be expensive. Containers are heavy when filled.

18

Acclimatizing Houseplants

Most foliage plants available for sale in North Carolina are grown in production nurseries in other states, such as Florida. They are grown under optimal production conditions that are quite different than conditions in the typical home or office. To produce a quick crop, nursery workers maintain a production environment with high light, high humidity, frequent watering, and high fertilizer rates. This push for quick growth creates a lush yet tender plant. Newly purchased plants need a period of time to adjust to the drastic environmental differences between a production nursery and the average indoor setting. To help reduce shock, gradually reduce a plant's light, humidity, growing media moisture, and fertilizer levels. This process of adaptation is called "acclimatization," and it provides time for plants to modify their leaf cellular structure to better adapt to a new light environment. If plants produced under high light are not properly acclimatized to low light conditions, the plants begin to starve and gradually decline. A newly purchased plant may have food reserves built up, so its decline may take a few months. But it eventually shows stress symptoms due to the abrupt decrease in light intensity. Acclimatization is also required when potted plants are moved from the outside to the inside and vice versa. When moving plants inside, place them in an indoor area of the highest light intensity and humidity. Gradually move them to their winter location over a period of four to eight weeks.

As mentioned earlier, all plants need the same, basic environmental conditions to survive. Light, water, temperature, air movement, humidity, fertilization, and proper growing medium are the key factors that affect plant growth. When growing tropical foliage plants indoors, gardeners find that light is often the most limited interior resource of all the factors that affect plant growth.

Light

Light is necessary for plants to manufacture their own food. Three specific aspects of light affect plant growth: light intensity (the amount of brightness plants receive), light quality (the colors in the light stream or "spectral distribution"), and light duration (how long plants are exposed to that intensity and quality). Optimal levels of all three aspects ensure healthy, beautiful houseplants.

Light Intensity

Light intensity is the amount of light given off at a certain brightness or strength. The higher the light level is surrounding a plant, the greater the supply of food. So the quantity of light a plant receives greatly affects its growth and overall health. The amount of light emitted indoors can vary drastically from room to room (as well as in different areas of the same room), so it is essential to determine the light intensity for each interior space. Our eyes are not good indicators of light intensity because they automatically adjust to differing light levels. Light intensity is measured in foot-candles (fc). One foot-candle is the amount of light cast by a candle on a flat surface at a distance of 1 foot. Various hand-held, simple-to-use, light meters are sold at reasonable costs by horticultural supply companies. Light meter "apps" are also available for smart phones, some of which are free. Once light levels are measured, select plants that thrive in those levels.

Not all houseplants require the same light intensity. In fact, an intensity range that is ideal for one species may damage another. Plants are typically categorized by the number of foot-candles required, grouped as low, medium, or high light-requiring. The foot-candle values for each range are defined in Table 18–10.

The lower ranges in each category are needed to maintain plant growth. The higher ranges are suggested to increase plant growth. Use these ranges as general guidelines. A healthy, growing plant is the best indicator that the environmental conditions are agreeable.

The light requirements for many houseplants have been researched and conveniently categorized for us. After light intensity values are obtained (Table 18–11), it is easy to find those plants that require the light intensities a particular interior space has to offer. This ensures the greatest growing success.

Plant food production (photosynthesis) is governed by light intensity and light duration. If the rate at which a plant produces food is equal to the rate at which it consumes its food (respiration), the plant simply maintains its relative size. This means that new plant tissue is produced at the same rate as old tissue dies. For a plant to grow, it must manufacture more food than it consumes, meaning there is more tissue being generated than there is tissue dying. For some species, longer day-length can make up for low-light intensity. Research has shown that the average houseplant needs approximately 85 fc for 12 hours a day to maintain its original quality for a year. Table 18–12 quantifies the survival expectancy of certain houseplant species under differing light conditions.

If a light meter is not available and sunlight is the primary light source, the following descriptions help determine the light in the space:

- **Low light:** Areas more than 8 feet away from a window; dimly lit corners; the center areas of rooms, hallways, or rooms facing north. In addition, spaces that receive only artificial light are usually low-light situations.
- **Medium light:** Indoor spaces that are 4 feet to 8 feet away from south and west windows and west windows that do not receive any direct sun.
- **High light:** Areas within 4 feet of large windows that face south, east, or west.

But what light intensity levels can we expect indoors? For reference, Table 18–13 lists light levels for various indoor and outdoor environments.

Factors Influencing Light Intensity

The amount of light a plant receives indoors is influenced by various factors. The dimensions of windows and doors, as well as the direction these openings face, affect the amount of light that enters a room. As seasons change, so does the angle of the sun. At midday in the summer, the sun's light energy hits the earth at a 90° angle, spreading the sun's energy out over a localized area. In the wintertime the angle of the sun is lower and hits the earth at a lower angle, spreading the sun's energy out over a larger area and making the light less intense at any given point.

Table 18–10. Foot-candle Values for Light Intensities

Light Intensity	Foot-Candles to Maintain Growth	Foot-Candles to Promote Growth
Low light	25 – 74	75 – 300
Medium light	75 – 149	150 – 1,500
High light	150 – 999	1,000 – 3,000+

During these seasonal changes, plants may need to be moved to lower or higher light intensities to provide them with the correct amount of light. Windows that face south, east, and west allow more light indoors than windows that face north. Draperies, shades, and sheers can reduce the amount of natural light that can enter. Keeping windows clean and removing window screens can increase light penetration by as much as 30%. Plant placement in relation to doors and windows also affects the light levels plants receive (Figure 18–19).

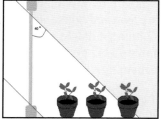

Figure 18–19. Plant placement in relation to a window influences light intensity levels.

Less obvious factors such as wall and floor colors can lighten or darken a room. Mirrors reflect sunlight back into a room, as do pools, natural bodies of water, and even nearby buildings. Roof overhangs, outside awnings, buildings, trees, and other outdoor structures can shade or block incoming light.

Symptoms of Inadequate Light Intensity
If a plant is not thriving, inadequate light intensity could be the problem. Plants that are grown under optimal light intensities generate new growth and have a compact, bushy **habit**. Overall leaf color is vibrant, leaves are normal size, stems are turgid, and flowering is promoted.

- **Too Low:** Plants grown under light intensities below optimum have leaves that do not expand to their full potential size. Leaf color is pale, and **internodes** are long (the stems are essentially stretching to reach higher light). This results in a spindly, leggy appearance. Leaves may detach from the stems because there is little stored energy to support them. The plant may cease flowering to conserve energy.

- **Too High:** In their native habitats, many tropical houseplants grow as understory plants beneath the forest canopy. Trees overhead diffuse direct sun, letting in only dappled, filtered light. When plants are grown in light intensities above optimum, chlorophyll can be destroyed, resulting in yellow leaves. Plants produce smaller leaves, reducing leaf surface area in an effort to minimize the amount of sunlight absorbed and the amount of water lost through **transpiration**. If the intensity is severe, leaves detach from the plant to save energy for new growth and to reduce water loss. Large brown patches of dead tissue may develop. This phenomenon is called "leaf scorch."

Strategies for Increasing Light Intensity
Because low light intensities are more likely to be a problem than high light levels, use the following techniques to increase light levels indoors:

- Rotate plants monthly between higher and lower light areas to give plants with low food reserves the chance to build up enough energy to survive when placed back into lower light conditions.
- Move plants closer to a light source.
- Install artificial lights, which can also serve to extend the day-length (see light duration) and can increase light intensity.

If increasing the light intensity is not an option, incorporate these cultural practices to extend the life of the plants:

- Do not overwater; provide just enough to keep plants from wilting.
- Reduce the amount and frequency of fertilization.
- Lower the air temperature a few degrees by adjusting your home's thermostat.

Light Quality
In addition to light intensity, plant growth is influenced by the quality of light received. Light is a blend of different colors, measured in wavelengths, as seen when light passes through a prism. The distribution of these colors is known as light quality (Figure 18–20). Some wavelengths (ultraviolet, infrared) cannot be seen by the human eye, but are nonetheless important for plant health.

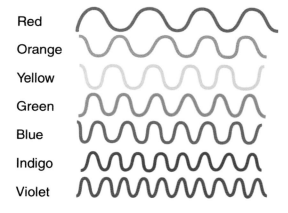

Visible Light - Wavelength

Figure 18–20. Light is a blend of different colors measured in wavelengths. The distribution of these colors is called light quality.
NASA, CC0

Different wavelengths affect plant growth in different ways. Plants use the blue and red portions of the light spectrum to manufacture their own food (photosynthesis). Plants grown strictly under blue light are compact, thick stemmed, have dark green leaves, and few flowers. The red and far-red wavelengths encourage flowering, stem elongation, and expansion of plant parts. The green and yellow portions of the spectrum are used in only small quantities, thus these are the colors we see reflected back from the leaves and stems.

Table 18–11. Light Intensity Requirements for Select Houseplants

Common Name	Scientific Name	Light Intensity	Temperature[a]	Comments
African violet hybrids & cultivars	*Saintpaulia* spp.,	High to medium	Warm	High humidity
Aloe vera	*Aloe barbadensis*	High	Average	
Aluminum plant	*Pilea cadierei*	High to medium	Warm	
Anthurium	*Anthurium* spp.	Medium	Warm	Keep moist
Aralia Balfour	*Polyscias balfouriana* 'Aralia Balfour'	High to medium	Warm	High humidity
Aralia, False	*Plerandra elegantissima*	High	Average	High humidity, keep moist
Aralia, Ming	*Polyscias fruiticosa*	High	Warm	High humidity
Arrowhead vine	*Syngonium podophyllum*	High	Average	Keep moist
Begonia, Rex	*Begonia* rex hybrids	High	Average	High humidity, keep warm
Bloodleaf	*Iresine herbstii*	High	Average	Keep moist
Botanical wonder	x *Fatshedera lizei*	High to medium	Average	
Bougainvillea	*Bougainvillea glabra*	High	Warm	
Burro's tail	*Sedum morganianum*	High	Average	
Caladium	*Caladium* × *hortulanum*	High	Warm	High humidity
Calathea	*Calathea picturata*	Medium	Average	
Cast iron plant	*Aspidistra elatior*	Medium to low	Average	
Chenille plant	*Acalypha hispida*	High	Warm	High humidity
Chinese evergreen	*Aglaonema commutatum*	Medium to low	Average	High humidity, keep moist
Coffee plant	*Coffea arabica*	High	Average	High humidity
Coleus	*Coleus blumei*	High	Average	
Corn plant	*Dracaena fragrans*	High to medium	Average	
Croton	*Codiaeum variegatum* var. *pictum*	High	Warm	High humidity, keep moist
Cyclamen	*Cyclamen persicum*	High	Cool	
Dieffenbachia, Gold	*Dieffenbachia maculata* 'Rudolph Roehrs'	Medium	Average to warm	
Dracaena, Gold dust	*Dracaena surculosa*	High to medium	Average	
Dracaena, striped	*Dracaena deremensis*	High to medium	Average	High humidity
Dragon tree	*Dracaena marginata*	High to medium	Average	
Dumbcane, giant	*Dieffenbachia amoena*	High to medium	Average	
Dumbcane, spotted	*Dieffenbachia maculata*	High to medium	Average	
Fatsia, Japanese	*Fatsia japonica*	High	Cool	
Fern, asparagus	*Asparagus plumosus*	High to medium	Average	
Fern, bird's nest	*Asplenium nidus*	Medium	Average	High humidity, keep moist
Fern, Boston	*Nephrolepis exaltata* 'Bostoniensis'	High to medium	Average	Keep moist

(continued)

18

Table 18–11. Light Intensity Requirements for Select Houseplants *continued*

Common Name	Scientific Name	Light Intensity	Temperature[a]	Comments
Fern, rabbit's foot; Golden polypody	*Polypodium aureum*	Medium	Average	Keep moist
Fern, Southern maidenhair	*Adiantum capillus-veneris*	High to medium	Average	High humidity, keep moist
Fern, staghorn	*Platycerium bifurcatum*	High	Average	High humidity
Fig, creeping	*Ficus pumila*	Medium to low	Average	High humidity
Fig, fiddle-leaf	*Ficus lyrata*	High to medium	Average	
Fig, weeping	*Ficus benjamina*	High to medium	Average	
Firecracker flower	*Crossandra infundibuliformis*	High	Warm	High humidity
Flame violet	*Episcia cupreata*	High	Warm	High humidity, keep moist
Friendship plant	*Pilea involucrata*	High	Warm	High humidity
Fuchsia	*Fuchsia × hybrida*	High	Cool	High humidity
Gloxinia	*Sinningia speciosa*	High	Warm	
Gold dust plant	*Aucuba japonica* 'Variegata'	High to medium	Average to cool	
Grape ivy	*Cissus rhombifolia*	High to medium	Average to cool	
Hibiscus, Chinese	*Hibiscus rosa-sinensis*	High	Average	
Ivy, English	*Hedera helix*	High to medium	Average to cool	
Jacob's coat	*Acalypha wilkesiana*	High	Warm	High humidity
Jade plant	*Crassula argentea*	High	Average to cool	
Joseph's coat	*Alternanthera ficoidea*	High	Average	
Kaffir lily	*Clivia miniata*	High	Average to cool	
Kangaroo vine	*Cissus antarctica*	High to low	Warm to cool	
Lipstick plant	*Aeschynanthus radicans*	High	Warm	High humidity, keep moist
Mandevilla	*Dipladenia sanderi*	High	Average	High humidity
Mosaic plant	*Fittonia verschaffeltii*	High to medium	Average to cool	High humidity
Moses-in-the-Cradle, Oyster plant	*Rhoeo spathacea*	High	Average	
Norfolk Island pine	*Araucaria heterophylla*	High to medium	Average	High humidity
Palm, Areca	*Dypsis lutescens*	High	Warm to average	High humidity
Palm, Bamboo	*Chamaedorea erumpens*	High to low	Average	
Palm, Fishtail	*Caryota mitis*	High to medium	Average	
Palm, Kentia	*Howea forsteriana*	High to medium	Average	
Palm, Parlor	*Chamaedorea elegans*	High to medium	Average	Low to high humidity, keep moist
Palm, Ponytail	*Beaucarnea recurvata*	High	Average	
Peace lily	*Spathiphyllum* spp.	High to medium	Average	Keep moist
Peacock plant	*Calathea makoyana*	Medium	Average	High humidity, keep moist
Peperomia, Watermelon	*Peperomia argyreia*	High to medium	Average	

(continued)

Table 18–11. Light Intensity Requirements for Select Houseplants *continued*

Common Name	Scientific Name	Light Intensity	Temperature[a]	Comments
Peperomia, Emerald ripple	*Peperomia caperata*	High to medium	Average	
Peperomia, oval-leaf; Baby rubber plant	*Peperomia obtusifolia*	Medium	Average	
Philodendron	*Philodendron selloum*	High to medium	Cool	
Philodendron, Heart leaf	*Philodendron scandens*	High to medium	Average	
Philodendron, Split-leaf	*Monstera deliciosa*	Medium to low	Average	
Piggyback plant	*Tolmiea menziesii*	High to medium	Average to cool	Keep moist
Podocarpus	*Podocarpus macrophyllus*	High	Average to cool	
Polka dot plant	*Hypoestes phyllostachya*	High	Average	
Pothos	*Epipremnum aureum*	High to low	Average	
Prayer plant	*Maranta leuconeura*	High	Average	High humidity
Purple heart	*Setcreasea pallida*	High	Cool	
Purple velvet plant	*Gynura aurantiaca*	High to medium	Average	Keep moist
Ribbon plant	*Dracaena sanderiana*	High to medium	Average	
Rubber plant	*Ficus elastica*	Medium	Average	
Schefflera	*Schefflera actinophylla*	High	Average	High humidity
Schefflera, dwarf	*Heptapleurum arboricola*	High	Average	High humidity
Screw pine	*Pandanus tectorus* 'Veitchii'	High	Warm	High humidity
Shrimp plant	*Justicia guttata*	High	Average to warm	
Snake plant	*Sansevieria trifasciata*	High to medium	Average	
Spider plant	*Chlorophytum comosum*	High to medium	Average	
Sprengeri asparagus fern	*Asparagus densiflorus* 'Sprengeri'	Medium	Average	
Strawberry geranium	*Saxifraga stolonifera*	High	Cool	Keep moist
Ti plant	*Cordyline terminalis*	High	Warm	
Umbrella palm	*Cyperus alternifolius*	Medium	Average	
Wandering Jew, Inch plant	*Tradescantia zebrina*	High to medium	Average	Keep moist
Wandering Jew, Small-leaf spiderwort	*Tradescantia subaspera*	High	Average	Keep moist
Wax plant	*Hoya carnosa*	High	Average	High humidity
Zebra plant	*Aphelandra squarrosa*	High	Average to warm	High humidity, keep moist

[a] Warm-temperature plants grow best at 70°F – 80°F during the day and 64°F – 70°F at night.

Average-temperature plants grow best at 60°F – 65°F during the day and 55°F – 60°F at night.

Cool-temperature plants grow best at 50°F – 60°F during the day and 45°F – 55°F at night.

18

Table 18–12.
Number of Months Plants Remain Attractive under Various Light Levels

Plant	15 to 20 fc[a]	25 to 50 fc	50 to 75 fc	75 to 100 fc
Aucuba	12	24	36	38
Begonia	…	12	…	…
Bromeliad	…	12	…	…
Cast iron plant	12	24	36	38
Chinese evergreen	12	36	36	…
Dieffenbachia	12	12	12	…
Dracaena	30	36	36	38
Peace lily	…	…	…	12
Peperomia	…	12	…	…
Philodendron	12	30	36	36
Pothos	…	…	30	36
Rubber plant	…	…	…	12
Snake plant	12	…	…	…
Syngonium	12	…	…	…

[a] fc = foot-candle

Table 18–13.
Average Light Intensities for Various Indoor and Outdoor Environments

Environment	Foot-candle levels
Library, classroom	20
Office	50
Supermarket	100
Light shining into a window	100–5,000
Outdoors—overcast	1,000
Outdoors—full sun	10,000

Light sources

The light sources available to houseplants are natural sunlight, artificial lights, or a combination of both. Natural sunlight is ideal because it supplies all of the colors of the light spectrum that plants need to develop properly. If natural sunlight levels are inadequate, artificial lights can be an acceptable complement. In addition to increasing light intensity, artificial lights also make it possible to manipulate day-length. Plants need a dark period to develop properly and so should not be grown under light for 24 hours a day. Unfortunately, with artificial lights, the light intensity decreases dramatically as the plant is moved away from the light source. Figure 18–21 shows the light intensity is significantly greater for a plant placed 1 foot away from an artificial light source than 10 feet away. With natural sunlight, the difference in light intensity within a span of 10 feet is very slight—unless the illumination path is blocked.

The most common types of artificial lighting are incandescent, fluorescent, and LED. Incandescent lights, although suitable for human purposes, are not ideal for growing houseplants. They generate mostly red light waves and some infrared light but are very low in the blue range. In addition, incandescent lights produce a great deal of heat, so plants must be placed at a safe distance to reduce the risk of burning foliage. Incandescent lights are approximately three times less energy-efficient than fluorescent lights, and their bulb life is much shorter. Finally, the decrease in light intensity as distance increases is greater for incandescent lights than for any other light source.

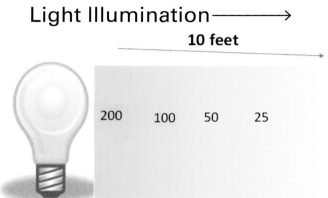

Light Illumination⟶

10 feet

200   100   50   25

Foot Candles

Figure 18–21. Light intensity from an artificial light source rapidly decreases as distance increases.

Fluorescent lights are the most economical and commonly used lighting in offices, banks, stores, and malls. Generic fluorescent lights produce mostly blue light, and are low in red light. Foliage plants grow well under these fluorescent lights, but blooming plants require extra infrared, which can be supplied by incandescent lights or special horticultural fluorescent lights. These "full-spectrum" lights emit all wavelengths and are quite effective if artificial lights are the only source of light for growing plants. Fluorescent lights are very energy-efficient and give off little heat. Plants can be placed close to these lights without the risk of burning the plant. Typically, a fluorescent light fixture is positioned approximately 12 inches above the plants. As with other artificial light sources, the light intensity levels decrease as the distance between the plant and the light source increases. A 40-watt fluorescent tube produces 120 foot-candles at a distance of 1 foot, but only 75 foot-candles at a distance of 2 feet. Ceiling fluorescent lights provide limited benefit for plants on the floor. As fluorescent tubes or bulbs age, their brightness decreases. When replacing fluorescent lights, remember to acclimatize plants to the new, brighter bulbs to prevent light shock to plants that have become accustomed to the older, dimmer bulbs.

LEDs (light-emitting diodes) are low-heat artificial lighting fixtures (when cooled properly) that are gaining in popularity. Horticultural LED grow-lights are available that emit only the wavelengths used by plants and last much longer than conventional lights, making them very energy-efficient and economical.

Natural Sunlight and the Seasons

As with light intensity, seasonal changes also regulate the light duration of natural sunlight. In summer, the sun's path is higher above the horizon, the day-length is longer, and natural sunlight is more intense than in other seasons. For many plants this is their peak growing period. In winter the sun's path is lower in the sky and farther to the south, the day-length is shorter, and the sun's intensity is weaker than in other seasons, so plants receive fewer hours of less intense sunlight due to the sun's southern angle (Figure 18–22). Because the amount of light plants receive in winter is both less intense and shorter in duration, plant growth decreases or stops during the winter. Therefore plants need less watering and fertilization at this time of the year.

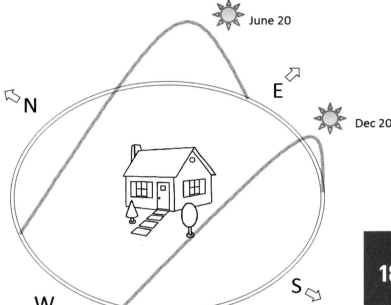

June 20

E

Dec 20

N

S

W

Figure 18–22. The sun's path in the summer is higher than in the winter.

Light Duration

The third aspect of light that effects plant growth is light duration (also called "day-length"). The length of time that plants are exposed to a light source, within a 24-hour period, can trigger physiological responses such as dormancy and flowering. This phenomenon is called **photoperiodism**. To be more exact, it is the amount of darkness that plants receive that brings about these responses.

Plants are categorized by their photoperiodic sensitivity. Plants that require long hours of darkness in their daily cycle to trigger these responses are called "short-day" plants. Plants that need short periods of darkness are called "long-day" plants (Figure 18–23). The number of hours needed is species-specific. Plant species in which physiological activity is not governed by photoperiod are called "day-neutral" plants.

Figure 18–23. Photoperiod demonstration on Poinsettia 'Prestige Red'. Short Day exposure (right): More than 12 hours of darkness in a 24-hour period. Long Day exposure (left): Less than 8 hours of darkness in a 24-hour period.
Diane Mays, CC BY - 2.0

Light and Temperature

Light and temperature are two closely interwoven aspects of plant growth. Photosynthesis (food production) is regulated by light intensity and light duration, while respiration (food consumption) is regulated by temperature.

Higher temperatures speed up the respiration process, and when air temperatures rise, so does a plant's demand for food. Many **interiorscapes** maintain low light intensities and high temperatures, which results in small amounts of food produced, yet large amounts of food consumed. Therefore, if low light is all that is available, maintaining a lower temperature (within a suitable range) will lower plant respiration and prolong life.

Temperature

The tropics have relatively consistent temperatures throughout the year, making tropical species ill-equipped to handle abrupt temperature changes. Most houseplants can tolerate normal, gradual temperature fluctuations, but sudden drops or rises can be detrimental. Houseplants cannot survive outdoors during North Carolina's winters. Many species experience **chilling injury** at temperatures below 55°F, while others can withstand temperatures as low as 45°F. Most houseplants grow best in day temperatures around 70°F and night temperatures around 60°F.

Detecting damage in plants exposed to a slight decrease or increase in temperature can be difficult. In many cases, the symptoms do not become apparent until weeks after exposure. Plants exposed to abrupt, significant temperature changes, however, develop symptoms very quickly. Severely cold-damaged leaves and stems appear

"water-soaked" due to a breakdown of the plant's cellular structure. Excessively low or high temperatures can hinder plant growth, cause leaf and flower drop, yellowing, **necrosis**, wilting, an increased susceptibility to diseases, and ultimately death. The lower the temperature is and the longer the exposure, the greater the damage.

When growing flowering houseplants, decreasing nighttime temperatures intensifies flower color, prolongs flower life, and decreases water loss. To produce these effects, adjust the thermostat to 55°F to 60°F at night.

Indoor Temperature Microclimates

Temperatures can differ from room to room, as well as in different areas of the same room, creating indoor **microclimates**. Consider these temperature variations when placing plants. Problems arise when temperature differences are undetected or not understood. A minimum/maximum thermometer helps pinpoint such differences.

Although the window sill is a popular place to grow houseplants, sunlight shining directly through a window can result in temperatures high enough to damage tender plant tissue. Conversely, energy-inefficient windows can allow temperatures to drop too low for tropical plants. Moving plants in toward the room and 6 inches away from a window is usually enough distance to protect plants from excessive heat or intense cold.

Plants are subject to blasts of hot or cold air when placed near exterior doors. In addition, the extra air movement at building entrances can increase plant transpiration, requiring an increase in watering and possibly resulting in tissue damage. Dramatic, eye-catching planters are often positioned at business entrances or in home foyers as showcase pieces. Tropical plants, however, can suffer chilling injury if exposed to cold air. Place planters far enough away from outside doors to prevent cold damage. Use temperate plants where cold-temperature blasts are possible.

Temperatures in unheated sunrooms can fluctuate so drastically within a 24-hour period that houseplants do not have time to adjust. If the outdoor daytime temperatures are suitable, it may be necessary to bring plants into heated areas at night. Fireplaces, radiators, appliances, and electronics make risky display areas due to the generated heat. The potting mix in a plant container placed on a warm refrigerator or television can dry out quickly, making more frequent watering necessary. Root tissue may even experience burns if the heat given off is too high.

Do not place plants on or near heat registers, radiators, or air conditioners. The air emitted from these devices is too extreme for plants.

Temperature Acclimatization

When moving tropical plants outdoors for the summer, wait until the nighttime temperatures are consistently above 60°F and protect plants from cold winds. In the winter, bring plants inside before the nighttime temperatures drop below 60°F. Move plants to an indoor area where the temperature and light exposure are similar to that of the outdoor location. Then ease the plants slowly into the new environment.

Not all houseplants have the same temperature requirements. Temperature preferences for houseplants are categorized as follows:

- **Warm:** Day temperatures 70°F to 80°F, night temperatures 64°F to 70°F
- **Moderate:** Day temperatures 60°F to 65°F, night temperatures 55°F to 60°F
- **Cool:** Day temperatures 50°F to 60°F, night temperatures 45°F to 55°F

Relative Humidity

As with light (intensity, quality, and duration) and temperature, houseplants require certain humidity levels in the surrounding air to flourish. Relative humidity is the amount of water vapor (moisture) in the air, expressed as a percentage, compared to the maximum amount of moisture the air can hold at that temperature.

Foliage plants native to tropical rainforests are accustomed to average relative humidity levels of 60% to 90%, and levels during nursery production are often kept as high as 85% to 95%. Many houseplants can grow well in relative humidity levels of 40% to 60%. In our buildings and homes, however, we maintain average relative humidity levels of only 10% to 15%. This is due to the increased drying effects of heating and air-conditioning systems.

The rate of plant transpiration (water lost from plant surfaces) is influenced by both relative humidity and the temperature in the surrounding air. Low relative humidity and high temperatures increase the rate of transpiration. Increased transpiration increases a plant's need for water, so high temperature and low humidity conditions require more frequent watering.

Conversely, the cooler the air is, the higher the relative humidity is and the lower the transpiration rate. So care should be taken not to overwater in these conditions. Providing an environment with moderate temperatures and high relative humidity slows transpiration, helping to maintain overall plant hydration.

Low relative humidity can affect both humans and plants adversely. To minimize human health problems caused by poor indoor air quality, the Occupational Safety and Health Administration, OSHA, recommends that buildings be maintained at a relative humidity of 30% to 60%. Plants grown in low relative humidity conditions exhibit such stress symptoms as leaf yellowing, curling, drop and marginal necrosis, dead spots or dead tips on leaves, flower bud death, and flower drop.

Although indoor humidity levels are often too low for most houseplants, there are various ways to increase indoor humidity levels around plants:

- **Humidifiers:** The most effective way is to place a humidifier in the immediate growing area. In tightly closed buildings, keep humidity from rising above 60% to prevent mold or mildew growth.
- **Pots of water:** Place a nonflammable container full of water on a hot radiator or a wood stove. The heat evaporates the water, adding moisture to the air.
- **Grouping:** Grouping plants closely together forms a canopy of leaves. The leaves transpire and create moisture but also trap moisture from the air, creating a humid microclimate around the plants (Figure 18–24). Maintain air circulation around the group to reduce the possibility of foliar diseases.
- **Pebbles in a saucer filled with water:** Fill the saucer with water just below the surface of the pebble layer (Figure 18–25). As the water in the saucer evaporates, the humidity in the air increases. Do not allow the plant container to contact the water in the saucer. Fertilizer that is flushed out of the pot becomes concentrated as **leachate** in the saucer. If the pot contacts the leachate, it can be absorbed back into the potting mix and may burn the roots. In addition, the pot can become water-logged, causing the plant to develop root rot.

18

Figure 18–24. Grouping plants helps keep relative humidity high.
Diane Mays, CC BY - 2.0

18-28

Figure 18–25. Pebbles in a saucer help keep relative humidity high.
Kathleen Moore, CC BY - 2.0

Misting plants with a spray bottle is not useful as it raises the relative humidity for only a short time. If mist is necessary, spray plants early in the morning so that there is enough radiant heat during the rest of the day to dry the foliage. Water remaining on foliage, accompanied by cool, damp night conditions, creates an ideal environment for disease development. Also, rooms such as kitchens, bathrooms, and laundry rooms are often touted as providing higher humidity than other rooms in the home. This may be true for short spurts of time, but foliage plants require consistent humidity levels as opposed to levels that fluctuate. Oscillating humidity levels impart as much damage as constantly inadequate levels.

Lastly, there are many species grown as houseplants that prefer low humidity. Plants such as cacti, succulents, and bromeliads grow well in low relative humidity. These plants have thick, fleshy, waxy, or hairy leaves that are adapted for maintaining plant hydration. This is typical of species native to climates that are consistently dry or exhibit long periods of drought.

Air Circulation

Outdoor plants are intermittently exposed to winds and breezes that help reduce diseases, encourage insects to relocate, build strong roots for anchorage, blow dead leaves and branches out of plant canopies, and dry out moist potting mixes.

Houseplants can also benefit from air circulation. Provide supplemental air movement via a ceiling, floor, or table fan to maintain constant temperatures throughout a room, disperse drafts, lower disease potential, and vent gases that develop from heating systems. Avoid aiming fans directly at plants, as this will dry them out. Instead, maintain a low volume of constant, indirect air flow, which will provide enough ventilation for houseplants.

Grooming

Grooming (cleaning and pruning) houseplants periodically is necessary to remove dust, keep them attractive and in desirable shape, and rid them of pests. This entails washing dust-coated dirty leaves, removing dead plant tissue, shaping up unruly growth habits, and watching for insects and diseases.

Leaves of indoor plants can become coated with a heavy layer of dust in a surprisingly short amount of time. Indoor dust and grime that accumulate on leaf surfaces will clog stomates, reducing transpiration and restricting gas exchange. Dust buildup also blocks sunlight, reducing photosynthesis, and is very unattractive.

Wash leaves every two or three months to keep houseplants beautiful and healthy. To clean **glabrous** leaves, wash upper and lower leaf surfaces with a soft, moistened cloth. Use a make-up or soft painters brush to clean dust from **pubescent** leaves. Place plants in the shower to wash away dust. Or, in warm weather, rinse them outside with a garden hose. Use warm water between 60°F to 75°F to prevent damaging the plant with excessively hot or cold temperatures. Avoid using leaf-shine products to clean foliage because these products attract dust, clog **stomata**, and slow growth.

To protect plant health, remove dead, damaged, or diseased leaves, stems, and flowers as quickly as they appear.

Pruning can also restore a plant's initial growth habit, reduce plant size, thin-out overgrowth, or artistically shape plants into desired forms. Always use sharp, sanitized pruners so as not to fray plant tissue when cutting and to prevent the spread of diseases by contaminated pruner blades.

Whether pruning to promote health or beauty, always cut stems just above a node (Figure 18–26) or where they attach to a larger branch. Remove undesired leaves where they attach to the stem. If less than a third of a leaf is damaged, trim off all but a slight amount of the dead leaf-tips. This will prevent the leaf from continuing to die back from the tip (Figure 18–27).

It is normal for aging leaves and flowers to abscise, or detach, when they are old. Dead plant tissue that falls onto the potting mix, however, is fodder for diseases. Dispose of all detached plant tissue promptly to decrease disease development.

18

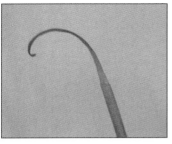 

Figure 18–27. Prune off at leaf tip leaving a small margin of dead tissue to prevent the leaf from continuing to die back.
Kathleen Moore, CC BY - 2.0

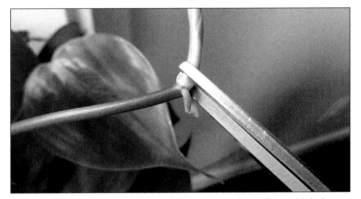

Figure 18–26. Prune stems above a node to a branch to which they are attached to prevent disease from entering extraneous internode tissue.
Kathleen Moore, CC BY - 2.0

Plants that receive light predominantly from one direction often lean toward the light source to maximize light absorption. This is called phototropism. To encourage uniform growth, rotate plants by a turning the container clockwise about 90 degrees (a ¼ turn) every three months.

Lastly, look for signs of insect and disease problems when grooming. Such signs include sticky leaves (**"honeydew"**), white cottony masses (scale or mealy bugs), brown bumps on stems (armored scale), and gray fuzzy growth on leaves (gray mold or powdery mildew). Eradicate infestations using methods described in the "Pest Management" section of this chapter and chapter 8, "IPM."

Integrated Pest Management

Insects

For insect management, the best defense is to **scout** often and take immediate action to eradicate if pests are found. Most insects harbor in inconspicuous areas of the plant to hide from predators. Because of this, insects are often overlooked until the plant shows a decline in health. Each insect species prefers to feed on and live in a particular plant part or parts. Learning an insect's favored locations greatly increases the ability to control the population.

Aphids are soft-bodied, piercing-sucking insects commonly found in clusters along stems, on tender growing tips, and on the undersides of leaves (Figure 18–28).

Aphids come in an array of colors—peach, green, and black are the most common. Often the cast-off skins (seen as white flecks) and excreted honeydew (sticky, clear mucilage) are more noticeable than the aphids themselves. Aphids are often difficult to manage because they can wedge deeply into developing, unfurling growing tips and are thus protected. Their soft bodies, however, make them somewhat easier to manage than other pests. Spray plants outside with a strong stream of water or use a soapy water spray. Be sure to cover undersides of leaves. Insecticides are rarely warranted.

Figure 18–28. Aphids feeding on plant tissue.
Mike Keeling, Flickr CC BY-ND - 2.0

Scales cover themselves with coating materials for protection. Two common types are found on houseplants. Soft scales are covered by a waxy secretion, and armored scales develop dark-brown shell-like coverings. Soft scales are round, flat, light brown or cream-colored insects that feed on the undersides of leaves and along

Figure 18–29. Soft scale insects.
Gilles San Martin, Flickr CC BY-SA - 2.0

18

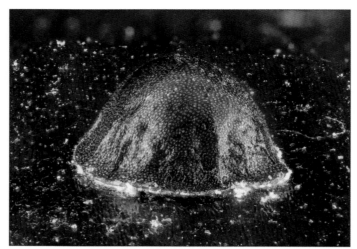

Figure 18–30. An armored scale.
USGS Native Bee Inventory and Monitoring Labratory CC0

stems (Figure 18–29). They produce chlorotic spots on leaf surfaces and along stems as chlorophyll is sucked from the plant. The adult armored scales are oval insects, covered with a dark-brown shell, resembling a humped horseshoe crab (Figure 18–30). They are usually found in a procession on plant stems. Scales do not have wings and move by crawling. Therefore, distancing plants from each other prevents crawlers from easily moving from plant to plant. Control can be accomplished by blasting the scales with a fine, pressurized (but gentle) stream of water. Although laborious, removing the insects by hand is one eradication technique. But hand removal is effective only when the population is small. Brushing the insects with a soft toothbrush dipped in isopropyl alcohol can be effective. A heavy infestation is best eradicated by spraying with horticultural soap or oil as per label instructions. Scales can require repeated treatments, so be thorough and persistent.

Mealybugs are oval-shaped, peach-colored insects often concealed under a soft, cottony covering that gives them a mealy appearance (Figure 18–31). The covering can protect both adults and eggs from pesticides. Mealybugs

Figure 18–31. A mealybug.
Matt Bertone

wedge themselves into crevices on the plant—such as leaf axils and the undersides of leaves. If the population is small, mealybugs can be removed by dabbing each insect with a cotton swab dipped in isopropyl alcohol. Mealybugs can also be blasted off outside with a hose. Set the stream of water to a gentle pressure, and aim directly at the insects, being careful not to damage plant tissue. As with scale, persistence and regular treatments are necessary to eradicate mealybugs.

Thrips are very small, slender, brown insects that burrow into immature growing tips and flower buds, feeding on the tender tissue, pollen, and petals (Figure 18–32). Damage includes brown, distorted, unattractive flower petals, distorted leaf growth, and chlorotic hash marks on leaf surfaces. Although thrips mostly prefer to feed on flowers, occasionally they infest the foliage of houseplants and bedding plants, resulting in necrotic leaf tissue and holes in leaves. To manage, remove all infected flowers, buds, and plant debris and discard. Use a sticky card to trap adults. Severe infestation may warrant a registered bacterial insecticide.

Figure 18–32. Thrips.
Matt Bertone

Spider mites are not insects but relatives of spiders. They suck chlorophyll out of plant cells from the underside of the leaf, causing tiny spots to appear on the upper leaf surface (Figure 18–33). If the population is abundant, spider mites feed on the upper leaf surfaces and growing tips. It is at this time that small, thin webs are seen at the growing points. Spider mites prefer a dry environment and can be prompted to move along by misting infested plants regularly. Perform misting outside so mites do not relocate to a different indoor houseplant. If plants become heavily infested and washing mites off is not working, discard plants.

Figure 18–33. Spider mite damage.
Scot Nelson, Flickr CC0

Fungus gnats are black insects, approximately 1/8-inch long. The adult fungus gnat looks like a miniature mosquito with dark wings, long legs, and antennae (Figure 18–34). The maggots produced by fungus gnats have these characteristics: a round, shiny-black head and a white body. Fungus gnats inhabit moist, shady areas and prefer a soil that includes peat as a component. They lay their eggs on the surface of moist potting mix, where the maggots, when hatched, feed on young roots and stems. Prevention is key and can be accomplished by using a potting mix composed primarily of bark and allowing it to dry between watering. Avoid the use of compost on affected plants, and use a sticky trap to capture adult gnats. Sanitize all gardening tools and containers to prevent infestation. A registered insecticide is rarely needed but can be used to kill the adults.

Figure 18–34. A fungus gnat.
Matt Bertone

Shore flies are often found on overwatered plants. Shore flies prefer warm, wet conditions and breed in algae growing on potting mix surfaces. The adult shore fly looks like a miniature house fly and is slightly larger than the adult fungus gnat (Figure 18–35). Unlike fungus gnats, neither the adult nor larvae harm plants. However, shore flies relieve themselves on foliage, leaving behind unattractive specks of black droppings. Apply the same management practices as for fungus gnat infestations: Allow media to dry out as much as possible without harming the plant, avoid the use of compost on affected plants, and use a sticky trap to catch adult flies.

Figure 18–35. Shore fly.
Matt Bertone

Diseases

Many houseplant diseases are caused by bacteria and fungi. Often the primary cause is plant stress due to unfavorable growing conditions. The best management methods are proper watering, sanitation, and prevention. Clean and sanitize pots, pruners, trowels, and other garden tools with a non-bleach household disinfectant product.

Fungal leaf spots first appear as small yellow spots. The spots enlarge, and the center turns light-tan to dark-brown (Figure 18–36). The diseased areas may run together. Sometimes, fungal, threadlike strands may appear in the affected area. Avoid wetting or misting the foliage. Isolate the plant, and remove the diseased leaves with a pair of scissors. Clean the blades between each cut by dipping them into a freshly made solution of a non-bleach household disinfectant product and then wiping off any excess with a clean cloth. This avoids spreading the disease.

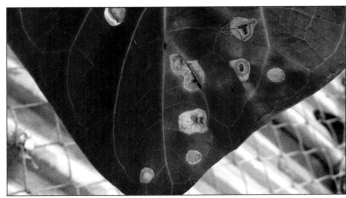

Figure 18–36. Fungal leaf spots.
Scot Nelson, Flickr CC0

18

Fungal root rots favor cool, wet potting mixes. These fungi enter the plant by attacking small roots, and can spread through most of the root system in a few days. Symptoms produced by infected plants include little or no new top growth, a change in color from green to yellow, and sometimes spotting and drying of the foliage (Figure 18–37). Prevention is the best control method; control after the fact is nearly impossible. Discard infected plants as they are unlikely to recover.

Figure 18–37. Root rot on a Yucca spp.
Scot Nelson, Flickr CC0

Bacterial foliar diseases can occur with high humidity, high temperatures, and plants crowded closely together, reducing air circulation. Misting the foliage is a major cause. Foliar symptoms include tip burn, leaf spots, leaf blight, rot, or collapse of plant tissue. Leaf spots are often angular lesions bordered by leaf veins (Figure 18–38). Spots are often light-green, translucent, and/or water-soaked with a yellow halo. As the disease spreads, the centers of the spots turn light-brown to dark-brown. Infected plants do not recover and should be discarded.

Figure 18–38. Bacterial foliar disease.
Scot Nelson, Flickr CC0

Sooty mold is a grey-black mold usually found on the leaves of plants that are infested with honeydew-excreting insects. The spores of the sooty mold germinate in the sweet, excreted droppings of the insects, often covering the leaf surface (Figure 18–39). Sooty mold is not directly harmful to plants. In fact, it can prove to be a helpful indicator of a honeydew-secreting-insect infestation. The detriment comes when the sooty mold is so thick that it interrupts the leaf's photosynthetic process. Clean sooty mold off with a sponge and warm water, and manage the honeydew excreting insects.

Figure 18–39. Sooty mold on a croton (*Codiaeum variegatum*).
Scot Nelson, Flickr CC0

Record Keeping

As with other hobbies and important tasks, keeping a journal or record of what was done and how it worked is helpful. The information can be reviewed later and assist in assessing future strategies. Records can be kept in a notebook or on a garden calendar. Items that can be included are container size and description, plant varieties, dates of planting, how many species were planted and how many survived, descriptions of diseases or pests with any actions taken and their effects, dates of harvest, amount of rain, amount and type of fertilizer used, evaluation of overall results, ideas for next year, and photographs of plants. See Appendix A, "Garden Journaling," for more information on recordkeeping.

Plant Problems and Possible Causes

Rapid leaf drop:
- Extreme temperature or light changes
- Root loss from transplanting
- Overwatering
- Underwatering

Gradual leaf drop:
- Insufficient light
- Insufficient fertilizer
- Overwatering
- Underwatering

Wilting of the entire plant:
- Exposure to cold
- Excess fertilizer
- Overwatering
- Underwatering

Loss of leaf color:
- Excess light
- Insufficient light
- Insufficient fertilizer
- Overwatering
- Underwatering
- Spider mite damage

Spotted leaves:
- Leaf scorch
- Sunburn
- Cold water on leaves (particularly African violets)
- Bacterial or fungal disease
- Air pollution
- Overwatering
- Spider mite damage

Leaf droop or curl:
- Air pollution
- Underwatering
- Aphids

Leaf tips turning brown:
- Low humidity
- Incorrect potting mix pH
- Air pollution
- Poor water quality (fluoride, sodium)
- Excess fertilizer
- Overwatering
- Underwatering

Stunted plants:
- Excess fertilizer
- Overwatering
- Underwatering
- Root-bound
- Insufficient light intensity
- Insufficient fertilizer

Pale and spindly new growth:
- Insufficient fertilizer
- Insufficient light
- Underwatering

Wilted or blackened new growth:
- Cold or hot drafts
- Sunburn
- Temperature too warm
- Temperature too cold
- Excess fertilizer
- Underwatering

White spots on leaves:
- Spider mites

Cottony masses on stems:
- Mealybugs and some scale species

Dark bumps on leaves or stems:
- Armored scales

Sticky spots under the leaves:
- Honeydew excreted by aphids, mealy bugs, scale, or white flies

Frequently Asked Questions

Outdoor Containers

1. How can I grow vegetables if I live in an apartment (or if I am short on space)?

Read the "Outdoor Containers" section of this chapter, and also refer to the following NC State Extension publications:

AG-753, *How to Create a Container Garden for Edibles in the North Carolina Piedmont.* This publication provides good information regarding container selection; planting media; plant selection; designing a vegetable container garden; and light, water, and nutrient requirements for vegetables, herbs, and fruits.

AG-748, *Container Garden Planting Calendar for Edibles in the NC Piedmont.* This publication provides a calendar with the time of year for planting different types of vegetables, herbs, and fruits.

2. I just found a beautiful ceramic pot, but there are no drainage holes in the bottom. Can I still use it?

The best thing to do would be to drill a hole or holes in the bottom of the pot. If that is not possible, you still may be able to use it if you find a smaller pot that has holes in the bottom and will fit inside the decorative pot. Remove the small pot containing the plant when you want to water, and put it back in the decorative pot after the water drains away.

Indoor Containers

1. My houseplant is dying! Am I overwatering or underwatering it? What can I do to save it?

How much and how often are you watering the plant? Thoroughly wet the potting mix when you water, and then allow the potting mix to dry out before watering again. To check for underwatering or overwatering, remove the plant from the pot and examine the roots. An underwatered plant's roots are white and the potting mix will be very dry. Fully soak the root ball in water and repot. Be sure the plant is not root bound. It may need to be in a larger pot. If the plant is being overwatered, the roots will be brown and soft and may have an odor if they are beginning to rot. It may or may not be possible to save the plant. Trim off the brown roots and repot the plant, possibly putting it in a smaller container. Make sure any pot used has drainage holes.

2. I have very little light in my home; which houseplants would you recommend?

Try cast iron plants (*Aspidistra elatior*), pothos (*Epipremnum aureum*), Chinese evergreen (*Aglaonema modestum*), or Algerian ivy (*Hedera canariensis*).

3. I moved my weeping fig (Ficus benjamina) to another room, and now it is dropping leaves. What is wrong?

You moved it! All plants tend to drop a few leaves when they are moved to a new environment. *Ficus benjamina* has a reputation for dropping leaves even if the environment is the same. As long as the light conditions in the location are the same and you are continuing your same watering and fertilizing schedule, the leaf drop should stop within a few weeks. After a few weeks if you are still noticing leaf drop, be sure to check that there are no drafts or other environmental changes in the new location that could be negatively affecting the plant.

4. Why are there never any flowers on my African violet (Streptocarpus spp.)?

There could be many reasons why your African violet is not blooming, but the most common reason is not enough light. Try moving it to a brighter location. Not enough humidity can cause flower buds to drop off before they bloom. Overfertilizing and underfertilizing can also affect flowering. It can be difficult to know the triggers for making a houseplant flower. Mimicking conditions in the plant's natural habitat, potting mix moisture fluctuations, and temperature fluctuations may be necessary to get a plant to flower.

5. There are little black bugs flying around my plant near the surface of the potting mix. What causes the bugs, and how can I rid myself of the problem without harming the plants?

Those bugs are probably fungus gnats. Frequent or excessive watering encourages their development. You can usually get rid of them by reducing the frequency of watering and allowing the potting mix to dry more between watering. They are not very harmful to plants; they are mostly a nuisance to people.

6. How can I get my poinsettia (or Christmas cactus) to bloom again?

Both of these species are short-day plants, meaning they need short days and long nights to trigger flowering. You can recreate these short days by putting a box over your plant or putting it in a closet for part of the day. Both plants need to be in good strong light during the part of the day when they are not covered. Poinsettias (*Euphorbia pulcherrimia*) need 11 hours or less of light for 10 weeks to initiate flowering. Christmas cactus plants (*Schlumbergera* spp.) need days of 11 hours of light or less for six weeks and require temperatures between 65°F to 70°F. Christmas cactus are quite sensitive to temperature. Several weeks at 55°F initiates flowering no matter the day length. If temperatures are above 70°F, flowers will never form.

Further Reading

Creasy, Rosalind. *Edible Landscaping*. 2nd ed. San Francisco, California: Sierra Club Books, 2010. Print.

Dewolf, Gordon P. *Taylor's Guide to Houseplants.* New York: Houghton Mifflin Company, 1987. Print.

Dole, John M., and Harold F. Wilkins. *Floriculture: Principles and Species.* 2nd ed. Upper Saddle River, New Jersey: Prentice Hall, Inc., 2004. Print.

Hastings, Don. *Month-By-Month Gardening in the South: What to Do and When to Do It.* 2nd ed. Atlanta, Georgia: Longstreet Press, 1999. Print.

Hessayon, D. G. *The House Plant Expert.* London: Expert Books, 1993. Print.

Hessayon, D. G. *The House Plant Expert Book Two.* London: Expert Books, 2005. Print.

McGee, Rose Marie Nichols, and Maggie Stuckey. *McGee & Stuckey's Bountiful Container: Create Container Gardens of Vegetables, Herbs, Fruits, and Edible Flowers.* New York: Workman Publishing Company, Inc., 2002. Print.

Miracle-Gro Complete Guide to Houseplants. Hoboken, New Jersey: John Wiley & Sons Inc., 2008. Print.

Ortho All about Houseplants. Hoboken, New Jersey: John Wiley & Sons Inc., 2007. Print.

Pleasant, Barbara. *The Complete Houseplant Survival Manual: Essential Know-How for Keeping (Not Killing) More than 160 Indoor Plants.* North Adams, Massachusetts: Storey Publishing, 2005. Print.

Reich, Lee. *Landscaping with Fruit.* North Adams, Massachusetts: Storey Publishing, 2009. Print.

Schuler, Stanley, ed. *Simon & Schuster's Guide to House Plants.* New York: Simon & Schuster Inc., 1986. Print.

Wolverton, Dr. B. C. *How to Grow Fresh Air: 50 House Plants That Purify Your Home or Office.* New York: Penguin Books, 1997. Print.

18

For More Information

http://go.ncsu.edu/fmi_containergardens

Contributors

Authors:
Diane B. Mays, Department of Horticultural Science
Kim Richter, Department of Horticultural Science
Lucy Bradley, Assistant Professor and Extension Specialist, Department of Horticultural Science
Julie Sherk, Assistant Professor, Department of Horticultural Science
Mark Kistler, Associate Professor, Department of Agricultural and Human Sciences
Joe Neal, Professor and Extension Specialist, Department of Horticultural Science

Artwork: Mary Archer, Department of Horticultural Science; Renee Lampila, Extension Master Gardener Volunteer

Contributions by Extension Agents: Donna Teasley, Michelle Wallace, Paige Patterson, Randy Fulk, Thomas Glasgow, Ben Grandon

Contributions by Extension Master Gardener Volunteers: Jackie Weedon, Karen Damari, Connie Schultz, Edna Burger, Kim Curlee, Renee Lampila, Joanne Celinski

Content Editors: Lucy Bradley, Professor and Extension Specialist, Urban Horticulture, NC State University; Director, NC State Extension Master Gardener program;
Kathleen Moore, Urban Horticulturist

Copy Editors: Barbara Scott, Debbi Braswell

Chapter 18 Cover Photo: Efraimstochter, Pixabay CC0

How to Cite This Chapter:
Mays, D., K. Richter, L.K. Bradley, J. Sherk, M. Kistler, and J. Neal. 2022. Plants Grown in Containers, Chpt 18, In: Moore, K.A. and L.K. Bradley (eds), *North Carolina Extension Gardener Handbook,* 2nd ed. NC State Extension, Raleigh, NC <https://content.ces.ncsu.edu/extension-gardener-handbook/18-plants-grown-in-containers>

18

Landscape Design

Objectives

This chapter teaches people to:

- Explain the basic principles of landscape design.
- Describe the process of creating a landscape design.
- Recognize the environmental factors that influence landscape design.
- Identify design opportunities for water, energy, and wildlife conservation.
- Recommend appropriate plants for a landscape given site and design conditions.
- Understand the history of landscape design.

19

Introduction

Landscape design is both an art and a purposeful process. It is the conscious arrangement of outdoor space to maximize human enjoyment while minimizing the costs and negative environmental impacts. A well-designed home landscape is aesthetically pleasing and functional, creating comfortable outdoor spaces as well as reducing the energy costs of heating and cooling the home. It offers pleasure to the family, enhances the neighborhood, and adds to the property's value. With a little forethought and planning, the designer can maximize the property's use and people's enjoyment of it; establish a visual relationship between the house, its site, and the neighborhood; and contribute to a healthy local ecosystem.

The planning process, possibly the most important aspect of residential landscaping, is often neglected. We can see the effects: overcrowded and overgrown plantings, lawns with scattered shade trees, a narrow concrete walk, trees and shrubs planted too close to structures (Figure 19–1), every plant a different species, or too many of the same plant. The result can be unattractive and may not serve the family's needs. Good landscape design creates a satisfying environment for the user while saving time, effort, and money and benefiting the environment.

Figure 19–1. Mature size should always be taken into consideration when selecting plants. This tree is far too large for this tiny front yard, and is completely overpowering the landscape and the house.
Scott S (scott*eric), Flickr CC BY - 2.0

Design Principles

When we develop and implement a landscape design, we rely on a dynamic process that addresses all aspects of the land, the environment, the growing plants, and the user's needs. This process ensures a pleasing, functional, and ecologically healthy design. Fundamental design concepts—scale, balance, unity, perspective, rhythm, and accent—form the basic considerations in design development. Simplicity, repetition, line, variety, and harmony are organizing principles. We use these principles to apply design concepts to landscape features, such as plants and hardscape materials. Understanding spatial organization is also integral to the art of landscape design. The resulting design is implemented in three-dimensional space. The space changes as we use it, as plants grow, and as nature contributes its full range of environmental conditions.

Figure 19–2. Scale is an important element to consider. The cannas are tall enough to be a background plant in this bed. If the lantanas (seen in the foreground) were moved to the back they would be visually lost in the design.
Lucy Bradley, CC BY - 2.0

Design Concepts

These basic concepts underlie a design's composition: scale, balance, unity, perspective, rhythm, and accent.

Scale is the proportion between two sets of dimensions—for example, the height and width of a tree compared to a house, or the size of a plant container compared to an entryway. Carefully consider both the mature height and spread before including a plant in the landscape (Figure 19–2). If the full-grown size is too large, a plant can overwhelm the design. If plants remain small at maturity, they may look inappropriate as a background border.

Balance refers to creating equal visual weight on either side of a focal point, creating a pleasing integration of elements. There are two types of balance: symmetrical and asymmetrical. Symmetrical balance describes a formal balance with everything on one axis, duplicated or mirrored on both sides. Symmetry is commonly seen in formal gardens (Figure 19–3). Asymmetrical balance describes an equilibrium achieved by using different objects. For example, if a large box is placed on one side of a scale, it can be counterbalanced by several smaller boxes placed on the other side. Asymmetrical balance occurs in landscaping when a large existing tree or shrub needs to be balanced out by a grouping or cluster of smaller plants (Figure 19–4). Balance can also be achieved by using color or texture.

Figure 19–3. Symmetry is seen here with the mirror image fence posts, hedges and shrubs. Symmetry in a garden is a more formal style.
Leimenide, Flickr CC BY - 2.0

Figure 19–4. Asymmetrical elements of the tree and bench on the left balance out with lower growing begonias and a sundial on the right to form a pleasing design.
Susan Strine, CC BY 4.0

Unity is achieved when different parts of the design are grouped or arranged to appear as a single unit. The repetitions of geometric shapes, along with strong, observable lines (Figure 19–5), contribute to unity. Ground covers and turfgrass act as unifying elements in a landscape. A unified landscape provides a pleasant view from every

angle. A landscape with too many ideas in a small space lacks unity. Too many plant varieties, accent plants, lawn accessories with contrasting forms, textures, or colors violate the principle of unity by distracting the viewer from a coherent visual theme that unites the landscape's individual elements.

Figure 19–5. Unity is demonstrated using lavender (*Lavandula angustifolia*) to line a path.
Old_Man_Leica, Flickr CC BY-ND - 2.0

Perspective is our visual perception of three-dimensional space. Certain techniques can make a space appear small, while others can make a space seem larger. Usually the goal in residential landscaping is to make a space appear larger. A strong accent in the center of a space can draw one's eye and make the space seem larger (Figure 19–6). Overhead tree canopies or structures make the

Figure 19–6. The decorative gate draws the eye to the back of this small side landscape making it appear larger.
J Brew (brewbooks), Flickr CC BY SA 2.0

19

space feel more confined or smaller. Many backyards have an area of grass surrounded by a border of shrubs. The border brings the eye to a boundary and makes the space appear confined.

Effective use of color can expand the space. Distant objects appear fine-textured and gray to the eye, so using gray, fine-textured plants at the landscape boundary can expand the apparent distance between the viewer and the plant. Tapering walkways or plantings toward a vanishing point can also create an illusion of distance. Using strong colors and coarse textures in the front of a border help to expand the area. To make the space appear smaller, reverse this concept and use strong colors and coarse textures in the rear and softer colors and finer textures in the front.

Rhythm is the repetition of design elements. Repetition helps draw one's eye through the design. Rhythm results when elements appear in a definite direction and in regular measures. Both color and form can be used to express rhythm (Figure 19–7).

Figure 19–7. Rhythm is seen in this landscape by repeatedly using the dome-shaped boxwood (*Buxus sempervirens*) and the weeping cherry (*Prunus cerasus*).
Marcia Boyle, CC BY - 4.0

Accent is the inclusion of an element that stands out in an orderly design. For example, silvery leaves stand out against a background of fall red maple leaves (Figure 19–8). Without accent, a design may be static or dull. An accent can be a garden accessory, plant specimen, a plant composition, or a water feature. Boulders are often used as accents, but they can be overused. To look natural, boulders should be partially buried. Water does not spring from the highest point of land in nature. So to appear most natural, water features should have their source below grade of other landscape features.

Figure 19–8. The silvery leaves of this blue star juniper are accented against the fall color of Japanese maple leaves.
Kathleen Moore, CC BY - 2.0

Understanding Space in Landscape Design

We customarily use paper or a computer to create a landscape plan. When we implement the plan, we build a three-dimensional space in which people engage. People engage in the world and are affected by it every time they venture outdoors. Landscapes are dynamic spaces—they are always changing. Plants change with the seasons, grow, age, flower, reproduce, and provide habitat for other creatures and species. In a well-calculated landscape plan, the designer addresses elements of space and change. Beyond this, our experience in a landscape becomes a major factor in the overall impact a place has on our lives. In landscape planning, better outcomes and richer environments can be achieved when we understand spatial definition and the importance of transition between different land uses and different planes of space.

The world consists of three different planes of space that affect human experience. As we engage in the world, we are always surrounded by these three planes—horizontal, vertical, and overhead. As the volumes of these different planes change, the way we experience the space changes. In the landscape, for example, an enclosed space created by a dense canopy has a different feeling than an open pasture. One space is shaded and dark, while the other is sunny and open. Our purpose in understanding these differences is not to pass judgment on them. Rather, it is to accept that these different kinds of spatial experiences exist. We recognize that the more transitional spaces a person goes through in moving from a completely enclosed environment to a completely open environment, the more seamless and connected the experience becomes.

Addressing the hierarchy, or order, of space and scale is also important. Specifically, land use can be determined by the scale of a space. Roads, for example, have a defined hierarchy. All lanes may be a standard size (large enough to accommodate one vehicle), but streets are designed to accommodate a certain amount of traffic. As such, a level one road such as an interstate may have four lanes in each direction. A level two road has only three lanes in each direction. A level three road has two lanes in each direction, and a level four road may have only a single road in one direction. By developing a hierarchy of land uses within a landscape, different landscape elements can be appropriately scaled to accommodate different activities and to create different experiences. For example, a level one path to the front of the house should be scaled to accommodate at least two individuals (4½- to 5-feet wide). As paths connect, they should gradually scale down in size. So all the paths that connect to the main entrance path should be level two (2½- to 3-feet wide). And paths in the landscape meant for an individual experience should be level three (1- to 2½-feet wide). Likewise, space designed for an individual is smaller than space for a small group or a large party.

Spatial definition of the three planes of space also helps to enhance our experience. The more clearly defined the plane, the easier it is to interpret. For example, a walkway that is defined using a hardscape such as brick clearly sends a message to people that this surface is for walking. What prevents someone from walking on this path? If the horizontal ground plane is clearly defined, then people intuitively understand where they should walk and where they should not. What prevents someone from cutting through a landscape? A designer can change the horizontal ground plane to reduce unintended land use by planting a tall ground cover. The increased vertical plane makes cutting through the landscape and not using the designated path undesirable.

Understanding three-dimensional space in landscape design is essential. Each plane of space and the transitions between planes are discussed in more detail below. We also discuss how to organize landscape spaces during the design process by using garden rooms, focal points, patterns, and geometry to create functional, appealing spaces.

Figure 19–9. A horizontal ground plane changes from a stone path to wooden platform.
Michelle Wallace

Horizontal Ground Plane

The ground plane functions as the floor of the landscape. Examples include lawns, patios, terraces, decks, and walkways. This plane influences the route by which people move through and experience the landscape. Materials can vary significantly, including compacted soil; plant materials such as lawn or moss and ground covers; crushed gravel; man-made products such as concrete, bricks, and rubber; and wood surfaces and products like lumber, mulch, and bark chips. Figure 19–9 illustrates the use of different materials to define the horizontal ground plane for walking through the landscape. The lower path is defined using irregular flagstone set in screenings, while the upper path is constructed of wood. Note the elevation change of a single step. People risk tripping and falling when an elevation change is one step or less. To intuitively heighten our attention, the designer has changed the materials of the ground plane. In addition, the ground covers on either side of the path begin to build up the vertical plane. The path, therefore, is clearly defined. Imagine

19

someone moving through the landscape and reaching the point before he or she steps up to a new height. Notice how the tree helps to create a gateway by increasing the vertical plane and adding an overhead plane. Our senses are heightened to pay attention to change. Notice how the elevated walkway is further defined with small posts that mark the walkway's edges by a subtle increase in the vertical plane. As we pass through this gateway, notice how the vegetation that flanks the path also increases in height. This further defines the pedestrian corridor. We know where to walk.

Vertical Plane

Vertical planes create the outdoor walls, enclose the space, and serve as a backdrop to enhance other elements within the space. Vertical elements frame certain views both inside and outside of the space and terminate the sightline. Examples in the landscape include trees, shrubs, walls, fencing, lampposts, and pillars. The vertical plane is defined by building facades that create an outdoor hallway. The transition from the ground plane (defined by a lawn or walkway) to the vertical plane is created through the use of edging, ferns, and vines (Figure 19–10). Breaking down the space into its elements, the ground plane is defined by the brick walkway. Moving from the horizontal plane to the vertical plane, the vertical plane is built up with the introduction of edging on either side of the path, then with the ferns along with the vines and the brick. The walls terminate our sightline and direct our vision toward the terminus in the path and the change in land use up ahead.

Figure 19–10. This vertical plane is defined by the two brick building facades. With a clearly defined path, this space can be called an outdoor hallway.
Michelle Wallace

Vertical planes in the landscape do not need to be continuous to define space. For example, a repeating allée of trees, which can be used to define both a pedestrian and a vehicle corridor, is not a solid wall. The viewer mentally fills in the blanks in the allée to create the feeling of entering a tunnel. When trees and plants are used in succession and repeated, movement is created (Figure 19–11). One's eye continuously moves to the next set of trees, and the user is propelled forward.

Figure 19–11. The trees define the vertical walls of this space. The trees were selected for human scale in this pedestrian path. This same pattern is often used to define vehicular corridors for cars but the trees are scaled larger for vehicles.
Michelle Wallace

Overhead Plane

The overhead plane defines the ceiling of an outdoor area that we often feel more than see. This plane serves as protection from the elements. Psychologically it provides a sense of shelter and protection. The feeling of "being under" creates a strong sense of enclosure. The overhead plane can provide an exceptional sensory experience from the character and color it creates as sun and shade patterns land on leaves. Our sensory experience also changes as the height of the overhead plane rises or falls with the tree canopy, with steps or paths that move up or down within the horizontal ground plane, and with the gradual transition that happens as we move from a completely open to a completely closed environment. Examples of overhead planes include tree canopies, overhead structures, awnings, and umbrellas. In Figure 19–12, the overhead plane is established by a continuous trellis with a repeating motif inspired by carrots. The trellis that creates the overhead plane includes colored plexiglass that casts a colored reflection on the walkway. The reflection changes as the sun moves across the sky. As the planted vines fill out seasonally, one's experience of walking under the gigantic carrot trellis changes. Someone may even identify with a rabbit and wonder what it must be like to run through the garden undetected. The space goes from being open to being enclosed.

Figure 19–12. An overhead plane defined by these iron sculptures. These sculptures will act as trellises as vines grow to cover and shade the walkway.

Michelle Wallace

Transitional Spaces

Transitional spaces are the spaces that connect one outdoor area to the next; examples include doorways, hallways, and platforms. These spaces also provide transitions between the different planes of space. Well-defined transitional spaces use exposure to similar materials (such as plants and paving) to gradually introduce new spaces to people from one outdoor area to the next. Examples of transitional spaces or transitional elements include entrance gates, paving changes, planted alleys, gateway arbors, edging, and bridges.

Figure 19–13 illustrates the use of a gateway as a major transitional element within a garden. Transitional spaces help to set the stage for the adventure of being in the landscape and moving from one place to the next. The scale of this gateway intuitively suggests that we are leaving one type of garden space and going into another with a different character. In the foreground, the horizontal ground plane changes as the Chapel Hill gravel paving meets the granite edging. The edging is still a part of the horizontal ground plane. As the paving meets the granite curbing, it begins building up the vertical plane. The vertical plane continues to grow with the increase in height created by plants. The paving also changes under

the gateway to a gray flagstone paving pattern. As we move out of the structure, the horizontal ground plane transitions into informal gray crushed granite fines. Note that the gray color helps to create a transition among all these different elements. The large structure completely encloses the user. Despite the large size, the structure is scaled to human size and the volume of space is considerably smaller than the next space you enter. As we exit the structure, the volume of space increases as the overhead plane is determined by the height of the tree canopy. This is a very common pattern used in architecture. The feeling generated by this space is used in churches across the world. Imagine entering a church. The entrance corridor usually has a low ceiling. Then the overhead plane is elevated in the main body of the church, rising to become a cathedral ceiling that evokes an emotional response in the user, frequently one of awe.

Figure 19–13. This archway is a transitional space inviting you to step through and experience another part of the landscape.

Michelle Wallace

Garden Rooms

A room can be defined as a space enclosed by walls, a floor, and a ceiling, as well as a place where activities happen. This same definition applies when describing an outdoor room, with one difference. The materials used to define an outdoor space are dynamic and in some cases lack a ceiling or overhead plane. Garden rooms are the destinations within a landscape. Even small properties have enough space to accommodate a single room.

The scale should be determined by the room's function. Is the space used for entertainment? Or is the space used by a single individual—say for reading? Who is using this space—young children, teenagers, adults? The character of the space can be defined using materials that address both the function and the users. Each plane of space should be defined. The furniture in the room should address the users' needs and express the character that distinguishes the space. Examples of garden rooms include an outdoor dining room, vegetable garden, reading room, entertainment space, kitchen, fire pit, and playground. Figure 19–14 is a large outdoor room. We enter the room through a doorway created by a bump out of the building façade on one side and a half wall made of the same material on the other side. The ground plane consists of a different stone material. The mounted wall fountain is centered on the entrance into this garden room to grab our attention and entice us into the room. The fountain also muffles the sounds of voices as people engage in conversations. As we enter the room, the ground plane increases, the walls are moved back, and the volume of the space increases. The rhododendron planted above the wall further affects the scale of the space and increases the feeling of enclosure. The furniture color is influenced by the blue hues of the plants and stone. Figure 19–15 is an outdoor dining room for two. In this residential outdoor dining area scaled for two, the ground plane is defined with flagstones set in granite fines. The ground plane is defined differently from the walkway because the material has changed and the space has increased in volume. The edges of the patio are transitioned into the vertical plane with the granite curb edging. The plants immediately surrounding the patio are low growing and increase in size moving away from the patio. Both the perennials and the trees help to define the scale of the space. Notice how the ceramic pots repeat the color of the furniture.

Figure 19–15. An intimate outdoor dining area scaled for two people.
Michelle Wallace

Focal Points

Focal points consist of carefully placed objects that direct a person's line of sight. Their purpose in the garden is to propel movement and entice the user to make a decision: How do I proceed at this bend in the path? Do I continue down the path that offers the same experience or choose the one that teases the senses by offering a sculpture, a specimen tree, a bridge, or an interesting boulder? When a focal point is well-placed on a user's journey, he or she does not feel manipulated. The journey through the garden is like a story that starts when one enters the garden. The story continues as one moves through twists and turns along a path, guided by focal points that foreshadow what happens next. Eventually a climax in the garden journey occurs at a destination—the garden activity room. The story, however, is not over. It resumes as one leaves the room and the gradual transition out of the space begins to move to the next destination or to leaving the garden.

Figure 19–14. A large outdoor garden room that can accommodate several people.
Michelle Wallace

Figure 19–16. A distant focal point, note the intriguing building at the far end of this path.
Michelle Wallace

Figure 19–17. This is the focal point destination.
Michelle Wallace

In Figure 19–16, notice the intriguing building in the distance centered on the path. The building has an interesting roof line with a wind vane on top. Although we cannot see what it is, the wind vane grabs our interest from far away. More than likely, curiosity drives us to discover what is ahead. Figure 19–17 is our focal point destination. On arriving at the wind vane, we discover the quaint colorful building, which houses the restroom for the garden. While the building is a strong focal point that functions as a driving force within the garden, smaller objects within the garden—such as garden art or plant specimens—also serve to propel us on a journey.

Pattern Language

Pattern language is a philosophy developed by Christopher Alexander (Professor Emeritus of Architecture at the University of California, Berkeley). Pattern language describes recognizable patterns in nature and human society that have developed over the ages and impact the way people live. Dr. Alexander defined the concept of a pattern language in the 1970s and spent his career studying patterns in the landscape created by nature and in society that influence lifestyles, communities, and architecture. His books, including The Timeless Way of Building and A Pattern Language: Towns, Buildings, Construction, have influenced the way designers (architects, landscape

Figure 19–18. A window garden pattern.
Michelle Wallace

architects, interior designers, and planners) create the spaces we use in daily life. As a result, Professor Alexander's ideas have affected millions of people. The number of patterns that can be observed and experienced daily is innumerable. Incorporating patterns into the garden experience enhances the user experience.

In Figure 19–18, a window garden is a pattern that brings the outdoor environment closer to home. A window garden breaks up the built outdoor facade, and it changes the view of the outdoor environment from the outside and inside of the building. The human eye is trained to see what is in the foreground and tends not to notice the things faraway as much. In Figure 19–19, an edible garden is a pattern built on humanity's agrarian roots and driven by activity. To live, people must eat. The ability to sustain ourselves by growing food is empowering. Figure 19–20 provides a bench in the garden for sitting. It seems like such a simple pattern. Yet magical life experiences take place on benches—engagements, first kisses, lunch. A bench provides an opportunity to become a part of the garden, not just an observer in the garden. A garden seat is used if there is a view, something of interest around it. It is not used if a view does not exist.

Garden Geometry

Geometry is part of the everyday world and influences the places where we live. A direct relationship exists between two objects on a plane. Because this relationship exists, a landscape designer must pay attention to the architecture before situating new objects or creating new spaces. Regardless of the geometry selected (for example, rectilinear, curvilinear, radial, or arctangent), the space and proposed objects must relate to the existing architecture (Figure 19–21a-d). The first image is a bubble diagram used for determining best locations for required activities and how much space those activities need, and for studying the relationship and circulation between activities and locations. The next step is determining which layout (geometry) is most appropriate. The following geometries are all based on the same bubble diagram. Note that everything in the bubble diagram remains the same. Only the SHAPE of each element changes.

Invisible guidelines extend out of the building at different angles of different degrees. A grid can be formed using known points on the architecture, such as the corner of the building, the center line of the window or door, and the edge of a porch. Objects placed in the landscape should have a direct geometric relationship with the building and with each other. For example, by placing a specimen tree on the centerline of a bay window, the designer ensures that the tree becomes a focal point for users looking outside into the garden from within a building.

It is important to understand that there are many ways of creating space in landscape design. No one method works for each landscape plan. A carefully laid out landscape plan with defined planes and transitions combined with good geometry and including objects that relate to garden features and buildings enriches our experience and the environment.

Figure 19–19. A vegetable garden pattern.
Michelle Wallace

Figure 19–20. Garden seating as a pattern.
Kathleen Moore, CC BY - 2.0

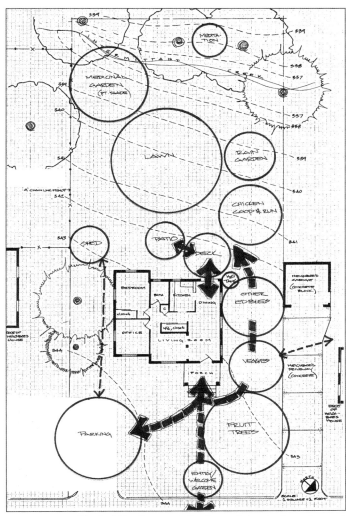

Figure 19–21a. The bubble diagram is for determining the best size and location for wanted elements and traffic patterns. Figures 19–21b-d play with the SHAPES. Notice all the bubble elements stay in the same place, and they stay fairly consistent in size.

Anne Spafford

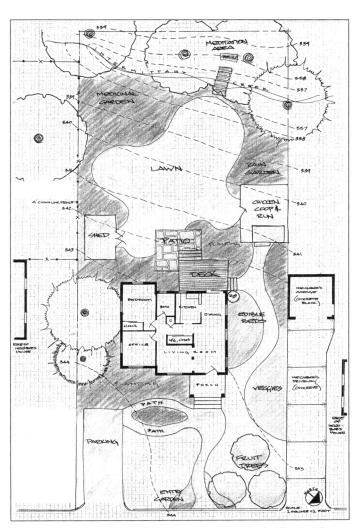

Figure 19–21b. A curvilinear layout having rounded lines and pathways to the items shown in the bubble diagram Figure 19–21a.

Anne Spafford

Applying Design Principles

Simplicity, repetition, line, variety, and harmony are used in landscape design to create a visually appealing composition.

Simplicity strives to create spaces, not fill them. "Less is more." Not every square foot of the landscape must be filled. Most residential landscapes consist of limited space, so the number of tree and shrub species used should also be limited. It is more effective to incorporate groups of one type of plant than to install one or two each of a wide variety of plants. Create simple lines and curves that add interest rather than irregular lines that might detract from the design (Figure 19–22).

Repetition in the landscape should not be confused with monotony. Repetition contributes to unity and simplicity. It makes a strong foundation for the landscape design like the chorus repeated in a song (Figure 19–23).

Figure 19–22. Perennial plants like woolly thyme (*Thymus pseudolanuginosus*), evening primrose (*Oenothera* spp.), and red feather reed grass (*Calamagrostis* × *acutiflora* 'Karl Foerster') do not overwhelm this tiny backyard.

Patrick Standish, Flickr CC BY - 2.0

Line forms real and imaginary lines in the landscape and plays an important role in the creation of small and large spaces. Draw the viewer's eye through the landscape by grouping plants or hardscape elements (Figure 19–24). The eye is unconsciously influenced by the way groupings fit and flow on both horizontal and vertical planes.

Variety created through diverse and contrasting forms, textures, and colors is a hallmark of good landscape design. By avoiding uniformity, variety reduces monotony in a design. Adding elements with opposite qualities or contrast heightens visual interest and increases viewer satisfaction with the design (Figure 19–25).

Harmony balances the other design principles by pulling the individual components together and creating a cohesive whole, ensuring that all parts of the design relate to and complement each other (Figure 19–26).

Figure 19–23. Various colors of azaleas (*Rhododendron* spp.) are repeated throughout this landscape.

Pixabay, vonpics CC BY0

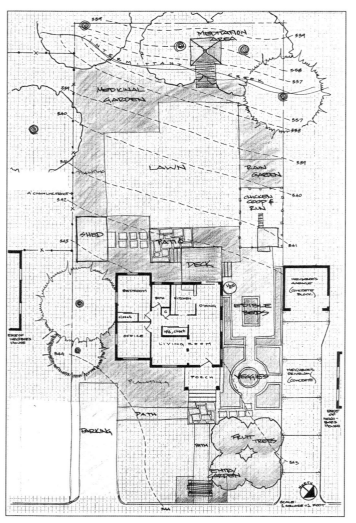

Figure 19–21c. A rectilinear layout using straight lines and angled pathways to represent the items shown in the bubble diagram Figure 19–21a.

Anne Spafford

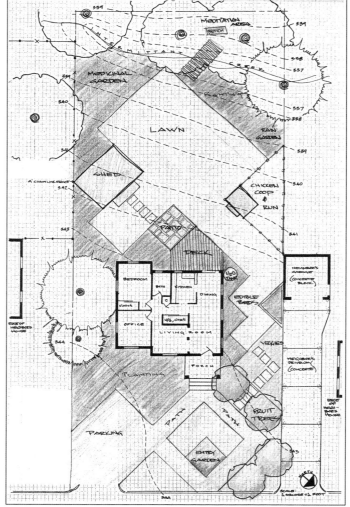

Figure 19–21d. An angled rectilinear layout uses the straight lines of Figure 19–21c but on the diagonal.

Anne Spafford

19

Figure 19–24. There are sweeping curvy lines in this landscape.
Kathy Sill, CC BY - 4.0

Figure 19–25. There is a wide variety of leaf textures, sizes, and colors that keep this small space interesting.
John Weiss, Flickr CC BY-ND - 2.0

Figure 19–26. Harmony is seen in this Japanese garden, all the design components relate to each other to create a cohesive whole.
John Weiss, Flickr CC BY-ND - 2.0

Six Steps to a Landscape Design

In the first part of this chapter, we introduced the principles and concepts that underlie landscape design. In this section, we focus on the mechanics of developing a landscape plan. Planning a residential landscape begins with evaluating the entire space and the overall desired effect of the final design. We begin the design process by determining the user's needs and desires and the site's environmental and physical conditions. With this information, the desired features—such as trees, shrubs, grass, walkways, parking areas, a vegetable garden, patio, deck, mailbox, screening wall, and outdoor lighting—can be organized into a cohesive design. By using the following six steps, we can take a straightforward, organized approach to developing and implementing a landscape that reflects the user's wants and needs and allows for future growth and change.

Step 1: Develop a Base Plan and Site Inventory

A base plan is a bird's eye view of the site drawn to scale. A plot plan of the property, as shown in Figure 19–27, is an excellent place to start. Sometimes a plot plan is provided when property is purchased. If not, check with the local county assessor's office or the NC County GIS, Tax and Deed website. The plot plan should include property lines, show the placement of the house on the property, and indicate the driveways, easements, and any other limitations. Be sure to check for any setbacks or streams on the property that could have their own set of legal parameters. Locating the exact property boundaries is important when a fence is part of the final design. Most property boundaries do not extend all the way to the road. Plants or hardscape installed in a state, county, or city right-of-way, such as between a sidewalk and the road, may be torn up for roadwork or to access utilities.

Next, gather and record information on the property's history. What was there before the current house was built? What is the history of land care? Was the property previously farmland? Have old buildings been removed, potentially leaving lead paint or plumbing behind? See AG-439-78, *Soil Facts: Minimizing Risks of Soil Contaminants in Urban Gardens*, for specific design strategies.

Use the plot plan to develop an up-to-date inventory of existing built features (such as the house, power lines, septic tanks, underground utilities, exterior lighting, and roof overhangs) as well as existing plants and beds, landscape features, and hardscape locations on the site. The height, style, and exterior elements of the home, as well as the construction materials used, should be noted to

19

help with design decisions. Measure and note on the plot plan any other structures and hardscapes that may have been added, such as patios, driveways, or sidewalks.

When all of the information has been gathered and marked on a rough sketch, transfer it to a final base plan. Make sure to draw to scale. Depending on the size of the property, a suitable scale, for an average homeowner landscape, is 1 inch equals 10 feet (or 1/10-inch scale). For a small property or courtyard a 1/4-inch scale may be more appropriate. Other popular landscape scales are 1:4, 1:5, 1:8, 1:10, 1:16 and 1:20. Scales of 1:4, 1:8 or 1:16 match the common increments used on a conventional ruler, but scales of 1:10 and 1:20 are used by engineers and landscape architects. Suggested symbols are shown in Figure 19–28. Be sure to indicate a north arrow on the plan. Locate any existing features on the property and the house, and be sure to include the following items:

- Aboveground and underground utilities (see "Locating Utilities")
- Windows, doors, and other openings, including height off the ground
- Existing healthy, meaningful vegetation that makes an impact (to accurately note the location, use a triangulation method. See sidebar.)
- Other vegetation that may be moved to a different location (eyeball this vegetation, but do not bother to triangulate.)
- Utility meters, drainpipes, water spigots, outlets, septic tank
- Features on or near the property line
- Anything else prominent on the existing site

Mark these features on the base plan as shown in Figure 19–29.

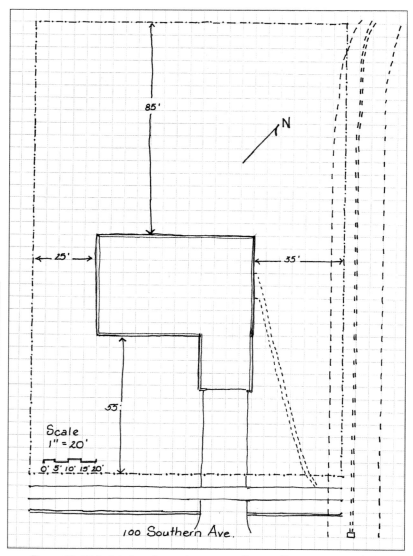

Figure 19–27. A plot plan shows the property lines, utility easements, the layout of the house. A plot plan should also contain a scale, a north arrow, and the address of the property.
Renee Lampila

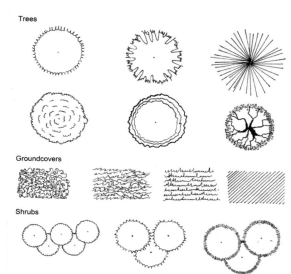

Figure 19–28. Any symbols can be used on a plot plan. These are some options.
Kathleen Moore, CC BY - 2.0

19

19-13

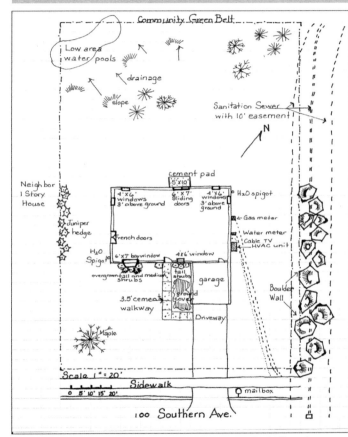

Figure 19–29. Existing features on the property including plants, hardscape elements, topography and features to take into consideration, such as drainage and the view of the neighbor's house.

Renee Lampila

Locating Utilities

Call 811, a free utilities location service, before you complete the base plan and 48 hours before digging is scheduled (Figure 19–30). This service notifies the electrical, phone, gas, water, and sewer utilities to come and mark the property. A different color spray paint is used for each utility. Generally, the utility line is located underground in a 5-foot zone around the marked line, 2.5 feet on either side of the line. These areas should be considered "no digging zones." Utilities should be marked when the base plan is being developed as some design decisions may be based on where lines run. The service must return and mark again before landscape installation if the lines have faded. Figure 19–31 is an example of what can happen when utility lines and right-of-ways are ignored by a gardener.

Figure 19–30. It is free to have utility lines marked. Call 811 before any digging occurs.

Cynthia Wagoner

Figure 19–31. These raised garden beds needed to be moved because they were planted in the right-of-way.

Danelle Cutting

Tips for Drawing on a Base Plan

- Have adequate paper to write on. Or better yet, make several enlarged copies of the plot plan to draw on and record measurements.
- Enlist the help of a partner. Having two people hold and read a measuring tape is much easier.
- Use a long measuring tape or invest in an inexpensive measuring wheel if the property is large. Piecing together measurements because the tape is too short can lead to errors. A 100-to 200-foot tape measures most things in an average yard.
- Record measurements carefully and legibly to avoid having to re-measure.

Inventorying the property and recording existing structures and features of the landscape also provides an opportunity to identify the positive and negative aspects of the existing landscape. One goal of effective landscaping is to create a definite relationship between the house and its environment. Note plants that should be retained and worked into the new landscape or planting. Some trees and shrubs may simply require pruning, while others may need to be relocated or removed entirely. Any neighborhood association guidelines and restrictions need to be considered. After locating the existing plants and beds on the plot plan, identify individual plants. A detailed evaluation of the negative and positive aspects of the existing landscape includes the following considerations.

Consider the house and existing hardscape:
- What is the architectural style or character?
- Is this new or established construction?
- Is it one story or two (or more)?
- Is it rustic or formal, modern, or traditional?
- What are the construction materials? What color?
- Are there walkways, walls, fences, patios, and decks that are improperly sized, in the wrong location, or in disrepair?

Consider the views:
- What are the views both within and beyond your property line?
- Where are the locations from which the landscape is viewed from inside and outside the home? Examples include views through a kitchen or sitting room window or from an existing porch or the street.
- Are the current views pleasing, or would additional plantings or hardscape add more interest to that area?
- Do any views need screening?

Consider plant density:
- Are there "overplanted" beds or areas that should be thinned?

- Are there sparse areas that would benefit from the addition of plants?
- Are there random individual or small groups of plants scattered incoherently across the site?
- Is there too much lawn or not enough?

Consider mature size of existing plants:
- Are there plants that are or will become oversized, creating a hazard or high maintenance?
- Are there undersized plants that look lost or out of scale and need to be moved or combined in a mass for better visibility?

Consider environmental benefit of existing plants:
- Do the plants properly address the impact of sunlight on summer cooling and winter heating for the residence?
- Are there any long-lived, native woody ornamental species, like willow oak (*Quercus phellos*), red maple (*Acer rubrum*), or bald cypress (*Taxodium distichum*), which are desirable and should be preserved?
- Do the existing plants offer a biodiversity of species that benefits the local ecosystem?
- Are any of the existing plants invasive species like privet (*Ligustrum sinense* or *L. japonica*), Japanese wisteria (*Wisteria floribunda*), Chinese wisteria (*W. sinensis*), or English ivy (*Hedera helix*) that should be removed?

Consider health of plants:
- Do plants require minimal pruning, spraying, and fertilizing?
- Are plants placed in ideal growing conditions—proper light conditions, soil type, and drainage?
- Are plants showing signs of disease, chronic insect depredation, or environmental stress such as poor or stunted growth, foliage discoloration, or dieback?
- Are the plants sited so that they do not compete for nutrients, water, and air circulation, which results in plant stress and disease?
- Do any plants always seem to have one problem or another throughout the year, making them candidates for removal?

Consider the landscape in the evening:
- Are there dark areas that could benefit from exterior lighting?
- Would evening-blooming plants that have white blossoms or attract nighttime pollinators add interest to the yard?

Consider design contributions of existing plant material:
- Do existing plant forms, textures, and colors contribute to coherent, unified design?
- Do existing plants offer seasonal interest?

19

Step 2: Conduct Site Survey to Identify Environmental Factors

Understanding the environmental factors that exist on a site is critical to designing a functional, healthy landscape. By accurately incorporating knowledge of site-specific environmental considerations into the design, we can create a landscape that is easier to install and maintain and is more ecologically friendly. The site needs to be carefully studied for more than one season. The environmental features, including sun and wind exposures, sight lines, sound transmission, soil conditions, water flow and drainage issues, and existing landscape, must be analyzed. The results can be noted on an overlay created by taping a sheet of tracing paper over the plot plan.

Sun and Shade

The way the sun affects the house and site at different seasons greatly influences the overall design. Good plant placement is based on knowing the sun's direction at different times throughout the day as well as at different times of the year. The yard needs to be observed throughout the day to determine which areas receive full sun (more than six hours a day), partial sun, and primarily shade. Understanding sun exposure helps us make design decisions like planting trees to provide shade to a patio in the summer or recognizing that putting a vegetable garden in an area that receives only partial sun results in little fruit when it comes time to harvest. Assessing winter and summer sun angles, as shown in Figure 19–32, tells us where to leave open areas that allow the winter sun's rays to heat the house and outdoor living areas.

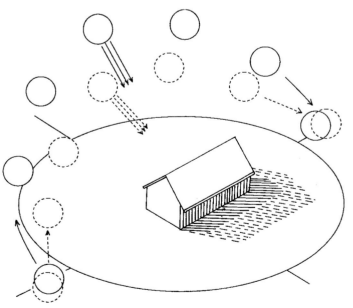

Figure 19–32. The angles the sun tracks across the sky. In the summer, it is higher and has a more sweeping arch (solid circles) and in the winter it is lower (dotted circles).

Wind

Knowing the direction of prevailing winter winds is crucial for deciding where to locate a windbreak, which can be especially important in the mountains or on the coast. Understanding wind patterns is also important to refrain from including structures or plants in the design that block summer breezes from outdoor living spaces. Mark the source and direction of winds on the plan overlay to visualize where a protective wind screen should be added or where breezes should be allowed to enter the landscape unimpeded.

Sights and Sounds

Walk the property to note what is visible in various directions. Standing on the front step, is the view pleasant? What is the view from the deck in the backyard? Also note the source of any objectionable noise on the site analysis overlay. Think, too, about the views from inside the home and looking out into the yard. On the site analysis overlay, identify views on which attention should be focused, as well as those that should be screened.

Soils

The native soils in North Carolina vary from light sand to heavy clay. In addition, many families are confronted with the difficult task of landscaping in "urban soils" that may include mortar, bricks, sheetrock, plywood, plastic, and other leftovers from construction. Often during the construction of a home, the top layer of soil is removed, leaving compacted subsoils mixed with construction debris that are unsuitable for plant growth. Have the soil tested, and on the site plan make note of both the soil type and the topsoil depth. Evaluate the soil in several sections of the property as soil types can change over a short distance, particularly if there is a change in elevation.

Water

Review a topographical map of the site and walk the property to examine stormwater patterns. Look for evidence of erosion and note any poorly drained or low areas that remain wet for several days after a rain. For the areas with evidence of erosion, examine rainwater harvesting options to reduce the amount of water flowing through these areas after a rain event. Use cisterns or rain barrels to harvest roof runoff and store it for later use (Figure 19–33). Consider contouring slopes to slow the runoff, minimize erosion and provide time for water to soak into the soil. Design options for addressing low-lying areas include installing an underground drainage system, building raised beds, grading, or planting a rain garden.

Overall, by addressing these environmental factors, we can create a design that is in harmony rather than in conflict with the observed natural patterns. This strategy leads to a successful, attractive, low maintenance, and ecologically beneficial landscape.

Figure 19–33. A rain barrel is filled with a PVC pipe attached to a roof downspout. This barrel is close to the garden for easy access to water vegetables.
Kathleen Moore, CC BY - 2.0

Step 3: Identify Activities and Uses for Landscape

To design a landscape that is aesthetically pleasing, enjoyable, and functional, we need information from the people who will use the space. What are their personal needs and wants, what functions do they want the space to fulfill? What activities will occur regularly in the future landscape? Checklist 19–1 is a printable list of possible uses and activities to consider when planning a landscape. Ultimately, the activities identified for a given landscape provide direction toward a design that suits all the users.

Planning Enough Space for a Deck or Patio

A landscape wish list may be long. Adequate space to comfortably incorporate the items on the list is essential. In the case of decks and patios, it is better to go too large rather than too small. A deck or patio for outdoor entertaining should comfortably accommodate the maximum number of guests who will be using the space. Wall seating around the edge of a patio and built-in benches for a deck take advantage of space and limit the need for extra furniture (Figure 19–34). Measure outdoor furniture planned for the space and allow 2 to 3 feet of walking room around chairs.

Checklist 19–1. Possible Landscape Activities and Uses

Users:
- ☐ Adults—How many _____
- ☐ Children (ages)—How many ___ Ages: _____
- ☐ Elderly or handicapped—How many _____
- ☐ Pets—How many _____ Types: _____

Access:
- ☐ Walks—width and appearance
- ☐ Driveway—surface and turnaround space
- ☐ Parking:
  - ☐ for family members
  - ☐ for guests
  - ☐ for campers
  - ☐ for boats
  - ☐ for bicycles

Activities:
- ☐ Outdoor entertaining:
  - ☐ Cooking/grilling
  - ☐ Dining
  - ☐ Seating
    - ☐ conversation
    - ☐ relaxation
- ☐ Gardening:
  - ☐ Ornamental flowers
  - ☐ Edible gardening:
    - ☐ vegetables
    - ☐ fruit trees or bushes
    - ☐ herbs

- ☐ Raised beds
- ☐ Containers
- ☐ Composting
- ☐ Other
- ☐ Children's play area
- ☐ Sports and recreation:
  - ☐ swimming pool
  - ☐ tennis court
  - ☐ basketball court
  - ☐ putting green
  - ☐ other

Other Uses:
- ☐ Dog pen/run
- ☐ Storage:
  - ☐ firewood
  - ☐ gardening and lawn care equipment
  - ☐ outdoor toys
  - ☐ sports equipment
  - ☐ lawn furniture/cushions
  - ☐ garbage receptacles
- ☐ Irrigation:
  - ☐ spigots
  - ☐ irrigation system
  - ☐ rain barrel

Using the plot plan scale, cut out paper patio furniture pieces sized to scale. Place and move pieces on the plot plan to help find an ideal location. People are accustomed to more elbowroom outside. Stake off the space to see if it is the right size, if the planned location takes advantage of good viewpoints in the yard and beyond, and if the site is out of direct traffic patterns to and from the house.

Figure 19–34. This small patio area extends its seating options by providing a flat topped wall.
Field Outdoor Spaces, Flickr CC BY - 2.0

Step 4: Locate and Develop Use Areas

A residential landscape consists of areas that are used for different purposes. In this step, we divide the site into several separate areas—each serving a purpose, but all combining into the overall design.

In residential landscapes, three general areas—public, private (family), and service (utility)—are used to organize activities and uses. Each area is developed to meet the user's needs and priorities (Checklist 19–2). After categorizing the activities, we can locate these areas for various

uses on the plot plan. Try to provide enough space for each activity within a given use area. Using another overlay sheet of tracing paper taped over the plot plan, note these use areas. Drawing bubbles to indicate use areas on the overlay helps to loosely define spaces for each activity (Figure 19–35).

The public use area is usually in the front of the house. The private use or family area is often in the back of the house. And the service area is generally in the backyard or side yard. It is important to locate and then develop each area so that it meets user needs, contributes to an attractive overall landscape, and addresses environmental factors identified in Step Two.

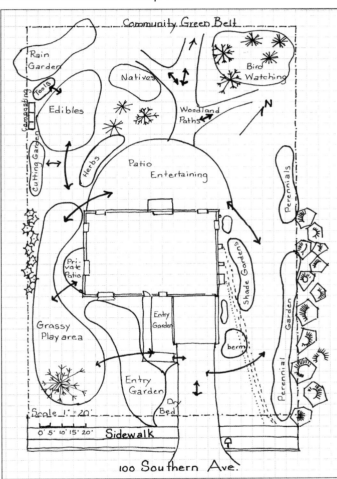

Figure 19–35. A bubble diagram helps loosely define activities and traffic flow in a landscape.
Renee Lampila

Public Use—Entrance Areas and Front Yards

The public use area is most often seen by passersby and guests and usually includes the front yard, drive, walks, and main entrance to the home. A first consideration is to direct visitors to the front door. This can be accomplished with several landscape features.

First, consider the front walk. This walk should be comfortable for two people walking side by side—a minimum of 4½ feet is recommended. The front entrance can be enhanced by a walkway with an interesting surface texture, such as brick, slate, concrete pavers, aggregate, or stained concrete (Figure 19–36).

Figure 19–36. The arbor and low-growing heather are inviting features leading visitors directly to the front door on this flagstone walk way.
Kathleen Moore, CC BY - 2.0

Outdoor lighting improves safety and directs pedestrian traffic to the entrance after dark. Low, indirect lighting can safely light paths. Municipalities and other government agencies are moving toward decreasing light pollution. For these reasons, incorporate appropriate light schemes into the landscape, including down-lighting of specimen plantings and hardscape. Another environmentally sustainable solution is solar lighting.

To help guide visitors to an entrance area add a focal point—for example, an interesting tree with ground cover underneath or a planter with a specimen shrub. Trees, shrubs, and grass can be used to focus attention on the entryway. Hardscape elements, including rocks, planters, trellises, arbors, and water features can also draw focus to the entryway.

Vehicle parking needs to be considered. If off-street parking is needed to accommodate visitors' cars, consider locating these spaces where they are easily accessible to the front entrance. Allow enough room for a door to swing open and a surface where someone exiting a vehicle can stand.

When planning the foundation areas, consider the mature size, color, texture, and number of plants needed. Consider the individual character of a plant so that as it matures it grows without major maintenance. Modern house foundations are often attractive and do not need to be hidden by dense borders of plant material.

If trees are desired near the house structure, choose a tree with a small canopy when fully grown so the branches do not interfere with the porch or roof. Placing tall trees in the backyard, and medium or small ones on the sides and in front, highlights the house (Figure 19–37). Examples of small canopy trees are dogwood (*Cornus florida*), Japanese flowering apricot (*Prunus mume*), Japanese maple (*Acer palmatum*), eastern redbud (*Cercis canadensis*), sourwood (*Oxydendrum arboreum*), and serviceberry (*Amelanchier* spp.). Tree-form evergreen shrubs are also useful, such as yaupon holly (*Ilex vomitoria*), camellia (*Camellia japonica*), inkberry holly (*Ilex glabra*), or wax myrtle (*Myrica cerifera*). When selecting trees or shrubs to frame a front entry, consider each plant's texture, color, shape, and size at maturity. The goal is to enhance the total visual effect while not blocking doors or windows or creating future maintenance issues from either plant root systems or branches and foliage.

Figure 19–37. This Japanese maple with a modest canopy is the right scale for this small front yard.
Lara604, Flickr CC BY - 2.0

While a front lawn is a very common feature, consider reducing the amount of area planted with turfgrass. Unless there are designated uses for a turf area in the front yard, the costs, labor, and chemical inputs often involved in maintaining a lawn can be avoided by planning a turf-free front landscape. Incorporate masses of ground covers or mulched areas in the front landscape to create interesting lines. A front yard without a lawn can be beautiful and inviting, more easily maintained than a lawn, and contribute to a sustainable, environmentally friendly landscape (Figure 19–38).

Figure 19–38. No one misses the lawn in this inviting front yard that incorporates a stone path, shrubs, perennials, and ground covers.
Kathleen Moore, CC BY - 2.0

Private Use—Family Activity Areas

When designing areas to be used privately by the family, refer back to the needs identified in Step 3. With North Carolina's pleasant climate, outdoor activities can be enjoyed most of the year, so decks, patios, and terraces should be considered an integral part of the residential landscape. The outdoor living areas should be easily accessible to the indoor living and kitchen areas of the home and should include private areas with attractive views.

Hot tubs, swimming pools, plant containers, raised beds for edibles, flower and woody ornamental gardens, water features, and sculptures are features that enhance an outdoor living area. Be sure to include space for recreation and sports. Some families enjoy basketball, tennis, or swimming, which requires special planning. If adding a large recreational feature like a tennis court or a swimming pool is not affordable with the initial landscape installation but is desired for the future, be sure to leave enough space in the private use area.

Consider children's needs for landscape space (Figure 19–39). Sandboxes, swing sets, playhouses, and toys should be located in the family activity area. Consider how children's needs and the use of that space will transition as the children grow up. Because play spaces are generally placed in major sight lines from the house, they are ideal for future focal points, such as a water feature or specimen plant.

Figure 19–39. These children are enjoying a natural play space made from tree rounds.
Lucy Bradley, CC BY - 2.0

Utility or Service Use Areas and Side Yards

Every residential landscape requires an area where gardening equipment, garbage cans, firewood, bicycles, and other items can be stored. Often these items end up at one side of the garage, behind the back porch, or under the deck. Set aside a certain amount of space for these necessities. Try to provide space for an outside utility building that is easily accessible (Figure 19–40).

Figure 19–40. A garden shed can be attractive as well as functional. It is the ideal place to store garden tools and potting supplies but it can also become a feature in the landscape as seen here with the cut-end logs decorating the walls.
Henry Burrows (foilman), Flickr CC BY-SA 2.0

Remember to keep the back of the site accessible to vehicles. Access facilitates major landscape maintenance tasks (like tree removal) or the addition of new landscape features, such as a concrete patio or a swimming pool.

If desired, spaces for gardening such as a greenhouse, beds for vegetables, or a compost pile can be provided in this area. As noted above, however, edibles can be integrated into the private use areas. If unsightly utility areas are visible from the house or patio, a screening wall or hedge may be needed (Figure 19–41). Do not forget to screen off unsightly areas from the neighbors.

A side yard is often the location for house utilities, including electricity and natural gas meters, cable access, or air-conditioning units. Homeowners do not typically spend a lot of money on their side yards because they do not spend a lot of time there. These utilitarian spaces can still be incorporated into the overall landscape at little cost by using attractive, functional access paths and screening materials. Be sure to keep plants and any screening structures away from utilities, both for ease of maintenance and to ensure good air flow.

Figure 19–41. This lattice is masking a power utility box with Italian Clematis (*Clematis viticella*) and Red Raspberry (*Rubus idaeus*) vines. These are deciduous vines that are easy to prune back, maintaining access around the box.
Kathleen Moore, CC BY - 2.0

19

Checklist 19–2. Developing Use Areas

PUBLIC USE ENTRANCE AND FRONT AREAS

Identify strategies to accent entryway:
- ☐ Alter the pathway: widen or change surface
- ☐ Add a featured plant
- ☐ Add a hardscape feature
- ☐ Add lighting

Assess house number visibility:
- ☐ Visible from a car driving both ways down street
- ☐ Visible traveling both ways on the sidewalk
- ☐ Visible at night
- ☐ Evaluate how visitors enter the home:
- ☐ Adequate parking for visitors:
- ☐ Off-street – include in landscape with easy access to entry
- ☐ On-street – easy access to entry
- ☐ Pathway to front door:
- ☐ Wide enough
- ☐ Well lit
- ☐ Free from tripping hazards
- ☐ Entry area visible and well lit

PRIVATE USE FAMILY ACTIVITY AREAS

Consider for outdoor entertainment space:
- ☐ Patio, deck, or terrace: _____
- ☐ Number of people to accommodate in space: _____
- ☐ Dining space adequate for desired table size
- ☐ Fireplace or fire pit
- ☐ Lighting of entertainment spaces
- ☐ Outdoor cooking space:
- ☐ BBQ pad
- ☐ Built-in gas grill
- ☐ Burners
- ☐ Ventilation
- ☐ Access to water

Consider hedges or screens for privacy:
- ☐ Outdoor entertainment spaces
- ☐ Unsightly areas on landscape site
- ☐ Neighboring properties
- ☐ Plant screen
- ☐ Hardscape screen (fences or walls)

Consider for children's play area:
- ☐ Playground equipment
- ☐ Sandbox
- ☐ Playhouse

Consider for recreation/sports areas:
- ☐ Lawn
- ☐ Basketball court/net
- ☐ Tennis court
- ☐ Swimming pool
- ☐ Lighting
- ☐ Other _____

Consider for pathways:
- ☐ Accessibility to activity areas
- ☐ Connectivity between activity areas
- ☐ Lighting

Consider for edible garden:
- ☐ Raised beds
- ☐ In-ground garden
- ☐ Fruit, nut trees and shrubs
- ☐ 6–8 hours of sunlight
- ☐ Greenhouse
- ☐ Evaluate soil type
- ☐ Good drainage; no low spots where water accumulates
- ☐ Good air circulation
- ☐ Protection from heavy winds
- ☐ Near good location for a compost pile
- ☐ Close to the kitchen
- ☐ Out of major sight lines
- ☐ Close to potable water source

Consider for pets:
- ☐ Identify pet(s) use of landscape
- ☐ Adequate turf grass meet for pets' needs
- ☐ Outdoor shelter for your pet(s):
- ☐ Kennel
- ☐ Dog house
- ☐ Dog run
- ☐ Shady areas for outdoor pet(s)
- ☐ Fencing
- ☐ Lighting

UTILITY OR SERVICE AREAS:

Considerations for exterior household utilities:
- ☐ Accessible for maintenance
- ☐ Adequate room for air flow
- ☐ Lighting

Storage:
- ☐ Garden and lawn equipment
- ☐ Garbage cans
- ☐ Bicycles
- ☐ Outdoor toys
- ☐ Sports equipment
- ☐ Lawn furniture/cushions

Screening for service areas:
- ☐ Plants
- ☐ Hardscape

Step 5: Design

Once the site has been analyzed, the activity wish list made, and bubble diagrams drawn (Figure 19–35) to best locate the activities and elements, the landscape layout can be determined. A landscape can be informal, formal, or a combination of the two. Informal landscapes tend to have curvilinear lines and winding paths. Formal landscapes have more formal planting beds and pathways with rectilinear lines.

A combination landscape might have a formal layout, but informal, loose plantings within the framework. Selecting the overall landscape layout is critical because it helps set the mood and energy of the space. It is important to get the layout right the first time as it can be time consuming and expensive to start over. The overall goal of this step is to get all the pieces of design to fit together like a puzzle so the final landscape, even after multiple installation phases, appears to be a unified, well-thought-out design.

Landscaping guided by a series of arbitrary "rules" such as "always plant shrubs in groups of three or five" and "never plant annuals in the public area" does not consider the needs of individual families and sites. Such landscaping rarely results in good design. Good design does not have to be limited by such so-called rules. Our objective in designing a landscape is not only creating good visual relationships. A successful landscape provides meaningful and useful spaces for people and their animals that fit with a family's desired aesthetic preferences. And a successful landscape promotes environmental stewardship. Developing a landscape design requires an understanding of the dynamic nature of the landscape. When we create a final design plan, we rely on basic design considerations, environmental design considerations, plant selection guidelines, and plan preparation instructions.

Basic Design Considerations
Emphasize by Grouping Plants

Rhododendrons, azaleas, dogwoods, or other woody ornamentals and herbaceous perennials can be mass-planted in informal beds (Figure 19–42). Try to locate the plants so that a natural scene develops as they mature. Plant the shrubs or trees together in one large bed and mulch well. Planting woody perennials en masse also provides winter structure for the landscape. Consider adding bulbs or borders that have masses of herbaceous perennials or annuals for seasonal color.

Provide Privacy

If the site analysis reflects a need to screen unsightly views, provide a noise barrier, or create privacy, plant evergreen shrubs or build a fence (Figure 19–43). If room and time allow, a natural evergreen hedge is a good screening option. Vines on trellises create effective screens in tight spaces. Many trees, shrubs, and vines that make good screens grow very well in North Carolina. Although deciduous plants lose their leaves in the fall, investigate their stem size and arrangement because a densely branched deciduous shrub can work as an effective and interesting screen even after its leaves have dropped.

Figure 19–42. Azaleas and bluebells in this lovely natural landscape.
denisbin, Flickr CC-BY-ND 2.0

Figure 19–43. A privacy hedge screens view, reduces noise, and adds beauty, wildlife habitat, and cooling.
Dean Thompson (Dean+Barb), Flickr CC-BY 2.0

Specimen Plants

In selecting specimen plants, consider quality—not quantity. By definition, specimen plants are plants grown alone for ornamental effect, rather than being massed with other plants as are bedding plants or edging plants (Figure 19–44). Specimen plants are located in the design to create focal points and draw attention to a specific area.

19

Figure 19–44. This Japanese maple (*Acer palmatum*) is a specimen plant with its finely divided leaves and striking fall color. It draws our eyes and is a focal point in the garden.
Jay Huang (Jaykhuang), Flickr CC BY - 2.0

Succession

We must design for time, or succession, when dealing with living, growing plant material. The initial planting should be based on the mature size of the plants. Although the entire space will not be filled, young, new plants should be placed so they will have space to grow and attain their mature size. Plan for the in-between areas in the newly planted garden so these open areas do not become weed-filled. One option is regular mulching with an organic material, such as pine fines, shredded leaves, or double-hammered hardwood mulch. All of these mulches suppress weeds, look attractive, conserve moisture, and protect and build healthy soil. Gaps can also be filled temporarily with annuals for a few years as long as they do not overcrowd or compete with permanent plantings.

Do not overcrowd plants during initial planting to create an "instant landscape" (Figure 19–45). Planting twice as many as needed, thinking they will be thinned out in a few years, doubles the cost of the job, and often the thinning never happens. Plants become overcrowded and compete for water and nutrients. Stressed, overcrowded plants are more susceptible to depredation by insects

Figure 19–45. These shrubs were overplanted and their mature size is much to large for this tiny garden. The branches are now overhanging the wall and can be a hazard to pedestrians.
Alan Stanton, Flickr CC BY-SA - 2.0

and plant diseases. Pests lead to unattractive, mainte-nance-intense plants that eventually need to be removed because they are unhealthy.

Ecologically Based Design Considerations

Residential landscapes are part of a larger landscape and ecological community. When we design an environ-mentally friendly landscape, we protect the site's natural elements and treat the landscape as a living system. We consider reducing energy, water, and material inputs, and avoid the use of toxic or prohibited materials. The following environmentally friendly design techniques and considerations are based on valuing ecosystem services in the landscape.

Designing for Water Conservation

Traditional landscape designs often incorporate the removal of all water offsite as quickly as possible. In an ecologically based design, water is not treated as a waste product to be captured and conveyed offsite. Instead, we view water as a resource to be captured and used in the landscape. The idea is to balance water inputs from pre-cipitation, surface flow, and piped-in sources with outputs from evapotranspiration, runoff, and water that infil-trates into the soil. This balance helps prevent negative environmental effects such as erosion and surface and groundwater pollution. We rely on the following design techniques and concepts to achieve water conservation and balance:

- **Hardscapes** create a slight slope on driveways and sidewalks to allow water to flow into the landscape rather than being diverted to the stormwater system. Where possible, use permeable surfaces for sidewalks, patios, and driveways (Figure 19–46) to allow water to soak into the ground.

Figure 19–46. This driveway uses permeable pavers that allow grass to grow in between and catch rainwater before it runs off.
Bradley Gordon (bradleygee), Flickr CC BY - 2.0

- **Earthworks** such as earthen berms and swales are used to contour the land to slow and capture rainwater, allowing it to infiltrate the soil. A swale is a trench dug perpendicular to the slope of the land. They are most effective on gentle slopes of less than 30 degrees. Begin installing swales as high in the landscape as possible, capturing water before it builds momentum and causes erosion. Continue building swales down the slope to promote infiltration and minimize stormwater runoff. A berm is a mound of soil that holds water in a plant's root zone. Terracing can also slow down water movement (Figure 19–47).

Figure 19–47. A simple terrace like this one made out of wood with dirt piled against it will help slow rainwater down so it has a chance to soak into the soil.
Irene Kightlye (hardworkinghippy : La Ferme de Sourrou), CC BY- SA 2.0

- **Rain gardens** are designed to capture and infiltrate rainwater into the landscape (Figure 19–48). Select a location in full or partial sun that is at least 2 feet above the water table. The site should also be between the source of stormwater runoff (roofs and hardscapes) and where the water leaves the property. Do not place the rain garden within 10 feet of the house foundation or within 25 feet of a wellhead or a septic system drain field. Avoid underground utilities. Use "Sizing Your Rain Garden," a sizing chart from the NC State Extension Stormwater Program, to calculate the size of water garden needed to manage a site's stormwater. Dig a hole 4 to 6 inches deep with a slight depression in the center. Use the soil removed from the hole to create a berm along the side of the rain garden opposite the side into which the water flows. Cover the berm with mulch or grass to prevent erosion. Create a filter bed by slightly recessing the garden and adding compost to whatever soil is already on site. Compost works well with all soil types, adding valuable nutrients and microbes. In sandy soils it slows infiltration rates, and in clay soils it improves infiltration and pore space. Do not add sand to a filter bed as it can cause clay soils to become brick-like. Install plants that can withstand both short periods of standing water and periods of drought. Then cover with 2 to 3 inches of hardwood mulch.

Figure 19–48. Rain garden designed in a parking lot median to mitigate stormwater runoff.
Meg Molloy, CC BY 4.0

19

- **Green roofs** or a living roof are partially or completely covered with vegetation and some type of growing medium, planted over a waterproof membrane. It may also include additional layers such as a root barrier and drainage and irrigation systems. Green roofs yield several important environmental benefits, including reducing stormwater runoff, restoring the natural water cycle in urban settings, enhancing biodiversity, and lowering outside building temperatures (Figure 19–49). In addition, green roofs increase awareness of stormwater management issues.

Figure 19–49. This shed incorporates a living green roof.
Christoph Rupprecht (Focx Photography), CC BY-SA 2.0

- **Rain barrels** and cisterns are containers placed under downspouts to capture and store rainwater until it is needed for landscape irrigation. These containers prevent uncontrolled runoff. They can also be used to collect condensate from air conditioners, allowing the water to be used as needed for landscape irrigation and conserving water, energy, and money. This reliable, high-quality source of water is available during summer months when irrigation needs are highest. In the best-case scenario, rain barrels can be used in concert with rain gardens, directing any runoff from barrels to a rain garden.

- **Gray water** is water discharged from bathtubs, showers, wash basins (except the kitchen sink), dishwashers, and clothes washers. Using gray water saves money by reducing the amount of tap water purchased for use in the garden and landscape as well as the energy that would have been used to treat and transport tap water. Using gray water also saves the energy that would have been used to transport and treat the gray water if it had entered the wastewater treatment system. A person who lives in a newer home with water efficient fixtures generates approximately 35 gallons of gray water per day (12,320 gallons per year), while a person in an older

home generates approximately 46 gallons per day (16,192 gallons per year). To protect groundwater and public health, rely on these requirements for safe use of gray water:

- The water must be used on the residential property where it was discharged. It must not be allowed to run off onto adjoining property, roadways, or into ditches or storm drains.
- The water must be applied to the landscape as soon as practical (within 24 hours of production).
- Apply the water directly to the ground. Do not spray it.
- Do not use gray water when laundering diapers, dying clothes, or when using any detergents, solvents, or other products that might be hazardous to the environment.
- Do not use gray water if any resident of the house has an infectious disease, such as diarrhea or hepatitis, or if any resident has internal parasites.
- Do not drink or apply gray water to edible crops (except those with a heavy rind like citrus and nuts).
- Include the capacity to divert gray water to the sewer system when desired.
- Check current state laws, local ordinances, and homeowner association covenants and restrictions prior to installing a gray water system.

A 1,000 square foot roof produces 630 gallons of runoff in a 1-inch rainstorm.

Other recommended design practices for water conservation include:

- Group plants according to water needs, such as "high water use" or "no supplemental water."
- Reduce the size of the lawn. As much as half of all the water used outdoors by the average homeowner goes to lawn irrigation.
- Install a multi-zone irrigation system with a rain sensor or soil moisture monitor.
- Avoid watering buildings, driveways, streets, and sidewalks.

Applying good design practices to conserve water in the landscape also conserves the energy that would have been required to provide that water.

Designing for Energy Conservation
Landscape plants provide shade (protection from radiant heat), minimize air movement (insulation), and cool the air through transpiration (release of water from leaves which then evaporates, a process that consumes energy and results in heat reduction).

The passive energy-conserving impact of a plant species depends on its size, whether it is deciduous or evergreen, the shape of its canopy, and the density of its foliage. Trees, shrubs, and vines are all effective, although arbors or trellises have to be included for vines or to espalier shrubs and trees.

Locate deciduous trees where the greatest benefit is derived from summer shade and winter sun—on the western side to protect the home from noon to sunset. There is also some benefit to planting on the eastern side to protect from sunrise to noon. Shade not only structures but also outdoor seating areas, walls, and hardscapes. Pay particular attention to shading windows, which are most vulnerable to heat gain. Shading air conditioners can reduce the air temperature inside the home, but be sure to allow for adequate air flow around the unit. Use trees to shade the walls rather than the roof of the house. Tree limbs over the roof shed litter that clogs rain gutters. If heavy limbs fall during a storm, they can damage the house.

Create a windbreak by identifying the prevailing winter wind and installing evergreen trees upwind from the house. One row of trees is effective, but a windbreak of up to five rows that includes several different species is more effective. The windbreak also serves as a privacy screen. A biodiverse windbreak (or screen) consisting of native plants also provides sources of food and shelter for beneficial insects and wildlife, including birds.

Do not over-plant! Too many trees and shrubs near the house can cause moisture problems that lead to mildew, mold, and high humidity. The wind and the sun should periodically dry the area around the home. Over-shading a home may result in higher energy and maintenance bills because lights have to be used more often and an air conditioner may be needed to control humidity.

Carefully positioned trees, shrubs, and vines can save up to 25% of a typical household's energy consumption for cooling and heating. Combining these landscape ideas with proper insulation and conservation habits should produce a significant decrease in energy consumption.

Designing for Wildlife Conservation

Landscapes are ecosystems. Ecosystems require a diversity of plants in various layers or levels to provide adequate habitat for wildlife. Consider including a water feature with shallow edges to provide drinking and bathing water for wildlife. Selecting native plants helps to attract birds, pollinators, and beneficial insects to the yard. See chapter 20, "Wildlife," for specific tips on attracting and managing wildlife in the landscape.

Designing for Food Security

Incorporating edibles into the entire landscape instead of only in a vegetable garden is a way to make the landscape more eco-friendly. Doing so also makes more efficient use of space by incorporating plants that perform multiple functions (add beauty to the garden, provide food and cut flowers, and attract pollinators). It is not necessary to substitute edible plants for all ornamentals, but many edible woody landscape plants have high ornamental value. The goal is to progress from the typical backyard vegetable garden and develop a plan that uses edible plants to solve functional landscape problems. Plan for year-round harvest by selecting a variety of plants that ripen at different times throughout the year.

Edibles are available that meet most plant selection design criteria. For trees, consider fruit and nut trees. Most deciduous fruit trees (including apple, fig, pear, cherry, peach, and plum) come in a variety of sizes ranging from a mature height of 8 feet to a mature height of 30 feet. Select one to fit the space. Be sure to provide adequate sunlight as fruit trees require 6 to 7 hours a day. For seasonal color, instead of purchasing annual flowers consider colorful vegetable plants. The bright stems of rainbow chard spruce up any planting bed. Kale comes in many varieties that have interesting colors and textures (Figure 19–50).

Instead of planting ornamental ground covers, think about planting strawberries or evergreen raspberries. An area

Figure 19–50. Edibles do not need to be relegated to vegetable gardens, this dinosaur kale is right at home in this perennial bed.
Lucy Bradley

with well-drained soil that receives at least 6 to 7 hours of direct sunlight produces strawberry plants with lush green foliage, spring blossoms, and early summer fruit. Rosemary, thyme, oregano, lavender, and many other herbs offer a variety of design options. Some are evergreen, some are shrublike, some create creeping ground covers, and all have colorful blooms and unique fragrances.

Blueberry bushes are a good substitute for a privet (*Ligustrum* sp.) or hedges of Asian hollies (for example, *Ilex cornuta* 'Burfordii'). Rabbiteye cultivars are more widely adapted to different soils than highbush cultivars. Rabbiteye blueberries do not tolerate the cold climate of the mountains but grow well in full sun all across the NC piedmont and coastal plain. Acid soil (with a pH of 4.5 to 5.5) usually promotes the best growth. Include two or more cultivars in the design to ensure proper pollination. Read more in chapter 14, "Small Fruits."

Designing to Minimize Maintenance

To make the landscape more efficient and less frustrating to maintain, consider these design suggestions:

- Avoid sharp angles, tight corners, narrow lawns, and irregular edges that are hard to mow and water.
- Reduce turfgrass areas—lawn is labor and material intensive, requiring regular mowing and other maintenance tasks plus irrigation, fertilizer, and other chemicals.
- Choose plants whose growth habit and mature size meet the design requirements to minimize pruning and shearing to maintain the desired size and shape.
- Look for plants that are drought-tolerant, wind-resistant, and adapted to low fertilization to save on maintenance.
- Group plants with the same water needs together to save time and money on irrigation.
- Locate the compost bin near where the green waste is generated.
- Consider minimizing the removal of organic material from the landscape in the design. Practice the law of return. For example, leave grass clippings on the lawn to enrich and protect soil, which feeds the grass, saves the labor of collecting and bagging clippings, and conserves the energy expended to truck them away. Plant deciduous trees and shrubs in large beds where leaves can accumulate and biodegrade to enrich and protect soil. This practice also conserves water, labor, and energy.

Designing for Wildfire Resistance

If wildfire is a potential problem, create at least a 30-foot defensible space around the house (more if the house is on a slope or if the surrounding vegetation is particularly flammable) by removing flammable material from the area surrounding the building. Identify the prevailing wind, which is the direction from which the fire is most likely

to approach. Be sure not to design storage for firewood, building materials, or other flammable landscape materials on that side of the yard. Remove any dead vegetation within the defensible space. Eliminate fuel ladders, plants of varying heights located near each other, which provide a means for the fire to jump to the canopy. Leave open space between plants or groups of plants within the defensible space. Do not plant within 5 feet of any structure or use dense masses of plants.

> *To learn about* **Permaculture**, *another ecologically based approach to landscape design, see Appendix G.*

Plant Selection

Plants are the dynamic heart of a landscape, and thoughtful plant selection is essential to developing a beautiful, earth-friendly landscape. Proper plant selection and placement create an appealing landscape, improve property value, beautify the community, and build a healthy local ecosystem. Selecting the right plant for the right place reduces the need for irrigation water, fertilizer, herbicides and pesticides, and labor.

Plants can be selected for their aesthetic or ecological value to fulfill specific functions such as screening or noise control. Plants are incorporated into the design to fill several visual and sensory roles in the landscape. Plants form a structural framework for the garden and yard, establish horizontal and vertical diversity and transition, and provide focal points. They can be used for screening and creating seasonal impact with foliage, bloom, twig color, or trunk architecture. Many plants add fragrance to the environment. Selections based on ecological value can reduce lawn area, control erosion, and add biodiversity by attracting, hosting, and feeding pollinators, beneficial insects, and other wildlife—including birds.

Native plants or cultivars of native species benefit the local ecosystem in a myriad of ways including by supporting insects, the primary food source for nesting birds and other native fauna. In addition, they attract native pollinators, including birds, bats, butterflies, bees, and moths as well as providing preferred food, shelter and habitat for wildlife. Native plants also enhance the beauty of all types of gardens—from formal to informal designs—and provide a sense of place and regional history. An extensive variety of native plants occur in North Carolina and they can be used to incorporate elements of local natural systems. See chapter 12, "Native Plants" for more information. There are also a variety of non-native ornamental species that thrive in North Carolina. When selecting non-natives make sure they are well adapted to the site's growing conditions but are not designated as weedy or invasive or considered a threat to natural habitats.

19

Avoid invasive plants such as English ivy (*Hedera helix*), privet (Japanese and Chinese *Ligustrum* spp.), Japanese and Chinese wisteria (*Wisteria floribunda* and *W. sinensis*), and Japanese honeysuckle (*Lonicera japonica*), all of which are detrimental to the local landscape and environment, including undeveloped natural areas. For lists of invasive plants, see the NC Invasive Plant Council, Going Native: Urban Landscaping for Wildlife with Native Plants, or the NC Native Plants Society.

To put the right plant in the right place, we must understand each plant's environmental requirements and its design characteristics. For example, choose drought-resistant or low-moisture plants for a location with limited available water. Or select a mounding, low-growing broadleaf evergreen for a low hedge next to a walkway.

Environmental requirements of the plant to consider include:
- Moisture needs
- Light exposure:
  - Full sun: at least 6 full hours of direct sunlight
  - Part sun/part shade: terms often used interchangeably to mean 3 to 6 hours of sun each day, preferably in morning and/or early afternoon
  - Full shade: less than 3 hours of direct sunlight each day with filtered sunlight during rest of day
- Insect and disease resistance
- Heat and wind tolerance
- Soil type preference

A plant's designated USDA Hardiness Zone (the USDA has an interactive zone map on their website) is a starting point for understanding its environmental requirements. Plant tags at nursery centers also provide environmental information. For the most accurate, research-based information on specific plants, use plant databases from credible websites such as the NC State Extension Gardener Plant Toolbox or other university extension programs as well as books by reputable horticulturists, botanists, and ecologists.

Key design factors to consider in plant selection include plant growth habit, mature size, bloom cycle, and seasonal interest.

A plant's growth habit determines its mature form, shape, and texture, which dictate how a plant occupies and accents the space and integrates into the landscape layout. Texture, form, shape, and size are physical characteristics of plants that provide interest, variety, and aesthetic appeal in a landscape. Based on these characteristics, some plants have more visual value in relation to the surroundings. Some are more functionally dominant, and some dominate simply by size. Select plants with upright forms and coarse textures for high visual impact. Low or prostrate forms and fine textures are less dramatic and have lower visual impact. When selecting plants for specific locations in the design, consider that the visual value also depends on the viewing distance, the season, light conditions, and adjacent plant material and structures.

Knowing the mature plant size is critical for spacing plantings to accommodate both mature height and width. Also consider mature sizes of nearby plants and distance from any nearby structures. Plants near buildings should be located half their mature width plus a minimum of 1 foot away from the structure. For example, a shrub that grows to be 5 feet wide should be planted 3½ feet (2½ feet + 1 foot) away from a structure. Choose plants that have the desired mature size versus ones that require constant pruning and maintenance to keep it the desired size.

Choose plants with different bloom cycles and foliage color to provide year-round color and to attract pollinators. Flowering trees provide pastels in spring. Beds of perennials and annuals furnish vivid hues in summer, and hellebores offer bursts of color in late winter. Many plants have more attractive foliage than flowers. In addition to innumerable shades of green, plants offer leaves of other colors. Many plants have variegated leaves with multiple colors on each leaf. Some variegated leaves have stripes of different colors (usually white, cream, or yellow and green). Others have patches or blotches of color, including combinations of white, cream, or yellow and green; pink, purple, and green; or yellow, orange, red, copper, and green.

To create seasonal interest, consider bloom color and time, foliage texture and color, fruit color and time, and twig and bark texture and color to achieve visual accents in every season. For example, evergreens add winter color and unity. When possible, select plants that provide year-round interest. A river birch (*Betula nigra*), has attractive spring flowers, beautiful fall or midsummer color, and exfoliating (shedding) bark for winter interest. Concentrate color where accent is desired, but when considering plant colors, remember that more is not necessarily better. In a good design, the main plant colors are the shades of green that set off the seasonal accent colors. Be wary of using too many evergreens as they can be visually "heavy" and not provide as much seasonal change as deciduous plants.

When selecting plants for a landscape, choose the woody ornamentals (trees and shrubs) first because they establish the borders, hedges, and specimen plantings that give structure and form to the green portion of the landscape. Create groups of shrubs and trees with similar environmental needs in mulched beds with curved edges rather than scattering plants throughout a lawn. Woody ornamentals often have extensive feeder root systems, and large trees can have feeder roots that extend twice the canopy diameter. These roots compete for resources with other plants, including turfgrass. Using large sweeps of perennials and ornamental grasses achieves winter form and interest.

Make sure final plant selections are appropriate for the site and the design. For example, choose a tall evergreen like a native arborvitae cultivar (*Thuja occidentalis*) and locate several to establish a screen or a windbreak. Select large deciduous trees planted well away from the house foundation on the south and west exposures to mitigate hot summer temperatures. For shady areas, consider masses of herbaceous shade-tolerant perennials like Indian pink (*Spigelia marilandica*), foamflower (*Tiarella cordifolia*), white wood aster (*Eurybia divaricata*), and green-and-gold (*Chrysogonum virginianum*) around shade-tolerant evergreen plants such as Christmas fern (*Polystichum acrostichoides*) or anise tree (*Illicium floridanum*).

Prior to this step, the plants in a design are abstract concepts that fulfill design specifications: a 30-foot by 20-foot deciduous shade tree or a 4-foot by 4-foot evergreen shrub. Delineating the environmental conditions where each plant will be placed allows us to select the genus and species for each spot. Again the NC State Extension Gardener Plant Toolbox is a valuable resource for identifying recommended options.

Once the specific plants are selected, they can be drawn to scale at their mature size on the plan as shown in Figure 19–51. Drawing plants to scale on the plan is an accurate way of determining quantities needed of each plant. Use symbols on the plan to clearly convey information about the plants and to allow the inclusion of details in the design. Figure 19–28 provides some commonly used symbols. Trees should be drawn with symbols that are transparent so the elements under the tree's canopy can be seen easily. In contrast, ground covers can be darkly or densely drawn as nothing is planted underneath them. Evergreen versus deciduous trees and shrubs should be graphically easy to distinguish.

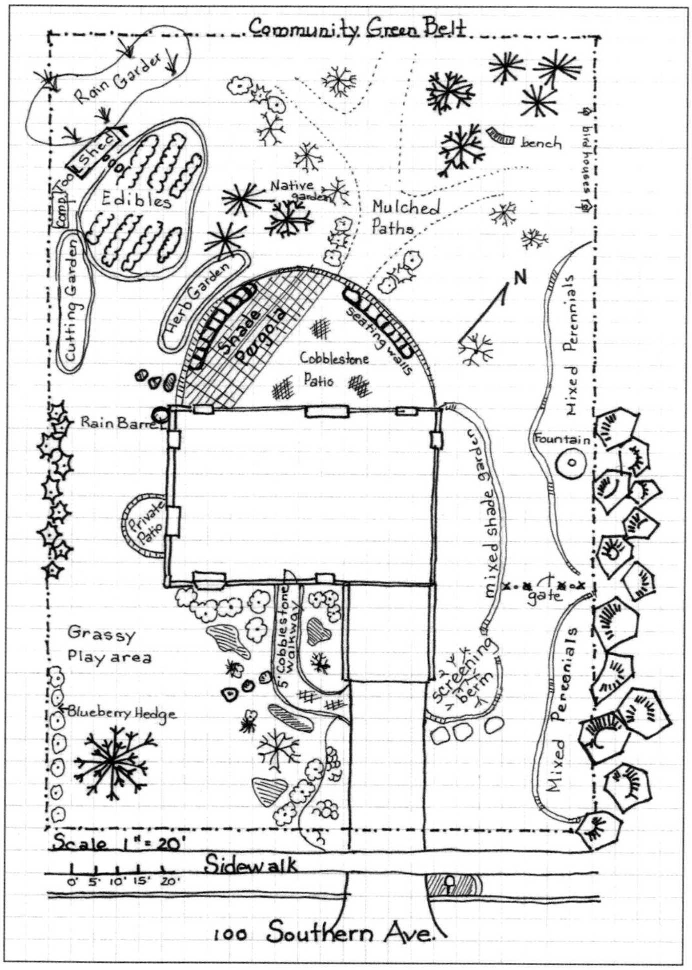

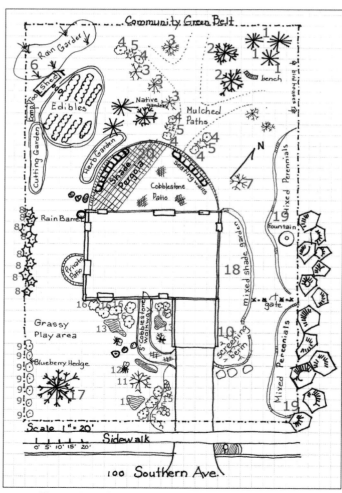

Figure 19–51. The final plot plan.
Renee Lampila

Figure 19–52. Plants labeled with numbers that correspond to Table 19–1.
Renee Lampila

Table 19–1. Plant Details for Plants in Figure 19–52

Plot Plan Reference	Plant Type Indicated in Plot Plan	Botanical Name	Common Name(s)	Cultivar(s)	Mature Height	Mature Spread
1	Evergreen tree (max spread 15'–20')	*Magnolia virginiana*	Sweetbay Magnolia		20'–50'	15'–20'
2	Deciduous tree (max spread 15'–20')	*Amelanchier × grandiflora* (*A. arborea × A. laevis* hybrid)	Serviceberry; Juneberry	'Autumn Brilliance' 'Ballerina,' 'Princess Diana'	20'–25'	15'–20'
3	Deciduous shrub/ small tree (max spread 15')	*Ilex verticillata*	Winterberry Holly	'Winter Red' with 'Southern Gentleman'	10'–12'	10'–12'
4	Deciduous small shrub (max spread 5')	*Itea virginica*	Sweetspire	'Little Henry' 'Merlot' 'Saturnalia'	3'–5'	3'–5'
5	Evergreen shrub (max spread 5')	*Myrica pumila* syn *M. cerifera* (dwarf)	Dwarf Wax Myrtle	'Don's Dwarf' 'Don's Other Dwarf'	4'–6'	4'–6'
6	Rain garden plants	*Viburnum rufidulum*	Blackhaw Viburnum		10'–20'	10'–15'
6	Rain garden plants	*Rudbeckia hirta*	Black-Eyed Susan		2'–3'	8"–10"
6	Rain garden plants	*Chelone glabra*	Turtlehead		1'–3'	1'–2'
6	Rain garden plants	*Asclepias incarnata*	Swamp Milkweed		2'–4'	2'–3'
6	Rain garden plants	*Chasmanthium latifolium*	River Oats		2'–5'	1'–2.5'
6	Rain garden plants	*Clethra alnifolia*	Sweet Pepperbush; Summersweet	'Ruby Spice' 'Sixteen Candles'	4'–10'	4'–6'
7	Deciduous tall shrub/ small specimen tree (max spread 15')	*Chionanthus virginicus*	Fringe Tree		12'–20'	12'–20'
8	Evergreen screening hedge tall shrub/tree (max spread 5')	*Ilex vomitoria*	Yaupon Holly	'Will Fleming' 'Scarlet's Peak'	10'–20'	3'–5'
9	Deciduous hedge shrub (max spread 5')	*Vaccinium corymbosum* syn *V. ashei*	Highbush or Rabbiteye Blueberry	'Climax' 'Premier' 'Tifblue'	6'–12'	8'–12'
10	Deciduous screening hedge tall shrub	*Aesculus parviflora*	Bottlebrush Buckeye		8'–12'	8'–15'
11	Deciduous small specimen tree (max spread 15'–20')	*Cercis canadensis*	Eastern Redbud	'Forest Pansy' 'Hearts of Gold' 'Ruby Falls'	15'–20'	15'–20'
12	Ornamental grass	*Muhlenbergia capillaris*	Pink Muhlygrass		2'–3'	2'–3'
13	Mixed groundcovers	*Mazus reptans*	Mazus; Cupflower	'Alba'	4"–6"	6"–12"
13	Mixed groundcovers	*Chrysogonum virginianum* *C. virginianum* var *australe*	Green and Gold; Goldenstar	'Allen Bush' 'Eco-Lacquered Spider'	4"–8"	1'–2'

(continued)

19

Table 19–1. Plant Details for Plants in Figure 19–52 *continued*

Plot Plan Reference	Plant Type Indicated in Plot Plan	Botanical Name	Common Name(s)	Cultivar(s)	Mature Height	Mature Spread
14	Deciduous small specimen shrub (max spread 5')	*Hydrangea quercifolia*	Oakleaf Hydrangea	'Pee Wee' 'Ruby Slippers' 'Munchkin' 'Sykes Dwarf'	2'–4'	3'–5'
15	Deciduous or evergreen small shrub (max spread 5')	*Fothergilla gardenii*	Dwarf Fothergilla	'Mount Airy' (*F. gardenii* × *F. major* hybrid)	3'–5'	3'–5'
16	Deciduous or evergreen small shrub (max spread 5')	*Loropetalum chinense*	Chinese Fringe-Flower	'Shang-hi' (Purple Diamond™), 'Shang-lo' (Purple Pixie™)	2'–5'	4'–5'
17	Deciduous large specimen tree (existing)	*Acer rubrum*	Red Maple		40'–60'	25'–45'
18	Mixed shade garden	*Aquilegia canadensis*	Columbine		2'–3'	1'–1.5'
18	Mixed shade garden	*Carex flaccosperma*	Blue Wood Sedge		6"–12"	6"–12"
18	Mixed shade garden	*Eurybia divaricata*	White Wood Aster		1'–2.5'	1.5'–2.5'
18	Mixed shade garden	*Geranium maculatum*	Wild Geranium		1.5'–2'	1'–1.5'
18	Mixed shade garden	*Gillenia trifoliata*	Bowman's Root		2'–4'	1.5'–2'
18	Mixed shade garden	*Heuchera america*	Alumroot/Coral Bells		1'–2'	1'–1.5'
18	Mixed shade garden	*Illicium floridanum*	Florida Anise Tree	'Pink Frost,' 'Halley's Comet'	5'–8'	5'–8'
18	Mixed shade garden	*Iris cristata*	Dwarf Crested Iris	'Alba'	6"–8"	6"–12"
18	Mixed shade garden	*Osmunda cinnamomea*	Cinnamon Fern		3'–5'	2'–3'
18	Mixed shade garden	*Polygonatum biflorum*	Solomon's Seal		1'–3'	1'–1.5'
18	Mixed shade garden	*Polystichum acrostichoides*	Christmas Fern		1'–2'	1'–2'
18	Mixed shade garden	*Silene virginica*	Fire Pink		1'–1.5'	1'–1.5'
18	Mixed shade garden	*Spigelia marilandica*	Indian Pink		1'–2'	1'–2'
18	Mixed shade garden	*Stylophorum diphyllum*	Celadine Poppy		1'–2'	1'–2'
19	Mixed herbaceous perennial garden	*Asclepias tuberosa*	Butterfly Milkweed		1'–2.5'	1'–1.5'
19	Mixed herbaceous perennial garden	*Baptisia alba*	White Wild Indigo		2'–4'	1'–2.5'
19	Mixed herbaceous perennial garden	*Baptisia tinctoria*	Yellow Wild Indigo		2'–3'	2'–3'

19

(continued)

Table 19–1. Plant Details for Plants in Figure 19–52 *continued*

Plot Plan Reference	Plant Type Indicated in Plot Plan	Botanical Name	Common Name(s)	Cultivar(s)	Mature Height	Mature Spread
19	Mixed herbaceous perennial garden	*Coreopsis auriculata*	Lobed Tickseed		6"–8"	6"–12"
19	Mixed herbaceous perennial garden	*Coreopsis lanceolata*	Lance-Leaf Tickseed		1'–2'	1'–1.5'
19	Mixed herbaceous perennial garden	*Echinacea purpurea*	Coneflower		2'–5'	1.5'–2'
19	Mixed herbaceous perennial garden	*Eutrochium fistulosum*	Joe Pye Weed	'Atropurpurea'	4'–7'	2'–4'
19	Mixed herbaceous perennial garden	*Helenium flexuosum*	Purple-Headed Sneezeweed		1'–3'	1'–2'
19	Mixed herbaceous perennial garden	*Hibiscus coccineus*	Scarlet Rose-Mallow		6'–8'	3'–5'
19	Mixed herbaceous perennial garden	*Hibiscus moscheutos*	Crimson-Eyed Rose Mallow		3'–6'	2'–4'
19	Mixed herbaceous perennial garden	*Iris virginica*	Virginia Blueflag		1'–3'	1'–3'
19	Mixed herbaceous perennial garden	*Liatris spicata*	Blazing-Star		2'–4'	9"–18"
19	Mixed herbaceous perennial garden	*Lobelia cardinalis*	Cardinal Flower		2'–4'	1'–2'
19	Mixed herbaceous perennial garden	*Monarda didyma*	Bee Balm		2'–4'	2'–3'
19	Mixed herbaceous perennial garden	*Panicum virgatum*	Switchgrass		3'–6'	2'–3'
19	Mixed herbaceous perennial garden	*Penstemon digitalis*	Tall White Beardtongue	'Husker Red'	2'–3'	1'–2'
19	Mixed herbaceous perennial garden	*Schizachyrium scoparium*	Little Bluestem		2'–4'	1.5'–2'
19	Mixed herbaceous perennial garden	*Solidago rugosa*	Golden Rod	'Fireworks'	2.5'–3'	2.5'–3'
19	Mixed herbaceous perennial garden	*Stokesia laevis*	Stokes' Aster	'Peachies Pick' 'Colorwheel' 'Mary Gregory' 'Alba'	1'–2'	1'–1.5'
19	Mixed herbaceous perennial garden	*Symphyotrichum oblongifolium*	Aromatic Aster	'October Skies'	1'–3'	1'–3'
19	Mixed herbaceous perennial garden	*Veronicastrum virginicum*	Culver's Root		4'–7'	2'–4'
20	Shade pergola	*Lonicera sempervirens*	Coral Honeysuckle	'Major Wheeler'	15'–20'	3'–6'

19

Preparing Final Plan

Using the fundamental design principles outlined at the beginning of this chapter and applying the results of Steps 1 through 5, we can develop the final landscape design plan that incorporates the design considerations and plant selections outlined in the first part of Step 6. This final plan (Figure 19–51) shows all changes to be made to existing site features like walks or driveways and any additions, such as a deck, pool, or patio. The final plan also shows the location of all plant material. Figure 19–52 assigns numbers to the plants on the plot plan and Table 19–1 gives a suggested plant list. Learn more about each of the plants listed on the NC State Extension Gardener Plant Toolbox. In selecting plant size on the plant list, resist the temptation to have an "instant landscape." Small plants establish faster and are more economical. Large trees and shrubs may achieve an instantaneous effect, but transplant stress increases with plant size.

Step 6: Installing the Landscape

The final plan ensures that all landscape work done on a property blends over time into the desired final outcome, creating a harmonious composition and providing physical and psychological comfort. Even with a completed plan, landscape development can be a long-term process. There is no need to develop an entire property at once. Completing the landscape over a period of several years might be economically more feasible and may ultimately improve the overall design. An extended installation time frame allows more opportunity to evaluate plants as they grow and mature and consider the impact and desirability of planned hardscape features. The additional time can also help better identify those parts of the landscape that supply essential functions and those that have to be installed before other elements of the landscape can be incorporated. By establishing priorities, we can implement the landscape in stages (for example, front yards versus backyards or hardscapes; then large plant material; then small).

When you prioritize elements for installation in a landscape, consider user needs and budgetary constraints. Budget should always be kept in mind as costs of installing various landscaping features can vary greatly. If shade is needed for a patio area, the least expensive is to plant a shade tree and wait several years. At an in-

creased cost, an arbor can be installed for instant shade. A large standing umbrella can be purchased at a modest cost. If the design calls for a grassy play area, a lawn can be started from seed in the fall or spring (depending on the turfgrass selected), and you can wait a season for it to be ready for use. For quicker results, you can choose the more expensive option of laying sod, allowing the grass to be ready for use much sooner.

A landscape installation can be very simple or extremely complicated. Homeowners should evaluate the skills and materials needed for installation and associated costs to determine whether these are DIY projects or whether money and time would be better spent by hiring a professional. Permanent structures or large hardscape elements, including irrigation systems, outdoor lighting, stone walls, decks, pools, and patios, may require skills that go beyond those of the average homeowner. When the job seems too big, call in a professional, licensed landscape contractor. North Carolina state law requires that anyone using the title "landscape contractor" must be registered by the Landscape Contractors Registration Board. A landscape contractor must pass exams covering soils, grading, plants, and various other topics. Be aware, however, that anyone who thinks they can do landscape work can set themselves up in business as a "landscaper," "landscape installer," or "landscape designer." Be sure to check references, visit other installations by the contractor, and check with the Better Business Bureau to make sure the contractor is licensed and bonded.

Construction Materials

We often think of landscaping and planting as synonymous. But landscaping also includes the incorporation of several important hardscape features, such as walls, patios, outdoor lighting, walks, and decks that are integral to a design. Although most people evaluate the success of landscape development in terms of the selection and condition of the plant materials, most well-designed landscapes contain a balance of construction and plant materials. Carefully designed and executed paved surfaces, fences, walls, overhead structures, and edging materials are attractive, and they can reduce routine maintenance.

Factors that influence the choice of materials include existing architectural and landscape features, cost, and sustainability. When selecting hardscape material, consider the principles of unity, rhythm, accent, and repetition. If possible, repeat materials and colors already used on the home. This achieves a major objective of good landscaping design: to establish a visual relationship between the house and the site. Use building materials that blend well in the local natural environment and relate to the home. For example, use wood shingles on a gazebo roof that match the home's roof on a wooded site, or select stone for retaining walls that reflects a stone chimney in an area where the stone is found naturally. Natural construction materials often combine well with resource efficient landscapes. Weathered wood, natural stains, concrete, and earth tones in brick usually blend with existing construction materials and relate to the natural environment.

The landscape materials can contribute to sustainability when we select renewable, local, and low-energy input materials. Explore options for using recycled materials and energy efficient materials in the landscape. Used bricks or broken concrete can be used for retaining walls. Recycled plastic material may be an appropriate choice for decking or fences. Consider the safety of re-purposing items before including them in the landscape. For example, the chemicals in creosote-impregnated railroad ties or lumber treated with chromated copper arsenate (CCA) can leach into the soil. Better options exist, such as untreated cedar, for use in gardens and near food crops.

Consider any potential environmental impact of selected materials, both the impact of using them and the impact of their production, packaging, and marketing. Limit the amount of impermeable surfaces, which collect heat and increase stormwater runoff. Consider using a permeable paving system—such as gravel or pavers that have open centers for planting grass—for patios, walkways, and driveways to promote infiltration, improve drainage, and limit runoff. Select energy-conserving construction materials. Remember that light pollution is a problem in urban and suburban areas and even affects migrating birds, moths and butterflies. Eco-friendly lighting schemes use down-lighting and solar power, and turn off automatically when not needed. Irrigation systems may include precipitation gauges so they automatically shut off when nature provides water.

Wood
Wood construction offers a readily available and relatively simple way to create functional, pleasing outdoor garden features. Try to find lumber that is not warped or splintered and that has the fewest knots. Painting, staining, or sealing wood decks and fences prolongs their life. Selecting the proper kind of wood is important because the finished product must withstand adverse weather and insect attacks.

The heartwood of a decay-resistant species such as redwood, cypress, or western red cedar is optimal for landscaping construction. Various outdoor grades of these woods are available, but all are quite expensive. Pressure-treated lumber is more economical and can be satisfactory for most wood projects. This lumber must meet certain standards for various uses and is marked

accordingly. Several yellow pine species native to the South are used for treated lumber.

The primary concern with using pressure-treated wood in raised-bed gardens has been with the arsenic in wood treated with CCA, chromated copper arsenate. In 2004, the EPA restricted the use of CCA, and it is no longer available to the public. ACQ is an alternative wood-treatment chemical that contains no arsenic, chromium, or any other chemical considered toxic by the EPA.

Review safety guidelines for the use of pressure-treated wood available where you purchased the lumber. Some key recommendations include the following:
• Do not breathe the dust.
• After handling wood, wash hands before eating, drinking or using tobacco products.
• Wash clothes separately before reuse.
• Do NOT burn scraps of pressure-treated wood.

Wood Alternatives
Durable and low maintenance wood-alternative products made with recycled wood plastics and sawdust are commercially available. These products do not need to be painted, stained, or sealed and are as easy to cut and install as real wood. The use of composite wood materials made from recycled plastic for decks and screening walls is very popular in modern landscaping. It is often three times the cost of pressure-treated wood, but it requires little to no maintenance.

To save material when designing a structure to be built with lumber or a wood alternative, try to use the entire board. Common lumber lengths are 8, 10, and 12 feet. Longer boards are progressively more expensive. A deck designed to be built with 10-foot lumber would be much less expensive than a deck built 10 feet 8 inches long. Also, remember that the structure must work with the outdoor scale. Instead of an 8-foot ceiling and walls 12 to 15 feet apart, outdoor spaces might be defined by a 25-foot-tall tree canopy or the backyard fence 75 feet away. Try to buy just the amount of pressure-treated wood needed as it cannot be recycled.

Brick
Brick is one of the easiest construction materials to use and is readily available. Building a simple walk, terrace, or patio can be a weekend do-it-yourself project. Laying brick on sand (with or without mortar) is an acceptable landscape practice. Aggregate concrete also makes excellent terraces and patios.

Always keep in mind the life of the landscape. Products that cost more upfront often outlast cheaper alternatives.

Case Study—Think IPM: Failing Tree

You have a sick eastern redbud tree. It has black spots on the leaves and many leaves are dying and falling off. You are wondering if you can give it some type of fertilizer or if there is something that can be sprayed on it to get rid of the black spots?

Review the five IPM steps and conduct some background research on the eastern redbud (*Cercis canadensis*).

1. Monitor and scout to determine pest type and population levels.
2. Accurately identify host and pest.
3. Consider economic or aesthetic injury thresholds. A threshold is the point at which action should be taken.
4. Implement a treatment strategy using physical, cultural, biological, or chemical management, or combine these strategies.
5. Evaluate success of treatments.

1. Monitor and scout to determine pest type and population levels.

This tree has been struggling for some time, but recently a noticeable black spot problem has appeared on the leaves. A sample could be sent to a diagnostic lab to determine which disease may be causing the black spots. But a more cost effective response simply requires digging a little deeper to reach the root of the problem.

2. Accurately identify pest and host.

Use the steps outlined in chapter 7, "Diagnostics" to help you identify the problem. Once the tree species is confirmed, examine both the healthy and damaged leaves carefully. The following questions will help you accurately identify the problem. Responses are included in italics.

Step 1. Identify the plant: *I looked up "redbud" on the NC State Extension Plant Finder. I also checked some gardening books I own and I have a* Cercis canadensis *tree.*

Step 2. Describe the problem: *The black spots started showing up three weeks ago and are spreading rapidly. The tree looks very sick.*

Step 3. Identify what is normal:

What does the healthy part of the plant look like? *Bright green, lush leaves, with no spots.*

What does the unhealthy part of the plant look like? *Leaves have between 3 and 20 black spots. The leaves are turning yellow or brown and are falling off.*

Have you had a soil test? *No.* (For information on how to submit a soil test see "Soils and Plant Nutrients," chapter 1.)

Step 4. Cultural practices:
Age and history of plant: *It has been in the ground three years and over the last two years it has been declining.*

Irrigation: *I watered the tree for the first summer, but now I don't water at all.*

Fertilizer: *I put some organic fertilizer on the last two springs but not this year.*

Maintenance: *I prune off any dead branches in the fall and rake the leaves. I also put a layer of compost around the roots each fall.*

Figure 19–53. A photograph taken after the rain. The redbud tree is at the corner by the neighbor's fence.
John Whitlock (johnwhitlock), Flickr CC BY - 2.0

Step 5. Environmental conditions:
Are there any significant water issues? *Yes, we do get standing water for a day or so after significant rainfall* (Figure 19–53).

What is the soil like? *It is a clay soil, very red.*

Describe the light. How many hours of sunlight? *It is planted in a shady corner of the yard at the corner of the property. This part of the yard gets only 3 to 4 hours of filtered sun a day.*

Describe any recent changes or events: *Sun exposure has stayed the same, but the neighbors installed a fence last spring that is about 2 feet away from the tree.*

Step 6. Signs of pathogens and pests:
On the leaves: *There are round black spots on the leaves and in the center of some there appears to be a small structure.*

On the stems: *I do not see any evidence of insects or fungus on the stems.*

On the roots and in the soil: *There is an ant nest near the base of the tree and I saw a cluster of eggs. There were also a few beetles crawling around. I detected a foul odor when digging near the roots.*

Step 7. Symptoms:
On the leaves: *The leaves are wilted and some are turning yellow or brown and falling off.*

On the buds/flowers: *It is not flowering yet.*

On the stems: *The branches where leaves have fallen off are dead and appear to have brown streaks inside.*

On the roots: *I did not remember how deeply I planted it. When I scraped back the soil, I was able to remove 3 inches before I got to the "root flare" on the trunk. The roots were dark colored and slimy feeling.*

Step 8. Distribution of damage in the landscape:
Are other plants in the landscape affected? *No.*

Step 9. Distribution of damage on the plant and specific plant parts:
Where is the damage seen on the plant? *In approximately 50% of the canopy.*

Step 10. Timing:
When did you notice this problem? *The tree never took off after planting. It has been declining over the last two years and this spring it has really started to look bad.*

You hypothesize this plant is suffering from a disease because there were signs of disease and though you saw insects, none of them were actually on the plant itself. Because there are symptoms on the leaves, stems, and roots, you suspect that it is primarily a vacsular problem. It is not affecting any other plants in the landscape. Though you could send of a sample to the NC State Plant Disease and Insect Clinic for a diagnois of the disease, based on the facts gathered, poor cultural practices are likley at fault. The location of the tree is a primary concern.

C. canadensis prefers well-drained soil and full to partial sun, not shade. You found three inches of soil before the root flare which indicates that this tree was planted too deeply. The heavy clay soil, and the fact that there is standing water for several days means the soil is compacted and that leads to root and vacular problems. The addition of a concrete path could have further exacerbated the root compaction. This tree is planted in the wrong place.

3. Consider economic, aesthetic, and injury thresholds.
Although you would like this tree to live, it is not a prize tree that you are willing to make heroic efforts to save. Furthermore, from looking at the samples, the injury is severe enough to warrant investigation. The tree is not going to survive without intervention.

4. Implement a treatment strategy using physical, cultural, biological, or insecticide control, or combine these strategies.
Physical. It is a diseased tree and would probably not survive transplanting to a more appropriate location. It should be removed from the site. Review the steps to completing a proper site analysis outlined in this chapter. A good site analysis can help avoid these types of problems in the future. Contouring a yard can help mitigate standing water problems.

Cultural. Many other plants thrive in shady, damp growing conditions. Matching a plant to the site is essential. Conduct a soil test and properly amend the soil before planting. Plant at a proper depth and provide regular maintenance including mulching, pruning, and fertilizing.

Biological. There are no recommended biological controls.

Chemical. There are no recommended chemical controls.

5. Evaluate treatment success.
You have started a folder with your site analysis and landscape design ideas. Your garden journal helps you keep track of any new plants chosen as well as how they and existing plants are growing.

19

Frequently Asked Questions

1. Do you have anyone who can draw up a landscape plan for me?
No. We cannot make a recommendation due to the time required and conflict of interest with members of the community providing that service in the green industry. NC State Extension has several resources to help you get started with planning a landscape. These resources are available on the NC State Extension website. Check your local Cooperative Extension center website for a list of upcoming classes related to landscaping design.

2. Where can I get a list of plants that grow well in this area?
NC State Extension has a searchable plant database that lists plants appropriate for various regions in North Carolina. You can search by height, light requirements, flower color, leaf color, what a plant attracts, zones, and much more.

3. What is the difference between a landscape architect, a landscape contractor, and a landscape designer?
A *landscape architect* is an individual who holds a professional license to practice landscape architecture through the NC Board of Landscape Architects (NCBOLA). A list of licensed landscape architects is available on the NCBOLA website. Landscape architects who are licensed in North Carolina must have graduated from a college program approved by the Landscape Architect Accreditation Board (LAAB) and have four years of experience in landscape architecture. A landscape architect has a seal bearing his or her name, certificate number, and the legend "NC Registered Landscape Architect." *Landscape contractors*, who often also do design work, are licensed by the state of North Carolina. *Landscape designers* are not licensed or regulated by the state but there are other certifications they can earn. They may draw up plot plans, but hardscape elements or alteration of sites, including grading and drainage plans, should be prepared by a licensed professional. Anyone doing irrigation work has to be certified by the state.

4. Where should I place trees to maximize their potential to conserve energy?
Trees help us save energy in many ways. To block solar heat in the summer but let much of it in during the winter, use deciduous trees. Deciduous trees with high, spreading crowns can be planted to the south of the home to provide maximum summertime shading. Trees with crowns lower to the ground are more appropriate to the west, where shade is needed from lower afternoon sun angles. Use allées of trees to channel summer breezes toward the home. To deflect winter winds, create windbreaks of dense evergreen trees or shrubs between the house and direction from which prevailing winds originate. Consider shading outdoor air conditioning units for maximum energy savings. Plant all trees far enough away from the home so that when they mature, their root systems do not damage the foundation and branches do not damage the roof.

Further Reading

Alexander, Rosemary. *The Essential Garden Design Workbook: 2nd Edition.* Portland, Oregon: Timber Press, Inc., 2009. Print.

Bales, Suzy, ed. *Suzy Bales' Down to Earth Gardener: Let Mother Nature Guide You to Success in Your Garden.* Emmaus, Pennsylvania: Rodale Press, Inc., 2004. Print.

Bender, Steve, and Felder Rushing. *Passalong Plants.* Chapel Hill, North Carolina: The University of North Carolina Press, 2002. Print.

Bender, Steve, ed. *The Southern Living Garden Book.* Birmingham, Alabama: Oxmoor House, Inc., 2004. Print.

Booth, Norman K., and James E. Hiss. *Residential Landscape Architecture: Design Process for the Private Residence.* 6th ed. Upper Saddle River, New Jersey: Prentice Hall, Inc., 2012. Print.

Bost, Toby, and Jim Wilson. *The Carolinas Gardener's Guide.* Franklin, Tennessee: Cool Springs Press, 2005. Print.

Chaplin, Lois Trigg. *The Southern Gardener's Book of Lists: The Best Plants for All Your Needs, Wants, and Whims.* Lanham, Maryland: Taylor Trade Publishing, 1994. Print.

Chatto, Beth. *The Damp Garden.* 1982. London: Orion Books Ltd, 1998. Print.

Chatto, Beth. *The Dry Garden.* 1978. London: Orion Books Ltd, 2002. Print.

Cornelison, Pamela, and the Editors of Sunset Books. *Landscaping Southern Gardens.* Menlo Park, California: Sunset Publishing Corporation, 2006. Print.

Cox, Martyn. *Big Gardens in Small Spaces: Out-of-the-Box Advice for Boxed-in Gardeners.* Portland, Oregon: Timber Press, Inc., 2009. Print.

Creasy, Rosalind. *Edible Landscaping.* 2nd ed. San Francisco, California: Sierra Club Books, 2010. Print.

Darke, Rick, and Doug Tallamy. *The Living Landscape: Designing for Beauty and Biodiversity in the Home Garden.* Portland, Oregon: Timber Press, Inc., 2014. Print.

Eddison, Sydney. *Gardening for a Lifetime: How to Garden Wiser as You Grow Older.* Portland, Oregon: Timber Press, Inc., 2010. Print.

Fell, Derek. *Vertical Gardening: Grow Up, Not Out, for More Vegetables and Flowers in Much Less Space.* Emmaus, Pennsylvania: Rodale Press, Inc., 2011. Print.

Francko, David A. *Palms Won't Grow Here and Other Myths: Warm-Climate Plants for Cooler Areas.* Portland, Oregon: Timber Press, Inc., 2003. Print.

Halpin, Anne Moyer. *Gardening in the Shade.* Des Moines, Iowa: Better Homes and Gardens Books, 1996. Print.

Hastings, Don. *Month-By-Month Gardening in the South: What to Do and When to Do It.* 2nd ed. Atlanta, Georgia: Longstreet Press, 1999. Print.

Heriteau, Jacqueline. *The National Arboretum Book of Outstanding Garden Plants: The Authoritative Guide to Selecting and Growing the Most Beautiful, Durable, and Carefree Garden Plants in North America.* New York: Simon & Schuster Inc., 1990. Print.

Ingels, Jack. *Landscaping Principals & Practices.* 7th ed. Independence, Kentucky: Cengage Learning, 2009. Print.

Kellum, Jo. *Ortho's All about Landscaping.* Des Moines, Iowa: Meredith Books, 1999. Print.

Messervy, Julie Moir. *Home Outside: Creating the Landscape You Love.* Newtown, Connecticut: The Taunton Press, Inc., 2009. Print.

Pick the Right Plant: A Sun and Shade Guide to Successful Plant Selection. Alexandria, Virginia: Time-Life Books, 1998. Print.

Polomski, Bob. *Month-By-Month Gardening in Carolinas.* Franklin, Tennessee: Cool Springs Press, 2006. Print.

Reed, Sue. *Energy-Wise Landscape Design: A New Approach for Your Home and Garden.* Gabriola Island, British Columbia, Canada: New Society Publishers, 2010. Print.

Reich, Lee. *Landscaping with Fruit.* North Adams, Massachusetts: Storey Publishing, 2009. Print.

Shafer, Karleen, and Nicole Lloyd. *Perennial Reference Guide.* St. Paul, Minnesota: The American Phytopathological Society, 2007. Print.

Smith & Hawken: *The Book of Outdoor Gardening.* New York: Workman Publishing Company, Inc., 1996. Print.

White, Hazel. *Sunset Hillside Landscaping: A Complete Guide to Successful Gardens on Sloping Ground.* 2nd ed. Menlo Park, California: Sunset Publishing Corporation, 2007. Print.

Young, Beth O'Donnell. *The Naturescaping Workbook: A Step-by-Step Guide for Bringing Nature to Your Backyard.* Portland, Oregon: Timber Press, Inc., 2011. Print.

19

For More Information

http://go.ncsu.edu/fmi_landscapedesign

Contributors

Authors:

Anne Spafford, M.L.A., Associate Professor, Department of Horticultural Science and Adjunct Faculty Member Department of Landscape Architecture, NC State University

Michelle Wallace, M.L.A., Extension Agent, Durham County

Cyndi Lauderdale, Extension Agent, Wilson County

Lucy Bradley, Professor and Extension Specialist, Urban Horticulture, NC State University; Director, NC State Extension Master Gardener program

Kathleen Moore, Urban Horticulturist, Department of Horticultural Science

Contributions by Extension Agents: Travis Birdsell, Donna Teasley, Julie Flowers, Susan Brown

Contributions by Extension Master Gardener Volunteers: Renee Lampila, Margaret Genkins, Barbara Goodman, Jackie Weedon, Karen Damari, Connie Schultz

Based on text from the 1998 Extension Master Gardener manual prepared by:

M.A. Powell, Extension Specialist, Department of Horticultural Science

Erv Evans, Extension Associate, Department of Horticultural Science

Chapter 19 Cover Photo: Pixabay CC BY0

How to Cite This Chapter:

Spafford, A., M. Wallace, C. Lauderdale, L. K. Bradley, K. A. Moore. 2022. Landscape Design, Chpt 19. In: K. A. Moore and L. K. Bradley (eds). *North Carolina Extension Gardener Handbook,* 2nd ed. NC State Extension, Raleigh, NC. <https://content.ces.ncsu.edu/extension-gardener-handbook/19-landscape-design>

19

Wildlife

Objectives

This chapter teaches people to:

• Create a wildlife habitat in their own landscape.

• Identify the positive and negative aspects of wildlife in home landscapes.

• Identify common wildlife pests, game, non-game and migratory birds and techniques to prevent and minimize damage.

• Understand the conservation laws that regulate wildlife in urban and suburban areas.

20

Introduction

Wildlife can bring endless enjoyment to a gardener. Many gardeners find no greater pleasure than relaxing outdoors watching hummingbirds sip **nectar** from trumpet flowers (*Bignonia capreolata*) (Figure 20–1) or bumble bees busying themselves on an aster vine (*Ampelaster carolinianus*). With development increasing across North Carolina and the loss of open lands, many wild species have adapted to survive in close proximity to humans. Yards are their new habitat, and wildlife visits bring opportunities for animal sightings that may not have been possible otherwise. There is more land in backyards than all the national parks combined (Emrath, 2006). Individual backyards are islands that can be connected within neighborhoods and cities to provide viable habitat for frogs, bats, birds, bees, lizards, salamanders, moths, migratory birds, and butterflies. There are many easy, inexpensive ways to make a yard a wildlife sanctuary.

Figure 20–1. A hummingbird sipping nectar from a trumpet flower.
Kelly Colgan Azar, Flickr CC BY-ND - 2.0

Planning a Wildlife Habitat

Creating an effective wildlife habitat requires a thoughtful plan. Trees and shrubs are more difficult to rearrange in a yard than are furniture or artwork in a home. Careful evaluation of the desired use of the yard and how it can better support wildlife results in a beautiful, functional landscape that increases the property value and the owner's enjoyment.

Please refer to "Landscape Design," chapter 19, for a step-by-step guide to creating an inviting outdoor space. A basic plan that meets human needs can also incorporate elements that support wildlife. Wildlife require four major resources to be successful: cover, food, water, and a place to raise young. Including each of these four elements in the landscape increases the presence of wildlife.

Journaling

The first step in any big project is observing the current situation. Keep a log or notebook and record any wildlife sightings in the yard. Be sure to indicate the number of individuals, time of day, season, weather, and any plants or structures used by wildlife. As a gardener moves through a project, the log book becomes an excellent tool to see how changing the landscape affects the number and variety of wildlife seen. Keeping good records also helps in expanding the habitat. Making a note that a nesting pair of cardinals used a maple tree last spring might inspire you to select another maple when you decide to plant another tree. See Appendix A for more on garden journaling.

Plan for Year-Round Food

The best way to meet the food requirements of wildlife is to include a wide variety of plants. To encourage greater wildlife diversity, extend food availability by selecting plants that bloom and fruit at different times of the year. Plants provide food through their leaves, flowers, nectar, fruits, seeds, and nuts. Plants that are native to North Carolina are the best choices for North Carolina wildlife. Native plants offer the food and cover sources to which native wildlife have adapted over many years. Also, using native plants reduces the likelihood of introducing exotic **invasive** species. Invasive species out-compete native plants and may leave wildlife with no food source. In addition to selecting plants to provide food for wildlife, it is important to manage the plants to maximize their output. Unmown grass provides seeds for many species of birds and small mammals. Consider insects, worms, and spiders as food for wildlife and leave them alone. It may be necessary to protect young plants until they are established and can become a **sustainable** food source for wildlife. In the meantime, begin attracting wildlife by providing feeders.

Black oil sunflower seeds, thistle seeds, and millet are recommended for songbirds. Black oil sunflower seeds are preferred because they have more nut meat and less hull than the black and white striped sunflower seeds and they attract a wider variety of birds. Follow these steps to keep bird feeders clean and free of mold and disease.

- Once a week, rake up waste food, husks, and other accumulated material below feeders on the ground and add it to compost.
- Consider providing multiple feeders, spaced apart in the landscape.

Wildlife require four major resources: food, cover, water, and a place to raise young.

- Use feeders that do not have sharp points or edges. Bacteria and viruses on contaminated surfaces can infect healthy birds through even small scratches.
- Clean and disinfect feeders at least once every two weeks, and more often if sick birds appear. Allow the feeder to air dry before refilling.
- Do not dispense food that smells musty, feels wet, looks moldy, or has fungus growing on it.

Feeding Hummingbirds

Hummingbirds are attracted to bright colors, so select a feeder that has red parts (Figure 20–2). Yellow, however, attracts insects, so avoid feeders that have yellow. Fill the feeder with a mixture of 4 cups water to 1 cup sugar (4:1 ratio). Do NOT use honey. Do not use red food coloring in the solution. Red feeders are enough to attract the birds. Feeders can be left up year-round but should be cleaned weekly with a toothbrush and mild detergent to prevent the spread of bacteria or disease organisms to hummingbirds visiting the feeder. Most hummingbirds leave North Carolina in mid-October and return in late March.

Figure 20–2. A hummingbird feeder. Red parts will attract the birds. There is no need to dye the sugar syrup red.
Francesco Veronesi, Flickr CC BY-SA - 2.0

Cover

Wildlife need adequate cover from **predators** and protection from the elements. Cover allows animals to use less energy as it protects them from cold winter winds or rain and shades them in the summer. Also, cover provides a place to build a nest or den or just to sleep or rest. Providing several layers in your landscape through the use of ground covers, shrubs, and low and high **canopy** trees can assure a variety of places for wildlife to hide. Rock outcroppings are another cover option. Consider leaving piles of brush in corners of your yard as they are excellent cover for birds and small mammals. Snags, or dead trees, make excellent places for animals to find food and cover (Figure 20–3).

Figure 20–3. A snag was left in this landscape providing cover for many birds and beneficial insects. Water, another essential component to a wildlife habitat, is also seen here.
Kathleen Moore, CC BY - 2.0

Water

Although many wildlife species obtain all the water they need from their food, a clean drink of water is always welcome. Despite North Carolina's rivers, streams, lakes, and ponds, a water source may not be nearby. In that case, consider adding one to increase the chances of wildlife sightings. A man-made pond can provide a beautiful centerpiece to your landscape and water for wildlife. Ponds should slope to allow animals to drink without the risk of drowning. Birdbaths are another and less expensive option. They can be purchased from a garden center or created using any shallow container, such as a garbage can lid or a terracotta saucer. Birdbaths should be shallow, no more than 3 inches deep, and should have non-slippery sides and bottoms (Figure 20–4). Stones and sticks can be placed in the birdbath to give birds and butterflies places to perch while they take a drink or bathe. Placing a birdbath under a tree provides cover against predators and a place birds can fly to after they bathe to preen their feathers. Water should be kept fresh and changed every few days to avoid the hatching of mosquito larvae and spreading of disease organisms. Clean the bath with a bristle brush and dish detergent once every week. Every

20

two weeks after cleaning the bath, sanitize it by filling it with a solution of one part bleach to ten parts water and letting it stand for 3 minutes. Then empty the bath down the sink and rinse well.

Figure 20–4. A shallow birdbath with nonslippery sides and bottom. Kathleen Moore, CC BY - 2.0

Place to Raise Young
Building birdhouses or leaving a snag helps cavity-nesting birds. Prevent invasive bird species such as starlings or house sparrows from outcompeting native songbirds for nesting boxes by ensuring the entry holes are too small for these non-native birds and by removing all perches from birdhouses. Be sure to include a metal plate around the opening so that squirrels cannot make the opening wider for themselves. For proper nest box construction measurements, check with a local Cooperative Extension center or visit nestwatch.org.

The resource list at the end of this chapter includes publications and Internet sources with additional ways to attract wildlife.

Certified Backyard Wildlife Habitat
After providing the necessary resources for wildlife in the backyard and following the principles and guidelines outlined in previous chapters for maintaining soil, air, and water quality, a gardener can register with the National Wildlife Federation to become a "Certified Backyard Wildlife Habitat" (Figure 20–5). Be sure to share

Figure 20–5. A certified backyard wildlife habitat sign. Connie Schultz

Ways to Attract Nocturnal Animals to the Garden

There is nothing quite like sitting on the porch at dusk watching bats perform aerial acrobatics while snatching mosquitos out of the sky, or listening to male frogs serenade their potential mates with a cacophony of croaks. Like their daytime counterparts, **nocturnal** animals have these basic requirements: food, water, and places to rest and raise young. Here are some tips to help attract species large and small:

1. **Grow the nectar plants that night-shift pollinators prefer.**
   Good candidates for moths include native night bloomers such as evening primroses, yuccas, and phlox (Figure 20–6). To attract giant silk moths, grow the host plants of their caterpillars, such as oak, sassafras, maple, birch, ash, willow, and cherry. Think of the caterpillars as baby silk moths and recognize they must eat leaves to grow. Tolerate some damage now to enjoy the magnificent adults later.

2. **Avoid pesticides,** which can harm insect pollinators and amphibians.

3. **Offer a drink.** Like many other animals, bats everywhere are drawn to garden ponds and other water features.

4. **Supplement nature's offerings with man-made habitat elements.**
   Buy or build a bat house (plans are available at Bat Conservation International). Or construct a nest box for owls
   (see the website of the Cornell Lab of Ornithology for proper dimensions).

Figure 20–6. Plants that bloom at night, like this primrose, or have pale colors can attract nocturnal pollinators like bats or moths. SyGrnwd, Wikimedia Commons CC BY- SA 4.0

20

new knowledge and encourage neighbors to provide increased habitat. Multiple connected yards with good resources are much more effective at sustaining wildlife than a single lot. The gardener is a habitat manager and through collaboration with neighbors can profoundly benefit the wildlife that share neighborhood living spaces. If neighborhood residents are on board, they can register their neighborhood and become certified by the National Wildlife Federation.

Do Not Make These Common Mistakes

- Plant flowers for the adult butterflies, but no plants to feed the baby butterflies (caterpillars).
- Plant flowers to attract adult butterflies, and then spray the caterpillars (baby butterflies) that hatch from the eggs laid by the adults.
- Spray for pests and accidentally kill honey bees. If you must use pesticides, never spray blooming plants and spray only in late afternoon when bees are done foraging for the day.

Injured Wildlife

A gardener may encounter injured wildlife. Knowing the steps to take helps make this time less stressful for the humans and the animals.

No Help Needed

Leave these animals undisturbed. They are able to care for themselves, or their mother is probably hiding nearby:
- White-tailed deer fawns
- Fledgling (young bird, fully feathered)
- Rabbit whose body is at least 4 inches long
- Opossum whose body (not including tail) is at least 9 inches long
- Squirrel who is nearly full size

Might Need Help?

These animals may need help:
- Brought by a cat or a dog
- Injured (bleeding, broken limb, concussion)
- Covered in insects
- Nearly featherless bird
- Shivering or cold to the touch
- Parents are dead

How to help

- Put children and pets inside to protect them and the wildlife.
- Note exactly where and when the animal was found so it can be returned.
- Baby birds or squirrels—put featherless chicks and baby squirrels back in their nests. If the nest is too high, or not visible, create a temporary nest using a small plastic container with holes in the bottom. Fill with pine

straw, grass, or leaves and attach to a tree near where the baby was found. Place the baby in the nest and watch from a distance to see if the parents return. If they do not return within two hours, place the baby in a small covered box with air holes and transport it to a nearby certified wildlife rescue organization or Wildlife Rehabilitator. DO NOT give it food or water. The hole at the back of their tongues leads directly into their trachea and they can be drowned accidentally when water is put in their mouth. It is illegal to possess or raise wild birds without state and federal permits.

- Bird stunned after flying into glass—place the bird on several paper towels in a small box with small holes in the top for ventilation. Tie the box closed and place in a dark, quiet room. In 20 minutes, or sooner if the bird stirs, take the box outside, point it toward an open area, and release the bird. If the injury occurs within 1⁄2-hour before sunset, keep the bird in the box until morning. DO NOT provide food or water.
- In North Carolina rabies occurs most often in raccoons, bats, foxes, and skunks. DO NOT handle these animals.
- Injured and diseased animals may be more aggressive; be extremely cautious.
- For more information and to identify a Wildlife Rehabilitator in your county, contact the NC Wildlife Resources Commission—Injured/Orphaned Wildlife.

Wildlife Interactions

The adage *"if you build it they will come"* is certainly true for wildlife habitats. Providing food, cover, water, and a place to raise young attracts many desirable wildlife species as well as some unexpected wildlife. When wildlife help themselves to carefully tended gardens or ornamental plants, or dig tunnels through pristine lawns, they can frustrate a homeowner. Forethought and careful management can prevent these species from becoming pests. Gardeners must be tolerant and balance the fact that we reside in former wildlife homes with the desire to maintain a beautiful yard and garden.

Preventing wildlife damage is much easier than dealing with established problems, but not all conflicts can be prevented. Here are some simple integrated pest management (IPM) techniques that can help prevent and manage common wildlife-related issues.

1. **Assess the damage.** Determine how much damage to tolerate before intervening. Sighting a single pest does not always mean control is needed.
2. **Identify and monitor pests.** Most organisms are innocuous, and many are beneficial. Properly identifying a pest and closely monitoring the pest and the damage helps lead to appropriate control decisions. Not all pests require control.

3. **Prevention is a first line of defense.** IPM programs work to manage the landscape to prevent pests from becoming a threat to plants or structures. Prevention can be cost-effective, conserve time, and present little to no risk to people or the environment. Here are some prevention techniques:

- Secure or remove food sources such as dog food or birdseed. Feed pets indoors.
- Remove any brush or wood piles near buildings.
- Block off decks, porches, and roof and basement access points with wire netting or a combination of steel wool and spray foam.
- Seal garbage cans.
- Create barriers around prized plants or beds with fencing or bird netting for cover.

4. **Scare tactics can be used temporarily to keep animals out of the yard.** Flash tape, noise makers, scary eyes, or scarecrows are most effective when they are moved to a new location every few days. Motion lights can startle when they first come on, but eventually the animal gets used to the light. Flashing or strobe lights work best. A motion sensor on a garden hose that sprays when an animal triggers the sensor can be very effective. Although scare tactics may be temporarily effective, little scientific evidence exists on their long-term effectiveness.

5. **Manage effectively.** Preventative methods and scare tactics are often effective at addressing wildlife problems, however, when those options fail, legal lethal techniques can be implemented to address the ongoing damage.

All wildlife have protections under the law, so be sure to consult the resources in this guide and/or the state Wildlife Resources Commission for guidance on legal lethal methods that can be used for a given species. Certified Wildlife Damage Control Agents can also be hired to assess and carry out legal lethal and non-lethal damage management. You can find a list of these agents online.

6. **Evaluate the strategy.** If further monitoring indicates the chosen strategy is not working, then additional pest control methods can be employed.

Intentionally attracting one type of wildlife can also unintentionally attract undesired wildlife. For example, birdseed put out to attract songbirds can fall on the ground below bird feeders and attract mice. Damage caused by wildlife can be costly and discouraging to gardeners. Unfortunately, there are no single, quick, or guaranteed solutions to most animal pest problems. The information below focuses on the most common wildlife problems, the relevant laws and regulations, and suggested management strategies.

Legal Requirements

Virtually all species of wildlife are protected at some level and are regulated by state and/or federal laws and regulations. Local ordinances, such as those regarding the discharge of firearms, may apply to wildlife management. The legal requirements under both federal and state laws apply, and compliance with one does not negate the requirements of the other.

Table 20–1. Mammals That May Visit a Yard

Common Name	Scientific Name
Armadillo, Nine-banded	*Dasypus novemcinctus*
Coyote	*Canis latrans*
Fox, Gray	*Urocyon cinereoargenteus*
Groundhog	*Marmota monax*
Mole, eastern	*Scalopus aquaticus*
Mole, star-nosed	*Condylura cristata*
Nutria; Coypu	*Myocastor coypus*
Skunk	*Mephitis mephitis*
Squirrel, Eastern gray	*Sciurus carolinensis*
Squirrel, Southern flying	*Glaucomys volans*
Vole, meadow	*Microtus pennsylvanicus*

Common Name	Scientific Name
Beaver, North American	*Castor canadensis*
Deer, White-tailed	*Odocoileus virginianus*
Fox, Red	*Vulpes vulpes*
Mink, American	*Mustela vison*
Mole, hairy-tailed	*Parascalops breweri*
Muskrat	*Ondatra zibethicus*
Raccoon	*Procyon lotor*
Squirrel, Carolina northern flying	*Glaucomys sabrinus coloratus*
Squirrel, Fox	*Sciurus niger*
Vole, pine	*Microtus pinetorum*

State Regulations

When wildlife causes substantial damage to a landowner's or lessee's property, he/she can apply for a permit from the NC Wildlife Resources Commission (NCWRC) to remove individuals of the species involved. Permit requests or questions about state laws and regulations should be addressed to the NCWRC (see box below). No depredation permits can be authorized for the taking of wildlife on someone else's property.

The permit can be used only by the landowner, lessee, or someone named on the permit by the landowner/lessee, when the necessary control cannot be obtained without capturing or killing the animal(s). The permit must specify whether the animal(s) will be killed or trapped and may place certain restrictions to limit the taking to the intended purpose. Trapping animals for depredation comes under statewide trapping law, G.S.113-291.6.

NCWRC
Centennial Campus
1751 Varsity Drive
Raleigh, NC 27606
866-318-2401

Table 20–2. Birds That May Visit a Yard			
Common Name	**Scientific Name**	**Common Name**	**Scientific Name**
URBAN ADAPTERS			
European starling	*Sturnus vulgaris*	Rock pigeon	*Columba livia*
House sparrow	*Passer domesticus*		
SUBURBAN ADAPTERS			
House Finch	*Haemorhous mexicanus*	Red-bellied woodpecker	*Melanerpes carolinus*
Northern mockingbird	*Mimus polyglottos*	White-breasted nuthatch	*Sitta carolinensis*
Mourning dove	*Zenaida macroura*	Northern flicker	*Colaptes auratus*
American robin	*Turdus migratorius*	Eastern phoebe	*Sayornis phoebe*
American crow	*Corvus brachyrhynchos*	Gray catbird	*Dumetella carolinensis*
Common grackle	*Quiscalus quiscula*	Eastern towhee	*Pipilo erythrophthalmus*
Brown-headed cowbird	*Molothrus ater*	Eastern bluebird	*Sialia sialis*
Blue jay	*Cyanocitta cristata*	Chipping sparrow	*Spizella passerina*
Carolina chickadee	*Poecile carolinensis*	Song sparrow	*Melospiza melodia*
Tufted titmouse	*Baeolophus bicolor*	Brown-headed nuthatch	*Sitta pusilla*
Chimney swift	*Chaetura pelagica*	Purple martin	*Progne subis*
Northern cardinal	*Cardinalis cardinalis*	Ruby-throated hummingbird	*Archilochus colubris*
Carolina wren	*Thryothorus ludovicianus*	Red-winged blackbird	*Agelaius phoeniceus*
Brown thrasher	*Toxostoma rufum*	Hairy woodpecker	*Picoides villosus*
Pine warbler	*Setophaga pinus*	Eastern screech owl	*Megascops asio*
American goldfinch	*Spinus tristis*	Common nighthawk	*Chordeiles minor*
Downy woodpecker	*Picoides pubescens*	Red-shouldered hawk	*Buteo lineatus*
Note: *birds are arranged in order of occurrence, reading down each column by habitat*			

20

Table 20–2. Birds That May Visit a Yard *continued*

Common Name	Scientific Name	Common Name	Scientific Name
URBAN/SUBURBAN AVOIDERS			
Field sparrow	*Spizella pusilla*	Red-cockaded woodpecker	*Picoides borealis*
Red-headed woodpecker	*Melanerpes erythrocephalus*	Acadian flycatcher	*Empidonax virescens*
Great crested flycatcher	*Myiarchus crinitus*	Yellow-throated vireo	*Vireo flavifrons*
Wood thrush	*Hylocichla mustelina*	Yellow-billed cuckoo	*Coccyzus americanus*
Red-eyed vireo	*Vireo olivaceus*	American redstart	*Setophaga ruticilla*
Killdeer	*Charadrius vociferus*	Yellow warbler	*Setophaga petechia*
Orchard oriole	*Icterus spurius*	Hooded warbler	*Setophaga citrina*
Summer tanager	*Piranga rubra*	Louisiana waterthrush	*Parkesia motacilla*
Blue-gray gnatcatcher	*Polioptila caerulea*	Blue grosbeak	*Passerina caerulea*
Pileated woodpecker	*Dryocopus pileatus*	Eastern meadowlark	*Sturnella magna*
Eastern kingbird	*Tyrannus tyrannus*	Loggerhead shrike	*Lanius ludovicianus*
Eastern wood-pewee	*Contopus virens*	Kentucky warbler	*Geothlypis formosa*
Northern parula	*Setophaga americana*	Veery	*Catharus fuscescens*
Baltimore oriole	*Icterus galbula*	Yellow-breasted chat	*Icteria virens*
Scarlet tanager	*Piranga olivacea*	Grasshopper sparrow	*Ammodramus savannarum*
Yellow-throated warbler	*Setophaga dominica*	Horned lark	*Eremophila alpestris*
Indigo bunting	*Passerina cyanea*	Black-throated green warbler	*Setophaga virens*
White-eyed vireo	*Vireo griseus*	Prairie warbler	*Setophaga discolor*
Ovenbird	*Seiurus aurocapilla*	Northern bobwhite	*Colinus virginianus*
Black-and-white warbler	*Mniotilta varia*	Prothonotary warbler	*Protonotaria citrea*
Common yellowthroat	*Geothlypis trichas*	Swainson's warbler	*Limnothlypis swainsonii*
SUBURBAN WINTER SPECIES			
Yellow-rumped warbler	*Setophaga coronata*	Hermit thrush	*Catharus guttatus*
Dark-eyed junco	*Junco hyemalis*	Blue-headed vireo	*Vireo solitarius*
Yellow-bellied sapsucker	*Sphyrapicus varius*	Golden-crowned kinglet	*Regulus satrapa*
House wren	*Troglodytes aedon*	Purple finch	*Haemorhous purpureus*
White-throated sparrow	*Zonotrichia albicollis*	Evening grosbeak	*Coccothraustes vespertinus*
Ruby-crowned kinglet	*Regulus calendula*	Pine siskin	*Spinus pinus*

Note: *birds are arranged in order of occurrence, reading down each column by habitat*

20

Common Name	Scientific Name	Common Name	Scientific Name
Table 20–3. Amphibians That May Visit a Yard			
FROGS AND TOADS			
American toad	*Anaxyrus americanus*	Fowler's toad	*Anaxyrus fowleri*
Southern toad	*Anaxyrus terrestris*	Northern cricket frog	*Acris crepitans*
Southern cricket frog	*Acris gryllus*	Cope's gray treefrog	*Hyla chrysoscelis*
Green treefrog	*Hyla cinerea*	Squirrel treefrog	*Hyla squirella*
Spring peeper	*Pseudacris crucifer*	Upland chorus frog	*Pseudacris feriarum*
Eastern narrowmouth toad	*Gastrophryne carolinensis*	American bullfrog	*Lithobates catesbeianus*
Green frog	*Lithobates clamitans*	Pickerel frog	*Lithobates palustris*
Southern leopard frog	*Lithobates sphenocephalus*		
SALAMANDERS			
Marbled salamander	*Ambystoma opacum*	Spotted salamander	*Ambystoma maculatum*
Eastern newt	*Notophthalmus viridescens*	Southern two-lined salamander	*Eurycea cirrigera*
Blue Ridge two-lined salamander	*Eurycea wilderae*	Northern dusky salamander	*Desmognathus fuscus*
White-spotted slimy salamander	*Plethodon cylindraceus*	Atlantic Coast slimy salamander	*Plethodon chlorobryonis*

If the landowner is unable or unwilling to control the problem, a number of private individuals or companies are authorized by the NCWRC to handle wildlife damage complaints. The NCWRC (919-707-0010) provides a list of Wildlife Damage Control Agents.

Permits are very rarely issued for endangered or protected species and must meet strict criteria. The executive director for the NCWRC may issue permits to take or possess an Endangered, Threatened, or Special Concern species according to regulations and policies in place (see 15A NCAC 10I .0102 for more information). However, when game animals cause substantial property damage during hunting season, landowners or lessees may obtain a hunting license and take animals on the property by any lawful means. During no-hunting seasons, game animals in the act of causing substantial property damage can be taken, without a permit, only by using firearms. Local ordinances, such as those regarding firearms within city limits, should be checked because they may have a bearing on choice of control method.

When an animal is killed, it must be buried or otherwise disposed of in a safe and sanitary manner. The killing and disposal methods for bears and alligators taken must be reported to the NCWRC within 24 hours. 15A NCAC 10B .0106 (F).

Federal Regulations
A permit is normally required to take migratory bird species: water fowl, mourning doves, hawks, blackbirds, woodpeckers, and most species of songbirds. The United States Department of Agriculture (USDA) and the Animal Plant Health Inspection Service (APHIS) Animal Control Office should be contacted for control information and permit application forms:

USDA-APHIS/ADC
6301 E. Angus Drive
Raleigh, NC 27613 (919-856-4124)

Mail permit application forms to:

USFWS
PO Box 49208
Atlanta, GA 27613 (404-679-7070)

Table 20–4. Reptiles That May Visit a Yard

Common Name	Scientific Name	Common Name	Scientific Name
SNAKES			
Worm snake	*Carphophis amoenus*	Black racer	*Coluber constrictor*
Ringneck snake	*Diadophis punctatus*	Corn snake	*Pantherophis guttatus*
Rat snake	*Pantherophis alleghaniensis*	Eastern hognose snake	*Heterodon platirhinos*
TURTLES			
Common snapping turtle	*Chelydra serpentina*	Painted turtle	*Chrysemys picta*
Eastern box turtle	*Terrapene carolina*	Yellowbelly slider	*Trachemys scripta*

Management Strategies to Reduce Damage

Many strategies exist that can be implemented and quite effective in managing a nuisance wildlife species. If these strategies are implemented in the following order, often chemical or lethal controls become unnecessary.

- **Habitat modification**—changes in habitat to make it less appealing, including removal of food or shelter
- **Exclusion**—creating physical barriers to wildlife
- **Repellents**—frightening, sound, taste, odor, or tactile sensation
- **Trapping**—capturing the animal
  Keep in mind that trapping may only be conducted during the legal trapping season for a given species or under an appropriate depredation permit. Trapped animals may be released alive at the site of capture; however, rules restrict the release of certain species onto other properties, and no releases are permitted onto federal or state owned lands. Consult the NC Wildlife Resources Commission for guidance prior to considering trapping as a management option.
- **Lethal control**—killing the animal
  Legal means vary by species and may include take during hunting seasons, take under a depredation permit, or take during the act of causing substantial property damage. See information below or consult the NC Wildlife Resources Commission for species-specific guidance.

Animals Commonly Encountered in Gardens, Lawns, and Landscapes

BIRDS—CROWS

Crows are 17 to 21 inches tall, shiny black, and make a distinctive "caw-caw" sound (Figure 20–7). Crows may pull up newly planted seeds or seedlings in the garden and eat ripe fruit and seeds. However, about a third of the crow's diet is animal matter, including grasshoppers, caterpillars, grubs, spiders, and millipedes.

Figure 20–7. A crow is 17 to 21 inches tall, shiny black, and makes a "caw-caw" sound.
Cristiano Betta, Flickr CC BY - 2.0

In North Carolina, pigeons are non-native and unprotected. Pigeons are crow-sized birds with slate-blue feathers and two black bars on the wings. The neck feathers have a greenish-purple sheen (Figure 20–8). Pigeons feed and roost in flocks. These birds can become a nuisance when they soil buildings, sidewalks, or window ledges with their droppings.

Figure 20–8. A pigeon is about the size of a crow with gray body feathers and iridescent purple-green neck feathers.
grendelkhan, Flickr CC BY-SA 2.0

Red-winged blackbirds are one of the most abundant birds in North America. They are 7 to 9 inches tall with a conical bill (Figure 20–9). Red-winged blackbird males have shiny black feathers and gold and red shoulder patches. Females have brownish feathers that can be mottled. Red-winged blackbirds may pull up newly planted seeds or seedlings in the garden and eat ripe fruit and seeds.

Figure 20–9. A red-winged blackbird.
Pixabay, Meister199 (Rick Tremblay) CC0

In North Carolina, starlings are non-native and unprotected. Starlings are about robin-sized with yellow beaks and gold-flecked, iridescent blue-black feathers (Figure 20–10). Their wings have a delta shape when in flight. They are found in all communities in North Carolina—from rural farms to more urban settings. They nest in holes in trees or other cavities. Starlings may pull up sprouting corn and other small grains and feed on insects, peanuts, fruits, berries, grains, and sunflowers. Most damage occurs in early morning and late afternoon. However, starlings also eat insects that may be harmful to plants such as larvae of Coleoptera (beetles) and Lepidoptera (moths and butterflies).

Figure 20–10. A starling has flecked, blue-black, iridescent feathers and a long conical yellow beak.
Koshy Koshy, Flickr CC BY - 2.0

Management Strategies for Bird Species Listed Above (Management recommendations for woodpeckers are listed separately in the next section)

Habitat Modification
- Thinning or pruning tree branches can discourage bird roosting.
- Spike strips can be placed where birds are known to roost (Figure 20–11).

Figure 20–11. Habitat modification: you can use spikes to prevent birds from roosting.
Tomasz Sienicki, Wikimedia Commons CC BY SA 3.0

20

- Corn hybrids with long husk extensions and thick husks are more resistant to damage by birds than other hybrids. Sunflower cultivars with heads that turn downward as they mature and seeds with thick hulls are less likely to be damaged.

Exclusion
- In some situations, birds can be excluded by using chicken wire or netting. Netting should totally enclose the plants (Figure 20–12) because even a small hole can allow birds to enter and become trapped.

Figure 20–12. Exclusion: bird netting must extend all the way around the crop as it does on these grapes. Any holes in the netting can cause birds to become trapped.
Kathleen Moore, CC BY - 2.0

Repellents
- Visual. Scarecrows, plastic flags on posts, mylar foil streamers, effigies such as plastic snakes or owls (Figure 20–13), and predator balloons may offer temporary control.
- Noisemakers. Propane exploders, shell crackers, electronic sound devices. Local ordinances against noise pollution could prevent the use of this technique.
- Chemical repellents. See the *North Carolina Agricultural Chemicals Manual* for recommendations.

Figure 20–13. Repellent, visual: using frightening devices like these plastic owls or falcons can deter birds. They must be moved frequently.
Kathleen Moore, CC BY-2.0

Trapping
- Not advised for crows or red-winged blackbirds.
- Mesh live traps baited with grain can be effective for trapping and removing pigeons and starlings.

Lethal control
- Firearms may be used to take crows and red-winged blackbirds in the act of destroying a landowner's or lessee's property.
- There is a legal hunting season for crows.
- There is no legal hunting season for red-wing blackbirds.
- To take crows out of season, and red-winged blackbirds not in the act of destroying property, property damage must be verified and a depredation permit obtained from NCWRC. (Refer to "Legal Requirements.")
- Pigeons and starlings have no protection under state laws. No permit is required, and there are no restrictions on the time of year they can be hunted. Be sure to observe local ordinances.

BIRDS — WOODPECKERS

There are several species of woodpeckers that are commonly found in the Southeast. Woodpeckers range in size from the crow-sized, red-crested, pileated woodpecker (Figure 20–14) to the 6-inch-long downy woodpecker (Figure 20–15). Most woodpecker damage is inflicted by the northern flicker or "yellow hammer," which is about 12 inches long. Male and female flickers have a brown and black striped back, white rump, a red patch on the head, and yellow under the wings and tails; the adult male has a black "mustache" not found in adult females (Figure 20–16). Other species causing damage in the Southeast are the red-bellied woodpecker (Figure 20–17), red-headed woodpecker (Figure 20–18), yellow-bellied sapsucker (Figure 20–19), and, occasionally, the hairy woodpecker (Figure 20–20).

Figure 20–14.
A pileated woodpecker, the largest and most spectacular woodpecker, can be found all over North Carolina. The cartoon character "Woody Woodpecker" is based on this type.
Kathleen Moore, CC BY - 2.0

Although woodpeckers may damage fruit, nut, and berry crops, these problems do not seem to be widespread. Also, because they eat insects, woodpeckers can be considered beneficial. Sapsuckers, which are considered a keystone species by many ecologists, often drill

Figure 20–15. A downy woodpecker is small with black feathers and white dots on the wings. The males have a red spot on their heads.
Eugene Beckes, Flickr CC BY-ND-2.0

Figure 20–16. A male northern flicker. Note the black "mustache" and yellow feathers on the tail.
Kelly Colgan Azar, Flickr CC BY-ND-2.0

Figure 20–17. A red-bellied woodpecker has red on the head and a blushing of red feathers on the belly (that are often difficult to see).
Kelly Colgan Azar, Flickr CC BY-ND-2.0

Figure 20–18. A red-headed woodpecker has a completely red head and black and white body.
tink tracy, Flickr CC BY-ND - 2.0

Figure 20–19. A yellow-bellied sapsucker is a migratory bird that breeds only in high elevations of the North Carolina mountains.
Michael (Michael Hart Photography), Flickr CC BY-ND - 2.0

Figure 20–20. A hairy woodpecker is a medum-sized woodpecker, larger than a downy but with similar coloring.
Ano Lobb, Flickr CC BY - 2.0

numerous ¼-inch holes in healthy trees to feed on sap as well as insects (Figure 20–21). Tree sap is flowing in a difficult time of year for birds to find food so many other bird species such as kinglets, warblers, phoebes, and even hummingbirds follow behind sapsuckers and lap up sap or insects.

Problems caused by woodpeckers are most often related to damage to buildings and annoying noise. Male woodpeckers "drum" (peck) to proclaim a territory and attract a mate. Metal flashing, guttering, television antennas, and wooden surfaces on a house may serve as resonators and amplifiers for this drumming sound and may be selected by a woodpecker over trees.

Woodpeckers peck holes in natural wood siding such as cedar, juniper, cypress, and redwood. When nesting, woodpeckers may pull out some insulation from between walls and lay eggs in this space. A woodpecker that mistakes its reflection for a trespasser in its territory may attack a window. Woodpecker damage can usually be avoided without killing the birds if a property owner or lessee begins control measures early.

Management Strategies for Woodpeckers

Woodpeckers are classified as migratory nongame birds and are protected by the Federal Migratory Bird Treaty Act. In addition, the red-cockaded woodpecker is fully protected as an endangered species. Endangered species

20

may not be killed or harassed. It is possible, however, to get a permit to kill other types of woodpeckers. Permits are issued by the US Fish and Wildlife Service upon recomendation of USDA-APHIS-Wildlife Services personnel. A strong case must be made to justify issuance of a permit. In addition, a state permit may also be required for measures that involve lethal control or nest destruction.

Figure 20–21. A red-cockaded woodpecker feasts on a bug.
U.S. Fish and Wildlife Service Southeast Region (USFWS/Southeast),
Flickr CC BY - 2.0

Endangered species may not be disturbed. Other species, however, may be managed with the following techniques:

Habitat Modification
- If you suspect that insect infestation of home siding is attracting woodpeckers to a house, have the siding treated before trying to repel the birds. The drumming sound on metal and wooden surfaces can be deadened by placing padding behind a regularly used drumming board or covering metal drumming sites with burlap.
- Locate nest boxes and suet feeders in trees nearby to lure the woodpeckers away from the home.
- Building an alternate drumming site may reduce the amount of damage to the house. Securely fasten a cedar board to the pecking site and loosely attach a second board to one end of the first board. These two boards should overlap to form a flexible resonating surface. A simple hollow box may serve as an effective substitute.
- To stop woodpeckers from pecking on windows, pull down the shades or blinds or block the bird's reflection with cardboard.

Exclusion
- It is important to cover holes with sheet metal or ¼-inch mesh hardware cloth as soon as the holes are detected. Wood putty should not be used as it will probably be pecked out.

- Staple polypropylene netting or screen wire near the rain gutter and angle it down toward the house to close off an area from woodpeckers.

Repellents
- **Scare tactics**—Rubber snakes, hawk silhouettes, pie pans, tin can lids, mylar or aluminum foil streamers, and small windmills (suspended by string or fishing line under the eaves) may repel woodpeckers from houses as well as fruit and nut trees. A loud-playing radio in a window may scare the birds away. Place concave (enlarging) mirrors near damaged areas.

Lethal Control
- Woodpeckers are federally protected migratory species. A federal permit is required to take these birds for control of depredation.
- NCWRC does not require the issuance of a concurrent state depredation permit when a federal permit has been obtained nor do they require that the federal permit be countersigned by a NCWRC official.
- Birds killed for depredations must be turned over to a representative of the US Fish and Wildlife Service (USFWS).
- The red-cockaded woodpecker is classified as an endangered species and may not be taken.

CATS

Domestic cats (*Felis catus*) include indoor-only, free-ranging indoor/outdoor, and feral cats (referred to as outdoor cats). Outdoor cats often use garden beds as litter boxes, which can create health risks to humans and wildlife by spreading parasites and diseases.

Domestic cats are not native to the United States and, when allowed outdoors, can be harmful to native wildlife. They are skilled predators, contributing to the extinction of at least 63 species and killing over 2.4 billion birds and 12.3 billion mammals each year in the United States. Do not create wildlife habitat to lure birds and other wildlife to areas where there are outdoor cats.

Management Strategies for Cats
The best management strategy is to keep cats indoors and ask neighbors to keep their cats indoors. Open communication can prevent and resolve many conflicts.

Habitat Modification
- Minimize the outdoor availability of water, food, and shelter.
- Avoid feeding birds if outdoor cats are present.
- Place trash in an enclosed area with lids tightly secured.
- Remove items that can be used as shelter.
- Mow grass and vegetation to reduce habitat for rodents.

Exclusion
- Fences must be at least 6 feet high with 2-inch by 2-inch mesh and a curved 2-foot overhang.
- Limit hiding areas and travel routes.

Frightening Devices/Repellents
- Motion-activated sprinklers can be effective, but most frightening devices are not.
- Although a few chemicals have US Environmental Protection Agency approval for repelling cats, there is no scientific evidence that they are effective.

Trapping
- Cage traps are generally effective without being lethal.
- Before attempting to trap cats, contact the local animal control agency, humane society, county animal shelter, and/or wildlife damage control agent for options.

Other Management Measures
- Contact the local animal control agency, humane society, county animal shelter, and/or wildlife damage control agent when considering other management strategies.

DEER, WHITE-TAILED

White-tailed deer may damage farm crops, gardens, trees, and shrubs. The severity of the problem varies with the deer population and the availability of other food. Deer browse on the tips, buds, branches, and foliage of ornamental trees, shrubs, and forest tree seedlings. Also, deer feed on corn, small grains, and vegetable crops, usually eating small, tender plants (most of the damage occurs during the first 10 days after germination). Because deer have no incisor teeth in the upper jaw, they tear vegetation away rather than cut cleanly. Vegetation damaged by deer has a jagged appearance (Figure 20–22). The split, sharp hooves of deer also leave distinctive hoofprints (Figure 20–23). Deer feed primarily at dawn, dusk, and nighttime, retreating to heavy cover the rest of the day. They feed exclusively on plant materials, and plantings near forest edges are most vulnerable.

Management Strategies to Minimize Deer Damage
Habitat Modification
- Unless very hungry, deer may not select medicinal plants, sticky or hairy leaves and stems, and foliage with a lemony or minty fragrance.

Figure 20–22. Deer browsing.
Kathleen Moore, CC BY 2.0

Figure 20–23. A deer footprint.
Sean, Flickr CC BY ND 2.0

- Planting some of these plants near the garden borders may help deter deer.

Exclusion
- Plastic tree cylinders or woven-wire cylinders can be used to protect young trees and shrubs.
- Fencing significantly reduces deer damage if installed and maintained properly (Figure 20–24). The most effective type is a high-tensile electric fence. See the NCWRC for more information on fencing options.

Figure 20–24. Exclusion fencing to keep deer out. Fences must be high enough (6 feet or more) to keep deer from jumping over.
Kathleen Moore, CC BY - 2.0

20

Repellents

- Although human hair is an odor repellent that has provided limited success, no scientific evidence exists on its effectiveness.
- The faint rotting odor derived from mixing four eggs in a gallon of water and spraying the mixture on plants may repel deer. Fortunately, the smell is too faint for humans to detect.
- A formulation of 1 to 2 tablespoons of Tabasco sauce in 1 gallon of water has been shown to have limited effectiveness.
- Recent studies have shown ordinary bars of soap can reduce deer damage. Suspend a bar of soap from a tree using a mesh bag or pantyhose (Figure 20–25). Each bar protects an area of 1 square yard.

Figure 20–25. Repellent: a bar of soap in a tree to repel deer.
Kathleen Moore, CC BY - 2.0

- See the *North Carolina Agricultural Chemicals Manual.* Be sure to read the label carefully as not all formulations are safe for use on food crops.
- The effectiveness of all repellents depends on the weather, the deer's appetite, and whether other food is available. New foliage that appears after treatment is unprotected. All chemicals should be applied according to the label's directions.
- Subsequent rain reduces a chemical's effectiveness and requires retreatment.
- Repellents are more effective if they are applied before deer become accustomed to foraging on garden plants.
- Do not use mothballs. Mothballs (naphthalene) have been used by some gardeners trying to control deer and rabbits. This practice is illegal and potentially dangerous. It is illegal to use any pesticide in a manner inconsistent with the product label. Deer and rabbits are not listed on the label for mothballs. Small children and pets can be poisoned by eating mothballs.

Lethal Control

- There are specified seasons when it is a legal to hunt deer.
- To take deer out of season, property damage must be verified and a depredation permit obtained. (refer to "Legal Requirements"). Deer taken under a depredation permit must be taken according to restrictions outlined on the permit itself.
- The only legal way a deer may be taken out of season, without a depredation permit, is if the deer is shot with a firearm while in the act of causing property damage. Refer to "Legal Requirements" and/or contact the NCWRC for additional information.
- Live trapping and removal of deer is not a practical way to control deer damage. The amount of labor, number of traps, and time necessary to remove enough of the herd to influence the problem are prohibitive. The welfare of target and non-target animals is also a challenge when dealing with live traps and relocation.
- An annual harvest (shooting) of does (female deer) and bucks (male deer) maintains a population within the carrying capacity of the herd's range. Landowners should provide sufficient opportunity to allow hunters to harvest the deer. Shooting is effective either by legal hunting during the open deer season (which requires a hunting license), by the landowner or lessee when deer are caught in the act of depredation, or as authorized by a wildlife depredation permit.

GROUNDHOGS (WOODCHUCKS)

The groundhog, also known as a woodchuck, is a lowland creature living along the edge of the woods or in open plains (Figure 20–26). Groundhogs are found in both the mountain and piedmont areas of North Carolina. They hibernate during the winter. Groundhogs are usually brownish-gray, but some individuals may be white or black. Their tails are relatively short, hairy, and somewhat flattened. A groundhog's body is supported by strong stout legs. Black claws on the front feet are long and curved to make digging through the soil easy. They are good climbers and may be seen in trees, surveying their surroundings or escaping from predators. Their primary predators include hawks, owls, foxes, coyotes, dogs, bobcats, weasels, and humans.

Groundhogs are mostly vegetarian. Groundhogs select trees, legumes, vegetables, and grasses. They can also gnaw on the bark of ornamental shrubs and fruit trees and in some situations cause enough damage to kill the plant. They will, when necessary, feed on the occasional insect or worm.

Their burrows are quite large, averaging 10 to 12 inches in diameter. The amount of dirt excavated when digging a burrow can be substantial and unsightly in a landscape.

These burrows and the tunnels that accompany them can cause problems like twisted ankles or broken legs for humans, livestock, or pets.

Figure 20–26. A groundhog, or woodchuck.
EIC, Wikimedia Commons CC-BY-SA-3.0

Management Strategies to Minimize Groundhog Damage

Habitat Modification
- High levels of human activity can keep groundhogs away from a property.
- Once a groundhog is gone, fill in the den and tunnels to prevent another groundhog, skunk, or rabbit from taking up residence.

Exclusion
- Practical for small home gardens, but not for a large acreage.
- Fencing has the added advantage of keeping out rabbits, dogs, cats, and raccoons.
- Groundhogs are good climbers, so fences must be electric, woven, or made of welded wire, and extend at least 3 to 4 feet tall with a 45-degree angle at the top to discourage groundhogs from climbing over (Figure 20–27).
- The fence should also be buried 12 inches to 14 inches underground to prevent groundhogs from digging under.
- Either the fence material can be bent at a 90-degree angle to the outside (away from the protected area) and extend for 6 inches or a separate piece of fencing material can be buried perpendicular to the fence and extended away from the garden 30 inches.
- In some cases, electric wire alone placed 4 to 5 inches above the ground has been effective.

Repellents
- Using frightening devices such as effigies (scarecrows or plastic owls) can be somewhat effective, but they must be moved regularly.
- Some people claim that fox urine, ammonia, or smells of other predators may repel groundhogs. There is no research-based information to support these claims.

Lethal Control
- Groundhogs can be shot year-round. There is no closed season or bag limit.
- During the legal trapping season, a North Carolina trapping license is required to use a body-grip trap or to trap and shoot groundhogs. Outside of the legal trapping season a depredation permit is required to use a body-grip trap or for trap and shoot for groundhogs.
- Groundhogs can be released alive at the site of capture, but cannot be relocated off site.

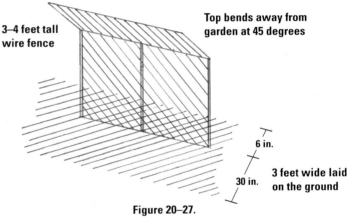

3–4 feet tall wire fence

Top bends away from garden at 45 degrees

6 in.

30 in.

3 feet wide laid on the ground

Figure 20–27.
A groundhog (woodchuck) fence. The fence must rise into the air 3–4 feet and bend away from the garden at a 45-degree angle. Having the fence not securely fastened to the posts will make it wobbly and difficult for woodchucks to climb.

MOLES— EASTERN, HAIRY-TAILED, AND STAR-NOSED

Three species of moles occur in North Carolina: the eastern mole (Figure 20–29), the hairy-tailed mole (Figure 20–29), and the star-nosed mole (Figure 20–30). Both the eastern mole and the hairy-tailed mole are classified as pests in North Carolina when tunneling in managed turf in the following areas: residential, commercial, government property (excluding federal and state parks), golf courses, driving ranges, golf instruction facilities, sod farms, athletic fields or visitor centers, and cemeteries. Pastures are not considered managed turf.

All moles are similar in appearance. The head has a long, hairless, pointed snout; lacks external ears; and has small, barely noticeable eyes. Moles have a short neck, and the muscular front legs support broad, heavily clawed feet. The animal's hind legs, feet, and tail are

20

small. The fur is short, velvety, dark-gray to black, and covers most of the animal. Total length ranges from 5 inches to 8 inches. Contrary to popular belief, moles are not in the rodent family.

Figure 20–28. Eastern mole with its long, hairless snout, small eyes, and heavily clawed feet.
Bert Cash, Flickr CC BY - 2.0

Figure 20–29. A hairy-tailed mole.
Andy Wright, Flickr CC BY - 2.0

Figure 20–30. A star-nosed mole.
US National Parks Service (US NPS), Wikimedia Commons CC BY0

Moles are seldom seen aboveground, but their presence can be observed by ridges in lawns, gardens, and ornamental beds created by the moles tunneling in search of food. Moles must cover a wider area than most underground animals to satisfy their food needs. Most runways are shallow burrows dug just beneath the surface and may or may not be used again. Slightly deeper tunnels are reused as main highways between the mole's home and feeding grounds. Other animals may use the tunnels made by moles.

Many gardeners consider moles an asset in the landscape as moles loosen the soil and feed on garden pests. Moles are **insectivorous**, which means they eat insects—not vegetation. A mole can eat daily almost its own weight in food, which consists almost entirely of earthworms and insects, including white grubs, ants, beetles, and other subterranean insects. Roots, bulbs, and tubers are not eaten by moles but may be damaged during digging activity. Extensive tunneling may lead to drying out of shallow-rooted lawns, flowers, vegetables, and shrubs or expose them to later attack by small rodents.

Moles are more active during rainy periods in summer. Tunnels made during dry weather tend to be shallow because moles follow the courses of earthworms.

The eastern mole, the probable culprit when lawns and gardens are damaged, is usually solitary; although the female shares her burrow with her young while they mature (approximately eight weeks).

Management Strategies for Eastern and Hairy-Tailed Moles
Habitat Modification
- Packing the soil down where tunnels are evident destroys burrows and can kill moles if done in the early morning or late evening.
- Reducing soil moisture by holding off on irrigation can be somewhat effective.

Exclusion
- Exclusion methods are generally effective only in small, high-value areas.
- A sheet metal or hardware cloth fence may be used to protect areas such as seedbeds. The fence should start at the ground surface and go to a depth of at least 12 inches and then bend outward an additional 10 inches at a 90-degree angle (Figure 20–31).

Repellents
- Although some electronic, magnetic, and vibrating devices are advertised to frighten or repel moles, none are shown to be effective.
- Placing hair, chewing gum, bleach, razor blades, broken glass, thorny rose branches, and other sharp objects in

mole tunnels has not been shown to be effective and is not recommended.

- The so-called mole plant (caper spurge) has been advertised as a living mole repellent, but there is no research to support the claims.

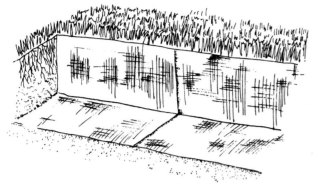

Figure 20–31. Moles are seldom seen above ground. A subterranean mole fence made of hardware cloth or sheet metal should be buried to a depth of 12 in. and then extend at a 90-degree angle away from the garden bed for 10 in.

Lethal Control

- A depredation permit is required prior to trapping Eastern and Hairy-Tailed moles. A frequently used runway can be located by caving in short sections of visible tunnels and checking them daily to see which ones are re-opened. Runways tend to be long straight tunnels, and there is no need to set traps on short, twisting tunnels. Set a spear-type trap (Figure 20–32) over a depressed portion of the surface tunnel. As a mole moves through the tunnel, it pushes upward on the depressed tunnel soil and trips the trap's trigger. One or two traps should be enough for the average lawn because the tunneling is probably caused by only a few moles.
- There are approved mole Rodenticides registered with the Environmental Protection Agency and the North Carolina Department of Agriculture. Registered pesticides can be found by going to www.kellysolutions.com/nc or Chapter IX of the *North Carolina Agricultural Chemicals Manual*, "Animal Damage Control." Also, landowners may contact the NC Department of Agriculture, Pesticide Section or their local NC Cooperative Extension center for information on currently approved pesticides and legal application. Rodenticides used to control these species must be applied in specifically protected bait stations to minimize the hazards to non-target species (including children and pets). Before purchasing and using a pesticide read the DIRECTIONS FOR USE on the actual label.

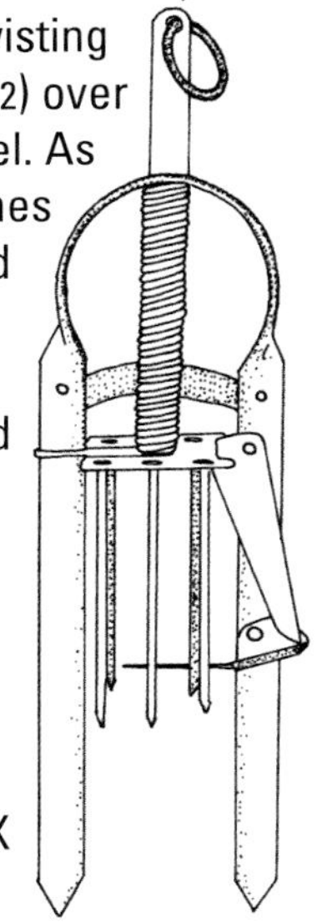

Figure 20–32. A spear-type mole trap.

The star-nosed mole has a distinctive flesh-colored ring of tentacles around its nose. Its tail is also distinctive with concentric rings of short, coarse hair. The star-nosed mole is a state listed species of Special Concern and has not been classified as a pest so management options are different.

Management Strategies for Star-nosed Moles
Habitat Modification

- Packing the soil down where tunnels are evident destroys burrows and can kill moles if done in the early morning or late evening.
- Reducing soil moisture by holding off on irrigation can be somewhat effective.

Exclusion

- Exclusion methods are generally effective only in small, high-value areas.
- A sheet metal or hardware cloth fence may be used to protect areas such as seedbeds. The fence should start at the ground surface and go to a depth of at least 12 inches and then bend outward an additional 10 inches at a 90-degree angle (Figure 20–31).

Repellents

- Although some electronic, magnetic, and vibrating devices are advertised to frighten or repel moles, none are shown to be effective.
- Placing hair, chewing gum, bleach, razor blades, broken glass, thorny rose branches, and other sharp objects in mole tunnels has not been shown to be effective and is not recommended.
- The so-called mole plant (caper spurge) has been advertised as a living mole repellent, but there is no research to support the claims.

Lethal Control

- There is no open hunting or trapping season for star-nosed moles.
- A depredation permit obtained from the Executive Director of the NCWRC is required to trap star-nosed moles and is only issued when substantial damage has occurred. (Refer to "Legal Requirements.") Contact NCWRC 866-318-2401.

Eastern cottontail rabbits eat a wide variety of plants, including grasses, clovers, carrots, lettuce, peas, beans, strawberries, and beets (Figure 20–33). They do not seem to like corn, squash, cucumbers, tomatoes, peppers, potatoes, and gourds, which could be planted near the garden edges. Rabbits gnaw the bark on the stems and lower limbs of ornamentals and fruit and forest trees. Rabbits

20

select apple, raspberry, blackberry, cherry, and plum. Ornamental plants that are often damaged include sumac, rose, tulip, basswood, dogwood, honey locust, red maple, sugar maple, and willow. Rabbits may completely **girdle** stems, thus killing the tree or shrub. The thicker, rough bark of older trees often discourages rabbits.

Figure 20–33. An eastern cottontail rabbit.
Ketzirah Lesser & Art Drauglis (Ketzirah & Art), Flickr CC BY-SA - 2.0

Rabbits have incisors in both the upper and lower jaws so that rabbit-damaged vegetation is cut cleanly (Figure 20–34) rather than torn away. Deer-damage vegetation has a jagged appearance (Figure 20–22).

Rabbits feed just before sunrise and just after sunset, but may be active during the day. They live in fence rows or at the edge of fields and rarely live in dense forests.

Figure 20–34. Cleanly cut leaves from rabbit predation.
Kathleen Moore, CC BY - 2.0

Management Strategies for Rabbits
Habitat Modification
- Rabbit habitat can be reduced by removing brush piles, weed patches, dumps, stone piles, and other debris.
- Controlling vegetation along ditch banks and fence rows should help.

Exclusion
- Small areas such as gardens can be protected from rabbits with a 1-inch mesh wire fence at least 18 inches to 24 inches high. If snow depth nears or exceeds the height of the fence, it will be ineffective. The bottom edge of the fence should be staked or buried at least 6 inches to prevent burrowing.
- Electric fences with strands placed at 4, 8, and 12 inches from the ground may also be effective.
- Trees can be protected by cylinders of ¼-inch mesh hardware cloth set firmly in the ground surrounding the trunk (Figure 20–35). The cylinders should be at least 18 to 24 inches high, but again, average snow depth must be considered. Commercial tree wraps and plastic guards may be used to prevent gnawing damage.

Figure 20–35. A cylinder of wire can protect trees from rabbit damage.
Chris Alberti, CC-BY-2.0

Repellents
- Dried blood meal sometimes protects flower beds, but it could attract dogs.

Lethal Control
- Lethal control of rabbits is very rarely necessary.
- Usually, exclusion solves the problem.
- An open hunting and box-trapping season is established for rabbits. Annual harvest during the open season may help avoid high populations that increase damage problems.
- A North Carolina hunting license is required to take rabbits during the legal hunting season. To take rabbits out of season, property damage must be verified and a depredation permit obtained. (Refer to "Legal Requirements.")

20

RACCOONS

Raccoons may eat grains, acorns, nuts, fruits, or vegetables (melons). They are heavy predators of corn, especially when the kernels are in the milking stage. Raccoons are omnivorous: they eat snails, frogs, insects, small mammals, garbage, birds, and eggs. They are active mainly at night and spend the day in hollow logs, rock cavities, culverts, and sometimes burrows. They primarily occupy areas near streams, lakes, and marshes. Raccoons are attracted to gardens, pet food, bird food, and garbage (Figure 20–36).

Figure 20–36. A raccoon is attracted to unsecured birdseed.
Robert Engberg, Flickr CC BY - 2.0

Management Strategies for Raccoons
Habitat Modification
- Removing a raccoon's day cover (hollow trees and logs) from areas immediately next to the control areas may force them to find cover and food elsewhere.
- Be aware that removal of snags, or dead trees, has the negative effect of reducing native bird habitat.
- Always feed pets indoors. Store pet food, bird food, and garbage inside or in sealed containers that cannot be opened by raccoons.
- Immobilize garbage cans, secure the lids, and follow proper sanitation methods.
- Raccoons actively use bird feeders. If there is a raccoon problem, consider a temporary suspension of bird feeding.

Exclusion
- A 2-inch mesh wire fence with an electrified strand can be used around gardens. The fence should be 4 feet high and run 6 inches below ground level and 18 inches outward at the base to prevent burrowing (Figure 20–37).

- Bags or netting can be placed over ripening crops such as corn cobs or peaches (Figure 20–38).

Repellents
- No repellents recommended.

Lethal Control
- Raccoons are considered a furbearing animal in North Carolina.
- A North Carolina hunting or trapping license is required to take raccoons during the legal hunting or trapping season.
- To take raccoons out of season, property damage must be verified and a depredation permit obtained. (Refer to "Legal Requirements.")

Figure 20–37. A fence can be used to keep raccoons out of a garden. It should extend into the air at least 4 feet and be buried in the ground 6 inches. The fence should extend underground 18 inches away from the garden to prevent burrowing.
Renee Lampila

Figure 20–38. Each peach on this tree has been individually bagged to protect it from predation. This can be a time consuming but effective option.
Bjarke Liboriussen (Ningbo Ningbo), Flickr CC BY - 2.0

20

Rodents can be a challenge in both urban and rural settings, but, vigilance in applying integrated pest management strategies can keep populations low. Knowing some of the key characteristics of rats helps in developing a management plan. They can climb most surfaces and jump up to 36 inches. They are shy, but also inquisitive, initially avoiding new objects, but in time investigating them. Rats are nocturnal—out from dusk until dawn. They are not active the entire time but have multiple periods of activity at night. Their poor eyesight causes them to rely on hearing, touch, and scent. Rats' incisors grow so rapidly they must constantly gnaw on everything to wear them down. Rats begin to breed at three months of age, producing up to 12 rats per litter and four to six litters per year. A pair of rats and their offspring could produce 1,500 more rats in only one year if they all survived. Their average lifespan is one year. Adult Norway rats (*Rattus norvegicus*) range from 12 to 18 inches long, nose to tail tip (Figure 20–39). Their gray to brown bodies are compact and heavy. They have relatively small eyes and ears, and their tails are generally about half their body length. Norway rats are prodigious burrowers. They eat garbage, meat, fish, cereals, seeds, pet food, and a wide variety of other substances. To determine if there is a problem, look for these signs: evidence of gnawing, rat droppings (capsule shaped and ½-inch to ¾-inch long), tracks, and large burrows along building walls.

Figure 20–39. A Norway rat, or brown rat (*Rattus norvegicus*). oatsy40, Flickr CC BY - 2.0

Management Strategies for Norway Rats

These strategies are most effective when there is a community-wide effort.

Habitat modification
- Minimize nesting sites by removing junk and storing materials 12 to 18 inches off the floor and away from walls.
- Limit food by storing bulk birdseed, chicken feed, and other potential sources of food in metal containers.
- Store chicken feed in a metal container each night.
- Feed pets indoors. Remove spilled seed from beneath bird feeders.
- Clean up spilled food. Use a tight lid on garbage cans.
- Practice good sanitation. Well-swept floors and mowed turf make it easier to detect problems and also force rats into exposed settings, making them more vulnerable to predators such as dogs and owls.

Exclusion
- Make structures rodent proof. Seal off all potential entryways.

Repellents
- None proven effective.

Lethal Control
- Rodent-killing, as the only control strategy, is expensive and effective for only a short while. Unless the conditions that allowed the rats to thrive are changed, new rats will soon move in.
- Control is most effective in winter when rat populations are lowest.
- Unless the rodent infestation is severe, it is best to sanitize and rodent-proof prior to killing rodents.
- When trapping, traps may be baited or not. Bacon, peanut butter, bread, and nutmeats make suitable baits. Place traps in areas of rodent activity, 15 to 30 feet apart, in places that are inaccessible to pets and children. Traps have several advantages over rodenticides:
  1. They are more affordable as they can be used many times.
  2. There is no chance of accidentally poisoning a child, a pet, or another non-target animal.
  3. The rat is killed instantly in the trap.
  4. There is no chance that the trapped rat will provide an unintended dose of poison to a hawk, owl, or another predator.
  5. There is no chance a trapped rat will crawl inside a wall to die and decompose.
- To use chemical bait, see the *North Carolina Agricultural Chemicals Manual*. All chemicals should be applied according to the label's directions.

Figure 20–40. A copperhead snake.
John Gerwin

SNAKES

Snakes in the garden may cause concern for some people, but often the snake is not causing any harm and may be one of the gardener's best friends. Snakes help keep rat, mice, vole, and rabbit populations in check. Snakes are seen most often in the spring or fall as they search for food or move to and from hibernation areas. They are frequently associated with small mammal habitats because rodents are primary food sources for many snake species.

Several venomous snakes, including the copperhead (Figure 20–40), cottonmouth (also known as water moccasin), three rattlesnake species, and eastern coral snakes are found in North Carolina.

When snakes are observed on your property, we recommend keeping a safe distance unless you can positively identify the species as being non-venomous. Wild snakes often bask in the sun and this is when they become highly visible. In most cases, the snake will move on by itself. It can be very difficult to differentiate between venomous and non-venomous snakes. As a general guideline, the three rattlesnake species are pit vipers and can be identified by a pit between and slightly below the eye and nostril, long movable fangs, a vertically elliptical pupil, and a triangular head (Figure 20–41). Nonvenomous snakes have two rows of scales on their tails, while venomous snakes have one row of scales. The coral snake is another venomous snake that can sometimes be found in the southeastern part of the state, although it is extremely rare. It is recognized by its distinctive pattern of red and black rings separated by a yellow ring (Figure 20–42). We do not recommend handling or killing any snake. For help in identifying snakes, Davidson College has created a free app for Apple iPhones (it can be downloaded from iTunes) and has multiple pictures of each species of snake in North Carolina.

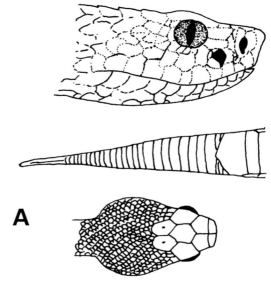

A

Figure 20–41. Characteristics of venomous and nonvenomous snakes.
A. Venomous: elliptical pupils, pit between eye and nostril, one row of scales on the tail, and a triangular-shaped head.
B. Nonvenomous: round pupils and two rows of scales on the tail.
John Gerwin

B

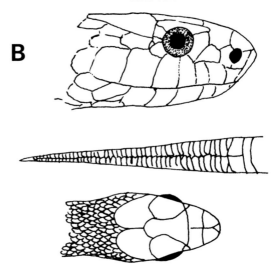

20

Figure 20–42. A coral snake; notice that the red and black are separated by yellow rings.

Evan Bench (austinevan)

Strategies for Discouraging Snakes
Habitat Modification

- Reduce cover and food supply by mowing closely around homes, gardens, and storage buildings.
- Store firewood and lumber away from the house and preferably elevated off the ground.
- Reduce mulch layers around shrubs to discourage small animals.
- Close cracks and crevices in buildings and around pipes and utility connections with ¼-inch mesh hardware cloth, mortar, or sheet metal.

Exclusion

- Small areas can be protected with a snake-proof fence made of ¼-inch mesh wire screening built up 30 inches and buried 6 inches underground. It is slanted at a 30-degree angle from top to bottom (Figure 20–43). The supporting stakes must be inside the fence, and any gate must fit tightly.
- The cost of the fence can make it impractical to protect the entire garden or yard. Tall vegetation just outside the fence must be removed.

Repellents

- Repellents are not effective.

Trapping

- Not advised or effective.

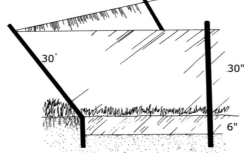

Figure 20–43. A snake fence should extend into the air 30 in. and into the ground 6 in. The fence should bend away from the garden at a 30-degree angle.

SQUIRRELS

The four most abundant tree squirrels (Figure 20–44) in North Carolina are the gray squirrel, fox squirrel, red squirrel, and southern flying squirrel. Gray squirrels are about 16 to 20 inches long with gray fur and a lighter underside. Fox squirrels are 19 to 29 inches long and have three basic color phases: red, gray, and black. Red squirrels are 11 to 14 inches long and have reddish fur and a white belly. Southern flying squirrels are 9 to 14 inches long with brown fur and white underside. In North Carolina, gray and flying squirrels usually cause depredation problems. Squirrels are agile and can jump 6 to 8 feet laterally. This makes control more difficult.

Squirrels eat a variety of foods including fruits, seeds, nuts, buds, shoots, insects, and fungi. They also pull or dig up corn plants and eat stored corn. In late winter and early spring, they often destroy the growing tips of young trees and shrubs. Much of their diet is made up of tree seeds (nuts), which are often stored. Broken and half-eaten nutshells beneath pecan and other nut trees indicate squirrel (or possibly blue jay) depredation. Studies show that squirrels do not "remember" where nuts are buried but happen to smell them while foraging. Nuts that are left covered often germinate and grow.

Squirrels eat from bird feeders. When other foods are in short supply, squirrels may damage trees by debarking and cutting an excessive number of buds. Squirrels usually build nests from leaves or den in natural tree cavities or crotches of branches. Squirrels sometimes den in buildings and cause damage by gnawing through siding and electrical wires (creating a fire hazard) and breaking weather seals. Although squirrels do not hibernate, they may remain in the nest for days during adverse weather. Most are **diurnal**, with the greatest activity in the early morning or late afternoon hours. The flying squirrel, however, is nocturnal (active at night).

Management Strategies to Minimize Squirrel Damage
Habitat Modification

- Use squirrel-proof bird feeders. Some have domed tops that prevent access (Figure 20–45). Others have a weighted cage on the outside that slides down over the holes in the feeder when a squirrel hangs from it to feed. Birds are too light to make the cage slide down.
- To reduce squirrel access to roofs and homes, remove overhanging branches and trim limbs at least 6 feet from homes and buildings.

Exclusion

- Isolated, high-value trees can be "squirrel proofed" by placing 2-foot-wide metal bands around the tree, 6 feet

Figure 20–44. Most commonly found tree squirrels in North Carolina.
Left to right: Gray squirrel, fox squirrel, red squirrel and southern flying squirrel.

off the ground (Figure 20–46). Trim overhanging branches to prevent access from nearby trees. This method does not work when trees are closely planted and have overlapping branches.

- High-value crops can be protected by building a fence of 1-inch mesh wire. The fence should be at least 30 inches high and extend 6 inches below the ground with an additional 6 inches bent outward (at 90 degrees) to discourage burrowing. At least two electrified strands (one 2 to 6 inches above the ground and the other at the fence height) should be set off the fence about 3 inches.
- Newly planted bulbs can be protected with 1-inch mesh poultry wire. Dig a trench slightly deeper than the desired depth of planting and fit the poultry wire in the bottom. Add soil and plant the bulbs. Place another strip of poultry wire over the plantings so that the bulbs are completely encased, then finish covering with soil.

Figure 20–45. Habitat modification: a baffle over a bird feeder will help stop predation by squirrels.

Repellents
- No repellents recommended.

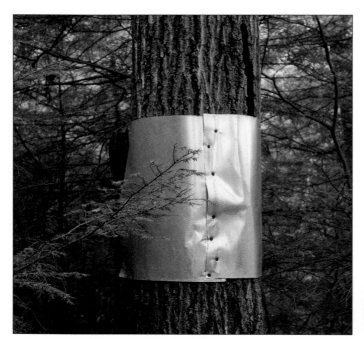

Figure 20–46. Sheet metal can be wrapped around a tree to prevent squirrels from climbing it. The metal must be adjusted periodically so as not to girdle the tree as it ages.

Nicholas A. Tonelli (Nicholas_T), Flickr CC BY - 2.0

Trapping

- With proper depredation permits, squirrels can be live trapped with wooden or wire box traps for relocation.
- Bait the traps with peanut butter rolled in oats, nut meats, pumpkin or sunflower seeds, or dried prunes. Tie the trap door open for several days to get squirrels accustomed to feeding in the trap. Wear gloves and do not handle the squirrel. Squirrels can be released onto other private property with written permission of the landowner. They cannot be released onto any government properties or onto other private property without permission.

Lethal control

- North Carolina hunting seasons are established for fox and gray squirrels, although some counties prohibit the hunting of fox squirrels. A hunting license is required during the open season.
- During the closed season, a landowner or lessee may apply for a depredation permit if they are experiencing squirrel damage. (Refer to "Legal Requirements.")

VOLES—PINE AND MEADOW

Four kinds of voles occur in North Carolina: pine, meadow, rock, and red-backed. These small mammals, commonly mistaken for mice, live in fields, orchards, and shrub habitats. Only pine and meadow voles causing damage in or immediately adjacent to cultivated lands—forest plantations, ornamentals nurseries, orchards, or horticultural plantings in institutional, recreational, and residential areas—are classified as pests (Figure 20–47 and Figure 20–48). These voles are becoming more common as the use of natural areas in the landscape increases. In horticultural plantings, pine and meadow voles can cause damage by eating flower bulbs, girdling the stems of woody plants, and gnawing roots. Plants not killed outright may die later due to root damage or disease organisms that entered through wounds created by the vole.

Pine voles have small eyes and ears that are hidden by their reddish-brown fur. A pine vole's tail is shorter than its hind legs. The adult pine vole is about 3 inches long and weighs 1 ounce or less. Pine voles spend most of their life underground in burrow systems. Unlike moles, voles are herbivores and feed on plant roots, flower bulbs, and the growing tissue (**cambium**) of tree roots. They eat bark primarily in fall and winter.

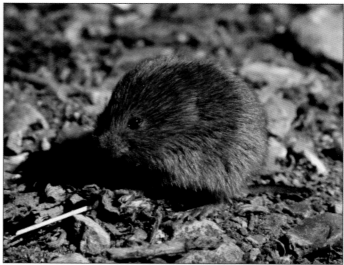

Figure 20–47. Pine voles have small eyes and ears that are hidden by their fur. The tail is shorter than the hind legs. The fur is reddish brown. The adult pine vole is about 3 inches long and weighs 1 ounce or less.

Peter Trimming (Peter G. Trimming), Flickr CC BY - 2.0

A pine vole tends to stay in an area as small as 1,000 square feet for its entire life. At night, they come aboveground and feed on fruit and tender green vegetation. Soils with substantial clay content are more likely than sandy soils to support pine vole populations because clay permits relatively permanent tunnel systems and nest chambers.

Pine voles damage trees and plantings below the ground (Figure 20–49). When the damage to a particular plant is extensive, the plant will be severely weakened and may die. The trunks of small trees or shrubs may be severed from the roots, making it possible to pull the top of the plant out of the soil. Or the plant may fall over by itself.

Upon close inspection of the plant, gnawing marks can be seen just under the soil line. In apple orchards, the damage to the tree may not be sufficient to kill the tree, but damaged trees produce less fruit. Careful observation

20

beneath the tree may reveal piles of earth (3 to 4 inches wide) and tunnels that are about 1½ inches in diameter. If pine voles are living under the tree, a network of tunnels approximately 3 inches under the soil can be located by probing with a ½- to ¾-inch diameter stick or rod.

Figure 20–48. A meadow vole is slightly larger than a pine vole; eyes and ears are visible. Voles can sometimes be confused with mice but their tails are shorter and their snouts are more blunt.
Greg Tally, Wikimedia Commons CC BY-SA - 3.0

The meadow vole's eyes are not covered by fur, and its ears (partly covered by hair) are visible. The tail is longer than the hind legs. The fur is dark brown, often silvery on the underside. The adult meadow vole ranges from 3½ to 5 inches long and weighs 1 to 2½ ounces. Meadow voles spend most of their lives aboveground, living in and feeding on grasses. They have larger home ranges than pine voles and may travel as far as ¼-mile in a week. The typical habitat for meadow voles is a grassy meadow, particularly in places where grasses grow in clumps. Tall fescue areas in orchards, lightly grazed pastures, and old fields are typical habitats. Signs of meadow voles are found mostly aboveground in taller grasses and cover. Look for trails in the grass and grass clippings, and check for feces at the base of large clumps of grass. The feces, shaped like wheat grains, may be brown or green in color and are frequently left in small piles. Typically, meadow voles girdle trees and saplings at the ground line (Figure 20–50). Close inspection of the damage reveals paired grooves left by their chisel-like teeth. The grooves are about ¹⁄₁₆-inch wide. Girdling completely around the tree trunk kills the plant, so any indication of aboveground damage is cause for instituting a control program.

Rabbits chew on young trees, but their girdling begins several inches above the soil line. Rabbits have much larger incisor teeth than voles, which is reflected in the size of grooves on the girdled tree. Rabbit damage can be controlled with a plastic tree guard, but these devices do not prevent meadow vole damage.

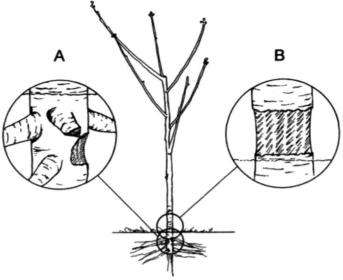

Figure 20–49. Plant damage. A) Below ground damage is generally pine vole. B) Above ground damage is meadow vole.

Figure 20–50. Damage to trees usually occurs near the ground line. Voles can easily girdle small trees.
Peter Linehan (P_Linehan), Flickr CC BY - 2.0

Testing for Voles

The apple sign test was developed to monitor vole populations in commercial orchards. The test permits the grower to detect the vole populations before the damage becomes severe. It also reduces the exposure of nontarget animals to control activities. Because the test shows where control is needed, areas without voles are not treated, saving time, money, and environmental risk. Conduct the apple sign test in the fall and spring each year. Sketch a map of the grounds, especially if plantings are extensive. Prepare enough brown shingles or 1- to 2-inch thick pieces of board (painted to match the background color of the flower garden or plantings) to scatter them strategically along the edges and throughout plantings at 15-foot intervals.

20

Place a shingle on the ground, if possible over a hole caused by a vole. To monitor for meadow voles, the shingle must be rounded in a tent-like fashion or propped up 3 to 4 inches off the ground so that the animal can go under it. After five days, place a ½-inch cube of apple under each shingle. After 24 hours, check to see if the apple has been removed or eaten. Leave the shingles in place for future monitoring. When monitoring has been completed, a control action can be directed to the locations where vole damage may occur rather than to the entire planting.

Management Strategies for Voles
Habitat modification
- Remove mulch from within a foot of the trunk of a plant. This prevents the vole from sneaking in under the mulch. Instead, the vole must use an exposed approach that is more dangerous and less attractive to it.
- Reduce or remove grass thatch to deter meadow vole populations. Close mowing prevents meadow voles from hiding from their predators (hawks, owls, foxes, cats, and dogs) and may prevent populations from becoming established.
- Soil cultivation disturbs burrows and reduces plant cover.

Exclusion
- Wrapping seedlings and young trees in hardware cloth cylinders can exclude voles. The mesh should be ¼-inch or less. Bury the wire 6 inches to keep voles from burrowing under the cylinder.
- Creating a gravel barrier several inches wide on the bottom and sides of the plant's root zone may provide protection.

Repellents
- None proven effective.

Lethal Control
- A depredation permit must be obtained from the NCWRC before trapping voles. Trapping is an effective way to determine if one or both kinds of voles are present.
- A snap-type mouse trap using a small piece of apple as bait works well. The trap should be placed under a shingle. To trap pine voles, some excavation is needed to place the trap down into the run. Place the trap at a right angle to the run. Bend the shingle to form an arched roof over the trap so the spring can clear the shingle (Figure 20–51).
- Meadow voles can be caught by setting traps at right angles to their runways in the grass. No excavation is necessary because meadow voles live aboveground. It takes persistence as well as skill to be a successful trapper. Remember, when trapping pine voles, no light must reach the trap site. A bait is not necessary if the trap is set across the runway and the trap trigger is

expanded. To do this, fix a piece of cardboard (such as that found on the back of a writing tablet) to the trigger. The new trigger should be just slightly smaller than the trap's wooden base. Traps should be set at 10-foot intervals throughout the damaged planting.
- Traps should be checked daily and reset until no voles are caught for a week. In large landscaped areas, concentrate trapping in a particular plant bed, achieve control, and then move the trapping effort to another area.
- Meadow voles have much larger home ranges than pine voles, making it impractical for homeowners to control meadow voles by trapping.
- There are approved Rodenticides for voles. Rodenticides used to control voles must be registered with the Environmental Protection Agency and the North Carolina Department of Agriculture. Registered pesticides can be found by going to www.kellysolutions.com/nc or the *North Carolina Agricultural Chemicals Manual*, go to Chapter IX, "Animal Damage Control." Also, landowners may contact the NC Department of Agriculture, Pesticide Section, or their local N.C. Cooperative Extension center for information on currently approved pesticides and legal application. Rodenticides used to control these species must be applied in specific protected bait stations to minimize the hazards to non-target species. Before purchasing and using a pesticide read the DIRECTIONS FOR USE on the actual label.

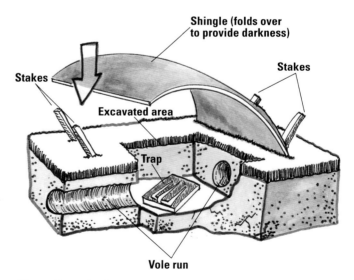

Figure 20–51. A vole trap set in the ground with a shingle over top.
Renee Lampila

WOODCHUCKS (see Groundhogs)

Frequently Asked Questions

1. The deer are eating my hostas and everything else! How can I stop them?

Most people enjoy watching deer in the wild, but deer can be a problem when they feed on landscape plants. Be sure you are not over-watering or over-fertilizing your plants as new growth is especially attractive to deer. Exclusion is generally the most effective technique for dealing with deer predation. Covering your flower bed or garden with poultry wire or a metal mesh cage supported by landscape stakes can keep deer out. Chemical deterrents generally work only before predation is established and need to be applied regularly. Scare tactics such as lights or sounds can be effective but need to be changed up regularly. While no plants are safe from hungry deer, consider replacing their favorites with deer-resistant plants identified on the NC State plant database.

2. I would like to attract birds and butterflies to my garden. What plants do you recommend for this?

Many native plants provide great habitat and food sources for birds and butterflies. Read more about "Native Plants" in chapter 12. Be sure to consider planting not only food sources for adult butterflies but caterpillar, or larval, food sources. Choosing plants that have different canopy heights provides different levels of cover and nesting sites for a wide range of birds. Providing year-round food by selecting plants that flower and fruit at different times of the year is another way to ensure diversity. Read more about attracting butterflies to your backyard in NC State Extension publication *Butterflies in Your Backyard* (AG 636-02) and about plants that attract birds in *Managing Backyards and Other Urban Habitats for Birds* (AG 636-01).

3. Are snakes bad? What should I do to get rid of them?

There are six venomous snakes in North Carolina and about 31 nonvenomous snakes. Davidson College has an excellent online snake identification key. Venomous snakes often have triangular shaped heads, vertical pupils (like a cat), and a heat sensing pit between the eyes and the nostrils. Snakes provide natural pest control in our gardens by keeping rodent populations in check. Reduce habitat by keeping landscape plants trimmed and away from buildings and removing debris piles that could provide shelter. Store firewood away from buildings and elevated off the ground. Sealing off cracks and holes in buildings with wire mesh or stainless steel can keep snakes out. It is not necessary to kill any snake in North Carolina. Leave snakes alone.

4. How do I deal with voles?

First, make sure you correctly identify that you have a vole problem. Encourage natural predators such as owls by placing owl boxes in your yard. Forcing voles to expose themselves leaves them vulnerable to predation. Remove mulch within a foot of the plant's trunk. This prevents the vole from sneaking in under the mulch. Reduce or remove grass thatch to deter meadow vole populations. Close mowing prevents meadow voles from hiding from their predators (hawks, owls, foxes, cats, and dogs) and may prevent populations from becoming established. Wrapping seedlings and young trees in hardware cloth cylinders can exclude voles. The mesh should be ¼-inch or less. Bury the wire 6 inches to keep voles from burrowing under the cylinder.

20

Further Reading

Adams, George. *Birdscaping Your Garden: A Practical Guide to Backyard Birds and the Plants That Attract Them.* Emmaus, Pennsylvania: Rodale Press, Inc., 1994. Print.

Beane, Jeffrey C., et al. *Amphibians and Reptiles of the Carolinas and Virginia.* 2nd ed. Chapel Hill, North Carolina: The University of North Carolina Press, 2010. Print.

Emrath, Paul. *Residential Land Use in the U.S. Washington, D.C.*: National Association of Home Builders, 2006. PDF file.

Hall, E. Raymond. *The Mammals of North America.* 2nd ed. 1981. Caldwell, New Jersey: The Blackburn Press, 2001. Print.

Ortho's All about Attracting Hummingbirds and Butterflies. Westminster, Maryland: Ortho Books, 2001. Print.

Potter, Eloise F., et al. *Birds of the Carolinas.* 2nd ed. Chapel Hill, North Carolina: The University of North Carolina Press, 2006. Print.

For More Information

http://go.ncsu.edu/fmi_wildlife

Contributors

Authors:
Christopher DePerno, Professor, Department of Forestry and Environmental Resources; Fisheries, Wildlife, and Conservation Biology
Christopher Moorman, Professor and Coordinator of the Fisheries, Wildlife, and Conservation Biology Program
Lucy Bradley, Professor and Extension Specialist, Urban Horticulture, NC State University; Director, NC State Extension Master Gardener program
Kathleen Moore, Urban Horticulturist, Department of Horticultural Science

Contributions by Extension Agents: Travis Birdsell, Sam Marshall, Michelle Wallace, Katy Shook, Wendi Hardup

Contributions by Extension Master Gardeners: Bethany Sinnott, Jackie Weedon, Karen Damari, Lee Kapleau, Ann Barnes, Chris Alberti, Connie Schultz, Caro Dosé

Reviewed by NC Wildlife Resources Commission: Jessie Birckhead, Colleen Olfenbuttel, Evin Stanford, Jeffrey Hall, Tammy Rundle

Copy Editors: Barbara Scott, Elizabeth K. Suits

Based in part on text from the 1998 Extension Master Gardener manual prepared by:
Erv Evans, Extension Associate Department of Horticultural Science
Peter Bromley, Extension Specialist, Department of Zoology
Adapted from North Carolina Animal Damage Control Manual.

Chapter 20 Cover Photo: Deer. Pikist, CC BY0

How to cite this chapter:
DePerno, C., C. Moorman, L.K. Bradley, K. Moore. 2022. Wildlife, Chpt 20. In: K.A. Moore and L.K. Bradley (eds). *North Carolina Extension Gardener Handbook,* 2nd ed. NC State Extension, Raleigh, NC. <https://content.ces.ncsu.edu/extension-gardener-handbook/20-wildlife>

Youth, Community, and Therapeutic Gardening

Objectives

After reading this chapter you can:

1. Explain the role of a volunteer educator in a community, youth, or therapeutic garden.
2. Identify effective steps to start and sustain a successful group garden.
3. Develop specific strategies for record keeping and evaluation in group gardens.

21

Introduction

Unlike the other chapters in this handbook, this chapter will not provide extensive information on how to garden. Instead, we focus here on how to serve as an effective educator, coach, and mentor to others in three primary arenas: community gardens, youth gardens, and therapeutic gardens.

Community Gardens (Figure 21–1). These gardens are generally organized as either plot gardens or cooperative gardens. Some community gardens, however, are a combination of both plot and cooperative areas. Plot gardens subdivide the land into family-sized plots—ranging in size from 100 to 500 square feet—where each individual (or family) gardens in their own plot. Sometimes a section of the garden is reserved as shared space to grow crops too large for individual plots (such as corn, pumpkins, watermelons, fruit trees, grapes, and berries). Gardeners divide the bounty from these shared plots.

Figure 21–1. This community garden is divided by plots.
Donna Teasley CC BY-SA - 4.0

In a cooperative garden, the entire space is managed as one large garden through the coordinated efforts of many community members. Produce from the garden is sometimes distributed equitably to all the member gardeners. Often, however, these cooperative gardens are associated with communities of faith, civic groups, or service organizations that donate part or all of the produce to charitable organizations such as food banks and soup kitchens.

Youth Gardens (Figure 21–2). With the increasing interest in science and nutrition education, many schools and youth organizations in the United States are planting gardens to serve as outdoor learning laboratories. In the garden, everyone is transformed into a scientist, actively participating in research and discovery. Besides providing a motivating, hands-on setting for teaching skills in virtually every basic subject area, the garden is a wonderful place to learn responsibility, patience, pride, self-confidence, curiosity, critical thinking, and the art of nurturing. In schools, raised-bed gardens, or sections of the school landscape, are customarily assigned to classes. Hands-on curricula and activities are selected to supplement and support the standard course of study for science and nutrition for specific grade levels. In some cases, school gardens require extensive volunteer support so that classes may be split into small groups of children to work in the garden.

Figure 21–2. Harvesting kale and amaranth in a school garden.
USDA, Lance Cheung, Flickr under Public Domain Mark 1.0

Figure 21–3. Therapeutic gardens often use raised beds with high sides for those who have trouble bending or are in wheelchairs.
Gloria Polakof CC BY - 2.0

Therapeutic Gardens (Figure 21–3). Still other gardens focus on horticultural therapy: using plants to improve the social, educational, psychological, and physical well-being of the gardeners and their caregivers, family, and friends. Located in hospitals, nursing homes, assisted living facilities, retirement communities, outpatient treatment centers, botanical gardens, and other settings, therapeutic gardens are generally designed to be accessible to people with physical limitations. Therapeutic gardens may be designed for active gardening programs or as quiet spaces for reflection. These gardens may include raised beds and firm pathways to provide access to participants in wheelchairs, Braille signage for gardeners with sight impairments, special ergonomically designed tools for gardeners with limited physical strength, and other helpful accommodations. Therapeutic gardens are often designed with plant material selected for texture, color, sound, taste, and scent to appeal to all five senses.

Ways Volunteer Educators Can Help

Volunteer educators can support all three kinds of gardening programs by sharing information, providing resources, promoting communication, supporting fund development, encouraging volunteer management, facilitating community development (connecting to community partners), teaching the value of record keeping, and assisting with evaluation. Some of the topics volunteer educators might cover include composting, pest management, soil stewardship, food safety, nutrition, and health.

> *"A good organizer (as well as a good facilitator) provides the framework and structure for groups to flourish."*
> (Abi-Nader, Dunnigan, and Markley, 2001)

The following lists describe ways that volunteer educators can support gardening programs. These activity suggestions reflect both volunteer experiences with gardening programs and the latest research about what makes a gardening program succeed or fail. See the References and Resources list at the end of this chapter for further reading.

Share Information
- Building exhibits
- Giving talks (Figure 21–4)
- Hosting workshops
- Visiting sites
- Consulting, mentoring, or coaching

Figure 21–4. This garden facilitator is presenting information before school children begin working in the garden.
Donna Teasley

Provide Resources
- Developing publications, such as online or printed newsletters and websites
- Growing vegetable transplants (Figure 21–5)
- Setting up a tool "lending library" (Figure 21–6)
- Supporting soil testing (including interpretation of results)
- Consulting about garden design consultation
- Designing a water collection system (Figure 21–7)
- Managing a community garden library
- Growing gardens seed bank
- Emailing tips on specific problems during the growing season
- Assisting with fund development, including grant writing

Figure 21–5. A garden mentor can help by growing transplants to be used in a youth, community, or therapeutic garden.
Lucy Bradley CC BY - 2.0

Figure 21–6. A tool lending shed allows garden workers to check out tools, use them and put them back. This saves money as well as time and effort carrying tools to the garden each day.
Lucy Bradley CC BY - 2.0

Figure 21–7. A colorful rain barrel collects water from the tool shed roof and provides a free water source for the garden.
Tim Mathews CC BY - 2.0

Promote Communication, Networking, & Public Relations
- Creating bulletin boards (Figure 21–8)
- Developing a directory of gardens
- Promoting the garden through social media
- Helping to coordinate tours (Figure 21–9)
- Assisting with planning effective meetings
- Soliciting positive media attention

Figure 21–8. A bulletin board allows gardeners to communicate with each other and the community.
Tim Mathews, CC BY - 2.0

Support Fund Development
- Assisting with a clear vision, mission statement, budget, and business plan and elevator speech
- Pointing groups in the direction of where to look for in-kind gifts
- Eliciting donations (individual, corporate, crowdfunding online)
- Establishing fees
- Planning and coordinating events (plant sales, silent auctions, educational and social events) (Figure 21–10)
- Applying for grants—from writing a proposal through implementation

Encourage Volunteer Management
- Recruiting volunteers
- Tracking volunteers and potential contacts (contact information, service organizations)
- Communicating with volunteers (bulletin board, listserv, gatherings, written schedule of events)
- Encouraging positive feedback and recognition

Figure 21–9. School children going on a tour of a community garden.
Donna Teasley CC BY-SA - 4.0

Figure 21–10. A plant sale can help raise funds for a garden.
Donna Teasley CC BY-SA - 4.0

American Community Gardening Association

Growing Communities Principles

- Engage and empower those affected by the garden at every stage of planning, building, and managing the garden project.
- Build on community strengths and assets.
- Embrace and value human differences and diversity.
- Promote equity.
- Foster relationships among families, neighbors, and members of the larger community.
- Honor ecological systems and biodiversity.
- Foster environmental, community, and personal health and transformation.
- Promote active citizenship and political empowerment.
- Promote continuous community and personal learning by sharing experience and knowledge.
- Integrate community gardens with other community development strategies.
- Design for long-term success and the broadest possible impact.

Core Beliefs of Community Garden Organizing

- There are many ways to start or manage a community garden.
- In order for a garden to be sustainable as a true community resource, it must grow from local conditions and reflect the strengths, needs, and desires of the local community.
- Diverse participation and leadership, at all phases of garden operation, enrich and strengthen a community garden.
- Each community member has something to contribute.
- Gardens are communities in themselves, as well as part of a larger community.

(Abi-Nader, Dunnigan, and Markley, 2001)

Steps to Creating a Successful Community Garden

Community gardens come in all shapes and sizes and can be found in neighborhoods, private yards, parks, school-yards, places of worship, or even on rooftops. The tasks of establishing and maintaining a successful community garden require a dedicated group of people with common interests and goals.

> *"Community organizing is successful when a community has taken charge of the process and project."*
> (Abi-Nader, Dunnigan, and Markley, 2001)

How do volunteers go about organizing a community garden for success? The following 10-step approach is based on the latest research about successful community gardens.

1. Set an informational meeting. Invite any interested parties—including neighbors, tenants, maintenance personnel, or local garden groups. Determine if a garden is needed and wanted by the group and set criteria for the garden. Will it be a community-maintained plot and harvest, or will individuals maintain their own plots and harvest their own crops? What are the criteria for who can be a member of the garden (such as must live within walking distance)? Will there be any fee associated with the garden? Can flowers be grown or just vegetables? Is this an organic garden? How will excess produce be distributed—to other neighbors or to local food banks? Will there be community tools, and where will they be stored?

2. Create committees. Dividing the group into committees helps distribute work and ensure that the garden criteria list becomes a reality. Not all of these committees are necessary to a successful garden. A Planning Committee composed of dedicated, organized, and enthusiastic members will take the wish list and help guide the group in making the garden a reality. A Communications Committee will include tech-savvy group members who can help with a website or blog, newsletter, flyers, and signage, and will keep the group up-to-date about the latest garden happenings. A Construction Committee should be formed of able-bodied group members who are willing and able to move dirt and mulch, erect fences, and create garden beds. A Funding and Partnership Committee will be comfortable asking for help from the community, whether it is in the form of writing grants or asking for community support from local vendors. This committee may also identify the people and organizations in the community who would be good garden partners because of benefits to the garden and the partner.

3. Assess assets and identify resources. Conduct an asset assessment by interviewing all members of the group to discover skills and knowledge within the group that can be leveraged to build and maintain a garden. Identify city contacts, those who could help in locating a garden site or handle questions about irrigation or zoning. Contact local garden groups and the county Extension Center for access to gardening experts. See Appendix H for sample asset assessment forms.

Figure 21–11. A water source is an imperative part of any garden. This community garden has a cleanup sink for gardeners to rinse produce and dirty hands.
Kathleen Moore, CC BY - 2.0

Figure 21–12. Design the garden to include divided beds, pathways, water access, and tool storage.
Scot Nelson, Flickr CC BY - 0 1.0

4. Identify financial needs. The Funding and Sponsorship Committee can help create a budget that outlines the funding needed to make the garden a reality. Money may be needed to purchase or rent space and for tools, seeds, and garden construction materials (such as soil amendments, mulch, fencing, lumber). Approaching a community sponsor may be a way to get a large donation. Applying for garden grants is another option. Requiring a fee to garden may provide some long-term income, but usually a large sum is needed up front. Hosting a fundraiser in the community can produce a large income in a short period of time. A plant sale, garden dinner, or selling fence posts or bricks imprinted with sponsors' names are some ideas.

5. Choose the site. Choosing the right site is extremely important. Is the land available, and can the group get a lease from the owner for at least five years? If the garden will grow vegetables, six hours of sunlight minimum is needed. A soil test should be completed (see chapter 1, "Soils and Plant Nutrients") to make sure the plot has suitable nutrients for growing vegetables and to get recommendations for needed nutrients. Is the site close enough that garden members can access it easily? Is there access to water (Figure 21–11)? Can tools be stored in a secure location? Will liability insurance be necessary?

6. Develop the site. Most plots need quite a bit of work to be transformed into a vibrant garden. Have the Construction Committee organize work parties to help remove debris and weeds, and amend the soil.

7. Design the garden. The Planning Committee can put the final touches on the garden's design, including how it will be divided, where pathways will be through the garden, water access, compost bins, tool storage, and signage (Figure 21–12). Consider planting a border of shrubs and perennials that give a tidy appearance that pleases neighbors and city code enforcers—even when the garden is resting for the winter.

8. Plan for children. A garden, no matter what its size, is a magnet for children. It is also a wonderful way to introduce young people to the magic of growing plants and where their food comes from (Figure 21–13). Creating a space or plot just for children allows them to experiment and experience the joy of gardening (Figure 21–14). When everyone feels a sense of pride and ownership in the garden, theft and vandalism are greatly reduced.

Figure 21–14. Think about incorporating a place for children to enjoy physical activity in the garden.
Lucy Bradley, CC BY - 2.0

Figure 21–13.
This children's garden has a welcoming sign, wandering pathways and spider web trellis inviting guests to walk through and explore.
Kathleen Moore, CC BY - 2.0

21

9. Finalize rules and put them in writing. Having the entire group create the ground rules ensures compliance. Making sure everyone in the group is on the same page and knows what is expected of them makes things run more smoothly. How will plots be assigned? What happens if a member does not maintain a plot? How will the money be handled? How often will the group meet? How will basic maintenance be handled? The Communication Committee can help disseminate the final rules to the group.

10. Create community. A community garden is all about sharing the joy of gardening with others. The Communication Committee can help create open lines of communication within your group to be sure news about the garden reaches every individual. Some groups have websites, blogs, an email distribution list, a phone tree, or a newsletter. Installing a waterproof bulletin board in the garden is a great way to announce news. Hosting potlucks or other social events in the garden helps individuals make connections with other gardeners.

(These guidelines are adapted from those established by the American Community Gardening Association.)

Asset-Based Community Development

Asset-based community development focuses on developing a sustainable community based on its members' strengths and potentials. The goal is to create a community that endures and extends a positive effect on both its members and the local environment. This approach is applicable to community gardening because a successful gardening effort requires a wide range of supplies (from seeds to land and tools), ample knowledge about gardening, and willing workers. The following lists describe how community garden volunteers and members can identify assets (both materials and talents), categorize them, and manage them effectively to create and sustain a garden.

Capacity Inventory
- Identify all available local assets and connect them with one another in ways that multiply their effect.
- Base the inventory on what the group has rather than on what the group needs.
- Stay internally-focused.
- Be relationship-driven.

Categories of Assets
- Individual gifts
- Associations
- Institutions
- Land and buildings
- The local economy

Mapping Reciprocal Partnerships Activity (See Appendix H)
- On a large sheet of paper, draw a circle in the middle and write "Gardening Project" inside the circle.
- On the outside edges of the paper, write the names of partners or potential partners and draw a box around each name.
- Brainstorm ways that each partner can help the garden project.
- Draw an arrow connecting each partner to the "Garden Project" box.
- Brainstorm about what the garden project can offer each partner.

Design

Although the role of a volunteer educator is not to create a garden design or to work directly with the design committee, it is important that each volunteer has a basic understanding of design guidelines. These concepts help create a lasting, functional garden space.

Accessibility
Table beds, planter boxes, hanging baskets, vertical gardens and large flowerpots can all be used to make gardening more "accessible" (EPA, 2011). Listed below are some of the applicable Americans with Disabilities Act (ADA) requirements for making gardens accessible.

Handicap parking: One of every 25 parking spaces must be "accessible," and a sixth of the accessible spaces must be "van-accessible."

Raised beds: At least one raised bed must be 24 to 30 inches high and 48 inches wide.

Table beds: These beds must be 27 to 34 inches high and 48 inches wide for adults and 24 to 30 inches high and 48 inches across for children (Figure 21–15).

Figure 21–15.
This table bed is accessible to wheelchairs.
USDA, Lance Cheung, Flickr
Public Domain Mark 1.0

21

Paths to and through the garden:
- Each path's surface must be firm and stable, and a minimum width of 36 inches.
- Passing space should meet ADA Accessibility Guidelines (ADAAG). Where the path is less than 60 inches wide, passing spaces shall be provided at maximum intervals of 200 feet.
- Passing spaces shall be either a minimum of 60 inches by 60 inches or an intersection of two walking surfaces that provide a T-shaped space complying with ADAAG 4.2.3, provided that the arms and stem of the T-shaped space extend at least 48 inches beyond the intersection.
- Cross slope should be a maximum of 1:33.
- Running slope should adhere to one or more of the following provisions:
  - 1:20 or less for any distance.
  - 1:12 maximum for 50 feet. Resting intervals shall be provided at distances no greater than 50 feet apart.
  - 1:10 maximum for 30 feet. Resting intervals shall be provided at distances no greater than 30 feet apart.
- Resting intervals should be a minimum length of 60 inches, have a width at least as wide as the widest portion of the trail segment leading to the resting interval, and have a slope not exceeding 1:33 in any direction.
- Where edge protection is provided, the edge protection shall have a minimum height of 3 inches.

For more detailed information as well as allowable exceptions, see the United States Access Board.

Plan for Shade and Seating
Although vegetable beds do best in full sun, gardeners do not. Shade trees on the north side of the garden can provide a protected retreat, as can vine-covered pergolas. Provide seating in the shade for gardeners to rest and visit (Figure 21–16).

Design Help
Design classes at community colleges, universities, and botanical gardens are excellent sources of information about designing a garden.

Figure 21–16. Provide a shady spot for gardeners to rest.
Gloria Polakof, CC BY - 2.0

Record Keeping and Evaluation

Record keeping and evaluation of garden programs are essential to keeping a project moving in a positive, sustainable direction over the long term. Good documentation helps with garden planning, demonstrating impacts, and applying for grants.

Record Keeping
Store community garden records in a location accessible to multiple garden members, such as in a notebook that stays secured at the garden or via an online shared drive.

At a minimum, track the following items:
- Plant varieties grown
- Garden maps
- Weight of garden harvests
- Photographs of garden at regular intervals
- Number of volunteers and volunteer hours
- Monetary donations and in-kind gifts
- Documentation of thank-you notes written and contact information of donors
- Number of individuals served by the garden

Evaluation
Set up a uniform evaluation strategy to ensure that your groups are evaluating the same measures in a consistent way every season. At the end of the year, data can be aggregated and garden results can be compared. Help garden members do the following:
- Identify what to measure.
- Select how to measure.
- Gather data.
- Analyze the data.
- Report to members, donors, and sponsors.

See Appendix H, Instructions for Tracking the Gardener Harvest, for more information on how to accurately measure crop yields.

Key Components of a Successful Mentor/Consultant Program

Any community garden depends on volunteer and member efforts. Volunteer educators who serve as mentors and consultants need ongoing training and networking to be successful and to feel supported by their peer group of volunteers. Experienced volunteers and researchers affiliated with the American Community Garden Association recommend the following components to a successful volunteer educator program:

21

Mentor training
- Introduction to community gardening
- Tours of existing community gardens, with opportunities to talk to garden leaders on site

Matching mentors to gardens

Networking: among mentors, gardeners, gardens
- Quarterly educational and social meetings and potlucks
- Website, listserv, social media
- Annual countywide spring kick-off and fall harvest festival

New community garden development

Support of existing community gardens

Policy advocacy

For more information on community gardening see *Collard Greens and Common Ground: A Community Food Gardening Handbook.*

Youth Gardening

Each garden is unique based on children's needs, the population served, the amount of space available for gardening and equipment storage, the degree of irrigation, any coursework requirements, and other such differences. A community garden that involves children can be sponsored by a school or church, a scouting group, or another youth organization.

A community garden at a school may require approval from teachers and administrators. Extension Master Gardener Volunteers (EMGVs) who volunteer at a school garden do not work with children except under the direct supervision of a teacher. An EMGV may be required to register as a volunteer with the school district and to have a background check prior to working with children. Some EMGVs may serve in a mentor role working with adult leadership rather than youth.

Other youth organizations may also require a background check on volunteers. The guidelines offered here are general recommendations for creating a successful youth garden based on the research of Cromwell, Guy, and Bradley (1996). These recommendations can be adapted and tailored to the group being served.

Form a Team
- Include faculty, administrators, custodians, cafeteria staff, students, and parents.
- Welcome members with a wide variety of skills, not just gardening know-how.
- Have teacher(s) create a list of goals for the garden.
- See Appendix H Application for Community Garden Assistance from EMGVs.
- Discuss goals and objectives, and develop a vision.
- Build a budget, and seek in-kind and monetary support.

- Create a calendar for the year.
- Determine how children and teachers will be engaged.

Cultivate Support
- Make the garden a showcase.
- Keep administrators, maintenance crew members, and sponsors informed.
- Celebrate the garden and its supporters via newsletters, websites, and school news bulletins.

Create the Garden
- Select a highly visible site with access to sun, water, and classrooms.
- Begin with these characteristics in mind: small, beautiful, and manageable.
- Clear the site.
- Design garden.
- Use turf-paint to draw the beds and walkways. Invite students in to pretend they are gardening, and then modify the plan based on experience managing a classroom in the space.
- Create the beds.
- Install irrigation, a compost bin, a tool shed, and other garden amenities as needed.

Plant
- Use a planting calendar to plan for harvest while school is in session.
- Have the soil tested and amend it according to test recommendations at least a week before planting.
- Plant seeds and transplants.
- Keep track of what you planted to facilitate crop rotation in the future.
- Mulch to minimize evaporation and weeds and to foster soil improvement.
- Check regularly for weeds, insects, and diseases.
- Keep records of what works and what does not work. This applies to crops and gardening techniques.

Develop a Plan for the Summer
Think of ways to keep the soil healthy, and the area attractive, while school is out of session and the garden is unattended. For example, plant a cover crop to improve soil while minimizing weeds and maintenance, or solarize the soil under clear plastic to reduce weeds, disease organisms, and nematodes. Consider scheduling volunteers to water, weed, and harvest.

Working with Children
Both research and practice indicate that children respond well to educators who are flexible, fascinating, and fun. This is especially true when the classroom is a garden, where kids can explore and get dirty. Waliczek (1998) offers the following tips for working with children in a garden based on his work with the KinderGARDEN effort at Texas A&M University.

Figure 21–17. Children learn best when they can actively participate.
Kathleen Moore

- Show them, instead of telling them (Figure 21–17).
- Ask lots of questions. "What would happen if?" "I wonder …."
- Plan for a short attention span. Get children started on a task quickly, and keep them busy.
- Never underestimate the fascination of digging a hole.
- Children are used to instant gratification. Provide it when you can (plant radishes).
- Getting dirty is essential. Let parents know to send "work" clothes.
- Serve as a coach or facilitator—not as a lecturer.
- Foster guided discovery.

Figure 21–18. The garden is full of creatures children find fascinating.
Amy Rozycki, CC BY - 2.0

- Creepy crawly critters are cool—model fascination, not revulsion (Figure 21–18).
- Create opportunities for ownership, responsibility, and leadership.
- Involve students in planning and construction.
- Be flexible. Capitalize on teachable moments.
- Get organized ahead of time so work time flows smoothly when children arrive.
- Never use weeding as a punishment.
- Recap garden experience by having children journal.
- Use age-appropriate techniques, including coloring and writing.
- Have fun!

Figure 21–19. Divide the children into small manageable groups.
Kathleen Moore

Managing a Class in the Garden

How can volunteers accomplish their educational goals with a group of children when so many distractions can occur in a garden? Small groups, multiple volunteers, and well-organized work stations can help to keep the class fun and purposeful. Cromwell, Guy, and Bradley (1996) explain how to create a learning oasis with these tips:

- Depending on class and garden size, split the students into groups, with only part of the students in the garden at a time (Figure 21–19).
- Have multiple volunteers to assist.
- Set up stations in the garden, each staffed by an adult or an older child, and have students cycle through the stations.

21

- Use a stopwatch to time sessions and keep on track.
- Place a rectangular trellis flat on the garden bed to define individual squares for students to plant.
- Have students create signage to designate planting areas.

Garden Etiquette

As does any other classroom, a youth garden requires mutual respect among educators and learners to accommodate everyone. The following rules of garden etiquette can help young gardeners and educators accomplish their mutual goals of having fun safely and learning in a garden (Cromwell, Guy, and Bradley, 1996).
- Walk on the pathways between the beds to avoid crushing plants or compacting soil.
- Ask before you pick anything.
- Harvest only from your own class plot.
- Wash everything before eating.
- Keep tools out of the path to avoid tripping.
- Hold tools below the waist.
- Place sharp edges or points of tools face down.
- Clean tools before putting them away.
- Deposit trash and recycling in designated receptacles.
- Compost plant waste.
- Wash hands after gardening.
- Share gardening information learned with family and friends.

Horticultural Therapy

Sally Haskett, Horticultural Therapist—Registered (HTR)

Since ancient times, gardens and nature have been recognized as holding the potential for solace and fulfillment. Millions of people worldwide engage in gardening for its benefits to their health and outlook on life. The process of therapeutic horticulture taps into this potential by using horticultural activities to improve human health and well-being. In the presence of a trained therapist with specific goals for clients, this process becomes the clinical practice of horticultural therapy (HT). Both therapeutic horticulture and HT are practiced in a wide variety of settings, including community, healthcare, institutional, and residential settings. Horticulture provides a medium for positive change in the realms of physical health, cognitive processes, social engagement, and emotional well-being.

The American Horticultural Therapy Association supports and advances the HT profession.

Potential activities for use in a therapeutic horticulture program are many and varied. Traditional gardening activities—such as preparing beds, sowing seeds, planting, maintenance, and harvesting—can be performed by people of all ages and abilities, with task adaptations and environmental modifications (Figure 21–20). Connections to nature evolve through gardening. These connections inherently provide opportunities for activities that teach about the cycle of life, and the activities provide endless occasions for delight with the insects and animals that inhabit our garden spaces.

Plants give prompt feedback if their needs are overlooked. Plant care and maintenance activities can be vehicles for personal growth by developing one's sense of purpose, self-esteem, and respect for other forms of life. Simply being in the garden and observing nature can be a beneficial activity.

Volunteer educators can get involved with existing therapeutic horticulture and HT programs, or they can start a program. Current programs exist in the following arenas:
- Continuing care retirement communities
- Healthcare and rehabilitation facilities
- Hospitals
- Schools
- Public gardens
- Community gardens
- Correctional facilities

For information on existing programs and to learn about ways to get connected, check out NC State Extension Therapeutic Hotriculture portal at therapeutic-hort.ces.ncsu.edu/get-connected.

Program commitments vary depending on the facility. At the North Carolina Botanical Garden (NCBG) in Chapel Hill, options range from a monthly commitment of two hours to a weekly commitment of four hours. For more information on volunteering in therapeutic horticulture programs at NCBG, for activity ideas, or to inquire about periodic trainings, please contact the NCBG.

Figure 21–20. A horticultural therapy program working with students who have disabilities.
Dr. Beverly J. Brown, Natashamariesilva, Wikimedia Commons
CC BY SA 4.0

Frequently Asked Questions

1. I want to start a community garden. Will Extension Master Gardener Volunteers (EMGVs) be able to help me build and maintain it?
An EMGV's role in a community garden is as a mentor and guide. These volunteers can connect you to resources and coach you through the steps necessary to establish and maintain a successful garden. They can facilitate meetings of your garden group and help identify problem areas. They are educators, not laborers.

2. Can I apply for grant funding to start my garden?
Depending on the type of garden and the people it will serve, there are many grant programs for starting and maintaining a garden. There are grants for garden supplies as well as seeds. Be sure your garden meets the criteria outlined in the grant and that you are capable of submitting any reporting requirements. Pay careful attention to any deadlines before you apply.

References and Further Reading

Abi-Nader, J., K. Dunnigan, and K. Markley. 2001. *Growing communities curriculum: Community building and organizational development through community gardening.* American Community Gardening Assoc., Columbus, OH.

Baldwin, K., D. Beth, L. Bradley, N. Davé, S. Jakes, and M. Nelson. 2009. *Eat smart, move more, weigh less: Growing communities through gardens.* NC Dept. of Health and Human Services, Div. of Public Health, Raleigh.

Boekelheide, D. and L.K. Bradley. 2016. *Collard greens and common ground: A North Carolina community food gardening handbook* (AG-806). NC State Extension, NC State Univ., Raleigh.

Bradley, L. and K. Baldwin. 2013. *How to organize a community garden (AG-737).* NC State Extension, NC State Univ., Raleigh.

Brennan, M.J. 2013. *Forsyth community gardening.* N.C. Cooperative Extension, Forsyth County Extension Center, Winston-Salem.

Bucklin-Sporer, Arden, and Rachel Kathleen Pringle. 2010. *How to Grow a School Garden: A Complete Guide for Parents and Teachers.* Portland, Oregon: Timber Press, Inc.

Chaifetz, A., L. Driscoll, C. Gunter, D. Ducharme, and B. Chapman. 2012. *Food safety for school and community gardens: A handbook for beginning and veteran garden organizers: How to reduce food safety risks.* NC State Extension, NC State Univ., Raleigh.

Cohen, Whitney. 2010. *Kids' Garden: 40 Fun Indoor and Outdoor Activities and Games.* Cambridge, Massachusetts: Barefoot Books.

Cromwell, C., L. Guy, and L. Bradley. 1996. *Success with school gardens: How to create a learning oasis in the desert.* Arizona Master Gardener Press, Phoenix, AZ.

U.S. Environmental Protection Agency. 2011. *Elder-accessible gardening: A community building option for brownfields redevelopment.* Solid Waste and Emergency Response, U.S. EPA, Washington D.C.

Gooseman, G. 2005. *Money for community gardens.* p. 118–124. In ACGA Community Greening Review, 2004–2005 Special Edition. American Community Gardening Association, College Park, GA.

Kite, L. Patricia. 1995. *Gardening Wizardry for Kids.* Hauppauge, New York: Barron's Educational Series, Inc.

Nashville Public Health Department, Communities Putting Prevention to Work. 2009. Community garden ADA (Americans with Disabilities Act) guidelines: Accessibility guidelines for gardens on metro owned or leased property. Dept. of Health and Human Services, Nashville, TN.

Peters, Elizabeth Tehle and Ellen Kirby, eds. 2008. *Community Gardening.* Brooklyn, New York: Brooklyn Botanic Garden.

Waliczek, T. 1998. *KinderGARDEN: Some basic tips for gardeners working with kids.* Dept. of Horticulture, Texas A&M Univ., College Station.

21

For More Information

http://go.ncsu.edu/fmi_communitygardens

Contributors

Author: Lucy Bradley, Professor and Extension Specialist, Urban Horticulture, NC State University; Director, NC State Extension Master Gardener program

Contributions by Extension Agents: Karen Neill, Danny Lauderdale, Kelly Groves, Colby Griffin, Pam Jones, Tim Mathews, David Goforth

Contributions by Extension Master Gardener Volunteers: Gloria Polakof, Jackie Weedon, Karen Damari, Connie Schultz, Joanne Celinski, Kim Curlee

Content Editor: Kathleen Moore, Urban Horticulturist

Copy Editor: Barbara Scott

Chapter 21 Cover Photo: Kathleen Moore

How to Cite This Chapter:
Bradley, L., 2022. Youth, Community, and Therapeutic Gardening, Chpt 21, In: K. A. Moore, L.K. Bradley (eds), *North Carolina Extension Gardener Handbook,* 2nd ed. NC State Extension, Raleigh, NC. <https://content.ces.ncsu.edu/extension-gardener-handbook/21-youth-community-and-therapeutic-gardening>

Figure 21–21. Gloves provide children some protection from exposure to urban soil contaminants.
Kathleen Moore

Garden Journaling
Garden Journals—A Powerful Tool for Success

Gardening provides exercise, stress relief, enjoyment, beauty, and a satisfaction that continues to grow as plants do. To maximize the benefits, keep a garden journal and record information and observations about plants, weather events, soil conditions, and wildlife encounters. A well-used garden journal is a powerful resource for any gardener.

Garden journals are as varied as the perennials in a garden. They may be a simple hardbound (Figure A–1) or spiral notebook (Figure A–2), recorded on graph paper notebook (Figure A–3), collected in a three-ring binder, or come in scrapbook form. If traditional paper formats do not appeal to you, consider recording data and observations in one of the countless digital formats (Figure A–4, Figure A–5) available online for free or purchase. Selecting a style is a matter of preference, choose a format you are comfortable with and committed to using on a regular basis. By recording information over a long period of time, you will create an invaluable source of information about your yard and garden that will guide you in making any future decisions about plants, problems, or design.

Figure A–3. Graph paper notebook.
Pixabay, SteveRaubenstine CC0

Capturing information about the site, seasonal factors, plants, pests, projects, and expenses will provide the data necessary to make informed decisions and have a successful thriving garden now and in the future.

Figure A–1. A hardbound notebook.
Pixabay, Oldiefan (Christiane) CC0

Figure A–4. Collecting information digitally.
Pexels, Pixabay CC0

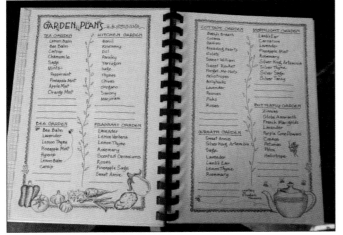

Figure A–2. A spiral notebook.
Kathleen Moore, CC BY - 2.0

Figure A–5.
A digital garden journal.
Karen Damari, EMGV

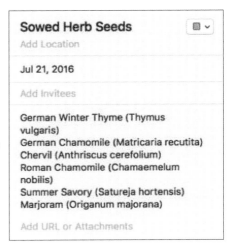

Sowed Herb Seeds

Add Location

Jul 21, 2016

Add Invitees

German Winter Thyme (Thymus vulgaris)
German Chamomile (Matricaria recutita)
Chervil (Anthriscus cerefolium)
Roman Chamomile (Chamaemelum nobilis)
Summer Savory (Satureja hortensis)
Marjoram (Origanum majorana)

Add URL or Attachments

1. Site Characteristics

Understanding site characteristics is critical to selecting plants that will thrive in a specific location. Take time to observe patterns of sun and shade. Identify the time of day the site is in shade and the level of shade (dappled, dense). Notice the direction slopes and swales face. How does wind affect the site? Every location has its own unique microclimate. Making the most of a location's strengths and avoiding known problems will lead to a more successful gardening experience. Recording details about different locations in the garden will serve as a guide for plant replacements, future projects, or expansions.

- Creating a drawing to scale using graph paper (Figure A–6) or a computer software program (Figure A–7) is especially helpful when designing a garden space. Be sure to include the location of all buildings, utilities, hardscapes, and plants. Make the drawing large and detailed enough to recognize plants later. Drawing in pencil allows you to make adjustments if you lose a plant or transplant something.
- Make note of the wet and dry areas of your yard.
- Follow the sun throughout the season noting areas of shade throughout the day. Remember that over time some sunny locations may transition into partial sun or even full shade so be sure to update your maps on a regular basis.
- Documenting all of the plants and hardscape elements in a location helps you to analyze their interactions—are your Carolina rhododendrons (*Rhododendron minus*) struggling under the shade of a pin oak (*Quercus palustris*) tree? Are the roots of your obedient plant (*Physostegia virginiana*) choking out your tulip (*Tulipa* spp.) bulbs? Is that western wall reflecting heat and burning the leaves of your American beautyberry (*Callicarpa americana*) shrub?

- Plants can outgrow their locations. Recording their appearance helps you understand why a plant that once thrived might be suffering now.

Soils

Conduct a soil test when you first begin to garden and every few years thereafter. This information will help you identify plants that will thrive in your specific setting as well as provide recommendations for fertilizers and soil amendments. Keep track of all soil test results in your garden journal. Preparing a table will allow you track changes over time and color-coding the cells makes it easy to decipher. (Table A–1). Note the dramatic increase in copper and zinc in where a huge load of uncertified compost was applied. Remember to document any soil amendments including brand names, nutrient amounts, amount applied, garden location, and dates.

2. Seasonality

Many events like plants blooming, pollinators visiting, or leaves turning color, happen in a cycle in the garden. While we have the best intentions of recalling the details, without writing down the dates and our own reflections, much of this information is lost. By capturing the month, day, year, and time in each journal entry we can create a body of information that allows us to reflect and learn from our triumphs and mistakes.

Information to collect

Weather: Collect environmental data like rainfall, temperature, humidity, day length, cloud cover, frost events, and storm damage. This data allows you to see the effect of the environment on your plants and guide you in plant and pest management decisions.

Keeping track of weather and weather patterns in your area will help you become a more knowledgeable gardener.

Figure A–6. A to-scale landscape drawing.
Amy Rozycki, EMGV

Figure A–7. A landscape design done on the computer.
Pixabay, MALCOLUMBUS (Malcolm Brook) CC0

Table A–1. Organizing Soil Test Results in a Meaningful Way

Scaled Index
deficient ≤50   excess ≥100

Location	Year	pH	Phosphorus	Potassium	Manganese	Sulfur	Zinc
Vegetable garden (raised beds)	2008	6.1	17 D	14 D	131 E	27 D	52 S
	2015	7.5	343 E	190 E	342 E	418 E	1562 *
Berries (side yard)	2008	6.9	33 D	37 D	406 E	25 D	167 E
	2015	7.2	450 E	164 E	240 E	190 E	1451 *
Herbs (main plot—top left)	2008	5.7	0 D	29 D	40 D	115 E	11 D
	2015	6.5	151 E	43 D	165 E	113 E	452 *
Fruit trees (main plot—center)	2008	5.7	0 D	29 D	40 D	115 E	11 D
	2015	7.6	300 E	99 S	275 E	333 E	1212 *
Flower beds (main plot—top right)	2008	5.7	0 D	29 D	40 D	115 E	11 D
	2015	6.2	19 E	48 E	178 E	39 E	161 *
Fruit trees (main plot—bottom right)	2008	5.7	19 D	27 D	109 E	20 D	29 D
	2015	6.3	40 D	40 D	179 E	33 D	223 *
Fruit trees (main plot—bottom left)	2008	5.7	19 D	27 D	109 E	20 D	29 D
	2015	6.2	204 D	65 S	153 E	45 D	586 *

D = Deficient

S = Sufficient

E = Excessive

* = dramatic increase in copper and zinc due to use of uncertified compost

By capturing weather data you can identify if your microclimate typically sees a later than average last frost or gets higher than average temperatures in the summer. This type of data can help you decide when to plant your tender annuals or find a plant that can withstand your high summer temperatures. Table A–2 is an example of gathering weather data like maximum, minimum, and mean temperatures, precipitation, cooling, and heating hours, along with historical climate data.

Chores: Develop a calendar either on paper (Figure A–8) or digitally (Figure A–9) with a seasonal chore lists of typical garden work like planting, fertilizing, pruning, deadheading, seed collection, weeding, mulching, and pest management. Creating a seasonal chore list spreads garden work throughout the year and allows for planning of future tasks. Winter may be a quiet time in the garden but it is the perfect season for planning and researching the next garden project. Spring is a very busy time in the garden so moving the construction of a tool shed to the fall might be a better use of your growing season. If you find useful information or a new technique in a book, on a website, or from a fellow gardener, make a reminder in your journal to try this new technique when the season permits.

Figure A–8. A hard copy calendar.
Pixabay, stevepb (Steve Buissinne) CC0

PLANT
Add Location

Jan 1, 2017
Repeats Yearly

Add Invitees

Onion, Pea,

Add URL or Attachments

Figure A–9.
A digital calendar
reminder.
Karen Damari, EMGV

Seasonal Plant Characteristics: Having color and interest every season provides enjoyment year-round. A simple list of the months and which plants are blooming will show you where you may have holes in your landscape. If drawing on graph paper, consider using transparent sheets over your main map to indicate how the plants and landscape change through each of the four seasons. Notice plant features including attractiveness to wildlife, edibility, fragrance, and leaf and bark color. Recording the location of plants that go seasonally dormant allows you to recognize bare areas and plan for year-round interest.

3. Plants

Getting to know the plants in your yard or garden and their individual requirements will help you identify where they will thrive and allow you to follow the popular gardening mantra "the right plant in the right place." Plants arrive in your garden from a variety of locations, whether they are volunteers that germinate unexpectedly from the soil, divisions from a generous neighbor, seeds shared by a friend, or pots purchased from a local nursery. Some plants may have plant tags with a great deal of information like Latin and common names, sun preferences, bloom times, and watering requirements, while mystery plants, with no tags,

Table A–2. Climate at Raleigh State University 1971–2000													
	Jan	**Feb**	**Mar**	**Apr**	**May**	**June**	**Jul**	**Aug**	**Sept**	**Oct**	**Nov**	**Dec**	**Ann.**
Normal Monthly Maximum Temperature	48.8° F	53° F	61.2° F	70.6° F	77.5° F	84.4° F	87.9° F	85.9° F	80° F	69.8° F	61.3° F	52.1° F	69.4° F
Normal Monthly Minimum Temperature	30.1° F	32.3° F	39.8° F	47.8° F	56.7° F	65° F	69.4° F	68.1° F	61.9° F	49.4° F	41.6° F	33.5° F	49.6° F
Normal Monthly Mean Temperatures	39.5° F	42.7° F	50.5° F	59.2° F	67.1° F	74.7° F	78.7° F	77° F	71° F	59.6° F	51.5° F	42.8° F	59.5° F
Normal Monthly Precipitation	4.46 in.	3.53 in.	4.46 in.	2.98 in.	4.03 in.	4.06 in.	4.35 in.	4.3 in.	4.27 in.	3.78 in.	3.06 in.	3.21 in.	46.4 in.
Normal Cooling Degree Days	0	0	2	17	114	295	422	371	189	41	5	0	1456
Normal Heating Degree Days	792	626	450	191	49	4	0	0	11	207	412	689	3431
Highest Mean Temperature	48.7° F	50.2° F	55° F	65.1° F	71.9° F	79.2° F	82.6° F	80.5° F	74.7° F	66.7° F	60° F	50° F	82.6° F
Median Monthly Mean Temperature	38.6° F	42.5° F	50.6° F	59.1° F	66.8° F	75.4° F	78.4° F	77° F	71.1° F	59.7° F	51.6° F	42.6° F	59.4° F
Lowest Mean Temperature	27.9° F	33.6° F	45.6° F	55.6° F	63.3° F	70.5° F	75.7° F	74.1° F	68.3° F	54.3° F	44° F	33.7° F	27.9° F
Year of Highest Mean Temperature	1974	1990	1997	1985	1991	1981	1986	1988	1980	1984	1985	1971	1986
Year of Lowest Mean Temperature	1977	1978	1996	1983	1992	1979	2000	1992	1974	1976	1976	1989	1977
Source: State Climate Office of North Carolina													

must grow large enough to produce identifying features such as mature leaves or flowers before you can look up their descriptions. Keeping records of where plants are obtained, the cost, any information from the label, or gathered from books or the internet, is an important part of any garden journal.

Plant Profiles

Creating plant profiles for an individual plant or family of plants will assist you in becoming more familiar with the plants in your yard. Plant profiles include:

1. Latin and common names as well as plant family to help with crop rotation or in the case of pests or diseases. You may want to include a pronunciation guide.
2. Information about where the plant was purchased or found and its cost.
3. The date it was planted.
4. Its expected mature height and width.
5. Your observations about the plant, its foliage, flowers, fragrance, color.
6. Any known or observed problems.
7. Activities around the plant such as pruning, fertilizing, or pest management, and the date completed.

Images

Continually capture various images of your garden from many angles and throughout the seasons. Images can be photographs or illustrations if you are artistic. These images will not only assist in identifying plants but also gives you a reference for observing how plants change through the seasons and the years. Remember to take "before" photos of the landscape as well as "in progress" photos. Capture both macro photos of plant details as well as large scale landscape photos. Taking photos of plant labels and seed packets is another way to record data without manually entering it into your journal.

Creating pressed plant specimens (Figure A–10) as part of your plant profile is an alternative to photographs or drawings and helps you become more familiar with your plants. Pressed, dried plants allow you to study their leaf, stem, and flower structures and give you a reference point even when the plants are dormant.

Harvests

Keeping track of fruit, vegetable, or nut harvests will help you plan for future crops.

Collecting and storing seeds is a fun hobby that helps make gardening more economical. Keeping track of which seeds are stored, dates of storage, and information about germination rates helps you get the most out of your seed bank.

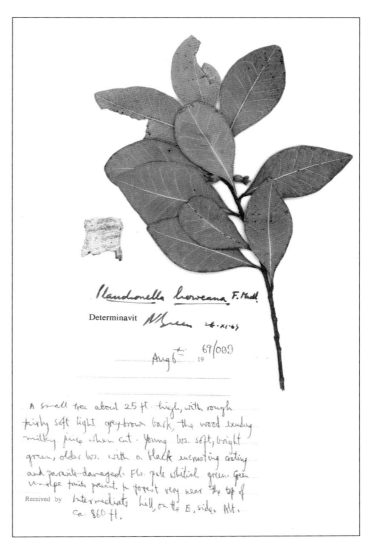

Figure A–10. A pressed plant specimen.
John Game, CC BY - 2.0

4. Pests

While good management practices minimize the presence of pests and pathogens in a garden, every gardener inevitably encounters them. "Scouting," or regularly examining plants including the bark, under the leaves, and around the soil helps with early identification of problems. Creating detailed records assists with the proper identification of the pest and proper management strategies. Read more in chapter 8, "IPM."

1. **Plant:** Record the plant description, symptoms, and signs.
2. **Environment:** Capture the location, season, and weather when the problem occurred.
3. **Pest:** Accurately identify the insect, disease or animal that is causing a problem.
4. **Action Taken:** Describe cultural, mechanical, biological, and chemical management strategies.
5. **Results:** Document any outcomes.

5. Projects

Having an area of your journal dedicated to special garden projects will not only help you keep to your budget and deadlines but will help you avoid repeating mistakes. Capture information including start and stop dates, supply lists, contact phone numbers and sources, any obstacles encountered, and notes about how they were overcome. Leave room to make detailed drawings of any building projects (Figure A–11) so you can take your journal with you when you pick up materials.

6. Expenses

Budgeting and keeping track of expenses is an important part of any garden project. Tracking the date purchased, quantity, source, item information, and evaluation of the product will help you evaluate successes and failures and assist in making better purchases over time. Photographing products and price labels is a quick and easy way to capture a lot of information that saves you time when it comes to entering budget information.

7. Tips

- Creating a space in your journal for simple observations is a great way to form connections and help you identify patterns in your garden. "I saw" pages help you record creatures, plants, people, relationships, connections, symptoms, and signs.

- Leave room for jotting down questions or tips learned from other gardeners.
- No matter how much we pamper our plants, there will always be casualties. Record the plant name, the circumstances under which it died, and any recommendations for next time.
- Consider including some fun elements in your journal, like envelopes for collecting specimens, gluing in old seed packets or product labels, and pasting in photos or illustrations from magazines or books.
- Using clear page protectors prevents wear and tear, and adding tabs to your journal helps you quickly locate the section you are looking for.
- Drawing conclusions from observations and data collection is an important part of your garden journal. Making notes about what worked or did not work guides future decisions.

Summary

No matter what format your garden journal takes—from a three-ring binder to an app on your phone or tablet—the simple process of observing and recording will provide you with invaluable information to guide you in creating the garden of your dreams.

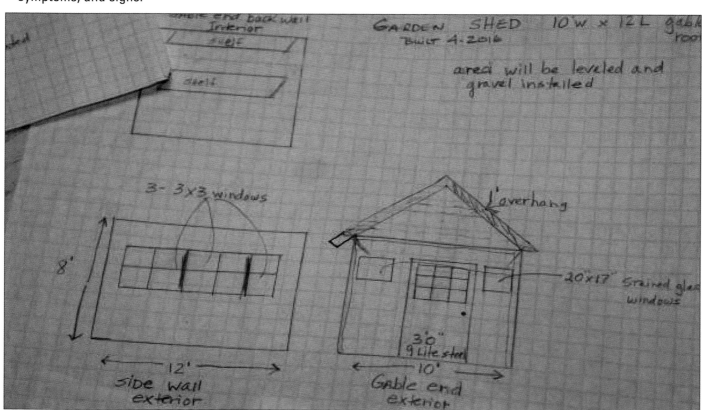

Figure A–11. A detailed drawing of a garden shed project.
Amy Rozycki, EMGV

Contributors

Authors: Lucy Bradley, Professor and Extension Specialist, Urban Horticulture, NC State University; Director, NC State Extension Master Gardener program
Kathleen Moore, Urban Horticulturist

Contributions by Extension Master Gardener Volunteers: Lise Jenkins, Sandy Ritter, Chris Alberti, L. Amy Rozycki, Jackie Weedon, Karen Damari, Jayne Boyer

Content Editors: Lucy Bradley, Professor and Extension Specialist, Urban Horticulture, NC State University; Director, NC State Extension Master Gardener program
Kathleen Moore, Urban Horticulturist

Graphic Design: Premila Jayaratne

Copy Editor: Barbara Scott

Plant Selection for Year Round Interest

Plant Name Botanical/Common	Winter Wildlife	Winter Edible	Winter Color	Winter Fragrant	Spring Wildlife	Spring Edible	Spring Color	Spring Fragrant	Summer Wildlife	Summer Edible	Summer Color	Summer Fragrant	Fall Wildlife	Fall Edible	Fall Color	Fall Fragrant
Trees																
Shrubs																
Groundcovers																
Perennials																

Gardening Expenses

Garden Location: _____ Season(s): _____ Year(s): _____

Item Description Brand Name & Where Purchased	Date	Notes (Strengths, Weaknesses, Rating)	Price $	Quantity	Total Spent

Grand Total:

A-8

Harvest Record

Plant: _____

Date Harvested	Quantity	Weight	Quality	Notes
Total				

Individual Plant Profile

Common Name(s) _____
Botanical Name _____ Family _____

Date Planted _____ Location _____ Exposure _____

Flower Color _____ Leaf Color _____ Mature Height _____ Width _____

Known Potential Problems/Symptoms
_____
_____
_____

Management Recommendations
_____
_____
_____
_____

Soil Preference
_____

Propagation Method
_____

Harvest Guidelines
_____

Pollinators/Wildlife Potential
_____
_____

Dated Photographs & Sketches

Notes _____

NC STATE
EXTENSION

Garden Projects

Task	Start Date	Notes, Contacts, Sources, Descriptions, Obstacles	Budget	Completion Date
Description:				
Steps 1.				
2.				
3.				
4.				
5.				
Description:				
Steps 1.				
2.				
3.				
4.				
5.				
Description:				
Steps 1.				
2.				
3.				
4.				
5.				

NC STATE

EXTENSION

What's Blooming in the Garden

DATE	*(trees, shrubs, bulbs, perennials, annuals, herbs, groundcovers)*
January	
February	
March	
April	
May	
June	
July	
August	
September	
October	
November	
December	

Pesticides and Pesticide Safety

Introduction

This appendix provides information on selecting the proper pesticides and using them safely, effectively, and legally. The inclusion of any pesticide name is for educational purposes and does not imply an endorsement of that product. We do not attempt to give specific chemical recommendations, but we do summarize basic concepts and principles for gardeners to use when considering the use of pesticides.

Pesticides are substances or mixtures of substances used to manage pests. The suffix "cide" means to kill, and "pest" refers to an unwanted living organism. Pesticides include **herbicides**, **insecticides**, **fungicides**, **miticides**, **nematicides**, and other such formulations. The first syllable of each word for these pesticide types indicates the intended target. For example, insecticides kill insects, herbicides kill weeds, and rodenticides kill rodents. Pesticides can also kill nontarget organisms. For example, some insecticides can kill earthworms, fish, or plants when misused. Some types of pesticides don't have the "cide" suffix. Examples include repellents and pheromones.

Safe handling of pesticides involves a combination of knowledge, common sense, and the ability to read and follow directions. Misuse of pesticides can result in poisoning of the gardener, family members, neighbors, pets, and/or the environment. Pesticides should only be applied as part of a comprehensive integrated pest management (IPM) program.

Read more about IPM in chapter 8. Before applying any pesticide, answer several questions:

- Which pests or pest problems exist?
- Is the problem the result of an unfavorable environment?
- Can the problem be corrected using other methods?
- Which pesticide will effectively manage the pest, will cause the least damage to **beneficial insects** and the environment, and will be least hazardous for the applicator to use? Have you considered runoff potential, chances of **leaching** into groundwater, chemical half-life(how rapidly it degrades), and toxicity to nontarget organisms?
- When and how much pesticide should be applied?

Many home gardeners do not know the answers to these questions. As a consequence, some gardeners may make too many pesticide applications or apply the wrong material at the wrong time, in the wrong manner, and in the wrong amount. In addition to wasting money and time, improper pesticide use can endanger the environment by killing beneficial insects, poisoning wildlife, and contaminating soil, water, and air. Problems such as these have led to many new regulations, including banned use and

General Pesticide Safety Guidelines

1. Use pesticides as part of an IPM program.
2. Follow label directions.
3. Wear protective clothing while using pesticides.
4. Do not eat, drink, or use tobacco while using pesticides.
5. Store pesticides in a secure location, in the original container, and away from food, feed, or fuel.
6. Dispose of empty pesticide containers properly.
7. Do not mix more than you can apply at one time.
8. Use the proper pesticide application equipment.
9. Be alert for pesticide poisoning, and seek help if symptoms appear.

Types of Pesticides

One way that pesticides are grouped is their chemical nature. In chemistry, "organic" refers to carbon-based molecules. This is different than the way "organic" is commonly defined by gardeners and by the National Organic Standards Board. In other words, organic as a production method has nothing to do with organic as a chemical term. The most common pesticide groups are inorganics, plant-derived organics, microbials, and synthetic organics. Additional pesticides include horticultural oils, soaps, and byproducts.

Inorganic Pesticides
These pesticides are made from minerals such as arsenic, copper, boron, lead, sulfur, tin, and zinc. Copper and sulfur are commonly available in garden supply shops.

Plant-Derived Organic Pesticides
These pesticides consist of natural compounds that come directly from plants. A common example is pyrethrum, which is made from the flowers of some Chrysanthemum species. Other plant-derived products include neem, nicotine, and red squill. Be careful with all pesticides; natural products can be as toxic to humans and other organisms, or even more toxic, than some man-made pesticides.

Microbial Pesticides
These pesticides consist of microscopic organisms—including bacteria, fungi, nematodes, and viruses—that attack pests. Most of these can be applied with conventional application equipment. A few microbial insecticides multiply and spread after application and may become established in the garden or lawn, but most of them require repeated applications to be effective. The most commonly encountered microbial pesticide is the bacterium *Bacillus thuringiensis* (Bt), which is often applied to control caterpillars. Bt does not spread after application, whereas *Paenibacillus popilliae*, used to manage Japanese beetle grubs, can. In general, microbial pesticides are less toxic than other pesticides for gardeners, beneficial insects, and the environment.

Synthetic Organics
Synthetic organics, those that are man-made, are the largest group of pesticides used by gardeners and farmers. An example is permethrin which is a synthetic compound similar to the plant-derived pyrethrum.

Some Pesticide Definitions
Contact pesticides kill pests that touch them. Most synthetic organic pesticides work in this manner. Insects are affected simply by walking across a treated surface.

Fumigants are gaseous pesticides that kill the pest when it inhales or absorbs the chemical. Fumigants are toxic to people and animals.

Nonselective pesticides are toxic to the targeted pest and many other plants or animals. Most synthetic organic insecticides are nonselective. For example, a pesticide containing carbaryl can be used to kill Colorado potato beetles, but it also kills bees and many other types of insects. Herbicides containing the **active ingredient** glyphosate kill nearly any type of plant. Gardeners must exercise extreme caution when using nonselective pesticides and always follow labeled instructions.

Protectants are applied to plants, animals, structures, and products to prevent entry or damage by a pest. To prevent termite damage, for example, termiticides are typically applied to the soil surrounding a building before termites are discovered.

Selective pesticides are more toxic to some kinds of plants or animals than to others. For example, a broadleaf herbicide kills **dicot** weeds but not grasses. Microbial pesticides often affect specific species of insects.

Stomach poisons must be eaten by the pest to be effective. They are generally effective if you are trying to encourage beneficial insects that do not feed on the sort of plant you have treated. Some stomach poisons, however, can also kill by contact.

Systemic pesticides are soluble in water and can be absorbed by a plant and transferred through some, or all of, the plant's tissues, including its leaves, stems, roots, flowers, nectar, and pollen. The pesticide then poisons any insects that feed on the plant. Neonicotinoids are nicotine-based systemic insecticides.

Pesticide Formulations

The mixture of active and inert ingredients included in a product is called a pesticide formulation. The active ingredient in a pesticide product is the substance that actually controls the pests. Inert ingredients, also known as "inactive" or "other" ingredients, may make the active ingredient easier to mix with water, safer to handle or apply, or allow the pesticide to be applied with various types of equipment. Inert ingredients are regulated to a limited degree but can also pose a hazard to the person applying the pesticide or to plants. Formulations may be liquid, gaseous, or solid. Some formulations are ready-to-use, and others must be diluted with water. Many pesticides are available in more than one formulation.

Liquid-type Formulations

Solutions are pesticides containing active ingredients that dissolve readily in liquid, such as water or a petroleum-based solvent.

Aerosol pesticides consist of liquids that contain active ingredients in solution or emulsion. The liquid solution or emulsion forms fine droplets when driven through a small nozzle by a pressurized gas. Aerosols often contain more than one active ingredient in low concentrations. Many aerosols come in disposable dispensers. Aerosols are most frequently used indoors, but a few are sold for outdoor use. Based on the amount of active ingredient, ready-to-use aerosols are typically expensive in comparison to other ways to purchase pesticides.

Dry Formulations

- **Dusts** are typically ready-to-use and combine the active ingredients with a dry inert material, such as talc, clay, nut hulls, or volcanic ash. The amount of active ingredients usually ranges from 1% to 10%. Some active ingredients are formulated as dusts because they are safer for crops in that form. Although they resemble wettable powders, dusts must always be used dry. Dusts drift easily; be careful not to let the chemical drift into nontarget areas, and wear goggles and a dust mask to avoid inhalation. Dusts leave visible residues that may be objectionable in some situations.
- **Wettable powders** are dry, finely ground pesticide formulations that look very similar to dusts. Unlike dusts, however, they are made to mix with water and are applied with a sprayer. Most wettable powders are more concentrated than dusts. They contain 15% to 95% active ingredient and often include 50% or more active ingredient. Because wettable powders form a suspension in water rather than a true solution, good agitation (shaking) is needed in the spray tank. Most wettable powders are less toxic to plants and people, but they leave a visible residue that may be objectionable in some situations.
- **Granules and pellets** are created in the factory by applying a liquid formulation of the active ingredient to coarse particles (granules) of some porous material, such as clay, corn cobs, or walnut shells. The pesticide is absorbed into the granule or coats the outside of it, or both. Granule particles are larger than dusts. The amount of active ingredient ranges from 2% to 15%. Granular formulations are less likely to drift than sprays or dusts. Many types of granules, however, can present hazards to birds. Granular formulations are most often used as soil treatments, and they may be applied either directly to the soil or over plants. They do not cling to plant foliage but may be trapped in the whorls (spiral growth) of some plants. With the exception of water dispersible granules, granular formulations should never be mixed with water. Some granules may need rain or irrigation after application for activation of the pesticide. Pellet formulations are very similar to granular formulations, except that particles are generally larger and have a consistent size and shape.
- **Baits** are edible or attractant substances mixed with a pesticide. The bait attracts pests, and the pesticide kills them after they eat the formulation. Baits are commonly used to control slugs, snails, rodents, ants, and some other insects. The amount of active ingredient in most bait formulations is less than 5%. Nontarget animals should be restricted from any area where bait traps are set. Baits are often put in bait stations to prevent access by all but the target pest. Household pets, squirrels, and chipmunks will eat bait designed for rats and mice. Dogs and cats are also attracted to slug bait.

To determine the best buy, look at both the concentration and quantity of active ingredient. A formulation with 10% active ingredient has twice the concentration as one containing 5% active ingredient. A frequent error that most home gardeners make is to purchase too much product. Do not purchase more than that needed in one season. Some pesticide products deteriorate with time. Excess products can create safety problems in storage and disposal.

Pesticides may be combined with other products. Weed-and-feed fertilizers are classified as pesticides. They are mixtures with relatively small concentrations of pesticides (herbicides) added to a fertilizer. Many pesticides are available in more than one formulation.

Landscape fabrics can be impregnated with pesticides, or pesticides can be sprayed on mulch. Check the labeling (the label and any pamphlets that come with the product) to find out what pesticide has been added and how to use the product.

Adjuvants

An **adjuvant** is a chemical already added to the pesticide formulation or spray mixture to increase its effectiveness or safety. A suspension agent added to a spray solution helps mix oil and water so they can be sprayed on plant surfaces. Some of the most common adjuvants are **surfactants** that alter the dispersing, spreading, and wetting properties of spray droplets. Examples of adjuvants include the following:

- **Wetting agents** enable wettable powders to be mixed with water.
- **Emulsifiers** enable petroleum-based pesticides to be mixed with water.
- **Spreaders** enable pesticides to form a uniform coating over the treated surface by reducing the surface tension of the spray droplets.
- **Stickers** improve the pesticide's ability to adhere to plant surfaces. Some stickers protect the spray from the effects of wind and rain, thus extending the active life of the pesticide. Most fungicides benefit from the use of stickers.

Making Pest Control Decisions

Adopt an IPM method that prevents or manages a problem using the most effective, environmentally friendly, and economical control measure(s). Research confirms that cultural, mechanical, physical, biological, and chemical management techniques exist for most pest problems. Begin with mechanical, physical, cultural, and biological management techniques, which are generally more cost-effective and environmentally friendly. Quick-acting chemical treatments, with the exception of some emergency fungicide treatments, should not be treated as a substitute for sound gardening practices.

When pesticides are applied is as important as what is applied. Review information for the best time of day, time of year, or point in a pest's life cycle for treatment. Read the label. Remember it is illegal to use or recommend the use of a product in a manner, rate, or on plants inconsistent with the label. Do not use pesticides on a fruit or vegetable plant unless the pesticide is specifically labeled for use on that crop or is labeled for use on all fruits and vegetables. Be sure to review the label to identify the safe minimum interval between spraying and harvest.

Labels and Labeling

The "label" refers to the printed information on or attached to the pesticide container (Figure B–1). Often there is more information available than will fit on the product package. The term "labeling" includes the label plus all information that is received from the company or its agents about the product. This includes supplemental brochures or flyers that accompany the product. Following the directions on the label is required by law.

Figure B–1. A pesticide label.
Chris Alberti, CC BY - 2.0

Pesticide labeling can be complicated, but it is important to understand the directions and precautions to use the product safely and correctly. Read the labeling with each purchase of a pesticide product. Instructions, precautions, and restrictions may have changed since the last time the product was used. Certain information must appear on the pesticide labeling. Items required are listed here and described in the sections that follow:

- Brand name, type of pesticide, and formulation
- EPA registration and establishment number
- Ingredient statement
- **Signal words** and symbols
- Hazards to humans and domestic animals
- Environmental hazards
- Physical or chemical hazards
- First Aid
- Directions for use
- Waiting period (if any)

- Preparation instructions and directions for use
- Protective clothing needed (Figure B–2).
- Storage and disposal
- Name and address of manufacturer

Figure B–2.
Pesticide label personal protective equipment.
Chris Alberti, CC BY - 2.0

Brand Names

Each company has a brand name for each of its products. The brand name is used in advertising; it appears plainly on the front panel of the label. Most companies register each brand name as a trademark and do not allow other companies to use that name. Manufacturing brand names are sometimes useful but can also be deceptive in identifying the active ingredient. For example, Liquid Sevin® refers to the active ingredient carbaryl. Sevin® is the manufacturer's name for carbaryl. Brand names such as Black Flag Ant and Roach Killer® or Ortho Flying Insect Spray® are not associated with a particular active ingredient. In other words, the U.S. EPA does not register products by brand name.

Type of Pesticide and Formulation

The type of pesticide is usually listed on the front panel of the pesticide label. This short statement indicates in general terms what the product controls.
Examples:
1. Insecticide for control of certain insects on fruit, nuts, and ornamentals.
2. Herbicide for the control of woody brush and weeds.

Some labels will also indicate the product formulation. The formulation may be named or abbreviated.

Ingredient Statement

Every pesticide label must list the active ingredients and the percentage of each active ingredient found in that product. Inert ingredients are not usually named, but the label must show what percentage of the total contents they make up. The ingredient statement must list the

official chemical names or chemical names of the active ingredients.

The chemical name identifies the chemical components and structure of the pesticide's active ingredient. Because chemical names are usually complex, many are given a shorter common name. Only those common names officially accepted by the EPA may be used in the ingredient statement on the pesticide label. The EPA requires that a particular common name be associated with a specific active ingredient. The official common name is usually followed by the chemical name in the list of active ingredients. Purchase pesticides according to the common or chemical names to be certain of getting the right active ingredient, no matter what the brand name or formulation.

EPA Registration Number and Establishment Number

An EPA registration number must appear on all pesticide labels (except minimum risk Section 25(b) products). This number indicates the pesticide product has been registered and its label approved by the EPA.

An EPA establishment number (for example, EPA Est. No. 122-NC-2) must also appear either on the pesticide label or container to identify the facility that produced the product. This is necessary if a problem arises or the product is found to be adulterated in any way. The "NC" in the establishment number indicates the product was manufactured in a specific facility in North Carolina.

Signal Words and Symbols (Table B-1)

The signal word and symbol on the pesticide labeling tells how toxic the pesticide is to humans. It is important to become familiar with the meaning of signal words and symbols.

Scientists determine the dosages that will cause death of laboratory animals when swallowed, when applied to the skin, or when inhaled, as well as levels that will cause irritation to the skin or eyes. The exposure route by which the product is graded the most toxic to humans will determine the signal word that must appear on the label. Additionally, the labeling of all highly toxic materials usually carries a skull and crossbones, along with the words "Danger" and "Poison". These products are rarely available to consumers.

The amount of pesticide that will injure or kill a pet or a child may be much less than the amount that will injure or kill an adult. All products must bear the following statement: "Keep out of reach of children."

Table B–1. Signal Words and Their Level of Toxicity

Signal Word	Toxicity	LD50[a]	Approximate Amount Which, When Swallowed, Will Kill the Average-Sized Adult
Danger - POISON	Indicates extremely toxic compounds when consumed, inhaled or absorbed through the skin or eyes. (Label must have skull and crossbones symbol.) Fatal at very low doses.		
Danger	Highly toxic	Up to and including 50mg/kg	A taste to a teaspoon
Warning	Moderately toxic	50–500mg/kg	A teaspoon to two tablespoons
Caution[b]	Slightly toxic	>500mg/kg	An ounce to more than a pint

a **LD50 is the approximate amount, which when swallowed will kill 50% of the animals tested.**

b **There is an additional category less toxic than Caution. No signal words are required on pesticide products which are determined by the EPA to be exempt or minimum risk. These are generally regarded as safe.**

Precautionary Statements

Hazards to humans (and domestic animals). This section of the label indicates the ways in which the product may be poisonous to people and animals. It will contain statements such as these: "Harmful if absorbed through the skin," or "Avoid contact with skin or eyes." The label will also specify any special precautions that the user needs to take, such as the kind of protective clothing recommended.

Environmental hazards. Some pesticides are particularly hazardous to bees, fish, birds, or other wildlife. This portion of the labeling warns of environmental damage that may be caused by the pesticide. Examples include the following warnings: "Do not apply when runoff is likely to occur." "Do not apply when bees are active."

Physical and chemical hazards. Certain pesticide formulations may be flammable, explosive, or present special chemical risks. Common statements in this section are "Keep away from heat, sparks, or open flame," or "Do not incinerate."

First Aid (Figure B–3). If a pesticide can be harmful, this segment of the labeling provides instructions for first aid. It will also advise when medical attention is necessary in case of exposure to the pesticide. Always consult the label before administering first aid to poison victims because the wrong first aid measures can cause additional injury. This section of the label may also instruct

physicians on how to treat poison victims. If a poison victim needs to be taken to a hospital, always take the pesticide label.

Directions for Use

To use any pesticide product safely and effectively, follow the pesticide instructions or directions for use (Figure B–4). This section of the label will include a reminder that it is a violation of federal law to use or recommend the use of a pesticide in a manner inconsistent with the labeling. The directions for use will include the following information:

• Pests that the product can be used to control. It is illegal to apply the pesticide to pests not listed on the label.

• The crop, animal, or other sites for which the product is registered. It is illegal to apply pesticides to sites not listed on the label.

Figure B–3. Pesticide label first aid.
Chris Alberti, CC BY - 2.0

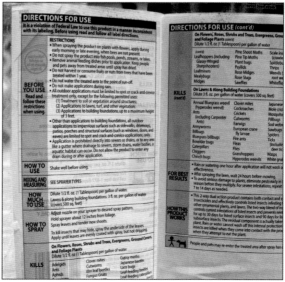

Figure B–4. Pesticide label directions for use.
Chris Alberti, CC BY - 2.0

- How to mix the pesticide and how much to apply. It is illegal to apply a pesticide at greater than the labeled rate.
- Application below the labeled rate is allowed but may not provide effective control.
- How to apply the pesticide, including when and where to apply. Pesticides must not be applied in a manner contrary to these instructions.
- How often to apply. Pesticides may not be applied more often than the label allows.

Most pesticides packaged for home use will indicate how many level teaspoons or tablespoons of pesticide are needed per gallon of water. Some labels may indicate how many ounces of pesticide are needed per gallon of water. Those labels will also state that 1 fluid ounce equals 2 tablespoons.

Waiting Period

Read the label to see how long people and pets should be kept out of the treated area (the re-entry interval or REI). If no time is listed, keep people and pets away at least until the sprays have thoroughly dried. If the pesticide was applied to a food crop, check the label to see how long to wait before harvesting (the pre-harvest interval or PHI); this is the time required for the residue to degrade to safe levels for consumption.

Equipment

Select the right equipment, use it correctly, and maintain it properly.

Compressed air sprayers (Figure B–5). Compressed air sprayers are inexpensive and simple to operate, but the sprayer needs to be shaken regularly to provide agitation. Look for a tank with a large opening; it will be easy to fill and clean. Sprayers come in several sizes from 1 quart to 5 gallons; buy the size most appropriate for specific needs. Sprayers can be made of plastic, stainless steel, or galvanized metal. Galvanized metal sprayers have to be cleaned carefully or they will corrode.

Fill the tank not more than three-quarters full of spray material. This leaves an air space at the top for building up air pressure with the pump.

Figure B–5. A compressed air sprayer.
Chris Alberti, CC BY - 2.0

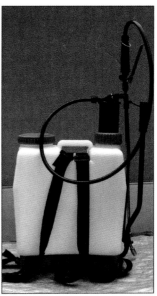

Figure B–6.
A backpack sprayer.
Chris Alberti, CC BY - 2.0

Compressed air sprayers are easy to understand, and most homeowners can repair them. Look for replacement parts at local garden supply stores. Use caution when opening the sprayer if any pressure remains in the tank. After each use, flush out the tank, lines, and nozzles. Wash out the sprayer with detergent and water when switching pesticides to avoid contamination. Make sure to wear protective clothing when using a compressed air sprayer.

Phenoxy herbicides, such as 2,4-D, are active in very low concentrations; residues that remain in the tank even after cleaning can still injure plants. It is best not to apply other pesticides with a sprayer that has been used with phenoxy herbicides. One strategy is to have a separate sprayer for herbicides and another one for insecticides and fungicides.

Backpack sprayers (Figure B–6). These are compressed air sprayers that are carried as a backpack. The capacity of these sprayers is usually 3 gallons to 4 gallons. All models have a built in spray pump handle that makes it easier to maintain good pressure while spraying. Some disadvantages of backpack sprayers are (1) they require more care about leaks because the sprayers rest on the body, and (2) they cost more than other sprayers. As a result, backpack sprayers usually are not practical unless a large area is to be sprayed. Make sure to wear protective clothing when using a backpack sprayer.

Hose-end sprayers (Figure B–7). These are small, inexpensive sprayers designed to be attached to a garden hose. A small amount of pesticide is mixed with water and placed in the container attached to the hose. All hose-end sprayers should be equipped with an anti-siphon device to prevent backsiphoning of toxic materials into the water supply.

Figure B–7.
A hose-end sprayer.
Chris Alberti, CC BY - 2.0

Problems can result from poor spray distribution and clogged nozzles. Also, the pesticide-water mixture can be inaccurate because it is determined by water pressure. In general, hose-end sprayers are not encouraged because of their inaccurate application rate and the likelihood of chemicals being applied in areas where they are not needed. Make sure to wear protective clothing when using a hose-end sprayer.

Figure B–8. A hand duster.
Kathleen Moore, CC BY - 2.0 (left) and Wayne Buhler (right)

Hand dusters (Figure B–8). Hand dusters may be as simple as a shaker can or may include a squeeze bulb, bellows, or a fan turned by a hand crank. Pesticides applied as dusts require no mixing, and dusts penetrate well into tight spaces. It is difficult, however, to obtain good coverage of foliage, and the dust drifts with a slight breeze. Make sure to wear protective clothing, including a face mask, when using a hand duster.

Granular applicators (Figure B–9). For home use, granular applicators usually consist of a shaker can for small areas or a spinning disk powered by a hand crank, or the wheels on a push spreader, for broadcast applications. Granular formulations are ready-to-use, do not drift as easily as some powder formulations, and are relatively

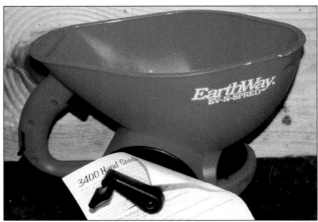

Figure B–9. A granular applicator.
Chris Alberti, CC BY - 2.0

easy to use. Make sure to wear protective clothing when using a granular applicator.

Personal Protective Equipment

Body covering (Figure B–10). Wear at least a long-sleeved shirt and long trousers or coveralls and socks and shoes or boots when applying pesticides. The clothes should be made of closely woven fabric . Do not wear leather clothing because leather tends to absorb and retain pesticides. Wear trousers outside boots to keep pesticides from getting inside.

Figure B–10.
A protective smock made of tightly woven fabric.
Chris Alberti, CC BY - 2.0

Gloves (Figure B–11). Most pesticide exposure occurs through the hands and forearms. Hot, sweaty skin with cuts or abrasions allows more rapid penetration. When handling concentrated or highly toxic pesticides, wear liquid-proof, chemical resistant, neoprene gloves that are long enough to protect the wrists. Unlined gloves are preferred. Unless spray is being directed upward, wear sleeves outside of the gloves to keep pesticides from running down the sleeves and into the gloves. Glove lining is hard to clean if a chemical gets on it. If spray is being directed upward, the sleeves should be inside the gloves to prevent pesticides from running into the sleeves.

Figure B–11. Long gloves protect the hands and arms from pesticide exposure.
Chris Alberti, CC BY - 2.0

Labels are constantly updated with new safety information. Older labels do not always mention the use of gloves and goggles when mixing and applying pesticides.

Goggles (Figure B–12). Eyes readily absorb and are very sensitive to the chemicals in some pesticide formulations, especially concentrates. Wear shielded safety glasses or goggles when mixing pesticides or spraying pesticides upward. Older labels do not always mention the use of gloves and goggles when mixing and applying pesticides. Use gloves and goggles anyway to be safe.

Figure B–12. Tight-fitting goggles protect the eyes from pesticide overspray. Chris Alberti, CC BY - 2.0

Shoes (Figure B–13). Wear liquid-proof boots or cover shoes with liquid-proof material. Leather and cloth absorb pesticides, and both leather and cloth are very difficult to clean.

Figure B–13. Waterproof protective shoes. Kathleen Moore, CC BY - 2.0

Preparation and Application

Mixing is usually considered the most dangerous pesticide activity because mixing involves working with concentrated material. Be sure to wear gloves and safety glasses. Never eat, drink, or use tobacco while handling pesticides.

Before mixing a pesticide, always read the labeling. Inspect the sprayer, duster, or spreader to see that it is functioning properly. There should be no loose or leaking hoses or connections. The cover gasket on a sprayer should fit securely. Partially fill the sprayer with water, and test it to make sure that the nozzles are not clogged. Make sure there are no leaks and that the tank holds pressure.

When preparing a wettable powder for spraying in a compressed air or pump-type applicator, place the required rate of pesticide into a quart jar half filled with water and mix well. Pesticides that contain surfactants (spreader-stickers, wetting agents) make mixing easier by helping to maintain the homogeneity of the mixture.

Table B–2. Conversion Table for Use of Pesticides on Small Areas

| Liquid Materials Approximate Rate | | |
per Acre	per 1,000 Square Feet	per 100 Square Feet
1 pint	2¼ teaspoons	¼ teaspoon
1 quart	4½ teaspoons	½ teaspoon
2 quarts	3 tablespoons	1 teaspoon
1 gallon	6 tablespoons	1¾ teaspoons
25 gallons	4⅔ pints	14⅔ tablespoons
50 gallons	9¼ pints	1⅞ cups
100 gallons	9¼ quarts	3⅔ cups
200 gallons	18⅓ quarts	7⅓ cups
300 gallons	27½ quarts	5½ pints
400 gallons	9¼ gallons	7⅓ pints
500 gallons	11½ gallons	9¼ pints

| Dry Materials Approximate Rate | | |
per Acre	per 1,000 Square Feet	per 100 Square Feet
1 pound	0.37 ounce 10.41 grams	0.037 ounce 1.04 grams
2 pounds	0.74 ounce 20.8 grams	0.08 ounce 2.08 grams
3 pounds	1.1 ounces 31.2 grams	0.11 ounce 3.12 grams
4 pounds	1.47 ounces 47.7 grams	0.147 ounce 4.17 grams
5 pounds	1.84 ounces	0.18 ounce

Next, pour the solution into a sprayer tank containing three-quarters of the water needed to spray the intended area. For example, if 4 gallons of spray solution are needed, put 3 gallons of water in the tank, add the quart of water-pesticide solution, and then finish filling the tank with water to make the 4 gallons of spray solution. Shake the tank thoroughly before spraying and agitate it frequently while spraying to keep the pesticide from settling. Apply to foliage until just before it drips off; covering all surfaces.

When mixing pesticides for hose-end applicators, place the required amount of pesticide and a small amount of water into the reservoir jar of the applicator. Stir until thoroughly mixed. Fill the unit to the desired volume, agitate, and spray according to directions. Keep the mixture agitated during spraying. After use, clean and store the application equipment properly.

Soil application often involves using soil drenches, granules, or dusts. Incorporate dry formulations (granules) into the soil with a rototiller or rake. For drenches, mix by adding the required amount of pesticide and water in a bucket. Create a small dike, 3 inches to 4 inches high, just beyond the leaf zone (dripline) of the plant. The dike should help keep the solution within the desired area.

Compatibility

Two or more pesticides that can be mixed together for a single application are said to be compatible. Sometimes the pesticides are formulated together by the manufacturer. Not all pesticides are compatible with each other. Some mixtures may be toxic to plants. Check the pesticide label first to see if there are any restrictions or allowable mixtures. Only mix pesticides if mixing them is recommended on the label.

Calibration

When a pesticide is applied to a given area, the usual approach is to mix a certain amount of material and apply the spray to the problem area. Some pesticide labels give application rates per 100 or 1,000 square feet. Make calculations to convert the rate given to determine how much to use on a small area using Table B–2. Be sure to pay attention to coverage statements. Mixing and applying can be confusing when the labeling does not state the number of gallons to use over a specific area.

To make sure the correct amount of pesticides is being applied, calibrate the sprayer. Keep in mind that spray volume varies with sprayer nozzle size, walking speed, and spray pressure. Calibration of drop and rotary spreaders can be found on the website for the spreader manufacturer. Follow the steps below to calibrate a compressed air sprayer.

When applying pesticide to an area measured in square feet, calibrate the sprayer by staking out a 1,000-square-foot test plot on a surface similar to the treatment site.

Step 1. Fill the sprayer tank half full with water (no pesticide).

Step 2. Record the number of seconds it takes to spray the test plot evenly while walking at a comfortable, steady pace. Consider spraying the test plot in this manner two or three times and average the times.

Step 3. Fill the sprayer half full with water and spray into a container for the average time from Step 2. Measure this water in ounces. The number of ounces equals the amount of spray used to cover 1,000 square feet.

This number helps calculate the amount of pesticide and water needed to treat the target area.

Example 1, Lawn Treatment: After using IPM techniques, you determine your lawn area needs to be sprayed with a fungicide.

1. Calculate square footage to be treated: The lawn area is 45 feet by 80 feet, or 3,600 square feet.

2. Identify the application rate: The labeled application rate for the fungicide is 2 ounces per 1,000 square feet.

3. Calibrate the sprayer using a 1,000 square foot test plot area. It takes 90 seconds to cover the plot. The amount of water collected in 90 seconds is 65 ounces. The sprayer output is 65 ounces per 1,000 square feet.

4. Determine the total spray mixture needed:

$$\frac{X \text{ oz}}{3{,}600 \text{ sq ft}} = \frac{65 \text{ oz}}{1{,}000 \text{ sq ft}}$$

X = 234 oz of mixture to cover 3,600 sq ft

5. Determine the amount of fungicide needed:

$$\frac{X \text{ oz}}{3{,}600 \text{ sq ft}} = \frac{2 \text{ oz}}{1{,}000 \text{ sq ft}}$$

X = 7.2 oz of fungicide to cover 3,600 sq ft

6. Determine the amount of water:

234 oz of total mixture - 7.2 oz of fungicide = 226.8 oz of water to cover 3,600 sq ft

$$\frac{X \text{ gallons}}{226.8 \text{ oz}} = \frac{1 \text{ gallon}}{128 \text{ oz}}$$

X = 1.77 gallons of water

Answer: To treat the lawn, add a little more than 7 ounces of fungicide to 1.75 gallons of water.

Example 2, Ornamental Treatment: After using IPM techniques, you determine your fruit trees need to be sprayed with an insecticide. The labeled rate for your insecticide is 4 ounces per gallon of water. You have six trees to treat. First calculate how much water needs to be sprayed to treat one tree: Add water to your tank and spray the tree as if you are spraying paint, timing the number of seconds it takes. You want adequate coverage, but do not want the insecticide to drip off the plant. Averaging the number of seconds it takes for a few sprays gives you more accurate results. Now spray the water into an empty container for that same number of seconds and measure the amount of water in ounces.

Number of trees to treat = 6

Seconds to spray one tree = 45 seconds

Amount of water collected in 45 seconds: 30 ounces

1. Determine the total amount of mixture needed by multiplying the number of trees by the amount of water required to treat one tree.
   - A. 6 trees × 30 oz = 180 oz
     - a. Convert ounces to gallons: 180 oz divided by 128 oz = 1.4 gallons of mixture
2. Determine the amount of insecticide needed by multiplying the labeled rate by the total spray mixture.
   - A. 4 oz per gal × 1.4 gal = 5.6 oz of insecticide
     - a. Determine the amount of water needed by subtracting the amount of insecticide from the total amount of mixture 180 oz total mixture minus 5.6 oz. of insecticide = 174.4 oz of water

Convert to gallons:

$$\frac{X}{174.4 \text{ oz}} = \frac{1 \text{ gallon}}{128 \text{ oz}}$$

$$X = 1.36 \text{ gallons of water}$$

Answer: Add a little more than 5½ ounces of insecticide to a little more than 1⅓ gallon of water.

Disposal, Cleanup, and Storage

Pesticide Disposal

There is no good method for disposing of excess spray materials. Dusts and granules can be saved for the next application, but not liquids. The best solution is to mix only as much as needed for one application session. If, however, pesticide remains in the tank after a spray job is complete, use it up. Spray it on other crops or sites listed on the label. Never pour pesticides down a drain. It is possible for pesticides to stop the bacterial action in a septic tank or contaminate a municipal sewage system, surface water, or groundwater. Pouring pesticides in a storm drain or ditch will cause environmental damage.

Thoroughly clean the pesticide application equipment immediately after each use. Dust or granular spreaders can corrode rapidly if pesticide residue remains. Rinse sprayers three times, and spray a portion of the rinse material through the nozzle. A small amount of detergent in the first rinse helps remove any residue. Do not dump the rinse water in one place where it will be concentrated and may become a pollutant. Spray the rinse water over a broad area (listed on the label) so that the pesticide will be further diluted. Never pour rinse water down the drain or in a ditch or storm drain, as rinse water is toxic.

Once the sprayer is clean, disassemble the nozzle, remove the tank cover, make sure the hose and spray mechanism are drained, and allow the sprayer to air dry.

After drying, reassemble the sprayer and store in a clean, dry location. Never clean nozzles with wire, knives, or other hard objects. They can damage the nozzle, which may change the spray pattern and delivery rate. Soft wood objects (such as toothpicks) or liquid solvents are recommended for cleaning nozzles.

Empty Pesticide Containers

Rinse empty pesticide containers at least three times. Pour rinse water into spray tanks and apply the pesticide-contaminated water to plants or the site as part of the spray solution. For glass and most plastic containers, replace the lid and place in the trash. If possible, punch holes in the containers and crush them to prevent further use.

Pesticide Information Sources

If you need more information on pesticides, contact these sources:

- **Regulations, violations:** The NC Department of Agriculture and Consumer Services, Structural Pests and Pesticide Division, (919) 733-3556
- **Pesticide Safety Education Program:** Pesticide Safety Education Specialist, NC State University, (919) 515-3113
- **Disposal advice:** NC Department of Agriculture and Consumer Services, Hazardous Waste Disposal, (919) 733-3556
- **Emergency medical advice:** Carolina's Poison Center, 1-800-222-1222 (24-hour response)

Excess Pesticides

Any pesticide for which the uses have not been suspended or canceled should be used if possible. If a pesticide has been suspended or canceled, or if the product cannot be used, call the NC Department of Agriculture and Consumer Services at (919) 733-3556 for disposal advice. The department may be able to pick up certain pesticides that cannot be legally used.

Cleanup

Clean up any spills immediately. Vermiculite, oil absorbents, and even kitty litter can be used to soak up liquid spills. Report any large spills that cannot be easily managed to the NC Department of Agriculture and Consumer Services, Structural Pests and Pesticides Divsion, by calling (919) 733-3556. For example, a spill of a liter of premixed imidacloprid in a driveway can probably be hosed off into the surrounding landscape. Thirty pounds of lawn pesticide spilled in a shed or on a lawn requires a call to the NC Department of Agriculture.

Personal Cleanup

The pesticide labeling will advise the kinds of protection that must be worn to avoid pesticide exposure. Shower after working with pesticides. Be sure to wash the entire body, including the hair. Wash immediately after any spill on the body.

Washing Clothes

Consider all clothing worn while handling or applying pesticides as contaminated. Handle with gloves. Wash separately from the family wash. Pre-rinse clothes worn during application of pesticides before washing them to help remove pesticide particles from the fabric. Wash the clothes in hot water with detergent. Wash only a few items at a time to allow for maximum agitation and water dilution. Do not wash other clothes with the clothing worn while applying pesticides. If only slightly toxic pesticides were used, one wash cycle is adequate. Run the washer through one additional cycle without clothes, using hot water and detergent to clean the machine. Line-dry clothes outside in the sun, if possible, to avoid contaminating the dryer. If the clothes are heavily contaminated with pesticide, dispose of them.

Storing Pesticides

Read pesticide labels for specific storage instructions. Check your state's pesticide storage regulations as many require pesticides to be stored in a place away from children and pets. A secure wood or metal cabinet or closet will serve the purpose.

Always store pesticides in their original containers, never in unmarked containers or containers that have held food or drink. Place dry products above liquid products (Figure B–14). Check pesticide containers often for leaks or breaks. If a container is damaged, replace it with another container that held exactly the same pesticide or with a new container. If a new container is used, transfer the labeling from the old one.

Store pesticides away from combustible materials, such as gasoline or oily rags. Do not weld or burn near the storage area. To prolong the effectiveness of a pesticide, store in dry, cool (but above freezing) conditions, out of direct sunlight, with the container properly closed. Extreme heat can reduce the effectiveness of pesticides.

Figure B–14. Store pesticides properly in original containers, dry products above liquids, in a secure wood or metal cabinet, away from children and pets.
Kathleen Moore, CC BY - 2.0

Pesticide Failures and Plant Damage

Pesticide Failures

Some pest populations have become resistant to and are no longer killed by certain pesticides. Pesticide resistance develops from overuse of pesticides or continued use of the same or closely related pesticides. Such use results in killing all of the susceptible pests, leaving only the resistant ones to mate—resulting in a resistant population. When target pests develop resistance, formerly effective pesticides no longer work and pests become much more difficult to manage.

In the home garden, most pesticide failures are the result of not following labeling instructions, using the wrong chemical for the pest, spraying at the wrong time, or applying an inadequate amount. If the pesticide has not worked satisfactorily, ask these questions:

- Has the pest been correctly identified?
- Has the correct pesticide been used? Is the pesticide out of date? Was it stored correctly? Check the label.
- Has the correct dosage been applied? Check the label. Check the calculations used when mixing the pesticide.
- Has the pesticide been applied correctly? Check the label. Was spray coverage adequate and evenly applied? Was the pesticide applied at the wrong time or with the wrong equipment? The pest may have been in a life cycle stage that was not susceptible.

When a pesticide is applied to a crop or treatment site, a tiny proportion of the pest population (for example, one insect or weed in 10 million) may survive exposure to the pesticide due to its genetic makeup. When the pests that survive breed, some of their offspring will inherit the genetic trait that confers resistance to the pesticide. These pests will not be affected the next time a similar pesticide is used. If the same pesticide is applied often, the proportion of less-susceptible individuals in the population will increase. To prevent resistance, rotate between pesticides that use different modes of action. For example, after using an insecticide that interrupts the insect's reproductive cycle, switch to an insecticide that acts as stomach poison.

For more information on pesticide resistance, click on the "Resistance" tab on the Pesticide Stewardship website.

Pesticide Damage

Selecting the least toxic appropriate material and following label directions can prevent most potential damages. Improperly used pesticides can damage plants and harm people and the environment.

Phytotoxicity

Phytotoxicity is injury to plants, which can range from slight burning or browning of leaves to death of the entire plant. Signs of chemical injury often do not appear until several days after exposure to the pesticide and can be confused with other plant problems. The likelihood of plant injury resulting from the use of a pesticide varies, depending on several factors:

- **Chemical used:** Some plants are sensitive to certain chemicals.
- **Formulation:** Emulsifiable concentrates, which contain solvents, are more likely to cause injury than wettable powders.
- **Concentration:** There is more room for error when using high concentrations.
- **Combination of chemicals:** Some mixtures cause injuries, whereas the same materials applied separately do not.
- **Method of application:** High-pressure applications may cause injury, whereas low-pressure applications would not.
- **Amount applied:** If too little is applied, the pest is not managed. Too much may cause plant damage.
- **Growing conditions:** Plants growing under stressful conditions (such as in a wet spot or in shallow soil) are more susceptible to injury than healthy plants growing in a location to which they are adapted.
- **Growth stage or condition of the plant:** Young, tender new growth tends to be more susceptible to injury than older growth. Some cultivars are more sensitive than others.
- **Weather conditions at the time of application:**
  - Heat and drought stress can increase plant injury or reduce plant tolerance.
  - Wind can increase drift, resulting in damage to non-target plants.
  - Rain can wash pesticide off, reducing effectiveness, and stormwater runoff can move pesticide into non-target areas.
- **Persistence:** Some pesticides remain active in the soil or can be taken up into the plant and remain effective even after plant parts have been composted.

Injury can take several forms:

- Dead, burned, or scorched spots on or at the tips of leaves
- Misshapen fruit, leaves, or plants
- Unusual color
- Stunting
- Delayed maturity
- Poor germination
- Death of the plant

Potential Harm to Humans

The chance of being poisoned by a pesticide depends on the toxicity of the pesticide and the amount of exposure. Consider both of these factors whenever applying a pesticide.

There are two general types of toxicity, acute and chronic. Acute toxicity refers to the ability of a pesticide to cause illness or injury as the result of a single or short-term exposure. If illness occurs shortly after applying a pesticide, it may be acute toxicity or perhaps heat stress, which causes some similar symptoms. Chronic toxicity refers to the ability of a pesticide to cause illness or injury as the result of repeated, long-term exposure.

Some people can develop allergic reactions to certain pesticides just as some people are allergic to certain foods, fragrances, or pollens. Allergic reactions are not thought to occur during the first exposure to a pesticide. The first exposure may cause the body to develop a histamine response to a particular substance. A later exposure—sometimes a much later exposure—results in the allergic reaction. Certain people seem to be more chemically sensitive than others. These people are more likely to develop allergies to pesticides.

Pesticides enter the body by four main routes: through the mouth (by being swallowed), through the lungs (by being inhaled), through the skin (through wounds or direct penetration), or in the eyes (through contact).

Many pesticides can enter the body through the skin. Oil-based pesticides enter skin more easily than dusts or wettable powders. Because oil-based pesticides often have a high concentration of the active ingredient, use extra caution when mixing the concentrated material for application. Insecticides are generally more toxic to humans than fungicides or herbicides because many insecticides are designed to disrupt the nervous systems of animals.

Symptoms and First Aid

Early symptoms of poisoning by some of the common pesticides are similar to those of food poisoning or flu. Heat stress can cause symptoms that may be confused with pesticide poisoning. Become familiar with the "Statement of Practical Treatment" on the label before using the pesticide. Pesticides are most hazardous when handling concentrated forms (during mixing) but can still be hazardous during application. Heed the precautions listed on the labeling.

First Aid Procedures

- If someone is exposed to a pesticide, take immediate action.

- If a pesticide is spilled, remove any contaminated clothing right away and wash skin thoroughly with soap and water. DO NOT use an abrasive cleaner, as this may allow the pesticide to penetrate the skin more easily.
- If pesticide enters the eyes, rinse the eye with clean water for 15 minutes.
- If the exposure is to pesticide vapors, get fresh air quickly.
- If someone exposed to a pesticide stops breathing, start artificial respiration immediately.
- If the pesticide is swallowed, read the label to see if you should induce vomiting. This is recommended for after swallowing some pesticides but is harmful after swallowing others. Never give anything by mouth to an unconscious individual.
- If you suspect that someone has been poisoned by a pesticide, follow the first aid advice on the pesticide label and IMMEDIATELY call a doctor or take the person to a hospital. Take all pesticide labeling, removing it from the container if possible. The doctor will need the information on the label to determine the proper treatment. The doctor may want to call the Carolina's Poison Center (1-800-222-1222) for specific information on treatment for pesticide poisoning.

Initial Symptoms of Pesticide Poisoning
1. Fatigue
2. Excessive sweating or salivation
3. Headache
4. Nausea and vomiting
5. Stomach cramps
6. Blurred vision
7. Diarrhea

Advanced Symptoms of Pesticide Poisoning
1. Difficulty in walking
2. Muscle twitching
3. Secretions from mouth
4. Chest pains
5. Difficulty in breathing
6. Dilated pupils
7. Unconsciousness and coma

Pesticides in the Environment

Pesticide Movement
After application, a variety of things can happen to a pesticide. Pesticides that move away from the release site may cause environmental contamination. Pesticide movement by air is usually called "drift." Pesticide particles, whether from dusts, sprays, or vapors, may be carried off site in the air. Drift can be reduced by following label instructions,

reducing pressure, and not spraying during windy periods. Volatilization of a pesticide occurs when it changes from a solid or liquid to a gaseous state after application. Following temperature recommendations on the label can reduce loss by volatilization. Because high temperatures increase volatilization, spray during the coolest part of the day.

Pesticide particles and liquids can also move off site because of spills, leaks, and improper equipment cleanup and pesticide disposal. Pesticides washed down a sink or storm drain could end up in the surface water supply.

A heavy rain after application increases the likelihood of surface water contamination by washing pesticides off the plant or from the soil. Sprays are less likely to cause problems from runoff than dusts or granular pesticide formulations. This is especially true if the spray has had time to dry before a rain. Soil runoff occurs when rainfall or irrigation rates exceed the rate at which water can be absorbed by the soil. Pesticides absorbed on soil particles move, too, when soil erosion occurs. Improving soil aeration, adding organic matter, reducing erosion, and paying attention to weather forecasts can help reduce pesticide contamination.

Leaching is the downward movement of pesticides and nutrients through the soil. Leaching is influenced by the solubility of the pesticide and by soil composition; pesticides are absorbed more readily by soils high in clay and organic matter and less so in sandy soils. Organic matter in soils can reduce pesticide activity to the point that higher rates are needed to achieve good pest control. Some pesticides become tightly held to soil particles and are not likely to move out of the soil and into water systems.

Pesticide Degradation
Pesticides vary in the rate at which they break down and in the length of time they remain in the environment. Some are active for only a short period of time before being changed into other chemical compounds that are almost always less harmful than the original material. Persistent pesticides break down slowly and stay in the environment for long periods. Most persistent pesticides have very limited uses or have been removed from the market.

Once absorbed by plants, most pesticides are broken down into less toxic materials. When the plant or plant part dies, any remaining residues can serve as a food source for soil microorganisms, which break down the pesticides. This is the most common means of pesticide degradation. Warm, moist, well-aerated soil with a pH of 6.5 to 7.0 encourages high microbial activity. Through a process called photodecomposition, energy from the sunlight can also alter and degrade the chemical properties of pesticides.

Pesticide Safety around Bees and Other Pollinators (Figure B–15)

After cultural needs of the plant are properly addressed and other IPM techniques have been exhausted, sometimes a pesticide is necessary. Pesticides can affect more than just the intended target, killing pollinators and natural predators. If you choose to use pesticides, take these precautions to protect beneficial insects:

- Check for "Bee Hazard" and other pollinator warnings in the Environmental Hazards section and in the directions for use on the pesticide label.
- Avoid spray drift and spraying on windy days.
- Avoid applying when there is dew formation as dew rewets pesticides and prolongs exposure to beneficial insects.
- Spray late in the day after pollinators are done foraging.
- Do not spray blooming plants.
- Select pesticides that are less toxic to bees. See the chapter on insect management in the North Carolina Agriculture Chemicals Manual for information on the relative toxicity of pesticides and reducing the risk of pesticide poisoning to honey bees.
- For honey bees, granular applications are safer than liquid sprays, which are safer than dusts, which are safer than microencapsulated pesticides.
- Avoid spraying natural areas and hedgerows, which provide habitat for native pollinators.

Figure B–15. A bumble bee on a bee balm (*Monarda* sp.) plant.
Danelle Cutting

Frequently Asked Questions

1. Is this pesticide hazardous to humans or pets?
When used according to the label, pesticides are considered to have an acceptable risk.

2. How long will this pesticide last on the shelf? (Is a pesticide I have on the shelf still usable?)
Store pesticides in original containers, according to their label, in a cool, dry place. Most pesticides should have an expiration date printed on the label. Do not use a cancelled pesticide. Do not use pesticides if physical changes are noticed. For example, dry pesticides may lump or discolor, while liquid pesticides may crystallize or separate. Pesticides may degrade if frozen during storage.

3. How long will this pesticide be effective once it is mixed?
Pesticides cannot be saved after they have been mixed with water. The length of active time will depend on the quality of the water.

4. How do I dispose of excess pesticides?
It is best to use all of the pesticide in the appropriate manner. The NC Department of Agriculture and Consumer Services has a pesticide disposal assistance program. For more information on the program, please call (919) 733-3556 or your local government's household hazardous waste program. If possible, avoid future pesticide storage problems by using an alternate control method that does not require a pesticide purchase. If pesticides must be purchased, buy the smallest quantity that will treat the area.

5. How do I dispose of extra spray that has already been mixed?

It is best to use the mixed spray on a site the pesticide is labeled to manage. Once mixed, the product cannot be stored.

6. When can my pets go back in the yard after I have sprayed?

The re-entry interval (REI) is listed on the label. Remember, the label is the law

Contributors

Authors:

Wayne Buhler, Professor and Extension Specialist, Department of Horticultural Science

Steven Frank, Associate Professor and Extension Specialist, Department of Entomology and Plant Pathology

Contributions by Extension Agents:

Alison Arnold, Danelle Cutting, Tim Mathews, Pam Jones, David Goforth

Contributions by Extension Master Gardener Volunteers:

Linda Alford, Patty Brown, Marjorie Rayburn, Jackie Weedon, Karen Damari, Louise Romanow, Kim Curlee

Content Edits:

Lucy Bradley, Professor and Extension Specialist, Urban Horticulture, NC State University; Director, NC State Extension Master Gardener program

Kathleen Moore, Urban Horticulturist

Copy Editor: Barbara Scott

Based in part on text from the 1998 Extension Master Gardener manual prepared by:

• Erv Evans, Extension Associate, Department of Horticultural Science
• Mike Linker, IPM Coordinator, Department of Crop Science
• Steve Toth, Extension Specialist, Department of Entomology

What information is required for a pesticide to be registered?

To be legally sold or used, pesticides must be registered by the Environmental Protection Agency (EPA). In evaluating a pesticide registration application, the EPA assesses a wide variety of potential human health and environmental effects associated with use of the product. Under the Food Quality Protection Act of 1996, the EPA must find that a pesticide poses a "reasonable certainty of no harm" before it can be registered for use on food or feed. For all pesticides other than reduced risk or food grade products used as pesticides, EPA requires the manufacturers to submit test data on the effects on humans and the environment.

Diagnostic Tables

These diagnostic tables review common problems with turf, woody ornamentals, small fruits, tree fruit and nuts, and vegetables.

Turf
Table C–1. Problems Common to Turf

Symptoms	Possible Causes	Management and Comments
Round or elongated lesions with tan centers are visible. Turf thins out. Affects primarily bermudagrass, bluegrass, and ryegrass and is common in wet spring weather.	Leaf spot	Avoid drought stress and light or frequent watering. Reduce **thatch** buildup and avoid spring fertilization with soluble nitrogen sources. Reseed with improved turf cultivars.
Leaf lesions occur that are light tan or white with dark borders and hourglass shaped. Affects all turfgrass species except tall fescue. Common in late spring or in turf under low fertility.	Dollar spot	Avoid drought stress. Prevent thatch buildup and soil compaction via regular **aerification**. Maintain adequate nitrogen fertility, and reseed with improved turf cultivars.
Elongated tan lesions have dark borders. Circular brown patches continue to spread in hot, wet weather and are most severe on tall fescue and ryegrass.	Brown patch	Keep nitrogen levels low during the summer on tall fescue. Mow at the proper height. Test soil to determine pH and phosphorus levels. Reseed in the fall with improved cultivars.
Develops when soil temperatures decline to 70°F in the fall, but the symptoms do not necessarily appear at this time. Symptoms are most evident during periods of cool, wet weather in the fall and spring. Symptoms are typically large circular patches of brown or tan turf. Each patch sometimes has a reddish ring. Sheath lesions are typical. Affects all warm-season turfgrasses.	Large patch	Bermudagrass rarely sustains significant damage and grows out of the symptoms quickly when the disease does occur. In contrast, centipedegrass, seashore paspalum, St. Augustinegrass, and zoysiagrass often sustain serious damage and recovery can take several weeks or months. Do not apply nitrogen to warm-season grasses in the fall and spring. Avoid establishing these grasses in low-lying areas that remain saturated for extended periods of time.
Only affects bermudagrass and zoysiagrass. Symptoms appear in circular patches from 6 inches to several feet in diameter that remain dormant as the turf greens up in the spring. These patches eventually die and collapse to the soil surface. The roots, stolons, and rhizomes are dark and rotten in affected areas. Patches recur in the same spot each year and increase in size by up to several inches each season.	Spring dead spot	Do not apply nitrogen within six weeks of winter dormancy. Reduce thatch buildup and relieve soil compaction through aggressive aerification and vertical mowing. Affected areas should be hollow-tine aerified at least three times per year during the summer when these grasses are most actively growing. Once the symptoms appear, the only means of control is to encourage the spread of the turf into the affected patches. Frequent spiking or aerification is recommended to break up the mat of dead turf in affected patches. Preemergent herbicides such as DNA herbicides will slow recovery significantly and should not be used in sites with history of this disease.
Circular straw-colored patches range from 3 inches to 12 inches in diameter. Patches occur in bluegrass and fine fescue lawns two years or older, July to September.	Summer patch	Avoid excessive nitrogen, especially in spring, and use slow-release nitrogen sources. Increase mowing height. Avoid light, frequent watering. Reduce thatch buildup.
Straw-colored patches are surrounded by a ring of dark green turf.	Animal urine; may resemble some diseases; may kill the crown tissue	Heavy irrigation will promote recovery of spots by leaching salts from the soil.

Table C–1. Problems Common to Turf continued

Symptoms	Possible Causes	Management and Comments
Early symptoms include small, yellow flecks that develop on the leaves and stems. The flecks expand over time into raised pustules, orange or red in color, that rupture to release powdery masses of yellow, orange, or red spores. Infected plants become yellow and are more susceptible to environmental stress. Heavily infected areas become thin and exhibit clouds of orange dust (rust spores) when the foliage is disturbed. The rust pustules on infected leaves turn black during the fall in preparation for overwintering. Primarily affects Kentucky bluegrass, tall fescue, St. Augustine-grass, and zoysiagrass.	Rust	Plant rust-resistant turfgrass varieties whenever possible to reduce injury. When planting cool-season turfs, use blends and mixtures of multiple species and/or varieties whenever possible. Plant shade-tolerant grasses, and raise mowing heights in heavily shaded areas. Prune trees and remove unwanted undergrowth to improve air movement and reduce prolonged leaf wetness. Mow at recommended heights and on a regular basis, removing no more than 30% to 40% of the foliage in one mowing. Collect and dispose of clippings from infected areas to slow the spread of the disease. Fertilize to meet the nutritional needs of the turf.
Large rings or arcs of dead or very green grass are bordered by zones of darker green grass; mushrooms may be present. This disease is more common on droughty sites and poorly nourished turf and occurs on all turf cultivars year-round.	Fairy ring	Aerate turf frequently. Maintain adequate nitrogen fertility. Irrigate during dry periods.
Turf comes up easily and obviously lacks roots. Turf can sometimes be rolled up like a carpet. Infestations can be severe on bluegrass, ryegrass, and fine fescues.	White grubs; C-shaped grubs found in soil usually in spring and fall	Avoid excessive irrigation and fertilization, particularly organic fertilizers, when adults are active (June through July). If necessary, use a labeled insecticide to target early instars in midsummer to late summer.
Turf blades can be pulled easily from sod. Light tan, sawdust-like pockets can be detected in soil in damaged areas.	Hunting billbugs; small, white, legless grubs found near crowns and roots; majority active from June through August but can be found in soil all year	Water and fertilize grass to stimulate regrowth if damage occurs. If necessary, use a labeled insecticide to control adults in April to mid-May; a second application may be required in mid to late June.
Defined "edge" or border can be detected between damaged and healthy turf (armyworm). Irregular brown patches occur with white moths flying over the turf (sod webworms).	Caterpillars (armyworms, cutworms, and sod webworms); light brown banded caterpillars may be found at soil surface feeding on blades (armyworms) or in the thatch (cutworms, sod webworms), active July through Sept. (armyworm), June through Aug. (sod webworms), and April through May (cutworms)	Bermudagrass can regenerate within a few days with adequate irrigation. Newly-established turfgrass may require reseeding (armyworm). High-cut turf rarely shows signs of sod webworm or cutworm damage. Both turf types outgrow feeding damage in spring (sod webworm or cutworm) and fall (sod webworm).
Irregular or circular patches occur in open turfgrass; damage increases in size from year to year. Turf struggles to recover, and area may become infested with weeds.	Ground pearls: tiny white shell ("pearl") or small (0.06 inch) pink-orange scale with well-developed claws	Promoting healthy turf growth using adequate fertility and irrigation practices can mask symptoms of ground pearl damage. Reseeding or sodding is not effective. Some zoysiagrass cultivars are resistant.
Turf appears dry and bluish-green. Footprints remain after walking on turf, and grass wilts.	Drought	Irrigate turf.

Table C–1. Problems Common to Turf continued

Symptoms	Possible Causes	Management and Comments
Large mounds (less than 18 inches in diameter) are created from excavated soil in open areas.	Fire ants, medium-sized ($\frac{1}{16}$ inch to $\frac{1}{4}$ inch) red and black ants; active spring-fall	In heavily-infested areas, chemical treatment may be necessary. Mound treatments can involve drench method (high traffic areas) or the use of bait stations. Avoid moisture for 24 hours after positioning bait stations or product will turn rancid.
Localized yellow or brown areas can be detected during dry weather. Damage usually occurs in sunny, well-drained locations.	Chinch bugs, tiny black insects with shiny white wings found on crowns and stems	Generally only an issue in St. Augustinegrass, and often controlled by natural predators such as big-eyed bugs. Use low to moderate rates of nitrogen when fertilizing, and clean equipment if moving from lawn to lawn.
Banded streaks or irregular patterns occur. Grass may appear to be stimulated at the margins with dark green and fast-growing areas.	Fertilizer or chemical injury; may kill the crown tissue	Calibrate spreaders and sprayers for uniform and accurate application of materials.
Black or dark spots or patches occur on lawn.	Oil or gasoline damage from leaking lawn mower	Severe oil leak or spill requires removal of affected soil. Small gasoline leaks or spills volatilize quickly.
Large yellow area occurs near a swimming pool.	Chlorine damage from pool water	Leach chlorine through soil with water and replant.
Scalped grass occurs over high spots, and crowns of plants are exposed.	Mower injury	Level the terrain, and raise mower blade or change mowing direction.
Shredded blade tips can be detected. Tips appear gray and then turn tan.	Dull mower injury	Sharpen mower blades.
Patches of dead or dormant grass occur, often following a dry period.	Buried debris, insect injury, or thick thatch	Check for causes.
Turf is pale green to golden-yellow. Yellow streaks may form parallel to leaf veins.	Chlorosis; iron or nitrogen deficiency	Maintain adequate fertilizer levels.
Black or greenish crust is visible on bare soil or in thin turf. Crust occurs in poorly drained or compacted areas and is usually more severe in shade.	Algae growth; soil pH may be low	Increase drainage and establish thicker stand of turf. Aerate compacted areas, and increase sunlight in shaded areas.
Small green plants are growing on bare soil or in thin turf.	Moss; occurs in poorly drained or compacted areas, usually more severe in shade at low fertility and in low pH soil	Increase drainage and establish a thicker stand of turf. Aerate compacted areas, and increase sunlight in shaded areas. Apply fertilizer and lime according to soil tests.
Large areas grow poorly or wilt rapidly in sandy soil. Turf grows slowly and does not respond well to fertilizer and irrigation. Root system is poor.	Nematodes	Fertilize and irrigate more frequently to compensate for the compromised root system. This does not mean fertilize and water more, just more often. For example, if you normally apply 1 lb N/1,000 sq ft/ month during the growing season for your lawn, you may want to apply ½ lb N/1,000 sq ft/ every two weeks instead. Do the same with watering; if you normally irrigate 1 inch per week, you may need to irrigate ½ inch every three days to four days during dry periods. Submit samples to the NCDA&CS for an assay to determine if levels are high enough to cause damage and warrant treatment.

Woody Ornamentals

Table C–2. Problems Common to Many Ornamental Trees and Shrubs

Symptoms	Possible Causes	Management and Comments
Many small twigs broken off	Squirrel damage	Squirrels prune twigs for nest building and often prune more than they need.
	Wind, ice, or hail breakage	Prune to remove weak branches.
	Twig pruner; twig girdler (insects)	Rake up and destroy fallen twigs.
	Construction damage to trees; soil compaction	Protect trees during construction. Choose species adapted to heavy soils. Observe proper planting practices.
Large areas of split bark; no decay evident	Cold injury (typically at base of main stem, but can be elsewhere in sensitive plants like pittosporum)	Allow plants to go dormant in the fall by avoiding practices that promote late flushes (late fertilization and late heavy pruning).
	Sunscald (damage on south or west side)	Cambium of thin-barked, young trees is damaged by temperature fluctuations on extremely cold days. Use tree wrap or block sun with boards on bright winter days.
	Mechanical injury (lawn mower, weed trimmer)	Dig up or kill grass and replace with mulch to avoid mowing too close to tree base.
	Lightning injury	Monitor condition of tree going forward.
Large areas of split bark; decay evident in wood	Secondary decay from wounds described above	No adequate controls. Remove loose bark. Water and fertilize tree at appropriate times.
	Fungal or bacterial canker (any of several)	Submit sample to local Extension agent or NC State's Plant Disease and Insect Clinic (PDIC) for laboratory diagnosis. Prune out and destroy affected stems where possible.
Conks or mushrooms growing from branches or trunk	Fruiting structures of wood-decay fungi	Control is usually not possible. Consult a professional; branch or tree removal is recommended if damage is extensive and tree is a hazard to persons or property. Note that fungal structures are not present on all trees with decay.
Gelatinous, orange masses coming from needles, stems, trunks, or woody galls of juniper species in the spring	Gymnosporangium rust fungi	Spores formed here will infect different groups of woody rosaceous hosts, depending on the species. If feasible, galls and dead branches can be pruned out. Do not plant crabapples and junipers within 2 miles of each other.
Gray-white powdery growth on leaves; leaves may be distorted	Powdery mildew (fungal disease)	Improve air circulation. Rake up and destroy leaves in fall. Use labeled fungicides if aesthetics are severely impaired and plant is not too large.

Table C–2. Problems Common to Many Ornamental Trees and Shrubs continued

Symptoms	Possible Causes	Management and Comments
Black, sooty growth on leaves and/or stems that comes off when rubbed with thumb	Sooty mold fungi that grow on honeydew secreted by insects	Identify insect pest (aphid, scale, psyllid, whiteflies, mealybugs). Optimize irrigation and fertilization. Dislodge insects with strong stream of water. Use horticultural oils or labeled insecticides as a last resort.
Brown, dead areas on leaf margins	Leaf scorch (caused by insufficient transport of water to leaves)	Water deeply during dry periods. Scorch is usually caused by hot, dry weather, but root rots or other root damage can also be involved.
	Bacterial leaf scorch (particularly on syca-more, pin oak, and sometimes redbud)	This systemic and chronic infection by a xylem-inhabiting bacterium has no cure.
	Dessication by winter winds	Water or shade plant in winter. Consider moving plant to a protected area.
	Chemical injury	Injury can occur where herbicides are used too close to plants on windy or hot days or when roots grow into an herbicide-treated area.
Plant wilted; may have poor color; limited new growth	Dry soil	Water deeply during drought.
	Root rot (fungal disease)	Improve drainage, and provide optimum growing conditions. Submit sample to the PDIC to determine which root-rot organism is involved to better choose resistant or tolerant plants.
	Nematodes	Submit soil sample to NCDA&CS for an assay to determine if nematodes are present. If so, use resistant plants, and provide optimum growing conditions. No chemical control is effective.
	Vascular wilt diseases	Submit sample to local Extension agent or the PDIC for laboratory diagnosis.
	Waterlogged soil	Improve drainage.
	Plant is root-bound	Cut root ball in several places before transplanting so roots will grow out into soil.
	Girdling roots	Plant's own roots have grown around base of trunk and strangled plant. Plant properly, and do not plant or mulch too deeply.
	Transplant shock	Do not transplant excessively large trees. Water often and deeply until established. Avoid excessive fertilization.
	Bark beetles and other borers	Prune out and destroy dead or dying wood. Keep trees healthy and growing vigorously. Beetles and borers are often secondary problems. Protect nearby trees of the same species with a labeled insecticide.
Bags constructed from plant material hanging from branches	Bagworms	Prune out affected branches. Handpick and destroy bags. Spray with a labeled insecticide in late spring when bags are barely visible.

Table C–2. Problems Common to Many Ornamental Trees and Shrubs continued

Symptoms	Possible Causes	Management and Comments
Scattered twig and branch dieback	Borers (holes and tunnels in branches)	Provide optimum growing conditions. Submit sample to local Extension agent or the PDIC for diagnosis before attempting chemical control. If possible, prune out and destroy affected branches.
	Cankers	Prune out affected branches, going several inches into clean wood. Destroy clippings.
Dark or sunken lesions on woody stems	Cankers	See above.
Interveinal yellowing of leaves; no wilting	Nutrient or mineral deficiency	Complete a soil test. Improve drainage.
	Waterlogged soil resulting in poor transport of nutrients to leaves	Improve drainage, and choose well-adapted species.
Large, rough, woody galls at base of tree and on roots	Crown gall (bacterial disease)	Depending on the species, the tree or shrub may continue to perform for years despite the disease.
Few or no flowers	Cold injury	Protect during cold (if practical).
	Improper pruning	Some plants flower only on old wood. Prune spring-flowering plants after they finish flowering—not in the fall. Drastic pruning can reduce flowering.
	Overfertilization with nitrogen	Nitrogen fertilization stimulates leaf production and reduces flower production.
	Excess shade	Grow plants in proper amount of light.
	Incorrect fertility	Complete a soil test.
	Young plant	Some plants will not flower until they reach a certain age or until they become established following transplanting.
Galls on branches	Various fungal and bacterial diseases	Prune out and destroy galled branches. Submit a sample local Extension agent or the PDIC for laboratory diagnosis.
	Various insects	Most galls are harmless. Prune out galled branches.
Rapid dieback of new growth; blackening or browning of leaves; plant appears scorched	Fire blight (bacterial)	This blight occurs only on rosaceous hosts, such as pear, cotoneaster, and flowering quince. Prune out and destroy infected branches to a foot below discoloration. Reduce nitrogen fertilizer. Remove water sprouts. Use resistant species or cultivars.
Webs or tents on foliage and small branches; numerous worms	Eastern tent caterpillars (spring) or fall webworms (late summer to fall)	Disturb the web; prune out and destroy affected areas. Remove egg masses during winter. Use Bacillus thuringiensis (Bt) sprays or a labeled insecticide.

Table C–2. Problems Common to Many Ornamental Trees and Shrubs continued

Symptoms	Possible Causes	Management and Comments
Proliferation of branches at specific points on the plant, forming a "witches' broom" effect	Insect injury	Prune out and destroy affected areas.
	Fungal, viral, or mycoplasma disease or certain herbicides	Prune out and destroy affected areas. If seen in roses and other symptoms of rose rosette are present, pruning is not reliably effective, so remove and destroy the plant. See "Diseases and Disorders," chapter 5.
Yellow or orange pustules on leaves, stems or fruit; infected leaves may drop; rusty colored spores on lower leaf surface	Rust (fungal diseases)	Replace with a resistant species or cultivar. Use a labeled fungicide in certain cases. Do not plant junipers and crabapples within 500 feet of one another.
Brown, gray, green or yellow crusty, leaf-like growths on trunk and branches	Lichens	Lichens are a combination of algae and fungi; they grow in moist, shady areas and do not harm the plant. Their presence in abundance on smaller plants indicates that the plant is unthrifty for other reasons.
White frothy material on foliage	Spittlebugs	Control is usually not necessary.
Early leaf drop or early fall color	Environmental stress such as drought, compacted soil or transplant shock	Improve soil conditions. Water if dry, and apply mulch. Do not fertilize with a high-nitrogen fertilizer.
	Various insects or diseases	Submit sample to your local Extension agent or the PDIC for laboratory diagnosis.
Browning of tips of conifer needles; faint yellow bands about ⅛-inch wide across groups of needles	Ozone injury	No control needed. New growth should be okay.
Sour-smelling sap oozing from cracks in tree bark	Slime flux (bacterial disease)	Provide optimum growing conditions. Avoid wounds to roots, which are entry points for the bacteria. Remove any loose bark.
Yellow and green mottle or mosaic pattern on leaves; leaves may be distorted	Viral disease; particularly common in nandinas, camellias, and roses	In most cases symptoms are not sufficiently severe to impair the aesthetics. Removal of plant may be necessary, especially in the case of rose rosette (see "Diseases and Disorders," chapter 5).
Oozing sap on trunk	Environmental stress	Drought or waterlogging can cause trees to ooze excessively.
	Mechanical injury	Prevent lawn mower and weed trimmer injury.
	Disease or insect damage	See information on specific diseases.
Brown leaf spots	Fungal or bacterial disease (any of several)	See information on specific diseases, or submit sample to your local Extension agent or the PDIC for laboratory diagnosis. Late in the season, diseases can be secondary as leaves senesce.
	Herbicide injury	Avoid using herbicides on hot, windy days, and follow label directions.

Table C–2. Problems Common to Many Ornamental Trees and Shrubs continued

Symptoms	Possible Causes	Management and Comments
General browning of conifer needles	Drought	Water deeply during drought, and apply mulch.
	Salt injury	Do not use de-icing salt on sidewalks or roads near trees or shrubs.
	Pine wood nematode	Submit a sample to NCDA&CS for an assay to determine presence of nematodes. Remove and destroy affected trees. This nematode is severe only on nonnative species, particularly Japanese black pine.
	Waterlogged soil	Improve drainage.
	Transplant shock	Do not transplant excessively large trees. Water often and deeply until established, and avoid excessive fertilization.
	Girdling roots	Plant's own roots have grown around base of trunk and strangled plant. Plant properly, and do not plant or mulch too deeply.
	Plant is root-bound	Cut root ball in several places before transplanting so roots will grow out into soil.
	Animal urine injury	Heavy irrigation will promote recovery of spots by leaching salts from the soil to reduce concentration.
	Fungal canker	Check trunk and branches for cankers. Prune out and destroy affected branches, going several inches into clean wood.
Leaves chewed or completely eaten	Various caterpillars, sawflies, or leaf beetles	Tolerate some damage. Keep plants healthy with water and fertilizer. Identify the insect, and use *Bacillus thuringiensis* (Bt) or labeled insecticide while insects are small and before damage is extensive. If the insect is cankerworm, apply metal bands around tree.
Waxy, scalelike structures tightly attached to leaves, twigs, or branches	Various scale insects	Submit sample to local Extension agent or the PDIC for laboratory diagnosis. Use dormant oil or horticultural oil.
Young leaves puckered, curled or distorted; clear, sticky substance on leaves; clusters of small insects on undersides of leaves	Aphids	Encourage natural predators. Dislodge with strong stream of water. Use horticultural oil or a labeled insecticide.
Serpentine trails or blotches in leaves	Leafminers	Management is not usually necessary.
Galls (abnormal growths on leaves, stems, or other tissues)	Various insects or mites	There are no chemical management options for gall insects, but the plants will not be seriously harmed. Prune off and destroy galls.
Water sprouts; suckers	Environmental stress; excessive pruning (on dogwoods in mountains may indicate dogwood anthracnose)	Pull or cut off water sprouts and suckers.

Table C–2. Problems Common to Many Ornamental Trees and Shrubs continued

Symptoms	Possible Causes	Management and Comments
Leaves stippled (pinpoint yellow spots); leaves off-color (gray, silver, white, or yellowish); varnish-colored specks on underside of leaf; may appear to be dirty due to fine webbing and dust that collects	Lacebugs, spidermites	Spray undersides of leaves; a strong stream of water will dislodge some of the pests. Use horticultural oil or a labeled insecticide.

Small Fruits

Table C–3. Problems Common to Small Fruits

Symptoms	Possible Causes	Management and Comments
DAMAGE NOTICED ON LEAVES AND STEMS		
Purplish or brown spots on leaves	Fungal or bacterial leaf spot (any of several)	Submit sample to local Extension agent or the PDIC for laboratory diagnosis.
	Chemical injury	Prevent by not overspraying. Follow labeled directions.
Plants wilt; leaves may drop or may turn brown at margins	Root or crown injury or disease; fertilizer burn; water stress (drought or overwatering)	Examine roots and crowns for insect damage. Submit sample to local Extension agent or the PDIC to test for root rot disease. Avoid overfertilizing. Use good water management practices to avoid overwatering or underwatering. Plant in raised beds to provide a well-aerated root zone.
White or gray crusty material covering leaves, stems, and/or fruits	Slime mold (fungus)	Slime molds grow on plant surfaces during wet weather and disappear again in dry weather. No management is necessary.
Small white, frothy masses on stems and leaves	Spittlebug	No management is necessary.
Chewing injury on leaves	Caterpillars, beetles	Foliar damage must be extensive to result in yield loss. For small areas of damage, hand removal of insects may be sufficient.
DAMAGE NOTICED ON FRUIT		
Gray, fuzzy mold on flowers or fruits, especially during wet periods	Gray mold (fungal disease)	Do not crowd plants. Use labeled fungicides; apply fungicides preventively in cool and wet seasons.
Fruit is soft with discolored, sunken, or moldy spots; may be leaking juice	Fungal or bacterial fruit rot (any of several)	Mulch around plants to cover old infected fruit and to inhibit rain-splashing of spores. Improve air circulation through pruning. Use a labeled fungicide.
Berries soft or dark; no visible mold; berries may be leaking juice	Fruit overripe or mishandled	Timely, complete harvest and rapid postharvest cooling will prevent most fruit quality problems. To avoid mold of harvested fruit, only harvest when dry—do not pick or handle fruit wet with dew or rain.

Table C–3. Problems Common to Small Fruits continued

Symptoms	Possible Causes	Management and Comments
Ripening berries covered with tufts of gray, green, white, orange, or black moldy growth	Fungal fruit rot (any of several)	Pick berries regularly and cool immediately. Remove mummied berries to prevent fungus from overwintering. Prune to increase air circulation. Submit sample to local Extension agent or the PDIC for laboratory diagnosis. Use a labeled fungicide.
Insect larvae found in ripening and ripe fruit	Spotted wing drosophila (*Drosophila suzukii*) (in all soft-skinned fruit)	Larvae are brown and have a distinct pair of breathing horns on one end. Eggs may be seen on fruit with a magnifying glass; they have two thread-like breathing tubes on one end. See case study at the end of chapter 14, "Small Fruits."
	Various insects, often crop-specific	Send images or submit samples to local Extension agent or the PDIC for laboratory diagnosis.
DAMAGE NOTICED ON ENTIRE PLANT		
Stunted, weak plants; poor yield	Various root and crown feeding insects; nematode injury	Examine roots and crown for signs of injury. Remove infected plants. Do not plant into newly tilled grass or sod. Submit soil to NCDA&CS for an assay for nematode analysis. Install new plants in a different location
	Poor site selection or poor site preparation; lack of adequate care	Evaluate soil properties, site preparation, drainage, soil fertility, and pH. Review plant requirements, and adjust fertility and watering to optimize growth.
	Wrong crop, cultivar, or species	Some cultivars or species of small fruit crops are not suitable for growing in North Carolina. Consult publications and your county Extension center for advice on plants that grow well in your area.
Stunting, leaf discoloration, deformed plant parts (leaves, flowers or fruit)	Virus disease	Submit samples to local Extension agent or the PDIC for laboratory diagnosis. Test for viruses and if found, remove infected plants and start in new area with virus-free plants.
	Herbicide injury	Evaluate recent herbicide use. Look for evidence of herbicide injury or drift from adjacent fields.

Tree Fruit and Nuts

Table C–4. Problems Common to Many Fruit and Nut Trees

Symptoms	Possible Causes	Management and Comments
Many small twigs broken off	Small-animal damage (squirrels, raccoons, possums); twig girdlers	Squirrels prune twigs for nest-building and often prune many more than they need. Pick up fallen twigs as a measure against twig girdlers.
	Wind breakage	Prune to remove weak branches.
	Environmental stress	Drought or waterlogging can cause branches to die and break off.

Table C–4. Problems Common to Many Fruit and Nut Trees continued

Symptoms	Possible Causes	Management and Comments
Premature fruit drop	Natural thinning	Many trees produce more fruit than they need and thin themselves.
	Spring frost	Frost often kills developing fruits or buds.
	Poor pollination	Tree may require other cultivars nearby to cross-pollinate.
	Environmental stress	Drought, cold or heat can cause fruit drop, especially for figs.
	Use of insecticide containing carbaryl	Carbaryl causes some fruit thinning if used within 40 days of fruit set; do not misuse; follow label directions.
	Insect and disease pressure	Submit sample to local Extension agent or the PDIC for laboratory identification.
Reduced yield and misshaped fruit	Inadequate pollination; adverse weather	Tree may require other cultivars nearby to cross-pollinate. Do not apply insecticide during bloom.
	Biennial bearing	Apples, pears, and pecans naturally bear a heavy crop one year and few fruits the following year if not properly pruned or thinned.
	Improper pruning	Do not prune off fruit-bearing wood during the dormant season.
Fruit deformity, pitting	Catfacing (from piercing-sucking insects)	Remove weeds from surrounding area. Use a labeled insecticide as a last resort.
Fruit drop, misshaped fruit	Frost injury	Monitor weather, and select optimum site to minimize crop loss.
Small fruit	Failure to prune or thin excess fruit	Peaches, nectarines, plums and apples tend to produce many small fruits if not pruned or thinned properly; consult pruning in chapter 11, "Woody Ornamentals" for proper pruning.
	Poor soil fertility	Test soil and follow amendment recommendations.
Large areas of split bark; no decay evident	Sunscald	Bark of trees (young ones) can split when exposed to intense sunlight; use tree-wrap or paint the trunk with white latex paint to reduce temperature swings on bright winter days.
	Mechanical injury (e.g., lawn mower, weed trimmer)	Remove grass around trunk, and do not mow too closely to base of tree.
	Lightning injury	Monitor condition of tree going forward
Gray-white powdery growth on leaves; leaves and fruit may be distorted or be russeted (weblike rough skin on fruit)	Powdery mildew (fungal disease)	Use recommended fungicide. Prune for optimal light and air penetration.

Table C–4. Problems Common to Many Fruit and Nut Trees continued

Symptoms	Possible Causes	Management and Comments
Oozing sap on branches or trunk	Natural process	Cherries, plums, and peaches naturally ooze sap at the site of injury.
	Environmental stress	Drought or waterlogging can cause fruit trees to ooze excessively.
	Mechanical injury	Exercise care when using tools. Remove surrounding vegetation and use mulch.
	Fire blight	Bacterial disease most commonly observed following bloom on rosaceous hosts (most often apple and pear) but can be observed throughout season. Ooze is actually bacteria but may be mistaken for sap. If on branches, prune at least 12 inches from the leading edge of a canker during spring. Can apply copper at bud break (first green tissue), but copper can lead to phytotoxicity at high rates and when applied after green tip. Apply biological or antibiotic like streptomycin sulfate for control.
Large areas of split bark; decay evident in wood, or fruits may be russeted (weblike rough skin on fruit)	Secondary decay of any of the wounds described above	No adequate controls are available. Remove loose bark; water and fertilize tree when necessary. Maintaining minimal stress on trees is the best defense.
	Fungal or bacterial canker (any of several)	If only twigs or scaffold limbs are affected, prune them out. Remove loose bark. Water and fertilize tree when necessary. Maintaining minimal stress on trees is the best defense.
Black, sooty growth on leaves, stems, and/or fruit	Sooty blotch or sooty mold (fungus that grows on honeydew, a substance secreted by aphids and other insects)	Remove brambles, which are alternate hosts. Thin canopy for increased air movement. Thin fruit. Cool ripe fruit after picking. Use a labeled fungicide. To manage aphids, water and fertilize trees, and encourage natural predators. Manage with labeled insecticide.
Brown, dead areas on leaf margins	Leaf scorch, caused by insufficient transport of water to leaves	Water tree deeply during dry periods. Scorch is usually caused by hot, dry weather, but root rots or other root damage can also be involved.
	Pesticide application during high temperatures	Avoid applying pesticides in high temperatures. Take steps to avoid overspray.
	Cold injury leading to bark splitting on branches	Do not prune or fertilize in late summer or fall.
Flying insects around ripe fruit	Yellow jackets, hornets, bees	Do not allow fruit to become overripe. Pick up and destroy fallen fruit. Use traps baited with pheromones or meat.

Table C–4. Problems Common to Many Fruit and Nut Trees continued

Symptoms	Possible Causes	Management and Comments
Wilted leaves, may have poor color	Dry soil	Water deeply during drought.
	Root-knot or other root-feeding nematodes	Submit soil sample to NCDA&CS for an assay and recommendations.
	Various fungal, bacterial, or viral diseases	Wilting may be due to a disease issue in the vascular (xylem) tissue of the plant. Wilting is due to water not being transported efficiently from soil upwards. Issue could be due to root rot disease, so consider improving drainage. Identify disease problem or submit sample to local Extension agent or the PDIC for diagnosis and recommendations.
	Root rot	Prevention is best; purchase root-rot-resistant, disease-free plants. Plant in well-drained areas or use raised beds. A labeled fungicide may reduce spread to other plants but will not kill fungus in infected plants.
	Waterlogged soil	Improve drainage.
Interveinal yellowing of leaves; no wilting	Nutrient or mineral deficiency	Complete a soil test, and use foliar analysis to determine any deficiencies.
	Waterlogged soil, resulting in poor transport of nutrients to leaves	Improve drainage.
	Herbicide injury	Avoid using herbicides too close to the tree.
	Virus	Send to diagnostic clinic. Viruses cannot be cured.
Large, rough and woody galls at base of tree and on roots	Crown gall (bacterial disease)	Some galls can be pruned out, but it is best to consult an arborist. Trees may live for many years in spite of galls. Disinfect shears between trees when pruning. If symptoms occur on apple, plant rootstocks with resistance or that are less susceptible to crown gall.
Young leaves curled and distorted; clusters of insects on undersides of leaves	Aphids	Encourage predatory insects like ladybird beetles and lacewings. If necessary, use a high pressure sprayer to apply a labeled insecticide, thoroughly covering the undersides of leaves.
Silk tents in branch crotches in spring	Eastern tent caterpillar	Physically remove tents or use labeled insecticide when caterpillars are small. Remove egg masses when pruning.
Silk tents on ends of branches in midsummer or late summer	Fall webworm	Physically remove tents or use labeled insecticide when caterpillars are small. Remove egg masses when pruning.
Leaves with tiny white flecking or stippling; often dirty with webbing; leaves gray	Spider mites	Prevent water stressed plants. Tolerate some damage. Encourage natural predators. Use insecticidal oils or soaps or a labeled miticide.

Vegetables

Table C–5. Problems Common to Many Vegetables

Symptoms	Possible Causes	Management and Comments
Poor fruit yield; fruit may be small and have poor flavor	Uneven moisture	Supply water during dry periods.
	Poor soil fertility or micronutrient deficiencies	Test soil and amend as recommended. Use complete fertilizers.
	Improper temperature	Check soil temperature. Plant at the appropriate season and time for your area.
	Poor pollination (primarily cucurbits)	Maintain optimal growing conditions, and hand-pollinate if needed. Only use pesticides when bees are not flying (evening hours).
Plants grow slowly; leaves light green	Insufficient light	Thin plants. Do not plant in shade.
	Cool weather	Use plastic or row covers in early spring.
	Poor soil fertility (this can include improper pH)	Test soil and amend as recommended. Use complete fertilizers.
	Improper pH	Test soil and amend as recommended.
	Excess water	Do not overwater. Improve drainage.
Seedlings do not emerge	Dry soil	Supply water.
	Seeds washed away	Replant.
	Damping-off (fungal disease)	Do not overwater. Use seed treated with a labeled fungicide.
	Slow germination due to weather	Delay planting until soil warms.
	Old seed	Store seed in a dry, cool place, and use current season's seed. Conduct germination tests on wet paper towels for heirloom seeds that are saved over from previous years.
	Seedcorn maggot	Plant shallowly. Wait until soil warms to plant.
General leaf yellowing, no wilting	Nutrient or mineral deficiency	Test soil and amend as recommended. Add nitrogen fertilizer. Apply complete fertilizer at planting.
	Insufficient light	Thin plants. Move garden location.
Wilted seedlings; seedlings fall over	Dry soil	Supply water.
	Damping off (fungal diseases)	Do not overwater. Treat seeds with a labeled fungicide. Have disease diagnosed before completing any fungicide treatment.
	Cutworms	Place a physical barrier, such as a cardboard collar or foil collar, around the plant. Use a registered insecticide.

Table C–5. Problems Common to Many Vegetables continued

Symptoms	Possible Causes	Management and Comments
Chewed seedlings	Rodents, rabbits, or birds	Place fence around garden. Cover plants with netting.
	Slugs	Use slug bait (either beer in a dish or commercial bait).
	Slow germination due to weather	Replant after soil warms.
	Root maggots	Avoid planting in soil with uncomposted materials (manure). Avoid successive plantings of the same crop in the same place. Use a labeled soil insecticide.
Wilted plants; bottom leaves may turn yellow	Dry soil	Supply water
	Root rot (fungal disease)	Plant disease-free seeds or healthy transplants. Do not overwater. Remove old plant debris. Rotate crops to different areas of the garden each season.
	Southern wilt (bacterial disease, mainly affecting tomato)	Use grafted rootstock with wilt resistance. Rotate crop away from plants in the *Solanaceae* family.
	Vascular wilt (fungal disease, mainly affecting tomato, potato, eggplant, pepper)	Plant resistant cultivars. Next season rotate crops away from *Solanaceae* family plants. Use soil solarization. Submit sample to local Extension agent.
	Root-knot nematode	Submit soil sample to NCDA&CS for an assay to determine presence of nematodes. Plant resistant cultivars and rotate crops. Solarize soil.
	Waterlogged soil	Improve drainage.
Leaves stippled with tiny white spots	Spider mites	Monitor cultural problems (including water and fertilizer). Spray mites off with soapy water. Encourage natural predators (other mites, thrips, minute pirate bugs, big-eyed bug, lacewing larvae). Treat with labeled miticide.
	Harlequin bug	Handpick bugs or eggs. Eliminate groundcovers or weedy areas (especially mustards). Destroy old cole crops or mustards (breeding areas). Natural parasites and predators may assist in management.
	Air pollution (ozone)	No control available. Damage is temporary.
Leaves with yellow and green mosaic or mottle pattern; leaves may be puckered and plants stunted	Virus disease	Choose resistant cultivars. Use disease-free seeds and healthy transplants. Practice weed control. Remove infected plants, and remove and destroy old plant debris.

Table C–5. Problems Common to Many Vegetables continued

Symptoms	Possible Causes	Management and Comments
Leaf margins turn brown and shrivel	Dry soil	Supply water.
	Leafhopper burn	Use good cultural practices. Use a labeled insecticide.
	Salt damage	Do not place garden where de-icing salt may have been applied on nearby concrete. Irrigate with clear water to flush root zone.
	Fertilizer burn	Get a soil analysis completed before season starts. Apply recommended fertilizer at recommended rates; do not over-apply fertilizers. Irrigate with clear water to flush root zone.
	Potassium deficiency	Test soil and amend as recommended or use complete fertilizer.
	Cold injury	Protect plants.
Discrete brown spots on leaves; some spots may have coalesced	Fungal or bacterial leaf spot disease	See management strategies under specific diseases. Choose resistant or tolerant varieties. Plant disease-free seeds and healthy transplants. Submit sample to local Extension agent or the PDIC for laboratory diagnosis.
	Chemical injury	Do not apply chemicals that are not labeled for use on the plant, and apply chemicals at labeled rates. Some chemical injury occurs from drift.
White powdery growth on upper leaf surfaces	Powdery mildew (fungal disease)	Plant resistant cultivars. Use healthy transplants. Improve air circulation. Recognize that mildew occurs at the end of season. Use a labeled fungicide.
Leaves shredded or stripped from plant	Hail damage	No control available. Damage is usually temporary.
	Rodents	Place fence around garden. See chapter 20, "Wildlife."
	Slugs	Handpick slugs from plants and throw them in soapy water. Use slug bait (either beer in a dish or commercial bait).
	Various insects	Identify insects, and use integrated pest management techniques.

Table C–5. Problems Common to Many Vegetables continued

Symptoms	Possible Causes	Management and Comments
Leaves curled, puckered, or distorted	Herbicide injury (common on tomato and cucumber)	If lawn herbicides are used, do not apply under windy conditions. Do not apply herbicides if temperature is above 85°F.
	Virus disease	Plant resistant cultivars if available. Practice weed control. Remove infected plants, and remove old plant debris.
	Aphids	Keep plants healthy. Spray aphids off regularly with soapy water. Encourage predators like ladybird beetles, hoverfly maggots, predatory wasps and lacewings (and their larvae aphid lions).

Contributors

Author: Mike Munster, Diagnostician, NC State Plant Disease and Insect Clinic

Contributions by Extension Master Gardener Volunteers: Jackie Weedon, Joanne Celenski, Jayne Boyer

Content Editors: Lucy Bradley, Professor and Extension Specialist, Urban Horticulture and Director of the Extension Master Gardener Volunteer program; Kathleen Moore, Urban Horticulturist; Terri Billeisen, Extension Associate, Department of Entomology and Plant Pathology; Rick Brandenburg, Co-Director, Center for Turfgrass Environmental Research and Education; Department of Entomology and Plant Pathology; Hannah Burrack, Associate Professor and Extension Specialist, Department of Entomology and Plant Pathology; Lee Butler, Extension Coordinator, Department of Entomology and Plant Pathology; Shawn Butler, Research Technician, Department of Entomology and Plant Pathology; Bill Cline, Researcher and Extension Specialist, Department of Entomology and Plant Pathology; Lina Quesada-Ocampo, Assistant Professor, Vegetable Pathology, Department of Entomology and Plant Pathology; David Ritchie, Professor and Extension Plant Pathologist, Department of Entomology and Plant Pathology; Sara Villani, Extension Assistant Professor, Department of Entomology and Plant Pathology

Copy Editor: Barbara Scott

Garden Tools

Gardening is much easier if you use the proper tools. Various kinds of gardening equipment are described in the following section. It is not necessary, however, for home gardeners to own all of these tools. A few of them are more useful for some crops than others. All are readily available at garden supply stores. Only buy what you need, and always buy the best tool you can afford. Quality tools last longer, do the job better, and are easier to use. Soon you will have a useful collection.

Types of Tools

Spades for digging and lifting
- A round-pointed shovel is a good all-purpose tool that is useful for digging and turning soil and can also be used to harvest crops such as Irish potatoes and sweet potatoes.
- A spade with a sharp edge is used for cutting and digging heavy soil, removing sod, and incorporating organic matter.

Forks for turning and carrying
- A garden fork with thick, square tines is good for mixing a compost pile or loosening soil.
- A pitchfork with longer, thinner tines is good for moving light, loose material, such as straw.

Rakes for smoothing and gathering
- A bow rake is good for smoothing out soil, removing stones, and breaking up clods.
- A straight rake is designed so that its back can be used to smooth the seedbed and to compact soil over freshly sown seed for improved germination.
- Rakes can also be used to gather dead or spent crop materials into piles.

Hoes for cultivating and weeding
- A common hoe, also called a square-blade hoe, works for most garden jobs.
- A pointed hoe, also called a Warren hoe, is good for opening a furrow and for cultivating between plants.
- A scuffle hoe, made in several patterns with a flat bottom, cuts weeds off under the soil surface as it is pushed back and forth between the rows. It breaks up the crust layer on top of the soil without bringing weed seeds to the surface.

Trowels for transplanting vegetable plants

Bypass pruning shears for cutting
- Shears can be used to prune plants and harvest produce.

Irrigation equipment
- A watering can is useful for gently watering transplants.
- Drip irrigation places water exactly where and when you want it.
- Garden and soaker hoses are good for general watering.

Compressed-air sprayer
- This is the most popular piece of equipment for applying chemicals because it gives good coverage, especially to the underside of plant leaves.

String and stakes
- Helps with aligning straight rows.

Measuring stick
- Useful for determining the distance between plants and rows.

Wheelbarrow or garden cart
- Either of these makes moving mulch, compost, soil, stones, tools, and harvested vegetables much easier than doing so by hand.

Spreaders to apply lime and fertilizer
- A drop spreader covers less area than a broadcast spreader with each pass over the site, but the area covered is easier to detect.
- A rotary or cyclone spreader applies materials uniformly, although the margins of the area covered may be difficult to see.

Tiller
A tiller makes soil preparation easy for gardeners who use it enough to make the purchase worthwhile. Three types are available, all of which are driven by gasoline or electric motors. On the most common and least expensive type, the tines are mounted in front. A second type has the tines mounted in the rear. Although more expensive, the rear-tine tiller is easier to operate. Many tillers with rear-mounted tines have a reverse gear that makes it possible to work in cramped areas. A third type is the center-mounted or mid-tine tiller, which combines the advantages of the other two types.

Maintenance

Once you have selected the right tools, it is important to provide regular maintenance. Clean tools after each use. Keep your tools sharp, as sharp tools are safer and more effective than dull ones. Regularly tighten loose nuts and screws. To prevent splinters, sand rough handles. Store tools in a dry, protected space, organized in a way that enables you to find what you need. Caring for the quality tools you have selected ensures that your investment lasts for many years.

Author:
Chris Gunter
Extension Vegetable Specialist and Associate Professor
Department of Horticultural Science

Season Extenders and Greenhouses

For centuries, gardeners have used a wide variety of techniques for sheltering plants from cold weather—both in early spring and fall—to extend the growing season for a longer, larger harvest. Ambitious gardeners can harvest greens and other cool-weather crops all winter by providing the right conditions. Warm-season crops like tomatoes and cucumbers can get as much as a month's head start in the spring or last a month longer in the fall than their conventionally planted counterparts. There are many ways to lengthen the growing season, depending on the amount of time and money invested.

A continuum of season extenders from simplest to most complex:
Cloches
Low tunnels and row covers
Cold frames and hot beds
High tunnels
Greenhouses

Cloches
The cloche was originally a bell-shaped glass jar set over delicate plants to protect them from the elements and help them get an early start in the spring or extend the fall garden as long as possible. The definition has expanded, however, to include many types of portable structures that shelter plants from drying winds and cold air. They trap solar radiation and keep moisture from evaporating from the soil and plants. Cloches are generally lightweight, portable, and reusable. A cloche can be a wax-paper cone, a water-filled plastic cylinder, or simply a cut-off plastic milk container (Figure E–1). It is preferable to have a design that can be closed completely at night to prevent frost damage, and opened or completely removed during the day for good air circulation. Cloches should be anchored or heavy enough that they do not blow away.

Figure E–1.
Garden cloches made from cut plastic bottles protect plants from frost.
Mandy Prowse, Flickr
CC BY-ND - 4.0

Row Covers and Low Tunnels
Row covers and low tunnels employ a spun-bond polyester fabric or plastic laid over an entire row or rows of a crop and sealed along the edges to trap heat and block wind (Figure E–2). Covers and low tunnels are often used in conjunction with plastic mulch and drip irrigation. These two systems differ only in that the "tunnels" in the low tunnel system are created with the use of wire hoops pushed into the soil to hold up the fabric so it does not come in contact with plant foliage. Both of these methods can offer 4°–5°F of frost protection and have the added benefits of screening out some damaging insects and diseases so that yields are not only earlier and larger, but often of better quality. Be aware that some insects may be trapped under the cover because they are already present in the soil or on the plants.

Figure E–2. Row cover made from polyester fabric.
Kathleen Moore, CC BY - 2.0

For those crops that are sensitive to heat or require pollination, care must be taken to remove these covers in a timely manner. Daytime opening is necessary for crops such as tomatoes and peppers if the temperature under the cover is expected to exceed 90°F for several hours. Under such conditions, the easiest way to ventilate quickly is to make long slits at the top of the low tunnel—but this should be done in anticipation of the high temperatures, not after the fact. Cucurbits (melons, cucumbers, and squash) are more tolerant of high temperatures.

Cold Frames and Hot Beds

Cold frames and hot beds are relatively inexpensive, simple structures that provide a favorable environment for growing cool-weather crops in early spring, fall, and into the winter months (Figure E–3). Some are elaborate and require a large investment, but most are reasonably priced for those who are serious about extending the season of fresh vegetables.

Cold frames rely on the sun as their sole source of heat. During the day the soil is heated by the sun; at night a cover can be used to slow the loss of heat. Hot beds supplement the heat from the sun with heating cables or with fresh manure buried beneath the rooting zones of the plants. The ideal location for a cold frame is a southern or southeastern exposure with a slight slope to ensure good drainage and maximum solar absorption. A sheltered spot with a wall or hedge to the north provides protection against winter winds. Sinking the frame into the ground also provides some protection and insulation. Some gardeners make their cold frames lightweight enough to be moved from one section of the garden to another.

In early spring a cold frame is useful for hardening seedlings that were started indoors or in a greenhouse. The cold frame provides a transition period for gradual adjustment to the outdoor weather. It is also possible to start cool-weather crops in the cold frame and either transplant them to the garden or grow them to maturity in the frame.

Use cold frames in spring and summer for plant propagation. Young seedlings of hardy and half-hardy annuals can be started in a frame many weeks before they can be started in the open. The soil in a portion of the bed can be replaced with media suitable for rooting cuttings, such as sand or peat moss.

Fall is also a good time for sowing some cool-weather crops in frames. If provided with adequate moisture and fertilization, most cool-season crops continue to grow through early winter in the protected environment of the cold frame. Depending on the harshness of the winter and whether additional heating is used, a frame may continue to provide fresh greens, herbs, and root crops throughout the cold winter months.

Cold frames can be built from a variety of materials. Wood and cinder block are the most common. If wood is used, choose a species that resists decay, such as a good grade of cedar. Never use wood treated with CCA, creosote, or pentachlorophenol, because these substances are harmful to growing plants. Wood frames are not difficult to build. Kits may also be purchased and easily assembled. Some kits even contain automatic ventilation equipment.

There is no standard-sized cold frame. The dimensions of the frame depend on the amount of available space, desired crops, and permanency of the structure. Do not make the structure too wide for weeding and harvesting; 4 to 5 feet is about as wide as is convenient to reach across.

Insulation may be necessary when a sudden cold snap is expected. A simple method is to throw burlap sacks filled with leaves, old blankets, or tarps over the frame at night to provide some protection and aid heat retention. Bales of straw or hay may also be stacked against the frame.

Ventilation is most critical in the late winter, early spring, and early fall on clear, sunny days. A thermometer in the cold frame can be used to monitor the daily maximum and minimum temperatures. On warm days, the sash should be raised partially to prevent the buildup of extreme temperatures inside the frame. Lower or replace the sash early enough each day to conserve some heat for the evening.

A few special precautions must be taken with cold frames and hot beds. In summer, extreme heat and intensive sunlight can damage plants. This damage can be avoided by shading with lath sashes or old bamboo window blinds. Also, the nearly airtight cold frame slows evaporation, so it is easy to overwater. To help reduce disease problems caused by overwatering, water early in the day so that plants dry before dark.

Convert a cold frame to a hot bed:

1. Dig out an area 8 or 9 inches deep (deeper if gravel is added for increased drainage).

2. Add an 18-inch layer of fresh horse manure.

3. Cover with 6 inches of good soil.

Figure E–3. Herbs and lettuce growing in a cold frame. Chris Alberti, CC BY - 2.0

High Tunnels

High tunnels are sometimes referred to as "hoop houses." They are constructed of PVC or metal bows that are attached to metal posts that have been driven into the ground about 2 feet deep. The PVC or metal bows are covered with one to two layers of 6-mil greenhouse-grade polyethylene and allow a gardener to walk inside (Figure E–4). Tunnels are ventilated by manually rolling up the sides each morning and rolling them down in early evening. High tunnels are a nice compromise between unheated low tunnels and a heated greenhouse. They enhance plant growth, yield, and quality. Although they do provide some frost protection, their primary function is to elevate temperatures a few degrees each day over a period of several weeks.

Figure E–4. A high tunnel is tall enough for a gardener to walk in.
Kathleen Moore, CC BY - 2.0

Remember to remove covers!

For crops requiring bee pollination, the covers are removed about the time that the first female flowers appear. For primarily wind-pollinated crops (tomato, pepper, eggplant), removal of covers is based on temperature, with a goal that the temperature not exceed 90°F for more than a few hours when the flower buds begin to open.

Greenhouses

Greenhouses can vary widely in design, durability, and cost. Location of the structure, whether it will be free-standing or attached to the home, and if it will be heated are important considerations. It can be a simple inexpensive PVC structure covered with plastic or an elaborate glass conservatory. Placing a greenhouse in a location with adequate sun exposure is extremely important. Delays in watering, or lack of adequate and timely heat, ventilation, or pest control, can lead to disappointing results. The more technology one invests in, the lower is the level of daily care that may be required. When deciding on the type of structure, be sure to plan for adequate bench space, storage space, and room for future expansion. Large greenhouses are easier to manage because temperatures in small greenhouses fluctuate more rapidly. In small greenhouses, the air volume inside is relatively small. So when the door is open, there can be a huge gain or loss of heat.

Lean-to. A lean-to greenhouse is a half greenhouse, split along the peak of the roof to lean against another structure, such as a house, shed, or garage (Figure E–5). A lean-to greenhouse is useful where space is limited to a width of approximately 7 to 12 feet and is the least expensive greenhouse structure. The disadvantages include some limitations on space, sunlight, ventilation, and temperature control.

Figure E–5. A lean-to greenhouse.
Robert Brook, Wikimedia CC BY - 2.0

Free-standing structures. Free-standing greenhouses are separate structures; they can be set apart from other buildings to get more sun and can be made as large or small as desired (Figure E–6).

Figure E–6. Free-standing greenhouse.
A S Morton, Flickr CC BY - 2.0

Structural Materials

Many kinds of commercial greenhouse frames and framing materials are available. The frames are made of wood, galvanized steel, or aluminum. Build-it-yourself greenhouse plans are usually for structures with wood or metal pipe frames. Plastic pipe materials generally are inadequate to meet snow and wind load requirements. Greenhouse coverings include long-life glass, fiberglass, rigid double-wall plastics, and film plastics with one-year to three-year lifespans. All of these have advantages and disadvantages.

Glass. An aluminum frame with a glass covering provides a maintenance-free, weather-tight structure that minimizes heat costs and retains humidity. Tempered glass is frequently used because it is two or three times stronger than regular glass. Small prefabricated glass greenhouses are available for do-it yourself installation, but most should be built by the manufacturer because they can be difficult to construct. The disadvantages of glass are that it is easily broken, initially expensive to build with, and requires much better frame construction than fiberglass or plastic. A good foundation is required, and the frames must be strong and must fit well together to support heavy, rigid glass.

Fiberglass. Fiberglass is lightweight and strong. A good grade of fiberglass should be used because poor grades discolor and reduce light penetration. Use only clear, transparent, or translucent grades for greenhouse construction. Light penetration is initially as good as glass but can drop off considerably over time with poor grades of fiberglass.

Double-wall plastic. Rigid double-layer plastic sheets of acrylic or polycarbonate are separated by webs. They are durable and are usually coated by a UV-inhibitor to extend their life.

Film plastic. Film plastic coverings are available in several grades of quality and several different materials. Generally, these are replaced more frequently than other covers. Structural costs are very low because the frame can be lighter and plastic film is inexpensive. The films are made of polyethylene (PE), polyvinyl chloride (PVC), copolymers, and other materials. A utility grade of PE that lasts about a year is usually available at local hardware stores. Commercial greenhouse grade PE has ultraviolet inhibitors in it to protect against ultraviolet rays, and it lasts 12 to 18 months. Copolymers last two to three years.

Heating

The heating requirement of a greenhouse depends on the desired temperature for the plants grown, the location and construction of the greenhouse, and the structure's total outside exposed area. The heating system must be adequate to maintain the desired day or night temperature.

Heating systems can be fueled by electricity, gas, oil, or wood. The heat can be distributed by forced hot air, radiant heat, hot water, or steam. For safety purposes and to prevent harmful gases from contacting plants, all gas, oil, and wood-burning systems must be properly vented to the outside. Unvented heaters (no chimney) using propane gas or kerosene are not recommended.

Air Circulation

Installing circulating fans in your greenhouse is a good investment. During the winter when the greenhouse is heated, you need to maintain air circulation so that the temperature remains uniform throughout the greenhouse. Without air-mixing fans, the warm air rises to the top and cool air settles around the plants on the floor.

Small fans with a cubic-foot-per-minute air-moving capacity equal to one-quarter of the air volume of the greenhouse are sufficient. For small greenhouses (less than 60 feet long), place the fans in diagonally opposite corners but out from the ends and sides. The goal is to develop a circular (oval) pattern of air movement. Operate the fans continuously during the winter. Turn these fans off during the summer when the greenhouse needs to be ventilated.

Ventilation

Ventilation is the exchange of inside air for outside air to control temperature, remove moisture, or replenish carbon dioxide (CO_2). Natural ventilation uses roof vents on the ridge line with side inlet vents (louvers). Warm air rises on convective currents to escape through the top, drawing cool air in through the sides.

Mechanical ventilation uses an exhaust fan to move air out of one end of the greenhouse while outside air enters the other end through motorized inlet louvers. Exhaust fans should be sized to exchange the total volume of air in the greenhouse each minute.

Ventilation requirements vary with the weather and season. One must decide how much the greenhouse will be used. In summer, one to one-and-a-half air volume changes per minute are needed. Small greenhouses need the larger amount. In winter, 20% to 30% of one air volume exchange per minute is sufficient for mixing in cool air without chilling the plants.

Cooling

Air movement by ventilation alone may not be adequate in midsummer; the air temperature may need to be lowered with evaporative cooling. Also, the light intensity may be too great for the plants, so shade cloth or paint may be necessary. Shade materials include roll-up screens of wood or aluminum, vinyl netting, and paint.

Controllers and Automation

Automatic control is essential to maintain a reasonable environment in the greenhouse. On a winter day with varying amounts of sunlight and clouds, the temperature can fluctuate greatly; close supervision would be required if a manual ventilation system were in use.

Thermostats can be used to control individual units, or a central controller with one temperature sensor can be used. In either case, the sensor or sensors should be shaded from the sun, located about plant height away from the walkway, and have constant airflow over them.

Water Systems

A water supply is essential. Hand watering is acceptable for most greenhouse crops if someone is available when the task needs to be done, but many hobbyists travel. A variety of automatic watering systems are available to help do the task over short periods of time. Timers or mechanical evaporation sensors can be used to control automatic watering systems.

Other Resources

Season Extension: Introduction and Basic Principles by Debbie Roos and Doug Jones

Author:

Chris Gunter, Extension Vegetable Specialist and Associate Professor, Horticultural Science

History of Landscape Design

A Brief History of Land Development and Its Influence on Landscape Design

Through the history of human civilization, land development has been an integral factor in our progress as a species. We are connected to the land. As humans went from being hunters and gatherers to gardeners and farmers, we forged a connection to the land. Likewise, as societies have evolved, so have the patterns that have influenced land development. Land formations and the environment, cultural heritage, religion, politics, war, and innovation (transportation methods, electricity, utilities, communication) as well as population growth have all played a major role in influencing architecture and the layout of the land. Many of the original influences of a particular landscape style may no longer play a role in modern society. This, however, has not prevented today's landscape design from being influenced by historical landscape styles and themes.

As civilization developed and rulers with their soldiers traveled from place to place, new ideas for land management were developed and integrated into the travelers' landscapes. Egypt introduced advanced methods of irrigation, geometric planning, walled cities, and the labyrinth, which later influenced the development of mazes, a popular element in medieval and Renaissance gardens. Assyria introduced the idea of large wooded hunting parks with small pavilions used for meditation and leisure. Persian gardens were influenced by the walled cities of Egypt, the hunting lands of Assyria, and other gardens in foreign lands. Because water was a precious commodity in these hot and arid locations, it played a central element in the garden with fountains usually centrally located.

The rise of Islam in the seventh century emphasized that paradise was a garden. Islamic gardens were designed to be looked on from above and to tease all of the senses through the incorporation of fragrant plants, colors, textures, and water features. In Spain, the Moors reintroduced, expanded, and improved irrigation and water was brought into the landscape in large quantities as a central focal point. In China, large parks with expansive water features included islands to attract mythical immortals so that people could discover the secret of long life. These imperial gardens could only be implemented by the emperor, while other Chinese gardens were more modest. During the T'ang dynasty, China and Japan exchanged ideas and goods. This led to an increased exchange of plants. Japan was heavily influenced by Chinese gardens. Being smaller, however, Japan adapted the major features of Chinese gardens to small-scale Zen gardens. The Zen philosophy influenced the Japanese garden movement with the introduction of features that were symbolic of natural elements. These included carefully placed boulders in screened sand, suggesting islands amid a body of water. The gardens were designed to encourage contemplation and self-exploration.

Greek gardens revolved around a combination of orchard, vineyard, and floral display with a fountain as a focal point. Greek mythology heavily influenced the introduction of sculpture to the garden. Rome was influential in the design and layout of modern cities. Romans developed the initial elements of urban design and spatial organization. Romans were also responsible for the introduction of topiary. After the fall of the Roman Empire, medieval gardens became primarily utilitarian with a heavy focus on food production and medicine.

During the Italian Renaissance, gardens were designed with humanistic as opposed to naturalistic values. Mathematics, geometric patterns, and a strong relationship between the villa and the garden formed the basis of this garden movement. Designers would use changes in elevation and incorporate elaborate water features to create waterfalls and pools. In France, André Le Nôtre, designer of Vaux-le-Vicomte and Versaille, influenced the layout of Paris, considered the model of civic design and land planning for the entire world during the nineteenth century. Le Nôtre introduced concepts of perspective and scale to visually expand the space. This was achieved by using an increased scale of planting incorporating parterres on broad terraces, placing sculpture, and installing grand water features. In England, the temperate climate encouraged the introduction of new plants and plant explorations in foreign lands. Some designers moved to designing landscapes based on pictorial art. Charles Bridgman, William Kent, and Lancelot (Capability) Brown influenced the development of the English romantic pastoral landscape scheme. Designers using this approach to landscape design worked with the natural features of the landscape to create more natural settings and sustainable landscapes.

Thomas Jefferson influenced the development of the American landscape. The funding of the Lewis and Clark expedition led to the Louisiana Purchase and the expansion of the United States. Expansion made a major impact on plant exploration. Plant collecting was a major interest of Jefferson's and resulted in thousands of newly documented plant species. These plants were then introduced to English plant collectors, and a prospering horticultural industry developed in the new world. Jefferson's design of the University of Virginia's campus, influenced by his stay in France, affected the design of college campuses throughout the United States. Andrew Jackson Downing influenced the establishment of landscape architecture in the United States. He introduced the English concept of a romantic or naturalistic style landscape to America and went on to influence other notable designers, including Frederick Law Olmsted, considered by many to be the father of modern landscape architecture in America.

Our landscapes will continue to evolve and change as we incorporate technology and innovation into our gardens to address issues such as stormwater management, water conservation, local food and plant trends, and population growth. Some of the elements influencing landscape design were introduced here because it is important to understand that history plays an important role in design decisions. If a house is built in a certain style, the surrounding landscape should respond to that. It is not necessary to replicate an Italian or formal English garden, but the essence of that garden style should be considered in a way that makes the landscape "at home." There is no single right approach or method. Multiple solutions and infinite design possibilities can be applied to create a beautiful, functional, environmentally beneficial landscape.

Author:
Michelle Wallace, N.C. Cooperative Extension Agent, Agriculture – Horticulture, Durham County

Permaculture Design

Permaculture was founded by Australians Bill Mollison and David Holmgren in the early 1970s. In their seminal book, *Permaculture One* (1981), they explain that permaculture melds *permanent* and *agriculture*, and is defined as *"consciously designed landscapes which mimic the patterns and relationships found in nature, while yielding an abundance of food, fiber and energy for provision of local needs."* The definition of permaculture has expanded to include people, communities and organizations, and so has evolved to permanent (or sustainable) culture.

Permaculture Is Grounded in Three Ethics

1. **Care for the earth.** The discipline looks to nature as a model for design. Permaculture includes replicating and restoring natural systems. With this ethic, permaculture emphasizes organic and sustainable methods of working with the land. It promotes the use of naturally occurring and locally available materials for design, installation and maintenance.

2. **Care for people.** One primary goal of permaculture is to provide for people's basic needs, including food, shelter, human connection, education, and a sense of purpose and place. A permaculture designer aims to produce both food and pleasure.

3. **Share in the surplus.** The third ethic is to share the surplus once basic needs are met. In alignment with natural systems, excess yield is transferred to another system or person. Waste becomes an asset to be repurposed.

Applying Permaculture Design Skills

Apply the following three tactics to design within a basic permaculture framework.

Tactic 1: Observe and interact with natural patterns

The first step in permaculture is to observe. The goal of permaculture is to learn from, and mimic, nature and natural systems. Take note of the natural systems that occur on your land. Pay attention to how and where water naturally runs and pools. Consider the ways people walk through the space because sometimes water or topography can dictate human paths. Notice where the site receives sun at different times of day. Be mindful of what types of trees are present, when and how they lose their leaves, and what you do with those leaves once they fall. All of this information is useful to understand existing assets and needs. Permaculture incorporates existing patterns and materials. For example, by observing how people navigate the space, you can locate pathways based on natural patterns. Noticing the amount of leaf fall in autumn and how quickly the leaves decompose allows you to consider leaves as an asset—a free, on-site mulch for any garden beds. Noticing sun location can help you create sunny outdoor rooms and understand where to place deciduous trees to allow passive solar heat in the colder months while blocking solar heat in the warmer seasons.

Tactic 2: Focus on energy efficiency

Mimic natural systems to decrease the human energy required to maintain a landscape. Choose and place elements to provide basic needs on-site and decrease the time, energy, and money spent acquiring the resources necessary to fuel a productive site.

Another tactic for energy-efficient planning is using a zone system based on how often tasks are performed (Figure G–1). Zone zero is the house itself. Zone 1 is closest to the house, and zones 2 through 5 are located increasingly further away.

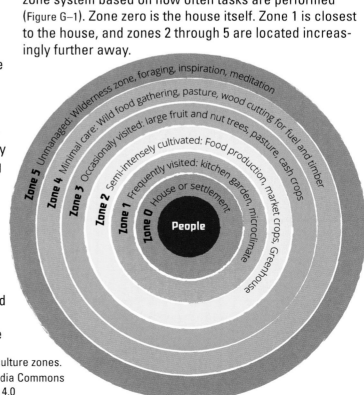

Figure G–1. Permaculture zones.
Felix Müller, Wikimedia Commons
CC BY-SA 4.0

Zone 1 includes the most intense activities that need to be performed several times a day and related elements that need to be accessed quickly. Examples include compost containers for kitchen scraps and kitchen herb gardens. Place a kitchen herb garden as close to the kitchen entrance as possible to facilitate leaving the kitchen while cooking, cutting some herbs, and returning to the stove quickly. Zone two includes activities that need to be performed about once a day. Zone three involves things that happen several times a week. Zone four includes activities that happen monthly or seasonally, such as harvesting building materials or foraging seasonal wild foods. Zone five is an area that is not managed at all, but is a place to observe and learn from nature.

Note that some activities may need to be placed in different zones for different users. Also note that zones often are shown as concentric circles. This may not always be the case, depending on the site (Figure G–2).

Tactic 3: Use permaculture principles as a guide to mimic nature

There is not one single list of principles. Rather, each practitioner has created a set of principles, very similar in concept, but with slight differences in focus. The principles delineated below are based on the principles stated by Bill Mollison in *Introduction to Permaculture* (1997), David Holmgren in *Principles and Pathways Beyond Sustainability* (2002), and well-known North American permaculturalist and author of *Gaia's Garden*, Toby Hemenway (2009). Permaculture designers strive to incorporate each of the principles described below.Included are explanations and examples of ways to apply permaculture principles as elements or techniques.

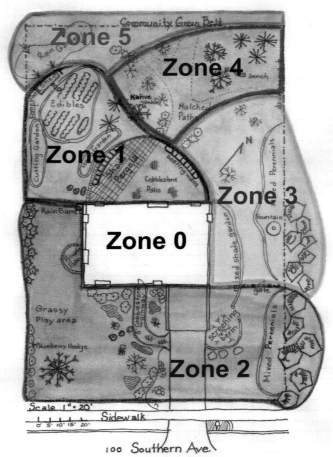

Zone 0 - House
Zone 1 - Daily use, private, high maintenance, vegetables
Zone 2 - Daily use, public, lower maintenance
Zone 3 - Monthly use, fruit and nut trees, high yield for low work
Zone 4 - Minimal care, hardy, drought tolerant plants
Zone 5 - Unmanaged, wildlife habitat

Figure G–2. Zones in non-concentric circles overlaid on a piece of property.
Renee Lampila

Table D–1. Each Zone and Its Recommended Activities

	Average frequency of visits	**Some appropriate elements**
Zone 1	Multiple times each day	Kitchen/herb garden, potted plants, chickens, kitchen compost
Zone 2	Daily	Vegetable gardens, chickens, early blooming fruit trees, trash containers, cold frames
Zone 3	Weekly	Fruit orchard, perennial shrubs
Zone 4	Visited monthly/seasonally	Mushrooms, cane harvesting, long term compost, woodland foraging, nut tree crops
Zone 5	Visited to observe & learn	Nature/Wilderness/Mature forests

Permaculture Principles

1. Observe and Interact
Learn to recognize natural patterns and relationships. Continual thoughtful observation is the key to good design. It is ideal, although not always possible, to observe a site in all four seasons before making design decisions about the space. When long-term observation is not an option, tools and calculations are available to assess the presence of sun and shade in various seasons, average monthly rainfall, first and last frost dates, and other data. Keep a garden journal (see Appendix A) to record weather, actions in the garden, and observations. Begin to recognize patterns and relationships between events such as temperature variations and disease, drought stress and insect problems, and day length and flowering.

2. Catch, Store, and Cycle Energy
Catch natural energy and use it as many times as possible within the site. Natural energies include sun, wind, water, and many natural cycles that we can work with and within to lessen the human energy necessary to maintain a landscape. Harnessing or catching the energy at its highest level is the first step. For example, installing **berms** and **swales** throughout the landscape ensures that rainwater is slowed and sinks into the earth as a natural reservoir rather than running off. Another example is to use tall **cisterns** that reach up to the roof to capture rainwater and that have outlets high enough that gravity can be used for distribution. We can also use a solar pathfinder to identify how much sun is available on a site during different seasons and where best to site and install solar panels.

Storing this energy is crucial to a site's long-term sustainability. Catchment containers and batteries must be big enough to capture the energy available. There are several rainwater catchment calculators available online. Similar calculations can and should be done with solar energy.

The final step is to cycle the energy. Once you have captured energy, use it in as many different ways as possible before it becomes a waste product or is cycled offsite. One example of energy cycling might be multiple uses of water. Catch water in a pond at the top of a slope. Use the pond as habitat for wildlife, a source of irrigation water in the heat of the growing season, and for soaking mushroom logs. When the water needs to be cycled out, drain the pond using gravity and have the soil catch that water to supply plants in drought. You have caught water on the site and used it in at least four different ways before it leaves the site. This is energy efficient cycling.

3. Relative Location
Identify which elements are connected, and place them accordingly. When we place related elements together, we reduce the human energy needed to complete tasks. Using the zone system helps with placement. One example of relative location is the placement of chickens, water, and compost in the landscape. Chickens need water, and they are very useful in breaking down a compost pile. Free-ranging chickens will gravitate toward the compost pile as a preferred hangout. Also, the material collected from cleaning a chicken coop can be added to the compost pile. These elements benefit one another, and their proximity makes our management of each element less intensive.

4. Stack Functions
Each element supports many different tasks and needs. Create elements that serve many different purposes, making the most efficient use of the materials and space used. A Belgian fence (Figure G–3) is one example of an element that stacks functions. The fence, made from espaliered fruit trees, acts as a space divider as well as a food source. An apple tree is a productive specimen in a garden, especially in the South. A fig tree placed at the north side of a vegetable garden in proximity to a house or work shed, and pruned around a ladder or tree house, becomes more than a source of food. It is also a climbing gym for children, a shade source in the summer, an easily managed harvest using the built-in platform, and wattle fence material from winter pruning. In this vein, think about placement and plant choice to optimize the number of different functions one element can play.

Figure G–3. A Belgian fence is espaliered fruit trees in a diamond pattern. This fence not only helps define the garden but also provides fruit.
Malcolm Manners, Flickr CC BY - 2.0

5. Stock the Most Important Functions
The most important needs in a site are supplied by multiple elements. Include backups in the system, alternate sources for important inputs, especially for the most important elements. For annual vegetables, have multiple sources of water collection and storage: in ponds, in cisterns, and in the soil. For soil, have multiple ways to continuously add nutrients and build soil: compost on site, grow and mulch with cover crops, and rotate crops.

6. Use and Value Diversity

Within the site, place importance on having many different species and elements. A diversity of crops allows for resilience in a landscape and helps to support a more dynamic ecosystem including both beneficial and pest animals, insects, and plants. Consider including different varieties of the same plant as well as including many different types of plants: annuals, perennials, edibles, and pollinator plants. This will offer the landscape resilience against disease organisms and pests, and it will create a more interesting look and feel.

7. Optimize Edges and Value the Marginal

Notice, learn from, and use the complexity that exists at the edges. In nature, the richest ecosystems occur where two different bioregions meet. The soil where the forest and the field meet is dense with minerals and leaf mulch, the area is an excellent mixture of sun and shade, and there is animal activity from both the field and the forest. Look for and create these types of edges in the landscape by creating curves and using plants as borders. The keyhole garden (Figure G–4) is a good example of increasing the edge in a landscape. Creating gardens in a keyhole shape increases the number of different types of plants that adjoin one another. A keyhole shape also creates an efficient use of space where many plants can be tended from one location.

Figure G–4. A keyhole garden allows a gardener to access many parts of the bed from a single location.
VLCinéaste, Flickr CC BY 2.0

Similarly, value what are often considered marginal plants and animals. This may require reconsidering what is identified as a "weed." For example, a dandelion is an early succession plant that reveals where soil needs care, a plant that is actively restoring poor soil by pulling up minerals from deep in the ground with its taproot, a wild green that we can harvest before it flowers, and a mineral-rich green naturally occurring in our landscape.

8. Use Small and Slow Solutions

Test new ideas on a small scale. Become comfortable and knowledgeable before expanding. Permaculture encourages us to use small tools and processes that may be slower, but make us conscious of local sourcing for materials. Some examples of small and slow alternatives include digging garden beds by hand rather than tilling soil, building with natural materials like cob or straw bale rather than synthetic materials with a bigger ecological footprint, and using a broad fork to turn soil rather than till each season. Another example would be building a small pond to understand how to site, install, and maintain the system before digging a large pond that does not drain or cycle.

9. Creatively Use and Respond to Change

Learn from and apply cycles as symbols of constant change, as in nature. Expect change to happen. Design and manage from this mindset. Nature is in constant flux—growing, dying, and rebuilding all of the time. This process can be referred to as succession. Work to facilitate succession in a space, transitioning a grassy lawn into a multi-story food forest in a matter of a few years through tactics such as sheet mulching, cover cropping, and planting in several different stories. Start with a ground floor, and slowly add taller and larger plants as the initial story matures. Factor in the succession of a space to create systems that work for seedlings as well as mature trees, shrubs, and understory plantings. Consider the change of seasons in the design, and create spaces and make plant choices that allow for year-round harvest and interest. Also consider the unexpected changes that nature presents, such as unexpected amounts of heat, cold, wind, and water. Build landscapes that are flexible, and be open to transitioning a design over time. As noted in the sixth principle, building in a diversity of plants creates resilience that can withstand sudden changes more readily than a landscape that includes very few types of plants and wildlife.

10. Produce No Waste (or Create Closed Loops)

Much of the work of permaculture, especially in an urban setting, is to identify and create uses for what are usually considered waste products. When we observe the landscape and day-to-day activities, we see a lot of waste (paper cups, coffee grounds, and yard clippings). Some examples of using waste in the landscape include collecting leaves in the fall and using them as mulch, connecting with the local coffee shop to collect spent coffee grounds for use in the garden, and considering garden pruning as a resource for mulch and compost rather than yard waste. Fruit tree prunings can be used to create wattle fences. If plant selection is done well, many green cuttings of plants trimmed in the garden can be placed directly onto other beds as mineral-rich mulch (dynamic accumulators). Enrich the system and lower costs by re-imagining so-called waste products as resources available for other systems and needs in the landscape. For example, weeds and caterpillars are chicken food, and chicken feces can be composted into fertilizer.

11. Design Interconnections Among Elements

Permaculture is more about connections within a system than about the individual elements within that system. Support each element (for example, a pond, a bee hive, mushroom logs, or chickens) with related elements, and understand how one element is needed as well as supported by other elements. This is the true application of permaculture, and the key to creating landscapes that are more self-sufficient, resilient, and continuously productive. An example of this on a small scale is a fruit tree guild (Figures G–5 and G–6). In a fruit tree guild, when a tree is planted, several other plants are planted around the base of that tree. Each of the plants is chosen and placed intentionally for its ability to support the tree and surrounding plants in some way. A guild might include a productive fruit tree, a mulching plant, a plant whose roots slow erosion and hold soil, a plant that attracts beneficial insects, and a plant to block the wind.

Figure G–6. An apple tree guild with pollinator attracting crown vetch (*Securigera varia*), a dynamic accumulator comfrey (*Symphytum* spp.), and human attracting strawberries planted below.
yaquina, Flickr CC BY - 2.0

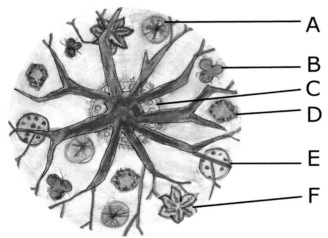

Figure G–5. A tree guild. In the center is an apple tree.
Kathleen Moore CC BY 2.0

A) Bee attractants: bee balm (*Monarda* spp.), borage (*Borago officinalis*)

B) Nitrogen fixers: clover, legumes

C) Bulbs to inhibit grass: garlic, onions, daffodils (*Narcissus* spp.)

D) Pest repellent herbs: mint (*Mentha* spp.), oregano (*Origanum vulgare*), lavender (*Lavandula* spp.)

E) Human attractants: berries

F) Dynamic accumulator, mulch plant: comfrey (*Symphytum* spp.)

Conclusion

In summary, permaculture is a mindful application of techniques for managing energies and resources, including wind, water, sun, soil, nutrients, animals, and people. Some energies are lacking and will need to be enhanced (which is often so for water). Other energies are in oversupply and may need to be mitigated or dispersed. Our ultimate goal in

Figure G–7. A spiral herb garden takes advantage of rainfall allowing water to seep down to lower levels. It takes up less space than a traditional bed because it uses vertical space.
Lucy Bradley, CC0

permaculture is to create connections among design elements so that the landscape is a cohesive and resilient system. Once principles are considered, work to ensure that principles and elements support and connect with one another.

Figure G–7 shows a garden made using multiple permaculture principles. If you are interested in more information, there are many books about permaculture as well as workshops and permaculture designer certification courses across the country.

Author:

Abbey Piner, Urban Horticulturist, Horticultural Science

Community Garden Resources

Photo credits: Left, Kathleen Moore; Right, Amy Rozycki

Tools, Forms, and Tracking for Youth, Community, and Therapeutic Gardens

The forms listed below are available online at the following URL, and the first five are reprinted here for your convenience: http://go.ncsu.edu/appendixH

- Application for Community Gardening Assistance

- Community Garden Asset Inventory

- Asset-based Community Development: Mapping Reciprocal Partnerships—Blank

- Asset-based Community Development: Mapping Reciprocal Partnerships—An Example

- Instructions for Tracking the Garden Harvest

- Tracking the Harvest: Measurement Guide for Counting or Weighing Vegetables (online only)

- Garden Harvest Tracking Sheet (online only)

Authors:

Mary Jac Brennan, Extension Agent, Forsyth County

Susan Jakes, Associate State Program Leader CRD, Extension Assistant Professor ANR/CRD

Application for Community Gardening Assistance

Name: _____

Address: _____

Phone#: _____

E-mail: _____

Your role in the garden: _____

Status of the Garden:

_____Just beginning to plan

_____Ready to build

_____Established

Type of Garden:

_____Individual Plots   _____Cooperative   _____School/Youth   _____Combined

Size of Garden:

_____< ¼ acre   _____¼– 1 acre   _____1–2 acres   _____> 2 acres

Please list the name of any organizations this project is connected with: _____

_____

How many people do you expect to be involved? _____

What is the address of the community garden? _____

_____

Who owns the land? _____

Do you have written permission to use the land for six or more years? _____

Application for Community Gardening Assistance (continued)

Do you have water available on the site? If no, how do you plan to get water? _____

_____

Do you know what the land was used for in the past? _____

_____

Have you done a soil test? _____

Did the soil test indicate any significant remediation? _____

How do you plan on funding the community garden? _____

_____

Community Garden Asset Inventory

Hello, I am with _____. We are talking to local people about their skills and experience in their communities. With this information, we hot to help people contribute to improving the neighborhood. My I ask you some questions about your skills, abilities, and experiences?

Community Involvement

Have you ever participated in the following community activities?

☐ Youth organizations   ☐ Community meals   ☐ Faith-based organizations   ☐ Community gardens

☐ Youth camps   ☐ Community fundraisers   ☐ Bingo   ☐ School-parent association

☐ Sports teams   ☐ Community groups   ☐ Field trips   ☐ Political campaigns

☐ Music groups   ☐ Neighborhood association   ☐ Rummage sales   ☐ Other groups

Have you ever been the leader of a local organization?

What was your leadership role (president, secretary, treasurer, etc.)?

Which description sounds most like you?

☐ Connector: know someone for every occasion, love to connect friends and acquaintances together to get things done.

☐ Administrative: love to organize/lead getting things done behind the scenes.

☐ Spokesperson: love to talk to new people and be in the forefront.

☐ A "doer": will do whatever is asked, do not wish to be in charge.

☐ Organizer/leader: want to be in front of the group, in charge and call the shots.

Skills Information

Now we will talk about a list of skills. It is an extensive list, so please bear with me. I'll read the skills and you just say "yes" when we get to one you have. These skills may have been learned through experience in the home, with your family, in the community, your place of worship, or your job.

Gardening

☐ Planting   ☐ Composting   ☐ Fertilizing   ☐ Harvesting   ☐ Preparing food   ☐ Pruning

☐ Raised beds   ☐ Weeding   ☐ Managing pests   ☐ Canning   ☐ Serving food

Construction

☐ Painting   ☐ Electrical   ☐ Concrete   ☐ Irrigation system

☐ Demolition   ☐ Masonry   ☐ Carpentry   ☐ Fences

☐ Plumbing   ☐ Welding   ☐ Pavers

Operating Equipment and Repairing Machinery

☐ Small appliances ☐ Forklifts ☐ Utility trailers ☐ "Bobcat" ☐ Handtrucks

☐ Auto repair ☐ Dump truck ☐ Farm equipment ☐ Mower

Business

☐ Writing reports ☐ Project mgt. ☐ Grant writing ☐ Selling products ☐ Email

☐ Filing forms ☐ Budgeting ☐ Interviewing ☐ Web design ☐ Spreadsheets

☐ Delegation ☐ Recordkeeping ☐ Property mgt. ☐ Social media ☐ Word processing

Are there any other skills you have that we have not mentioned?

Priority Skills

When you think about your skills, what three things do you do best or enjoy the most?

1. _____

2. _____

3. _____

Are there any of these skills you would like to teach?

What skills would you most like to learn?

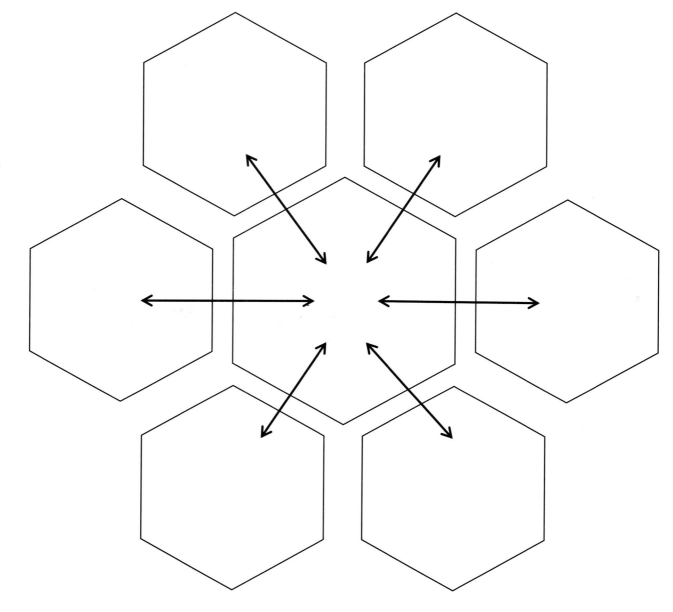

Mapping Reciprocal Partnerships—An Example

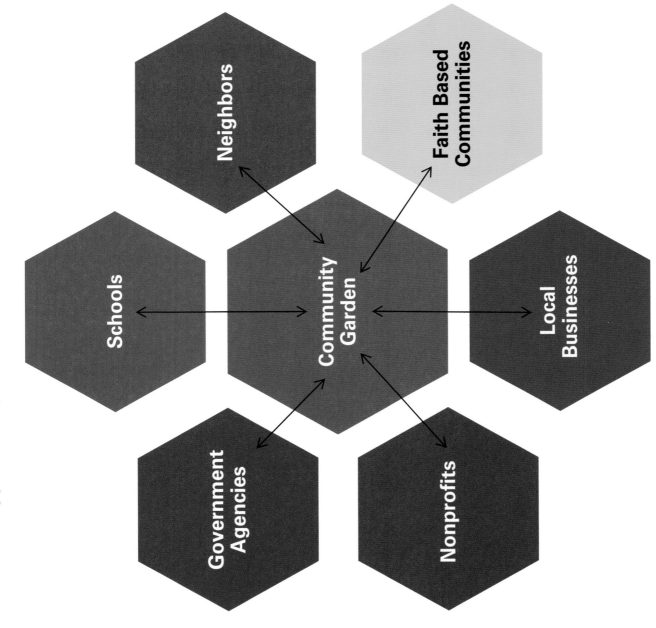

Instructions for Tracking the Garden Harvest

You may either weigh or count your produce. Select which method you prefer and use it to measure all the produce through the season. (Do not switch back and forth between the two methods, which makes it difficult to compile information). Refer to the Vegetable Measurement Guide online (https://go.ncsu.edu/appendixH) to identify what the count for each type of produce or which unit of measurement to use (pounds or ounces) when weighing your produce. If you do not have a scale, use the counting method.

Step 1. Harvest and Measure

- Pick vegetables or herbs from your garden.

- Use the online vegetable measurement guide to estimate the amounts you have picked (http://go.ncsu.edu/appendixH).

  For example:

  Basil is measured by 2 cupped hands. If you pick enough basil to fill 2 cupped hands 3 times, record "3" on your chart.

  Beets are measured by the plant. If you pull 20 beets, record "20" on your chart.

  Cucumbers are measured by the fruit. If you pick 22 cucumbers record "22" on your chart.

Step 2. Record Vegetable Measurement Amounts

- Record your harvest on the tracking sheet.

Step 3. Add Up Totals

- At the end of each 2-week period, add up the amount harvested and record at the end of the line in the "Total" column.

Step 4. Turn in Tracking Sheet

Glossary

A

Abiotic disease. A condition caused by nonliving, nonparasitic, or noninfectious agents.

Abscisic acid (ABA). Is considered a "stress hormone." It is a signaling molecule that induces stomatal closure under drought or extreme temperature stress conditions.

Abscission. The dropping of leaves, flowers, or fruit by a plant. Can result from natural growth processes (e.g., fruit ripening) or from external factors such as temperature or chemicals.

Abscission layer. Specialized cells, usually at the base of a leaf stalk or fruit stem, that trigger both the separation of the leaf or fruit and the development of scar tissue to protect the plant.

Absorption. The intake of water and other materials through root or leaf cells.

Accumulated heat units. Number of heat units in a growing season. Usually calculated at temperatures above 50°F, but can be calculated at other temperatures, depending on the crop. A day's heat units are calculated as:
Max temp (°F) + Min temp (°F) divided by 2 - 50°F.

Acid soil. Soil with pH below 7 on a pH scale of 1 to 14. The lower the pH, the more acid the soil. (See also pH.)

Actinomycete. A bacterium of an order of typically nonmotile filamentous form. They include the economically important streptomycetes, and were formerly regarded as fungi.

Active ingredient. The chemical in a pesticide formulation that actually kills the target pest.

Additive. A substance that, when added to a pesticide, reduces the surface tension between two unlike materials (e.g., spray droplets and a plant surface), thus improving adherence. Also called an adjuvant or surfactant.

Adhesion. The force of attraction that causes two different substances to join.

Adjuvant. See Additive.

Adventitious. Growth not ordinarily expected, usually the result of stress or injury. A plant's normal growth comes from meristematic tissue, but adventitious growth starts from nonmeristematic tissue.

Adventitious bud. A bud that develops in locations where buds usually do not occur. An example would be buds found on root pieces used for propagation; roots do not have buds.

Adventitious root. A root that forms at any place on the plant other than the primary root system.

Aeration or aerification. The practice involving removal of cores or turf plugs and soil with the purpose of reducing compaction and improving air flow.

Aerial root. An unusual type of root that develops on stems above ground.

Aerobic. Active in the presence of free oxygen.

After-ripening. The seed maturation process that must be completed before germination can occur.

Aggregate. Soil aggregates are groups of soil particles that bind to each other more strongly than to adjacent particles. The space between the aggregates provide pore space for retention and exchange of air and water.

Aggregation. The process by which individual particles of sand, silt, and clay cluster and bind together to form soil peds.

Agriculture. The science or practice of farming.

Agronomy. The science of land cultivation, soil management, and crop production.

Air drainage. The downward flow of air through the soil caused by gravity; also, as cold air is heavier than warm air, it flows downhill and often fills hollows which become frost pockets.

Alkaline soil. Soil with pH above 7 on a pH scale of 1 to 14. The higher the reading, the more alkaline the soil. (See also pH.)

Allée. A walkway lined with trees or tall shrubs.

Allelopathy. The excretion by some plants' leaves and roots of compounds that inhibit the growth of other plants.

Alternate leaf arrangement. Leaves are attached at alternating points from one side of the stem to the other.

Ammonium. A plant-available form of nitrogen contained in many fertilizers and generated in the soil by the breakdown of organic matter. (See also Nitrogen cycle.)

Anaerobic. Active in the absence of free oxygen.

Analogous. In landscaping, use of adjacent colors on the color wheel such as blue, violet, and red.

Anatomy. In botany, the study of plant structure.

Angiosperm. Flowering plants. Plants that have a highly evolved reproductive system. Seeds enclosed in an ovary such as a fruit, grain, or pod.

Anion. Negatively charged ion, for example, chloride.

Anion exchange. A chemcial process in which an anion is replaced by one or more other anions. Anion exchange capacity (AEC). The sum total of exchangeable anions that a soil can absorb expressed in meq/100g (milliequivalents per 100 grams) soil.

Annual. Plants started from seed that grow, mature, flower, produce seed, and die in the same growing season.

Anoplura. A major order of insects that have two pairs of wings, or are wingless, and piercing-sucking mouthparts (sucking lice).

Anther. The pollen-bearing part of a flower's male sexual organ. The filament supports the anther; together they are referred to as the stamen.

Anthracnose. Plant disease characterized by black or brown dead areas on leaves, stems, or fruits.

Anvil pruner. A pruning tool that cuts a branch between one sharpened blade and a flat, anvil-shaped piece of metal. Has a tendency to crush rather than make a smooth cut.

Apex. The tip of a stem or root.

Apical dominance. The inhibition of lateral bud growth by the presence of the hormone auxin in a plant's terminal bud. Removing the growing tip removes auxin and promotes lateral bud break and subsequent branching, usually directly below the cut.

Apical meristem. Area of the plant shoot and root tips where cells actively divide to provide more cells that will expand and develop into the tissues and organs of the plant. Also called shoot meristem.

Arboretum. An area devoted to specimen plantings of trees and shrubs.

Asexual propagation. Reproduction of a plant using its own vegetative parts. (See also Vegetative propagation.)

Aspect. Direction of exposure to sunlight.

Assimilation. Building of cell matter from inorganic (minerals) and organic (carbohydrates and sugars) materials.

ATP (adenosine triphosphate). A molecule that is used in a number of metabolic reactions in plant cells to carry out cellular work.

Attractant. A material that lures pests.

Auricle. A claw-like appendage projecting from the collar of the leaf.

Auxin. One of the best known and most important plant hormones. Most abundantly produced in a plant's actively growing tips. Generally stimulates growth by cell division in the tip region and by cell elongation lower down the shoot. Growth of lateral buds is strongly inhibited by the normal concentration of auxin in the growing tip.

Available water supply. Soil water that is available for plant uptake. Excludes water bound tightly to soil particles.

Axil. The upper angle formed by a leaf stalk (petiole) and the internodes above it on a stem.

Axillary bud. An embryonic shoot which lies at the junction of the stem and petiole of a plant. As the apical meristem grows and forms leaves, it leaves behind a region of meristematic cells at the node between the stem and the leaf, an undeveloped shoot or flower at the node. Also called the lateral bud.

B

Bacillus thuringiensis. A bacterium used as a biological control agent for many insects pests.

Bacterium. A single-celled, microscopic organism having a cell wall but no chlorophyll. Reproduces by cell division.

Balled and burlapped. A plant dug with soil. The root ball is enclosed with burlap or a synthetic material.

Band. To apply a pesticide or fertilizer in a strip over or along each crop row.

Bare-root. A plant with little or no soil around its roots; deciduous plants and small evergreens are commonly sold bare-root.

Basal. (1) At or near the base of a branch or trunk. (2) At or near a plant's crown.

Basal break. New growth that develops at the base of a branch or near a plant's crown.

Beneficial fungi. Fungi used in controlling organisms that attack desirable plants.

Beneficial insect. An insect that helps gardening efforts. May pollinate flowers, eat harmful insects or parasitize them, or break down plant material in the soil, thereby releasing its nutrients. Some insects are both harmful and beneficial. For example, butterflies can be pollinators in their adult form but destructive in their larval (caterpillar) form.

Berry. The fleshy fruit of cane fruits, bush fruits, and strawberries.

Biennial. Plants that take two years, or a part of two years, to complete their life cycle.

Biennial bearing. Producing fruit in alternate years.

Binomial. A biological species name consisting of two names: the genus name and specific epithet.

Biological insect control. The use of beneficial organisms to control pest insect populations.

Biosolids. A by-product of wastewater treatment sometimes used as a fertilizer, also known as municipal sewage sludge.

Blackleg. Darkening at the base of a stem.

Blade. The flat portion of the grass leaf above the sheath. Also the flattened, green portion of a leaf.

Blanch. To exclude light from plants or parts of plants to render them white or tender. Often done to cauliflower, endive, celery, and leeks. Also used to promote adventitious root formation on stems.

Blend, seed. A combination of two or more cultivars of the same species, for example Rebel and Falcon tall fescue.

Blight. Rapid death of leaves and other plant parts.

Blotch. A blot or spot (usually superficial and irregular in shape) on leaves, shoots, or fruit.

Bole. See Trunk.

Bolting. Producing seed or flowering prematurely, usually due to heat. For example, cool-weather crops such as lettuce bolt during summer; leaf crops are discouraged from bolting by removal of flower heads. (See also Deadhead.)

Bonsai. One of the fine arts of horticulture; growing carefully trained, dwarfed plants in containers selected to harmonize with the plants. Branches are pruned and roots trimmed to create the desired effect.

Botanical insecticide. An insecticide, such as rotenone or pyrethrum, derived from a plant. Most botanicals biodegrade quickly. Most, but not all, have low toxicity to mammals.

Botanical maturity. In fruits, refers to a final stage of development when the fruit is still on the plant and cell enlargement and the accumulation of carbohydrates and other flavor constituents are complete.

Botany. The science that studies all phases of plant life and growth.

Botrytis. A fungal disease promoted by cool, moist weather. Also known as gray mold or fruit rot.

Bract. A modified leaf, usually small, but sometimes large and brightly colored, growing at the base of a flower or on its stalk. Clearly seen on dogwoods and poinsettias.

Bramble. A spiny cane bush with berry fruits (e.g., raspberries and blackberries).

Branch. A subsidiary stem arising from a plant's main stem or from another branch.

Branch collar. See Collar.

Break. (1) Any new growth coming from a bud. (2) See Bud break.

Broadcast. (1) To sow seed by scattering it over the soil surface. (2) To apply a pesticide or fertilizer uniformly to an entire, specific area by scattering or spraying it.

Broadleaf evergreen. A non-needled evergreen.

Broadleaf plants. Also written as "broad-leaved" are dicot plants with leaves that have a flat, relatively broad surface as distinguished from plants with needle- or scale-like leaves. Broadleaf can be evergreen or deciduous.

Brown rot. Soft rot of fruit covered by gray to brown mold.

Bryophytes. Plant scientists recognize two kinds of land plants, bryophytes (nonvascular) and tracheophytes (vascular). Bryophytes are small, non-vascular plants, such as mosses, liverworts, and hornworts. They play a vital role in regulating ecosystems because they provide an important buffer system for other plants, which live alongside and benefit from the water and nutrients that bryophytes collect.

BTU. British thermal unit. Amount of heat required to raise the temperature of 1 pound of water 1°F.

Bud. A small protuberance on a stem or branch, sometimes enclosed in protective scales, containing an undeveloped shoot, leaf, or flower.

Bud break. The resumption of growth by resting buds.

Bud head. A swollen or enlarged area where a bud was grafted to a stock.

Bud leaf. First emerged leaf of a grass plant.

Bud scale. A modified leaf that forms a protective covering for a bud.

Bud sport. See Mutation.

Bud stick. A shoot or twig used as a source of buds for budding.

Bud union. The suture line where a bud or scion was grafted to a stock. Sometimes called a graft union.

Budding. A method of asexual plant propagation that unites one bud (attached to a small piece of bark) from the scion to the rootstock.

Buffer capacity. The maximum amount of either strong acid or strong base that can be added before a change of one pH unit occurs.

Bulb. A below ground stem (e.g. a tulip) that is surrounded by fleshy scale-like leaves that contain stored food.

Bulbil. A small bulblike organ that sometimes forms on aerial plant parts.

Bulblet. (1) An underground bulb formed in the leaf axis on a stem. (2) A tiny bulb produced at the base of a mother bulb.

Bunchgrass, bunch-type growth. Plant development in the absence of rhizome and stolon production; a non-spreading grass.

C

Calcium carbonate. A compound found in limestone, ashes, bones, and shells; the primary component of lime.

Callus. Tissue that forms over wounds.

Calorie. Amount of heat required to raise the temperature of 1 cubic centimeter of water 1°C.

Calyx. The entire set of sepals on a flower. The highly colored portions of the flower that protect the inner reproductive structures. Often attract insects with their color or may contain osmophores which are scent structures (both of which facilitate pollination).

CAM or Crassulacean Acid Metabolism. CAM allows plants to keep their stomata closed during the hot part of the day to prevent water loss. These plants can open their stomata at night and save the collected carbon dioxide for the next day when sunlight is available.

Cambium. A layer of meristematic tissue that produces new phloem on the outside, new xylem on the inside, and is the origin of all secondary growth in plants. The cambium layer forms the annual ring in wood.

Candelabrum. A strong, dominant rose cane with accelerated growth that originates from a bud union and explodes with many blooms.

Candle. On a pine tree, new terminal growth from which needles emerge.

Cane. The externally woody, internally pithy stem of a bramble or vine.

Canker. A plant lesion where part of the plant quits growing and the surrounding parts continue to grow. Sunken, discolored, dead areas on twigs or branches, usually starting from an injury, wound, or pathogen.

Canopy. (1) The top branches and foliage of a plant. (2) The shape-producing structure of a tree or shrub.

Capillary action. The force by which water molecules bind to the surfaces of soil particles and to each other, thus holding water in fine pores against the force of gravity.

Capitulum. (1) A dense, short, compact cluster of sessile flowers, as in composite plants or clover. (2) A very dense grouping of flower buds, as in broccoli.

Causal organism. The organism (pathogen) that produces a given disease.

Caterpillar. See Larva.

Catfacing. Disfigurement or malformation of a fruit. Fruits typically affected include tomatoes and strawberries. Catfacing is caused by insects or adverse weather during fruit development, as well as other unknown factors.

Cation. Positively charged ion. Plant nutrient examples include calcium and potassium. (See also Anion.)

Cation exchange capacity (CEC). A soil's capacity to hold cations as a storehouse of reserve nutrients.

Cell. A structural, functional unit of a plant.

Central leader. (1) A trunk or stem extending up through the axis of a tree or shrub and clearly emerging at the top. (2) A system of pruning that uses the central leader as a basic component. (See also Leader.)

Cercus (Cerci plural). A threadlike or sometimes forceps-like tail near the tip of an insect's abdomen (usually a pair) which are used to help them sense and detect their environment.

Chelate. A complex organic substance that holds micronutrients, usually iron, in a form available for absorption by plants.

Chemical insect control. The use of chemicals, or insecticide, to control insect populations.

Chilling injury. A description of plant damage to tropical and sub-tropical species, caused by temperatures that are cold but not freezing, generally ranging from 33 to 59°F.

Chimera. A plant or plant part that is a mixture of two or more genetically different types of cells.

Chitinous. Chitin is a tough, semitransparent substance that is the main component of the exoskeletons of arthropods, such as the shells of crustaceans and the outer coverings of insects. Chitin is also found in the cell walls of certain fungi and algae. Chemically, it is a nitrogenous polysaccharide (a carbohydrate).

Chlorophyll. The green pigment in plants responsible for trapping light energy for photosynthesis.

Chloroplast. A specialized component of certain cells. Contains chlorophyll and is responsible for photosynthesis.

Chlorosis. Yellowing or whitening of normally green tissue, due to a lack of chlorophyll.

Cistern. A reservoir, tank, or container for storing or holding water or other liquid.

Clay. The smallest type of soil particle (less than 0.002mm in diameter).

Climber. A plant that climbs on its own by twining or using gripping pads, tendrils, or some other method to attach itself to a structure or another plant. Plants that must be trained to a support are properly called trailing plants, not climbers.

Cloche. A plastic, glass, or Plexiglas plant cover used to warm the growing environment and protect plants from frost.

Clone. A plant group whose members have all been derived from a single individual through constant propagation by vegetative (asexual) means, e.g., by buds, bulbs, grafts, cuttings, or laboratory tissue culture.

C:N ratio. The ratio of carbon to nitrogen in organic materials. Materials with a high C:N ratio (high in carbon) are good bulking agents in compost piles, while those with a low C:N ratio (high in nitrogen) are good energy sources.

Cohesion. The sticking together of like molecules. Cohesion allows water to form drops.

Cold composting. A slow composting process that involves simply building a pile and leaving it until it decomposes. This process may take months or longer. Cold composting does not kill weed seeds or pathogens.

Cold frame. A plastic-, glass-, or Plexiglas-covered frame or box that relies on sunlight as a source of heat to warm the growing environment for tender plants.

Cole crops. A group of vegetables belonging to the cabbage family; plants of the genus Brassica, including cauliflower, broccoli, cabbage, turnips, and Brussels sprouts.

Coleoptera. A major order of insects that have two pairs of wings, or are wingless, and chewing mouthparts (beetles, weevils).

Collar. A swollen area at the base of a branch where it connects to a trunk. Contains special tissue that prevents decay from moving downward from the branch into the trunk. The place to make a proper pruning cut. (See also Shoulder ring.)

Collembola. A major order of hexapods that are wingless and have chewing mouthparts (springtails).

Compaction. Pressure that squeezes soil into layers that resist root penetration and water movement. Often the result of foot or machine traffic.

Companion planting. The practice of growing two or more types of plants in combination to discourage disease and insect pests.

Compatible. Different varieties or species that set fruit when cross-pollinated or that make a successful graft union when intergrafted. (See also Pollinizer.)

Complementary. In landscaping, use of opposite colors on the color wheel such as red and green, orange and blue, and yellow and violet.

Complete fertilizer. A fertilizer that contains all three macronutrients (N, P, K).

Complete metamorphosis. A type of insect development in which the insect passes through the stages of egg, larva, pupa, and adult. The larva usually is different in form from the adult. (See also Simple metamorphosis.)

Compost. The product created by the breakdown of organic waste under conditions manipulated by humans. Used to improve both the texture and fertility of garden soil. (See also Humus.)

Compound bud. More than one bud on the same side of a node. Usually, unless growth is extremely vigorous, only one of the buds develops, and its branch may have a very sharp angle of attachment. If it is removed, a wider angled shoot usually is formed from the second (accessory) bud. Ashes and walnuts are examples of plants that typically have compound buds.

Conifer. A cone-bearing tree or shrub, usually evergreen. Pine, spruce, fir, cedar, yew, and juniper are examples.

Conk. A fungal fruiting structure (e.g., shelf or bracket fungi) formed on rotting woody plants.

Contact herbicide. A chemical that will harm a plant, when it comes into contact with green plant tissue.

Cool-season grasses. Turf species that have optimum growth at temperatures between 60 and 75°F.

Cordon. (1) A method of espaliering fruit trees, vines, etc., to horizontal, vertical, or angled wire or wooden supports so the maximum branch surface is exposed to the sun, resulting in maximum fruit production. (2) A branch attached to such a support.

Coriaceous. Leaf textures that are leather-like and tough.

Coring. See Aerification.

Cork cambium. On woody plants, the layer of cells that produces bark, or cork, located just below the bark layers.

Corm. A below ground stem that is solid, swollen, and covered with reduced, scale-like leaves (for example, in crocus).

Cormel. A small, underdeveloped corm, usually attached to a larger corm.

Cornicle. A short, blunt horn or tube (sometimes button like) on the top and near the end of an aphid's abdomen. Emits a waxy liquid that helps protect against enemies.

Corolla. Part of a flower; all of the petals together.

Cortex cells. Found beneath the epidermis, these cells help move water from the epidermis and are active in food storage.

Corymb. A usually flat-topped flower cluster in which the individual flower stalks grow upward from various points on the main stem to approximately the same level.

Cotyledon. A seed leaf, the first leaf from a sprouting seed. Monocots have one cotyledon, dicots have two.

Cover crop. A crop planted to protect the soil from erosion, improve soil structure, and increase organic matter content.

Crawler. An early stage of insect developement (nymph) that is mobile.

Creeping growth habit. Plant development at or near the soil surface that results in lateral spreading by rhizomes, stolons, or both.

Crop rotation. The practice of growing different types of crops in succession on the same land chiefly to preserve the productive capacity of the soil by easing insect, disease, and weed problems.

Crop seed. Any seed grown for profit, often including undesirable grassy weeds, such as orchard grass.

Cross-pollination. The fertilization of an ovary on one plant with pollen from another plant, producing an offspring with a genetic makeup distinctly different from that of either parent. (See also Pollinizer.)

Crotch angle. The angle formed between a trunk and a main scaffold limb. The strongest angles are 45 to 60°.

Crown. (1) Collectively, the branches and foliage of a tree or shrub. (2) The thickened base of a plant's stem or trunk to which the roots are attached. (3) Compressed aboveground stems as occurs in grasses. The portion of a grass plant that includes the stem apex, un-elongated internodes, and lower nodes from which secondary roots begin.

Crown gall. A specific disease caused by the bacterium Agrobacterium tumefaciens that causes excessive, undifferentiated growth that may girdle roots, stems, or branches.

Cultipack. To firm and pulverize (a seedbed) with a corrugated roller.

Cultivar. A cultivated variety of a species. Propagation of cultivars results in little or no genetic change in the offspring, which preserves desirable characteristics.

Cultivation. In turf, the working of the soil without the destruction of the turf.

Cultural insect control. Controlling an insect population by maintaining good plant health and by crop rotation and/or companion crops.

Curlytop. Rolling and curling of leaves at the growing point. May indicate a viral infection.

Cuticle. (1) A waxy layer on the epidermis on a leaf. (2) The outer layer of an insect's body.

Cutin. (1) A waxy substance on plant surfaces that tends to make the surface waterproof and can protect leaves from dehydration and disease. (2) A waxy substance on an insect's cuticle that protects the insect from dehydration.

Cutting. One of several forms of asexual propagation.

Cyme. A flower stalk on which the florets start blooming from the top of the stem and progress toward the bottom.

Cyst. The swollen, egg-containing female body of certain nematodes. Can sometimes be seen on the outside of infected roots.

Cytokinins. A class of plant growth substances (phytohormones) that promote cell division, or cytokinesis, in plant roots and shoots, and promote the growth of buds.

D

Damping off. Stem rot near the soil surface leading to either failed seed emergence or to the plant's falling over after emergence.

Day-neutral plant. A cultivar or species capable of flowering without regard to day length. (See also Short-day plant, Long-day plant.)

Deadhead. To remove individual, spent flowers from a plant for the purpose of preventing senescence and prolonging blooming. For effective results, the ovary behind the flower must be removed as well.

Deciduous. A plant that sheds all of its leaves annually.

Decomposers. The microorganisms and invertebrates that accomplish composting.

Decomposition. The breakdown of organic materials by microorganisms.

Defoliation. The unnatural loss of a plant's leaves, generally to the detriment of its health. Can be caused by several factors such as high wind, excessive heat, drought, frost, chemicals, insects, or disease.

Dehorning. A drastic method of pruning a neglected tree or shrub. Entails the removal of large branches, especially high in the crown, a few at a time over several seasons.

Depredation. Causing damage or loss.

Dermaptera. A major order of insects that have two pairs of wings, or are wingless, and have mouthparts (earwigs).

Desiccation. Excessive dryness or loss of moisture resulting in drying out the plant tissues.

Determinate. A plant growth habit in which stems stop growing at a certain height and produce a flower cluster at the tip. Determinate tomatoes, for example, are short, early fruiting, have concentrated fruit set, and may not require staking. (See also Indeterminate.)

Determinate inflorescence. In determinate inflorescences, the youngest flowers are at the bottom of an elongated axis or on the outside of a truncated axis. A terminal bud forms a terminal flower and then dies out, stopping the growth of the axis. The other flowers then grow from lateral buds below it.

Dethatch. To remove thatch (a tightly intermingled layer of stems and roots, living and dead, that forms between the soil surface and green vegetation of grass).

Devigorating. The opposite of invigorating.

Diatomaceous earth. The fossilized remains of diatoms (a type of tiny algae) used to kill insect pests, snails, and slugs.

Dichotomous key. A tool that allows the user to determine the identity of items in the natural world, such as trees, wildflowers, mammals, reptiles, rocks, and fish. Keys consist of a series of choices that lead the user to the correct name of a given item.

Dicot. See Dicotyledon.

Dicotyledon. Plants with two seed leaves. Also referred to as dicot.

Dieback. Progressive death of shoots, branches, or roots, generally starting at the tips.

Differentiation. A change in composition, structure, and function of cells and tissues during growth.

Dioecious. Plants that have male and female flowers occurring on separate plants (e.g., holly).

Diptera. A major order of insects that have one pair of wings and sucking or siphoning mouthparts as adults and chewing mouthparts as larvae (mosquitoes, flies, and gnats).

Direct seeding (direct sowing). Planting seeds into garden soil rather than using transplants.

Disbud. The selective removal of some flower buds so remaining buds receive more of the plant's energy and produce larger, showier flowers. Roses, chrysanthemums, and camellias often are disbudded.

Distorted growth. Twisted or misformed growth.

Diurnal. Active during the day.

Division. The breaking or cutting apart of a plant's crown for the purpose of producing additional plants, all genetically identical to the parent plant.

DNA. Deoxyribonucleic acid is the genetic information that dictates all cellular processes. DNA is organized into chromosomes and is responsible for all characteristics of the plant.

Dormancy. An annual period which causes the resting stage of a plant or ripe seeds during which nearly all manifestations of life come to an almost complete standstill.

Dormant. Resting or not growing. A deciduous tree is dormant in the winter.

Dormant bud. A bud formed during a growing season that remains at rest during the following winter or dry season. If it does not expand during the following growing season, it is termed latent.

Dormant oil. An oil applied during the dormant season to control insect pests and diseases.

Double, semidouble. A flower with more than the normal number of petals, sepals, bracts, or florets. May be designated botanically by the terms flore pleno, plena, or pleniflora.

Double worked. Grafted twice, i.e., grafted to an intermediate stock.

Downy. Leaf textures that are covered with very short, weak, and soft hairs.

Downy mildew. Known best by its common name, downy mildew is caused by the oomycete. It is an obligate parasite of vascular plants, meaning that it cannot survive outside of a living host. It does not produce overwintering oospores, but survives from year to year on living plants. These organisms are distinctly different from the powdery mildews.

Drainage. The ability of soil to transmit water through the surface and subsoil.

Drain tile system. Tiles installed in the ground that act as a piping system to collect and redirect subsurface water that moves down into and through the soil.

Dripline. An imaginary line on the ground directly beneath the outermost tips of a plant's foliage. Rain tends to drip from leaves onto this line.

Drip zone. The area from the trunk of a tree or shrub to the edge of its canopy. Most, but not all, of a plant's feeder roots are located within this area.

Drupe fruit. See Stone fruit.

Dwarfed. Restricted plant size without loss of health and vigor.

E

Ecology, plant. The study of the complex relationships of plants in biological communities.

Economic threshold. The level at which pest damage justifies the cost of control. In home gardening, the threshold may be aesthetic rather than economic.

Ecosystem services. Provisioning services such as food and water; regulating services such as flood and disease control; cultural services such as spiritual, recreational, and cultural benefits; and supporting services such as nutrient cycling that maintain the conditions for life on earth.

Elytra. Hardened opaque outer wings of a beetle.

Emasculate. To remove a flower's anthers.

Embryo. The tiny plant that is formed inside a seed during fertilization. It has two growing points, the radicle (a tiny root) and the plumule (a tiny shoot).

Embryo dormancy. Common in seed of woody perennial plants. A physiological condition in the embryo that prevents it from growing. This type of dormancy can be overcome by stratification.

Enation. Epidermal outgrowths on leaves or stems.

Endemic. Belonging exclusively or confined to a particular place.

Endoskeleton. The internal body support found in most animals outside of the insect kingdom.

Endosperm. The tissue surrounding the embryo of flowering plant seeds that provides nutrition to the developing embryo, or the food-storage area in a seed for the growing embryo.

Enzyme. A biological catalyst that aids in conversion of food and other chemical structures from one form to another.

Epidemic. A widespread and severe outbreak of a disease.

Epidermis (leaf). The outer cell layers on the top and bottom of the leaf.

Epidermis (root). The cells that protect the root surface. The epidermis contains the root hairs and is responsible for the absorption of water and minerals dissolved in water.

Epidermis (stem). In non-woody plants, the outer single layer of surface cells that protect the stem. As in leaves, this layer is usually cutinized, or waxy, and on young stems it has stomata.

Epinasty. An abnormal downward-curving growth or movement of a leaf, leaf part, or stem.

Erect. Caneberries that have arching, self-supporting canes.

Espalier. The training of tree or shrub to grow flat on a trellis or wall. Espalier patterns may be very precise and formal or more natural and informal.

Ethylene. Is the only hormone that is a gas. It speeds aging of tissues and enhances fruit ripening.

Etioliation. Long internodes and pale green color of plants growing under insufficient light or in complete darkness.

Evergreen. A plant that never loses all its foliage at the same time.

Excise. To remove or extract, as an embryo from a seed or ovule.

Excurrent. A tree form in which the main trunk remains dominant with small more or less horizontal branches. Fir and sweetgum are examples.

Exfoliating. Peeling off in shreds or thin layers, as in bark from a tree.

Exoskeleton. An insect's outer body support.

Exotic. Of foreign origin or character; not native; introduced from abroad, but not fully naturalized

F

Fallow. To keep land unplanted during one or more growing seasons.

Family. A sub-order in the classification of plants.

Fasciation. Distortion of a plant that results in thin, flattened, and sometimes curved shoots.

Fastigiate. (of a tree or shrub) having the branches sloping upward more or less parallel to the main stem

Feeder roots. Fine roots and root branches with a large absorbing area (root hairs.) Responsible for taking up the majority of a plant's water and nutrients from the soil.

Fertility (soil). The presence of minerals necessary for plant life.

Fertilization. (1) The fusion of male and female germ cells following pollination. (2) The addition of plant nutrients to the environment around a plant.

Fertilizer. Any substance added to the soil (or sprayed on plants) to supply those elements required in plant nutrition.

Fertilizer analysis. The amount of nitrogen, phosphorus (as P2O5), and potassium (as K2O) in a fertilizer expressed as a percentage of total fertilizer weight. Nitrogen (N) is always listed first, phosphorus (P) second, and potassium (K) third.

Fertilizer ratio. The smallest whole number relationship among N, P2O5, and K2O.

Fibrous root. A root system that branches in all directions, often directly from the plant's crown, rather than branching in a hierarchical fashion from a central root. (See also Taproot.)

Field capacity. The amount of soil moisture or water content held in the soil after excess water has drained away and the rate of downward movement has decreased. This usually takes place 2–3 days after rain or irrigation in pervious soils of uniform structure and texture.

Field signature. The distribution pattern of the disease over all plants of the same species.

Filament. The stalk supporting a flower's anthers.

Flag or Flagging. Loss of turgor and drooping of plant parts, usually as a result of water stress. Can be seen as branch loss in a tree.

Floating row covers. Covers, usually of a cloth-like material, placed over growing plants and used to protect the plants growing beneath from undesirable pests and climate.

Floricane. Second-year growth of cane berries. Produces fruit on laterals.

Flower bud. A type of bud that produces one or more flowers.

Foliar fertilization/feeding. Fertilization of a plant by applying diluted soluble fertilizer, such as fish emulsion or kelp, directly to the leaves.

Foot-candle. A unit of measure of the intensity of light falling on a surface, equal to one lumen per square foot and originally defined with reference to a standardized candle burning at one foot from a given surface.

Force. To bring a plant into early growth, generally by raising the temperature or transplanting it to a warmer situation. Tulips and paper whites are examples of plants that often are forced.

Form. (1) A naturally occurring characteristic different from other plants in the same population. (2) The growth habit (shape) of a plant.

Formal. (1) A garden that is laid out in precise symmetrical patterns. (2) A flower, such as some camellias, that consists of layers of regularly overlapping petals.

Frass. The excrement of insect larvae.

Frond. Specifically, the foliage of ferns, but often applied to any foliage that looks fernlike, such as palm leaves.

Fruit. The enlarged ovary that develops after fertilization occurs.

Fruiting habit. The location and manner in which fruit is borne on woody plants.

Fumigation. The application of a toxic gas or other volatile substance to disinfect soil or a container, such as a grain bin.

Fungicide. A compound toxic to fungi.

Fungus (Fungi). A plant organism that lacks chlorophyll, reproduces via spores, and usually has filamentous growth. Examples are molds, yeasts, and mushrooms.

G

Gall. A growth on plant stems or leaves caused by abnormal cell growth stimulated by the feeding of some insects (e.g., aphids) or by viral, fungal, or bacterial infection or genetic abnormality.

Genetically modified. A plant or animal that has had genetic material introduced to its genome from other organisms through artificial means.

Genus. A subdivision of family in the classification of plants. Plants of the same genus share similarities mostly in flower characteristics and genetics. Plants in one genus usually cannot breed with plants of another genus.

Geography, plant. The study of the distribution of plants throughout the world.

Geotropism. The turning or curving of a plant's parts in response to gravity. A root growing downward is an example. Geotropism is controlled largely by the hormone auxin.

Germination. The processes that begin after planting a seed that lead to the growth of a new plant.

Gibberellins (GAs). Plant hormones that regulate growth and influence various developmental processes, including stem elongation, germination, dormancy, flowering, sex expression, enzyme induction, and leaf and fruit senescence.

Girdled or girdling. The damaging, cutting, removing, or clamping of cambium all the way around a trunk or branch. Sometimes, girdling is done deliberately to kill an unwanted tree, but often it results from feeding by insects or rodents. Wires and ties used to support a tree can cause girdling, as can string trimmers.

Girdled roots. A root system that has outgrown its pot to the extent that the roots are encircling the inside of the pot, restricting nutrient uptake.

Glabrous. Leaf textures that are hairless, smooth.

Glaucous. Covered with a grayish, bluish, or whitish waxy coating that is easily rubbed off. Blue spruce needles are an example of glaucous leaves.

Gradual metamorphosis. See Simple metamorphosis.

Graft union. See Bud union.

Grafting. A method of asexual plant propagation that joins plant parts so they will grow as one plant.

Gravitational water. Water in excess of a soil's capacity. Drains downward to groundwater.

Green cone. An enclosed composting unit often used for composting food waste.

Green manure. An herbaceous crop plowed under while green to enrich the soil.

Ground color. The color of a fruit before it ripens.

Groundcover. Plants used for holding soil, controlling weeds, and providing leaf texture.

Growing season. The period between the beginning of growth in the spring and the cessation of growth in the fall.

Growth regulator. A compound applied to a plant to alter its growth in a specific way. May be a natural or synthetic substance. (See also Hormone.)

Guard cells. A pair of specialized parenchyma cells that border the pore, responsible for regulating the size of the opening. They swell to open the stoma and shrink to close it.

Gymnosperm. Plants that have seed not enclosed in an ovary (e.g., conifers).

Gynoecium. The female portion of the flower, the pistil is also referred to as the gynoecium or "female house." The gynoecium is the innermost whorl of (one or more) pistils in a flower and is typically surrounded by the pollen-producing reproductive organs, the stamens, collectively called the androecium.

H

Habit. The growth, shape, and form of a plant.

Half-hardy. Plants able to withstand some cold, damp weather but will be damaged by frost.

Halteres. Modified hind wings that are reduced in size and used for stabilization during flight.

Hardening off. (1) The process of gradually exposing seedlings started indoors to outdoor conditions before transplanting. (2) The process of gradual preparation for winter weather.

Hardpan. An impervious layer of soil or rock that prevents root growth and downward drainage of water.

Hardy. Frost or freeze tolerant. In horticulture, this term does not mean tough or resistant to insect pests or disease.

Harrow. An implement consisting of a heavy frame set with teeth or tines that is dragged over plowed land to break up clods, remove weeds, and cover seed.

Haustorium. A modified hyphal branch of a parasitic plant. Grows into a host plant's cell to absorb food and water.

Head. (1) To cut off part of a shoot or limb rather than remove it completely at a branch point. (2) The part of a tree from which the main scaffold limbs originate.

Heartwood. The central cylinder, often dark colored, of xylem tissue in a woody stem.

Heeling in. The temporary burying of a newly dug plant's roots to prevent their drying until a new planting site is prepared. Nurseries heel in bareroot berries, trees, and shrubs.

Hemiptera. A major order of insects that have two pairs of wings and piercing-sucking mouthparts (bed bugs, stink bugs, cinch bugs).

Herbaceous. A soft, pliable, usually barkless shoot or plant. Distinct from stiff, woody growth.

Herbaceous perennial. A plant that dies back in the winter and regrows from the crown in spring.

Herbicide. A chemical used to kill undesirable plants.

Herbicide, contact. Herbicide that injures only those portions of a plant with which it comes into contact.

Herbicide, nonselective. Herbicide that kills or injures all plants. Some plant species may exhibit more tolerance than others. Examples include glyphosate, and glufosinate.

Herbicide, postemergence. Herbicide that needs to be applied after weeds emerge to be effective.

Herbicide, pre-emergence. Herbicide that needs to be applied before weeds emerge to be effective. Can be applied before or after turf establishment. Rainfall or irrigation is often needed to move the chemical into the top few inches of the soil for best activity.

Herbicide, selective. Herbicide that kills or injures some plants without harming others.

Herbicide, systemic. Herbicide that is taken up through contact with the leaves or through the soil (via contact with the roots) and is moved throughout the plant to kill the whole plant.

Heterozygous. Having mixed hereditary factors, not a pure line.

Homoptera. A major order of insects that have two pairs of wings, or are wingless, and piercing- sucking mouthparts (aphids, leafhoppers, scales, mealybugs).

Homozygous. Pure for a trait, breeds true.

Hirsute. Leaf textures that are pubescent with coarse, stiff hairs.

Hispid. Leaf textures that are rough with bristles, stiff hairs, or minute prickles.

Honeydew. A sticky substance excreted by aphids and some other insects.

Hormone. A naturally occurring compound that alters plant growth in a specific manner. (See also Growth regulator.)

Horticultural oil. An oil made from petroleum products, vegetable oil, or fish oil used to control insect pests and diseases. Oils work by smothering insects and their eggs and by protectively coating buds against pathogen entry.

Horticulture. The science of growing fruits, vegetables, flowers, and other ornamental plants.

Host. A plant on which an insect or disease completes all or part of its life cycle.

Host plant. A plant that is invaded by a parasite.

Host range. The various plants that may be attacked by a parasite.

Hotbed. An enclosed bed for propagating or protecting plants. Has a source of heat to supplement solar energy.

Hot composting. A fast composting process that produces finished compost in 4 to 8 weeks. High temperatures are maintained by mixing balanced volumes of energy materials and bulking agents, by keeping the pile moist, and by turning it frequently to keep it aerated.

Humus. The end product of decomposing animal or vegetable matter. (See also Compost.)

Hybrid. The results of a cross between two different species or well-marked varieties within a species. Hybrids grown in a garden situation will not breed true to form from their own seed.

Hydathode. A modified pore, especially on a leaf, that exudes drops of water.

Hydrophobic. Having little or no affinity for water.

Hydroponics. A method of growing plants without soil. Plants usually are suspended in water or polymers, and plant nutrients are supplied in dilute solutions.

Hymenoptera. A major order of insects that have two pairs of wings, or are wingless, and chewing mouthparts (wasps, bees, ants, sawflies).

Hypha (or hyphae). A single filament of a fungus.

Hypocotyl. The seedling stem that develops below the cotyledons.

I

Imbibition. The portion of the germination process that involves the absorption of water, causing the seed to swell, and that triggers cell enzyme activity, growth, and the bursting of the seed coat.

Imbricate. A type of true bulb that does not have the tunic (papery covering) to protect the fleshy scales.

Immobilization. The process by which soil microorganisms use available nitrogen as they break down materials with a high C:N ratio, thus reducing the amount of nitrogen available to plants.

Immune. A plant that does not become diseased by a specific pathogen. (See also Resistance, Tolerant.)

Imperfect flower. Flowers lacking one or more of the sexual parts.

Included bark. "Ingrown" bark tissues which often develop where two or more stems grow closely together, causing weak, under-supported branch angles.

Incompatible. Kinds or varieties of a species that do not successfully cross pollinate or intergraft.

Incomplete flower. Structurally, flowers consist of four main parts: sepals, petals, stamens, and pistils. Any flower that does not have one or more of these parts is considered to be an incomplete flower.

Incomplete metamorphosis. See Simple metamorphosis.

Incubation. A period of development during which a pathogen changes to a form that can penetrate or infect a new host plant.

Indeterminate. A plant growth habit in which stems keep growing in length indefinitely. For example, indeterminate tomatoes are tall, late-fruiting, and require staking for improved yield. (See also Determinate.)

Indeterminate inflorescence. An indeterminate inflorescence may be a raceme, panicle, spike, catkin, corymb, umbel, spadix, or head. In a raceme, a flower develops at the upper angle (axil) between the stem and branch of each leaf along a long, unbranched axis. Each flower is borne on a short stalk, called a pedicel.

Indigenous. See Native plant

Infection. The condition reached when a pathogen has invaded plant tissue and established a parasitic relationship between itself and its host.

Infiltration. The movement of water into soil.

Inflorescence. The flowering portion of a plant. The arrangement of flowers on an axis or stem or a flower cluster.

Inflorescence collective. A group of individual flowers. The grouping can take many forms, such as a spike (flowers closely packed along a vertical stem, e.g., snapdragons), an umbel or corymb (flowers forming a flattened dome, e.g., yarrow), a panicle (a complex hierarchical arrangement of flowers, e.g., hydrangeas), or a capitulum (tightly packed disc flowers, e.g., the center of a daisy).

Inoculation. The introduction of a pathogen to a host plant's tissue.

Inoculum. Any part of the pathogen that can cause infection.

Inorganic. Being or composed of matter other than plant or animal.

Insectary plant. A plant that attracts beneficial insects.

Insecticidal soap. A specially formulated soap that is only minimally damaging to plants, but kills insects. Usually works by causing an insect's outer shell to crack, resulting in its interior organs drying out.

Insecticide. A chemical used to control, repel, suppress, or kill insects.

Insectivore. An animal or plant that feeds mainly on insects. Any of various small, usually nocturnal mammals of the order Insectivora that feed on insects and other invertebrates.

Instar. The stage of an insect's life between molts.

Integrated control. An approach that attempts to use several or all available methods for control of a pest or disease.

Integrated insect control. The use of a variety of insect control methods, beginning with simpler.

Integrated pest management. A method of managing pests that combines cultural, biological, mechanical, and chemical controls, while taking into account the impact of control methods on the environment.

Intensive gardening. The practice of maximizing use of garden space, for example, by using trellises, intercropping, succession planting, and raised beds.

Intercalary meristem. Found mostly in monocots, these cells divide and provide the growth of the leaf from the base of the plant.

Intercropping/Interplanting. The practice of mixing plants to break up pure stands of a single crop.

Interiorscape. An interior planting, usually referring to professional designs installed in commercial buildings.

Internode. The area of the stem that is between the nodes.

Interstem/Interstock. The middle piece of a graft combination made up of more than two parts, i.e., the piece between the scion and the rootstock. Often has a dwarfing effect.

Invasive. Growing vigorously and outcompeting other plants in the same area; difficult to control.

Ion. An electrically charged particle. In soils, an ion refers to an electrically charged element or combination of elements resulting from the breaking up of an electrolyte in solution.

Isolation. The separation of a pathogen from its host by culturing on a nutrient medium or on an indicator plant.

Isoptera. A major order of insects that have two pairs of wings, or are wingless, and chewing mouthparts (termites).

J

Joint. A node; the place on a stem where a bud, leaf, or branch forms.

Juvenile stage. (1) The early or vegetative phase of plant growth characterized by the inability to flower. (2) The first stage of an insect's life cycle after the egg, either a larva or a nymph. (3) The immature stage of an organism.

K

K. See Potassium.

Key, dichotomous. A tool for plant or animal classification and identification. Consists of a series of paired statements that move from general to specific descriptions.

Knot garden. A formal garden in which two or more kinds of plants with different-colored foliage, often herbs, are planted and pruned so they interweave and form an intricate design.

L

Labellum. The spongy tip on sponging mouth parts found in house flies, flesh flies, and blow flies, used to suck up liquids or readily soluble food.

Larva. (larvae is plural) The immature form of an insect that undergoes complete metamorphosis. Different from the adult in form, a caterpillar for example. The newly hatched, wingless, often wormlike form of many insects before metamorphosis.

Latent bud. Buds that do not grow for long periods of time and can become embedded in the enlarging stem tissue. These buds grow only when conditions necessary for their growth occur, such as drastic pruning. Not all plants have latent buds.

Lateral. A branch attached to and subordinate to another branch or trunk.

Lateral bud. An undeveloped shoot or flower that is found at the node. Also called the axillary bud.

Lateral meristem. Cylinders of actively dividing cells that start just below the apical meristem and are located up and down the plant. Includes the vascular cambium and the cork cambium.

Layering. A method of stimulating adventitious roots to form on a stem. There are two primary methods of layering. In ground layering, a low-growing branch is bent to the ground and covered by soil. In air layering, moist rooting medium is wrapped around a node on an above-ground stem.

Leachate. A liquid that has passed through unprocessed organic material. May contain pathogens, phytotoxins, and anaerobic microorganisms that could be harmful to plants.

Leaching. Movement of water and soluble nutrients down through the soil profile.

Leader. A developing stem or trunk that is longer and more vigorous than the laterals. (See also Central leader.)

Leaf-axil. The area between the leaf or petiole and the stem.

Leaf curl. Rolling and curling of leaves.

Leaflet. A single division of a compound leaf

Leaf scar. A visible, thickened crescent or line on a stem where a leaf was attached.

Leaf scorch. Damage to a leaf, due to adverse environmental conditions such as high temperatures, that causes rapid water loss resulting in dead tissue.

Lenticel. A small opening on the surface of fruits, stems, and roots that allows exchange of gases between internal tissues and the atmosphere.

Lepidoptera. A major order of insects that have two pairs of wings and sucking or siphoning mouthparts as adults and chewing mouthparts as larvae (moths, butterflies).

Lesion. A localized area of discolored or dead tissue.

Life cycle. The successive stages of growth and development of an organism.

Lignen. A complex organic substance in cell walls that makes firm and rigid.

Ligule. A thin projection from the top of the leaf sheath in grasses; it may be a fringe of hairs, membranous, or absent.

Lime. A rock powder consisting primarily of calcium carbonate. Used to raise soil pH (decrease acidity).

Living mulches. Any plant that is used to cover an area of soil and add nutrients, enhance soil porosity, decrease weeds and prevent soil erosion.

Loam. A soil with roughly equal proportions of sand, silt, and clay particles.

Lodge. To fall over, usually due to rain or wind. Corn and tall grasses are examples of plants susceptible to lodging.

Long-day plant. A plant requiring more than 12 hours of continuous daylight to stimulate a change in growth, e.g., a shift from the vegetative to reproductive phase. (See also Short-day plant, Day-neutral plant.)

M

Macronutrient. Collectively, primary and secondary nutrients.

Macropore. A large soil pore. Macropores include earthworm and root channels and control a soil's permeability and aeration. . In a substrate, the larger spaces (or pores) that lies between component particles that hold air.

Mallophaga. A major order of insects that are wingless and have chewing mouthparts (chewing lice).

Mandible. The first pair of jaws on insects: stout and tooth-like in chewing insects, needle or sword-shaped in sucking insects. The lateral (left and right) upper jaws of biting insects.

Maturity. (1) In fruit, ripeness, usually the state of development that results in maximum quality. (2) The flowering phase of plant growth.

Mechanical insect control. Manual removal of insects and eggs from infested plants

Meristem. Plant tissue in the process of formation; vegetative cells in a state of active division and growth, e.g., those at the apex of growing stems and roots and responsible for enlarging stem diameter.

Mesophyll. In between the epidermis layers, where photosynthesis occurs.

Metamorphosis. The process by which an insect develops. The term is a combination of two Greek words: meta meaning "change" and morphe meaning "form." Metamorphosis is a marked or abrupt change in form or structure, like a caterpillar turning into a butterfly. (See also Complete metamorphosis, Simple metamorphosis.)

Microclimate. Climate affected by landscape, structures, or other unique factors in a particular immediate area.

Micronutrient. A nutrient, usually in the parts per million range, used by plants in small amounts, less than 1 part per million (boron, chlorine, copper, iron, manganese, molybdenum, zinc, and nickel).

Micropore. A fine soil pore, typically a fraction of a millimeter in diameter. Micropores are responsible for a soil's ability to hold water. In a substrate, the smaller spaces (or pores) between component particles that are occupied by water or air.

Microscopic. Organisms so small that they can be seen only with the aid of a microscope.

Mixed buds. Buds that produce both shoots and flowers.

Mixed fertilizer. A fertilizer that contains at least two of the three macronutrients (N, P, K).

Mixture, seed. A combination of seeds of two or more species, for example Kentucky bluegrass and perennial ryegrass.

Modified central leader. A system of pruning used primarily on fruit trees. The central leader is encouraged for the first few years, then suppressed. This system allows for well-placed scaffolds and strong crotches, but keeps the tree's crown relatively close to the ground for easy harvesting.

Molt. The shedding of exoskeleton during insect growth The form assumed between molts is called an instar.

Monochromatic. In landscaping, use of the various tints, shades, and hues of only one color.

Monocot. See Monocotyledon.

Monocotyledon. Plants with one seed leaf. Also referred to as monocot.

Monoecious. Plants that have imperfect flowers (male and female) occurring on the same plant (e.g., corn).

Morphology. The study of the origin and function of plant parts.

Mosaic. Non-uniform foliage coloration with a more or less distinct intermingling of normal green and light green or yellowish patches.

Mottle. An irregular pattern of light and dark areas.

Mulch. Any material placed on the soil surface to conserve soil moisture, moderate soil temperature, and/or control weeds. Wood chips, bark chips, and shredded leaves are mulches that eventually add organic matter to the soil; inorganic materials such as rocks are also used.

Mutation. A genetic change within an organism or its parts that changes its characteristics. Also called a bud sport or sport.

Mushroom. The fruiting structure of certain families of fungi characterized by gills.

Mycelia. Masses of fungal threads (hyphae) that make up the vegetative body of a fungus.

Mycology. The study of fungi.

Mycoplasma. See Phytoplasm.

Mycorrhizae. Beneficial fungi that infect plant roots and increase their ability to take up nutrients from the soil.

N

N. See Nitrogen.

Nativar. A plant that is a cultivar of a native plant.

Native plant. A plant indigenous to a specific habitat or area.

Naturalize. (1) To design a garden with the aim of creating a natural scene. Planting generally is done randomly, and space is left for plants to spread at will. (2) The process whereby plants spread and fill in naturally.

Necrosis or necrotic tissue. Death of cells resulting in necrotic or dead tissue.

Nectar. A sweet liquid secreted by plants to attract pollinators.

Nectaries. Cells of the petal of a flower that secrete nectar.

Nematicide. A material that kills or protects against nematodes.

Nematode. Microscopic roundworms that live in soil and living tissue, as well as water, and survive as eggs or cysts.

Netted veins. Having branched veins that form a network, as the leaves of most dicotyledonous plants.

Nitrate. A plant-available form of nitrogen contained in many fertilizers and generated in the soil by the breakdown of organic matter. Excess nitrate in soil can leach to groundwater. (See also Nitrogen cycle.)

Nitrifier. A microbe that converts ammonium to nitrate.

Nitrogen. A primary plant nutrient, especially important for foliage and stem growth.

Nitrogen cycle. The sequence of biochemical changes undergone by nitrogen as it moves from living organisms, to decomposing organic matter, to inorganic forms, and back to living organisms.

Nitrogen fixation. The conversion of atmospheric nitrogen into plant-available forms by rhizobia bacteria living on the roots of legumes.

Nitrogen, quick release. Readily available sources of nitrogen that exhibit fast turf greening, short residual, and high burn potential, such as ammonium nitrate.

Nitrogen, slow release. Slowly available sources of nitrogen that exhibit slow turf green-up, long residual, and low burn potential, such as IBDU, urea formaldehyde.

Nocturnal. Active at night.

Node. The area of the stem that bears a leaf or a branch. A joint where leaves, roots, branches, or stems arise.

Nomenclature. The assigning of names in the classification of plants.

Nonpoint source. A relatively small, nonspecific source of pollutants that, when added to other sources, may pose a significant threat to the environment. (See also Point source.)

Nonselective pesticide. A pesticide that kills most plants or animals.

Nonviable. Not alive; nonviable seeds may look normal but will not grow.

Noxious weed. (1) Weeds that have been declared by law to be a species having the potential to cause injury to public health, crops, livestock, land, or other property. (2) A very invasive, difficult to control plant.

N-P-K. Acronym for the three major plant nutrients contained in manure, compost, and fertilizers. N stand for nitrogen, P for phosphorus, and K for potassium.

Nucleus. The organelle within a cell that contains chromosomes and thus controls various cellular processes, including division into new cells.

Nutrient. Any substance, especially in the soil, that is essential for and promotes plant growth. (See also Macronutrient, Micronutrient.)

Nymph. The immature form of those insects that do not pass through a pupal stage. Nymphs usually resemble the adults, but are smaller, lack fully developed wings, and are sexually immature but eat the same food, and reside in the same environment.

O

Ocelli. There are two types of insect eyes: simple and compound. Simple eyes (called ocelli) have one lens that perceives light intensity but does not produce an image.

Offset. A new shoot that forms at the base of a plant or in a leaf axil.

Oil. See Horticultural oil.

Ooze. A mixture of host fluids, bacteria, yeast, and/or fungi.

Open-pollinated seed. Seed produced from natural, random pollination so that the resulting plants are varied.

Opposite leaf arrangement. Two leaves are attached at the same point on the stem, but on opposite sides.

Organelle. A structure within a cell, such as a chloroplast, or mitochondria that performs a specific function.

Organic. (1) Relating to, derived from, or involving the use of food produced with the use of feed or fertilizer of plant or animal origin without employment of synthetically formulated fertilizers, growth stimulants, antibiotics, or pesticides. (2) Being or composed of plant or animal matter. (3) A labeling term that refers to an agricultural product produced in accordance with government standards.

Organic fertilizer. A natural fertilizer material that has undergone little or no processing. Can include plant, animal, and/or mineral materials.

Organic matter. Any material originating from a living organism (peat moss, plant residue, compost, ground bark, manure, etc.).

Organic pesticide. Pesticides derived from plant or animal sources.

Organic production. The production of food using accepted naturally occurring materials.

Organism. A living being.

Ornamental plant. A plant grown for beautification, screening, accent, specimen, color, or other aesthetic reasons.

Orthoptera. A major order of insects that have two pairs of wings, or are wingless, and chewing mouthparts (grasshoppers, crickets, and cockroaches).

Osmosis. Passage of materials through a membrane from an area of high concentration to an area of lower concentration.

Outer seed coat. The protective outer shell for the seed.

Ovary. The part of a flower containing ovules that will develop into seeds upon fertilization. Along with the style and stigma, it makes up the pistil (female sexual organ).

Ovipositor. Egglaying organ.

Ovule. Within the ovary, a tissue/structure that will develop into a seed after fertilization.

Oxidative respiration. The chemical process by which sugars and starches are converted to energy. In plants, known as respiration.

P

P. See Phosphorus.

Palisade mesophyll. The cells just beneath a leaf's upper epidermis that contain most of the leaf's photosynthesis.

Palmate or palmately compound. (1) A leaf whose veins radiate outward from a single point somewhat like the fingers of a hand. (2) A form of espalier training.

Panicle. A panicle is a much-branched inflorescence. In an indeterminate inflorescence a panicle is a branched raceme in which the branches are themselves racemes (e.g., *Yucca recurvifolia*). A panicle can also be a compound indeterminate inflorescence, a branched raceme in which each branch has more than one flower, as in the astilbe (*Astilbe* x. *arendesii*).

Parasite. An organism that lives in or on another organism (host) and derives its food from the latter.

Parasitic seed plant. A plant that lives parasitically on other seed plants. An example is mistletoe.

Parent material. The underlying geological material (generally bedrock or a superficial or drift deposit) in which soil horizons form.

Parterre. A formal garden in which shrubs, flowers, and paths form a geometric pattern of matched pairs.

Parthenocarpic. Development of fruit without fertilization.

Pathogen. Any organism that can cause a disease.

Pathology. The study of plant diseases.

Ped. A cluster of individual soil particles.

Pedicel. The stem of an individual flower.

Peduncle. The main stem supporting a cluster of flowers (as opposed to a pedicel, which is the stem of an individual flower).

Pendulous. Hanging loosely; suspended as to swing or sway.

Perennial. A plant that lives more than two years and produces new foliage, flowers, and seeds each growing season.

Perfect flower. A type of flower with both stamens and pistils.

Perianth. Collectively, sepals and petals form the perianth.

Permanent wilting point. The point at which a wilted plant can no longer recover.

Permeability. The rate at which water moves through a soil.

Persistent. (1) Adhering to a position instead of falling, whether dead or alive, e.g., flowers or leaves. (2) A pesticide that retains its chemical properties in the soil for a long time.

Petals. Highly colored portions of the flower, inside the sepals, that protect the inner reproductive structures. Often attract insects with their color or may contain osmophores which are scent structures both of which facilitate pollination..

Petiole. The stalk that joins a leaf to a stem; leafstalk.

pH. The acidity or alkalinity of a solution on a scale of 0-14, with a value of 7 signifying neutral, values below 7 signifying acidic, and values above 7 signifying alkaline. Relates to the concentrations of hydrogen (H+) ions in the soil. pH values are logarithmic.

Phenological stage. Crop development stage.

Phenoxy. Herbicides work to mimic IAA or auxin in broadleaf plants causing uncontrolled growth and eventual death.

Pheromone. A vapor or liquid emitted by an insect that causes a specific response from a receiving insect. Some pheromones are used to find a mate. Synthetic pheromones are used as attractants in insect traps.

Phloem. The principle nutrient-conducting structure of vascular plants.

Phosphate. The form of phosphorus listed in most fertilizer analyses.

Phosphorus (P). A primary plant nutrient, especially important for flower production. In fertilizer, usually expressed as phosphate.

Photoperiod. The amount of time a plant is exposed to light.

Photoperiodism. Plant responses to light and dark periods that induce certain physiological reactions.

Photosynthate. A food product (sugar or starch) created through photosynthesis.

Photosynthesis. (1) The process in which green plants convert light energy from the sun into chemical energy in order to produce carbohydrates. (2) Formation of carbohydrates from carbon dioxide and a source of hydrogen (as water) in the chlorophyll-containing tissues of plants exposed to light.

Phototropism. The phenomenon of plants growing toward the direction of a light source.

Physiographic. The geological terrain that defines the range in which some plants occur, such as alpine plants that occur only in decomposed granite high on the slopes of mountains and survive extreme cold and winds, or desert plants which grow in sand and live on less than 10 inches of rain a year and survive temperatures over 100 degrees.

Physiology. The study dealing with the functioning of plants, their mechanisms of response, and their physical and biochemical processes.

Phytoplasm. Microscopic, single-celled organisms that lack distinct cell walls and that cause destructive diseases in plants.

Phytotoxic. Toxic to a plant.

Picotee. A pattern of flower petal coloration in which the edges of the petal are in a color that contrasts with the flower body.

Pinch. To remove a growing tip from a stem, thus causing axillary shoots or buds to develop. (See also Deadhead, Shear.)

Pine fines. Finely ground pine mulch also sold as a soil conditioner. A byproduct of the bark mulch industry, pine fines are too small to be sold as bark mulch, but make an excellent mulch for flower beds and container plantings (direct-seeded annual flowers can still push up through) and an excellent soil amendment to introduce organic matter into heavy clay soil.

Pinnately compound. An arrangement of leaflets attached laterally along the rachis of a compound leaf.

Pinnatifid. A leaf shape cleft nearly to the midrib in broad divisions not separated into distinct leaflets.

Pistil. The female component of the flower. It is in the center of the flower and has three parts, the stigma, the style, and the ovary.

Pistillate. Female flowers; flowers with no stamens (pistils only), also called imperfect because they lack the stamen.

Plant classification. The scientific grouping and naming of plants by characteristics.

Plant disease. Any lasting change in a plant's normal structure or function that deviates from its healthy state.

Plant growth regulator. See Growth regulator.

Plant nutrition. A plant's need for and use of basic chemical elements. (See also Macronutrient, Micronutrient.)

Plant pathology. The study of diseases in plants: what causes them, what factors influence their development and spread, and how to prevent or control them.

Plant tissue culture. Plant material grown in vitro under sterile conditions in an artificial medium. A primary means of rapidly increasing the number of plants from a single mother plant.

Pleach. To intertwine branches of trees, vines, or shrubs to form an arbor or hedge.

Plug. 2- to-4-inch chunks of sod, either round or square, with soil around their roots.

Pleniflora. A term used in botanical names to indicate a double-flowered cultivar. (See also Double.)

Plumule. The shoot portion of an embryo.

Point source. A single, identifiable source of pollutants such as a factory or municipal sewage system. (See also Nonpoint source.)

Pollard. A method of tree pruning that involves heading back severely to main branches each year so as to produce a thick, close growth of young branches.

Pollen. A plant's male sex cells, which are held on the anther for transfer to a stigma by insects, wind, or some other mechanism.

Pollen tube. A slender tube growing from the pollen grain that carries the male gametes and delivers them to the ovary.

Pollination. The first step in fertilization; the transfer of pollen from anther to a stigma.

Pollinator. An agent such as an insect that transfers pollen from a male anther to a female stigma.

Pollinizer. A plant whose pollen sets fruit on another plant. (See also Cross-pollination.)

Polychromatic. In landscaping, use of all the colors and their tints, shades, and tones.

Pome fruit. A fruit having a core, such as an apple, pear, or quince.

Pomology. The science of fruits and the art of fruit culture, especially tree fruits.

Porespace. The spaces within a rock body or soil that are unoccupied by solid material.

Postemergent. A product applied after crops or weeds emerge from the soil.

Potash. The form of potassium listed in most fertilizer analyses.

Potassium (K). A primary plant nutrient, especially important for developing strong roots and stems. In fertilizers, usually expressed as potash.

Powdery mildew. Fine, white to gray, powdery fungal coating on leaves, stems, and flowers.

Power raking. Using fixed knife-type blades that slice thatch as opposed to ripping it out.

Predator. An animal that eats another animal.

Preemergence. A product applied before crops or weeds emerge from the soil.

Preharvest interval. The amount of time that must elapse (legally) after application of a pesticide before harvest takes place.

Preplant. A product applied before a crop is planted.

Prickle. A rigid, straight, or hooked outgrowth of bark or stems. Often called a thorn, but technically different. Roses are examples of plants with prickles. (See also Thorn.)

Primary growth. Growth that occurs via cell division at the tips of stems and roots.

Primary nutrient. A nutrient required by plants in a relatively large amount (nitrogen, phosphorus, and potassium).

Primocane. First-year growth, usually vegetative, on cane berries. Only fall-bearing raspberries produce fruit on primocanes in late summer.

Processed fertilizer. A fertilizer that is manufactured or refined from natural ingredients to be more concentrated and more available to plants.

Production. Nursery or greenhouse growing area used before plants are put up for retail sales.

Prolegs. Are plump, fleshy, and often hooked to allow the caterpillar to hold onto a plant

Propagate. To start new plants by seeding, budding, grafting, dividing, etc.

Propagule. Any structure capable of being propagated or acting as an agent of reproduction.

Protozoa. Any of a diverse group of eukaryotes, of the kingdom Protista, that are primarily unicellular, existing singly or aggregating into colonies.

Provenance. An area within a plant's native range that seed or propagation materials such as cuttings were collected.

Prune. To remove plant parts to improve a plant's health, appearance, or productivity.

Pseudobulb. A thickened, aboveground, modified stem that serves as a storage organ. Found in some orchids.

Psocoptera. A major order of insects that have two pairs of wings, or are wingless, and chewing mouthparts (barklice, booklice).

Pubescent. Leaf textures that are hairy.

Pupa. The stage between larva and adult in insects that go through complete metamorphosis.

Pupae. An insect in the non-feeding stage between the larva and adult, during which it typically undergoes complete transformation within a protective cocoon or hardened case. Only insects that undergo complete metamorphosis have pupal stages.

Q

Quarantine. A regulation forbidding sale or shipment of plants or plant parts, usually to prevent disease, insect, nematode, or weed invasion in an area.

Quick-release fertilizer. A fertilizer that contains nutrients in plant-available forms such as ammonium and nitrate. Fertilizer is readily soluble in water.

Quiescent. In a state or period of inactivity or dormancy.

R

Raceme. A flower stalk on which the florets start blooming from the bottom of the stem and progress toward the top.

Rachis. The rachis is the midrib of a leaf. It is usually continuous with the petiole and is often raised above the lamina or leaf blade. On a compound leaf, the rachis extends from the first set of leaflets (where the petiole ends) to the end of the leaf. The stem of a plant, especially a grass, bearing flower stalks at short intervals.

Radial spacing. The horizontal spacing of branches around a trunk.

Radicle. The root portion of an embryo.

Raking, power. Removal of debris with rapidly rotating vertical tines or brush.

Ray flowers. In a composite flower head of the daisy family any of a number of strap-shaped and typically sterile florets that form the ray. In plants such as dandelions, the flower head is composed entirely of ray flowers (also called florets).

Receptacle. The base of the flower stalk that holds the sexual organs of a flower.

Region of maturation. The area of the root where the enlarged root cells turn into the various root tissues.

Regulatory insect. Term used to describe insects that have an unknown impact in a new environment to which they may be moved.

Relative humidity. The percentage of moisture saturating the air at a given temperature. The ratio of water vapor in the air to the amount of water the air could hold at the current temperature and pressure.

Repotting (or "transplanting"). The process of moving previously potted plants into new containers, usually of larger size.

Resistance. The ability of a host plant to prevent or reduce disease development by retarding multiplication of the pathogen within the host.

Respiration. The process of burning sugars to use as energy for plant growth. The process by which carbohydrates are converted into energy. This energy builds new tissues, maintains the chemical processes, and allows growth within the plant.

Reversion growth. A stem that originates from and has the characteristics of the plant's rootstock. (See also Sucker.)

Rhizobia bacteria. Bacteria that live in association with roots of legumes and convert atmospheric nitrogen to plant-available forms, a process known as nitrogen fixation.

Rhizome. A stem that forms the main axis of the plant. An underground creeping stem that can produce roots and shoots at each node. (adj. rhizomatous)

Rhizosphere. The thin layer of soil immediately surrounding plant roots.

Root bound. A condition in which a plant's root system has outgrown its pot resulting in root constriction. Typically, the roots begin to encircle the pot's outer edge. Further growth is prevented until the plant is removed from the container.

Root cap. The cells that protect the root tip as it pushes through the soil. These cells slough off and are replaced by others as roots grow downward.

Root cutting. An asexual method of propagation that involves removing a section of root from a 2- to 3- year-old plant during the dormant season and placing it into growing medium.

Root hair. Thin hair-like structure that grows from the epidermis of the region of maturation of the root. This structure absorbs water and nutrients from the soil.

Root knots. Swelling and deformation of roots.

Root meristem. A type of apical meristem located at the tips of roots. Provides for elongation of the roots and produces the cells that will become the epidermis, cortex, xylem, cambium, and phloem of the mature root.

Root and stem rot. Soft and disintegrated roots and lower portions of the stem; sometimes results in death of the plant.

Root pruning. The cutting or removal of some of a plant's roots.

Rootstock. The portion of a plant used to provide the root system and sometimes the lower part of the stem for a grafted plant.

Root sucker. See Sucker.

Rosette. A small cluster of leaves radially arranged in an overlapping pattern.

Rot. Decomposition and destruction of tissue.

Rotation (rotate). The practice of growing different plants in different locations each year to prevent the buildup of soil borne diseases and insect pests.

Row cover. A sheet of synthetic material used to cover plants in order to retain heat and exclude insect pests.

Rugose. Wrinkled.

Rogue. To uproot or destroy diseased or atypical plants.

Runner. See Stolon. (Examples of runners are strawberries and spider plants.)

Russet. Yellowish-brown or reddish-brown scar tissue on the surface of a fruit. Also naturally occurring tissue on potato tubers.

Rust. Fruiting structure of certain family of fungi. Raised pustules on leaves, stems, and fruits; contain yellow-orange or rust-colored spore masses.

S

Sand. The coarsest type of soil particle.

Sanitation. The removal and disposal of infected plant parts; decontamination of tools, equipment, hands, etc.

Saprophyte. An organism that can subsist on non-living matter.

Sapwood. The newly formed lighter outer wood located just inside the vascular cambium of a tree trunk and active in the conduction of water.

Scab. Slightly raised, rough areas on fruits, tubers, leaves, or stems.

Scabrous. Leaf textures that are rough to the touch; texture of sandpaper.

Scaffold branches. The principal branches of a tree or shrub arising from the trunk or another main branch to form the plant's framework.

Scaffold whorl. The first three to four branches on a trunk uniformly spaced.

Scale. (1) A modified leaf that protects a bud. (2) A type of insect pest.

Scalping. Excessive removal of turf leaves by close mowing, resulting in a brown, stubbly appearance.

Scarification. Artificial methods to soften the seed coat including scratching or rupturing the seed coat with sandpaper, nicking it with a knife, or degrading it with concentrated acid.

Scion. The portion of a plant or cultivar that is grafted onto a separate rootstock, consisting of a piece of shoot with dormant buds that will produce the stem and branches.

Sclerites. Insects' bodies are separated into segments, and the cuticle of each segment is formed into several hardened plates called sclerites.

Sclerotia. Seed-like, compact masses of fungal tissue that allow fungi to survive unfavorable conditions.

Scout. Assessing pest pressure and plant performance. The first step in any IPM plan.

Secondary growth. Growth that increases the girth of stems or roots without elongating them. Secondary growth is seen in some dicots but not in monocots.

Secondary nutrient. A nutrient needed by plants in a moderate amount: calcium, magnesium, and sulfur. (See also Macronutrient, Primary nutrient.)

Secondary root. A type of root system that forms after the primary root emerges from a seed and branches outward.

Seed. Matured ovule that occurs as, or in, mature fruits.

Seed, certified. A seed lot inspected to meet minimum standards and to ensure trueness to type for a given cultivar.

Seed coat. The protective outer layer of a seed that provides protection for the enclosed embryo.

Seed coat impermeability. Caused by a hard seed coat that is impermeable to water, preventing the seed from germinating.

Seed dormancy. An adaptive feature of some plants to keep the seeds from germinating until conditions exist that favor seedling survival.

Seed leaf. See Cotyledon.

Seed scarification. Involves breaking, scratching, or softening the seed coat so that water can enter and begin the germination process.

Selective pesticide. A pesticide that kills only certain kinds of plants or animals; for example, 2,4-D kills broadleaf lawn weeds but leaves grass largely unharmed.

Self-fertile. A plant that produces seed with its own pollen.

Self-fruitful. A plant that bears fruit through self-pollination.

Self-pollination. Pollination that can occur when the anther and stigma are in the same flower or if the anther and stigma are in different flowers on the same plant or in different flowers on different plants of the same species, variety, or cultivar.

Self-sterile. A plant that needs pollen from another species, variety, or cultivar (e.g., cross-pollination).

Self-unfruitful. A plant that requires another variety for pollination. (See also Pollinizer.)

Semi-trailing. Caneberries that are fully trailing the first year but become more erect the following year.

Senescence. The aging process. Also used to describe a plant that is in the process of going dormant for the season, although technically only the parts that are dying (the leaves) are becoming senescent.

Sepal. The outer covering of the flower when it is in the bud stage. They are leaf-like in structure and usually green; however they can be colored and look like petals, as in tulips. They may fold back as in roses or remain upright as with carnations. Together, all the sepals form the calyx.

Separation. A term applied to a form of propagation by which plants that produce bulbs or corms multiply.

Sessile. Sessile means "sitting" or "resting on the surface." A characteristic of plant parts which have no stalk. Flowers or leaves are borne directly from the stem or peduncle, lacking a petiole or pedicle. Stalkless flowers, as in a spike with sessile flowers attached directly at the base.

Sexual propagation. The deliberate, directed reproduction of plants using seeds or spores. (See also Asexual propagation.)

Shear. To cut back a plant (as opposed to selective pruning or deadheading). Often used to regenerate plants with many small stems, where dead-heading would be too time consuming.

Sheath. The basal portion of the leaf surrounding the grass stem. In grass plants, it is usually split with overlapping edges.

Shoot. One season's branch growth. The bud scale scars (ring of small ridges) on a branch mark the start of a season's growth.

Shoot meristem. The apex of a shoot where cells actively divide to provide more cells that will expand and develop into the tissues and organs of the plant. Also called apical meristem.

Short-day plant. A plant requiring more than 12 hours of continuous darkness to stimulate a change in growth, e.g., a shift from the vegetative to reproductive phase. (See also Long-day plant, Day-neutral plant.)

Shot-hole. Roughly circular holes in leaves resulting from the dropping out of the central dead areas of spots.

Shoulder ring. One of the ridges around the base of a branch where it attaches to a trunk or to another branch. (See also Collar.)

Shrub. A woody plant that grows to a height of 3 to 12 feet. May have one or several stems with foliage extending nearly to the ground.

Side-dress. To apply fertilizer to the soil around a growing plant.

Sign. The part of a pathogen seen on a host plant; the physical evidence of something that has attacked a plant.

Signal word. An indication of toxicity on pesticide labels. Pesticides labeled "caution" are the least toxic, those labeled "warning" are more so, and those labeled "danger" are the most toxic.

Silt. A type of soil particle that is intermediate in size between sand and clay.

Simple metamorphosis. A type of insect development involving three stages: egg, nymph, and adult. The nymph usually resembles the adult. (See also Complete metamorphosis.)

Siphonaptera. A major order of insects that have two pairs of wings, or are wingless, and piercing-sucking mouthparts as adults and chewing mouthparts as larvae (fleas).

Slicing. Penetration of turf in a vertical plane by a series of solid flat tines.

Slime flux. A type of ooze specific to trees where the fermentation of plant fluids creates pressure.

Slime mold. A 'primitive' class of fungi called Myxomycetes. Slime molds are saprophytic fungi that live on dead organic matter, such as wood mulch, and appear in several different colors. Also called Dog Vomit mold, the spores are widespread and it usually appears in spring or early summer after soaking rains.

Slit seeder. A gasoline-powered machine that slices even rows into the soil, and drops grass seed directly into those rows to improve seed-soil contact. Slit seeders are most typically used to apply seed over an existing lawn, where mature grass or weeds may get in the way of the new seed.

Slow-release fertilizer. A fertilizer material that must be converted into a plant-available form by soil microorganisms.

Smut. Black masses of spores produced by fungi that may form on stems, ears of corn, etc. A specific type of fungus that grows in the grain heads.

Soft pinch. To remove only the succulent tip of a shoot, usually with the fingertips.

Soft rot. The water soaked appearance of cells that don't get enough oxygen.

Soil. A natural, biologically active mixture of weathered rock fragments and organic matter at the earth's surface.

Soil horizons. A soil horizon is a layer generally parallel to the soil crust, whose physical characteristics differ from the layers above and beneath. Each soil type usually has three or four horizons. Horizons are defined in most cases by obvious physical features, chiefly color and texture.

Soilless mix or substrate. Components used in potting mixes that are not true soils, such as vermiculite, perlite, peat, bark, sand, gravel, sphagnum moss used in container growing mixes but no real soil.

Soil salinity. A measure of the total soluble salts in a soil.

Soil solution. The solution of water and dissolved minerals found in soil pores.

Soil structure. The arrangement of soil particles or their aggregates.

Soil texture. How coarse or fine a soil is. Texture is determined by the proportions of sand, silt, and clay in the soil.

Solitary flower. A plant that forms a stalk that bears a single flower, such as a tulip.

Soluble salt. A mineral (salt) often remaining in soil from irrigation water, fertilizer, compost, or manure applications.

Sonic repeller. A sonic wave-emitting unit said to disrupt the activities of small mammals or insects but not proven to be effective.

Sooty mold. Common name given to a condition that is not truly a disease, but a black coating on leaves, branches and fruit made up of a fungal growth that is usually dark colored and powdery-like, giving it the name sooty mold. These fungi are saprophytic, that is, they do not feed on live plant tissue, but rather thrive on insect secretions, known as honeydew, that are high in sugars.

Sori. A cluster of sporangia borne on the underside of a fern frond.

Species. A group of individual plants interbreeding freely and having many (or all) characteristics in common.

Species-specific. Limited to effecting one species or a certain group of species.

Specific epithet. The second word in a Latin binomial. Sometimes called trivial name.

Specimen. An individual plant with outstanding characteristics (leaves, flowers, or bark), generally used as a focal point in a landscape.

Spiking. Penetration of turf in a vertical plane by series of solid round tines.

Spines. Are modified leaves, leaflets, petioles or stipules. Blackberries or wintergreen barberry (*Berberis juliane*) have spines.

Spiracles. Circular tubes in the exoskeleton of insects that allow air into the trachea. In an insect's respiratory system, tracheal tubes deliver oxygen directly to tissues.

Split complementary. In landscaping, use of a pure color and a color from either side of its complementary counterpart.

Spongy parenchyma. The lower layer of cells in the mesophyll.

Spore. (1) The reproductive body of a fungus or other lower plant, containing one or more cells. (2) A bacterial cell modified to survive in an adverse environment. (3) The reproductive unit of ferns.

Sport. See Mutation.

Spot treatment. To apply a pesticide to a small section or area of a crop.

Sprig. A stolon or rhizome used to establish turf.

Spur. Short, stubby stems common on fruit trees such as apples and pears. These spurs produce the flower buds.

Stamen. The male, pollen-producing part of a flower consisting of the anther and its supporting filament.

Stamens or staminate. The male fertilizing organ of a flower, typically consisting of a pollen-containing anther and a filament; flowers with no pistil (stamens only), also called imperfect because they lack the pistil.

Standard. A plant pruned so that it consists of a single bare vertical stem, atop which a shaped mass of foliage, usually globular, is maintained.

Stem cutting. A section of a stem prepared for vegetative propagation; forms adventitious roots on the stem.

Sterile. (1) Material that is free of disease organisms (pathogens), as in potting medium. (2) A plant that is unable to produce viable seeds.

Stigma. The receptive surface on a pistil that receives pollen.

Stipules. A pair of appendages found on many leaves where the petiole meets the stem.

Stock. See Rootstock.

Stolon. An above-ground creeping stem that can produce roots and shoots at each node. This horizontal stem can be either fleshy or semi-woody.

Stoloniferous. Producing or bearing stolons.

Stoma, stomate, stomata (plural). Any pore or opening on the surface of a leaf or stem through which gases (water vapor, carbon dioxide, and oxygen) are exchanged. This pore is an opening into a leaf that is formed by specialized epidermal cells on the underside (and sometimes upper sides) of the leaf.

Stomatal complex. The term is also used collectively to refer to an entire stomatal complex, both the stomatal pore itself and its accompanying guard cells.

Stone fruit. A fleshy fruit, such as a peach, plum, or cherry, usually having a single hard stone that encloses a seed. Also called a drupe.

Strain. A variation within a cultivar or variety.

Stratification. Chilling seed under moist conditions. This method mimics the conditions a seed might endure after it falls to the ground in the autumn and goes through a cold winter on the ground.

Style. On a pistil, a tube connecting the stigma and the ovary.

Stylet. A nematode's lance like or needlelike mouth-part. Used to puncture and feed from plant cells.

Subapical meristem. Aids in formation of shoots and flowering stalks.

Subspecies. A major division of a species, more general in classification than a cultivar or variety.

Succession. The progression of a plant community to a stable mixture of plants.

Succession planting. (1) The practice of planting new crops in areas vacated by harvested crops. (2) Several smaller plantings made at timed intervals.

Succulent. Leaf textures that are fleshy, soft, and thickened in texture; modified for water storage.

Sucker. A shoot or stem that originates underground from a plant's roots or trunk, or from a root- stock below the graft union. (See also Reversion growth.)

Summer annual. Annual plant in which the seed germinates in the spring, and the plant develops, matures, and produces seed by the end of the growing season.

Summer oil. A light refined horticultural oil used during the growing season to control insect pests and diseases.

Sun scald. Winter or summer injury to the trunk of a woody plant caused by hot sun and fluctuating temperatures. Typically, sun scalded bark splits and separates from the trunk.

Surfactant. See Additive.

Susceptibility. The condition of a plant in which it is prone to the damaging effects of a pathogen or other factor.

Sustainable gardening. Gardening practices that allow plants to thrive with minimal inputs of labor, water, fertilizer, and pesticides.

Suture. A line of junction of contiguous plant parts.

Swale. A low place in a tract of land, usually moister than the adjacent higher land. A valleylike intersection of two slopes in a piece of land.

Symbiotic. Mutually beneficial.

Symptom. A plant's response to an attack by animal or pathogen; a visible reaction of a plant to disease such as wilting, necrosis, abnormal coloration, defoliation, fruit drop, abnormal cellular growth, or stunting.

Synthetic fertilizer. Chemically formulated fertilizers, mainly from inorganic sources.

Synthetic pesticide. Chemically formulated pesticide, mainly from inorganic sources.

Systemic. Spreading internally throughout the plant.

Systemic pesticide. A pesticide that moves throughout a target organism's system to cause its death.

T

Taproot. A type of root system that grows straight down with few lateral roots.

Taxonomy. Classification or naming of plants or animals.

Temporary branch. (1) A small shoot or branch left on a young tree's trunk for protection and nourishment. (2) A low lateral allowed to remain until a tree is tall enough to have scaffolds at the desired height.

Tender. Not tolerant of frost and cold temperatures. In horticulture, tender does not mean weak or susceptible to insect pests or diseases.

Tendril. A slender projection used for clinging, usually a modified leaf. Easily seen on vines such as grapes and clematis.

Terminal. The tip (apex), usually of a branch or shoot.

Terminal bud. The bud that is found at the tip of shoots.

Thatch. A tightly intermingled layer of undecomposed roots, stems, and shoots located between the soil surface and the green vegetation of the turf grass. The brown, fibrous, spongy layer located between the soil and the grass blades.

Thermoperiod. The change in temperature from day to night.

Thermophilic. Growing at high temperatures, as in microorganisms that break down organic matter in a hot compost pile.

Thin. (1) To remove an entire shoot or limb where it originates. (2) To selectively remove plants or fruits to allow remaining plants or fruits to develop.

Thorax. The thorax is made up of three segments (prothorax, mesothorax, and metathorax). Each segment has a pair of legs, and the wings are attached to the last two segments, which also have spiracles or circular openings used for breathing.

Thorn. A hard, sharp-pointed, leafless branch. A modification of a stem or branch which means they can be branched or not, have leaves or not and they arise from a bud. A black locust tree (*Robinia pseudoacacia*) or hawthorn (*Crataegus oxycantha*) is an example of a plant that produces thorns. (See also Prickle.)

Threshold. The point at which plant aesthetic quality or injury leads a gardener to decide action should be taken.

Thysanoptera. A major order of insects that have two pairs of wings, or are wingless, and rasping-sucking mouthparts (thrips).

Thysanura. A major order of insects that are wingless and have chewing mouthparts (silverfish, firebrats).

Tiller. A grass plant shoot arising in the axes of leaves in the unelongated portion of the stem. A shoot that arises from a plant's crown.

Tilth. The state of aggregation of a soil especially in relation to its suitability for crop growth.

Tissue culture. The process of generating new plants by placing small pieces of plant material onto a sterile medium.

Tolerant. A plant that will produce a normal yield even if infested by a disease or insect pest. (See also Immune, Resistance.)

Tomentose. Leaf textures that are covered with matted, wooly hairs, like Lamb's Ears (*Stachys byzantina*).

Top-dressing. 1) The practice of spreading a thin layer (¼ inch) of soil, compost, humus, or a sand and peat mix over the turf or soil. 2) For turf: A sand or prepared soil mix applied to the turf to help smooth the surface, enhance establishment, and reduce thatch buildup.

Topiary. A tree or shrub shaped and sheared into an ornamental, unnatural form, usually a geometric shape or the shape of an animal.

Totipotency. The ability of any cell to develop into an entire plant.

Trace element. See Micronutrient.

Tracheophytes. Any plant that has elaborate tissues with water- and nutrient-conducting tissue termed "vascular tissue" including roots, stems and leaves. Some tracheophytes reproduce with seeds and some with spores.

Trailing. Cane berries that are not selfsupporting and have low yields.

Transpiration. The loss of water through the leaf stomata. The transpired water comes from the photosynthetic process and also from water in the cells.

Trap Crop. A trap crop is a plant that attracts agricultural creatures usually insects, away from nearby crops. This form of companion planting can save the main crop from decimation by pests without the use of pesticides.

Triadic. In landscaping, use of three colors that are at equal distances from each other on the color wheel.

Trichomes. The "hairs" that are extensions of the epidermal cells on a leaf.

Tropism. The tendency of a plant part to turn in response to an external stimulus, either by attraction or repulsion, as a leaf turns toward light. (See also Geotropism, Phototropism.)

Trunk. The main stem of a tree. Also called a bole.

Trunk taper. The degree to which a tree's stem or trunk decreases in diameter as a function of height above ground.

Truss. A flower cluster, usually growing at the terminal of a stem or branch.

Tuber. (1) A below ground stem used for food storage (e. g., potato). (2) For turf: An underground stem modified for food storage that is attached to the root system as found in yellow nutsedge.

Tuberous root. An underground storage organ made up of root tissue. Sprouts only from the point at which it was attached to the stem of the parent plant. Dahlias are an example.

Tuberous stem. A below ground stem consisting of a swollen hypocotyl, lower epicotyl, and upper primary root (for example, in tuberous begonias).

Tunicate. A tunicate bulb has a paper-like covering or tunic that protects the scales from drying and from mechanical injury. Examples of tunicate bulbs include: tulips, daffodils, hyacinths, grape hyacinths (muscari), and alliums.

Turf. A covering of mowed vegetation, usually a grass.

Turfgrass. A species or cultivar of grass, usually of spreading habit, which is maintained as a mowed turf.

Tolerance, turf. Ability of a turf species to withstand application of a pesticide (herbicide) at the normal dosage without being killed or injured. Specific tolerance may be associated with an anatomical or physiological characteristic in the plant.

Turgor or turgor pressure. Cellular water pressure; responsible for keeping cells firm.

Twig. A young stem (1-year-old or less) that is in the dormant winter stage (has no leaves).

U

Umbel. A group of flowers growing from a common point on a stem, like Queen Anne's Lace (*Ammi majus*).

Understock. See Rootstock.

USDA zones. Areas derived by the USDA that indicate average-low winter temperatures. Used as a plant hardiness indicator. Other plant hardiness zones developed by other entities use different numbering systems.

V

Vacuole. A membrane-bound cavity within a cell, often containing a watery liquid or secretion.

Vaporization. The evaporation of the active ingredient in a pesticide during or after application.

Variegated. Having patches, stripes,, or marks of different colors.

Variety. In the wild, a plant growing within a species that is different in some particular characteristic from other members of that species. When grown from seed, a variety will maintain all of its particular characteristics. Also called a botanical variety.

Vascular pathogen. A disease-causing organism that invades primarily the conductive tissues (xylem or phloem) of the plant.

Vascular system. The internal structure of the stem that transports water, minerals, and sugars throughout the plant.

Vascular tissue. Water, nutrient, and photosynthate-conducting tissue. (See also Xylem, Phloem).

Vector. A living organism that is able to transmit or spread a pathogen.

Vegetative bud. A type of bud that develops into shoots.

Vegetative propagation. The increase of plants by asexual means using vegetative parts. Normally results in a population of identical individuals. Can occur by either natural means (e.g., bulblets, cormels, offsets, plantlets, or runners) or artificial means (e.g. cuttings, division, budding, grafting, or layering).

Venation. (1) The pattern of veins in leaves. (2) In insects the arrangement of veins in wings.

Vermicomposting. Composting with worms. Although there are over 6,000 species of worm, only seven have been found suitable for bin composting. One in particular, *Eisenia fetida* (common name: red wiggler), is the most widely used.

Vernation. The arrangement of new leaves within an older leaf sheath (e.g., on a grass plant).

Vertical mower. Also known as a dethacher or power rake, a machine used to remove thatch from grass by cutting it vertically.

Vertical spacing. The vertical space between branches on a tree.

Vertical Shoot Position (VSP) trellis. Vine shoots are trained upward in a vertical, narrow curtain with the fruiting zone below.

Vestigial. Of an organ or part of the body, degenerate, rudimentary, or atrophied, having become functionless in the course of evolution.

Viability. A seed's ability to germinate.

Viable. Alive; seeds must be alive in order to germinate.

Virulent. Capable of causing severe disease.

Virus. An infectious agent composed of DNA or RNA, too small to see with a compound micro-scope; multiplies only in living cells.

W

Warm-season grasses. Turf that has its optimum growth at temperatures between 80 and 95°F.

Water-holding capacity (WHC). The ability of a soil's micropores to hold water for plant use.

Watering-in. The initial watering after plants have been potted or repotted into new containers.

Water-soaking. Lesions that appear wet and dark and usually are sunken and or translucent. Often a symptom of bacterial disease.

Water sprout. A vigorous shoot originating above the ground on a plant's trunk, older wood, or bud union. Usually breaks from a latent bud, often the result of heavy pruning.

Weed. A plant growing where it is not wanted.

Weed-and-feed. A combination fertilizer and herbicide sometimes used on lawns.

Weediness. Likelihood of seeds germinating into unwanted plants that must be removed.

Wetting agent. A chemical that aids in liquid-to-surface contact.

Wetwood. Another name for slime flux.

Whorled leaf arrangement. Three or more leaves are attached at the same point on the stem.

Wilt. Loss of cell turgor; drooping and drying plant parts due to interference with the plant's ability to take up water and nutrients.

Wilting point. Point at which the water content within plant cells is low enough that cellular turgor is lost and the plant wilts.

Winter annual. Annual plant in which the seed germinates in the fall, producing a plant that over-winters, matures, and produces seed the following growing season.

Witches' broom. A plant condition suspected to be caused by genetic mutation or a virus where all adventitious buds in a certain part of the plant start growing, resulting in a lot of tiny stems; abnormal brush-like development of many weak shoots.

Woody perennial. A plant that goes dormant in winter and begins growth in spring from above-ground stems.

Woundwood. After wounding, callus forms. Woundwood is a tough, woody tissue full of lignin that grows behind callus When woundwood closes wounds, then normal wood continues to form.

X

Xeric. A plant or landscape that conserves water. Most xeric plants need minimal supplemental water after an establishment period (18 to 24 months after planting) unless there is extreme drought.

Xylem. The principal water conducting tissue of vascular plants.

Y

Yield. Refers to both the measure of the yield of a crop per unit area of land cultivation, and the seed generation of the plant itself.

Z

Zone of elongation. The area of the root where the cells expand.
Credits
Compiled by NC State Extension Master Gardener Volunteer Connie Schultz.

This glossary is based, in part, on the glossary from the *Idaho Master Gardener Handbook*.

Index

B

Extension Gardener—Your Gardening Resource.

NC State Extension provides reliable resources for all your gardening needs through our Extension Gardener web portal: extensiongardener.ces.ncsu.edu.

The Extension Gardener program covers everything from home gardening and food production to community gardening and therapeutic horticulture.

Your contribution to the Extension Gardener fund will help support the gardening program and provide useful resources to gardeners across North Carolina.

Make your gift online: go.ncsu.edu/donate-extensiongardener

Help Make Extension Better—Contribute to Our Publications.

NC State Extension helps to strengthen North Carolina families and communities every day through our mission and outreach programs. Our publications and communications enhance Extension's statewide, regional, and county programmatic efforts. Your contribution will support the production of these publications, help empower people, and provide solutions.

Make a secure gift online: go.ncsu.edu/ExtPublications

Mail a check: Please make checks payable to the North Carolina Agricultural Foundation, Inc. and note Account #011893.

Other gift options: Send us your contact information so we can contact you about making your gift in bank drafts or appreciated stocks:

NAME   PHONE

ADDRESS   EMAIL

Mail checks or contact information to CALS Advancement
NC State University
Campus Box 7645
Raleigh, NC 27695-7645

Fundraising efforts for Extension Publications/Communications operate under the auspices of the North Carolina Agricultural Foundation, Inc., a 501(c)3 non-profit (Tax ID# 56-6049304). You will receive an official receipt for your tax-deductible donation.

Please contact cals_advancement_business@ncsu.edu or 919.515.2000 with questions regarding donations.